CW00341288

A-Z ENCYCLOPEDIA OF FISHING IN THE BRITISH ISLES

A-Z ENCYCLOPEDIA OF FISHING IN THE BRITISH ISLES

CONSULTANT EDITOR ROY WESTWOOD

CHANCELLOR
PRESS

Consultant Editor
Roy Westwood

Contributors
Dave Coster
Andy Little
Dr Barrie Rickards
Dave Cooling
Chris Ogborne

Editor
Julian Brown

Art Editor
Chris Pow

Designed on D.T.P.
Tony Truscott Designs

Production Controller
Cheryl Cooper

Acknowledgements
All photographs by Roy Westwood
Artwork by Oxford Illustrators

First published in 1991
This 1994 edition published by Chancellor Press
an imprint of Reed Consumer Books Limited
Michelin House, 81 Fulham Road, London SW3 6RB
and Auckland, Melbourne, Singapore and Toronto

Copyright © 1991 Reed International Books Limited

ISBN 1 851 52584 X

All rights reserved. No part of this publication may be reproduced, stored in a retrieval system, or transmitted in any form or by any means, electronic, mechanical, photocopying, recording or otherwise, without the permission of the copyright holder.

Produced by Mandarin Offset
Printed in China

CONTENTS

Angler's Mail

COARSE

The cult of coarse angling has inspired a flood of tackle innovations in the last decade – particularly in the field of carp and match fishing. All the latest gear is listed in this section together with full descriptions of the baits, species and basic techniques for rivers and lakes.

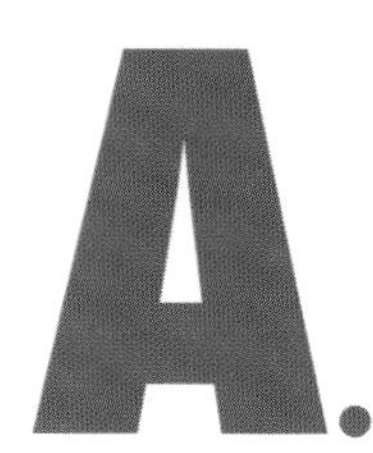

■ Additives

Liquid or powder mixtures which are added to hookbaits or groundbait. Some liquid attractors are prepared for individual species like bream and roach and appear to boost catches if applied sensibly to baits and groundbaits.

Slightly more complex are powdered additives specifically developed to blend with groundbaits. An unexpected bonus has been the way these highly concentrated powders work when sprinkled over baits like maggot, or mixed into bland breadcrumb groundbaits.

Other types of additives include the appetite stimulators or bait enhancers which have evolved from successful boilie mixes used by carp anglers.

■ Add-on weights

Add-on weights are designed to semi-load, or to completely modify, bottom-end waggler floats into self cockers. Rather than fully weighting large wagglers with bulbous, unwieldy locking shot the add-on weight creates a far more streamlined effect. It becomes part of the float and reduces the size of the shot needed to trap it on the line.

These floats tend to out-distance conventional, shot-locked bottom-enders, and they will also slice through awkward winds, leading to far better accuracy. The only possible disadvantage with weighted floats is their tendency to dive deep – if care is not taken – as they land in the water. This problem can be overcome by slightly adjusting casting technique. After the float has been cast and just before it lands, the line is feathered off the reel. This lays the float and tackle gently on the water, eliminating splash and too much submersion.

Add-on weights are made in both brass and tungsten. The latter is much smaller, size for size, but is also more expensive. Both types of weight are usually sized up in similar fashion to larger shot in BB, AAA and SSG units, or multiples of these.

The brass add-ons are normally pushed onto the bottom eye fixture of the float and are held in place with a small piece of silicone tubing, just leaving the eye showing for the line to be attached. Tungsten weights, which have a taper at both ends, are applied slightly differently. One end is pushed into a short piece of silicone tubing which is also anchored over the bottom eye of the float. A swivel float adaptor, or one of the smaller silicone float adaptors, is then slid over the end of the weight.

A third adjustable weighting option is to invest in a set of loaded Drennan Crystal wagglers with specially moulded tungsten polymer bases which allow a sensible amount of extra shot to be added. These

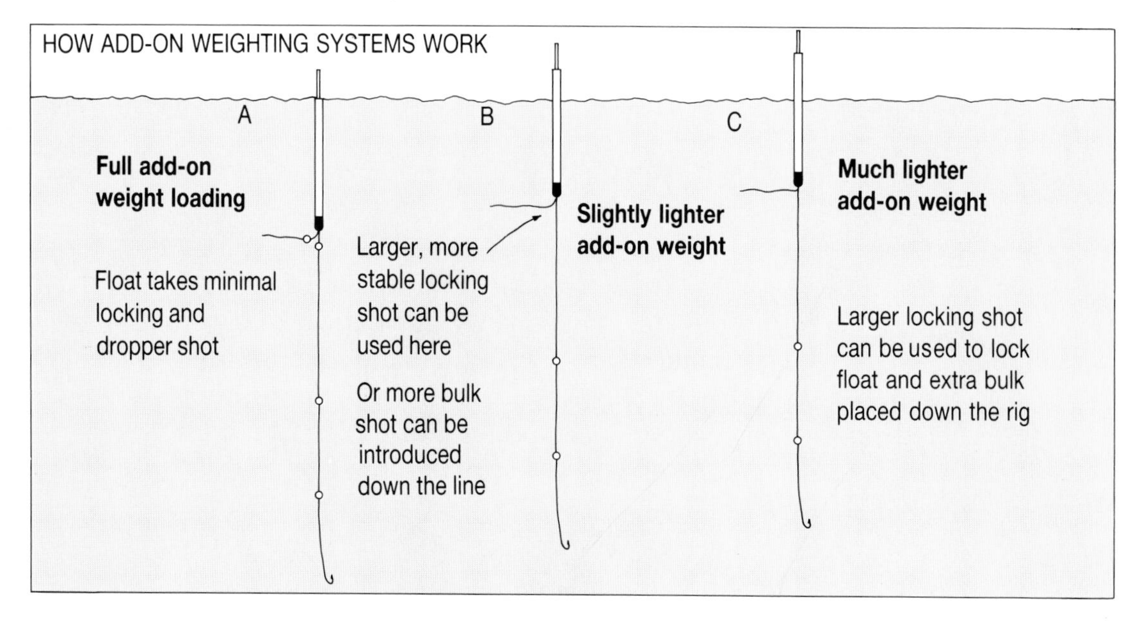

weighted bases can also be unplugged and fitted to different sized floats within the range, to give differing degrees of buoyancy.

Whichever add-on weighting system you choose, take into account its suitability for adapting conventional wagglers into very good bottom-end sliders. The best bottom-end sliders require approximately a third of their weight carrying capacity in the base of the float. After selecting the correct add-on weight to suit, a small Inter-fishing Link is fitted to the base eye on the float. This gives the correct eye size to stop against a sliding float stop.

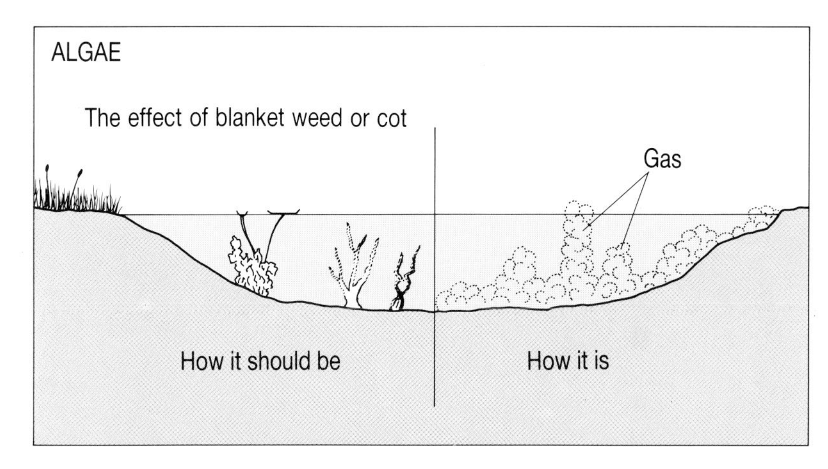

■ Algae

Algae are the most primitive form of plant life and rely upon chemical nutrients for their well-being. Give them an excessive supply and they multiply excessively, until the decay of their own waste products becomes toxic and kills them – and any other aquatic life that happens to get in the way. Algae include seaweeds, both floating and submersed algae (phytoplankton), and also silk-weed and blanket weed.

Algae are vital to the well-being of any fishery but in excess they can be disastrous. Microscopic algae have bloomed, due to excess nutrients, and killed off fisheries wholesale. Examples of this include the Norfolk Broads where Prymnesium repeatedly strikes.

Waters thrive best when there is barely enough nutrient supply to sustain algae. This gives the other plant life a chance. Generally, our waters are too nutrient-rich – they have too high values for nitrate and phosphate.

■ Antenna

The thin sight tips found on delicate stillwater float designs and ultra sensitive pole floats. On running line floats the antenna is normally quite long to help in spotting lift and on-the-drop bites. Pole floats usually have quite short, highly visible nylon antenna.

■ Anti-reverse

The anti-reverse mechanism is built into all fixed spool reels, the majority of modern closed face reels and many centrepins. Quite simply, when the anti-reverse is switched on it prevents the reel backwinding and releasing extra line – it can only retrieve line. The only way line can be released from the reel in this mode is to open the bale arm or slacken off the clutch so line can be pulled from the spool under tension.

The main idea behind the anti-reverse is to allow the angler to fish and strike one-handed. And if the rod is positioned in rests, the anti-reverse allows a quick one-handed movement to lift the rod and strike. With a correctly adjusted clutch setting, the hook can be set against the reel's immobility with the anti-reverse engaged. Line will only pull off the reel if a big fish runs hard away from the angler, causing the clutch to rotate.

Many experienced anglers prefer to tighten the clutch right down so it cannot give line either. Again, with the anti-reverse engaged, the strike is made and the rod is left to cushion all the impact if a good fish is hooked. This technique is only recommended for anglers who are thoroughly familiar with their tackle. It requires a very deft touch indeed to quickly disengage the anti-reverse in order to

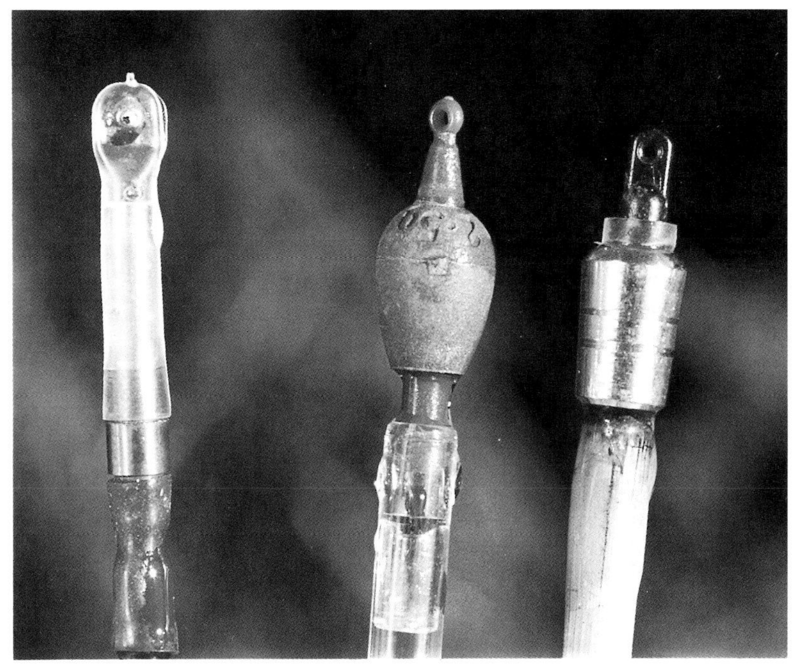

Three ways of loading the base of a waggler (from left): tapered tungsten weight secured by silicone tubing, Crystal waggler with tungsten polymer unit and brass add-on.

backwind line to prevent a breakage against a powerful running fish. See Reels.

■ Anti-tangle rigs

See Carp fishing; Legering,

■ Arlesey bomb

The most widely used legering weight. Its streamlined shape casts well and also does not make too much disturbance on landing. Traditional Arlesey bombs range in size from just 1/8 oz up to 1.25 oz. A similar profile of weight has been adapted for moulding heavier carp bombs.

Generally, the Arlesey is used for straight legering or paternostering. It has a swivel head which is fixed to the reel line when paternostering or through which the line is left to run freely for straight legering. The attachment eye will also accept a swivel link for quick change purposes.

A good selection of different sized Arlesey bombs is essential for quivertipping and swingtipping. See Legering.

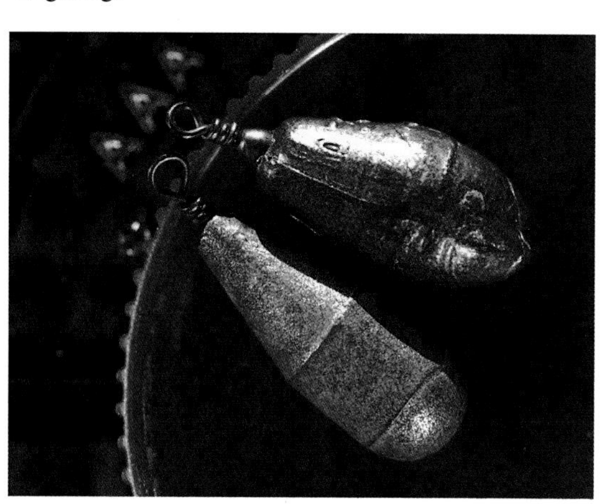

Right: **Streamlined Arlesey bombs.**

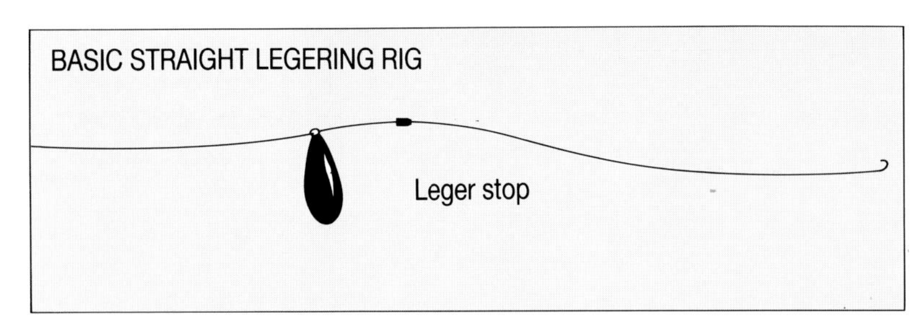

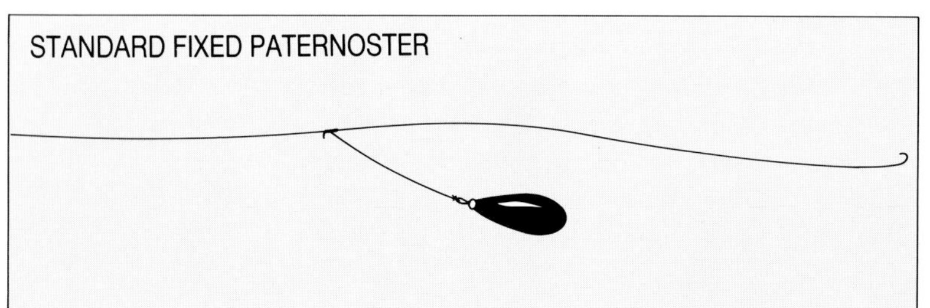

■ Atmospheric pressure

The general assumption is that a rising barometer spells improved weather – and good fishing - which usually proves to be the case. In winter, a rising barometer means a return to milder weather and south-west winds and nothing could be better for pike feeding. The fish generally become more active as the barometer rises and will fall to a variety of techniques.

But in recent years, much more has been attributed to air pressure. Cambridge pike expert Barrie Rickards maintains that in periods of low pressure the fish become less active, and if they feed at all it will be in a desultory fashion down near the bottom. Flies have to be deep-sunk and retrieved slowly, and pike fall to deadbaits lying static on the bottom.

Explanations for this have so far eluded anglers. But it is known that under high air pressure oxygen dissolves more readily in the surface layers of the water with the opposite happening in low pressure conditions. There will always be a tendency towards de-oxygenation when the barometric pressure is low. This fact alone may control the activity of fish.

■ Atomiser spray

Atomisers are very useful for finishing off groundbait mixes to exactly the right consistency. Their fine spray does not overload the groundbait with moisture and helps to keep a nice fluffy texture.

The Atomiser bottle is either filled with plain water at the bankside, or a flavouring can also be added to further enhance groundbaits and feed baits. Where atomisers really score is with pure breadcrumb mixes for fishing a cloudy consistency with punched bread on the hook. It is now possible to purchase special white punch crumb which does not bind together or go stodgy if mixed with the atomiser.

Atomisers are also extremely useful for slightly dampening jokers which have been treated with leam. They give just the right amount of moisture to form a small ball of leamed-up jokers for feeding. A couple of sprays will also help to keep jokers and bloodworm in tip top condition when storing them in dampened newspaper.

■ Avon float

This float is designed for running water and has a buoyant balsa body, pronounced sight tip and normally a cane stem. See Floats.

■ Back lead

A secondary weight slid down the main line after the baited hook has been cast out. It pins the line tightly to the bottom between the point where it comes to rest and the main weight. The method was developed in carp fishing to make the line less obvious to easily spooked fish and prevent them touching it as they move into the baited area.

On many waters where the carp have become educated, they associate the line with danger and will often dash out of the swim if their body makes contact with it. The back lead is usually lighter than the main bomb, weighing between one eighth of an ounce and half an ounce. It is attached to a link swivel or purpose-made clip and slid down the line after tightening up to the terminal rig and positioning the rod back up the bank.

At close range up to about 25 yards, the back lead doesn't need to be any more than about a rod length or two out from the bank. But at longer range, once the back lead has been slid down the line, the rod is picked up and held high against a taut line to slide the lead further down nearer the main rig.

■ Back shot

The back shot is a simple but ingenious way of stabilising float rigs in awkward, downstream winds. It entails placing a small shot anything from six inches to two feet above the float to help anchor the line. In light wind, a No.8 shot will normally be sufficient, stepping up to a No. 4 or even a No.1 in a severe blow.

Without back shotting, a downstreamer will blow the reel line in front of a top and bottom attached float, pulling it off line, or speeding it unnaturally down the swim. The idea of the back shot is to keep the line in a straight line, behind the float, not only for better presentation but also for a cleaner, more direct strike. Back shotting works with stick floats, Avons, balsas, and top/bottom attached pole floats.

■ Back wind

There are three ways of giving line when a good fish has been hooked:

1. Most reels have clutches which can be slackened off so line will be pulled free when a certain amount of pressure is applied.
2. Line can also be released, under direct fingertip control, with the bale arm open.
3. Probably the most direct and satisfactory method of playing a good fish is to disengage the reel's anti-reverse mechanism and release extra line by back winding as required. If a large fish makes a really fast, unstoppable run – this is normal with barbel, carp and pike – it's often best to release the handle completely. Control is brought back by gently touching the outside of the drum with a finger of the rod hand.

■ Bait apron

These are useful accessories when wading. By wearing the apron around the waist, loose feed and hookbaits are kept dry and easily accessible, eliminating the need for a bait tray or waiter which are difficult to position on many waters anyway.

■ Bait dropper

A metal or plastic bait dropper deposits loose baits on the bottom, without the need for groundbait. It is attached directly to the hook on the rig being used

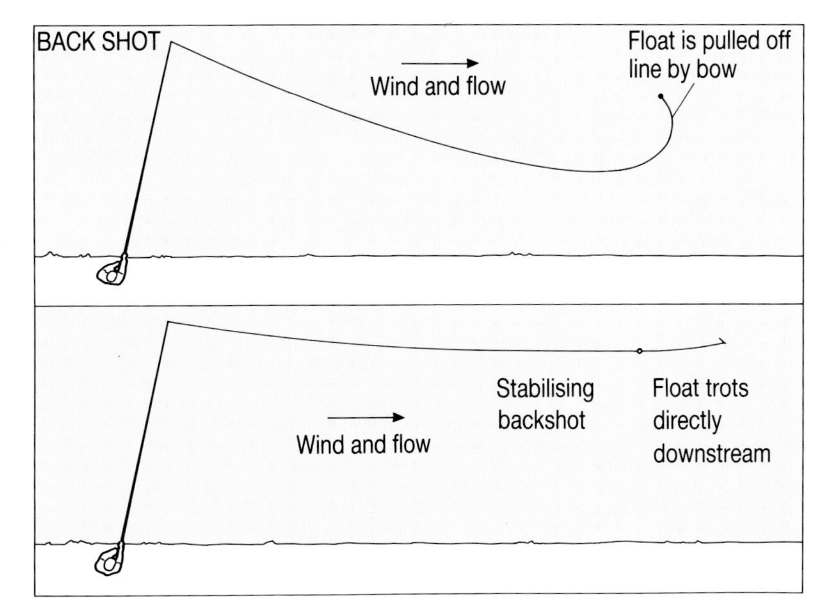

A bait dropper makes it possible to spread a bed of loose baits on the bottom in fast water swims.

and filled with baits like hempseed, maggots, casters, pinkies, squatts, bloodworm or jokers.

Once the dropper hits bottom, a weighted plunger protruding from the base is forced upwards and triggers a hinged door to open, depositing free samples of feed very accurately. Bait droppers work best at close range, when pole fishing or laying on with float gear just off the rod tip. The dropper is particularly effective at spreading a bed of particle baits on the bottom in fast water for species like barbel. It guarantees bait stays in the swim!

■ Bait waiter

The basic type of bait waiter consists of a flat tray which screws into a supporting bank stick. It places the bait boxes and groundbait bowl within easy reach when wading. Commercially produced waiters are made to take a specific type of round or square bait box. It's common to find recesses for three or four bait boxes and perhaps a small extra compartment for handy implements like scissors and disgorger.

Most bait waiters can also be used when sitting on the bank to position the bait boxes at waist level – providing it's possible to push a bankstick into the ground. All bait waiters have a standard three eighth of an inch BSF thread so they will fit any commercially produced bankstick.

An interesting development is the miniature, alloy platform with four adjustable legs. This lightweight platform is more commonly used by the canal angler on hard concrete banks where it is impossible to use a bankstick. Primarily, the bait platform is designed to present baits and groundbaits at sitting height.

■ Baiting needle

Chiefly used by carp anglers for mounting boilies on a hair rig. Commercially made needles usually have an injection moulded handle and stainless steel shaft with a barb or hook on the end to pull the hair through the bait. The needle is pushed through the boilie and the loop of the hair pulled back through the bait and trapped on the other side by a boilie stop.

Needles with a forked end simply push the hair loop through the boilie and out the other side. Some

Below: The choice of bait waiters includes this stable platform designed with towpath anglers in mind.

Right: Crochet hook (left) and other purpose-made baiting needles for mounting boilies on a hair.

of the specialist needles have an internal, hollow chamber which accepts an isotope to help baiting up at night.

A size 0.75 crochet hook works equally well as the purpose-designed needles and with its smooth contours will not damage the fine filaments on delicate hair rig fibres.

■ Baits

There is a massive choice of baits for coarse fishing but maggots undoubtedly remain the most popular. Other long established baits like worms, bread, luncheon meat, cheese and hemp also continue to be very effective. Bloodworms and jokers are controversial newcomers and only became widely available in the last decade. These natural baits have proved so effective for catching small fish that they are now banned on many club waters.

Whatever you decide to stick on the hook, the most important maxim is that fresh bait, in tip top condition is always likely to catch more fish.

Boilies The boilie is a universal carp bait, being more selective than most of the other alternatives. It consists of fine food powders which are mixed together and added to eggs, forming a paste. It is then rolled into balls and boiled to form a hard skin on the outside.

Colours and flavours are added to improve the bait's attraction to carp. Boilies are normally round in shape so they can be catapulted accurately over long distances. But flat boilies have their uses – for example when presenting a bait on top of a soft bottom or weed. Boilies are produced commercially in frozen or shelf-life packs in diameters ranging from about 8 mm to 22 mm. See Carp fishing.

Bread A very versatile bait that can be used in crust or flake form on large hooks, shaped from a paste for medium sized hooks, or compressed with a punch for smaller patterns. Crust makes a good surface bait and fished on a big size 2 or 4 hook will account for carp on stillwaters and chub on rivers. It's also a good choice for weedy waters because its slow sinking qualities keep it visible above bottom debris.

Flake can also be used with big hooks, but more generally it is combined with size 8 to 14 long shank models for species like chub, bream and big roach. Both crust and flake are at their best when taken from a freshly baked loaf.

Most anglers prefer a thick sliced, fresh white loaf for their punch fishing. Thicker slices compress slightly harder into a punch head and stay on the

Brightly coloured boilies - the supreme carp bait.

BAIT CHART

Bait	Species	Recommended hook size/pattern
Maggots	Barbel, bleak, bream, carp, chub, dace, eels, gudgeon, perch, roach, rudd, ruffe, tench.	Single: 18-24, fine wire. Double: 14-18, forged. Multiple: 8-12, forged.
Casters	Barbel, bream, carp, chub, dace, eels, roach, rudd, tench.	Single:16-20, fine wire. Double: 14-18, forged. Multiple: 10-12, forged.
Pinkies	Bleak, skimmer bream, dace, eels, gudgeon, perch, roach, rudd, ruffe, tench.	Single: 20-24, fine wire. Double: 20, fine or forged.
Squatts	Bleak, bream (and skimmers), dace, gudgeon, perch, roach, rudd, ruffe, tench.	Single: 22-24, fine wire. Double: 20-22, fine wire.
Worms	Barbel, bream, carp, chub, eels, perch, roach, ruffe, tench.	Lobs: 2-12, forged. Brandlings: 8-16, forged. Reds: 14-18, fine wire.
Bloodworms	Bleak, bream, skimmers, gudgeon, perch, roach, rudd, ruffe, tench.	Single: 20-26, fine wire. Double: 18-24, fine wire.
Breadpunch	Bleak, skimmer bream, gudgeon, roach, rudd.	16-24, fine wire.
Breadflake and crust	Barbel, bream, carp, chub, roach, tench.	Large pieces: 2-12, forged. Small: 12-16, fine wire.
Luncheon meat	Barbel, carp, chub, tench.	Large pieces: 4-10, forged. Small: 12-16, forged.
Boilies	Barbel, bream, carp, chub, tench.	Standard: 6-10, forged. Mini: 10-14, forged.
Hemp	Barbel, bream, carp chub, roach, rudd, tench.	Big fish: 14-18, forged. Roach, etc: 14-20, fine wire.
Tares	Barbel, bream, carp, chub, roach.	Big fish: 12-18, forged. Roach, etc: 14-18, fine wire.
Sweetcorn	Barbel, chub, dace, roach, rudd.	Single: 12-16, forged. Multiple: 8-12, forged.

Above: **Four sizes of bread punch.**

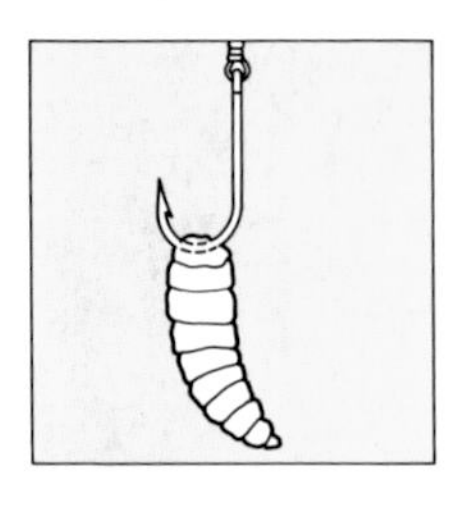

Above: **Single maggots must be mounted so they wriggle away from the point of the hook.**

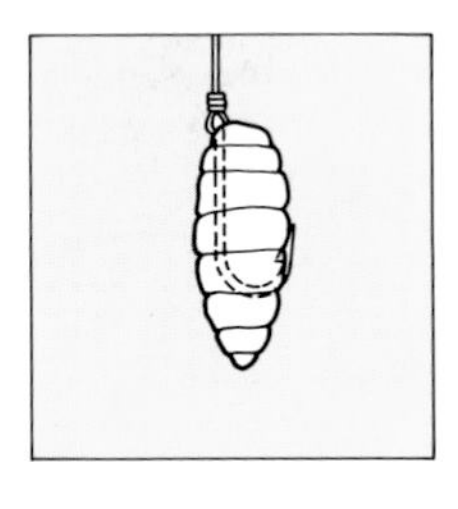

Above: **The correct way to hook a single caster is to bury the hook until it is almost hidden.**

hook longer. It's also possible to gain much the same effect with thinner slices by steaming and rolling them with a round, heavy object before going fishing. This gives the slices a sticky, pasty quality.

All bread intended for use with the bread punch should be kept moist and fresh in an air tight container or wrapper. Punched bread is mainly suitable for smaller, size 14 to 24 hooks.

Punched bread is an excellent canal or stillwater bait and works particularly well when used with a cloudy groundbait in clear water conditions. A good bait for species like roach, skimmers, crucian carp and rudd.

Paste is the only bread bait which cannot be formed successfully from a fresh loaf. The bread needs to be three or four days old, giving it time to dry out. It will then absorb a little water, allowing the bread to be kneaded-up readily into a paste. Paste is best mounted on size 6 to 14 hooks.

When making up a paste many anglers add a little flavouring. Something sweet like custard powder or a few drops from a concentrated liquid flavouring are good ideas. Paste baits are excellent at close range when laying on for fish like bream, tench, big roach and carp.

Maggots The plain, white maggot is a superb bait and will take most species of freshwater fish. But it's definitely profitable to experiment with coloured maggots. There are occasions when species like roach and chub show a marked preference for bronze maggots. Tench, perch and bream often seem to get excited by reds while yellow can pull roach, bream and dace – on difficult waters.

There are several maggot types. Normal shop-bought maggots are often called big maggots. They are widely available in tackle shops as whites, bronzes, reds and yellows. Sometimes you can also obtain greens and blues. The big maggot is suitable for many forms of floatfishing and,of course, many maggot swimfeeder designs.

Pinkies are roughly half the size of the normal, big maggot. In their natural state, as the name suggests, they have a pinkish tinge to their off white colour. Pinkies are also available dyed, mainly in red, bronze and fluorescent pink colours. This is a favourite bait of the match angler and is good for catching small fish on light tackle. It's also a good change bait for bigger fish like bream, perch and roach when the going is hard.

Squatts have a much wider use nowadays compared to their original role as a feed bait for bream. These tiny maggots are half the size again of pinkies and have always been favoured for bream fishing because of the sluggish way they lie on the bottom after being fed in groundbait. Pinkies and maggots have a habit of crawling out of sight on weedy or stony bottoms.

While the squatt is still very popular for bream fishing, it is now a premier canal and lake bait. By loose feeding squatts, matchmen found they could get brilliant results with fish like bream, roach, perch, and gudgeon on pole or light waggler tackle. Usually, one or two squatts, or a pinkie is used on the hook.

Red squatts are becoming increasingly popular on waters where bloodworm has been banned. Although a poor substitute in many ways, they can work quite well, mainly when the water is a little coloured.

Right: **Bronze maggot (left) and pinkie - the matchman's favourite.**

Finally, there are gozzers, a type of maggot which you're less likely to see in a tackle shop because they cannot be reared commercially. They must be home bred on a medium sized heart from the butcher's shop. The gozzer can be fed up until it is twice as big as a commercial maggot and combined with its very soft skin, this makes it a superb bream, tench and roach bait.

Gozzers must be planned in advance by at least ten days before a fishing trip. First, the heart is sliced in several places to open up the muscle, then it is placed in a large tin containing a bed of clean bran. The container is left in a dry, shady spot outdoors with a lid placed slightly ajar, just enough for a fly to get in and lay its eggs in the heart. This process is called the blow.

After a few days there should be a few patches of eggs showing on the cuts made in the heart. At this stage if big gozzers are required, surplus blows are scraped away, just leaving two or three. Too many blows and there'll be insufficient feed to go around resulting in gozzers which are on the small side.

Once you're satisfied the right amount of eggs are laid on the heart, it is wrapped up in newspaper to help prevent smells and returned to the container. It can also be completely covered with bran. A week later, the gozzers should be ready for riddling off, after which they need to be stored in fresh, damp bran in a closed bait box to prevent escapees.

If you do not have the time to breed your own hook maggots, shop-bought samples can certainly be improved. Indifferent bait is revitalised by removing the sawdust with a small maggot riddle, then adding fresh sawdust and a sprinkling of fine maize flour. To clean and soften up hook baits, store a handful in a closed bait box containing a small amount of dampened bran for a couple of days.

All the different types of maggots can be hooked in similar fashion. The best way is to mount a single maggot through the tiny flap of skin at the tail or blunt end. This won't impede the maggot's movement, in fact if will wriggle even more enticingly.

Position the bait with the head pointing away from the hook point so it won't turn over and mask the point. When fishing with double maggot, it's best to hook one through the head and the other through the tail to prevent the hooklength spinning up on the retrieve.

Generally, fine wire hooks from 18s to 24s are used for single maggot, while 14s or 16s are better for double, perhaps using a forged model if big fish are expected.

Casters An important bait which derives from the maggot is the caster or chrysalid. This is the form the maggot eventually turns into before hatching out as a fly. When maggots first turn into casters several days after purchase they are a light brown or bronze colour. At this stage they will sink and are termed as true casters – a brilliant big fish bait. If the casters are exposed to the air for too long they become a much deeper brown, eventually turning almost black. They are then known as floaters because they become buoyant.

Most tackle shops turn their own casters to a high standard, but because of the work involved in constantly riddling them off, they are quite expensive. Caster maggots have to be run through riddles once or twice a day to catch the casters and seal them in airtight containers before they become too advanced and turn into floaters.

Casters are best stored in a fridge in an airtight plastic bag. If they are to be kept for a few days it's advisable to open the bag at least once every 24 hours to allow the bait to breathe. This keeps it alive and prevents the casters from losing their crispness and attractive colour. Suffocated casters take on burn marks from plastic bags and turn a horrible

Casters and hemp - a winning combination.

grey colour when opened up to the air. They become much less effective in this state.

Unlike maggots, there are two good ways of hooking the caster. They can be mounted like a maggot, when the fish are showing little caution, but often it's better to completely bury the hook inside. For a normal sized caster, an 18 hook is about right, inserting the point through the fat tail end and inverting the hook carefully until it is completely inside. To keep the hook in position, its point is gently pushed very slightly out of the side of the bait. This stops it slipping off the hook on the cast.

Casters will sort out quality fish on most venues. Double caster is particularly favoured for big chub, barbel, bream, tench and medium sized carp. Single baits are better for dace, roach, skimmers and rudd.

Meats Luncheon meat is a well established bait, particularly for barbel and chub. It has probably taken more specimen sized fish of these species than any other bait. Being rather soft, luncheon meat tends to fly off on the cast and for security it should be wedged on the hook with a makeshift pad or V-shaped plastic boilie stop.

To do this, a cube of meat is selected to match the size of the hook. Then the hook is pushed carefully through the middle until the bend is exposed the other side. The boilie stop is slipped under the bend and the hook pulled back trapping it in place against the meat. Fixed in this way, the soft bait will not fly off on the cast. Instead of the boilie stop, a short length of grass stem, piece of macaroni or anything similar will also hold the meat secure.

Sausage meat is another effective bait for chub and barbel. It usually needs to be stiffened into a paste with bread dough and then it will hold on large hooks both on the cast and in powerful currents. A recent craze on the River Trent has been the use of chopped up steak for chub. The tactic is to feed with chopped up stewing steak and then offer a sliver of real steak on the hook! On the right day, the chub go wild for this strange combination which works on float or feeder tackle.

The choice of seeds

Hemp The most popular seed bait is hemp which is now used widely throughout the season. To prepare for a day's fishing, tip a pint or so of the seeds into a large saucepan and cover them with about an inch of water. Bring to the boil with the lid removed. Then once the water has reached boiling point, let the hemp simmer for 30 minutes with the saucepan lid not quite covering the pan to keep the heat in.

Check every ten minutes or so that the water has not evaporated away and top up with the odd cupful if necessary. The bait is ready when white shoots emerge from most of the seeds. At this stage any water left is strained off and the bait stored in a plastic bag or bait box. It is best to keep hemp frozen after cooking, or at least fridged if it's not to be used immediately.

Hemp is a superb feed bait and can be used with most other popular baits. In the warmer summer and autumn months it can be lethal for roach and after perhaps an hour of constant feeding will often result in a bite a cast, if used on the hook once the fish arrive in numbers.

As autumn gets a hold and the days become colder, hemp loses its effectiveness as a hookbait, but will still draw fish into a swim and hold them there. It can be fed along with maggots and casters – a combination that works well for chub, barbel, roach, dace, perch, tench, carp and bream.

As a hookbait, hemp fits well on a size 18 short shanked pattern. Simply push the bend of the hook into the opening where the white shoot emerges. If the fish, particularly big ones, are really mopping up the seeds then an even larger hook is a good idea. Once fish have gained a taste for hemp, they won't even be put off by a size 12 hook!

Tares Tares are bigger than hemp when cooked and much softer skinned. It is a good hookbait to use with hemp and a handful will be sufficient for a day's fishing. They can be cooked with the hemp for convenience.

Hemp and tares - pulls in the roach.

When fully cooked, the tare should feel soft to the touch. If you cook hemp and tares together, the tares will be ready to use when the hemp is considered ready.

Tares cook up into a natural, light brown colour. If you want them to look like the darker hempseed, they can be treated with soda to create an all black hookbait.

Size 12, 14, 16 or 18 short shanked hooks are needed for tares. Use fine wire patterns for roach and dace fishing and forged when after chub, barbel and carp.

Sweetcorn Sweetcorn, straight from the tin, is a very good summer bait for species like tench, bream, carp and big roach. It should be used on a size 10, 12 or 14 hook, preferably gilt in colour. This is a good bait to fish overdepth on the float, but it can also be legered or used successfully with an open-end swimfeeder. Some anglers dye sweetcorn red on hard fished waters. This is a good ploy which often brings extra fish.

Worms The three common types of earth worms found in the British Isles are all popular for freshwater fishing.

Brandlings are the easiest to obtain in large numbers and are actually farmed commercially. When hooked they ooze an evil looking yellow body fluid but this does not seem to affect the brandling's appeal when used as a hookbait but it's advisable only to use this worm as a last resort when chopping up worms to feed in groundbait.

Brandlings vary in size dramatically. The larger ones can do justice to a size 8 or 10 hook, while anything between a 12 and 18 can be matched with the smaller ones. This bait is suited to tench, skimmer, bream, perch and chub fishing.

Redworms tend to be on the small side and are very lively on the hook. They make superb baits for fussy fish like big roach, bream, tench and rudd. Redworms are also good for chopping up into groundbait when after tench and bream. Canal anglers find chopped red worm work well for perch, introduced neat to the swim with a pole cup. Generally, a small hook is recommended for this bait – use 10s to 14s for a full sized worm and 16s to 18s for a tiny piece.

Lobworms are not always easy to find until the weather gets really damp from September onwards. They're an excellent bait for chub and tench, fished on big size 2 - 6 hooks. Smaller sections of this worm can also be lethal in coloured water for big roach, perch and eels using smaller hooks to match.

The lobworm is a brilliant fish attractor when chopped up into groundbait. Perch and bream particularly will home in from quite considerable distances once they get the scent!

Matchmen reach for the bloodworm when the going gets tough.

Bloodworm and joker These are the larvae of midges which live in the bottom mud of many waters. Jokers are a little more difficult to locate, usually being found in great numbers in sewage effluent streams and settling ponds.

Both baits are difficult to collect which makes them expensive over the tackle shop counter. But in winter particularly, the bloodworm and joker combination will bring bites when all else fails.

Jokers are very lively in water and they're usually mixed in groundbait or leam to feed and attract fish, holding them in the swim. The bloodworm is three or four times larger and is used on the hook but can also be fed if bigger fish like bream, perch and good roach are expected. Primarily these are canal and lake baits, most effective when colder weather makes the fish inactive and less likely to feed on conventional baits like maggots.

For bigger fish, bunches of bloodworm can be effective on a fine wire size 18 or 20 hook. More normally, 22s and 24s are about right for single or double worm. Sometimes size 26 or smaller hooks are used in desperation with a single joker – by winter league anglers trying to snatch vital team points on a poor section! Most bloodworm fishing is confined to the pole because of the ultra fine tackle these fragile baits require.

■ Bale arm

The bale on a fixed spool reel directs the line on to a free-running roller to avoid damaging the mono when retrieving under pressure. It is opened to release line from the spool and closed to retrieve it. Automatic bales on match reels flip open when pressed downwards or are activated with a trigger mechanism. See Reels.

■ Balsa

The slimmer, conventional all-balsa float has a slightly tapering sight tip, but still takes a good weight loading for extra stability. Fatter, cigar-shaped models are specifically designed to carry large baits in powerful currents. See Floats.

■ Bank stick

Bank sticks accept a standard three-eighths of an inch BSF thread which is common to all rod rest heads, bait waiters, keepnets, angle locks, pole rollers, landing nets and target boards. Most anglers carry at least a couple of 36 inch long plain bank sticks for use with a back rod rest and their keepnet. A pair of medium length but adjustable telescopic sticks are also invaluable for precisely positioning a target board, bait waiter or pole roller.

To support the front rod rest, it is preferable to select a robust, adjustable four foot bank stick which will extend to almost twice its length. This is handy when the front rest has to be fixed out in the water, or when the rod needs to be propped up high for legering in fast currents.

■ Barbel

The barbel is a cyprinid, that is a member of the carp family. Other species of barbel exist elsewhere in Europe and Asia, but in the UK there is only one species. It grows to a weight in the mid-teens, possibly a little beyond that, but for most keen barbel anglers a 10 lb fish is the dream. Its distribution is from Yorkshire to Hampshire and it is absent from Scotland, Ireland and Wales.

The barbel is primarily a river fish, but is stocked in a few stillwaters. The main rivers are the Yorkshire Ouse, Swale and Ure, Dorset Stour, Hampshire Avon, Severn, Thames, Kennet, Lea and the Bristol Avon.

The underside of the fish is more or less flat, for hugging the bottom, and the dorsal line is gently arched and hydrodynamically shaped with heavy shoulders and a wristy tail region. Its colour is essentially a dark brown dorsally to a rich deep golden brown on the flanks and distinctly paler beneath. The ventral and pectoral fins particularly may have

The barbel is built to survive in the swiftest of currents.

a pinkish or orange tinge, which greatly aids the fish-spotting angler in clear waters.

Branched barbules The fish has four fleshy barbules, two located on the 'nose' above the underslung mouth, and two rooted at the backward corners of the upper lip. In some waters, barbel may have more than this, and some show branching of the barbules.

The barbules are sensory organs and the fish tastes for its food which consists of animal matter such as insects, larvae, and worms, but also vegetative matter. At spawning time, as with the common bream and the tench, they seem to have a predatory phase and will eat small fish.

No fish fights better than the barbel or, at least, no fish fights to the last gasp in such a way. The British record stands at 14 lb 6 oz and was captured from the Hampshire Avon's Royalty Fishery in 1934.

■ Barbless

The use of hooks without barbs is now mandatory on some waters because they penetrate the fish's mouth more cleanly and can be removed with the minimum of damage to tissue. Pike anglers have taken to barbless hooks in a big way. See Hooks.

■ Bars

An area of the lake bed that rises higher in the water than the surrounding bottom and more commonly found in gravel pits than ponds, lakes or rivers. They are formed during excavation of the pit and are generally clear areas with less natural food than the troughs alongside.

But fish shoals, including carp, love to follow the line of the bars up and down the pit and it's often worth presenting a bait on them. Some bars have sheer sides rising quickly up from the deeps which cause considerable abrasion to line if there is a layer of sharp grit or mussel shells.

The shallowest bars warm up fastest in summer and carp will bask on them in large, heavily fished pits where they have been driven out from the margins.

■ Beachcaster rig

See Carp fishing.

■ Beads

Small plastic beads are useful anti-tangle devices when incorporated in the majority of legering and feeder fishing rigs. It is advisable to place a bead between the leger stop and any free-running feeder or weight. This will prevent the hook length twisting around the weight and act as a shock absorber, making the stop less likely to slip on the cast.

■ Bedchair

On many waters carp fishing is a waiting game and the length of the sessions vary from a day and a night up to several weeks at a time. The long-stay angler demands comfort and specialist bedchairs fit the bill. A cushioned mattress and adjustable legs and back rests are features of the top selling models.

■ Bite

Bites vary from very positive disappearances of the float or a savage jerk on the quivertip to an almost imperceptible tremble on the float tip.

Experience tells an angler when to strike at a bite because it's difficult to set hard and fast rules. Obviously, a sailaway movement on any indicator warrants a fast strike in response. But on some occasions the half-hearted take, or bite, is best left alone until the fish gains confidence and begins to move away with the hookbait, eventually causing a definite indicator movement.

Another type of bite which can prove very frustrating is the line bite, or liner. This is caused by fish swimming into the line while legering and often results in a fierce pull on the swingtip or quivertip. A series of missed bites with the hookbait remaining intact normally tells you something is wrong. Usually the answer is to fish slightly closer in.

Bite indicators There are numerous visual and audible devices on the market to help in spotting bites

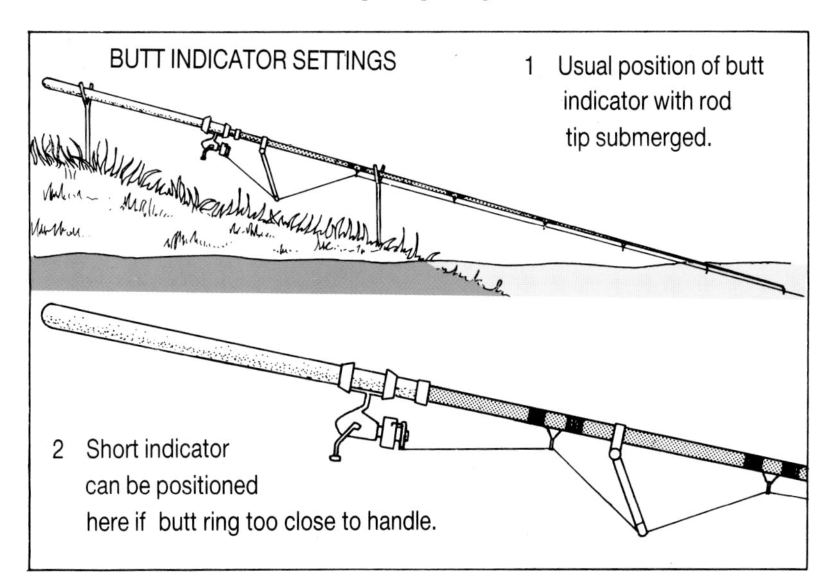

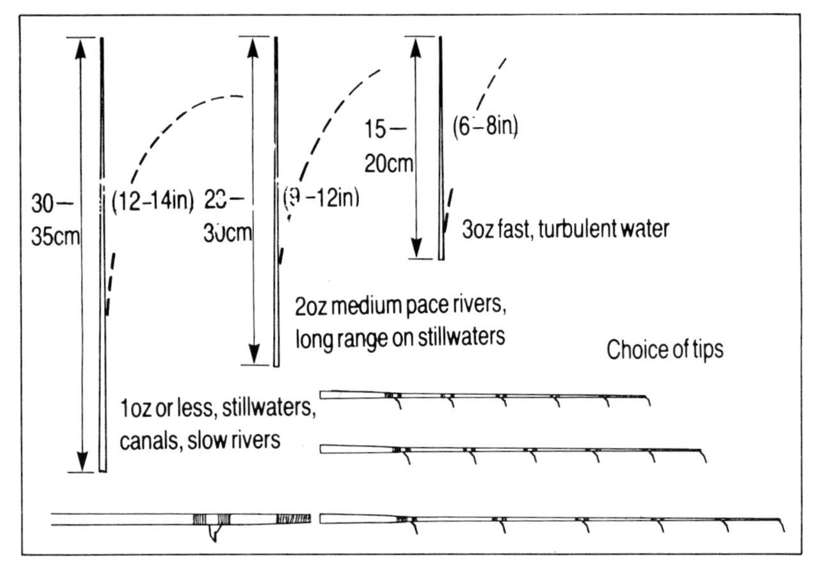

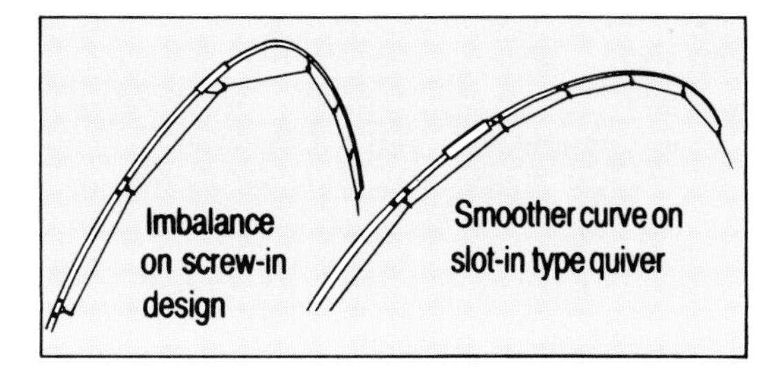

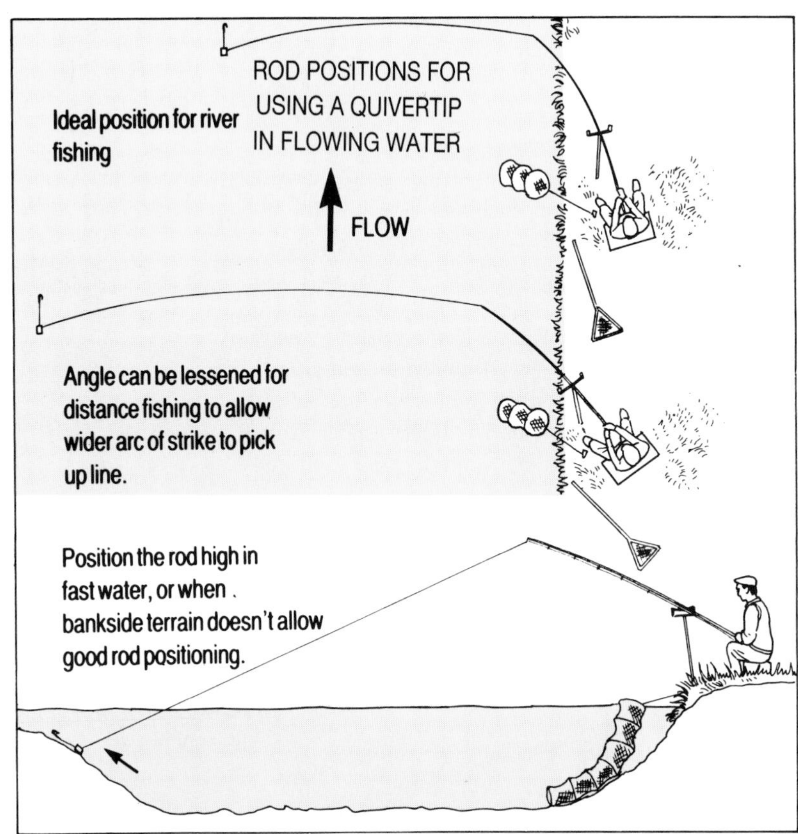

Top and top right: **Many rod manufacturers are producing custom-made quivertip rods that take up to three or four slot-in quivers.**

Above: **Rod positions for using a quivertip in flowing water.**

while legering. Generally, the system you choose is dictated by the target species, type of venue or weather conditions.

Butt indicator The butt indicator fits on the rod just above the handle by means of a Terry clip. The idea is to try and keep the device sheltered from the elements. Butt indicators are used most when strong winds cause standard swingtips or quivertips to sway uncontrollably, making it difficult to spot bites.

With a butt indicator, the rod tip can be sunk up to two feet beneath the surface to prevent the wind from battering it around. This indicator works in similar fashion to the swingtip and offers only a fraction more resistance because the line runs through the rod rings before registering a bite.

Generally, a nine inch long butt indicator is about right for positioning above the rod handle, before the butt, or first rod ring. Some rods have badly positioned butt rings which are slightly too close to the handle. If this is the case, a shorter six inch indicator will work better, fitted between the butt ring and the first intermediate.

Any normal casting technique suits the butt indicator method. The rod should be positioned in two rests and pointed directly towards the end rig so it presents minimum resistance to a fish making off with the bait. The tip of the rod can be slightly submerged, or pushed quite deep under the water. The best setting is the one which keeps it most stable.

The indicator is adjusted by first tightening up the line to the end tackle. Then a little slack is given, allowing the indicator to fall back to a 45 degree angle with its base eye pointing upwards. Fixed in this way, both drop-back and normal forward bites will show up clearly. The butt indicator can be weighted to counteract slight flows, but mainly it is a stillwater method.

Quivertip The quivertip is by far the most popular bite indicator and at its most basic is readily available as a simple screw-in accessory marketed in several test curve ratings. This type simply tightens into a threaded tip eye – the only pre-requisite needed to fit them on leger, or shorter match rods.

Screw-in indicators vary by length and taper with the shorter, stiffer ones for fast flows and the longer, finer tapering designs for sensitive stillwater work. A good selection of different strength quivertips is required to deal with varying flow rates.

Multi-tip legering rods are sold with a selection of their own different actioned quivertips which simply plug into the top section of the rod. Some manufacturers are now making the base of these universal in diameter, so it is even possible to switch tips between rods in their ranges. In many ways, the multi-tip idea is superior because there is a far more natural curve where the quiver meets the blank proper.

A third quivertip option is the built-in, or permanently spliced tip. This probably provides the most satisfactory union between quivertip and blank but there are obvious limitations. The rod will only be suitable for conditions where the tip is capable of showing up bites making it a very specialist design.

When quivertipping, it is essential to position the rod at an angle to the end tackle. At close to medium range it needs to be about 35-40 degrees while for long range, a slightly lesser angle, something like 25-30 degrees, is better. More line must be picked up to set the hook at long range and that demands the strike must be made through a greater arc. There is no advantage to be gained by pointing the rod anywhere near where the end rig is positioned, because bites will not show up.

Stiffer-actioned quivertips are used for fast currents, because the flow would pull lighter ones around too far for tiny indications to register. The faster the water, the higher the rod must be positioned, in order to lift as much line out of the flow as possible. This prevents the current dragging the tackle out of place.

A downstream-pointing position is preferred when setting the quivertip rod up in rests. This makes for a better, more positive strike, working with the current to set the hook.

Swingtip In the right hands, this remains a good indicator for bream fishing on stillwaters or sluggish rivers and drains. The swingtip is very good for species like bream because it offers such little resistance – important in not spooking these fickle fish as they so often mouth a bait, before laboriously deciding whether or not to take it.

Another useful advantage of using this type of indicator is the way the rod can be positioned, pointing outwards towards the end tackle, giving a wider arc of striking distance. Again, this helps in setting the hook when fishing a bomb rig at long range.

Swingtips are manufactured from a variety of materials including sarkandas reed, plastic, cane, fibre-glass and carbon. Length and material determine the weight of the swingtip with lighter tips for calm conditions and no flow, heavier to combat drift, flow and wind.

The lighter swingtips made from sarkandas, plastic and cane can also be fitted with pre-formed, rigid rubber connectors to help combat drift and wind. With the light to medium tips, if this trick fails against worsening conditions, another way out is to fix a weight to the bottom of the tip. Lead wire is often used as a stabiliser.

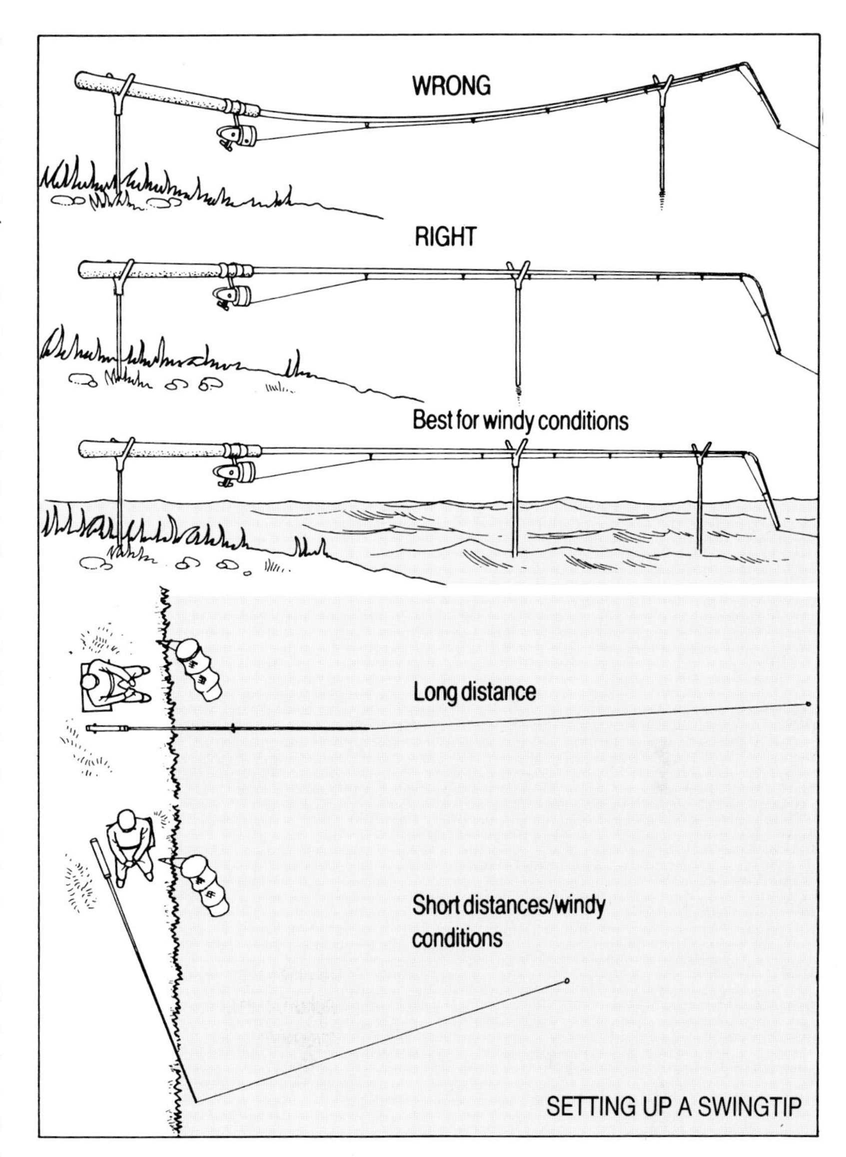

SETTING UP A SWINGTIP

More experienced swingtip anglers can often be seen using longer, reverse taper models up to 18 inches long to increase weight and stability. These are normally made from glass or carbon. The extra weight does not spoil the method as long as the tip is just heavy enough to counter the drift or flow.

Longer swingtips perform better with one or two intermediate eyes which help prevent tangles, by stopping the line from wrapping back round them. The angler soon knows when maximum length and weight of the swingtip has been reached because the cast becomes impeded.

Positioning of the rod is also important. The rests should be placed very carefully to prevent any bellying, or sag on the rod which will impair its striking power. Sometimes it is better to use three rests to really steady the rod when it is a bit windy.

When casting over 40 metres, it is best to position the rod pointing directly towards the terminal tackle

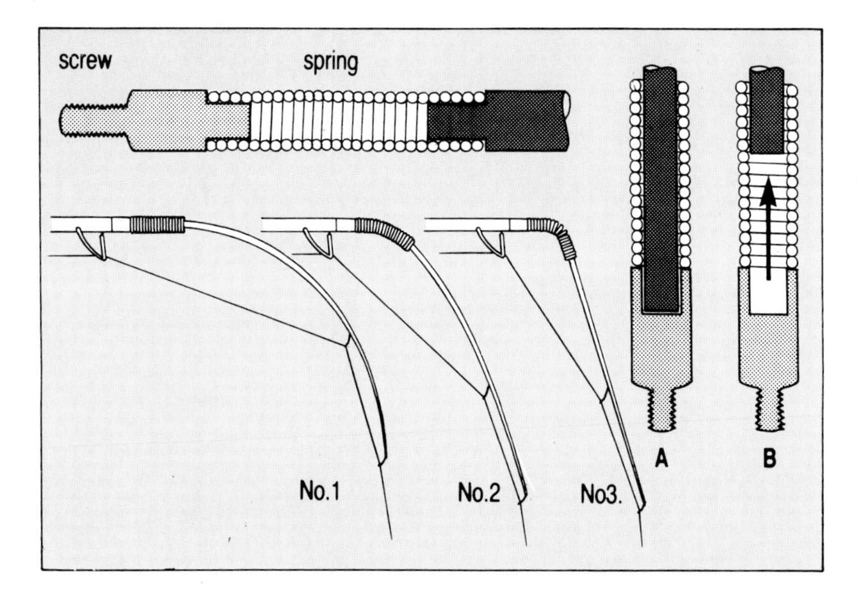

Above: **Springtip.**
1. Tip too soft and bends before spring.
2. Tip bending slightly in unison with the spring.
3. Tip bending before spring is affected. If you are buying a springtip go for type 3 action. With dual purpose spring / quiver you will probably have to settle for action 2. With action 1 you might as well be fishing with a quivertip, as the spring is only cosmetic.
A. Quivertip. Tip pushed home in the housing.
B. Springtip. Tip detached from housing.

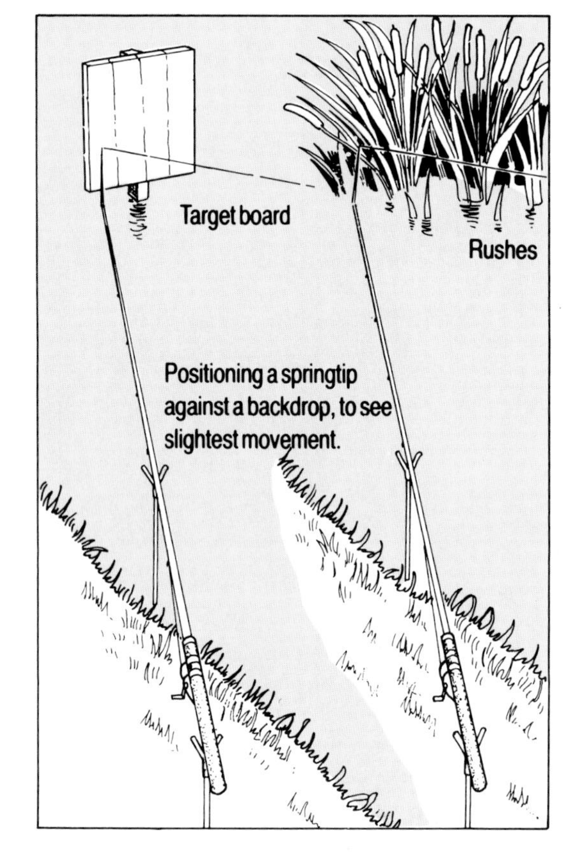

for full striking power. This is not so crucial for shorter distances, where much less effort is needed to set the hook and the rod can be fixed set more sideways on. Pick a swim with the wind on your back if possible to shield the sensitive tip as much as possible.

Springtip The springtip is intended for use on hard venues with little flow where bites are expected to be at a premium. It is adjustable and if weather conditions worsen you can adjust its sensitivity accordingly. Springtips look similar to quivertips but generally they are slightly stiffer in their action. But in actual use they become far more sensitive, because the whole tip leans over on a coiled spring which joins this indicator to its screw-in attachment.

It is something of a cross between a slightly tensioned swingtip and a sensitive quivertip. The spring gives a little stabilising resistance, but bends the split second you get a bite, magnifying the movement on the stiffer tip. If its sensitivity is impaired by a sudden gale, you can push the tip's base back through the centre of the spring, locking it into a housing. This bypasses the spring action completely making it into a normal quivertip.

The rod is best positioned sideways on, creating a 45 degree angle where the line leaves the top eye. This results in the slightest flicker showing up well – and far more dramatically than on a standard quivertip. This is why it is such a popular bad weather, or hard venue indicator.

For optimum effect, the springtip needs to be tightened into ever so slightly after the cast so it is just bending forward and will register drop-back bites. A dark background helps show more timid bites so a target board is a good idea.

Drop-off indicator Drop-off indicators have been increasingly popular since the early 1970s. Originally, they comprised a table tennis ball into which a hairgrip was glued so that the two ends of the grip stuck out at each side of the ball. String was attached to

Right: **Drop-off indicator with electronic alarm.**

the closed end of the grip and tethered to the back rod rest. The ball was then clipped to the reel line just below the reel spool and the line tightened to the bait. Following a bite, the line pulled clear of the clip and the indicator dropped off and fell to the ground.

All modern drop-off indicators developed from this principle. The string has now been replaced by a stiff bar, the clip on the ball greatly improved from the hairgrip, and an electronic alarm is often fitted to the end of the bar that attaches to the rod rest.

The disadvantages of the system are few, but real. One is that on rivers especially, a run may occur without registering either a pull-off or a drop-back bite and, in theory, this is possible in stillwaters too. All that happens is that the running pike maintains exactly the same distance from the rod and its run circumscribes a part of a circle – an arc.

Electronic There are two main types of electronic indicator – the antenna models and those which are operated by a rotating vane wheel. Both are screwed into a bank stick and serve as the front rod rest.

The vertically mounted antenna indicator emerges from the top of the box unit immediately underneath the rod. The line runs alongside and to the right of the antenna. As the line tightens following a bite, it applies pressure against the antenna pulling it to a more upright position and triggering the alarm.

This is activated by a make and break set of contacts at the base of the box which are set in the open position before the line tightens up. As the antenna moves, the contacts are brought together completing the circuit, sounding a buzzer and illuminating an LED. The internal contacts are adjustable for varying degrees of sensitivity.

The top selling indicator featuring the rotating vane wheel is the Optonic – an accessory that has achieved cult status in carp fishing. Once the rod is resting in the Vee of this indicator, the line is automatically directed into a slot which makes contact with the wheel. When a bite develops, the wheel rotates and a vane on its spindle will cut through the beam of a photo electric cell or bring a magnet and reed switch into contact to complete the circuit. Again, this activates a buzzer and LED.

The rotating vane wheel will sense movement in either direction so if a carp swims towards the angler the line will fall slack causing a dropback on the monkey climb system and sounding the buzzer. Some models have latching facilities with a second LED remaining illuminated for several seconds after a bite has occurred. This is helpful when only a small amount of line is taken and the run does not fully develop. It allows the angler using several rods to rcognise immediately which one produced the slight movement.

The rotating vane wheels are made in varying sensitivities depending on the number of blades fitted on the spindle. The more blades, the more sensitive the Optonic. In blustery conditions it gives you the option of switching over to a minimum two vane wheel to overcome false bleeps caused by the wind rocking the set-up or catching the line.

Compact Optonics are self-contained units but it's possible to fit extension leads and a sounder box so the angler can sit in the comfort of a bivvy and instantly hear a run developing.

■ Bite off

This is sometimes a problem in carp fishing when the baited hook is taken beyond the pharyngeal or throat teeth and the trace bitten through. It should be avoided at all costs but is rarely experienced with modern hair-rig methods.

The danger time is when fishing with mass baits which persuade the carp to gorge themselves in a small, heavily baited area. A shorter hook link – usually less than six inches – should solve the problem but if the bite-offs persist a frightener will be needed.

This consists of a two inch length of Biro tube mounted lengthways across the hook link so about an inch is protruding either side. This is fixed between two and four inches from the hook and

Left: **Optonic with ears to hold the rod steady in high winds.**

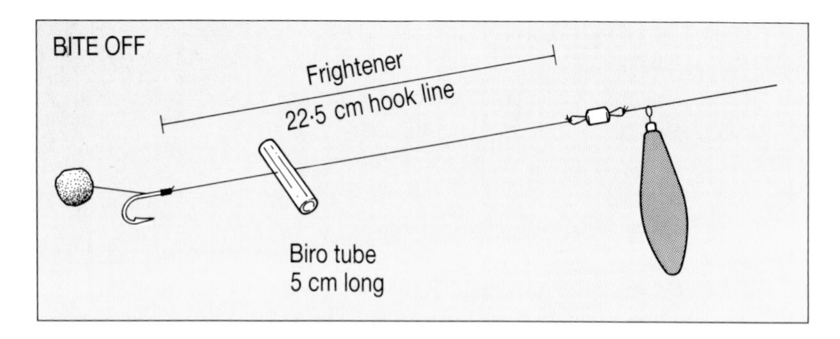

when the bait is sucked in will hit up against the carp's mouth causing it to panic.

■ Bivvy

The long session carp angler needs protection from the elements and the bivvy provides just that. Basically, it's an umbrella with an overwrap that pins to the ground right around the perimeter providing complete protection from wind and rain. The other alternative is to purchase bivvy sides which are attached around the umbrella edge with velcro and eyelets. These are not as stable as the overwrap but are useful to carry in the bottom of the rucksack for emergencies.

Bivvys permanently fixed to the umbrella to form a one-piece unit are becoming increasingly popular with long session anglers.

■ Blank

Most modern rods are made from carbon cloth which is cut out into pre-determined shapes and wrapped around tapered steel mandrels which are then baked. The process is highly complex, particularly if it involves a mixture of materials. The basic hollow tubes which emerge from this process are known as the rod blanks.

A roomy bivvy with the side walls permanently welded to the edge of the umbrella.

But a plain blank offered for sale without rings would normally have the ferrules or spigots already fitted and perhaps an inserted parallel tube at the handle end. Corks or duplon would be needed to form the finished handle.

The term blank still applies if the handle and reel fittings are already in place. It is possible to purchase both plain and customised blanks, but the transformation into a finished rod only occurs once the rings have been whipped on and varnished in place.

■ Blanket weed

Blanket weed, or cot, is a direct result of high nutrient values giving a rich food supply for this alga. The menace often completely coats the bottom of water shallower than eight feet. This suppresses insect life, bloodworm sites, and retards macrophyte growth. It is an ecology destroyer, and there is little doubt that the bream fishing on many Fenland rivers and drains has declined simply because the shoals do not now have the acreage of muddy bottom to browse over. See Algae.

■ Bleak

This surface-loving fish grows to only a few ounces and anglers' catches are usually dominated by fish weighing about half-an-ounce each. They occur in vast shoals in rivers and are quite widely distributed in England and Wales. However, they seem to be absent in Scotland and the Lake District, as well as Ireland.

They fall most readily to tiny baits on tiny hooks, fished shallowly or down to mid-water. The bites are often like lightning and the technique for hitting them seems to vary from day to day.

The bleak has a distinct green sheen down its silvery flanks. Their diet is largely aquatic and airborne insect life, though they eat some plant matter if it is carried on the current as plankton. The British record is 4 oz 4 dr and was set on the River Monnow, Monmouthshire in 1982.

■ Blockend feeder

The blockend deposits loose feed directly around the hookbait and is essentially a small plastic cylinder with exit holes. It is totally enclosed with a removable cap at one or both ends. This type of feeder is exclusively for maggots, hemp and casters and may have varying sized exit holes, for different rates of feed. See Swimfeeders.

■ Bloodworm

See Baits.

■ Blown bait

A bait that has become unacceptable to carp. It happens when a single bait gains popularity on a water with a high percentage of the anglers using it virtually exclusively. Most of the stock eventually get caught on the favoured offering – some of them several times – and gradually the carp associate it with danger and actively avoid it. But when baits become less effective and are forgotten for two or three seasons they can be reintroduced.

■ Bobbin

The most basic form of bite indicator is a dough bobbin formed from a piece of bread or paste moulded into a ball and squeezed onto the line between reel and butt ring. Suspended on a little slack line, the bobbin will show up lift and drop-back bites when legering or free-lining.

Bobbins only work on stillwaters in calm conditions. It is possible to purchase plastic ones which clip on the line and release easily on the strike. These have a facility to take extra weight to combat drift and can be tethered to a bank stick to avoid losing them when the strike is made.

■ Bodied waggler

Floats with a buoyant, bulbous base and long stem which carry plenty of shot for fishing at range. See Floats.

■ Boilie

See Baits; Carp fishing.

■ Bolt rig

A self-hooking rig popular in carp fishing. The baited hook is tied to a short hook link between five and ten inches in length and a free running or semi-fixed, heavy leger weight of more than two ounces run directly on the main line. The line between leger weight and rod tip is kept very tight and usually secured under a line clip.

This creates considerable resistance which the carp feels immediately it moves off with the bait because it has very little freedom of movement. It takes fright, bolts off and hooks itself giving a blistering run.

The fast darting bleak feeds chiefly on the surface.

■ Boron

Rod manufacturers found boron both strengthened and mellowed the action of carbon rod blanks but it is now chiefly confined to the production of fly rod blanks.

■ Bottom-end float

Any type of waggler float which is attached to the reel line by its bottom eye only is described as a bottom-ender. Normally these floats are locked on the line with large shot for security and to make them cast well. Rarely does a bottom-end float have less than two thirds its weight loading trapping it on the line. Any less causes an imbalance and results in tangles on the cast. Distance is also sacrificed.

Bottom-end floats are the first choice for running line tackle on stillwater venues because it allows the line to be totally submerged all the way back to the rod tip. This helps beat drift and keeps the tackle stationary, or at least stable. When the line has been submerged with a bottom-ender, a sideways strike is necessary to set the hook.

On flat calm days or when fishing flowing water, a floating line can be used with bottom-end float designs. This allows a fractionally clearer upward strike and a little more tackle control when trotting.

■ Bow wave

A carp moving just below the surface sets up a noticeable wake. The activity is most common in summer and is at its most spectacular when a fish is hooked on the surface with a floater. Bow waving is also common at spawning time as the fish race around in small groups.

■ Bow method

The bow method is normally used when feeder fishing on running water. It is a way of feeding line out

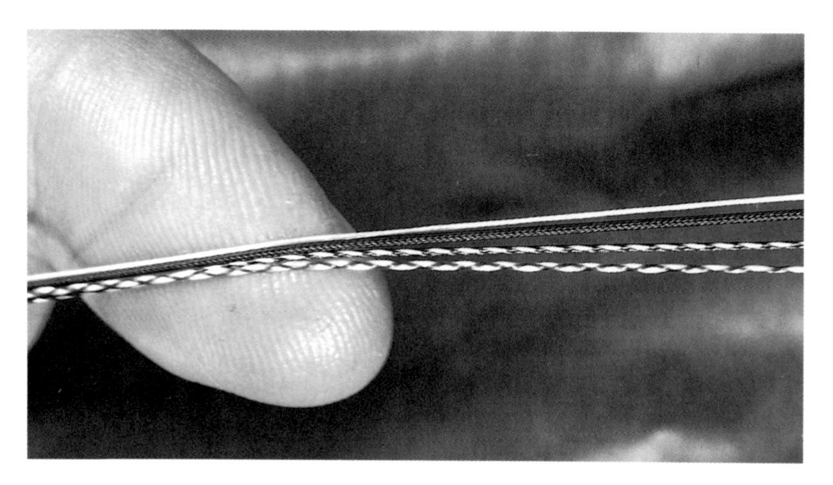

Choice of hook link materials for carp (from bottom): two braids from the Silkworm stable, Dacron and multi-strand.

into the water to reduce the effect of flow or water pressure on the tackle. See Legering.

■ Braids

These have made a huge impact in carp fishing during the last decade as hook links. Materials include nylons, polyesters and Terylenes as well as other high performance synthetics. Numerous fine filaments are braided together to form a strong and supple hook link which out-performs more rigid lengths of nylon.

The tighter the braid, the stiffer it becomes. This is known as 'picks per inch' and varies between 12 on the very supple braids to 40 on the slightly stiffer ones. It is possible to braid super soft and high abrasion resistant fibres together to produce super reliable, supple hook links.

■ Brandlings

See Baits.

■ Breadflake

See Baits.

■ Breaking strain

The pressure which a fishing line will withstand before it breaks, expressed in pounds and percentages of a pound.

But anglers are now thinking more in terms of diameters following the introduction of new, low diameter lines. A finer diameter line for any given breaking strain offers clear advantages in deceiving fish. But it is also possible to take out extra insurance against breakages by selecting the same thickness of low diameter line as would normally be used – but with the benefit of a higher breaking strain.

Referring to monofilaments by breaking strain will be a hard habit to break because standard lines like 1.1 lb, 1.7 lb and 2.6 lb are still extremely popular for hook lengths.

An accurate 3 lb line should withstand 3 lb of pressure being applied in its dry state, but may lose several ounces when knotted or wet. For these reasons it is best to regard breaking strain as a rough guide, or to use it together with diameters, which should be clearly marked on the spool. See Line.

■ Bream

There are two species of bream in British waters, the bronze and silver. The bronze bream, which may exceed 16 lb in weight, is distributed over much of the British Isles, occurring in many types of water, including trout streams. But the silver bream, possibly exceeding 3 lb at a maximum, is restricted to eastern England and to the slower moving rivers, drains and stillwaters.

The distinction between the two is important. Small bronze bream are rather pale in colour and are often incorrectly called silver bream. Silver bream, for their part, are rarely recognised for what they are by anglers, and are usually dismissed as hybrids. The main features that distinguish the two species are as follows:

1. For fish of the same size the eye of the silver bream is much larger.
2. The silver bream's colouring is rather like that of the bleak, being green dorsally. But larger silvers, over 1 lb, have a dark green to brown back and a distinctly blue hue to the flanks seen through the overall silver colouration.
3. Bronze bream have a substantial mucous layer, and silver bream, in most waters, relatively little slime.
4. It is often said that the silver bream is more slender than the bronze. This needs qualification. At equal weights, say 1 lb, the silver bream is closer in outline to a roach or rudd, rather than having the depth of a bronze bream at that weight.

In addition, there are slight differences in the scale counts, and the silver bream has fewer branched rays in the bream-like anal fin. But different authorities give different measurements, so these cannot be heavily relied upon.

The throat teeth are different in the two breams, the silver having two rows of denticles and the bronze just one.

Two-tone bream The characteristic bronze flanks of the larger of the two species appears when the fish is between 1 lb and 2 lb. When the fish are in excess of

10 lb, every angler's dream fish, the colour can be a deep, rich, burnished brown.

Two-tone bream, in which one quarter of the fish is pale coloured, are more common than in any other species but this does not seem to otherwise affect the health of the individual.

The bream is a mud-grubber par excellence. As it feeds its mouth parts extend in a conspicuous tube, and they suck and blow at the soft sediment. They eat all forms of insect life, some plant material such as algae, and during the spawning period are carnivorous and cannibalistic.

The British bronze bream record was set at 16 lb 6 oz on a private Staffordshire fishery in 1986. The silver record of 15 oz came from a fishery in Suffolk in 1988.

■ Bristle

Bristle is another term for antenna. The fine nylon sight tips on pole floats are commonly known as pole float bristles. Thin tipped running line floats are usually called antennas.

■ Bubblers

Carp rooting in the bottom for food release gases locked in the mud and expel air through their gill covers. The effect at the surface is like a miniature witch's cauldron! A bait cast into the path of a bubbler gives a good chance of a take.

■ Bulk shot

When split-shot are pushed or grouped together in order to get the hookbait down fast, they are known as bulk shot. The term is also used when placing the majority of a waggler's weighting around its base. These are really locking shot but in this form they can also be said to be bulk-shotting the float.

■ Bullhead

Although still widely found in the British Isles the bullhead's habitat has been seriously depleted, due to abstraction partially reducing current flow, and excess nutrients causing a slimy coating of algae over the pebbles it needs to live under.

The shape of the bullhead – large, flattish head and wide mouth – is ideal for squeezing under stones where it hides for much of the day. Another common name for it, in country districts, is the Miller's Thumb, referring to the broad, flattened head. It is a savage predator, eating anything that moves, up to a size fairly close to its own. Once it gets its mouth clamped on them there is little chance of the prey escaping. They are cannibalistic at times.

The bronze bream shoals tightly and has a reputation for toying with the bait.

The mouth is probably bigger in proportion to the fish than any other freshwater species, including the catfish. The other striking feature of the fish is its huge pectoral fins, which it often uses for walking on the bottom, and propping itself up. There is a British record for this species – just 1 oz.

■ Butt foam

A piece of foam wedged in the butt ring to create resistance on the reel line when fishing over gravel bars and across weed beds. Without it, the line may fall slack following a take and a running fish could drag it over rough bars or tangle it in weed. The foam will keep the line taut and high in the water.

There are times when a hook will bounce out of a carp's mouth when it slows down after making a fast run. The use of foam on these occasions maintains constant pressure on the line and in theory improve the chances of retaining a hookhold.

■ Butt indicator

See Bite indicators.

■ Buzzer bar

A screw-in support bar for the rods which is mounted on a single bank stick. It simplifies the set-up by cutting down on the number of bank sticks and rod rests when fishing two rods or more. The buzzer bars are used in pairs with the front one being slightly wider than the rear to achieve a straighter line from rod tip to leger weight.

Stainless steel bars are more durable than aluminium and they are all fitted with three eighths of an inch BSF threads to accept rod rest heads or electronic indicators.

C

■ Cage feeder

The cage feeder is an open-end design for use with groundbait. It is more versatile than conventional perspex feeders because its wire frame will hold very sloppy groundbait mixes on the cast. See Swimfeeders.

■ Carbon fibre

The majority of fishing rods are made from carbon fibre. The slim, lightweight blanks produce an overall action and feel which is superior to any other material. It is also favoured for top quality, lightweight poles which retain rigidity over long lengths. There are some very good carbon composite rods at a budget price for those seeking an inexpensive entry into the sport.

As a general guide, the more expensive the carbon rod or pole, the higher the carbon content. The precise carbon content is often specified on top-of-the-range models and it can make a huge difference. A 12 foot fibre-glass match rod may weigh as much as a pound – a real handful for a day's fishing! – while a carbon composite could halve that weight. But a top class, full-carbon match rod may only register 4 oz, a featherweight by comparison!

Carbon improves poles in the same way but always treat it with respect, especially near power lines where it can turn into a killer. Never fish with carbon fibre rods or poles within 20 metres of high voltage overhead wires. Carbon is a highly conductive material and electricity can arc several feet.

The regular scale pattern on a gravel pit common carp.

■ Carp

The wild carp was first introduced to the UK over 500 years ago and reared in monastery stewponds for food. There are few true wildies left today because of inter-breeding with other strains. The wild carp has similar-sized scales covering its entire body in uniform lines. It is slender, chub-shaped and seldom exceeds 10 lb. Unless you are certain of a lake's stocking history there is no guarantee that wild carp exist in the water. Under-nourished commons tend to get mistaken for wild carp.

There are probably fewer than a dozen waters in which true wildies have survived. Most are tiny farm ponds that have been unfished for years and where access is difficult or impossible. Wild carp will make the most of any natural food source available, the most common being bloodworm. It is supplemented with pea snails, shrimp, crayfish and other small crustaceans.

Any weed or broad-leaved plant will be exploited and they certainly have a liking for Canadian pondweed. It's not known if they actually eat the weed or suck at the insects clinging to the leaves. Wild carp grow slowly but selective breeding produced the King carp from which the following fast-growing strains have evolved.

Common carp The nearest equivalent in terms of appearance to the wildie. It has the same uniform scales covering its entire body but it attains much heavier weights and its body shape is much deeper.

Mirror carp The mirror has scales scattered haphazardly over its body and they vary in shape and size. Larger groups are clumped around the root of the tail and invariably there's a line along the fish's back. The linear mirror has two perfect rows of scales on either side of its body. One runs along the back from just behind the gill cover to the root of the tail while the other follows the whole length of the lateral line.

The fully-scaled mirror has scales covering its whole body but they are much larger than those on the common carp and not a uniform size.

Leather carp A strain that is also known as the nude carp because it is completely devoid of scales.

Crucian carp Much smaller in size than the King carp and completely different in appearance. It is a shorter, plumper looking fish with a high back and no barbules around its mouth. Any crucian over 4 lb is an excellent specimen. They are delicate feeders and the best baits are maggots, small pieces of breadflake or a single grain of sweetcorn.

Grass carp A rarity in the UK and the only water containing grass carp that offers reasonable access is the Leisure Sport Horton fishery to the west of London. They are chub-like in appearance and were originally introduced to private, enclosed waters on an experimental basis by Ministry scientists. They feed extensively on weed and were regarded as possible replacements for chemical treatment on waters clogged by rampant weed growth.

They grow to 30 lb on the Continent but a ten-pounder is a specimen. Grass carp are known to take a wide range of conventional baits including maggots and boilies. Their upturned mouth suggests they are primarily surface feeders.

Carp fishing

The sheer size and fighting ability of carp has made them Britain's most prized coarse fish. They are widely distributed throughout the country and thrive in just about every type of water from fast flowing rivers to silted pools. But they appear to do best in gravel pits, especially in the south. The abundance of natural food and good quality water in these freshly-dug pits results in fast-growing fish that attain their maximum size.

Carp scaling more than 30 lb are now commonplace and 40-pounders are captured every season. But there has only ever been one fish over 50 lb – the record-breaking 51 lb 8 oz specimen captured by Chris Yates from Redmire Pool.

Behaviour and location On many waters there's little difference between catch rates in summer and winter so the whole season can be devoted to carp fishing.

Top: **A mirror carp captured in early winter positively glows with good health.**

Above: **It's obvious why the leather is also known as a nude carp.**

A tubby crucian hooked on maggots.

There's nothing complex about the basic attractions of carp fishing. The fish run big and fight all the way into the net.

Spawning usually occurs around the end of June to the beginning of July and in a hot summer will be repeated several times. Water temperature is the trigger and spawning usually takes place in some of the shallowest parts of a fishery, particularly where there is good weed cover.

For several weeks running up to spawning, carp can be positively sexed from their external features. Males develop tubercles around the head, gill cover and pectoral fins and are rough to the touch around the head area. The tubercles resemble thousands of tiny, greyish white spots. Other carp caught at this time which have plump stomachs and no tubercles are almost certainly females. During the rigours of spawning, carp inflict damage on themselves and are in their worst condition.

In the warm months, the carp spends a great deal of time on or near the surface giving the chance to select out fish and present a floating bait. As summer draws on, the carp start to regain lost body weight and their spawning injuries such as split fins, body scratches and even missing scales start to heal.

In autumn, the water temperatures are falling and the carp feed for much longer periods. This is the time when bottom fishing with boilies is most productive. Weight gain is at its highest and the carp are moving into tip-top condition.

Towards the end of autumn and the onset of winter, the carp reach their heaviest weights of the year. Their colours are very vivid and they're unrecognisable as the tatty specimens caught in early summer.

They feed less each day in winter and seek out safe sanctuary areas of the lake such as beneath fallen trees and around dying weed beds. Location at this time of year must be spot on, rigs selected with great care and baiting kept to a minimum. The fact that the fish's activity has slowed down with the drop in water temperature, makes them more vulnerable to parasite infestation. By the end of winter they look drab and almost grey in appearance.

Then Spring arrives again and the natural food larders are replenished – and so, too, is the carp's body weight. They return to pristine condition and the females, in particular, pack on weight as the eggs inside their bodies mature.

Tackle and accessories Carbon rods of 11 ft or 12 ft and test curves ranging from 1 lb 8 oz through to 3 lb meet the requirements in carp fishing. A soft, all-through action rod is best suited to close-range work with light lines of around 8 lb matched to the lighter test curves. In the heavier test curves, lines of 10 lb and more will be needed, stepping up for heave and hold tactics when fishing tight against snags.

Fast taper rods are ideal for launching baits to long distance and it's unusual for this type of rod to have a test curve of less than 2 lb. For ultimate distance work with heavy leads up to three ounces, a shock leader of a higher breaking strain than the main line must be used to avert crack-offs. A minimum of 15 lb breaking strain and a leader of at least three rod lengths is considered safe.

Fixed spool reels with long, conical spools give perfect line lay tapering from the front to the rear, and are fine for long-distance casting. Smoothly-operating rear drags are a common feature and the Baitrunner and free spool systems have been a major breakthrough. These make it possible to fish with a closed bale arm while the spool is in a free-running mode. A quick turn of the reel handle re-engages the spool and because the bale arm remains closed throughout the operation it is the ultimate system to ensure tangle-free operation.

A 36 or 42 inch span landing net is required for carp with a sturdy six foot pole and deep, soft meshing for safely lifting the carp from the water to the bank.

The rods spend most of the time sitting in rests waiting for the next take and the set-up must be rock steady. Quality bank sticks and buzzer bars are essential and for hard, impenetrable banks, rod pods make life a lot easier. Monkey climbs provide a visual check to a developing run and the electronic buzzer signals audible indication, allowing the angler to look away from his tackle and scan the lake for signs of fish.

Basic set ups

1. To fish with an open bale arm, the monkey climb needles are positioned about two inches in front of the reel spool. The tops of the needles must touch the rod itself to ensure the monkey body is trapped on the needle. After casting out and tightening up to the lead, the line is trapped in the monkey climber clip and the bale arm opened. The weight of the indicator will prevent line spilling uncontrollably from the spool.

When a take develops the monkey rises up the needle, pulling line from the open spool. With a fast take, the monkey body will hover on the needle just below the spool. If the runs stops, the indicator drops down the needle, trapping and controlling the line in the process. Lifting the rod from the rests to execute a strike automatically pulls the line free from the monkey climb system.

2. The monkey climb needles are moved forward to within two inches of the electronic bite alarms on the front rests when fishing with a closed bale arm off the clutch or with a Baitrunner type reel. The needles do not need to touch the rod because the line is now under control with the bale arm closed. The Baitrunner or clutch is set with just the right amount of tension to allow line to be pulled relatively freely from the spool. The monkey body is allowed to drop to the bottom of the needle by rotating the spool and releasing line. When a take occurs, it will rise to the top and stay there as line is given by the clutch or Baitrunner.

3. A similar system can be used for inducing the carp to bolt on a very tight line or for drop-back indication on a semi-fixed lead. The monkey climb needles are positioned just in front of the electronic bite alarms as before but the line is held in a clip attached to the rod handle. The taut line between the clip and leger weight keeps the monkey climb at the top of the needle.

Top: **The open bale set-up with the indicators at the bottom of the needles.**

Above: **Closed bales with the needles forward and indicators held high.**

When fishing with a semi-fixed lead and the carp moves towards the angler, the take is signalled by the monkey climb body dropping down the needle. But if it moves away it will feel the resistance of the line held in the clip, causing it to bolt and resulting in a screaming run. For this type of dropback set-up it is an advantage to use a much heavier monkey climb body. This takes up the slack line much quicker when a fish heads towards the bank after taking the bait.

Bottom rigs The basic set-up for fishing with a bottom bait for carp is relatively straightforward. The leger weight is used free-running on the main line with a bead acting as a buffer against the hook link swivel. The length of the nylon or braided hook link varies between 5 and 18 inches. Shorter links are ideally suited to hard bottomed lakes or gravel pits and longer ones to softer, silty bottoms or fishing over bottom weed.

A hair rig is tied to a suitably sized hook. As a rule of thumb, a size 10 matches well with a 14 mm boilie, a size 8 to a 16 mm and size 6 with 18 mm. If a larger hook is selected for a snaggy swim then double up on the hookbait. For example, use two 16 mm baits with a size 4.

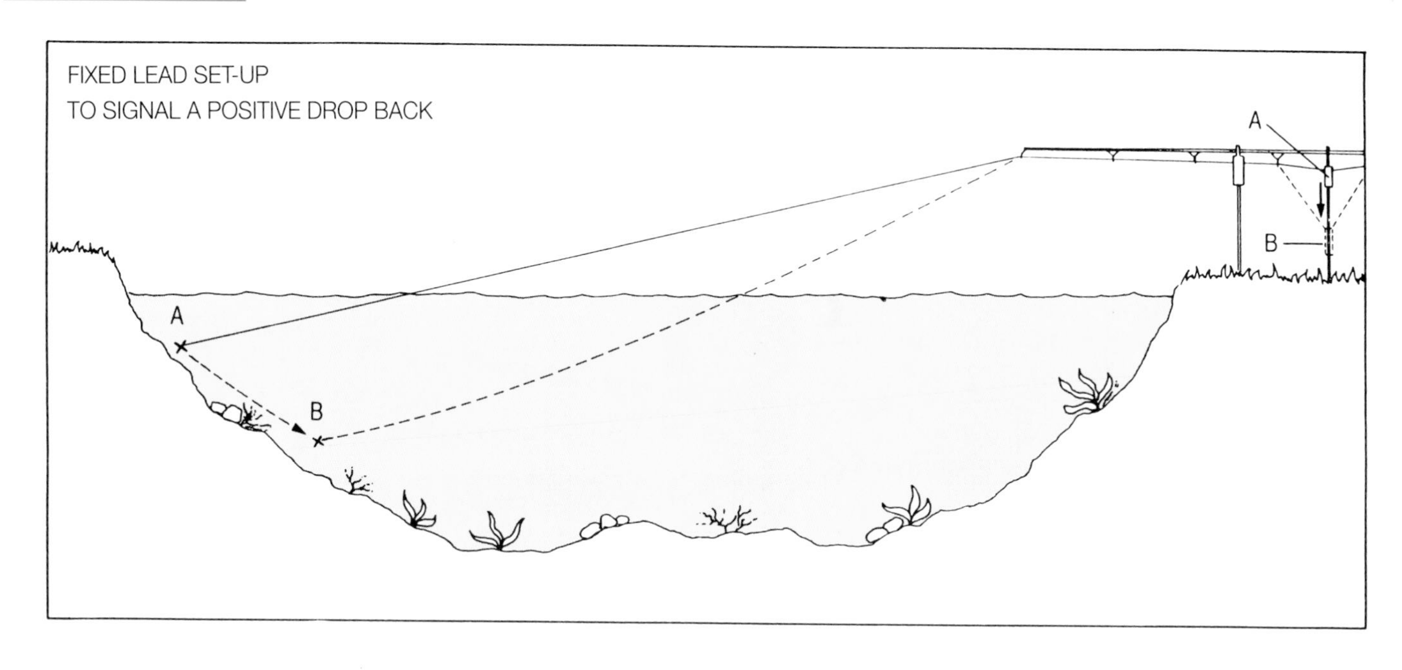

The softest hook links have parallel strands of fine filaments and are highly prone to tangling during the cast. This is overcome by introducing a length of rig tubing on the main line just above the hook link swivel. Weights with a large enough swivel eye can be wedged on the tubing about an inch or so back from one end. The main line is threaded through the tubing with the weight nearest the hook end and then the hook link attached in the normal way.

The length of the anti-tangle tubing must be slightly greater than the hook link, again for tangle-free casting. The lead will fly through the air followed by the stiffened tube which pushes the hook link out to one side.

Below right: **Simple free-running leger with a bead buffer.**

Below: **Helicopter anti-tangle rig with rotating hook link.**

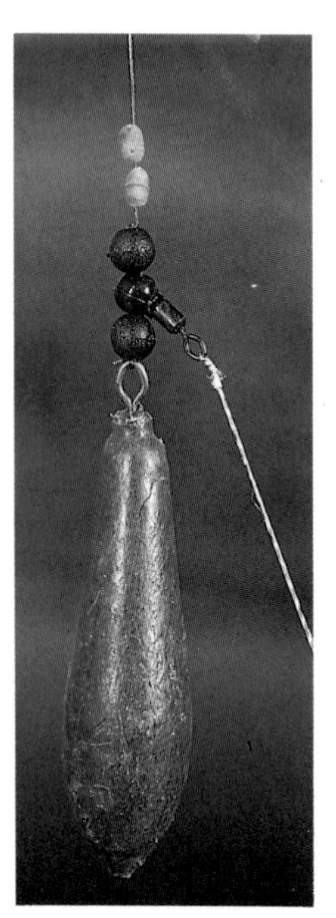

Another anti-tangle system for use with the softest hook links is known as the helicopter or rotary rig. This time the weight is tied directly to the end of the reel line. A swivel bead with the hook link attached sits directly above the weight with beads either side for easy rotation. It is trapped in position just above the weight by a couple of rubber float stops.

If the bottom is excessively silty and there's a danger of the hook link being buried then an additional pair of float stops are inserted between the leger weight and the bottom bead allowing the hook link to be positioned further back up the line. This will probably be no more than six or nine inches. Always leave a small gap between the beads to ensure they turn freely. The helicopter is classed as a semi-fixed lead and this must be borne in mind when deciding on the bite indicator set-up as dropback bites are almost a certainty.

Surface rigs The surface controller rig is most popular when fishing with small floating baits – particularly pet food biscuits. The bait is far too light to be cast out on its own but the controller in its various sizes means distances of up to 75 yards are easily reached.

If the main line is being tied direct to the hook, it is first passed through a swivel mounted in the top of the controller which is then trapped by a leger stop fixed either side for short to medium range fishing.

For longer range or where a different hook link material is being used then the controller rests against the swivel of the link with a float stop or leger stop holding it in place. When carp wise up to

Left: **Chum Mixer floater on a supple, floss hair.**

At its most basic, a boilie is simply paste rolled into a ball and dropped in boiling water for a few minutes to give it a hard, protective skin. Just about any form of food can be liquidised, ground up, mixed with binders and attractors and made into a boilie. Pre-mixed ingredients are available to roll your own and there's a superb range of ready-made boilies in handy packs. These are the most convenient option as shelf-life packets are simply left in the tackle bag between trips – or frozen bags stored in the freezer. Shelf-life and frozen boilies are made in 18 mm, 14 mm, 10 mm and 8 mm diameters.

Favourite boilie flavours that have proved themselves repeatedly over the years include Maple, Tutti Frutti, Peanut Pro, Honey Yucatan, Black Cherry, Blue Cheese, Strawberry Yoghurt, Peach Melba and Caribbean Cocktail.

nylon hook links, the multi-stranded materials take over as the fine filaments are difficult to detect.

To present a dog biscuit, first drill a hole through the middle and feed through a dental floss hair which is attached to the eye and the bend of the hook. Any free play between the hook and the biscuit must be kept to a minimum for the best presentation.

Eventually, the carp may also grow wary of this rig and the next alternative is the beachcaster set-up. With this system, no hook link touches the water at all. Instead, it is suspended from the main line which runs from an anchored pike float through to the rod tip.

The beachcaster rig is made up by tying a leger weight of at least two ounces to the end of the main line. A pike float is fixed on the line between one and two feet overdepth. About 18 inches to two feet above the float, a three-way swivel is inserted into the main line and a mono hook link tied to the central eye.

The length of the hook link is critical. It must be adjusted so that it only just touches the water when the line is taut between the pike float and the rod tip which is propped upright against a long rest.

There are purpose-made rod rests for beachcaster-style fishing. Clearly, the higher the rod is off the ground the more acute the angle of the line and the greater the distance which can be fished. About 70 yards out in eight feet of water is the maximum.

Baits Boilies are the No.1 bait in carp fishing because they are selective and cannot be taken by most smaller, unwanted species. Being perfectly round, they catapult extremely well with great accuracy. The boilie can be any colour, flavour and size you want if you make your own.

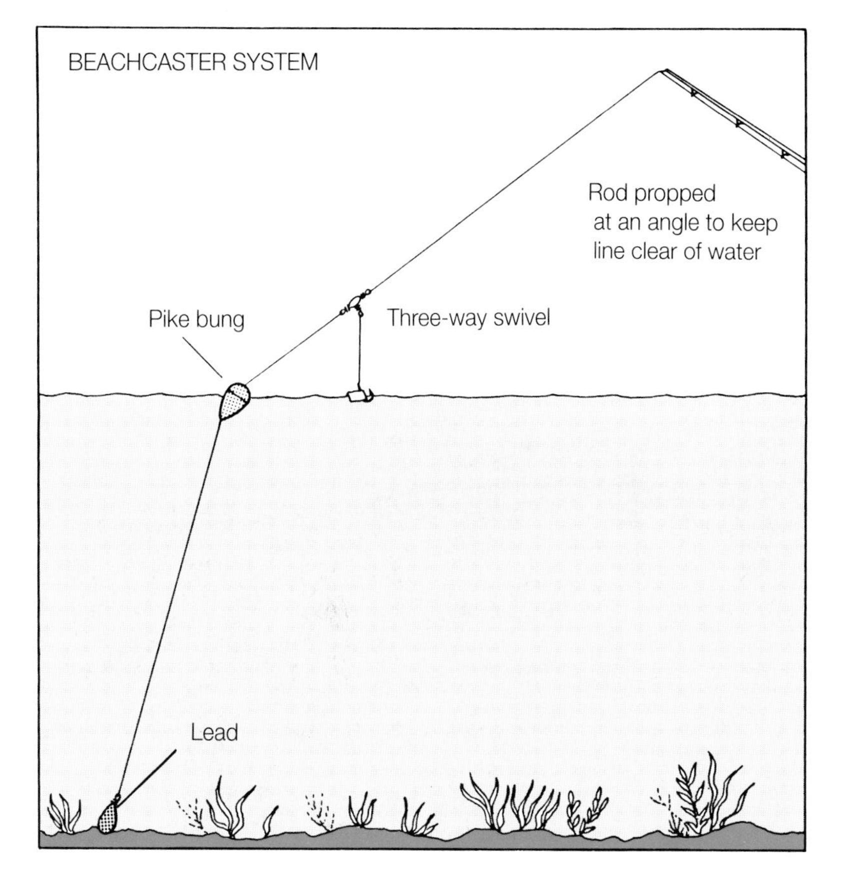

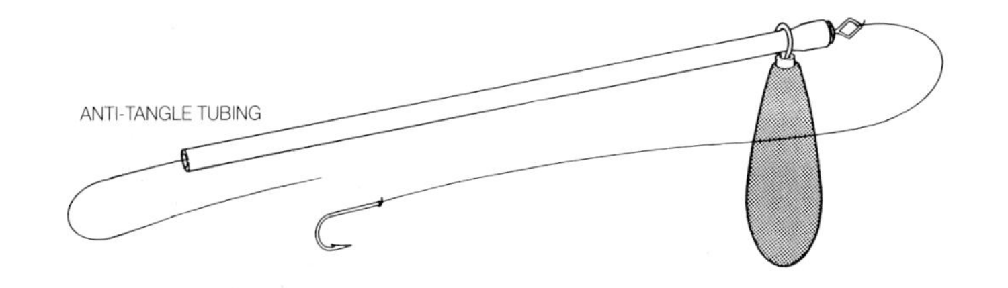

Starter boilie recipes A high nutritional bait consists mainly of milk powders and a good starter recipe for a protein bait could contain the following ingredients: 5 oz casein; 2 oz lactalbumin; 1.5 oz calcium caseinate; 1 oz gluten to act as a binder and 0.5 oz Equivite which is a mineral supplement.

Once all the dry ingredients have been thoroughly mixed together, they are added to beaten eggs with colours and flavours. Pay attention to the dosage levels and follow the maker's recommendations. The ball of paste is rolled out into long sausages of equal diameter and it is a good idea to rub margarine or lard between the palms to prevent the mix sticking to your hands.

Break a couple of paste slugs from a sausage and roll between the palms to produce two boilies simultaneously. Repeat the process until all the strips are used up. The next step is to give the boilies a hard skin in a saucepan of boiling water. It is important that the water never goes off the boil otherwise the baits will soak it up like a sponge and become mushy.

The easiest method is to immerse just a few baits at a time in a flour sieve. Give them about two minutes in the boiling water before shaking off the excess water and allowing the hot baits to dry off on a towel. Once they have cooled down, store them in a plastic bag in the freezer.

Bird foods and bird food supplements also make good ingredients for HNV baits. A typical recipe could comprise the following: 5 oz Nectar Blend; 2 oz PTX; 1.5 oz Robin Red; 1 oz gluten and 0.5 oz wheatgerm.

As previously, the mixed powders are added to beaten eggs and the result is a paste that has a distinctive smell and taste all of its own. Initially, it will not require any extra flavour or attractor. But as its efficiency falls away it can be perked up again with additional flavours and enhancers.

Another category of HNV baits is based around fish meals. A good recipe is 3 oz whitefish meal; 2 oz shrimp meal (preferably red); 2 oz anchovy or razorfish meal; 2 oz gluten and 1 oz Codlivine. Obviously, this recipe is heavy in oils and unless emulsifiers are added fish meals are better used in higher water temperatures to obtain most benefit. Sweet flavours such as peach melba and strawberry yoghurt are now being mixed with the fish meals and the results have been devastating on some waters.

The final category of mixes could loosely be described as carbohydrates with a good recipe based around 4 oz semolina; 4 oz ground rice; 1 oz gluten and 1 oz Vitamealo. It is again added to eggs but as the mix is bland it's essential to use good flavours, sweeteners and enhancers.

Labour saving rolling devices are available to take some of the tedium out of making your own.

Natural baits Maggots are probably the most instant carp bait and introduced in large quantities they'll send the fish into a feeding frenzy. They are useful for stalking individual fish or when the going gets tough in winter. Maggots are normally fished in multiples directly on a small hook or on a hair with a large hook close to snags.

Red maggots work particularly well when the carp are preoccupied on bloodworm. In summer, floating maggots account for good catches when the fish are basking in the surface layers.

Brandlings or redworms can be used for stalking bubblers with a float and a freelined lob draped over a lily pad has captured many fine carp.

Meats Luncheon meat used straight from the can has been a consistent catcher of carp for many years. It is cut into cubes of varying size up to one inch square and mounted directly on the hook or a hair with a baiting needle. Over silty bottoms, two and three inch long slivers of meat are worth trying, cut so they are about half an inch wide and an eighth of an inch thick. Meat rests gently on the bottom and can be made to float by gently frying both sides in a shallow pan for a couple of minutes.

Cheeses Hard cheeses are cubed and fished the same way as luncheon meat. Soft varieties are best made into a paste by mixing with a little rice powder. Mould the paste around the hook leaving the point free and fish it on a hair-rig.

Pastes Liquidised pilchards or sardines make an excellent paste with a binder added. Fine semolina or rice powder in equal proportions with calcium caseinate or casilan produce a nice, smooth bait. Trout pellets and pet biscuits can be ground up into a fine powder, using a coffee mill but again require a binder. With all ground powders, water must be added to hold the paste together.

Handling and weighing Carp should never be allowed to touch anything that is dry. It is essential to douse all the weighing equipment with water before handling the fish. The rate at which water percolates through weigh slings and sacks should be checked. Once they have been filled with water, they should empty in seconds and not minutes. Some sacks are fitted with mesh corners to stop the carp sucking the soft sack material into its mouth.

Unhooking mats are needed to lay out the fish for unhooking and recent examples include a model with inflatable sides which effectively traps the carp on the cushioned base.

Weigh bags should be zeroed in on the scales before the carp is carefully placed inside. Always suspend the scales from the support eye or bar – never clasp the body as this can give an inaccurate recording.

When moving the carp from landing net to unhooking mat, keep it as low as possible to the ground and try to support it in your hands. If the carp starts to thrash about never pin it to the ground – it could cause internal damage.

Stake out the sack securely in deep water, if possible, among shade. The carp must be in an upright position and never retain more than one fish in a single sack.

Organisations to join The two major carp fishing organisations are the Carp Anglers' Association and the Carp Society. Both publish magazines and newsletters as well as staging conferences and regional meetings.

The British Carp Study Group is aimed at the more dedicated carp angler with more than ten years experience of fishing for the species. Contact addresses and telephone numbers are published regularly in Angler's Mail.

■ Casein

A milk powder sold in various grades with a protein level of 95 per cent which is used in the production of boilies for carp fishing.

■ Cast

Accurately positioning the float or leger weight in the swim involves the mastery of a number of co-ordinated casting actions. When using a top and bottom attached float at close range, a variety of casts work well. It is possible to flick the tackle out underarm, from the side, or even overhead. This gives plenty of scope to find a way around bankside obstructions.

But the underarm cast will not work with the bottom-end waggler. This float requires a sideways casting technique when attempting to place the float under far side cover on narrow waterways. The overhead cast is far more accurate for long range work.

Casting is even more limited with leger or feeder tackle. The rod must be kept reasonably high to launch the weight with some precision. An overhead cast is the most accurate, but in awkward surroundings it is possible to cast one-handed, slightly from the side and with a fair degree of efficiency.

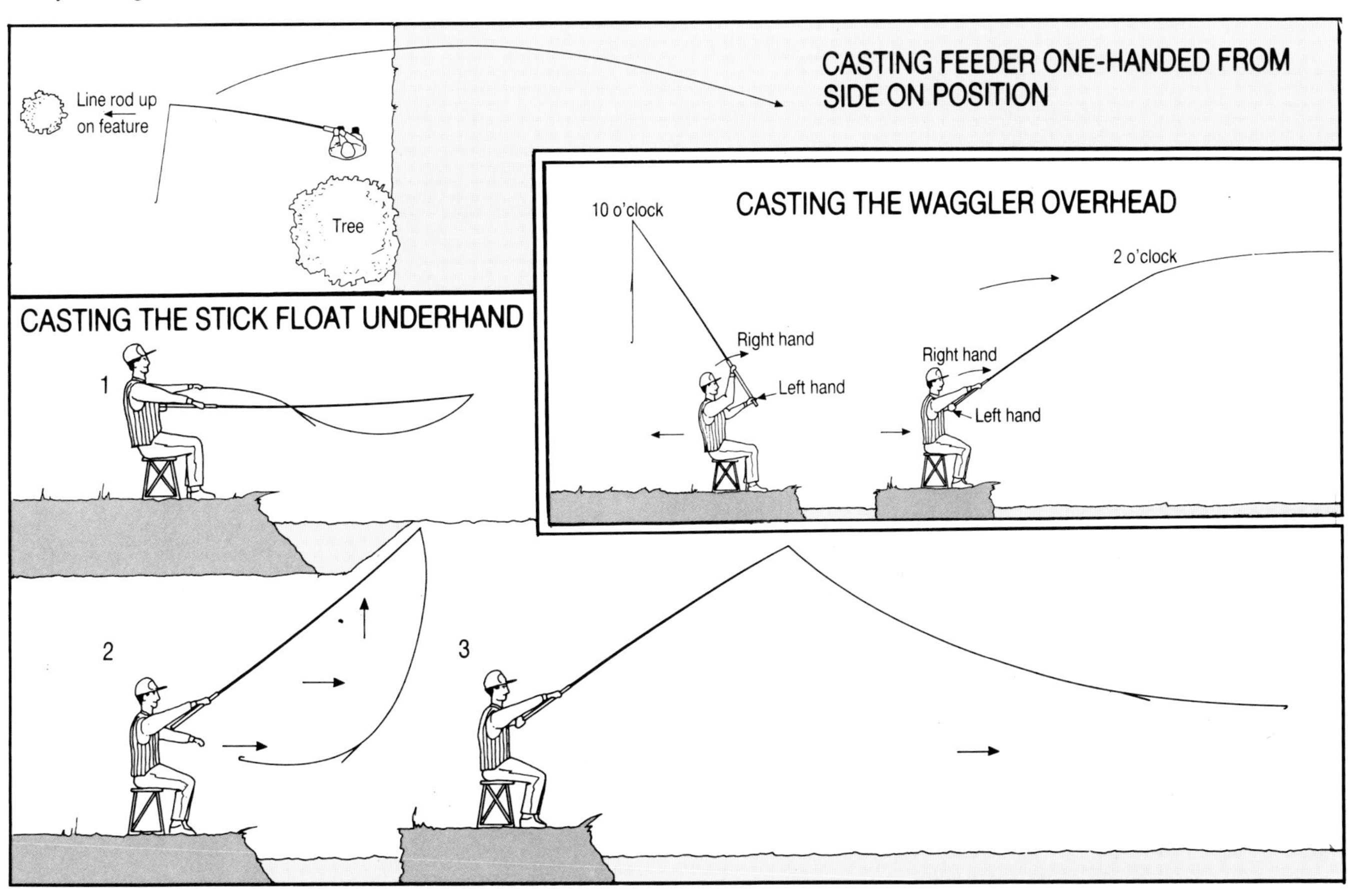

Casting the feeder The ideal way to cast the feeder, or a bomb rig, is from a position behind the head with the rod pointing at about 10 o'clock. One hand supports the reel seating with the reel positioned at the top of the rod's handle. The other hand steadies the butt of the handle.

From a stationary position the rod is brought forward, over the head, in a short punchy manner, releasing the line at approximately 2 o'clock. It is best to maintain the rod in this position until the tackle is near its destination, then the hand by the reel can be used to slightly feather the line to soften the touch down.

On short to medium length casts, about two feet of line between rod tip and terminal tackle is about right. For long distance casting it's possible to wind the end tackle within an inch or two of the rod tip to gain extra leverage.

If a conventional overhead cast is out of the question, the bomb or feeder can also be cast one-handed. This type of cast is usually carried out from a sitting position, sideways to the water, lining up a point directly behind and in line with the desired target area. The rod is kept slightly lower for this cast and is brought round staying on an imaginary 10 o'clock line.

Casting the waggler If the objective with a waggler rig is to tuck the float under far bank cover on canal or small river fisheries, a very low, sideways cast is preferable. The hook length is held in the free hand while the rod is held directly above the reel with the other hand. From a seated position, the best stance is to turn in the direction of the free hand, so the hookbait, with the rod held a foot or so above it, is to the side. The rod is then moved forward in a sweeping movement, letting go the terminal tackle a split second before the rod is pointing at the target. A fraction later the line is also released from the rod hand, keeping the rod parallel with the water until the tackle lands.

The more conventional waggler cast is overhead, lining the target up with the rod pointing back at 10 o'clock. A clean punching cast forward, releasing the line at 2 o'clock – should send the tackle directly out on a straight trajectory. For extra range, the hand supporting the butt of the rod should be pulled sharply into the chest to flex the rod's action fully and gain those vital extra yards.

Casting the stick float The underhand cast is the easiest to use with the stick or any top and bottom attached float. The line is held with the free hand, just a couple of inches above the hookbait, while the rod hand points the rod directly out over the water.

Keeping the rod low to the surface at the start of the cast, it is then flicked upwards to about 10 o'clock as the hookbait is released. Watching the tackle travel out in an arc, the reel line is released just as the arc is completed – so the tackle is on a straight line moving away from the rod tip. The rod hand then dictates how much line is released from the reel and also is used to slightly feather the reel line as the tackle lands. This keeps it in a straight line and prevents tangles.

Once the tackle is on the water the float's passage through the swim can be regulated by bringing the free hand up to the reel to feed or brake the line.

Wide gape catapult with quick-change elastics.

■ Casters

See Baits.

■ Catapults

The catapult is essential for feeding bait well beyond throwing distance. There are many specialist designs for loose feed, boilies and groundbait and experienced anglers carry several 'pults for different venues and baits.

Most popular is the maggot catapult which can also be used for firing out hemp, casters, sweetcorn, pinkies and squatts. Commercial models tend to have plastic or alloy frames and both are good. There are also various forms of hollow and solid elastic or latex and it is up to the individual to select the right strength for his needs.

Loose feed pouches differ in size. The smallest pouches are intended for stretchy elastics and help provide accurate feeding of small amounts of bait. Medium to large pouches are better for more powerful elastics. They contain the bait well when stretching the catapult to its limit for extra distance.

Boilie 'pults usually have a very small pouch for feeding one bait at a time. Some specialists use the very powerful Black Widow or Diablo target catapults for this purpose. These can launch a boilie 100 metres!

The groundbait catapult needs an alloy frame – plastic is not really rigid enough for long distance firing as it flexes too much. Look for a wide gape which aids accuracy. The best groundbait pouches are formed with a rigid base, to stop the groundbait breaking up.

With loose feed catapults it is often easier to hold them upside down, keeping your arm straight out from the body, when firing. This gives better accuracy and stops the pouch bouncing back and hitting your knuckles.

Groundbait catapults with soft elastics for short range feeding can be used in the same way. But heavy duty groundbait 'pults should be held upright, with the elbow joint locked out straight. When firing these make sure the elastic is tensioned back parallel with the arm supporting the catapult. The supporting arm should never be moved while firing the bait, otherwise nasty injuries could be inflicted on the catapult hand if the cup or pouch flies round and hits the knuckles.

For pinpoint accuracy when using any catapult, it is always best to line up a far bank feature as a marker. Make a mental note of how far the elastic has been stretched when firing, for consistency of distance.

■ Catfish

One of the most powerful fighters known to anglers. The head is flattened and wide with a huge mouth. The upper jaw is adorned with two long feelers and the lower jaw with four smaller barbules. These feelers and barbules are sensory detectors which may help substitute for the catfish's tiny eye and presumed poor eyesight.

Although of restricted distribution at one time, it is clearly spreading by various means, some legal, some not. Now it occurs in various waters in several counties. It is also capable itself of working through the river systems, and one fish was recently trapped in the tidal Great Ouse by water authority officials.

Catfish, or Wels, are both scavengers and predators, and will fall to live and deadbaits as well as other baits such as worms and boilies. Although of generally blotchy colouration, the actual colouration is quite variable from blotchy greens, greys, browns and blacks, through to pale-coloured fish and golden albinos. The British record specimen of 43 lb 8 oz was hooked from Tring Reservoirs, Hertfordshire in 1970.

■ Centrepin

See Reels.

■ Charr

A left over from the last ice age. The fact that populations have been isolated from one another in different lakes, has led some past authorities to give them different species and subspecies status. In the Arctic, the charr (or char) is migratory, but in the UK is restricted to certain lakes in the Lake District and North Wales and also in Ireland.

As a species in the UK, it rarely much exceeds a foot in length, the majority of those netted in Lake Windermere being around 8-10 inches. Charr have whitish body spots, and lack the brown and black spots of trout. But more importantly they have a beautiful vermilion flash along the belly and lower flanks, something that is far more striking, for example, than on a rainbow trout. This colouration extends to the pectoral, pelvic and anal fins and less so to the caudal fin and is typical of the breeding season.

Fishing for charr is highly specialised and may involve worm, spinner, or fly, often at great depths using down-rigger systems. Charr feed on minute phytoplankton and zooplankton and migrate diurnally relative to the food supply. British record is 7 lb 7 oz – a fish taken in 1990 from Loch Arkraig, Inverness-shire.

■ Chub

This pugnacious, omnivorous species is distributed widely in the UK, including parts of Scotland, and in a variety of habitats. It is prepared to eat virtually anything and this no doubt contributes to its success in different habitats. It is absent from Ireland, parts of Wales and some parts of south west England.

The chub can be caught on most hookbaits but it is a notoriously cunning fish, to the extent that its enthusiasts have combined in the Chub Study Group.

It is a much more solid and chunky fish than the roach and has a large mouth with conspicuous white lips. Fish spotters often detect the presence of big chub by the movements of their lips! The flanks of the fish are often bronze when the fish is bigger, but

The chub prefers to sit tight under bushes and other protective canopies waiting for food to drift down on the current.

otherwise the species has no striking colouration features except perhaps for the delicately tinted anal and pelvic fins which are often pinkish.

The chub is a fine fighter on most waters, and is peculiar in that on its first run for freedom it will bolt directly at a snag or weedbed, rather than vaguely in the general direction of safety. Small chub are not unlike dace, but are more solid at all weights and have clearly rounded dorsal and anal fins. Any chub over 4 lb is a good fish and few over 6 lb are caught. A 1913 Hampshire Avon chub of 8 lb 4 oz stands as the British best.

■ Chum Mixer

Famous brand of dog biscuit which rates as the No.1 surface bait in carp fishing. A small bait drill is used to channel a hole through the centre so the hard, dry biscuit can be mounted on a hair. Used straight from the bag, Mixer will catapult about 25 yards and it usually takes several pouch loads to get the carp feeding on them. They absorb water quite quickly and swell up in size. If they lose their effectiveness in their natural state, Mixers can be flavoured with a diluted boilie flavour and water.

This is done by putting about 1 lb of dry Mixer into a large polythene bag. Add about 10 ml of flavouring to 150 ml of water and pour inside the bag. Blow air into the bag and shake for several minutes to evenly distribute the liquid over every Mixer.

■ Churner

The backward rotation of the reel caused by a take from a carp. This style of fishing with a closed bale arm was popular before the Baitrunner and free spool systems became available. Many modern fixed spools are not suitable for churner fishing because they are too free-running and spill line from the spool causing bird's nests.

■ Close Season

The purpose of a Close Season is to allow fish to breed without being disturbed by anglers. The coarse fish Close Season has, traditionally, extended from March 15 to June 15. Most species spawn in this period but tench and carp frequently spawn after it, and some like pike and zander spawn before it on occasion.

Variations in the Close Season do occur. For example, some of the old water authority areas allowed Close Season fishing in stillwaters unconnected to the river drainage system.

The game fishing Close Season is over the winter period between October and March because these species spawn at that time. The Close Season has been scrapped in some areas for rainbow trout fishing, because they do not generally breed in UK stillwaters.

■ Closed-face

See Reels.

■ Clutch

A clutch mechanism is incorporated in all open-faced reels and the majority of closed-face models. Clutch adjustment varies the pressure needed to pull line from the spool without opening the bale arm on open-faced reels or releasing the pick-up pin on closed-face models.

On some reels the clutch adjustment is located on the face of the line spool, but the majority have rear clutch or drag tensioning ratchets. The clutch is a fail-safe device which should be tensioned at the beginning of a session so that it only concedes extra line under reasonable pressure. This will prevent break-offs on the strike and while playing good fish. See Reels.

■ Continental groundbait

See Groundbait.

■ Controller

A form of self-cocking float used for presenting a small, light bait to surface feeding carp. Most are injection moulded from plastic or machined balsa wood and have a counterbalancing weight in the base with a swivel in the top. See Carp Fishing.

■ Corks

The majority of rod handles are still formed with round sections of cork which slide on the butt of the blank where they are glued in place and sanded down to a uniform size. Cork is also incorporated in certain float designs, such as pike bungs, grayling floats and quill Avons.

■ Counter-balanced bait

A highly successful way of presenting a bait that neither really floats or sinks to suspicious carp. The bait to be counter-balanced is made to float by cooking or inserting a piece of rig foam within it. It is then counter-balanced out by the weight of the hook alone or possibly with the addition of a small split-shot or a tiny piece of sinking putty. If the balance is exactly right, a vortex caused by the carp in the vicinity of the bait will induce it to rise several inches at a time which most fish find hard to resist.

■ Crochet hook

See Baiting Needle.

■ Crucian

See Carp.

■ Crumb

The most popular freshwater groundbait is white and brown bread crumb. There are many types of crumb including heat-dried white, which will not turn stodgy when mixed with water. This is used when fishing punched bread and simulates liquidised fresh bread.

It is possible to find different grades of crumb ranging from fine to coarse which makes it possible to mix up all sorts of groundbait consistencies. Crumb can be used on its own but also makes a good bulking agent for use with more expensive Continental mixes.

Brown crumb gives a cloudy soft consistency, ideal for on-the-drop fishing, or for bulking out slightly stodgy bottom feeds. White crumb in its natural form is a good binder, or a good cloud bait when treated. A popular development has been to feed fresh white bread into a food liquidizer. This creates a lovely fluffy consistency which will sink very slowly. It's an excellent form of crumb for punch or flake fishing.

White and brown crumb can be mixed together for a basic bottom mix. Mixed 50-50 it will break down quickly. More white is added for a slower breakdown.

■ Crystal bend

These are widely recognized as premier maggot hooks because the bend is accentuated towards the point. This stops the lively bait from wriggling off on the cast, or in the water. In reality, the crystal bend is a very good all-round hook, suited to most baits and methods. See Hooks.

Self-cocking controller for punching out tiny, light baits into the path of surface feeding carp.

D

Thames dace hooked from the highly oxygenated shallows.

■ Dace

Primarily a fish of streamy waters, though not the high mountain streams. It has a wide distribution but is missing from Scotland, West Wales and Cornwall, and is of restricted distribution in the Lake District.

The dace is quite closely related to the chub but can easily be distinguished from it by the fact that the edges of the dorsal and anal fins are slightly concave or level, rather than convexly rounded. This silver fish rarely has any pigmentation of the fins which are more or less transparent though darker in bigger fish.

The dace is a varied feeder, often in the surface layers looking for flies, which it takes readily. But it also bottom feeds and quite large dace can be caught on worm baits fished hard on the bottom. Traditionally, dace fall to small hooks and baits fished long trotting.

In recent decades the Little Ouse has possibly been the most prolific producer of big dace. The Hampshire Avon and Dorset Stour still yield big dace and many other rivers have high quality dace fishing if not the giants of 1 lb or more. The British record of 1 lb 4 oz 4 dr came from the Little Ouse in 1960.

■ Dacron

Trade name for braided Terylene which is available in many diameters, breaking strain and colours.

■ Day ticket

Some club and privately-owned waters welcome visiting anglers but a day permit must be purchased in advance – usually from a tackle shop local to the venue – or on the bank, when a bailiff does his round. The day ticket entitles the angler to fish from sunrise to sunset, unless fishery rules dictate otherwise.

■ Dental floss

A good hook link material for carp and superb when used as a hair. Floss is made from many fine filaments laying parallel with each other and gently twisted. The floss strands are easily separated to construct very supple hairs. Dental floss is white straight from the dispenser but soon takes on the colour of the bottom as the strands open up in water and catch small, suspended particles of debris.

■ Disgorger

For small hooks, the most popular disgorger is the plastic, slit-head type. These have no sharp edges and will not damage the fish if it has swallowed the hookbait. The slit is used to engage the nylon above the hook, then keeping the nylon taut, the disgorger is run down into the fish's mouth until it hits the bend of the hook. Slight pressure, or a twist will dislodge the hook and allow it to be retrieved.

There are similar alloy disgorgers which work just as well and slot on the line. The advantage of plastic models is that they are brightly coloured and float – making them easy to retrieve if you accidentally drop them. Never use the V-shaped metal disgorger which can damage fish and easily slip off the line when trying to locate the hook.

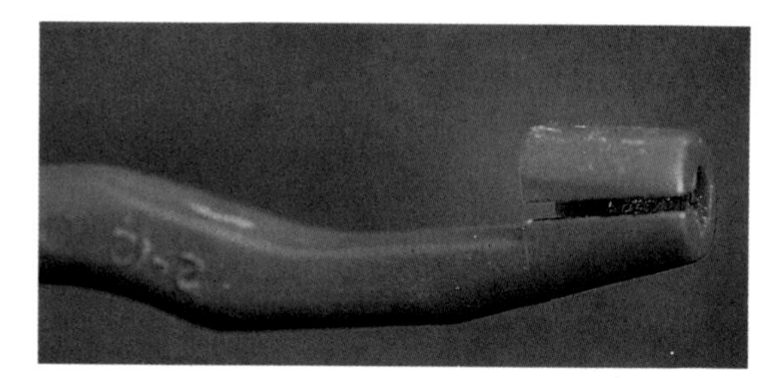

Right: The design of disgorger which every angler must carry.

There are also plastic disgorgers for larger eyed and spade end hooks. These have more bulbous heads and a larger slit to fit over the hook shank. With bigger fish it is sometimes easier to remove large hooks with a pair of surgical forceps.

■ Domed top

Certain stick float designs have domed tops. This shape makes them slightly more buoyant by holding up well in the surface tension. A useful shape when dragging overdepth, or trotting in turbulent water.

■ Dotting down

This means sufficient weight has been added to the rig for the correct amount of tip to be left showing above the surface. It is also possible to dot a float down below this level if the fish are really cagey.

■ Double rubber

Floats attached to the line with silicone sleeves placed both at the top and bottom are called double rubber models. The double rubber is mainly used on flowing waters with a floating line for better control.

■ Drag system

Another term for a clutch. It is possible to have front or rear drags on open-faced reels, which can be adjusted to regulate line flow when the bail arm is closed.

■ Drift

Surface drift refers to the top layer of water moving faster than the deeper layers. This can occur on still, sluggish or pacey venues. Unless tackle is modified to cope, good presentation is lost and the angler is unlikely to catch.

It is also possible to use wind, or drift, to your advantage, by making float tackle behave in a manner that is likely to attract bites from certain species. On stillwaters a floating line will pull the float along in drift, sometimes a good ploy when the fish are active and willing to chase a bait. Pike anglers often use drift to sail their baits out to long range.

■ Drip feed

When fishing reasonably close in with pole or running line tackle, an excellent way of feeding groundbait is to drip feed. This entails throwing small offerings at the float regularly, sometimes every cast.

Wet or dry groundbait can be used and the objective is to make the fish expect the regular offerings. Match anglers particularly favour this method when fishing groundbait with small baits like bloodworm, squatts and bread punch. It is mainly a small fish approach.

■ Drop off

An area of the lake which falls away into deeper water. It can be the side of a steep bar, the edge of a dam or a slightly sloping margin. Food items tend to collect at the foot of a drop-off making it a good spot to present a bait.

■ Duplon

When cork became rather scarce and more expensive in the early 1980s, many rod manufacturers began to look at all types of synthetic substitutes. The material that emerged as a front runner was duplon, a rubbery, slightly spongy substance.

The consistency of duplon used on quality carp and pike rods today is very much improved. It is more tightly formed and will not absorb water so readily.

■ Dust shot

Number 8 shot or smaller are known as dust shot. The sizes run from 8 down to minute number 15s which are so small as to be rarely used. Most serious anglers might carry a selection of 8s, 10s, 11s and 12s – ample for most fine rig variations.

Because they are so small dust shot are used on gossamer hooklengths. They can also be bulked to dot down tiny pole floats. In larger sizes these shot are also popular on stick float rigs. Being made from lead, they are much smaller than non-toxic shot and hang slightly more centrally on the line. Number 8s are often grouped in twos and threes instead of fixing larger shot.

On the majority of venues it is legal to use lead shot weighing 0.06 grams or less. These are not thought to present any problems to wild life.

■ Dyes

Dyes are used to colour maggots and the process is now mostly carried out on bait farms. Offal is treated with dye so the maggots absorb it completely. It is possible to dye maggots bronze, red, yellow, fluorescent pink, even blue or green! Safe food dyes are often added to groundbaits to make them more attractive.

E

■ Eel

In the UK there is only one species of eel which is migratory and reputed to return to the Sargasso Sea to spawn and die, after remaining in freshwater for up to 80 years in some cases. Eels occur everywhere. In some waters which have no connection at all with the river systems, it is claimed that the eels travel over land, during thunderstorms to both reach such waters initially, and leave them eventually.

During the migratory phase, in the estuaries, the eel becomes a silver eel, and has larger eyes, in contrast to the green, yellow or brown eels when they are resident in freshwater. Eel angling enthusiasts often distinguish different morphotypes, including fish with small heads and others with large mouths.

The eel has no pelvic fins, a neat pair of small pectorals, and extremely elongate anal and dorsal fins which connect at the tail end. The lateral line of the fish is marked by a slight depression along the flanks and the muscle packs are clearly visible.

The eel populations are exploited as never before, by highly efficient, almost hi-tech systems. How long they can survive such pressure remains to be seen, but it is worth noting that the level of removal of eels from some fisheries may have totally altered the ecological base of those fisheries, probably for the worse.

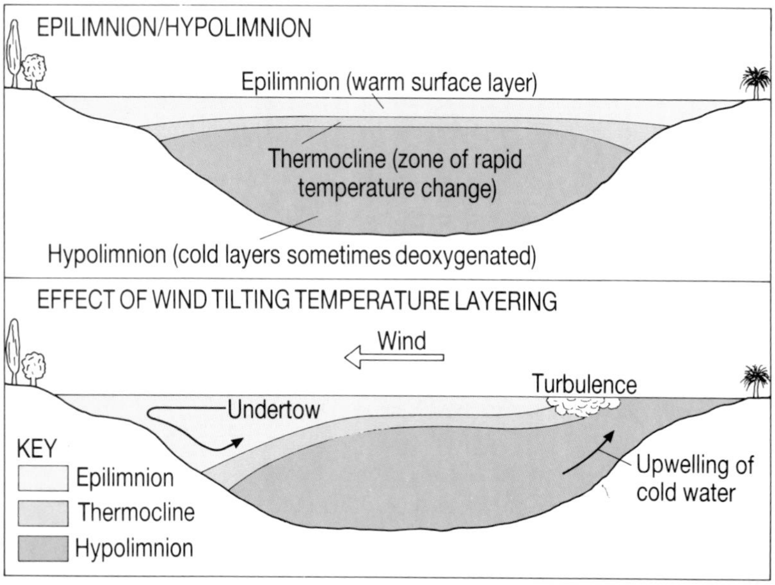

Eels are both scavengers and crafty predators and are more or less omnivorous except that they take little in the way of vegetative matter except for anglers' baits. A 4 lb eel is big, but they do reach double-figures.

They enjoy living in bolt-holes in the bottom sediment, or old oil drums, and any tangle of debris, provided that the water is clean. They can be caught on worms, fish baits and boilies, and the larger-sized eels fight extremely doggedly, testing any tackle to the limit.

The problem of handling eels, real wrigglers and strong with it, is ever present. The keen eel anglers quickly stroke the flanks of an eel, unbelievable though this may seem, and this nearly always quietens them down sufficiently to remove the hook.

Although a great deal is known about the eel it is still a puzzling and mysterious fish, and possibly some of the things we know are merely assumptions. But there is no doubt about the British record – a fine 11 lb 2 oz specimen captured from a Hampshire lake in 1978.

■ Echo-sounder

These have been used by sea anglers afloat, for many years, as a direct offshoot from commercial sea fishing. Today, with a huge range of very portable echo-sounders available, they are increasingly used by specimen hunters and game fishermen.

There are broadly two kinds of sounder. The first type displays the bottom contours, weed, fish, or all three. Others produce a graph of sorts, which may or may not have a print-out facility. It takes little experience to be able to distinguish the different types of bottom, read the depth, or recognise weed, logs, and fish.

They are an invaluable aid to the boat angler, and most especially those that give a print-out which can be stored and studied. Each sounder usually has two components. One is a transducer, which is lowered over the side of the boat, and which sends out and receives the echo, usually over a conical search area. The other is the console, screen and battery housing, which sits inboard in a convenient position for the angler to read.

■ Epilimnion

Thermal stratification takes place in many still waters during the milder months of the year. The epilimnion is the surface layer of warmer water, heated by the sun's rays. Because there is an upper warm layer there is, naturally, a lower colder layer, and this is called the hypolimnion. Between the two is a transition zone called the thermocline, where a rapid change in temperature takes place over a small depth.

Under the influence of summer breezes, the two main layers can operate independently of each other in terms of undertow and water mass movements. This will then obviously affect the position of phytoplankton, zooplankton and the movement of such food items.

The lower layer can become deoxygenated during the summer as a result of decayed plant and animal matter sinking below the thermocline. The layers themselves can be tilted under the influence of stronger winds.

In winter, this thermal layering is lost and a more uniform temperature exists throughout the lake. But at one stage of cooling, when the water reaches 39°F, the bottom will be the warmest place because water is at its heaviest at that temperature and thus sinks. Below that temperature water is lighter again – which is why ice floats on top of the lake rather than sinking to the bottom!

■ Eutrophic

Waters described as eutrophic are those rich in dissolved nutrients, the opposite being oligotrophic. The latter is, or was, typical of many mountain lakes. Eutrophism of waters in British lowlands has increased dramatically in the last few decades, partly as a result of the stress on the sewage system, and partly as a result of excess use of fertilisers. See Algae; Blanket Weed.

■ Eye fluke

Eye fluke is the larval stage of a parasitic organism – the life cycle involves snails (eaten by fish), fish (eaten by birds) and birds. The larva infects the eye lens of the fish, often causing blindness, and occasionally death, especially with rainbow trout.

■ Eyed hooks

See Hooks.

F

■ Feathering

It is possible to ease back on the trajectory of the float or leger during the cast by gently braking or feathering the line with a finger as it flows from the reel spool. This is done to avoid overshooting the target area or more usually to make the tackle land gently on the water and avoid excessive disturbance to the swim. It ensures the end tackle lands in a straight line.

The term feathering also applies to the tactic of slightly retarding the flow of the line with the fingers when trotting. This slows the tackle down causing the float to hold back against the flow.

■ Feeding

Learning to feed a swim correctly with groundbait, loose offerings, or a combination of both is vitally important in the quest for good fishing. Anglers who are good at feeding their swim usually assess its possibilities carefully taking note of depth, water clarity, temperature, wind and light intensity.

Groundbaiting policies Groundbait tends to work well when fishing for species like tench, bream, carp and roach in coloured stillwater venues. Several large balls introduced into the swim at the start of a session may hold a big shoal of fish for several

hours. Usually, the groundbait is laced with enticing baits like casters, squatts, hemp or chopped worms.

Further feeding following the initial bombardment is dictated by how the fish react. After a good catching period, a slowing down of bites, or a period of total inactivity will often signal the need for more groundbait to bring the fish back.

Fair quantities of groundbait, mixed quite firmly to carry free offerings like casters and squatts, frequently score in summer and autumn when water temperatures are high and the fish active. But this is drastically reduced in winter as the fish's metabolism slows down and waters become clear. Many anglers resort to minimal amounts of groundbait in an open-ended feeder at this time of year.

Groundbait can also be a deadly attractor in cloudy form, or mixed to a softish consistency so it breaks up as it nears the bottom. Unlike the more heavy mixes which tend to bring best results in coloured water, a cloud mix can bring to life clear stillwater venues and is particularly effective on difficult canal venues.

Feeding small quantities of cloud every cast or certainly every few minutes is called drip feeding. This is a method developed to a fine art by match anglers, when using baits like squatts, bread punch and bloodworm. The idea is to constantly maintain a cloudy haze in the swim so the fish become used to the groundbait and expect it to be introduced at regular intervals. If the feeding was more irregular there's a danger it could spook the shoal.

With any form of groundbait, you've got to feel your way into the session. If you think the fish will respond, give them an initial good helping, then feed according to the response. But if you suspect it's going to be a tough day, then only feed a small amount of groundbait at the start to check on the response. If it appears to work, try feeding again, but always be prepared to stop groundbaiting. Small amounts will do little harm for long, too much groundbait can kill a swim for days!

Loose feed techniques Knowing when not to use groundbait is more difficult. Mainly it is a case of loose feeding for a response. Keep the feed going in regularly if bites continue but slow it down if the reverse happens. Often, loose feed works better on the little and often principle, rather like the drip feeding with groundbait.

But there are days when occasional loose feeding works better. For some reason the bait falling through the water scares the fish off for a short period. It is a matter of gauging how much feed you can safely introduce to keep the shoal happy for the longest period.

Loose feed and groundbait combinations can work well when the fish are moving in and out of the swim or are reluctant to feed well. By experimenting with light groundbait to pull the fish in, the trick is then to loose feed over the top while bites are coming regularly. Groundbait is only used again to attract the fish back once the loose feed ceases to hold them.

Straight loose feeding is more a river method for species like chub, roach, dace and barbel and can involve one or two baits being fed. Hemp and maggots, or hemp and casters are often introduced together. Casters are rarely fed on their own, unlike maggots. Loose-fed baits may be introduced by hand, catapult, bait dropper or pole cup.

Obviously, there will be golden days when whatever you throw at the fish the float keeps diving under. But these are the exceptional outings and consistent results depend more on careful feeding and the ability to step up or down when necessary.

Gradually, good and bad results combined should help provide the necessary insight into feeding techniques. A sudden change in conditions from very bright to overcast, a rise in temperature, the wind picking up or changing direction – all these factors, if read properly, can be used to your advantage. A fast change of tactics will often turn a biteless day into a hectic session!

■ Ferrule

Few rods are now constructed with ferrule type joints between the sections although the dictates of fashion are fickle and it's possible they could make a comeback.

■ Fibre-glass

Once the most popular rod material, fibre-glass, has been superseded by carbon-fibre which is considerably lighter. There are still budget-priced glass match rods on the market and the material is used for the production of soft-actioned spinning rods and certain sea models.

Glass remains a popular choice for the softer, more sensitive quivertips used with carbon leger and feeder rods. That's because solid carbon tips have proven slightly too stiff for registering delicate bites.

■ Fisheries

Fisheries can be enormously variable in size and type but the term implies that these waters can be fished productively, over a period, as either a commercial or sporting enterprise. A small stream with only minnows and bullheads would not be regarded as a viable fishery, but possibly as a nursery or spawning site adjacent to a fishery proper.

That said, the variety of fisheries includes streams and rivers of all kinds and sizes, estuaries and, of course, sea fisheries. Canal and drain systems produce good fisheries very often. Of the stillwater variety there are man-made clay pits, gravel pits, borrow pits, reservoirs, farm ponds, flooded mine workings; and of natural stillwaters, glacial lakes, marshes, dew ponds and so on.

All these may have good fishing, and may be managed, whether a tiny farm pond with crucian carp and tench, or a vast loch with salmonids.

■ Fixed spool

See Reels.

■ Flavourings

Highly concentrated liquid flavourings are added to baits like maggots, groundbaits and sometimes even rubbed into the hands by smokers to avoid tainting the hookbait. Fruit flavours are most effective with maggots, masking the pungent ammonia smell. Savoury flavours tend to magnify it.

Boilies are nearly always flavoured and there is a massive choice of aromas. On hard venues, anglers may also add a few drops of flavouring to groundbait mixes.

■ Flick tip

See Pole Fishing.

■ Float adaptors

If a waggler is fixed directly on the line, the whole rig must be broken down to change the float. But this can be avoided by using an adaptor on the line which will fit over the base of any bottom-end float and hold it tight by suction. It means the float can be changed in seconds without breaking the line. Probably most popular are the all-silicone adaptors but for long range fishing the swivel type or Inter Fishing Links are a little safer because the line cannot cut through them. Adaptors fold over on the strike, cutting down on resistance.

■ Float caps

Float caps are small sections of rubber or silicone tubing, in various diameters which strap top and bottom style floats on the line. Select larger bores for the thicker tops and finer tubing for the narrow bases. It is worth taking care to get the sizes just right for a snug, secure fit. Longer lengths of tubing are available which can be trimmed as desired.

■ Float stops

In flowing water, anglers often place a small shot under top and bottom floats to act as a marker and prevent the float from slipping on the strike. When slider fishing, the stop is above the float. This can be a small piece of knotted nylon, which holds against the tiny eye of the sliding float, when its weighting pulls the line down as far as the stop. There are also commercially-produced sliding float stops – small pieces of rubber which transfer onto the reel line and behave in the same manner.

■ Floatant

Silicone sprays are often used in top and bottom float fishing to keep the line buoyant. These first came into the sport through fly fishing where they are used to treat surface flies. The silicone spray is just as effective on nylon line.

■ Floats

The basic function of any float is to signal that a fish has taken the hookbait. For maximum sensitivity, it is weighted down with the appropriate size of split-shot until just the tip of the float is showing. The idea of different float shapes and materials is to combine the job of bite indication with the correct

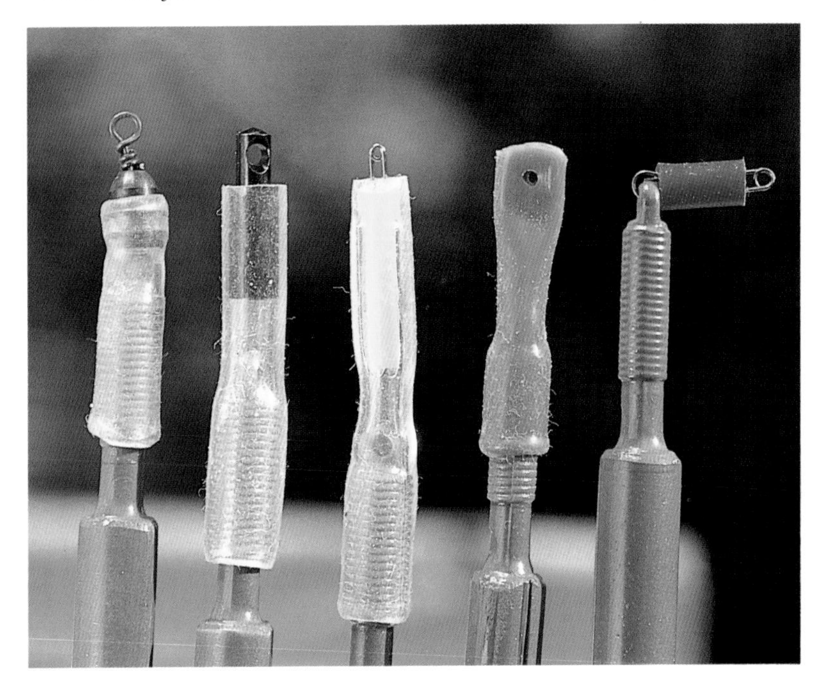

A range of quick-change float adaptors.

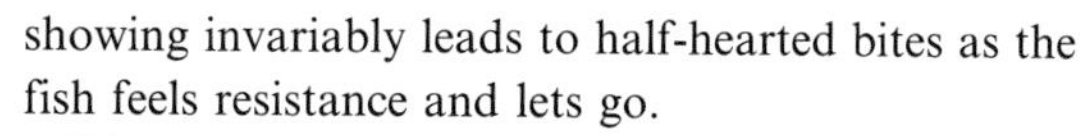

bait presentation, to attract attention from the fish in the first place.

Certain float shapes perform better in stillwater, others in flow. Some floats are more suited to shy biting fish because their finer sight tips require less of a pull to drag them under. Float selection is a matter of common sense and it does not take long to appreciate which pattern should be strapped on the line to suit the circumstances.

Shotting systems Another similarity all floats have in common is that they will only work well when shotted up or weighted correctly. Leaving too much float showing invariably leads to half-hearted bites as the fish feels resistance and lets go.

Floats to cope with fast water and big baits (from left): balsa, cane and wire stem Avons and Chubber.

Floats can be weighted by bulking the shot, spreading it out down the line or, in the case of wagglers, using it to lock the float in position.

Bulk shotting entails grouping the majority of the weight the float can carry somewhere down the line, near the hook. This gets the hookbait down to the fish quickly in deep or fast flowing water.

Spread shot are more versatile in medium to slow flowing rivers or stillwaters. Fixing shot at regular intervals down the line, between float and hook, results in a slow descent of the hookbait, which approximately corresponds to the rate at which loose offerings fall through the water. It follows that a hookbait that behaves naturally is more likely to be snapped up by a fish.

Locking shot are large shot used to trap bottom-end waggler floats on the line. By using up to 95 per cent of the float's weight carrying capacity directly around its base, long-distance, tangle-free casting is possible. Normally, no less than two thirds the carrying capacity should be used to hold the float, otherwise tangles will result on the cast.

Whatever shotting or weighting arrangement you choose, it is essential to try and make the hookbait behave as naturally as possible. If fishing overdepth, then the hookbait should be anchored as securely as possible.

In order to detect the tiniest of indications, an important factor is the dropper, or tell-tale shot. This is the shot placed nearest the hook and it's the last weight to register on the float as it cocks. If the float does not cock correctly then a fish has intercepted the hookbait on the drop and a strike should be made. Similarly, a dropper shot can be set to rest on the bottom, so the float lifts if a fish picks up the hookbait – a tactic known as laying on.

The bodies on running water floats tend to be more bulbous towards the top, or are certainly made with slightly more buoyant sight tips. Too fine a tip will be pulled under by the current.

Stillwater floats have much thinner tips for greater sensitivity, because there is less need to stop them dragging under. Their bodies are more liable to be fatter at the base, tapering up to a slim neck, again to prevent unnecessary resistance. To sum up, body-up floats are primarily designed for flowing water and body-downs for stillwater.

Avons The traditional Avon float has a balsa body mounted on a cane stem. Modern patterns have wire or glass stems. There are also balsa on quill specials called Toppers. All the Avon variations have been designed to fish streamy water at long range, or

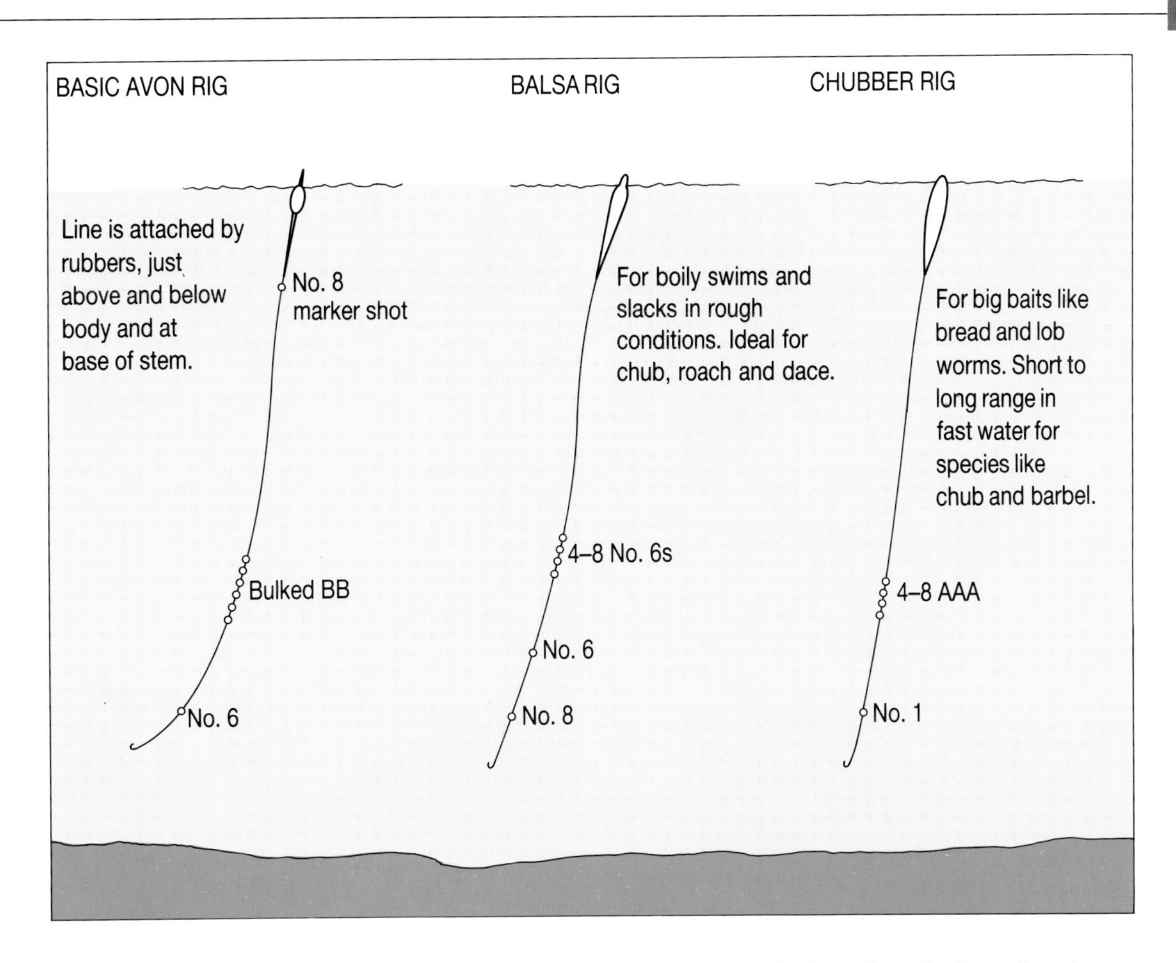

deeper running water where a fair degree of stability is required.

The tip of an Avon float stands slightly proud of the main body for improved visibility at distance. These floats normally work best bulk-loaded with strings of BB shot – anything from three to a dozen depending on the size of float and depth of swim.

Avons take over from the popular stick float and balsa designs in conditions where these floats would lose control or not be as visible. They are mostly used for species like chub, dace, roach, grayling and barbel.

Balsas and chubbers All balsa floats are attached to the line top and bottom style and fall into two main categories. There are slimmer models with a slightly stepped-down neck which are selected when more weighting than the stick float can carry is needed. Usually extra depth, flow or surface drift dictates the change.

Fatter, cigar-shaped balsas are better when using large baits like bread, luncheon meat and lobworms in pacey rivers. These floats take considerably more weight and can be controlled well at long range. They have more buoyant tips to hold up bigger baits and are often called Chubbers because they are used widely on fast rivers like the Wye for this species.

Chubbers made from clear plastic perform just as effectively as the all-balsa designs.

Pole specials

• Body-up – river pole floats with bodies tapering down towards a wire or cane stem provide better buoyancy in fastish water. They also hold back well without pulling the float too far over sideways.

• Body down – these taper towards the tip for more sensitivity and are chiefly stillwater floats designed to carry a reasonable to heavy loading in deeper water.

• Conventional – slim all-balsa pole floats, without any prominent body shape. These are very sensitive and are used in shallow to medium depths in calm conditions.

• Wire stem – short to long wire stems can be found on a large variety of pole floats, both bodied and slim in shape. The wire stem is a stabiliser, helping to hold the float steadily in wind or flow. It also helps cock the float quickly when speed fishing or taking fish on the drop. Primarily, wire stems are fished on a short line.

• Cane stems – these are found on a wide range of body patterns. They are better for long lining, or fishing to hand. The cane stem, being lighter than wire, does not affect the float when it is cast on a

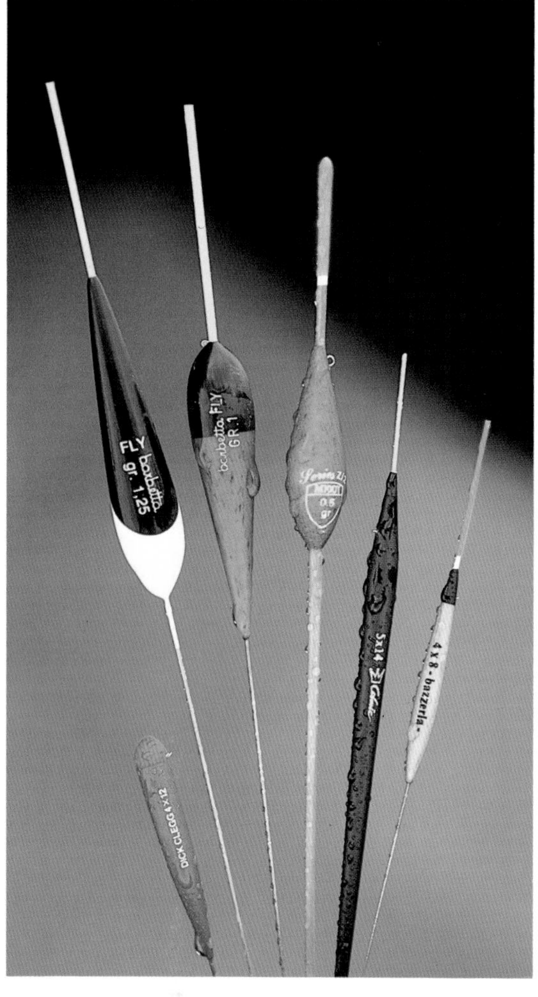

Right: **Set of pole floats for all occasions (from left): mini pattern to fish the far bank shallows with a long pole; body down for still-waters; body up model to ride the current on rivers; cane stem float for fishing to hand; all-rounder pattern with slim body; ultra-fine float for use with bloodworm and squatt.**

Far right: **Specials to carry in the float box (from left): quill and balsa, loaded float and two canal models for presenting squatt and caster with great finesse.**

long line, but still offers a good degree of stability.

• Giant pole floats – floats that take weightings of between four and 16 grams have been specially developed for fishing on long lines to hand style with the long pole. They are popular with British matchmen in Ireland and Denmark where fish are plentiful and it is often essential to speed fish with ten metres of pole to hand. A big, stable float is required to do this effectively, and sometimes it must be very heavy to get the bait down fast, or to beat windy conditions.

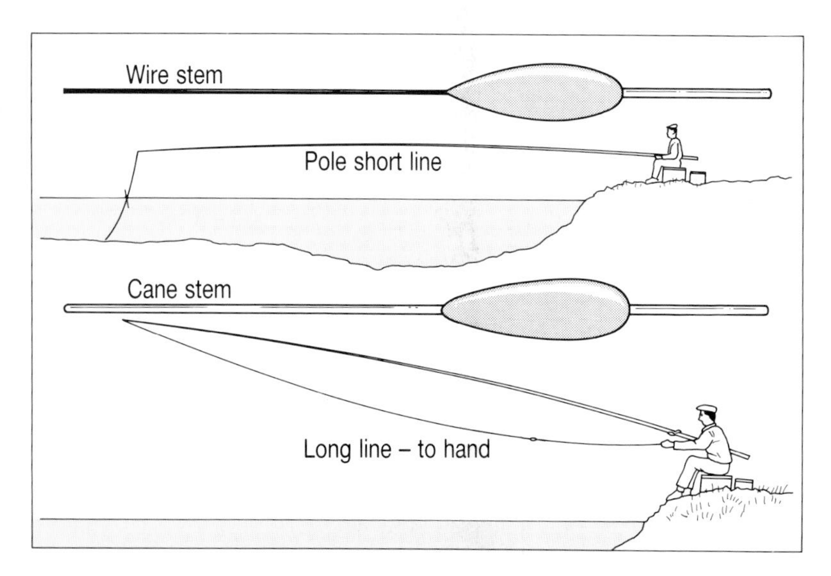

• Miniature pole floats – tiny pole floats are eagerly snapped up by long pole enthusiasts. These are often used on short lines with ten to 14 metres of pole when fishing the very shallow far bank shelf of canal venues. Floats only two or three inches long are used in depths down to six inches, often pushing them under far bank cover.

This highly successful method accounts for some exceptional catches of small and big fish which hug the far side to escape heavy boat traffic and towpath disturbance. Mini pole floats may only take the absolute minimum of shotting. This keeps the rigs simple and less likely to tangle when fishing shallow water.

Canal specials Canal anglers have the choice of special bottom-end floats for fishing with a running line in very clear, shallow water. The floats are best described as mini wagglers and are usually crafted from balsa wood with a sensitive, tapering sight tip.

The best designs of canal specials have little if any paint on their surface as this would limit the weight they could carry. Instead, the balsa is usually dyed to darken it and then sealed with a waterproof varnish.

Canal specials cause very little surface commotion on the cast and work best on light 1.5 lb to 2 lb reel lines. Many anglers use tiny Styl weights as droppers to enhance their performance. This gives the hook-bait a very slow fall and often takes a lot of fish on the drop.

When used with relatively short 11 ft or 12 ft soft-actioned canal rods, these floats help produce large weights of small fish when sport is good.

Self-cockers Commercial self-cocking, or loaded wagglers come in several sizes, with different sized plug-in or push-on weights to suit each float.

This is a flexible system as the loadings can be switched between the floats. It permits bigger, more secure locking shot to be used or alternatively more bulk weight down the rig. Of course, the option for minimal shotting still exists for the rare occasions it is wanted.

The advantage of self-cocking floats lies in the extra distance they achieve on the cast and the accurate way they slice through a side wind. They are also very stable in the water. Loaded floats are less likely to tangle without large amounts of shotting to dot them down.

Sliders Where the depth is greater than the rod length, the solution is to use a slider float. There are two possibilities, the top and bottom slider for

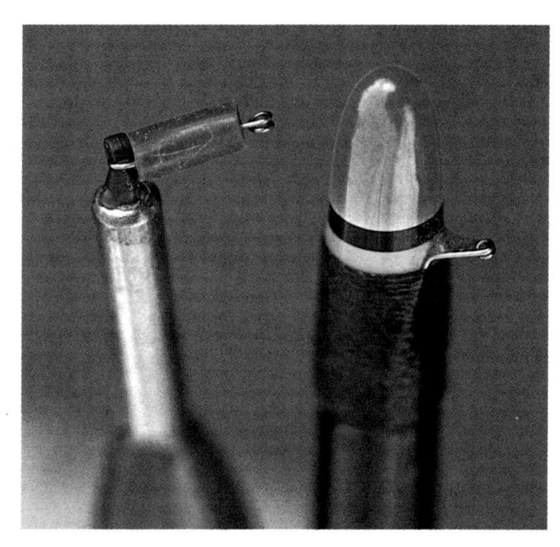

Inter-Fishing link on a bottom-end slider (left) and the specially whipped eye on a top and bottom version.

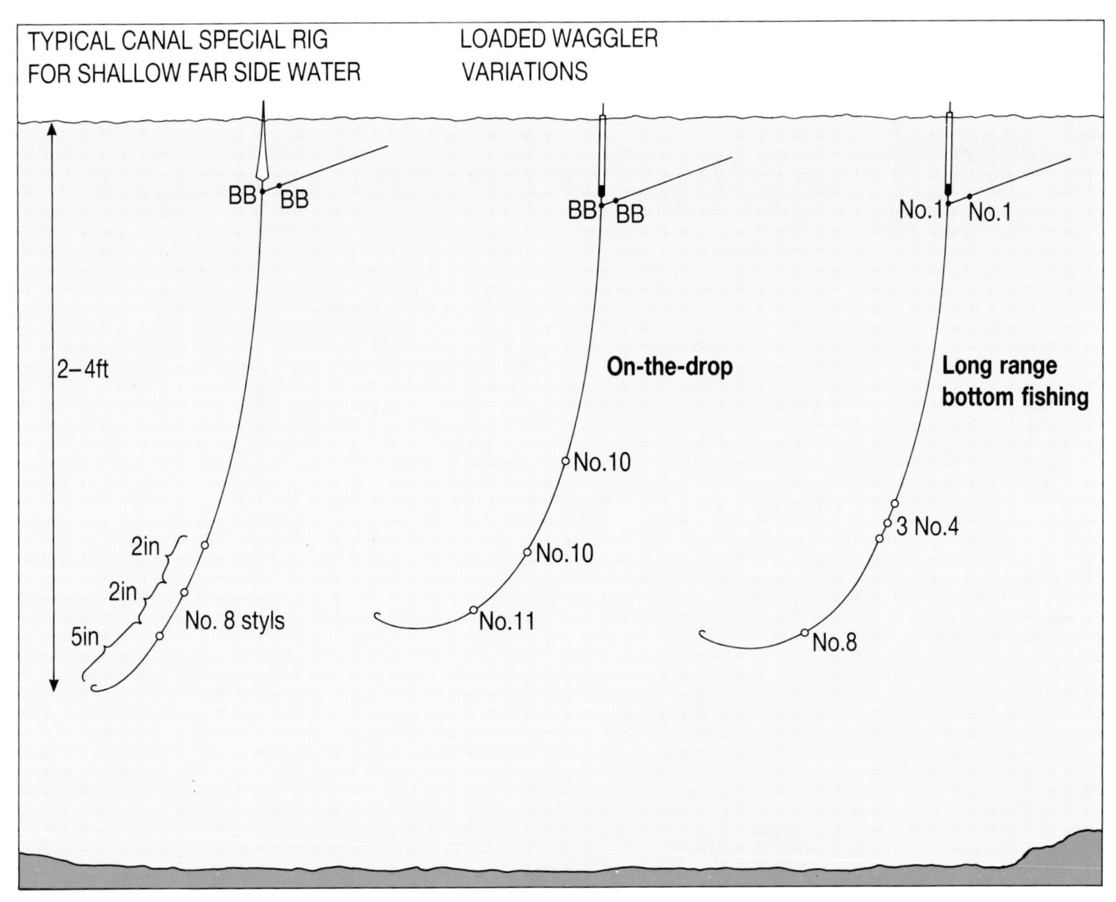

A selection of typical canal rigs.

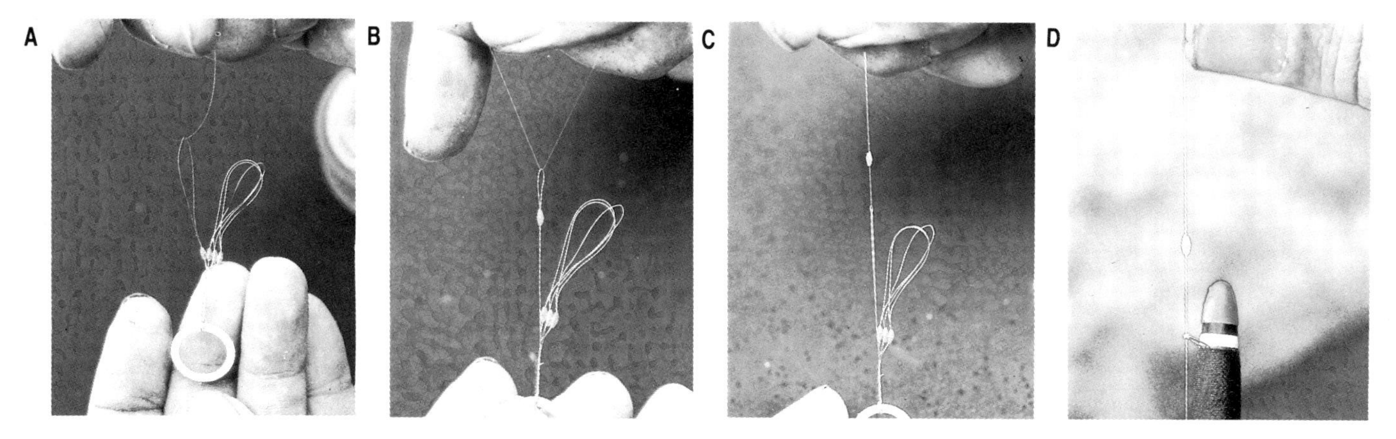

Above: **How to use a rubber float stop.**
A. Feed the reel line through the wire loop holding the rubber stop.
B. Push the rubber stop towards the end of the retaining wire.
C. Clasp the line as shown and slide the stop off the loop and onto the nylon. Withdraw loose end of the line from the rubber stop.
D. Move the stop up line to the required depth for fishing the slider.

flowing water, or close range and the bottom-ender for still, or sluggish water.

Running water sliders have an extra side eye. These all-balsa floats are fished in similar fashion to conventional top and bottom attached models. The only difference is that they cannot be held back hard as the stop knot which rests against the top eye would be pulled out of place, shallowing up the float's depth setting.

The way to slow down a top and bottom eye slider is to step-up in float size and weighting. This slows its progress nicely when trotting.

The waggler slider attached bottom-end only is normally bodied and may also be partly weighted in the stem section. This aids the float on the cast, stopping it from veering off target. These floats have a tiny wire base eye or a small swivel adaptor to stop against the sliding float knot.

Shotting for both floats is remarkably similar. The tell tale, set eight inches from the hook, can be anything from a No. 4 shot to a No. 1. The bulk shot is positioned two feet above this, then four to five feet above, another No. 4 shot to stop the float sliding down to the bulk. A sliding float stop or special rubber sliding stop is fixed in position above the float at the right depth.

The only stipulation when casting a bottom-end slider at distance is to feather the line as it lands to prevent tangles. This puts the bulk shot in front of the float. The float stop is also crucial in preventing tangles.

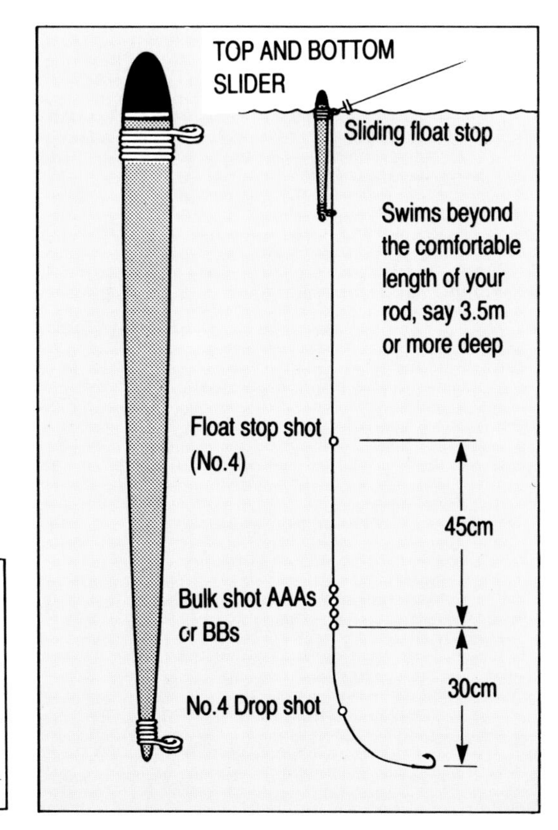

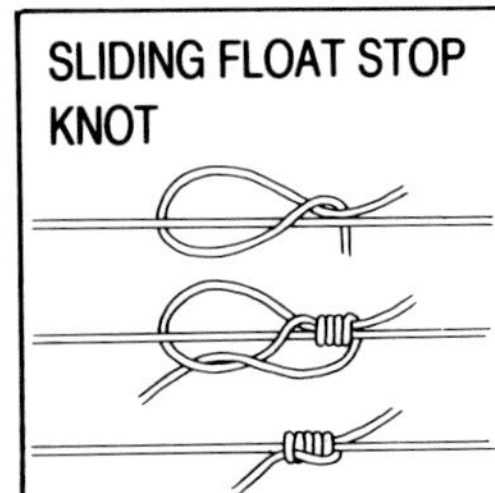

Sticks The stick must always be attached to the reel line top and bottom. Many anglers also secure it in the middle to prevent slippage.

Stick floats have balsa bodies and a cane, glass or wire stem. Conventional cane stems are very versatile for on-the-drop and normal trotting work. Glass stems give the float a fraction more stability while wire offers good control in faster currents, or windy conditions.

Cane and glass stemmed sticks are perhaps the best models for combining with strung out shotting, to make the most of on the drop presentation. Wire sticks also work well set like this but are equally proficient with bulked shot when fishing tight to the bottom.

Whatever the target species, if the stick float can cope with the range being fished – usually one to four rod lengths – it is the most versatile running line, river float.

Other options to look for when selecting a stick are how the tip has been formed. The choice lies between domed tops for pacey currents, stepped tops for slightly finer presentation and pointed for really delicate bites.

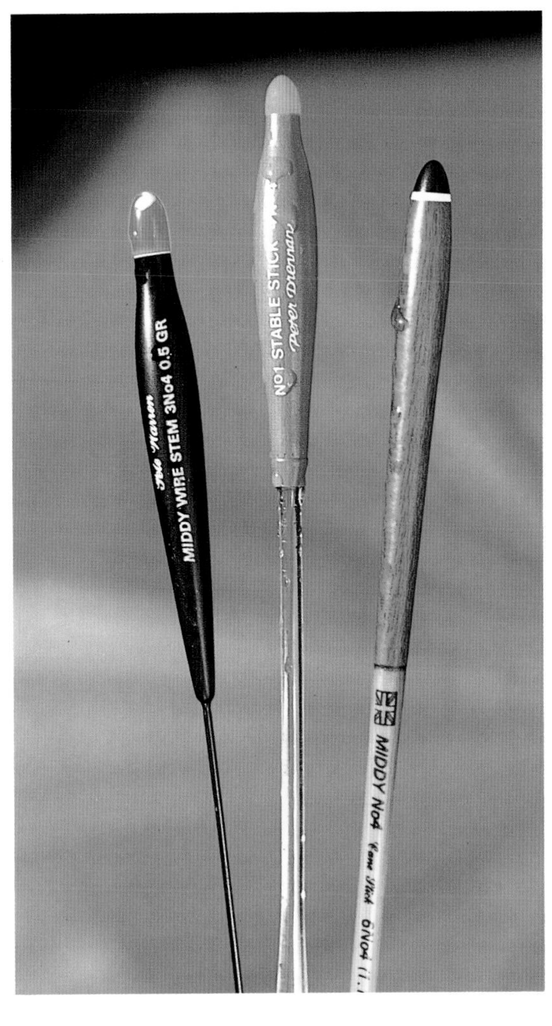

Far left: **Wire and glass stemmed stick floats and traditional wood model.**

Left: **The waggler family (from left): bodied, loaded, Crystal insert, peacock insert and straight peacock.**

It is important to use a floating line with this float. It aids and gives a clean, resistance-free strike. Many anglers carry a silicone floatant spray just in case the line begins to sink after a while. These sprays will make it buoyant again in seconds and the effect will last for several hours.

Wagglers The main waggler models are inserts, straights and bodied. As the name suggests, inserts have a much finer sight tip – in relation to the general diameter of the float. This increases the sensitivity of the design and makes it good for far bank fishing on small rivers and canals. It is also suitable for on-the-drop, or mid-water fishing. The insert waggler is the first choice float for any middle distance stillwater fishing – it is that versatile.

Generally, the bodies of these floats are made from peacock quill, balsa, sarkandas or hollow plastic. All have their good points. Shotting lies within normal guidelines. At least two thirds of the float's capacity are weighted as locking shot, with various options down the line depending on bottom fishing, or up-in-the-water requirements.

Inserts are good drift beaters if fished with a sinking line. They will also team well with a surface line in calm conditions and this may fractionally aid the strike.

The insert design begins to fail when there is a need to drag the tackle well overdepth, either on drift-affected stillwaters, or river venues. That's the time for a switch to the straight waggler which is similar apart from its much fatter, buoyant tip. This prevents the float constantly dragging under by presenting more resistance to the surface tension.

Straights tend to require a little extra shotting down the line, to help stabilise them. With a little experience it is possible to anchor them completely in drifting stillwater by feeding the right amount of line out to hold them – in unison with shot resting on the bottom.

Bodied wagglers are long distance floats. They are really an extension of the insert and straight designs, except their balsa bodies offer greater shot carrying capacity. Because these floats require a positive casting action, they need very stable locking shot. It is best to anchor at least two large shot either side of the float for this purpose.

Below: **A bottom-end slider rig for stillwaters.**

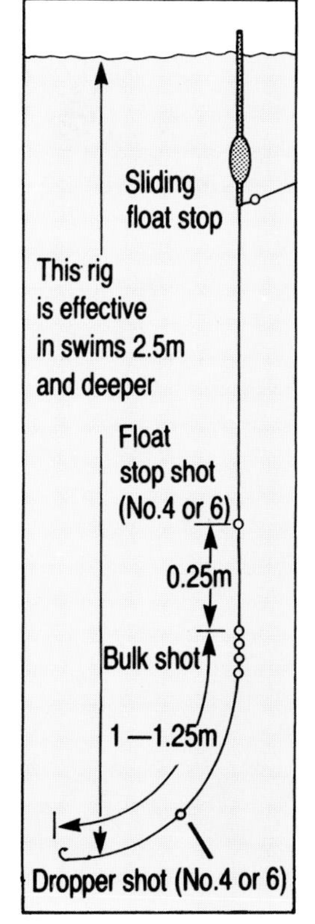

Right: **Stick floats and how they behave on landing.**

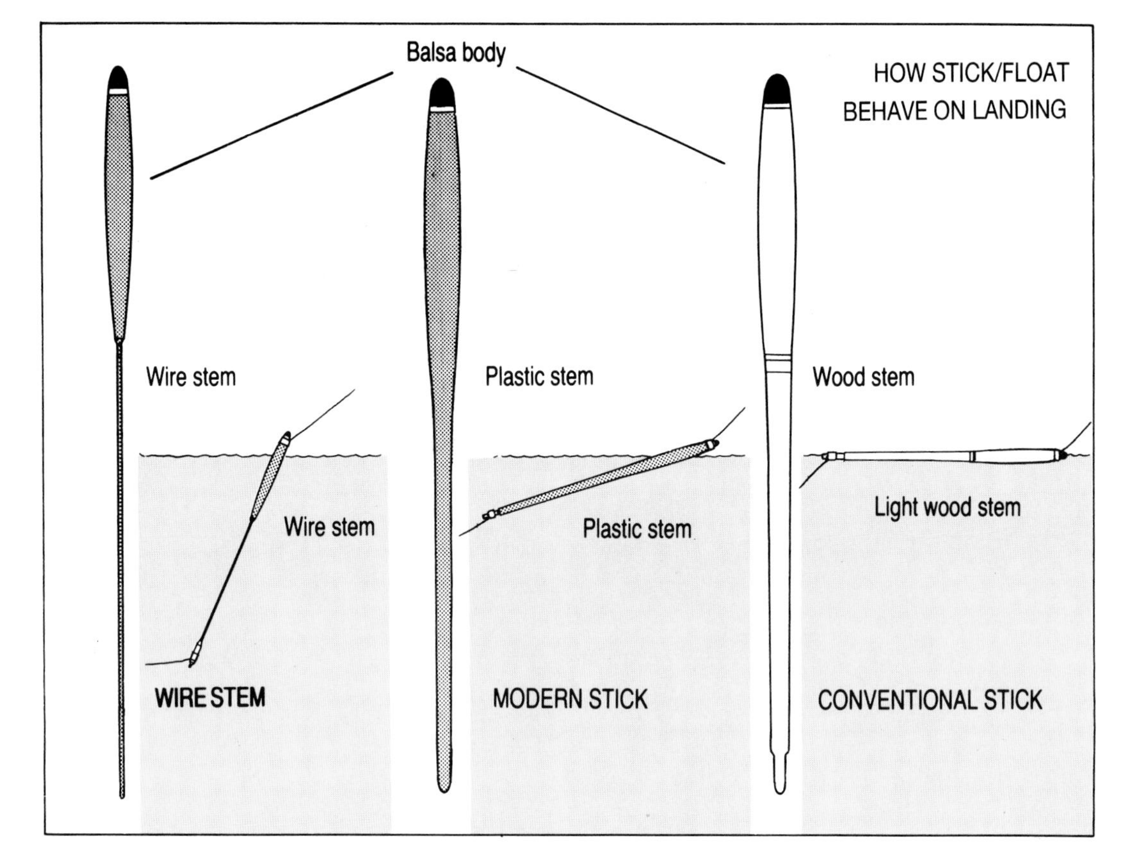

Light stick rigs.
Below left: **This set-up is the starting point and can satisfy a variety of styles, including on-the-drop and dragging over depth.**
Below right: **When fish are feeding near the bottom the rig is modified to bulk shotting.**

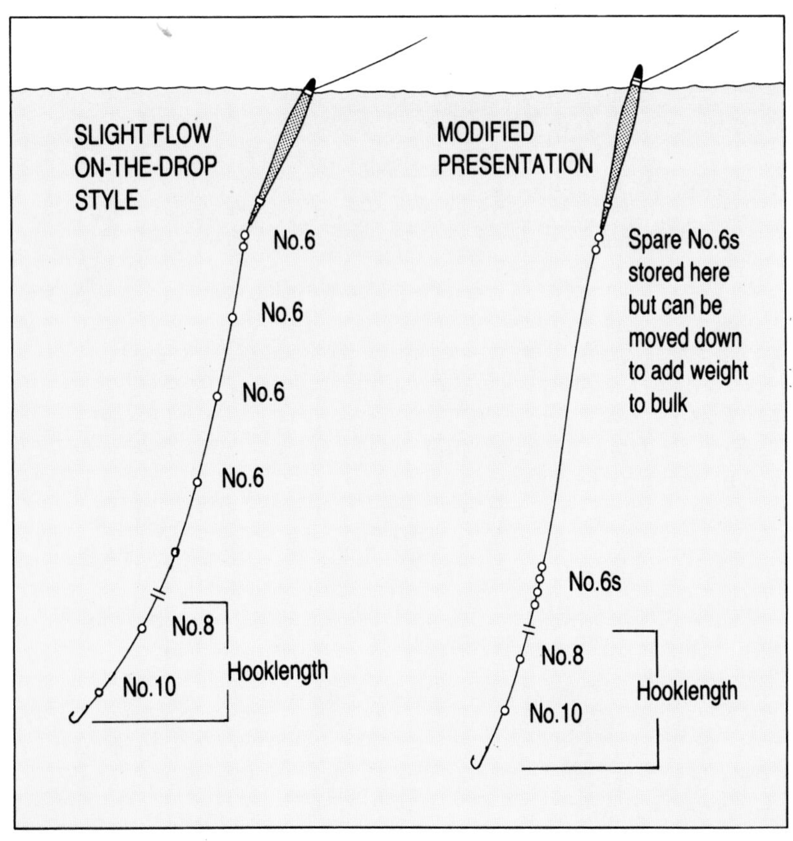

The bodied design is normally used with a groundbait catapult to get the feed out on the same line. Extra large, home-made versions sometimes have large weights Araldited into the base. They can be cast up to 50 yards! Anglers have found these floats very effective for long range carp fishing on stillwaters with light match tackle.

Smaller bodied wagglers have been superseded by loaded crystals nowadays. Because of their greater body mass, the bodied design is also worth considering as an excellent drift beater. It is not unknown to fish a float twice the size needed to reach a set distance, simply because these types hold so 'well against awkward surface drift.

Windbeaters A further variation on the bodied waggler is the windbeater. It looks the same as a bodied waggler apart from its inflated bulbous sight tip. This is extra buoyant to hold up in really bad drift. It also makes them more visible in very choppy conditions.

■ Floaters

Surface baits for carp. Breadcrusts were probably the first but floating dog biscuits – notably Chum Mixer – have become everybody's first choice. Oven-baked boilie mixes containing twice the amount of

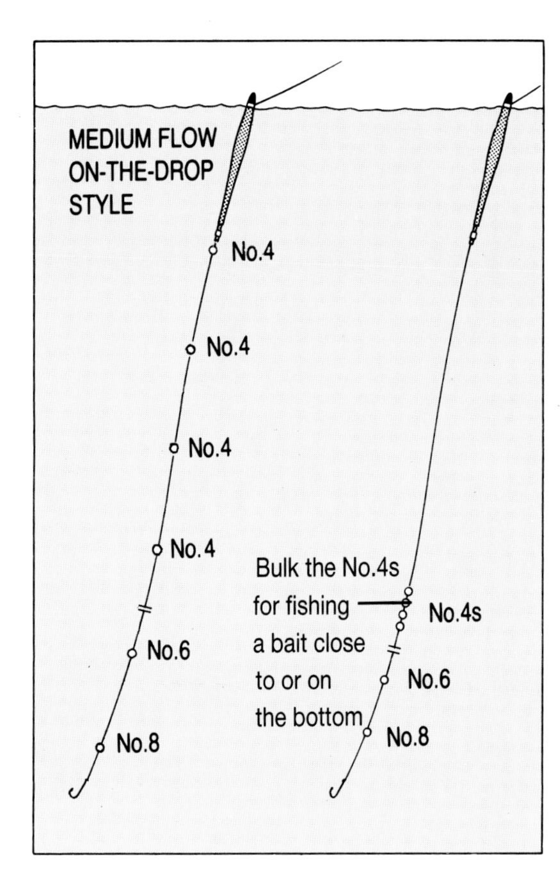

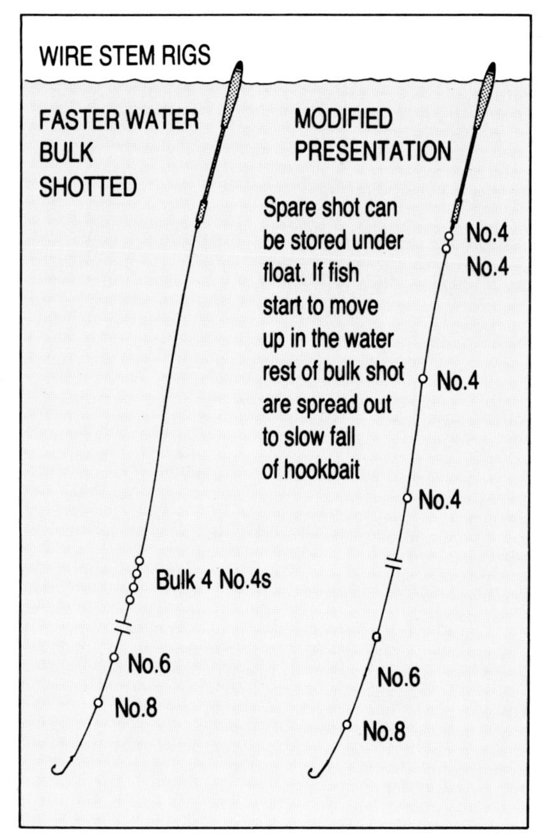

Far left and left:

Conventional stick rigs.

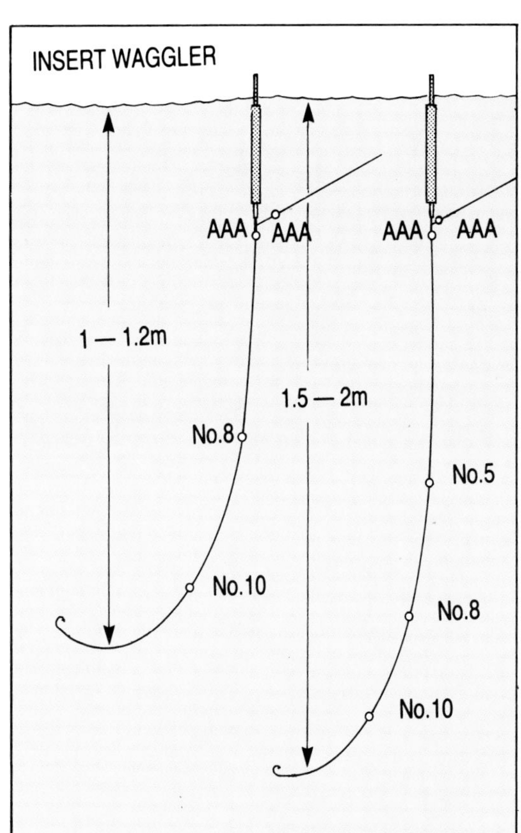

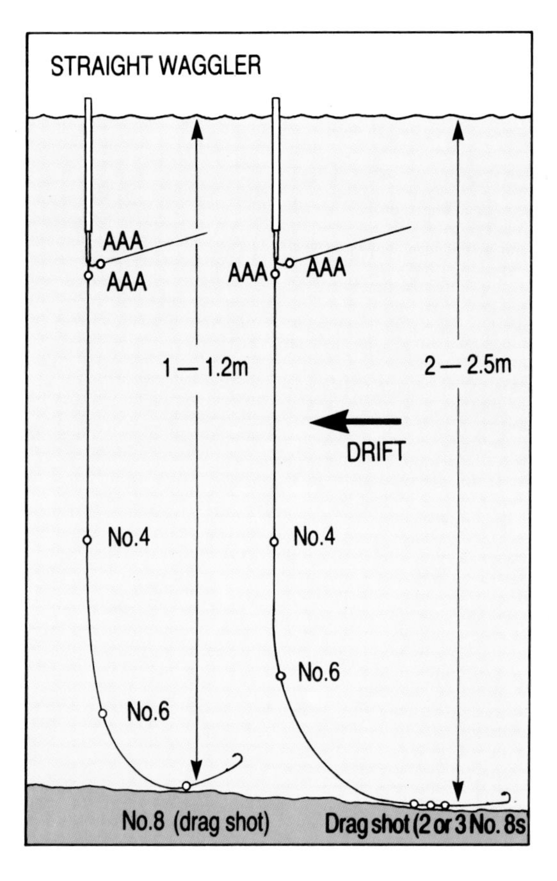

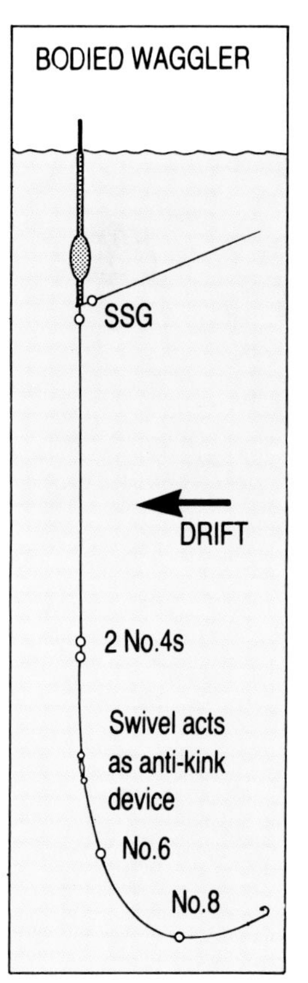

eggs are also occasionally used. This produces a thick, soupy mix to which baking powder is added to make it rise. A tough loaf of specialist floating cake has its own individual flavour and colour.

■ Food chain

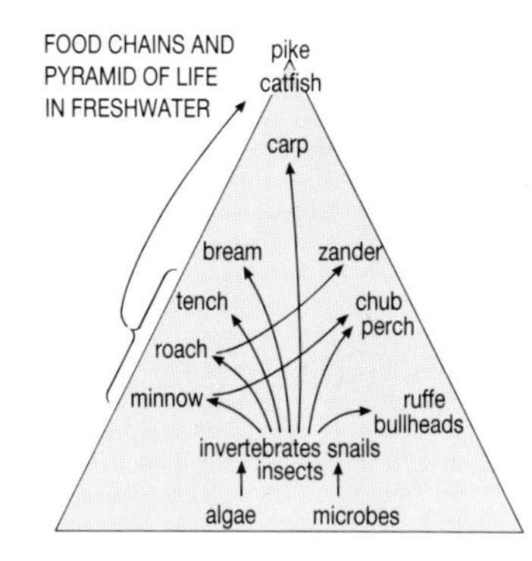

All life is connected in a kind of dog-eat-dog situation, with the vastly abundant lower forms of life, such as algae and microbes, being eaten by slightly larger forms of life, and so on up to elephants, whales and lions. The continuous nature of the chain is vital. Should one link be broken the consequences can be widespread, affecting creatures well away from the break itself – it has a knock-on effect.

For this reason, the best fisheries are those with a rich diversity of plant and insect life, and an equally diverse fish and animal life. The most suspect fisheries, the most vulnerable to disease for example, are those with low diversity and where one species of fish depends upon one food item for its survival.

In any fishery, there should be enough small fish or fry to supply food to the predators such as eels, perch and pike, as well as to grebes and cormorants. Equally, enough of them must survive the fry stage to become adult cyprinids feeding on weed and insects. Below the fry in the hierarchy must be plenty of invertebrates such as snails and insects, as well as plant and animal plankton to nourish the little fish. And so on, up and down the food chain – each link in the chain is as important as the next.

■ Fry

This is simply a term embracing the shoals of small fish in a fishery. These may be the young of one species or the adults of another smaller species. All are fry.

■ Fully scaled Mirror

See Carp.

G

■ Golden tench

An albino tench, usually of a striking yellow colour, though retaining all other features of a normal tench including the jewel red eye. They occur in the wild rarely, but are more common in aquatic collections as a result of artificial selection during breeding.

They retain their albino appearance if stocked, and are a spectacular addition to a fishery. When small their colouration may make them easy prey, which explains why the more camouflaged normal tench has been selected during evolution. Golden tench are exactly the same species as normal green tench.

■ Gozzer

See Baits.

■ Gravid

This is the term used to describe a fish which is not merely containing spawn – they do this for several months anyway – but one which is conspicuously in spawn and perhaps about to spawn. Many species, such as tench and pike, can be quite bloated at this time and may exude eggs from the vent, when handled.

■ Grayling

Widely distributed in Britain but lacking in northern Scotland and Ireland. Its preferred habitat is fast-flowing, cold streams and it occurs in some lakes. It is a well-loved fish of many anglers especially of northerners where the Yorkshire rivers can provide fine sport. Others regard it as inferior to the trout as a sporting fish, which is a pity.

The grayling has a huge, soft, dorsal fin which distinguishes it from other species As a member of the salmonids it has a small adipose fin between the main dorsal and the tail. The large fin is related, in part at least, to spawning activity.

Another interesting feature of the grayling is its pear-shaped pupil which makes it unique among British fishes. The flanks of the fish have a mauve

Golden tench netted from Zyg Gregorek's Anglers' Paradise lakes in Devon.

sheen and dispersed, dark spots while the underparts are pale, sometimes faintly golden. It is one of the most delicately beautiful fish in freshwater, but rarely exceeds 4 lb. A 2 lb fish would be excellent.

Grayling are often taken on fly tackle, and they have an unusual habit of rising from the bottom, vertically upwards, to intercept the offering. There is a whole school of fishermen who use floats, long trotting, and worms to capture grayling. The British record is 4 lb 3 oz hooked from the Dorset Frome in 1989.

■ Groundbait

The most basic form of groundbait is white or brown breadcrumb. Unless specially treated, white tends to be on the stodgy side while brown gives a nice fluffy consistency. Mix the two together for greater versatility.

Plain crumb works well with baits like punched bread or on venues where the fish are not fussy, such as well populated Irish and Danish waters. But when bites are at a premium, plain breadcrumb has its limitations. Crumb swells to twice its size in water and quickly fills up the fish. Even brown and white mixtures are rather limited in what they can achieve.

Continental groundbait has become incredibly popular because it offers a wide range of consistencies and is a great attractor and holding agent – all rolled into one. Most importantly, it does not overfeed the fish, mainly because its ingredients are non-absorbing and contain little if any bread.

The majority of experienced anglers opt for a compromise, carrying a mixture of breadcrumb and Continental groundbait. There is nothing wrong in mixing the two but take care not to use excessive breadcrumb if there is any suspicion the fishing might be a little less than easy.

Plain crumb mixers Plain brown crumb forms a cloud when mixed dry or wet. A dry mix is better for fishing at close range with baits like punched bread,

Dampen Continental groundbait with a sponge to obtain perfect consistency.

squatts and pinkies. A wetter, more sloppy consistency gives a little extra weight for feeding small balls accurately at greater range – such as when fishing the long pole with punched bread.

Brown crumb is also a good bulking agent when a lot of groundbait is required. It is relatively cheap and can be bound together with a small percentage of one of the heavier Continental mixes.

The only white breadcrumb which forms a cloud successfully on its own has been specially heat treated and is known as punch crumb. It is also often mixed in with fresh liquidised bread to provide a little weight and aid feeding accuracy.

Normal white crumb is unusable on its own, being far too stodgy. When wet, it is only used as a binding agent to keep other mixes together for fishing at long range or in fast turbulent waters.

Continental consistencies The best starting point with Continental brands is to begin by looking at consistencies. Many manufacturers are helpful on this score, naming their blends as lake, river, bottom, feeder or cloud mixes. Other recipes are designed for particular species but this is not as important as achieving the right consistency to suit the method and baits you will be using. Think of the groundbait as a medium to attract fish and as a way of introducing free offerings where they cannot be loose fed. With this line of attack, you will not go far wrong.

All the leading Continental brands have mixes ranging from the extremely light to very heavy. Light and heavy recipes can be mixed together to form a medium consistency, or a medium mix purchased off the shelf.

Light mixes are used for on-the-drop, surface and mid-water fishing and to induce bites on clear or difficult venues. They give a lovely slow sinking cloud and are less likely to spook fish. A good cloudy mix can be fed little and often, even on every cast.

Speed fishing for gudgeon has been developed into a fine art by many top canal matchmen.

Medium consistencies are used for feeding baits like bloodworm, jokers, squatts, pinkies and casters in small helpings either by hand or soft-actioned catapult. In this case, the chief job of the groundbait is to get the feed out accurately.

Medium consistency groundbaits can be mixed to produce a fluffy ball which breaks up as it nears the bottom. A wetter consistency creates a cloud as it hits the water. Mixed very dry the same applies – but the groundbait will float for a second or two before exploding into an attractive cloud.

Heavy mixes are mainly used to bind largish balls of feed together so they can be fed at long range without fear of breaking up. Bream anglers pack the balls of feed with plenty of squatts and casters and perhaps chopped worms to try and hold a shoal for a long period. Heavy mixes are also used to get feed baits down to the bottom quickly in powerful currents.

The heavy consistency is also useful when fishing with baits like bloodworm and jokers. Several large balls, containing these baits, will take a long time to break down on the bottom. By slowly releasing small amounts of the feed baits, as the groundbait dissolves away, an initial groundbait bombardment can keep a swim ticking over for several hours.

Continental groundbaits contain numerous additives and base ingredients. Obvious inclusions like ground hempseed – a great favourite – do help to hold fish in the swim. More often, bland ingredients like biscuit flour and maize meal are included as bulking agents, while other types of flours are there to give the right clouding and binding effects.

■ Gudgeon

The gudgeon grows to only a few ounces yet may occur in profusion in many waters, making a sizeable catch possible. In times gone by, gudgeon parties were organised on the Thames when hundreds would be caught and cooked. It occurs throughout Britain and Ireland except northern Scotland, usually in rivers and streams, but also in lakes and ponds. It is a highly adaptable species, feeding on most food items, animal and vegetable.

The species has a distinctive pair of barbules at the corners of the mouth. The body is soft, but muscular, and the flanks have a bluish sheen, often, and with vague spot markings along the lateral line – rather like salmon parr markings only fainter.

All the standard techniques for small cyprinids work well for gudgeon: indeed, at times, they seem to work too well! The British record of 4 oz 4 dr came from a Welsh pond in 1977.

■ Hair-rig

The greatest leveller of all time in carp fishing. Inventor Lennie Middleton first attached a boilie to a hook by tethering it on a human hair in 1979 – and that's how the rig got its name. His aim was to deceive the carp into thinking that the bait was just another free offering with no hook attached.

Lennie's theory that the carp would confidently pick up a hair-rigged bait proved correct and many thousands of anglers have benefitted as a result. For best effect, the hair should hang from halfway along the shank of the hook. This is achieved by tying it to the eye and then sliding a short length of silicone tubing over the top to midway on the shank. This is the perfect pivot point, allowing the bend of the hook to be drawn into the carp's mouth. On rejection, it tries to leave eye first and at a slight angle giving the best chance of the hook point catching inside.

There have been endless experiments with hair lengths and materials but nothing beats a few strands of fine dental floss which is adjusted so the boilie just touches the bottom of the bend.

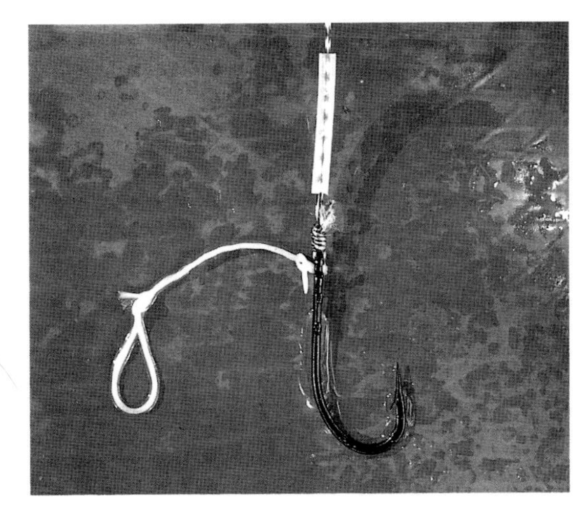

Dental floss hair on which the boilie is threaded and then secured with a boilie stop trapped in the loop. The silicone sleeve is slid down over the eye to midway along the shank.

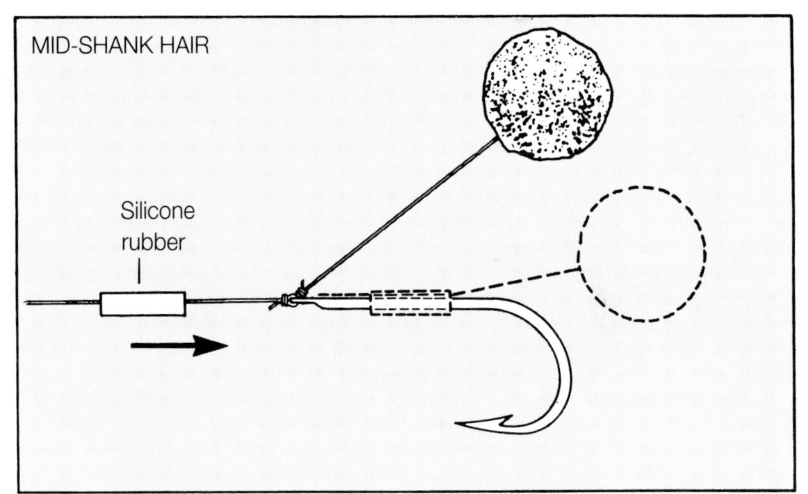

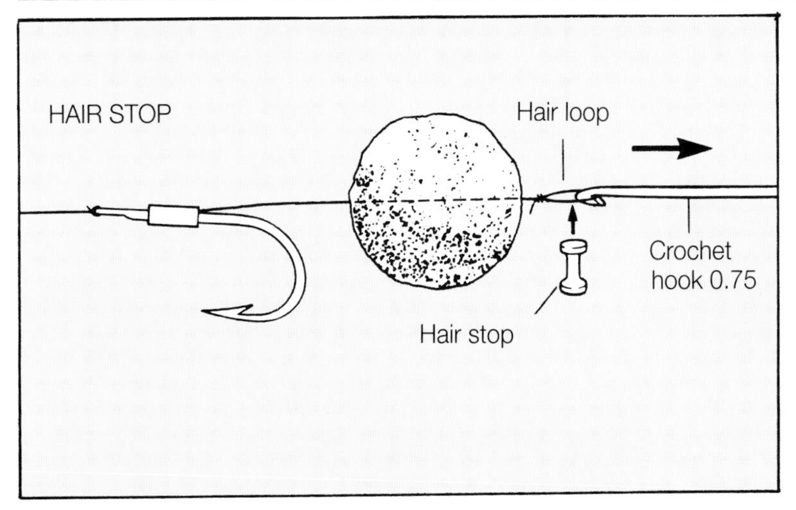

■ Handling fish

Many fish have the scales covered in a layer of slime or mucous as protection against injury or disease. When handling fish, it is important that as much of the mucous layer as possible is left intact. Wet hands remove far less mucous than dry hands, and also have a more calming effect on the fish, making it less liable to leap. It is for the same basic reason that fish should always be unhooked on a soft background – grass, cloth or polythene – and never on sand or gravel.

Fish should be held firmly with wet hands, or a wet net, until they stop flexing, and the hook can then be removed with forceps, disgorger, or the fingers. Never hold a fish where there is a risk of it flipping free of your grasp onto a hard surface – like the bottom of a boat. And never keep a fish out of water for longer than strictly necessary.

Keepnets should be staked out carefully in deep, and preferably, shaded water and fish placed inside, not thrown or dropped into them. The best keepnets unfasten at their base to release the fish. They should not be tipped along the net like peas in a tube. Keepsacks are used for some species, such as carp and keep tubes have been designed for pike.

Return big fish By and large it is better to return larger fish to the water as soon as possible, retaining them only occasionally. They have a greater oxygen demand than small fish and may become distressed in nets, sacks or tubes in warm weather. This is especially true during the night when there is an oxygen minimum period just before dawn in summer.

All large fish are best unhooked in the folds of a wet net, or in one of the unhooking mats now available. Pike should be unhooked with the angler wearing gloves of thick, soft material and forceps should be used to remove the hooks.

Holdalls with strong shoulder straps and outer pockets for bank sticks and brolly.

■ Hempseed

See Baits.

■ High protein bait

A carp bait with a protein value of more than 60 per cent. For example, a typical boilie mix of milk powders could easily work out to 85 per cent protein. In theory, baits with higher protein levels should be more beneficial to the carp but there are many other factors involved and the case has not really been proven either way. The success of these mixes rests on the belief that the carp associate them with a feeling of well being and eventually seek them out in preference to baits with a lower protein content.

■ Holdall

Angling luggage basically falls into three categories. There are rod holdalls, net and bait carryalls, and for those who do not favour the solid type of tackle box, the rucksack.

Rod holdalls are made in varying lengths and capacities. Longer padded versions are popular for two-piece carp rods. Match anglers tend to prefer shorter, but much more spacious holdalls which will hold several rods, poles, umbrella and a variety of bank sticks.

Basic keepnet and landing net carryalls have just one compartment. But the new jumbo carryalls also offer storage room for bait boxes, flask and a host of other accessories including catapults, bait waiter and groundbait mixing bowls. The larger carryalls are usually fitted with a padded shoulder strap.

Rucksacks are more popular with specialist anglers, particularly carp enthusiasts who may need to carry a great deal of gear down to the water's edge for a three or four day session.

■ Hooks

Traditionally, hook sizes were evenly numbered from the largest size 2 through to the smallest size 26 which is almost exclusively used in match fishing. But a recent trend which originated on the Continent has seen the introduction of odd numbered hooks between 12 and 26.

Bigger hooks from 2s to 8s are best used with big baits like lumps of bread, luncheon meat, lobworms and boilies. The same types of bait, scaled down in size, suit hooks in the middle range from size 10 to 16. These are also suitable for baits like sweetcorn and groupings of maggots and casters.

Smaller hooks from 18 down, are for baits like maggots, casters, hemp, tares, breadpunch and bloodworm.

Odd sized hooks from 15 through to 25 offer the angler more choice when stepping up or down in hook size. This can make a crucial difference in hitting shy bites, or in actually getting a bite in the first place, when the going is tough.

Spade or eyed? Apart from hook size, there's a number of other hook choices starting with spade-end or eyed patterns. The spade requires a more complicated knot but it provides superior presentation of the bait – particularly in the smaller sizes. The spade-end has a flattened top to its shank which prevents the knot, which is formed on the shank, from pulling free.

Eyed hooks are formed with a complete bend at the top of the shank through which the line is first threaded before being knotted with a tucked Half-Blood or Grinner. It can also be tied to the shank.

Eyed patterns are preferred in larger hook sizes because they are less prone to damaging the line under severe pressure. A spade-end can be quite sharp and cut through the line like a razor if a big fish bolts into weed.

The last resort is the ready-tied hook. There is a really good range available – with every imaginable breaking strain of line to match the hook sizes. Normally, ready-tied hooks come in packets of six or ten.

Barbless are kind on fish Barbless hooks are now mandatory on some private fisheries because the owners consider they are kinder on the fish. Matchmen have also taken to barbless patterns in a big way as it cuts down on unhooking time.

Barbed hooks are still popular where they are allowed because they hold baits like maggots very securely on the cast and there's less chance of a fish slipping the hook.

Ever conscious of fish conservation, most hook manufacturers produce micro barbs. If removed with care, these will not do any damage to the mouth of a fish.

Types of wire Hook patterns vary mainly to suit different types of bait. The most common patterns are crystal and round bend. Live baits like maggots stay on the crystal bend patterns better on the cast and also do not tend to ride up, masking the hook point. Round bend hooks give more hooking power when sinking, or at least partly submerging, the hook into an inanimate bait like bread, tares and hemp.

Above: **Fine wired hooks for delicate baits.**

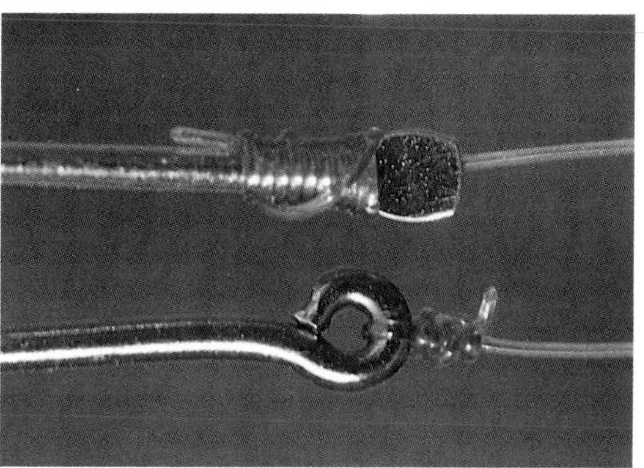

Left: **Spade-end or eyed? The choice of pattern starts with the size of the target fish.**

Forged hooks are made of stronger, flattened wire and are the first choice for bigger fish, or for amassing large catches when the fish are feeding freely. Fine wire patterns must be used with care but often produce bites when the going is tough because they are so light.

Of course, the thickness of a hook must also be related to the bait being used. A forged hook, even in a small size, would burst a fragile bloodworm. Baits like this can only be presented correctly on very fine wire patterns.

Modern hook manufacturing processes are, in fact, narrowing the gap between fine wire and forged hook strengths. Carbon hooks are extremely sharp but even the finest wire models possess amazing strength. Some of the best patterns can be straightened out completely and then bent back to their original shape without breaking!

The chemically sharpened or etched hook offers a superior point, generally both sharper and stronger than its predecessors. Once the hook point has been cut to shape, it is etched down even smoother in a chemical bath which also has the effect of honing the point.

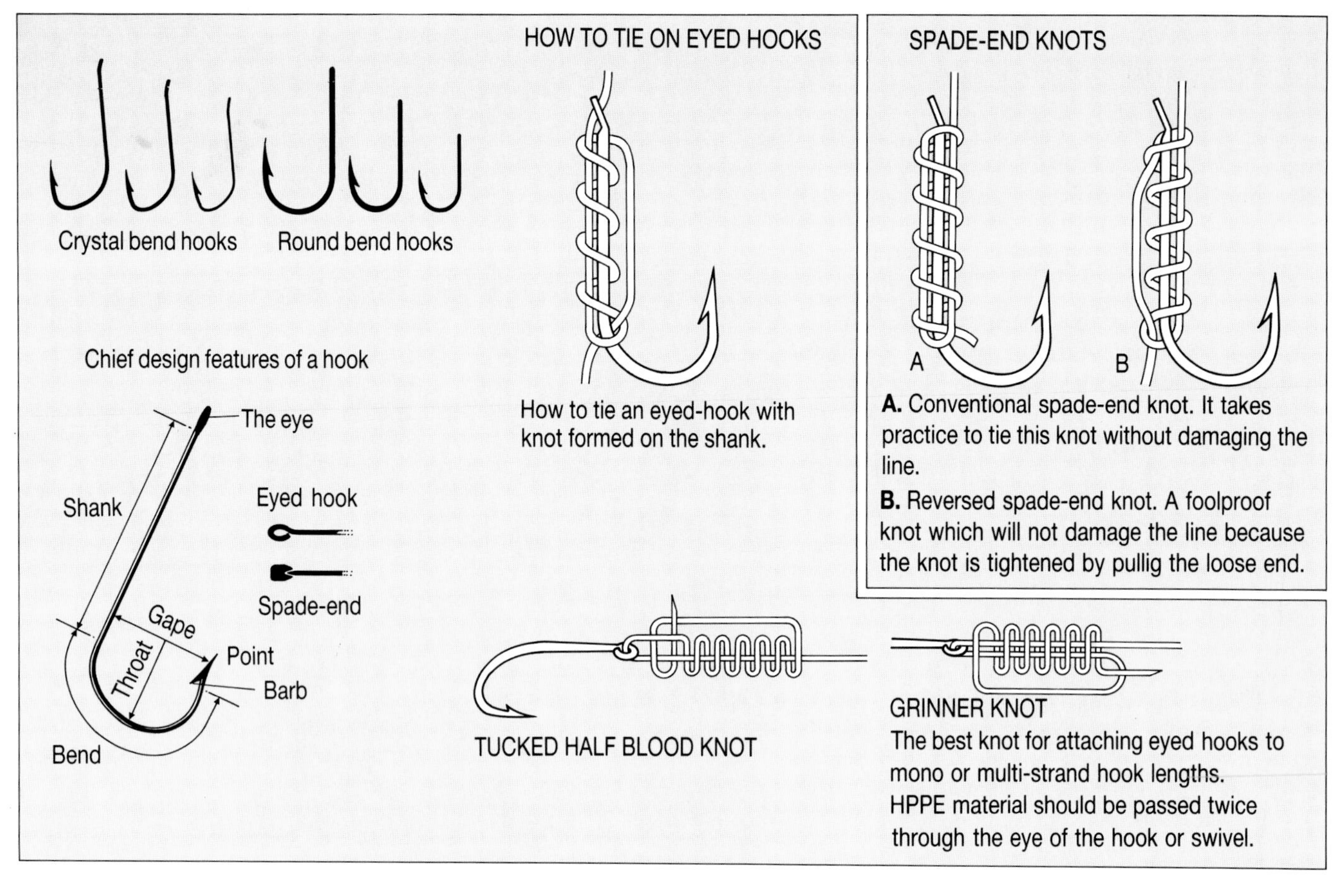

Never be afraid to change up a size if bites are confident and fish are being bumped off on the strike. Similarly, a change to a smaller hook can make a huge difference if the fish are only pecking at a bait, without taking it completely down.

Hooks - trebles Treble hooks are widely used in salmon and pike fishing. The use of some artificial lures would be impossible without trebles – large plugs for example. In other circumstances single hooks can be substituted but in the case of pike the treble gives a surer purchase, initially, in a bony mouth.

Snap tackle with a sliding Ryder hook on the wire trace. Only one of the points on each treble is barbed for holding the bait - the others are barbless.

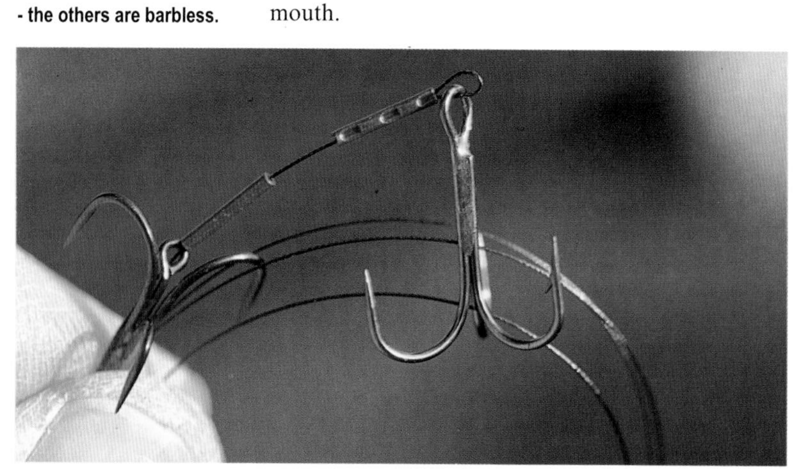

Once the fish is hooked, a single is as good as a treble – unless it pulls free, when its chances of relocating are three times less than that of a treble hook.

Treble hooks comprise, roughly speaking, three single hooks brazed back to back, so that each is at 120 degrees to the axis or shank. Usually they have an eye for attachment of the trace, but may also be tapered for binding. The hook bends are as variable as for single hooks, and the hook points and barbs are the same.

Having three hooks enables the barbless hook fanatic to use semi-barbless hooks – one hook has a barb for bait holding and the other two are barbless. Most treble hooks have barbs that are too rank and too deeply cut. In the future, there's likely to be a move to microbarbs.

Treble hooks can be used singly, or in tandem on Jardine snap tackles. Some long-shank trebles are available for binding a bait like a prawn. Other trebles have a slit along the shank, right up to the eye, enabling easy changes on trebles.

■ Hook link

The hook link or length is a short piece of monofilament or HPPE material tied to the hook and attached to the main line by the loop method, blood knot or a connecting swivel. It must always be a lower breaking strain than the main line.

By keeping the hook link short, the minimum amount of line will be lost with the hook attached if the tackle gets snagged up. Lighter hook length line also gives much better bait presentation.

Whether pole or running line fishing, it is unwise to tie the main line direct to the hook. If a snag is found, there is no telling where the line might part – many yards of tackle could be lost and present a real hazard to wildlife.

■ Hotspot

There are areas on any fishery where the fish always seem to shoal up and provide good catches. These prime swims are known as hotspots. Sometimes, hotspots are created by anglers deliberately baiting up just one spot to draw in the fish. Swims close to the access gates on many of the fisheries also tend to fish well simply because they are a short walk from the car park and bait is going in constantly.

Normally, a feature on the lake or an abundant source of food is responsible for the hotspot. Depth may have something to do with it and different hotspots emerge as the season rolls on and water temperatures start to dip. Bankside cover, underwater gravel bars, moored boats, wider sections on narrow canals and rivers – all these factors can provide a haven for fish.

Wherever you fish, a well-trodden section of bank will tell you a swim has something special to offer.

■ HPPE

Kryston Products pioneered the use of high performance polyethylene in carp fishing by making it available in multi-strand form and as a more manageable braid known as Silkworm. HPPE is strong and supple but incredibly low in diameter making it perfect for hook links.

For maximum knot strength, two turns of HPPE should be passed through the eye of the swivel or hook followed by a four or five-turn Grinner knot. Sharp scissors must be used to trim the material cleanly.

Multi-strand is 100 per cent HPPE yarn and its fine fibres lay parallel to each other making it tricky to tie with rough hands. But it's worth persevering as the fine filaments fan out in water and blend in with the bottom. Silkworm has an HPPE core with a polyester wrap around the outside. It still remains very limp and is much easier to handle than multi-strand.

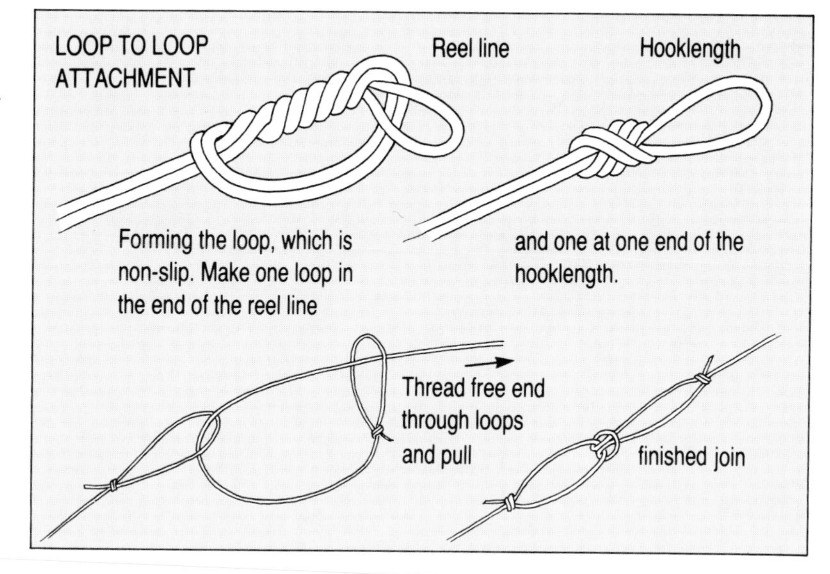

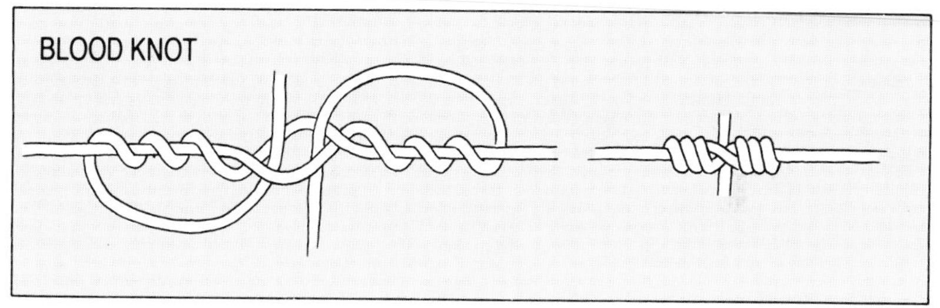

Top: **Loop to loop attachment. The most popular way of attaching a hook length to the reel line. Above: Blood knot. An alternative method of securing the hook length to the reel line. This knot is often preferred by match anglers.**

■ Hybrid

A hybrid is a cross between two different species. The hybrid is usually sexually sterile, but the fish may be very vigorous in growth and strength. All hybrids show some intermediate characters between the two parents. Hybridisation is fairly common among closely related species, and less common among widely separated species.

Bream and roach, roach and rudd, rudd and bream hybridise regularly, partly because their spawning sites may be similar, as may their spawning times. But perch and pike, belonging to totally unrelated families of fish, do not hybridise. Incidentally, the zander is not a hybrid between pike and perch, but is another member of the perch family.

Tricky to identify The more closely related are the hybridising species, the greater the chance that the hybrid progeny might be fertile. Naturally this cannot happen frequently in a water otherwise the two parent species would totally merge! So, fertile hybrids are not common, but when they do occur, they can back-breed with one of the parent species.

The progeny of such a cross is likely to have three-quarters of the features of one (original) parent species, and one-quarter of the other. It almost goes without saying that they would be difficult to identify. Crosses of this kind are even less likely to be fertile than the 50:50 crosses.

Very careful examination of the scale counts, pharyngeal teeth and other indicators are usually sufficient, in expert hands to determine whether a fish is pure. But then it has to be dead!

IJ

■ Indicators

See Bite indicators.

■ Insert waggler

See Floats.

■ IPN

Infectious pancreatic necrosis (IPN) is a virus which comes in several strains, some of which are relatively passive, others more active. Adult fish are the carriers, but it is dangerous to young fish, and it may be fatal to young trout. If the fish live in a stressed environment, even the passive forms of the virus may prove fatal.

■ Isotope

A slim, glass tube filled with a radioactive gas which glows brightly in darkness. It is taped to the rod tip for legering at night, attached to a float or glued into a monkey climber body for carp fishing. The gas is harmless and emits no more radio activity than the illuminated numbers on a watch face.

Isotopes are graded from 200 to 500 microlamberts. The more powerful units are most suited to carp fishing. They can even be glued into the spreader blocks of some landing nets and to protect the fragile isotope tube, it's a good idea to fix it in place with bathroom sealer.

■ Jokers

See Baits.

■ Keepnet

Fishery byelaws dictate a minimum length and diameter for keepnets and all meshing must be knotless. There have been vast improvements in design over recent seasons, particularly for matchmen who retain their catch for several hours and weigh the lot.

If used correctly, the keepnet should have no ill effects. But it is most important that as much of the net as possible is submerged to give the fish the maximum amount of space. On stillwaters, it is best to stake the net out with bank sticks at both ends to prevent it from collapsing. On flowing water the current tends to support the net in one direction so it need not be staked out – unless the nearside is very shallow.

Mesh sizes There are three knotless mesh sizes, usually made from a soft, multi-filament polyester material netting. Gudgeon mesh is the largest and only tends to be used by the specimen angler, or where large catches of fish like bream may be expected on very prolific waters. It's claimed that the wider mesh offers more oxygen to a larger mass of fish.

Minnow mesh is about half the size of gudgeon mesh but fine micro mesh is more popular. It will not let even the tiniest fish escape, which is why it is preferred by match anglers.

There are square and circular framed keepnets with a minimum length of six feet and to be fair on your catch it is best to spend a few extra pounds on a larger net than you actually require. There will always be occasions where the bank is awkward and an extra couple of feet is needed to suspend enough net into the water.

Square nets are a better proposition on venues with shallow margins as these nets will sit lower in the water and offer the fish a greater area in which to swim. Round nets are fine so long as you can get them staked out in a reasonable depth.

While short canal keepnets of six to eight feet in length may be acceptable on these venues, a good all-round net should be at least ten feet long.

■ Kevlar

Lightweight material, often used to strengthen carbon rod and poles. Kevlar combines well with carbon and is usually incorporated as an external weave which supports, stiffens and certainly strengthens hollow carbon blanks.

■ King carp

See Carp.

■ Kiting

Carp hooked on a long line often swim straight for the margins, kiting resolutely towards obstructions and making it very difficult for the angler to exert control with possibly as much as 60 yards of line between him and the fish.

Heavy side-strain, keeping the rod low to the water and pulling hard in the opposite direction, will sometimes succeed in turning the carp's head. But if it actually reaches the bank then the best tactic is to plunge the rod tip far below the surface to try and keep the line away from obstructions. It is then a matter of winding as hard as possible until the carp is out of the danger zone.

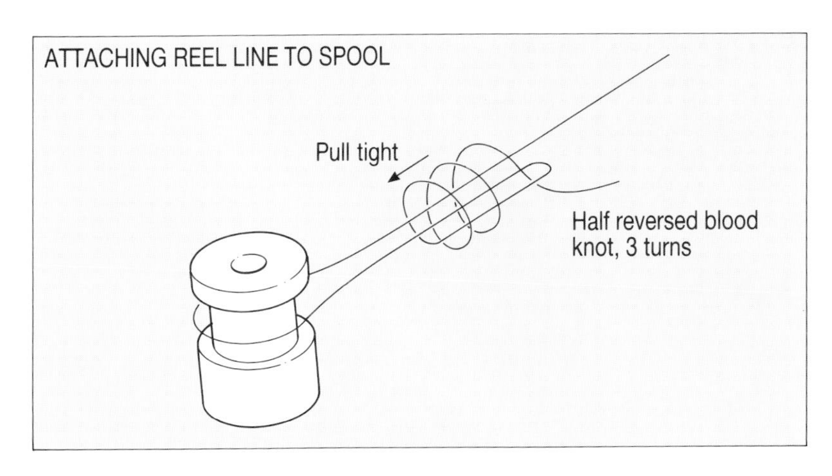

■ Knots

- Blood Knot for tying hook lengths to reel line. See Hook Link.
- Grinner for attaching eyed hooks and swivels to mono or HPPE hook lengths. See Hooks.
- Loop to Loop for attaching hook lengths to the reel line. See Hook Link.
- Sliding Stop Knot for sliding floats. See Floats.
- Spade-end tying. See Hooks.
- Tucked Half-Blood for tying on eyed hooks. See Hooks.
- Water or Cove Knot for joining lines of unequal strength. See Trout Fishing section.
- Knot for attaching reel line to spool (see diagram).

Rectangular framed keepnet gives fish more freedom when staked out in shallow canal margins.

L

■ Lake fishing

Sizing up a stillwater is not always that difficult. In the warmer months these fisheries tend to be at their most productive and an early or late session will often reveal plenty of signs of fish movement – a vital pointer to good sport.

Tackling up for coloured waters A highly coloured water indicates that there's a good head of fish, probably including larger species like tench and carp which keep the bottom sediment suspended in their constant search for food.

This type of venue will normally respond to an attacking approach. It is a fair bet the pole, fished to hand style at a length of four to five metres, will sort out good numbers of small fish. Plenty of groundbait, fed in a soft consistency, is bound to draw in lots of fish. Squatts and pinkies will also help to hold them, switching between pinkies and big maggots on the hook. Later in the session a switch to loose fed casters could well bring some bonus fish.

If the venue holds lots of small carp and large tench another excellent method is the waggler. Fish on-the-drop style, feeding soft groundbait and spray plenty of maggots or casters over the float. This should draw a good head of fish into the swim.

When the fish are very active it is often possible to get them boiling for loose feed on the surface. Double maggot or caster on the hook are the best killing baits.

Clear water methods Features are not of prime importance on the heavily coloured stillwater, but they come into their own on the deeper, clear type of venue. In bright, sunny conditions the fish will be found tightly hugging weed or overhead cover. Seek out swims within casting distance of heavily over-

High summer on a Sussex lake which has been coloured up by tench and carp filtering out food from the bottom mud.

grown islands and tuck your bait, either on waggler or legering gear, as close as possible.

Another obvious spot is alongside thick surface weed or through gaps in weedy areas. This is where the long pole can score really well, using a heavy gauge elastic and strong line to bully powerful fish like tench out quickly.

Carp and bream will be more likely from shaded areas, while a delicate running line float rig will often find species like roach and rudd if you fish into the slightly darker looking water – just off any shallower areas. A canal waggler rig is ideal for this type of fishing.

Clear water pits can be very difficult to master and often dictate a long range approach to find the fish. The secret of these waters is to really familiarise yourself with the bottom contours. Gravel excavations produce a network of bars and these are the main key to fish location.

In such clear water, the shallower areas will almost certainly be more weedy with the clearer spots in the deeper water. Fish usually shoal in the deeper channels between the bars but in warmer weather often move on to the tops of the bars.

On clear pits the long range waggler can be excellent for species like bream and tench. The open-end feeder and straight bomb also work well, but feel your way with groundbait as the fish might not take large quantities.

Prolific shallows Wind direction is another important gravel pit guideline. Often the wind stirs up sediment on the shore it is blowing into, which in turn dislodges food. Coloured water is always worth investigating.

More consistently coloured pits are often prolific fisheries. The colour is a good thing because it prevents weed growth from getting out of hand and the fish tend to be more widely spread.

Searching out underwater bars is just as important on this type of fishery, but unlike the clearer pits, in the warmer months the fish are much more inclined to seek out the shallower water over the gravel bars. The water is richer in food in these areas and the fish probably feel more secure because of the darker, murkier water.

When fishing the shallows like this, big stable wagglers are needed to beat the wind, but shotting down the line is kept minimal, because fish will often take a bait on-the-drop. Loose feed works well if you can reach the desired spot, otherwise a very soft groundbait mix is used to carry out squatts and casters by means of a soft actioned catapult. Red maggots are a prime hookbait on this sort of water. Casters, worms and sweetcorn are also worth a try.

After a good spell of catching on the waggler, bites often tail off after a couple of hours. A switch to the straight bomb can pull odd bonus fish, but usually a small, open-end feeder is better and if bream, tench and small carp are about, bites start coming thick and fast again after a few casts.

Depending on how coloured the water is, the short pole can produce well on gravel pit fisheries, normally when there's a good surface ripple which encourages the fish to venture nearer to the bank.

The long pole is also viable but has a tendency to take fish in short bursts. It is a good idea to have another swim on the go further out, chopping and changing between the two lines will bring much better results than flogging one method all day on the same line.

Winter cutbacks Water clarity is much clearer in winter, even on the stillwaters which were very coloured in summer. This tells you the fish will not take so much loose feed, and groundbait must also be used very sparingly.

On lake venues where the short pole brought an immediate response, bites are at a premium. The pole angler has to fish much further out into the deeper water, with a short line between pole tip and float. Bites will often only register as tiny movements on the delicate float tip. The fish are much more lethargic and less likely to bury the float out of sight.

With conventional baits like maggots and casters, only half a dozen free offerings every ten minutes or so are needed so as not to overfeed the fish. Smaller baits like bloodworm and breadpunch may well be essential to gain a response.

The waggler, too, will need modifications, with the fish requiring much less feed and more time to inspect a hookbait. Tackle has to be fished overdepth with the hookbait anchored hard on the bottom. Often a couple of small helpings of groundbait will be enough for several hours fishing, the trick being to find deeper water within range of the catapult so very small amounts of loose feed can be introduced to keep the fish interested.

If the float looks like being defeated by the distance required to locate the fish in deeper water, one of the best winter lake methods is the open-end feeder. Much less groundbait is used to hold a mixture of casters and squatts. Hemp can be added as well to cut down on the groundbait. It is also a good idea to use a much smaller sized feeder than the model that scored so well in the warmer months.

The first barrier to cross is in getting an initial response, so it is a good idea to begin a session with a small hook and double pinkies. It is surprising how

Round landing net with a finer mesh copes with most coarse fish.

Triangular landing nets designed for carp fishing.

quickly a small bait like this brings bites while larger maggots and casters are ignored. Get a few fish coming on the pinkies and as your confidence builds, try switching to bigger baits as the day progresses.

Whatever method you choose for your winter lake fishing, always remember the quality fish often come on the feed during the last hour of daylight. It is well worth hanging on for this period no matter how poor sport has been. A degree or two rise in water temperature is all that is needed to provoke some hectic action.

■ Lamprey

The three British species are the sea, river and the brook lampreys. The brook is an entirely freshwater species but the first two spawn in freshwater and the progeny eventually return to the sea to pursue parasitic life styles.

The brook lamprey is non-parasitic, but it uses its sucker for attachment to stones and other objects. Lampreys are primitive, jawless fishes and possess a sucker in the adult stage, instead of jaws.

The suckers of sea and river lampreys attach to a host – various fish species – from which they get their sustenance. Lampreys have no scales, no paired fins, and the skeleton is cartilaginous rather then bony.

■ Landing net

Round or pan landing nets are much favoured by match anglers because they are relatively shallow and it is an easy job to remove even quite large fish once they are on the bank. Small pan nets with diameters down to as small as 12 inches are made for the pole angler who is only expecting fish up to 12 oz. A more average size is 18 inches which will cope with fish up to around 6 lb.

Specimen sized pan nets are gaining popularity and are good for the roving angler who wants to strap one to his back, without having to re-assemble the net once a fish is hooked. This type normally has quite deep netting, so a good fish can be quickly weighed within the confines of the net.

Triangular nets fold down for easy storage and lightweight models with glass arms are most popular. These nets usually have a thick cord drawstring tensioning the arms and work very well as long as big fish are not lifted in them. Specimen sized triangular nets are much deeper making it possible to lift hefty fish by gathering the mesh under the frame.

Fine mesh landing nets are kind on the fish and work well on stillwaters or slow flowing rivers. A wider mesh is easier to manoeuvre in the current on faster rivers and will not feel as heavy.

■ Laying on

A float fishing method normally associated with big fish where the hookbait is anchored on the bottom. Many anglers fix a large shot like a No.4, No.1 or BB between six and 12 inches from the hookbait. The float is set another 12 inches overdepth and after the tackle has been cast out, the line is tightened up until just the tip of the float is showing.

If normally loaded, bites usually register on the float by lifting the tip further out of the water,

Quivertipping for bream with the rod positioned at the correct angle for maximum sensitivity.

before it then gradually sinks away. This is the time to strike!

Another method is to over-shot the float by the weight of the last shot, which rests on the bottom. When a fish picks up the hookbait and lifts the extra weight, it sinks the float straight away. Strike immediately!

■ Leam

A fine powdered clay which is used to weight and bind groundbaits together. It is also very good for holding jokers together. Just a light dusting helps form jokers into a ball for feeding – all that is required is a quick spray from an atomiser.

Dry leam is sold in grey and gold colours. Dampened leam is very heavy and is a darker brown. This is used by pole anglers to gain extra distance when feeding small helpings of jokers. Damp leam is also excellent for storing bloodworm and jokers and keeps the baits fresh for several days.

■ Legering

A leger weight pins the hookbait firmly to the bottom. This often brings good results when float tackle is not achieving the correct presentation – too much flow could be pulling the hookbait through too fast, or surface drift dragging it out of the feed area.

The leger works equally well in flowing and stillwaters and is normally combined with a quivertip, swingtip, springtip or butt indicator.

Types of weight The most widely used leger weight is the Arlesey bomb which is fitted with a swivel so it can be run directly on the reel line for straight legering techniques. The alternative is to tether it to a short link of nylon for paternoster style fishing. Another trick when switching between the bomb and feeder is to clip the Arlesey to a quick-change swivel link, or American snap swivel as they are sometimes called.

Simple link legers comprise a number of split-shot pinched on a small link, or boom of nylon which can be fixed paternoster style, or left free running if a swivel is utilised.

Drilled bullets and coffin weights are threaded on the reel line and then simply anchored on their

Assortment of non-toxic leger weights.

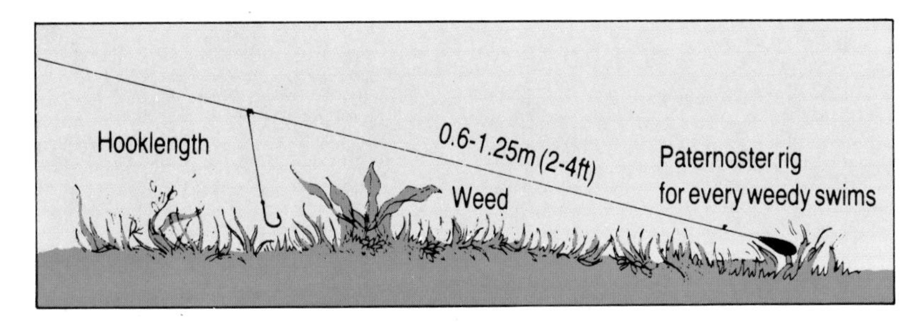

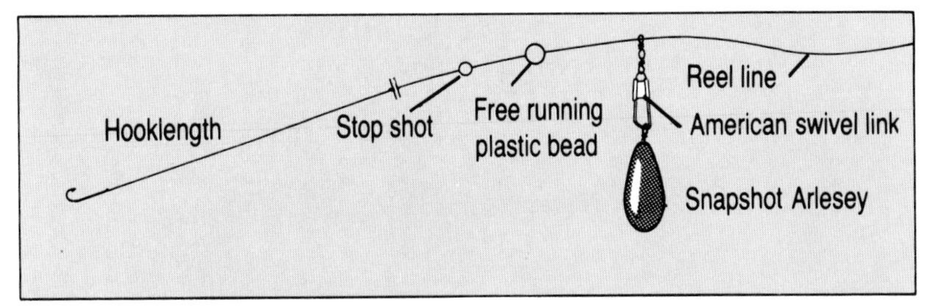

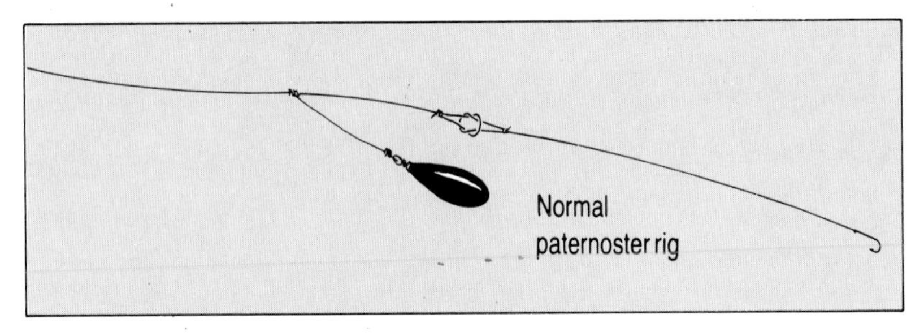

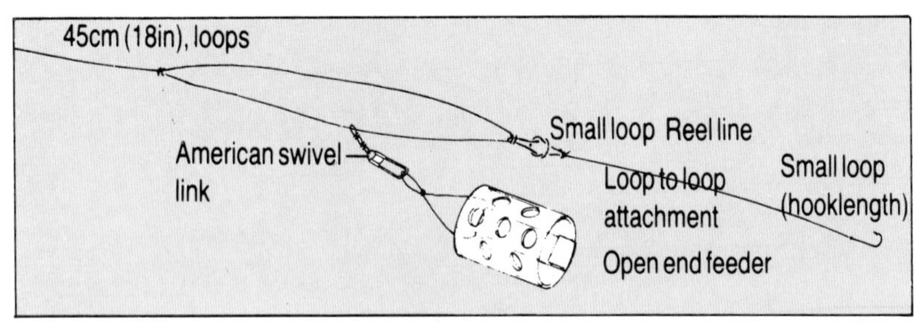

There's an abundance of set-ups for leger rigs but these are the most common.

downside with a split-shot, or leger stop. Below this is fixed a short hook length. The drilled bullet is round so it can be induced to roll in flowing water – a good trick when trying to search out fish on big baits like luncheon meat. Flat coffin weights are designed to hug the bottom when a stationary bait is required in strong currents.

A recent development has been inter-changeable link legers which screw into a moulded nylon link. Once the link is attached to the rig, the weights can be switched up or down in size without dismantling the tackle.

Free-running rig For close range legering, a very basic free-running weight, stopped 12 to 24 inches from the hookbait, works quite well if the bottom is not weedy or snaggy. But a vast improvement is made by attaching the leger weight to a swivel link and inserting a small plastic bead on the line as a buffer against the leger stop. Now the end tackle is much more versatile. The leger weight can be changed in seconds for a different sized bomb or a swimfeeder. The bead acts as an anti-tangle device, pushing the hook length away from the leger weight. It also stops fine weed from clogging up the free running swivel link.

Paternosters Free-running leger rigs fail miserably on weedy bottoms. Even the bead will not stop the weight from constantly snagging solid on the line. This is hopeless because a taking fish will feel resistance and reject the hookbait.

The answer is to fish one of the paternoster rig variations. One good way of keeping the hookbait clear of weed is to attach the leger weight to the bottom of the reel line, then fix a short hook length two to four feet back up the reel line.

The more conventional paternoster involves the leger weight being tied to a nylon boom which comes off the reel line just above the hook length. Being fixed, weed and debris will not affect the weight and bites register directly to the indicator – because of the play the leger boom affords.

The loop system An excellent weight attachment method is the loop. A 12 to 18 inch loop is formed at the base of the reel line, on which is left a free running swivel link. At the base of the large loop, a smaller one inch loop is formed to which the hook length is attached. Once the leger weight is clipped to the swivel link, the small hook length loop is pushed away to prevent tangles. There is also enough room on the large loop for bites to register without the leger weight moving. The great feature of this system is that there are no stops to cause tangles or slipping. This method is also suitable for long range feeder fishing.

Rod positioning is vitally important when legering. A target board helps show up delicate bites while quivertipping, especially in winter when registrations are more lethargic.

The bow method The bow method is a useful tactic to keep in reserve when bites prove difficult to hit. On stillwaters, it entails feeding a little line out into the surface drift, after the end tackle has settled. Until the drift takes up the slack, causing a slight bow, the line is studied for any quick indications. If a bite does come at this stage it is normally a savage, unmissable one because the fish feels no resistance against the slack.

Once the bow has formed, a taking fish will still feel less resistance than if it had snatched the bait against a straight line from end rig to rod tip.

The bow is even more effective on flowing water. Again, it's a matter of feeding line out into the current after the end tackle has settled to create the bow. This will help stop the flow from dragging the end tackle out of place. More importantly, if the end tackle is just weighted sufficiently to hold bottom, a pull on the hook link from a fish is invariably enough to upset the delicate balance – the leger weight moves and the fish is on!

The bow method is used with a quivertip indicator on flowing water. The quivertip should be slightly tensioned by the pressure of the current on the line. Bites often show up as slight tremors to begin with, but any steadier pull will move the end tackle and the tip falls back violently. It is then a case of lifting the rod and gently tightening into the fish. Often the force of the current on the bow will set the hook home automatically. This method works just as effectively with feeder tackle.

Leger stop Commercially-made leger stops are supplied in two sizes, mini and standard. They consist of a small plastic peg which plugs into a plastic collar. The collar is first threaded on the reel line to the required position, then the peg is firmly pushed home. The stop prevents a feeder or leger weight from sliding any further down the line on the cast. Split-shot can also be used as leger stops but slippage is a problem on long casts.

■ Leger weights

See Legering.

■ Licences

All anglers in freshwater require a rod licence from the National Rivers Authority in order to fish. Sea anglers do not need a licence, and neither is one required for some tidal estuaries. The upstream point at which licences become necessary is stipulated in the byelaws for the NRA of the relevant region.

The rod licence may entitle the angler to fish with one, two or more rods, providing that they are all fully attended and not left to fish for themselves. There is usually no age factor involved with licencing, although some authorities turn a blind eye at anglers under the age of 14 years. Strictly, they too require a licence to fish. In the Republic of Ireland, the game fishermen need a licence, but coarse and sea anglers do not.

In general then you cannot fish at all, in freshwater, unless you have an NRA licence. But taking out a licence does not mean you can fish where you like.

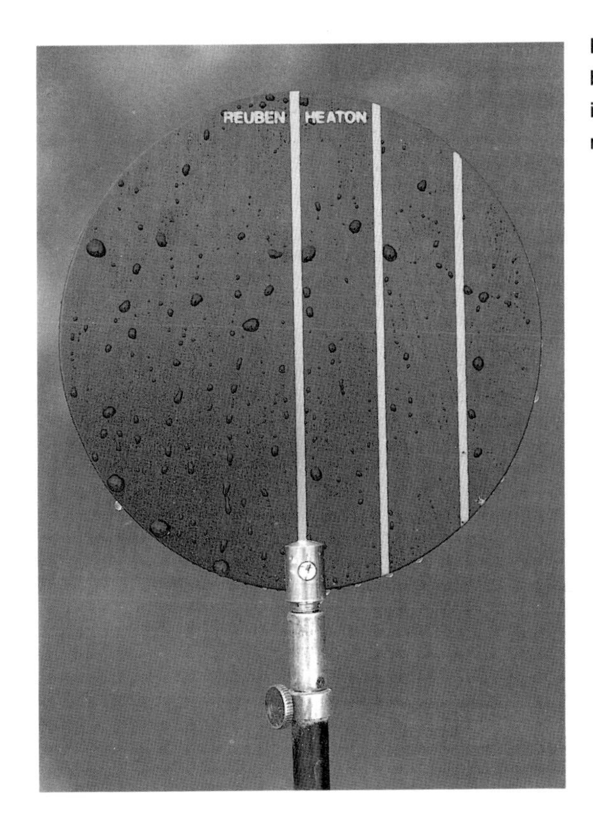

Line up the tip on a target board and the tiniest of indications will show up more clearly.

This is because all waters are owned by somebody, or the fishing rights leased. You may need a club permit or permission from the owner and for those permits you will need to pay a fee.

Most NRA licences are issued by fishing tackle shops, or the HQ of the NRA. The byelaws are usually printed on the reverse side, as are the Close Season dates. Club cards can be obtained from the fishing club secretary, or, on occasion, from the tackle shop.

If there is no counterfoil system in operation it pays to obtain a receipt, otherwise you lay yourself open to prosecution should your licence, or permit, be lost.

■ Lily pads

Leaves of the water lily, usually found floating on the surface, but with their equivalents under the water, looking soft and less regular, and commonly referred to as cabbages. Lily pads, if not in excessive development in shallow water, give ample cover for fish and are a favourite depository of snail eggs. Lift almost any lily pad and the gelatinous mass of snail eggs can be seen underneath them.

■ Line

Modern monofilaments range in breaking strain from just a few ounces to well in excess of 100 lb.

Improved technology has widened the choice of nylon lines to take in numerous, low diameter brands. Now it's possible to select specialist lines for individual species.

Lines may slightly differ in colour from brand to brand, but this is not critical when considering reel lines where floating and sinking characteristics are of greater importance.

Certain brands sink well and are well suited to waggler and legering methods where it is desirable to cut the monofilament beneath the surface. Other makes both float and sink – with a little coaxing.

Thirdly, there is the floating line, a useful quality to have when floatfishing with top and bottom float designs, like stick floats, balsas and Avons.

Most coarse anglers carry several spare spools for their reels loaded with different kinds of line for varying methods. Generally, if you inspect the lines on offer you will be looking for a matt finish for good sinking lines, while floaters are usually very shiny on their surface.

If you're in any doubt, it's possible to spray a sinking agent on the line to degrease it and cut through the surface film. Another device clips on the rod, just above the reel, and the line is wound back through a pad to coat the line with a sinking formulation.

Floatants, in the form of silicone sprays, are also very handy. Even a good floating line can begin to sink when it becomes slightly worn. A quick spray soon makes suspect line very buoyant again.

Low diameter lines Standard monofilaments are still the most widely used for reel lines, offering good stretchability and robustness.

The new breed of low diameter monofilaments, being rather expensive, largely lacking in stretch and rather less durable, are more popular for hook lengths. Many low diameter lines cannot take large locking shot without a silicone buffer. It is only really in the higher breaking strains, above 4 lb, where anglers are beginning to experiment with these on the reel. A large saving on diameter increases a line's casting distance, but without the safeguard of a stretch factor, a heavier shock leader is advisable.

The benefits of finer lines are considerable. They allow the hookbait to act more naturally and offer less resistance to a taking fish. They are possibly less visible, although this has not been proven, and are an advantage when the fishing is hard. When relating breaking strains and diameters to your fishing requirements, it is best to follow these guidelines:

1. Use a slightly heavier breaking strain than you think your reel line requires. This gives a buffer against the odd bad cast.
2. Go for the thinnest diameter you can find without totally eliminating stretch factor. Thinner lines cast further and easier but lack of stretch can cause break-offs.
3. Relate the reel line to the breaking strains of the hook lengths you will be using. A very slight variation in diameter makes for more secure knots. A big stepdown from reel line to hook length diameter can cause the thicker line to cut through the finer mono – no matter how proficient the knot!

As a starting point, a 2 lb sinking reel line, coupled with a 1.5 lb or 1.7 lb hook length is a good combination for general waggler fishing. Step up to a 2.5 lb reel line tied to a 2 lb hook length with really big floats or when fishing snaggy swims.

The stick float angler would probably fish a 2 lb floating reel line on a river like the Trent, with a 1.7 lb hook length if species like chub were expected. It would be quite feasible to drop down to a 1 lb hooklength, still keeping to 2 lb reel line – the diameter gap is still not too severe – if the going dictated a lighter approach, perhaps for a less powerful species like roach.

With the swimfeeder, 4 lb to 6 lb reel lines might be needed on a fast flowing river, because the line is going to take a lot of wear and tear, retrieving a weighty feeder against the powerful current. But on more sluggish, flowing water, it is perfectly acceptable to drop down to a 3 lb reel line, even when casting at long range. As long as the feeder is not too heavy for the line on the cast, distance will be achieved more easily with a lighter weighting and line combination.

■ Line clip

A line-retaining clip fitted to the rod handle directly above the reel spool. It is used to make a carp bolt on a very tight line or to keep the line taut through to a semi-fixed lead so that drop-back bites show up clearly.

Commercially-made models with a tensioning screw work fine but it's possible to make your own by cutting a two inch long sliver from an old carbon blank. It needs to be about three-eighths of an inch wide with one end tapered almost to a point for trapping the line. Electrical tape will bind the clip tightly to the corks or duplon.

■ Linear Mirror

See Carp.

■ Liner

A fish which has fouled the line between the angler and his rig producing a false indication. Line bites are common in bream fishing and tend to be more of a problem in shallow water. Sometimes it's a sign that a shorter cast is worth trying. Liners should be avoided in carp fishing to avoid spooking the fish. See Back lead.

■ Link leger

When a weight is attached to the rig by a short boom, or length of nylon it is called a link leger. The length of the link is usually between two and six inches. The weighting comprises a standard bomb or split-shot spread out along on the nylon link. It works better tied to a swivel which is free-running on the reel line.

■ Loaded float

See Floats.

■ Lobworm

See Baits.

■ Locking shot

Split-shot used to trap a bottom-end float on the line are known as locking shot. They position the float at the required depth and normally represent a large percentage of its loading.

■ Loop to loop

See Hook link.

■ Loose feeding

Throwing or catapulting loose baits like maggots, casters and hemp around the float to attract fish. They are also known as free offerings and scatter baits. Loose feeding is one of the most successful ways of drawing fish into a swim and holding them there. Baits should be fed little and often for greatest effect.

Above: **A commercially-made line clip for use in carp and pike fishing.**

Left: **Loaded waggler trapped on the line with locking shot.**

■ Luncheon meat.

See Baits.

■ Lures

Spinners, spoons and plugs used to attract predatory fish. All the game species take lures, as well as perch, pike, zander and chub. Very rarely, cyprinid species like bream grab spinners and spoons.

Six spoons that pike like to chew on (from left): home-made Norwich shape made from a tablespoon; Lucky Strike Lizard; an old Milbro Norwich; home-made Jim Vincent copper lure; Blair spoon and a Pikko.

Below: Carry a mixture of brightly coloured lures - one will often score where all others fail. From top: Shakespeare rubber lure with fluttering tail; Cisco; Kuusamo; DAM jointed plug and Rooster Tail.

Lure fishing is an extremely successful way of catching many species of fish, often in large numbers. When the fish are feeding well, huge catches can be made partly because no time is wasted baiting up. Coarse fish take lures best up to the end of October. After that, in colder weather, it is necessary to know your water, and also to fish in the right conditions.

It is wise to use a wire trace for lure fishing, even when the species with sharp teeth are not expected. Modern trace wire is fine and inconspicuous. The trace needs a link swivel on the business end, and a swivel for attachment to the reel line at the other.

Spinners tend to kink up the line, so an anti-kink lead can be added at the top of the trace. The Wye lead is probably the best of these, and it also gives extra casting or sinking weight where necessary with spoons and plugs as well as spinners.

Single hooks in weed The difficulty with lures is to know which to use – there are as many different lures as there are flies for the fly fisherman. If a water is heavily weeded then a surface plug or weedless, single-hooked Spinnerbait might well beat the weed. If distance and depth are needed then a small, heavy spoon such as a Toby might well be worth first try.

Where weed beds reach within two feet of the surface then try a shallow-diving floater over the top of the weeds – the predator will surge from its sanctuary when it sees the plug wobbling by.

For fishing in the middle of lily beds try a Spinnerbait, floating plastic spoon or a slow-sinking plastic spoon. Each of these has an inturned single hook which gives some protection from the weed. In sunken trees, a Spinnerbait can be fished in among the branches.

It pays to try small lures before large ones, say a plug or spoon of two to three inches or a spinner between one and two inches. Small baits disturb the water less, and spook the fish less easily. But with pike, a large six inch spoon will take fish when smaller ones fail. On occasion the same is true of plugs. So begin small, and work up.

Colour considerations Lures displaying a perch or pike overall colouration take plenty of fish. Silver and copper lures are also successful, presumably because of their resemblance to roach, rudd and carp. But black is another excellent colour, especially on gin-clear waters or on a bright sunny day.

Plugs which have a red head and white body succeed in drains with a bit of colour in them, and also at dawn and dusk. And then there are the garish colours like brilliant orange, crimson and yellow which all capture fish on their day and it's worth having a selection in your lure bag. As a generalisation, all lures should have a flash of red on them somewhere.

The keen lure angler would not set out with less than 30 lures in his bag. Top of any lure list should be Spinnerbaits with skirts of black, yellow and chocolate and orange. The blades can be copper-coloured and shaped like a pheasant's egg in outline, or willow leaf.

Next could be a Lucky Strike Lizard in nickel/copper colouration, about five inches long. Third might be a plug like Shakespeare's Big S, a shallow-diving floater. Fourth, another plug, this time the K12 Kwikfish in coachdog finish, which is a kind of spotted yellowish-white with flashes of red for the gills: a big plug, with a sinuous wobble and a real catcher of 20 lb pike.

Fifth, a choice of barspoons: Veltic, Ondex, the Shakespeare range – all are good. But one of the best is the Sonic Rooster Tail with yellow feathers on the treble. These come in various weights and colours. Then you'd need a selection of ordinary egg-shaped Norwich spoons – the Blare Spoon is a good one, though you can make your own out of table spoons. These cast well and are easy to paint in various shades.

If hunting perch, chub or trout, try smaller versions of each of the above, except for the Spinnerbaits which at half-an-ounce will take anything in sea or freshwater. Finally, perhaps a surface lure or two and here the Crazy Crawler is a must, together with a floating plastic spoon, and a Troubleshooter.

Great lures from the Barrie Rickards collection. Pictured at the top are a pair of Ryobi Muggers with a Troublemaker and Spinnerbait immediately below. The jointed plugs in the next row are a K12 Kwikfish and Rapala floater. Another Troublemaker and a Moss Boss Swamp Fox complete the line-up.

M

■ Maggots

See Baits.

■ Margin fishing

Fish will move close to the bank in coloured water or where there is a protective canopy of weed. A light float rig or freelined bait cast tight to the bank often produces surprising results and is known as margin fishing.

Top matchman Mark Pollard plays it cool under pressure as a big tench pulls the elastic shock absorber from his pole.

■ Marker

A highly visible float, chunk of polystyrene or film canister anchored by a length of line and heavy weight to pinpoint a hotspot or underwater feature in the swim. The best system is a marker float permanently attached to a spare rod as it makes for easy recovery at the end of the session.

A heavy, free running leger weight is threaded on first and then the marker float attached directly to the end of the line. The float and weight is cast out and if the hotspot is a bar or drop-off it can easily be felt as the lead rises and falls over the contours of the bottom. When in position, the line is sunk and the bale arm left open. The marker float will pop to the surface precisely pinpointing the feature.

■ Mass baits

Thousands of tiny baits spread in the swim to attract carp. Seeds like hemp, buckwheat and mini maples are normally used with the objective of persuading the carp to become preoccupied on the angler's offerings instead of naturally occurring food stocks like bloodworm.

Mass baits work best over silt as some of the seeds lay on top while others are churned into the bottom by the carp and virtually establish a perpetual supply of the same food source. Between 10 lb and 20 lb of seeds will be required in the swim and special droppers have been designed to cast these light baits over long distances.

■ Match fishing

The two basic tiers of competition fishing are club contests and the more demanding Open match circuit. Then there are the challenges of top flight team fishing in series like the Angler's Mail Super League which carries considerable cash sponsorship from Sundridge. Achieving success in Opens demands a greater commitment because of the higher standard of competition and the extra investment that's required on bait to meet every possible need.

Many thousands of matchmen fish two Opens or team contests every weekend and possibly a contest in midweek during peak season. Bait, transport, pools and entry fees combined make it almost impossible for the majority of matchmen to show a profit at the end of the season, unless they clean up in one of the classics and make a killing at the expense of a bookmaker.

Every match stretch is divided into equal sections for a more equitable spread of the pools incentives and starts with a sealed draw for the numbered pegs. Competitors must wait for the official start before introducing any baited hook or groundbait into their swim. The average match is fished over five hours and the angler with the heaviest net of fish is declared the winner.

Entry fees are fairly modest at between £1 and £2 which includes a peg fee to the club who control the fishing. Optional pools from £3 to £10 are divided between the top three or four anglers overall and section winners.

Open match fixtures are listed in Angler's Mail and it's normally possible to reserve a ticket on a first come, first served basis by telephoning the organiser. Club events are more informal although most of the important match dates through the season will be decided well in advance and listed in the membership book.

The showpiece team contests of the year are the National Championships staged by the National Federation of Anglers. There are a series of divisions with the pressures of promotion and relegation adding to the excitement.

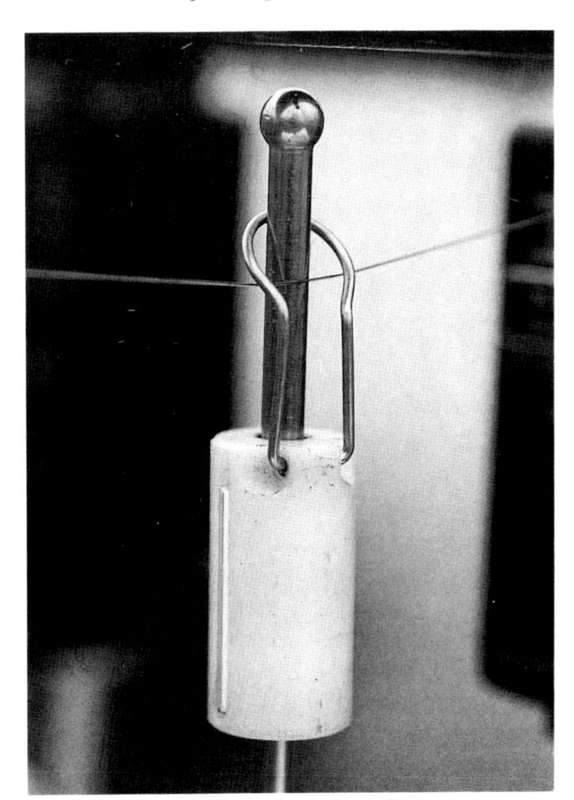

Left: **Monkey climber with internal isotope and flip-top line retainer.**

■ Mending the line

The action of straightening out the line between rod tip and float to prevent a belly forming and dragging the float off line. This technique applies more on running water when a floating line is being used with a top and bottom attached float.

After a few yards, the wind or surface current may catch the line and begin to drag the float off course or speed up its movement through the water. The angler must respond by lifting up the line and laying it back smoothly on the original course directly behind the float.

It's possible to mend the line without moving the float and this results in more fish.

■ Micro shot

See Split-shot.

■ Minnow

The British minnow is found all over these islands, but it is one of several European minnows. It is a tubby, soft fish, like a miniature chub in outline and fin shapes, and it has a series of vertical dark bars along the upper half of its flanks. The male in the breeding season has crimson underparts, the female being fat and silvery.

The minnow is not normally an angler's fish, but they will take a maggot on tiny hooks quite readily. They are considerably underrated in the sense that minnow stocks are vital as food for various predators, especially perch and trout, and young pike.

Traditionally, minnows are caught in special minnow traps, for they are widely used as bait. The trap consists of a plastic or glass bottle, transparent, with a conical,inward-pointing entrance at one end. Baited with pieces of bread, these traps can catch minnows by the dozen. The British record minnow scaled 13 dr and came from the River Calder, Lancashire in 1981.

■ Mirror carp

See Carp.

■ Monkey climber

Injection moulded indicator which slides on a stainless steel needle and is unaffected by wind. The best designs have PTFE bodies and snag-free metal clips to retain the line on the needle. These clips flip back out of the way, freeing the line, once the monkey climber is pulled to the top of the needle.

■ Mucous

See Handling fish.

■ Multiplier

See Reels.

■ Mussels

Shellfish which are also known as clams or bivalves. Within the two equal shells are a fleshy foot and body that many species of fish love to eat. Other freshwater mussels include the zebra, beds of which can be highly damaging to tackle. This mussel is the unusual host to the eggs of the bitterling, a species of fish rather rare in East Anglia and other parts of eastern England. The small pea mussel is eaten by various species.

N

■ National Anglers' Council (NAC)

The umbrella body for angling which was set up to represent the sport at government level. It was originally founded because government grant-giving bodies refused to negotiate with a diversity of angling federations.

The National Federation of Anglers, National Federation of Sea Anglers and Salmon and Trout Association are the leading organisations for coarse, sea and game fishing in this country.

■ National Federation of Anglers (NFA)

Formed in 1903 to pull together the many clubs and associations which proliferated at this time. Essentially, it represents the match anglers' interests, and it has staged the National Championships from 1906 until the present day. The NFA has been very active in anglers' battles to defend their sport.

■ National Rivers Authority (NRA)

The old water authority regions became regions of the new National Rivers Authority which started work in the autumn of 1989, after a run-up period of planning and rehearsal. Although the NRA regions can be said to replace the water authorities, and to stem directly from them, there are differences.

For example the NRAs now have a powerful anti-pollution role, and in 1990 many prosecutions were brought by them against polluters. The NRA is not responsible for sewerage works, nor for the large reservoirs in their regions, or water supply in general. That is the role of the privatised water companies. The main functions of the NRAs are as follows: guardians of the environment; flood defence; pollution control; recreation; navigation in some instances; and fisheries development.

Right: **Always draw a fish over the submerged net — never chase it around the swim.**

■ Needle

Stainless steel runner for the monkey climber indicator which is staked directly into the ground or screwed into an aerial bar holding other needles. The top of the needle is flattened or ball shaped to retain the monkey climber.

■ Netting

The simple rule is to submerge the net, keep it perfectly still and draw the fish smoothly over the top. Never chase a hooked fish with the net – it usually ends in disappointment.
See Landing nets; Playing fish.

■ Night fishing

Fish are inclined to feed more confidently at night and some carp become exclusively nocturnal feeders because of excessive fishing pressure in daylight hours.

There are numerous accessories for float fishing in the dark, the most popular being inexpensive chemical night lights. These glow for several hours once the tube is bent and the two liquids in their separate chambers mix together creating a chemical reaction. Several sizes are available and they simply fix to the float tip by a short length of silicone tubing. They are clearly visible up to 30 metres.

The more expensive isotopes are not as bright but have a life span of many years. They're excellent for whipping to the rod end or attaching to quivertips. Carp anglers fit them inside the indicators on monkey climbers and to their Optonics or even the boss of a landing net.

It's not necessary to fish at long range in darkness because the fish will move into the margins, particularly on hard fished waters where they're accustomed to picking up baits introduced in daylight.

■ Nude carp

Another name for the leather carp. See Carp.

■ Nylon

See Line.

O

■ Oils

These highly concentrated flavourings must be used very sparingly. Oil dips for boilies used on the hook have become hugely popular because it makes the bait far more potent than the loose offerings scattered around it. Fish oils are used by pike anglers to spice up deadbaits and leave a trail of flavour in the swim. Pilchard and smelt are the recommended predator attractors.

■ Olivette.

See Pole fishing.

■ Open-end feeder.

See Swimfeeders.

■ Open-faced reel.

See Reels.

■ Opercular

The larger cheekbone of most species of fish, covering and protecting the gills. Ageing of fish is more accurately carried out on sections of the bone which display growth increments, than by scale reading. But for an opercular reading to be taken the fish must be killed.

■ Orfe

The orfe or ide is quite closely related to the chub and the dace. It is perhaps halfway between a roach and a chub in overall outline, and all its fins red-tinted. There are two varieties, the natural, sometimes called silver orfe by aquarists, and the golden orfe, a beautiful red/yellow fish with occasional, irregularly positioned black patches.

Strangely it is the golden variety that occurs in some British waters, rather than the natural form, because the latter has been a prohibited import for a number of years. Lymm AC have the most famous

orfe waters and currently hold the British Record at 5 lb 5 oz. They grow up to more than 5 lb in the wild, but zoos have had much larger specimens.

Eventually, they should approach 10 lb in the UK Like the chub they are omnivorous, although possibly not to quite the same extent. It is possible that the natural form exists in some waters, for they were certainly stocked in the 1960s.

■ Overfitting joint

This type of joint eliminates the spigot fitting on rods and is believed to increase the overall strength of a blank. On poles it is known as put-over and makes it easier to locate the pole sections together. Overfitting joints are less likely to stick if they get a little dirty.

P

Above: **Orfe turn up in the most surprising places and reach a respectable size.**

Below: **The pugnacious perch - many fisheries hold vast shoals of stunted fish.**

■ Parrot mouth

A carp with a deformed mouth usually caused by poor unhooking techniques. Carp have quite hard, rubbery lips and hooks are often difficult to extract without pliers or forceps. With inturned hook points, it is possible to get double and treble hooking. This happens when the hook goes through the lip once, emerges from the other side and then goes back in again. If this occurs, cut up the hook into tiny sections and remove the segments.

■ Particles

Seeds, pulses, beans and nuts are chiefly associated with particle fishing for carp. Baits like black-eyed beans, chick peas and maples must be soaked in water overnight and then boiled for around 45 minutes. The soaking restores the dehydrated seeds to something like their original size and boiling softens them up and makes them easy to use. Other particles like sweetcorn and red kidney beans are ready to mount on the hook straight from the can.

Nuts which taken their fair share of fish include Brazils, cashews, almonds, hazel and tigernuts. They are prepared in much the same way as seeds and by taking on water they'll release more of their attractive oils once fired into the swim. Particles are chiefly used in summer and autumn.

■ Paternoster

See Legering.

■ pH

The concentration of hydroxoniumions in gram/ions per litre or in layman's terms, a measure of the acidity/alkalinity of water. pH7 is neutral. Anything less than that is acidic, anything more alkaline. pH3 is too acid for much life to exist in it; pH8 is typical of some of our best chalk streams. Waters with a high pH tend to contain a high diversity of shell life and fish.

■ Peacock

Highly buoyant quill used to manufacture floats. It doesn't require sealing and can be cut to length on the bank and fitted to the line with float rubbers.

■ Perch

The perch thrives over the whole of the UK and Ireland with the exception of the very tip of northern Scotland. Fish of 3 lb are very large indeed, and a 4 lb specimen is a giant by any standards. All perch seem bigger than they are simply because of their bristling pugnacity. On capture their sharp gill covers flare, and the dorsal spines become erect – a good defence mechanism if the predator is careless. Small perch have seven or more vertical stripes, adults fewer. Some of the stripes may bifurcate dorsally.

The flanks of the perch have a lot of green in them, and the pelvic and anal fins are often a brilliant red. In zander these are quite transparent. The dorsal side is darker, as is the tail fin, but with red tinges in parts. The first dorsal fin is very sharply spined, but the second is soft. The operculum is sharply pointed backwards and the first rays of the ventral fins are stiff rather than spiny.

Plague killed millions The species is predatory from an early age, and perch of 1 oz will take quite a large spinner.

They love clear water with extensive rush and reed beds as well as soft weeds. The weed beds are used for spawning and each spring the ribbons of perch spawn perhaps an inch wide and several feet long are not uncommon. In the 1960s the perch suffered a catastrophic disease which wiped out millions of fish nationwide. In the 1980s they recovered and it is clear that some large fish lived through the inexplicable plague. It affected only perch. The British record was set at 5 lb 9 oz and came from a Kent lake in 1985.

■ Permit

See Licences.

■ Pharyngeal

The throat teeth of carp-like species or cyprinids. They are deeply embedded in the throat muscles, as facing pairs, and crush food by the two working surfaces being ground together. Chub crush crayfish in these knobbly, knuckle-like teeth, as you will discover if you poke your incautious finger down the throat of a small chub.

The pike's role in maintaining a balanced fishery is now more widely appreciated and fish of this size are a valuable asset.

■ Pinkies

See Baits.

■ Pike

In the UK, we have only one type of pike – and we are part of the species' Northern Hemisphere, circum-polar distribution. Other species occur in North America and in eastern Siberia. It is absent in the most northerly tip of Scotland.

Right: **Pike sliders and weighted deadbait float.**

Top right: **Pike are attracted to oily sea fish baits like sardines, mackerel, smelt and herring. Dyed sandeels also provide a visual stimulant, but nothing compares with the pike's liking for eel sections.**

Centre right: **Long-nosed, surgical forceps are a vital investment to remove trebles as cleanly as possible.**

Below: **Hold the pike with a thick gardening glove and extract the hook with your free hand.**

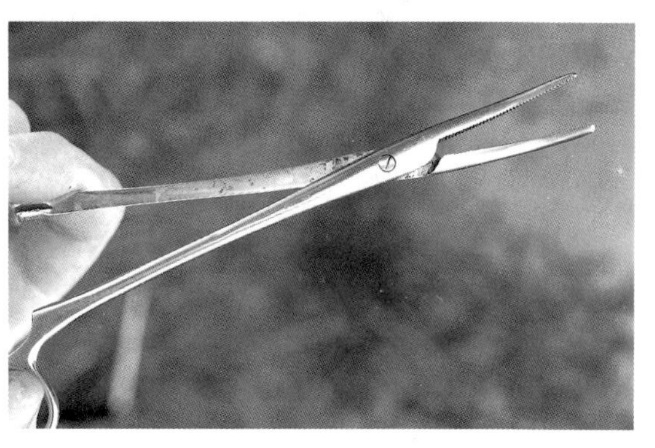

The pike is designed for hunting by extraordinarily rapid acceleration from a standing start. The body is elongate, and the dorsal, tail and anal fins are grouped at the rear of the fish to achieve this acceleration. The pectoral and pelvic fins control roll, steering and braking.

Colour varies considerably from pale in coloured waters, to green in very clear waters. But always there is a bar marking in young fish, changing to broken bars or spots in mature fish. The pike grows to 50 lb and more but there is dispute as to whether genuine 60-pounders have been caught. A 30 lb fish is very large indeed and a very successful pike angler might take several over 20 lb in a season.

The pike is most adaptable to habitat, and adjusts its food to whatever prey is available, tending to select those present in the greatest numbers. There are debates about the biomass of pike a water can stand. Everybody agrees that 10:1 down to 7:1 is satisfactory but there is some evidence that on very productive waters 3:1 is quite possible. That's to say that for every three tons of food fish, one ton of pike can grow successfully.

Pike have been on earth for about 80 million years or more, and there is no evidence at all that they have caused any other fish to become extinct by predation! The record pike of 45 lb 6 oz was captured from a Welsh trout reservoir in 1990.

■ Pike fishing

One of the most popular branches of the sport, and growing rapidly. The Pike Anglers' Club of Great Britain caters for the enthusiast. The increased popularity puts the pike, especially, at risk, for as a major predator it is at the top of the food chain. This means that it is numerically small, and also that it is affected by every change in the food chain leading up to it.

Accumulated poisons finally end up in the pike in heaviest concentrations, and in some countries the eating of pike has been declared a health risk.

Because the pike eats fish, primarily, the techniques for its capture can be summarised as follows: 1. livebait fishing (the singly most productive method); 2. deadbait fishing; 3. use of artificial lures. Whatever the method, a wire trace or traces is essential. Dead and livebaits are usually fished on multi-hook rigs comprising treble hooks and the methods vary from float paternoster, sunken float paternoster, to legering.

In modern times an excellent code of conduct has been devised in hooking, landing, and handling pike. The bite is struck relatively early with no deliberate attempt to gut-hook the fish as happened in the past. Secondly, the pike are landed in nets, the gaff having been outlawed on all NFA waters.

Thirdly, by means of thick, soft gloves and artery forceps, the hooks can be removed without putting the pike at risk during the process. Unhooking mats have also been marketed, and these help greatly, holding the fish firmly yet without damage. All this is to prevent damage not only to the individual fish, but to preserve the food chain or pyramid in its correct hierarchical form.

Double trace system Baits vary tremendously. There is a huge choice of deadbaits for example. In preferred order, these might be: sardine, mackerel, smelt, herring, sandeels, sprats, perch and roach. Livebaits are usually roach, dace, chub, perch, crucians and bream. Chub are probably the best livebait for pike, although all are successful enough.

Essentially, the same rigs are used for both forms of fishing, simply adjusting the depth of the sliding float stop, the weight and the position of the bait.

One of the latest developments in piking is to use two wire traces, one above the other, each being more or less a foot long. This double trace system is used in both dead and livebaiting.

The use of two traces prevents backlash of the bait during casting. If this occurs, and only one trace is in use, the hooks can tangle with the nylon reel line and a take by a pike results in a bite-off. A pike then has hooks and baits in its jaws and sometimes has no way of getting rid of them. The double trace method completely eliminates this problem.

■ Playing fish

When a sizeable fish is hooked at long range, the rod is kept low and slightly to one side. This tends to bring the fish up in the water and away from the shoal and potential snags. Line is gained by using the rod's shock absorbing qualities to pull the fish towards the bank. The curved rod is eased back and then line wound on to the spool as it is returned to

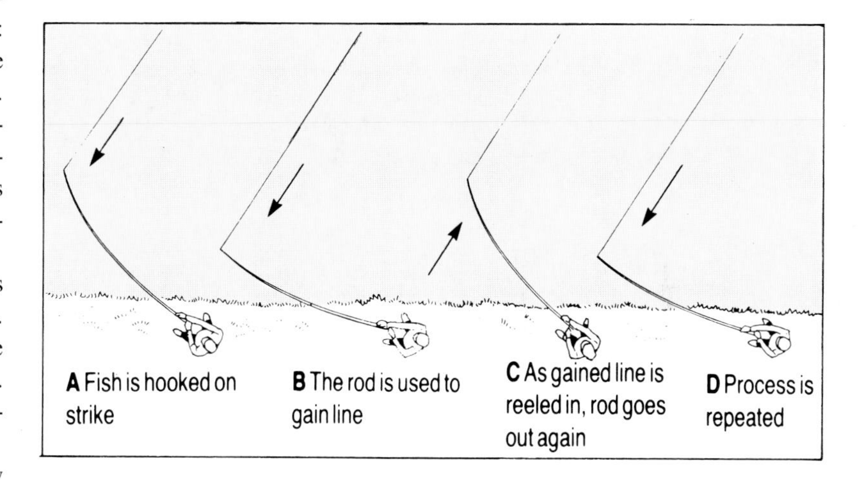

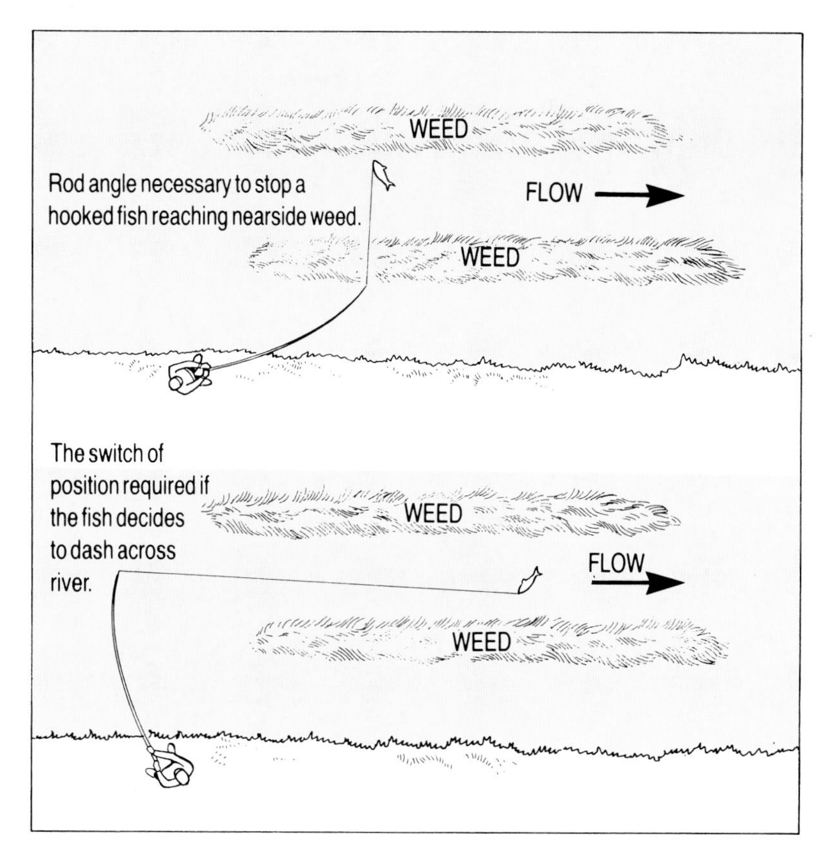

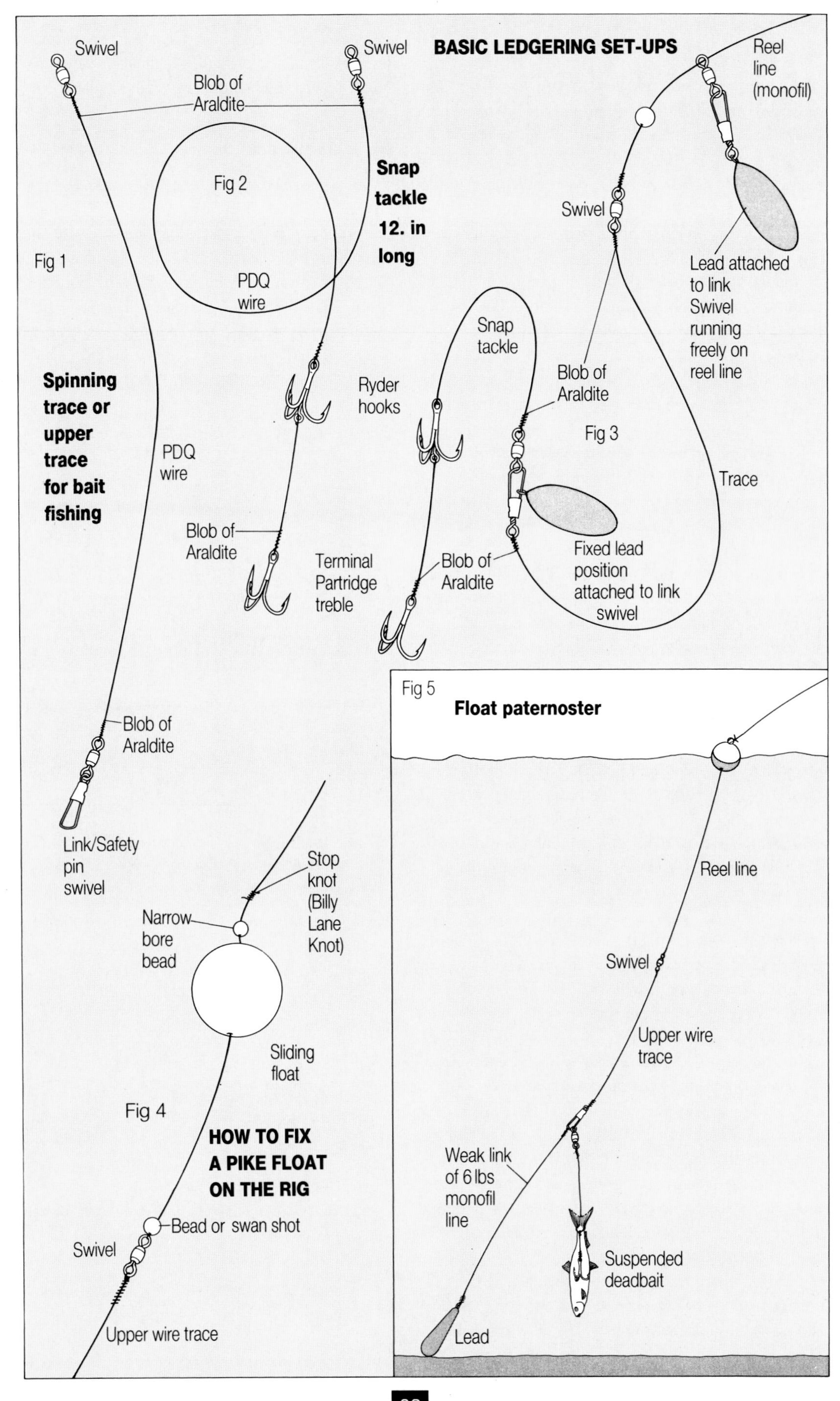
BASIC LEDGERING SET-UPS
Fig 1
Swivel
Blob of Araldite
Spinning trace or upper trace for bait fishing
PDQ wire
Blob of Araldite
Link/Safety pin swivel
Fig 2
Swivel
PDQ wire
Snap tackle 12. in long
Ryder hooks
Blob of Araldite
Terminal Partridge treble
Fig 3
Reel line (monofil)
Swivel
Lead attached to link Swivel running freely on reel line
Snap tackle
Blob of Araldite
Trace
Blob of Araldite
Fixed lead position attached to link swivel
Fig 4
Stop knot (Billy Lane Knot)
Narrow bore bead
Sliding float
HOW TO FIX A PIKE FLOAT ON THE RIG
Bead or swan shot
Swivel
Upper wire trace
Fig 5
Float paternoster
Reel line
Swivel
Upper wire trace
Weak link of 6 lbs monofil line
Suspended deadbait
Lead

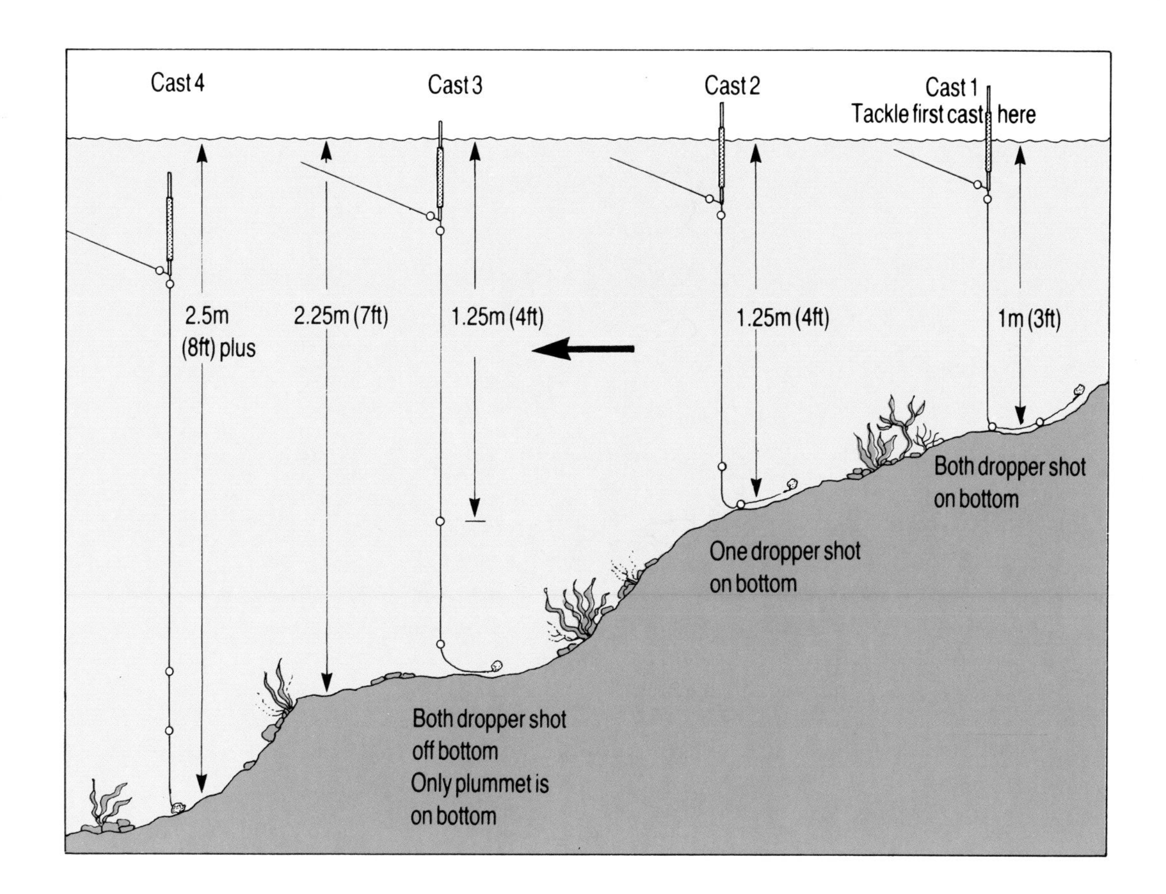

How to plumb the depth with a waggler rig when fishing a feature like an island or far bank shelf.
1 The first cast shows the depth is under 1.25m (4ft) because both dropper shot and plummet fail to register on the float.
2 The float sinks lower but one shot is still on the bottom as the depth is about 1,25m (4ft).
3 The float cocks correctly. Both drop shot must be off the bottom – leaving just the plummet touching.
4 The float sinks and, as the rig is set at 2.1m (7ft), the depth is obviously falling away.

its previous position, still under pressure. The procedure is repeated until the fish is within netting distance.

Sluggish species like bream hooked at distance on shorter leger rods can be gently wound in with the rod held high. The rod's lifting powers will probably only be needed when the fish nears the net.

Float fishing at close range usually requires the rod to be held high in the one or two o' clock position. This gives more control over the hooked fish, preventing it from darting into bankside cover. The rod's action is again used to recover line, reeling in as the rod is moved back in the direction of the fish.

Whatever playing technique is used, always maintain a slight angle between the rod tip and fish – then if it makes an unexpected lunge, the rod will cushion the impact. Never point the rod straight at the fish as all control is forfeited.

Submerge the landing net at the conclusion of the fight and lead the fish over the top on a tight line. Slowly lift the net rim clear of the water once the fish has been drawn completely over the meshing. Put the rod down, pull the net into the edge, and then grasp both sides of the net frame to lift the fish from the water.

If a fish dashes into weed or other snags and everything goes solid, slacken off the line for a minute or so to see if it swims out. The other alternative is to apply pressure from different angles such as downstream on a river.

■ Plugs

See Lures.

■ Plummet

A heavy weight fixed on the hook of a float rig to plumb the precise depth of the swim and check out the bottom contours. There are hinged clip-on plummets, conventional cork-based designs and more recent pole fishing models, where the hook is attached on a wire an inch or two from the weight – making it possible to accurately position the hookbait slightly off the bottom. A large split-shot, pushed over the bend of the hook will serve as a makeshift plummet, as will a small piece of tungsten putty, moulded around the hook.

Most times, the best place to present a floatfished hookbait is on, or just off bottom. This setting is easily achieved once float rigs have been correctly shotted up. After fixing the float at the estimated depth, the hook is fixed to the plummet and the tackle cast out. If the float lies flat on the surface the depth setting is too great, but if it sinks completely out of sight then it is too shallow. The tackle is adjusted each time until the float tip is just showing. This gives the correct depth of the swim at that point. It is then wise to check the depth at several other points in the swim to make certain there are not any deeper troughs.

■ Polarising glasses

Polaroids or polarising glasses eliminate reflected light from the water surface and make it possible to spot fish which ordinarily would be virtually invisible to the naked eye. Big fish anglers regard them as vital kit.

■ Pole fishing

A pole consists of lightweight tapering sections which fit together into lengths of up to 12 metres and more. There is no reel or rings – the line attaches direct to the tip of the top joint. This allows more control over the float than a running line and presentation of the hookbait is much superior.

Fishing with a short line, the pole tip is directly above the float and the tiniest of bites can be hit immediately. In deep water, or when fishing gaps in weed, the pole is unbeatable. Tackle can be fished at a greater depth with a fixed float and slotted into tiny gaps in weed. Long poles are brilliant for placing delicate end tackle within an inch of, or actually underneath, far bank cover, on canals and narrow rivers.

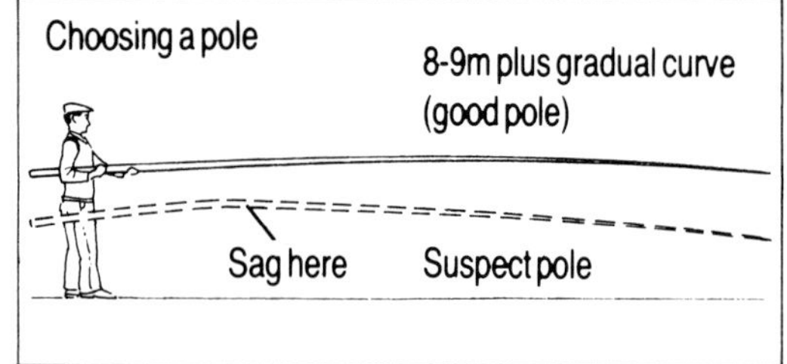
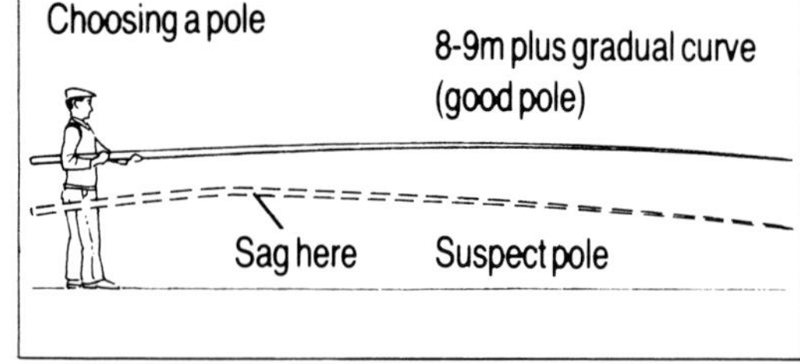

Choosing a pole The priority when purchasing a pole is to obtain the longest model you can afford. Stiff poles are better than soft actioned ones. Over certain lengths, longer poles are bound to droop slightly but look for a gradual curve as this will not transmit on the strike. A pole with any sag at its lower end will bounce when you try and lift it to hit bites and this will result in countless bumped fish.

Longer poles tend to be stiffer and lighter at shorter lengths – which you will often need. And a longer pole increases the fishing options – 11 or 12 metres will put your tackle across most canal venues, so you can fish tight-up to far bank cover. These longer lengths also allow you to chase fish out once they stop feeding closer in. Having a few spare sections to hand can make all the difference in stopping a big fish if it runs out into open water.

Most long poles have their weights marked on the butt sections. It is worth studying these because a 12 metre pole weighing between 700 and 800 grams will be easier to handle than 1,000 grams or more.

The majority of poles are now made from carbon-fibre, but at the cheaper end you will find carbon and fibre-glass mixes. These are only usually fishable at lengths up to nine or ten metres. Middle priced poles have a tendency to be very good up to 11 metres, while if models longer than this are required,

PTFE bush
Flick tip
plastic line adaptor
Elastic
pole section proper
plastic stop

Above: **Flick tip and second section of pole fitted with internal plastic.**

Reaching out with a pole to the far bank of a canal where the fish have shoaled up on the shallow ledge.

– along with lightness and rigidity – the price will increase accordingly. Many long carbon poles now have reinforcing, external kevlar weaves for improved stiffness and strength.

It is also important to look at joints before committing yourself to a pole. The easier they are to unship and push together, the better. Put-over joints are a distinct advantage in this respect and do not tend to jam up.

Flick tips and elastic systems Once you have a pole, there are two ways of setting it up. The most basic is the flicktip which usually has a spliced-in length of solid carbon. This is often used when fishing to hand style with the length of the line virtually matching that of the pole so that there is no need to unship the sections. Fish are then swung straight to hand.

The flick tip is used at longer lengths on a short line, when trying to hit lightning fast bites from small fish. The flick tip has a softish action and is the only buffer to cushion your tackle against the fish. It is only used when fish up to about a pound in weight are expected.

For bigger fish or as a safeguard when unshipping the long pole, an elastic shock absorber is often more satisfactory. Most favoured is the internal set-up which entails threading elastic through the top one or two sections of pole.

A hollow top section needs to be fitted to the pole, or the flick tip cut out at its splice. A friction-free PTFE bush is then fitted into the end to allow the elastic to pass out in a smooth manner.

Once installed, the elastic is tied off to a Stonfo adaptor to which the line can be hooked at the other end. This allows pole rigs to be switched over in seconds and also prevents tangles. Pole elastic is coded into breaking strains from very fine – for use with thin diameter lines – up to quite thick for heavier duty work and bullying fish out of tight corners.

Select the right float system Different rigs are needed with different lengths of pole and naturally enough to combat changes of venues and conditions.

The easiest method of fishing a short pole to hand warrants the rig being slightly shorter than the length of the pole. This allows the fish to be swung in comfortably while the pole tip is bending over. It is standard practice to use cane stemmed pole floats when fishing this way because they cast better on a long line.

Wire stem pole floats offer more stability on the long pole and can be held back, or worked through the swim more successfully on a short line. Float shapes are determined more by water conditions, body up for flowing water, body down for stillwater.

Choice of weights There are several ways of weighting a pole float rig. The most common is to use an olivette. This is a bulk weight which is most often placed above the hook length, approximately 12 to 18 inches from the hook. Olivettes come in carefully graded sizes, so it is always possible to find one to match a float, allowing a little leeway for a couple of extra dropper shot.

The olivette system of weighting is the most versatile and easiest to use. The olivette can be moved up to accommodate fish taking on-the-drop, or

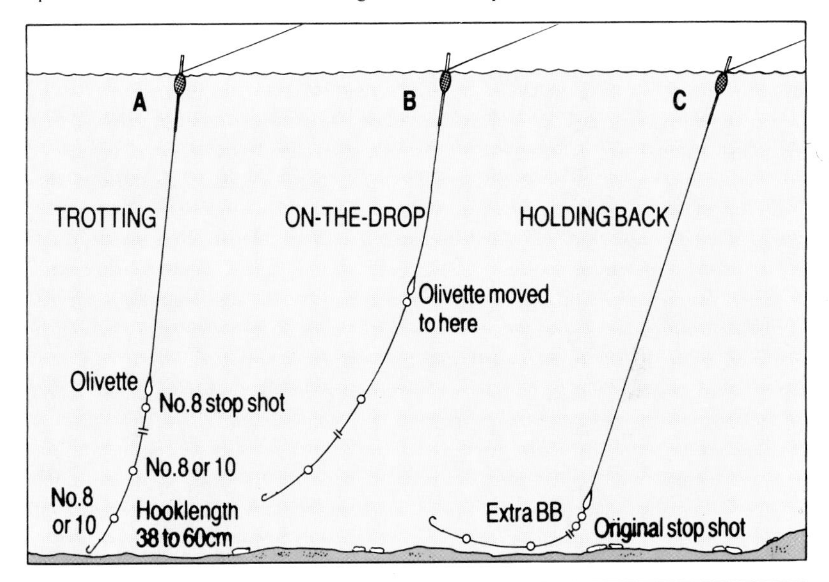

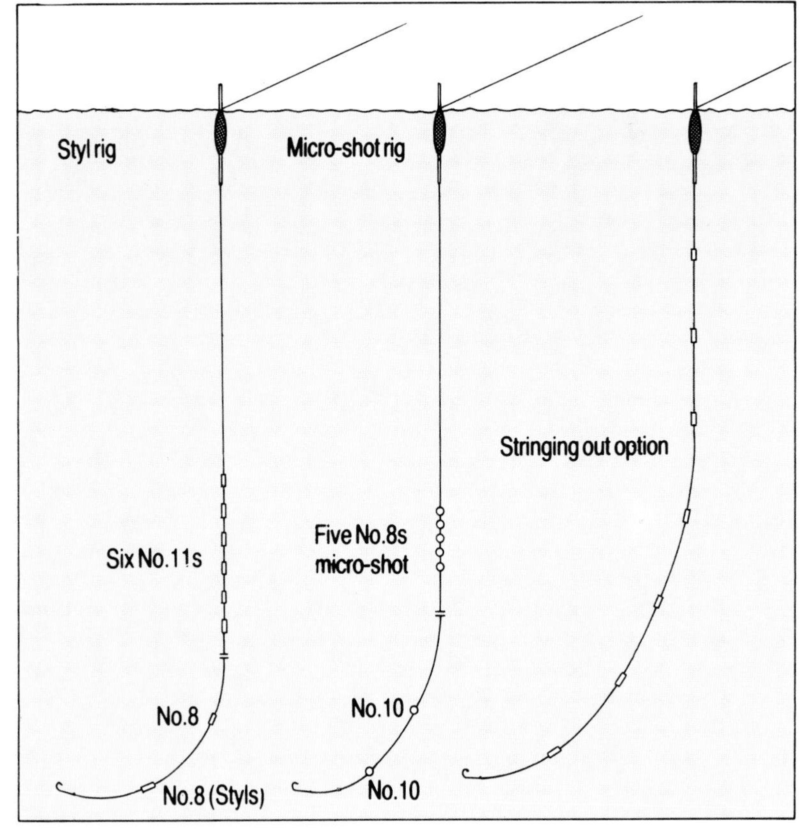

Styl weights present a slow falling hookbait.

pushed down to get the hookbait through small fish. Larger olivettes and correspondingly larger floats are used when fishing long poles to hand, or faster currents.

Micro shot are another vital pole fishing accessory. A range of 9s, 10s, 11s and 12s is useful in planning and balancing delicate pole rigs. Size 10s, 11s and 12s make useful dropper shot below the olivette to give the hookbait a slow fall as it nears the bottom. The smaller sizes are also handy for finely balancing the rig – placing the final ones that dot the float down, underneath the olivette where they will not interfere with the rig's performance.

Another delicate form of weighting is the Styl. These are very small elongated leads with a long cut in their side. A special pair of pincers are used to gently fix them in place on the line. The end result is a streamlined, slow sinking weighting system, perfectly suited for fishing off the bottom. or on-the-drop. Styls can be used on their own in a strung-out fashion, or just on the hooklength, below an olivette, or bulked shot.

Styls are also good for bulk weighting light rigs because they can pick up slight undertow and make a rig behave more naturally.

Long pole for river fishing
Pole broken down
4m (12ft)
1.25m-2m (4-6ft)
2m (6ft)

Deep swim in stillwater
Pole broken down
6m (18ft)
0.6-1m (2-3ft)
4.6m (14ft)

Shallow far bank
Pole broken down
2m (6ft)

Accessories Essential pole fishing accessories include winders for storing the end rigs. These are best made up at home. A pole float shotting-up device is a great boon. These clip on the base of the float, then in a container of water it is possible to see the exact weighting the float will take before fixing everything on the line.

Pole cups fit on the end of a long pole and after being filled with bait they are up-ended right over the float. A small bait dropper which will not strain the pole, is another useful feeding device.

There are some superb accessories to assist in handling the pole. They include rests which bolt on the side of solid tackle boxes to hold the pole steady, allowing you to release both hands for more accurate feeding. The pole roller, positioned slightly back from the fishing position, permits several sections of pole to be unshipped at once, in a smooth, flowing movement.

Work up from 8 metres Long poles take a little getting used to and it is better to first master seven to eight metres, then to steadily progress up to lengths in excess of ten metres.

Start on heavily stocked, small fish waters to get used to unshipping the pole after a fish has been hooked. Several hours of catching small fish will soon teach you the knack of unshipping several sections at once, always looking for smooth handling, so as not to knock fish off the hook. As handling techniques improve, it becomes possible to fish a shorter line for better presentation.

Whips for speed fishing Whips are shorter poles with lengths up to six or seven metres. They are primarily designed for speed fishing to hand and are thinner than long poles, even when placed side by side against the top sections.

Many anglers carry a whip or two along with their longer pole, so several rigs can be assembled on the bank. As their name suggests, shorter whips have a springier action, ideal for flicking out very light rigs and for picking up a long line smartly on the strike. Whips can be telescopic or part take-apart towards their lower sections.

■ Polyvinyl Alcohol (PVA)

PVA sheet dissolves in water and is marketed in tape, bag or string form to solve bait presentation difficulties. For example, in a densely weeded swim the entire end rig can be crashed safely through the canopy of leaves and stems by tucking it all inside a protective PVA bag. The bag quickly dissolves away leaving the bait perfectly presented. PVA tape is ideal for tying long hook links back against the main line to prevent tangling during the cast.

But the chief use of PVA is in stringer rigs for carp fishing. Several baits are threaded on a length of PVA string with the bottom one being tied on to act as a stop. The other end of the PVA is tied to the bend of the hook or swivel eye. When the rig is cast out and the PVA string melts it will leave free offerings where they are most needed around the hookbait.

■ Pop-up baits

A buoyant bait suspended at varying heights from the bottom. Pop-ups can be fished directly up from the lead on a shortish hook link of between six and 12 inches. The other method is to counterbalance the bait by fixing a split-shot which is large enough to sink it between one and six inches from the hook.

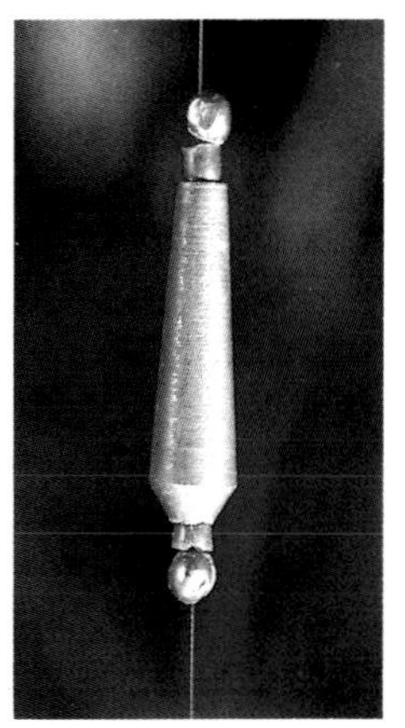

Above: **Olivette hurries the hookbait through small fish in midwater so it reaches larger specimens down below.**

Left: **Critically weighted pole float rigs stored on winders and ready for immediate action.**

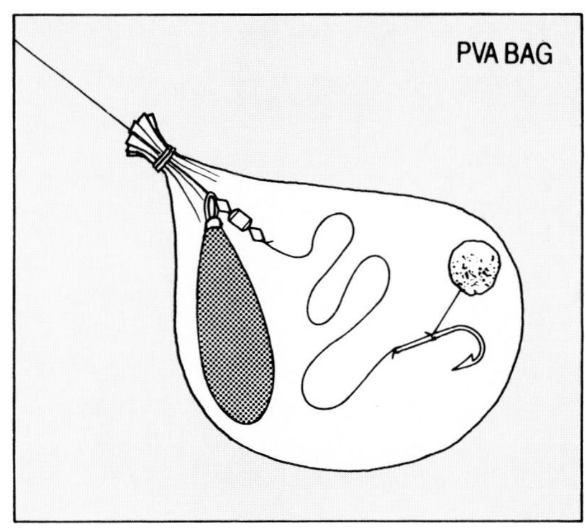

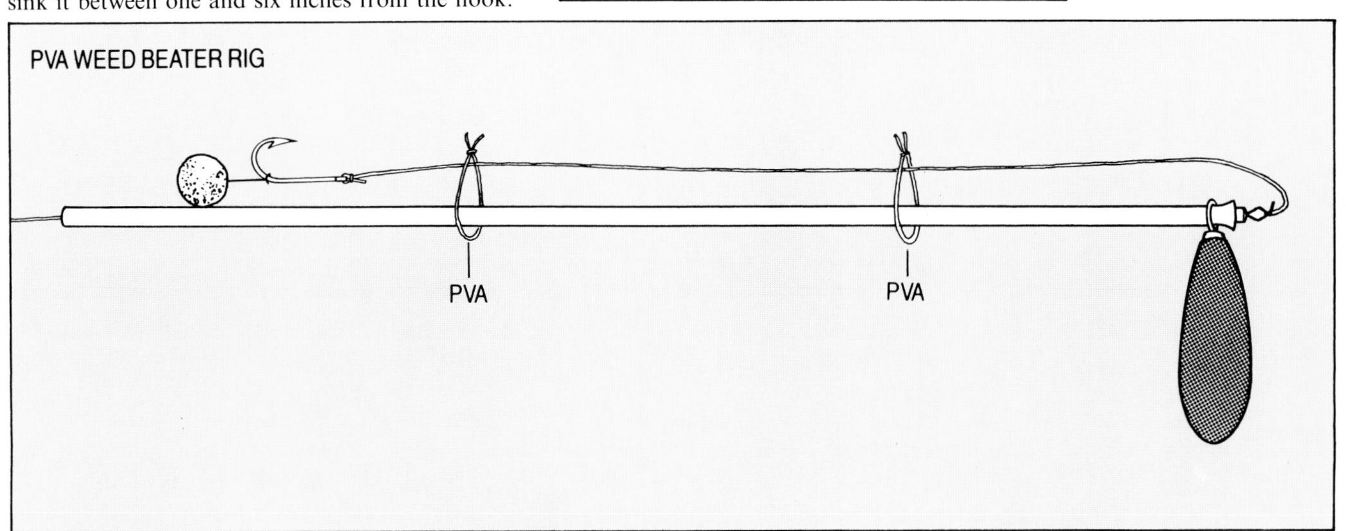

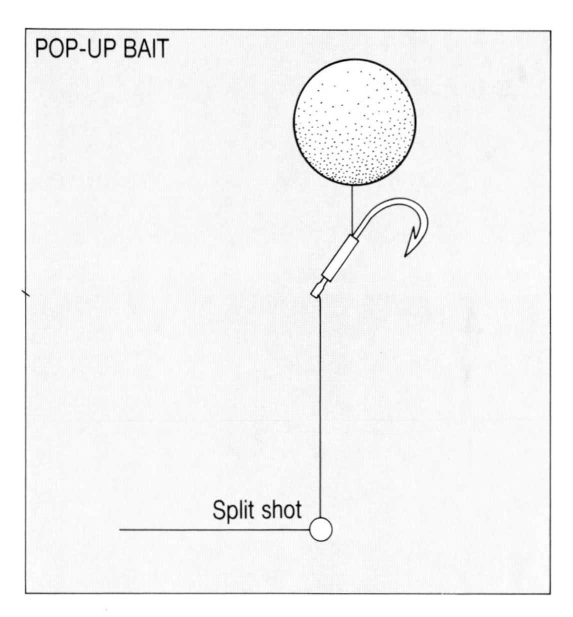

A boilie is made into a pop-up by inserting a piece of foam inside or cooking it to make it float. Pop-ups are used when there's a danger of a standard boilie disappearing from sight into a soft or weedy bottom. A pop is also more likely to be singled out by the carp than a boilie presented hard on the bottom when the swim has been heavily baited.

■ Pope

See Ruffe.

■ Prebait

Some anglers spend days or even months regularly baiting up a favourite swim or area of the lake. The objective of any prebaiting programme is to concentrate the fish within a tight area – or encourage them to feed freely on a certain type of bait. It is potentially time consuming and expensive but the results frequently prove spectacular.

■ Punched bread

See Baits.

■ Putty

Non-toxic putty is used as a lead substitute but unlike split-shot is obtainable in both sinking and floating versions. Floating putty is moulded around the top of the controller to give extra casting weight when casting out a surface bait. Sinking putty makes it possible to counter-balance a pop-up so that it only just sinks.

R

■ Records

The British Record (rod-caught) Fish Committee was set up in the 1950s to rationalise the national record list which at the time was something of a hotch-potch.

The Committee considers all the evidence on its merits, and reaches a subjective judgement. Photographs of the catch are acceptable. If you are lucky to catch a record-breaker, keep the fish alive for inspection or ensure good photographs are taken; secondly, muster as many witnesses as possible; retain the balance carefully and have independent witnesses to the reading on the balance at the time the fish was weighed; check that you were fishing legally with the correct rod licence and permit.

In general, hold the fish, pick up the telephone and ring Angler's Mail or the BRFC direct. If you fear for the well-being of fish, then take good photographs, including close ups in the case of roach, rudd and dace particularly, and return it if you wish.

■ Redworms

See Baits.

■ Reels

Fixed spool, or open-faced reels are fine for waggler, stick and leger fishing. The line flows unimpeded from the spool making these reels the No.1 models for long range fishing.

The forefinger should comfortably reach the forward lip of the spool so line can be feathered off the reel with the rod hand when trotting with an open bale arm. Check the bale arm flips over smoothly.

Above left: **Free-spinning centrepin.**

Above: **A top quality fixed spool offering immaculate line lay.**

Left: **Closed faced reel eliminates tangles in a facing wind.**

Below: **Lightweight multiplier built for spinning in freshwater.**

The bales on most reels will close manually and this helps prevent fish being bumped off the hook after striking when you need to engage the line cleanly to wind in.

Shallow, open-faced spools suit float fishing with fine 2-3 lb lines while deeper ones are available for legering and feeder fishing. Many reels are now sold with both types of spool.

The spools on closed-face reels are hidden from view inside a housing which makes tangles less likely in awkward, windy conditions. They are popular for stick float and balsa fishing because of the smooth way they pick up the line after the hook has been set. The only drawback is that the coils of line bed in after a good fish has been landed and long casting is not quite so smooth.

Sweet-running centrepin reels perform well in faster water where heavy Avon or big balsa floats pull line off the reel. Once set in motion, the large drum of the centrepin will automatically rotate line off with the slightest of pulls. This slightly slows down the tackle as it moves through the swim, giving ideal presentation as the float leans back. When a bite occurs, the reel is braked with a finger of the rod hand, as the rod is swept back into the strike. Centrepins are also used for laying on or legering at close range for big fish. This is chiefly because of the controlled manner in which they give line when a large fish bolts off.

Small freshwater multipliers are a favourite with lure anglers. They give a greater feeling of being in direct contact with the fish compared to the more remote sensation of a fixed spool. They're also handy for pike deadbaiting.

Reel seats including secure screw-up (centre) which is virtually standard on specimen rods.

■ Reel seat

The standard reel seat consists of two alloy or plastic collars which push onto the reel either side of its stem. This simple system is used on most float and leger rods.

Specimen rods are normally fitted with an independent, screw-type reel seat which is slipped over the blank and glued in place before the handles are formed around it. The reel's front foot pushes into a recess and then a collar is screwed up tight to secure the back foot. This is a more secure arrangement for long distance casting.

■ Returning fish

The angler's first responsibility is to treat his catch humanely. That means the bare minimum of handling to reduce the risk of mucus loss. Fish should always be placed gently back into the water and never thrown.

If a keepnet is used, it should be emptied at the end of the session by first gathering up the lower sections. Then the fish are released by submerging the open neck of the net so they can swim out.

When big fish are returned immediately after capture, they must be held upright in the margins, facing upstream. Wait for the fish to recover its strength and when it is ready, allow it to swim away from your hands.

A hefty roach of 2 lb 9 oz from the middle reaches of the Hampshire Avon.

■ Rigs

See Floats; Legering; Carp fishing; and Pike fishing.

■ River fishing

A more versatile approach is required for river fishing where fluctuations in flow, depth and width call for a wide range of rigs and techniques. Float tackle has to be worked skilfully through the flow, with an equally measured approach to the feeding of the swim.

Long trotting with light stick float rigs is a successful method on small rivers and streams, deliberately feeding downstream and taking fish from the edge of a shoal to avoid disturbance.

Loose feeding should be little and often with baits like maggots, hemp and casters on the smoother glides. Free-lining and legering are productive but be prepared to keep on the move, as one good fish can upset a shallow swim for several hours. Small rivers and streams normally contain chub, dace, roach, small pike and perch.

How to vary the attack Medium sized rivers offer more variety. In the deep water, species like bream, barbel, roach, perch and chub may be expected – there could even be carp. The shallows will be more likely to provide dace, roach and odd chub.

A standard stick float rig gives plenty of scope, perhaps beginning a session with a bulk shotting set-up. Feed requirements might be greater than the smaller river, perhaps three or four pints of maggots, or two pints of casters and two of hemp.

On a river at normal level, a couple of handfuls of feed at the start are followed up with regular small amounts of loose offerings every cast. The float is trotted through with the free baits. This should attract a steady string of bites during the first hour, by fishing the float just off the rod tip.

Gradually, the activity might dry up but by pushing the float overdepth and holding the tackle back, another brisk hour of sport is possible with this different presentation.

A couple of bites much higher up the swim, on-the-drop, signal it is time for yet another tackle change. The float is shallowed up and the bulk shot spread out for a slower fall of the hookbait.

By stepping up the feed slightly and holding back against the float as it hits the water, you should find yet another good spell should materialise as the fish move up in the water to intercept the constant flow of loose feed.

This simple stick float procedure works on many medium depth river swims. Later options could be to switch to a straight or small swimfeeder rig – often the float dries up completely. There is also the opportunity to switch the attack over to the far bank.

The waggler normally helps locate chub where there is overhanging cover on the far side, perhaps later switching to a small maggot feeder.

Flood water tactics Medium sized rivers are usually affected rapidly by rain water and might rise several feet very quickly. If the water colours up, fish will tend to move out of their normal haunts. It is then worthwhile searching out deeper, nearside slack areas where a larger, more stable all-balsa float can find a lot of fish. If the water is boiling, a bait dropper will get the bait down on the bottom better. A small feeder fished down the edge can also bring good results.

All the methods described for small and medium sized rivers can be applied to larger venues, perhaps with slight modifications. For instance, step up in float size to cope with increased casting distance.

Often three or four pints of feed will be enough for a session. But fishing a waggler into open water could use up a gallon of maggots to feed off small fish in the quest to pull larger species like chub into the swim.

Groundbait tends to work better on larger, flowing waters, both in softer form for float fishing with loose feed and in stiffer consistencies for legering at range.

Long range feeder tactics score heavily on some big rivers. Extra lead loadings and longer, more beefy rods are needed. Mainly, maggot feeders are used for this long range fishing with stronger reel lines and forged hooks. Features on narrower waterways such as overhanging far bank cover, are worth investigating.

With extra water on, these wider rivers can be explored at range with big top and bottom floats and baits like bread, luncheon meat and lobworms. On fast rising rivers, float tackle fished down the side, or a straight leger, sort out bonus fish when the going is hard.

Wading on a low level Thames to reach the streamier water where the roach and dace have shoaled up.

The pole is growing more popular as an alternative to the stick float, fished on a long line in normal conditions, or coupled with a big float for laying on in fast water.

Less bait is required in winter and a couple of pints is enough for a session. Fish are lethargic and inclined to take more stationary hookbaits. Laying on with pole tackle, holding back with running line rigs, fishing the straight bomb or feeder, are all better alternatives than trotting hopefully with the flow.

■ Roach

Surveys reveal that more anglers fish for roach than any other species. A 3 lb roach remains an epic

Right: **Feeder rod with inter-changeable tip sections makes it a versatile performer.**

Far right: **Hardened inserts prolong the life of rod rings.**

catch and very few 4 lb fish have ever been taken.

The roach is widely distributed in many kinds of water both still and moving, deep and shallow. It is absent from the north of Scotland, and has only a patchy distribution in Ireland, though it is spreading very rapidly.

The upper fins of the roach are red-brown and the pelvic and anal fins distinctly red. The dorsal part of the fish tends to be dark, even blackish or brown and blue, but always dark. On the flanks the dominant colours are silver and blue and the belly is white. The eye is relatively large, red, and the two lips meet equally at the anterior end of the fish, although the mouth as a whole gives the impression of being slightly underhung.

Roach grow best on a diet of insects and weed, and they prefer clear waters with a high pH. When roach grow very large the proportions of the body do change, and the shoulders get rather heavier. As so few anglers are familiar with giant roach, such a capture always raises questions as to the fish's pedigree.

At this stage recourse must be made to measurements like scale counts, the position of fins, and so on. These features can then be compared with those likely pretenders such as rudd, rudd-roach hybrids, roach-bream hybrids, rudd-bream hybrids, and chub.

Techniques for roach fishing include all those commonly applied to cyprinid fishing, including long trotting, laying on and legering. And the baits may be animal or vegetable or combinations of both. Big roach love boilies. The British record stands at 4 lb 3oz and was caught from the Dorset Stour in 1990.

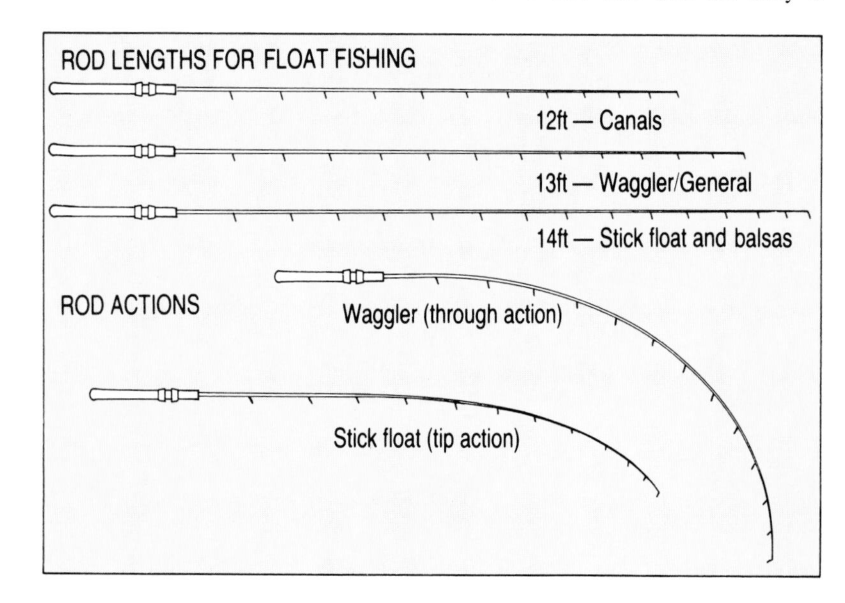

■ Rods

Fibre-glass offers the cheapest entry into fishing with leger rods costing as little as £15-£20 and float rods selling for under £30. But it is worth spending a bit extra on a more lightweight and responsive carbon fibre model.

It is possible to pay in excess of £100 for a carbon rod, but there are many excellent budget models for under £40. Middle-priced rods tend to have lined rings which last longer, and their higher carbon content makes for a thinner, lighter blank.

Top of the range carbons are slimmer and lighter again, because they are made from the highest quality cloth. Many have silicone carbide guides which will last a lifetime. They have also been designed by top anglers.

Spliced and hollow tips Match rods of 12 and 13 feet are preferred for float fishing with a spliced tip recommended if you're a regular stick angler. But hollow tipped rods with a more through-action are better for long-range waggler fishing. There is considerable cross-over between the two types of tip design but the hollow tip has the edge as an all-rounder. Spliced rods have more of a tip action which can be limiting.

Match rods of 14 feet give greater control when combined with top and bottom fixed floats on flowing water. Shorter canal rods adapt well to narrower waterways.

Leger and feeder rods vary in length from the very short 6 feet wand used for delicate, close-in legering up to 13 feet for a really high powered feeder blank.

A good all-round feeder and legering rod would be somewhere in the region of 10 feet 6 inches or 11 feet, while rods in excess of this are for long distance only.

Specialist rods are given test curve ratings. A 1 lb or 1.50 lb rod is classed as soft-actioned, while 2 lb to 2.5lb is a good all-rounder with a lot of power in reserve. Rods of 3 lb and upwards are used for very long-range casting or pike fishing with big deadbaits. Specimen rods range from 11 to 13 feet and are normally two-piece in construction.

■ Rod mats

Rectangular waterproof sheet with holes punched through to accept bank sticks and monkey climb needles. The mat protects the set-up from being splattered with mud during downpours which in dire circumstances could jam the indicators.

Tip action match rod sets the hook crisply.

Left: **Specialist rod rest heads for float fishing (top) and quivertipping.**

■ Rod rests

Front and rear rod rests support the rod in an easily-accessible position leaving the hands free for unhooking a fish, making fine tackle adjustments, or feeding with a catapult.

For legering, the rod rests are positioned even more accurately. They must hold the rod rock steady with its handle very close to hand. Rod rest heads have a standard thread and screw into any bank stick. There are different designs of heads for float fishing and legering.

■ Roller

A pole fishing accessory which makes it possible to unship several sections simultaneously. See Pole Fishing.

Pole roller makes it easier to unship the sections and protects the fragile carbon.

■ Rotary rig

Another name for the Helicopter rig. See Carp fishing.

■ Rudd

Broadly roach-like but with a much deeper body, the rudd is a common species in Ireland and Britain as far north as southern Scotland. But it is not all that common north of the Midlands except in selected waters where it has been stocked. In the south of England it is, like the perch, the free-biting dream fish of schoolboys. Big rudd are a quite different proposition and few anglers have fished successfully for rudd over 2 lb 8 oz.

The rudd is most adaptable to varied habitats, but prefers large stillwaters and ponds, being less than happy in fast waters. It feeds at all levels on insects and plant material, but has a tendency to feed more in the upper layers and at the surface than does the roach. Its lower jaw protrudes to assist upward sipping with the mouth.

Look for the protruding bottom lip on a rudd.

The rudd is a deeper bodied fish than the roach and is always heavier in the shoulder – the dorsal fin is set well back from a vertical line going upwards from the pelvic fin base. The rudd is always more golden. Indeed, golden rudd, are not uncommon in nature, as well as in the aquarists' tanks.

The fins are much redder than those of a roach, and the ventral part of the body has a distinctive hard keel which is absent in roach. Finally, there are two rows of throat teeth and not one as in the roach.

Problems of identification really only arise with hybrids or very big fish – and then it's best to call in an expert. It is a serious question, of course, because hybrids are often bigger than their parents, especially if sterile, when growth energy is not lost in mating each year. All they have to live for is food!

Tactics for rudd have been more specialist than for roach, and include fly fishing both wet and dry – any red coloured fly seems to work well. Floating crust is another technique and buoyant bait fished above a leger also works well.

Rudd have a habit of moving into very shallow, sun-warmed water, feeding among thick bulrush and reed stems. If these fish are located, they can often be caught. While small rudd are voracious biters, big fish can be quite careful, and will often swim along holding the bait between their lips, rather than mouthing it. Britain's biggest rudd of 4 lb 8 oz was captured in Norfolk in 1933.

■ Ruffe

The ruffe is a splendid little fish rarely exceeding 4 oz, but striving to be like his big brother the perch. It is widely distributed in England, Wales, and the border counties of Scotland. The ruffe has a sharp operculum and spiny first dorsal fin like the perch, but differs in lacking stripes, red fins and in having the first and second dorsals joined rather than separated.

The body colour tends to be blotchy brown or olive brown, with vague spots sometimes. The undersides are pale. The only species with which it might be confused are tiny zander. But the zander has two dorsal fins which are separated, and zander above one ounce have the stabbing teeth present in the upper and lower jaw. The British record stands at 5 oz 4 dr from a Cumbrian water in 1980.

■ Run

A term chiefly used in carp and pike fishing to describe the action of a fish picking up the bait and moving off. A dropped run is when a fish rejects the bait after initially taking line from the spool.

S

■ Sack

The only satisfactory way of retaining a carp is to stake it out in deep water inside a dark coloured sack made from heavy duty, industrial nylon and with many thousands of perforations to ensure water flows in and out very easily.

The fish will feel secure in the dark sack but the lanyard attached to the D-ring must be tied very securely to a bank stick with the fish in a comfortable, upright position. There are two chief designs of rectangular sack. One has an open end which is drawn together by a pull cord gathering the neck. The other has an opening along its longest side with a zip fastener.

■ Sarkandas

Sealed with a minimum of paint or varnish, this reed makes excellent straight and insert wagglers. In thinner diameters sarkandas is also used as the stem for bodied wagglers.

■ Scales

Most fish have scales which are usually secreted within the skin between layers of the epidermis. The outer layer actually covers the scale, but may often be worn off and damaged locally, even when the whole body has a full mucous layer.

There is clearly a protective function in scales – for example, a glancing blow may dislodge scales but prevent tissue damage, exactly the same principle as the crash helmet. But scales may also have hydrodynamic and other functions. Scales grow by incremental addition and in temperate to cold latitudes will have winter and summer growth rings, enabling rough ageing of the fish.

But when the fish stops growing in length, additions to the scales may cease, so a minimum age only may be possible. Big carp in excess of 40 years may have scales which indicate only 15 growth bands.

■ Shock leader

When you are casting heavier leads and sometimes weighty swimfeeders it is safer to use a shock leader of stronger line. The leader is tied to the reel line and wound on to the spool with a minimum of three revolutions of the handle. Then the leader runs the entire length of the rod and a yard beyond the tip before the terminal tackle is attached.

This strong line takes the strain of the cast far better than the weaker reel line, but once the short leader passes through the rod rings, the benefit of a lower diameter reel line comes back into play, for greater casting distance.

Tie a 6 lb shock leader to 3 lb or 4 lb reel line, for the swimfeeder, and a 15 lb leader with 8 lb reel line for casting long range with heavy leads.

■ Silicone tubing

Top and bottom floats like sticks are strapped to the line with short lengths of silicone tubing. It is sold in a range of diameters and colours to fit floats from thicker-bodied Chubbers down to delicate wire-stemmed pole floats.

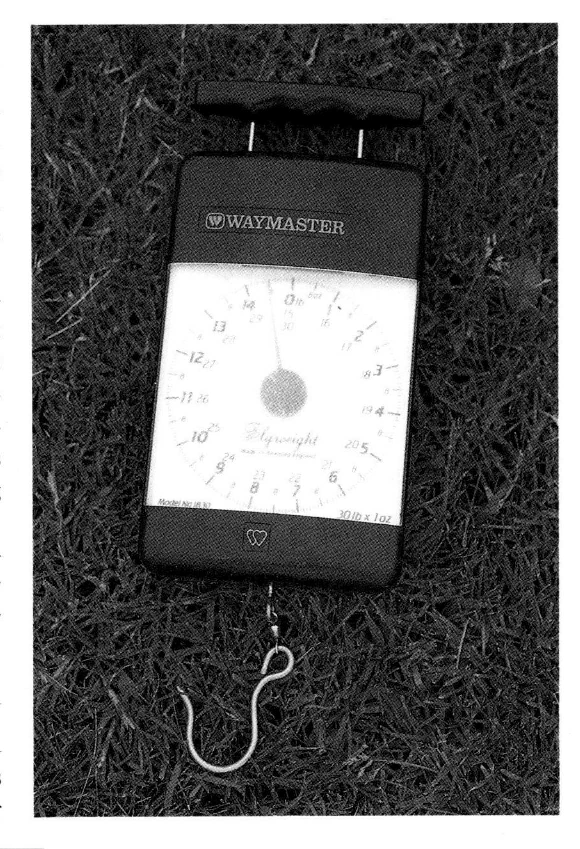

Lightweight dial scales.

This type of rubbery tubing is also good for covering nylon feeder links to help prevent tangles.

■ Ski lead

On some occasions the weighting built into swimfeeders is not sufficient to hold bottom. Ski leads are designed to slot under the conventional strip lead found on many types of feeder and provide the extra weight required. They are sold in different sizes, to suit different weighting requirements and can be positioned in seconds. The ski lead also holds the feeder more stable because of its double runners, which hold to the bottom well in fast currents.

■ Snap tackle

The most famous, and perhaps the best snap tackle is that invented by Alfred Jardine. This comprises a treble on the end of the trace, and one above it – a Ryder Hook – the position of which can be moved to suit the size of the bait. In Jardine's earliest versions this hook was fixed, and different size snap tackles then became necessary.

Later, he adopted a sliding upper treble and this system is much favoured by many experienced pike anglers today. The principle of the snap tackle is that a pike can be struck immediately, setting the hook in the jaw, rather than in the throat. This works well as long as the baits are 4 oz or less in size. Modern snap tackle enthusiasts tend to use smaller trebles than in the past, perhaps in 6-10. They are used for both dead and livebaits.

■ Spade end

See hooks.

■ Spawning

This is the action of laying the eggs by the female and the fertilisation of them by the male's milt. Spawning activity varies greatly from species to species, as to technique, time and place.

Most species spawn at a particular temperature – but that temperature is specific to the species. For example, tench spawn at a higher temperature than, say, roach and bream and, in consequence, tend to spawn later in the year.

Some fish scatter the eggs onto soft weeds or rushes, such as the pike. Perch exude a tube of eggs and leave it draped over weed stems. Trout and salmon dig a redd in gravel and bury the eggs in coarse gravel. Zander and sticklebacks stand guard over their eggs. One ingenious fish, the bitterling, injects its eggs into the zebra mussel's syphon system, ensuring a constant flow of water over them.

The eggs themselves vary in size and colour, and in the time taken to hatch. The number of eggs produced by a species tends to increase in proportion to the size of the individual, but overall varies from a few hundred to about half-a-million.

■ Specimen hunter

This is a term probably coined in the late 1940s or early 1950s and denotes an angler who hunts large specimens of whatever species he is after.

During the 1960s many specimen hunting groups were formed, and they were grouped into the National Association of Specimen Groups (NASG) founded by Eric Hodson and a few others. The NASG became NASA, the National Association of Specialist Anglers. Membership is open to anyone, club or individual, who specialises in a particular species or a particular style of fishing.

■ Spigot joint

Many rods have sections which join together by means of spigot joints. The lower section has an insert, slightly thinner in diameter, which protrudes by several inches. This part slots up into the next section and is often called the male half of the joint. The hollow section above is the female half. When fitted together, spigot joints normally leave up to one inch of the spigot, or male section showing. This is correct, allowing for a little wear and tear.

■ Spinners

See Lures.

■ Spliced tip

A slender length of solid carbon up to 36 inches long spliced into the tip of a float rod. The tip section of the blank is cut back to take the tip, which is then glued in place and rung-up with line guides.

Spliced tips often give a softer action than is possible with hollow sections, which have a tendency to flatten-off. They are used for close-in float fishing with finer lines, also for legering rods where the tip may be of fibre-glass construction, for an even softer action, to act as an indicator.

■ Split-shot

Originally, lead split-shot were a by-product from the manufacture of shot-gun cartridges. These lead pellets were graded in sizes which are still used today, although larger shot are now manufactured from non-toxic materials.

Split-shot are graded from 1s to 15s in their smaller sizes. The higher the number, the smaller the shot. Larger shot are also based on shotgun pellet sizes. The biggest are SSG, known as swan shot, then in decreasing sizes there are AAAs and BBs. These bigger samples are often called locking shot because they are used to weight and fix wagglers to the line.

Lately, one company has also released SA and AB sizes which conveniently slot in between the three larger sizes. This offers anglers greater options when weighting waggler rigs, because these harder, alloy based shot are difficult to trim down in the quest for accurate settings.

Medium sized shot have many applications. They are handy for fixing next to larger locking shot to finish off the weighting of a float, and also help to prevent the larger shot from slipping. Sizes from 1s to 5s are also used for shotting down the rig and when grouped together are often called bulk shot.

Smaller shot from 6s to 10s are more commonly used on the hook length and in this capacity are referred to as dropper shot. They are not so likely to damage finer lines, like their larger counterparts.

Micro shot – 11s to 15s – are chiefly used on delicate pole fishing terminal tackle, both in bulking floats and spread on gossamer hook lengths for on-the-drop presentation.

Lead shot are now only permissable in the very small sizes from 8s to 15s which are not thought to harm wildlife. Shot smaller than 12s are rarely used anyway Size 8s, 9s and 10s are often called dust shot.

Approximate split shot weights
(Weights vary slightly make by make)

SSG	1.60-1.68 grams
AAA	0.75-0.90 grams
BB	0.38-0.42 grams
No1	0.26-0.30 grams
3	0.18-0.20 grams
4	0.17-0.20 grams
5	0.15-0.16 grams
6	0.10-0.12 grams
7	0.08 grams
8	0.05-0.06 grams

■ Spook

Poor groundbaiting, bankside noise, a heavy cast, or too high a profile against a clear back-drop, can all spook fish in certain circumstances. It is also possible to spook a shoal if a fish is not quickly steered away, after it is hooked. A good fish which slips the hook can also take other fish out of the swim.

Thamesly shot were among the first of the non-toxic shot and have stayed the course.

Double Cut shot hang centrally on the line.

■ Spoons

See Lures.

■ Spring balance

See Scales.

■ Sterndrag

Clutch mechanism controlled by an adjustment knob at the rear of a reel.

Sterndrag with numbered tension settings.

■ Stick

See Floats.

■ Storm side

These attach to the sides of an umbrella and are pinned to the ground with spikes giving protection against the elements. They're virtually a halfway house between an umbrella and a bivvy and pack up into a small, lightweight roll.

■ Strike

The action of sweeping back the rod horizontally or vertically to set the hook after a bite.

■ Stringer

A method of attaching loose offerings to the rig using PVA string which dissolves in water. See Polyvinyl Alcohol.

■ Styl

See Pole fishing.

■ Style pincers

Tool for fixing styl weights onto the line.

■ Swimfeeder

The function of a swimfeeder is to release loose offerings or groundbait in close proximity to the hookbait. The swimfeeder is fixed, or left free-running on the line, usually between 12-36 inches of the hook, which makes for very accurate feeding of the swim.

Swimfeeders can be set up much the same way as straight legering rigs – replacing the leger weight. They work well free running with a leger stop for short range, but are better used on a paternoster set-up, or loop method for long range.

Open-end feeders are used for groundbait, which can hold other offerings like casters and squatts.

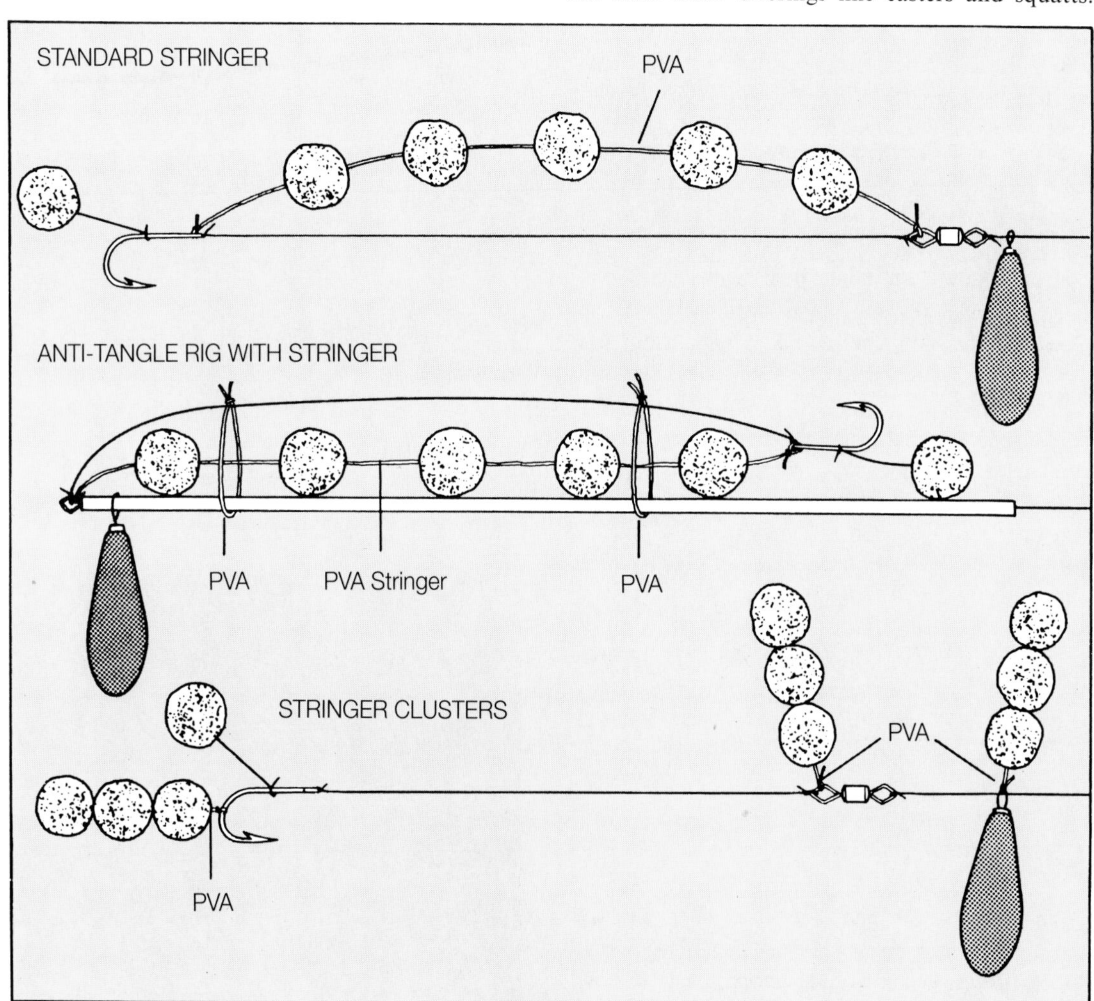

Far left: **Good quality rolling swivels.**

Left: **Swivel bead provides extra permutations on the terminal rig.**

There are standard perspex open-enders and cage feeders which are more versatile for feeding after groundbait mixes.

Blockend feeders are designed for loose offerings like maggots, hemp and casters. See Legering.

■ Swingtip

See Bite indicators; Legering.

■ Swivels

Swivels have free turning attachment eyes at both ends. They are a good way of linking a wire, or multi-strand trace to the main line, because a very secure knot can be tied to them. Swivels are also used free running to form link legers and paternoster style feeder rigs. Another use is as an anti-tangle device when placed between hook length and main line. This helps prevent the hook length spinning up as the tackle is retrieved.

American snaplink swivels.

■ Syndicate

Syndicates are usually formed on privately owned waters where the owner is anxious to exert tight control or obtain a good return for fishing which is rated above average. Costs are usually higher than club season tickets and membership is limited to a handful of anglers.

The three basic types of swimfeeder (from left): open-ended, cage feeders and blockends.

T

■ Tackle box

Cantilever plastic boxes which open out with numerous compartments are popular with pike anglers and other specialist anglers who carry a separate seat. Larger tackle, or seat boxes, start with toughened plastic containers fitted with shoulder straps. A smaller tackle box is usually stored within to hold floats, shot and other accessories.

Continental boxes normally have a padded seat, underneath which are various trays and drawers in which to store smaller accessories. Often the top part, consisting of three or four layers can be removed, or at least opened on hinges, to reveal a larger storage compartment in the base for carrying bigger items like reels.

A top of the range tackle box designed for pole fishing complete with its own stand and trolley wheels.

■ Tares

See Baits.

■ Target board

See Legering.

■ Tench

The velvet green/brown fish with the little red eye, is the species many anglers like to start the season with on 16 June. It is found throughout England, Wales, and southern Scotland, but is less common north of Yorkshire. It is widespread in Ireland, but not in every water by any means.

The species prefers lakes and weed-choked ponds, but is happy enough in slow moving rivers and drains. It feeds in the mud for the most part and it is not suited to gravelly or rocky rivers. But it exists in rocky parts of the River Inny in Ireland, so is fairly adaptable.

The fish has a silken feel to it, caused by the very tiny scales set in thick skin,and a layer of mucous covering them. The back is brown to greenish, shading down the flank to green with a yellow or golden sheen. The belly is usually yellowish and occasionally vermilion.

It has a pair of barbules at the mouth. The fins are rounded, brown and soft and the male's pelvics are conspicuously large with a thick root – it is thought they act as an aid to milt spreading during spawning. Male tench are smaller than females and fight more tenaciously, perhaps assisted by the large pelvics. Golden tench are not that rare, and usually they have a few black blotches on them.

Tench live primarily on grubs and insects and on bloodworms from the mud. But they are also partly vegetarian and can be carnivorous and cannibalistic round about the spawning season. Most cyprinid hunting techniques are applicable to tench fishing,

except that most are caught on the bottom. They do feed off the bottom as well, and this can be taken advantage of by the careful angler on occasion.

Tench into double-figures have increased in number in the last decade, but fish of 7 lb are still considered very large by any criteria. Britain's record tench scaled 14 lb 3 oz and was hooked from a Middlesex gravel pit in 1987.

■ Tenting

The lifting of surface weed by a carp's back. When growth is thick in summer, the carp are completely hidden from view in weed beds but any movement by a big fish immediately below the surface will push a tent-shaped piece of weed above the water surface.

■ Test curve

The power of a blank stated in pounds to the nearest quarter-pound. Assuming the rod butt is held rigid in the horizontal plane, the test curve rating is the loading required to pull the tip down so the rod bends into a quarter-circle.

■ Throwing stick

A length of aluminium tubing with a hand grip at one end and a swan-like neck at the other for firing boilies beyond catapult range. The boilie is dropped inside and rests on a plug down towards the handle. The tube is held at the 11 o' clock position then quickly thrown forward to one o' clock which hurtles the boilie from the end of the stick at great speed. It is possible to send an 18 mm boilie more than 100 yards using the Cobra swan-neck design.

■ Touch leger

Holding the line just above the reel to feel for bites. A highly sensitive method of legering.

■ Trace wire

Multi-strand or cabled wire is used to attach hooks in the bait, or the lure, when fish with sharp teeth are the quarry. Cabled wire comes in two types – a thicker, relatively soft wire like the PDQ and Alasticum brands or a very fine wire such as Tidemaster and Marlin Strand.

Tench weights have shot up in recent seasons and double-figure specimens are now a strong possibility in several southern waters.

Long walks with a mountain of tackle are made more bearable with a well designed trolley.

Fine wire is rather prone to spiral twisting and kinking but with care, all these wires can be twisted by hand at the waterside. All trace wires are improved by the addition of a blob of Araldite to hold the overlap ends.

Crimps are also used to hold the overlap, and the only drawback seems to be that the shoulders of the crimp may eventually weaken the wire adjacent to them, by repeated flexing at one point.

The latest trace wires are of steel and Kevlar mixtures. Some of these can be knotted, and they perform extremely well.

■ Trolley

Tackle trollies are used to pull large items like the tackle box, carryall and sometimes a rod holdall. There are several designs which usually fold down to a third of their size, or dismantle completely for easy storage in the car.

■ Trolling

The technique of pulling a lure or bait behind a moving boat. Modern trollers usually combine their boat fishing with the use of an echo-sounder. It is critical in trolling to know exactly what depth you are fishing, and how the lure is performing. Down-riggers get round the depth problem. A bite to a down-rigger system registers as a slack line bite, unlike traditional trolling where a thump on the rod tip indicates a take.

■ Tubercles

Several species of fish develop tubercles on their heads and parts of the body at spawning time. The bream is the most well known of freshwater fish exhibiting tubercles, but roach can also show the same feature.

U

■ Umbrella

Angling umbrellas normally range from 45 inches to 50 inches in length when furled. Smaller sizes still open out enough to offer reasonable shelter from wind and rain. Larger models are better for use with an overwrap or bivvy, when specimen anglers are staying by the waterside for long periods and want a more permanent and comfortable shelter. Most umbrellas incorporate a tilt device which allows them to be angled to the side to act as a wind shield.

■ Undertow

A strong wind often causes undertow several feet down where the water begins to move in the other direction. Undertow also occurs on rivers in deeper swims or eddies where a fast surface current pushes the lower layers of water backwards.

Fishing from a shore into a facing wind, there will be an undertow running away from you, at depth. Undertow can be used to draw the fish towards you by introducing attractants into the flow.

■ Unhooking

After a fish has been landed, the hook should be removed as quickly as possible. If the hook is visible, this may just be a case of withdrawing it by trapping the shank between thumb and finger and gently working it loose – an operation best carried out while larger fish are still within the confines of the landing net. If the hook is deep down inside the fish, a disgorger, or forceps are used.

■ Waders

Thigh length boots which allow the angler to fish out in the water. They are useful where the margins are very shallow. By wading out several yards, much better tackle presentation is possible and deeper water can be reached.

■ Waggler

See Floats.

■ Water temperature

This can be important as a trigger to set off fish spawning, and in its extremes it seriously influences behaviour and feeding of fish. More important than the actual figures in degrees, is whether the water is cooling or heating. In winter a cooling water is usually a poor bet. But in summer the opposite can apply. Barometric pressure is probably more important than temperature.

Thigh waders with sure-grip soles.

■ Watercraft

The art of reading the water and interpreting the correct tactical approach. This ability is acquired with experience and covers matters like swim selection and adopting a quiet, inconspicuous approach.

■ Weighing fish

Spring balances and dial scales are used extensively throughout the sport to weigh nets of fish or individual specimens. Large dial scales are principally needed in match fishing for recording down to at least half-an-ounce and sometimes mere drams for important fixtures.

For personal record-keeping, many anglers are happy to rely on a spring balance. These are inexpensive and give reasonable accuracy to within half-a-pound in the case of tubular models for big fish, weighing up to 40 lb and more. Smaller balances weigh to within an ounce or so.

The specimen angler takes his record-keeping more seriously and usually invests in dial scales to give accurate readings within half-an-ounce.

Soft, lightweight weighing slings protect fish from damage during weighing and must always be thoroughly soaked beforehand. The sling is hung on the balance, the dial zeroed, and then the fish is placed in the sling. The reading is accurate providing that the dial balance is not knocked after being zeroed. It is very easy to knock dial balances out of true, and then readjustment is necessary.

When using ordinary spring balances, the weight of the weighing sling should be deducted from the reading taken. Anglers still record in pounds and

This fish can come to no harm trapped inside a weigh sling and suspended low over a cushioned mat.

ounces, although the metric system has crept into match fishing. For real accuracy, a beam scale is preferred.

■ Weed rake

Metal rake head joined to a length of rope which is flung into a weed-choked swim and repeatedly retrieved until a clearing is scraped out. Two rake heads fixed back to back are most efficient. Tench will investigate a raked swim virtually before the disturbed clouds of sediment have settled.

■ Weigh-sling

Soft nylon sling with drain holes and support handles for hooking on the scales and weighing fish. It should always be thoroughly doused in water and zeroed on the scales before placing a fish inside.

■ Weight-length scales

The Mona's Scale for pike is one of the most famous weight-length scales. It is based on the supposition that a 40-inch pike weighs 20 lb and generally serves its purpose, which is simply to note whether your pike is overweight or underweight. No weight-length scale can actually be used to determine the weight of a fish, except when the scale is devised for the particular water in question and, what is more, allowance is made for the seasonal differences.

■ Weights

See Split-shot; Legering; Swimfeeders; Pole fishing.

■ Whip

See Pole fishing.

■ Wildie

See Carp.

■ Wind direction

Wind direction is often crucial in angling, for it influences where the fish will be in a water, controlling oxygenation, drift of food, and moving currents both at the surface and at depth. The wind may effectively cool or warm a water, remove ice, concentrate algae, and have a host of other effects, especially local effects such as wind funnelling.

Every angler should seriously note the wind on every trip, and attempt to deduce its effects. South west blows are usually beneficial to angling, and cold, easterly winds of any force are often detrimental.

■ Winder

See Pole fishing.

■ Zander

Because of the controversy surrounding the spectacular spread of zander in Fenland, more nonsense has been written about this species than any other in recent times. It is probably the only British 'pike-perch', for although walleye seem to have existed in the River Delph in the past, none seem to be present today.

The zander belongs to the perch family – it is an elongate perch which grows to close on 20 lb. It is not a cross between pike and perch. Zander have spread to at least 16 counties in England, but do not occur in Wales, Scotland, Ireland or the Lake District. Some of the spread has been natural, some not, but after the upsurge in the Fens, a wider distribution of the species was inevitable.

The characteristic features of the zander are its walleye-type eye which is blank, almost opaque in appearance, the stabbing teeth in both upper and lower jaws, at the front and the spiny first dorsal which is slightly separated from the second, soft dorsal. The pectoral and pelvic fins are very transparent. The body is rather nondescript, blotchy greens and browns arranged roughly in vertical bars but not as sharply defined as those of a perch.

The zander is an unusual predator in that it feeds well, even preferentially, in coloured water and at night. Its eyes are adapted specially for low light vision. They eat small fish mainly, but will tackle large fish quite often. When pack hunting they will attack larger fish than they can eat and there is some evidence that they will scavenge the carcasses later on.

Tackle and techniques for zander are scaled down versions of those used for pike. But when deadbaiting, it is essential to avoid sea fish baits, for they produce relatively few takes.

When lure fishing as close an imitation as possible to the fish they feed upon does seem to give an advantage to the angler. They seem rarely to fall for off-beat lures, unlike pike. The British record zander of 18 lb 8 oz was captured from a Cambridge water in 1988.

Angler's Mail

SEA

Here's a comprehensive guide to the tackle, baits and species that figure most prominently in boat and shore fishing around our challenging coastline. Tides, casting styles and specialist knots are all covered and there's first-rate advice on the opportunities in charter fishing.

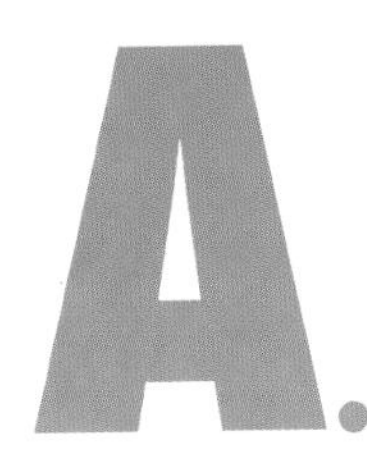

A

■ Aberdeen hook

A fine wire, long shanked hook with a round bend and straight eye. Traditionally, Aberdeens have been made from a soft wire so they can be pulled free from deeply hooked fish. But some recent patterns are being lightly tempered to produce a more rigid hook.

They are a popular choice for flatfish such as plaice and dabs, because the long shank is easier to extract from a deeply hooked fish. The length of shank also makes it easier to thread a long bait like worm or sandeel up the line. While they can be used for a wide range of other species, their springiness may cause problems with larger fish.

■ Albright knot

A special knot used to join a long monofilament leader to a wire line without impairing the passage of the line through the rod rings. A loop is formed in the end of the wire line, using a crimp in the case of multifilament wire or a haymaker twist with single strand wire. This is achieved by making the first turns holding the two strands at right angles to one another, at 45 degrees to the direction of the line. This ensures that both wrap equally around each other, preventing slippage.

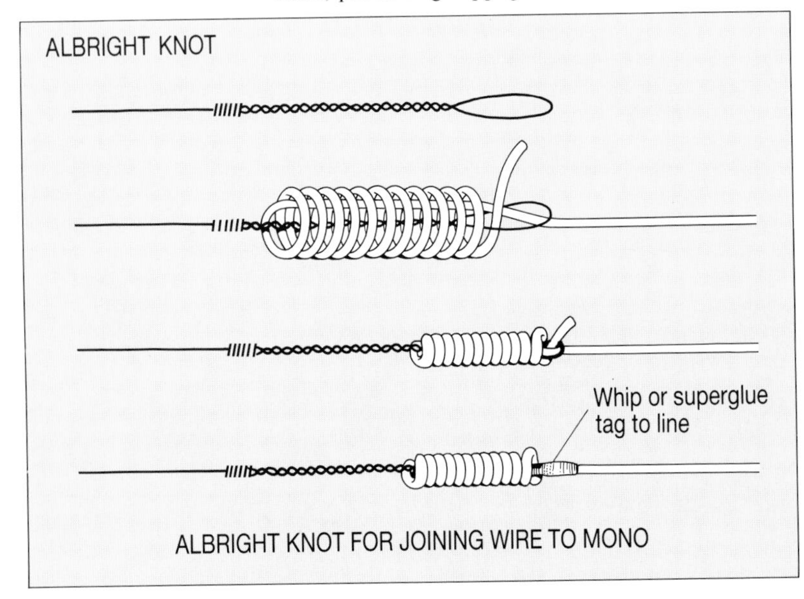

ALBRIGHT KNOT FOR JOINING WIRE TO MONO

A few turns of the free end at right angles around the standing line will finish the twist, and the end should be broken off by flexing it back and forwards. The monofil leader is fed through the loop and whipped back on itself over the loop. The free end is then fed back through the loop, the whole moistened and snugged down. The tag can be whipped down to give a smooth finish. This is the only reliable knot for joining wire and nylon, while the only other solution is to use a small, strong swivel.

■ Angler fish

This species is known to the commercial fisherman as the frogfish, or confusingly as monkfish. It is easily recognised by its immensely broad head and huge gaping mouth full of teeth. The curiously modified rays of the dorsal fin have flags of skin hanging from the tip which it waves over its mouth attracting prey into grasping range.

An important deep water commercial species with highly prized white flesh, it is found in depths to 550 metres over bottoms of mud, sand or gravel. It is also found occasionally in shallow water, especially when young, and adult fish have been observed drifting on the surface, supposedly stalking seagulls.

It appears to eat most species of fish, shellfish and squids. It occurs all round the United Kingdom, and is usually hooked by anglers drifting whole fish baits on the bottom near wrecks for species like ling. The British records are currently 94 lb 12 oz from a boat in Belfast Lough and 68 lb 2 oz from the shore at Canvey Island.

■ Attractor bead

A common ploy to add extra attraction to the bait is to slide a few brightly coloured beads on the line immediately above the hook. Plaice and other flatfish are the usual target, though they also work with predatory species including whiting. The importance of different colours is not fully understood, but the usual choices are 6 mm diameter fluorescent beads in white, yellow, green, orange or red.

■ Attractor spoon

Canadian salmon anglers have long made use of huge spoons or dodgers up to ten inches in length because they believe it helps attract fish to their bait. The role of the spoon is to simulate a fish trying to make off with the bait.

A similar technique is used for flounder fishing on this side of the Atlantic and recently boat anglers have started to incorporate the three inch white plastic flounder spoons in their rigs as attractors for cod. There would seem to be no reason why much larger spoons should not work over here. On a smaller scale, the same principles work with ragworm-baited Mepps spinners for thin-lipped mullet, and spinnerbaits tipped with mackerel strip for bass.

B

■ Bait

Probably the biggest problem facing the average angler is the need to obtain fresh, high quality bait. Many top anglers spend as much time digging for worms and scouring beaches for peeler crabs as they do fishing.

Boat anglers face similar problems obtaining fresh mackerel in these times of commercial overfishing. But it should never be overlooked that many tackle dealers situated near or on the coast still perform a sterling service in supplying bait, especially if anglers plan ahead and order well in advance.

Frozen bait, including lugworm and peeler crabs, calamari squid (intended for human consumption) and a wide variety of blast frozen fish ranging from sandeels primarily marketed for the sea angler to mackerel and herring will all catch fish if used properly.

Crabs Hard crabs are regularly found in the stomach of fish, but apart from smoothhounds and ballan wrasse, few fish find them acceptable as a bait. The time to collect crabs for bait is when they are just about to shed their shells. In this vulnerable state, they are known as peelers.

Mass moults occur in early summer and late autumn, but a few can be found throughout the warmer months. If no cracks in the shell are visible, pull the last segment from a leg. If the new segment is formed underneath then the crab is about to peel. But if just a few muscle fibres are visible then put it back.

Green shore crabs are most widely used, but velvet swimming crabs and edible crabs are favoured in some areas. Check the legal size limits for edible crabs, as they do apply to angler's bait.

Peeler crabs will keep easily in a fridge, providing they are put in seawater for a few minutes every other day. Kill them with a sharp knife and remove all the hard shell. In this state they can be frozen if required. Bind the flesh to the hook with knitting elastic and they make a top bait for bass, cod and flatfish.

Fish Almost any species of fish can be used as bait, but four reign supreme. Small fresh or live pouting are excellent baits for bass, cod or conger. Sandeel are used for bass, pollack, small-eyed ray, turbot, plaice and many others. They can sometimes be collected from a sandy beach at low water, but most anglers have to buy them if they want live baits.

Frozen sandeel is readily available at tackle shops. It is best fished on a fine wire hook, putting it either through the chin or in the mouth and out of the gill cover. Nick the hook into the skin of the belly just behind the pelvic fins.

Crab is an effective but expensive bait for wrasse.

Top: **Ragworm**

Top Right: **White rag**

Above: **Lugworm**

Herring can be bought if fresh enough, but mackerel should ideally be caught on the day.

Even the best frozen mackerel is not a patch on the real thing. Chunks cut across the body of either make good baits for whiting and thornback, and strips can be used to tip a cocktail bait.

Fillets of mackerel will catch almost any fish in the sea, though some sandeel feeders like pollack and turbot may prefer a thinner bait. Split the fillet in two lengthwise. A fillet hooked at the thin end, through the tough flesh that formed the wrist of the fish's tail, will flutter attractively in the water but not spin to cause twisting in the line.

A mackerel flapper is a good big bait for ling or conger and makes a better scent trail than a whole fish. Cut along either side of the backbone from just behind the head back to the tail, right through the body of the fish. The backbone can then be removed, leaving the head with both fillets attached.

Put an 8/0 O'Shaughnessy through the chin and out through the top of the head. A banjo is an economical alternative. This is the head, backbone and belly of the mackerel after other anglers have removed the fillets. Remove the tail fin as it can make the bait spin.

Lugworm Lugworm seems to be a more successful bait on the east and west coasts, though cod anglers everywhere swear by it. Blow lugworm live in U-shaped tubes and can be dug fairly readily by searching out the casts on sandy beaches. Yellowtail and black lugworm live in deeper straight tubes, and are very hard to dig out. A bait pump may work better with these varieties.

Tanking is of limited value with lugworm, and they are best kept wrapped in newspaper in a cool fridge.

Ragworm The centipede-like ragworm is the staple bait for many anglers especially in the south and south-west. It can be dug in mud or gravelly sand, and will keep if tanked in cool seawater. The very largest specimens, often 12 inches or more in length, are called king ragworm and make a fine bait for stingray, bass and mid-water pollack.

The small mud-dwelling harbour rag or maddies can be bunched on the hook for flatfish. White ragworm are often found in the sandier areas along with lugworm. These are very active worms, ideal for tipping off cocktail baits. Ragworm are usually threaded onto a long shanked hook, but it sometimes pays just to nick them through the head and leave the whole worm moving freely in the water as an added attraction.

Handle ragworm with care, gripping them just behind the head, as they can bite.

Shrimps Shrimps and prawns can be collected in rock pools for use as livebaits for wrasse, pollack and bass. They are best hooked near the tail and fished on light float tackle. Cooked prawns are favoured in some areas as a bait for flounder.

Shellfish Most species of shellfish have some value as bait. Razorfish can be collected by pouring salt down their keyhole-shaped blow holes at low water, or gathered with a long barbed spear. Alternatively they can be collected along with clams and slipper limpet from the debris after a storm.

Mussels can be gathered from rocks of pier pilings in many areas. All are rather soft baits when fresh, and some anglers salt them or leave them out of water for a day or two to toughen them up. The flesh is often tied to the hook with knitting elastic, small bits for pouting and flatfish, large helpings for bass or cod

Squid Squid and cuttlefish can be bought fresh or frozen from good fishmongers, and sometimes from tackle shops. Fished whole they are excellent for cod, bass and conger. Thinly cut strips make useful tips for cocktail baits, especially for plaice.

■ Bait clip

Casting distances are inevitably limited by a flapping bait which is often blasted off the hook by air resistance. The solution is to streamline the rig by using a bait clip which holds the baited hook against the line during the cast but then releases it on impact with the water.

The clip itself consists of a wire or plastic hook which engages with the baited hook. In theory, the bait can be clipped up the line or down, but in reality the best solution for distance casting is to clip the bait close behind the weight. A stop knot will ensure that a clipped down bait is not pushed up the line away from the hook.

■ Bait fork

In easy conditions, ragworm and shallow-dwelling lugworm can be dug using an ordinary garden fork. But when the worms are deeper, a proper potato fork with a narrow head and longer, flat tines is a much more effective tool.

■ Bait pump

This Australian idea is a relatively new arrival on the bait collection scene. It is a simple suction pump which is placed over the wormhole, and lifts out a core of sand, hopefully containing the worm. Black lugworm, which make straight, deep burrows, can often be very effectively collected with this tool.

■ Baitsafe

The Intakl Baitsafe is a coffin-shaped plastic box, with built-in lead for casting weight, grip wires, and a hollow chamber into which the baited hook can be placed. The lid of the box is designed to open on impact with the water. This device offers a viable solution to the problems of casting small, delicate baits over longish distances.

■ Ballan wrasse

This is the largest of our wrasses which is found in inshore waters all round the country. But it is of most importance to anglers on the rocky coasts of southern and western Britain where it will venture

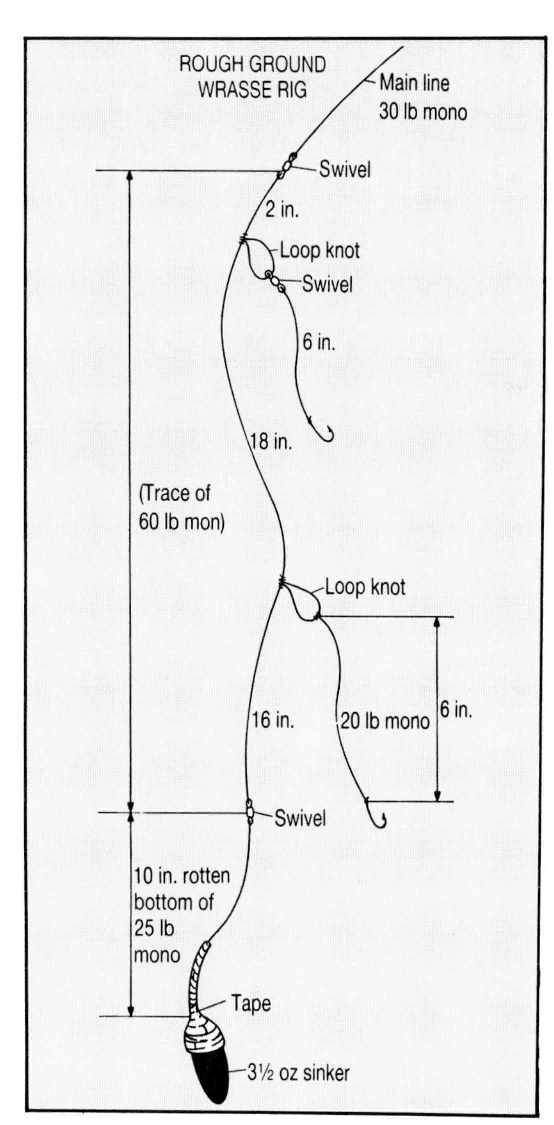

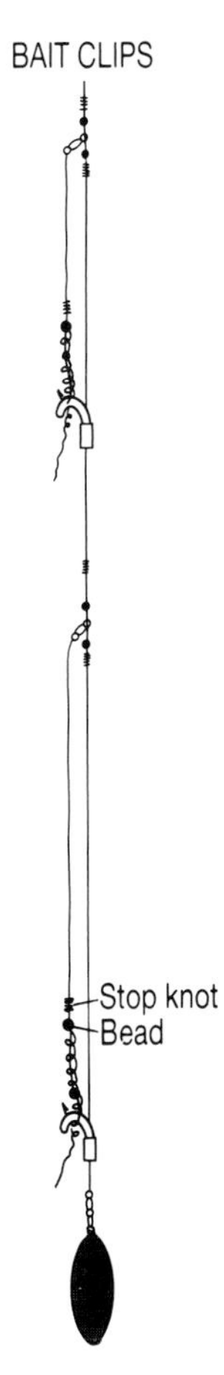

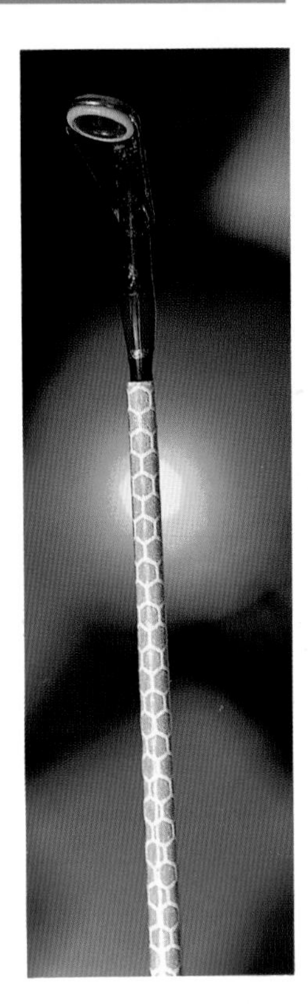

Luminous tape wrapped around the tip glows bright under a night light.

into very shallow water. The best specimens are usually captured where there's a reasonable depth and in colder weather it retreats into deeper water. Wrasse trapped in shallow water by cold weather will often perish in considerable numbers.

Conventional beachcasting tackle may sometimes be necessary to prise a specimen from a particularly rocky or kelpy area, but it's more enjoyable to tackle up with the kind of gear usually associated with carp angling.

Because of the rough nature of its habitat, float fishing or a paternoster with a rotten bottom is the preferred method. The top bait is crab followed by worm, prawn and shellfish. Ballans are one of the few fish which can consistently be captured on hard-backed crabs.

The British records are currently 9 lb 6 oz from a boat on the Eddystone, and 8 lb 6 oz from the shore on Guernsey.

■ Bass

The hard fighting bass is one of the finest tasting fish in European waters and is equally popular with the sea angler and commercial fisherman. It can be taken by a wide variety of methods from the shore and boats.

In Britain its main distribution ranges from Morecambe Bay in the north west to the Wash on the east coast. It has been recorded from both coasts of Scotland and ranges well to the south of Britain, as far as the Mediterranean and the Atlantic coast of North Africa.

Traditionally, bass are fish of inshore waters, living on open beaches, rocky shores and reefs, and often well into the estuaries of rivers. Recent research has also revealed the existence of large stocks of fish well offshore, especially in the winter months when the adults migrate from their shallower summer feeding grounds to deeper water. Spawning occurs offshore in the spring, but the juveniles move rapidly into estuaries where they spend about five years growing until they are mature at about 16 inches in length.

Many of these nursery estuaries now have some legal protection for the young fish. Bass are relatively slow-growing and occasional specimens as old as 25 years have been recorded. The British records are currently 19 lb 9 oz from a boat in Herne Bay, Kent, and 19 lb from the shore at Dover.

Bass are an active, hunting fish and will respond to a wide range of methods. These include beachcasting with sandeel, lugworm or crab baits, livebaiting with sandeels, pouting or other small fish, bottom fishing with large baits such as whole squid, large crab baits or sides of mackerel, and lure fishing with plugs, rubber eels or metal spoons.

The Bass Anglers' Sportfishing Society encourages the conservation, research and protection of bass. Membership is open to all, and details are available from the secretary, John Morgan, 30 Thomas Street, Port Talbot, West Glamorgan SA12 6LT.

■ Beachcaster

This term is sometimes used to describe an angler who fishes from the beach but it is more usually applied to indicate the type of rod he is using.

Modern beachcasters built from fibre-glass, carbon fibre or kevlar composites, tend to be tip-actioned, with a stiff butt, powerful mid section, and

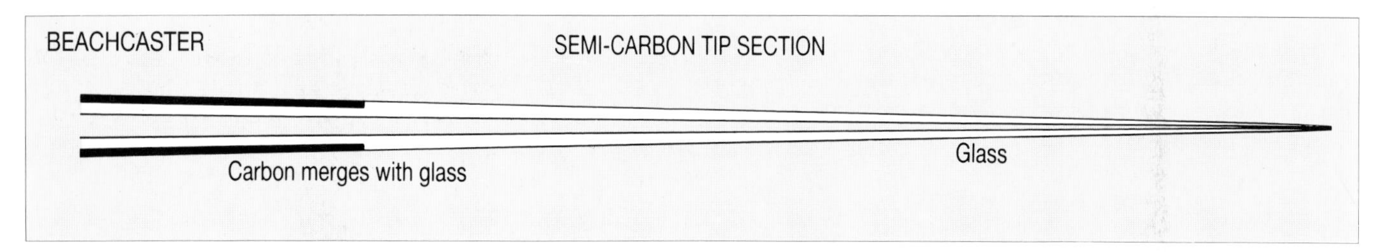

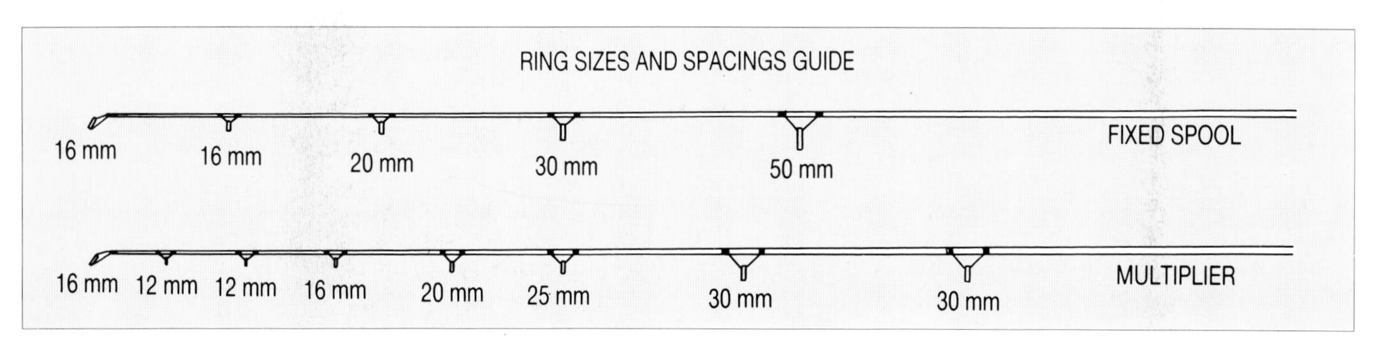

a soft tip often of plain fibreglass to enhance bite detection.

Length generally ranges from about 11 feet for the faster techniques like the pendulum cast with the reel at the top of the handle, to 13 or 14 feet for off-the-ground casting or with the reel set low on the handle. Lined rings are almost universal, with a tip diameter of about 16 mm allowing shock-leader knots and scraps of weed to pass through easily.

Ringing system For use with a multiplier, about seven rings up to 30 mm are used, while a fixed spool rod will probably only have four intermediate rings, but going up to 50 mm. Handles tend to be long and simply finished, with a carbon and steel fixed reel seat, or perhaps a snaplock or just coasters.

The large diameter of the butt means that only small grips are likely to be used, and many come with just a layer of plastic shrink-wrap tubing over the blank.

The standard rod is designed to cast a 5 oz weight which will cover most angling demands but it is possible to get specialist rods for casting 6 oz to 8 oz over rough ground, or so-called bass rods designed for 1oz to 4 oz.

■ Beach fishing

This term is often used to embrace all forms of shore fishing which is probably the last bastion of cheap angling in this country. There is still no licence for a sea angler to buy, though this does mean that there is no protection or management of the fishery for his benefit. Access to the shoreline is free in most places but there are some special cases where the foreshore is privately owned and access is restricted.

Plenty of challenges The shore-bound angler has a wide range of options depending on where he lives and how far he is prepared to travel. Small sandy coves in Cornwall offer a very different challenge from the wide and flat beaches of the east coast, or the steep shingle of Dorset's Chesil Beach, With care it is possible to choose a single outfit to manage all three, but over a period of time most anglers will acquire a range of tackle suited to each particular situation.

Piers and rocky shores offer challenges of their own, but again they can be managed on the same tackle. These places also offer a wider range of specialist approaches for the open-minded angler, with techniques like float fishing and lure fishing coming into their own.

Many shore anglers start off from a beach, but in reality it is not the easiest place to begin. Most beaches, whether flat or steep, sand or shingle, are rather featureless places, and the fish appear and disappear in confusing patterns. Research into the chosen beach is essential.

Watch the regulars Any beach worth fishing has its own group of regular anglers – if you walk the beach and see no-one fishing there may be a good reason for it. Watch for the times when people do go fishing, but do not be surprised if the most successful anglers are there during the hours of darkness. Walk along the beach and meet them, and when they are not busy ask about their catches and their fishing experiences.

Observe their choice of tackle and bait, and you will discover that the simple paternostered lugworm with a 5 oz lead is not universal. Read the catch reports in the local and national angling press, and talk to local tackle dealers.

Top: **A deep water mark like the Chesil Bank which is swept by strong tides will offer more variety of fish - and the chance of real heavyweights.**

Above: **A typical composite beachcaster capable of punching out baits to the 100 yard mark.**

Of all the forms of shore angling, beach angling places the greatest demands on the casting skills of the angler. Sooner or later, the ability to cast far out to sea will become necessary, and it is never too soon to start learning to cast properly. While it is possible to acquire a cheap fibreglass beachcaster and a fixed spool reel for approximately £60, these may not be capable of the demands that distance casting places upon them.

■ Bell lead

This is one of the traditional leads for boat angling, and while its flat-bottomed, conical shape confers neither a particularly smooth drop in the water nor stability on the sea bed, its ease of production especially in larger sizes from 1-3 lb ensures that it remains in regular use.

■ Bird's nest

A hideous tangle in the line which in sea fishing usually occurs when casting with a multiplier from the beach. It is nothing like as common a problem with fixed spool reels unless the spool is overfilled allowing the line to tumble off the front lip.

Bird's nests on the multiplier can usually be attributed to two different causes. Those which build up early in the cast are the most spectacular, often resulting in a potentially dangerous crack-off especially if the shock-leader has left the reel. This results from the spool accelerating faster than the lead can pull the line from the reel, and coils of mono lift off the spool in sheets, producing the most unbelievable mess. The solution in most cases is to alter the casting style, using a longer and slower technique and removing any snatch from the cast.

If the tangle comes at the end of the cast, then the lead is slowing down more than the spool of the reel producing an inevitable over-run. Solutions include increasing the casting drag on the reel by using larger brake blocks or thicker oil, and reducing the amount of line on the reel. If a magnetic controlled multiplier is being used then simply increase the effect of the magnets by dialling in a higher setting.

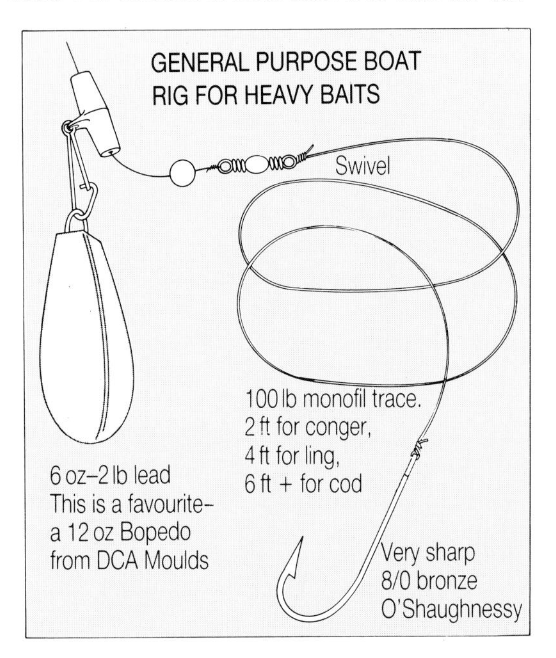

■ Blue shark

This is a rather slender, elegant shark with long pectoral fins and a beautiful, deep blue back over a white belly. The colour fades quickly if the fish has to be killed. It is an oceanic shark, only really common well offshore on the coasts of Cornwall and southern Ireland.

It can usually be fished for on the drift, using sporting tackle of 20 or 30 lb class. A long rubbing trace and a heavy wire biting trace are essential at the hook. The British record is currently 218 lb 9 oz from a boat off Looe in Cornwall.

■ Boat fishing

Buying your own boat demands a lot of careful research, for an unwise choice is a continuous drain on the finances, if not actually dangerous. Above all a boat needs to be safe in the situation it is being used in. Close to the shore, a compass, pair of oars, bailer, lifejacket and a couple of flares may cover most eventualities, but for venturing further out a radio, electronic position finder, navigation lights and possibly a spare engine become necessary, plus a lot higher standard of maintenance and seamanship. Remember that if you get into trouble, someone else will risk his life to rescue you.

Charter fishing opportunities Most ports have three levels of charter boats. First there are the casuals and pleasure boats. These may be commercial boats earning extra cash at weekends, or general purpose boats catering to the summer trade. They tend to stick to inshore marks and have only rudimentary fish-finding equipment. They are cheap and offer trips of short duration for those curious to find out a little about the sport.

Secondly there are the standard angling charter boats. These may be part-time commercial fishing boats, but increasingly they are the smaller, slower specialist angling boats. They cater for the more serious angler who wants to fish the inshore waters, usually out to about 12 miles. The skippers may be

extremely knowledgeable both about angling and about their waters.

Finally there are the big name boats, the high-speed specialists in deep water wrecking, who are also more than able to work inshore waters if required, either locally or increasingly for south coast boats, on the Channel Isles as part of a three day charter.

The skippers of these boats are full-time, making their living from keeping anglers happy. They have every worthwhile bit of technology in their cabins, and have an information grapevine that keeps them in touch with every catch in their area.

■ Boat rods

For general boat fishing a rod between six and eight feet is favoured – long enough to be able to flex to both enhance the sport and make it difficult for the fish to break the line, but short enough to be easily handled in the confined space. Long rods give a more pleasant action, but they are a less efficient lever against the fish and in heavy-duty situations like conger or shark fishing, or pirking, a shorter rod can be advantageous.

It is conventional to describe a rod by the class of line it is designed to be used with, though most rods are versatile enough to be used one class either way if conditions warrant it.

Different classes:

- 6 lb class rods are rarities, but a pleasure to use for fish like bream, plaice and bass.
- 12 lb class covers the same species with heavier leads, and also lighter fishing for pollack and codling.
- 20lb class is the all-rounder, suitable right up to light-tackle fishing for tope and small shark.
- 30 lb class is the heaviest that many boat anglers possess, and will cope even with most conger and other wreck fishing.
- 50 lb class is moving towards the big-game category, though it has some uses for big conger, skate, shark, and pirking on wrecks. Anything bigger is only really suitable for use in a fighting chair as most anglers couldn't bend it.

The majority of boat rods are still made on hollow glass or semi-carbon blanks, but carbon and carbon-kevlar composites are rapidly gaining in the

Left: **Beachcaster with multiplier ringing, custom-built model for long distance pendulum casting and heavy duty boat rod fitted throughout with rollers.**

Above: **The cabin of a top class charter boat fitted out with all the electronics for navigation and fish finding.**

A flat sea and little tide run makes it possible to use a lighter outfit.

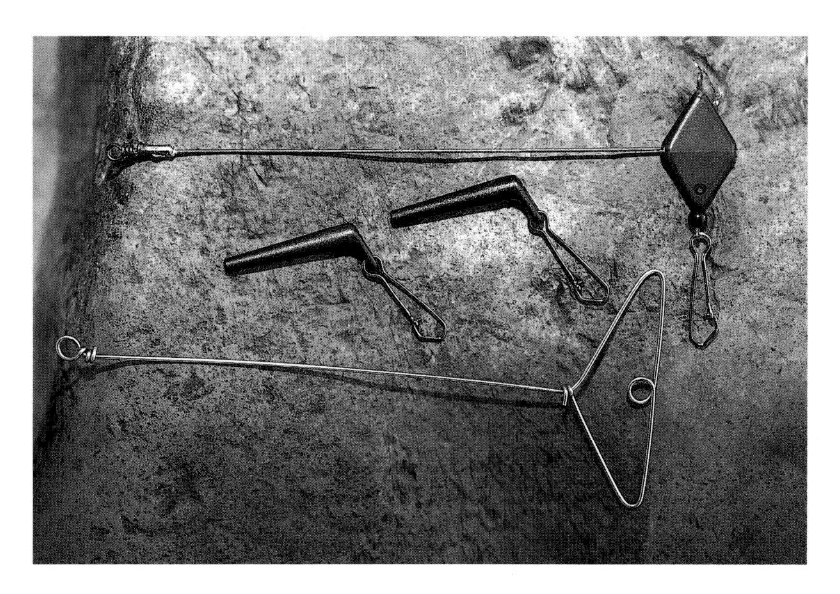

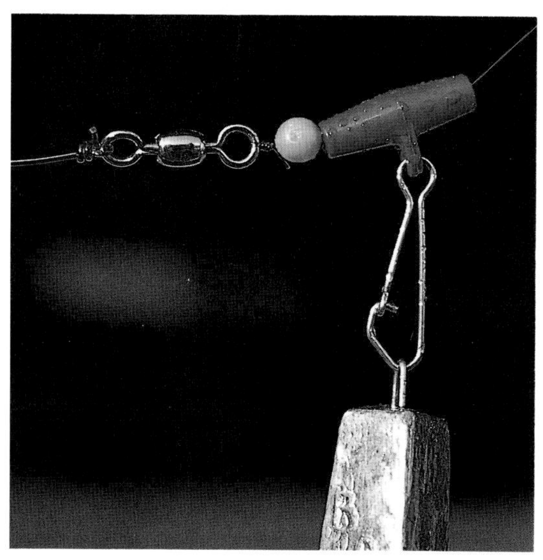

Above: **Wire booms and small sliders for making up boat rigs.**

Above right: **Free running leger with a Zip slider.**

marketplace. Traditional butts were wooden, but nowadays hollow glass is the usual choice with warm, comfortable Hyperlon grips.

Rods are usually jointed below a chromed brass reel seat, although there is now a lightweight Fuji boat seat suitable for rods up to 30 lb class. With rods up to seven feet it is possible to use a one-piece construction with a standard Fuji seat and avoid the joint altogether. For lighter rods Fuji rings are almost universal, but roller rings become worthwhile for heavier gear.

■ Boom

See Clements; French; Zip slider.

■ Brake blocks

Centrifugally braked casting reels have a number of small brake blocks which slide on bars inside the reel. These blocks are forced outwards by the spinning of the reel spool, and rub against a drum producing a braking effect. Smaller reels usually have bars for two blocks, while larger reels may have four. A tournament caster may only use one small block, while the average beachcaster will probably have two medium sized blocks for general use.

■ Breakaway

The original Breakaway design is a torpedo-shaped lead with swivelling grip wires. Each wire carries a bead which engages in a slot on the side of the lead, preventing the grip wire from releasing until it is given a relatively heavy pull.

The tension can be adjusted by bending the wires, or by winding an elastic band around them. But care must be taken not to convert the weight into a fixed wire lead with the inevitable problems of dragging it out of the sea bed, and avoiding snags on the retrieve. More recent variations have produced long-tailed leads for uptiding with nose wires and beach-casting, and use rollers rather than beads on the wires for a more controllable release.

■ Breakwater

Many of our major ports have enormous stone structures set offshore to give shelter to their harbours and coastal shipping. These breakwaters often date back to the Napoleonic period, and can provide excellent, sheltered deep water fishing if they can be reached easily by boat like those at Dover and Plymouth.

Other breakwaters including the structure at Portland in Dorset have the potential, but access is denied most of the time by the Ministry of Defence. In most cases, they offer a wide range of fishing opportunities with areas of very rough ground and fierce tides, and sheltered areas often with a sandy bottom.

All sorts of species come within range but float fishing for mackerel, garfish and mullet is particularly worthwhile.

■ Bream

Four species of fish are known as sea bream in Britain. The red bream is a summer and autumn resident, mostly on offshore reefs and wrecks along the south and west coasts. In winter it retreats to deeper water on the continental shelf. It has the typical deep body of a sea bream, with large eyes and a spiny dorsal fin, and its body and fins have a distinctive pinkish colour. It is a popular light-tackle sporting proposition and a fine eating fish.

Even in 200 feet of water, it is possible to drift a fish or squid strip bait on a small hook, using perhaps 8 lb line and a spinning rod with no more than a couple of ounces of lead. Sadly it is no longer as common as years ago. The British record is 9 lb 8 oz from a boat off Mevagissey, Cornwall, and 7 lb 8 oz from the shore at Alderney, Channel Islands.

The black bream is another summer visitor which frequents inshore reefs in the early summer, and may remain there until the autumn. It is also found on some offshore wrecks, and can be captured using the same methods as for red bream. Long flowing traces were favoured by the experts in days when it was abundant.

The colour is usually a bluish black with silver sides, and specimens often have vertical dark bars on their sides. The British record is 6 lb 14 oz from a Devon wreck, and 4 lb 14 oz from the shore at Alderney, Channel Isles.

The gilthead bream is a regular summer migrant to the south west coast, seeming to favour the area around Salcombe in Devon. It looks rather like a portly black bream, with a distinctive gold bar across the front of its head. The British records are 9 lb 8 oz from a boat, and 8 lb 6 oz from the shore, both at Salcombe.

The Ray's Bream is only a distant relative, and is a rare summer migrant which wanders usually up the west coast off Ireland, round Scotland and down into the North Sea. It is an exotic looking fish, with a bulbous head, elongate dorsal and anal fins lacking distinct spines, and a deeply forked tail fin. The British record is 6 lb 3 oz from a boat off Barra Head, Scotland, and 7 lb 15 oz from the shore at Hartlepool.

■ Brolly sheet

A weatherproof nylon sheet attached to the edge of the umbrella closing the gap between the rim and the ground. Loops or velcro strips attach it firmly to the umbrella, and pegs stake it to the ground. Pockets around the edges can be filled with pebbles or stones to anchor the sheet down against the wind.

The black bream moves on to the inshore reefs in early summer.

Roller rings are essential for wire.

■ Bulk spool

Nylon monofil is wonderful stuff, but its life expectancy is short in the saltwater environment. Bulk buying is the only realistic and economic solution. Even when sensibly stored in a cool, dark place, nylon has a finite life before it starts to weaken. Most anglers prefer to purchase 600 or 1,000 metre spools of fresh line as required.

■ Bull huss

This larger relative of the lesser spotted dogfish can be recognised by its widely separated nasal flaps, and usually larger spots. It occurs on rough ground around Britain, but mostly on the south and west coasts. Its food is mainly crabs and a wide variety of fish, and it is usually captured by anglers fishing with large fish baits.

In several parts of the country there is a distinct seasonal run of this species, usually in spring or autumn, when it becomes a worthwhile target for the beach angler. But captures from the shore are usually accidental. From inshore boats, it often features in mixed bags from rough ground. The British records are currently 22 lb 4 oz from a boat off Minehead, Somerset, and 17 lb 15 oz from the shore near Falmouth, Cornwall.

C

■ Cantilever box

One of the most efficient ways of storing sea tackle is to use a cantilever box. Access to the tackle is very good, and it is easy to see when stocks of a particular item is running low. But care must always be taken to keep saltwater spray out of the open compartments.

■ Casting

Every shore angler needs to master some form of casting although with modern tackle even the simple overhead thump can send 5 oz of lead towards the 100 yard mark. From piers or rocks this is usually more than adequate, but venture onto a beach and the day will soon arrive where anglers all around are taking fish at greater range.

Most anglers will master the layback cast from a book and some practise on the beach or in a playing field. For ultimate distance the pendulum cast is the solution, and the best recommendation is to seek out a competent casting instructor, either through a fishing club, a local tournament casting event or a tackle dealer.

Off the ground cast This is a useful cast for anyone who has trouble mastering the layback or pendulum casts. It is also good when using a particularly long rod or a heavier-than-usual casting weight. Because the terminal tackle starts on the ground, it is necessary to have a reasonably level and snag-free bit of beach to cast from, but even wired leads will lift off surprisingly well.

Imagine the clock face on the beach with 12 o'clock pointing to sea. Start with a lead drop of between half and three-quarters of the rod length. Lay the tackle out in a straight line on the beach pointing to 8 or 9 o'clock. The further round it is the more power will be generated.

Take up a position with the leader taut to the rod tip and the rod pointing towards the lead. The feet should be comfortably spaced with the left foot pointing along the beach to 3 o' clock and the body twisted from the hips so that the head is facing towards the lead. The rod butt should be held high near to the chin with the tip only a few inches off the ground.

The cast is executed by pivoting the body until it is facing the sea. At the same time pull the rod round with the left hand kept high at first but

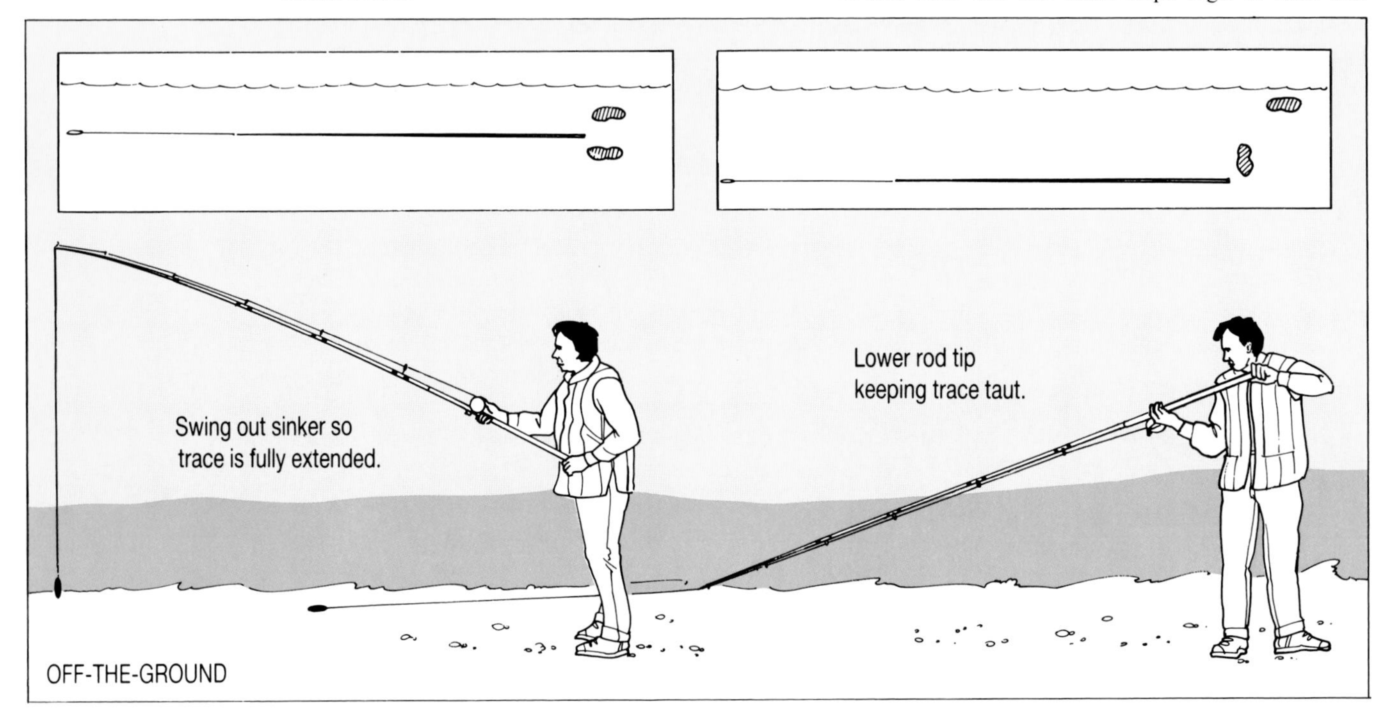

pulled down later to turn the rod over at the end of the cast. The right arm and shoulder will have to dip slightly to get under the rod to punch through the cast.

Layback cast In performance terms, the layback cast falls between the simple overhead thump and the powerful pendulum cast. It uses far more rotational power and a wider range of body muscles than the overhead, and is capable of reaching distances of over 150 yards with a 5 oz lead.

Again, imagine a clock face on the beach, with 12 o'clock pointing out to sea. A right handed caster should stand with his feet comfortably apart and parallel to the beach, facing 3 o'clock. Rotate the upper half of the body to face directly away from the sea, at 6 o'clock. Use a sinker drop of about half the length of the rod. Point the rod at about 5 o'clock to begin with, and sloping upwards at about 45 degrees. Push the rod away from the body so the lead swings out, and then back in to about the 9 o'clock position.

When the lead reaches the peak of its inswing, pull round and up with the left hand, straightening the body. As the rod comes round, the right hand can be used to push the rod up, and the left hand will then pull the butt down. Most anglers will find that as the body turns to fully face the sea, it will be easier to pivot on the left foot and bring the right foot round,so the cast ends with both feet facing the sea.

Once the basic cast has been mastered, the length of the stroke and the power of the cast, can be increased by starting with the rod pointing at 7 o'clock, and swinging the lead in towards the 10 o'clock position.

Pendulum cast The pendulum cast is the ultimate distance style and has produced all the tournament distance records. It is not an easy technique to learn and demands good co-ordination, a powerful rod and well tuned reel. Most importantly, the leader must be strong.

Executed properly, it will project a bait up to 180 yards – in tournaments, distances of well over 250 yards are achieved without baits. Badly done, it destroys baits and rods, produces the most horrendous bird's nests and is downright dangerous. If ever a method called for professional instruction, this is it.

As the layback cast extends the power arc of the overhead thump, so the pendulum extends that of the layback. Consider the clock face on the beach with 12 o'clock pointing out to sea. Start the cast facing away from the sea at 6 o'clock. The sinker drop should be longer, perhaps eight or nine foot from the rod tip, and the rod held high pointing to 9 o' clock. Reach out to push the rod away, starting the lead on a high swing which will end on the inswing with the leader almost horizontal and pointing at 3 o'clock.

As the lead pauses at the top of the inswing, the body pivot starts, leading with the head and following with the hips and feet until facing the sea. At the same time, the left hand pulls the rod right round at shoulder level, until the right hand comes under the rod and punches through, turning the rod over and completing the cast.

■ Catfish

The catfish or wolf-fish is an rather ugly, grey, elongate species with prominent dog-like teeth in the front of its jaws. It occurs throughout the North Sea and around Scotland, where it lives a solitary existence feeding on starfish, sea urchins, crabs and shellfish, all of which can be crushed in its formidable jaws.

Although it lives mostly in deep water, young fish are often found inshore in the summer. The British

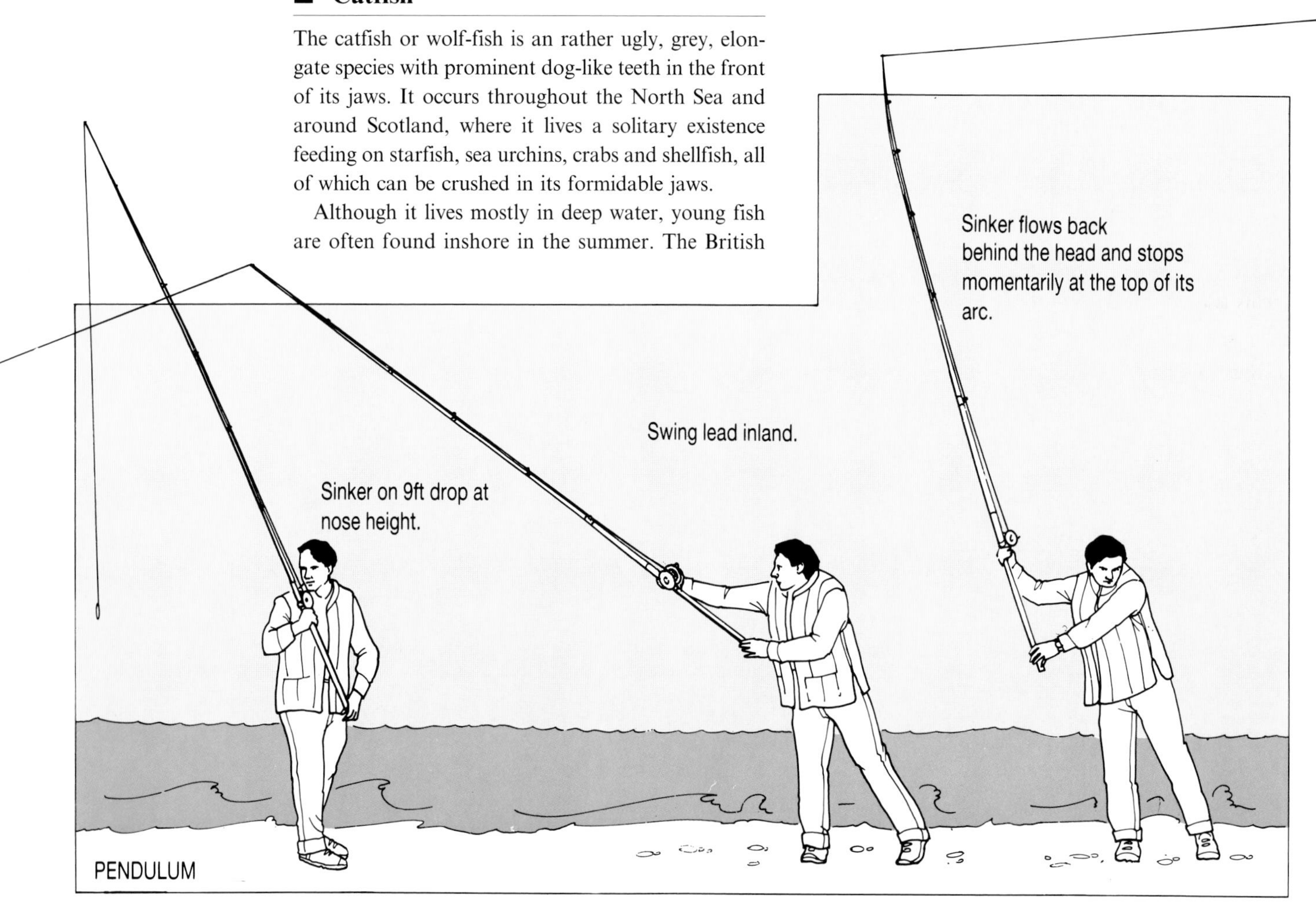

records are currently 26 lb 4 oz from a boat off Whitby, and 12 lb 12 oz from the shore at Stonehaven, Scotland.

■ Charter skipper

Whatever level you enter the charter boat market, it is important that you have a good relationship with the skipper. He should know what you expect from the trip, and what your level of skill is. You should feel comfortable taking his advice, and if need be his orders.

The wise angler recognises that he pays not only for the boat, but also for the skipper. And the wise skipper is only too happy to do all in his power to make the trip successful, not only by his seamanship and fish-finding skills, but also by advising and helping the angler during the day.

Far too many charter trips end in misery through some misunderstanding between the skipper and the anglers. Check in particular the booking conditions regarding cancellation. The normal rule is that if the skipper cancels, the money is returned in full less any for bait that has been purchased – but you should be offered the bait.

If you cancel then you pay – in full if it is at short notice, and only a generous skipper will return a deposit at any length of notice. When the decision about cancellation hinges on the weather, then you have to be able to trust the skipper's advice. If you cannot, then you have chosen the wrong skipper.

■ Clement's boom

This is a wire boom with a clip to carry the lead in a boat fishing leger rig. The Clement's boom has two eyes for the line, separated by several inches of wire, while its near relative the Kilmore boom has only a single eye. The eyes may be plain wire loops, or lined – in the early days with ceramic inserts but nowadays with nylon.

This type of boom is becoming less popular, with many anglers using one of the fine nylon sliders like the Zip, Eddystone, Ashpole or Mustad Knotless, or just a plain link swivel.

■ Clothing

Serious consideration should be given to the choice of suitable clothing, especially when going afloat. The key points to remember are warmth, waterproofing, buoyancy, mobility and visibility.

While trainers may be alright for a summer day, walking boots, wellingtons, waders or moonboots are the main choices of footwear, each having a role to play. Metal studded footwear has no place in sea angling, usually being downright lethal.

In summer, a tracksuit, or moleskin trousers and a canvas smock will be comfortable afloat or ashore. A peaked cap, lightweight waterproofs, and a fishing waistcoat complete the outfit. The waistcoat can be a fishing style one with pockets to carry tackle, or better still one of the designs with added buoyancy.

In winter, good thermal underwear, topped with a thermal pile suit and a set of quality waterproofs will cover both shore and boat angling. Good gloves and a balaclava helmet will keep the extremities warm. There are now many quality buoyancy suits available to the angler, which in addition to their lifesaving capabilities offer warmth and waterproofing. Afloat, safety is always be a serious consideration, and fluorescent colours should be chosen when available.

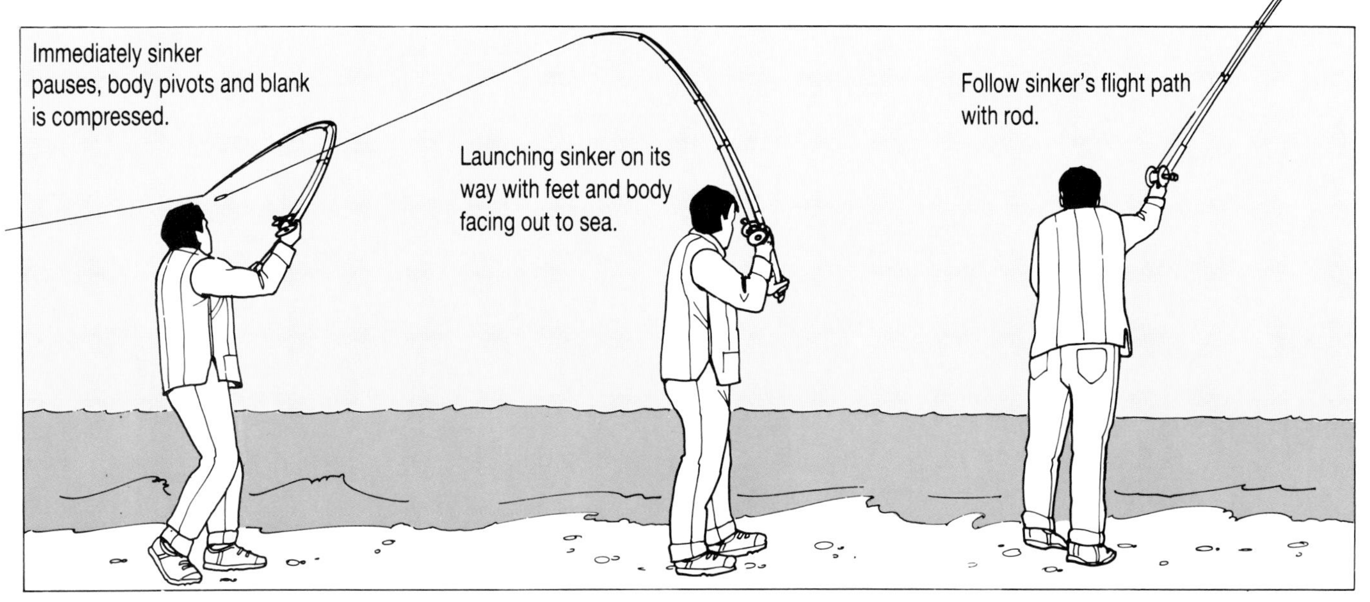

■ Coalfish

Large coalfish, with the closely related pollack, are considered by many to be among the best of Britain's offshore, sporting species. Both are active, predatory species and crash dive for the bottom repeatedly when hooked, testing tackle to its limits.

Coalfish can be recognised by their dark olive back which lacks the brassy tints of pollack and their conspicuous straight, white lateral line – that of the pollack is much darker and less conspicuous, and arches distinctly over the pectoral fin.

In general, coalfish have a more northerly distribution than pollack, though both species occur all round the British coasts, favouring rocky shores, offshore reefs and wrecks. From the shore, spinning, fly fishing or bait fishing with prawn, fish or worm baits in mid-water will produce small to mid-sized specimens, especially in the summer.

Offshore, the favourite method is a rubber eel fished on a flying collar rig, or a pirk, especially one of the slimmer Scandinavian designs worked rather more actively than might be the case for cod or ling. Although the Scottish coast and the North Sea are the areas of greatest abundance, fine specimens are captured regularly in the extreme south west, and the British records are currently 37 lb 5 oz from a boat off the Eddystone, Cornwall, and 20 lb 6 oz from the shore at Newquay, Cornwall.

■ Coasters

There are several efficient designs of reel seat for beachcasting rods but some anglers find they need to shift the reel's position and that rules out a fixed, screw-up fitting. For example, the reel might be moved nearer the butt of the rod to cope with casting very heavy weights. The solution is to use a coaster to clamp the reel in the required spot.

The cheapest coaster is a simple Jubilee clip but this is difficult to adjust on the beach. Several companies make proper coasters, usually incorporating a large padded knob which is easy to unscrew and provides a comfortable place to lock the forefinger around during casting.

■ Cod

This species must rank as one of the most popular with anglers because it runs to a good size, fights doggedly and makes good eating. It can be captured using almost any method and bait, at almost any venue on any ground. But this does not mean they are easy to catch.

Cod are active hunters with voracious appetites, but consistent success comes, as with most species, to those anglers prepared to do their homework.

Beach fishing for cod is mainly a winter pastime, when the shoals move inshore to feed. Large lugworm baits paternostered at long range at night are the favoured tactics on the shallower east and south coast beaches. Crab or squid baits fished at closer range often score in deeper water. Rigging a small worm bait alongside a flying hook will often snag a small pouting or whiting, making a fine livebait for the patient angler after a specimen fish.

The inshore movements of cod vary widely in different parts of the country, and it is essential to be familiar with the trends on local beaches, both in terms of time of year and state of the tide.

From the boats, many regions have developed their own methods. Large baits fished on the bottom are always a favourite. Mussels or lugworm tend to be the choice in the north, with crab, squid or cuttlefish in the south. Uptiding is favoured in shallow waters like the Thames estuary and the Bristol Channel, but conventional bottom fishing at anchor or on the drift is more widespread in other areas.

Wire line is needed in faster currents like the Isle of Wight waters. Unbaited pirks and muppets work over rough ground or wrecks, and rubber eels fished over wrecks on flying collar rigs account for some fine specimens every year, especially in the south west.

The British records are currently 53 lb from a boat off south Devon, and 44 lb 8 oz from the shore at Barry, Glamorgan.

■ Common skate

Despite its name, this leviathan of the seas is nowadays very much a rarity. Along with its similarly sized relatives, the long-nosed and white skate, the only venues with much promise seem to be the south of Ireland and the west coast of Scotland, where coincidentally many anglers return all the fish they catch as a conservation measure.

The usual tactics for these fish involves the use of heavy rods and reels – at least 50 lb class – and wire traces with large fish baits, coalfish often being the preferred species. The British records are currently 227 lb from a boat off Tobermory, Scotland, and 138 lb from the shore on the Isle of Lewis, Scotland. Specimens weighing more than double this size are known to exist.

■ Conger

One of our more robust sporting fish, the conger is a challenging species for anyone with access to rocky areas from boat or shore, particularly on the south and west coasts. They can be found all year round in deep water and on offshore wrecks. From the beaches, they are mainly a summer and autumn fish as they move to deeper water in the winter. Severe cold will often kill conger which have been unable to retreat offshore.

They are active hunters, and most specimens fall to fresh fish, squid or cuttlefish baits legered firmly on the bottom.

Wire traces are not normally necessary but heavy monofilament of at least 100 lb breaking strain is recommended, along with a stout hook from size 6/0 upwards according to the size of the bait. Conger are an ideal species on which to practice conservation, as their flesh, although very palatable, does not seem to suit the British taste.

They can usually be returned even to deep water without ill effects, and for that reason it is better to avoid stainless steel hooks, using bronze ones which will rust away if they have to be left in the fish.

The normal shore tactic is to use conventional beachcasting gear with a line of between 20 lb and 30 lb depending on the roughness of the ground. In cleaner conditions at close range, good sport is possible with smaller eels on a heavy carp or bass rod and lighter line. But care must be taken to prevent fish diving into snags and some losses are inevitable.

From a boat, 30 lb or 50 lb class tackle will cope with most specimens, though anyone with an ambition to heave a three-figure specimen from a wreck should select tackle with care – it is not enough to just keep buying stiffer rods and stronger line. Look instead to the new generation of big-game stand-up rods which coupled with a suitable harness give real lifting power to the angler. The British records are currently 109 lb 6 oz from a boat off South Devon and 67 lb 1 oz from the shore at Torquay.

■ Cool box

After investing time and money collecting quality bait it is foolhardy to waste it by letting it shrivel up on a hot, sunny day. A wide mouthed flask will keep a small supply of frozen baits cold – often well enough for unused ones to be returned to the freezer at the end of the day. But a cool box containing freezer packs is the most efficient way of keeping live and frozen bait cool and fresh.

■ Crimping tool

Shark, tope and similar toothy species must be tackled with wire traces to prevent them biting through the line, and others like conger and ling need at least heavy nylon traces. Wire can only be attached to hooks or swivels using crimps, and nylon over about 100 lb is best joined in this way, as it is very difficult to knot.

The line should go through the crimp, through the loop, back through the crimp and then fed back into the crimp so the end is tucked inside. In the smaller sizes, crimps can be secured with proprietary crimping pliers or even by the careful use of ordinary pair of pliers.

The finished join should be tested very carefully, as it is easy to damage the line by applying too much pressure. Heavy gauges of nylon and wire should be joined with special big-game or yacht rigging crimps applied with a specially designed tool.

D

Dab

This diminutive but tasty flatfish is an important species for the saltwater angler fishing anywhere in Britain on sandy beaches and offshore sandbanks, especially in autumn or winter.

The dab can be distinguished from other flatfish like plaice and flounders by the lack of orange spots, the strongly curved lateral line around the base of the pectoral fin, and the uniformly rough feel over the eyed side if the fish is stroked towards the head.

The food of dabs differs from that of plaice and flounders, as they mainly prefer shrimps, crabs and other small crustaceans. But most are captured by anglers using paternostered worm baits, though tipping the hook with a sliver of squid or fish will often attract the better specimens.

The British records are currently 2 lb 12 oz from a boat in Wester Ross, Scotland, and 2 lb 9 oz from the shore at Port Talbot, Glamorgan.

■ Dogfish

See Bull Huss and Lesser Spotted Dogfish.

■ Dropnet

Anglers fishing from piers and steep rock marks are often unable to get to the water's edge to land a fish using a net or gaff and a dropnet is needed. A bicycle wheel rim, or a specially-made metal ring, is attached by three or four strong cords to the end of a sufficiently long rope. A net is suspended from the ring with a weight in the bottom to ensure it sinks below the frame.

The net is lowered into the water and gently raised once the fish is drawn over it. Supplies of fresh bait like prawns and hermits crab can be collected in the net by lowering it to the bottom and leaving it there for a period with a lump of fish inside.

E

■ Eagle ray

This is a relative of the stingray which is only rarely taken by anglers on the south coast of England. It can be distinguished by its pointed wings and the small dorsal fin just in front of the spine. They are believed to feed on small molluscs and crustaceans. The British record is currently 61 lb 8 oz from a boat off the Isle of Wight.

■ Ebb tide

See Tides.

■ Electric ray

Two species of electric rays have been recorded from British waters, the electric ray and the much smaller marbled electric ray. They are easily recognised by their rounded body shape. The electric ray has a uniform grey or brown back, and the leading dorsal fin is much larger than the latter. The marbled species has a light mottling on its brown back, and the two dorsal fins are similar in size.

Both are active predators on bottom-living fish, and a powerful electric shock can be delivered, especially by larger specimens. They are rarely hooked

Commercially-made feathers.

by anglers, though they are not uncommon. The British records for the electric ray are 96 lb 1 oz from a boat and 52 lb 11 oz from the shore, both from Cornwall. The marbled electric ray records are 2 lb 8 oz from a boat and 5 lb 8 oz from the shore, both from Jersey.

■ Electronics

Electronic equipment plays an increasingly important role in boat angling. Safety is the most important consideration and the easiest way to summon help is to have a radio on board. VHF radio is the only one that is monitored by the emergency services, and this should be the first priority. A simple examination is required before it can be used legally; one day courses are run by the Royal Yachting Association. Sets are available for any working range, and even open dinghies can have waterproof hand-held sets at a very reasonable price.

Navigation is the next priority if the boat goes out of sight of land. Units which give the position of the boat to within about 100 feet using signals from land-based Decca stations are readily available. The facilities for larger boats are quite amazing, with techniques like displaying on screen the actual position of the boat on an electronic map of the area. Simple position finding is also available in weatherproof units for the larger dinghy.

Fish finding equipment has evolved out of the early sonar depth location systems. Nowadays the dinghy angler is offered a whole range of weatherproof liquid crystal display units, showing the depth and distribution of fish below the boat.

■ Feathers

Bare hooks with chicken feathers whipped to the shanks are the traditional way of attracting mackerel from boat and shore. They are also coupled with bait to tempt a variety of predatory species. Chicken feathers still score when action counts more than colour, but they have been supplemented with a variety of man-made tinsels and fluorescent colours.

Feathers are tied to short, stiff snoods about six inches long and spaced 12 inches apart so they do not tangle. For smaller fish, as many as six feathers may be fished on the trace, but for larger species, two or three is usual. White or silver feathers, about a inch or less in total length, will sometimes attract greater sandeels or launce for bait when worked near the bottom over sandbanks. For mackerel, red and silver feathers about 1.50 in. long are often best.

Check suspect knots From a boat, the trace is lowered on reasonably strong tackle, and the rod swept up and down rhythmically. A heavy lead – rarely less than 8 oz – is needed to give good control, and the whole depth of the water should be searched systematically until the fish are located.

Particular care should be taken when buying commercially produced feathers for casting from the shore. Mass produced knots are potentially suspect and they should be tested beforehand to avoid dangerous crack-offs. The trace must have a breaking strain of at least 30 lb for use with a 3 oz lead and 50 lb with a 5 oz weight.

Three inch long white chicken feathers with a piece of mackerel on the hook are usually chosen for cod, gurnard, whiting, and other small species, and they are fished near the bottom. For cod, the lead is often replaced with a pirk, and the feathers worked in the same way as Muppets.

■ Filleting knife

The traditional Swedish design of filleting knife with a long, slim, pliable blade is difficult to better for cleaning small to medium sized fish and preparing bait. The most sensible choice is a six inch blade in stainless steel, with a comfortable handle and a stout sheath of leather or plastic.

■ Finger stall

Trapping the line with an unprotected finger while powercasting with a fixed spool reel is asking for trouble. Nylon gripped under pressure cuts deep into flesh if there's the slightest slippage and line slap following release can also cause finger injuries. A leather or plastic finger stall sold by chemists provides the necessary protection.

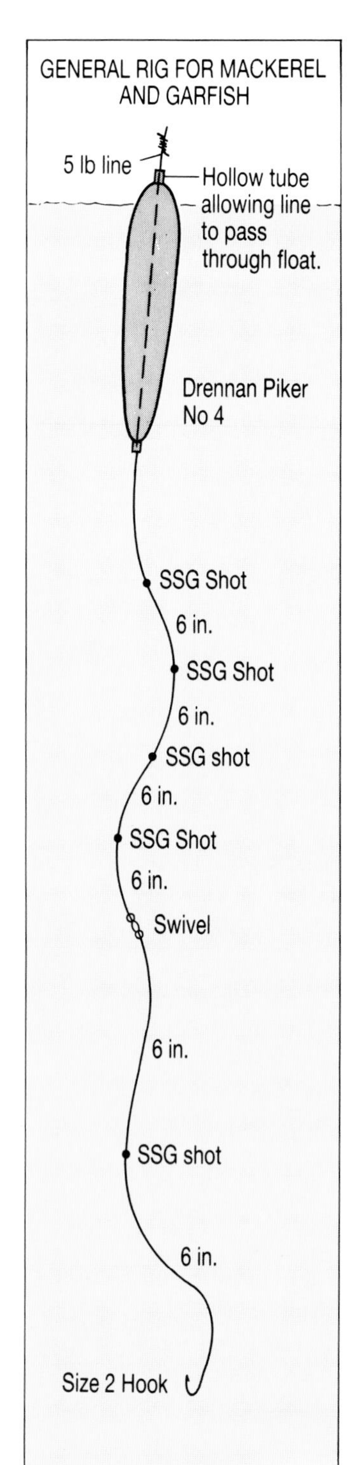

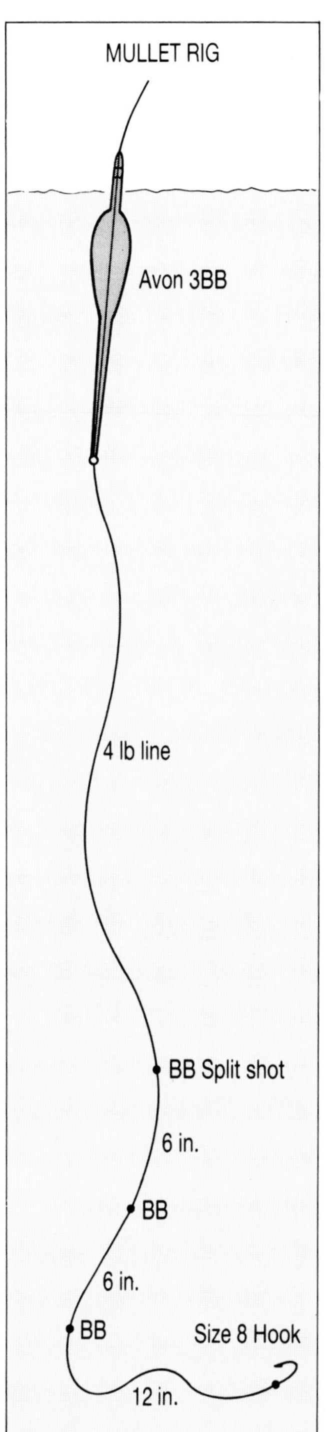

■ Fixed grip leads

Leads with fixed grip wires, rather than the swivelling wires of Breakaway sinkers, are the last resort in extreme conditions of tide or wind when no other weight will anchor the bait. They are awkward to use, being difficult to pull out of the bottom and inclined to snag any obstructions. The remedy is to use a lead-lift and high-speed reel, to get the end tackle planing towards the surface on the retrieve.

The strongest grip is achieved by fairly short, stout wires sticking out from the sides of the lead. Longer and springier wires, often from the nose of the lead and curved or bent outwards, will 'walk' over the sea bed once they have been dislodged.

■ Flat weights

Flattened leads plane up to the surface on the retrieve and are used over rough ground to avoid the snags. The simplest way of making a flat lead is to hammer out a bomb on a hard surface. Experienced anglers who turn out their own weights produce the required shape by using just one half of a commercial mould or an old spoon of suitable size firmly clamped to the work surface. On a slow drift over sandbanks, flat leads slide over the sea bed instead of rolling like a bomb.

■ Float fishing

The choice of floats for saltwater fishing is more complicated than in freshwater, not least because there is a shortage of custom-made models. For estuary and close range fishing for species like flounder and mullet, Chubbers and wagglers from the freshwater ranges are ideal, and if something bigger is needed then the smaller sizes of Drennan Pikers take some beating.

In the open sea, the larger Pikers and Zepplers will do most tasks, including acting as very efficient sliders for taking species like wrasse, pollack and garfish. For the very largest sizes, specialist tackle shops supply cylindrical sliding floats of cork or polystyrene taking up to 3 oz of lead. The only time anything larger is needed is to suspend a shark bait from a boat, and here a balloon or slotted lump of polystyrene will suffice.

■ Flood tide

See Tides.

■ Flounder

Flounder are fish of inshore waters, both on open sandy beaches and more typically in muddy estuaries where they can penetrate many miles into freshwater. They feed mainly on shrimps, crabs, molluscs – especially cockles – and ragworm. In late winter, usually March, they migrate offshore to spawn and when they return in early summer they are often in very poor condition.

The flounder is the mainstay of sport in regions like the north west.

On the open beach, any tackle baited with worm is likely to hook a flounder at some time. Its small mouth means that hooks of about size 2 are often best, and specialists favour a paternoster with lightweight nylon booms to give the bait movement. Fluorescent beads also add colour to the bait. Two or three hook rigs increase the rate of capture for match anglers, where this is allowed, and in some locations baits like peeler crab and shrimp are favoured.

Try light tackle In the calmer waters of estuaries, it is possible to use much lighter tackle such as carp rods with weights of 1 oz to 2 oz. Long distance casting might still be needed but the fish are often taken at close range in mere inches of water as they follow the tide onto the mudflats.

Float fishing is not widely used, but there could also be some potential for searching these areas with the vaned drifter floats used by pike anglers.

The flounder is closely related to the plaice and dab, and can be identified by its brown or green back being covered with smooth scales apart from patches of rough ones along the lateral line and at the bases of the fins. The British records are currently 5 lb 11 oz from a boat at Fowey, Cornwall, and 5 lb 3 oz from the River Teign in south Devon.

■ Flounder spoon

In summer, the flounder tends to be an active, hunter and is often difficult to tempt in estuaries on a static bait. During the 1920s and 1930s, a south coast dinghy angler called John Garrad perfected a technique for catching these fish by trolling a baited white spoon behind a boat being rowed gently with the tide.

His recommended spoon was about three inches in length and it was attached by a short link of swivels to a single hook baited with rag or lug.

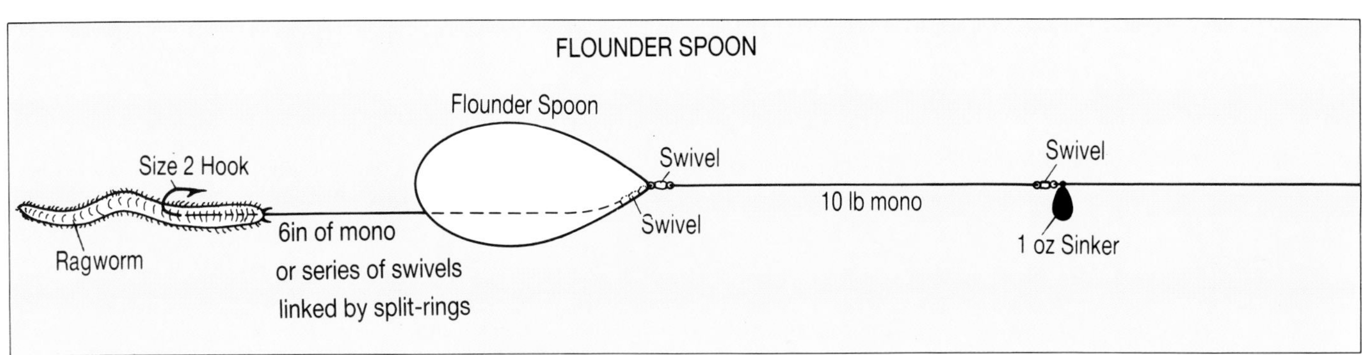

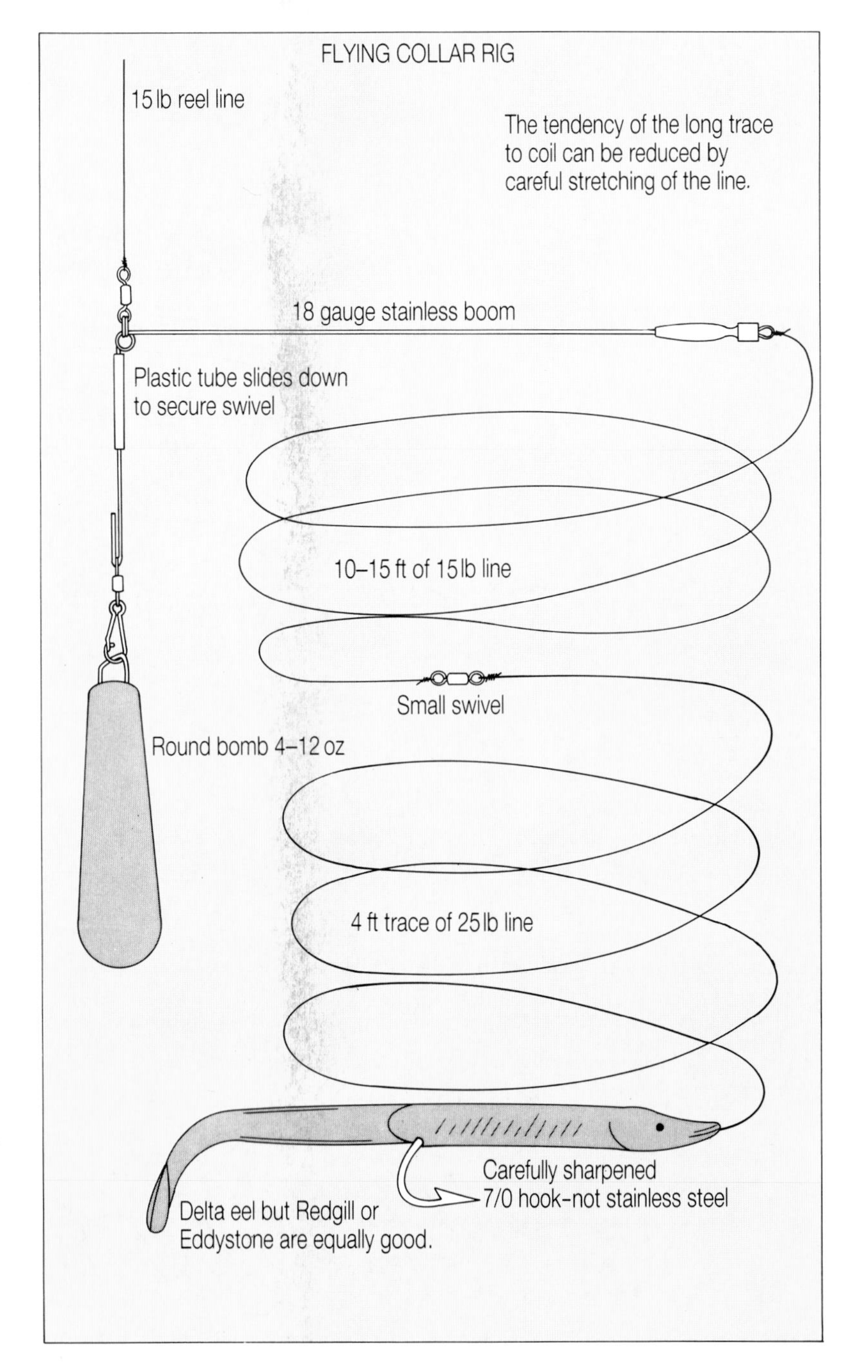

Chrome and red spoons were also favoured in some light conditions, and smaller chromed spoons, about one inch in length, were found to be very effective for eels. The method has lost its popularity but the introduction of near-silent electric outboards could reverse the trend. Similar spoons are still available and used as attractors for plaice and cod.

■ Fluorescent tape

Rod tip visibility is improved on beachcasters by wrapping brightly coloured tape around the top six or eight inches of the tip. Fluorescent orange tape is suitable for daytime but at night a highly reflective, fluorescent tape obtained from cycle shops is needed to make the tip stand out under lamplight. .

■ Flying collar rig

One of the standard boat rigs intended primarily for catching pollack and coalfish over wrecks or reef. It also accounts for cod, bass and sometimes ling. The rig was designed for use with rubber eels such as the Redgill and Eddystone brands, but it is also teamed with live or dead sandeel, large ragworm or thinly sliced strips of mackerel. The rig comprises a long trace, usually between ten and 20 inches in length, which allows the lure to be presented with an enticing movement. Because the fish are mostly hooked in midwater, it is possible to use relatively light line even to catch large specimens.

A long, forgiving rod combined with a well-adjusted lever drag reel provides fine sport on 12 lb or 15 lb line. But 20 lb or 30 lb line is a safer choice when the biggest specimens are on the wrecks in winter.

A stouter trace affects the lure's mobility but reduces the problems of tangling and provides protection from abrasion in the fish's mouth. It also helps in handlining the long trace when the fish is brought to the boatside.

Booms prevent tangles With longer traces, it is often wise to incorporate a swivel into the trace, and the smallest size compatible with the strength of the line should be chosen. A long boom, between six and 18 inches long, serves both to attach the lead and more importantly to push the trace line away from the reel line and avoid tangles on the long trip to the bottom.

The traditional French boom is widely used, along with home-made, L-shaped wire booms. Modern designs of fixed booms like those from Knotless Fishing Tackle are particularly efficient. Alternatively, a suitable sliding boom, like the larger Eddystone patterns or the tubular plastic ones popularised by freshwater anglers, may be used with a swivel to stop it in position.

The flying collar rig is mostly used from a drifting boat, though it is sometimes possible to anchor over a mark, allowing tidal movement to work the trace away from the boat.

The rig is lowered to the sea bed under careful control to avoid tangles, and then retrieved steadily until it reaches the surface or a level in the water where a strike is thought unlikely. Then it is lowered again, and the cycle repeated.

Fish can be very fussy about the rate of retrieve and the depth at which they will hit the lure. It is essential not to react when a fish strikes, but just to continue winding steadily until it hooks itself. The reel drag needs setting with great care, for when pollack or coalfish hit the lure they tear off many yards of line in a spectacular crash-dive.

■ French boom

The traditional stainless steel wire boom used with the flying collar rig and a whole variety of paternoster set-ups for boat fishing. It can be tied to the reel line for added security but the triangular base is designed so the line is twisted around it, producing a simple, easily adjusted stand-off paternoster.

G

■ Gaff

The gaff is still the most widely-used method of landing sea fish destined for the table, although nets are becoming more popular with species like plaice and pollack. The usual choice is a three inch gape stainless steel hook lashed to a stout four foot wooden pole. Some beach anglers favour the small telescopic gaffs designed for salmon anglers.

Screw threaded gaffs are not popular, as there is too great a risk of the fish spinning off the hook. The trick to good gaffing is to get the hook into a solid part of the fish, and lift it out of the water in a single movement. On a charter boat, the skipper will normally take charge of the gaff, and a lot can be learned from watching his technique from a safe distance.

The gaff should be avoided with fish that are to be returned to the water, though some like skate and monkfish can be carefully gaffed in the wing to get them into the boat. Generally it is better to leave fish like shark and conger in the sea while the hook is removed or the trace cut.

■ Garfish

It's impossible to mistake the garfish with its very elongate shape, vivid blue or green back, and long beak heavily armed with sharp teeth. This strange looking fish is a close relative of the flying fishes, and a second species has recently been recognised in British waters.

It is a popular fish with light tackle anglers especially along the south coast, and can be attracted to either feathers or spinners fished near the surface. It gives a spectacular fight, often clearing the water in an attempt to shed the hook. Indeed its presence may be revealed by its habit of leaping out of the water near flotsam.

Getting a hook to penetrate into the hard jaws of the garfish is difficult. The most successful way of catching it consistently is to floatfish with strips of fish on a very sharp, small hook. The British records are currently 3 lb from a boat off Penzance, and 2 lb 15 oz from the shore at Coverack, Cornwall.

■ Grey mullets

There are three species of these sporting fish in British waters. They are often seen nosing around near the surface in harbours and estuaries, and sometimes in the open sea, but are rarely captured on conventional sea angling tackle. Instead, they offer an exciting challenge on freshwater gear, float-fishing or legering with baits like worm, bread or fish strip, and sometimes employing specialised fly-fishing and spinning methods.

Long beaked garfish are spectacular fighters for their size.

They naturally browse over mudflats, grazing algae and small animals from the surface. They are opportunist feeders and often adapt to other available food including restaurant scraps and the debris around sewage outfalls.

Thick-lipped grey mullet The thick-lipped grey mullet is the largest and most widespread species. In summer and autumn, it is found in most inshore habitats from the freshwater zone near river estuaries into the open sea. It can be recognised by its thickened, upper lip which bears two or three rows of wart-like papillae. Bread or fish strip baits probably account for most captures but they are renowned for feeding on almost any soft animal or vegetable material.

A popular method along some parts of the south coast is to fly fish with maggots on the hook when they are feeding on naturally-occurring maggots washed out of piles of rotting seaweed. The British records are 10 lb 1 oz from a boat off Portland, Dorset, and 14 lb 2 oz from the shore in a lagoon at Aberthaw, Glamorgan.

Thin-lipped grey mullet The thin-lipped grey mullet is much less common but during the summer it frequents estuaries of many southern rivers. The most successful methods are floatfished ragworm, or spinning with a medium to large spinner baited with a piece of ragworm. The British records are 3 lb 7 oz from a boat in Christchurch harbour, Dorset, and 6 lb 4 oz from the shore in the River Rother, Kent.

Golden grey mullet Golden grey mullet are the least common of the three species, and prefer warm, shallow lagoons of sea water or similar open sea areas. They can be caught on baits of worm or fish strip. The British records are 1 lb 14 oz from a boat in Falmouth harbour, Cornwall, and 2 lb 12 oz from the shore on Alderney in the Channel Isles. The separation of these two species can be difficult, even for an expert.

The National Mullet Club was founded in 1975 to promote interest in the sporting capture and conservation of all three species. Membership is open to all, and details are available from the Secretary, David Rigden, 69 Powerscourt Road, North End, Portsmouth, Hampshire PO2 7JG.

The striking profile of a red gurnard.

■ Gurnards

There are seven species of gurnards in northern European waters, of which four are widespread if rarely abundant around the British coastline. They are distinguished by their heavily-armoured heads with strong spines, spiny dorsal fins, and the curiously-modified rays of the pectoral fins, which are detached from the main fin and are used to walk over the sea bed, feeling for food at the same time.

The tub or yellow gurnard is the largest. The British records are 11 lb 7 oz from a boat off Wallasey and 12 lb 3 oz from the shore at Langland Bay in Wales. It is a dull red or brown, with brilliantly coloured pectoral fins usually with bright blue margins. It is found in water of shallow to moderate depth over a sandy bottom where it feeds on shrimps, crabs and a wide range of other small animals.

The red gurnard is deep red on the back. Its fins have a yellowish tinge, and the lateral line scales are vertically elongated and soft. It is a shallow water species, and the British records are 5 lb from a boat off Rhyl, Wales, and 2 lb 10 oz from the shore at Helford River, Cornwall.

The grey gurnard is usually grey on the back though it is occasionally a dull red in colour The lateral line scales are small and sharply pointed. It is the most common species, and the British records are 2 lb 7 oz from a boat off Mull, and 1 lb 8 oz from the shore on the Isle of Man.

■ Groyne

Many stretches of coastline are protected from erosion by groynes of timber, concrete or stone. The area around the seaward end of the groyne usually experiences turbulence and scour which attract both surface and bottom dwelling fish.

Casting from the shoreline to the area just downtide of the end of the groyne will often produce much better success with flatfish and other bottom feeders than fishing the open ground nearby.

■ Haddock

This close relative of the cod is most often caught by anglers off the northern shores of Britain although occasional fish, often of specimen size, are found along the south coast. The lateral line is black while the cod lateral is white. The barbule is much smaller than on a cod and there is also usually a black mark above the base of the pectoral fin.

The haddock is a bottom dweller and although some small fish are eaten, it feeds mainly on brittlestars, worms and shellfish. Most are captured on bottom fished baits of lugworm or mussel. The British records are currently 13 lb 11 oz from a boat off Falmouth, and 6 lb 12 oz from the shore at Loch Goil, Scotland.

■ Hake

An important commercial species which is only rarely encountered by anglers. The hake is an elongate member of the cod family, which lacks any barbules. They live mostly in deep water well offshore, rising to midwater at night to feed on smaller fish and squids. The British records are currently 25 lb 5 oz from a boat in Belfast Loch, and 3 lb 8 oz from the shore at Port Talbot, Glamorgan.

■ Halibut

The halibut has a large predatory mouth like turbot and brill but is more closely related to plaice. The relatively thick but narrow body, with its dark green back and white belly, is unlikely to be mistaken in British waters, if its large size alone is not sufficient identification. Specimens to over eight foot long weighing 700 lb have been taken by commercial boats.

Captures on rod and line are very rare nowadays, though anyone with enough resources and time to troll large fish baits like coalfish or haddock of 3lb to 5lb or more in weight might strike lucky. Fishing in midwater over sand or gravel bottoms well off the Scottish coast is most likely to yield success, and beefy tackle is recommended – the Americans rate their Pacific halibut as one of their finer sporting propositions. The British record is currently 234 lb from a boat off Scrabster, Scotland.

■ Headlight

Quality lights, owing much of their development to caving, are available from companies like Petzl at prices between £15 and £30. A miner's headlight costing around £90 with heavy duty battery and charging unit is made by Oldhams who supply National Coal.

■ High water

See Tides.

■ Hooks

Almost all sea hooks use the same numbering system for sizes as in freshwater. Beyond a size 1, the hooks get larger from 1/0 to perhaps a 10/0, about the largest size in use in Britain. The problems of long-term rusting can be solved by using stainless steel hooks but many anglers avoid them because they

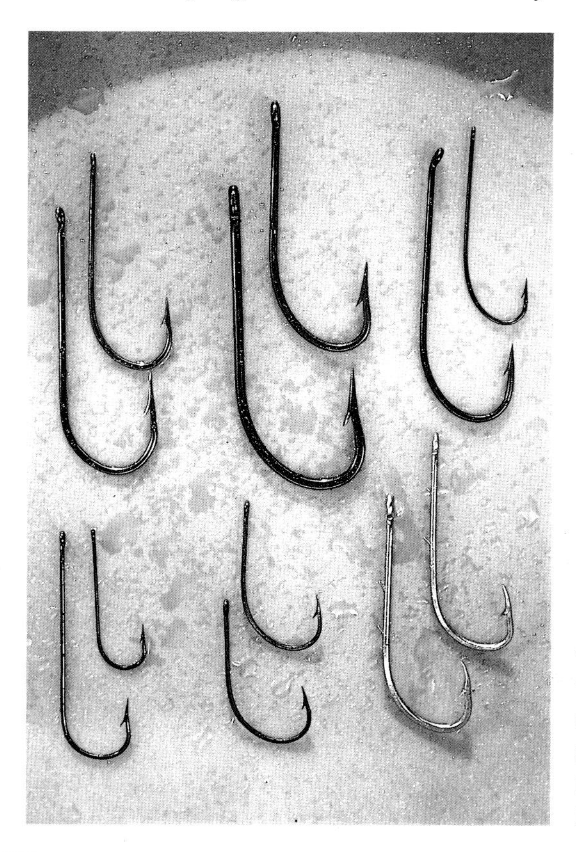

The basic hook choice. Top row (from left): Viking, O'Shaughnessy and Spearpoints. Bottom row: Aberdeen, Limerick and Baitholder.

can be difficult to sharpen and will not rust away if they are lost in the fish.

Chemically-sharpened hooks may be alright to use from the packet, but others will inevitably need sharpening before use, and both should be checked on every retrieve, and resharpened when necessary.

The hook should be of a suitable size and shape to present the bait and the required size, strength and design to hook and land the target species.

Different points Hooks with longer shanks, small barbs and long points penetrate most easily but may work loose in a lengthy struggle. Hooks with outturned or offset points tend to prick a fish, which may allow for the hook to be driven home. Those with inturned points may be slow to get a grip, but are very tenacious once in place.

Sea anglers often have to present big baits of fish, squid, or large quantities of worms or crab. The usual solution is to use progressively larger hooks, with 6/0s and 8/0s being quite commonplace on many rigs.

The advantages of two-hook Pennell rigs are becoming realised, often using a pair of 2/0 or 3/0 hooks for cod or bass. Other rigs of freshwater origin are starting to become accepted in some saltwater circles, a prime example being the use of hair-rigged eel sections when tope fishing.

It is still rare to see small double or treble hook rigs being used to present whole fish baits, but should anyone doubt their strength and ability to find a secure hold in a large mouth they need only watch a 30 lb pike being unhooked by a freshwater angler using size 8s.

See Aberdeen; Limerick; O'Shaughnessy; Spearpoint; Viking.

■ International Game Fish Association (IGFA)

This organisation is the parent body for sport angling in both salt and freshwater, and was founded in 1939 to 'establish ethical international angling regulations and to serve as a central processing centre for world record catch data'.

Membership is open to all, and details are available from IGFA, 3000 E. Las Olas Boulevard, Fort Lauderdale, Florida 33316-1616, USA.

■ Jubilee clip

See Coasters.

■ Kelp

Strictly speaking, kelp is the group of large seaweeds known as laminarians, the brown algae such as oarweed and seabelt which are anchored by their thick stipe or stem and a gnarled holdfast to rocky shores below the low water mark. But many anglers do not differentiate between these and the related wracks which are mostly less massive, and more typical of the intertidal zone. Together they provide shelter for a whole host of food items like crabs, shrimps and small fish, and many species like wrasse, pollack, conger and bass can be found feeding among their stems.

■ King ragworm

See Baits.

■ Knitting elastic

Soft baits like peeler crab and many fresh shellfish will not stay on the hook during hard casting. One solution is to whip the bait to the hook using knitting elastic or the coarser and less efficient shirring elastic.

■ Knots

In most situations, the knots used for nylon monofilament by the sea angler are exactly the same as those used in freshwater. A Grinner (Uniknot) or bloodknot will secure hooks or swivels, and allow lengths of line to be joined together.

The number of turns in these knots should be reduced in the heavier strains, and three turns will suffice for lines between 50 lb and 100 lb. Above this, suitable crimps should be used, as the line is too stiff to knot safely. Special knots are only needed for braided and wire lines, and situations where widely differing diameters have to be joined. See also: Albright knot; Leader knot.

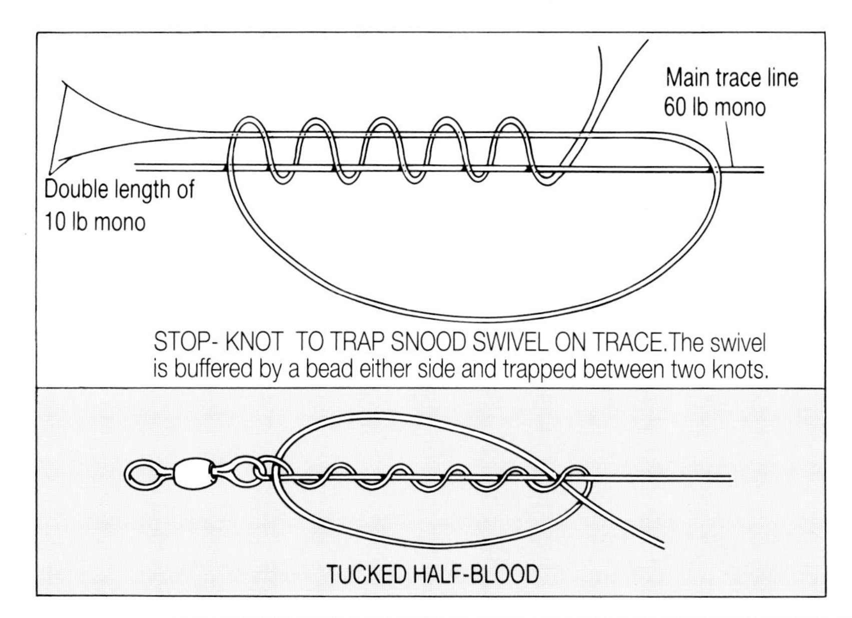

STOP- KNOT TO TRAP SNOOD SWIVEL ON TRACE. The swivel is buffered by a bead either side and trapped between two knots.

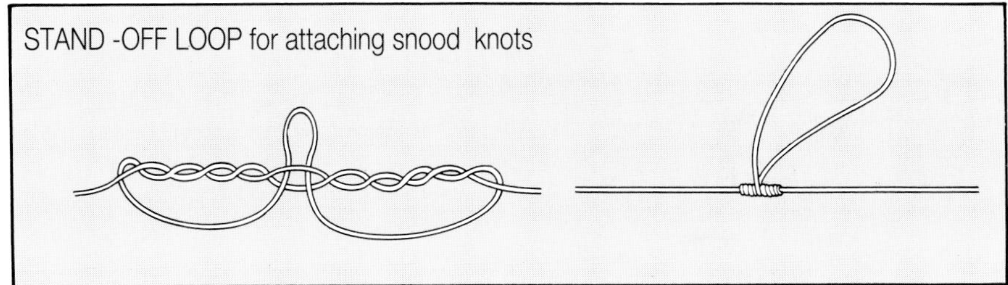

L

■ Lead lift

On snaggy ground, a lead lift fixed just above the lead helps the tackle plane up from the bottom as quickly as possible. It can be made by cutting out a kite-shaped piece of plastic about four inches by two inches from the side of a plastic container, with holes punched along the long axis through which the trace can be threaded.

Several companies produce commercial lead lifts of similar design or with a stout wire running through the centre to which the lead and trace is clipped.

■ Leader

A length of heavier line between the hook or trace and the reel line. This prevents the main line from making contact with the rough skin of certain fishes – the trace protects it from the teeth – but its chief use is as a shock leader to absorb the stresses of casting. A powerful cast with beach fishing tackle can propel five ounces of lead at speeds of around 100 mph, and if that breaks off then it is a potential killer. The safest way of incorporating a shock leader into the rig is to tie it directly to the reel line with a Mustad oval link at the other end to which

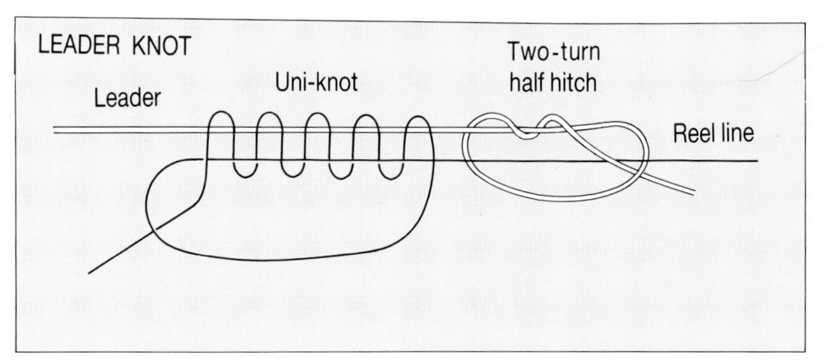

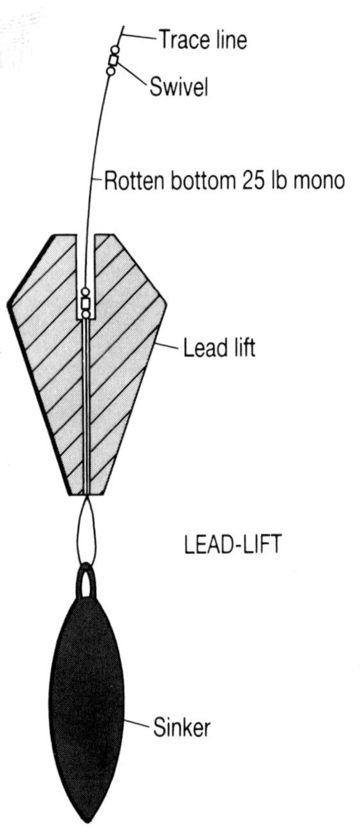

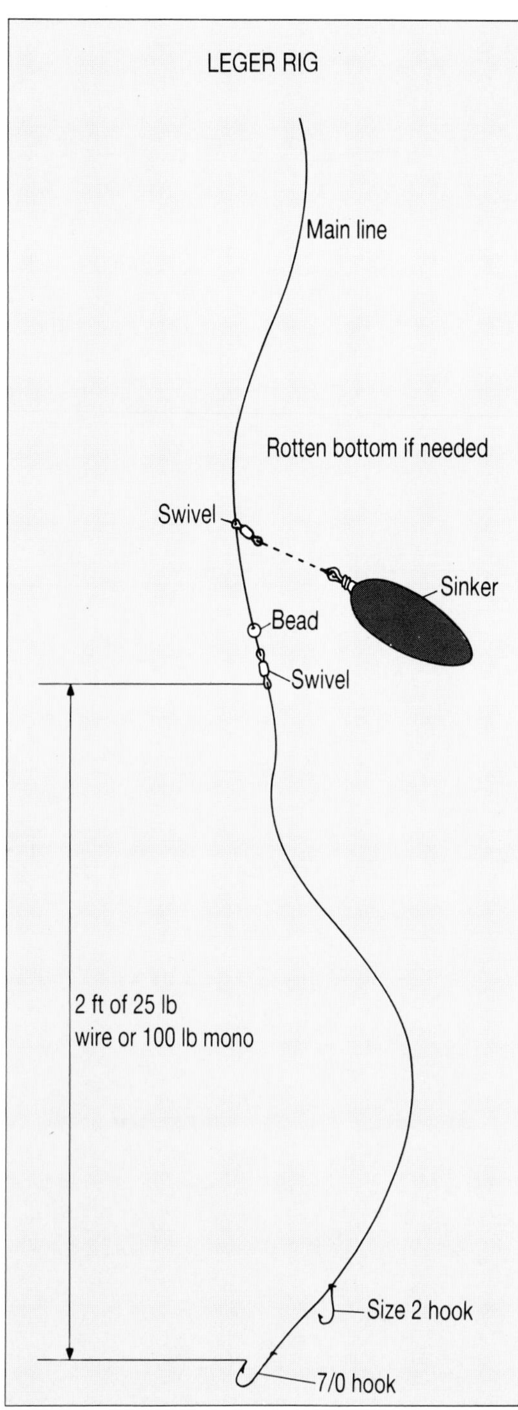

the lead is clipped. Snoods are attached paternoster fashion, tied to small swivels trapped between pairs of beads which are Superglued to the leader (effectively the same as the carp angler's helicopter rig).

The leader should be long enough for about six turns on the reel, then up through the rod rings and down for the desired drop for casting – usually about 20 feet in total. The breaking strain must be at least 10 lb for every ounce of weight to be cast – that's 50 lb breaking strain for a 5 oz weight.

■ Leads

For distance casting from the shore or uptide from a boat, the bomb or torpedo rules supreme. Its many forms, with a short loop or a long-tail, plain, side-wired or nose-wired fixed grip, or Breakaway give a range of adhesion for different conditions.

Make sure that the wire loop or tail is well embedded in the lead for power casting, and discard the weight if the loop becomes corroded.

For downtide boat fishing, the two most important factors are stability on the drop and mobility on the bottom. With midwater methods like the flying collar rig, stability on the drop is more important and round section plain bombs are best. On the bottom, square or diamond section bombs are less inclined to roll, and the Bell lead is still favoured for very heavy weights despite its poor performance on the drop.

Sea anglers are still allowed to use lead and it is relatively economical to produce them at home. Molten lead at about 350 degrees Centigrade is an extremely dangerous substance which can cause serious burns and explode on contact with water, so safety is the most important consideration. The lead, moulds and the workspace must all be dry.

Thick gloves and heavy duty shoes, long sleeves and goggles must also be worn at all times. An old saucepan with a strong handle and a pouring rim can be used to heat up to 10 lb of lead. A gas ring is the best heat source with the pan placed securely over the heat. Commercial lead moulds with clamps, and brass or stainless wire loops are essential. The wire must go deeply into the mould, with the ends bent over for extra safety.

See also Bell lead; Breakaway; Fixed grip leads; Flat weights; Long-tailed torpedo; Torpedo; Watch lead.

■ Leger rig

The sliding leger rig with the lead stopped above the hook by a swivel is used to present a bait on the bottom to a fish which is likely to run off. It is widely used in boat fishing, but much less so on the shore where only fish like bass and conger are likely to drop a bait if they feel resistance.

In reality, the line will only slide freely through the lead or lead link at fairly close range – the belly in the line caused by a tide flowing along the beach will soon produce too much friction. Furthermore, the rig does not cast well with the sort of large baits that sea anglers often use, and the hook length will become twisted round the line above the lead.

■ Lesser spotted dogfish

This small relative of the shark patrols fairly shallow water over sand, gravel or broken ground, hunting out whelks and other shellfish and crabs and shrimps plus any small fish that come their way.

Anglers usually catch them on worm, sandeel and mackerel baits which they can detect from a considerable distance using their incredible sense of smell. They do not grow to any great size, nor do they put up a great struggle.

The British records are currently 4 lb 1 oz from a boat off Newquay, Cornwall, and 4 lb 15 oz from the shore at Kirkcudbright, Scotland.

■ Level-wind

Most small multipliers owe their origins to freshwater spinning where a level-wind mechanism which automatically spreads the line evenly on the reel is invaluable, especially if it does not interfere too much with the casting performance.

When these same reels are taken onto the beach, the level-wind prevents the angler from getting a good grip on the spool, catches on the leader knot, and increases the resistance of the reel reducing casting distance. Removing the level-wind is a reasonably skilful, engineering task because the reel cage will need strengthening to keep its precise alignment. Conversion kits are widely available, but leading companies are starting to market beachcasting multipliers built without a level-wind mechanism.

The beachcasting novice with a level-wind multiplier should pause before removing the mechanism. If casts of less than 100 yards are involved, the problems of drag and grip are not likely to be severe. The more precise line lay may actually improve the cast and the extra resistance will often limit over-runs.

■ Lever drag

On a multiplier reel there are two basic systems to control the rate at which a fish can take line from the reel, the lever drag and the star drag. The lever drag is operated by a single sliding lever below the handle on the reel. This can be moved from free-spool at one end of its travel, to a central notch where the drag exerts the optimal drag setting for the line on the reel, through to the other end of the travel where the spool is locked solid. A small knurled knob allows the settings to be adjusted to suit different line strengths.

Internally, the lever brings a single large disc to bear directly against the spool. The mechanism is simple, sensitive and easy to adjust, though difficult to build on a small framed reel, and is the usual choice for boat reels where fast running fish are the target.

■ Lights

When fishing at close range in the dark it is often better to avoid all lights. On beaches where it is necessary to fish at ranges of 80 yards or more the fish

The miner's headlamp is probably the most versatile form of night light on the shore.

will not be scared by the light, and the comfort and convenience of a good lamp cannot be overstated. There are a few electric lamps capable of producing acceptable light levels, and headlights are invaluable for tackling up and landing fish.

For their main light source, most anglers choose the power and economy of quality paraffin or petrol pressure lamps. These have an candle power output of between 300 and 500 and give off a good bit of heat as well. Take good care of the lamp and it will last many years. Wipe any sand and salt off after a trip, use clean fuel, and protect it from sharp knocks which may break the gauze mantle prematurely – or even the glass. A stand which clamps the lamp several feet off the ground will increase the illumination considerably.

■ Limerick hooks

The Mustad Limerick is a popular hook available in eyed or spade-end versions. It is a short shanked, lightly forged pattern with a relatively wide gape and a reversed offset point. The proportions make it a good choice for fishing bulky baits like crab, whether small chunks on a size 2 for eels and pouting, or large lumps on a 4/0 for cod and bass.

It can also be used to present big baits like mackerel fillets or squid for bass and cod, either nicked through the end of the bait hair-rig style if distance casting is not important, or else Pennell fashion.

■ Line

Braid, wire and nylon are all used in modern sea fishing. Least common is braided Dacron with its low stretch for the big-game angler after surface swimming fish. Wire lines, available in both single and multi-strand, are best suited to deep water and fast tides. Nylon monofilament is almost universal, but with a vast range of different kinds available it is important to understand something of their characteristics and uses.

The all-round sea angler may use 4 lb nylon for mullet fishing, 8 lb for plaice, light tackle pollacking and spinning for bass or mackerel, 12 lb for baitfishing for bass, 15 lb for all-round beachcasting and fishing the flying collar rig for pollack, 25 lb for general boat fishing and heavy beachcasting, 40 lb for wrecking, 50 lb for beachcasting shock leaders, and even 100 lb and upwards to make traces for conger and ling.

Assuming that a nylon monofil is of good quality and has been stored in a cool, dry and dark environment so it will not deteriorate, its ability to perform these tasks will depend on its composition, diameter, abrasion resistance and stiffness, as well as the breaking strain.

■ Ling

The ling is a member of the cod family, most obviously shown by the conspicuous barbule on the lower jaw. It is almost eel-like in profile and has a long second dorsal and anal fin. The colour is a mottled brown or grey on the back, shading to almost white below. It is common on rough ground, reefs and wrecks, living near the bottom in depths over 100 feet and right down to 1,000 feet or more. The mouth full of sharp teeth is a clear indication that it is predominantly a fish feeder.

High abrasion resistance is the key quality in any sea line.

Imitation sandeels, pirks and Muppets - they score heavily from the boats.

Below: Shore lures from the Dave Cooling collection. Pictured are a jointed Rapala, imitation Rebel Crayfish, Rebel jointed plug and a see-through Bomber lure.

Mackerel fillets or flappers fished on leger tackle or paternosters with hooks of 6/0 and upwards is the usual ling tactic. Stout traces of 100 lb monofil or even wire are needed to defeat the sharp teeth. On wrecks, ling will also be taken frequently on pirks and Muppets.

Ling can be taken virtually all round the British coast, but the best opportunities for large specimens exist off the north east coast, and the wrecks of south Devon. The British records are 59 lb 8 oz from a boat off Bridlington, Yorkshire, and 19 lb 4 oz from the shore on Jersey.

■ Long-tailed torpedo weight

Torpedo leads, or bombs, with a three or four inch wire tail are very popular. It is claimed that they are more stable in flight for long-distance casting. Where the lead is fitted with grip wires, the tail will push the body of the lead off the sea bed, encouraging the grip wires to bite more firmly into the bottom.

■ Low tide

See Tides.

■ Lugworm

See Baits.

■ Lure fishing

Fishing with an artificial lure requires careful

thought and confidence in the method, otherwise chances of success are slim. Yet there is no doubt that a well-chosen lure, be it spoon, spinner, pirk, plug or rubber eel, is capable of producing fine catches in a wide range of conditions. The flounder spoon, rubber eels with a flying collar rig, Muppets and pirks are mainly boat fishing methods, and are covered separately.

While it may be possible to fish a small pirk from a steeply shelving shore with a beachcasting rod, most lure fishing involves casting weights from half-an-ounce to two ounces. A carp rod or a freshwater spinning rod combined with a fixed spool reel and line between 8 1b and 12 1b will cope with mackerel, garfish, pollack, bass and just about anything else that comes along, and give a lot of fun at the same time. The mobility of the method means that a lot of ground can be covered in search of fish.

In deeper water, the usual lures are metal spoons like the Tobis and Toby, whose design and weight means they can be cast a good distance and fished at a range of depths according to the speed of retrieve. Alternatively, a rubber sandeel can be used with a lead fixed on the trace. In shallow water, these lures will snag the bottom too readily, and the floating, diving plug comes into its own. These cannot be cast very far because of their weight and design – about 30 yards is the limit in most situations. It surprises many anglers how often large bass and wrasse can be taken from this narrow strip along the shoreline.

■ Mackerel

If the average mackerel weighed 10 lb instead of 1 lb, this miniature tunny would be the most popular species in Britain, for it is a fine fighter and a superb eating fish. Most anglers seek it out purely for use as bait, tackling up with feathers and heavy gear which prevents it from showing its true potential. If the chance ever arises, spin for it with a single-handed rod and 5 lb line, or even a fly rod and a small-silver reservoir fly. Float fishing with a carp rod and small slivers of mackerel skin for bait is about as near as most anglers can get to such a sporting ideal.

Despite the enormous commercial fishing pressure on this species, shoals still move onto the south-western shores in Spring and spread themselves all around the coast during the summer and autumn, to drop back offshore as the weather cools. In mild winters, some fish may be found within casting range of south Devon and Cornwall all year round. The British records are currently 6 1b 2 oz from a boat off Penberth Cove, Cornwall, and 5 lb 11 oz from the shore at Brixham.

■ Maddies

See Baits.

■ Maintenance

Anything metal should be washed in warm, fresh water after every trip, and left out to dry thoroughly. Even fittings made of stainless steel can still rust. Putting the rods and reels under the shower for a few minutes is one simple solution.

Most anglers can perform a basic strip-down and lubrication on a reel. Just take the side plates off, oil the workings lightly and put a smear of Vaseline or

Mackerel are crucial to the food chain in the seas.

similar grease on the inside surfaces, and the life of the reel will be prolonged. This should only be needed about four times a year.

Large hooks are worth re-using, and should be treated in the same way as the rest of the tackle. Light surface rusting can be removed with a wire brush, especially the ones on hobbyist's power tools. Sharpen them carefully afterwards.

■ Measuring stick

A simple ruler made from wood or metal which is chiefly used in shore matches to confirm whether a fish is of takable size for the species concerned according to the size-limits. The fish is measured from the snout to the tip of the tail and if found to be undersized it must be returned.

Statutory Ministry size-limits are imposed on the trawling industry and they also apply to rod and line fishing from shore and boat. The National Federation of Sea Anglers issue their own list of minimum lengths for individual species and in many cases these exceed the Ministry size-limits. It is an offence to take an undersized fish from the sea and spot checks along the shoreline are not unknown. The purpose of the regulations is to protect immature stocks from over-exploitation.

Commercially-produced measuring sticks are available, but it is easy to make your own. A piece of aluminium or similar metal about 18 inches by two inches is ideal. Bend about one inch of the metal up at a right angle, and mark out from the bend in inches, using an indelible pen or a metal scribe. The names of the common species can be written on the rule at the appropriate position. Place the nose of the fish against the upturned end, and if the tail reaches the relevant mark then the fish is sizable.

■ Miner's headlight

See Headlight.

■ Monkfish

The monkfish or angel ray is a bottom-dwelling member of the shark family, although its flattened form might suggest a closer relationship to the rays. In warm weather, they may move into water as shallow as six feet on sandy beaches where they feed on flatfish and crabs. South and west Wales, and the south coast of Ireland are prime monkfish locations and mackerel baits are favoured.

They tend to be very localised and sensitive to overfishing, but with care they can be returned alive. Sometimes the fight is very sluggish, and the fish do not appear to realise they have been hooked. At the boat these individuals may wake up and provide a spectacular and dangerous display of their true strength. The British records are currently 66 lb from a boat off Shoreham, Sussex, and 52 lb 14 oz from the shore in North Wales.

■ Monopod

The ideal monopod rod rest is a five foot long alloy pole, with a strong, flared point, and preferably a footrest at one end to help drive it into the sand or shingle on the beach. At the top is a deep vee or horseshoe-shaped rest, set at an angle to the pole to cradle the rod. A cup at the base holds the butt and is movable so that the height of the rod can be adjusted to suit the conditions.

These rests cannot be used on solid surfaces, and it is difficult to position the rod at a low angle. Now that very high quality tripod rests are freely available and more and more anglers favour the use of paired rods, the monopod rest is becoming less common on the beach.

■ Mullet

See Grey mullets; Red mullet.

■ Multiplier

The multiplier is a revolving spool reel with a train of gears to rotate the spool faster than the handle is turned. The higher the gear ratio, the faster the retrieve for a given spool diameter, but it will require more leverage to turn the handle and there is more risk of damage to the gears if they are forced against a heavy load.

Ratios may be as low as 2:1 for a boat reel designed to lift heavy fish, and up to 6:1 for a high speed beachcasting reel.

A good multiplier is a precision tool. The spool can accelerate up to 40,000 rpm when distance casting from the beach. Careful lubrication and tuning are necessary to achieve this sort of performance, and regular maintenance is needed.

Casting with a multiplier demands a degree of skill and many novices will prefer to stick to a fixed spool which is easier to master. At night, when the lead cannot be watched, or when casting into a head wind – two occasions when over-runs are a strong possibility – then the fixed spool still finds favour with experienced anglers. It is also obviously difficult to cast with a multiplier using light spinning or float fishing tackle.

The multiplier is used almost exclusively from

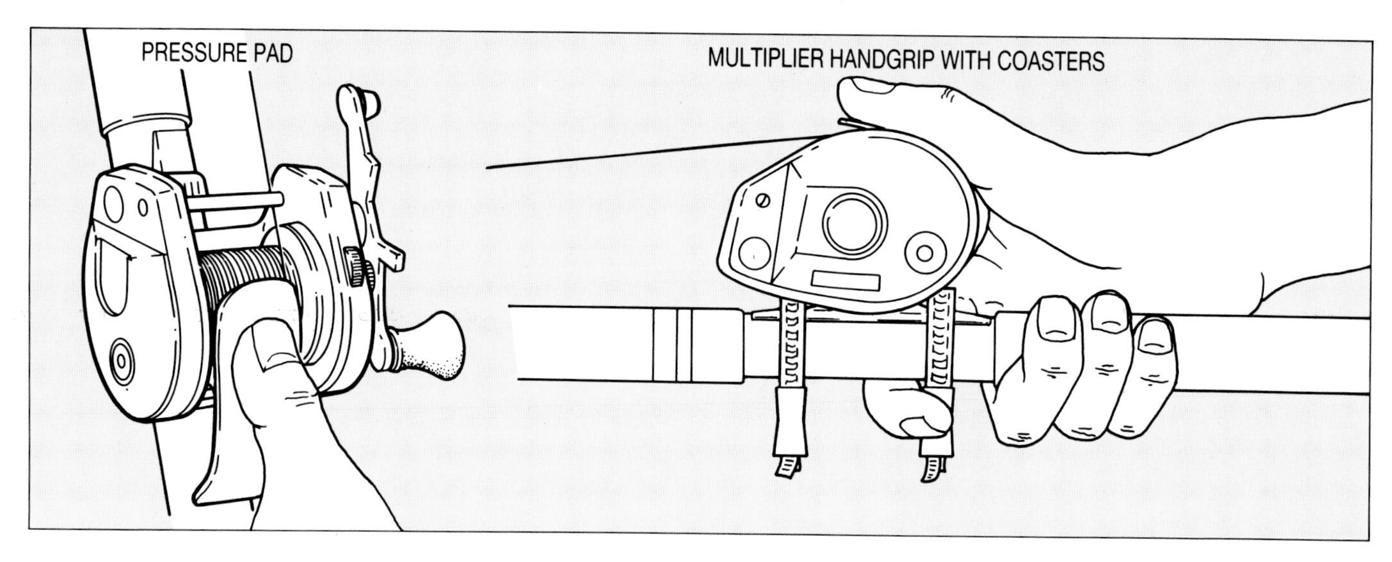

boats. It is much stronger than the fixed spool reel, and copes far better with heavy tackle and large fish. The line capacity and the quality of the drag mechanism become the most important factors. When using heavy gear, it is important to ensure that the spool is made of metal rather than plastic which can be crushed by the load.

■ Muppet

The Muppet is a soft, plastic squid-shaped lure usually sold in sizes between three inches and eight inches long. A wide range of colours is available in both luminous and fluorescent materials. Luminous green, fluorescent red, blue and black seem the most popular.

For wreck fishing, between one and three Muppets are rigged on a strong trace above a pirk, in what is often called a killer rig. A short, stiff snood of at least 5O lb nylon is threaded through the head of the Muppet, a bead slipped on, and then a 6/0 or 8/0 hook tied on. This is often baited with a fillet of mackerel or strips of squid, but cod in particular will take them unbaited. Smaller Muppets can be used as attractors for fish like whiting and codling in the same way as fluorescent beads.

N.O

■ National Federation of Sea Anglers

The NFSA is the parent body for sea angling in England and there are similar federations in Wales, Scotland and Ireland. Clubs join their regional division, and are represented at national level. There is no individual membership, though there is a Personal Members Club. More information from the Development Officer, David Rowe, 14 Bank Street, Newton Abbot, Devon TQ12 2JW

■ Neap tide

See Tides.

■ O'Shaugnessy hook

This is probably the standard pattern for larger fish, both from the beach and the shore. It is a strong, heavy-wire, forged hook with a straight eye. The medium-length shank is ideal for presenting big baits of fish or squid, but the large eye can make it difficult to thread fillets up the trace. The O'Shaughnessy is the usual choice for conger, cod and ling, and indeed most other sizable species.

■ Over-run

See Bird's nest.

■ Paternoster

The rig is usually described as a paternoster when the hook is attached higher on the trace than the lead. In boat and pier fishing, this gives the opportunity to present a bait off the sea bed. From the shore, the hook will still be on the bottom because of the angle of the line.

It is possible to tie up a running paternoster where the lead is fastened to a long dropper from a sliding swivel on the trace, but the paternoster is usually a fixed lead rig. The snood is attached to the leader with a knot, boom or tied to a swivel trapped between two beads which are locked in place with knots, crimps or Superglue.

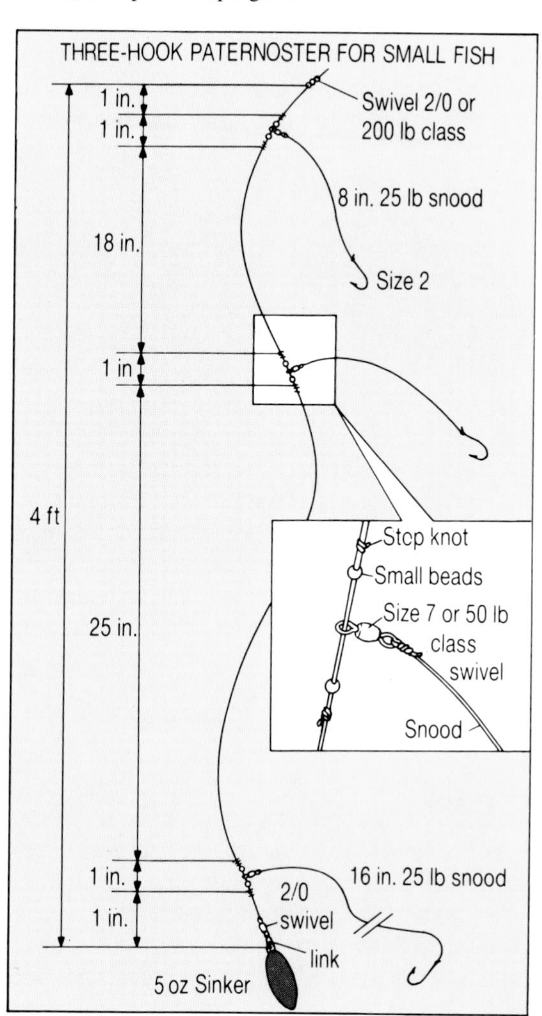

The fish cannot run off freely with the bait but whichever way it moves it is likely to hook itself, either by the tension of the line to the rod tip or the weight or grip of the lead.

■ Peeler crab

See Baits.

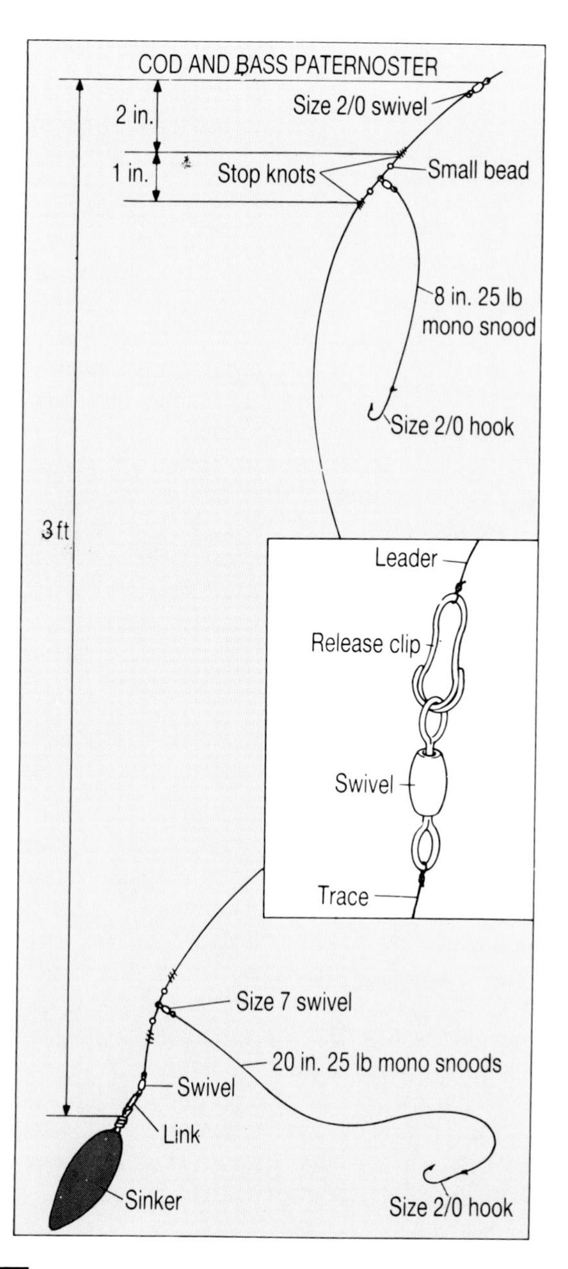

The majority of our Victorian piers have crumbled into the sea but the structures which survive provide fascinating fishing.

■ Pennell rig

A two hook rig originally designed for freshwater fishing to support a worm at both ends. It prevents the bait sagging and ensures the fish is hooked whichever end of the worm it grabs. It is now widely used by sea anglers for worms and other long baits like mackerel fillets and whole squid.

The snood is passed through the eye of the top hook which is allowed to slide and tied to the bottom hook as normal. The upper hook is positioned to suit the length of the bait and then secured in place by wrapping the snood four or five times around the shank. A Pennell rig often means smaller hooks which offer improved penetration can be used.

■ Pier fishing

While the number of piers steadily declines and restrictions are increasingly being imposed on angling from those that survive, they still offer a fascinating opportunity to sea anglers.

Some piers offer a platform to deeper water over a sandy bottom, with summer flatfish and winter codling. Here the tackle is much the same as on the beach, but without the need for distance casting so rods can be shorter and rigs more varied.

Other piers give extra opportunities with the weed-strewn boulders and pilings on which they rest. These provide rich pickings for mid-water feeders like pollack, bass or mullet, and surface predators like mackerel and garfish.

Float fishing is undoubtedly the most enjoyable way of tackling them, using a spinning rod or even a freshwater float rod if you can get near enough to avoid straining the tackle while landing the fish. A dropnet is a must where better fish are expected.

■ Pirk

The traditional angler's pirk is a length of one inch chromed tubing between eight and 12 inches long, filled with lead and armed with a treble hook. The Wilmek Nobbler is a clever variation on this theme, consisting of a plastic cylinder inside which a variety of leads up to 1 lb are inserted according to conditions. The finish is metallic or fluorescent.

Pirks are used mainly in deeper water for cod and ling, though pollack and coalfish will sometimes be taken. They are usually fished on 30 lb or 50 lb line, with a trace of 50 lb to 100 lb monofil, on which two or three Muppets or rubber eels may be added on short paternosters. The rig is lowered to the seabed, and jerked vigorously just off the bottom to attract the fish. The hooks may be baited with sides of mackerel, especially if ling are the target.

■ Plaice

A species found all around the British Isles, especially where the sea bed is composed of coarse sand or fine gravel. It is enormously popular with anglers and commercial fishermen alike, grows to a good size, makes excellent eating, and on light tackle is a fine sporting proposition.

The plaice rates as one of the most popular summer migrants.

Plaice live inshore, or on offshore sandbanks, except when they move to deeper water in the Spring to spawn. They feed mainly on shellfish, especially mussels, and crustaceans like shrimps and small crabs, though larger specimens will often take sandeels. From the beach, they'll fall to worm baits fished on a paternoster rig. Cocktails of worm and peeler crab often tempt the better specimens.

Many sandy estuaries and offshore sandbanks are important sport fisheries for plaice. It is often possible to use light 6 lb and 8 lb tackle on the drift. A flounder spoon fished with worm is popular in some areas, but a long flowing trace is the usual method.

The trace may be up to 20 foot at times, with a size 2 hook baited with a cocktail selected from worm, slipper limpet, razorfish, hermit crab or peeler crab, and tipped with a thin sliver of squid. Give the fish plenty of time to get such a large bait down. If the boat is drifting, remember to pay out slack line as the bite develops, so the bait is not pulled away from the fish.

Plaice are usually identified by the rich orange spots on their backs, though this is not always reliable. The scales on the back of a plaice feel uniformly smooth when stroked towards the head, even along the lateral line and at the fin bases. The British records are currently 10 lb 3 oz from a boat in Longa Sound, Scotland, and 8 lb 6 oz from the shore at Bournemouth.

■ Pollack

The pollack is very similar in appearance to the coalfish, being distinguished by its brassy flanks and dark, curved lateral line. It is also very similar in behaviour, but tends to be more common on southern and western coasts, while the coalfish is more common in the north and east.

Pollack spend their first couple of years in shallow rocky water, and are often taken by anglers on worm bait or spinners. Older fish move into deeper water, often on reefs or wrecks where they feed predominantly on fish, particularly sandeels, sprats and herring.

The favourite method for these sporting opponents is the Redgill or rubber eel fished on a flying

A breakwater pollack hooked on white feathers.

Plump pouting that made short work of a cod-sized bait.

collar rig, though some are caught on pirks, baited feathers or fish baits on the bottom. A few large fish seem to exhibit a winter migration onto the beaches, and specimens can be taken at locations like Dorset's Chesil Beach.

In American books, the fish they call a pollock is actually our coalfish. The British records are currently 29 lb 4 oz from a boat off Dungeness, Kent, and 18 lb 4 oz from the shore on Chesil Beach, Dorset.

■ Porbeagle shark

This is the most common of the large sharks of British waters, and may be found all around our coasts. It is present at all times of year, though it is more common in the summer due to a northward migration of fish. The porbeagle is predominantly a surface dwelling shark which feeds on fish, especially mackerel, herring and members of the cod and dogfish families.

Boat fishing for porbeagles is mainly concentrated around the Isle of Wight, Devon and Cornwall, the mid Wales coast, and the west coast of Scotland. They are not uncommonly found over wrecks in deep water, feeding on the shoals of fish attracted by that wreck. They will also come into water as shallow as 12 feet, especially in tidal races off rocky headlands.

While the average size of fish taken by anglers is about 100 lb, there is always the chance of one a lot bigger. Boat tackle in the 30 lb and 50 lb classes is most widely used, with float fished mackerel baits on a 15 foot long wire trace to protect the line both from teeth and the abrasive skin. The British record is currently 465 lb from a boat off Padstow, Cornwall.

■ Pouting

The characteristic rattling bite of a pouting is welcomed by match anglers as a few more reliable ounces for the scales, but by many others as yet another wasted bait in the search for better things.

On some big cod venues, a successful tactic is to rig a worm on a small hook, with a much larger hook as a flier. When a pouting or small whiting takes the worm and hooks itself, it is left out as a livebait for the cod. Conger and bass also show a liking for this species.

This small member of the cod family, often called bib or just pout, can be present in enormous numbers on sand or shingle beaches, and also in rather larger sizes on wrecks and reefs offshore.

Though they appear to feed mainly on shrimps and small crabs, they are usually caught on worm or fish baits, and indeed almost anything else. The British records are currently 5 lb 8 oz from a boat off Berry Head, Devon, and 3 lb 6 oz from the shore near Minehead.

■ Quick release clip

These clips are used whenever it is necessary to change end tackle regularly, and more quickly than a knot allows. In shore match fishing, a spare trace can be baited up while waiting for a bite.

On the retrieve, the used trace is unclipped, and the new one clipped on and cast out immediately. Then the fish can be sorted out and measured, and the trace rebaited ready for the next cast. On a boat, it is often easier to unclip the trace when dealing with toothy fish like conger or tope. The hook can be removed without the hindrance of the reel line and lead dragging about. If it is to be eaten it may even be easier to leave the hook in the fish until it is being gutted.

It may seem obvious, but never use a clip that is weaker than the trace to which it is attached. Specialist clips like the Berkley McMahon specify the tested strengths printed on the label. The Mustad oval split rings, and their newer Easy-links, appear to be virtually indestructible in normal usage.

■ Ragworm

See Baits.

■ Rapala

In the 1930s, a Finnish fisherman called Lauri Rapala started hand-carving wooden plugs, paying special attention to imitating the action of prey fish in the water. Rapala lures are still made of lightweight woods – usually balsa – to give the maximum movement in the water, and are built around a strong, wire frame to ensure the hooks cannot be pulled out.

They are mostly designed for trolling or close range fishing, as they cannot be cast very far. Their action places them in a class of their own however, especially for bass. A wide range of patterns, colours and sizes are available, and they are renowned world-wide for all predatory fish, right up to big-game species like marlin and tunny.

■ Rays

There is no biological difference between rays and skate – it is just conventional to refer to the smaller species as rays, and the larger as skate. Like the related dogfish, they rely heavily on their sense of smell to find their prey. Once it has been tracked down, they flop on it, pressing it to the sea bed while they get it into their mouth. This leads to a long drawn-out bite, before the fish moves off positively with the bait in its mouth.

Blonde ray In terms of the average size of captured fish, this is the biggest our of the rays. It can be recognised by its sandy coloured back with small black spots which go right to the edges.

It is usually found on the south and west coasts, favouring the same sandy ground as plaice and turbot. The usual tactic is a sandeel or slim fillet of mackerel fished on a long flowing trace. The British records are 37 lb 12 oz from a boat off Start Point, Devon, and 32 lb 8 oz from the shore on Alderney.

Cuckoo ray This small ray is easily identified by the distinct black and yellow marbled marking on each wing. It is very abundant but only rarely encountered by anglers.

The British records are 5 lb 11 oz from a boat off the Causeway Coast, Northern Ireland, and 4 lb 10 oz from the north Cornwall shore.

Small eyed ray The small eyed or painted ray is a popular species with shore anglers on sandy beaches in the south and west of the country. It is almost exclusively captured on sandeel legered at long range.

It can be recognised by its brown back patterned with pale lines and blotches. The British records are currently 16 lb 6 oz from a boat off Minehead, Somerset, and 14 lb 8 oz from the shore at Stoke Point, Devon.

Spotted ray Small blonde rays are often confused with large spotted (or homelyn) rays, but the spots on this species are much larger and do not reach the edges of the wings. It is common along the south and west coasts, and is usually taken by boat anglers

using fish baits, but its main food source appears to be crabs and shrimps. The British records stand at 8 lb 3 oz from a boat off the Isle of Whithorn, Scotland, and 8 lb 5 oz from the shore at Mewslade Bay, south Wales.

Thornback ray The thornback or roker is our most common inshore ray, occurring all around the coast on all types of ground. Larger specimens are almost primarily fish eaters and are most often taken on fresh mackerel or herring, though they will often take crab or worm baits. The dorsal surface has a blotched or marbled pattern of fawn and brown, and is very variable. The British records are 38 lb from a boat off Rustington, Sussex, and 21 lb 12 oz from the shore in Kirkcudbright, Scotland.

Undulate ray This is an offshore ray of the south coast, living on sandy bottoms in a moderate depth of water. Its back is a light brown with pale spots and long wavy dark-brown markings. The British records are 21 lb 4 oz from a boat off Swanage, Dorset, and 21 lb 4 oz from the shore on Jersey.

■ Redgill

After the Second World War, Alex Ingram produced the two-piece Mevagissey eel, used with spinning and trolling gear for bass and pollack. This was such a success that a company was set up to manufacture them, and subsequently the Redgill eel. Although a brand name, this has come into common usage to describe a number of similar products which all share the rigid, hollow rubber body enclosing the hook, and a pliable rubber tail bearing swimming vanes.

Between the Redgill, Eddystone and Delta stables, an enormous range of sizes and colours are available. Dark colours like red and black find most favour with deep-water coalfish and pollack on flying collar rigs. Lighter colours, like the natural sandeel finishes and the blue back on a white body seem to be more popular for shallow trolling for bass.

They can also be used from the shore providing sufficient weight is added for casting. A barrel lead can be inserted into the body with the hook, or a lead attached several feet up the trace.

For shallow water, a self-weighted float or controller can be used to keep the lure near the surface.

■ Red mullet

The red mullet or goatfish is easily recognised by its pinky-red coloration and the two extremely long barbules beneath the lower jaw. A regular summer migrant to British waters, it is mostly found on broken ground along the English Channel. The bulk of its food is shrimps, worms and small molluscs, but most rod-caught specimens fall to worm baits.

The British records are currently 3 lb 7 oz from a boat, and 3 lb 10 oz from the shore, both at Guernsey, Channel Isles.

■ Reducer

It is becoming increasingly popular to fix a multiplier reel right at the butt of the rod, especially when using the pendulum cast with rods of over 12 foot in length.

While this gives a better balance during the cast, its makes the retrieve very awkward, and one solution to the problem is to have an extension piece for the handle, known as a reducer. This is about 15 inches long, and can be slipped into the end of the butt to effectively move the reel away from the body for the retrieve.

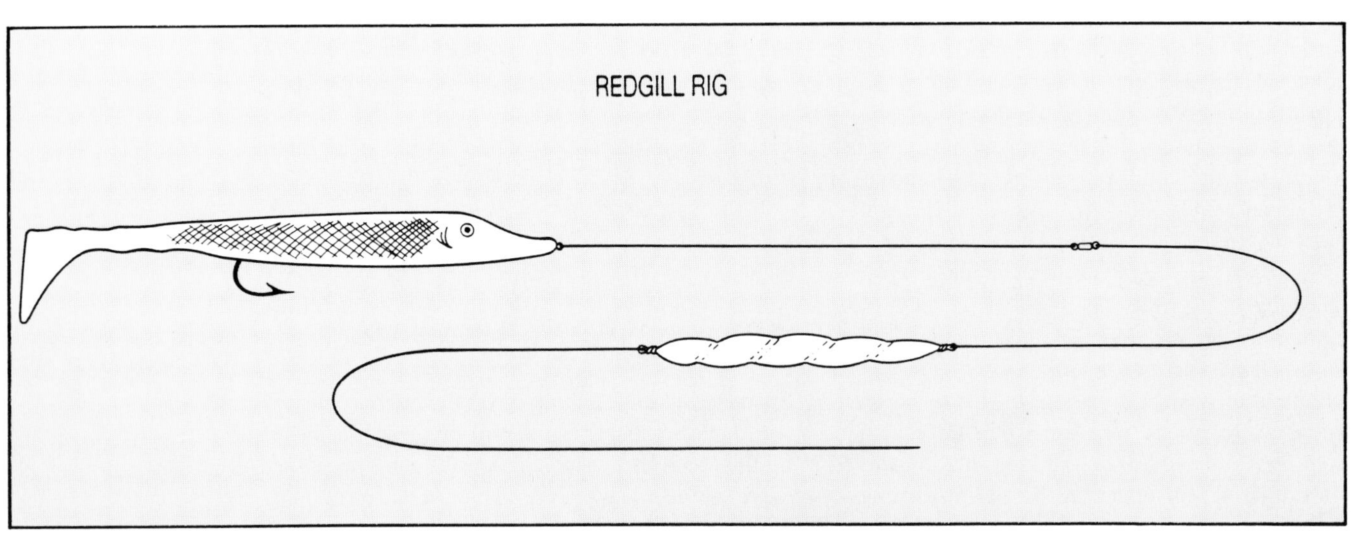

Beach multipliers fitted with level winds (top) and larger capacity boat models.

■ Reels

There are three basic types of fishing reels, and all have a place in the sea angler's armoury. The multiplier is so widespread in its use that it is listed separately.

Centrepin reels are still used for shore fishing on rocky coasts, where their sheer lifting power may outweigh their casting limitations. For the boat angler, the combination of lifting power and the fast retrieve offered by the larger sizes gives them a certain merit, usually for cod fishing with bait or pirks.

The fixed spool reel is essentially a shore angler's tool, since the gearing is not suited to hauling heavy leads and heavier fish from the sea bed. On the shore, small freshwater models are used for mullet and mackerel, and mid-sized ones for bass, wrasse and pollack.

Beachcasters who favour the fixed spool are starting to find properly designed saltwater mangles to suit their needs. As well as a substantial construction and robust gears, and a good measure of corrosion resistance, the caster needs a coned spool of about three inch diameter to give an effective capacity for distance casting, a bale arm that will not snap over during the cast, and a drag that can be locked solid to prevent line slip during the power phase of the cast.

Such a reel offers a rate of retrieve fast enough to lift the tackle over snags, and an almost foolproof casting system which even multiplier experts favour for night fishing or casting into a head wind.

■ Rig wallet

Several sea-angling specialists now produce rig wallets containing a number of self-sealing plastic envelopes in which terminal rigs can be individually stored in loose coils. They allow the angler to pre-

Fixed spool for shore casting with a manual bale.

The famous Pulpit Rock at Portland - home of huge ballan wrasse.

pare a number of alternative rigs in advance, and to store a number of spares to cover the inevitable losses.

■ Rock fishing

Rock fishing offers a wide range of opportunities. It may be that the rocks are just a comfortable ledge onto a clean sandy bottom and conventional beach tackle is the obvious choice, but it can mean fishing 100 feet of water from 100 feet up a cliff where tackle more like a crane is needed.

Where a rocky shore gives onto a rocky sea bed the fish will usually be found at closer range than on a beach, even if the water is not much deeper. The jumble of boulders and weeds at the angler's feet will hold a rich store of shrimps, crabs and small fish, and predators will move close in to feed on them.

Lure fishing or float fishing are often the best tactics, but large baits on the bottom may produce the biggest fish providing the tackle is robust and has been selected to be snag-free, perhaps using lead lifts, flat weights or rotten bottoms.

Safety should always be a major factor in rock fishing. Steep cliffs and narrow ledges always provide the risk of a fall even when dry, and it is characteristic of such marks that they are inevitably far from help. When they are wet or covered in weed or slimy algal growths, footwear should be chosen with care, and slow progress is the order of the day. Never wear studded waders – rubber cleated boots or climbing boots are the best choice.

If there is any danger of a cliff-fall, wear a safety helmet. Take a companion at all times, and make sure someone at home knows where you are and when you are expected back. Carry a torch even if you intend getting back before dark, make sure that you have an escape route suitable for all states of the tide, and set up your fishing position well above not only the expected high water, but any rogue waves that might come your way.

■ Rockling

Sooner or later, most anglers will find their offering of worm or fish has been taken by a small fish rather reminiscent of a ling. It has the same elongate dorsal and anal fins, and a single barbule under the chin identifying it as a member of the cod family.

The colour will be brown or dark red, often with distinct blotches, and there are between three and five extra barbules above the mouth. The captive will be one of the five rocklings which occur around our coasts, and is of little value beyond a few more ounces to the match angler, or a possible bait for better things.

■ Rod rest

See Monopod; Tripod.

■ Rods

See Beachcaster; Boat Rods; Lure fishing; Wire line.

■ Rogue wave

The classic rogue wave is an unwelcome feature of exposed Atlantic coasts. Arising far offshore, they come crashing onto rock marks well above the usual high-water level, sweeping away all in their path. Anglers on any exposed shore should make sure that they are aware of how far the tide is likely to come up – look for the line of debris at the high-water level – and check that there is a safe route away from the mark.

■ Roller rings

There will always be friction between the rod rings and the line. This may only be of passing interest to the beach angler who is more worried about resistance to wear and impact. To the boat angler who often has to pump heavy fish from the sea-bed, reducing this source of friction can substantially increase the life of his line.

Most boat rods for 20 lb line and above are fitted with a roller tip ring, which is the point of greatest friction. It is worth seeking out the better quality rings like AFTCO and the British made ones from Hopkins and Holloway. A roller ring that sticks or traps the line down the side is worse than useless. For 50 lb rods and upwards, and any rod designed for use with wire line, you should have roller rings throughout despite the cost.

■ Rotten bottom

Fishing on really rough ground and wrecks will inevitably lead to tackle losses. Rather than risk losing the whole trace or worse still the fish, the lead can be attached to the trace by a rotten bottom. This is a length of lighter line which will break before anything else, restricting the loss to the weight which can often be an old steel bolt or even a stone tied up in the foot from an old pair of tights. About 6 lb or 8 lb line will reduce unnecessary losses but is easy to break out when it is needed.

This rig is not suitable for casting beyond a gentle lob, and when distance is needed the lead must be supported during the cast. A hook with the point and barb cut off can be tied on the end of the leader. The lead is hung on the hook, but drops off on impact with the water leaving the lead attached by the rotten bottom.

Alternatively, tie a four inch loop in the end of the leader, and push the loop just through the eye of the lead. A stout metal pin will keep it in place during the cast, but drop out in the water.

S

■ Shark

About fifteen species of shark have been recorded in northern European waters, but only three are common – the blue shark, porbeagle and thresher, which is unmistakable with its enormous tail almost as long as its body.

There does not seem to be the same enthusiasm for this branch of the sport as is found elsewhere in the world. While most ports along the south and west coasts have at least one skipper prepared to take out a shark angling party, there is a lack of the specialist boats and tackle usually associated with big-game angling.

Hook a smoothhound in the shallows from the shore and watch the line pour from the spool!

Equipment tends to be robust rather than refined, and the emphasis is on drift fishing with mackerel baits suspended below large floats. In reality, a good 30 lb class outfit with a lever drag reel should cope with most British shark and 50 lb class is only necessary for the very biggest specimens.

■ Shock leader

See Leader.

■ Sinker

See Leads.

■ Smoothhound

There are two British species of smoothhound, the common and the starry, but in most respects they can be considered as one. Rounded white spots are numerous on the starry, and more or less absent on the common smoothhound. Both are small, slim, grey-backed sharks, distinguished from the spurdog by the absence of spines on the dorsal fins, and from small tope by the lack of distinct teeth.

The smoothhounds have flattened grinding plates in their mouths, rather like rays. These are used to crush the shells of crabs which are their main food. Most species of crabs and lobster are eaten, but peeler shore crabs and hermit crabs are usually chosen as bait.

They are widespread but only common at a few favoured locations, where they are highly rated by beach and inshore boat anglers for their fast and furious fight.

The British records for the smoothhound are currently 28 lb from a boat off Heacham, Norfolk, and 17 lb 8 oz from the shore at Sowley Sedge, Hampshire. For the starry smoothhound, the records are 28 lb from a boat off Maplin Sands, Essex, and 23 lb 2 oz from the shore at Bradwell-on-Sea, Essex

■ Snood

The snood is the sea angler's hook length or trace. The choice of snood is a compromise between good presentation, freedom from tangles, and abrasion resistance. Apart from special situations like flounder, plaice and mullet, sea anglers rarely go below 15 lb for snoods, with 25 lb to 40 lb favoured for larger species or those like rays with abrasive mouths.

Within this range, some situations demand long snoods of special, limp nylon to enhance presentation, while others favour short, stiff snoods which are much less likely to tangle on casting. Really heavy materials are saved for big cod, ling, conger and of course tope and other sharks.

■ Sole

The soles are in a different family from all the other British flatfish. The mouth is at the side of the head rather than the front, and is surrounded by lots of little sensory papillae. There are several species in European waters, but only the Dover sole is of interest to the angler.

The Dover sole is found all around the British Isles, but is perhaps most common on the south and south-east coasts. It favours a bottom of sandy mud, in which it buries itself during the daytime, coming out at night to feed on worms, shrimps and small molluscs.

On some beaches they live very close to the shore, and lugworm baits presented on size 4 hooks just 20 to 40 yards out can be the most productive method. The British records are 3 lb 12 oz from a boat off the Isle of Wight, and 6 lb 1 oz from the shore on Alderney.

■ Spearpoint

The Spearpoint series of hooks are another product from the Breakaway Tackle Development Company designed by Nigel Forrest. The shore hooks are fine wire and lightly forged, and come with spade ends or small ring eyes, while the heavier wire boat hooks have turned down eyes. They have small barbs and a short, sharp, needle point which is a very effective combination.

Recent changes in design have led to them becoming rather longer in the shank, improving their qualities as a worm hook. Spearpoints are rather smaller than corresponding sizes from other makers, and they are an excellent choice for small fish. They are effective for larger species like bass, pollack and cod.

■ Split ring

Split rings are made in two distinct forms, oval and round. Mustad oval rings, and their newer Easy-links, provide the ideal quick-release clip for attaching leads or swivels to a leader.

Round rings are used almost exclusively for attaching hooks to lures, and should be chosen with care as many are not corrosion resistant. About 5 mm or 6 mm diameter is right for small spinners and plugs, but rings up to 25 mm or 30 mm diameter are favoured for pirks. A few anglers still use small split rings as sliding links on traces.

■ Spring tide

See Tides.

■ Spurdog

This is an easy member of the dogfish group to identify, especially if picked up carelessly. It has a grey back with distinct white spots, and large, very sharp spines at the leading edges of the two dorsal fins. While these spines are not venomous, they will penetrate the skin easily and deeply, and the wounds often become infected.

Spurdog are found in large shoals containing fish of the same size and sex. They range over all kinds of terrain, at any depth where food is available. Food means almost any locally abundant fish or other animals. The larger fish are mostly females, and tend to be found in deeper water.

When they are present, it is often difficult to avoid catching spurdog on any tackle, though anglers aiming for this species use chunks of mackerel or herring on baited feathers or paternosters, with snoods sufficiently robust to withstand their rough teeth.

The British records are 21 lb 3 oz from a boat off Porthleven, Cornwall, and 16 lb 12 oz from the Chesil Beach in Dorset.

■ Star drag

This is the most common form of drag mechanism on a multiplier reel. Its presence is indicated by a four or five pointed star lever below the reel handle, which is tightened to increase the resistance of the drag to a running fish.

Instead of the single, large disk of the lever drag, the star drag uses a stack of several soft washers sandwiched between steel disks. This makes the assembly more compact and suitable for smaller reels, but it is less efficient at dissipating heat so will not run at peak smoothness for as long. It is also less easy to adjust in action, and most anglers set the drag at the start of the day and leave it alone, using thumb pressure on the spool to increase the drag if necessary.

■ Stingray

This is a relatively unmistakable ray, with its thick body and smooth olive or grey back. The wings are rounded, and the tail is long and whip-like. At the base of the tail is one or occasionally two large spines which, in addition to the physical damage they can do, secrete a venom from a groove along their rear edge.

Anyone who is unfortunate enough to be stabbed by this formidable weapon should seek medical attention immediately, as the reaction is rapid and extremely painful, and can be very serious. Hot water applied to the wound is about the only field treatment which will help.

Stingrays migrate northwards in the summer, and move into shallow sandy waters all around our coasts, but they are only become abundant in areas like the Thames estuary, the Solent and some Hampshire beaches, and also in the Bristol Channel. They are something of a cult fish, as they grow to a very good size and fight extremely well for a ray, though they have no culinary value and should be returned alive to the sea.

Studies have suggested that they feed on a wide range of bottom animals, especially molluscs, crabs and small fish. Anglers however invariably catch them on large legered ragworm.

The British records are 65 lb 8 oz from a boat off Bradwell-on-Sea, Essex, and 53 lb 8 oz from the shore at St. Osyth, Essex.

■ Storm beach

A storm beach is one that faces directly into the prevailing wind. On the east coast it is generally one facing east and likely to yield dabs and codling, and on the west coast faces west or south-west and produces bass and flounder. Typically, it consists of hard-packed, rippled sand, and has a surf running in all but the calmest of conditions.

It will usually only produce fish when a moderate surf is running. If there is too little, fish will not move into the shallow water as there is nothing being scoured out for them to feed on. Too much surf will make it impossible to fish, though just after a storm often produces the best sport.

■ Swivels

Twists form in the line if the terminal tackle turns in the water, whether on the retrieve, dropping down to the sea bed on the cast, or just sitting in the tide on the sea bed. These twists may actually weaken the line, but most obviously the twists will cause tangles when the line gets slack. Swivels are needed to take the twists out of the line as soon as possible after they form.

Even the best swivels barely work when the twists actually occur because the tension in the line prevents them from rotating. But slack line allows the swivel to spin and removes the twists rather than making the line tangle. Use only the best swivels, because they turn more freely and are stronger.

Always choose the smallest swivel that is stronger than the line you are using but use a larger size if the wire of the swivel is appreciably smaller than the diameter of the line – otherwise it may cut into the mono. Quality swivels invariably indicate their breaking strain on the packaging.

T

■ T bar

This strange looking device is often the best way of removing a hook from a large fish, providing it is not too far down its throat. It saves having to hold the fish down, and with practise can be carried out over the side of the boat so species like conger can be returned without ever leaving the water.

Grab the trace about two feet from the hook, and catch the trace near the fish in the small hook at the end of the T bar. Pull up with the T bar, and push down with the trace until the hook on the T bar engages on the hook in the fish's mouth. At this point, your hook should be point down, with the fish hanging on the barb. A sharp jerk and the weight of the fish should dislodge even the most solid hookhold.

■ Tide tables

Tides rule the sea angler's life, and the tide table should be his bible. A yearly tide table can be purchased from a local tackle shop for under a pound and is the best investment around. By itself it will not tell you when the fishing will be good, but it will tell you when similar tide conditions can be expected to those on other successful days.

When the exact details of local tides are less important it is possible to estimate them from the London tables published in Angler's Mail every week, adding or subtracting the time factor for your nearest venue. A big tide in London will be a big tide everywhere on the coast.

The local table will have been corrected for local variations and contains the local tide heights. Normally it will show the times and heights of high waters, but for bait gathering or boat launching the times and heights of low waters are also important. If they are not printed in the local angler's tide table, try a boat chandler instead.

Remember that the table contains the predictions for the tide, and what happens on the beach will also depend on the prevailing wind and atmospheric pressure.

Steel T-bar for removing the hooks speedily.

■ Tides

A basic understanding of the tides is essential to a successful sea angler, because it influences both the movement of fish and the availability of bait. The movement of the water is a result of the positions of the sun, earth and moon. The rotation of the earth relative to the others causes the twice daily surge of water in and out, the parts of the cycle being known as the rising or flood tide, the high water slack, the falling or ebb tide, and the low water slack.

How far the tide comes in each day is determined by the relative positions of the three bodies. When all three are in line, at new or full moon, the gravitational pull is greatest, and the tides are large, or springs. They come higher up the beach at high water, and go further down the beach at low water.

About a week after the spring tides, the moon will be at right angles to the sun, at first and last quarter. Then the tides will be small or neap, moving less up and down the beach. The very biggest tidal

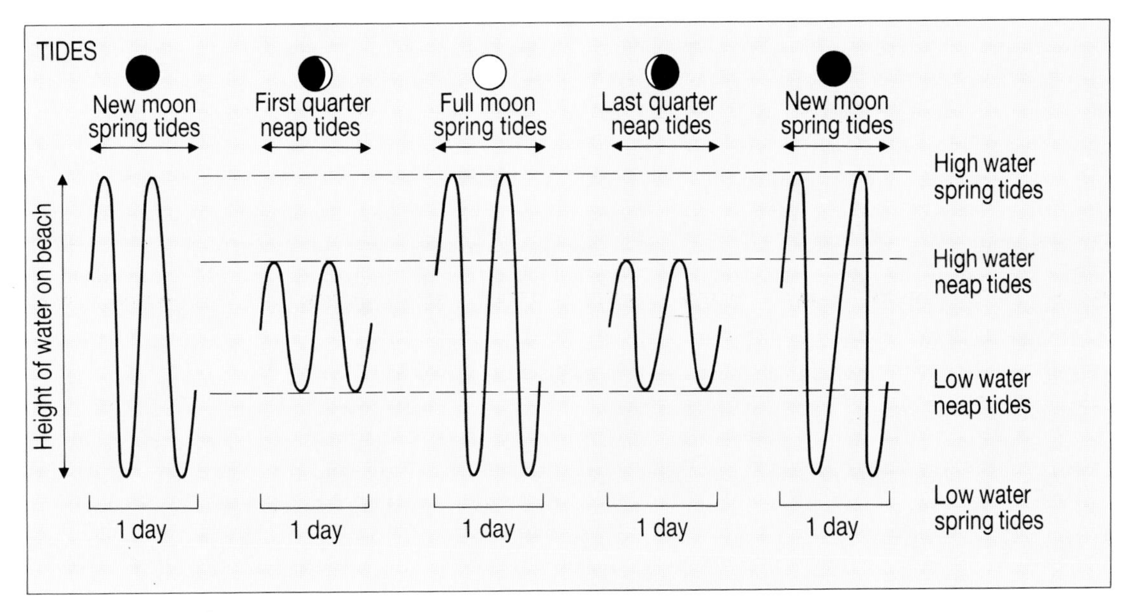

ranges in the year are experienced at the equinoxes, around March 21 and September 23.

Springs are favourite The timing of a particular state of tide falls back by about 25 minutes on each cycle, so high water one day will be almost an hour later than on the preceding day. The tidal range experienced on a beach varies enormously around the British Isles, with places like the Bristol Channel and the Channel Isles experiencing ranges in excess of 40 feet from low water to high, while places like Dorset may experience an average of only a few feet.

There is no simple rule to tell the best tide for a particular beach, but there is no doubt that the tidal conditions are one of the most important factors. Find the right conditions for a particular beach and the fish are likely to be present whenever those conditions are repeated.

Spring tides are often favourite on a sandy beach, with the first few hours of the flood being best. On a rocky beach, the period up to high water springs may be best, but shingle or cobble beaches often fish best on neap tides when the exact state of the tide may be less important.

■ Tope

The technique of uptiding has produced an enormous upturn of interest in tope fishing in recent years, not least because the combination of shallow water and light tackle allows this sporting small shark to give its best performance. Tope live all around the British Isles, and spend the summer in shallow water with a gravel or sandy bottom, moving to deeper water offshore for the winter. Areas like the Thames estuary, the Solent and the west Wales coast are well-known for their excellent summer tope fishing.

Few tope are caught from the shore, though in some places it is possible providing a suitable trace is used and there is enough line on the reel to cope with their searing runs. From a boat, 15 lb or 20 lb tackle is sufficient whether fishing uptide or down.

The best baits are sides or flappers of mackerel, small flatfish, or three to four inch sections of silver eel. A sharp hook about size 6/0 is attached to a 12 inch length of wire, and then a six foot rubbing trace of stout nylon. The wire is a protection from the impressive teeth, and the nylon from the abrasive skin common to all sharks and dogfish.

Tope are a valuable sporting resource, but of little use in the kitchen. They should always be returned alive. Never use a gaff – tope can be netted, but a salmon tailer or hand tailing is easier with practise. The biggest fish are females in pup, invariably caught at the beginning of the summer, and should be handled with particular care.

The British records are 79 lb 12 oz from a boat off Bradwell, Essex, and 58 lb 2 oz from the shore in north Devon.

■ Torpedo weights

As distance casting emerged as a priority for many beach anglers, so the torpedo or bomb became the standard weight. There is no doubt that its streamlined shape will give the best casting distances, and it is also stable on the drop in boat fishing which is especially important with rigs like the flying collar.

The standard bomb will roll on the bottom in the tide, which can be used to the angler's advantage to seek out fish or fish-holding depressions in the sea

Triggerfish have become regular visitors to the south coast - confirmation that our coastal waters are getting warmer.

Below: **Lightweight tripod gives excellent support.**

bed. On a congested beach, or in situations where a static bait or a self-hooking rig is desirable, either Breakaway or fixed grip wires can be used.

■ Triggerfish

Recent hot summers have seen increasing numbers of this warm-water exotic from further south in the Atlantic and the Mediterranean. It usually turns up from July onwards on southern and western beaches, with Dorset's Chesil Beach being perhaps the most prolific venue.

It is not a strong swimmer and usually drifts along on the prevailing current, but gives a surprisingly good account of itself when hooked. The British records are 4 lb 9 oz from a boat off Weymouth, Dorset, and 4 lb 6 oz from the Chesil Beach.

■ Tripod

In recent years a new generation of sophisticated aluminium tripods have appeared on the market, offering support for pairs of rods on any surface. They are adjustable for rod height off the beach and the angle the rods are held at, so the rods can be lowered in high winds.

Attachment points under the tripod can support bags of sand or shingle to hold the rest steady in rough conditions, or to store ready baited spare traces.

■ Trolling

Trolling a bait or lure behind a boat under power can be very effective for some species like bass and pollack. Lures such as Redgills, Rapala and live or dead sandeels are used most frequently, with a barrel lead several feet above the lure.

It is often necessary to keep the tackle a long distance behind the boat, up to 100 feet if the fish are wary, and to troll at speeds so slow that some petrol engines cannot cope.

Two rods can be fished over the stern of a boat with care, but if more are desired then outriggers should be used to space out the tackles. These are aluminium or fibreglass poles between 12 and 30 feet long supported at right angles from the side of the boat. The line goes from the rod to a tension clip at the end of the pole, keeping the rig well away from those fished over the stern.

A pulley system can be rigged to the end of the outrigger, so the tackle can be fed out to the end without having to ship the outrigger pole.

For deep trolling the answer is the downrigger. This is a winch to lower a lead weight of up to 10 lb on a wire line over the stern of the boat to the desired depth. The rod line is clipped to the downrigger wire near the lead, and the line is paid out as the lead is lowered.

The lure will be fished at the chosen depth until a fish hits it, when the clip will release the line and the fish can be played out without the hindrance of a heavy weight on the line.

■ Turbot

The turbot and its close relative the brill can be distinguished from the other common flatfish by their large mouths which clearly identify them as fish eaters. The turbot has a rather angular diamond shape, whereas the smaller brill is a more elongate oval. Both live on sandy bottoms on offshore banks, though smaller specimens can sometimes be taken from the beach and turbot may crop up on the sandy areas around deepwater wrecks.

The favoured method for their capture is a long flowing trace baited with sandeel or mackerel fillet, either from an anchored or drifting boat. The British record turbot are 33 lb 12 oz from a boat off Salcombe, south Devon, and 28 lb 8 oz from the shore in Suffolk. The brill records are 16 lb from a boat off the Isle of Man, and 7 lb 7 oz from the shore on Guernsey.

UV

■ Uptiding

Uptiding or boatcasting is a method which evolved for fishing shallow waters like the Thames estuary. Its development since the 1970s is primarily associated with the exploits of Bob Cox and John Rawle, two charter skippers at Bradwell-on-Sea, Essex, although it had been used since at least the 1920s.

They realised that in shallow water fish avoided swimming under the boat, probably because of the noise from the hull. By casting the tackle away from the boat, it would lie in the path of the fish.

Casting from a boat is not easy, and can be dangerous if not done sensibly. The ideal rod is between nine and ten feet long, with a soft tip, powerful mid section, and stiff butt. The tip flexes to avoid disturbing the lead, the middle provides the power to control the big fish often encountered, and the stiff butt gives leverage for casting.

Combined with a multiplier holding 15 lb to 20 lb line, this outfit will handle stingrays, thornback, bass, cod, tope and many other species. The technique is viable in depths up to 75 feet, but the usual recommendation is to cast at least three times the depth of the water, at an angle uptide.

Grip leads are essential, and a shock leader should be used in most situations. A simple paternoster or leger rig is used, but the trace is adjusted according to the species being targeted. With a trace of any length, the baited hook can be hung on the grip wires during casting to avoid hitting other anglers on the boat.

After the lead hits the water, pay out a large belly of line which will help hold the lead down on the bottom. The rod should be placed in a rest, and the tide will bend the soft tip over. Bites will usually be slack-liners, with the fish hooking themselves against the grip wires. Wind down until the weight of the fish is felt, and then the fight begins.

■ Viking hooks

If an angler were so unwise as to demand a single pattern of hooks to cope with all sea angling demands, then the Mustad Viking would be the best choice available. Pattern 79515 has a tapered-wire straight eye which is neat enough to slip most baits over without too much damage.

It is a medium wire forged hook which is strong enough to handle anything less than big conger and sharks, but will take a sharp enough point to be ideal for bass and cod from the shore. Sizes range from 6/0 down to freshwater sizes which are excellent for wrasse.

■ Watch lead

Years ago the Polo-like watch lead was used by sea anglers everywhere. It fell out of favour as distance casting became the vogue because it most certainly is not aerodynamic. Many experienced sea anglers keep a few around however, as they grip a clean sandy bottom well and do not roll about. They can be useful for boat fishing, or even pier fishing at close range.

■ Weevers

There are two species of these unpleasant small fish in British waters. Both are elongate, brown backed fish with upturned eyes and long anal and second dorsal fins. At the back of the head is a spiny, erect, black first dorsal fin. These spines, and the sharp edges of the gill covers, inject a poison which is extremely painful and may be dangerous.

Weevers bury themselves in shallow sandy water, and although they do take angler's baits they are more likely to be encountered by bathers or bait collectors.

■ Weights

See Leads.

■ Whiting

When winter cod are not around, the whiting is the staple species for most beach and inshore boat anglers. It is a member of the cod family though its chin barbule is very small. It has distinct silvery sides, a long and rather pointed snout, and a mouth full of small sharp teeth.

Larger specimens are predominantly fish eaters, and a paternoster baited with chunks of herring or mackerel, or a worm bait tipped with fish strip are

Selection of shore sinkers including plain torpedoes, flat leads, Breakaways and a weight incorporating a planing device.

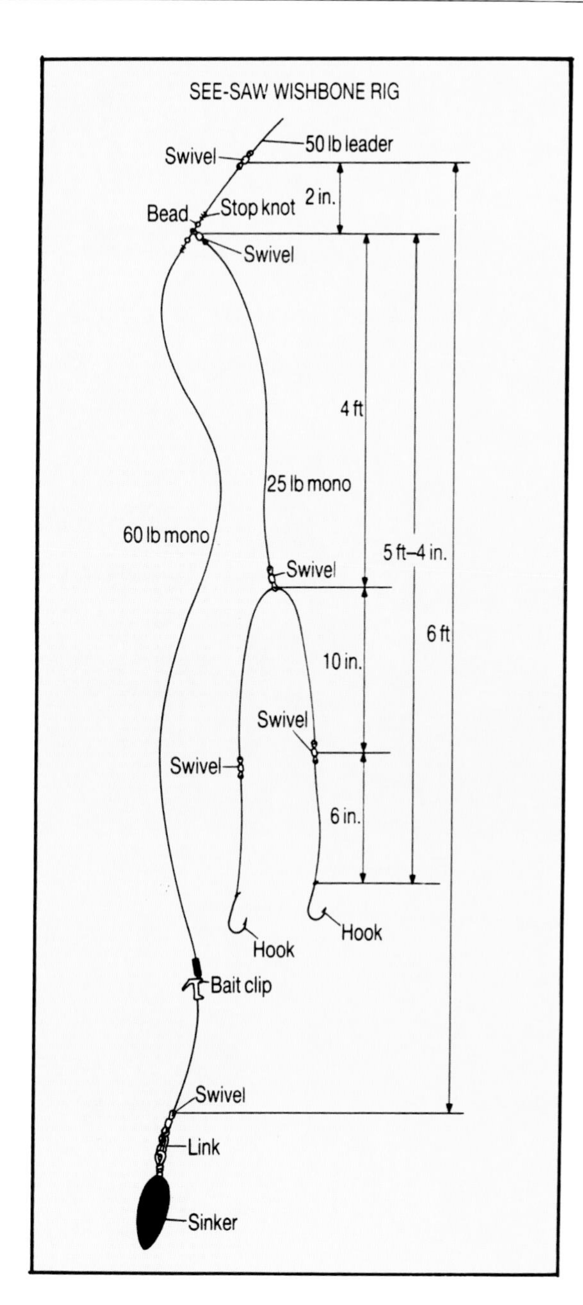

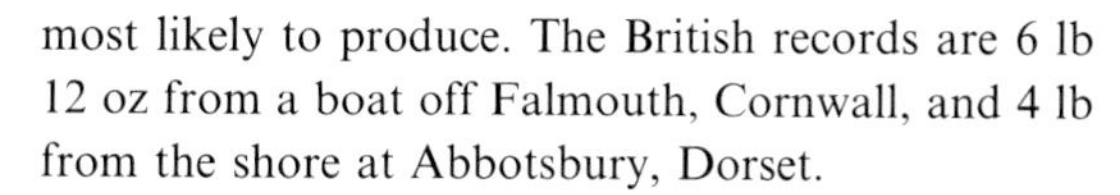
most likely to produce. The British records are 6 lb 12 oz from a boat off Falmouth, Cornwall, and 4 lb from the shore at Abbotsbury, Dorset.

■ Wire line

When the combined effects of depth and current demand 2 lb or more of lead to hold bottom from a boat, fishing with nylon line becomes almost impossible. The only realistic solution is to change to a wire line. The weight of the line and its reduced diameter mean that only about half the lead will be needed to hold bottom, and the lack of stretch means that even the gentlest bite can be felt.

Wire lines come in two forms, braided wire which is much easier to handle but inclined to fray, and single strand which is even thinner for a given strength but inclined to kink.

Tangles in wire lines are very difficult to resolve, especially when the other lines involved are nylon, or worse still Dacron. Charter skippers will often insist that everyone on the boat uses wire, or no-one.

The best rod for wire line is a fast taper 30 lb or 50 lb class rod, seven foot or longer, with roller rings throughout. Use a multiplier with a narrow, metal

Top: **Whiting accompany cod inshore and liven up winter sessions.**

Above: **Bell, watch and torpedo weights for holding in the tide race from a boat.**

Above: **Ballan wrasse must be held hard because they dash into the kelp in a flash.**

Right: **The sun sets on a successful wrecking session and there's a moment to reflect on the sporting qualities of a small coalfish.**

spool, and put a couple of hundred yards of nylon on the spool to protect it from the wire. A long leader of heavy nylon is recommended, to add some elasticity to the rig and to carry the lead boom.

Finally, take a 12 foot length of broom handle, or similar, to wrap the line around when you need to break out of the bottom.

■ Wishbone rig

This is a two hook rig which allows baits to be presented side by side, instead of one above the other. It concentrates the scent trail in one place, and looks like one large bait should a bigger fish come along while allowing smaller fish to take the individual baits, thereby offering the angler two chances.

The simplest way of producing it is to tie a large loop in the end of the snood, cut this in the middle, and put a baited hook on each end. Alternatively, tie a small swivel on the end of the snood, and thread another piece of line through the other eye. Tie the hooks on both ends of this second piece of line and it is a see-saw wishbone.

The travel of this second snood can be limited by putting swivels, leger stops, or Mustad KF line stops at the desired distance above the hooks.

■ Wrasse

In addition to the ballan wrasse, there are at least six other species found around the British shores. They all share the same basic lifestyle, feeding on crustaceans and molluscs on weedy, rocky shores. Apart from the cuckoo wrasse, they are all very small and of little interest to the angler. See Ballan Wrasse.

■ Wreck fishing

Many charter boats are not licensed to fish the distant wrecks, and only a few skippers are capable of getting the best out of them. So if a wreck fishing trip is being planned, make sure you get the right skipper.

Your skipper will have a fast and seaworthy boat, with clear decks to maximise the fishing area. The cabin will be full of the latest electronics, for safety as well as to locate the wreck precisely, and he will know which are the most productive wrecks at the time of the trip.

Wreck fishing means a certain amount of hardship, and the wise angler is well prepared for what is in store. There will be many hours of travelling, with little to pass the time apart from watching the seagulls. Make sure your clothing is warm, dry and comfortable enough to cope with this as well as the actual fishing. Remember that the weather is usually worse offshore than on dry land. Take plenty of food and suitable drinks. And take twice as much tackle as you expect to use, because there are no tackle shops 40 miles out to sea.

There are three main methods for wreck fishing but the flying collar rig for pollack, coalfish or cod is many people's favourite, as it combines light tackle with fighting fish. Fishing pirks and Muppets for cod and ling can be very productive, but the continual jigging is very demanding on the stamina of the angler.

Finally there is bait fishing. While it is possible to have wonderful light-tackle sport fishing for bream on a wreck, most anglers concentrate on the heavyweights like cod, ling and conger, using large baits like mackerel flappers, squid or whole cuttlefish. Unlike the other two methods, bait fishing is much more likely to be carried out from anchor, so check beforehand that the tides are suitable.

Z

Zip slider

The most reliable weight carrier for a boat fishing leger rig on the market. It is a robust, red plastic slider with a large stainless steel clip to take the lead. Use it for conger, ling, cod, skate and any other heavy bottom fishing.

MERCUR

Angler's Mail

TROUT

The range of tackle you need for a day's trout fishing is expertly detailed in the following pages with practical advice on where and how to find the fish. A select number of flies have been picked out from the hundreds on offer as being the all-time best deceivers of rainbows and browns.

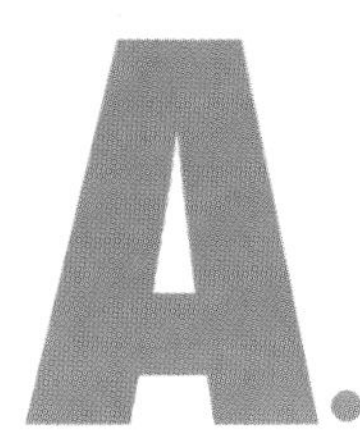

A

■ Ace of Spades

One of the best lures for the opening weeks of the season, but also takes fish through the whole year. Devised by Dave Collyer, the fly is tied Matuka style with the body rib taken through the wing feathers. It has built-in 'life' which allows it to be fished very slowly.

■ AFTMA

A scale of line weights from 1 to 12 devised by the American Fishing Tackle Manufacturers' Association. The higher the number, the heavier the line. The scale is based on the weight of the first 30 feet of fly line. By matching the number of the line to a rod designed to cast that weight, perfectly balanced tackle is achieved.

Reel manufacturers also usually specify the capacity of their reels on the AFTMA scale. For example, a reel may be described as holding a forward taper AFTMA 6 line, plus 100 yards of backing. In practice, most quality rods will team with two line sizes. The most exacting rod specifications even allow for a WF (weight forward) or a DT (double taper) AFTMA rating.

In general, line weights up to AFTMA 5/6 are considered best for stream fishing, with AFTMA 5 to 9 preferred on stillwaters. Salmon anglers use lines from 8 to 12 on the big rivers.

■ Appetiser

A fry imitator which rates as one of the best. The wing is white marabou overlaid with a pinch of squirrel tail. It is mostly used in the summer on brighter days and fishes well at all depths. But it is most effective when stripped fast through the surface. A relatively easy fly to tie, and one that has many variations – but the original is still the best.

B

■ Baby Doll

Regarded as a lure pattern, the Baby Doll has evolved into one of the most successful competition flies, tied on smaller size 10 and 12 hooks. It is one of the simplest flies to tie, consisting almost entirely of fluorescent white wool.

The tying is 'tight' and there is no natural movement to the fly itself, and so it must be fished with a lot of movement and life. Variations on the original theme are many, most notably the Peach Doll which is tied with a bright pink/peach wool.

■ Backing

Backing line is wound on the reel underneath the fly line to fill out the spool. Without it,the coils of fly line would be too tightly laid producing a corkscrew effect when pulled off the reel. Backing also provides a reserve of line when a fish makes a long run. Most backing consists of braided dacron which is very fine and strong. As a rule of thumb, 50 yards of backing is the absolute minimum and 150 yards is needed for big river or salmon fishing.

■ Bag limit

The maximum number of fish that can be taken in a day's fishing, according to fishery rules. Bag limits vary but the average permit gives the right to take between four and eight trout after which you must stop fishing.

On some trout waters, an extra ticket can be purchased when the limit is reached making it possible to continue fishing and take additional trout. Other venues may impose a bag limit of one brace, with extra fish being paid for at the market rate per pound.

Compared to the wide open spaces of a reservoir, the smaller stillwaters like Stafford Moor in Devon give you much more confidence that fish are within sight of the fly.

■ Bank fishing

Virtually all major reservoirs issue bank fishing permits and in most cases they are excellent value for money. The huge number of smaller stillwater fisheries offer sport at a wide range of prices, often with a real chance of confronting an exceptional specimen. Reservoirs probably represent the greater challenge with literally miles of bank to choose from.

Smaller stillwaters might appear less intimidating but this can be misleading. They are frequently difficult, especially in high summer. Rather than the long distance casting generally required on the big lakes, it is far better to adopt the stalking approach here, walking the banks and using rushes and reed beds for camouflage, and picking off individual fish. Polarising glasses are essential and short casting with a small weighted nymph gives the best results.

Because of their great size, and the large numbers of anglers fishing them, the big lakes are stocked with a smaller average size of fish. This contrasts with many smaller waters which are stocked with much larger trout to attract the specimen hunters. An average size of 5 lb may be advertised in which case you can expect many of the trout to weigh much heavier. Inevitably, the high cost of rearing these larger trout means there is a premium to pay for this kind of sport.

When bank fishing on large or small stillwaters, always look for the features that will hold fish. Choose a spot with bankside trees, weed beds or an area of rushes. Try to pick a place with contrasting depths, or near to a known underwater feature like, a ledge or shelf. On the larger lakes, there will probably be submerged river beds, lines of old tree stumps, or old roads or hedges – all these will be fish-holding spots.

On the smaller lakes, search out any inlet flows or springs. Areas of stone or gravel among weed beds should prove productive and so will shady spots where trees overhang the water. Remember that places that are easily reached will be the most heavily fished. Those features which are impossible to reach with a fly will be under-fished and will almost certainly act as a sanctuary for the trout. A difficult spot is nearly always a good one.

Watercraft plays a major part on any fishery. Cautious wading will always be rewarded. Fish the close margins first, wading progressively out to deeper water. The same applies on smaller lakes. In early morning, when freshly stocked fish are less likely to be spooked, you can catch them by short casting – four or five yards of line are plenty. Use bankside features to keep concealed from the fish whenever possible. Trout are far from being the stupid creatures that some would have you believe.

Above: **England international Chris Ogborne gives line to a Chew rainbow that crash dived as it neared the boat.**

Above right: **The well equipped boat fleet at Chew Valley Lake.**

There is always a temptation on the bank of a major reservoir to envy the boat anglers, thinking that they have the better deal. More often than not, the reverse is true. The bank angler has just as much flexibility in choosing his fishing spot, and can employ a whole range of floating and sinking line tactics.

■ Bass bag

A lightweight bag used to retain the catch and keep it fresh. The traditional straw bass has largely been replaced by canvas or lighter synthetic materials. An absolute essential on a hot summer's day, to prevent the fish from cooking prematurely.

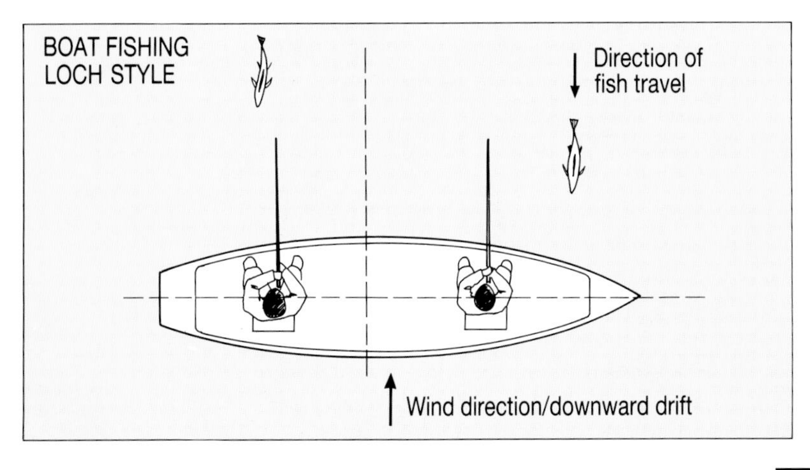

■ Bibio

One of the classic top dropper flies, particularly in early season. The fly is palmered with a black hackle, over a body of predominantly black seal's fur, with a touch of red fur tied in centre body. A genuine all-water fly.

■ Black and Peacock Spider

Attributed to that great stillwater angler, Tom Ivens, this is one of the true originals. It has been suggested that it is tied to represent a snail, but this is stretching things a bit far. It is far closer to being a general suggestive pattern in the midge and sedge families, and when tied with a soft hen hackle it has wonderful 'life' at the water surface. Best fished slowly, right on the top, and in the evening rise. At other times, particularly darker cloudy days, it makes a superb choice for the top dropper.

■ Blae and Black

A fly with its origins a long way north of the border, on the lochs and rivers of Scotland. It is a wet fly of very bland appearance, but is deceptively good in the water. One of the best patterns for grayling, but effective when any dark flies are on the water, or emerging.

■ Boat fishing

Inevitably confined to larger stillwaters and not really practical on lakes of less than 100 acres. Costs are at least double the bank permit because of the need to maintain the boat fleet and engines if fitted. There are frequently long booking lists at the premier fisheries like Chew and Grafham.

The essence of boat fishing is freedom. You can escape the land for a day, and have total freedom to explore thousands of acres. Sometimes you might fish at anchor, near a known underwater feature like an old river bed or some semi-submerged withies. But the real pleasure – and arguably the most effective way of fishing – is to drift. This is the classic loch style method, casting in front of a freely drifting boat, and covering many acres with long drifts downwind.

It is best practised with two people in a boat, when both have a casting angle of 90 degrees from the middle line. A broad sweep of water is covered on each drift. Fish in open water generally move upwind, and with the boat drifting towards them the flies are worked up and across their line of travel. All sorts of patterns can be used, from the traditional wet flies, with wings and palmered hackles, through to lures and attractors.

Similarly, by using lines of varying densities a whole range of depths can be explored. The actual depth of fishable water is really only governed by the speed of drift, which in turn is determined by wind strength. On gentle days it will be possible to work the flies at considerable depths, but with a big wind it will only be practical to reach around five or six feet, even with a Hi-D line.

Fishing at anchor allows really deep water to be explored, but fish quickly become accustomed to seeing a boat above them, and will move out of range. A heavy, lead core line can also be used to drift fish over the deeps.

Dry fly is becoming an increasingly popular method from the boats. Teams of dries, chosen as much for their silhouette as anything else, are combined with a long leader. On really fussy days, like a flat calm for example, a single dry fly can be the only way of preventing a blank.

Dapping is another form of dry fly fishing, and again it has a long and honourable pedigree on the lochs of Scotland and Ireland. It involves using a blow line, normally of floss, which carries the fly downwind and daps it on the water ahead of the boat. This has a teasing, but very lifelike motion, and is especially effective when the daddy longlegs are about.

Larger fish tend to shun the margins and shallow water, only venturing in at dusk. But in open water they move more freely, and fishing from a boat you never know when something really big is going to head towards you from the deeps.

No fundamental changes in tackle are required for boat fishing. And there are only two accessories which could be regarded as musts – a purpose-made boat seat and a drogue. The seat is particularly helpful if you have long legs. It fits across the thwarts, and as well as giving more freedom of movement it provides extra height. This can be very crucial in spotting fish.

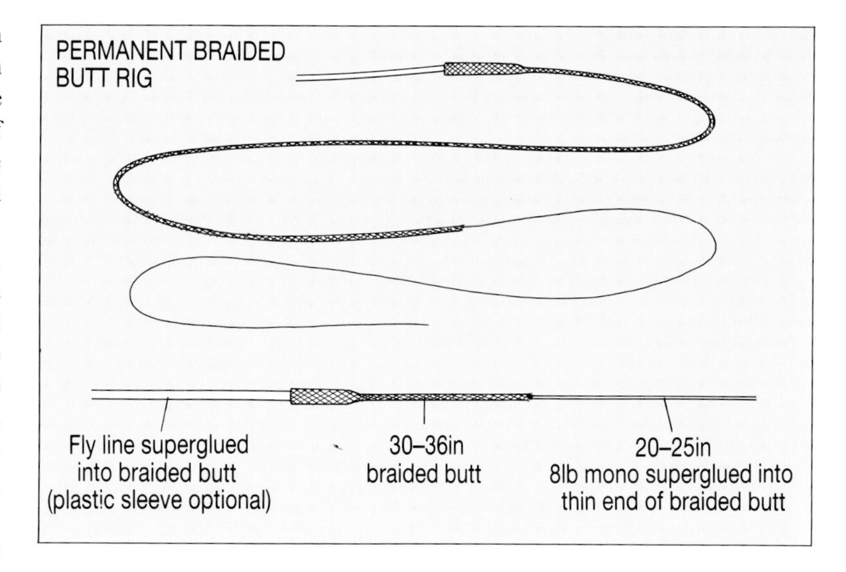

The drogue is something no serious boat fisher can afford to be without. It is a simple, parachute-like device that trails behind the drifting boat, and acts like a sea anchor. On rougher days it slows the drift very noticeably, allowing more contact with the flies and a more controlled retrieve.

■ Braided leader

Possibly one of the greatest tackle innovations of the last generation. A braided leader consists of a tapering length of nylon braid that attaches to the end of the fly line. It tapers down to the diameter of nylon monofilament and perfectly transfers the energy from an unfurling line into the leader itself. The normal leader can then be made up in the usual way.

Most anglers prefer to restrict themselves to a braided butt, which is actually the top 30 inches of the braided leader. A length of about 20 inches of straight mono – usually 8 lb breaking strain – is either needle-knotted or Superglued to this, forming a permanent butt rig. A butt rig made up in this way normally lasts a complete season.

■ Brook trout

The native trout of Britain and a far cry from the stockie browns and rainbows of today's stillwaters. Sadly, angling pressure has reduced their numbers but they continue to thrive in the moorland streams of Devon, Cornwall and Yorkshire, as well as the rivers and lochs of Scotland and Ireland. They are easily recognised by the bright red spots down the flanks and rarely reach any great size. A 1 lb fish is unusual. They should not be confused with the American Brook Trout, which is another introduced species.

Brown trout are much slower growing than rainbows and cost more to stock.

■ Brown trout

Also native to Britain, brown trout are the traditional game species of river and lake. On most stillwaters, local strains have been augmented, most notably by Loch Leven strains from Scotland, to produce fish with improved fighting qualities. They are more expensive to rear than their rainbow cousins, as they have a slower growth rate.

On the famous Bristol waters, a rainbow of one year can be stocked at almost 1 lb. It will take a brownie two years to reach that size but they tend to live much longer and quickly settle in to a new environment. If a brownie remains uncaught it may live for as long as ten or twelve year. Rainbows rarely survive more than two seasons after stocking.

The fighting qualities of big browns are legendary, as they keep their heads down and dive for the bottom.

■ Butcher

Not so much an individual fly as a collection of patterns, as the well known variations of Silver, Bloody, and Kingfisher Butcher illustrate. It is basically an attractor fly and is most certainly not imitative in any way. It relies on colour and flash for its attractor properties and is probably best as a middle dropper in a three fly team.

■ Butt

The term used to describe the end of the leader nearest the fly line. Leader butts can be either straight or braided mono and form the link between the fly line and the chosen leader material. Mono butts are attached to the line in various ways, the best being a nail knot, which can be over-whipped for neatness.

■ Buzzer

This is the name given to all flies that represent the midge pupae, in a whole range of colours and sizes. There are many ideas as to what represents an ideal Buzzer pattern, and there is a huge variation in styles. Some Buzzers are suggestive, with the emphasis only on shape or outline. Others are a very close copy, with a perfect colour match for the natural insect, complete with breather tubes and emergent wing buds.

All can have their day, depending on the conditions. Most are designed to be fished right on the top, preferably in a hatch, and movement is usually very slow.

■ Caenis

A natural insect known as the angler's curse for very good reasons. This tiny, up-winged fly hatches in great profusion on most stillwaters, usually in the hotter summer months. Like all up-winged flies it has three tails but is still only half-an-inch long. It is virtually impossible to imitate at the tying bench.

The reason why fish are so difficult to catch in a Caenis hatch is probably due to their huge numbers. When literally thousands of naturals are on the surface, the odds against the angler's imitation being taken are just impossibly long.

■ Casting

The art of casting a fly or flies onto the water. The aim is to present the fly in the most lifelike manner, in the right place, at the right time. This is achieved by a series of fluid movements, combining the action of the rod with both the fly line, and the leader configuration. It is a skill that can only be perfected by long practise, preferably with at least an introductory session of professional tuition.

Good presentation of the fly is achieved through accuracy and delicacy – the two are irretrievably linked. Accuracy involves gauging the position of the fish in the water, including its speed and direction of travel. The fly is then presented ahead of that position. Delicacy means presenting the fly without fuss or water disturbance, in such a way that the fish genuinely believes it to be a food item.

Many forms of casting have evolved for different purposes. Double haul is the most popular on stillwater. Greater distances are achieved by increasing line speed with a double haul on both hands. Roll casting, usually with a longer rod, throws the line out without needing a back-cast. Other more specialised casts – for instance the Spey and Steeple casts – are for very specific angling circumstances, and should be learned with help from an established expert.

■ Casts

Also known as tippets or leaders. The cast, normally of nylon monofilament in various breaking strains, is the final link between the angler, his tackle, and the fish. The diagrams show various leader systems but several golden rules should always be observed:

1. Always use the very best leader material – it is false economy to buy the cheap stuff.
2. Gear the breaking strain to the type of fishing. In early season, and in conditions of big wind and wave, you can raise the breaking strain. In flat calms, and when fishing for experienced or fussy fish, finer nylon will be needed.
3. Generally, use the lightest nylon with which you feel comfortable and confident. For beginners, or anyone in doubt over leader construction, pre-tied leaders are available.

LEADER CONSTRUCTION
The following leaders should be attached to your permanent butt consisting of 30 in braided section, or 30 in of 10 lb nylon. All lengths quoted are exclusive of this permanent section.

1. STANDARD LEADER (Two Fly) (All sections same breaking strain)

Butt — 36 in — Dropper — 60 in — Tail Fly

2. Standard Wet Fly Leader (Three Fly) (All sections same breaking strain)

Butt — 36 in — Top Dropper — 45 in — Middle Dropper — 72 in — Tail Fly

3. Stepped down Leader construction

Butt — 36 in of 6 lb — Dropper — 45 in of 5 lb — Dropper — 72 in of 4 lb — Tail Fly

In all cases, dropper lengths should be around 6–8 in maximum. Do not join lengths of say 10 lb and 5 lb together, as the diameters are not compatible and this produces too much strain on the knot. Step down leaders in smooth, progressive drops.

Above: **Standard overhead cast.**

1. Adopt a relaxed position with the feet spaced about 18 inches apart and facing square to the direction in which you wish to cast. The rod is held parallel to the water surface and there needs to be about five or six yards of line extending from the tip out into the water. With the line held firmly in the left hand, begin to raise the rod towards the vertical.

2. Continue with a smooth move to the vertical, pulling downwards with the left hand to increase the line's speed of travel.

3. Increase the movement with the right hand to 'snap' the rod to the vertical and allowing its natural momentum to flex it backwards to around 20 degrees. The line will form a loop in the air which is the back cast. As this straightens out behind, you'll feel a gentle pull indicating that the line is straight and you are ready to start the forward cast.

4. Push forward smoothly and firmly to the 12 o' clock position, at the same time pulling down again with the left hand to increase line speed. All the power in the casting motion is applied between the 10 and 2 o' clock positions as the spring or flex in the rod is transmitted within this arc.

5. As you reach the 2 o' clock position, hold the line firmly in the left hand until it moves in the forward loop at about head height.

6. As the line passes your head, release the left hand completely and allow the rod to drift down to the 3 o' clock position. The momentum of the line will straighten it out, as well as pulling the shooting line with it to complete the cast.

Note:

False casting, which takes place between stages 3 and 5, helps to build up line speed. It is possible to perform the cast in one movement but most anglers make two or three false casts before the release in stage 6.

The crucial phases in the cast are between 10 and 2 o' clock and the arm,wrist and rod should move in the same plane. This gives good line speed and is vital in achieving accuracy and presentation. The real power should come from the flex in the rod and not from brute strength on the part of the caster.

Above right: **Double haul.**

1. The stance is the same as in the overhead cast although many anglers find it better to stand more at an angle with the forward foot pointing in the direction of the cast.

2. As the line clears the water, the rod speeds up on the back cast and the left hand pulls down as far as possible. This must be co-ordinated to gain maximum line speed in the back loop.

3. The rod stops in the 20 degree position and as the line straightens out it drifts back a little, in order to gain maximum thrust on the forward stroke. At the same time, the left hand comes up to shoulder height.

4. As the line fully straightens behind, the left hand allows another two or three yards of line out and the elbow bends,

almost to chin level.

5. Once the 'back stop' is felt, the forward cast is punched out, stopping at the 2 o' clock position. To gain line speed, the left hand is hauled down again. The angler will be aiming at an imaginary point, about head height above the water, some 30 yards distant.

6. The left hand then releases the line which shoots forward under its own momentum. The rod can be raised to shoulder height for extra distance.

Note:

Just as with the overhead cast, all the power is transmitted by themovement of the rod between the 10 and 2 o'clock positions. Once again at least two or three false casts will be needed to build up the momentum. Extra distance is achieved by generating greater line speed and by throwing a tighter loop of line on both the forward and back casts.

Presentation is improved by stopping the line just before it reaches the end of the 'shoot.' This has the effect of straightening the leader and causing a tighter turn-over of the flies. Accuracy and good presentation need not be lost when going all out for maximum distance.

Right: A short, accurate cast alongside a weed raft puts the fly within tempting range of the fish hiding deep under the canopy.

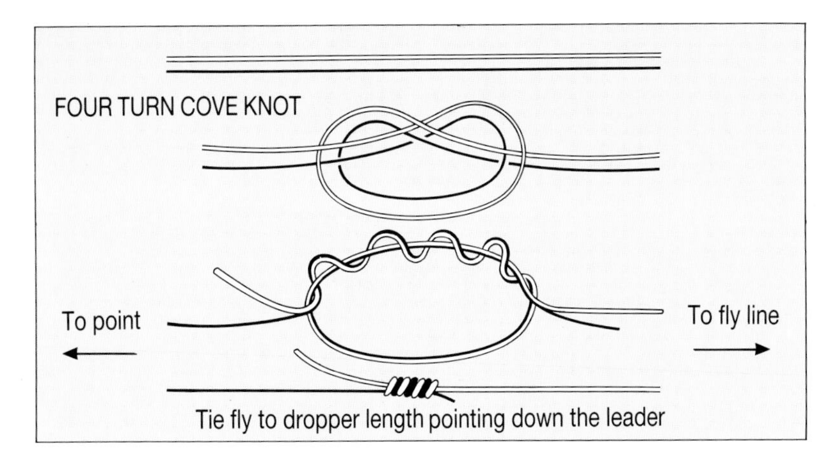

■ Cheetah

A hybrid species of trout, initially reared for stillwaters by crossing rainbows with American brook trout. The cross only achieved a very limited success, as the fighting qualities of the hybrid were not as good as either of the originals. Very limited availability.

■ Corixa

One of the important food items in the diet of most stillwater trout. It is aquatic – originating in the water – and prefers shallow (4-6 feet) rather than deep water. It is also known as water boatman but the Latin name is most often used. Imitations are relatively easy to tie, the important element being the silver rib or body, which simulates the air bubble that covers the body of the natural insect as it swims to and from the surface to replenish its air supply. The natural is most prolific in the months of September and October, when they migrate between stretches of water.

■ Cove Knot

Otherwise known as the Water Knot, this is arguably the best and safest knot for tying droppers into a leader system. Quick and simple to tie, this knot is vastly superior to the traditional Blood Knot, and is an absolute must when using low diameter nylon.

■ Cranefly

Also known as the Daddy, or Daddy Longlegs, this is one of the biggest insect food items of stillwater trout. It is terrestrial – which means it originates on land rather than in water – and is blown onto the water by the wind, most often in September and October. It is best imitated by flies like the Hopper, or the Wet Daddy which represents the waterlogged or drowning insect.

D

■ Daddy Longlegs

See Cranefly.

■ Damsel

Fly pattern and natural insect – both referred to by the same name. Damselflies are the beautiful electric blue or green insects that look rather like scaled-down dragonflies. They abound on most waters in the British Isles, both still and running, and appear throughout the summer, from late May onwards.

The nymph is a drab olive green colour, free swimming, and very active. They are copied by various artificial nymphs, some of which are close-copy while others are general suggestive patterns, like the Pheasant Tail. Damsel nymph patterns are often weighted, and are best fished in areas of reed beds and rushes.

■ Dapping

The art of Dapping an artificial fly on the water, ahead of a drifting boat. An ultra-lightweight, floss blow line is used, allowing the fly to be fished ten to 15 yards from the boat. See Boat Fishing.

■ Degrease

The removal of shine from leader material with a degreasing compound which helps the line penetrate through surface film. The compound is smeared on a pad through which the leader is drawn. Leaders become dirty by the adhesion of floatant from the fly, or by water debris. It is removed by substances based on a Fuller's Earth mix, sometimes with detergent or glycerin as extra components.

■ Diawl Bach

A Welsh fly pattern, literally translated to mean Little Devil. A simple pattern to tie, consisting of a ribbed, peacock herl body and a hackle fibre tail and beard. Deadly in the evening rise, this is a fly that has risen to fame on the Bristol waters, primarily as a suggestive Buzzer pattern. It needs to be fished very slowly, right on the top.

■ Dog Nobbler

A lead-headed lure with a long, wriggling tail of marabou feathers. The basic principle of all the Nobbler variants is that they are highly mobile lures with a prominent lead head for vertical travel. They are fished fairly fast, and their effectiveness relies as much on provoking aggression in the trout as anything else.

■ Double taper

A fly line which tapers evenly from the fine tip section though to the thicker centre of the line. It then tapers off evenly again to the end of the line. In effect, this gives two identically tapered lengths of fly line which can be reversed if the front taper is damaged.

Less popular than the Forward Taper, or Weight Forward profiles, DT lines are more widely used on running water where distance casting is not a major consideration. Modern WF lines now offer comparable presentation, and some Long Belly WF tapers are undoubtedly superior to the DT lines. See Fly lines.

■ Drag

The dragging motion of the fly line on the water surface. Any drag in running water is highly detrimental to presentation, but it also has great relevance to stillwater fishing, particularly in flat calm conditions. Drag is easily recognised by a wake-like ripple, coming from the line or fly.

■ Drift fishing

See Boat fishing.

A special dropper dispenser containing ready made-up casts.

■ Dropper

A fly that forms part of a cast of two or more flies. It also sometimes refers to the short length of nylon that attaches that fly to the main leader. Droppers are used in both river and lake fishing, when a team of flies is required in preference to a single pattern.

The leader is broken down into varying lengths, as the diagrams explain, the joins being made with Grinner or Water knots. Although teams of four flies can be used, the best presentation is achieved with three, or in some cases only two flies. The breaking strain of the nylon can be stepped down in stages, tapering progressively to the point fly. Alternatively, a level length of the same breaking strain nylon can be used.

■ Dry fly

See Flies.

■ Dubbing

General term used for various substances that form the body of a fly pattern. Typically, seal's fur is a traditional dubbing material, but is now being replaced by synthetic blends. The fur is dubbed to the fly, with individual fibres sometimes being picked out with a dubbing needle.

■ Dunkeld

One of the most ancient patterns originating from Scotland where it started life as a salmon fly. One of the great attractor patterns, it is just as effective in the smaller sizes for trout. It is a traditional style winged fly, best tied fairly slim and fished as part of a team.

E

■ Entomology

The study of fly life. It is virtually impossible to know and recognise all the insect orders that are relevant to fly fishing. But this complex subject can be simplified by breaking down the main categories such as midges and sedges.

The study of the principal food items and the subsequent copying of them at the tying bench is one of the most rewarding aspects of trout fishing, and one that should improve the catch rate.

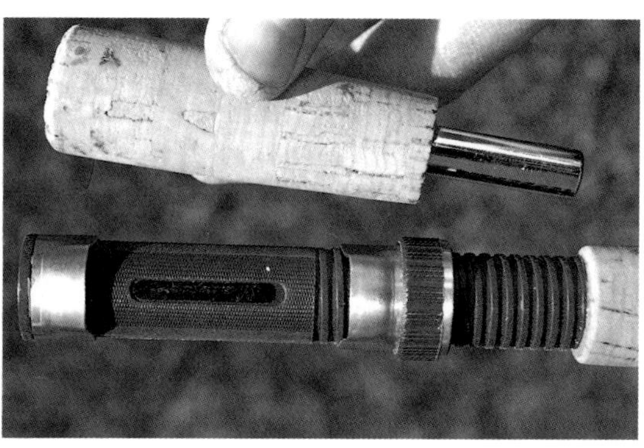

Extension butts are fitted to some trout rods for extra wrist support.

■ Extension butt

A short, removable extension which plugs or screws into the bottom of the rod. It is most often found on rods over 11 feet in length. Butts vary from two inches to around six inches and provide extra wrist support, but are not normally used in the casting action. Rods used for salmon fishing have integral butt sections, that are part of the rod itself and require a double-handed casting technique.

F

■ Figure - of - eight

Method of retrieving the line which imparts a very slow movement to the fly. The figure-of-eight retrieve can be very fluid and continuous in motion, or a series of tiny inch-long pulls. The line is held in overlapping coils in the retrieve hand or allowed to fall free to the ground.

■ Fish location

It is possible to narrow the odds on any water by following a logical sequence of actions in order to locate the fish.

1. On arrival at the Lodge or ticket hut, ask the bailiff or warden for advice. By the very nature of his job, he will know the most likely spots to fish, and should be able to give up-to-the-minute advice on flies.
2. Look in the lodge for the contour map, and identify areas of deep or shallow water. Look also for natural features like woods, hedges and such like. Then match this to the prevailing wind direction, which will tell you where to find either shelter or ripple, depending on the wind's strength.
3. Then look at the water itself, and see where most other anglers are heading. The bush telegraph works very well in angling circles, and news of stock fish or any hotspots will spread very quickly.
4. Once on your chosen stretch of bank, don't rush straight in to your wader tops and start thrashing. Take a look at the water surface. Is there any fly life visible, that may give clues as to what is hatching beneath the surface? Are there any terrestrial flies being blown onto the water? Are there any trees or bushes overhanging the bank, to provide both food and shelter for the fish? Is there a hedge, or a ditch, or a weed bed, or any other feature? Finally, you will be ready to start. Fish the margins first, and only then start to wade out to fish deeper water.

If all else fails, and there are absolutely no hints as the where to go or what to fish with, try the 'percentage approach.' This involves fishing for 30 minutes with a floater, then 30 minutes with the Intermediate and so on, until you have explored all the available depths.

Within those half hour sessions, try different retrieve rates, and then different fly patterns, using nymphs, attractors, and finally lures. Even if fish are not showing at all at the surface, there will often be a certain depth where they are feeding quite avidly, and only by investigating different water levels will you have a chance of finding them.

■ Flies

Artificial flies fall into many categories, but the main divisions are nymphs, traditional wet flies, attractors, lures, and dries.

Nymphs are tied to suggest or represent the nymphal stages of various insect orders. They are all fished sub-surface, almost always as the point or tail fly in a team. Recommended patterns to form the basis of a starter box of flies are: Pheasant Tail, Damsel Nymph, Stick Fly, Buzzer, Ombudsman, Hare's Ear Nymph.

Traditional wets include winged flies like the Dunkeld and Peter Ross. Some are semi-imitative, suggesting the outline or shape of a hatching midge or sedge, while others rely on their colour or speed of retrieve. Recommended: Dunkeld, Mallard and Claret, Invicta, Silver Invicta, Connemara Black, Peter Ross.

Attractors are smaller lure type flies, tied to place the accent on attraction rather than any particular food item. They feature strongly in competition fishing. Recommended: Soldier Palmer, Bibio, Viva variation, Peach Doll, Black Tadpole, Clifton.

Lures are larger flies, usually tied on long-shank hooks, with the emphasis on mobility and movement. Some imitate small fish fry, but most are designed to provoke an aggressive or territorial reaction from the fish. Recommended: Appetiser, Ace of Spades, Jack Frost, Missionary, Muddler, Whisky Fly.

Dry fly or Emerger patterns are fished in or on the water surface. Recommended: Grey Duster, Hopper, Emerger, Raider (Emerger variant), Shuck Fly, Legged Emerger.

Methods of presentation and retrieve vary, not only within these categories but also from one pattern to another. These factors are discussed within the entries for individual flies in this Encyclopaedia. In all cases, a Clinch knot is used to attach the fly to the leader.

Successful nymph tyings from the Ogborne vice. Left from top: Ombudsman, Pheasant Tail and Green Tag. Right: Hare's Ear, Damsel and Buzzer.

Traditional wet flies. Left from top: Dunkeld, Mallard and Claret and Invicta. Right: Silver Invicta, Connemara Black and Peter Ross.

Attractor flies are small lures favoured by competition anglers. Left from top: Soldier Palmer, Bibio and Viva variation. Right: Peach Doll, Black Taddy and Clifton.

Anatomy of the flies The terminology used to describe the various parts of flies can be misleading, particularly when changing from one category to another. For instance, a wing can be anything from four complete feathers on a lure to just a few wisps of feather fibres on a wet fly.

The diagrams illustrate most of these variations, showing how the standard terms are applied to each style of fly. But the one word that causes most confusion is probably hackle as this applies to many different uses of what is essentially the same item – a feather. To simplify things, the following should serve as a useful guide:

- A hackle is a single feather, usually taken from a hackle cape.
- Throat hackle (also called false hackle or beard hackle) consists of a small pinch of hackle fibres tied in beneath the head.
- Tail hackle is a pinch of hackle fibres tied in at the tail.
- Palmered hackles are full feathers, wound down the whole length of the body.
- Head hackles are wound around the head of the fly, as with most typical dry flies.
- Parachute hackles are tied in parallel to the hook shank, enabling the fly to settle absolutely flat on the water surface. Parachute hackles are normally tied with the use of a Gallows tool and a major feature of these flies is that they invariably land the right way up on the water, making significant improvements in presentation. But they are fairly difficult to tie and are not for the beginner to fly tying.

Right: **Lures intended to provoke an aggressive response.**
Left from top: Ace of Spades, Muddler and Appetiser.
Right: Jack Frost and Whisky.

Below: **Recommended dry fly patterns.**
Top: Black Hopper, Shuck Fly and Grey Duster.
Bottom: Emerger, Raider and Legged Emerger.

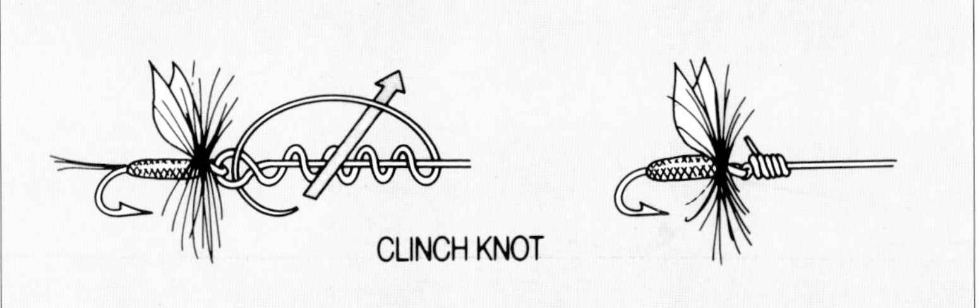

■ Floss

See Boat fishing; Dapping.

■ Floatant

A liquid or gel used to make either fly or line sit on the water surface. Most floatants have a silicone base, which is highly water-repellant. Popular brands include GINK and the long-established Mucilin. The golden rule is to apply floatant sparingly – too little is far better than too much.

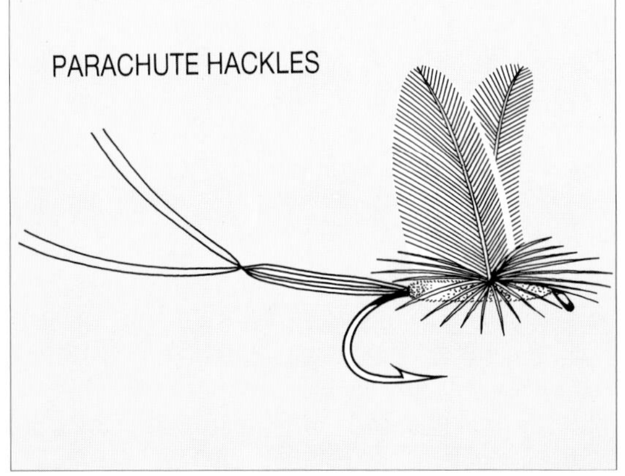

■ Fly box

Storage systems for flies are a matter of personal preference, but every angler needs a fly box. Some prefer a large reservoir storage box for the whole collection, and then use a small box for the day's selection. Others carry pocket sized boxes for each category of nymphs, lures and so on which is arguably more practical.

Fly boxes should display the flies clearly for quick reference and selection. They must also store them safely, in such a way that they will not rust, or become damaged by being squashed.

Inadequate storage can ruin an otherwise excellent fly collection, by damaging fibre and feather, spoiling wings and squeezing hackles out of shape. You will also need to choose between clips to retain the flies or a box lined with ethafoam. Foam is better for hook points, repelling water and avoiding rust.

■ Fly lines

It is easy to argue that the fly line is the most important single item of tackle, ranking even above the rod itself. Good casting, presentation and accuracy all depend on the quality of the line.

Every fly line is rated on the AFTMA scale so that it can be perfectly balanced with both rod and reel. The rating system also refers in part to the style of fishing for which each line is intended. The lightest lines are used for trout fishing in streams and the heaviest for the big salmon rivers. Most serious anglers require lines in at least three densities – floater, slow sink, and very fast (HI-D) sinking.

The full range embraces the following densities: floater, intermediate (sometimes called neutral density), slow sink, fast sink and very fast sink (Hi-D).

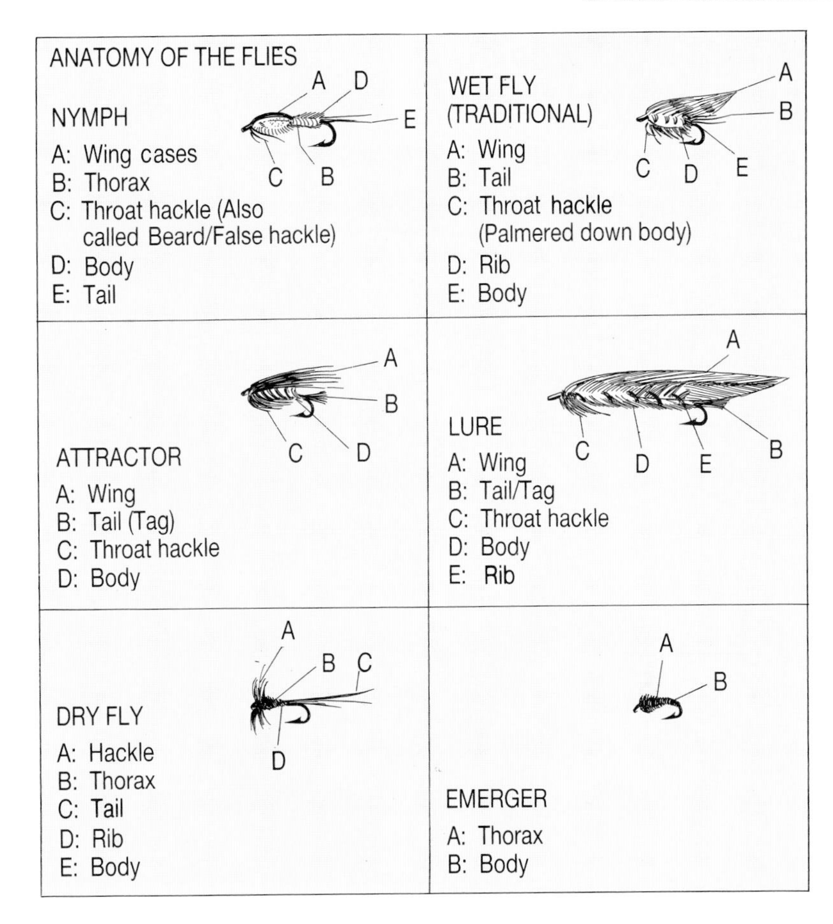

Some very fast sinkers are classed as lead core lines, and these have a comparable sink rate with the Hi-D.

The explorable depths possible with each line type are shown in the diagram. The line profile or taper like double taper and weight forward also contribute to presentation. DT lines are arguably better for river anglers, while WF tapers are preferred on lakes as greater distances can be achieved.

Below left: **Combination fly box with protected compartments for dry flies and ethafoam in the lid.**

Below: **Floating lines in pale colours are most popular.**

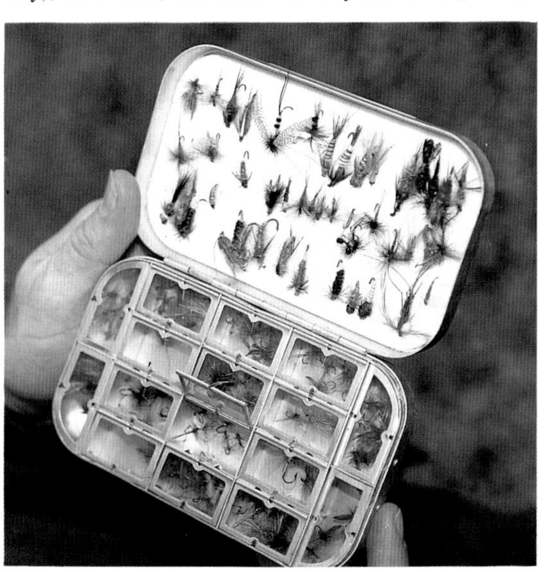

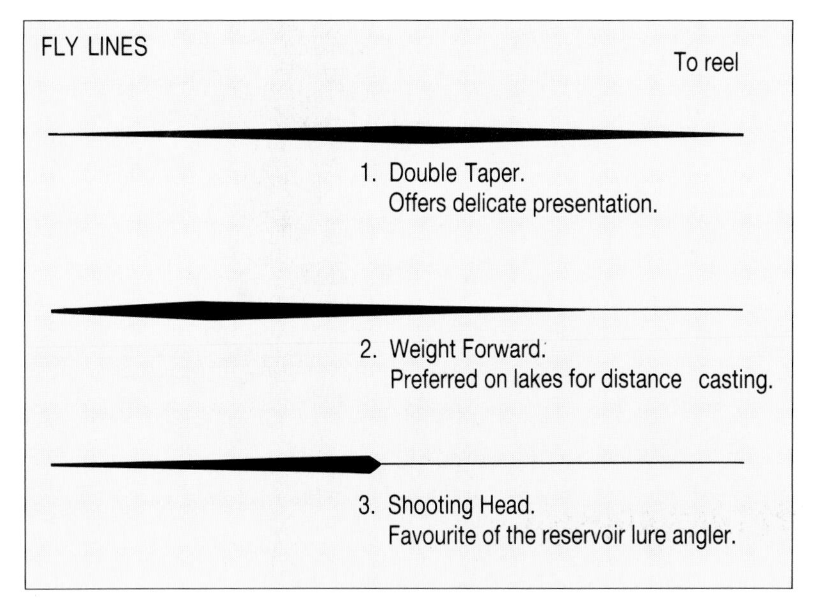

The longest casting lines are shooting heads. These are normally ten to 12 metres in length and are attached to a thin running line which is either thin braid, monofilament, or even flattened monofilament. This shoots through the rod rings with the minimum of friction, once the front ten metres have been aerialised. But distances are usually only achieved at the expense of presentation, and shooting heads are really only of significance to reservoir lure fishermen.

LINE SINK RATES

Exporable water in most practical fishing circumstances.

Floater — Surface

Intermediate — 1–6 ft

Slow sink — 2–8 ft

Fast sink — 3–10 ft

Hi-D or lead core very fast sinkers — 5–20 ft

Note: By using weighted nymphs the floating line can also explore same depths.

Before the line is attached to the reel, a bed of backing line must be wound on. The amount of backing varies according to the reel capacity, and also the style of fishing to be undertaken. In all cases, the backing is attached to the reel with an Arbor Knot, and then the line itself is joined to the backing with a nail knot. This gives total security.

Modern plastics are developing at such a rate that a new generation of fly lines has emerged incorporating the principle of low-stretch or non-stretch. These lines are claimed to cast better and give more immediate and positive contact with the fish. This is another area where personal preferences hold sway since some anglers actually like the cushion of a stretchy line finding it more forgiving of smash takes.

The colour of fly lines is rife with age-old arguments. Most sinkers are sold in darker colours, with which few people would argue. The debate really starts with the floaters. Should they be dark or light?

The argument that carries most weight is that the bellies of most fish-eating birds are white, and that this stands out less against the predominantly light background of the sky. Consequently, floaters that are either white, or in very pale colours, are by far the most popular.

■ Fly reels

One of the essentials in the flyfishing outfit where it's worth spending a little extra to buy a lot more. A well engineered reel can provide a lifetime of use, and will not jam or let you down at the crucial moment. Traditional fly reels, mostly in aluminium alloy, are relatively simple. They are machined in two parts, the spool and cage, and have an audible ratchet system. Some have an exposed rim, which permits fingertip control when playing a fish.

Geared reels offering faster line recovery are also available but it's at the expense of extra weight. Plastic and graphite reels have become popular recently but some anglers find that they do not possess sufficient weight to balance the rod in the hand.

Essentially, the reel's function is to act as a storage reservoir for the fly line. It must be fitted with a positive drag and be capable of retrieving the line smoothly, particularly if you prefer to play fish directly from the reel rather than by hand.

The drag control on some reels is little more than a cosmetic feature as it does little to increase tension on the line. Like the ratchet, it is more traditional than functional. Only those reels with an expanding drum brake system offer genuine drag control, and these are considerably more expensive.

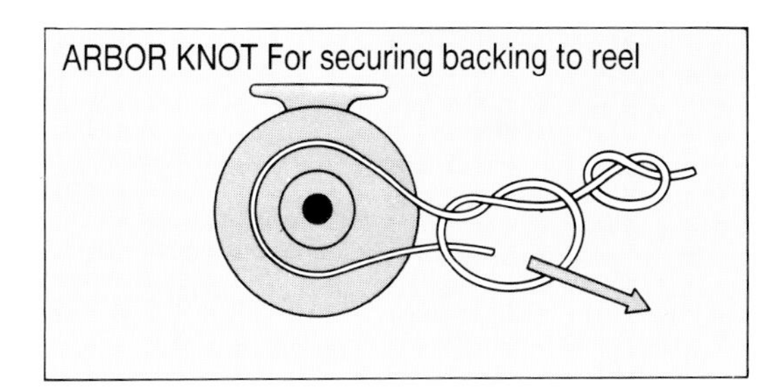

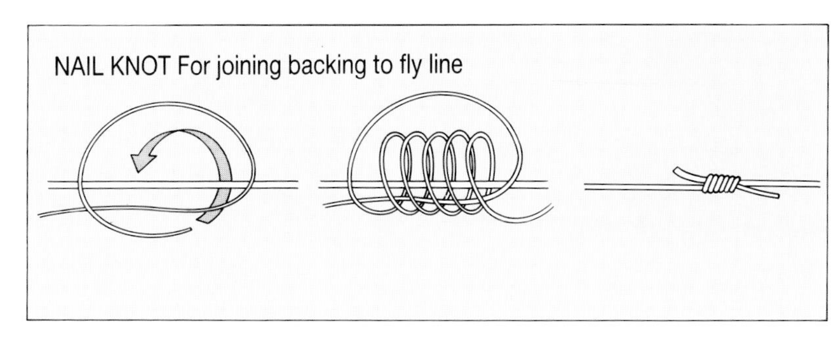

The best way of cutting down on reel costs is to buy two reels, and several spare spools. In this way you can house all your varying fly line densities, without the expense of buying four or five complete reels. Most reels offer very quick and easy spool release. This is a low-cost option that makes a lot of sense.

■ Fly tying

There is nothing quite like the thrill of catching a fish on a fly of your own design, or your own tying. The best fly fishermen are almost all fly tyers as well. Fly tying is a skill that requires a little tuition, and then a lot of practise.

The basic kit of a vice and simple tying tools is not expensive, and most tyers find that they build up a collection of fur, feather and materials over the years. Neither does a fly have to be perfect to catch a fish – some of the scruffiest and most untidy creations are among the best. Fly tying can be an exacting science, particularly when the object is to create an exact copy of an insect, but it can also be very relaxed. The basic lures and suggestive patterns do not require any great level of skill, and no-one should be deterred from fly tying because they think it to be too technical.

Fur and feathers are now available in greater profusion than ever before and many companies offer tyers an almost baffling choice.

The essential tools required by the fly tyer are a vice, scissors, bobbin holder, dubbing needle and hackle pliers. A base kit of materials comprises the following: hooks; tying silks; hackle capes of badger, red game, white and black; peacock, swan and ostrich herl; orange, black and white marabou plumes; pheasant tails and if possible a complete pheasant skin; packet of mixed colour wools; seal's fur substitute in various colours; flat, oval, silver and gold tinsels; various colours of chenille.

Aluminium fly reel and top selling model from the economical Dragonfly series.

G

■ Gallows tool

Device for tying parachute-style hackles, on dry flies. Very much a technique for advanced fly tyers.

■ Gold Ribbed Hare's Ear

A fly with a long pedigree, the origins of which go back to the 19th century. It is also a fly of many versions, either a nymph or dry, weighted or unweighted, large and small. In the smaller sizes it is a great Olive imitation when fished dry or wet, and is a much-loved pattern on the chalk streams. On stillwater the preferred sizes are 10 to 14, where it makes a good all-round suggestive nymph. The weighted version is an ideal single fly for stalking the small stillwater fisheries, when casting at individual trout.

■ Green Peter

This is an Irish pattern, originally tied to represent a big natural sedge of the same name. A big, bushy fly, best fished on the top dropper in a good wave. In Ireland, they often treat it with floatant and fish it right on the top, where it will even catch fish in Mayfly time.

It is not a fly for flat calms, and it has only marginal application on the bank. Essentially, it's a boat fishing pattern for days when the wind really blows. As such, it is probably one of the best wake flies ever.

■ Greenwell's Glory

One of the greatest dry fly patterns of all time, being a good copy of both stream and pond Olives. In fact, it works when virtually any Olives are hatching, often better than even a close copy pattern. Like all successful flies it has been copied and varied, and there are now Greenwell's nymphs, as well as traditional wets based on the original. The stillwater variation is a wet fly, with a heavier flat gold tinsel rib, ideal as middle dropper in a three fly team.

■ Grey Duster

This is one of the few patterns that comes even close to being effective when there is a hatch of Caenis on the lakes. It is a dry fly with a very light grey overall appearance, and the use of a stiff badger or grizzle hackle means that it really sits up on the water. This aspect can be further enhanced by tying the hackle parachute fashion which gives a better profile to the fly. An excellent pattern for both still and running water.

■ Grip

Term used for the cork rod handle often with the specification of its shape. These vary from the full scroll, to the half-scroll (also called half-Wells) and the Cigar shape. Most experts agree that the Half-Wells grip is the best all-round handle.

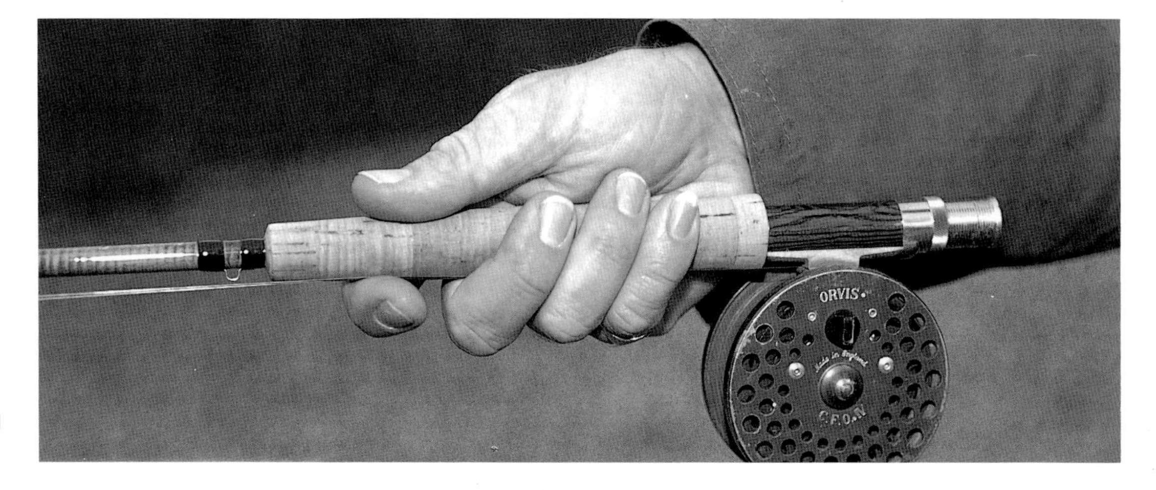

The classical grip with the thumb pointing along the top of the rod. In theory, this makes it easier to move the rod through the same plane on the forward and back cast.

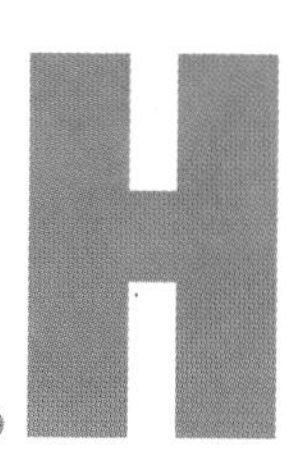

■ Hackle

A hackle is actually a single feather from a hackle cape, but the term hackling or to hackle is more common. Fly tying manuals describe various forms of hackle as they refer to a definitive part of the dressing of a fly.

Hackle feathers are used in various ways. A full collar hackle involves winding the feather round the hook one or more times – usually three or four – to form a stiff circle of fibres. Alternatively, a false hackle involves using a few fibres at the throat, perhaps to suggest legs. And then there is the palmered hackle, which is generally used as a body, over-ribbed with dubbing.

Hackles are obtainable in a host of different colours, both natural and dyed, and are one of the top five fly tying materials. They also vary in stiffness with cock hackles being very stiff compared to hen hackles which are soft and flowing, adding life to a fly. Hackle pliers are a useful tool for applying the hackle to the fly.

■ Hawthorn

Fly pattern and natural insect. Hawthorns are quite unmistakeable insects, appearing during the month of May, usually on warm and sunny days. They are predominantly black, with a pair of abnormally long legs trailing down behind them in flight. As their name suggests, they frequent Hawthorn bushes, but can be found on or near any hedgerow or clump of bushes.

They are terrestrial insects but often get blown onto the water by even a gentle breeze, and the trout really love them. The best artificials are fished semi-dry, sitting in rather than on the surface. The wings are tied spent, so that they lay in the film, with legs trailing well beyond the hook bend. Best sizes are l0s and 12s.

■ Hooks

There are specialist hooks for dry fly, wet fly, nymph or lure tying. The diagram right illustrates the main features.

Hooks are available in various different bends – round, Sproat and Limerick – but these are not nearly as important as wire gauge, which can have a fundamental effect on how the fly actually fishes. A fine wire hook is needed for dry fly work, with medium fine for wet flies and some nymphs. Other nymphs, particularly those designed to fish at some depth, need a heavy gauge wire to help them sink.

Larger lures and streamers are generally tied on heavier wire gauges for strength, as well as to help them 'swim' properly.

THE CHIEF HOOK TYPES

DRY FLY
1. Standard shank length
2. Fine wire gauge
3. Round bend

WET FLY
1. Standard shank length
2. Fine to medium wire gauge
3. Sproat bend

NYMPH
1. Standard and long shank
2. Medium to heavy wire gauge
3. Limerick/ Sproat/Round bend
(Including some tailor-made nymph shapes like the Partridge Living Nymph hook.

LURE/STREAMER
1. Long and Extra Long shank
2. Heavy gauge wire
3. Ring Eye (optional)
4. Round bend

I

■ Imitative flies

A category of artificial flies tied to specifically represent individual insects, or other items in the diet of trout.

■ Invicta

Another traditional wet fly that is equally at home on rivers and stillwaters. The Invicta is truly one of the all-time greats. On stillwaters it is said to represent or suggest the confused outline of a hatching sedge, and there is little doubt that the palmered hackle helps in this respect. But the Invicta works at any time, whether there are sedge about or not, so its appeal is far wider than this description would suggest.

It works well in a big wave, pulled along through the surface, and yet is just as effective when fished much deeper, as part of a team. It is a marvellous bob fly and in bigger sizes does well on the point. On the river, the Invicta is tied more sparsely, but the overall tying remains the same. Variations exist, most notably the Silver Invicta, but the original is still the best by far. One of the top 20 essential flies.

JK

■ Jack Frost

Lure pattern devised by Northampton expert Bob Church as a fish fry imitator. The combination of white marabou and a red tag and hackle provide all the trigger points for the trout, and the mainstay of the fly is its mobility – it has a lovely, pulsing motion, no matter how slow the retrieve.

■ Keeper ring

Small ring, usually just above the rod's cork grip, to keep the fly secure while the rod is not in action.

■ Knots

See Clinch (Flies); Cove or Water; Arbor (Fly Lines); Nail or Needle (Fly Lines).

L

■ Landing net

The net should have a diameter of at least 20 inches, or if triangular in shape, 20 inches across the arms. Some nets designed for bank fishing are not entirely suitable in the boat, as the handle can get in the way. Yet this same handle is vital on the bank where it doubles as a wading staff. It can even be a life saver in areas of soft mud, or submerged ditches.

Some bank anglers prefer a folding net, which clips to the belt for ease of carrying. This type is also more suitable in the boat.

■ Larva

Stage in the insect life cycle, usually between egg and pupa. For example, bloodworm is the larval stage of the midge.

■ Lift off

The act of lifting the fly line off the water's surface and the moment when many trout choose to seize the fly.

■ Line tray

Bowl-shaped device for storing line as it is retrieved, keeping it clear of the water or undergrowth. It clips to the belt, or front of the jacket. The tray usually has a net base or drain holes so water can seep away, and the line lays in open coils in the bottom. This helps in shooting the line greater distances, particularly when a shooting head is used.

■ Location

See Fish location.

■ Loch style

See Boat fishing.

■ Lures

See Flies.

■ Mallard and Claret

Among the best known of all lake patterns and one of the supreme wet flies of all time. The Mallard and Claret is a fly for all waters, seasons and conditions. Its shape suggests various insects in the hatching stage, but it is the overall outline that holds the key to success. Deceptively simple to tie, it should be fished as part of a team and is best in the middle dropper position.

It is useful as a bob fly, works well in windy or calm conditions, and is even good in the middle of the evening rise. It's not a question of knowing when to put one on, but rather of when to take it off.

■ Mending

The action of mending the fly line, normally associated with river fishing, to maintain direct touch with the flies. Wind and wave action on the line moves it across the water at quite a speed, causing a large bow in the belly of the line. This is mended by raising the rod to 45 degrees and throwing the half-loop back upstream or against the wind. This reduces the bow and produces a straighter line between the rod tip and flies.

■ Missionary

A long established fly that was one of the very first stillwater specials used at Blagdon 80 years ago. It is part lure and part attractor, with the teal wing definitely showing shades of the Peter Ross in its pedigree. It can be fished at all depths, on all density lines, but is particularly good in the summer months when the fish fry are about.

■ Montana

The Montana is an American nymph pattern that has found favour with brown and rainbow trout in Britain. It is normally fished weighted, and is very deadly on smaller stillwaters. Although normally tied on a long shank 10, it can also be scaled down to International size with no loss in its effectiveness. The predominantly black colour makes it especially useful in early season.

■ Muddlers

Not a single fly, but a whole family of patterns that make use of spun and clipped deer hair at the head. This forms a tight ball which is quite buoyant, allowing the lure to be fished right at the surface, although it is more commonly used with sinking lines at various depths. Smaller versions are used as 'wake' flies, as they make a great commotion when stripped fast through the surface.

N O

■ Needle Knot

See Fly lines.

■ Nymphs

See Flies.

■ Over-wintered

The term used for fish that have survived over the Close Season, implying their residential status in the lake or river.

P

Chris Ogborne steers a rainbow to hand on the top lake at Avington.

■ Pheasant Tail

The original was invented as a chalk stream fly by Frank Sawyer, but the pattern has been copied, changed and varied to the extent where it is scarcely recognisable today. Again, this is really a whole family of flies, tied to the same general principle of using a Pheasant Tail fibre body and wing case, and then varying the rib, thorax and hackles.

The original nymph is still superb on running water. Its lake counterpart is better on a longer shank hook and is an excellent imitator of pin fry, damsels, and even sedge. As a general suggestive pattern, it is without peer.

■ Playing trout

The way in which you handle a hooked fish will, to a certain extent, dictate the way in which it fights. Some favour a gentle touch, keeping the fish below the surface and gradually coaxing it to the net. Others prefer a spirited approach, with much aerobatics. This will tire the fish more quickly, but is more prone to danger. The main argument is whether to play from the hand, or from the reel. Most anglers these days favour the former, as you have greater control and can react more quickly to any sudden run.

■ Polystickle

A lure developed in the immensely strong Midlands school of fly fishing, essentially as a fish fry imitator. The slim profile is intended to be fished fairly fast, and like most fry patterns it is best in the surface layers. It is most definitely a seasonal fly, with its top months being late summer when the fry have reached a size of around two inches in length.

■ Priest

Simple device for despatching fish cleanly, with a sharp tap on the head. Most are functional, but some are of lead-filled hardwood which can be objects of some beauty. Often sold with an integral marrow scoop for examining the stomach contents. It should be a matter of conscience for all anglers to despatch their fish quickly and cleanly, without causing any undue suffering.

■ Pupa

The stage in an insect's life cycle between larva and adult. The most commonly known example is the midge pupa, or buzzer.

R

■ Rainbow trout

This species was introduced to Britain from America just after the turn of the century, and has thrived in all our waters since then. Without rainbows, pressure of angling would almost certainly have reduced the stocks of native browns to seriously low levels. Rainbows now form the backbone of stillwater sport across the country.

They grow almost twice as fast as browns, and are less temperamental to breed. Selective breeding has produced a high average size, to the extent where it is now possible to stock with two year old fish that weigh more than five pounds. Cock rainbows can be in poor condition in early season, so some fisheries now experiment with triploids – sexless fish that are in peak condition at all times.

Rainbows have a very poor record of natural breeding and without good fishery management they would certainly not thrive as they do. Selective breeding has also produced some monster fish, well into the 20 lb class.

■ Reels

See Fly reels.

■ Reel seat

The bottom part of the rod handle, either in wood or cork, shaped to hold the foot of the reel. This is secured by a winch fitting, or in the case of very light rods a sliding band.

■ Ripe fish

Term applied to a trout that is ready to spawn.

■ Rise forms

Fish feeding at the water surface often give clear indication of their presence in rise forms. These vary

Freshly caught rainbow from Avington lakes in Hampshire.

Single leg and snake rings.

from the full-blooded head and tail rise where virtually the whole fish leaves the water, to the barely discernible sip of a trout removing a surface insect with hardly any disturbance at all.

Recognising rise forms will give many clues as to the fish's feeding pattern and direction of travel. A methodical rise form, where the trout moves in a predictable line and takes regularly, indicates that it is feeding on one particular insect, probably pupae in the surface film.

A splashy rise is probably to adult insects, whereas a slashing rise in the shallows is usually associated with fry bashing.

■ Rods

While remaining a matter of personal choice, there are some quality factors that relate to all rods and these are worth remembering when in the tackle shop, and faced with a baffling array.

First, what fishing are you most likely to be doing? If you mostly fish from the bank, will the rod cast good distances, and with accuracy? Is it powerful enough for your requirements, and will it cast the range of line sizes needed for your style of fishing?

There are no great demands on boat rods for distance casting, but accuracy is possibly of greater importance. The rod must not be unduly tiring to use for a whole day, yet it must be versatile enough to lift the line over your boat partner's head on every cast.

The rings on a fly rod must guide the line cleanly and quickly from butt to tip with a minimum of friction. Any amount of friction reduces line speed and impairs casting. It is not commonly appreciated that the spacing of the rings is critical to rod design. The very best rods are designed for a specific casting action with a particular line weight and this is complemented by the right number of rings correctly spaced along the rod.

The butt or stripping ring is normally 30 inches along the butt section and takes a lot of pressure during the cast. For that reason, it is usually fitted with a ceramic insert for strength and good shooting performance. Intermediate rings are normally either of the ceramic type such as Fujis and Seymos or made from stainless steel or hard chrome.

Ceramics tend to have a small bridge and can be single or double leg. Metal rings are snakes which is effectively a half twist with the two legs being whipped to the rod. There is great debate as to whether ceramics offer superior casting performance but it is significant that the world's finest rods all use top quality snake rings. It is claimed that the reduced area of contact with the line results in better casting. The tip ring takes a great deal of the casting pressure like the butt and is again engineered from ceramic or hard chrome.

Graphite rods need not cost the earth – £50 to £70 will currently buy a very acceptable model. The most important thing is that it suits you, as an individual, and your own style of fishing. Many anglers require an armoury of rods, for different sorts of fishing, and here the choice is limitless.

There are specialist rods for dapping, long rods for the big lochs of Scotland and Ireland, and stiff uncompromising tools built only for long distance casting, or trolling.

S

■ Seal's fur

One of the most popular dubbing materials and an integral part of the dressing of many flies. Availability is now very restricted due to the ban on the import of seal products, but some dealers may still have supplies.

The fur is used in many dyed colours, and it has a wonderful natural sheen that no substitute can quite match. Substitutes are usually available, most notably the Antron fibre mixes, and these are very fair. Antron is often mixed with a natural fur, such as Hare or Rabbit, to make it look even more lifelike.

■ Season

There was a time, less than 20 years ago, when the trout season was clearly defined across the whole country. Typically, it would start on April 1 and finish on October 1, and that was more than enough for most fish – and fishermen. Nowadays, the season is less clearly defined. Most of the big reservoirs open around April 1 and close between October 15 and 30 , but there are a host of numerous local exceptions.

Many rivers do not start until May 1 and close on October 1. Some, most notably the smaller stillwaters, have no Close Season at all, remaining open as all-year-round fisheries. This is achieved by stocking only with rainbow trout, which unlike the brownies have no formal close season.

■ Sedge

Second only to the midges, sedge are the most prolific fly species on most stretches of water. Also known as caddis, they form a major part of the diet of most stillwater trout, and many fly patterns are tied to imitate or suggest the various forms of sedge.

The natural insects are easy to recognise. In pupa form, they create little cases for themselves, and these can be found under almost any rock or stone. When the time comes to hatch, they break out of the cases, swimming freely to the water surface where they hatch into adults. The adult insects are characterised by their roof-shaped wings, and also by long, forward-facing antennae. Most are about half-an-inch long, a size that is doubled if you count the antennae.

■ Selective feeding

Feeding pattern whereby trout become pre-occupied with one specific food item, often to the exclusion of all else.

■ Shrimp

Natural food item, and fly pattern. Shrimps abound in freshwater all over Britain, often in great numbers. It is also true to say that the trout consume them in equally great numbers.

Artificial shrimp patterns are much more popular on running water, and on the smaller stillwaters, where they can be used to 'target' individual fish. They should be well leaded, and fished very close to the bottom with a slow twitch retrieve.

■ Shuck

The empty case out of which the fly – usually sedge or midge – has hatched. After a big hatch of insects, you will often see literally thousands of shucks on the water.

■ Smash Take

The term applied to a full-blooded take, where the fish grabs the fly and rushes off, all in one movement. Because the take is so savage, anglers are often broken on the strike. It is difficult to cushion these takes, even with a very soft rod

■ Soldier Palmer

One of the all-time greats, and well up in the top 20 flies on stillwaters. The Soldier Palmer combines many trigger factors as it is pulled through the water surface, often forming a wake with its bushy palmered hackle. Although best on the top dropper position, it can be fished almost anywhere, and is sometimes even used with sinking lines to good effect. Many variations exist, but the basic original is still unbeatable and is normally the first choice for any day's loch-style fishing.

■ Spent fly

An adult insect that has completed its life cycle, and is shortly to die. Most spent flies display a splayed wing position on the water, as they struggle feebly with wings outstretched in the film.

■ Spinner

A stage in the life cycle of up-winged insects, most notably the Ephemerids (Mayfly-type flies). After the flies change from the nymphal aquatic stage and hatch into adults they go through a further transformation. The first is the Dun, and the second is the Spinner. The insect is then fully mature and can breed, finally falling exhausted to the water for the final, spent stage.

■ Spoon

The spoon, or marrow spoon to give its full name, is a simple device for examining the stomach contents of a fish, enabling the angler to assess the food items on which it is feeding. The marrow spoon is pushed into the trout's mouth, given a half-turn, and then withdrawn. The contents of its last meal will then be clearly visible giving vital clues to fly selection.

■ Stick fly

A classic standby nymph pattern for all stillwaters, and one of the best general representations of the caddis pupa. Normally tied with a green or red tag at the tail, the Stick Fly is very simple to tie, and even easier to fish. It can be inched along the bottom, pulled at mid-water, or stripped across the top – all methods catch fish, proving the total versatility of the fly. One of the top 20 patterns.

■ Striking

The action of lifting or striking as the fish takes the fly, to give a firm hook-hold. This is either achieved by smoothly raising the rod, pulling with the line hand, or by a combination of both. Striking should never be too sharp. It should be a positive fluid motion, allowing the rod to act as a cushion as the line tightens into contact. Too quick a strike will result in broken leaders, while too slow a reaction will give the fish time to reject the fly.

■ Stripping

The action of stripping the line back in a fast – or sometimes very fast – retrieve. Although normally associated with lure fishing, stripping is often required in the boat, particularly when drifting rapidly downwind in a big wave. This retrieve pattern leaves little room for subtlety, and contact with the fish can be very positive indeed.

■ Suggestive flies

A category of fly patterns designed to suggest insects or other food items, rather than to imitate them by close-copy.

T

■ Tackle bag

Few anglers can do without a tackle bag and it needs a good size. It must hold everything from reels and spare jackets through to a packed lunch and Thermos flasks. More importantly, it should hold all the gear in some sort of rational order, so that items like spare reel spools are easily found.

Tandem lure for use with heavy lines in the deeps.

■ Tail

Fly tails are an integral part of many dressings. They can be of fur, feather, wool or one of the many synthetic fabrics now available.

■ Tandem lure

One fly, but consisting of two hooks tied in tandem. Normally the rear hook, which is attached by either wire or nylon braid to the front hook dressing, is simply a kind of detached body. Some tandem lures are genuine 'doubles', like the original Worm Fly. Tandems have limited application, but can sometimes be responsible for an above-average fish.

■ Terrestrial flies

Any insect that originates on land, rather than water. During the season, many flies get blown onto the water and become major food items for the fish. The best known terrestrials are probably the daddies, hawthorns and ants.

■ Thorax

The neck and throat area of a fly, usually just behind the head. In artificial flies, the thorax can be made up of various materials, often overlaid with imitation wing cases.

■ Tiger trout

This is another hybrid strain of trout with mixed parentage. The cross features American brook trout, but is not found too often due to its somewhat dubious fighting qualities.

■ Tippet

Another term for the leader, or the leader material. In fact,tippet is something of an Americanism and the word is not nearly as common as cast or leader.

■ Triploid

These products of specialised breeding programmes are sometimes called hybrids but they are still 100 per cent rainbows. The process results from extensive research with hormone sex-reversal with fingerlings at some of the best fish farms in Britain. It produces trout that do not exhibit the early season problems of most cock fish which are often dark and gravid well into May and lack the fighting powers of hen rainbows.

■ Trolling

The art of trailing a fly or flies behind a boat, often at considerable depth. Not all fisheries allow trolling, and many anglers consider it to be an unsporting way of catching trout. But in lakes where it is permitted, it is often responsible for some big fish, which can brought up from the depths by the use of a very long trolling line.

■ Turn-over

The action of the unfurling fly line as the loop turns over at the very end of the cast. Correct turn-over is critical to good casting, particularly for accuracy and presentation. It can be greatly improved by the use of a braided butt leader. See Casting, page and Leaders.

■ Viva

The Viva is probably one of the best-known of all stillwater flies, yet it is difficult to categorise. It falls neatly between attractor and lure, having most of the advantages of each and few of the drawbacks. Its predominantly black colour makes it a good early season pattern, but really it is a genuine fly for all seasons, all waters, and all depths of fishing.

■ Waistcoat

Another genuinely essential accessory. The fishing waistcoat used to be considered the badge of office of all serious anglers. Nowadays, almost everyone realises the convenience that it offers, as it is perfectly feasible to carry tackle for a complete day's fishing in the pockets.

Most waistcoats actually have more pockets than most of us need, and there is room for fly boxes, spare spools, leader dispensers – in fact the list is endless.

■ Walker's Mayfly

A large mayfly nymph pattern invented by that legend of our sport, Richard Walker. In fact, there is an adult mayfly pattern that carries the same name, but it is the nymph that most people recognise in the first instance. It can be fished weighted or otherwise, and is just as good on running water as it is on still. Neither is it restricted to mayfly time, proving the genuine versatility of the pattern as a year-round suggestive fly.

■ Water Knot

See Cove.

A fishing waistcoat holds everything you need for a day's trout fishing.

■ Wet flies

Category of fly patterns, usually associated with the whole series of winged traditional patterns. But the term wet flies will include patterns for still and running water, both winged and spiders, as well as some that might also be called attractors.

■ Whisky fly

A very bright hair-wing fly that is most definitely in the lure category. Originally designed to be fished fast in the surface, it is now known to be effective at almost any depth, with the key feature undoubtedly being the hot orange colouration. This is not an early season fly, being best in the months of July and August.

■ Wind knot

The term applied to almost any knot or tangle that occurs while casting. Wind knots seriously reduce the strength of the leader, and on windy days you should check for them at regular intervals. They can be untied, but it is always better to re-tie the complete leader, or at least the affected section of leader.

■ Wind lanes

A phenomenon that occurs on most waters, in a variety of wind conditions. The acceptable theory is that they are caused by the confluence of surface currents or water movements, but whatever the reason there is no doubting their importance. These long strips of calm in an otherwise rippled surface are like a magnet to all types of fish, and they should always be fished very thoroughly. Boat anglers in particular find them extremely productive, but they are just as relevant when they are reachable from the bank.

In a wind lane, fish can see the food item more clearly, without the confusion of background ripple, and that's probably the real secret. In fact, they probably do not contain any more food than the surrounding rippled area – it is just that the calm backdrop makes it easier for the fish to see.

■ X – rating

There was a time when leader breaking strain was given in a series of X ratings, such as 3X. But this has always been a source of confusion, and the vast majority of anglers prefer to quantify their nylon by its breaking strain. Despite the fact that leader diameter is of far more importance than its breaking strain, it seems that most anglers have more confidence in the 'poundage' system.

INDEX

Page numbers in *italic* refer to the illustrations

CW00341002

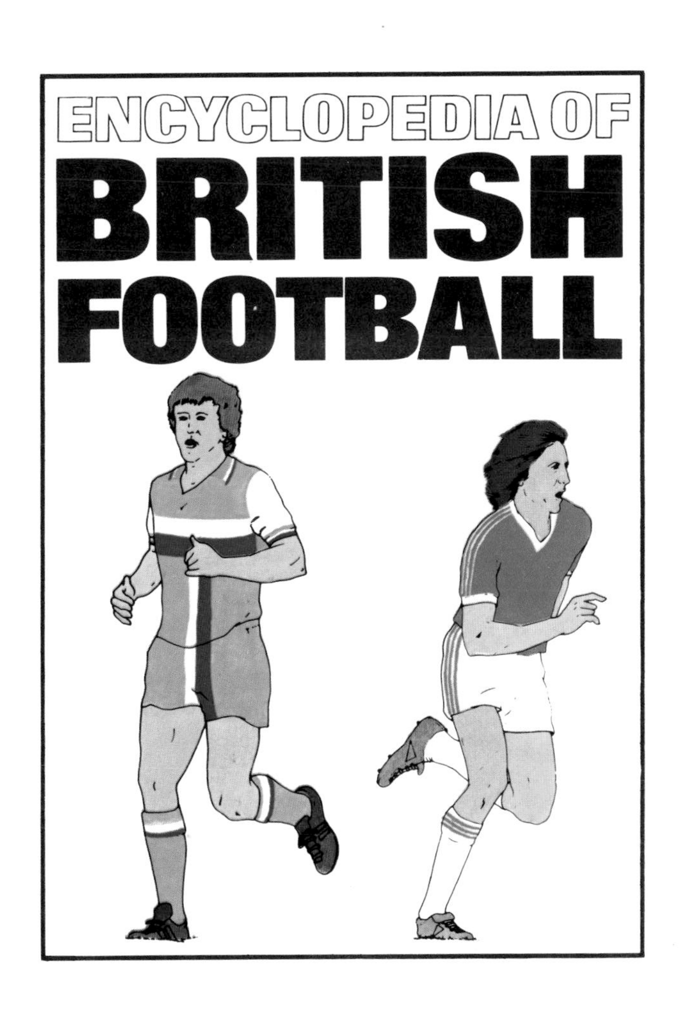
ENCYCLOPEDIA OF
BRITISH
FOOTBALL

ENCYCLOPEDIA OF BRITISH FOOTBALL

Phil Soar · Martin Tyler

WILLOW BOOKS
Collins
8 Grafton Street, London W1
1983

Endpapers: *'If Spurs had bought Batman and Robin they could scarcely have created more interest,' said Brian James of Keith Burkinshaw's purchase of Ossie Ardiles and (seen here) Ricky Villa. But even Burkinshaw could not have foreseen the heights and depths of two FA Cup wins, Villa's amazing final goal against Manchester City and the repercussions of the Falklands War.*
Title page: *Kenny Dalglish, centre-point of Liverpool's staggeringly successful spell in the late 1970s and early 1980s. Now Scotland's most capped player he scored the winning goal in the 1978 European Cup final in his first season with the club.*
Right: *Asa Hartford and Brian Kidd, key figures in the highly-rated Manchester City side of the late 1970s. A disastrous second flirtation with Malcolm Allison and the collapse of the transfer market left City deep in trouble just a few short years later.*
Contents page: *Brian Clough, the only man to challenge Liverpool's domination of the 1970s. With Derby County and Nottingham Forest he equalled Herbert Chapman's feat of managing two separate clubs to the League Championship, and then went on to the decade's most unexpected success when unfancied Forest won two European Cup finals.*
Page 8: *David Webb's 'Golden Shoulder' deflects a Hutchinson throw-in over the line to win the 1970 FA Cup final replay for Chelsea. The 2-2 draw with Leeds at Wembley was the first Cup final to fail to be decided there and the replay was the first final to be held outside London since 1915, when the Wartime final also took place at Old Trafford. In 1915 Chelsea had lost that final 3-0 to Sheffield United; in 1970 they beat another Yorkshire side, Leeds United, 2-1.*

Edited by Phil Soar and Martin Tyler

Written by Jonathan Culverhouse, Phil Soar, Martin Tyler and Richard Widdows

Designed by Jackie Tulloch

Artwork by Paul Buckle

© Marshall Cavendish Limited 1971, 1972, 1973, 1974, 1977, 1979, 1982, 1983

British Library Cataloguing in Publication Data

Soar, Phil
Encyclopedia of British football.—4th ed.
1. Soccer—Great Britain—History—Dictionaries
I. Title II. Tyler, Martin.
796.334'0941 GV944.G7

ISBN 0-00-218049-9

Some of this material was first published in the partwork *Book of Football*

First printing by William Collins in 1974
First updating and revision 1977
Second updating and revision 1979
Third updating and revision 1983

Printed and bound in Hong Kong by Dai Nippon

Introduction

As Sir Walter Scott said nearly two centuries ago, life is but a game of football: for so many people football is not just a sport, more a preoccupation, and for everyone who feels that way, young or old, the Encyclopedia of British Football is an invaluable companion. Here, in a unique pictorial history, are all the facts and figures that even the most fanatic follower could ever need.

Encyclopedia of British Football was the first publication ever to reproduce all of the English and Scottish tables since the Leagues began. Add to that each and every club's complete Cup and League history, a unique record of every single international ever played by each of the Home Countries, a history of all the major competitions, and you have an unequalled storehouse of football fact and minutae.

Yet again we have brought all of the records relevant to the domestic and international game up to date with season 1982-83, correcting errors, introducing new features and covering all of the game's recent developments in a whole series of new comprehensive articles. We hope you enjoy reading them as much as we enjoyed putting them together.

Phil Soar　　　　Martin Tyler

Contents

THE ORIGINS OF FOOTBALL

NOBODY INVENTED FOOTBALL. As soon as an Egyptian, or Assyrian, or Chinese had first kicked or bounced or rolled an object to a companion the seeds of football had been sown. Once the war-games of Greek youths had been adapted to include a ball, all the principles of the modern game had been established—a conflict in which one crowd of combatants tries to force the ball through the territory and into the base guarded by an opposing crowd of combatants. It really is as simple as that, and always has been, whether Association or Rugby, American or Gaelic, Australian Rules or the Eton Wall Game.

Football is, at its simplest, so instinctive and attractive a pastime that it is not surprising to find it growing at numerous points quite independently. Both in China and in ancient Mexico they played a sort of target football, kicking or heading a ball with immense skill through holes in silk screens or through rings set high in a wall. These were games played at royal command, for military training, or at religious festivals. To win a casket of gold and jewellery was not unknown, though the equivalent of the loser's medal was often even more striking—occasionally the losing team was executed on the spot!

Acrobatic artistry and delicate skills still survive in a charming game played in Burma, where groups of men kick a wicker-work ball between them, the ball never stopping, never touching the ground: there are no goals, no winners or losers—just applause and appreciation of the grace and ball control involved.

The war-games of the Greeks were very different in spirit; they were adapted, as so many things Greek, by the empire-building Romans and were eventually spread throughout the Empire under the name of *harpastum*: two teams on a rectangle of land trying to kick or carry a ball over their rivals' base line.

Inevitably, the game came to Britain. The Britons and Celts adapted it in their own way—there is the legend that the first game played among the Anglo-Saxons was a victory celebration, using the severed head of a defeated Dane as a ball. And so British football evolved in a form that was barely to change for 1,500 years. Every Shrove Tuesday at Ashbourne, in Derbyshire, they still play the ferocious cross-country village game that some historians have traced back as far as the year AD217. Conflicts of this sort, between hordes of players representing two neighbouring villages or, as in the case of Ashbourne, two halves of the same town, were the norm until the call for stricter and more uniform rules came towards the end of the 18th century.

The Normans, too, had a tradition of football, also adapted from the time of the Roman occupation, which they brought over with them. And within 100 years of William the Conqueror's arrival football had taken root both as a pastime among the Norman ruling elite and as a rampage among their subjects.

In medieval times the game developed very slowly, if at all. Skills took second place to vigour, and no one seems to have been anxious to establish real rules. Twice, between 1280 and 1325, it

The oldest annual match which is still played is held in the Piazza Della Signoria in Florence. It dates, like this print, from the 16th century, though the town represented here is probably Siena.

is recorded that footballers died through falling on their daggers; it is not recorded whether this was done on purpose after conceding a goal, nor whether the daggers were worn as part of the conventional football kit of the day, for discreet use in the thick of the scrimmage.

Indeed, the only rules that the game did attract at this time were those expressly forbidding it. Edward III, Richard II and Henry IV, all of them concerned with maintaining a strong army against the French, each decreed that football was bad training for battle and that, in any case, its popularity was getting in the way of regular archery practice. The game was banned time and again, both in England and Scotland, without any lasting effect. Then, as the years passed, the game became a natural target for the killjoys; the Puritans furiously condemned the 'bloody and murthering practice'; one Philip Stubbs, in proclaiming that the end of the world was just round the corner, put a fair measure of the blame on 'football playing and other develishe pastimes' on the Sabbath. But the game survived—as 'football' in the English towns and villages, as 'hurling' in Cornwall, and 'knappan' in parts of Wales. It became accepted as part of the English scene on holidays and at festival time.

It was about now that football received the shot in the arm that was eventually to make it the most popular game in the world. The early 19th century saw a tremendous upsurge in education for the privileged; it was the era of the public schools, whose teaching methods impressed the aristocracy and the new industrialists alike. The boys at these schools had little time and even fewer facilities for the more extravagant pastimes of country-house living—no riding, no fishing, no hunting, no horse-racing. But they quickly adapted the principles of the town and village games—all they needed were two teams and a ball—to the fields or the yards round their school buildings; and they played these games at every opportunity.

And, conveniently for the game, this passion among the boys for the rough, invigorating games of the 'lower classes' coincided with the triumphant peak in the career of that great educationalist, Dr Thomas Arnold of Rugby School. Arnold himself was not a great supporter of the games cult but, seeing that the boys were determined to organize and play games, he brought discipline and a sense of purpose into their pursuit, just as he had done into every other facet of school life. Arnold's followers, and there were many of them, accepted the idea of organized games with enthusiasm. So suddenly, after centuries of official censure and puritan disapproval, people were actually *encouraging* boys to play football!

There was no stopping the game now. In every great public school football of one kind or another became part of the tradition. The rules, as yet, varied drastically from school to school. There was no such thing as the inter-school match, so there was absolutely no need for any one school to play the game to anything like the same rules as the school in the next county. Some of the games that evolved were bizarre in the extreme. At Charterhouse, 20-a-side matches were played in the only space available—a long brick cloister, open at one end, blocked in by a wall at the other: no long kicks were allowed, no handling the ball, no passing forward—dribbling was the order of the day. At Harrow, where the game had to be adapted to the veritable bog that the winter rains formed in the fields below the hill on which the school stands, a big heavy ball was needed, and rules that encouraged movement. The ground was comparatively big—some 150 yards by 100 yards, and high kicking and catching the ball (though not carrying) were permitted.

At Eton, of course, the Wall Game flourished—on an extraordinary pitch 120 yards long and just six yards wide, with, in the early days, 18 or 20 on each side; the goals were a tree at one end and a garden door at the other; progress upfield was painfully slow and very muddy, tries (or 'shies' as Etonians called them) were rare, and converted goals much rarer. The Wall Game still appears to give a lot of Etonians and a lot of newspaper photographers pleasure at the annual St Andrew's Day match; but only two goals have been scored this century!

And at Rugby, too, football was steeped in tradition even before Dr Arnold—a wide-running game with plenty of space, long scrimmages, 'offside' given against a player getting in front of the ball, handling allowed only for a fair catch . . .

Until, that is, the afternoon in 1823 when a Manchester-born boy called William Webb Ellis, later a clergyman and later still to die in obscurity in the South of France, broke all the conventions by catching the ball, tucking it under his arm, and running with it to the opponents' goal line.

This little act of defiance, which might very easily have been shrugged off and forgotten, caused a lot of hard thinking at Rugby School. Eventually, 'running in', as it was called, was accepted into their rules and, in time, led to the basic distinction between the two codes of football.

While boys were still at school, the fact that they played to a strange set of rules hardly mattered. When, however, they left for the universities or for business in the provinces, it became clear that if they were to continue playing football they were going to need a universal set of rules, acceptable to all teams. Up until the 1850s, two teams at, say, Oxford, would only be playing on familiar ground if every player had been to the same school; as things turned out, a major game was often preceded by a long correspondence and lengthy argument about the conventions. Was handling to be allowed? How many players on each side? How long should the pitch be? How wide the goals? Would carrying the ball be permitted? ('Yes', would say all the Old Rugbeians; 'No', would say almost everyone else.) And even when the game got under way, confusion and protests would necessitate long midfield conferences between the two captains.

In time it became usual for the Rugby men, and their small but growing company of followers from other schools, to play on their own, and for the others, from Westminster, Charterhouse, Shrewsbury, Harrow and so on, to come to some compromise over the rules of the 'dribbling' game.

Few of these early codes of rules have come down to us intact, but snatches from them give a clear idea of the patterns of the early game, and in particular how boring it must have been to stand in the cold and watch.

In almost every case the game was won or lost (if indeed any goals at all were scored in the one, or two, or three afternoons laid aside for it) in the interminable, seething scrimmage. The aim of the game was, by dint of skilful footwork, to dribble the ball solo through the opposing team, who would all gang up in a scrum to defend. If one man was tacked (and tackling was usually unceremonious and often brutal), another would gather the ball and perform his own solo run until possession was lost and the opposition forwards started the same process in reverse.

The first serious attempts at laying down the rules of football went some way to improving it as a spectacle. In 1848, at Cambridge, 14 men representing Eton, Harrow, Winchester, Rugby and various other public schools, after a seven-hour session, produced the so-called 'Cambridge Rules'—rules that were adapted and tightened up twice in the 1850s.

Goals were awarded for balls kicked between the flag posts and under the string; goal kicks and throw-ins were given much as today (though throw-ins, taken with one hand only, might travel as far as a kick); catching the ball direct from the foot was allowed, provided the catcher kicked it immediately (no running with the ball, despite that delegate from Rugby); and there was a much more workable offside law—a man could play a ball passed to him from behind, so long as there were *three* opponents between him and the goal.

The game was now established on a common foundation. Competition was possible, and winning became important. By 1855 rules like these were the basis of inter-university matches, and the legendary inter-school matches of public school fiction had begun to blossom.

Amid all this activity in the leisurely atmosphere of the universities and the public schools there emerged, almost out of the blue, the first recognizable 'football club'.

The old, hard, ruthless town football had been played in Sheffield for many years, but sometime in 1854 or 1855 (though the oldest existing rulebook is dated 1857), after Sheffield Cricket

The early forerunners of modern day matches were timeless brawls between neighbouring parishes or villages; this is a representation of one around the 15th century. The term 'Derby' comes from an annual match played in that town between the parishes of St Peter's and All Saints and last contested on Shrove Tuesday 1846.

Club had inaugurated a new ground at Bramall Lane, one of the cricketers—William Prest—and some friends from the Collegiate School in Sheffield formed the Sheffield Football Club.

They wrote a constitution and a set of rules (not unlike the Cambridge Rules, though a bit rougher—pushing with the hands was allowed) and specified that every member should have two caps—one red, one dark blue—to distinguish the teams in games played among themselves.

This small band of old school acquaintances, with no apparent encouragement from the gentlemanly scholars from 'down South', had laid the foundations of football in the North of England. Within five years there were 15 different clubs in the Sheffield area, and an 1861 match between the two great local rivals, Sheffield and Hallam, drew a gate of 600 spectators. (Seventy-five years later, at that same Bramall Lane, Sheffield United crammed in 68,000-plus for a Cup-tie.)

Meanwhile, back among the law-makers, rules and regulations were being hammered out, published, revised, re-negotiated and re-published in a thoroughly confusing burst of activity. At Uppingham School in Rutland, where football was distinguished by an enormously wide goal (with, incidentally, a cross-bar rather than tapes between the posts), another great Victorian educationalist, J. C. Thring, issued the rules for what he called *The Simplest Game*. They were indeed very simple, and provided a very straightforward game—no violence, no kicking at the ball in the air, nobody allowed in front of the ball, etc. They were unadventurous, but they provoked great interest, and a number of schools agreed to adopt them.

And at Cambridge, things were moving again. The rules for a match between Cambridge Old Etonians and Cambridge Old Harrovians, in November 1862, specified 11-a-side, an umpire from each side plus a neutral referee, goals 12ft across and up to 20ft high, an hour and a quarter's play only, and the three-man offside rule. These rules were said to have worked well; in the following year they formed a vital part of the revised Cambridge Rules and, in the following months, those of the newly formed Football Association.

In the month of October 1863 football, in the South at least, came of age. The eager young gentlemen of Cambridge University issued their definitive set of rules, but almost at once the control of the game passed from the scholars to the clubs, where it has remained ever since.

The formation of the Football Association was bitter and often ill-tempered, and a certain stubbornness on both sides ensured that the split between the Rugby code and the dribbling code became too wide ever to be mended. The real divergence was not over running with the ball, but over 'hacking'. Rugby men felt it was manly and courageous to tackle an opponent by kicking him on the shin; the dribbling men did not, and voted it out. The Rugby men called the dribbling men cowards, and walked out of the Football Association for ever.

In 1863, football was still far from the game we know today. Every player was still allowed to handle the ball, and when he caught it he could 'make a mark' and so win a free kick; there was, in the first FA laws, a 'touch-down' rule, allowing a free kick at goal after a ball had been kicked over the opposing goal line and touched down (the Rugby 'try', in fact); there was still disagreement over offside, and the FA started off with the Rugby-style 'no one interfering with play in front of the ball' rule.

But within a few years soccer rejected all the distinctive Rugby conventions. Soon only the goalkeeper could handle the ball, the touchdown was abolished, forward passing became the essence of good attacking play and of good entertainment for the spectators. By the early 1870s, England and Scotland were playing internationals and the FA Cup had begun its distinguished and glamorous career. It was only a matter of time before football was to become the most popular pursuit that Britain—and the world—had ever known.

THE BEGINNINGS OF LEAGUE AND CUP

THE MOST IMPORTANT date in the history of football is 26 October 1863. That was the day on which the Football Association came into being and the point at which 'modern' football can be said to have begun.

In a sense, the most interesting thing about that meeting in the Freemasons' Tavern, Great Queen Street, Holborn, was not the teams that were represented but those that were not. There was, for instance, no one from the main provincial centres of the game—Sheffield, Glasgow and Nottingham—nor, more surprisingly, from Cambridge, where the first formal laws had been drawn up in 1848. As a result it was 20 years before the whole country accepted uniform procedures.

The thirteen laws that were eventually approved are indicative of the origins of the men who drew them up. They were, basically, the laws of the game as played at Harrow and by the teams of Harrovian Old Boys—particularly No Names (of Kilburn) and Forest School, who became the famous Wanderers in 1864.

The Blackheath Club, which played to the rules of the game at Rugby, had broken away by the end of 1863, though that alternative game did leave behind it one significant innovation—the more precise name for its competitor. The story may not be true, but one Charles Wreford-Brown, who later became a notable official of the FA, was asked by some friends at Oxford whether he would join them for a game of 'rugger'. He refused, claiming that he was going to play 'soccer'—evidently a play on the word association. The name caught on.

There was no immediate attempt by the new Football Association to integrate all the various other codes around the country. Not until Charles Alcock, who had been at Harrow from 1855 to 1859, joined the committee did some sort of impetus build up. The rigorous offside law, basically that still employed in rugby, was revised when Westminster and Charterhouse schools joined, but the most important step was the arrival of Yorkshire representatives in 1867.

Yorkshire is the home of the oldest of all football clubs—Sheffield FC. The first written evidence of the club's existence dates from 1857—though it may have been founded by Old Boys of the Collegiate School in Sheffield as early as 1854. By the later date, however, it had its own rules and its secretary approached the newly formed FA in 1863 with a view to integration. The FA did not even bother to reply.

The north Midlands generally was to the provinces what Harrow was to the Home Counties. It was here that the first of the present League clubs originated—Notts County (often referred to as Nottingham before 1882) in 1862, Nottingham Forest in 1865 and Chesterfield in 1866. There have been suggestions that a Stoke club was established by a group of Old Carthusians in 1863—but 19th century records give the date as no earlier than 1867.

The first hint of a game that the modern supporter might be able to identify with was the Notts County–Nottingham Forest clash of 1866. The only score of the day came at the end of a 'negative scoreless afternoon' (shades of the present day) when 'there was a sort of steeplechase across the goal-line and over the grandstand railings ... where W H Revis, of the Forest, touched down. The place-kick, 15 yards at right angles from the goal-line was taken by the same player.' The ball had merely to go between the posts as there was no cross-bar.

As can be deduced, the Nottingham game was a hybrid, relying on a mixture of Rugby, Sheffield and London rules, but with the expansion of the FA to accommodate Sheffield uniformity was not far away. As Alcock himself wrote, '... the objects of the Association are to still further remove the barriers which prevent the accomplishment of one universal game.'

By 1870 Alcock, now secretary of the FA, had established

£10 REWARD.

STOLEN!

From the Shop Window of W. Shillcock, Football Outfitter, Newtown Row, Birmingham, between the hour of 9-30 p.m. on Wednesday, the 11th September, and 7-30 a.m., on Thursday, the 12th inst., the

ENGLISH CUP,

the property of Aston Villa F.C. The premises were broken into between the hours named, and the Cup, together with cash in drawer, stolen.

The above Reward will be paid for the recovery of the Cup, or for information as may lead to the conviction of the thieves.

Information to be given to the Chief of Police, or to Mr. W. Shillcock, 73, Newtown Row.

FOOTBALL.—Last evening a meeting of the captains or other representatives of the football clubs of the metropolis was held at the Freemasons' Tavern, Great Queen-street, Lincoln's Inn-fields. Mr. Pember, N. N. Kilburn Club, having been voted to the chair, observed that the adoption of a certain set of rules by all football players was greatly to be desired, and said that the meeting had been called to carry that object into effect as far as practicable. Mr. E. C. Morley (Barnes) moved, and Mr. Mackenzie (Forest Club, Leytonstone) seconded, the following resolution:—"That it is advisable that a football association should be formed for the purpose of settling a code of rules for the regulation of the game of football." Mr. B. F. Hartshorne said that though he felt it was most desirable that a definite set of rules for football should be generally adopted, yet, as the representative of the Charterhouse School, he could not pledge himself to any course of action without seeing more clearly what other schools would do in the matter. On the part of the Charterhouse he would willingly coalesce if other public schools would do the same. Probably, at a more advanced stage of the association, the opinion of the generality of the great schools would be obtained. The chairman said every association must have a beginning, and they would be very happy to have the co-operation of the last speaker at a future meeting. The resolution for the formation of the association was then put and carried. The officers were elected as follows:—Mr. A. Pember, President; Mr. E. C. Morley (Barnes), Hon. Secretary; Mr. F. M. Campbell (Blackheath), Treasurer. The annual subscription was fixed at one guinea, all clubs being eligible if of one year's standing, and to be entitled to send two representatives to the yearly meeting, to be held in the last week in September, when the rules would be revised, and the general business arrangements carried out.

ST. GEORGE'S-IN-THE-EAST.—The arrangement which has been for some time past in progress for an ex-

unofficial internationals between England and Scotland (or rather a team of Scots resident in London) and a regular London-Sheffield encounter. The growing competitiveness of the game encouraged him to add another suggestion in 1871—a challenge cup 'for which all clubs belonging to the Football Association should be invited to compete'. The idea was unashamedly based on the interhouse knock-out competition at Harrow—the winners being referred to as the 'Cock House'.

The holders of the new trophy, known as the FA Challenge Cup, were to enjoy two invaluable advantages—they were exempt until the Final and they could choose where it was played. Fifteen clubs entered in the first year, though only twelve competed. Of these, two, Maidenhead and Marlow, have entered in each and every subsequent year. The real attraction was the appearance of Queen's Park, the Glasgow side that had been formed in 1867 and had still not had a single goal scored against them. They drew with the Wanderers, at the Oval, in the semi-final but could not afford to return for a replay and the Wanderers went on to beat Royal Engineers in the Final at the same venue. The only goal of the match was scored by Matthew Betts, playing under the assumed name of A H Chequer—meaning that he was a member of the Old Harrovian side Harrow Chequers—and 2,000 people paid the not insubstantial sum of one shilling to watch. Captain of the Wanderers was one Charles W Alcock.

The Wanderers won again the following year, beating Oxford University at the early hour of 11 am so that the event would not clash with the Boat Race. The days of football pre-eminence were still far in the future! Queen's Park again had to withdraw at the semi-final stage though they had been given a bye that far. The Cup was dominated for a dozen years by a handful of southern clubs—Wanderers, Royal Engineers, Oxford University, Old Etonians and Clapham Rovers—but the writing was on the wall for these gentlemen amateurs as early as 1877.

In that year, as a result of correspondence between Manchester FC and Marlborough College, the authority of the FA rules was generally accepted throughout the country. Thus the Sheffield version passed into oblivion, but not before it had had a significant effect on the game. The throw-in was used in Yorkshire some five years before the FA accepted it and the free-kick was an innovation from Sheffield; so was the cross-bar. Before 1866 there had been no height restriction on the goal at all—as was seen in that first Nottingham match.

The duration of the game had finally been determined at 90 minutes by 1877, and handling the ball had been restricted to the goalkeeper. In addition neutral referees and umpires (later linesmen) were now an established part of the game and even more so a year later when the familiar blast of the referee's whistle was heard for the first time during a match between Nottingham Forest and Sheffield Norfolk. Before 1878 officials had been forced to attract attention in any way they could—usually by waving a handkerchief.

It is never easy defining the exact moment when a new trend affects any discipline. Yet a casual observer could not fail to have been struck by unusual qualities of the 1878-79 FA Cup competition. It was won by Old Etonians, who beat Clapham Rovers 1-0, but there was nothing remarkable in that fact. A glance at the earlier rounds, however, reveals one very significant feature—the success of two provincial clubs. Nottingham Forest reached the semi-finals and beat Old Harrovians, the real successors to the previous year's Cup winners Wanderers, who had lost most of their players to the Old Boy's clubs on the way.

But the real interest was reserved for Old Etonians' fourth-

Far left: The Aston Villa side which won the League and Cup Double in 1896-97. It was to be 64 years before the feat was repeated.

Left above: Two years previously, Aston Villa had made history by winning the Cup and losing it in the same year to thieves who apparently melted it down. Villa were fined £25 and the money was used to purchase an identical trophy.

Left: The Times *of 27 October 1863 gave just three column inches to the arrival of organized football with the foundation of the Football Association. Only one other paper* (Bell's Life) *reported the event.*

round tie with Darwen. The Lancashire side were who trailing 5-1 with only 15 minutes left, suddenly came to life with a four-goal burst, and were robbed of their likely reward when the Etonians refused to play extra-time. £175 was raised to dispatch Darwen back to London—the result being a 2-2 draw and a second replay which the southerners won 6-2.

Football came late to the major industrial conurbations. Aston Villa came into being in 1874 with neighbours Small Heath (to be renamed Birmingham) following a year later. In Lancashire Blackburn and Bolton both saw the light of day in 1874 and the Newton Heath side (later Manchester United) was founded at the Lancashire and Yorkshire Railway Company's engine depot of that name in 1878.

It was a time of hope for Lancashire. After the near starvation of the 1860s—when cotton supplies were cut off during the American Civil War—and the economic depression of the early 1870s, an industrial boom was absorbing all who needed work. Immigrants flocked in from the agricultural areas and the Celtic fringes and football turned this to its advantage. Advertisements in the Glasgow papers attracted the Scottish 'professors' who taught the English the 'passing' as opposed to 'dribbling' game. Some teams, notably Preston, took on so many Scots that English players felt positively lonely and it is to this era and not the reign of Shankly at Liverpool that we owe the oft-repeated cry of the overlooked, 'you need to wear a kilt to get into that team.'

There were, of course, inducements. A Scot named J J Lang claimed he was the first ever professional when Sheffield Wednesday paid him to move from Glasgow in 1876. By 1880, while most of the players had other jobs, they received substantial remuneration from playing the game—not unlike the 'shamateurs' of the 1960s and, in consequence, football was taken much more seriously than in the south. The days of the gentlemen amateur were almost over.

The 1881 Cup Final—between Old Etonians and Old

Carthusians—was the last of the all-amateur finals and, indeed, the last all-southern Final until Spurs met Chelsea in 1967. Old Carthusians later went on to become the first club to win both the FA Cup (1881) and the Amateur Cup (1894 and 1897).

While Etonians managed to defeat Blackburn Rovers the following year, the inevitable happened in 1883 when Blackburn Olympic became the first club to take the trophy out of the Home Counties. It would have been difficult to devise a better pair of teams to illustrate the differences between the game, and the life, in the South and the North. The Old Etonians speak for themselves—representatives of all that was privileged in the South of England; gentlemen amateurs with the time and income to allow their devotion to the game when they thought fit. Blackburn Olympic came from the most industrialized area in the world—the dingy terraces that crawl like centipedes up and down the valleys of the mid-Lancashire weaving towns breeding many of the players that were not imported from Scotland.

Olympic even had a manager, once a travelling organizer of exhibition matches, one Jack Hunter. Like many managers after him, he took his team away to Blackpool to prepare for the Final. Of the players, two were weavers, one a spinner, one a plumber, one a metal-worker and two had no apparent means of support—apart from football.

'The blossom might be in the South, but the roots are in the North' goes the old economic adage, but in football the reverse was nearer the truth. Had the FA not wisely decided to accept professionalism the game must have developed very differently and might even have fallen into the sad split that has contributed to rugby never becoming a world-wide game. The North could never have competed with the South had it accepted the amateur strictures. A working man at the top of his craft might earn £2 for a six-day week; a farm labourer no more than 15/- (75p) at the time. Without some sort of financial inducement no working man could devote the requisite time and energy to the game. The vital decision was approaching; either the South accepted professionalism and kept the game under a single authority or insisted on the amateur ethic and caused the inevitable split.

As it happened the South had very little say on the field for a long time. The Cup stayed in Blackburn for a record four years—Blackburn Rovers following up the short-lived Olympic's success and equalling Wanderers' three successive wins. The Old Etonian success in 1882 was the last by a southern club until Spurs dramatic intervention in 1901. In fact, between Etonians' last win and Spurs 'double' in 1961, the Cup returned south on only seven occasions.

But to return North. The problem of 'professionalism' so worried the Lancashire FA that they forbade the signing-on of Scots in 1881 and in 1883 Accrington were expelled from the FA for giving an inducement to a particular player. Matters came to a head after a drawn Cup game between Preston North End and Upton Park on 19 January 1884. The London club protested that Preston had paid and played professionals and the Lilywhites were thrown out of the competition. Suspensions on members of the playing staffs followed for Great Lever and Burnley in Lancashire, Walsall and Birmingham St George's in the Midlands and Hearts in Scotland.

William Sudell, the founder of Preston North End, subtly suggested the formation of a British Football Association as a result of these suspensions. In October 1884 he received the support of 26 Lancashire clubs plus Aston Villa and Sunderland.

It was a strange forerunner of the similar situation which was

Left: *Since the formation of the League in 1888 only one non-League side has ever won the FA Cup, Spurs in 1901. Their centre-forward, Sandy Brown, scored a record 15 goals in the competition that year, including three in the two finals. Before a 114,815 crowd at Crystal Palace he is being congratulated on the first of those three—a 25th minute header from a John Kirwan (far side of field) cross. Note the old pitch markings, changed a year later.*
Left below: *The first FA Cup final victory by a northern side came in 1883, when Blackburn Olympic defeated Old Etonians at The Oval. Etonians were captained by Arthur Kinnaird, who appeared in 9 finals.*
Below: *The programme from the 1897 final, which Villa won 3-2 to clinch the last Double for 64 years. All the goals came within the space of 25 minutes, from Devey, Campbell and Crabtree for Villa and Bell and Hartley for Everton.*

NOTHING BETTER THAN
John Piggott's Cup Tie Football PRICE 9/3

JOHN PIGGOTT.
Please send for my Football and General Lists.
117, CHEAPSIDE, AND MILK STREET, E.C.

HIT OF THE SEASON.
John Piggott's Surrey Driver Bat PRICE 15/9

SCOTCH WHISKY,
"BERTRAM BLEND."
EIGHT YEARS OLD.
Per 42/- Dozen.
Bottles and Case included.
Sample Flasks on the Ground, 1/-.
BERTRAM & CO., LONDON & LEITH, N.B.

MANFIELD'S BOOTS.
WHITE CRICKET BOOTS,
WITH STOUT DAMP-PROOF SOLES.
LEATHER LINED, 13/6.
THE "M" CYCLING SHOES,
4/11, 5/11, 8/11, 10/6.
PHOTO PRICE LISTS FREE.
SAMPLE PAIR POST FREE.
67 & 68, CHEAPSIDE; 376 & 377, STRAND,
ETC., ETC.
AND IN ALL LARGE TOWNS.

WELCOME ALWAYS,
KEEP IT HANDY,
GRANT'S MORELLA
CHERRY BRANDY.
The best Tonic for Football Players
(See Captain Boyton's letter.)
MOST COMFORTING in CHILLY WEATHER.
Ask for GRANT'S and don't be put off with inferior makes.

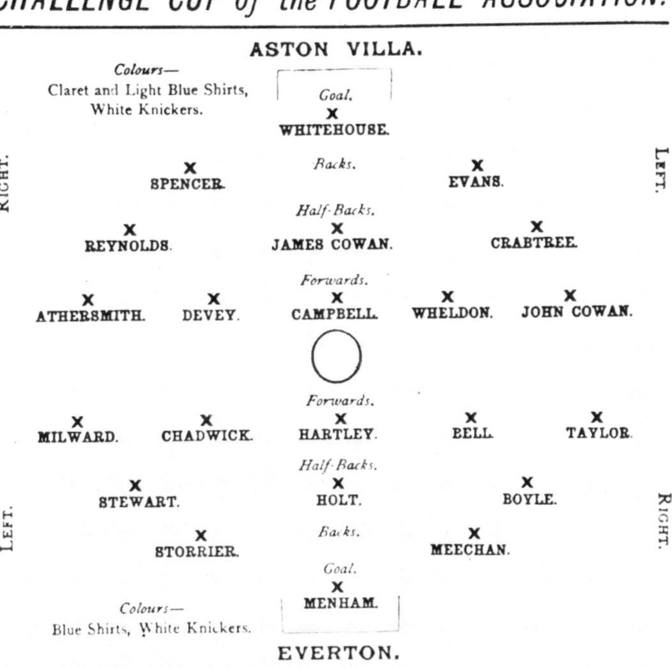
CRYSTAL PALACE.
Saturday, April 10th, 1897.
FINAL TIE
FOR THE
CHALLENGE CUP of the FOOTBALL ASSOCIATION.

ASTON VILLA.
Colours—
Claret and Light Blue Shirts,
White Knickers.

RIGHT. / LEFT.

Goal.
WHITEHOUSE.

Backs.
SPENCER. EVANS.

Half-Backs.
REYNOLDS. JAMES COWAN. CRABTREE.

Forwards.
ATHERSMITH. DEVEY. CAMPBELL. WHELDON. JOHN COWAN.

Forwards.
MILWARD. CHADWICK. HARTLEY. BELL. TAYLOR.

Half-Backs.
STEWART. HOLT. BOYLE.

Backs.
STORRIER. MEECHAN.

Goal.
MENHAM.

LEFT. / RIGHT.

Colours—
Blue Shirts, White Knickers.
EVERTON.

Referee—J. LEWIS (Lancashire). Linesmen—J. HOWCROFT (Redcar). A. SCRAGG (Crewe).

Official Programme. ONE PENNY.

ELLIMAN'S FOR BRUISES

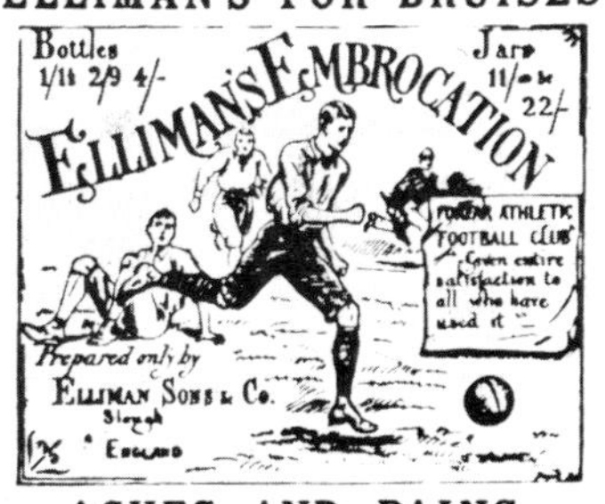

ACHES AND PAINS.
Miss ROSE ALPHONSINE, Spiral Ascensionist, writes:
"When doing my Spiral Ascension at the Jardin de Paris my feet and knees became swollen and very sore. I tried your Embrocation, and after two good rubbings I was able to perform. I now use it after every ascension, and will always keep some by me."
23, Helix Gardens, Brixton Hill, S.W., London,
October 29th, 1894.

1d. ARE YOU A FOOTBALLER? 1d.
We presume so, or you wouldn't be at this Match!
Perhaps you also run a bike?
WELL
SPORTS
IS THE PAPER YOU WANT.
(Illustrated. 32 pages.)
People Swear by it,
Rivals Swear at it,
Agents Pant for it,
The Public Fight for it,
And you can Buy it EVERYWHERE.
Nothing succeeds like
SPORTS!

CARTERS Used at Lord's, Oval, Crystal Palace, Aston Villa, etc. GRASS 237, 238, & 97, HIGH HOLBORN, LONDON. LISTS POST FREE. SEEDS.

to confront the Rugby Union in Huddersfield a decade later, only on the latter occasion the parent body decided that amateurism was more important than unity and the Northern Football Union (Rugby League) was the result.

The *Manchester Guardian* read the crisis of 1884 thus: 'The first effect of any change (the legalization of professionalism) will be to make the Rugby game the aristocratic one, and the Association game will probably almost die out in the south of England, where it is already declining in favour.'

By the start of the 1885-86 season a special general meeting of the FA had legalized the payment of players, basically on the same lines of those employed in cricket (Alcock was also secretary of Surrey CCC).

But it was not harmony everywhere. The Scots banned all professionals from ever playing north of the border and eventually took things further when, in 1887, they decreed that 'clubs' belonging to this (the Scottish) Association shall not be members of any other National Association.'

It was something of a blow for the better Glasgow sides—Queen's Park had reached the Cup Final in 1884 and 1885 and the emerging Rangers had been beaten by Aston Villa in an 1887 semi-final at, of all places, Crewe. It was sad in another way for had the Scots maintained contact for just another year that utopia of so many administrators—a British League—might have come into being.

The Scots, nevertheless, had done a great deal for the English game. Before 1872 it was a 'dribbling' game. The public school boy had been taught to exhibit his individual excellence by simply running at the opposition until he lost the ball. As a result most English sides played with a goal keeper, two backs and eight 'dribbling' forwards. The early contacts with the Scots showed just how inefficient the English system was. Though Royal Engineers and Sheffield had both been noted for a 'combination' style of operation, it was the Scots who had elevated the 'passing' game to a fine and impressive art, depending more on skill and perception than mere force and speed. And it was not only on the field that the Scots were to improve the English game. It was William McGregor, an exiled committee man at Aston Villa, who first devised a plan for the Football League at a time when fixture lists were becoming increasingly disorganised.

It was not inappropriate, either, that McGregor, first president of the Football League, should have been associated with Aston Villa. Secure in their vast, redbrick mausoleum north of Birmingham ('worth a goal start' as James Cowan used to say of it), Villa won the Championship six times and the Cup on five occasions before the First World War.

Control of that era fell to very few clubs; primarily Aston Villa and Sunderland, with Manchester United, Newcastle United and the two club sides in both Sheffield and Liverpool providing the main opposition. The first 27 Championships were shared by only ten clubs—those eight plus Preston and Blackburn Rovers. It was to be some years before there was a significant shift of power towards the South. By the end of the First World War, London's trio of Arsenal, Chelsea and Spurs had at last all made their mark and the Southern League was absorbed as the Third Division in 1920.

But all this was in the future when Villa director William McGregor sent his famous letter to Blackburn, Bolton, Preston, West Bromwich and the secretary of his own club, Villa, on 2 March 1888. It had become increasingly difficult for the major clubs to guarantee fixtures; opponents either failed to turn up or were forced to complete postponed or replayed cup ties on dates which were already booked. The real concern, of course, was that gates were dropping off as a result. McGregor saw the great need for a definite list of fixtures—as well as the added attraction of competitive football—which would guarantee spectators the game they expected to see.

The initial meeting was held on the eve of the Cup Final, Friday 23 March 1888, at Anderton's Hotel, in London. McGregor's suggestion for a name, the Association Football Union, was rejected because of a possible confusion with the rugby code while McGregor's own objections to the name Football League (because he thought it would be confused with the unpopular and politically extreme Irish National and Land Leagues) were felt to be irrelevant.

The business was not concluded until 17 April at the Royal Hotel in Manchester, a far more appropriate setting as no southern club had taken any part in the discussions. There it was found that no more than 22 dates could be set aside for fixtures and the League would therefore have to be confined to 12 members. Thus Nottingham Forest, the Wednesday from Sheffield (who did not adopt the present title until 1929) and a long since defunct Lancashire League club called Halliwell went away empty handed while the remaining 12 became the founder members of the oldest League in the world.

Six were from Lancashire: Accrington, Blackburn Rovers,

Below: *The major problem facing the embryonic Football Association in the 1860s and 1870s was the vast divergence of rules still operating. At Uppingham, where J C Thring had drawn up 'The Simplest Rules' in 1862 (around when this picture was taken), teams numbered 15-a-side and attacked a goal stretched right across the pitch. Uppingham's was probably the first code to employ a crossbar, but did not allow the ball to go above waist height.*
Above right: *A cavalcade of fans leaving Kingsway, London, bound for the 1906 final between Everton and Newcastle United.*

Bolton Wanderers, Burnley, Everton and Preston North End, five from the loosely-defined Midlands: Aston Villa, Derby County, Notts County, West Bromwich Albion and Wolverhampton Wanderers and one, Stoke, came from the no-man's land between the two. The twelve have been remarkably durable—only Accrington and Notts County spending the greater part of the first 80 years out of the First Division.

McGregor explained: 'It appeared to me that a fixed programme of home-and-away matches between the leading clubs in the country, such fixtures to be kept inviolate, would produce football of a far more interesting nature than we then saw.' It was a fitting prologue.

The first season was dominated by Preston North End; 'Proud Preston', the 'Old Invincibles' that had emerged from the North End Cricket Club in 1881 and whose president was the William Sudell who had forced the professionalism issue with his openly illegal payments.

Sudell's team consisted largely of talented Scots, but in John Goodall he had the finest English centre-forward of his day (albeit an Englishman with Scots parents). Preston's inaugural double was completed without losing a game in the League or conceding a goal in the Cup. They thus became the first—and most likely the last—League side to go through a season without losing a game. But it was a brief flowering. Though they won the Championship the following season, Preston have not won it since, and have only one other Cup success to their credit, in 1938, and then it took a last minute penalty which went in off the bar to take a trophy back to Deepdale.

The Aston Villa story has its similarities, but they were always a far grander club than Preston. Between 1892 and 1905 Villa won five Championships and reached four Cup Finals, winning three of them. That included a double—in 1896-97—which, for 64 years, seemed destined to be the last of all time. Despite all the trophies they won in this period Villa are probably better remembered for one they lost—the FA Cup. After beating neighbours West Bromwich in the 1895 Final, Villa allowed a local boot and shoe manufacturer, William Shillcock, to display it in his shop window. It disappeared on the night of 11 September, and never reappeared in any recognizable form. The FA fined Villa £25, and used the money to buy a new trophy.

The midlanders' great rivals in this period were Sunderland. The north-easterners' rise to fame was astonishingly fast. They relied on Scottish players who cost them no more than a signing-on fee, but the most famous Scotsman to join their ranks proved more expensive. Ned Doig—Arbroath's goalkeeper—was deemed ineligible after his first match, and Sunderland forfeited £50 and two points. The problem was resolved, and Doig proved his worth—between the start of the 1890-91 and 1896-97 seasons they lost only one home game. The results of such defensive excellence were the League Championships of 1892, 1893 and 1895, followed by further successes in 1902 and 1913.

On the last of those five occasions Sunderland finally managed to reach their first Cup Final—only to see their double hopes disappear with a Tom Barber header that gave the trophy to rivals Villa. Early on in the game Clem Stephenson—the Villa forward who was later to captain the great Huddersfield side of the 1920s—told Sunderland's Charlie Buchan that he had dreamed Barber would head the only goal. As well as being accurate it was appropriate—neither club had much more than dreams to live on for the next 60 years.

The Cup had been growing in importance since the founding of the League. By 1893 Surrey County Cricket Club, worried about the size of the crowds, had to withdraw the Oval as the venue and that year the Final was played at Fallowfield, Manchester. The official attendance was 45,000, though at least twice that number managed to get in. Wolves won for the first time, defeating Everton, despite having lost a League game 4-2 to a team of Everton reserves the previous week. The 1894 Final was played at Goodison, Notts County becoming the first Second Division side to take the trophy, but the season after that the wide

When Sunderland won the League for the fourth time in 1902, this commemorative lapel button was produced for the supporters' club. Known as the team-of-all-the-talents, Sunderland then depended on Scots acquired from north of the border for little more than their signing-on fee. They were particularly strong at home, losing only once at Newcastle Road between September 1890 and the same month six years later.

open spaces of Crystal Palace staged the game for the first time.

Londoners still tended to be a little scathing about the whole event. This was partially because of the sudden invasion from the alien North ('a northern horde of uncouth garb and strange oaths' as the Pall Mall Gazette described Blackburn Rovers' supporters in 1885), but largely because southern clubs had little say in affairs.

But in 1901 Tottenham Hotspur, of the Southern League, became the first and only non-Football League team to win a post-1888 Cup Final—and an amazing affair it turned out to be. The 114,815 crowd still stands as the third largest attendance (after the 1913 and 1923 Finals) at a football match under any code in England and they were treated to one of football's most celebrated disputed goals.

As *The Times*, in typically subdued fashion, said, '... the result was not a true reflection of the run of the game. The second goal by Sheffield was the chief incident of the match. Clawley (the Spurs goalkeeper) fumbled a shot slightly but got it away. The referee decided that the ball was over the line and therefore a goal. Clawley says that this was impossible as he must have been behind his line for a goal to have been scored ...' Most of the crowd it seemed, agreed with Clawley. The game ended at 2-2, but justice was seen to be done at Bolton when Spurs won the replay 3-1. To be fair, the Spurs team consisted of one Irishman, two Welshmen, three northern-Englishmen and five Scots and can hardly be credited with reviving football south of the Trent.

That distinction belongs more fairly to Arsenal. Founded in 1886 by a Scotsman called David Danskin and a group of workmates at the Woolwich Arsenal, the club was originally called Dial Square. The name was changed to Royal Arsenal, then Woolwich Arsenal, The Arsenal and, finally, plain Arsenal. Adopting professionalism in 1891, they found that the southern opposition was simply not strong enough and began to organize fixtures against teams from further north. In 1893 Arsenal became the first southern club to be elected to the Football League.

In 1892 the League had absorbed the rival Football Alliance and now had two divisions and 28 clubs, none south of Birmingham. Until 1898 there was no automatic system of promotion and relegation—the bottom clubs in the First Division and the top clubs in the Second playing 'test' matches to decide which were worthy of the premier places. In that year Stoke and Burnley reasoned that a draw in the last of these test matches would give them both First Division places. The resulting goalless game aroused more than a few suspicions and the system was abolished.

Arsenal's election to the Second Division in 1893 was followed by promotion to the First eleven years later. The subsequent relegation in 1913 proved a blessing in disguise for it led to chairman Henry Norris deciding to move right across London, from south of the river Plumstead to Highbury. Their arrival incurred the wrath not only of the local residents, who thought Arsenal an utterly undesirable neighbour, but of nearby Tottenham, to whom the Gunners were not only undesirable but a positive threat.

Norris's machinations mysteriously gained Arsenal admittance to the First Division after the First World War and joining them were the third of London's great trio, Chelsea. Created out of nothing by the son of a builder—H A Mears—Chelsea FC started with a ground in 1905, bought a team and then began looking for someone to play.

The Football League were somehow persuaded that it was in their best interests to take in a club that had yet to play a game—and in two years Chelsea had been promoted. 'Chelsea will stagger humanity!' wrote one journalist—though he was referring to the ground. Built in the style of the great Glasgow stadia, with hopes that it would hold 100,000, Stamford Bridge was privileged to hold the first three post-war Cup Finals but has rarely staggered anyone.

The same could never be said about Manchester United's new stadium. In 1910 they finally moved across Manchester from Clayton—where the grandstand expressed its dismay and collapsed soon afterwards—to Old Trafford where, bettering Chelsea, it was hoped to seat 100,000. United had finally emerged as the major force they were to remain, winning the League in 1908 and 1911 and the Cup in 1909. The quality of Old Trafford was also soon realized. It staged the 'Khaki' Final (so called because of all the soldiers in the crowd) in 1915, the only time in the 20th century that the Final has been initially fought for outside London.

The last few years before the First World War have aptly been called 'those strange years of hysteria'. Though Victoria was dead, the era contained the dying vestiges of Victoriana. All in all, it was a very bizarre period. These were the years of the suffragettes, the first great nationwide strikes, a state of open warfare between the political parties over Ireland, the first feeble attempts to create a welfare state and, of course, the inexorable approach of the corporate madness that was the First World War. In its small, strange way football somehow managed to reflect the atmosphere of that era.

If Oldham Athletic, of all clubs, had won their last game of the 1914-15 season they would have become League Champions. In the Cup Bristol City were finalists in 1909, Barnsley in 1910 and then Bradford City and Barnsley both won the trophy, in 1911 and 1912. None of those four clubs had done anything of note before and none has done anything since. In 1911, in between her Cup Final appearances, Barnsley had to seek re-election. It was a strange time, but it was also a tribute to the strength in depth of the football of the times and a comment on the inability of the bigger clubs—like Villa—to automatically buy success. There were Final replays in 1910, 1911 and 1912 and extra time was therefore instituted in 1913. It was fifty-eight years before another replay was needed.

After the war, in 1920, the Southern League, founded by the professional club at Millwall, became the new Third Division. A year later a northern section was added, initially of 20 clubs but increased to 22 in 1923 and the League structure still in existence half a century later had been established.

THE F.A. CUP

'I'VE GOT A LEAGUE Championship medal, a Fairs Cup medal, a League Cup medal and dozens of caps—but sometimes I think I'd swap the lot for a place in a Cup winning side.' The words were those of Billy Bremner before Leeds United's long-awaited success at Wembley in 1972, but they could have come from any of a large number of professionals, that enormous group who have never been lucky enough to carry the Cup around the arena after the highlight of the English season.

The FA Cup has an undeniable aura about it. Not only is it the oldest football competition in the world, not only is its Final watched by hundreds of millions of people *outside* Britain, not only is it the annual showpiece for Britain's national sport, but it has been elevated far beyond that. It is now a ritual, different from a royal wedding or a moon-landing only in that it occurs at more predictable intervals.

In 1971 the BBC published a list of the biggest audiences for single programmes in the history of British television. Four of the top ten were Cup Finals. And despite all the protestations about the League Championship being the ultimate test of professional ability, there is the sneaking suspicion that no-one would sacrifice an FA Cup winners medal for a League Championship equivalent.

For, in the last resort, football must be a game about eleven men against eleven, about one team leaving the field victorious and the other vanquished, about a packed stadium saluting just one team—just one winner.

In its ultimate simplicity the FA Cup is the forerunner of competitions all over the world. But in a sense it is a lot more than that, for the hundred-year history of the FA Cup is also the history of English football.

It was in the offices of *The Sportsman*, a London newspaper, on 20 July 1871, that seven men took a hesitant step and made football history. The central figure was 29-year-old Charles Alcock, secretary of the FA and the man who suggested that: '... it is desirable that a Challenge Cup shall be established in connection with the Association ...' Among the other six present were Matthew Betts, who scored the first ever Cup Final goal, and Captain Francis Marindin, later president of the FA, who appeared in two Finals and refereed another eight.

Alcock had pinched the idea for his competition from his old school, Harrow, where there was a simple knock-out tournament among the houses, the winner being known as the 'Cock House'. The FA ordered a Cup from Martin, Hall and Company; it cost a mere £20 and stood just 18 inches high.

Fifteen clubs entered the first year—all but Donington School, Spalding, and the great Queen's Park of Glasgow coming from the home counties. In fact Donington scratched without playing a game and never entered again, thus establishing some kind of record.

The strict knock-out principle was not yet in operation; four clubs played in the third round and four in the next, in part through byes and in part through a rule which allowed teams which drew to both go through to the next round.

The Cup's beginnings were undoubtedly humble. Just 2,000 people turned out for the Final to see men dressed in trousers and caps (Royal Engineers wore 'dark blue serge knickerbockers'), who changed ends every time a goal was scored and who won throw-ins by touching the ball down in rugby fashion if it went out of play. The Kennington Oval pitch would have hardly been recognizable to present-day supporters—there was no centre-circle, no half-way line, no penalty area and a tape instead of a cross-bar. Alcock's team, the Wanderers, beat the Engineers 1-0.

The century that followed can be roughly divided into four phases—largely determined by the geographical location of the Final. Firstly there was the amateur era, then the Northern takeover, the Crystal Palace period and, finally, the post-1923 Wembley era.

Ten years after that first Final the Old Etonians beat Blackburn Rovers at the Oval. When the final whistle blew, the victorious captain, Arthur Kinnaird, of the red beard and long white trousers, stood on his head in front of the pavilion. It was appropriate that his should be the final gesture of an age ready to be confined to the history books; he appeared in nine of the first twelve Finals, five times on the winning side. Only James Forrest of Blackburn Rovers and C H R Wollaston of the Wanderers received so many winner's medals.

Kinnaird's winning appearances were with Old Etonians in 1879 and 1882, and Wanderers, in 1873, 1877 and 1878. His first for the Wanderers was the only occasion on which the Final was contested on the challenge basis that was written into both the competition's title and its original rules. The Wanderers, being the holders, not only had the solitary game to play—the Challenge Final in which they beat Oxford University 2-0—but they were also allowed to choose the venue of that match, which is the reason for Lillie Bridge's one moment of sporting significance.

The Wanderers also entered the records in a unique way in 1878—they won the Cup for the third consecutive time and thus,

What fans were prepared to do to get into the first ever Wembley final, between Bolton and West Ham in 1923. The crowd for the famous White Horse final was certainly in excess of 200,000, making it the largest attendance at any game ever played, anywhere.

according to the rules, outright. It was, however, returned with the proviso that it should never again be handed to one team in perpetuity. In fact the scene was a little more comical than that. Charles Alcock, as secretary of the Wanderers, handed back the Cup and asked that it should never be won outright. Charles Alcock, now in his role as secretary of the FA was only too happy to agree.

In the years that followed only one club—Blackburn Rovers between 1884 and 1886—has repeated the feat, and they were presented with a special shield which still hangs in their boardroom.

It was to Blackburn, in fact, that the Cup fled when it left the gentlemen amateurs of the South. That Lancastrian cotton-weaving town had two fine clubs in the 1880s—Olympic, who became the first side from outside the home counties to win the trophy, in 1883, and Rovers, who won it in the subsequent three seasons.

But the Blackburn clubs were not the first 'outsiders' to make their mark on the competition. In 1879 Nottingham Forest became the first of England's northern sides to reach the semi-finals—and at their first attempt—but more significant was the performance of Darwen, a neighbour of Blackburn, the same year. In the previous round they had held Old Etonians to two draws, the first by scoring four times in the last 15 minutes, but had gone down 6-2 on their third visit to the capital.

Darwen were unlucky that the rule under which all ties after the second round had to be played at the Oval was still in force. No semi-final was contested outside London until 1882, when Blackburn Rovers drew with Sheffield's The Wednesday at Huddersfield and beat them in Manchester, but for the next few years—before the Irish and Scottish FAs banned their clubs from entering—ties were played all over the United Kingdom. As a result Linfield captured the unique record of never having lost a Cup tie. They drew 2-2 with Nottingham Forest in 1889, and then withdrew before the replay, never to enter again.

Forest had actually arrived in Ireland and played a friendly instead, but it helped create an odd record for them as well, for they are the only club to have been drawn to play FA Cup ties in all four home countries. In 1885, after a drawn game at Derby, Forest had replayed a semi-final with Glasgow's Queen's Park at Merchiston Castle School, Edinburgh, the only semi-final ever contested outside England.

But to return to Darwen, whose performance was in no small way due to the presence of two Scots, Fergus Suter and James Love, both of whom had been 'mislaid' by Partick Thistle on a tour of England. They were, of course, among the first of the professionals that were soon to take over the competition and football south of the border.

The issue of payment did not actually come to a head until January 1884, when Preston North End drew with mighty Upton Park, one of the original entrants in 1872 and still staunch supporters of the lily-white amateur game. The Londoners protested that Preston had included professionals in their team, North End admitted as much, and were disqualified.

Just over a year later the FA sensibly bowed to the inevitable and professionals were allowed provided, among other clauses, they were: '. . . annually registered in a book to be kept by the committee of the FA . . .'

At least Preston had the satisfaction of seeing Upton Park humbled in the next round by neighbours Blackburn Rovers, on their triumphant march to the first of a hat-trick of wins. At the time Blackburn were also midway through a record of 24 Cup games without defeat, which lasted from a 1-0 setback at the hands of Darwen in the second round of the 1882-83 competition to the December of 1886.

But it was not Rovers who first brought the Cup to Lancashire, rather a long since defunct outfit called Blackburn Olympic. When their captain, Warburton, got back to a deserved civic reception in 1883, he declared to the crowd: 'The Cup is very welcome to Lancashire. It'll have a good home and it'll never go back to London.' He was quite right. In the next twelve years it went no further south than Birmingham where, in 1895, it was stolen from the window of a football-boot manufacturer William Shillcock and was never seen again.

In an edition of the *Sunday Pictorial* in February 1958 one Harry Burge, at the age of 83, admitted to having stolen the Cup and melted it down for counterfeit half-crowns. If that is true it is a sad commentary on the economics of the times—the Cup contained less than £20 worth of silver and could hardly have justified the effort.

Fortunately for the FA the chairman of Wolverhampton Wanderers had presented his players with scaled-down replicas when they won the trophy in 1893, and it was therefore possible to create an exact reproduction of the original.

That same Wolves victory was on the occasion of the first Final to be contested outside the capital. Surrey CCC, alarmed at the size of the crowd for the 1892 Final, withdrew the Oval as a venue and, in recognition of Lancashire's supremacy, the game's premier event switched to the country's second city, Manchester. There the Fallowfield ground was besieged by a crowd which broke down the barriers and fell through the wooden terracing in a remarkable harbinger of both the first Wembley Final, 30 years later, and the Ibrox disaster, then less than ten years away.

A week earlier Everton's reserve team had thrashed Wolves 4-2 in a First Division game but this time it was a different story with the Midlanders' captain Allen scoring the only goal of the match. The next season saw an equally surprising result. Second Division Notts County beat Bolton, 4-1 at Goodison Park, after reasonably protesting that it was virtually a home game for Bolton, and their centre-forward Jimmy Logan scored a hat-trick to equal William Townley's 1890 feat for Blackburn Rovers.

After the 1894 Final the FA must have concluded that London was the only rightful place for the showpiece of the season, and it has been played there with only one exception (1915) ever since. The obvious choice was Crystal Palace—though the FA's decision to move the game to London can be viewed a little cynically in the light of the fact that only one of the finalists who

Below: The programme for the second of the Cup Final meetings between West Bromwich Albion and Aston Villa, in 1892. This was the last final to be played at The Oval (Surrey CCC thought the crowds had grown too big). Villa and WBA are the only clubs to have met in three separate finals—1887, 1892, 1895.
Far right: Two Welsh international keepers, two similar FA Cup Final mistakes. In 1927 Arsenal's Dan Lewis fumbled a simple shot from Cardiff's Ferguson and let the ball slip over the line for the only goal of the match—the Cup hence leaving England for the one and only time. Forty three years later **(bottom)** *Gary Sprake dives over the top of Peter Houseman's speculative effort and Chelsea are back in the controversial 1970 Cup Final. Eventually Leeds and Chelsea drew 2-2 and the game went to a replay at Old Trafford, the first replay since the event moved to Wembley.*

ever played at the Palace was a London club—Spurs, in 1901—and only two others, Southampton and Bristol City, came from south of Birmingham.

Crystal Palace in 1895 was already a Victorian weekend playground—something like a cross between Battersea Fun Fair and Brighton beach—and it had a huge natural bowl which was used for sporting events. Terracing as it is known today was never built there; most of the 80 or so thousand who attended Finals stood on the steep grassy slopes of the east side.

The first Final at the Palace (not, incidentally, the present home of Crystal Palace) was the third clash between Birmingham rivals West Bromwich and Aston Villa—they are still the only clubs to have met each other three times in a Final. At kick-off both had won once each, but Villa went on to take the Cup this time, promptly lost it to Mr Burge, but were back again two years later to carry off the new trophy after a Final which must rank along with 1948 and 1953 as one of the greatest ever.

It was also a particularly significant game for it gave Villa a League-Cup Double which looked, for 64 years, like being the last of all time. Villa had won the League by the massive margin of eleven points (there were only 16 clubs in the division) and at the Palace defeated Everton 3-2, all the goals coming in the 25 minutes before half-time.

The club that took Villa's mantle of 'the team of all the talents' was Newcastle United—possessors of what is surely the oddest of all Cup Final records. In five Finals at the Crystal Palace they did not win one game, yet they did not lose at Wembley until their sixth match there!

The Geordies' record between 1905 and 1911 is startling in its consistency. They reached the Final in 1905, 1906, 1908, 1910 and 1911. In 1910 they admittedly managed to draw with Second Division Barnsley, and beat them in the replay at Goodison to record their only pre-First World War win. In 1909 they lost a semi-final by the game's only goal to Manchester United, so the only year in the seven between 1905 and 1911 that they did not reach the last four was 1907.

That season—one in which they won the League—Newcastle suffered a first round knock-out at St James' Park to a club then languishing at the bottom of the Southern League. And the name of that club whose feat must rank alongside the giant-killing exploits of Walsall and Colchester? Irony of ironies ... Crystal Palace. It was almost as if the very name made the Northumbrians go weak at the knees.

When the two great sides of the era—Villa and Newcastle—

FA CUP SUCCESS 1872 — 1983

	Cup Final wins	Cup Final appearances	Semi-final appearances
*Tottenham Hotspur	7	7	11
Aston Villa	7	9	17
Newcastle United	6	11	13
Blackburn Rovers	6	8	16
West Bromwich Albion	5	10	18
*Wanderers	5	5	3
Arsenal	5	11	16
Manchester United	5	9	16
Wolverhampton Wanderers	4	8	13
Manchester City	4	8	10
Bolton Wanderers	4	7	12
Sheffield United	4	6	10
Everton	3	7	18
Sheffield Wednesday	3	5	14
West Ham United	3	4	5
Preston North End	2	7	10
Old Etonians	2	6	6
Liverpool	2	5	13
Sunderland	2	3	10
*Nottingham Forest	2	2	9
*Bury	2	2	2
Huddersfield Town	1	5	7
Derby County	1	4	13
Leeds United	1	4	6
Oxford University	1	4	6
Royal Engineers	1	4	4
Chelsea	1	3	10
Burnley	1	3	8
Portsmouth	1	3	4
Blackpool	1	3	3
Southampton	1	2	8
Notts County	1	2	4
Cardiff City	1	2	3
Clapham Rovers	1	2	3
Barnsley	1	2	2
Charlton Athletic	1	2	2
*Ipswich Town	1	1	3
*Old Carthusians	1	1	3
*Blackburn Olympic	1	1	2
*Bradford City	1	1	1
Leicester City	—	4	7
Birmingham City	—	2	9
Queen's Park (Glasgow)	—	2	4
Brighton	—	1	1
Fulham	—	1	5
Bristol City	—	1	2
Luton Town	—	1	1
Queen's Park Rangers	—	1	1
Millwall	—	—	3
Stoke City	—	—	3
Swifts	—	—	3
Crystal Palace	—	—	2
Darwen	—	—	2
Grimsby Town	—	—	2
Swansea City	—	—	2
Swindon Town	—	—	2
Cambridge University	—	—	1
Crewe Alexandra	—	—	1
Derby Junction	—	—	1
Glasgow Rangers	—	—	1
Hull City	—	—	1
Marlow	—	—	1
Norwich City	—	—	1
Old Harrovians	—	—	1
Oldham Athletic	—	—	1
Port Vale	—	—	1
Reading	—	—	1
Shropshire Wanderers	—	—	1
Watford	—	—	1
York City	—	—	1

*Undefeated in Finals

met in 1905 they drew a crowd of 101,117 to a game that seemed to have little appeal for the Londoner—but even this figure had been surpassed four years earlier for a game that will surely remain unique for all time.

Since the Final returned in 1895 Londoners had regarded it, more than a little disdainfully, as an affair for provincials—rather like an Agricultural Exhibition at Earls Court is regarded today. In fact London had only one League club—Arsenal—at the turn of the century and had never had a professional interest in the Final.

Then, in the first year of the new century, came a record-breaking Final. 1901 saw Tottenham become the only non-League club to win the Cup since the Football League was founded, though they needed a replay against Sheffield United—winners two years before—to do it. The attendance printed in the following day's papers—114,815—was the largest ever at a football match and has been surpassed in England only twice since—at the 1913 and 1923 Finals.

Sandy Brown, who scored twice at Crystal Palace and once in the replay at Bolton, became the first man to score in every round of the Cup (a feat not equalled until 1935) and his total of 15 Cup goals has yet to be surpassed.

And on top of all this was a violently disputed goal which only the referee and the Sheffield United team of the hundred thousand present though was justified. The incident was no doubt quite comical to non-partisan spectators. Clawley, the Spurs goalkeeper, clashed with Bennett, a Sheffield forward, and the ball ran behind. Clawley appealed for a goal-kick, Bennett for a corner and the referee silenced them both by awarding a goal. He apparently judged Clawley to have been *behind* his own goal-line

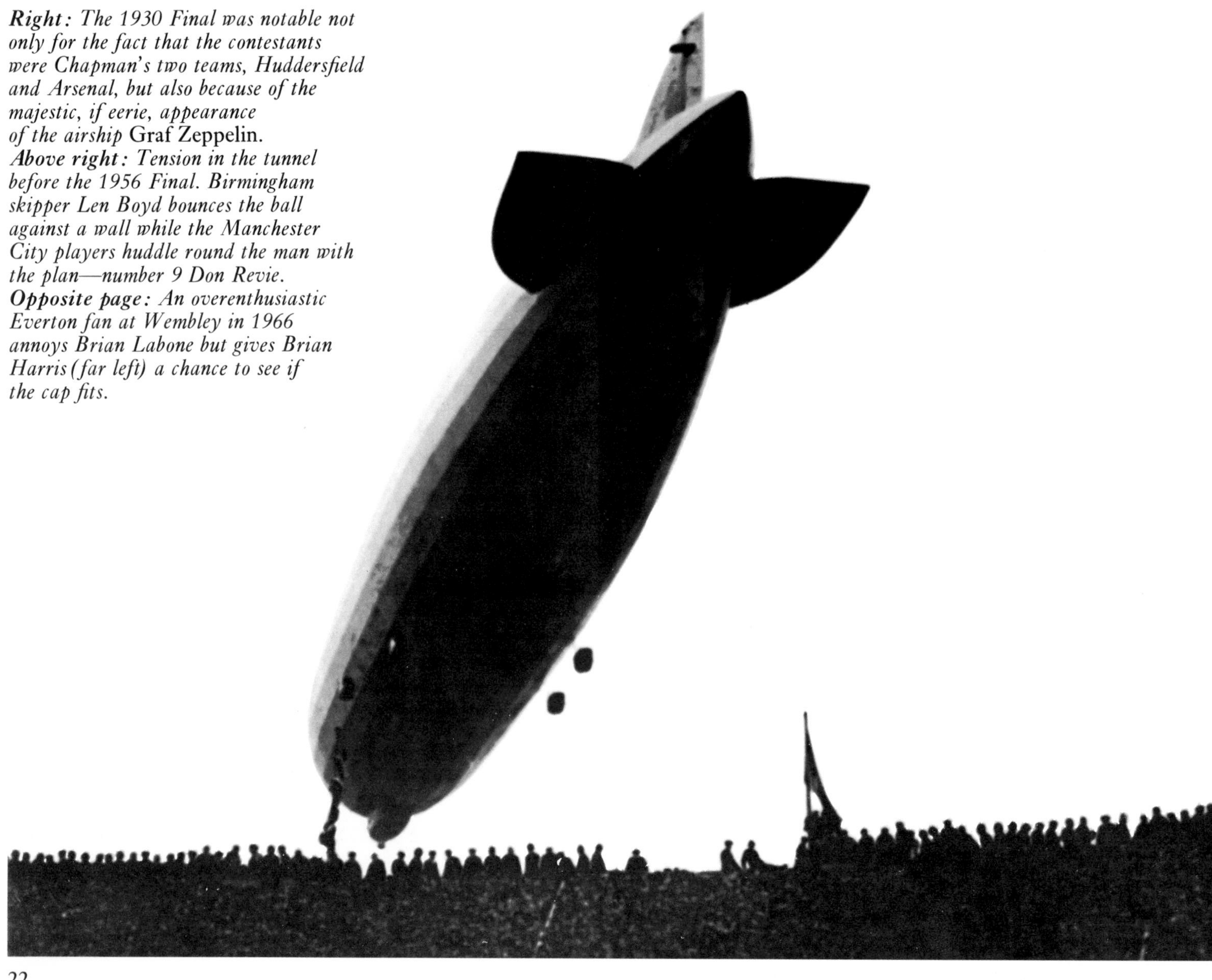

Right: *The 1930 Final was notable not only for the fact that the contestants were Chapman's two teams, Huddersfield and Arsenal, but also because of the majestic, if eerie, appearance of the airship* Graf Zeppelin.
Above right: *Tension in the tunnel before the 1956 Final. Birmingham skipper Len Boyd bounces the ball against a wall while the Manchester City players huddle round the man with the plan—number 9 Don Revie.*
Opposite page: *An overenthusiastic Everton fan at Wembley in 1966 annoys Brian Labone but gives Brian Harris (far left) a chance to see if the cap fits.*

before carrying the ball out and being challenged by Bennett.

London's star fell as quickly as it had risen and the capital did not have another representative in the Final until 1915, when Chelsea lost in the muted atmosphere of a wartime Old Trafford, to the side their fellow Londoners had defeated—Sheffield United.

The Yorkshiremen, however, did not carry off the same trophy Spurs had deprived them of. The design of the latter had been pirated for another competition in Manchester and so the second of the three FA Cups was presented to Lord Kinnaird—whose nine Final appearances is still a record—to mark his 21 years as President of the Football Association.

The present trophy, weighing 175 oz and 19 inches high, was ordered from Fattorini and Sons of Bradford and, appropriately if strangely, Bradford City were its first holders. Strangely, because neither Bradford club had been near a Final before and neither has been near one since.

As remarkable as the ability of some clubs to keep coming back and taking the Cup is the inability of others to get near it. Take Sunderland for instance. By the time they finally took the trophy back to Wearside in 1937, they had won the League Championship six times. But near neighbours and rivals Newcastle already had seven Final appearances to their credit—and another three soon to follow. Sunderland's only previous Final was another of the classics—the 1913 game that attracted a crowd even bigger than at the 1901 Final. They assembled for a decisive game, for it was the only Final in the first hundred years of the Cup to be contested by the clubs that finished first and second in the League. In the end honours were shared, Sunderland winning the League and Villa the Cup.

Seven years later several Villa players provided an illusion of continuity when they again collected winners medals. In the interim Europe had been at war for four years and the Crystal Palace had been requisitioned as a service depot. There was no prospect of it being available before 1923 and the FA had to look elsewhere for a venue for the highlight of the season.

Having decided that London was still the only possible home for the Cup Final—a contentious conclusion that was not particularly well received in Manchester, Birmingham or Liverpool—the FA were left with only one choice. The White Hart Lane and Highbury of 1919 were far from the imposing stadiums they are today, and the dreary Stamford Bridge was alone in being large enough.

So Chelsea's impersonal arena it was—a decision that nearly caused the FA a lot more criticism. By the semi-final stage the arrangements for the Final itself were far too advanced for the venue to be changed—but the Chelsea side that had reached the last pre-War Final were alive and well, third in the League, and favourites to reach the first post-War Final as well. The Pensioners went to Bramall Lane for their semi-final against Aston Villa with the prospect of a home tie in the Final—though it was technically against the rules of the competition.

It was Billy Walker who saved the FA's face. He scored two goals, Villa won 3-1 and went on to beat Huddersfield at Stamford Bridge.

The three Stamford Bridge Finals were among the most anonymous ever. All three were won by the only goal of the match, and the attendances in 1920 and 1922 were among the lowest of the century, coming nowhere near to filling the ground.

The 1922 game was called the most forgettable of all time, but suddenly acquired a new significance after a sequel 16 years later. The earlier game was a lamentable affair—even the FA minutes commented on the conduct of the players. It was appropriate that it should be decided by a disputed penalty when Preston's right-back Hamilton brought down Huddersfield's winger Billy Smith on the edge of the area, though many said outside it. After a lengthy and heated discussion between the Preston players and the referee, Smith himself took it and scored.

The 1938 game was equally drab, and the contestants were—Huddersfield and Preston. At least it was better tempered and had reached the last minute of extra-time without a goal when Huddersfield's centre-half Young tripped George Mutch and Mutch himself converted the penalty. The story goes that Bill Shankly—then playing for Preston—told Mutch to 'shut your eyes and hit it'. He had obviously been coached in something like that vein, for the ball hit the bar on its way in.

But back in 1923 no doubt everyone was glad to get away from Stamford Bridge to Wembley, where the FA had co-operated in a scheme to incorporate a vast new stadium in the British Empire Exhibition, scheduled to open in 1924. The Empire Stadium was ready a year earlier and public enthusiasm was enormous. Unfortunately the FA were lulled by the below capacity crowds at Stamford Bridge and thought that Wembley—capable of holding 127,000 according to the Exhibition authorities—would be more than big enough.

They were perhaps unlucky in that one of the contestants was West Ham, then leading the Second Division and the darlings of East London. In the end the FA publicly thanked a policeman called George Scorey and his white horse Billy that the game took place at all. West Ham were less pleased with the behaviour of the FA's equine saviour. Their game relied on the use of fast-running wingers Richards and Ruffell and, as trainer Charlie Paynter said afterwards: 'It was that white horse thumping its big feet into the pitch that made it hopeless. Our wingers were tumbling all over the place, tripping up in great ruts and holes.' Maybe, but it did not stop Ted Vizard having an excellent game on the left-wing for Bolton. The FA were more generous to PC Scorey, regularly sending him tickets for later Finals—but he was not much interested in football and, in fact, never went to another match.

When Arsenal returned to Wembley for the centenary Cup Final in 1972 they at least had statistics on their side. Newcastle had won in 1951 and 1952, Spurs in 1961 and 1962 and Arsenal had taken the trophy in 1971. But the portents were to be overcome by Leeds in their third FA Cup Final, for Allan Clarke scored the only goal of the match and Arsenal became the very first holders to return to Wembley and lose.

It was a defeat which reminded their followers of the inter-War period. Mighty Arsenal were the giants who strode across the thirties, winning the League five times but having a strangely chequered history in the Cup. True, they did win it twice, but far better remembered are the two occasions when they lost. The first of these was in 1927, when Cardiff with eight internationals and only one Englishman in their side took the Cup out of England for the first and only time. The solitary goal of the game came from a speculative shot by Cardiff's centre-forward Ferguson. The ball seemed to be easily gathered by Arsenal's Welsh international goalkeeper Dan Lewis, but he seemed to indulge in a grotesque parody of his trade, the ball slipping away from his

FOOTBALL ASSOCIATION CHALLENGE CUP FINALS 1872 — 1983

Year	Venue	Winners		Scorers	Runners-up		Scorers	Attendance
1872	Kennington Oval	Wanderers	1	*Betts*	Royal Engineers	0		2,000
1873[1]	Lillie Bridge	Wanderers	2	*Kinnaird, Wollaston*	Oxford University	0		3,000
1874	Kennington Oval	Oxford University	2	*Mackarness, Patton*	Royal Engineers	0		2,000
1875*	Kennington Oval	Royal Engineers	1	*Scorer not known*	Old Etonians	1	*Bonsor*	3,000
Replay	Kennington Oval	Royal Engineers	2	*Renny-Tailyour, Stafford*	Old Etonians	0		3,000
1876	Kennington Oval	Wanderers	1	*Edwards*	Old Etonians	1	*Bonsor*	3,000
Replay	Kennington Oval	Wanderers	3	*Hughes (2), Wollaston*	Old Etonians	0		3,500
1877*	Kennington Oval	Wanderers	2	*Heron, Kenrick*	Oxford University	1	*Kinnaird (o.g.)*	3,000
1878[2]	Kennington Oval	Wanderers	3	*Kenrick (2), Wace*	Royal Engineers	1	*Scorer not known*	4,500
1879	Kennington Oval	Old Etonians	1	*Clarke*	Clapham Rovers	0		5,000
1880	Kennington Oval	Clapham Rovers	1	*Lloyd-Jones*	Oxford University	0		6,000
1881	Kennington Oval	Old Carthusians	3	*Page, Wynyard, Parry*	Old Etonians	0		4,500
1882	Kennington Oval	Old Etonians	1	*Anderson*	Blackburn Rovers	0		6,500
1883*	Kennington Oval	Blackburn Olympic	2	*Matthews, Costley*	Old Etonians	1	*Goodhart*	8,000
1884	Kennington Oval	Blackburn Rovers	2	*Brown, Forrest*	Queen's Park (Glasgow)	1	*Christie*	4,000
1885	Kennington Oval	Blackburn Rovers	2	*Brown, Forrest*	Queen's Park (Glasgow)	0		12,500
1886	Kennington Oval	Blackburn Rovers	0		West Bromwich Albion	0		15,000
Replay[3]	The Racecourse, Derby	Blackburn Rovers	2	*Brown, Sowerbutts*	West Bromwich Albion	0		12,000
1887	Kennington Oval	Aston Villa	2	*Hunter, Hodgetts*	West Bromwich Albion	0		15,500
1888	Kennington Oval	West Bromwich Albion	2	*Woodhall, Bayliss*	Preston North End	1	*Dewhurst*	19,000
1889	Kennington Oval	Preston North End	3	*Gordon, Goodall, Thompson*	Wolverhampton Wanderers	0		22,000
1890	Kennington Oval	Blackburn Rovers	6	*Townley (3), Lofthouse, Southworth, Walton*	The Wednesday	1	*Bennett*	20,000
1891	Kennington Oval	Blackburn Rovers	3	*Southworth, Townley, Dewar*	Notts County	1	*Oswald*	23,000
1892	Kennington Oval	West Bromwich Albion	3	*Nicholls, Geddes, Reynolds*	Aston Villa	0		25,000
1893	Fallowfield, Manchester	Wolverhampton Wanderers	1	*Allen*	Everton	0		45,000
1894	Goodison Park	Notts County	4	*Logan (3), Watson*	Bolton Wanderers	1	*Cassidy*	37,000
1895	Crystal Palace	Aston Villa	1	*Devey*	West Bromwich Albion	0		42,560
1896[4]	Crystal Palace	The Wednesday	2	*Spiksley (2)*	Wolverhampton Wanderers	1	*Black*	48,836
1897	Crystal Palace	Aston Villa	3	*Campbell, Devey, Crabtree*	Everton	2	*Bell, Hartley*	65,891
1898	Crystal Palace	Nottingham Forest	3	*Capes (2), McPherson*	Derby County	1	*Bloomer*	62,017
1899	Crystal Palace	Sheffield United	4	*Bennett, Beers, Priest, Almond*	Derby County	1	*Boag*	78,833
1900	Crystal Palace	Bury	4	*McLuckie (2), Wood, Plant*	Southampton	0		68,945
1901	Crystal Palace	Tottenham Hotspur	2	*Brown (2)*	Sheffield United	2	*Bennett, Priest*	114,815
Replay	Burnden Park, Bolton	Tottenham Hotspur	3	*Cameron, Smith, Brown*	Sheffield United	1	*Priest*	20,740
1902	Crystal Palace	Sheffield United	1	*Common*	Southampton	1	*Wood*	76,914
Replay	Crystal Palace	Sheffield United	2	*Hedley, Barnes*	Southampton	1	*Brown*	33,068
1903	Crystal Palace	Bury	6	*Leeming (2), Ross, Sagar, Plant, Wood*	Derby County	0		63,102
1904	Crystal Palace	Manchester City	1	*Meredith*	Bolton Wanderers	0		61,374
1905	Crystal Palace	Aston Villa	2	*Hampton (2)*	Newcastle United	0		101,117
1906	Crystal Palace	Everton	1	*Young*	Newcastle United	0		75,609
1907	Crystal Palace	The Wednesday	2	*Stewart, Simpson*	Everton	1	*Sharp*	84,584
1908	Crystal Palace	Wolverhampton Wanderers	3	*Hunt, Hedley, Harrison*	Newcastle United	1	*Howie*	74,967
1909	Crystal Palace	Manchester United	1	*Turnbull A*	Bristol City	0		71,401
1910	Crystal Palace	Newcastle United	1	*Rutherford*	Barnsley	1	*Tufnell*	77,747
Replay	Goodison Park	Newcastle United	2	*Shepherd (2 inc a penalty)*	Barnsley	0		69,000
1911[5]	Crystal Palace	Bradford City	0		Newcastle United	0		69,098
Replay	Old Trafford	Bradford City	1	*Spiers*	Newcastle United	0		58,000
1912	Crystal Palace	Barnsley	0		West Bromwich Albion	0		54,556
Replay*	Bramall Lane	Barnsley	1	*Tufnell*	West Bromwich Albion	0		38,555
1913	Crystal Palace	Aston Villa	1	*Barber*	Sunderland	0		120,081
1914	Crystal Palace	Burnley	1	*Freeman*	Liverpool	0		72,778
1915	Old Trafford	Sheffield United	3	*Simmons, Kitchen, Fazackerley*	Chelsea	0		49,557
1916-1919		*Competition suspended*						
1920*	Stamford Bridge	Aston Villa	1	*Kirton*	Huddersfield Town	0		50,018
1921	Stamford Bridge	Tottenham Hotspur	1	*Dimmock*	Wolverhampton Wanderers	0		72,805
1922	Stamford Bridge	Huddersfield Town	1	*Smith (penalty)*	Preston North End	0		53,000
1923[6]	Wembley	Bolton Wanderers	2	*Jack, Smith J R*	West Ham United	0		126,047
1924	Wembley	Newcastle United	2	*Harris, Seymour*	Aston Villa	0		91,695
1925	Wembley	Sheffield United	1	*Tunstall*	Cardiff City	0		91,763
1926	Wembley	Bolton Wanderers	1	*Jack*	Manchester City	0		91,447

fumblings and rolling slowly over the line.

Lewis blamed the incident on his new jersey, and to this day Arsenal always wash goalkeepers' jerseys before they are used, to get rid of any surplus grease. It was a pity that they could not wash away their Cup luck as easily.

Still, there was nothing contentious about Arsenal's 2-0 win over Huddersfield in the 1930 Final, a game remembered for the moment when the *Graf Zeppelin* appeared over the Stadium. The airship—pride of a re-emergent Germany—dipped in salute and passed on sedately.

Two years later Arsenal were back to suffer the greatest of all Cup Final controversies. Their opponents were eternal Cup runners-up Newcastle, and the losers medals seemed destined to make their familiar trek to the North East as early as the fifteenth minute when John put Arsenal ahead. But it was not to be.

Davidson, the Newcastle centre-half, sent a long ball along the right, Richardson went for it but it appeared to be hit too hard for him and looked to have bounced out of play before he hooked it back across the goal. The Arsenal defence stopped and Allen was left free to flick the ball into the net.

The referee, a Mr Harper, carved himself an everlasting niche in soccer history by allowing the goal and Newcastle went on to win via another by Allen. That particular incident—and the photographs of the day tended to support the view of the Arsenal defence rather than that of the referee—probably ranks as the most arguable Cup Final goal ever.

For a time it was quite impossible to keep Arsenal out of the Cup headlines. In the third round the following season they went to Walsall, a club of no great pretensions, and lost 2-0 in a game that still ranks above Yeovil-Sunderland and Colchester-Leeds as the greatest of all the giant-killing acts. The reasons are emotional rather than analytical. What more needs to be said than that Arsenal spent more on their boots in 1933 than Walsall had paid in transfer fees for their whole team?

The little clubs can indeed add drama, and one of the most appealing things about the Cup is the periodic appearance of the giantkillers. On occasions it has even gained a club admission to the League—Peterborough after their successes in the 1950s and Hereford and Wimbledon after their exploits in the 1970s are perhaps the best examples. Often enough it has cost managers of League clubs their positions. When amateur Blyth Spartans defeated both Crewe and Stockport in successive rounds of the 1971-72 competition, the managers of both the Fourth Division clubs lost their jobs the following week.

Victories by non-League clubs over their League brothers are common enough of course—in 1956-57 it happened as many as eleven times. But since the League added a Third Division in 1920 there have been only five instances of a non-League club beating a First Division side, only one away from home. Hereford did well in the third round of 1972, drawing at Newcastle and winning the replay. *Old Moore's Almanac* for the year had predicted that a non-League side would win the Cup and Hereford certainly did their best to oblige—drawing with West Ham in the next round before going down 3-1.

Superstititon seems to play a big part in the Cup, where Portsmouth were the arch-adherents. In 1934 they employed manager Jack Tinn's lucky spats to bring them fortune and comedian Bud Flanagan to tell them jokes in the dressing room before the game with Manchester City. It did no good, City coming back to win 2-1 after losing the 1933 Final. City did the

927	Wembley	Cardiff City	1	*Ferguson*	Arsenal	0		91,206
928	Wembley	Blackburn Rovers	3	*Roscamp (2), McLean*	Huddersfield Town	1	*Jackson*	92,041
929	Wembley	Bolton Wanderers	2	*Butler, Blackmore*	Portsmouth	0		92,576
930	Wembley	Arsenal	2	*James, Lambert*	Huddersfield Town	0		92,448
931	Wembley	West Bromwich Albion	2	*Richardson W G (2)*	Birmingham	1	*Bradford*	92,406
932	Wembley	Newcastle United	2	*Allen (2)*	Arsenal	1	*John*	92,298
933	Wembley	Everton	3	*Stein, Dean, Dunn*	Manchester City	0		92,950
934	Wembley	Manchester City	2	*Tilson (2)*	Portsmouth	1	*Rutherford*	93,258
935	Wembley	Sheffield Wednesday	4	*Rimmer (2), Palethorpe, Hooper*	West Bromwich Albion	2	*Boyes, Sandford*	93,204
936	Wembley	Arsenal	1	*Drake*	Sheffield United	0		93,384
937	Wembley	Sunderland	3	*Gurney, Carter, Burbanks*	Preston North End	1	*O'Donnell*	93,495
938*	Wembley	Preston North End	1	*Mutch (penalty)*	Huddersfield Town	0		93,497
939	Wembley	Portsmouth	4	*Parker (2), Barlow, Anderson*	Wolverhampton Wanderers	1	*Dorsett*	99,370
940-1945		*Competition suspended*						
946*	Wembley	Derby County	4	*Turner H (og), Doherty, Stamps (2)*	Charlton Athletic	1	*Turner H*	98,000
947*	Wembley	Charlton Athletic	1	*Duffy*	Burnley	0		99,000
948	Wembley	Manchester United	4	*Rowley (2), Pearson, Anderson*	Blackpool	2	*Shimwell (penalty), Mortensen*	99,000
949	Wembley	Wolverhampton Wanderers	3	*Pye (2), Smyth*	Leicester City	1	*Griffiths*	99,500
950	Wembley	Arsenal	2	*Lewis (2)*	Liverpool	0		100,000
951	Wembley	Newcastle United	2	*Milburn (2)*	Blackpool	0		100,000
952	Wembley	Newcastle United	1	*Robledo G*	Arsenal	0		100,000
953	Wembley	Blackpool	4	*Mortensen (3), Perry*	Bolton Wanderers	3	*Lofthouse, Moir, Bell*	100,000
954	Wembley	West Bromwich Albion	3	*Allen (2 inc a penalty), Griffin*	Preston North End	2	*Morrison, Wayman*	100,000
955	Wembley	Newcastle United	3	*Milburn, Mitchell, Hannah*	Manchester City	1	*Johnstone*	100,000
956	Wembley	Manchester City	3	*Hayes, Dyson, Johnstone*	Birmingham City	1	*Kinsey*	100,000
957	Wembley	Aston Villa	2	*McParland (2)*	Manchester United	1	*Taylor*	100,000
958	Wembley	Bolton Wanderers	2	*Lofthouse (2)*	Manchester United	0		100,000
959	Wembley	Nottingham Forest	2	*Dwight, Wilson*	Luton Town	1	*Pacey*	100,000
960	Wembley	Wolverhampton Wanderers	3	*McGrath (og), Deeley (2)*	Blackburn Rovers	0		100,000
961	Wembley	Tottenham Hotspur	2	*Smith, Dyson*	Leicester City	0		100,000
962	Wembley	Tottenham Hotspur	3	*Greaves, Smith, Blanchflower (penalty)*	Burnley	1	*Robson*	100,000
963	Wembley	Manchester United	3	*Law, Herd (2)*	Leicester City	1	*Keyworth*	100,000
964	Wembley	West Ham United	3	*Sissons, Hurst, Boyce*	Preston North End	2	*Holden, Dawson*	100,000
965*	Wembley	Liverpool	2	*Hunt, St John*	Leeds United	1	*Bremner*	100,000
966	Wembley	Everton	3	*Trebilcock (2), Temple*	Sheffield Wednesday	2	*McCalliog, Ford*	100,000
967[7]	Wembley	Tottenham Hotspur	2	*Robertson, Saul*	Chelsea	1	*Tambling*	100,000
968*	Wembley	West Bromwich Albion	1	*Astle*	Everton	0		100,000
969	Wembley	Manchester City	1	*Young*	Leicester City	0		100,000
970*	Wembley	Chelsea	2	*Houseman, Hutchinson*	Leeds United	2	*Charlton, Jones*	100,000
eplay*	Old Trafford	Chelsea	2	*Osgood, Webb*	Leeds United	1	*Jones*	62,000
971*	Wembley	Arsenal	2	*Kelly, George*	Liverpool	1	*Heighway*	100,000
972	Wembley	Leeds United	1	*Clarke*	Arsenal	0		100,000
973	Wembley	Sunderland	1	*Porterfield*	Leeds United	0		100,000
974	Wembley	Liverpool	3	*Keegan (2), Heighway*	Newcastle United	0		100,000
975	Wembley	West Ham United	2	*Taylor A (2)*	Fulham	0		100,000
976	Wembley	Southampton	1	*Stokes*	Manchester United	0		100,000
977	Wembley	Manchester United	2	*Pearson, Greenhoff J*	Liverpool	1	*Case*	100,000
978	Wembley	Ipswich	1	*Osborne*	Arsenal	0		100,000
979	Wembley	Arsenal	3	*Talbot, Stapleton, Sunderland*	Manchester United	2	*McQueen, McIlroy*	100,000
980	Wembley	West Ham United	1	*Brooking*	Arsenal	0		100,000
981*	Wembley	Tottenham Hotspur	1	*Hutchison (o.g.)*	Manchester City	1	*Hutchison*	100,000
eplay	Wembley	Tottenham Hotspur	3	*Villa 2, Crooks*	Manchester City	2	*Mackenzie, Reeves (pen)*	92,000
982*	Wembley	Tottenham Hotspur	1	*Hoddle*	Queen's Park Rangers	1	*Fenwick*	100,000
eplay	Wembley	Tottenham Hotspur	1	*Hoddle (pen)*	Queen's Park Rangers	0		90,000
983*	Wembley	Manchester United	2	*Stapleton, Wilkins*	Brighton & Hove Albion	2	*Smith, Stevens*	100,000
Replay*	Wembley	Manchester United	4	*Robson 2, Whiteside, Muhren (pen)*	Brighton & Hove Albion	0		92,000

*After half-an-hour's extra time. Extra time became compulsory in 1913. [1]Challenge system. The holders, Wanderers, were exempt until the Final.
[2]Wanderers won the trophy outright but restored it to the Association. [3]Blackburn Rovers were also awarded a special shield to mark their third consecutive win.
[4]After the Cup had been stolen in 1895, the FA ordered a replica. The 1896 Final was the first time it was awarded.
[5]After the Cup's design had been duplicated for another competition, it was withdrawn and presented to Lord Kinnaird on his completing 21 years as President of the Football Association. The present trophy was first awarded in 1911. [6]Official attendance figure. Actual attendance was probably in excess of 200,000. [7]Substitutes allowed for the first time.

same thing in 1956, beating Birmingham with the 'Revie plan' after losing to Newcastle in 1955.

The 1934 Final was the occasion on which Frank Swift fainted. He said that the tension of the last few minutes, when he spent his time between the posts musing on how difficult it would be to clean the Cup and listening to the photographers counting down the seconds, was simply too much and he collapsed as the final whistle went.

Portsmouth's rituals proved luckier five years later. Their opponents Wolves arrived at Wembley as the hottest favourites of the century and full of a publicity seeking course of 'monkey glands'. Portsmouth preferred to rely on the spats again and, when the signature book came round, were heartened to see that Wolves players were so nervous that their signatures were barely legible.

Portsmouth won the Cup easily and proceeded to hold it for the longest period ever—seven years. This, however, was less due to their prowess than the outbreak of the Second World War.

After that lengthy intermission the Cup re-appeared in unfamiliar form. Because of the lack of a League programme, the FA decided to hold the Cup on a home-and-away basis—for the first and only time. It was not really a success, but it created its talking points.

Bradford PA lost 3-1 at home to Manchester City in the fourth round and then went on to win 8-2 at Maine Road, while Charlton became only the second team to *lose* a Cup game and still reach the Final. Fulham beat them 2-1 in the third round at Craven Cottage but Charlton had already won the first leg 3-1 and went through. One previous occasion when this had happened was the second part of a three-match quarter-final fiasco in 1890. Wednesday beat Notts County 5-0 in the first part. County protested to the FA, the game was replayed and County won 3-2. This time it was Sheffield's turn to protest and the eventual result was a 2-1 win for Wednesday—who went on to lose the Final rather ignominiously 6-1 to Blackburn Rovers.

The 1946 Final was almost as high scoring a game—Derby winning 4-1. That surprised no one for it took Derby's tally for the competition to 37, the highest aggregate since 1887-88 when Preston beat Hyde 26-0. Charlton's Bert Turner was the central figure of the game, scoring an own goal for Derby and within a minute equalizing with a free-kick which went in off Doherty's legs.

There followed two years later one of a pair of great Finals that have to be regarded in tandem. In the first the League runners-up, Manchester United, beat Blackpool 4-2 in what has always been regarded as the 'purest' of the Wembley games. Blackpool reached Wembley twice more in the next five years, losing to Newcastle in 1951 and facing Bolton in 1953, a game consigned to legend as 'the Matthews Final'. Blackpool came back from 3-1 down 20 minutes from time and 3-2 down with just three minutes of normal time left to win 4-3 in the game which will probably always rank—whatever its merits—as *the* Cup Final.

It was a game in keeping with the heady atmosphere of 1953, of the Coronation, of Everest, of Gordon Richards' Derby win, of the Hungarians visit to Wembley. Yet tacticians point to Bolton's strange response to left-half Eric Bell's injury in the first half. Bell moved to the left-wing. Inside-left Harry Hassall, no great tackler, moved to left-half and, when left-back Ralph Banks went down with cramp twenty minutes from the end, he was left marking Matthews. As a result, Matthews' right-wing was left as open as the proverbial barn door and Bolton paid the price.

Bell's injury was a portent for the next decade. Between 1952 and 1961 only two Finals—1954 and 1958—were not marred by some vital injury. And, significantly, only two of the teams that suffered—Manchester City in 1956 and Nottingham Forest in 1959—eventually won the Cup. The phenomenon, dubbed 'the Wembley hoodoo', was generally attributed to the turf.

Danny Blanchflower explained after the 1961 Final: 'It was a lush trap; the ideal pitch should have a little give in it. But Wembley is too soft. It pulls at the lower muscles of the leg, braking some efforts and ruining the natural timing.' After that particular game—in which Len Chalmers of Leicester suffered torn ligaments—the hoodoo seemed to die away. Substitutes were first introduced in 1967 and it was never an issue again. Perhaps cutting the grass a little shorter made the difference.

Wolverhampton were the great team of the fifties, winning three Championships, yet their two Cup wins were in the last year of the previous decade and the first of the next. And they were against, perhaps, the two worst post-War finalists. In 1949 Leicester arrived at Wembley with the sole distinction of being the worst placed League club (they finished nineteenth in the Second Division) ever to reach the Final. In fact with one point less they would have been playing Third Division football in the August of the same year. Leicester's 3-1 defeat was the prelude to three more in the next 20 years—leaving them with the undisputed position of chief bridesmaid.

Wolves' 1960 opponents were in some ways even more ragged. Blackburn Rovers received a transfer request from centre-forward Derek Dougan on the morning of the match, left-back Dave Whelan broke a leg and right-half McGrath scored an own goal. It was the most one-sided of all the Wembley Finals and, while promising to herald in an even more successful decade than the one before for the Midlanders, it was in fact manager Cullis's swansong. Five years later Wolves were playing Second Division football.

Manchester United's post-war record is far sadder. Despite their wins in 1948, 1963 and 1977, it is the games of 1957 and 1958 that they must be remembered by. Not only did United become the first club to lose successive finals at Wembley, but they did so in tragic circumstances.

United approached Wembley in 1957 as League Champions, having reached the semi-final of the European Cup, and on the verge of becoming perhaps the best British club side ever. Real Madrid had beaten them in the European Cup, but it had disheartened nobody, and Busby had said: '... the only difference between the teams was in their experience, and we shall soon acquire that ...' To add spice to the Cup Final their opponents were Aston Villa, the last club to do the double that United seemed to have so firmly in their grasp.

But within minutes Villa's outside-left McParland had crashed into the United keeper Ray Wood and fractured his cheekbone. Wood went off, Jackie Blanchflower had to take over, and the machine was disturbed. McParland scored two goals to give Villa a record seventh win. As one journalist put it the next day: 'McParland was the man of the match—bagging two goals and one goalkeeper.'

But if 1957 could be called tragic for United, then 1958 was cataclysmic. That was, of course, the year of Munich. Six of the 1957 Wembley side—Byrne, Colman, Edwards, Whelan, Taylor and Pegg—were dead. Two—Johnny Berry and Jackie Blanchflower—survived but never kicked a ball again. And what happened next has become a legend.

The FA waived its rules to allow Stan Crowther, a member of the Villa side that had beaten United in 1957, to play for United after having turned out for Villa already in the competition. Ernie Taylor, already a successful Cup Finalist with Blackpool and Newcastle, was brought to hold the team together. And as if partaking in some medieval ritual, the crowd support bordered on religious fanaticism. Wherever the new United appeared gates were closed. In the Cup Sheffield Wednesday were the first to fall before this uncanny force, then the favourites West Bromwich, then Second Division Fulham after two semi-final games which ended at 2-2 and 5-3.

And so they arrived at the gates of Wembley, where their opponents were to be Bolton. Poor Bolton. Five years earlier every uncommitted observer had wanted them to lose so that Stanley Matthews could get his winner's medal. This time they must have had a sneaking suspicion that even their own fans would not have minded too much if the Cup had ended up just five miles down the road at Old Trafford.

But the fates had let things go far enough. Within three minutes a very unghostly Nat Lofthouse put Bolton one up and, early in the second half, made it two with a charge that bundled both the ball and goalkeeper Gregg into the back of the net.

The myth has grown up that it was Lofthouse's charge that lost United the game. That is unlikely. In many ways they had looked what they were—a team carried along on a wave of fanaticism that could not, in the end, disguise the makeshift nature of the effort. After all, only Foulkes and Charlton had played in both Finals. In the space of six years and three Finals in the 1920s

Right above: *After the party's over; Manchester City have beaten Leicester City 1-0 in the 'After the goal rush' final of 1969 and Tony Book holds the Cup while Glyn Pardoe clings onto his medal.*
Right below: *'Happy' Harry Hampton scores one of the two goals with which Villa beat Newcastle in the 1905 Final. It was the first year of a disastrous spell for the Geordies; beaten 1905 and 1911 they appeared in five Finals at Crystal Palace and did not win there once.*
Opposite page: *Ricky George's extra-time shot flies past Newcastle United keeper Iam McFaul and Hereford thus become the first non-League side to defeat First Division opposition for nearly a quarter of a century. It was this win which effectively gained Hereford a place in the Fourth Division in the same year, 1972.*

Bolton had used just 17 players. United had been forced to use 20 in successive appearances.

Manchester's Yorkshire counterpart—Leeds—have a record almost as sad. The team that Don Revie brought from the shadows became the first to take second place in both major competitions on two separate occasions, 1965 and 1970. What was sadder was the universal opinion that, in the latter Final, Leeds were the better of the two sides. But then the best side is surely the one that scores most goals and Chelsea did precisely that in the first replay since the Final moved to Wembley.

One club with a very satisfactory post-War Cup record is Tottenham. They have won five Finals, to bring their total to seven appearances and a record seven wins. The third, fourth and fifth of these came within the space of six years—1961, 1962 and 1967—and the first, a 2-0 win against Leicester, earned Spurs the first double for 64 years.

The first season of the decade seems to have a fascination for White Hart Lane. Spurs won the Cup first in 1901, next in 1921, the League for the first time in 1951, the Double in 1961, the League Cup in 1971 and the FA Cup again in 1981.

Newcastle have been almost as successful at Wembley. In seven appearances they have won five times and they share with the North Londoners the distinction of being the only club to win in consecutive seasons there. The Magpies were successful in 1924, 1932, 1951, 1952 and 1955, and were not beaten until Liverpool and Manchester City overcame them in the 1974 FA Cup and 1976 League Cup. The fact that they beat Arsenal twice—1932 and 1952—only serves to stress how poor London's record has been in an event that the FA have always insisted should be held there.

But Spurs' Double in 1961 was the precursor of a remarkable run of success for the capital—the more so in comparison with what had gone before. Between 1961 and 1982 London clubs won eleven of the 22 finals. In the previous 60 years they had won just six.

Arsenal's Double was the more remarkable of the two if only for its unpredictability. With Spurs in 1961 the possibility had been discussed from very early on in the season. Arsenal came through at the last moment in both competitions—overhauling Leeds after being six points behind with just six weeks to go, taking 27 points from their last 16 matches, and scoring a last-minute penalty to draw with Stoke in the semi-final.

On the Monday of Cup Final week they beat Spurs—appropriately as their North London neighbours were then the only 20th-century Double winners—to take the League, and five days later squeezed past Liverpool at Wembley to deprive Spurs of their uniqueness. It was Arsenal's 64th game of the season.

Strangely it was left to Arsenal to try and prevent yet another Double the following season. They failed, after a dour game which, if nothing else, epitomized the football of the early seventies and ended in its most familiar score—1-0. Leeds were in no way dispirited by the manner of their victory—it was third time lucky for both the club and for Allan Clarke, the man who scored the only goal of the Final.

Having won the one that had eluded them for so long however, Leeds went to Wolverhampton just two days later needing a single point for the elusive double. But they lost 2-1.

Leeds defeat the following year, 1973, by Sunderland was the most emotional of the post-War finals (excluding perhaps 1953) and was the first of several Second Division successes. Fulham were beaten by West Ham in 1975, Southampton beat Manchester United in 1976, Arsenal went down to West Ham in 1980 and QPR took Spurs to a replay in 1982. West Ham have the odd distinction that all their finals have featured Second Division clubs—they were in that League in 1923 and 1980, as were their opponents in 1964 and 1975. Certainly the appearance of five non-Division I sides in the last ten finals suggests a convergence of standards, though perhaps those of elaborate defensive tactics rather than forward skill. Sunderland, Southampton and West Ham all won their finals 1-0, conclusions which mirror the increasing ability of teams throughout the game to score a single goal and hold onto that lead against apparently superior opponents. It was a trend that hopefully reached its peak in the European Cup with Nottingham Forest's defeat of SV Hamburg and Aston Villa's conquest of Bayern Munich.

As the 1970s went on, the most surprising feature of the Cup was the way the South came to dominate it. Between 1975 and 1982, only one northern club, Manchester United in 1977, actually took the trophy back to its traditional home. Even worse, only 5 of the 16 finalists in that period were from Lancashire and none at all came from the Midlands, North East or Yorkshire. Strangely, this was not mirrored in the League or League Cup—competitions then dominated by Liverpool, Nottingham Forest and Aston Villa with scarcely anyone else getting a look in.

Though Manchester United's denial of Liverpool's treble in 1977 was surely the most unexpected of results, the finals of 1978 and 1981 were the ones that appealed to the public. Ipswich had long been seeking a Cup final win to go with their lone League

GIANT-KILLING BY NON-LEAGUE CLUBS 1919-1983

Victories over First Division sides

*Cardiff City	2	Oldham Athletic	0	1919-20
*Sheffield Wednesday	0	Darlington	2 (after 0-0 draw)	1919-20
†Corinthians	1	Blackburn Rovers	0	1923-24
Colchester United	1	Huddersfield Town	0	1947-48
Yeovil Town	2	Sunderland	1	1948-49
Hereford United	2	Newcastle United	1 (after 2-2 draw)	1971-72
Burnley	0	Wimbledon	1	1974-75

Victories over Second Division sides

*Coventry City	0	Luton Town	1 (after 2-2 draw)	1919-20
*Fulham	1	Swindon Town	2	1919-20
*Plymouth Argyle	4	Barnsley	1	1919-20
*Wolverhampton W	1	Cardiff City	2	1919-20
Wolverhampton W	0	Mansfield Town	1	1928-29
Chelmsford City	4	Southampton	1	1938-39
Colchester United	3	Bradford PA	2	1947-48
Yeovil Town	3	Bury	1	1948-49
†Bishop Auckland	3	Ipswich Town	1 (after 2-2 draw)	1954-55
Lincoln City	4	Peterborough United	5 (after 2-2 draw)	1956-57
Notts County	1	Rhyl	3	1956-57
Worcester City	2	Liverpool	1	1958-59
Ipswich Town	2	Peterborough United	3	1959-60
Newcastle United	1	Bedford Town	2	1963-64
Blyth Spartans	3	Stoke City	2	1977-78
Harlow Town	1	Leicester City	0 (after 1-1 draw)	1979-80

Biggest victories over League sides

Carlisle United	1	Wigan Athletic	6	1934-35
†Walthamstow Avenue	6	Northampton Town	1	1936-37
Derby County	1	Boston United	6	1955-56
Hereford United	6	Queen's Park Rangers	1	1957-58
Barnet	6	Newport County	1	1970-71

Progress to last sixteen (present fifth round)

*1919-20 Cardiff City
*1919-20 Plymouth Argyle
1947-48 Colchester United
1948-49 Yeovil Town
1977-78 Blyth Spartans

*The Third Division did not come into being until 1920. In the 1919-20 season the best Southern League clubs were of a comparable standard with Second Division sides. †Amateur club.

Championship, and when it came against Arsenal it had to be worked for. The woodwork kept Ipswich at bay for so long that it seemed certain Wembley was watching another 'lucky Arsenal' display, with the Gunners sneaking a last minute winner. In the end it was not to be, Roger Osborne scoring the only goal and going off straight afterwards with mental rather than physical exhaustion.

Spurs virtually made Wembley their home ground in 1981 and 1982, appearing there seven times in 18 months. Both the 1981 final against Manchester City and the 1982 version against QPR had to be replayed, the only occasions replays had taken place at Wembley. Spurs were lucky to draw with Manchester City at all, Glenn Hoddle's 81st minute free-kick going in off Tommy Hutchison's shoulder and giving Hutchison the distinction of scoring for both sides, only the second time this had happened. The replay of this, the Centenary final, lived up to its billing, with one of the best games in the competition's history. Spurs won 3-2 in the end, the final goal coming from Ricky Villa's memorable dribble, a moment reckoned to be the best individual Cup Final goal in living memory.

Hoddle scored again the following year—twice. His was Spurs' only goal of a 1-1 draw, then he converted a sixth minute penalty to win the replay 1-0. QPR were the better team and unlucky to go away with the losers' medals, but Spurs were clearly exhausted at the end of a terrible season for them. After bravely contesting four trophies, the Cup Final was their final hope and was preceded by the loss of their two Argentinians—Ardiles and Villa—because of the Falklands War.

A less publicized aspect of the 1982 Cup Final replay was its similarity to the 1923 'White Horse' Final. This was not so much because a Second Division London side was playing, but because it was the only other time that it had been possible to turn up and buy a ticket at the gate. The attendance was only 90,000 and the unheard of had happened—empty seats at the Cup final. It was a sign that not even the game's premier event was immune from the cold winds of recession blowing over the nation's soccer fields. But while the recession was certainly felt at the top, football at other levels had never been healther. That was fortunate for the FA Cup, for in many ways it is a competition for the 600 or so little clubs who set off in the 36 first qualifying round groups well before summer turns to autumn.

A club like Boden Colliery Welfare, playing in the North-Eastern Geographical Division in September 1983 is faced with 15 rounds before reaching Wembley. Of course, hardly any of the clubs which start at this early stage even reach the First Round proper. Twenty-four of the best non-League sides are exempt until the Fourth (the last) Qualifying Round, and the winners from that round go on to the First Round proper where they are joined by the Third and Fourth Division clubs and the previous season's FA Challenge Trophy finalists. After two rounds this number has been cut to twenty, who are joined by the 44 big boys—the First and Second Division clubs.

The Cup, however, has a place for the likes of Abergavenny Thursdays and Irthlingborough Diamonds. It started, and remains, a competition for all the clubs affiliated to the Football Association—and it is a place they guard manfully.

Really it is a competition—and most certainly a Final—for the fan. It is the fan who pays £100 for black market tickets, who turns mortals into immortals simply because they scored a goal, who talks about it, dreams about it and relives it for months, who would not give away a Final ticket for a fortune, because the most valuable thing a fortune can buy is a Cup Final ticket.

Danny Blanchflower puts it the players' way: 'In truth we are brainwashed about the Cup Final. A player hears so much about it before he gets there ... the "majestic" twin towers ... the "hallowed" green turf ... the "royal" greeting ... the crowd singing "Abide With Me" ... It all sounds like some distant religious ceremony that takes place at the end of the season in the promised land. The reality of it can never live up to the dream. The dream is not for the player, it is for the fan ... the lover of the game who doesn't really know what it is like out there and never *will* know. It is the fan's day, which is why some 400 million of them all over the world tune in on Cup Final day.

Spurs' Glenn Hoddle beats QPR's Peter Hucker easily with a 6th minute penalty in the 1982 Cup Final replay. It was the only goal of the game. Hoddle had three scoring shots in the four games which made up the 1981 and 1982 finals. In the first 1981 game his free-kick was deflected by Tommy Hutchison, in the first 1982 game his shot was deflected by Tony Currie (but Hoddle was awarded the goal) and this penalty won the replay.

THE LEAGUE CHAMPIONSHIP

On 7 October 1978 Nottingham Forest established a new record of 35 League games without defeat by beating Wolves 3-1. Their last League defeat had been on 19 November 1977 at Leeds, the supplanted record holders. A month later, on 4 November 1978, their goalless draw with Everton established another record—that of 36 consecutive first-class competitive games without defeat. The beaten record, held by Blackburn Rovers, had been established all of 96 years previously, in 1881-82. Since that defeat by Leeds, Forest had played 59 first-class games (six FA Cup, nine League Cup, four European Cup, the FA Charity Shield and 39 First Division) and had been beaten just once (on 11 March 1978) by West Bromwich Albion in an FA Cup quarter-final. Their next game, a 3-2 victory at Everton in the League Cup on 7 Nobember 1978, was also their 18th consecutive *away* first-class game (excluding matches on neutral grounds such as Wembley) without defeat—also a record. The following Saturday, their 3-1 win at Tottenham was their 21st consecutive away League game without defeat—and another record.

Forest's astonishing run remains the most remarkable sustained performance in the history of English League football. It finally came to an end on 9 December 1978 at, appropriately, Anfield, where Forest went down 2-0. They had, however, gone undefeated for over a year and for a complete season of matches—42. It was the first time a club had gone a whole season without defeat since Preston had won the first Championship in 1889 without losing a match—but the Lancastrians had played only 22 fixtures.

Forest had broken virtually every record in the book—longest undefeated run, longest undefeated League run, longest run of away matches without defeat, most away League matches without defeat—and they went on to win the European Cup undefeated at the first attempt. And yet they did not win the Championship at the end of that season, Liverpool finishing eight points clear with a record of 68, the highest ever achieved by the Champions during the two points for a win era. Forest finished with 60 points, a total surpassed by only 12 of the League Champions in the 35 seasons between the War and the introduction of three points for a win.

It was a perfect illustration of the unfortunate truth about the League Championship—that it is as much what your contemporaries do as what you achieve yourself that determines the difference between success and failure.

Hence Leeds could win the Championship in 1969 by scoring 66 times (one fewer than the number of points they got), while forty years earlier Manchester City mustered 23 goals more and were relegated! Even worse was to come for City in 1938, when they scored 80 goals, more than any other club in the First Division, and were relegated again. In 1928-29, by comparison, Cardiff City conceded fewer than any other club in the First Division and finished bottom of the table for their troubles.

Leeds' 66 goal tally—one less than the record 67 points they amassed—was perfectly respectable in a climate of defensive football. City's 1926 total of 89, however, was not—unfortunately for them—as extraordinary then as it would have been forty years on.

For those years saw the decline and fall of positive attacking football. Preventing goals is easier than scoring them, and the 'smash-and-grab' type of football, with goals on the quick break out of defence as introduced by Herbert Chapman during his reign at Arsenal, rapidly became the favoured tactic.

That style of play was perhaps best seen at its peak when the Gunners themselves played against Aston Villa in 1935. Territorially outplayed, Arsenal were restricted to just nine shots at goal, eight of them from their England centre-forward, Ted Drake. The score? Aston Villa 1 Arsenal 7. Drake scored all seven Arsenal goals and struck the cross-bar with his eighth shot.

In the early days of the League, Sunderland, for example, won the 1893 title with 100 goals—and 48 points—from just 30 matches. But defences quickly became more sophisticated and the offside trap, brought to a fine art by Bill McCracken of Newcastle in the middle twenties, showed itself as early as 1909. In that year, Newcastle won the title with only 65 goals.

It is interesting to speculate what might have happened if the Football League's original intention to award points only for wins had been carried through. The mind boggles at the goals there might have been had a drawn game remained valueless in terms of points! However, it was not to be, for after 10 weeks of the first season it was decided that drawn games should be worth a point to each side.

At the end of the first season, Preston North End were champions. That inaugural season, 1888-89, when Preston also won the FA Cup without conceding a goal, their League record was so outstanding that it remains an imperishable landmark in soccer history.

In their 22 League matches, they won 18 times and drew four, scoring 74 goals against 15. They are the only British club ever to have gone through a season without a defeat in either League or Cup.

Preston were champions again in the League's second season, though they were beaten four times. In 1890-91, however, they finished second. It was Everton who took the title away from them, and who were to become the most consistent League club, spending all but five of the next 74 seasons in the top division. The record for unbroken membership belongs to Sunderland who, up to their relegation in 1958, had been 57 consecutive seasons in the top bracket.

Considering that the North East has produced only three major clubs, Sunderland, Newcastle and Middlesbrough, the area has done well in terms of First Division membership—at least one of the three was there until 1962—especially as none of those was an original League member.

There were twelve of those: Wolves, Everton, Preston, Burnley, Derby, Notts County, Blackburn Rovers, Bolton, Stoke, Accrington, Aston Villa and West Bromwich Albion. The North East was not the only region with no representative in the first League. Not one of that dozen came from London or the South.

By 1983, the story was different. The Home Counties had five clubs in the First Division, the Midlands as many as seven, Lancashire was down to four and Yorkshire and the once mighty North East had only Sunderland. The five remaining clubs—Ipswich, Brighton, Norwich, Swansea and Southampton—came, needless to say, from elsewhere, though Luton and Watford might be added to the list of the relatively unfamiliar. But that fact is important. Very few First Division teams have come from elsewhere. In the League's first 80 seasons, just twelve clubs have been situated outside the traditional areas of football power—London, the Midlands, Lancashire, Yorkshire and the North East—areas which contain some 80 percent of the country's population.

They are Grimsby (who joined Division One in 1901), Bristol City (1906), Cardiff (1921), Portsmouth (1927), Luton (1955), Ipswich (1961), Southampton (1966), Norwich (1972), Carlisle (1974), Brighton, Swansea and Watford.

But if that signifies any shift in the balance of power, it has been so slight as to be negligible. After all, apart from Portsmouth in 1949 and 1950, and Alf Ramsey's Ipswich in 1962, the Championship has never left the pockets of soccer strength.

This is not because the industrial areas produce the best players, but because they provide more spectators. Crowds paying money at the gate means money to spend on new players. It is a harsh fact of football life that the clubs with the best support tend to get the best players. There are exceptions—of which Aston Villa and Newcastle have been examples since the War.

It was different in 1888 when the League started. Professionalism had been legal for only three years; money was not yet all important. Then, the best players came from those parts of the country where there were most young men. And with Lancashire and the Midlands centres of heavy industry, they were able to attract young men from Scotland, Ireland and Wales, where jobs were few. Many a skilful footballer emerged from kickabouts with his workmates.

But as industry began to spread, so did the quality and scope of the game. It is no coincidence that the first team from the South to join the League was a works team—Woolwich Arsenal. The Crimea had made a munitions factory on the banks of the Thames important to the country's war effort. More was to come from that factory than shells.

Not that Arsenal were the first 'outside' club to penetrate the monopoly of the Midlands and Lancashire. Arsenal did not really emerge until 1904, when the League was 16 years old.

The first 'newcomers' were Sunderland, in 1890, who won the Championship in 1891 and 1892, when Sheffield's Wednesday joined the First Division, a year ahead of the other Sheffield club, United.

The arrival of these three was no surprise. Sunderland had a fine team drawn from a mixture of local Northerners and Scotsmen who had been tempted over the border, while Sheffield was one of the first towns in which organized football was played. Indeed, the Sheffield amateur club, formed in 1857, is the oldest in the world.

Sunderland had been champions six times when they were relegated in 1958, which, when added to Newcastle's four, gives the North East an impressive record considering its population. Lancashire, of course, boasting the Liverpool and Manchester clubs in addition to earlier giants of the League such as Blackburn, Preston and Burnley, have easily the best record with 33 of the first 80 Championships.

There have been few discernable patterns with regard to the winning of the League, except perhaps for the years 1963-70. Then the title seemed to be the preserve of the North. Champions in those years were Everton, Liverpool, Manchester United, Liverpool, United again, Manchester City, Leeds and Everton. Eight Championships, and seven of them won by Lancashire's two major cities.

Below: *The First Division was enlivened in 1982 by the arrival of two sides who were not from the traditional strongholds of the game but whose tactics were designed to bring fans back to their matches. Chiltern neighbours Watford and Luton soon became the First Division's leading scorers, although the policy did not immediately bring them any honours. Watford rose from the Fourth to the First Division in the space of five years (1978-82) and their off-field publicity was almost as good as that on the park. Chairman Elton John added some undreamed-of glamour, here handing out gold discs to his principle strikers Luther Blissett and Ross Jenkins. Both had been with the club since the Fourth Division days and Blissett even managed to score a hat-trick on his first full England appearance, late in 1982 against Luxembourg.*

Right: *Luton, under David Pleat, were less flashy than their neighbours but just as entertaining, particularly early on in the 1982-83 season when, among other results, they drew 3-3 at Anfield. Seen here on the way up in 1979, Alan Birchenall, Ricky Hill and Alan West form the wall at a free-kick.*

Leeds' 1968-69 success was their first. Yorkshire neighbours Huddersfield, however, collected three in consecutive seasons during the twenties, under the guidance of the famous Herbert Chapman, later to build the Arsenal team that became the only club to emulate Huddersfield's feat.

Huddersfield's first Championship they won dramatically. For at the end of the 1923-24 season Cardiff City also had 57 points, and the two clubs' goal averages were remarkably similar. Huddersfield had scored 60 goals against 33, Cardiff 61 against 34. That in fact gave Huddersfield a microscopic advantage but under today's goal difference Cardiff would have been top.

And that was tragic for Cardiff. For in their last game of the season, the Welshmen had been awarded a penalty in the last minute at Birmingham. No one wanted to take it, but eventually Len Davies stepped up. He missed it, the game ended in a goalless draw and Huddersfield were champions.

If Huddersfield's climb to the top had been dramatic, Cardiff's rise—and their subsequent decline—was even more spectacular. Admitted to the Second Division in 1920, they won promotion in their first season. Curiously, they were then only a 200th part of a goal behind Birmingham in first place.

Within seven years, Cardiff had been Championship runners-up, beaten FA Cup Finalists, and Cup winners in 1927. Within another seven, they were seeking re-election after finishing bottom of the Third Division South.

That same season, 1933-34, Huddersfield scored more goals than any of their First Division rivals. Perhaps that was some atonement for their poor tally that had deprived Cardiff of what would have been their first and only Championship success. For those 60 goals Huddersfield scored in 1923-24 comprised the lowest aggregate since the War.

The War seemed momentarily to have arrested the trend of fewer and fewer goals, and even the advent of the 'policeman' centre-half, the result of the offside law change in 1925 and exemplified by Arsenal's Herbie Roberts, could do little to stop the surge in goalscoring. In 1931, when the Championship was Arsenal's, they scored 127 goals, while Aston Villa, runners-up that season, themselves scored a record 128.

After the Second World War, football boomed but goals like everything else were in short supply. That was until the great young Manchester United side of the mid-fifties. In 1957, just before the Munich disaster, they scored 103 goals, as did Wolves the next year. In 1959, Wolves surpassed themselves with 110.

But with the Spurs team that won the double in 1960-61 came one of the last centuries before the massed defences took over. Though Tottenham scored a conspicuous 111 goals in 1962-63, Everton's 84 gave them six more points and thus the title. No club has scored 100 First Division goals since that year.

The fall-off in goalscoring can be clearly seen at the other end of the table. While Spurs won the double, Newcastle went down with 86 goals to their credit. Compared with the miserable 27 Huddersfield scraped together when they were relegated just over a decade later, Newcastle might well curse their misfortune.

In the 1970s goals were even tighter. From 1960 to 1965 Spurs scored 115, 88, 111, 97 and 87 League goals in the five seasons. A decade later, in a period when they reached four Cup finals, their goal scoring figures went 54 (3rd), 63 (6th), 58 (8th), 45 (11th) and 52 (19th). Their League positions and Cup finals show that they were by no means an unsuccessful team. The margins had, however, become much tighter with fewer goals being scored. A draw when you are 1-0 down is a lot easier to achieve than when the deficit is 4-1. Fewer goals lead, inevitably, to more low scoring draws and the possibility, if not likelihood, or the poorer teams sneaking an undeserved win. At the most extreme, teams could still survive and barely score at all. The most absurd example of this came from Second Division Orient in 1974-75. They finished 12th with a point a game record of 42 points. And yet they scored only 28 goals—an average of $1\frac{1}{2}$ points per goal!

The First Division in recent years has suffered from the dominance of Liverpool. The Merseysiders won 7 of the 11

Liverpool's remarkable run of success between 1973 and 1983—seven Championships, three European Cups, one FA Cup, three League Cups, two UEFA Cups and, amazingly, finishing only once below second in the first Division—was the most sustained and impressive performance in the history of English football. The only negative feature was that it did have the tendency to depress interest elsewhere in the country.

Opposite top: *The Liverpool players celebrate David Johnson's goal at Leeds on 17 May 1979. It was Liverpool's 85th of the season and established a record goal difference of 69 goals for League Champions. They conceded only 16 goals all season, another modern record (Preston conceded 15 from 22 games in 1888-89), and led the First Division from the first day of the season to the last.*

This page: *David Johnson in action again, against WBA.*

Opposite bottom: *Another trophy for Liverpool, the Charity Shield of 1979. Appearing as League Champions, Graeme Souness, Alan Hansen and Kenny Dalglish celebrate their 3-1 victory over Arsenal. Liverpool have held the Shield a record 10 times, on three occasions jointly.*

Championships that followed Derby's surprise success of 1972. In that year Liverpool should have won the trophy as well. They went to Arsenal for the last game of the season needing a win to clinch it, but only drew 0-0. On the same evening Leeds needed just a draw at Wolves and they, in their turn, would have been champions. The result of a game destined to feature in future lawsuits was 2-1 to Wolves so Derby, who had completed their fixtures and all gone off to Majorca sure they would be caught, were unexpectedly declared Champions for the first time.

Derby's manager was, of course, Brian Clough and the only real challenge Liverpool have had in the last decade has come from Clough and his East Midland clubs Derby and Forest. Though Clough had left, Derby won another Championship in 1975 (albeit with only 53 points) and the East Midlands connection had been cemented after ex-Derby captain Dave Mackay moved from Nottingham Forest as manager. Clough took the vacant chair at the City Ground, gradually built his squad, and, between April 1977 and May 1979 Forest moved from a team on the fringe of promotion in the Second Division, through the First Division championship to becoming worthy, and by no means lucky, European Champions. It was the fastest rise in football history. Promoted only third behind Wolves and Chelsea, they became the only club to win the First Division Championship immediately after being promoted other than as Second Division champions.

Liverpool were, of course, second that year. In ten seasons, Liverpool have finished other than first or second only once—fifth behind Aston Villa in 1981. And they won the European Cup that season to compensate! The Liverpool phenomenon is a remarkable one, but it has made the League less interesting. To maximize national involvement, and to motivate the fans, the honours have to be shared around. Even in Liverpool in 1983 football fans were bored. It had happened too often. They had even won the European Cup three times—what else was there to achieve? And, after all this, attendances at Anfield were dropping fast. Minor sides were scrapped, the full-time staff was cut to just enough for two teams. It made little difference to the club's consistency in the League. For the 7th time in 11 years the Merseysiders walked away with the Championship, having established such a massive lead at the half-way point that the rest of the season was academic except for speculation on whether Liverpool would become the first side for nearly two decades to score 100 First Division goals. In Bob Paisley's final year, little had changed since his first.

LEAGUE CHAMPIONSHIP

	Winners	Runners-up
1888-89	Preston North End	Aston Villa
1889-90	Preston North End	Everton
1890-91	Everton	Preston North End
1891-92	Sunderland	Preston North End
1892-93	Sunderland	Preston North End
1893-94	Aston Villa	Sunderland
1894-95	Sunderland	Everton
1895-96	Aston Villa	Derby County
1896-97	Aston Villa	Sheffield United
1897-98	Sheffield United	Sunderland
1898-99	Aston Villa	Liverpool
1899-1900	Aston Villa	Sheffield United
1900-01	Liverpool	Sunderland
1901-02	Sunderland	Everton
1902-03	The Wednesday	Aston Villa
1903-04	The Wednesday	Manchester City
1904-05	Newcastle United	Everton
1905-06	Liverpool	Preston North End
1906-07	Newcastle United	Bristol City
1907-08	Manchester United	Aston Villa
1908-09	Newcastle United	Everton
1909-10	Aston Villa	Liverpool
1910-11	Manchester United	Aston Villa
1911-12	Blackburn Rovers	Everton
1912-13	Sunderland	Aston Villa
1913-14	Blackburn Rovers	Aston Villa
1914-15	Everton	Oldham Athletic
1915-19	No competition	
1919-20	West Bromwich Albion	Burnley
1920-21	Burnley	Manchester City
1921-22	Liverpool	Tottenham Hotspur
1922-23	Liverpool	Sunderland
1923-24	**Huddersfield Town	Cardiff City
1924-25	Huddersfield Town	West Bromwich Albion
1925-26	Huddersfield Town	Arsenal
1926-27	Newcastle United	Huddersfield Town
1927-28	Everton	Huddersfield Town
1928-29	Sheffield Wednesday	Leicester City
1829-30	Sheffield Wednesday	Derby County
1930-31	Arsenal	Aston Villa
1931-32	Everton	Arsenal
1932-33	Arsenal	Aston Villa
1933-34	Arsenal	Huddersfield Town
1934-35	Arsenal	Sunderland
1935-36	Sunderland	Derby County
1936-37	Manchester City	Charlton Athletic
1937-38	Arsenal	Wolverhampton Wanderers
1938-39	Everton	Wolverhampton Wanderers
1939-46	No competition	
1946-47	Liverpool	Manchester United
1947-48	Arsenal	Manchester United
1948-49	Portsmouth	Manchester United
1949-50	**Portsmouth	Wolverhampton Wanderers
1950-51	Tottenham Hotspur	Manchester United
1951-52	Manchester United	Tottenham Hotspur
1952-53	**Arsenal	Preston North End
1953-54	Wolverhampton Wanderers	West Bromwich Albion
1954-55	Chelsea	Wolverhampton Wanderers
1955-56	Manchester United	Blackpool
1956-57	Manchester United	Tottenham Hotspur
1957-58	Wolverhampton Wanderers	Preston North End
1958-59	Wolverhampton Wanderers	Manchester United
1959-60	Burnley	Wolverhampton Wanderers
1960-61	Tottenham Hotspur	Sheffield Wednesday
1961-62	Ipswich Town	Burnley
1962-63	Everton	Tottenham Hotspur
1963-64	Liverpool	Manchester United
1964-65	**Manchester United	Leeds United
1965-66	Liverpool	Leeds United
1966-67	Manchester United	Nottingham Forest
1967-68	Manchester City	Manchester United
1968-69	Leeds United	Liverpool
1969-70	Everton	Leeds United
1970-71	Arsenal	Leeds United
1971-72	Derby County	Leeds United
1972-73	Liverpool	Arsenal
1973-74	Leeds United	Liverpool
1974-75	Derby County	Liverpool
1975-76	Liverpool	Queen's Park Rangers
1976-77	Liverpool	Manchester City
1977-78	Nottingham Forest	Liverpool
1978-79	Liverpool	Nottingham Forest
1979-80	Liverpool	Manchester United
1980-81	Aston Villa	Ipswich Town
1981-82	Liverpool	Ipswich Town
1982-83	Liverpool	Watford

** League title won on goal average

THE MILK CUP

'It's a joke. It can never get off the ground. Within three years it'll be scrapped.' That was the reaction of one First Division manager to the news that the move for a Football League Cup had been given official approval.

The millions who saw the passion, excitement and urgency generated by Stoke and West Ham in the four-match semi-final of 1972, or saw the expressions on the faces of the Stoke and Chelsea players as they climbed the Wembley steps a few weeks later, would find it difficult to believe that remark had been made only 12 years before.

'The League Cup has become one of the highlights of the domestic soccer calendar,' asserted Football League secretary Alan Hardaker, who initiated the idea. And the statistics then backed him up.

Yet for some time it appeared that the pessimists were the realists. The Cup, voted in at the annual meeting of the League in 1960 by a majority of only 15, was a very sickly infant, and the reception it received in some quarters was, to put it kindly, lukewarm. British managers, players and crowds were just beginning to adjust to the thought of European competition and here was another tournament, created to help the smaller sides and not particularly lucrative, to clog up the fixture list still further. It was not right to expect footballers to play 60 times a season.

Five clubs, including those who had finished second, third, fourth and fifth in the First Division the previous season, refused to enter, thus devaluing the competition before it had even started. The following year the number of absentees swelled to 10, including seven of the top ten.

The early, two-legged finals were hardly affairs to shake the football world and in 1962, when it was played out between a Second and a Fourth Division side, the two games pulled in barely 30,000 spectators. So, as the big clubs continued to view it with contempt and the smaller ones entered almost as a matter of form, as the press and the public looked on with detachment, the League Cup went stuttering on.

Hardaker remained the most ardent of its few committed supporters. He had always been obsessed with what was essentially his idea though, as he points out, he could not and did not implement it. 'It's been called Hardaker's baby and even Hardaker's folly,' he explains, 'but I did not take the decision to introduce it. Like everything else done by the League it was a matter for the clubs to vote on.'

Hardaker's early optimism was based on comparisons with the competition's much older sister, the FA Cup. 'Every worthwhile development in football has faced initial problems and criticism, and the League Cup was no exception. The early history of the FA Cup shows that it too had to face a variety of problems for several years, not least lack of interest. It was strongly criticized on its inception because it introduced a competitive element into amateur football, namely the winning of a trophy. There were 15 entries. After ten seasons there were 73.'

But the FA Cup was the first national competition. It was the natural result of the enthusiasm and aspirations of an emerging sport. The League Cup, by contrast, was anything but; money was its motivating force. It had to be created, and then it took several severe changes—with more commercial carrots being dangled—to drag it from a struggling child into a promising adolescent. They came in 1966.

The previous season the eight absent clubs had included seven from the top eight in the First Division—among them League Champions Manchester United, FA Cup holders Liverpool and, most indicative of all, Chelsea, the holders of the League Cup itself. Tommy Docherty apparently thought the Fairs Cup a good deal more important. Attendances, though slightly improved, remained mediocre.

There were two major changes. First, the awkward home and away final was abolished in favour of a more romantic (and lucrative) Saturday climax at Wembley. Second, the Fairs Cup committee decided to accept the winners as entrants for its competition the following year—provided they were a First Division side. (Though an obvious incentive this move never actually promoted an entrant: in 1967 and 1969 the winners, Queen's Park Rangers and Swindon, were both Third Division sides, in 1968 Leeds—who were to win the Fairs Cup later that season—qualified by coming fourth in the League, and in 1970 Manchester City went on to win the Cup Winners Cup, thus defending that trophy the following year. Spurs, in 1971, were the first club able to take up the offer, and by then the actual Fairs Cup was no more.)

The changes completely revitalized a flagging League Cup. All but League Champions Liverpool and Cup winners Everton now entered, and the converts included four sides who had remained aloof from the start—Arsenal, Sheffield Wednesday, Spurs and Wolves. Perhaps there was a certain justice in the fact that all four of them went out to sides of lesser standing in the League, and not one of them reached the last 16—that is, won more than one game.

In fact West Ham, who had seen something in the League Cup from the start, were responsible for the elimination of the two North London sides who had just joined the fold. They then beat Leeds (7-0) and Blackpool but were stopped short of Wembley by WBA—in a repeat of the previous year's two-legged final—after crashing 4-0 at The Hawthorns.

Albion's opponents were QPR, then running away with the Third Division championship. Rangers had started as they meant to go on with a 5-0 win over Colchester, but they had only one game against a First Division club on the way, beating Leicester 4-2. The match at Wembley, in danger of being a one-sided anti-climax, proved to be the opposite. Lowly QPR, down two goals by an ex-player of their's, Clive Clark, were faced with an apparently impossible task against a club separated from them by about 30 places in the League. But they did do it, with goals from Roger Morgan, Rodney Marsh (a splendid effort that, with the help of television, made him a household name by the Monday morning) and Mark Lazarus.

Had the League Cup come of age? From some quarters came an honest conversion, from others came grudging acknowledgement. Cynics pointed out the fact that no Third Division club had reached the FA Cup Final in the 47 years that section had been in existence, let alone won it, and said that the big sides were still loath to take it at all seriously. But 98,000 at Wembley and millions more in their armchairs thought differently.

The moves had apparently done the trick. Though some clubs committed in Europe continued to opt out—notably Manchester United—the competition grew in stature over the next few years and the average attendance (all for mid-week games except the final) soared from just over 11,000 in 1965-66 to over 19,000 in 1971-72.

In 1968 Leeds at last won a domestic honour, with a laboured 1-0 victory over a re-emerging Arsenal on a dreadful Wembley pitch. The following year Arsenal were back (this time on an even worse Wembley surface, thanks to the Horse of the Year Show) to face Swindon, who had played 11 matches to reach the final.

Swindon were trying to repeat Queen's Park Rangers' double of League Cup and promotion to the Second Division, and they succeeded. Brilliant goalkeeping from Peter Downsborough and two goals from Don Rogers helped them to a 3-1 win, though the effects of a recent 'flu epidemic at Highbury took its toll of the Arsenal players during extra time. Nine of the Arsenal squad appeared in both 1968 and 1969, among them Frank McLintock, who thus finished on the losing side at Wembley for the fourth time.

Extra time was again required in 1970, this time for Manchester City's 2-1 win over West Bromwich Albion. The tie of the competition, however, was the semi-final between the Manchester giants. City—promoted in 1966, League Champions in 1968, FA Cup winners in 1969, and now on their way to a European triumph—had been severely challenging the supremacy of a Manchester United side desperately trying to maintain the status achieved by the European Cup win over Benfica at Wembley in 1968, and a side competing in the League Cup for the first time since 1960-61.

For the first time, perhaps, a League Cup match apart from the final took on a significance outside the competition. The edited versions of both games were televised, and millions saw City confirm their suspicions with a 2-1 win at Maine Road and a 2-2 draw at Old Trafford, the second leg being played in front of 63,418—a record for the League Cup away from Wembley. 'Perhaps now they'll bloody well believe us,' said City wing-half Mick Doyle after the tie. The final, a dull, grinding affair, was a disappointment.

For those who thought the age of the lower clubs was over in the League Cup the 1970-71 competition was something of a revelation. Aston Villa, like QPR and Swindon chasing escape from the Third Division, reached Wembley. They were fortunate in meeting only one First Division side in their first five ties—a struggling Burnley in the second round—but when they did meet opponents of renown and calibre in Manchester United they proved nothing was missing. First they secured a 1-1 draw at Old Trafford and then, in front of 62,500, beat United 2-1 at Villa Park. But Wembley, Tottenham and Martin Chivers proved to be more difficult. Villa held Spurs for 80 minutes, but then two goals from the England man kept the League Cup firmly in the First Division.

There it was to stay in 1972, when Stoke beat Chelsea at Wembley in the final of what had been the first competition it had been compulsory for all 92 clubs to enter—a rather late and empty gesture at the 1971 annual general meeting. But, like the previous two seasons, it was the semi-final stage that stole the headlines.

While Chelsea and Spurs were battling out their tie, West Ham were trying to make the final an all-London affair by beating Stoke. They got off to a good start with a 2-1 win at the Victoria Ground, but John Ritchie pulled a goal back at Upton Park in the return and, in the dying minutes of extra time Gordon Banks (who had been beaten by a Geoff Hurst penalty in the first leg) made a brilliant save to stop his England colleague repeating the feat. A fine replay at Hillsborough produced no goals, and then in the second replay at Old Trafford there was the strange sight of Bobby Moore donning the goalkeeper's jersey while the injured Ferguson was off the field.

Stoke beat him once, with Bernard following up a penalty kick Moore had managed to save first time; then, with Ferguson restored, West Ham took the lead through Bonds and Brooking; Dobing pulled Stoke level before half-time and, as the two sides approached seven hours of battle, Conroy scored the winner.

The final didn't stand a chance. Three of the Stoke-West Ham clashes and both Chelsea-Spurs games had been covered by television and, though the pre-match publicity was as great as for

Garry Birtles scores Forest's third goal in the 1979 final. Also appearing in 1978 and 1980, Forest were the first team to contest three consecutive Wembley finals.

any FA Cup Final, the match was almost inevitably a come-down. Stoke, by no means standing on ceremony or overawed by Wembley, absorbed all Chelsea's subtle pressure and took their chances well to win 2-1. After 12 matches in the tournament that year they deserved some reward.

Following on the heels of Stoke's belated success, Norwich City reached the 1973 final (their first Wembley appearance) despite not having won any of their previous 12 League matches. After the final it was to be another 8 before they recorded a success. Just ten days before Wembley they had sold their star forward Jim Bone, and their resulting contest with Spurs produced a dreadful match. The only romance came from Ralph Coates who scored the game's only goal after coming on as substitute.

That final began a remarkable hat-trick for Ron Saunders, then the manager of Norwich. Twelve months later he led out Manchester City, his new club, to meet Wolverhampton Wanderers in the 1974 Final. Again he was loser. Yet remarkably 1975 saw Saunders in charge of a third League Cup finalist, Second Division Aston Villa—and this time he was a winner, ironically over Norwich City.

It was also ironic that the League Cup should gain in popularity just as the fixture list was becoming congested, with an increasing number of clubs entering Europe and the emergence of peripheral competitions: the Watney Cup, the Texaco Cup and the Anglo-Italian Tournament.

It may be that the League Cup provided the incentive; that officials and administrators saw the financial rewards to be reaped from competitive matches outside the two established folds. Certainly for a club stuck in the middle of the Third or Fourth Division and eliminated from the first round of the FA Cup in November, a run to the last eight or four can provide the only financial and psychological release during a mundane season.

No exercise can have started so badly as the League Cup. As Walter Pilkington, one of its most ardent advocates, was to put it later: 'It arrived as an apparent weakling, unwanted and shunned by the rich relations, regarded as an unnecessary affliction, derided by critics who gave it little or no chance of survival.'

It had not even been really intended. The idea was gently mooted in the 'Pattern of Football', published in 1957 by the Football League, with the main proposal being five divisions of 20 clubs. That, pointed out the smaller 'big' clubs who could not afford to lose a single fixture—Preston, Bolton, and the rest—would mean losing four valuable matches. The League Cup then gained favour as a compensation but, somewhere along the line, while that idea was accepted, the restructuring of the League went by the board.

The early tournaments did little or nothing to undermine the conviction that it would die an early death. The first season, for instance, the figures were arranged by mutual agreements of the clubs concerned—an arrangement that proved so cumbersome that the competition dragged on, in front of meagre crowds, for 11 long months, with the final being resolved in the September of 1961. The lowest attendance was 1,737 for a first round tie between Lincoln City and Bradford Park Avenue—a dismal record that stood until 1974. The 20 percent pool produced £29,982, or £354 for each competing club.

There were, however, more memorable events: such as Bradford City's 2-1 defeat of Manchester United, Chelsea's 18 goals in three games (including seven against both Millwall and Doncaster), and Gerry Hitchens' eleven goals for Villa before he joined Inter-Milan.

The second season, with the number of absentees doubling—Bill Shankly even kept his Second Division Liverpool out, and they won the title—the result was almost total apathy. The final was an irrelevant affair between Second Division Norwich and Fourth Division Rochdale. This was the only season when all the competing First Division clubs (bar Leicester, who won a bye) competed from the first round.

In the third season the First Division, though still represented by only twelve clubs, at last asserted its authority, Birmingham City beating Villa in the final. The top section retained their monopoly on finalists until 1967, despite the fact that their maximum presence in any year was only 14. Ironically in 1966-67, when all but Liverpool and Everton entered, the League Cup went to a Third Division side.

The competitions up till then were unlikely to have provided standard items for the serious reminiscences of football journalists. Goalscoring, perhaps, was the one thing that caught the eye: Tony Hateley's ten in six games for Villa in 1964-65; West Ham's 25 in eight games on the way to the 1966 final, including two fives against Cardiff in the semi-final and eleven of them to Hurst; WBA's 28 in nine games the same season, with eleven to Tony Brown; Orient's 9-2 win over Chester in 1962-63; Workington's 9-1 victory over neighbours Barrow in 1964-65 (amazingly, the competition's record win is between two clubs who are no longer in the League); and Leicester's 8-1 triumph against Coventry the same year.

Above left: Ron Harris, David Webb, Alan Hudson, John Dempsey and Paddy Mulligan can only watch helplessly as Terry Conroy heads Stoke in front against Chelsea in the 1972 League Cup Final—both clubs' second appearance in the final.
Above right: Arsenal's Bobby Gould (10) equalizes in the 1969 League Cup Final. But Swindon's Don Rogers scored twice in extra-time and the Third Division club, like Queen's Park Rangers in 1967, had beaten First Division opposition in the final.
Left: Jimmy Greenhoff celebrates after Conroy's goal. George Eastham (second left) went on to score Stoke's second to complete a 2-1 win—Stoke's 12th game of the competition and their first major success in a 109-year history.

The rise in popularity of the League Cup after 1966 cannot be put down solely to the introduction of a Wembley final and a promise of a place in Europe. For one thing there was a general stimulation of interest in the game after the World Cup; television coverage was becoming more and more frequent and the League Cup, with its important rounds being played between October and March, plugged the mid-week gaps left by a lack of FA Cup replays and European games; and the League Cup proved it produced goals, averaging 3.49 a game up to 1967 and keeping above three for the rest of the decade—well over the figures for the League and the FA Cup. As it rose in popularity the little clubs benefited: the share-out from the 20 percent pool was £327 for every participating club in 1963-64, but by 1972 it was over £2,000.

All the while 'Hardaker's baby' continued to progress, even though the finals rarely produced matches where skill overcame the electric atmosphere of a Wembley occasion. Perhaps the football public were conditioned by similar failings in most FA Cup Finals.

In 1974 Third Division Plymouth Argyle provided the spice by reaching the semi-finals of a competition that kept its interest even though the energy crisis restricted many kick-offs to midweek afternoons. Argyle finally fell to Manchester City after they had achieved sensational wins on the grounds of Burnley, QPR and Birmingham.

City's opponents were Wolverhampton Wanderers in their first Wembley appearance for 14 years. It proved a happy return for the Black Country club largely thanks to an afternoon of inspired goalkeeping by reserve Gary Pierce, on his 23rd birthday. City's flair from Summerbee, Bell, Lee, Law and Marsh wore a transparent look.

Though Bell equalized Wolves' first half goal from a mis-cued shot by Hibbitt, Wolves became League Cup winners when Richards scored nine minutes from time.

The competition emphasized its democracy in 1975, even if it produced another tedious final. Not one of the semi-finalists came from the First Division—the main giant-toppers being Chester of the Fourth. Manchester United, Aston Villa and Norwich City—the three clubs to be promoted from Division Two—were the other clubs in the last four with Villa and Norwich reaching Wembley. The game seemed destined for a goalless draw until Graydon missed a penalty in the 80th minute but scored from the rebound.

In 1977 and 1978 both Wembley finals produced goalless draws which were eventually resolved at Old Trafford. Aston Villa beat Everton in the second replay of the 1977 final to win the Cup for a record third time and in 1978 Nottingham Forest achieved a remarkable win over Liverpool—who they were to depose in the first round of the 1978-79 European Cup.

These were early days in the strange relationship between Liverpool and Forest. In fact, in the three seasons after Forest's promotion in 1977 the two clubs met 13 times in first-class matches. Liverpool won three, six were drawn and Forest won four. The League Cup final was the first of their major clashes and it followed the soon-to-become familiar pattern. Liverpool attacked a Forest side short of five regulars, and with teenage reserve Chris Woods in goal, for 120 minutes and didn't score. In the replay at Old Trafford, Phil Thompson brought John O'Hare down outside the penalty area, referee Pat Partridge gave a spot-kick which John Robertson converted and Forest won 1-0.

FOOTBALL LEAGUE AND MILK CUP FINALS 1960-1983

1960-61	**ASTON VILLA**				
First leg:	*Rotherham 22 August 1961 Attendance 12,226*				
	Rotherham United		2	**Aston Villa**	0
	Webster, Kirkman				
Second leg:	*Villa Park 5 September 1961 Attendance 27,000*				
	Aston Villa		3	**Rotherham United**	0
	O'Neill, Burrows, McParland				
1961-62	**NORWICH CITY**				
First leg:	*Rochdale 26 April 1962 Attendance 11,123*				
	Rochdale		0	**Norwich City**	3
				Lythgoe 2, Punton	
Second leg:	*Norwich 1 May 1962 Attendance 19,708*				
	Norwich City		1	**Rochdale**	0
	Hill				
1962-63	**BIRMINGHAM CITY**				
First leg:	*St Andrew's 23 May 1963 Attendance 31,850*				
	Birmingham City		3	**Aston Villa**	1
	Leek 2, Bloomfield			Thomson	
Second leg:	*Villa Park 27 May 1963 Attendance 37,921*				
	Aston Villa		0	**Birmingham City**	0
1963-64	**LEICESTER CITY**				
First leg:	*Stoke 15 April 1964 Attendance 22,309*				
	Stoke City		1	**Leicester City**	1
	Bebbington			Gibson	
Second leg:	*Leicester 22 April 1964 Attendance 25,372*				
	Leicester City		3	**Stoke City**	2
	Stringfellow, Gibson, Riley			Viollet, Kinnell	
1964-65	**CHELSEA**				
First leg:	*Stamford Bridge 15 March 1965 Attendance 20,690*				
	Chelsea		3	**Leicester City**	2
	Tambling, Venables (pen), McCreadie			Appleton, Goodfellow	
Second leg:	*Leicester 5 April 1965 Attendance 26,957*				
	Leicester City		0	**Chelsea**	0
1965-66	**WEST BROMWICH ALBION**				
First leg:	*Upton Park 9 March 1966 Attendance 28,341*				
	West Ham United		2	**West Bromwich Albion**	1
	Moore, Byrne			Astle	
Second leg:	*The Hawthorns 23 March 1966 Attendance 31,925*				
	West Bromwich Albion		4	**West Ham United**	1
	Kaye, Brown, Clark, Williams			Peters	
1966-67	**QUEEN'S PARK RANGERS**				
Final:	*Wembley 4 March 1967 Attendance 97,952*				
	Queen's Park Rangers		3	**West Bromwich Albion**	2
	Morgan (R), Marsh, Lazarus			Clark 2	
1967-68	**LEEDS UNITED**				
Final:	*Wembley 2 March 1968 Attendance 97,887*				
	Leeds United		1	**Arsenal**	0
	Cooper				
1968-69	**SWINDON TOWN**				
Final:	*Wembley 15 March 1969 Attendance 98,189*				
	Swindon Town		3	**Arsenal**	1
	Smart, Rogers 2			Gould	
1969-70	**MANCHESTER CITY**				
Final:	*Wembley 7 March 1970 Attendance 97,963*				
	Manchester City		2	**West Bromwich Albion**	1
	Doyle, Pardoe			Astle	
1970-71	**TOTTENHAM HOTSPUR**				
Final:	*Wembley 27 February 1971 Attendance 98,096*				
	Tottenham Hotspur		2	**Aston Villa**	0
	Chivers 2				
1971-72	**STOKE CITY**				
Final:	*Wembley 4 March 1972 Attendance 99,998*				
	Stoke City		2	**Chelsea**	1
	Conroy, Eastham			Osgood	
1972-73	**TOTTENHAM HOTSPUR**				
Final:	*Wembley 3 March 1973 Attendance 100,000*				
	Tottenham Hotspur		1	**Norwich City**	0
	Coates				
1973-74	**WOLVERHAMPTON WANDERERS**				
Final:	*Wembley 2 March 1974 Attendance 100,000*				
	Wolverhampton W.		2	**Manchester City**	1
	Hibbitt, Richards			Bell	
1974-75	**ASTON VILLA**				
Final:	*Wembley 1 March 1975 Attendance 100,000*				
	Aston Villa		1	**Norwich City**	0
	Graydon				
1975-76	**MANCHESTER CITY**				
Final:	*Wembley 28 February 1976 Attendance 100,000*				
	Manchester City		2	**Newcastle United**	1
	Barnes, Tueart			Gowling	
1976-77	**ASTON VILLA**				
Final:	*Wembley 12 March 1977 Attendance 100,000*				
	Aston Villa		0	**Everton**	0
	Hillsborough 16 March 1977 Attendance 55,000				
	Aston Villa		1	**Everton**	1
	Kenyon (og)			Latchford	
	Old Trafford 13 April 1977 Attendance 54,749				
	Aston Villa		3	**Everton**	2
	Nicholl, Little 2			Latchford, Lyons	
1977-78	**NOTTINGHAM FOREST**				
Final:	*Wembley 18 March 1978 Attendance 100,000*				
	Nottingham Forest		0	**Liverpool**	0
	Old Trafford 22 March 1978 Attendance 54,350				
	Nottingham Forest		1	**Liverpool**	0
	Robertson (pen)				
1978-79	**NOTTINGHAM FOREST**				
Final:	*Wembley 17 March 1979 Attendance 100,000*				
	Nottingham Forest		3	**Southampton**	2
	Birtles 2, Woodcock			Peach, Holmes	
1979-80	**WOLVERHAMPTON WANDERERS**				
Final:	*Wembley 15 March 1980 Attendance 100,000*				
	Wolverhampton W.		1	**Nottingham Forest**	0
	Gray				
1980-81	**LIVERPOOL**				
Final:	*Wembley 14 March 1981 Attendance 100,000*				
	Liverpool		1	**West Ham United**	1
	A. Kennedy			Stewart (pen)	
	Villa Park 1 April 1981 Attendance 36,693				
	Liverpool		2	**West Ham United**	1
	Dalglish, Hansen			Goddard	
1981-82	**LIVERPOOL**				
Final:	*Wembley 13 March 1982 Attendance 100,000*				
	Liverpool		3	**Tottenham Hotspur**	1
	Whelan 2, Rush			Archibald	
1982-83	**LIVERPOOL**				
Final:	*Wembley 25 March 1983 Attendance 100,000*				
	Liverpool		2	**Manchester United**	1
	A. Kennedy, Whelan			Whiteside	

It was an incident which led to one of football's most humorous interviews, when Peter Taylor, hugging the trophy (Forest's first under the Clough/Taylor management), was told that it certainly wasn't a penalty and Forest should therefore not have won. He rhetorically replied: 'Oh, who's got the Cup then?' and made off down the corridor with it.

Forest were back the next year, 1979, beating Southampton 3-2 in the final with two goals from Garry Birtles. In 1980 they made it a hat-trick of appearances, becoming the first club ever to appear in three consecutive Wembley finals. They had gone a record 25 games and 17 ties without defeat in the competition between September 1976 and March 1980. There the records ended after an absurd defensive mix-up between Peter Shilton and David Needham let in Andy Gray to score the only goal of the game and give Wolves a 1-0 victory.

Liverpool beat London opposition in the next two finals—West Ham after a replay in 1981 and Spurs 3-1 after extra-time in 1982. Spurs had led until three minutes from time and the defeat was their first in nine domestic cup finals, their first in nine games at Wembley and also broke an unbeaten run of 25 cup games.

The week before the Spurs v Liverpool final the competition had been renamed the Milk Cup. This was not a move calculated to enhance the stature of either the competition or milk, even though Liverpool gratefully accepted the award of not one but two trophies. In actual fact, the competition was slipping back into the 1960s again, being seen as something of an irrelevance compared with other fixtures in a crowded list and having lost some of its romance—the minor sides no longer progressed so far as the financial demands of the bigger clubs insisted that they did not slip up when it could be avoided.

In retrospect, the competition had reached its peak with those excellent semi-finals involving Chelsea and Stoke in 1972. At that time the Wembley finals were still a rare treat. In the decade that followed, the fact of having *two* finals a year at Wembley, plus a large number of replays (six in the two competitions) helped to rather devalue both events. For Liverpool, however, 1983 was a red-letter year. Beating Manchester United 2–1 in the final, they became the first club to win three consecutive Wembley finals and only the fifth to chalk-up a hat-trick in any domestic competition (Wanderers and Blackburn Rovers in the FA Cup, Huddersfield and Arsenal in the League being the others) and that was definitely a record to savour.

FROM THE GREAT WAR TO THE WORLD CUP

THE TWENTY YEARS between the First and Second World Wars has been called the era of the manager. That is not quite accurate. In truth it was the era of one manager; just one man, whose achievements found an appropriate setting halfway through two turbulent decades in the 1930 FA Cup Final. Those ninety minutes were, quite simply, a microcosm of the whole period.

The combatants were Huddersfield Town and Arsenal. Just eleven years earlier the Yorkshire club's directors had recommended that the organization move, lock, stock and barrel, to Leeds, support and success being sadly elusive in a Huddersfield obsessed with rugby league. The same year Arsenal crept into the First Division by means which could only be described as devious, being elected after finishing only fifth in the immediate pre-War Second Division.

Four years before the 1930 Final Huddersfield had become the first club ever to win three consecutive League Championships and, five years after it, Arsenal did precisely the same thing. During their great years both were managed by the same man, Herbert Chapman and, appropriately enough, the game in question was won by the club he then managed, Arsenal, over the club he had left, Huddersfield.

Herbert Chapman was born in the very far south of Yorkshire, at Kiveton Park, in 1873. His professional career in midfield with Spurs was distinguished largely by the lemon coloured boots he wore. In 1907 he became manager of the Southern League side Northampton Town and later moved to Second Division Leeds City, who were ignominiously thrown out of the League in 1919 for making illegal payments to players. Their place was taken by Port Vale—who were to suffer exactly the same fate half a century later. Vale, however, were re-elected. Leeds were not and Chapman—suspended though his only involvement was an alleged timely incineration of the club's books—took a partnership in an engineering firm.

Not for long though. Huddersfield, rather than move to Leeds as their directors were then threatening, managed to raise some cash and sign a number of players. When his suspension was lifted, Chapman joined Huddersfield as manager in September 1920. Here the story really begins. Chapman's first success was the FA Cup of 1922, albeit with a disputed Billy Smith penalty, and two years later Huddersfield won the League Championship on goal average from Cardiff. The next season they retained the title with a new defensive record—only 28 goals conceded—and went on to make it a hat-trick in 1926.

By that time, however, Chapman had gone. His success at Huddersfield was remarkable, for he had no great financial resources and the Yorkshiremen, facing the fierce competition of rugby league, had never drawn large crowds. His team had few outstanding players—most notable was Alex Jackson, one of the Scottish 'Wembley Wizards' that crushed England 5-1 in 1928. Jackson was technically a right-winger, though he actually wandered all over the park. England captains Clem Stephenson and Sam Wadsworth were valuable signings, while Sam Barkas was an excellent full-back partner for Wadsworth. Barkas, in fact, was one of Alf Ramsey's first boyhood idols.

Chapman's ability lay in choosing and moulding his players as parts of a whole—not just allowing them to function as individuals in the well-defined grooves laid down when 'positional' play was strict. He chose well at Huddersfield, but he was perhaps lucky in that his formation came right immediately. When he moved to Arsenal in 1925 it took rather longer to build a Championship side.

In a sense it was an appropriate time to move, for 1925 was also the year of the most significant tactical development since the 'passing' game had superseded the 'dribbling' game in the 1870s.

The immediate cause was the change in the offside law on 12 June 1925, when the '... fewer than three players between the attacker and the goal' clause was changed to '... fewer than two ...' The change had become desirable because so many teams were employing a very simple offside trap, bringing their defenders upfield to render lethargic forwards offside and sometimes confining play to a strip covering no more than 40 yards of the middle of the field.

The Notts County full-backs Morley and Montgomery had been guilty of this before the First World War, but it took their Newcastle counterparts McCracken and Hudspeth to elevate the 'offside game' to a fine art in the early 1920s. The pair became so identified with the ploy that when one side arrived at Newcastle Central station and a guard blew his whistle the centre-forward was heard to remark 'Blimey, offside already!'

When the trend became unacceptable the International

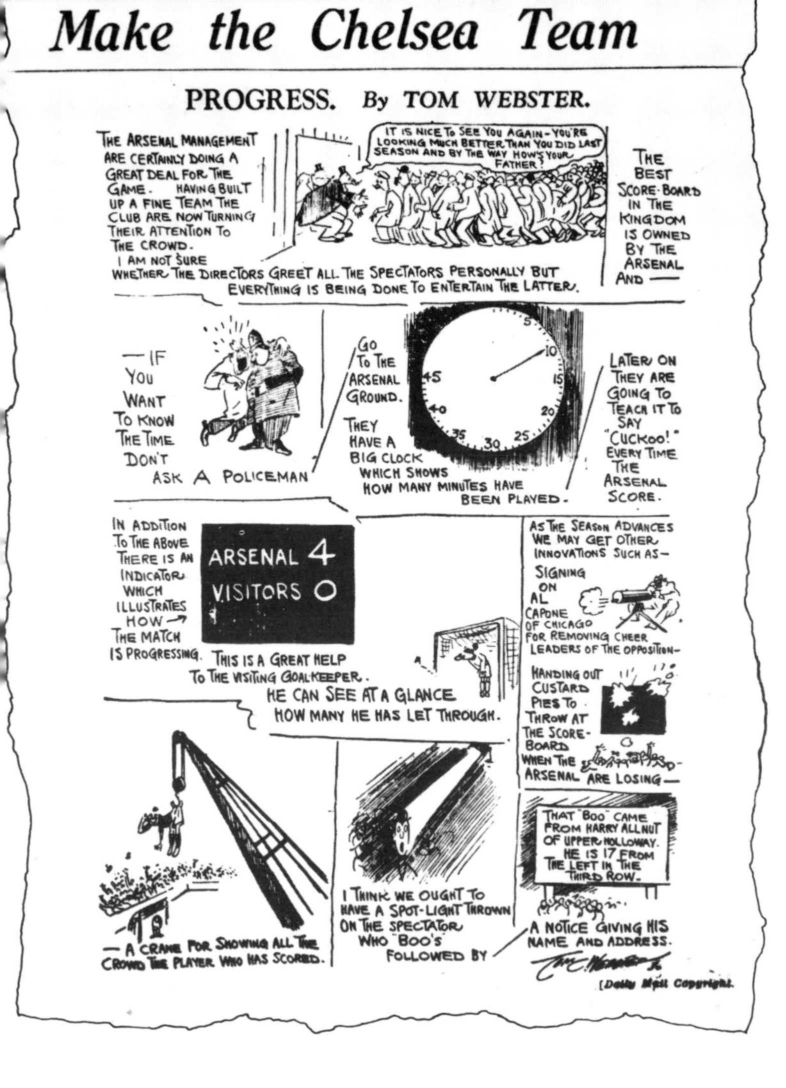

Left: Herbert Chapman's new approach to the whole field of club football prompted the Daily Mail *cartoonist Tom Webster to produce this strip in 1930. The famous south bank clock is still a feature of the ground.*

Board—the law making body—finally acted; and the results were startling. In the 1924-25 season 1192 goals were scored in the First Division. In the next season that figure read 1703—an increase of almost 50 percent, or, more graphically, an extra goal for every match played.

But while the immediate result was to move the advantage from defence to attack, the long term effect was probably negative, for the tactical result was, at its simplest, that one attacker became a defender.

Credit for devising the 'third-back game', as it became known, has never been adequately apportioned. Bob Gillespie of Queen's Park quickly made it his job to blot out the opposing centre-forward but folklore has it—with some concrete support—that the man behind the innovation was Herbert Chapman.

Chapman's first action on joining Arsenal had been to acquire a scheming inside-forward. His choice was Charlie Buchan from Sunderland, the man selectors said was 'too clever to play for England'. The fee was an imaginative £2,000 down and £100 for every goal he scored in the subsequent season. Buchan scored 19. But it was a transfer significant beyond its immediate impact and strange terms.

In 1929 Henry Norris, Arsenal's chairman, sued the FA for libel after he had been suspended for making illegal payments. The Buchan case was particularly mentioned and it was shown that Buchan had been offered other inducements to join the club. Norris lost his case and far more for, when he died in 1934, he was an exile from football and the club that he had dragged from obscurity.

Charlie Buchan's return to Arsenal, the club he had actually walked out on before the War over eleven shillings expenses, was not a very happy one. One of his, and Chapman's, earliest matches for the club was a humiliating 7-0 defeat at Newcastle on 3 October 1925. Buchan was so upset at such a return to his old home that he and Chapman organized an immediate tactical discussion. One or the other (accounts vary as to who it was) proposed that Arsenal's centre-half, Jack Butler, should adopt a purely defensive role and that one of the inside-forwards should drop back to supply the creative link between defence and attack that the centre-half could no longer provide.

Oddly enough Newcastle's centre-half, Charlie Spencer, claimed he had played just such a defensive role in that vital match, and the Arsenal plan may have come from observing Newcastle's success. Before 1925 the centre-half performed exactly the functions his title implied—he had played in the middle of the field helping in defence and instigating attacks.

Buchan expected to be given the creative inside-forward's job himself, but Chapman valued his goalscoring abilities too highly and detailed a reserve inside-forward, Andy Neil, to perform the midfield role at Upton Park the following week on Monday 5 October 1925. Arsenal won 4-0, with Buchan scoring twice.

Chapman gradually revised his team by pushing the full-backs out to mark the wingers, and using both his wing-halves (now free of their close-marking duties) to perform the midfield duties along with the withdrawn inside-forward. The scheme worked well enough, but was not perfected until Chapman purchased the vital creative link, Alex James, from Preston in 1929. Thus the team played in a formation which could loosely be described as 3-4-3 or 3-3-4, rather than the 2-3-5 of the pre-First World War era. Though most teams quickly copied Chapman's system, club programmes 45 years later were still putting down teams in the out-dated 2-3-5 pattern.

One of the secrets of good management is, of course, fitting systems of play to the men available. Some successful managers, like Stan Cullis at Wolves, managed to find just the players to operate a stereotyped formation. Some, like Ramsey at Ipswich, devise a system which suits the limited skills of the players available. Chapman's way was a combination of both, and his spectacular dips into the transfer market were basically a means of filling very specific gaps in both team and system.

Between 1925 and 1930 Chapman's team and tactics developed in step. Butler's successor as the 'policeman' centre-half was Herbie Roberts, acquired from Oswestry in 1926. His two full-backs were George Male and Eddie Hapgood, often partners for England. David Jack came from Bolton to replace Buchan for the first ever five figure fee (£10,370) in 1928 and, a year later, the key to the whole side arrived from Preston. Alex James was finally persuaded to adopt the midfield general role—spraying out long passes to the flying wingers Hulme and Bastin and to the unrefined but effective Jack Lambert at centre-forward.

That was essentially Chapman's great side of the early 1930s. Having lost the Cup Final of 1927, when Dan Lewis let the ball slide underneath his shiny new jumper and allowed Cardiff to take the Cup out of England for the first time, Arsenal returned to defeat Huddersfield 2-0 three years later.

The League was won for the first time in 1931 with 66 points (which remained a record until Leeds bettered it by one in 1969) and the following year Arsenal were at Wembley to lose by the famous 'over the line' goal to Newcastle: Allen's equalizing goal came from a cross which seemed well over the goal-line when Richardson made it. Between 1933 and 1935 Arsenal completed a hat-trick of League Championships, then beat Sheffield United in the Cup Final of 1936 and were champions again in 1938.

As Chapman died in 1934 he was neither with Huddersfield nor Arsenal when they completed their hat-tricks of Championships. He was succeeded at Highbury by George Allison, a radio commentator.

A simple recitation of Arsenal's successes in the 1930s, impressive though it is, tells only a part of the story. In a way that no other team, before or since, has ever approached, Arsenal somehow *were* football for a decade. In almost every way the Gunners' influence on the game was all-pervasive and Chapman's remarkable success on the field should never be allowed to conceal some remarkable achievements off it.

His skill as a public relations officer was certainly equal to his skill as a tactician. He claimed that as much energy had been expended getting the name of Gillespie Road tube station changed to Arsenal as had been exerted winning the Cup in 1930. He changed the name of the club from 'The Arsenal' to plain 'Arsenal' because, he explained, 'it will always be first in a list of

Above right: Complete with spectacles and plus-fours, Arsenal manager Herbert Chapman poses with his team at Hendon before the trip to Paris and the annual friendly with Racing Club.
Inset: The bust of Chapman at Highbury—a memorial to football's revolutionary thinker.
Above: But enthusiasm for the game in the late 1940s was not all for the good. A sixth round FA Cup tie at Burnden Park between Bolton and Stoke on 9 March 1946 attracted so many fans that closing the gates had no effect. They were broken down by the thousands outside with the tragic result that 33 were killed and hundreds injured when a wall collapsed.

clubs as well as on the field.' Appreciating the publicity value of the titled, he persuaded the board to accept Lord Lonsdale as one of their number and persuaded the Prince of Wales to open a new stand in 1932. He changed from the original Nottingham Forest colours to a red shirt with white sleeves because it was more distinctive, and later the red socks became blue and white hooped. This was so that the players could recognize each other without looking up in a melee and not, as Chapman had kidded, because 'red runs in the wash'.

Chapman was one of the first to experiment with numbering players—the FA finally accepted the idea for the 1933 Cup Final, five years after Chapman—and was in the forefront of schoolboy and youth training schemes.

In his trainer, Tom Whittaker, he appointed the first of the modern day physiotherapist coaches. Modern medical equipment, training routines and individual treatment all arrived at Highbury long before they had been considered anywhere else.

All in all, Arsenal were the very first of the wholly professional football clubs in the British Isles. Herein, perhaps, lies the key to the antipathy that followed, and still follows, the Gunners around the country. No story of the 1930s can be complete without considering this remarkable antagonism.

'Lucky Arsenal' was the cry that flitted across a decade. Time after time, Arsenal seemed happy to absorb the pressure of less talented attacks and win games by the simple expedient of the breakaway goal. It was difficult to convince the unsophisticated terraces or the ageing boardrooms of the 1930s that 80 minutes of unrewarded pressure was less valuable than one goal from a few sudden breaks by Hulme and Bastin. Indeed, it was to be another 30 years before British fans fully appreciated that the best of two teams is, by definition, the one that scores more goals.

It is, of course, impossible to view Arsenal out of historical perspective. The thirties were, for most of provincial Britain, arguably the worst decade for almost a century. In many of the textile towns unemployment reached a third of the workforce; in some places, like Jarrow, literally the whole town was on the dole for years on end. To these towns Arsenal came to represent the wealth, the affluence, and the unfair advantage that London seemed to have stolen from the rest of the country. It was not too unrealistic to see Arsenal as a symbol of the wealth earned in the North but spent and enjoyed in the South.

With the football ground being almost the only entertainment outlet available to the working-classes, it is not surprising that Arsenal became a subject of fierce emotional commitment—one way or the other. Walsall's defeat of Arsenal in the third round of the Cup in 1933 was a cause of widespread celebration all over the country, and the economic conditions of the times go no small way to explaining the peculiar position that one match still holds in the game's folklore—it was the perfect example of the poor, underfed weakling rising to humiliate a Goliath which had all the advantages.

On reflection Arsenal gained their reputation not by winning everything going—though they won a lot—but by always being the team to beat. They were really the first professionals to invade a world of semi-amateurs. They disturbed the cosy unthinking mood of the time where even the leading clubs were happy to meander along, appointing an old player as manager, reaching the odd semi-final here, the top five of the League there. This was success, this was football. Arsenal were simply of another generation. Instead of putting down men in chess-board formation—centre-forwards with iron foreheads and no feet, wingers on the touchline where they belonged—Arsenal experimented.

But Chapman's two great teams—Huddersfield and Arsenal—should not be allowed to disguise the fact that there were other sides of note in the inter-War period. Bolton, for instance, won

Left: Dixie Dean scores the second of Everton's goals in their 3-0 win over Manchester City in a 1933 FA Cup Final unique in the game's history. Not only was it the first time players were numbered but the only occasion on which they were numbered from 1 to 22. Numbering on shirts for League matches didn't come until 1939.

Right: The first day of League football for seven long years and a symbol to the British public that life was nearly back to normal. Spectators cheerfully queue in the rain outside Stamford Bridge on 31 August 1946. Hundreds of thousands of men were demob happy with money to spend and some years to make up.

the Cup in 1923, 1926 and again in 1929, the first being the occasion of the inaugural Wembley Final and the highest attendance ever at a British football match. West Bromwich won promotion from the Second Division and the FA Cup in 1931—a unique double—and the next year their promotion partners, Everton, went on to become only the second club to win the Second and First Division in consecutive seasons. With a Cup win in 1933, Everton were probably the closest rivals to Arsenal in the period. Dixie Dean had completed his remarkable 60-goal feat with a hat-trick in the last game of the 1927-28 season—against Arsenal—and went on to become a major attraction of the following decade.

On a wider front Britain was barely aware. While Cuba and the Dutch East Indies battled for the World Cup the Home Countries stood aloof from FIFA. England did not enter until 1950, when a traumatic game against the United States showed how 20 years of isolation could take their toll. Chapman may have built the strongest club side in the world, but that was far removed from the true international success that was so long coming.

For the English, then, the era meant Arsenal and in the end that must be Chapman's epitaph. Mention the club in any soccer conscious country in the world and it will produce instant recognition. The word no longer means a place where arms are kept, but rather the club that Herbert Chapman built. The name is a permanent memorial to the achievements of one man—and the club that had the good sense to appoint him.

Chapman's Arsenal team had faded by the time the Second World War began in 1939, but for many players their careers were ruined by the seven year suspension of football coinciding with their late twenties and early thirties. In 1939 Wolves appeared to have a team with a future—by 1946 they were all seven years older and Stan Cullis had to look for (and, as he did, find) new players to fit. That being said, the War also provided little opportunity for younger players to obtain the requisite experience, so the fixtures and the players on the first day of the season in 1946 bore an uncanny resemblance to that of the quickly aborted 1939-40 equivalent, which had lasted just three matches.

Of course, many names would appear no more, overtaken by age and tiring muscles. Others had been killed during the war, men like Tommy Cooper the great Liverpool full-back who met his end as a despatch rider, Albert Clarke, Blackburn Rovers' gifted inside-forward killed in Normandy on D-Day, Harry Goslin, pre-War captain of Bolton Wanderers, killed in action in Italy, Coen, that fine Luton goalkeeper shot down in a raid over the Ruhr Valley on a RAF bombing raid, or youngsters just making their way in the game in 1939 like Reynolds, transferred from Charlton to Torquay United a few days before war began, called up and killed in action before he had ever kicked a ball for his new club.

Others again were scattered all over the country, indeed all over the world, retained in the Forces and in essential industries. Consequently clubs gave League chances to men who before the war and again today would not have been allowed to lace a boot in a League dressing room.

In 1946-47 in the frantic bid to find and mould a decent combination clubs called on more men than ever before or since. Arsenal had 31 men on first team duty during the season, Huddersfield Town 32. In the Second Division Newport County's League roll call reached the astonishing figure of 41 and Bury, Leicester City, Manchester City, Millwall, Nottingham Forest and Sheffield Wednesday, all topped the 30 mark. Beating them all were Hull City, in the Third North. They fielded 42 men.

Yet Saturday 31 August 1946 was a symbol to the British people that life was nearly back to normal. On that day a full programme of first class League fixtures was played in the British Isles for the first time since 2 September 1939. In fact the 1945-46 FA Cup competition had been completed under unique rules which required the games to be contested on a home-and-away basis. One resulting oddity was that Charlton became the first side to reach the Final after undisputably *losing* an earlier game. Fulham beat them 2-1 in one of the third round matches but Charlton won on aggregate by taking the other match 3-1.

At the time hundreds of thousands of men were already demobbed with their gratuities burning a hole in their pockets and five or six years of their young lives to make up. Millions in factories and industry had been earning more money than ever before but as the war dragged on found less and less to spend it on. Now, with football back, there would be something exciting to help use up some of that cash, trips to be made by train and coach with meals to buy in towns not visited for many years, and wayside inns to dally at.

Rationing still blanketed all the civilizing amenities of life, cars and television sets for all were still a dream, you could not have a house built because of a word called licence. Another period as long as the war they had come through lay ahead before austerity began to fade from people's lives. But in the meantime, there was sport. The fact that once the light evenings had gone the government banned midweek matches in the drive to put the national economy back into a peacetime footing made the Saturday afternoon date all the more desirable.

Small wonder then that on 31 August 1946, when clubs opened their grounds to the public shortly after noon, there were long queues outside practically all of them. Small gates were the exceptions, not the rule. In the Third Division South, for example, only two clubs reported attendances of under 10,000. Crowds of 20,000 and 25,000 at this level were commonplace.

This was to be a unique season in many ways. The fixtures were a complete replica of those which had made for the 1939-40 campaign—a season which died after just seven days. This heightened the illusion that life had been taken up where it had left off. Ahead lay the terrible winter of 1946-47, by far the worst of the century and at a time when food and fuel were still heavily restricted. The winter struck late, and with floodlighting still another future dream, clubs could not get the alarming backlog of fixtures cleared. The season became the longest in history, lasting from 31 August to the following 14 June. The 1947-48 season began only 70 days later.

Both sides of the freeze-up, however, the crowds poured in. This was the time when a Jimmy Hill should have risen and forced through the no-maximum wage for footballers still 15 years or more in the future. Instead, after arbitration, the wage for the best First Division players was increased for the 1947-48 season to £12 a week maximum and £10 a week during the close season.

When the balance sheets for 1946-47 were presented all but

half a dozen clubs reported profits, many of them substantial. Stoke City led the way with £32,207, Burnley made £18,000, Liverpool over £17,000, Middlesbrough £15,000 and Wolves nearly £11,000. In Scotland, Rangers made £12,500; Queen of the South, whose home town Dumfries has a population of only 26,000, topped £11,000.

But it was not these figures which created a sensation in the soccer world, rather the £15,000 paid by Derby County to Morton, the Scottish club, for inside forward Billy Steel to succeed Peter Doherty.

On the field the defensive techniques of future years had not even begun to put in an appearance. Clarrie Jordan scored 41 goals for Doncaster Rovers, Wally Ardron of Rotherham United 38; Don Clark (Bristol City) and Dick Yates (Chester) 36 each; four of the Wolves' forwards reached double figures—Dennis Westcott 37, Jesse Pye 20, Jimmy Mullen 12 and Johnny Hancocks 10. Charlie Wayman netted 30 times for Newcastle United. Freddie Steele got 29 for Stoke City, Stan Mortensen 28 for Blackpool with Reg Lewis and Ronnie Rooke getting 49 between them for Arsenal. Jack 'Gunner' Rowley thumped 26 for Manchester United.

There were great names abroad in the land but at the end of an historic and colourful first post-War season such an authority as the late Ivan Sharpe was moved to write: 'More and more players—that's the need today.'

The 1946-47 season attracted some 35,000,000 spectators but this record was left far behind in the second post-War campaign. When all the figures were in, the attendance total in first-class football alone topped 40,000,000. This was five million more than ever before and it represented the taking of £4,000,000 at the turnstiles. England won the Home International Championship and against foreign opposition were invincible. This made it possible for Lord Athlone, President of the Football Association to deliver a speech at the annual meeting which smacked faintly of 'showing the flag'.

'At a time when exports are of paramount importance,' he said, 'football is far from being insignificant. A successful English referee in the Argentine or our international team in Italy is a way of speaking to other nations in a language ordinary people can understand.' For the first time the magic word 'television' came upon the scene. The FA was all for it, the Football League dead against it.

Two clubs dominated the English scene—Arsenal and Manchester United. United, for the first occasion in modern times rose to a national eminence which has surrounded Old Trafford ever since. Colchester United, then members of the Southern League, had their first glorious hour when they knocked First Division Huddersfield Town out of the FA Cup. In Scotland Hibernian took the Championship to Edinburgh for the first time since 1903. The team included Gordon Smith, Alec Linwood, Willie Ormond, Eddie Turnbull and an Englishman, Bobby Coombe. The most sensational transfer of the season came when Tommy Lawton, England's centre-forward, moved down to the Third Division, joining Notts County for a record £20,000 fee.

Surely 1948-49 could not see a new attendance record? In the event it did—easily. Leaving aside FA Cup games, internationals and the 30 major professional and amateur competitions outside the first class aegis, the number of people who attended League matches reached the never surpassed total of 41,271,424.

The defeat in the Cup of the then mighty Sunderland by

Below: *Bowlers, boaters, trilbies and cloth caps mingle in a section of the crowd for the 1921 Cup Final at Stamford Bridge.*
Below right: *The 1930 FA Cup Final and Huddersfield are hit by an Alex James free kick—the first of Arsenal's two goals.*

Yeovil Town of the Southern League on a sloping pitch down in Somerset was the most talked of event in the season. For the first time the Amateur Cup Final was staged at Wembley and a crowd of 95,000 paid over £20,000 to see Bromley beat Romford 1-0. Transfer fees continued to spiral upwards, Derby County paying Manchester United £25,000 for inside-forward Johnny Morris in March 1949.

As the 20th century came up to its half way mark football reached a watershed. The boom was a long way from over but 1949-50 was to be the last season in which total League attendances for a season topped 40,000,000. This, too, was the last season of the League in the form of 88 clubs equally divided into four sections, for at the annual meeting four new clubs—Colchester United, Gillingham, Scunthorpe and Lindsey United and Shrewsbury Town—were admitted, two each to both sections of Division Three. The election of Scunthorpe to the Northern group was one of the strangest quirks of post-War football. On the first ballot Shrewsbury were elected easily but Workington and Wigan Athletic tied for second place. Rather than just a straightforward vote between the two tied clubs, the League took it into its head to organize another open ballot—the result being that Scunthorpe defeated both of their seemingly stronger opponents. Workington replaced New Brighton the following year but it took Wigan 30 more years to achieve their goal and by that time their opponents Workington had come and gone, finally voted out.

The fifth post-War season, although it was not realized at the time, marked the real beginning in a change in public tastes and habits. At long last the all round austerity and drabness was disappearing. People could now think in terms of cars, clothes, furniture, new fabrics, new colours, television sets, holidays abroad. No longer did sport, and soccer in particular, represent one of the few worthwhile things on which to spend spare money and time.

The season's return for Football League attendances was still extremely good, topping 39,500,000 and it meant that in five campaigns the first-class game in England and Wales alone had attracted some 197,000,000. But impressive as the figures for 1950-51 were they represented the first small hole in the dyke. Not only were they one million down on the previous season and nearly two million down on 1948-49, but the League was now bigger by four clubs.

In other respects the sky was still the limit. A few days before the transfer deadline in March 1951, Sheffield Wednesday persuaded Notts County to accept £34,000 for Jackie Sewell which made the player literally worth his weight in gold.

Tottenham were perhaps the first club to perceive the need to meet the new challenge from outside Britain which was about to engulf the national elevens of the four home countries. Arthur Rowe, Spurs manager, a silver haired Cockney had instituted a style called 'push and run'. Briefly it meant doing the simple things quickly and accurately and it showed the benefits of a higher work rate than previously thought necessary from all eleven members of a side. Newly promoted from Division Two they cast a shadow of the worldwide greatness they were to earn a decade later by storming straight on to take the First Division title.

From that season the honeymoon between football and the fans was over. The game is still a crowd puller without parallel in any form of activity known to 20th-century man but it is unlikely ever to know again such a golden age at the turnstiles when in six years it was patronised by 236 million fans, a figure equivalent to the entire population of the United States or Russia. They were, indeed, the Golden Years.

1966 AND ALL THAT

An Englishman looking at football since the Second World War will inevitably focus on one of two moments in time. One is the evening of 6 February 1958 when the plane carrying Manchester United, undisputably Britain's best club side, crashed on take-off from Munich airport. The other comes eight years later, the afternoon of 30 July 1966, when the country that gave the world the game finally took its place as more than an also ran. After two decades of international mediocrity, a reputation had been re-established.

The World Cup win came at the midpoint of a decade which saw a complete change in the British game. The vital point was the abolition of the maximum wage in 1961. George Eastham had brought the whole question of players' conditions and contracts into the open and into the courts when Newcastle refused to give him a transfer. Victory for Eastham meant that men who had been restricted to a niggardly maximum wage of £20 a week could command three or four times that amount. Within a year Johnny Haynes, then captain of England, had become the first home footballer earning £100 a week.

It was perhaps unfortunate that this players' revolution should have occurred just as two other forces were changing the fabric of the game, a little more slowly to be sure, but just as vitally. One was the growth of private transport and an effective road system, allowing anyone within 40 miles of Manchester, say, to regard United as their local club.

The other factor was the introduction of regular televised games. This affected the game more subtly than the administrators had originally feared. Rather than simply staying at home to watch Spurs rather than going out to see Brentford—a matter of laziness—the really vital change was one of attitude. For spectators were persuaded that the football they wanted to see was that played by the major clubs and, in many cases, that alone.

And so the eventual effect of these changes was to strengthen those already strong and to weaken those already weak. Great old clubs like Bolton and Blackburn found that their reputations meant nothing beside the pull of George Best at Old Trafford. In 1971 Manchester United took a quite unprecedented step by making several of their League matches all-ticket. That was the result of 25 consecutive years as the greatest draw in Britain. Three times Sir Matt Busby built great sides—the 1948 combination that won the Cup, the 1958 'Babes' who died at Munich and the 1968 European Cup winning side. But it was not so much the success and hours of incomparable entertainment that has tied United to the hearts of the British people, rather it was a single incident at a German airfield when the team that has been called the greatest English club side ever was destroyed.

Over two decades later people who do not see a football match from one year to the next, religiously go along to their local ground when United play—simply because of the legend of Munich. It made United more than a football team—it made them an article of football faith.

There were other good club sides—the orthodox fast-running Wolves of the 1950s who first introduced the British to European

DAILY EXPRESS

No. 17,949 | FRIDAY FEBRUARY 7 1958 | 3 a.m. forecast: Cold; snow or sleet likely | Price 2½d.

ALIVE Blanchflower, Edwards, Berry, Scanlon, Morgans, Gregg, Wood, Charlton, Viollet, Foulkes; Busby

DEAD Byrne, Bent, Jones, Whelan, Colman, Pegg, and Tommy Taylor

SURVIVORS SPEAK

THREE TAKE-OFF ATTEMPTS—AND THEN DISASTER

Express Photo News SEE PAGES 2, 5, 6, 7 AND 16

Matt Busby called out: It's my legs, my legs...

Express Staff Reporters

MANCHESTER United footballers told last night the stark, dramatic story of how the airliner bringing them home from Yugoslavia had

Below: February 1958 and the story that stunned a nation. Though the Daily Express *correctly reports Duncan Edwards as being alive he was to die a few days later, the eighth player victim of the Munich air crash which created a legend around Manchester United.*

competition; the two North London 'double' sides of 1961 and 1971, so close geographically yet so far apart in style; Ipswich Town, the most unexpected winners in the history of the League and perfect proof that the age of method had arrived; Leeds United, 'the professionals', never giving anything away, never letting opponents relax, the worshippers of workrate yet destined to become seemingly eternal runners-up; Celtic, so utterly dominant under Stein's command in the 1960s that Scottish football became as predictable as the rising of the sun. And yet, for all this talent, British teams took a long time to make an impact in Europe.

The first steps into Europe had been as painful as the Common Market negotiations. Though Hibernian entered the European Cup in its inaugural season (1955-56), reached the semi-finals and made £25,000 from the venture (a large sum for a Scottish club at the time), the Football League, in traditionally short-sighted fashion, had 'advised' Chelsea not to enter. It is worth remembering that the League had only just begun to allow floodlit fixtures at this time, and they 'advised' Manchester United the same way the following year. But Matt Busby was more farsighted than his superiors and took no notice.

Revenge was swift. After the Munich crash in 1958 the organizing committee invited United to enter the European Cup the following year along with the League Champions, Wolves. A joint committee of the League and FA finally refused permission on the grounds that it was against the competition's rules (those already waived by the organizers). It was the shabbiest paragraph in a truly parochial chapter.

Europe was a tremendous catalyst for the British. Not only did Football and Scottish League clubs come to adopt entry into European competition as a major goal, but it changed the face of the game in these somewhat isolated Isles. It was not long before club sides realized that the good old-fashioned tackle from behind and charge on the goalkeeper were not going to be tolerated by crowds, opponents or referees in European matches. The less physical game gradually crossed the Channel and its advantages led to a growing rejection of the intimidating behaviour so characteristic of the 1950s. By 1971 the charge on the goalkeeper was no more than a memory and the Football Association felt strongly enough to try and cut out the equally contentious tackle from behind.

So Britain finally came to accept the discipline of Europe, just as she came to accept a new concept in tactics and coaching and the widespread influx of supposedly 'continental' systems. The combination of an emphasis on sheer physical fitness, leading to the 'perpetual motion' players of whom Alan Ball was probably the best example, and the rejection of the more strictly positional 'stopper' or '3-2-5' formation, with its familiar full-backs, inside-forwards and wingers, led to considerable confusion on the terraces in the 1960s.

That a man could wear a number seven shirt and *not* patrol the right touchline seemed quite revolutionary to many used to watching Matthews and Finney. Dick Graham achieved some early success with an all-purpose Crystal Palace side—once threatening to number his players in alphabetical order as he claimed numbers did not count any more (which assumes that they once did of course)—and Matt Gillies and Bert Johnson took Leicester to the Cup Finals of 1961 and 1963 with similarly revolutionary concepts on how the game should be played.

But while Alf Ramsey achieved the most obvious success with methodical rather than inspired football—neither his Ipswich side of 1962 nor the England of 1966 will ever be categorized among the world's great entertainers—a more appealingly influential figure in the English game of the period was Ron Greenwood, manager of West Ham from 1961. This, in part, was a result of his willingness to allow journalists a view of the inner workings of the football world and his propensity to sit and discuss the game for hours with those who could take his views outside the dressing-room.

Greenwood himself has often suggested that the real credit for the new ideas that gained so much currency in the 1960s should go to Walter Winterbottom. The Football Association's Chief Coach from 1946 to 1963, Winterbottom spent most of that period doubling-up as manager of England's various teams, roles whose compatability was not always obvious. While he is widely remembered for a relatively unspectacular spell as team manager, his work on the coaching side at Lilleshall is known only to those inside the game. His tactical appreciation, his encouragement of personal skills and his insistence on a team's corporate knowledge of its objectives are factors that no one who has taken an FA course could ignore. It was at Lilleshall, not Wembley, that the foundations of the 1966 World Cup win were laid.

Top left: *Euphoria on the bench as Geoff Hurst scores England's fourth goal in the 1966 World Cup final against West Germany. The only man still seated? Alf Ramsey. To the right stands a seemingly horrified Jimmy Greaves, the greatest goalscorer of his generation who had missed, initially through injury but finally because of Ramsey's gamble on Hurst, what should have been the highlight of his career. He was later to say that the match deeply affected his life.*
Left: *Bobby Charlton practises his skills under the watchful eye of Harold Shepherson during an England training session at Lilleshall. It was here, not Wembley, where the foundations of success were laid.*

Attitudes were changing. It was not that whether Wolves or Manchester United won the League became less significant, more that the most important consequence was that success gained entry to the European Cup. Whereas a climax used to occur every season—around the time of the Cup Final—it now seemed to occur only once every four years, at the time of the World Cup.

Before 1950 the British regarded the World Cup as an event competed for by foreigners. But the dispute with FIFA having been healed, the four home countries finally agreed to enter and FIFA accepted the Home International Championship as a qualifying competition. The first and second countries were to go through to the final rounds—virtually carte blanche for England and Scotland.

In the event, it provided the Scots with a fine opportunity to display that shortsighted foolishness which has often made the English FA appear prophetic visionaries by comparison. England beat Scotland 1-0 at Hampden in the deciding match and the losers, coming only second in the Championship, refused to go to Brazil for the World Cup.

So England went alone and came back even lonelier. At Belo Horizonte they suffered a footballing humiliation not surpassed before or since. The game against the USA was expected to be a canter. That vast country had never adopted the world's most popular version of football, preferring instead its own brutal perversion. The American coach—irony or ironies—was a Scotsman, Bill Jeffrey, and the night before the game his team were up until the early hours at a party; the only unanswered question was the size of the defeat.

Instead they won 1-0; one British press agency assumed the score was a mistake and printed the result as 10-1. To be fair to England, it was one of those days that every team sometimes has—nothing would go right. Looking back, paradoxically, the outcome was more of a disappointment to the Americans than the English. The latter lost 1-0 to Spain in the next game and went home having got nowhere. But the Americans sincerely believed that their victory was going to be the spark that ignited the game across the Atlantic. They could not have been more wrong.

In England the result was not treated seriously—in fact it was dismissed as the fluke it undoubtedly was and the tower of English self-confidence survived, if only for another three years. The main reason for that pride was 80 years of internationals in which England had never lost at home to foreign opposition.

True, Eire had won a poor game 2-0 at Everton in 1949, but as nine of their side were regular Football League players they can hardly be regarded as aliens. That record was threatened in November 1951 when England drew 2-2 with Austria thanks to an Alf Ramsey penalty. In October 1953 they were 4-3 down to a FIFA side in a full international with only one minute left. Mortensen collided with an opponent and England were awarded a penalty ('although it was still two months to Christmas' as a reporter put it). Ramsey scored again and England's record was safe—but for just four weeks.

The moment of truth arrived on the afternoon of 25 November 1953. Ramsey later said that the game against Hungary had a profound effect on him; it could hardly have had any other. While the game against the USA could be dismissed as a freak the defeat by Hungary was without excuse. A far better team had shown England that reputation was no longer enough.

Eighteen years later that same England side were gathered at a function also attended by Ferenc Puskas. Ramsey greeted his full-back partner that day, the late Bill Eckersley, rather quizically; 'Hello, it is Bill isn't it?' and Puskas was heard to remark: 'It was like that when they played us—the team hardly seemed to know each other's names.'

England lost 6-3. Far worse, they had made no plans when, six months later, they played a return in Budapest. That one was lost 7-1. England were totally exposed by a side that shamed them in ability, fitness and, above all, in tactical awareness.

English football had entered a period in the doldrums from which it was not to emerge for a dozen years. In the 1954 World Cup the Uruguayan side that had defeated Scotland 7-0 also put out England 4-2. In 1958 England failed even to reach the quarter-finals, losing to the USSR in a group play-off. England's style was summed up by Vittorio Pozzo when he described a goal by Kevan as being scored with the 'outside of his head', implying that England were still not one of the world's more thoughtful soccer nations. That year, at least, Northern Ireland and Wales reached the quarter-finals.

In 1962 England went out 3-1 to Brazil, again in the quarter-finals; Scotland, Wales and Ireland failed to qualify. That was the end of Walter Winterbottom's reign as team manager. Alf Ramsey took over what ought to have been one of the best teams in the world. The first game after his appointment was against France, who declined in the 1960s to the Third Division of European

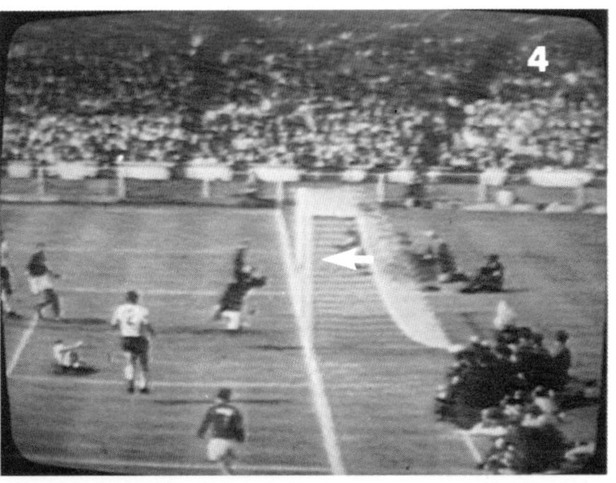

The most controversial goal scored in the history of British, and possibly World, football was England's third in the 1966 World Cup final against West Germany. Geoff Hurst turned on an Alan Ball pass, thumped the ball past defender Willi Schulz and onto the crossbar. The ball bounced down and out so fast that no-one could tell whether it was over the line or not. The body of keeper Hans Tilkowski obscured the line of vision of the television cameras while other cameras, there for the film Goal!, *were placed along the penalty line at an inconclusive angle. There was, however, another motor camera present which was almost exactly on the goal-line and the pictures above are taken from its frames. Referee Dienst asked his linesman, Bakhramov, to decide and the Russian said it was a goal. Judged by the sequence above, the linesman was wrong. Even allowing for the very slight angle, the ball is always in vision to the field side of the near post (arrows indicate the ball's position) and it is inconceivable that, at any point, the* whole *ball could have been over the line. The time sequence can be judged by the position of Tilkowski's falling body. Hurst's last minute goal, giving him a hat-trick and England a 4-2 success, helped still the uncertainty but the eventual result might have been very different had Dienst given the benefit of the doubt to the defending side.*

football. England lost that game 5-2, Ramsey declared that they would win the World Cup anyway and the rest is history.

The World Cup victory is not to be denigrated—but what really stands out from 1966 is how sceptical about England's abilities (after previous World Cups) supporters had become and how little chance England were given of winning. Look at the facts. England played six games, all of them at Wembley. In nearly 60 years of internationals against foreign opposition, England had lost only four times at home—to Eire in 1949, to Hungary in 1953, to Sweden in 1959 and to Austria in 1965. Not even Brazil had managed to win at Wembley. Of the 40 full international games England had played against her six opponents, Uruguay, Mexico, France, Argentina, Portugal and West Germany, she had lost only eight. Not a single one of those had been at home and none of those six countries had managed even a draw at Wembley.

In fact the Germans, the other finalists, had never beaten England anywhere, managing just one draw back in Berlin in 1930. Quite simply each of those six matches should have been won and had they been ordinary mid-week 'friendlies' no one would have expected anything but the eventual results. But it is easy to be wise after the event. At the time there was always Brazil, seeking a hat-trick of victories, a rampant Hungarian attack, Eusebio in startling form and the ever-present threat of West Germany, Russia and Italy.

Ramsey's strength was in his free hand. At long last the FA had realized that the system devised by Stanley Rous during the Second World War—whereby he did everything—was the most effective available. Thus, although there was still an international committee technically in existence, Ramsey was the only man who did any selecting. When asked by one of this committee at a cocktail party exactly what its official duties were, Ramsey is reputed to have replied: 'To come to cocktail parties.'

Being a defender himself, it is not surprising that Ramsey, like a successful First World War general, believed that defence was the key to victory. For the 1966 World Cup final England ended up with just two fulltime forwards, Hurst and Hunt, five defenders (Stiles playing an auxiliary defensive role wherever he was needed) and three providers.

The formation was substantially the same for the traumatic game in Leon four years later—except that now both Peters and Ball were required to be preoccupied in midfield—when it was proved beyond dispute that the best laid schemes of men, mice and Alf Ramsey can be thwarted by individual error.

Peter Bonetti, deputizing in goal for Banks, was adjudged to have been at fault for the first German goal and was possibly not blameless for the other two. It is sad that one display—albeit the most important of his career—will always be remembered before so many excellent ones elsewhere. Banks later speculated that he might even have been deliberately poisoned but the truth on the field was a little harder to take—it had been an excellent game but, in a sense, just one of those days. Though Bonetti might have saved Beckenbauer's goal, Seeler's back header was surely nothing more than a fluke and Ramsey was horribly unlucky.

The years 1953 and 1966 must be considered the landmarks of the post-War era for English soccer. The former had the effect of an earthquake—it overthrew all the misconceptions English football had about itself, though it took ten years for all the lessons to filter through. The second date was notable for an atmosphere more akin to VE-day. That was not necessarily inappropriate for it was, after all, the day the national game came in from the cold.

THE 1970s

THE FIRST HALF of the 1970s was a depressing time for England and the rest of the home countries, though Scotland were to enjoy a pocket of consolation in qualifying for, and doing themselves some justice at last, in the finals of the 1974 World Cup. For England, however, there was no consolation—failing in the latter stages of the 1970 World Cup, eliminated in the quarter-finals of the 1972 European Championship and failing to qualify for the 1974 World Cup finals—and, on 1 May 1974, Sir Alf Ramsey paid the traditional price for failure when he was sacked by the Football Association. Joe Mercer became England's caretaker manager through the 1974 home internationals and a summer tour during which England provided opposition for more fortunate nations warming up to contest the 1974 World Cup finals.

The Football Association then announced that Don Revie, fresh from Leeds' magnificent twenty-nine game unbeaten run at the beginning of the 1973-74 season, would be the new England team manager.

Yet Revie was to experience much the same difficulties as his predecessor. England failed to qualify for the quarter-finals of the 1976 European Championship and in the following post mortem there were some familiar points made: the length and toughness of the English season led to injuries and exhausted players, there was too much football, not enough co-operation between the League and the FA, and not enough time for preparation. Yet, with the wisdom of hindsight, Revie's policy also carried one major flaw. He continually altered his line-up and team work suffered badly. The only unchanged side he ever fielded was his last, against Uruguay in Montevideo. In July 1977, shortly after that match, Revie gave an exclusive interview to the *Daily Mail* in which he announced that he had resigned as England's manager. This was the first the FA knew about it. It provided an unsavoury end to his three-year term in succession to Ramsey, and with England on the brink of failing to qualify for the second successive World Cup, he had been rather less than successful.

Yet, with English football at its lowest ebb for years, with Don Revie's resignation and England's sorry goal-scoring attempts against Finland and Luxembourg, there was Liverpool. Marching magnificently through Europe and England, they were to become only the third English team to reach a European Cup final. The most remarkable moment of their run came in the second leg of the quarter-final against St Etienne. The French Champions, a goal clear from the home leg, scored at Anfield. Liverpool needed three to get through as a result. There seemed to be no chance, but they went on to win 3-1 (a victory reminiscent of Manchester United's 3-3 draw in Madrid in their 1968 semi-final). Their opposition in the semis—Zurich—proved little more than a formality for a team still attempting the treble.

So, Liverpool went to Rome to meet Borussia Monchengladbach having won the League Championship again, but having been surprisingly defeated by Manchester United in the FA Cup final five days earlier. It didn't affect them at all. Playing glorious football, McDermott, Tommy Smith and Phil Neal all scored to demolish the Germans 3-1. Keegan's display against the West German captain Berti Vogts was the outstanding feature—though for Keegan it was to be his last game for Liverpool before moving to SV Hamburg.

Below: *Gerd Muller completes West Germany's remarkable comeback in the World Cup quarter-final at Leon in Mexico. England had been 2-0 ahead but conceded fluke goals to Beckenbauer and Seeler. In extra-time Grabowski centred, Labone and Bonetti were left helpless and Muller made it 3-2.*

Four months later, Ron Greenwood, the new England team manager, included seven Liverpool players in the side to play Switzerland—yet England could manage no more than a goalless draw. More significantly his side, still based on Liverpool, failed to reduce the World Cup deficit with a meagre 2-0 victory in Luxembourg. England then had to achieve an expansive win over Italy to qualify, but they could do no more than reverse the Rome scoreline—Scotland were once again to be Britain's only representatives in the World Cup finals.

Liverpool, however, went on to confirm their status as the best side in Europe—retaining their title as European Champions. The highlight this time was their semi-final defeat of Borussia Monchengladbach, at Anfield, with Ray Kennedy performing quite brilliantly. The final itself was far less memorable—with Bruges playing defensively and Liverpool below their best.

In the first half of the decade, the minor European trophies had become almost resident in the boardrooms of the League clubs. Manchester City brought home the Cup Winners Cup in 1970, handing it over to Chelsea the following year.

From 1970, the UEFA Cup (once the Fairs Cup) was successively won by Arsenal, Leeds, Spurs, and Liverpool. In 1976, Liverpool repeated their double of 1973, winning both the UEFA Cup and League Championship. Both UEFA finals provided thrilling finishes. In 1973 Liverpool carried a three-goal lead to Germany for the second leg against Monchengladbach. Two superb goals by Jupp Heynckes before half-time seemed to have broken Liverpool's resistance, but no further cracks appeared and amidst electrifying tension they clung on.

In 1976 two brilliant counter-attacks from Bruges saw Liverpool two goals down at Anfield before a second half flourish produced a three-goal comeback. It seemed hardly enough for the second leg but Liverpool's consistency had produced just the sort of resilience that earned a winning draw in Belgium and a second UEFA trophy. How odd that Liverpool should meet the same teams again in her first two European Cup finals.

In domestic football, Arsenal became the fourth side in the history of the game to complete the League and Cup double. Their triumph in 1971 perhaps has more merit than the previous doubles of Preston, Aston Villa and Tottenham Hotspur. Their unceasing hounding of Leeds United in the League race and the character they showed in coming from behind to win the FA Cup in extra-time (after even more of a tightrope performance against Stoke in the semi-final) somehow compensated for the steamrollering style which was often more effective than pretty.

Stoke City added a little glitter to the League Cup when they beat Chelsea in the 1972 final. Appropriately enough for a team which has always recognized the value of age and experience, 35-year-old George Eastham shot the winning goal (his first for three years) and another veteran, Gordon Banks, won his first club medal.

But even Stoke's feat was eclipsed 14 months later by Stokoe's. As manager of Second Division Sunderland, Bob Stokoe was the key figure in the most dramatic of FA Cup finals. A solidly struck goal by midfield player Ian Porterfield created the biggest upset of the century by beating Leeds United, the odds-on favourites.

For Leeds, it was another of the bewildering occasions when they failed at the last hurdle. In four FA Cup finals under Don Revie, they had only once won. Five times they had been runners-up in the First Division; winners again only once.

Leeds United were the microcosm of the problems of the early seventies. Their gradual evolution into a strong team was based on physical play with an emphasis on defence. They were also roundly accused of overstepping the mark in terms of what is

Above left: *Frank McLintock holds aloft the FA Cup after Arsenal's 2-1 extra-time defeat of Liverpool in 1971. The significance was far greater, however, for it was the second leg of a Double which had been fought for week after week, game after game.*
Left: *A sign of the times in 1974 at Old Trafford. Manchester United were the first of the major clubs to erect barriers around their pitch, a result of their fans' continuing bad behaviour. But by the end of the decade most of United's contemporaries had followed.*

called professionalism, of setting a bad example from the top. Their disciplinary record was appalling, and at the start of the 1972-73 season their ground was closed because of the behaviour of the crowd (not for the last time either).

Yet there was a significant change at the start of the following campaign. The players, under the threat of the FA, behaved; not only did they win but they became a free scoring side. They extended a League record by going through their first 29 games of the season unbeaten. Then their character was put to a considerable test when they lost four matches in quick succession and a nine-point advantage over Liverpool had been whittled away. Yet, faced by the threat (and their supporters' expectation) of once again coming second, Revie's squad mustered a final effort and deservedly won their second Championship. It was to be the last success of an ageing side which had still to face the mortification of losing the 1975 European Cup final to Bayern Munich after dominating the game's opening half and having a seemingly good goal disallowed.

While Leeds were trying to rebuild under Jimmy Armfield in 1976, many of the side must have felt slightly better about their defeat by Sunderland when Second Division Southampton put paid to Manchester United in the 1976 Cup final.

It was United's first season back in the First Division after being relegated in 1974—ravaged by the retirements and declines of Charlton, Law, Best, Crerand and company. Tommy Docherty fielded a team of talented but very young players who for most of the season had chased the elusive League and Cup double—the League title going to Liverpool.

Queen's Park Rangers and Derby County had also challenged for the 1976 Championship, but Liverpool's swarming, supremely efficient teamwork proved too much. Their style and success had characterized both the 1960s and 1970s, but Bob Paisley's success in taking them to that record ninth Championship was generally regretted outside Merseyside. The other three contenders—QPR, Manchester United and Derby—had all contributed rather more originality.

A quite remarkable cog in the Liverpool machine was Ian Callaghan, winger in the 1965 Cup winning side and the 1966 World Cup finals, whose ageless midfield prompting earned him the Footballer of the Year award for 1974.

Liverpool also lifted the FA Cup that year—a convincing win over a Newcastle United side who mustered little challenge on the day—but they lost their Championship to Leeds and were runners up the following year to Derby.

County under Brian Clough had discarded the garb of Second Division also-rans for the cloak of League Champions in 1972. But in 1973 it was Clough himself who was discarded after an undignified boardroom feud.

Clough by this time had established a national reputation as a controversially outspoken pundit. When he and Derby County parted company the story led the front pages as well as the back. Derby's players, bemused and hurt by the incident, threatened a strike, which thankfully did not materialize. Dave Mackay, a former player, was brought back from Nottingham Forest in a successful attempt to quell the storm.

Ironically, both Clough and his assistant Peter Taylor were in charge of Nottingham Forest when Mackay himself was dismissed from County 18 months after his Derby side had achieved a second Championship of the decade. By that time the tide in the East Midlands was flowing rapidly back to Nottingham and Clough.

Manchester City moved towards the seventies with their 1969 Cup win when Neil Young's shot made Leicester runners-up for the fourth time in 20 years. City subsequently declined, gradually losing first Mercer, then Allison, then Johnny Hart through nervous exhaustion. Before he left in 1972, Allison made one of the most questionable decisions of the decade, buying the enigmatic Rodney Marsh when City seemed to have the Championship tied up. But the side fell apart, Derby crept through to the title, and Allison's reputation was scarred, if not permanently as far as City were concerned. As Joe Mercer commented: '£200,000 is a lot of money to spend just to lose the Championship.'

Under the brief reign of Ron Saunders, City lost the 1974 League Cup final, but under Tony Book they were successful in the same competition in 1976. Too often their fluid style could only be produced at Maine Road, and it was not until Bill Taylor, Fulham's coach in the 1975 Cup final, joined the staff that application allied to artistry began to produce away results.

North of the border, Celtic reached a second European Cup final in 1970, but contributed to the game's lack of appeal in Scotland by refusing to give up the League Championship. In

Above left: *Old father time waits for no man, particularly in professional sport; reduced circumstances for the two biggest names of the 1960s—George Best of Fulham and Billy Bremner of Hull—who were contesting a Second Division game in October 1976.*
Above and above right: *'If Spurs had bought Batman and Robin they could scarcely have created greater curiosity,' said Brian James in the* Daily Mail *when Keith Burkinshaw brought home two of Argentina's World Cup squad in 1978. The purchase of Ossie Ardiles (above, playing against Wolves) and Ricky Villa (right, passing Gordon Cowans of Aston Villa) was indeed the most remarkable transfer of the 1970s. Their effect on Tottenham was considerable, with the Spurs going on to win the FA Cup in consecutive years, 1981 and 1982, and their presence became even more significant with the outbreak of war in the Falklands.*
Right: *Viv Anderson, seen here with Forest team-mate Tony Woodcock, became the first coloured footballer to play for England when he appeared against Czechoslovakia on 29 November 1978.*

1974 they won their record ninth consecutive title—a whole generation of spectators had grown up without realising that Celtic at the top of the League was not an immutable law. More interesting, perhaps, was their series of consecutive defeats in the first four League Cup finals of the decade. In 1975, Rangers finally broke Celtic's hold on the Championship and went on to retain the title in 1976. They won it again in 1978, after Celtic had denied them a hat-trick in 1977.

In both England and Scotland, two of the reasons most often mentioned for the decline in attendances at first-class football matches over recent years have been televised games and hooliganism. By 1976, even mighty Leeds were only covering three-quarters of their £800,000 outgoings from gate receipts. In fact, only a handful of League clubs were actually operating in the black, something which once again reinforced doubts that the accepted League structure could survive—though legislation the following year allowed the use of lucrative lotteries to boost the ailing coffers. A more serious threat to football as a whole, however, came from violence on the terraces and around League grounds. Whilst accepting that a mindless minority were culprits, the spread of hooliganism—given impetus by its coverage in the media—grew in its intensity and regularity. Fences around grounds, strict segregation of fans and the actual banning of visiting supporters from Manchester United and Chelsea (two notable clubs whose reputations had been particularly scarred by the violent conduct of their so-called followers) helped a little to curb the disturbances within the stadia.

The loan of Birmingham and England forward Trevor Francis to Philadelphia of the North American Soccer League for the summer of 1978 highlighted a more direct threat to the quality of the game. Coinciding with the passing of the retain-and-transfer system (after years of negotiation, the clubs finally forfeited their rights to keep players once the period of an individual contract had elapsed), the lure of Europe and the United States took on an added glow. With the British tax system vastly penalising stars in all areas, who could blame the country's best footballers from following in the steps of businessmen, golfers and pop-stars?

Ten years earlier the NASL had been a rest-home for ageing professionals, a chance for one final pay-day. All that seemed to have changed when Pele joined New York Cosmos; no longer could players scoff at the standards. Pele became the catalyst who injected the League with excitement as well as credibility; the big-business that was attracted to invest ensured that the North American clubs could and would bid for the likes of Trevor Francis, at the height of their careers, and no longer for those who were fading into oblivion. With a supply of coaches like Gordon

Jago, Freddie Goodwin, Eddie McCreadie, and Ken Furphy they were certainly not short of contacts through whom to make the deals.

Clubs like Luton, whose creditors gave them just one month to live in 1975, were more than happy to off-load players to the States for the summer in order to ease inflated wage bills, even though these players would always miss pre-season preparation and often the opening League games. But, in fact, as League clubs became keener to loan, the American game declined. By 1983 only twelve of the 24 teams of seven years before survived in North America and the problem had become peripheral. The NASL had been a graveyard of hopes for more than a few British players and entrepreneurs. One of the most intriguing financial stories in British football during the decade was that of Coventry City's involvement with the game in America. Jimmy Hill, once the Sky Blue manager, had become chairman of the club and proved himself an excellent financial director. His policy of clearing the club's debts while transfer fees were still high and creating an all-seated stadium was widely applauded. His successes were not repeated across the Atlantic. The failure of the franchises in Detroit and Washington (despite the presence of Cruyff and Francis) left both the Hill family and Coventry City heavy losers.

Domestically clubs responded to all the threats to their survival with a little more enterprise, though Liverpool's Championship season of 1977 brought them only 15 goals from their 21 away games. A record number of sending-offs in the 1977-78 season told rather more about less tolerant refereeing than any sinister cynicism on the field. And in that season one club—or perhaps one man—gave the First Division a tremendous impetus.

By August 1977 Brian Clough had been out of the First Division for nearly three years, (following his sacking by Leeds United after a tempestuous reign of 42 days as their manager). Now his Nottingham Forest side had just sneaked into the third promotion spot of the Second Division, a point ahead of Bolton Wanderers and Blackpool.

Although Clough had been reunited with his assistant Peter Taylor, who had not been at Leeds with him, Forest were generally tipped for a rapid return from whence they came rather than honours. But Forest became a revelation. Clough strengthened the side for the new season by paying £270,000 for goalkeeper Peter Shilton, by bringing his former Derby midfield lynch-pin Archie Gemmill into the camp and by signing centre half Dave Needham from Queen's Park Rangers. All three transfers took place after the opening jousts in the League Cup competition. This cup-tied the new signings, but did not prevent Forest from winning the trophy—beating Liverpool, the European Champions, with a disputed John Robertson penalty after a draw at Wembley in one of the most one-sided games ever seen there.

After each League Cup-tie men like Frank Clark, John O'Hare, Ian Bowyer and 18-year-old Chris Woods, Shilton's stand-in, would lose their places, but the result was competition to be in the team that made Forest almost invincible in the League.

Forest's remarkable triumphs were good for the democracy in the game, as was Ipswich reaching their first ever FA Cup final; there they beat Arsenal 1-0, a more attractive if less disciplined side than that which won the double. The League was not over blessed with the creative skills of a Liam Brady, the all-round talents of a David O'Leary or the sheer presence of a Malcolm Macdonald. But where they did exist, the main problems of the future seemed, at the time, to be how to keep them from joining a gravy train abroad and how to ensure that those who wished to be thrilled by them could watch in safety. The 1980s, though, were to throw up far more difficult problems.

Left: Roberto Bettega scores Italy's second goal in her 2-0 defeat of England in Rome on 17 November 1976. Although England managed to reverse the scoreline in the return, it was this game which effectively put her out of the 1978 World Cup finals. The England defenders are Hughes, Cherry and McFarland.

Left: Despair in the dugout for the men of the 1970s, Brian Clough and Peter Taylor. During the decade they managed unfancied Derby to the Championship in 1972, left a team there good enough to win it again in 1975, and then took even less successful Nottingham Forest to the League in 1978 and the European Cup in 1979. They were, in effect, the only domestic challenge to Liverpool for most of the period.

THE CHALLENGE OF THE 1980s

On a sunny Saturday in September 1979 Bristol City defeated Wolves 2-0 before 18,835 people at Ashton Gate and moved into sixth place in the First Division of the Football League. It was the highest position they had achieved since the First World War. Exactly three years later, in September 1982, they took the field against York City. By this time they had lost nearly nine-tenths of their supporters and Bristol City, effectively bankrupt, were 92nd in the Football League, bottom of the Fourth Division. It was the fastest descent in history and City's troubles were a microcosm of those facing the whole business.

It was in 1981 that the realities of the new decade began to come home to the Football League. The signs had been there for some time, but not until the shakings rather than stirrings of recession were felt did matters accelerate. A string of clubs suddenly found bank managers more stony faced than before, and there was a rash of what would have been, in any other business, bankruptcies.

Bristol City, Hereford and Hull declared themselves as good as finished in their present form, Halifax and Derby were clearly on the edge, while Wolves, £2½ million in debt with no apparent means of clearing it and possessing a massive white elephant of a stand, virtually went over the brink.

All of these clubs, and others whose plights were less publicized, were saved in some way or another but, after the 1982 World Cup, matters took a dramatic turn for the worse. The problem was in large part outside football, a direct result of the appalling recession. The heartlands of British football—Glasgow, the North East, Lancashire and the West Midlands were all suffering 15 per cent unemployment rates and football was no longer at the top of most families' shopping lists.

The obvious effect was on attendances. Suddenly they dropped by a consistent 10 per cent, and a lot more in many cases. When Everton played Arsenal in a Milk Cup tie in November 1982, 13,089 were prepared to turn out and see it. Given that Everton have around 8,000 season ticket holders, it presumably meant no more than 6,000 had bothered to pay at the gate. Interestingly, 20,000 Evertonians turned out the same season for the Youth Cup final against Norwich. Two weeks earlier, West Brom, second in the League, had attracted just 6,000 for another Milk Cup tie against Nottingham Forest. And there was now a clutch of Division I clubs—Notts County, Birmingham, Coventry, Luton, Brighton—who could not expect to get as many as 10,000 for a run-of-the-mill match. Thirty years before many Third Division clubs would have turned their noses up at such a figure.

One result was the creation of a new industry—working parties on football's future. They seemed to appear everywhere. The most prestigious was, ironically, chaired by Norman Chester, who had prepared a similar, eminently sensible, report nearly 20 years before and seen all of his proposals rejected with barely a hearing.

There was no lack of reasons being put forward for the slump in gates—but a singular dearth of solutions acceptable to most people in it. And most of the arguments were sadly familiar.

Most significant, but least offered, was the simplest; that the world had changed. When football attendances were at their height, in the 1940s and early 1950s, the options facing the working man were remarkably limited by present day standards. He had money to spend perhaps, but little to spend it on. Even that simplest, now taken for granted, option of sitting in front of a television set was unavailable—there was no Saturday afternoon viewing. The opportunities, particularly with the gradual disappearance of Saturday morning work, have increased remarkably. It would, in fact, be a more pertinent question to ask how football has ever managed to retain half the attendances of the peak years of the 1940s, rather than why it has lost the rest.

The recession, beginning in 1979 and getting dramatically worse through to 1983 (and with few prepared to guess where the economy would be in 1990), was another major element. For a father with two sons, a Saturday football match was not likely to cost much less than £20, no small proportion of the average after tax take home pay of around £110 per week, and that was before considering the plethora of mid-week matches. By 1982 the more perceptive observers were beginning to note an age gap on the terraces. Life-long supporters, perhaps retired, or not so pressed for money later in life, still came along, as did teenagers and the unmarried with some disposable income. But those in their late 20s and 30s, with perhaps a mortgage and family, were dropping away. In hard times the money could be better spent elsewhere, and how, then, would *their* children develop the viewing habit?

Hooliganism was another reason for families to stay away from football grounds. Chanting had led to fighting, to forced segregation, violent pitch invasions and, eventually, deaths. Fatalities after fights outside grounds (and obviously totally outside the control of clubs) led to deaths in Cardiff, Coventry, Millwall, Middlesbrough and London. Interestingly, the real level of violence inside grounds had fallen away dramatically, partially because of segregation, partially because of an apparent decline in passions. There were some exceptions, notably Chelsea and Leeds whose supporters still seemed intent on having their clubs permanently banned from the League (to the benefit of everyone else, according to general public opinion), and the record of some English supporters abroad was appalling. But, in reality, the real level of violence at the vast majority of soccer matches was small, and even that was little more than a reflection of a changing social fabric. Football here was clearly suffering from an imbalance of unfavourable media coverage.

But those who live by television must accept the danger of dying by television. It was the growth of televised football that generated much 'copycat' violence. A televised invasion at a Sunderland v Leeds Cup tie in the mid-60s was the progenitor of numerous imitations, eventually causing most clubs (and Wembley) to fence off their pitches. And while local songs such as the Pompey chimes, 'On the Ball, City' at Norwich, 'You'll Never Walk Alone' at Anfield and 'Glory Glory' at White Hart Lane had been a central part of football's charm, now they were swamped by universal chants learned from 'Match of the Day'.

When Manchester United played Anderlecht in an European match, the Belgian club's chant was heard for the first time on television and, within a season, every club in the land was being 'encouraged' (or depressed) by the local equivalent of 'United, United, we are the Champions', even if they were 22nd in the League. Was there ever any reason why Third Division clubs should have had supporters who '... hate Nottingham Forest, we hate Liverpool too', or why the players of teams from Aberdeen to Plymouth should be reassured to know that they would never walk alone? The ultimate in television propagation was (hopefully) to be heard in 1981 when chants were increasingly taken from television advertising (e.g. 'We'll take more care of you ...' a British Airways theme from a national institution financially sicker even than football) and passed on down the League's kops by television again for a second time.

Television was no less guilty in spreading tactical ideas quickly (and perhaps inaccurately) and destroying the magic of the major personalities. A visit from Arsenal in the 1930s, or from Stanley

Matthews in the 1950s, was a moment to be savoured. It came round once a year and it was worth going to see. By 1982 a resident of Penzance could be reasonably sure of seeing Liverpool or Spurs at least once a fortnight on television, which was as often as the season ticket holder in Ormskirk or Enfield. It has to be stressed that television presenters themselves were in no way responsible for these developments; rather it was the way the medium itself tends to allow the viewer a simplified view of everything. Excellent presenters on both television networks worked hard to explain the game and to ensure that the viewer did not take away false impressions, while Jimmy Hill's tactical analyses added a new depth to the public's awareness of the sport.

The influence of the media has been the most debated and most emotional of all of the 'problems' facing the game. Much of the criticism, if not downright false, has tended to miss the point. It is foolish to ignore the fact that television has brought football to a wider audience and has placed the game more centrally on the national stage (just as it is foolish to forget that millions enjoy *playing* the game each weekend). It is obvious nonsense to suggest that television must damage live interest in a sport. American football games are televised twice a week, live in their entirety, during the season and yet virtually every match is a sell out (the critical points here probably being that there are a limited number of teams playing only 18 games a season and that the event is shown complete). Baseball attendances have risen fast at a time when it is possible in many American cities to watch the local team, live, at least three nights a week, and it is surely the case that televised one-day cricket has encouraged crowds and interest in a sport which was dying on its feet.

The real problems of football as a televised product are complex but revolve around three points—the loss of 'the magic', highlights and frequency. The familiarity with the legends of the game that television makes possible has been a crucial influence. It has not, in fact, greatly damaged the Tottenhams and Liverpools of this world, but it has dealt a major blow not only to Third and Fourth Division sides but also to the less celebrated clubs in the First. A child's vision of football must now largely be determined by what he sees on television. That is his or her first experience of the game. It is the Kevin Keegans and Glenn Hoddles that he associates with, whether he lives in Newcastle or Norwich, Tottenham or Torquay. They are far more real than the players at his local club, who advertise a poorer band of the same product and, because they don't appear on television, are not to be taken too seriously.

One of the more depressing aspects of watching children play football in, say, West London has been their allegiances—in the late 1960s boys who had never been north of St Albans swore undying allegiance to Leeds United, ten years later their younger brothers could not be persuaded that they did not have an inate, unbreakable link with Liverpool or even Nottingham Forest. Television has tended to damage, if not destroy, the essential provincialism of the game, the association of club and town, which was its source and has been its strength for so many

***Left:** John Robertson of Nottingham Forest, probably the only consistently successful winger of the 1970s. It was Robertson who made the only goal of the 1979 European Cup Final, a cross for Trevor Francis, and scored the only goal of the 1980 final.*
***Below:** Keith Cassells (left), Southampton's acquisition from Oxford United, on the attack during a game against Norwich City. These two clubs, while not exceptionally successful in the 1970s and 1980s, did both reach Wembley twice in the 1970s and are symbolic of a gradual change in the power base of the game. While many of the Northern clubs slowly decline, following the economic fortunes of their home towns, there is an increasing number of more southerly clubs with relatively small populations establishing themselves in the First Division.*

decades. Highlights and frequency are more technical matters and were the basis of the debates in April and May 1983. In an attempt to limit the damage television could do to crowds, the League and FA insisted around 1960 that games should not be shown in entirety, or live, but cut down to approximately 30 minutes at most and shown late in the evenings. This proved a perfect illustration of Brady's Law—that legislation tends to generate the exact opposite effect to that which was intended. Rather than making televised football less exciting or interesting, showing just highlights (particularly when action replays from two angles became the norm in the 1970s) has proved much more appealing than the real thing—particularly when it can be experienced from your own fireside. A child reared on televised football will inevitably find the real thing dull when he visits his local ground and has to watch all the parts that the TV scissors cut out—even if the atmosphere can make up for it a little.

Frequency is another side of the same coin. In 1983 it was usually possible to watch highlights of three matches on a Saturday night, two on a Sunday afternoon, the goals from up to ten more on Saturday lunchtime, plus perhaps four European or international games on a Wednesday evening. Major clubs, such as Manchester United, would almost certainly appear on television 20 times a year. All these programmes showed highlights only, further removing the potential spectator from the realities of the terraces.

Why it took so long for this large penny to drop is one of life's mysteries. There was one brief experiment of live League football in 1960, but it was chopped after one match—hardly a serious appraisal. The authorities seemed concerned, reasonably, that fans would not go to games if they knew they were being televised, but the problem seems less likely that fans won't turn up to watch a televised Liverpool v Everton, rather that they won't watch Brentford v Lincoln at the same time. It is a complex problem, but one that the FA and League had to tackle. Allowing the live televising of one full game once a week (chosen from, perhaps, six major clashes the same night but the televised game not being announced in advance, or with the game not being shown in the local television area) might cause a short term decline in attendances. The hope has to be, however, that if the product is good enough it will prove an adequate advertisement for the game and will lure people back—particularly those who, in the end, prefer 90 minutes of their local team to 90 minutes of two others.

The balance is delicate, particularly as the League and FA cannot prevent BBC or ITV showing internationals, European or Scottish games, but by mid-1983 the League were considering offers from video companies and hence taking weekly football off television screens completely. It should also be said that, if football and television are to pursue a symbiotic relationship, then football might extract more cash for its product. While the example of American football is not necessarily a good guide to what might happen elsewhere, in the early 1980s the 28 major clubs (roughly the equivalent of the First Division) negotiated a

*Bristol City's remarkable decline from First to Fourth Division in the space of three years was the fastest in football history. One moment they were at Anfield (**below** Kenny Dalglish scores for Liverpool against City on 6 October 1979) and, seemingly a blinking of an eye later, were struggling in the re-election zone of the Fourth Division. And yet, ironically, Bristol City were one of the few clubs to enthusiastically pursue many of the new marketing ideas which were being promoted as the long-term saviours of the game. They had a good rapport with their spectators, built a stand that could be used by the general public for other sports, and **(right)** went in for much of the American razzmatazz associated by British spectators with the new North American Soccer League. City were, indeed, the only club to regularly have its own cheerleader group, the Robins.*

package that gave them each $20 million per season in TV rights. That figure is approximately ten times the annual gate receipts of a successful First Division club today.

It is very easy, of course, for football to point to external problems and to ignore facts closer to home. As well as there being too much televised football in the early 1980s, there was clearly too much football full stop. The major clubs had long been playing far too many games—somewhere between 60 and 70 a season if they were in Europe—and destroying their chances as a result. Spurs, for instance, in pursuit of League, Cup and Cup Winners Cup, had to play 23 matches between 20 March and 27 May 1982. Several began moves in the same year to create a 'Super League' of 16 or 18 clubs. Arsenal appeared to be the prime mover, ironically as there were few outside North London who would be inclined to regard Terry Neill and Don Howe's Arsenal as super-anything.

Spectators were drifting away from the game because there was too much of it. As Brian James said in 1970, as soon as a fan decides he really doesn't want to see a League Cup tie on a cold Wednesday night, he has broken his habit. It's then much easier to decide that Birmingham City next Saturday can be given a miss as well. The plethora of mid-70s quick-buck inventions (Texacos, Anglo-Italians, Watneys etc.) had happily died by 1980—though there was something called, imaginatively, the Group Cup and then, confusingly, the Football League Trophy, skulking around for those clubs prepared to demean themselves. The decision to rename the also confusing Football League Cup in the image of its sponsor (the Milk Cup) was a further stage in that competition's declining relevance—even if the League managed to resist the temptation of reshaping the trophy in the shape of a milk bottle.

It was increasingly difficult to take seriously a competition which wavered drunkenly back and forth between one leg and two (why, if the second round must be two-legged, should the third be sudden death?) and which was concluded by constant exhortations to acquire 'a lotta bottle'. Spectators up and down the country understandably voted with their carpet slippers.

Even Europe was becoming less attractive. After six consecutive English wins (five of them 1-0), the European Cup had lost the magic of Real Madrid, Benfica and, more recently, Ajax. The smaller European sides attracted comparable attendances and Liverpool, in particular, had to adapt to a large fall in revenue from the heights of earlier years.

While European football at a club level could still bring in the crowds if the opposition was right, at a national level it suffered one disastrous experience at the beginning of the decade. In keeping with the previous two World Cups, blanket television coverage was to be the norm for the 1980 European Championship, held in Italy. The tournament proved to be extremely tedious, the worse for football because the games were shown live. England's performances were uninspired (eventually a 1-0 defeat by Italy eliminated her), none of the other home countries had qualified, the crowds were tiny when Italy was not playing and the finale was poor—a typically hard, last-minute winner performance from the Germans. As a curtain raiser to the decade it was a long-term disaster. The expanded 24-team World Cup in Spain two years later was better, but had its faults. Primarily it went on too long—for a month—and there were too many mediocre games. Scotland were eliminated on goal difference for the third time running, and while Northern Ireland's performances were interesting, if not overwhelming, England deflation at the end left a sense of intense disappointment. Not to score in either of the second series games and, worse, not to look like scoring, was a poor end after a promising beginning. At the finish the fact that the bad guys won (Italy and West Germany) and the good guys were eliminated (Algeria, Cameroons, Brazil, France) was not a great advertisement for football either. It showed that, at the highest level, cynicism, illegalities and 'professionalism' could pay off and we couldn't always rely on the Brazilian cavalry to come to the rescue.

'Cynical' and 'professional' were adjectives that were increasingly applied to many players in the domestic game as well—though more off the field than on it. Kevin Keegan's move from Southampton to Newcastle, coinciding with a court case over a contract with an agent, was not greeted with the interest (away from the banks of the Tyne) that his earlier perambulations had generated. While an authentic hero, and the only British player to be voted European Footballer of the Year in two consecutive polls, Keegan might arguably be judged by history as having failed at the critical moment—specifically with an easy

header in front of the Spanish goal 21 minutes from the end of England's World Cup. When salaries and promotional incentives of between £100,000 and £200,000 a year were being bandied around by the press at a time of 15 per cent unemployment, it was difficult to feel too much sympathy for Keegan's need for 'a new challenge'.

The criticism of Keegan was probably a little unfair and certainly overdone. Timing was all; Keegan, the most celebrated player of his generation, had largely become a symbol of a press and public backlash against player demands, transfer fees and some of the financial idiocies of the game. When members of Aston Villa's European Cup winning side (already reputably being paid the highest bonuses in the League) were publicly demanding 'loyalty bonuses' despite having signed favourable long-term contracts, they found little public support. At a time when there were so few outstanding players, it was not surprising that ambitious chairmen (rather than managers by the late 1970s) had bid up transfer fees and salaries. The problem was the knock-on—'If him, why not me?' The ubiquitous agent and lawyer came to dominate the scene—in one instance a major signing was seen to arrive for the ceremonies with a personal staff of three.

Clubs began to sell players, or just lay them off, simply to save the wages. Bristol City cancelled the contracts of eight of their most highly paid players, arguing that the alternative was going out of business. Transfer fees collapsed at the same time. Steve Daley, for whom Manchester City's Malcolm Allison had paid £1,450,000, went at a loss of £1 million a year later. Garry Birtles went from Nottingham Forest to Manchester United for over £1 million, didn't score for nearly a whole season, ended with just 11 goals and returned for a million pounds less. Justin Fashanu, who had cost Brian Clough another £1 million in 1981, could barely attract one-tenth of that sum a year later. Clubs would sell who they could where they could, just to obtain cash. The brightest and the best went abroad, where the wages were higher and the transfer fees were limited by the European Community (to a generally accepted limit of around £500,000). Manchester City were in such dire straits that they had to sell the jewel in their crown, Trevor Francis, to Sampdoria of Genoa for £400,000 less than they had paid a year before. Forest, in their turn, had sold Francis because his contract had only a year to run and, at the end of it, he would be a free agent and they would then receive so much less for him.

Individual players saw their colleagues move, receive £25,000, and sometimes more, as 'signing-on fees' and told themselves: 'My career's short, I might break a leg next week—why shouldn't I move for £25,000? What do I owe this club?' The public eventually became cynical. The true heroes, the great players of yesteryear who were seen to be honest, decent, loyal men, the Billy Wrights and Jimmy Dickinsons, were few and far between. Those that could be identified—like Steve Perryman or Joe Corrigan—began to be appreciated more for it, but the mood on the terraces and in the pubs was less enthusiastic, and attendances suffered because of it.

But, at the end of the day, the single most important reason why people were deciding not to go to football matches was that they were losing interest in the game. This was simply related to what happened on the field, the development of tactics since, say, the heyday of the great Spurs double side in the early 1960s, the fall in the number of goals scored and the increasing primacy of the more easily coached defence over attack.

In fact the tide was probably already turning as the decade began. The decision to award three points for a win (though not in Scotland) in 1981 was clearly a step in the right direction and in 1982 young managers such as David Pleat at Luton and Graham Taylor at Watford made it clear that they would not

Far left: Cyrille Regis is outjumped by Bob Hazell of Queen's Park Rangers during QPR's surprise defeat of West Bromwich in the 1982 FA Cup semi-final at Highbury. QPR won 1-0.
Left: Trevor Brooking (left), the hero of Budapest and the most cultured English player of his generation, brings the ball away from the attentions of the Watford defence.
Left above: Heartbreak at Hull; Stuart Croft heads away a Fulham cross during a Third Division game in 1980. The empty terraces bear witness to what had happened to many clubs in the 1970s and early 1980s and Hull were one of several to declare themselves effectively bankrupt and up for sale in the 1981-82 season. Interestingly, the only time during that season the ground was full was for a rugby league fixture.

Above: Spurs' new stand, completed in 1982 at a cost in excess of £5 million and the most expensive ever built at an English football ground. Controlling one of the game's most prudent clubs, the Spurs board was soon facing mounting criticism and the stand was one of the reasons quoted for the surprising boardroom struggle at White Hart Lane late in 1982. At Wolves, a similar new stand had clearly been a major factor in the club's bankruptcy the same year.
Right: 1980s marketing at nearby Highbury. The players seem unconvinced.

pursue the traditional apathy of newly promoted First Division clubs—play it tight and hope for enough home wins to finish around 15th. The two sides quickly raced to the head of the scoring tables, Watford being abundant at both ends; in October 1982 they recorded their highest victory with an 8-0 defeat of Sunderland. A month later they went down 7-3 to Nottingham Forest. It was certainly exciting stuff, though it appeared to have little immediate effect on attendances. Crowds in the 1982-83 season stayed stubbornly 10 per cent below the corresponding figures for 1981-82, a season which had only just topped an aggregate of 20 million.

The arguments about Alf Ramsey's effect on the English game after his remarkable successes at Ipswich in 1962, and in the World Cup four years later, will probably rage until the end of the century. The Ipswich Championship was a one-off, though Ramsey did use withdrawn wingers, but the World Cup was certainly a seminal influence. It should be remembered by critics of Ramsey's 'wingless wonders' that it was not Ramsey's choice to play without them. The simple fact was that the wingers Ramsey had available could not perform the job he required against the Latin American teams—Mexico, Uruguay and Argentina. England, still largely insulated from the world game, then had little experience of sides which drew midfield players back to mark wingers (thus providing a double barrier) and also added a sweeper as extra insurance. English wingers, used only to a marking full-back, were not experienced enough (or skilful enough) to play against this system (and, generally, still aren't) and Ramsey was forced to seek out other means of finding those elusive goals.

He was fortunate that Ron Greenwood had developed Geoff Hurst as a target man at West Ham (then a new tactic) and that he had the 20-year-old Alan Ball to act as the play anywhere dynamo, virtually giving England an extra man on the field and compensating for playing only two front men. That League teams began to adopt this system was more the result of their opponents using the extra man in midfield (particularly in European matches) than any belief that wingers were now obsolete. To begin with, only one winger was withdrawn, giving a system usually described as 4-3-3. But when teams who were either away from home, or did not have a recognized winger on their books, began to play 4-4-2, then it was soon discovered that packing the midfield with four men paid dividends. The one extra man helped cut out the flow to the remaining winger and he too had to start coming back, either to fill the midfield or just to get hold of the ball. It is probably not unfair to say that there was only one consistently successful winger in English football in the 1970s—John Robertson of Nottingham Forest, and he was hardly typical of the breed. It was very much the era of getting behind the ball, closing down space and playing it tight. Needless to say, it was an age of far fewer goals and far more midfield sterility.

It was declining attendances and constant criticism from the press and fans, whenever they were able to voice their views, that persuaded the First Division managers as a group that they had to act. The FA helped by insisting that the 'professional foul' was to be regarded as a sending-off offence, though this did cause some problems of interpretation by referees at the beginning of the 1982-83 season.

The likely solutions to the game's decline had long been known and were not going to come as any revelation to the various committees which had inefficiently split the task among themselves. It was possible to perm any number from less television; better, largely-seated, stadia; the closure of many kop-ends in a determined attempt to stamp out hooliganism; the gradual reduction of real wages and transfer fees; smaller divisions; less football; regionalized and semi-professional third, fourth and fifth divisions (it is surely absurd that teams now watched by 1,000 people per week should maintain a full-time staff); more incentives for goals and positive play.

The major problem with these obvious steps, apart from the inate conservatism of the League and the need for a 75 per cent majority on any vote, is that none of them offer a short-term solution. In virtually every case, it is jam tomorrow. Closing down the Shed at Chelsea, or other trouble spots, and building better stadia costs a lot of money today and, almost certainly, would reduce revenues in the short term. Letting players go if the wage bill is too high takes time and, as Bristol City discovered, the immediate effect is likely to be a worse team, worse results and fewer fans paying at the gate. Fewer matches might well mean higher standards and higher attendances in five years time—but not tomorrow.

And it was immediate survival that troubled most clubs, not the 1990s. Even if they transfer their highest paid players, they are still faced with the biggest financial headache—interest payments to the bank. They are not unlike the Mexicos and Argentinas of the world—they have borrowed too much to repay their debts from what is now actually coming in. The loans which had been advanced against the collateral of the value of the ground, or the transferability of the team (always a tenuous security when the only purchasers were other football clubs), were less safe at a time when property values were collapsing and no one was buying even the best players. So the banks were gently calling the loans in, and if not that then certainly not extending any more, and it seemed inevitable that more clubs would go the way of Chelsea and Wolves, both of them effectively going into temporary receivership burdened with seemingly unrepayable debts.

Where this leaves the Football League is anything but clear. There is no doubt that, given the will, the problems can be solved—but not for 92 clubs. On the other hand, if there are no changes, and if the recession continues through the 1980s, there seems only one way for most clubs—to simply disappear from public view. Norman Chester presented his report in March 1983. It had few surprises and the formula of a smaller First Division and regionalised lower divisions had been rejected before. The idea that home clubs should keep all their receipts was quickly branded as a means of the rich becoming richer, but might help still talk of a breakaway 'Superleague'. Almost immediately the opposition, lead by Fulham's Ernie Clay, gathered its forces and it did seem that the League's requirements for a 75 percent majority before major changes were introduced could again be a stumbling block.

At the beginning of 1983 there was perhaps only one certainty for the rest of the decade; that Liverpool, who had yet to capture either of the great prizes of the double or a hat-trick of championships, would go on winning trophies. And that was not necessarily a cheerful thought for chairmen up and down the land.

THE GAME IN SCOTLAND

THE HISTORY OF Scottish football, to be brutal, is the history of three very great clubs, of an epic series of internationals against the old enemy England, of a constant stream of talent leaving the country for richer rewards south of the border, and of very little else.

Despite occasional flashes from lesser clubs, Celtic and Rangers have dominated the field since the 1890s. And before the turn of the century, Queen's Park, perhaps the greatest amateur football club of all time, *was* Scottish football. They organized football north of the border from the first; excelled at it; beat the English, virtually on their own, time and again, and stamped their high-principled personality on the Scottish game.

Football had flourished in Scotland, of course, long before Queen's Park Football Club was founded. The Scottish game had grown in concert with that of Wales and Ireland and the English countryside, a game of violent celtic fervour characterized by uncompromising battles between neighbouring villages—clan against clan, as often as not, and with plenty of heads broken in the process.

As in England, the game provoked its share of royal disfavour. James I, James II, James III and James IV liberally scattered statutes banning football across the 15th century, and James VI, on ascending the English throne, expressly forbade his son Henry from 'rough and violent exercises at the foot-ball'. (James V was a notable absentee from this bunch of anti-football monarchs, but then he was only one year old when he succeeded to the throne.) Yet football never lost its popularity. By the beginning of the 19th century, while the schools were beginning to take up the game in England, Scottish football found a working champion in the novelist Sir Walter Scott, a fervent supporter of the traditional inter-village game.

Indeed, Scott was himself much in evidence at the most famous of all the matches to be held in football's Dark Ages north of the border. Sir Walter not only backed (financially) the Men of Selkirk against the Men of Yarrow (themselves backed, incidentally, by the Earl of Home)—he also wrote a ballad specially for the day. The game (in two legs, rather like the European Cup) ended even—one leg each; and the food and drink lying ready for the teams dissuaded them from playing a decider. At this date (1815), though, football in Scotland was generally recognized to be in decline, and even Scott himself was declaring that 'it was not always safe to have even the game of football between villages; the old clannish spirit is too apt to break out.'

Nevertheless, football survived in Scotland not through the influence of the public schools as it did in the south of England, but through the young artisans and professional men who recognized the game for the simple, energetic and enjoyable pastime that it was. The game had its greatest following in the industrial areas of Scotland's central lowlands, and in Glasgow the keenest players eventually gravitated, in the mid 1860s, to one of the city's three public parks—Queen's Park.

On 9 July 1867, together with YMCA members and caber-tossing Highlanders who also used the park for recreation, they met to form the 'Queen's Park Football Club', thus officially establishing the game in Scotland and founding a tradition in Glasgow which, for single-minded fanaticism, would be difficult to parallel anywhere but in Rio de Janeiro.

The early history of Queen's Park is one of virtually undiluted success. Between their formation in 1867 and 1872 not a single goal was scored against them; they did not lose a single match until February 1876, when they were beaten by London's Wanderers, and only in December of the same year, by which time Scottish competition had become extremely fierce, did they go down at home.

In the very early years, Queen's Park were so dominant that not only did they attract the best results—they also laid down the rules, which were obediently followed by early local opponents such as Thistle, Hamilton Gymnasium and Airdrie (all of whom, incidentally, played their football in the summer months).

In 1870, however, Queen's Park's reputation ensured the acceptance of Scottish football on the national map. Charles Alcock, the recently elected Secretary of the FA wrote a letter to the *Glasgow Herald* announcing that teams of English and Scottish players were to meet at Kennington Oval. He invited nominations from Scotland with a stirring call to arms: 'In Scotland, once essentially the land of football, there should still be a spark left of the old fire, and I confidently appeal to Scotsmen . . . etc. etc.'

It was a stroke of genius on Alcock's part. No one, least of all a gentleman footballer, could resist a provocative challenge like that. Queen's Park nominated one Robert Smith, a member of a famous Queen's Park family now based in London, as their player, and the teams met on 19 November 1870, England winning 1-0.

This was not, as yet, international football, or anything like it. The Scottish team was in reality composed of a lot of well-heeled young men who owed family name and background to Scotland,

***Right:** The Queen's Park side that won the first Scottish Cup in 1874. In the early years the club were so successful that not only did they attract the best results, they also laid down the rules, which were obediently followed by early local opponents.*
***Far right:** The Oval was the venue of the England–Scotland match for some years. Here England attack during the 1877 match—the first they lost at home, Scotland winning 3-1.*

but who were all living in or near, London, and had time on their hands. One of their number was an Old Rugbeian, who had presumably learnt his football in the handling tradition; another was the son of the Prime Minister W E Gladstone, and was himself an MP at the time of the match; yet another was Quintin Hogg, the grandfather of a later Lord Chancellor.

And, most illustrious of all, the Old Etonian Arthur Fitzgerald Kinnaird, aristocrat, football patriarch, successful banker, later Lord High Commissioner of the Church of Scotland—and a football fanatic, who played whenever he possibly could, and whose personality swayed the Football Association for five decades. His influence on the game is incalculable; that it came unscathed through the early troubled years of professionalism into the heyday of popularity in the years before the First World War is in considerable part due to this remarkable Scot and his 33 years as President of the Football Association.

***Right:** The programme for an 1875 friendly between Queen's Park and the Wanderers. As players did not wear numbers, they were identified by the colour of their caps or stockings. Queen's Park, despite their strange 2-2-3-3 formation, had still not lost a game since their formation eight years earlier.*
***Below:** A ticket for the first international football match, at Partick in 1872. The Scots included nine Queen's Park men but could only draw 0-0.*

INTERNATIONAL
FOOT-BALL MATCH,
(ASSOCIATION RULES,)
ENGLAND v. SCOTLAND,
WEST OF SCOTLAND CRICKET GROUND,
HAMILTON CRESCENT, PARTICK,
SATURDAY, 30th November, 1872, at 2 p.m.
ADMISSION—ONE SHILLING.
No. 806

This first encounter between 'England' and 'London Scottish', was followed by repeat performances on roughly the same lines, twice in 1871 (a 1-1 draw and 2-1 win to 'England') and once in February 1872 (1-0 to 'England').

It was the Queen's Park visit to London for the semi-final of the first FA Cup competition that really formalized inter-national football. Donating a guinea (one sixth of that year's income) toward the purchase of the Cup, Queen's Park drew with Wanderers but could not afford to return for a replay. Nevertheless their style impressed everyone present and also

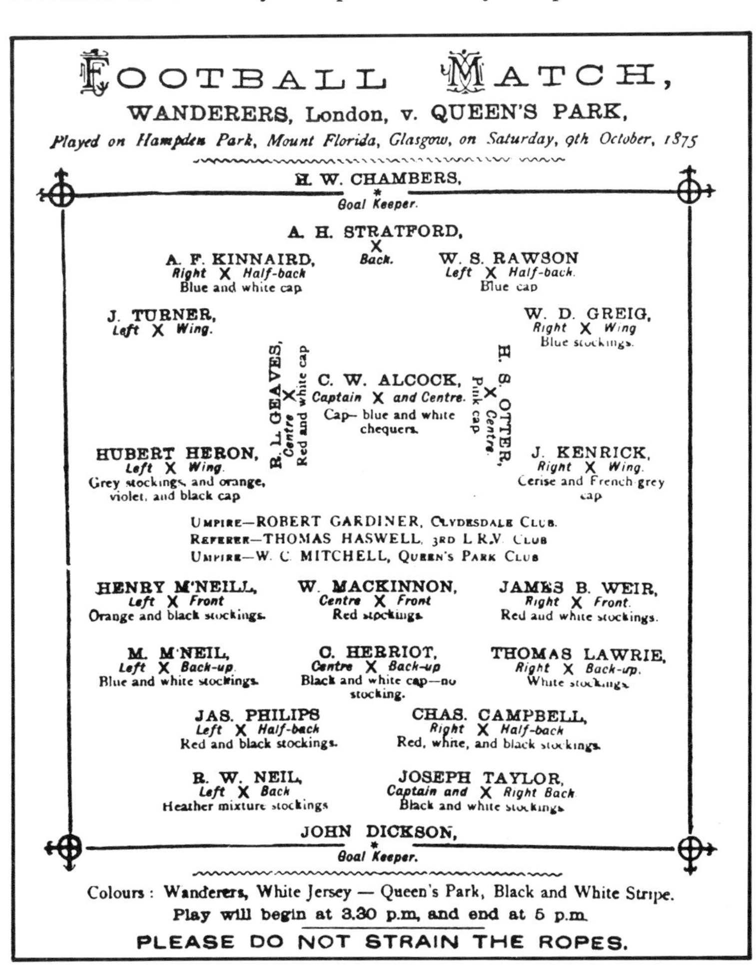

FOOTBALL MATCH,
WANDERERS, London, v. QUEEN'S PARK,
Played on Hampden Park, Mount Florida, Glasgow, on Saturday, 9th October, 1875

H. W. CHAMBERS,
Goal Keeper.

A. H. STRATFORD,
Back.

A. F. KINNAIRD, *Right* X *Half-back*, Blue and white cap
W. S. RAWSON, *Left* X *Half-back*, Blue cap

J. TURNER, *Left* X *Wing.*
W. D. GREIG, *Right* X *Wing*, Blue stockings.

R. L. GEAVES, *Centre* X, Red and white cap
C. W. ALCOCK, *Captain* X *and Centre.* Cap— blue and white chequers.
H. S. OTTER, *Centre.* X, Pink cap

HUBERT HERON, *Left* X *Wing.* Grey stockings, and orange, violet, and black cap
J. KENRICK, *Right* X *Wing.* Cerise and French grey cap

UMPIRE—ROBERT GARDINER, CLYDESDALE CLUB.
REFEREE—THOMAS HASWELL, 3RD L.R.V. CLUB
UMPIRE—W. C. MITCHELL, QUEEN'S PARK CLUB

HENRY M'NEILL, *Left* X *Front*, Orange and black stockings.
W. MACKINNON, *Centre* X *Front*, Red stockings.
JAMES B. WEIR, *Right* X *Front.* Red and white stockings.

M. M'NEIL, *Left* X *Back-up.* Blue and white stockings.
C. HERRIOT, *Centre* X *Back-up*, Black and white cap—no stocking.
THOMAS LAWRIE, *Right* X *Back-up.* White stockings.

JAS. PHILIPS, *Left* X *Half-back*, Red and black stockings.
CHAS. CAMPBELL, *Right* X *Half-back*, Red, white, and black stockings.

R. W. NEIL, *Left* X *Back*, Heather mixture stockings
JOSEPH TAYLOR, *Captain and* X *Right Back*, Black and white stockings.

JOHN DICKSON,
Goal Keeper.

Colours: Wanderers, White Jersey — Queen's Park, Black and White Stripe.
Play will begin at 3.30 p.m, and end at 5 p.m.
PLEASE DO NOT STRAIN THE ROPES.

Daily  

THURSDAY, JUNE 8, 1978

8p (CHANNEL ISLANDS 9p)

Jeers for Ally after World Cup disgrace

THE SHAME OF SCOTLAND

A typical newspaper headline the morning after Scotland's dismal 1-1 draw with Iran in the 1978 World Cup finals. A drugs scandal involving winger Willie Johnston completed a thoroughly miserable South American campaign for the Scotland squad.

made them aware that the 400 mile journey was not only feasible but might even be worthwhile. The result was the very first football international, played in 1872.

Alcock and Kinnaird probably had most to do with arranging the trip north—Alcock was originally chosen to play for England and Kinnaird for Scotland though neither actually performed—but, looking back, the most interesting feature was the patronizing attitude of the Londoners—that England were going north to show the Scots how to play the game.

Nothing could have been further from reality. Sadly lacking is a photograph of the teams—the players would not promise to buy prints so the official photographer refused to take any frames. At Kennington the following year there was more trouble over photographs—on that occasion they never materialized because the England players insisted on pulling faces.

The match was played at the West of Scotland Cricket Club's ground in Partick. The Scots included nine Queen's Park men (and two more, the brothers Smith, who had played for the club before moving to London a couple of seasons earlier). This provided an understanding between players that the scratch English team could not match, but skilfully though the Scotsmen played, neither side could score—and so the first England-Scotland match ended in a goalless draw. (It happened only twice more in the next century—in 1942 and in 1970.)

The success of the encounter—4,000 spectators turned up, 'including many ladies'—led Queen's Park to search for a suitable ground to play further fixtures. The following season Glasgow Town Council agreed to let 'Hampden Park, Mount Florida' to the club. Ten years later railway construction forced them to move to another site in Hampden Park. The present stadium was completed on yet another site in 1903.

In the spring of 1873, Scotland travelled south to take on the English giants at Kennington. Again the majority of their side was composed of Queen's Park men and again the crowd was enormous by contemporary standards, 3,000 of them at a shilling a head. They saw a splendidly contested match, with England's powerful dribbling earning them a 2-0 lead, which Scotland equalized only to allow England to score twice more in the closing stages.

The following year, 1874, was a great one for Scottish football. In the first place, Scotland now had its own Football Association, formed in 1873 not specifically to run football north of the border (Queen's Park were doing that very effectively at that time without help from outside), but to institute their own cup competition for the 1873-74 season. Of the original eight SFA members, only Queen's Park now survives (the others were Clydesdale, Dumbreck, Easter, Granville, Rovers, Vale of Leven and Third Lanark, the last to fade away as late as 1967). There were 16 entrants for the first Scottish Cup, which in 1874 was duly won by Queen's Park, as it was in the two following seasons as well.

And, on 7 March 1874, the Scots defeated England. There were 7,000 spectators to watch the 2-1 triumph, and a game which, by all accounts, was notable for its 'beautiful and scientific play'. The English, as usual, excelled in individual brilliance. The Scots, also as usual, knew each other's play (seven men from Queen's Park), and bewildered their opponents with their accurate, defence-splitting passes. The home side's winning goal was described as '. . . a scene which can never be forgotten as long as internationals are played'; Harry McNeil, the midfield wizard, was carried shoulder-high to the pavilion; and the first of Scottish football's 'finest hours' was complete.

The pattern was to be prepared in the coming years, all too often for the self respect of the English clubs. The two countries drew in 1875, Scotland won 3-0 in 1876, beat England in England for the first time in 1877, and thrashed them 7-2 at Hampden in 1878. Of the first eleven matches, from 1872 to 1882, England won two and Scotland seven; on four occasions Scotland scored five or more goals. There was no doubt about it, the Scots had taken on England at their own game and made them look silly.

Both sides were still, of course, amateur but Scotland were playing like professionals. There will always be a dispute about who first developed the passing game—the great Royal Engineers club, which had many successful seasons in London football in the 70s and 80s, claim some credit for 'the combination game', and Sheffield were also early to discover the weaknesses of the individualistic dribbling method, with eight forwards, one half-back, one back and one goalkeeper.

But it is traditionally held that Queen's Park were the first club

Top: A dispirited Ally MacLeod—the subject of most of the press criticism which followed Scotland's disastrous results in the 1978 World Cup finals. The national team manager's resignation inevitably followed and despite a lucrative job which he then took in club management, MacLeod never reversed his misfortune.
Above: The game goes on but the real Rangers–Celtic struggle is where it was often to be found—on the terraces.

to perfect football as a *team* game, rather than a game played by a group of individuals. And while the English gentlemen footballers of the 70s and 80s were still vainly dribbling solo at the opposing defenders—just as they had done at school—their undoubted skills were quite impotent when faced with the understanding and team work built up by the Glaswegians.

And this skilled passing game was not only effective, it was attractive too for it increased the scope of the game and the speed of the attacks, and it led to more goals. No wonder they were packing 12,000 into Hampden Park for the internationals as early as 1880.

The popularity of football in Scotland at the start of the 1880s, and the skill of the young footballers who flocked to the new clubs—long-forgotten names like Renton and Oxford Glasgow, still-familiar ones like Kilmarnock and Dumbarton—transformed the game. The non-London clubs were demanding universal laws. Rules for goal-kicks and corners were regularized into the form they have today; handling the ball was reserved for the goalkeeper alone; free-kicks for infringements were accepted. After a series of squabbles between English and Scottish clubs, the Scottish throw-in was adopted all over the country.

The rules were settled more or less amicably. The dispute over professionalism was not. The rumblings began at the end of the 1870s: rumours started over the alleged payment of players by some of the northern English clubs, and by the early 1880s a full-scale row was brewing. Teams with unashamed working-class origins were making themselves felt, especially as in many parts of the country factories and offices were beginning to close after noon on Saturday, allowing the working man a full half-day's leisure every week. And the teams emerging in the North of England—Darwen and Preston, Blackburn and Accrington—often fielded more Scots than Englishmen.

At first, perhaps, the chance of a job in the prosperous factories of Lancashire was as much a lure as the prospect of a weekly shilling or two for playing football, but soon the northern clubs were competing for the services of the Scottish football names and talent scouts were scouring the parks of Glasgow for a likely catch.

In 1885 England accepted professionalism, under strict supervision. Scotland held out against it for another eight years. It was a bad time for Scottish football. On the one hand their strong ideological principles forced them to reject the idea of paying sportsmen money; on the other, they saw quite clearly that the English clubs were ready to snap up those footballers whose principles were less rigid, and Scottish football could only suffer in consequence.

It is surprising, in fact, and a tribute to the deep wells of talent to be tapped in the Scottish Lowlands in those days, that the effect was not worse. The professionalism crisis soured the FA Cup, and the Scottish clubs who still competed. In 1886, the professionals of the fast-rising Preston North End thrashed the amateur Queen's Park 3-0 in Glasgow, and in a game of brutal tackling and foul temper. The next year (after a club called Rangers had reached the semi-finals of the FA Cup before going down to Aston Villa), the Scottish Association decreed that '... clubs belonging to this association shall not be members of any other national association.' Scotland had broken away, just as it seemed that the still-amateur South of England might be proposing to form a British League.

The decision of the Scottish clubs to form a Scottish League in 1891 (and so grant two seasons of glory to Dumbarton, who won the first two Championships) heralded the end of the first chapter in Scottish football. Although professionalism was still banned (until 1893, when the SFA bowed to the inevitable), payments to League players were made quite openly; Queen's Park, still fiercely amateur, refused to join the league until 1900, and the relentless advance of the hard, working-class clubs finally overshadowed these Scottish aristocrats. In 1896, the first year in which the 'Anglos' (the Scottish professionals playing in the English League) were allowed to be selected for Scotland, Queen's Park, for the first time, provided only one member of Scotland's team. But the balance was restored, Scotland's sorry run ended, and they started winning again. And there were 50,000 supporters there to see it.

For Queen's Park it had been a glorious run. In the years between their formation in 1867 and the coming of professionalism, they had, virtually alone, run Scottish football. Losing in two consecutive Finals, they had come closer than any Scottish team to taking the coveted FA Cup out of England; they had, again virtually alone, provided international teams to humble England; they had won the Scottish Cup nine times.

They had provided Scottish crowds with an attractive and fast-moving game which was supported with all the fervour of a new religion. What is more, it grew unopposed. Cricket had never really thrived in Scotland, and rugby was even more haughtily upper-class in Edinburgh and the Borders than it was in southern England. And against all odds and all predictions Queen's Park have remained both amateur and, relatively, talented. In the 1890s, with the advent of professionalism, Celtic and Rangers took over the commanding heights of Scottish football and, sadly perhaps, have shared the battle for supremacy ever since.

Maybe that was not so clear ninety years ago. 'You might as well attempt to stop the flow of Niagara with a kitchen chair as to endeavour to stem the tide of professionalism,' said the leading voice of one of the factions at the 1893 AGM of the Scottish Football Association. The speaker was J H McLaughlin of Celtic, a prime advocate of the issue at question, the legalization of professionalism in Scotland.

And from that meeting—the third inside a year when the question of allowing professionalism was the main item on the agenda—the motion was finally carried. And from that day in May, the story of Scottish football has virtually become the story of Rangers and Celtic. Indeed, of the next 80 Scottish First Division championships contested, only seven different clubs on only 14 occasions took the title away from Glasgow's 'Old Firm'.

Looking back on the first day of 1983, a casual observer would have seen that from 1893 Rangers and Celtic had been champions 66 times—Rangers 36, Celtic 30; their records in the Scottish Cup would be hardly less impressive—47 times they had lifted the trophy out of a possible 75.

Those figures reflect a situation that was prophesied as far back as 1890 by the almost clairvoyant members of the club which is now the last bastion of amateurism in the senior British game, Queen's Park.

In an aptly titled book, 'The Game for the Game's Sake' (the history of Queen's Park), Glasgow author Robert Crampsey depicts clearly and concisely the attitude of the Hampden club to professionalism at the time: 'Queen's also saw, and warned, that the certain effect of a moneyed game within Scotland would be to tip the scales far too heavily in favour of the big city clubs. As long as those intangible things called honour and prestige were all

FULL INTERNATIONALS PLAYED BY SCOTLAND 1870–MARCH 1983

Date		Venue	Opponents	Score
*19 November	1870	Kennington Oval	England	0-1
*28 February	1871	Kennington Oval	England	1-1
*18 November	1871	Kennington Oval	England	1-2
*24 February	1872	Kennington Oval	England	0-1
30 November	1872	Glasgow	England	0-0
8 March	1873	London	England	2-4
7 March	1874	Glasgow	England	2-1
6 March	1875	London	England	2-2
4 March	1876	Glasgow	England	3-0
25 March	1876	Glasgow	Wales	4-0
3 March	1877	London	England	3-1
15 March	1877	Wrexham	Wales	2-0
2 March	1878	Glasgow	England	7-2
23 March	1878	Glasgow	Wales	9-0
5 April	1879	London	England	4-5
7 April	1879	Wrexham	Wales	3-0
13 March	1880	Glasgow	England	5-4
27 March	1880	Glasgow	Wales	5-1
12 March	1881	London	England	6-1
14 March	1881	Wrexham	Wales	5-1
11 March	1882	Glasgow	England	5-1
25 March	1882	Glasgow	Wales	5-0
10 March	1883	Sheffield	England	3-2
12 March	1883	Wrexham	Wales	3-0
15 March	1884	Glasgow	England	1-0
26 March	1884	Belfast	Ireland	5-0
29 March	1884	Glasgow	Wales	4-1
14 March	1885	Glasgow	Ireland	8-2
21 March	1885	London	England	1-1
23 March	1885	Wrexham	Wales	8-1
20 March	1886	Belfast	Ireland	7-2
27 March	1886	Glasgow	England	1-1
10 April	1886	Glasgow	Wales	4-1
19 February	1887	Glasgow	Ireland	4-1
19 March	1887	Blackburn	England	3-2
21 March	1887	Wrexham	Wales	2-0
10 March	1888	Edinburgh	Wales	5-1
17 March	1888	Glasgow	England	0-5
24 March	1888	Belfast	Ireland	10-2
9 March	1889	Glasgow	Ireland	7-0
13 April	1889	London	England	3-2
15 April	1889	Wrexham	Wales	0-0
22 March	1890	Paisley	Wales	5-0
29 March	1890	Belfast	Ireland	4-1
5 April	1890	Glasgow	England	1-1
21 March	1891	Wrexham	Wales	4-3
28 March	1891	Glasgow	Ireland	2-1
4 April	1891	Blackburn	England	1-2
19 March	1892	Belfast	Ireland	3-2
26 March	1892	Edinburgh	Wales	6-1
2 April	1892	Glasgow	England	1-4
18 March	1893	Wrexham	Wales	8-0
25 March	1893	Glasgow	Ireland	6-1
1 April	1893	London	England	2-5
24 March	1894	Kilmarnock	Wales	5-2
31 March	1894	Belfast	Ireland	2-1
7 April	1894	Glasgow	England	2-2
23 March	1895	Wrexham	Wales	2-2
30 March	1895	Glasgow	Ireland	3-1
6 April	1895	Liverpool	England	0-3
21 March	1896	Dundee	Wales	4-0
28 March	1896	Belfast	Ireland	3-3
4 April	1896	Glasgow	England	2-1
20 March	1897	Wrexham	Wales	2-2
27 March	1897	Glasgow	Ireland	5-1
3 April	1897	London	England	2-1
19 March	1898	Motherwell	Wales	5-2
26 March	1898	Belfast	Ireland	3-0
2 April	1898	Glasgow	England	1-3
18 March	1899	Wrexham	Wales	6-0
25 March	1899	Glasgow	Ireland	9-1
8 April	1899	Birmingham	England	1-2
3 February	1900	Aberdeen	Wales	5-2
3 March	1900	Belfast	Ireland	3-0
7 April	1900	Glasgow	England	4-1
23 February	1901	Glasgow	Ireland	11-0
2 March	1901	Wrexham	Wales	1-1
30 March	1901	London	England	2-2
1 March	1902	Belfast	Ireland	5-1
15 March	1902	Greenock	Wales	5-1
5 April	1902	Glasgow	England	1-1
3 May	1902	Birmingham	England	2-2
9 March	1903	Cardiff	Wales	1-0
21 March	1903	Glasgow	Ireland	0-2
4 April	1903	Sheffield	England	2-1
12 March	1904	Dundee	Wales	1-1
26 March	1904	Dublin	Ireland	1-1
9 April	1904	Glasgow	England	0-1
6 March	1905	Wrexham	Wales	1-3
18 March	1905	Glasgow	Ireland	4-0
1 April	1905	London	England	0-1
3 March	1906	Edinburgh	Wales	0-2
17 March	1906	Dublin	Ireland	1-0
7 April	1906	Glasgow	England	2-1
4 March	1907	Wrexham	Wales	0-1
16 March	1907	Glasgow	Ireland	3-0
6 April	1907	Newcastle	England	1-1
7 March	1908	Dundee	Wales	2-1
14 March	1908	Dublin	Ireland	5-0
4 April	1908	Glasgow	England	1-1
1 March	1909	Wrexham	Wales	2-3
27 March	1909	Glasgow	Ireland	5-0
3 April	1909	London	England	0-2
5 March	1910	Kilmarnock	Wales	1-0
19 March	1910	Belfast	Ireland	0-1
2 April	1910	Glasgow	England	2-0
6 March	1911	Cardiff	Wales	2-2
18 March	1911	Glasgow	Ireland	2-0
1 April	1911	Liverpool	England	1-1
2 March	1912	Edinburgh	Wales	1-0
16 March	1912	Belfast	Ireland	4-1
23 March	1912	Glasgow	England	1-1
3 March	1913	Wrexham	Wales	0-0
15 March	1913	Dublin	Ireland	2-1
5 April	1913	London	England	0-1
28 February	1914	Glasgow	Wales	0-0
14 March	1914	Belfast	Ireland	1-1
4 April	1914	Glasgow	England	3-1
V26 April	1919	Everton	England	2-2
V 3 May	1919	Glasgow	England	3-4
26 February	1920	Cardiff	Wales	1-1
13 March	1920	Glasgow	Ireland	3-0
10 April	1920	Sheffield	England	4-5
12 February	1921	Aberdeen	Wales	2-1
26 February	1921	Belfast	Ireland	2-0
9 April	1921	Glasgow	England	3-0
4 February	1922	Wrexham	Wales	1-2
4 March	1922	Glasgow	Ireland	2-1
8 April	1922	Birmingham	England	1-0
3 March	1923	Belfast	Ireland	1-0
17 March	1923	Paisley	Wales	2-0
14 April	1923	Glasgow	England	2-2
16 February	1924	Cardiff	Wales	0-2
1 March	1924	Glasgow	N Ireland	2-0
12 April	1924	Wembley	England	1-1
14 February	1925	Edinburgh	Wales	3-1
28 February	1925	Belfast	N Ireland	3-0
4 April	1925	Glasgow	England	2-0
31 October	1925	Cardiff	Wales	3-0
27 February	1926	Glasgow	N Ireland	4-0
17 April	1926	Manchester	England	1-0
30 October	1926	Glasgow	Wales	3-0
26 February	1927	Belfast	N Ireland	2-0
2 April	1927	Glasgow	England	1-2
29 October	1927	Wrexham	Wales	2-2
25 February	1928	Glasgow	N Ireland	0-1
31 March	1928	Wembley	England	5-1
27 October	1928	Glasgow	Wales	4-2
23 February	1929	Belfast	N Ireland	7-3
13 April	1929	Glasgow	England	1-0
1 June	1929	Berlin	Germany	1-1
4 June	1929	Amsterdam	Netherlands	2-0
26 October	1929	Cardiff	Wales	4-2
22 February	1930	Glasgow	N Ireland	3-1
5 April	1930	Wembley	England	2-5
18 May	1930	Paris	France	2-0
25 October	1930	Glasgow	Wales	1-1
21 February	1931	Belfast	N Ireland	0-0
28 March	1931	Glasgow	England	2-0
16 May	1931	Vienna	Austria	0-5
20 May	1931	Rome	Italy	0-3
24 May	1931	Geneva	Switzerland	3-2
19 September	1931	Glasgow	N Ireland	3-1
31 October	1931	Wrexham	Wales	3-2
9 April	1932	Wembley	England	0-3
8 May	1932	Paris	France	3-1
17 September	1932	Belfast	N Ireland	4-0
26 October	1932	Edinburgh	Wales	2-5
1 April	1933	Glasgow	England	2-1
16 September	1933	Glasgow	N Ireland	1-2
4 October	1933	Cardiff	Wales	2-3
29 November	1933	Glasgow	Austria	2-2
14 April	1934	Wembley	England	0-3
20 October	1934	Belfast	N Ireland	1-2
21 November	1934	Aberdeen	Wales	3-2
6 April	1935	Glasgow	England	2-0
J21 August	1935	Glasgow	England	4-2
5 October	1935	Cardiff	Wales	1-1
13 November	1935	Edinburgh	N Ireland	2-1
4 April	1936	Wembley	England	1-1
14 October	1936	Glasgow	Germany	2-0
31 October	1936	Belfast	N Ireland	3-1
2 December	1936	Dundee	Wales	1-2
17 April	1937	Glasgow	England	3-1
9 May	1937	Vienna	Austria	1-1
15 May	1937	Prague	Czechoslovakia	3-1
30 October	1937	Cardiff	Wales	1-2
10 November	1937	Aberdeen	N Ireland	1-1
8 December	1937	Glasgow	Czechoslovakia	5-0
9 April	1938	Wembley	England	1-0
21 May	1938	Amsterdam	Netherlands	3-1
8 October	1938	Belfast	N Ireland	2-0
9 November	1938	Edinburgh	Wales	3-2
7 December	1938	Glasgow	Hungary	3-1
15 April	1939	Glasgow	England	1-2
WT 2 December	1939	Newcastle	England	1-2
WT11 May	1940	Glasgow	England	1-1
WT 8 February	1941	Newcastle	England	3-2
WT 3 May	1941	Glasgow	England	1-3
WT 4 October	1941	Wembley	England	0-2
WT17 January	1942	Wembley	England	0-3
WT18 April	1942	Glasgow	England	5-4
WT10 October	1942	Wembley	England	0-0
WT17 April	1943	Glasgow	England	0-4
WT16 October	1943	Manchester	England	0-8
WT19 February	1944	Wembley	England	2-6
WT22 April	1944	Glasgow	England	2-3
WT14 October	1944	Wembley	England	2-6
WT 3 February	1945	Villa Park	England	3-2
WT14 April	1945	Glasgow	England	1-6
V13 April	1946	Glasgow	England	1-0
23 January	1946	Glasgow	Belgium	2-2
15 May	1946	Glasgow	Switzerland	3-1
19 October	1946	Wrexham	Wales	1-3
27 November	1946	Glasgow	N Ireland	0-0
12 April	1947	Wembley	England	1-1
18 May	1947	Brussels	Belgium	1-2
24 May	1947	Luxembourg	Luxembourg	6-0
4 October	1947	Belfast	N Ireland	0-2
12 November	1947	Glasgow	Wales	1-2
10 April	1948	Glasgow	England	0-2
28 April	1948	Glasgow	Belgium	2-0
17 May	1948	Berne	Switzerland	1-2
23 May	1948	Paris	France	0-3
23 October	1948	Cardiff	Wales	3-1
17 November	1948	Glasgow	N Ireland	3-2
9 April	1949	Wembley	England	3-1
27 April	1949	Glasgow	France	2-0
WC 1 October	1949	Belfast	N Ireland	8-2
WC 9 November	1949	Glasgow	Wales	2-0
WC15 April	1950	Glasgow	England	0-1
26 April	1950	Glasgow	Switzerland	3-1
21 May	1950	Lisbon	Portugal	2-2
27 May	1950	Paris	France	1-0
21 October	1950	Cardiff	Wales	3-1
1 November	1950	Glasgow	N Ireland	6-1
13 December	1950	Glasgow	Austria	0-1
14 April	1951	Wembley	England	3-2
12 May	1951	Glasgow	Denmark	3-1
16 May	1951	Glasgow	France	1-0
20 May	1951	Brussels	Belgium	5-0
27 May	1951	Vienna	Austria	0-4
6 October	1951	Belfast	N Ireland	3-0
14 November	1951	Glasgow	Wales	0-1
5 April	1952	Glasgow	England	1-2
30 April	1952	Glasgow	USA	6-0
25 May	1952	Copenhagen	Denmark	2-1
30 May	1952	Stockholm	Sweden	1-3
18 October	1952	Cardiff	Wales	2-1
5 November	1952	Glasgow	N Ireland	1-1
18 April	1953	Wembley	England	2-2
6 May	1953	Glasgow	Sweden	1-2

that were at stake then a local lad might just as well play for his village or small town with which he at least had an affinity. Pay him, and he would sell his sword to the highest bidder.'

The principles which moved the members of Queen's at the time bear the closest scrutiny. Even before payments were legalized, many clubs were obviously practising a form of professionalism. Players would be paid for time off work and for travelling expenses, with sums that clearly exceeded what they were actually due. Queen's Park never did—and indeed still do not—hold with that sort of thing.

And while Queen's Park remained a drawing power right up till the Second World War—and old-time Hampdenites still talk nostalgically of the 'great' Queen's team of the late twenties—it is a fact that since 1893, when they held the Scottish Cup, they have not won a single major trophy.

So the signs of what was to come were manifestly clear to some way back at the very birth of professionalism. Fortunately Queen's Park were only partially right, for Aberdeen, the two Dundee clubs, Hearts and Hibs are also 'big city clubs'. So why have they never enjoyed a protracted run of success? And since there were six First Division teams in Glasgow—none of them, theoretically at least, enjoying a proportionate population advantage over the others—why have Partick Thistle, Clyde, Queen's Park and Third Lanark (sadly now defunct) not even taken a minor share of the 'Old Firm's' success?

The answer—in a word—must be religion. Rangers and Celtic very quickly became more than just football clubs. They were causes—to be fought for, defended, devoted to and, if the need arose, died for. And, but for the dedicated medical staff who man the casualty departments of Glasgow's infirmaries, the supreme sacrifice—martyrdom—would, over the years, have taken its toll of the city's population on many a drunken Saturday night.

Exactly when the religious rift between the two clubs occurred is strangely obscure. Certainly Celtic, founded in 1887 by Brother Walfrid, of the Catholic teaching order of Marist Brothers, had religious influences from the very first. Celtic Football and Athletic Club was formed principally to raise money for food for needy children in the missions of St Mary's, Sacred Heart and St

Date		Venue	Opponents	Score
WC 3 October	1953	Belfast	N Ireland	3-1
WC 4 November	1953	Glasgow	Wales	3-3
WC 3 April	1954	Glasgow	England	2-4
5 May	1954	Glasgow	Norway	1-0
19 May	1954	Oslo	Norway	1-1
25 May	1954	Helsinki	Finland	2-1
WC16 June	1954	Zurich	Austria	0-1
WC19 June	1954	Basle	Uruguay	0-7
16 October	1954	Cardiff	Wales	1-0
3 November	1954	Glasgow	N Ireland	2-2
8 December	1954	Glasgow	Hungary	2-4
2 April	1955	Wembley	England	2-7
4 May	1955	Glasgow	Portugal	3-0
15 May	1955	Belgrade	Yugoslavia	2-2
19 May	1955	Vienna	Austria	4-1
29 May	1955	Budapest	Hungary	1-3
8 October	1955	Belfast	N Ireland	1-2
9 November	1955	Glasgow	Wales	2-0
14 April	1956	Glasgow	England	1-1
2 May	1956	Glasgow	Austria	1-1
20 October	1956	Cardiff	Wales	2-2
7 November	1956	Glasgow	N Ireland	1-0
21 November	1956	Glasgow	Yugoslavia	2-0
6 April	1957	Wembley	England	1-2
WC 8 May	1957	Glasgow	Spain	4-2
WC19 May	1957	Basle	Switzerland	2-1
22 May	1957	Stuttgart	West Germany	3-1
WC26 May	1957	Madrid	Spain	1-4
5 October	1957	Belfast	N Ireland	1-1
WC 6 November	1957	Glasgow	Switzerland	3-2
13 November	1957	Glasgow	Wales	1-1
19 April	1958	Glasgow	England	0-4
7 May	1958	Glasgow	Hungary	1-1
1 June	1958	Warsaw	Poland	2-1
WC 8 June	1958	Vasteras	Yugoslavia	1-1
WC11 June	1958	Norrkoping	Paraquay	2-3
WC15 June	1958	Orebro	France	1-2
18 October	1958	Cardiff	Wales	3-0
5 November	1958	Glasgow	N Ireland	2-2
11 April	1959	Wembley	England	0-1
6 May	1959	Glasgow	West Germany	3-2
27 May	1959	Amsterdam	Netherlands	2-1
3 June	1959	Lisbon	Portugal	0-1
3 October	1959	Belfast	N Ireland	4-0
4 November	1959	Glasgow	Wales	1-1
9 April	1960	Glasgow	England	1-1
4 May	1960	Glasgow	Poland	2-3
29 May	1960	Vienna	Austria	1-4
5 June	1960	Budapest	Hungary	3-3
8 June	1960	Ankara	Turkey	2-4
22 October	1960	Cardiff	Wales	0-2
9 November	1960	Glasgow	N Ireland	5-2
15 April	1961	Wembley	England	3-9
WC 3 May	1961	Glasgow	Eire	4-1
WC 7 May	1961	Dublin	Eire	3-0
WC14 May	1961	Bratislava	Czechoslovakia	0-4
WC26 September	1961	Glasgow	Czechoslovakia	3-2
7 October	1961	Belfast	N Ireland	6-1
8 November	1961	Glasgow	Wales	2-0
WC29 November	1961	Brussels	Czechoslovakia	2-4
14 April	1962	Glasgow	England	2-0
2 May	1962	Glasgow	Uruguay	2-3
20 October	1962	Cardiff	Wales	3-2
7 November	1962	Glasgow	N Ireland	5-1
6 April	1963	Wembley	England	2-1
†8 May	1963	Glasgow	Austria	4-1
4 June	1963	Bergen	Norway	3-4
9 June	1963	Dublin	Eire	0-1
13 June	1963	Madrid	Spain	6-2
12 October	1963	Belfast	N Ireland	1-2
7 November	1963	Glasgow	Norway	6-1
20 November	1963	Glasgow	Wales	2-1
11 April	1964	Glasgow	England	1-0
12 May	1964	Hanover	West Germany	2-2
3 October	1964	Cardiff	Wales	2-3
WC21 October	1964	Glasgow	Finland	3-1
25 November	1964	Glasgow	N Ireland	3-2
10 April	1965	Wembley	England	2-2
8 May	1965	Glasgow	Spain	0-0
WC23 May	1965	Chorzow	Poland	1-1
WC27 May	1965	Helsinki	Finland	2-1
2 October	1965	Belfast	N Ireland	2-3
WC13 October	1965	Glasgow	Poland	1-2
WC 9 November	1965	Glasgow	Italy	1-0
24 November	1965	Glasgow	Wales	4-1
WC 7 December	1965	Naples	Italy	0-3
2 April	1966	Glasgow	England	3-4
11 May	1966	Glasgow	Holland	0-3
18 June	1966	Glasgow	Portugal	0-1
25 June	1966	Glasgow	Brazil	1-1
22 October	1966	Cardiff	Wales	1-1
16 November	1966	Glasgow	N Ireland	2-1
15 April	1967	Wembley	England	3-2
10 May	1967	Glasgow	Russia	0-2
21 October	1967	Belfast	N Ireland	0-1
22 November	1967	Glasgow	Wales	3-2
24 February	1968	Glasgow	England	1-1
30 May	1968	Amsterdam	Holland	0-0
16 October	1968	Copenhagen	Denmark	1-0
WC 6 November	1968	Glasgow	Austria	2-1
WC11 December	1968	Nicosia	Cyprus	5-0
WC16 April	1969	Glasgow	West Germany	1-1
3 May	1969	Wrexham	Wales	5-3
6 May	1969	Glasgow	N Ireland	1-1
10 May	1969	Wembley	England	1-4
WC12 May	1969	Glasgow	Cyprus	8-0
21 September	1969	Dublin	Eire	1-1
WC22 October	1969	Hamburg	West Germany	2-3
WC 5 November	1969	Vienna	Austria	0-2
18 April	1970	Belfast	N Ireland	1-0
22 April	1970	Glasgow	Wales	0-0
25 April	1970	Glasgow	England	0-0
EC11 November	1970	Glasgow	Denmark	1-0
EC 3 February	1971	Liege	Belgium	0-3
EC21 April	1971	Lisbon	Portugal	0-2
15 May	1971	Cardiff	Wales	0-0
18 May	1971	Glasgow	N Ireland	0-1
22 May	1971	Wembley	England	1-3
EC 9 June	1971	Copenhagen	Denmark	0-1
14 June	1971	Moscow	Russia	0-1
EC13 October	1971	Glasgow	Portugal	2-1
EC10 November	1971	Glasgow	Belgium	1-0
1 December	1971	Rotterdam	Holland	1-2
26 April	1972	Glasgow	Peru	2-0
20 May	1972	Glasgow	N Ireland	2-0
24 May	1972	Glasgow	Wales	1-0
28 May	1972	Glasgow	England	0-1
28 June	1972	Belo Horizonte	Yugoslavia	2-2
2 July	1972	Porto Alegre	Czechoslovakia	0-0
5 July	1972	Rio de Janeiro	Brazil	0-1
WC18 October	1972	Copenhagen	Denmark	4-1
WC15 November	1973	Glasgow	Denmark	2-0
14 February	1973	Glasgow	England	0-5
12 May	1973	Wrexham	Wales	2-0
16 May	1973	Glasgow	N Ireland	1-2
19 May	1973	Wembley	England	0-1
22 June	1973	Berne	Switzerland	0-1
30 June	1973	Glasgow	Brazil	0-1
WC26 September	1973	Glasgow	Czechoslovakia	2-1
WC17 October	1973	Bratislava	Czechoslovakia	0-1
14 November	1973	Glasgow	West Germany	1-1
27 March	1974	Frankfurt	West Germany	1-2
27 May	1974	Glasgow	N Ireland	0-1
14 May	1974	Glasgow	Wales	2-0
18 May	1974	Glasgow	England	2-0
1 June	1974	Bruges	Belgium	1-2
6 June	1974	Oslo	Norway	2-1
WC14 June	1974	Dortmund	Zaire	2-0
WC18 June	1974	Frankfurt	Brazil	0-0
WC22 June	1974	Frankfurt	Yugoslavia	1-1
30 October	1974	Glasgow	East Germany	3-0
EC20 November	1974	Glasgow	Spain	1-2
EC 5 February	1975	Valencia	Spain	1-1
16 April	1975	Gothenburg	Sweden	1-1
13 May	1975	Glasgow	Portugal	1-0
17 May	1975	Cardiff	Wales	2-2
20 May	1975	Glasgow	N Ireland	3-0
24 May	1975	Wembley	England	1-5
EC 1 June	1975	Bucharest	Rumania	1-1
EC 3 September	1975	Copenhagen	Denmark	1-0
EC29 October	1975	Glasgow	Denmark	3-1
EC17 December	1975	Glasgow	Rumania	1-1
7 April	1976	Glasgow	Switzerland	1-0
6 May	1976	Glasgow	Wales	3-1
8 May	1976	Glasgow	N Ireland	3-0
15 May	1976	Glasgow	England	2-1
8 September	1976	Glasgow	Finland	6-0
WC13 October	1976	Prague	Czechoslovakia	0-2
WC17 November	1976	Glasgow	Wales	1-0
27 April	1977	Glasgow	Sweden	3-1
28 May	1977	Wrexham	Wales	0-0
1 June	1977	Glasgow	N Ireland	3-0
4 June	1977	Wembley	England	2-1
15 June	1977	Santiago	Chile	4-2
18 June	1977	Buenos Aires	Argentina	1-1
23 June	1977	Rio de Janeiro	Brazil	0-2
7 September	1977	East Berlin	East Germany	0-1
WC21 September	1977	Glasgow	Czechoslovakia	3-1
WC12 October	1977	Liverpool	Wales	2-0
22 February	1978	Glasgow	Bulgaria	2-1
13 May	1978	Glasgow	N Ireland	1-1
17 May	1978	Glasgow	Wales	1-1
20 May	1978	Glasgow	England	0-1
WC 3 June	1978	Cordoba	Peru	1-3
WC 7 June	1978	Cordoba	Iran	1-1
WC11 June	1978	Mendoza	Holland	3-2
EC20 September	1978	Vienna	Austria	2-3
25 October	1978	Glasgow	Norway	3-2
EC29 November	1978	Lisbon	Portugal	0-1
19 May	1979	Cardiff	Wales	0-3
22 May	1979	Glasgow	N Ireland	1-0
26 May	1979	Wembley	England	1-3
2 June	1979	Glasgow	Argentina	1-3
EC 7 June	1979	Oslo	Norway	4-0
12 September	1979	Glasgow	Peru	1-1
EC17 October	1979	Glasgow	Austria	1-1
EC21 November	1979	Brussels	Belgium	0-2
EC19 December	1979	Glasgow	Belgium	1-3
EC26 March	1980	Glasgow	Portugal	4-1
16 May	1980	Belfast	N Ireland	0-1
21 May	1980	Glasgow	Wales	1-0
24 May	1980	Glasgow	England	0-2
28 May	1980	Poznan	Poland	0-1
31 May	1980	Budapest	Hungary	1-3
WC10 September	1980	Stockholm	Sweden	1-0
WC15 October	1980	Glasgow	Portugal	0-0
WC25 February	1981	Tel Aviv	Israel	1-0
WC25 March	1981	Glasgow	N Ireland	1-1
WC28 April	1981	Glasgow	Israel	3-1
16 May	1981	Swansea	Wales	0-2
19 May	1981	Glasgow	N Ireland	2-0
23 May	1981	Wembley	England	1-0
WC 9 September	1981	Glasgow	Sweden	2-0
WC14 October	1981	Belfast	N Ireland	0-0
WC18 November	1981	Lisbon	Portugal	1-2
24 February	1982	Valencia	Spain	0-3
23 March	1982	Glasgow	Holland	2-1
28 April	1982	Belfast	N Ireland	1-1
24 May	1982	Glasgow	Wales	1-0
29 May	1982	Glasgow	England	0-1
WC15 June	1982	Malaga	New Zealand	5-2
WC18 June	1982	Seville	Brazil	1-4
WC22 June	1982	Malaga	Soviet Union	2-2
EC13 October	1982	Glasgow	E. Germany	2-0
EC17 November	1982	Bern	Switzerland	0-2
EC15 December	1982	Brussels	Belgium	2-3
EC30 March	1983	Glasgow	Switzerland	2-2

* These matches were played by a team of Scots resident in London. They are not regarded as official.
†This match was abandoned after a disaster at the ground. It is not regarded as official.
‡Abandoned after 79 minutes. V – Victory games. J – Jubilee game. WT – War-time game. WC – World Cup. EC – European Championship.

Michael's in the impoverished east end of the city.

Rangers have no such deep-rooted affinity with Protestantism, although Ibrox Park, their wide-open stadium just south of the Clyde, has come to mean to Glasgow's Protestants almost what the Vatican means to the world's Catholics.

Rangers were founded by a group of enthusiastic rowers who used to 'kick the ball' after their strenuous work-outs on the Clyde. In fact, Rangers' first ground was at Glasgow Green, to this day the centre for rowing enthusiasts in the city. A Catholic is known to have played for Rangers in the twenties, and although they had since made 'mistakes' and signed one or two others (who were quickly released) it was only in 1976 that the religious discrimination—against 'left-footers' to use the Glasgow vernacular—was actually formally admitted and abolished.

Celtic, for their part, judge a man solely by his ability. Many of the greatest players in the club's history—John Thomson, Bobby Evans, Bobby Collins, Willie Fernie, and as many as four of the European Cup winning team of 1967 were Protestants. In fact Ronnie Simpson, the goalkeeper in the 1967 side, is the son of an ex-Ranger centre-half, Jimmy Simpson. And in 1965 Celtic appointed a Protestant team manager when they brought Jock Stein in.

But for all that, Celtic's supporters are 99 per cent Catholic. Much more to the point, they are Irish Catholic—or of Irish extraction. Those 'needy children' for whom the club was founded were largely the offspring of the droves of Irish workers who came to Glasgow at the end of the last century looking for work and enough to live on.

With a background like that Rangers and Celtic seem to be guaranteed the undying allegiance of tens of thousands. So has any provincial outfit a hope of competing with these two over the long term?

Nowadays, it seems extremely unlikely. Outside the 'Old Firm', with the occasional temporary exception, every club in Scotland faces an uphill struggle in the battle for economic survival. The money necessary to build, and maintain, a winning side just does not come in through the turnstiles any more.

So every player in the country outside Ibrox and Parkhead is available for transfer. Players don't have to ask away. If somebody comes along to buy a provincial player, he'll be allowed to go if the price is right; those clubs just can't afford to turn down big money.

Nor can they afford to offer a youngster with potential star quality the same kind of money as Rangers or Celtic. So, as a direct result of the bitter rivalry between two clubs and their fans, Glasgow is generally able to skim the cream of the country's talent.

In 1975 the Scottish League split into three divisions in an attempt to bring more competitiveness into the competition. The Premier League was restricted to the top ten clubs who played each other four times during the season. The First and Second Divisions each contained 14 clubs (with Meadowbank Thistle making up the even numbers). After an attempt to increase fixtures for the First and Second Division clubs by the introduction of a Spring Cup had failed, the clubs met each other three times in 1976-77 season. This new structure, very much on trial, was not helped by the results of its first season. Rangers became the first Premier Division winners—six clear points ahead of who else but Celtic, themselves five points above Hibernian. Even under a new system the old order prevailed with Rangers going on to complete the treble.

It wasn't always like that—until about 1960 the game was thriving in Scotland. It wasn't uncommon for crowds of 30,000 to turn up for a Third Lanark versus Hibs match at Cathkin Park. And, of course, in the years following the last War, the problem for most clubs was simply how quickly they could get people through the turnstiles. Yet Rangers and Celtic still managed to monopolize the top of the heap.

Joint runners-up in the League Championship stakes to the big two are Hearts and Hibs, with four wins apiece. But two of Hearts' victories were gained in the 1890s, and the other two in 1958 and 1960. Hibs won the League in 1902-3, and then three times in their halcyon days between 1948 and 1952. By 1977 Hibs were still the only club outside Rangers and Celtic to win the title in successive years. Those great Edinburgh teams of the early and late fifties were the nearest anybody ever came to sustaining a serious threat to the Glasgow stranglehold. But even they didn't last long.

Hearts, for instance, with the near-legendary Dave Mackay at wing-half and the formidable inside trio of Conn, Bauld and Wardhaugh up front, looked invincible in their heyday. But sandwiched between their two League titles was one by Rangers, who were only mediocre by comparison. The Old Firm refused to surrender.

Hearts did win a Scottish Cup and two League Cups as well as their League Championships, but never completed the big double in one season. So it was with Hibs. They won three League Championships in five years, with what many Scots still regard as the finest forward line in history (Smith, Johnston, Reilly, Turnbull and Ormond), but never won a cup. Indeed, in the 30 years since the Scottish League Cup became a major competition, only two seasons have gone by when the Old Firm failed to land one of the major trophies. They were 1951-52, when Hibs won the League, Motherwell the Scottish Cup, and Dundee the League Cup, and 1954-55 when Aberdeen won the League, Clyde the Scottish Cup and Hearts the League Cup. Fifteen years later no one expected to see such a season again.

The hopelessness of the provincials was put in a nutshell by the late Tom Preston, chairman of Airdrie. Tom, a great talker who played in Airdrie's Scottish Cup winning team of 1924, rarely

Kenny Dalglish (left) stretched his record number of Scottish caps to 89 when he played against Belgium on 15 December 1982. Far from bringing his international career to a full stop, the World Cup that year spurred him to show he was far from finished.

Scotland's traditional 'Second Division' clubs

1 Albion Rovers (Coatbridge)
2 Alloa Athletic
3 Berwick Rangers
4 Brechin City
5 Clydebank
6 East Stirlingshire (Falkirk)
7 Forfar Athletic
8 Hamilton Academicals
9 Montrose
10 Queen's Park (Glasgow)
11 Stenhousemuir
12 Stranraer
13 Arbroath
14 Ayr United
15 Clyde (Glasgow)
16 Cowdenbeath
17 Dumbarton
18 Dunfermline Athletic
19 East Fife (Methil)
20 Morton (Greenock)
21 Queen of the South
22 Raith Rovers (Kirkcaldy)
23 St. Mirren (Paisley)
24 Stirling Albion

Highland League clubs

25 Brora Rangers
26 Buckie Thistle
27 Caledonian (Inverness)
28 Clachnacuddin (Inverness)
29 Deveronvale (Banff)
30 Elgin City
31 Forres Mechanics
32 Fraserburgh
33 Huntly
34 Inverness Thistle
35 Keith
36 Lossiemouth
37 Nairn County
38 Peterhead
39 Ross County (Dingwall)
40 Rothes

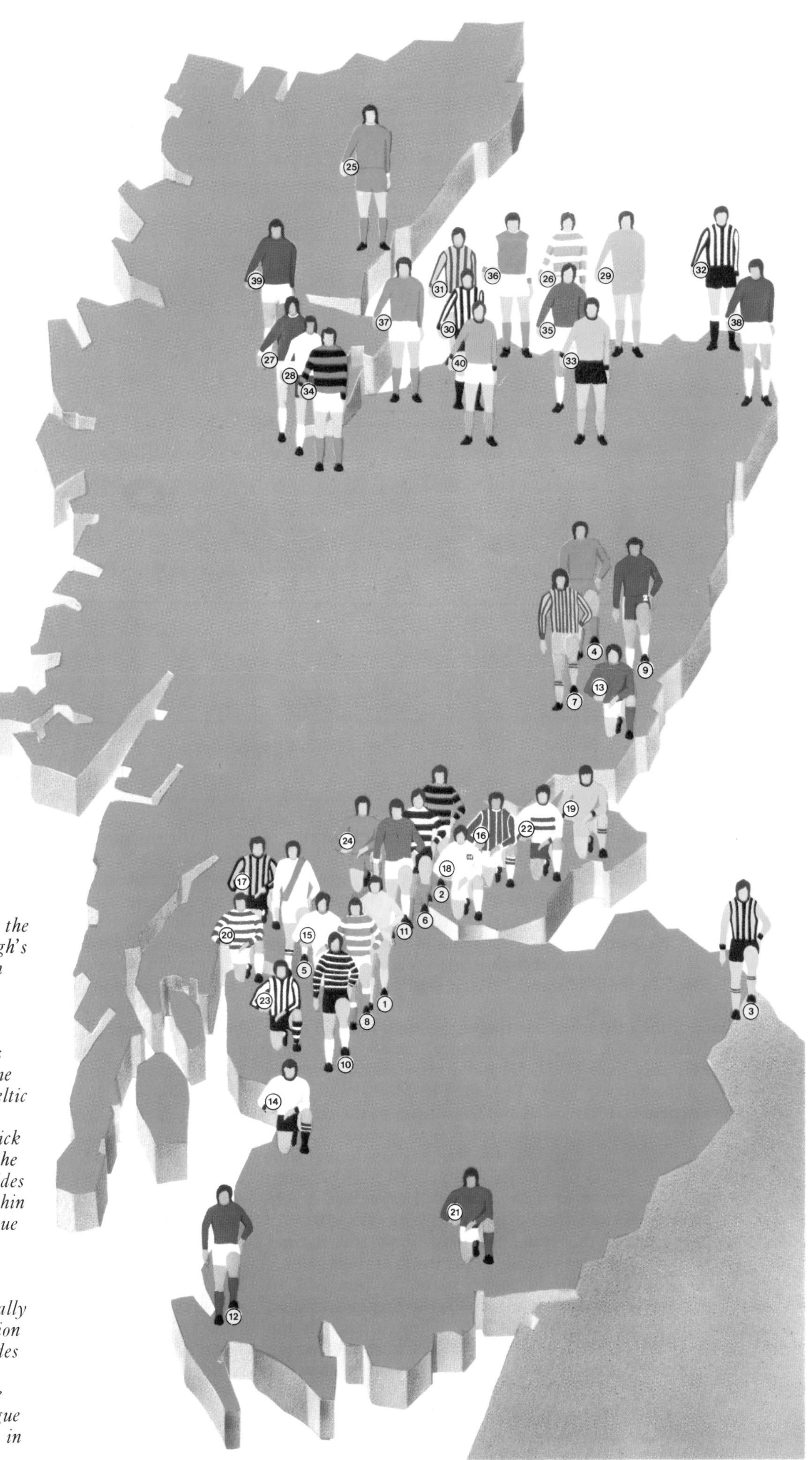

Forty one clubs traditionally make up the numbers in Scottish football (Edinburgh's Meadowbank Thistle are missing from the map); their geographical location gives a good guide to their problems. Because the great majority cluster around the Central Lowland belt, it is almost as easy for anyone in their home towns to head off to see Rangers or Celtic as it is to visit the local club. Only Stranraer, Queen of the South, Berwick and the four clubs that cluster round the Tay are outside the central belt and sides like Falkirk and East Stirling are within 60 miles of all but eight Scottish League teams. The Highland League operates independently, with only Aberdeen offering any opposition for crowds. Highland League attendances are usually higher than those in the Second Division and Cup wins by Highland League sides over the lesser senior clubs are commonplace. In the first round of the 1958-59 Scottish Cup Highland League Fraserburgh beat Dundee, then fourth in Division 1, 1-0.

SCOTTISH FA CUP FINALS

Year	Venue	Winners		Runners-up	
1874	Hampden Park	Queen's Park	2	Clydesdale	0
1875	Hampden Park	Queen's Park	3	Renton	0
1876	Hampden Park	Queen's Park	1:2	Third Lanark	1:0
1877	Hampden Park	Vale of Leven	0:1:3	Rangers	0:1:2
1878	Hampden Park	Vale of Leven	1	Third Lanark	0
1879[1]	Hampden Park	Vale of Leven	1	Rangers	1
1880	Cathkin Park	Queen's Park	3	Thornlibank	0
1881	Kinning Park	Queen's Park	3	Dumbarton	1
1882	Cathkin Park	Queen's Park	2:4	Dumbarton	2:1
1883	Hampden Park	Dumbarton	2:2	Vale of Leven	2:1
1884[2]	Hampden Park	Queen's Park		Vale of Leven	
1885	Hampden Park	Renton	0:3	Vale of Leven	0:1
1886	Cathkin Park	Queen's Park	3	Renton	1
1887	Hampden Park	Hibernian	2	Dumbarton	1
1888	Hampden Park	Renton	6	Cambuslang	1
1889	Hampden Park	Third Lanark	2	Celtic	1
1890	Ibrox Park	Queen's Park	1:2	Vale of Leven	1:1
1891	Hampden Park	Hearts	1	Dumbarton	0
1892[3]	Ibrox Park	Celtic	5	Queen's Park	1
1893	Ibrox Park	Queen's Park	2	Celtic	1
1894	Hampden Park	Rangers	3	Celtic	1
1895	Ibrox Park	St Bernard's	2	Renton	1
1896	Logie Green	Hearts	3	Hibernian	1
1897	Hampden Park	Rangers	5	Dumbarton	1
1898	Hampden Park	Rangers	2	Kilmarnock	0
1899	Hampden Park	Celtic	2	Rangers	0
1900	Ibrox Park	Celtic	4	Queen's Park	3
1901	Ibrox Park	Hearts	4	Celtic	3
1902	Celtic Park	Hibernian	1	Celtic	0
1903	Celtic Park	Rangers	1:0:2	Hearts	1:0:0
1904	Hampden Park	Celtic	3	Rangers	2
1905	Hampden Park	Third Lanark	0:3	Rangers	0:1
1906	Ibrox Park	Hearts	1	Third Lanark	0
1907	Hampden Park	Celtic	3	Hearts	0
1908	Hampden Park	Celtic	5	St Mirren	1
1909[4]					
1910	Ibrox Park	Dundee	2:0:2	Clyde	2:0:1
1911	Ibrox Park	Celtic	0:2	Hamilton Acad	0:0
1912	Ibrox Park	Celtic	2	Clyde	0
1913	Celtic Park	Falkirk	2	Raith Rovers	0
1914	Ibrox Park	Celtic	0:4	Hibernian	0:1
1915-19	*No competition*				
1920	Hampden Park	Kilmarnock	3	Albion Rovers	2
1921	Celtic Park	Partick Thistle	1	Rangers	0
1922	Hampden Park	Morton	1	Rangers	0
1923	Hampden Park	Celtic	1	Hibernian	0
1924	Ibrox Park	Airdrieonians	2	Hibernian	0
1925	Hampden Park	Celtic	2	Dundee	1
1926	Hampden Park	St Mirren	2	Celtic	0
1927	Hampden Park	Celtic	3	East Fife	1
1928	Hampden Park	Rangers	4	Celtic	0
1929	Hampden Park	Kilmarnock	2	Rangers	0
1930	Hampden Park	Rangers	0:2	Partick Thistle	0:1
1931	Hampden Park	Celtic	2:4	Motherwell	2:2
1932	Hampden Park	Rangers	1:3	Kilmarnock	1:0
1933	Hampden Park	Celtic	1	Motherwell	0
1934	Hampden Park	Rangers	5	St Mirren	0
1935	Hampden Park	Rangers	2	Hamilton Acad	1
1936	Hampden Park	Rangers	1	Third Lanark	0
1937	Hampden Park	Celtic	2	Aberdeen	1
1938	Hampden Park	East Fife	1:4	Kilmarnock	1:2
1939	Hampden Park	Clyde	4	Motherwell	0
1940-46	*No competition*				
1947	Hampden Park	Aberdeen	2	Hibernian	1
1948	Hampden Park	Rangers	1:1	Morton	1:0
1949	Hampden Park	Rangers	4	Clyde	1
1950	Hampden Park	Rangers	3	East Fife	0
1951	Hampden Park	Celtic	1	Motherwell	0
1952	Hampden Park	Motherwell	4	Dundee	0
1953	Hampden Park	Rangers	1:1	Aberdeen	1:0
1954	Hampden Park	Celtic	2	Aberdeen	1
1955	Hampden Park	Clyde	1:1	Celtic	1:0
1956	Hampden Park	Hearts	3	Celtic	1
1957*	Hampden Park	Falkirk	1:2	Kilmarnock	1:1
1958	Hampden Park	Clyde	1	Hibernian	0
1959	Hampden Park	St Mirren	3	Aberdeen	1
1960	Hampden Park	Rangers	2	Kilmarnock	0
1961	Hampden Park	Dunfermline Ath	0:2	Celtic	0:0
1962	Hampden Park	Rangers	2	St Mirren	0
1963	Hampden Park	Rangers	1:3	Celtic	1:0
1964	Hampden Park	Rangers	3	Dundee	1
1965	Hampden Park	Celtic	3	Dunfermline Ath	2
1966	Hampden Park	Rangers	0:1	Celtic	0:0
1967	Hampden Park	Celtic	2	Aberdeen	0
1968	Hampden Park	Dunfermline Ath	3	Hearts	1
1969	Hampden Park	Celtic	4	Rangers	0
1970	Hampden Park	Aberdeen	3	Celtic	1
1971	Hampden Park	Celtic	1:2	Rangers	1:1
1972	Hampden Park	Celtic	6	Hibernian	1
1973	Hampden Park	Rangers	3	Celtic	2
1974	Hampden Park	Celtic	3	Dundee Utd	0
1975	Hampden Park	Celtic	3	Airdrieonians	1
1976	Hampden Park	Rangers	3	Hearts	1
1977	Hampden Park	Celtic	1	Rangers	0
1978	Hampden Park	Rangers	2	Aberdeen	1
1979	Hampden Park	Rangers	0:0:3	Hibernian	0:0:2
1980	Hampden Park	Celtic	1	Rangers	0
1981	Hampden Park	Rangers	0:4	Dundee Utd	0:1
1982	Hampden Park	Aberdeen	4	Rangers	1
1983	Hampden Park	Aberdeen	1	Rangers	0

[1] Vale of Leven awarded the Cup after Rangers failed to attend the replay.
[2] Queen's Park awarded the Cup after Vale of Leven failed to attend the final.
[3] After Queen's Park protested at the first game, which Celtic won 1-0.
[4] Owing to riots the Cup was withheld after two drawn games (2-2, 1-1) at Hampden.

SCOTTISH LEAGUE CHAMPIONSHIP

Season	First	Pts	Second	Pts
1890-91	†Dumbarton	29	†Rangers	29
1891-92	Dumbarton	37	Celtic	35
1892-93	Celtic	29	Rangers	27
1893-94	Celtic	29	Hearts	26
1894-95	Hearts	31	Celtic	26
1895-96	Celtic	30	Rangers	26
1896-97	Hearts	28	Hibernian	26
1897-98	Celtic	33	Rangers	29
1898-99	Rangers	36	Hearts	26
1899-1900	Rangers	32	Celtic	25
1900-01	Rangers	35	Celtic	29
1901-02	Rangers	28	Celtic	26

thought, never mind spoke, about anything but football. A distinguished Scottish journalist recalls a walk through Airdrie with Preston: 'Two little boys about ten years old skipped past us. They were wearing Celtic scarves and woollen ski hats. Tom spread his hands and said, "See that? That's what we've got to compete with." He was, of course, referring to the fact that here were two local boys who, even at their age, were leaving the town to follow Celtic.' In the 1960s and 1970s it was the same all over the country.

Considered from a detached viewpoint, Scottish football often adopts the features of a farce. For instance, between the years 1905 and 1947, only once (1931-32) did a team outside the duo manage to win the Scottish First Division. The Motherwell of the thirties were generally regarded as the finest team in the country. Yet at the end of their purple patch that solitary League Championship was all they had to show. Rangers saw to that with an incredible eight wins in nine years. Motherwell were runners-up four times. It is almost as if the Scottish League had a rule prohibiting provincial clubs from even challenging Glasgow.

At the other end of the scale, for most First and Second Division sides surviving economically is the name of their game.

The secret of keeping heads above water, as practised so successfully by the Stranraers, the Brechins, the Stenhousemuirs, lies in these clubs' realistic attitude to life. They realize only too well that a town of 10,000 inhabitants—which is about average among the 'rabbits'—just could not support an ambitious football club.

Others, with even bigger populations, have tried to live with the Celtics and in the end all have failed spectacularly. Dunfermline Athletic are the latest and perhaps greatest example.

In the middle of the 1950s, the Fife club were determined to put themselves on the soccer map. By the end of the first decade they had made it to the First Division.

In 1961, under the management of Jock Stein, they won the Scottish Cup, beating Celtic in the final. There was no turning back now. By 1968, when they again won the Scottish Cup, they had proved themselves one of the most progressive—and one of the most feared—provincial clubs in the country.

But the strain of having to maintain their status inevitably proved too much. By season 1971-72 they were reduced to calling for public aid, saying they needed an immediate £50,000 to save the club from extinction. At the end of the same season they were relegated to the Second Division from whence they had come.

Most of the others have learned from these fatal errors over the years, and it would not be unfair to say that every season, from the dozen and a half clubs which form the division, only a handful are seriously looking for, or are capable of, promotion. Of course it was not always so. In fact, the Second Division was formalized at the end of season 1921-22 through the desire of lesser clubs to enjoy the pickings of the First Division.

From the introduction of professionalism in 1893 until the beginning of the First World War the Second Division was only semi-recognized by the Scottish League and promotion to the First Division was by election only.

An aspiring Second Division club had to have plenty of friends to be elected. On the other hand, a club like Queen's Park, whose fortunes faded around 1900, were saved several times from dropping to the Second Division because they had plenty of friends who voted that they stayed where they were.

The system sowed the seeds of discontent. There grew a feeling

1902-03	Hibernian	37	Dundee	31
1903-04	Third Lanark	43	Hearts	39
1904-05	‡Celtic	41	Rangers	41
1905-06	Celtic	49	Hearts	43
1906-07	Celtic	55	Dundee	48
1907-08	Celtic	55	Falkirk	51
1908-09	Celtic	51	Dundee	50
1909-10	Celtic	54	Falkirk	52
1910-11	Rangers	52	Aberdeen	48
1911-12	Rangers	51	Celtic	45
1912-13	Rangers	53	Celtic	49
1913-14	Celtic	65	Rangers	59
1914-15	Celtic	65	Hearts	61
1915-16	Celtic	67	Rangers	56
1916-17	Celtic	64	Morton	54
1917-18	Rangers	56	Celtic	55
1918-19	Celtic	58	Rangers	57
1919-20	Rangers	71	Celtic	68
1920-21	Rangers	76	Celtic	66
1921-22	Celtic	67	Rangers	66
1922-23	Rangers	55	Airdrieonians	50
1923-24	Rangers	59	Airdrieonians	50
1924-25	Rangers	60	Airdrieonians	57
1925-26	Celtic	58	Airdrieonians	50
1926-27	Rangers	56	Motherwell	51
1927-28	Rangers	60	*Celtic	55
1928-29	Rangers	67	Celtic	51
1929-30	Rangers	60	Motherwell	55
1930-31	Rangers	60	Celtic	58
1931-32	Motherwell	66	Rangers	61
1932-33	Rangers	62	Motherwell	59
1933-34	Rangers	66	Motherwell	62
1934-35	Rangers	55	Celtic	52
1935-36	Celtic	66	*Rangers	61
1936-37	Rangers	61	Aberdeen	54
1937-38	Celtic	61	Hearts	58
1938-39	Rangers	59	Celtic	48
1939-46	*No competition*			
1946-47	Rangers	46	Hibernian	44
1947-48	Hibernian	48	Rangers	46
1948-49	Rangers	46	Dundee	45
1949-50	Rangers	50	Hibernian	49
1950-51	Hibernian	48	Rangers	38
1951-52	Hibernian	45	Rangers	41
1952-53	*Rangers	43	Hibernian	43
1953-54	Celtic	43	Hearts	38
1954-55	Aberdeen	49	Celtic	46
1955-56	Rangers	52	Aberdeen	46
1956-57	Rangers	55	Hearts	53
1957-58	Hearts	62	Rangers	49
1958-59	Rangers	50	Hearts	48
1959-60	Hearts	54	Kilmarnock	50
1960-61	Rangers	51	Kilmarnock	50
1961-62	Dundee	54	Rangers	51
1962-63	Rangers	57	Kilmarnock	48
1963-64	Rangers	55	Kilmarnock	49
1964-65	*Kilmarnock	50	Hearts	50
1965-66	Celtic	57	Rangers	55
1966-67	Celtic	58	Rangers	55
1967-68	Celtic	63	Rangers	61
1968-69	Celtic	54	Rangers	49
1969-70	Celtic	57	Rangers	45
1970-71	Celtic	56	Aberdeen	54
1971-72	Celtic	60	Aberdeen	50
1972-73	Celtic	57	Rangers	56
1973-74	Celtic	53	Hibernian	49
1974-75	Rangers	56	Hibernian	49
1975-76	Rangers	54	Celtic	48
1976-77	Celtic	55	Rangers	46
1977-78	Rangers	55	Aberdeen	53
1978-79	Celtic	48	Rangers	45
1979-80	Aberdeen	48	Celtic	47
1980-81	Celtic	56	Aberdeen	49
1981-82	Celtic	55	Aberdeen	53
1982-83	Dundee Utd	56	Celtic	55

†Shared after indecisive play-off (2-2). ‡Celtic won play-off. *Goal average.

SCOTTISH LEAGUE CUP FINALS

1945-46	Hampden Park	Aberdeen	3	Rangers	2
1946-47	Hampden Park	Rangers	4	Aberdeen	0
1947-48	Hampden Park	East Fife	1:4	Falkirk	1:1
1948-49	Hampden Park	Rangers	2	Raith Rovers	0
1949-50	Hampden Park	East Fife	3	Dunfermline Ath	0
1950-51	Hampden Park	Motherwell	3	Hibernian	0
1951-52	Hampden Park	Dundee	3	Rangers	2
1952-53	Hampden Park	Dundee	2	Kilmarnock	0
1953-54	Hampden Park	East Fife	3	Partick Thistle	2
1954-55	Hampden Park	Hearts	4	Motherwell	2
1955-56	Hampden Park	Aberdeen	2	St Mirren	1
1956-57	Hampden Park	Celtic	0:3	Partick Thistle	0:0
1957-58	Hampden Park	Celtic	7	Rangers	1
1958-59	Hampden Park	Hearts	5	Partick Thistle	1
1959-60	Hampden Park	Hearts	2	Third Lanark	1
1960-61	Hampden Park	Rangers	2	Kilmarnock	0
1961-62	Hampden Park	Rangers	1:3	Hearts	1:1
1962-63	Hampden Park	Hearts	1	Kilmarnock	0
1963-64	Hampden Park	Rangers	5	Morton	0
1964-65	Hampden Park	Rangers	2	Celtic	1
1965-66	Hampden Park	Celtic	2	Rangers	1
1966-67	Hampden Park	Celtic	1	Rangers	0
1967-68	Hampden Park	Celtic	5	Dundee	3
1968-69	Hampden Park	Celtic	6	Hibernian	2
1969-70	Hampden Park	Celtic	1	St Johnstone	0
1970-71	Hampden Park	Rangers	1	Celtic	0
1971-72	Hampden Park	Partick Thistle	4	Celtic	1
1972-73	Hampden Park	Hibernian	2	Celtic	1
1973-74	Hampden Park	Dundee	1	Celtic	0
1974-75	Hampden Park	Celtic	6	Hibernian	3
1975-76	Hampden Park	Rangers	1	Celtic	0
1976-77	Hampden Park	Aberdeen	2	Celtic	1
1977-78	Hampden Park	Rangers	2	Celtic	1
1978-79	Hampden Park	Rangers	2	Aberdeen	1
1979-80	Hampden/Dens	Dundee Utd	0:3	Aberdeen	0:0
1980-81	Dens Park	Dundee Utd	3	Dundee	0
1981-82	Hampden Park	Rangers	2	Dundee Utd	1
1982-83	Hampden Park	Celtic	2	Rangers	1

that, as there were rewards for success, there should be a penalty for failure. That, in fact, there should be a promotion-relegation system between First and Second Division. But all was forgotten when the War began in 1914.

When hostilities ended four years later and football in Scotland began again the Second Division had vanished. In its place was the Central League, a rebel division comprised of clubs who had been in the pre-War lower grade and a few newcomers.

The breakaway League was an immediate success, a real money-spinner in Fife particularly, and clubs like Dunfermline and Cowdenbeath were able to tempt players away from Celtic and Rangers.

Very quickly the Scottish League realized their First Division was threatened, so the idea was hatched that the 'rebels' should be recognized as a Second Division.

'On our terms, though', said the Central League, who of course had been angling after a fair deal all along, anyway. And their terms were that there should be automatic promotion and relegation rather than the vaguaries of election.

The Scottish League agreed and in season 1921-22 the official Second Division came into being. The first movement came at the end of that term—Alloa were promoted and three clubs, including Queen's Park, were relegated in order to even the numbers of teams in both Divisions. At the end of the following season began the two-up–two-down system. From then until the Second World War, the only changes in the Second Division were those prompted by clubs dropping out. The number of clubs fluctuated but the overall set-up remained the same.

The entire League programme was suspended, of course, between 1939 and 1945. When normality was restored in season 1946-47 several changes had taken place.

For a start, the separate Leagues were called Division A and Division B as opposed to I and II. And eight teams had dropped from the 1939 Second Division into the newly-formed Division C, which was composed of 'non-League' clubs and reserve teams of the established clubs in the top two divisions.

Stirling Albion, formed only in 1945, were the first champions of 'C' Division and they were promoted to Division B. During the next few years they proceeded to yo-yo their way up and down from 'B' to 'A' and back to 'B'.

In the late forties, with the inevitable 'boom' which followed the War allowing more clubs to run reserve teams, Division C was split into two regionalized groups—South-West and North-East. With the bisection of 'C' Division, it meant the end of promotion to 'B' from that table, as had happened to Stirling previously. It was not until 1955 that the two division system was re-established.

The 'C' divisions were scrapped, and the Reserve League was formed. Five 'non-League' clubs from 'C' were elected to Division II.

And the top two teams in Division II were promoted to the First Division. To even up the teams in each Division, the bottom two in the First Division in 1955 were not relegated.

That is the way it stayed until 1975 when a major reorganization took place. The top ten clubs of Division One in 1974-75 formed a new Premier Division while the bottom eight along with the top six of Division Two formed the new Division One. The rest of the clubs remained in Division Two. Yet at the top, whatever the structure, the race was never difficult to predict—Rangers or Celtic first, the rest nowhere.

IRISH AND WELSH FOOTBALL

If there was ever a time for the contradictions, contrasts and sheer strangeness of international football in Ireland and Wales to be forever encapsulated, then 1982 was the year. As it began, tiny Northern Ireland found herself among 24 countries in the World Cup draw. In itself this was remarkable, for her qualification group performance had been by far the worst of all the countries present (and the worst of the five teams in the British Isles), with just six goals scored and nine points from eight matches. By contrast, Wales and the Republic of Ireland had managed 10 points each, had played in much tougher groups and apparently had, by any international standards, far better squads.

For both these countries, however, the World Cup was something of a tragedy. Both failed to proceed on goal difference—Eire largely because of two very debatable penalty decisions that went against her, Wales because, absurdly, she had failed to beat Iceland in Swansea.

On 27 May 1982, Billy Bingham brought his World Cup qualifiers to Wrexham for a Home International Championship (now more often known by the misnomer of British Championship) match and drew a crowd of 2,315, the lowest for any home international this century. Ireland played badly and lost 3-0. And yet, two months later, the Irish were contesting what was effectively a World Cup quarter-final tie with France and, had a perfectly good early goal by Martin O'Neill not been disallowed by an incompetent linesman, the Irish might have gone further. In the first qualifying group the Irish had drawn with Yugoslavia and then gone on to beat the hosts, Spain, in Valencia for what was probably the best international result in Irish history.

The world's—and Britain's—press wrote of the magnificent reception the players would surely get when they returned to Belfast, missing another critical point about the Irish. Alone of the qualifiers, they were not going home to the country they represented. Of the whole squad of 22, no more than half-a-dozen

FULL INTERNATIONALS PLAYED BY WALES 1876–FEBRUARY 1983

Date		Venue	Opponents	Score
25 March	1876	Glasgow	Scotland	0-4
15 March	1877	Wrexham	Scotland	0-2
23 March	1878	Glasgow	Scotland	0-9
18 January	1879	London	England	1-2
7 April	1879	Wrexham	Scotland	0-3
15 March	1880	Wrexham	England	2-3
27 March	1880	Glasgow	Scotland	1-5
26 February	1881	Blackburn	England	1-0
14 March	1881	Wrexham	Scotland	1-5
25 February	1882	Wrexham	Ireland	7-1
13 March	1882	Wrexham	England	5-3
25 March	1882	Glasgow	Scotland	0-5
3 February	1883	London	England	0-5
12 March	1883	Wrexham	Scotland	0-3
17 March	1883	Belfast	Ireland	1-1
9 February	1884	Wrexham	Ireland	6-0
17 March	1884	Wrexham	England	0-4
29 March	1884	Glasgow	Scotland	1-4
14 March	1885	Blackburn	England	1-1
23 March	1885	Wrexham	Scotland	1-8
11 April	1885	Belfast	Ireland	8-2
27 February	1886	Wrexham	Ireland	5-0
29 March	1886	Wrexham	England	1-3
10 April	1886	Glasgow	Scotland	1-4
26 February	1887	London	England	0-4
12 March	1887	Belfast	Ireland	1-4
21 March	1887	Wrexham	Scotland	0-2
4 February	1888	Crewe	England	1-5
3 March	1888	Wrexham	Ireland	11-0
10 March	1888	Edinburgh	Scotland	1-5
23 February	1889	Stoke	England	1-4
15 April	1889	Wrexham	Scotland	0-0
27 April	1889	Belfast	Ireland	3-1
8 February	1890	Shrewsbury	Ireland	5-2
15 March	1890	Wrexham	England	1-3
22 March	1890	Paisley	Scotland	0-5
7 February	1891	Belfast	Ireland	2-7
7 March	1891	Sunderland	England	1-4
21 March	1891	Wrexham	Scotland	3-4
27 February	1892	Bangor (Wales)	Ireland	1-1
5 March	1892	Wrexham	England	0-2
26 March	1892	Edinburgh	Scotland	1-6
13 March	1893	Stoke	England	0-6
18 March	1893	Wrexham	Scotland	0-8
8 April	1893	Belfast	Ireland	3-4
24 February	1894	Swansea	Ireland	4-1
12 March	1894	Wrexham	England	1-5
24 Marcb	1894	Kilmarnock	Scotland	2-5
16 March	1895	Belfast	Ireland	2-2
18 March	1895	London	England	1-1
23 March	1895	Wrexham	Scotland	2-2
29 February	1896	Wrexham	Ireland	6-1
16 March	1896	Cardiff	England	1-9
21 March	1896	Dundee	Scotland	0-4
6 March	1897	Belfast	Ireland	3-4
20 March	1897	Wrexham	Scotland	2-2
29 March	1897	Sheffield	England	0-4
19 February	1898	Llandudno	Ireland	0-1
19 March	1898	Motherwell	Scotland	2-5
28 March	1898	Wrexham	England	0-3
4 March	1899	Belfast	Ireland	0-1
18 March	1899	Wrexham	Scotland	0-6
20 March	1899	Bristol	England	1-4
3 February	1900	Aberdeen	Scotland	2-5
24 February	1900	Llandudno	Ireland	2-0
26 March	1900	Cardiff	England	1-1
2 March	1901	Wrexham	Scotland	1-1
18 March	1901	Newcastle	England	0-6
23 March	1901	Llandudno	Ireland	1-0
3 March	1902	Wrexham	England	0-0
15 March	1902	Greenock	Scotland	1-5
22 March	1902	Cardiff	Ireland	0-3
2 March	1903	Portsmouth	England	1-2
9 March	1903	Cardiff	Scotland	0-1
28 March	1903	Belfast	Ireland	0-2
29 February	1904	Wrexham	England	2-2
12 March	1904	Dundee	Scotland	1-1
21 March	1904	Bangor (Wales)	Ireland	0-1
6 March	1905	Wrexham	Scotland	3-1
27 March	1905	Liverpool	England	1-3
8 April	1905	Belfast	Ireland	2-2
3 March	1906	Edinburgh	Scotland	2-0
19 March	1906	Cardiff	England	0-1
2 April	1906	Wrexham	Ireland	4-4
23 February	1907	Belfast	Ireland	3-2
4 March	1907	Wrexham	Scotland	1-0
18 March	1907	London	England	1-1
7 March	1908	Dundee	Scotland	1-2
16 March	1908	Wrexham	England	1-7
11 April	1908	Aberdare	Ireland	0-1
1 March	1909	Wrexham	Scotland	3-2
15 March	1909	Nottingham	England	0-2
20 March	1909	Belfast	Ireland	3-2
5 March	1910	Kilmarnock	Scotland	0-1
11 March	1910	Wrexham	Ireland	4-1
14 March	1910	Cardiff	England	0-1
6 March	1911	Cardiff	Scotland	2-2
13 March	1911	London	England	0-3
28 March	1911	Belfast	Ireland	2-1
2 March	1912	Edinburgh	Scotland	0-1
11 March	1912	Wrexham	England	0-2
13 April	1912	Cardiff	Ireland	2-3
18 January	1913	Belfast	Ireland	1-0
3 March	1913	Wrexham	Scotland	0-0
17 March	1913	Bristol	England	3-4
19 January	1914	Wrexham	Ireland	1-2
28 February	1914	Glasgow	Scotland	0-0
16 March	1914	Cardiff	England	0-2
V11 October	1919	Cardiff	England	2-1
V18 October	1919	Stoke	England	0-2
14 February	1920	Belfast	Ireland	2-2
26 February	1920	Cardiff	Scotland	1-1
15 March	1920	London	England	2-1
12 February	1921	Aberdeen	Scotland	1-2
14 March	1921	Cardiff	England	0-0
9 April	1921	Swansea	Ireland	2-1
4 February	1922	Wrexham	Scotland	2-1
13 March	1922	Liverpool	England	0-1
1 April	1922	Belfast	Ireland	1-1
5 March	1923	Cardiff	England	2-2
17 March	1923	Paisley	Scotland	0-2
14 April	1923	Wrexham	Ireland	0-3
16 February	1924	Cardiff	Scotland	2-0
3 March	1924	Blackburn	England	2-1
15 March	1924	Belfast	N Ireland	1-0
14 February	1925	Edinburgh	Scotland	1-3
28 February	1925	Swansea	England	1-2
18 April	1925	Wrexham	N Ireland	0-0
31 October	1925	Cardiff	Scotland	0-3
13 January	1926	Belfast	N Ireland	0-3
1 March	1926	London	England	3-1
30 October	1926	Glasgow	Scotland	0-3
12 February	1927	Wrexham	England	3-3
9 April	1927	Cardiff	N Ireland	2-2
29 October	1927	Wrexham	Scotland	2-2
28 November	1927	Burnley	England	2-1
4 February	1928	Belfast	N Ireland	2-1
27 October	1928	Glasgow	Scotland	2-4
17 November	1928	Swansea	England	2-3
2 February	1929	Wrexham	N Ireland	2-2
26 October	1929	Cardiff	Scotland	2-4
20 November	1929	London	England	0-6
1 February	1930	Belfast	N Ireland	0-7
25 October	1930	Glasgow	Scotland	1-1
22 November	1930	Wrexham	England	0-4
22 April	1931	Wrexham	N Ireland	3-2
31 October	1931	Wrexham	Scotland	2-3
18 November	1931	Liverpool	England	1-3
5 December	1931	Belfast	N Ireland	0-4
26 October	1932	Edinburgh	Scotland	5-2
16 November	1932	Wrexham	England	0-0
7 December	1932	Wrexham	N Ireland	4-1
25 May	1933	Paris	France	1-1
4 October	1933	Cardiff	Scotland	3-2
4 November	1933	Belfast	N Ireland	1-1
15 November	1933	Newcastle	England	2-1
29 September	1934	Cardiff	England	0-4
21 November	1934	Aberdeen	Scotland	2-3
27 March	1935	Wrexham	N Ireland	3-1
5 October	1935	Cardiff	Scotland	1-1
5 February	1936	Wolverhampton	England	2-1
11 March	1936	Belfast	N Ireland	2-3
17 October	1936	Cardiff	England	2-1
2 December	1936	Dundee	Scotland	2-1
17 March	1937	Wrexham	N Ireland	4-1
30 October	1937	Cardiff	Scotland	2-1
17 November	1937	Middlesbrough	England	1-2
16 March	1938	Belfast	N Ireland	0-1
22 October	1938	Cardiff	England	4-2
9 November	1938	Edinburgh	Scotland	2-3
15 March	1939	Wrexham	N Ireland	3-1
20 May	1939	Paris	France	1-2
WT11 November	1939	Cardiff	England	1-1
WT18 November	1939	Wrexham	England	2-3
WT13 April	1940	Wembley	England	1-0
WT26 April	1941	Nottingham	England	1-4
WT 7 June	1941	Cardiff	England	2-3
WT25 October	1941	Birmingham	England	1-2
WT 9 May	1942	Cardiff	England	1-0
WT24 October	1942	Wolverhampton	England	2-1
WT27 February	1943	Wembley	England	3-5
WT 8 May	1943	Cardiff	England	1-1
WT25 September	1943	Wembley	England	3-8
WT 6 May	1944	Cardiff	England	0-2
WT16 September	1944	Liverpool	England	2-2
WT 5 May	1945	Cardiff	England	2-3
V20 October	1945	West Bromwich	England	1-0
19 October	1946	Wrexham	Scotland	3-1
13 November	1946	Manchester	England	0-3
16 April	1947	Belfast	N Ireland	1-2
18 October	1947	Cardiff	England	0-3
12 November	1947	Glasgow	Scotland	2-1
10 March	1948	Wrexham	N Ireland	2-0
23 October	1948	Cardiff	Scotland	1-3
10 November	1948	Birmingham	England	0-1
9 March	1949	Belfast	N Ireland	2-0
15 May	1949	Lisbon	Portugal	2-3
22 May	1949	Liege	Belgium	1-3
26 May	1949	Berne	Switzerland	0-4
WC15 October	1949	Cardiff	England	1-4
WC 9 November	1949	Glasgow	Scotland	0-2
23 November	1949	Cardiff	Belgium	5-1
WC 8 March	1950	Wrexham	N Ireland	0-0
21 October	1950	Cardiff	Scotland	1-3
15 November	1950	Sunderland	England	2-4
7 March	1951	Belfast	N Ireland	2-1
12 May	1951	Cardiff	Portugal	2-1

lived there. Many, by their own admission, never went there other than for international matches.

It was very easy to understand the annoyance of many other soccer nations that the British Isles have somehow managed to maintain five international teams, despite the fact that virtually all their players compete in just one League competition. After the declining attendances at home international matches (excepting England v Scotland) in recent years, it was also very difficult to argue that there was any obsessive domestic desire for all of these international teams. At Wrexham, the excuse for that 2,000 attendance was that the FA Cup final replay was on television; a threadbare one to be sure—why should a public that cared about Wales prefer to stay in and watch a Cup final between two sides from London?

The fact was that international football had lost much of its appeal over a fifteen year period in which the number of matches played had more than doubled and the inability of the Welsh and Irish to call on squads of genuinely first-class players had become increasingly obvious. Notwithstanding Ireland's amazing performance in Spain (which was surely the exception tending to prove the rule) an Ireland v Wales game was no better and no worse than an English Second Division match. Even when England and Scotland are the opposition, the power of the Irish and Welsh has tended to be that of frustrating their bigger brothers, that determined defence which has become so much less appealing to crowds in recent decades.

This is not to say that the two Irelands and Wales have not had their successes in recent years. In 1980 Northern Ireland won the Home International Championship outright for only the second time in her history (the first was in 1914), appropriately in the Irish FA's Centenary year. That being said, it was not an entirely glorious campaign—1-0 defeats of Scotland and Wales and a 1-1 draw at Wembley.

It was essentially the same squad that did so well in Spain, a team that had been denied any immediate opportunity of repeating its 1980 success when both England and Wales refused to travel to Belfast the following year at the height of the Maze hunger strikes. Rather than rearrange the matches elsewhere, the fixtures were dropped, giving rise to understandable suspicions that both managers were not entirely unhappy to lose one game from an extremely crowded club and country fixture list. For the first time in peacetime since it had been instituted in 1883-84 the Championship was left unfinished—a conclusion that drew forth surprisingly little comment.

The only organizations to show any great concern proved to be the Welsh and Irish FAs, who probably detected the thin end of the wedge. To both these bodies, the money they receive from the visits of England and Scotland is crucial to their administration—it is the largest single source of income—and the Championship has survived largely to provide this finance.

The move in the 1970s to play the whole competition at the end of the season eventually proved to be a footballing disaster. Players, generally drawn from the Football League, were exhausted; many of the better sides could not release their players

16 May	1951	Wrexham	Switzerland	3-2
20 October	1951	Cardiff	England	1-1
14 November	1951	Glasgow	Scotland	1-0
19 March	1952	Swansea	N Ireland	3-0
18 October	1952	Cardiff	Scotland	1-2
12 November	1952	Wembley	England	2-5
15 April	1953	Belfast	N Ireland	3-2
14 May	1953	Paris	France	1-6
21 May	1953	Belgrade	Yugoslavia	2-5
WC10 October	1953	Cardiff	England	1-4
WC 4 November	1953	Glasgow	Scotland	3-3
WC31 March	1954	Wrexham	N Ireland	1-2
9 May	1954	Vienna	Austria	0-2
22 September	1954	Cardiff	Yugoslavia	1-3
16 October	1954	Cardiff	Scotland	0-1
10 November	1954	Wembley	England	2-3
20 April	1955	Belfast	N Ireland	3-2
22 October	1955	Cardiff	England	2-1
9 November	1955	Glasgow	Scotland	0-2
23 November	1955	Wrexham	Austria	1-2
11 April	1956	Cardiff	N Ireland	1-1
20 October	1956	Cardiff	Scotland	2-2
14 November	1956	Wembley	England	1-3
10 April	1957	Belfast	N Ireland	0-0
WC 1 May	1957	Cardiff	Czechoslovakia	1-0
WC19 May	1957	Leipzig	East Germany	1-2
WC26 May	1957	Prague	Czechoslovakia	0-2
WC25 September	1957	Cardiff	East Germany	4-1
19 October	1957	Cardiff	England	0-4
13 November	1957	Glasgow	Scotland	1-1
WC15 January	1958	Tel Aviv	Israel	2-0
WC 5 February	1958	Cardiff	Israel	2-0
16 April	1958	Cardiff	N Ireland	1-1
WC 8 June	1958	Sandviken	Hungary	1-1
WC11 June	1958	Stockholm	Mexico	1-1
WC15 June	1958	Stockholm	Sweden	0-0
WC17 June	1958	Stockholm	Hungary	2-1
WC19 June	1958	Gothenburg	Brazil	0-1
18 October	1958	Cardiff	Scotland	0-3
26 November	1958	Birmingham	England	2-2
22 April	1959	Belfast	N Ireland	1-4
17 October	1959	Cardiff	England	1-1
4 November	1959	Glasgow	Scotland	1-1
6 April	1960	Wrexham	N Ireland	3-2
28 September	1960	Dublin	Eire	3-2
22 October	1960	Cardiff	Scotland	2-0
23 November	1960	Wembley	England	1-5
12 April	1961	Belfast	N Ireland	5-1
WC19 April	1961	Cardiff	Spain	1-2
WC18 May	1961	Madrid	Spain	1-1
28 May	1961	Budapest	Hungary	2-3
14 October	1961	Cardiff	England	1-1
8 November	1961	Glasgow	Scotland	0-2
11 April	1962	Cardiff	N Ireland	4-0
12 May	1962	Rio de Janeiro	Brazil	1-3
16 May	1962	Sao Paulo	Brazil	1-3
22 May	1962	Mexico City	Mexico	1-2
20 October	1962	Cardiff	Scotland	2-3
ENC 7 November	1962	Budapest	Hungary	1-3
21 November	1962	Wembley	England	0-4
ENC20 March	1963	Cardiff	Hungary	1-1
3 April	1963	Belfast	N Ireland	4-1
12 October	1963	Cardiff	England	0-4
20 November	1963	Glasgow	Scotland	1-2
15 April	1964	Swansea	N Ireland	3-2
3 October	1964	Cardiff	Scotland	3-2
WC21 October	1964	Copenhagen	Denmark	0-1
18 November	1964	Wembley	England	1-2
WC 9 December	1964	Athens	Greece	0-2
WC17 March	1965	Cardiff	Greece	4-1
31 March	1965	Belfast	N Ireland	5-0
1 May	1965	Florence	Italy	1-4
WC30 May	1965	Moscow	Russia	1-2
2 October	1965	Cardiff	England	0-0
WC27 October	1965	Cardiff	Russia	2-1
24 November	1965	Glasgow	Scotland	1-4
WC 1 December	1965	Wrexham	Denmark	4-2
30 March	1966	Cardiff	N Ireland	1-4
14 May	1966	Rio de Janeiro	Brazil	1-3
18 May	1966	Belo Horizonte	Brazil	0-1
22 May	1966	Santiago	Chile	0-2
22 October	1966	Glasgow	Scotland	1-1
16 November	1966	Wembley	England	1-5
12 April	1967	Belfast	N Ireland	0-0
21 October	1967	Cardiff	England	0-3
22 November	1967	Glasgow	Scotland	2-3
28 February	1968	Wrexham	N Ireland	2-0
8 May	1968	Cardiff	West Germany	1-1
WC23 October	1968	Cardiff	Italy	0-1
26 March	1969	Frankfurt	West Germany	1-1
WC16 April	1969	Dresden	East Germany	1-2
3 May	1969	Wrexham	Scotland	3-5
7 May	1969	Wembley	England	1-2
10 May	1969	Belfast	N Ireland	0-0
28 July	1969	Cardiff	Rest of Britain	0-1
WC22 October	1969	Cardiff	East Germany	1-3
WC 4 November	1969	Rome	Italy	1-4
18 April	1970	Cardiff	England	1-1
22 April	1970	Glasgow	Scotland	0-0
25 April	1970	Swansea	N Ireland	1-0
EC11 November	1970	Cardiff	Rumania	0-0
EC21 April	1971	Swansea	Czechoslovakia	1-3
15 May	1971	Cardiff	Scotland	0-0
18 May	1971	Wembley	England	0-0
22 May	1971	Belfast	N Ireland	0-1
EC26 May	1971	Helsinki	Finland	1-0
EC13 October	1971	Swansea	Finland	3-0
EC27 October	1971	Prague	Czechoslovakia	0-1
EC24 November	1971	Bucharest	Rumania	0-2
20 May	1972	Cardiff	England	0-3
24 May	1972	Glasgow	Scotland	0-1
28 May	1972	Wrexham	N Ireland	0-0
WC15 November	1972	Cardiff	England	0-1
WC24 January	1973	Wembley	England	1-1
WC28 March	1973	Cardiff	Poland	2-0
12 May	1973	Wrexham	Scotland	0-2
15 May	1973	Wembley	England	0-3
19 May	1973	Everton	N Ireland	0-1
WC26 September	1973	Katowice	Poland	0-3
11 May	1974	Cardiff	England	0-2
14 May	1974	Glasgow	Scotland	0-2
18 May	1974	Wrexham	N Ireland	1-0
EC 4 September	1974	Vienna	Austria	1-2
EC30 October	1974	Cardiff	Hungary	2-0
EC20 November	1974	Swansea	Luxembourg	5-0
EC16 April	1975	Budapest	Hungary	2-1
EC 1 May	1975	Luxembourg	Luxembourg	3-1
17 May	1975	Cardiff	Scotland	2-2
21 May	1975	Wembley	England	2-2
23 May	1975	Belfast	N Ireland	0-1
EC19 November	1975	Wrexham	Austria	1-0
24 March	1976	Wrexham	England	1-2
EC24 April	1976	Zagreb	Yugoslavia	0-2
6 May	1976	Glasgow	Scotland	1-3
8 May	1976	Cardiff	England	0-1
14 May	1976	Swansea	N Ireland	1-0
EC22 May	1976	Cardiff	Yugoslavia	1-1
6 October	1976	Cardiff	West Germany	0-2
WC17 November	1976	Glasgow	Scotland	0-1
WC30 March	1977	Wrexham	Czechoslovakia	3-0
28 May	1977	Wrexham	Scotland	0-0
31 May	1977	Wembley	England	1-0
3 June	1977	Belfast	N Ireland	1-1
6 September	1977	Wrexham	Kuwait	0-0
20 September	1977	Kuwait	Kuwait	0-0
WC12 October	1977	Liverpool	Scotland	0-2
WC17 November	1977	Prague	Czechoslovakia	0-1
14 December	1977	Dortmund	West Germany	1-1
18 April	1978	Teheran	Iran	1-0
13 May	1978	Cardiff	England	1-3
17 May	1978	Glasgow	Scotland	1-1
19 May	1978	Wrexham	N Ireland	1-0
EC25 October	1978	Wrexham	Malta	7-0
EC29 November	1978	Wrexham	Turkey	1-0
EC 2 May	1979	Wrexham	West Germany	0-2
19 May	1979	Cardiff	Scotland	3-0
23 May	1979	Wembley	England	0-0
25 May	1979	Belfast	N Ireland	1-1
EC 2 June	1979	Valetta	Malta	2-0
11 September	1979	Swansea	Eire	2-1
EC17 October	1979	Cologne	West Germany	1-5
EC21 November	1979	Izmir	Turkey	0-1
17 May	1980	Wrexham	England	4-1
21 May	1980	Hampden	Scotland	0-1
23 May	1980	Cardiff	N Ireland	0-1
WC 2 June	1980	Reykjavik	Iceland	4-0
WC15 October	1980	Cardiff	Turkey	4-0
WC19 November	1980	Cardiff	Czechoslovakia	1-0
24 February	1981	Dublin	Eire	3-1
WC25 March	1981	Ankara	Turkey	1-0
16 May	1981	Swansea	Scotland	2-0
20 May	1981	Wembley	England	0-0
WC30 May	1981	Wrexham	Soviet Union	0-0
WC 9 September	1981	Prague	Czechoslovakia	0-2
WC14 October	1981	Swansea	Iceland	2-2
WC18 November	1981	Tbilisi	Soviet Union	0-3
24 March	1982	Valencia	Spain	1-1
27 April	1982	Cardiff	England	0-1
24 May	1982	Hampden	Scotland	0-1
27 May	1982	Wrexham	N Ireland	3-0
2 June	1982	Toulouse	France	1-0
EC22 September	1982	Swansea	Norway	1-0
EC15 December	1982	Titograd	Yugoslavia	4-4
23 February	1983	Wembley	England	1-2

WC World Cup games
EC European Championship games
V Victory International WT War time International
ENC European Nations Cup games

Right: *The greatest moment in Welsh soccer history; Spurs winger Terry Medwin scores the goal which put the Welsh into the 1958 World Cup quarter-finals. Playing against Hungary, runners-up in 1954, in a group play-off game Ivor Allchurch and Medwin got the goals in a 2-1 win. In the quarter-final it was only a single goal from 17-year-old Pele in the last minute which eliminated Wales, their only defeat of the tournament. 1958 remains the only year Wales have reached the finals of the World Cup.*
Right below: *Mike England (left) at the heart of the Welsh defence against his namesake country in the early 1970s. A decade later he was the Welsh manager and took his side to the very fringes of the 1982 World Cup finals. In the end, they failed to qualify because of a 2-2 draw with Iceland in Swansea but the Welsh still obtained one more point than did England and Northern Ireland.*
Opposite bottom: *Port Vale's Sammy Morgan scores Northern Ireland's equalizing goal against Spain at Hull City's Boothferry Park in February 1972. A large number of Irish internationals in the 1970s had to be transferred from Belfast because of the security situation, a trend that reached a peak in 1981 when both England and Wales refused to play Home International Championship matches there and the tournament was left incomplete. In 1972 Boothferry Park was Irish manager Terry Neill's home ground.*

because of European commitments and spectators were increasingly tired of football as well. Only the England v Scotland match drew big crowds, and this was a problem in itself. In 1983, in an effort to frustrate the bi-annual Scots invasion, the match was arranged for midweek while the rest of the competition was spread around the season. Its value and its significance were now entirely nominal.

It was not always so. Until the mid-20th century the Welsh and the Irish had but one aim—to beat the English and the Scots. It was not until the early years of the century that the English, in particular, took the opposition at all seriously. In the 1890s the Corinthians were twice allowed to choose the whole England team against Wales, while on two other occasions England played Ireland and Wales on the same day. In the 1920s and 1930s it was normal to 'compensate' players who had just missed out on major honours with an odd appearance against the Welsh or Irish.

The situation was further complicated by the split after Irish home rule was bitterly fought for and conceded in 1921. It was hoped that, like rugby, a single association could be maintained, but this proved impossible. A Belfast winner of the Southern Irish version of the Cup (Alton United) was refused permission to carry the trophy across the border, while a whole string of Catholic versus Protestant incidents (and more than one death) at major matches just prior and after the First World War rendered such hopes stillborn. The split has proved a great tragedy for the game in Ireland—imagine what the Northern Ireland team might have done in Spain if it could have included the likes of Brady, Lawrenson, Daly and Stapleton.

Technically the Republic of Ireland can still choose Northern-born players for non-British Championship matches, while Belfast can choose Southerners to play against England, Scotland and Wales. In actual fact, this has not occurred since Johnny Carey (and others) played regularly for both countries after the Second World War (Carey played against England twice, representing both countries, in the space of three days). It was not until 1954 that Belfast was forced by FIFA to designate its teams Northern Ireland, although it still calls itself the Irish FA.

The Welsh have had a far less troublesome history, but only one real spell of success. That was in the 1930s, when Wales could only rely on players from their four affiliated League clubs (Cardiff, Swansea, Newport and Wrexham) because English sides had no obligation to release them.

The selfishness of the English clubs did, however, produce one memorable moment of glory. It came in 1930, when the Football League banned the release of all League players from Saturday afternoon internationals played by Wales, Ireland and Scotland and the Welsh had to travel to Hampden without any English League players.

That situation provided few problems for the Scots. At the

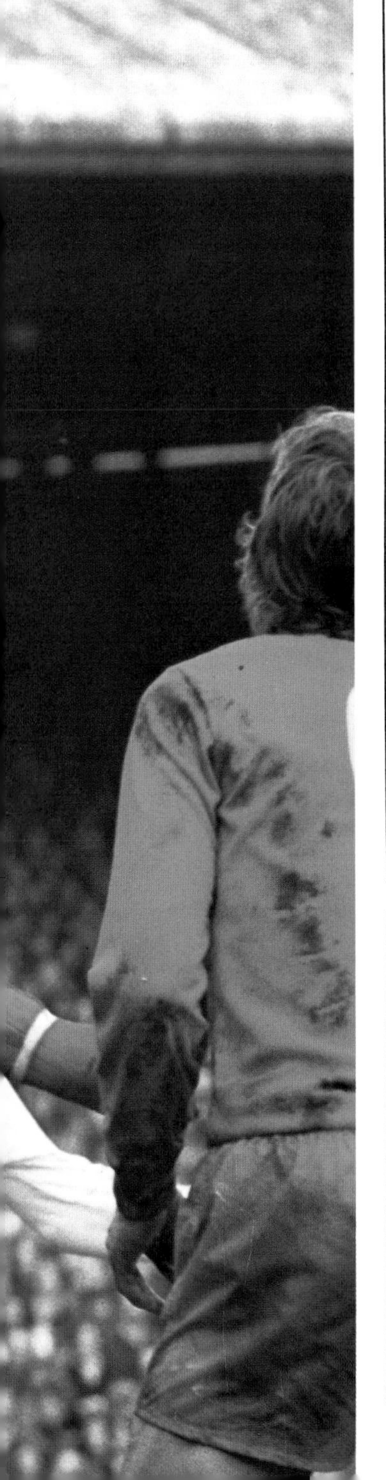

FULL INTERNATIONALS PLAYED BY EIRE 1924–MARCH 1983

Date		*Venue*	*Opponents*	*Score*
28 May	1924	Paris	Bulgaria	1-0
2 June	1924	Paris	Netherlands	1-2
3 June	1924	Paris	Estonia	3-1
16 June	1925	Dublin	USA	3-1
21 March	1926	Turin	Italy	0-3
23 April	1927	Dublin	Italy	1-2
12 February	1928	Liege	Belgium	4-2
20 April	1929	Dublin	Belgium	4-0
11 May	1930	Brussels	Belgium	3-1
26 April	1931	Barcelona	Spain	1-1
13 December	1931	Dublin	Spain	0-5
8 May	1932	Amsterdam	Netherlands	2-0
WC25 February	1934	Dublin	Belgium	4-4
WC 8 April	1934	Amsterdam	Netherlands	2-5
15 December	1934	Dublin	Hungary	2-4
5 May	1935	Basle	Switzerland	0-1
8 May	1935	Dortmund	Germany	1-3
8 December	1935	Dublin	Netherlands	3-5
17 March	1936	Dublin	Switzerland	1-0
3 May	1936	Budapest	Hungary	3-3
9 May	1936	Luxembourg	Luxembourg	5-1
17 October	1936	Dublin	Germany	5-2
6 December	1936	Dublin	Hungary	2-3
17 May	1937	Berne	Switzerland	1-0
23 May	1937	Paris	France	2-0
WC10 October	1937	Oslo	Norway	2-3
WC 7 November	1937	Dublin	Norway	3-3
18 May	1938	Prague	Czechoslovakia	2-2
22 May	1938	Warsaw	Poland	0-6
18 September	1938	Dublin	Switzerland	4-0
13 November	1938	Dublin	Poland	3-2
19 March	1939	Cork	Hungary	2-2
18 May	1939	Budapest	Hungary	2-2
23 May	1939	Bremen	Germany	1-1
16 June	1946	Lisbon	Portugal	1-3
23 June	1946	Madrid	Spain	1-0
30 September	1946	Dublin	England	0-1
2 March	1947	Dublin	Spain	3-2
4 May	1947	Dublin	Portugal	0-2
23 May	1948	Lisbon	Portugal	0-2
30 May	1948	Barcelona	Spain	1-2
5 December	1948	Dublin	Switzerland	0-1
24 April	1949	Dublin	Belgium	0-2
22 May	1949	Dublin	Portugal	1-0
WC 2 June	1949	Stockholm	Sweden	1-3
12 June	1949	Dublin	Spain	1-4
WC 8 September	1949	Dublin	Finland	3-0
21 September	1949	Everton	England	2-0
WC 9 October	1949	Helsinki	Finland	1-1
WC13 November	1949	Dublin	Sweden	1-3
10 May	1950	Brussels	Belgium	1-5
26 November	1950	Dublin	Norway	2-2
13 May	1951	Dublin	Argentina	0-1
30 May	1951	Oslo	Norway	3-1
17 October	1951	Dublin	West Germany	3-2
4 May	1952	Cologne	West Germany	0-3
7 May	1952	Vienna	Austria	0-6
1 June	1952	Madrid	Spain	0-6
16 November	1952	Dublin	France	1-1
25 March	1953	Dublin	Austria	4-0
WC 4 October	1953	Dublin	France	3-5
WC28 October	1953	Dublin	Luxembourg	4-0
WC25 November	1953	Paris	France	0-1
WC 7 March	1954	Luxembourg	Luxembourg	1-0
8 November	1954	Dublin	Norway	2-1
1 May	1955	Dublin	Netherlands	1-0
25 May	1955	Oslo	Norway	3-1
28 May	1955	Hamburg	West Germany	1-2
19 September	1955	Dublin	Yugoslavia	1-4
27 November	1955	Dublin	Spain	2-2
10 May	1956	Rotterdam	Netherlands	4-1
WC 3 October	1956	Dublin	Denmark	2-1
25 November	1956	Dublin	West Germany	3-0
WC 8 May	1957	Wembley	England	1-5
WC19 May	1957	Dublin	England	1-1
WC 2 October	1957	Copenhagen	Denmark	2-0
11 May	1958	Katowice	Poland	2-2
14 May	1958	Vienna	Austria	1-3
5 October	1958	Dublin	Poland	2-2
ENC 5 May	1959	Dublin	Czechoslovakia	2-0
ENC10 May	1959	Bratislava	Czechoslovakia	0-4
1 November	1959	Dublin	Sweden	3-2
30 March	1960	Dublin	Chile	2-0
11 May	1960	Dusseldorf	West Germany	1-0
18 May	1960	Malmo	Sweden	1-4
28 September	1960	Dublin	Wales	2-3
6 November	1960	Dublin	Norway	3-2
WC 3 May	1961	Glasgow	Scotland	1-4
WC 7 May	1961	Dublin	Scotland	0-3
WC 8 October	1961	Dublin	Czechoslovakia	1-3
WC29 October	1961	Prague	Czechoslovakia	1-7
8 April	1962	Dublin	Austria	2-3
ENC12 August	1962	Dublin	Iceland	4-2
ENC 2 September	1962	Reykjavik	Iceland	1-1
9 June	1963	Dublin	Scotland	1-0
25 September	1963	Vienna	Austria	0-0
13 October	1963	Dublin	Austria	3-2
11 March	1964	Seville	Spain	1-5
8 April	1964	Dublin	Spain	0-2
10 May	1964	Cracow	Poland	1-3
13 May	1964	Oslo	Norway	4-1
24 May	1964	Dublin	England	1-3
25 October	1964	Dublin	Poland	3-2
24 March	1965	Dublin	Belgium	0-2
WC 5 May	1965	Dublin	Spain	1-0
WC21 October	1965	Seville	Spain	1-4
WC10 November	1965	Paris	Spain	0-1
4 May	1966	Dublin	West Germany	0-4
22 May	1966	Vienna	Austria	0-1
25 May	1966	Liege	Belgium	3-2
ENC23 October	1966	Dublin	Spain	0-0
16 November	1966	Dublin	Turkey	2-1
ENC 7 December	1966	Valencia	Spain	0-2
22 February	1967	Ankara	Turkey	1-2
21 May	1967	Dublin	Czechoslovakia	0-2
22 November	1967	Prague	Czechoslovakia	2-1
30 October	1968	Katowice	Poland	0-1
10 November	1968	Dublin	Austria	2-2
4 December	1968	Dublin	Denmark	1-1
WC 4 May	1969	Dublin	Czechoslovakia	1-2
WC27 May	1969	Copenhagen	Denmark	2-0
21 September	1969	Dublin	Scotland	1-1
WC 7 October	1969	Prague	Czechoslovakia	0-3
6 May	1970	Dublin	Poland	1-2
9 May	1970	Berlin	West Germany	1-2
23 September	1970	Dublin	Poland	0-2
EC14 October	1970	Dublin	Sweden	1-1
EC28 October	1970	Malmo	Sweden	0-1
EC 8 December	1970	Rome	Italy	0-3
EC10 May	1971	Dublin	Italy	1-2
EC30 May	1971	Dublin	Austria	1-4
EC10 October	1971	Linz	Austria	0-6
11 June	1972	Recife	Iran	2-1
18 June	1972	Natal (Brazil)	Equador	3-2
21 June	1972	Recife	Chile	1-2
25 June	1972	Recife	Portugal	1-2
WC18 October	1972	Dublin	Russia	1-2
WC15 November	1972	Dublin	France	2-1
WC13 May	1973	Moscow	USSR	0-1
16 May	1973	Wroclaw	Poland	0-2
WC19 May	1973	Paris	France	1-1
6 June	1973	Oslo	Norway	1-1
21 October	1973	Dublin	Poland	1-0
5 May	1974	Rio de Janeiro	Brazil	1-2
8 May	1974	Montevideo	Uruguay	0-2
EC12 May	1974	Santiago	Chile	2-1
30 October	1974	Dublin	USSR	3-0
EC20 November	1974	Izmin	Turkey	1-1
EC10 May	1975	Dublin	Switzerland	2-1
EC18 May	1975	Kiev	USSR	1-2
EC21 May	1975	Berne	Switzerland	0-1
EC29 October	1975	Dublin	Turkey	4-0
24 March	1976	Dublin	Norway	3-0
26 May	1976	Poznan	Poland	2-0
8 September	1976	Wembley	England	1-1
13 October	1976	Ankara	Turkey	3-3
WC17 November	1976	Paris	France	0-2
9 February	1977	Dublin	Spain	0-1
WC30 March	1977	Dublin	France	1-0
24 April	1977	Dublin	Poland	0-0
WC 1 June	1977	Sofia	Bulgaria	1-2
WC12 October	1977	Dublin	Bulgaria	0-0
5 April	1978	Dublin	Turkey	4-2
12 April	1978	Lodz	Poland	0-3
21 May	1978	Oslo	Norway	0-0
EC24 May	1978	Copenhagen	Denmark	3-3
EC20 September	1978	Dublin	N Ireland	0-0
EC25 September	1978	Dublin	England	1-1
EC 2 May	1979	Dublin	Denmark	2-0
EC19 May	1979	Sofia	Bulgaria	0-1
22 May	1979	Dublin	West Germany	1-3
29 May	1979	Dublin	Argentina	0-0
11 September	1979	Swansea	Wales	1-2
26 September	1979	Prague	Czechoslovakia	1-4
EC17 October	1979	Dublin	Bulgaria	3-0
29 October	1979	Dublin	United States	3-2
EC21 November	1979	Belfast	N Ireland	0-1
EC 6 February	1980	Wembley	England	0-2
WC26 March	1980	Nicosia	Cyprus	3-2
30 April	1980	Dublin	Switzerland	2-0
16 May	1980	Dublin	Argentina	0-1
WC10 September	1980	Dublin	Holland	2-1
WC15 October	1980	Dublin	Belgium	1-1
WC28 October	1980	Paris	France	0-2
WC19 November	1980	Dublin	Cyprus	6-0
24 February	1981	Dublin	Wales	1-3
WC25 March	1981	Brussels	Belgium	0-1
WC 9 September	1981	Amsterdam	Holland	2-2
WC14 October	1981	Dublin	France	3-2
28 April	1982	Algiers	Algeria	0-2
22 May	1982	Santiago	Chile	0-1
27 May	1982	Uberlandia	Brazil	0-7
EC22 September	1982	Rotterdam	Holland	1-0
EC13 October	1982	Dublin	Iceland	2-0
EC17 November	1982	Dublin	Spain	3-3
EC30 March	1983	Valletta	Malta	1-0

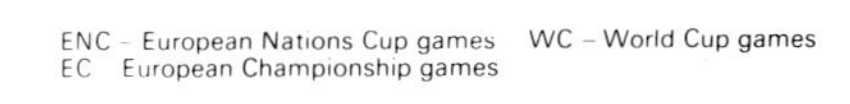

ENC – European Nations Cup games WC – World Cup games
EC European Championship games

time their domestic football had never been of a higher standard and they could call upon a powerful team of home-based players. But the harrassed Welsh selectors realized that their four clubs did not have sufficient players of quality and they were forced to delve deeply into the amateur ranks. So emerged, under the captaincy of Fred Keenor, 'the Welsh unknowns'. By any standards the team looked a strange one with Dewey of Cardiff Corinthians, Ellis of Oswestry and Collins of Llanelli all amateurs. Rightly, the team was dubbed Fred Keenor and 10 others.

Incredibly, Wrexham's Bamford shot Wales into the lead in five minutes but, when Battles put Scotland level in the 50th minute, everyone expected an avalanche of goals. But Wales, gallant little Wales, defending majestically, hung on to achieve one of the most remarkable results in soccer history.

How did it happen? Apart from the inspiring Keenor, one man deserves the credit: Ted Robbins, the doyen of football secretaries, who, from 1910, had guided the fortunes of what had often been a motley collection of players.

Robbins, with his white hair, astrakhan coat and Edwardian wing collar, did not appear, on the face of it, the man to establish a rapport with professional footballers. Yet, somehow, he injected fire and brimstone into the most ordinary players. A Third Division nonentity would go out like the traditional Welsh dragon.

Robbins and the red shirt of Wales worked a strange alchemy which turned pigmies into giants. But perhaps it was that Welsh dragon too. One of the oldest Welsh proverbs is 'Y draig goch d dyry gychwen' (The Red Dragon gives impetus).

Robbins, the human dynamo, devoted his life to the cause of Wales. He travelled everywhere pleading in his soft North Walian voice for a more open handed attitude from the English clubs. Ivan Sharpe, that great journalist, once recalled how Robbins would ring up on a Friday and say: 'I'm still two short for tomorrow's international. But I'm not worried. Wales are never whacked.'

Nor were they. The inspiration of that Hampden triumph—for, in the context, triumph it was—set the pattern for the arrival of the great Welsh side of the thirties which won the Home Championship outright three times (1933, 1934 and 1937) and was undefeated from 1932 to 1934. Ted Robbins and his men brought back a little of the pride to these men. The Welsh football team, triumphing over the English, was something in which they could believe. Unfortunately it was not an attitude which was always evident after the war. In the early seventies, for instance, Wales did not score a goal in a home international for twelve matches (between April 1970 and May 1974). In recent years the Welsh have tended to stumble at the final hurdle. They almost reached the European Championship semi-final of 1976, only to lose a quarter-final match to Yugoslavia when an East German referee denied a penalty and the crowd over-reacted and probably distracted the players. Two years later realistic World Cup hopes were dashed by another, even more absurd, penalty award when Joe Jordan handled the ball at Anfield and Scotland.

FULL INTERNATIONALS PLAYED BY IRELAND AND NORTHERN IRELAND

Date		*Venue*	*Opponents*	*Score*
18 February	1882	Belfast	England	0-13
25 February	1882	Wrexham	Wales	1-7
24 February	1883	Liverpool	England	0-7
17 March	1883	Belfast	Wales	1-1
9 February	1884	Wrexham	Wales	0-6
23 February	1884	Belfast	England	1-8
26 March	1884	Belfast	Scotland	0-5
28 February	1885	Manchester	England	0-4
14 March	1885	Glasgow	Scotland	2-8
11 April	1885	Belfast	Wales	2-8
27 February	1886	Wrexham	Wales	0-5
13 March	1886	Belfast	England	1-6
20 March	1886	Belfast	Scotland	2-7
5 February	1887	Sheffield	England	0-7
19 February	1887	Glasgow	Scotland	1-4
12 March	1887	Belfast	Wales	4-1
3 March	1888	Wrexham	Wales	0-11
24 March	1888	Belfast	Scotland	2-10
31 March	1888	Belfast	England	1-5
2 March	1889	Liverpool	England	1-6
9 March	1889	Glasgow	Scotland	0-7
27 April	1889	Belfast	Wales	1-3
8 February	1890	Shrewsbury	Wales	2-5
15 March	1890	Belfast	England	1-9
29 March	1890	Belfast	Scotland	1-4
7 February	1891	Belfast	Wales	7-2
7 March	1891	Wolverhampton	England	1-6
28 March	1891	Glasgow	Scotland	1-2
27 February	1892	Bangor (Wales)	Wales	1-1
5 March	1892	Belfast	England	0-2
19 March	1892	Belfast	Scotland	2-3
25 February	1893	Birmingham	England	1-6
25 March	1893	Glasgow	Scotland	1-6
8 April	1893	Belfast	Wales	4-3
24 February	1894	Swansea	Wales	1-4
3 March	1894	Belfast	England	2-2
31 March	1894	Belfast	Scotland	1-2
9 March	1895	Derby	England	0-9
16 March	1895	Belfast	Wales	2-2
30 March	1895	Glasgow	Scotland	1-3
29 February	1896	Wrexham	Wales	1-6
7 March	1896	Belfast	England	0-2
28 March	1896	Belfast	Scotland	3-3
20 February	1897	Nottingham	England	0-6
6 March	1897	Belfast	Wales	4-3
27 March	1897	Glasgow	Scotland	1-5
19 February	1898	Llandudno	Wales	1-0
5 March	1898	Belfast	England	2-3
26 March	1898	Belfast	Scotland	0-3
18 February	1899	Sunderland	England	2-13
4 March	1899	Belfast	Wales	1-0
25 March	1899	Glasgow	Scotland	1-9
24 February	1900	Llandudno	Wales	0-2
3 March	1900	Belfast	Scotland	0-3
17 March	1900	Dublin	England	0-2
23 February	1901	Glasgow	Scotland	0-11
9 March	1901	Southampton	England	0-3
23 March	1901	Llandudno	Wales	0-1
1 March	1902	Belfast	Scotland	1-5
22 March	1902	Belfast	England	0-1
22 March	1902	Cardiff	Wales	3-0
14 February	1903	Wolverhampton	England	0-4
21 March	1903	Glasgow	Scotland	2-0
28 March	1903	Belfast	Wales	2-0
12 March	1904	Belfast	England	1-3
21 March	1904	Bangor (Wales)	Wales	1-0
26 March	1904	Dublin	Scotland	1-1
25 February	1905	Middlesbrough	England	1-1
18 March	1905	Glasgow	Scotland	0-4
8 April	1905	Belfast	Wales	2-2
17 February	1906	Belfast	England	0-5
17 March	1906	Dublin	Scotland	0-1
2 April	1907	Wrexham	Wales	4-4
16 February	1907	Liverpool	England	0-1
23 February	1908	Belfast	Wales	2-3
16 March	1908	Glasgow	Scotland	0-3
15 February	1908	Belfast	England	1-3
14 March	1908	Dublin	Scotland	0-5
11 April	1908	Aberdare	Wales	1-0
13 February	1909	Bradford	England	0-4
20 March	1909	Belfast	Wales	2-3
27 March	1909	Glasgow	Scotland	0-5
12 February	1910	Belfast	England	1-1
11 March	1910	Wrexham	Wales	1-4
19 March	1910	Belfast	Scotland	1-0
11 February	1911	Derby	England	1-2
18 March	1911	Glasgow	Scotland	0-2
28 March	1911	Belfast	Wales	1-2
10 February	1912	Dublin	England	1-6
16 March	1912	Belfast	Scotland	1-4
13 April	1912	Cardiff	Wales	3-2
18 January	1913	Belfast	Wales	0-1
15 February	1913	Belfast	England	2-1
15 March	1913	Dublin	Scotland	1-2
19 January	1914	Wrexham	Wales	2-1
14 February	1914	Middlesbrough	England	3-0
14 March	1914	Belfast	Scotland	1-1
25 October	1919	Belfast	England	1-1
14 February	1920	Belfast	Wales	2-2
13 March	1920	Glasgow	Scotland	0-3
23 October	1920	Sunderland	England	0-2
26 February	1921	Belfast	Scotland	0-2
9 April	1921	Swansea	Wales	1-2
22 October	1921	Belfast	England	1-1
4 March	1922	Glasgow	Scotland	1-2
1 April	1922	Belfast	Wales	1-1
21 October	1922	West Bromwich	England	0-2
3 March	1923	Belfast	Scotland	0-1
14 April	1923	Wrexham	Wales	3-0
20 October	1923	Belfast	England	2-1
1 March	1924	Glasgow	Scotland	0-2
15 March	1924	Belfast	Wales	0-1
22 October	1924	Liverpool	England	1-3
28 February	1925	Belfast	Scotland	0-3
18 April	1925	Wrexham	Wales	0-0
24 October	1925	Belfast	England	0-0
13 January	1926	Belfast	Wales	3-0
27 February	1926	Glasgow	Scotland	0-4
20 October	1926	Liverpool	England	3-3
26 February	1927	Belfast	Scotland	0-2
9 April	1927	Cardiff	Wales	2-2
22 October	1927	Belfast	England	2-0
4 February	1928	Belfast	Wales	1-2
25 February	1928	Glasgow	Scotland	1-0
22 October	1928	Liverpool	England	1-2
2 February	1929	Wrexham	Wales	2-2
23 February	1929	Belfast	Scotland	3-7
19 October	1929	Belfast	England	0-3
1 February	1930	Belfast	Wales	7-0
22 February	1930	Glasgow	Scotland	1-3
20 October	1930	Sheffield	England	1-5
21 February	1931	Belfast	Scotland	0-0
22 April	1931	Wrexham	Wales	2-3
19 September	1931	Glasgow	Scotland	1-3
17 October	1931	Belfast	England	2-6
5 December	1931	Belfast	Wales	4-0
17 September	1932	Belfast	Scotland	0-4
17 October	1932	Blackpool	England	0-1
7 December	1932	Wrexham	Wales	1-4
16 September	1933	Glasgow	Scotland	2-1
14 October	1933	Belfast	England	0-3
4 November	1933	Belfast	Wales	1-1
20 October	1934	Belfast	Scotland	2-1
6 February	1935	Liverpool	England	1-2
27 March	1935	Wrexham	Wales	1-3
19 October	1935	Belfast	England	1-3
13 November	1935	Edinburgh	Scotland	1-2
11 March	1936	Belfast	Wales	3-2
31 October	1936	Belfast	Scotland	1-3
18 November	1936	Stoke	England	1-3
17 March	1937	Wrexham	Wales	1-4
23 October	1937	Belfast	England	1-5
10 November	1937	Aberdeen	Scotland	1-1
16 March	1938	Belfast	Wales	1-0
8 October	1938	Belfast	Scotland	0-2
16 November	1938	Manchester	England	0-7
15 March	1939	Wrexham	Wales	1-3
V15 September	1945	Belfast	England	0-1
28 September	1946	Belfast	England	2-7
27 November	1946	Glasgow	Scotland	0-0
16 April	1947	Belfast	Wales	2-1
4 October	1947	Belfast	Scotland	2-0
5 November	1947	Liverpool	England	2-2
10 March	1948	Wrexham	Wales	0-2
9 October	1948	Belfast	England	2-6
17 November	1948	Glasgow	Scotland	2-3
9 March	1949	Belfast	Wales	0-2
WC 1 October	1949	Belfast	Scotland	2-8
WC16 November	1949	Manchester	England	2-9
WC 8 March	1950	Wrexham	Wales	0-0
7 October	1950	Belfast	England	1-4
1 November	1950	Glasgow	Scotland	1-6
7 March	1951	Belfast	Wales	1-2
12 May	1951	Belfast	France	2-2
6 October	1951	Belfast	Scotland	0-3
14 November	1951	Birmingham	England	0-2
19 March	1952	Swansea	Wales	0-3
4 October	1952	Belfast	England	2-2
5 November	1952	Glasgow	Scotland	1-1
11 November	1952	Paris	France	1-3
15 April	1953	Belfast	Wales	2-3
WC 3 October	1953	Belfast	Scotland	1-3
WC11 November	1953	Liverpool	England	1-3
WC31 March	1954	Wrexham	Wales	2-1
2 October	1954	Belfast	England	0-2
3 November	1954	Glasgow	Scotland	2-2

Jordan's team, were given a ludicrous spot-kick and proceeded to Argentina.

Wales' World Cup hopes four years later were dashed by that 2-2 draw with Iceland and their only appearance on the world stage remains the 1958 World Cup finals in Sweden, when a Terry Medwin goal beat Hungary and took them to the quarter-finals. That year also saw Northern Ireland's other great triumph—a quarter-final place after a defeat of Czechoslovakia. The almost legendary side, containing Blanchflower, McIlroy and Bingham and managed by Peter Doherty, was savaged by injuries and went down to France 4-0. The coincidences were not missed when the Irish went down 4-1 to the same team 24 years later.

The Republic of Ireland has never appeared in the final stages of an international tournament, despite having in recent years an extremely competent and entertaining squad of players, though her recent international record has been confused by the tendency of managers Johnny Giles and Eion Hand to put out teams of essentially League of Ireland players under the national flag.

It was really only in the 1970s that the Republic emerged as a football force at all—prior to that decade the government-inspired restrictions on those who played the sport (in an attempt to preserve the strength of Gaelic football and hurling) spilled over into public ambivalence and indifference. At the same time, however, the relaxation of rules on eligibility gave the Irish, Welsh and Republic sides a significant increase in their pool of players and clearly made them more competitive internationally (at one extreme, Mick Robinson plays for Eire because of his great-grandmother's nationality). This had odd consequences—like the scrambles by international managers to 'sign' some overseas born players who could be eligible for any of the four countries.

While on the one side this was a clear plus, on the other it was probably a minus. Many Englishmen with a parent or grand-parent born in Wales or Ireland, and who had stood little chance of reaching the full England side, now had a chance of international football. It did seem a little distant from the traditional view of what a national team represented to suddenly find Bob Wilson wearing the Scottish keeper's jersey or Chris Hughton as left-back for the Republic; and it was perhaps a factor in the noticeable decline of interest in the performances of the home countries except at the highest level.

In the mid-1980s whether the independent home associations would survive the century was a genuine question. Northern Ireland's displays in Spain had probably stemmed the tide, but there was bound to be a revival of the subtle campaign to decrease the United Kingdom's numerical chances in major competitions. Paradoxically, it was a suggestion most people in the British Isles would probably welcome—ever since the days of Manchester United being able to win the European Cup with a squad containing George Best, Denis Law and Bobby Charlton, only to see them head off for different international sides, it had been clear that the United Kingdom's international chances were reduced rather than enhanced by the maintenance of this arguably outdated system.

FEBRUARY 1882–MARCH 1983

Date		*Venue*	*Opponents*	*Score*
20 April	1955	Belfast	Wales	2-3
8 October	1955	Belfast	Scotland	2-1
2 November	1955	Wembley	England	0-3
11 April	1956	Cardiff	Wales	1-1
6 October	1956	Belfast	England	1-1
7 November	1956	Glasgow	Scotland	0-1
WC16 January	1957	Lisbon	Portugal	1-1
10 April	1957	Belfast	Wales	0-0
WC25 April	1957	Rome	Italy	0-1
WC 1 May	1957	Belfast	Portugal	3-0
5 October	1957	Belfast	Scotland	1-1
6 November	1957	Wembley	England	3-2
4 December	1957	Belfast	Italy	2-2
WC15 January	1958	Belfast	Italy	2-1
16 April	1958	Cardiff	Wales	1-1
WC 8 June	1958	Halmstad	Czechoslovakia	1-0
WC11 June	1958	Halmstad	Argentina	1-3
WC15 June	1958	Malmo	West Germany	2-2
WC17 June	1958	Malmo	Czechoslovakia	2-1
WC19 June	1958	Norrkoping	France	0-4
4 October	1958	Belfast	England	3-3
15 October	1958	Madrid	Spain	2-6
5 November	1958	Glasgow	Scotland	2-2
22 April	1959	Belfast	Wales	4-1
3 October	1959	Belfast	Scotland	0-4
18 November	1959	Wembley	England	1-2
6 April	1960	Wrexham	Wales	2-3
8 October	1960	Belfast	England	2-5
WC26 October	1960	Belfast	West Germany	3-4
9 November	1960	Glasgow	Scotland	2-5
12 April	1961	Belfast	Wales	1-5
25 April	1961	Bologna	Italy	2-3
WC 3 May	1961	Athens	Greece	1-2
WC10 May	1961	West Berlin	West Germany	1-2
7 October	1961	Belfast	Scotland	1-6
WC17 October	1961	Belfast	Greece	2-0
22 November	1961	Wembley	England	1-1
11 April	1962	Cardiff	Wales	0-4
9 May	1962	Rotterdam	Netherlands	0-4
ENC10 October	1962	Katowice	Poland	2-0
20 October	1962	Belfast	England	1-3
7 November	1962	Glasgow	Scotland	1-5
ENC28 November	1962	Belfast	Poland	2-0
3 April	1963	Belfast	Wales	1-4
30 May	1963	Bilbao	Spain	1-1
12 October	1963	Belfast	Scotland	2-1
30 October	1963	Belfast	Spain	0-1
20 November	1963	Wembley	England	3-8
15 April	1964	Swansea	Wales	3-2
29 April	1964	Belfast	Uruguay	3-0
3 October	1964	Belfast	England	3-4
WC14 October	1964	Belfast	Switzerland	1-0
WC14 November	1964	Lausanne	Switzerland	1-2
25 November	1964	Glasgow	Scotland	2-3
WC17 March	1965	Belfast	Holland	2-1
31 March	1965	Belfast	Wales	0-5
WC 7 April	1965	Rotterdam	Holland	0-0
WC 7 May	1965	Belfast	Albania	4-1
2 October	1965	Belfast	Scotland	3-2
10 November	1965	Wembley	England	1-2
WC24 November	1965	Tirana	Albania	1-1
30 March	1966	Cardiff	Wales	4-1

Date		*Venue*	*Opponents*	*Score*
7 May	1966	Belfast	West Germany	0-2
22 June	1966	Belfast	Mexico	4-1
22 October	1966	Belfast	England	0-2
16 November	1966	Glasgow	Scotland	1-2
12 April	1967	Belfast	Wales	0-0
21 October	1967	Belfast	Scotland	1-0
22 November	1967	Wembley	England	0-2
28 February	1968	Wrexham	Wales	0-2
10 September	1968	Jaffa	Israel	3-2
WC23 October	1968	Belfast	Turkey	4-1
WC11 December	1968	Istanbul	Turkey	3-0
3 May	1969	Belfast	England	1-3
6 May	1969	Glasgow	Scotland	1-1
10 May	1969	Belfast	Wales	0-0
WC10 September	1969	Belfast	Russia	0-0
WC22 October	1969	Moscow	Russia	0-2
18 April	1970	Belfast	Scotland	0-1
21 April	1970	Wembley	England	1-3
25 April	1970	Swansea	Wales	0-1
EC11 November	1970	Seville	Spain	0-3
EC 3 February	1971	Nicosia	Cyprus	3-0
EC21 April	1971	Belfast	Cyprus	5-0
15 May	1971	Belfast	England	0-1
18 May	1971	Glasgow	Scotland	1-0
22 May	1971	Belfast	Wales	1-0
EC22 September	1971	Moscow	Russia	0-1
EC13 October	1971	Belfast	Russia	1-1
EC16 February	1972	Hull	Spain	1-1
20 May	1972	Glasgow	Scotland	0-2
24 May	1972	Wembley	England	1-0
27 May	1972	Wrexham	Wales	0-0
WC18 October	1972	Sofia	Bulgaria	0-3
WC14 February	1973	Nicosia	Cyprus	0-1
WC28 March	1973	Coventry	Portugal	1-1
WC 8 May	1973	Fulham	Cyprus	3-0
12 May	1973	Everton	England	1-2
16 May	1973	Glasgow	Scotland	2-1
19 May	1973	Everton	Wales	1-0
WC26 September	1973	Sheffield	Bulgaria	0-0
WC14 November	1973	Lisbon	Portugal	1-1
11 May	1974	Glasgow	Scotland	1-0
15 May	1974	Wembley	England	0-1
18 May	1974	Wrexham	Wales	0-1
EC 4 September	1974	Oslo	Norway	1-2
EC30 October	1974	Solna	Sweden	2-0
EC16 March	1975	Belfast	Yugoslavia	1-0
17 May	1975	Belfast	England	0-0
20 May	1975	Glasgow	Scotland	0-3
23 May	1975	Belfast	Wales	1-0
EC 3 September	1975	Belfast	Sweden	1-2
EC29 October	1975	Belfast	Norway	3-0
EC19 November	1975	Belgrade	Yugoslavia	0-1
3 March	1976	Tel Aviv	Israel	1-1
8 May	1976	Glasgow	Scotland	0-3
11 May	1976	Wembley	England	0-4
14 May	1976	Swansea	Wales	0-1
WC13 October	1976	Rotterdam	Holland	2-2
WC10 November	1976	Liege	Belgium	0-2
27 April	1977	Cologne	West Germany	0-5
28 May	1977	Belfast	England	1-2
1 June	1977	Glasgow	Scotland	0-3
3 June	1977	Belfast	Wales	1-1

Date		*Venue*	*Opponents*	*Score*
WC11 June	1977	Reykjavik	Iceland	0-1
WC29 September	1977	Belfast	Iceland	2-0
WC12 October	1977	Belfast	Holland	0-1
WC16 November	1977	Belfast	Belgium	3-0
13 May	1978	Glasgow	Scotland	1-1
16 May	1978	Wembley	England	0-1
19 May	1978	Wrexham	Wales	0-1
EC20 September	1978	Dublin	Eire	0-0
EC25 October	1978	Belfast	Denmark	2-1
EC29 November	1978	Sofia	Bulgaria	2-0
EC 7 February	1979	Wembley	England	0-4
EC 2 May	1979	Belfast	Bulgaria	2-0
19 May	1979	Belfast	England	0-2
22 May	1979	Hampden	Scotland	0-1
25 May	1979	Belfast	Wales	1-1
EC 6 June	1979	Copenhagen	Denmark	0-4
EC17 October	1979	Belfast	England	1-5
EC21 November	1979	Belfast	Eire	1-0
WC26 March	1980	Tel Aviv	Israel	0-0
16 May	1980	Belfast	Scotland	1-0
20 May	1980	Wembley	England	1-1
23 May	1980	Cardiff	Wales	1-0
11 June	1980	Sydney	Australia	2-1
15 June	1980	Melbourne	Australia	1-1
18 June	1980	Adelaide	Australia	2-1
WC15 October	1980	Belfast	Sweden	3-0
WC19 November	1980	Lisbon	Portugal	0-1
WC25 March	1981	Glasgow	Scotland	1-1
WC29 April	1981	Belfast	Portugal	1-0
19 May	1981	Glasgow	Scotland	0-2
WC 3 June	1981	Stockholm	Sweden	0-1
WC14 October	1981	Belfast	Scotland	0-0
WC18 November	1981	Belfast	Israel	1-0
23 February	1982	Wembley	England	0-4
24 March	1982	Paris	France	0-4
28 April	1982	Belfast	Scotland	1-1
27 May	1982	Wrexham	Wales	0-3
WC17 June	1982	Zaragoza	Yugoslavia	0-0
WC21 June	1982	Zaragoza	Honduras	1-1
WC25 June	1982	Valencia	Spain	1-0
WC 1 July	1982	Madrid	Austria	2-2
WC 4 July	1982	Madrid	France	1-4
EC13 October	**1982**	**Vienna**	**Austria**	**0-2**
EC17 November	**1982**	**Belfast**	**W. Germany**	**1-0**
EC15 December	**1982**	**Tirana**	**Albania**	**0-0**
EC30 March	**1983**	**Belfast**	**Turkey**	**2-1**

ENC – European Nations Cup games WC – World Cup games
EC European Championship games V – Victory International

ENGLAND ABROAD

'THE FOOTBALL ASSOCIATION requires applications from young men who would be prepared to play in an international match against Scotland in Glasgow on November 23.' Imagine the effect of that in the small ads column of a daily paper!

The applications would start pouring in at once—not only from Bryan Robson, Glenn Hoddle and Peter Shilton, but from just about every park player in the country—and then the task of choosing the final team would begin.

This massive labour would be accomplished single-handed by the FA Secretary. He would consult nobody and select himself as captain of the side. And, because FA funds would be low, he would suddenly find himself wondering how the visit to Scotland would be financed.

So there would be another newspaper advertisement, and a circular letter to every club in membership of the FA! 'Contributions are required from interested parties to pay the railway and hotel expenses of the England team to play Scotland.' Fantastic as it may seem, that was exactly what happened when Charles Alcock, the FA Secretary, first put forward the idea of an England v Scotland match in 1872.

Today, more than a century later, an international is planned more like a military operation. The players will meet at least four days in advance at a luxury hotel, all their expenses are paid and they receive £100 for the privilege of playing for their country. In addition they receive a £200 win bonus or £100 for a draw. All they need to bring are their boots, a personal towel and, of course, themselves. As one FA official put it, 'All we really need is a body. We provide the rest.'

How different it all was in the far-off days of the first international when, on a cold, wet, windy night in 1872, a group of officers and gentlemen gathered in the Royal Garrick Hotel in Glasgow. Instead of the frugal glasses of orangeade or coca-cola, and the starchless main meals, they tucked into a gargantuan feast with all the gusto of men who had endured the rigours of a train journey from London.

It had been a journey with nothing of the cushioned plushness of a modern Inter-City line. Limbs ached from the buffeting on the wooden austerity of the seats, and the acrid smell of smoke had the travellers still heavy with catarrh.

The game itself ended in a scoreless draw, a surprising result for the Englishmen, who had arranged the fixture, in the words of the FA minutes, 'In order to further the interests of the Association in Scotland'. There was to be ample opportunity to regret the condescending tone of that statement.

In the next 19 years England were to beat Scotland only twice but at least the significance of those defeats was not lost on 'Pa' Jackson, assistant secretary of the FA, who determined that England should create a team on the Queen's Park pattern. So, in 1882, Jackson formed his Corinthians from former public schools and university men and, in the next seven years, of the 88 players capped by England, 52 were Corinthians. On two occasions when the FA agreed to play Ireland and Wales on the same day, the entire Corinthians side was sent to represent England.

Yet the death of the Corinthians and the true-blue amateur tradition they represented was assured almost from birth. Professionalism was already taking root in the North, and by the end of the century it had completely changed the complexion of international football.

The FA, mainly through the influence of the perceptive Charles Alcock, bowed to the inevitable and, in 1885, James Forrest of Blackburn Rovers became the first acknowledged professional to play for England. Forrest's fee was ten shillings per match—£99.50 less than the FA offered their players in 1974.

At the start of professionalism, the paid players were treated with suspicion, and the amateur captain would always dine alone to avoid being tainted. At one Birmingham hotel, the manager even asked for guarantees from the FA ensuring that they would pay for any damage caused by professional members of the England team.

But from the day of Forrest's arrival in 1885, the eventual disappearance of the amateur player from the international scene was inevitable. The odd exception, such as Bernard Joy of Casuals and later Arsenal, served only to prove the point.

The amateur player might have had his day, but the amateur administrator most certainly had not. The first England team manager, Walter Winterbottom, did not emerge until after the Second World War and, even then, he was never accorded the right of selection. Perhaps that was not surprising, for the whole process had been haphazard from the beginning.

After the strange 'volunteering' process which selected the team for the original match, clubs were asked by the FA to nominate men for the second. A series of trial matches was held, during which a small army of 71 players was whittled down to the final eleven. As a result, only three men survived from the first international to the second.

The International Selection Committee, later to hold so much sway, was not formed until 1888. Originally it was composed of seven men but by the fifties this figure had risen to more than 30.

It was not until Alf Ramsey took over in 1963 that the team selection for full and Under-23 internationals was taken out of the hands of a committee.

Players were not so much selected as voted for. A committee enthusiast from, for example, south-east London would report that he had seen a promising player with Millwall. If he could lobby enough support, his discovery would go in to the exclusion of an established star. One interesting result, reflecting the fact that the FA is based in London, is that all the Third Division players who have ever appeared for England came from Third Division South clubs. Not one player hailed from the Third Division North.

Caps were won with all the unpredictability of pools dividends. In 1923, Bromley, the London amateur club, had a promising centre-forward called Frank Osborne, a clerk at Thomas Cooks, the travel agents. Fulham persuaded the youngster to join them as an amateur and, within a month, he was playing for England against France in Paris.

The statistics tell the whole story. In eleven seasons before the Second World War, England used 99 players; in the following eleven they used 145, 66 of whom never gained a second cap.

Ironically enough, there was much more continuity during the War itself when, with so many leading players serving abroad, the pool of stars available for internationals was restricted.

That meant that the same players—Swift, Scott, Hardwick, Denis and Leslie Compton, Soo, Franklin, Mercer, Matthews, Carter, Lawton, Finney—came up for selection time after time. In a sense they were the harbingers of the squad system of the 1960s.

A further important step came later in the War when Sir Stanley Rous, later to become President of FIFA, proposed to the FA, of which he was then secretary, that England should have a team manager.

The choice fell upon Walter Winterbottom, a schoolteacher who had been centre-half for Manchester United. A man of charm and insight, Winterbottom was well qualified, but he was to learn unhappily that he had been given responsibility without power. Winterbottom was asked merely to coach and prepare players, while the actual selection remained firmly in the hands of the selection committee. To have a team manager was one thing, but to allow him the licence to decide who should play for England was quite different.

It was in this pantomime atmosphere that England, grievously under-prepared, embarked on her first World Cup sortie to Brazil in 1950. The inglorious defeat at the hands of the USA was just one in a whole catalogue of disasters. Things had gone wrong from the very start when two of the England players—Matthews and Taylor—both missed the first game because they had been touring with an FA team in Canada when the England party arrived in Brazil.

That, however, was but one of Walter Winterbottom's problems. When the party took a dislike to the Brazilian food, he even found himself entrusted with the task of cooking. That defeat by the USA and Hungary's historic 6-3 win at Wembley three years later taught the FA what the world had long suspected—that the British were no longer the masters of football.

Something drastic should have been done, but the only significant change came during the 1954 World Cup when some of the senior players were invited to advise on team selection.

Preparations were still as chaotic as ever. The England party arrived in Sweden for the 1958 World Cup finals to find that no training camp had been laid on. The harassed Winterbottom, whose experience of World Cups seemed never less than horrific, was left to chase around for accommodation only days before the first game.

Chile was hardly any better. Incredibly, the England party travelled to the tournament without a team doctor, and the result was that Peter Swan fell ill and, after receiving the wrong treatment, almost died.

The man who achieved more than anyone to create a professional and realistic environment within England's international soccer was, of course, Sir Alf Ramsey. As the successful and unequivocal manager of Ipswich, he did not need to seek the England job when Winterbottom lost, as he was bound to do, his vain battle against administrative incompetence and selectorial vanity in 1962.

Although he was said to have been only third choice for the job, Ramsey could take the post on his own terms. He would not countenance the intolerable pressure which had been laid upon his hamstrung predecessor. He would pick the players and, if the selectors *had* to remain in existence, they would do so only as a rubber stamp.

Ramsey decided that if a man was selected to play for England, the player had to be first to be told. The committee, the press and the world could wait. How different from the days when the most frequent morning paper story was how Stanley Accrington came out of the cinema and read in the evening paper that he had been chosen for England!

It was a sign of the times when, in 1964, Bobby Moore complained of the strain of England's pre-match training. Ten years earlier they would hardly have tired a nicotine-besotten parks player but, come Ramsey, those days were clearly over. Stalag Lilleshall was the players' description of their training camp for the 1966 World Cup.

Ten to four-thirty, Monday to Thursday, Ramsey would be in his Lancaster Gate office, and he expected the same discipline and punctuality from everyone else. The awesome combination of Harold Sheperdson and Les Cocker—'as cuddly as a sack of cobblestones' said Max Marquis—were brought in as trainers and strict rules of conduct were laid down for the players.

What Ramsey accomplished for England needs little reiteration. He promised that England would win the World Cup in 1966 and they did. Consciously or otherwise, he succeeded by going back to 'Pa' Jackson's concept of running an international side on the same lines as a club.

His stubborn, unsmiling defence of his players did little on the field of public relations; yet on the field of play those players responded to his fierce loyalty. But for England's amazing quarter-final in Leon—quite out of character for a Ramsey side—the World Cup might have been retained, or at least lost to Brazil in the final.

Finally Ramsey paid the usual managerial price for failure—in his case England's failure to qualify for the 1974 World Cup. His

The two principle rivals for the title of midfield terror in the early 1970s clash at Hampden during the England v Scotland match on 27 May 1972. The conflicts between Billy Bremner (centre) of Scotland and Leeds and Peter Storey (right) of Arsenal and England were as real at club as at international level, their two sides being the main protagonists of the period. The Scots had an unhappy time against England in the 1970s, winning only three of the eleven clashes while England won seven, including the 1972 game 1-0.

FULL INTERNATIONALS PLAYED BY ENGLAND 1870–MARCH 1983

Date		Venue	Opponents	Score
*19 November	1870	Kennington Oval	Scotland	1-0
*28 February	1871	Kennington Oval	Scotland	1-1
*18 November	1871	Kennington Oval	Scotland	2-1
*24 February	1872	Kennington Oval	Scotland	1-0
30 November	1872	Glasgow	Scotland	0-0
8 March	1873	Kennington Oval	Scotland	4-2
7 March	1874	Glasgow	Scotland	1-2
6 March	1875	Kennington Oval	Scotland	2-2
4 March	1876	Glasgow	Scotland	0-3
3 March	1877	Kennington Oval	Scotland	1-3
2 March	1878	Glasgow	Scotland	2-7
18 January	1879	Kennington Oval	Wales	2-1
5 April	1879	Kennington Oval	Scotland	5-4
13 March	1880	Glasgow	Scotland	4-5
15 March	1880	Wrexham	Wales	3-2
26 February	1881	Blackburn	Wales	0-1
12 March	1881	Kennington Oval	Scotland	1-6
18 February	1882	Belfast	Ireland	13-0
11 March	1882	Glasgow	Scotland	1-5
13 March	1882	Wrexham	Wales	3-5
3 February	1883	Kennington Oval	Wales	5-0
24 February	1883	Liverpool	Ireland	7-0
10 March	1883	Sheffield	Scotland	2-3
23 February	1884	Belfast	Ireland	8-1
15 March	1884	Glasgow	Scotland	0-1
17 March	1884	Wrexham	Wales	4-0
28 February	1885	Manchester	Ireland	4-0
14 March	1885	Blackburn	Wales	1-1
21 March	1885	Kennington Oval	Scotland	1-1
13 March	1886	Belfast	Ireland	6-1
29 March	1886	Wrexham	Wales	3-1
31 March	1886	Glasgow	Scotland	1-1
5 February	1887	Sheffield	Ireland	7-0
26 February	1887	Kennington Oval	Wales	4-0
19 March	1887	Blackburn	Scotland	2-3
4 February	1888	Crewe	Wales	5-1
17 March	1888	Glasgow	Scotland	5-0
31 March	1888	Belfast	Ireland	5-1
23 February	1889	Stoke-on-Trent	Wales	4-1
2 March	1889	Everton	Ireland	6-1
13 April	1889	Kennington Oval	Scotland	2-3
†15 March	1890	Belfast	Ireland	9-1
†15 March	1890	Wrexham	Wales	3-1
5 April	1890	Glasgow	Scotland	1-1
† 7 March	1891	Sunderland	Wales	4-1
† 7 March	1891	Wolverhampton	Ireland	6-1
6 April	1891	Blackburn	Scotland	2-1
† 5 March	1892	Wrexham	Wales	2-0
† 5 March	1892	Belfast	Ireland	2-0
2 April	1892	Glasgow	Scotland	4-1
25 February	1893	Birmingham	Ireland	6-1
13 March	1893	Stoke-on-Trent	Wales	6-0
1 April	1893	Richmond	Scotland	5-2
3 March	1894	Belfast	Ireland	2-2
12 March	1894	Wrexham	Wales	5-1
7 April	1894	Glasgow	Scotland	2-2
9 March	1895	Derby	Ireland	9-0
18 March	1895	Queen's Club, Kensington	Wales	1-1
6 April	1895	Everton	Scotland	3-0
7 March	1896	Belfast	Ireland	2-0
16 March	1896	Cardiff	Wales	9-1
4 April	1896	Glasgow	Scotland	1-2
20 February	1897	Nottingham	Ireland	6-0
29 March	1897	Sheffield	Wales	4-0
3 April	1897	Crystal Palace	Scotland	1-2
5 March	1898	Belfast	Ireland	3-2
28 March	1898	Wrexham	Wales	3-0
2 April	1898	Glasgow	Scotland	3-1
18 February	1899	Sunderland	Ireland	13-2
20 March	1899	Bristol	Wales	4-1
8 April	1899	Birmingham	Scotland	2-1
17 March	1900	Dublin	Ireland	2-0
26 March	1900	Cardiff	Wales	1-1
7 April	1900	Glasgow	Scotland	1-4
9 March	1901	Southampton	Ireland	3-0
18 March	1901	Newcastle	Wales	6-0
30 March	1901	Crystal Palace	Scotland	2-2
3 March	1902	Wrexham	Wales	0-0
22 March	1902	Belfast	Ireland	1-0
‡ 5 April	1902	Glasgow	Scotland	1-1
3 May	1902	Birmingham	Scotland	2-2
14 February	1903	Wolverhampton	Ireland	4-0
2 March	1903	Portsmouth	Wales	2-1
4 April	1903	Sheffield	Scotland	1-2
29 February	1904	Wrexham	Wales	2-2
12 March	1904	Belfast	Ireland	3-1
9 April	1904	Glasgow	Scotland	1-0
25 February	1905	Middlesbrough	Ireland	1-1
27 March	1905	Liverpool	Wales	3-1
1 April	1905	Crystal Palace	Scotland	1-0
17 February	1906	Belfast	Ireland	5-0
19 March	1906	Cardiff	Wales	1-0
7 April	1906	Glasgow	Scotland	1-2
16 February	1907	Everton	Ireland	1-0
18 March	1907	Fulham	Wales	1-1
6 April	1907	Newcastle	Scotland	1-1
15 February	1908	Belfast	Ireland	3-1
16 March	1908	Wrexham	Wales	7-1
4 April	1908	Glasgow	Scotland	1-1
6 June	1908	Vienna	Austria	6-1
8 June	1908	Vienna	Austria	11-1
10 June	1908	Budapest	Hungary	7-0
13 June	1908	Prague	Bohemia	4-0
13 February	1909	Bradford	Ireland	4-0
15 March	1909	Nottingham	Wales	2-0
3 April	1909	Crystal Palace	Scotland	2-0
29 May	1909	Budapest	Hungary	4-2
31 May	1909	Budapest	Hungary	8-2
1 June	1909	Vienna	Austria	8-1
12 February	1910	Belfast	Ireland	1-1
14 March	1910	Cardiff	Wales	1-0
2 April	1910	Glasgow	Scotland	0-2
C29 June	1910	Durban	South Africa	3-0
C23 July	1910	Johannesburg	South Africa	6-2
C30 July	1910	Capetown	South Africa	6-3
11 February	1911	Derby	Ireland	2-1
13 March	1911	Millwall	Wales	3-0
1 April	1911	Everton	Scotland	1-1
10 February	1912	Dublin	Ireland	6-1
11 March	1912	Wrexham	Wales	2-0
23 March	1912	Glasgow	Scotland	1-1
15 February	1913	Belfast	Ireland	1-2
17 March	1913	Bristol	Wales	4-3
5 April	1913	Stamford Bridge	Scotland	1-0
14 February	1914	Middlesbrough	Ireland	0-3
16 March	1914	Cardiff	Wales	2-0
4 April	1914	Glasgow	Scotland	1-3
V26 April	1919	Everton	Scotland	2-2
V 3 May	1919	Glasgow	Scotland	4-3
V11 October	1919	Cardiff	Wales	1-2
V18 October	1919	Stoke-on-Trent	Wales	2-0
25 October	1919	Belfast	Ireland	1-1
15 March	1920	Highbury	Wales	1-2
10 April	1920	Sheffield	Scotland	5-4
23 October	1920	Sunderland	Ireland	2-0
C26 June	1920	Durban	South Africa	3-1
C17 July	1920	Johannesburg	South Africa	3-1
C19 July	1920	Capetown	South Africa	9-1
14 March	1921	Cardiff	Wales	0-0
9 April	1921	Glasgow	Scotland	0-3
21 May	1921	Brussels	Belgium	2-0
22 October	1921	Belfast	N Ireland	1-1
13 March	1922	Liverpool	Wales	1-0
8 April	1922	Villa Park	Scotland	0-1
21 October	1922	West Bromwich	N Ireland	2-0
5 March	1923	Cardiff	Wales	2-2
19 March	1923	Highbury	Belgium	6-1
14 April	1923	Glasgow	Scotland	2-2
10 May	1923	Paris	France	4-1
21 May	1923	Stockholm	Sweden	4-2
24 May	1923	Stockholm	Sweden	3-1
20 October	1923	Belfast	N Ireland	1-2
1 November	1923	Antwerp	Belgium	2-2
3 March	1924	Blackburn	Wales	1-2
12 April	1924	Wembley	Scotland	1-1
17 May	1924	Paris	France	3-1
22 October	1924	Everton	N Ireland	3-1
8 December	1924	West Bromwich	Belgium	4-0
28 February	1925	Swansea	Wales	2-1
4 April	1925	Glasgow	Scotland	0-2
21 May	1925	Paris	France	3-2
C27 June	1925	Brisbane	Australia	5-1
C 4 July	1925	Sydney	Australia	2-1
C11 July	1925	Maitland	Australia	8-2
C18 July	1925	Sydney	Australia	5-0
C25 July	1925	Melbourne	Australia	2-0
24 October	1925	Belfast	N Ireland	0-0
1 March	1926	Crystal Palace	Wales	1-3
17 April	1926	Manchester	Scotland	1-0
24 May	1926	Antwerp	Belgium	5-3
20 October	1926	Liverpool	N Ireland	3-3
12 February	1927	Wrexham	Wales	3-3
2 April	1927	Glasgow	Scotland	2-1
11 May	1927	Brussels	Belgium	9-1
21 May	1927	Luxembourg	Luxembourg	5-2
26 May	1927	Paris	France	6-0
22 October	1927	Belfast	N Ireland	0-2
28 November	1927	Burnley	Wales	1-2
31 March	1928	Wembley	Scotland	1-5
17 May	1928	Paris	France	5-1
19 May	1928	Antwerp	Belgium	3-1
22 October	1928	Everton	N Ireland	2-1
17 November	1928	Swansea	Wales	3-2
13 April	1929	Glasgow	Scotland	0-1
9 May	1929	Paris	France	4-1
11 May	1929	Brussels	Belgium	5-1
15 May	1929	Madrid	Spain	3-4
C15 June	1929	Durban	South Africa	3-2
C13 July	1929	Johannesburg	South Africa	2-1
C17 July	1929	Capetown	South Africa	3-1
19 October	1929	Belfast	N Ireland	3-0
20 November	1929	Stamford Bridge	Wales	6-0
5 April	1930	Wembley	Scotland	5-2
10 May	1930	Berlin	Germany	3-3
14 May	1930	Vienna	Austria	0-0
20 October	1930	Sheffield	N Ireland	5-1
22 November	1930	Wrexham	Wales	4-0
28 March	1931	Glasgow	Scotland	0-2
14 May	1931	Paris	France	2-5
16 May	1931	Brussels	Belgium	4-1
17 October	1931	Belfast	Ireland	6-2
18 November	1931	Liverpool	Wales	3-1
9 December	1931	Highbury	Spain	7-1
9 April	1932	Wembley	Scotland	3-0
17 October	1932	Blackpool	N Ireland	1-0
16 November	1932	Wrexham	Wales	0-0
7 December	1932	Stamford Bridge	Austria	4-3
1 April	1933	Glasgow	Scotland	1-2
13 May	1933	Rome	Italy	1-1
20 May	1933	Berne	Switzerland	4-0
14 October	1933	Belfast	N Ireland	3-0
15 November	1933	Newcastle	Wales	1-2
6 December	1933	Tottenham	France	4-1
14 April	1934	Wembley	Scotland	3-0
10 May	1934	Budapest	Hungary	1-2
16 May	1934	Prague	Czechoslovakia	1-2
29 September	1934	Cardiff	Wales	4-0
14 November	1934	Highbury	Italy	3-2
6 February	1935	Everton	N Ireland	2-1
6 April	1935	Glasgow	Scotland	0-2
18 May	1935	Amsterdam	Netherlands	1-0
J21 August	1935	Glasgow	Scotland	2-4
19 October	1935	Belfast	N Ireland	3-1
4 December	1935	Tottenham	Germany	3-0
5 February	1936	Wolverhampton	Wales	1-2
4 April	1936	Wembley	Scotland	1-1
6 May	1936	Vienna	Austria	1-2
9 May	1936	Brussels	Belgium	2-3
17 October	1936	Cardiff	Wales	1-2
18 November	1936	Stoke-on-Trent	N Ireland	3-1
2 December	1936	Highbury	Hungary	6-2
17 April	1937	Glasgow	Scotland	1-3
14 May	1937	Oslo	Norway	6-0
17 May	1937	Stockholm	Sweden	4-0
20 May	1937	Helsinki	Finland	8-0
23 October	1937	Belfast	N Ireland	5-1
17 November	1937	Middlesbrough	Wales	2-1
1 December	1937	Tottenham	Czechoslovakia	5-4
9 April	1938	Wembley	Scotland	0-1
14 May	1938	Berlin	Germany	6-3
21 May	1938	Zurich	Switzerland	1-2
26 May	1938	Paris	France	4-2
22 October	1938	Cardiff	Wales	2-4
26 October	1938	Highbury	FIFA	3-0
9 November	1938	Newcastle	Norway	4-0
16 November	1938	Manchester	N Ireland	7-0
15 April	1939	Glasgow	Scotland	2-1
13 May	1939	Milan	Italy	2-2
18 May	1939	Belgrade	Yugoslavia	1-2
24 May	1939	Bucharest	Rumania	2-0
C17 June	1939	Johannesburg	South Africa	3-0
C24 June	1939	Durban	South Africa	8-2
C 1 July	1939	Johannesburg	South Africa	2-1
WT11 November	1939	Cardiff	Wales	1-1
WT18 November	1939	Wrexham	Wales	3-2
WT 2 December	1939	Newcastle	Scotland	2-1
WT13 April	1940	Wembley	Wales	0-1
WT11 May	1940	Glasgow	Scotland	1-1
WT 8 February	1941	Newcastle	Scotland	2-3
WT26 April	1941	Nottingham	Wales	4-1
WT 3 May	1941	Glasgow	Scotland	3-1
WT 7 June	1941	Cardiff	Wales	3-2
WT 4 October	1941	Wembley	Scotland	2-0
WT25 October	1941	Birmingham	Wales	2-1
WT17 January	1942	Wembley	Scotland	3-0
WT18 April	1942	Glasgow	Scotland	4-5
WT 9 May	1942	Cardiff	Wales	0-1
WT10 October	1942	Wembley	Scotland	0-0
WT24 October	1942	Wolverhampton	Wales	1-2
WT27 February	1943	Wembley	Wales	5-3
WT17 April	1943	Glasgow	Scotland	4-0
WT 8 May	1943	Cardiff	Wales	1-1
WT29 May	1943	Wembley	Wales	8-3
WT16 October	1943	Manchester	Scotland	8-0
WT19 February	1944	Wembley	Scotland	6-2
WT22 April	1944	Glasgow	Scotland	3-2
WT 6 May	1944	Cardiff	Wales	2-0
WT16 September	1944	Liverpool	Wales	2-2
WT14 October	1944	Wembley	Scotland	6-2
WT13 February	1945	Birmingham	Scotland	3-2
WT14 April	1945	Glasgow	Scotland	6-1
WT 5 May	1945	Cardiff	Wales	3-2
WT26 May	1945	Wembley	France	2-2
V15 September	1945	Belfast	N Ireland	1-0
V20 October	1945	West Bromwich	Wales	0-1
V19 January	1946	Wembley	Belgium	2-0
V13 April	1946	Glasgow	Scotland	0-1
V11 May	1946	Stamford Bridge	Switzerland	4-1
28 September	1946	Belfast	N Ireland	7-2
30 September	1946	Dublin	Eire	1-0
13 November	1946	Manchester	Wales	3-0
27 November	1946	Huddersfield	Netherlands	8-2
12 April	1947	Wembley	Scotland	1-1
3 May	1947	Highbury	France	3-0
18 May	1947	Zurich	Switzerland	0-1
25 May	1947	Lisbon	Portugal	10-0
21 September	1947	Brussels	Belgium	5-2
18 October	1947	Cardiff	Wales	3-0
5 November	1947	Everton	N Ireland	2-2
19 October	1947	Highbury	Sweden	4-2
10 April	1948	Glasgow	Scotland	2-0
16 May	1948	Turin	Italy	4-0
26 September	1948	Copenhagen	Denmark	0-0
9 October	1948	Belfast	N Ireland	6-2
10 November	1948	Birmingham	Wales	1-0
2 December	1948	Highbury	Switzerland	6-0
9 April	1949	Wembley	Scotland	1-3
13 May	1949	Stockholm	Sweden	1-3
18 May	1949	Oslo	Norway	4-1
22 May	1949	Paris	France	3-1
21 September	1949	Everton	Eire	0-2
WC15 October	1949	Cardiff	Wales	4-1
WC16 November	1949	Manchester	N Ireland	9-2
30 November	1949	Tottenham	Italy	2-0
WC15 April	1950	Glasgow	Scotland	1-0
14 May	1950	Lisbon	Portugal	5-3
18 May	1950	Brussels	Belgium	4-1
WC25 June	1950	Rio de Janeiro	Chile	2-0
WC29 June	1950	Belo Horizonte	USA	0-1
WC 2 July	1950	Rio de Janeiro	Spain	0-1
7 October	1950	Belfast	N Ireland	4-1
15 November	1950	Sunderland	Wales	4-2
22 November	1950	Highbury	Yugoslavia	2-2
14 April	1951	Wembley	Scotland	2-3
9 May	1951	Wembley	Argentina	2-1
19 May	1951	Everton	Portugal	5-2
C26 May	1951	Sydney	Australia	4-1
C30 June	1951	Sydney	Australia	17-0
C 7 July	1951	Brisbane	Australia	4-1
C14 July	1951	Sydney	Australia	6-1
C21 July	1951	Newcastle NSW	Australia	5-0
3 October	1951	Highbury	France	2-2
20 October	1951	Cardiff	Wales	1-1
14 November	1951	Birmingham	N Ireland	2-0
28 November	1951	Wembley	Austria	2-2
5 April	1952	Glasgow	Scotland	2-1
18 May	1952	Florence	Italy	1-1
25 May	1952	Vienna	Austria	3-2
28 May	1952	Zurich	Switzerland	3-0
4 October	1952	Belfast	N Ireland	2-2
12 November	1952	Wembley	Wales	5-2
26 November	1952	Wembley	Belgium	5-0
18 April	1953	Wembley	Scotland	2-2
A17 May	1953	Buenos Aires	Argentina	0-0
24 May	1953	Santiago	Chile	2-1
31 May	1953	Montevideo	Uruguay	1-2
8 June	1953	New York	USA	6-3
WC10 October	1953	Cardiff	Wales	4-1
21 October	1953	Wembley	FIFA	4-4
WC11 November	1953	Liverpool	N Ireland	3-1
25 November	1953	Wembley	Hungary	3-6
WC 3 April	1954	Glasgow	Scotland	4-2
16 May	1954	Belgrade	Yugoslavia	0-1
23 May	1954	Budapest	Hungary	1-7
WC17 June	1954	Basle	Belgium	4-4
WC20 June	1954	Berne	Switzerland	2-0
WC26 June	1954	Basle	Uruguay	2-4
2 October	1954	Belfast	N Ireland	2-0
10 November	1954	Wembley	Wales	3-2
1 December	1954	Wembley	West Germany	3-1
2 April	1955	Wembley	Scotland	7-2
15 May	1955	Paris	France	0-1
18 May	1955	Madrid	Spain	1-1
22 May	1955	Oporto	Portugal	1-3
2 October	1955	Copenhagen	Denmark	5-1
22 October	1955	Cardiff	Wales	1-2
2 November	1955	Wembley	N Ireland	3-0
30 November	1955	Wembley	Spain	4-1
14 April	1956	Glasgow	Scotland	1-1
9 May	1956	Wembley	Brazil	4-2

Date		Venue	Opponents	Score
16 May	1956	Stockholm	Sweden	0-0
20 May	1956	Helsinki	Finland	5-1
26 May	1956	Berlin	West Germany	3-1
6 October	1956	Belfast	N Ireland	1-1
14 November	1956	Wembley	Wales	3-1
28 November	1956	Wembley	Yugoslavia	3-0
WC 5 December	1956	Wolverhampton	Denmark	5-2
6 April	1957	Wembley	Scotland	2-1
WC 8 May	1957	Wembley	Eire	5-1
WC15 May	1957	Copenhagen	Denmark	4-1
WC19 May	1957	Dublin	Eire	1-1
19 October	1957	Cardiff	Wales	4-0
6 November	1957	Wembley	N Ireland	2-3
27 November	1957	Wembley	France	4-0
19 April	1958	Glasgow	Scotland	4-0
7 May	1958	Wembley	Portugal	2-1
11 May	1958	Belgrade	Yugoslavia	0-5
18 May	1958	Moscow	USSR	1-1
WC 8 June	1958	Gothenburg	USSR	2-2
WC11 June	1958	Gothenburg	Brazil	0-0
WC15 June	1958	Boras	Austria	2-2
WC17 June	1958	Gothenburg	USSR	0-1
4 October	1958	Belfast	N Ireland	3-3
22 October	1958	Wembley	USSR	5-0
26 November	1958	Birmingham	Wales	2-2
11 April	1959	Wembley	Scotland	1-0
6 May	1959	Wembley	Italy	2-2
13 May	1959	Rio de Janeiro	Brazil	0-2
17 May	1959	Lima	Peru	1-4
24 May	1959	Mexico City	Mexico	1-2
28 May	1959	Los Angeles	USA	8-1
17 October	1959	Cardiff	Wales	1-1
28 October	1959	Wembley	Sweden	2-3
18 November	1959	Wembley	N Ireland	2-1
9 April	1960	Glasgow	Scotland	1-1
11 May	1960	Wembley	Yugoslavia	3-3
15 May	1960	Madrid	Spain	0-3
22 May	1960	Budapest	Hungary	0-2
8 October	1960	Belfast	N Ireland	5-2
WC19 October	1960	Luxembourg	Luxembourg	9-0
26 October	1960	Wembley	Spain	4-2
23 November	1960	Wembley	Wales	5-1
15 April	1961	Wembley	Scotland	9-3
10 May	1961	Wembley	Mexico	8-0
WC21 May	1961	Lisbon	Portugal	1-1
24 May	1961	Rome	Italy	3-2
27 May	1961	Vienna	Austria	1-3
WC28 September	1961	Highbury	Luxembourg	4-1
14 October	1961	Cardiff	Wales	1-1
WC25 October	1961	Wembley	Portugal	2-0
22 November	1961	Wembley	N Ireland	1-1
4 April	1962	Wembley	Austria	3-1
14 April	1962	Glasgow	Scotland	0-2
9 May	1962	Wembley	Switzerland	3-1
20 May	1962	Lima	Peru	4-0
WC31 May	1962	Rancagua	Hungary	1-2
WC 2 June	1962	Rancagua	Argentina	3-1
WC 7 June	1962	Rancagua	Bulgaria	0-0
WC10 June	1962	Vina del Mar	Brazil	1-3
ENC 3 October	1962	Sheffield	France	1-1
20 October	1962	Belfast	N Ireland	3-1
21 November	1962	Wembley	Wales	4-0
ENC27 February	1963	Paris	France	2-5
6 April	1963	Wembley	Scotland	1-2
8 May	1963	Wembley	Brazil	1-1
29 May	1963	Bratislava	Czechoslovakia	4-2
2 June	1963	Leipzig	East Germany	2-1
5 June	1963	Basle	Switzerland	8-1
12 October	1963	Cardiff	Wales	4-0
23 October	1963	Wembley	FIFA	2-1
20 November	1963	Wembley	N Ireland	8-3
11 April	1964	Glasgow	Scotland	0-1
6 May	1964	Wembley	Uruguay	2-1
17 May	1964	Lisbon	Portugal	4-3
24 May	1964	Dublin	Eire	3-1
27 May	1964	New York	USA	10-0
30 May	1964	Rio de Janeiro	Brazil	1-5
4 June	1964	Sao Paulo	Portugal	1-1
6 June	1964	Rio de Janeiro	Argentina	0-1
3 October	1964	Belfast	N Ireland	4-3
21 October	1964	Wembley	Belgium	2-2
18 November	1964	Wembley	Wales	2-1
9 December	1964	Amsterdam	Netherlands	1-1
10 April	1965	Wembley	Scotland	2-2
5 May	1965	Wembley	Hungary	1-0
9 May	1965	Belgrade	Yugoslavia	1-1
12 May	1965	Nurnberg	West Germany	1-0
16 May	1965	Gothenburg	Sweden	2-1
2 October	1965	Cardiff	Wales	0-0
20 October	1965	Wembley	Austria	2-3
10 November	1965	Wembley	N Ireland	2-1
8 December	1965	Madrid	Spain	2-0
5 January	1966	Everton	Poland	1-1
23 February	1966	Wembley	West Germany	1-0
2 April	1966	Glasgow	Scotland	4-3
4 May	1966	Wembley	Yugoslavia	2-0
26 June	1966	Helsinki	Finland	3-0
29 June	1966	Oslo	Norway	6-1
3 July	1966	Copenhagen	Denmark	2-0
5 July	1966	Chorzow	Poland	1-0
WC11 July	1966	Wembley	Uruguay	0-0
WC16 July	1966	Wembley	Mexico	2-0
WC20 July	1966	Wembley	France	2-0
WC23 July	1966	Wembley	Argentina	1-0
WC26 July	1966	Wembley	Portugal	2-1
WC30 July	1966	Wembley	West Germany	4-2
EC22 October	1966	Belfast	N Ireland	2-0
2 November	1966	Wembley	Czechoslovakia	0-0
EC16 November	1966	Wembley	Wales	5-1
EC15 April	1967	Wembley	Scotland	2-3
24 May	1967	Wembley	Spain	2-0
27 May	1967	Vienna	Austria	1-0
EC21 October	1967	Cardiff	Wales	3-0
EC22 November	1967	Wembley	N Ireland	2-0
6 December	1967	Wembley	USSR	2-2
EC24 February	1968	Glasgow	Scotland	1-1
3 April	1968	Wembley	Spain	1-0
8 May	1968	Madrid	Spain	2-1
22 May	1968	Wembley	Sweden	3-1
1 June	1968	Hanover	West Germany	0-1
EC 5 June	1968	Florence	Yugoslavia	0-1
EC 8 June	1968	Rome	USSR	2-0
6 November	1968	Bucharest	Rumania	0-0
11 December	1968	Wembley	Bulgaria	1-1
15 January	1969	Wembley	Rumania	1-1
12 March	1969	Wembley	France	5-0
3 May	1969	Belfast	N Ireland	3-1
7 May	1969	Wembley	Wales	2-1
10 May	1969	Wembley	Scotland	4-1
1 June	1969	Mexico City	Mexico	0-0
8 June	1969	Montevideo	Uruguay	2-1
12 June	1969	Rio de Janeiro	Brazil	1-2
5 November	1969	Amsterdam	Netherlands	1-0
10 December	1969	Wembley	Portugal	1-0
14 January	1970	Wembley	Netherlands	0-0
25 February	1970	Brussels	Belgium	3-1
18 April	1970	Cardiff	Wales	1-1
21 April	1970	Wembley	N Ireland	3-1
25 April	1970	Glasgow	Scotland	0-0
24 May	1970	Quito	Equador	2-0
WC 2 June	1970	Guadalajara	Rumania	1-0
WC 7 June	1970	Guadalajara	Brazil	0-1
WC11 June	1970	Guadalajara	Czechoslovakia	1-0
WC14 June	1970	Leon	West Germany	2-3
25 November	1970	Wembley	East Germany	3-1
EC 3 February	1971	Valetta	Malta	1-0
EC21 April	1971	Wembley	Greece	3-0
EC12 May	1971	Wembley	Malta	5-0
15 May	1971	Belfast	N Ireland	1-0
19 May	1971	Wembley	Wales	0-0
22 May	1971	Wembley	Scotland	3-1
EC13 October	1971	Basle	Switzerland	3-2
EC10 November	1971	Wembley	Switzerland	1-1
EC 1 December	1971	Athens	Greece	2-0
EC29 April	1972	Wembley	West Germany	1-3
EC13 May	1972	Berlin	West Germany	0-0
20 May	1972	Cardiff	Wales	3-0
23 May	1972	Wembley	N Ireland	0-1
27 May	1972	Glasgow	Scotland	1-0
11 October	1972	Wembley	Yugoslavia	1-1
WC15 November	1972	Cardiff	Wales	1-0
WC24 January	1973	Wembley	Wales	1-1
14 February	1973	Glasgow	Scotland	5-0
12 May	1973	Everton	N Ireland	2-1
15 May	1973	Wembley	Wales	3-0
19 May	1973	Wembley	Scotland	1-0
27 May	1973	Prague	Czechoslovakia	1-1
WC 6 June	1973	Katowice	Poland	0-2
10 June	1973	Moscow	USSR	2-1
14 June	1973	Turin	Italy	0-2
26 September	1973	Wembley	Austria	7-0
WC17 October	1973	Wembley	Poland	1-1
14 November	1973	Wembley	Italy	0-1
3 April	1974	Lisbon	Portugal	0-0
11 May	1974	Cardiff	Wales	2-0
15 May	1974	Wembley	N Ireland	1-0
18 May	1974	Glasgow	Scotland	0-2
22 May	1974	Wembley	Argentina	2-2
29 May	1974	Leipzig	East Germany	1-1
1 June	1974	Sofia	Bulgaria	1-0
5 June	1974	Belgrade	Yugoslavia	2-2
EC30 October	1974	Wembley	Czechoslovakia	3-0
EC20 November	1974	Wembley	Portugal	0-0
12 March	1975	Wembley	West Germany	2-0
EC16 April	1975	Wembley	Cyprus	5-0
EC11 May	1975	Limassol	Cyprus	1-0
17 May	1975	Belfast	N Ireland	0-0
21 May	1975	Wembley	Wales	2-2
24 May	1975	Wembley	Scotland	5-1
3 September	1975	Basle	Switzerland	2-1
EC30 October	1975	Bratislava	Czechoslovakia	1-2
EC19 November	1975	Lisbon	Portugal	1-1
24 March	1976	Wrexham	Wales	2-1
8 May	1976	Cardiff	Wales	1-0
11 May	1976	Wembley	N Ireland	4-0
14 May	1976	Glasgow	Scotland	1-2
23 May	1976	Los Angeles	Brazil	0-1
28 May	1976	New York	Italy	3-2
WC13 June	1976	Helsinki	Finland	4-1
8 September	1976	Wembley	Eire	1-1
WC13 October	1976	Wembley	Finland	2-1
WC17 November	1976	Rome	Italy	0-2
9 February	1977	Wembley	Holland	0-2
WC30 March	1977	Wembley	Luxembourg	5-0
28 May	1977	Belfast	N Ireland	2-1
31 May	1977	Wembley	Wales	0-1
4 June	1977	Wembley	Scotland	1-2
8 June	1977	Rio de Janeiro	Brazil	0-0
12 June	1977	Buenos Aires	Argentina	1-1
15 June	1977	Montevideo	Uruguay	0-0
7 September	1977	Wembley	Switzerland	0-0
WC12 October	1977	Luxembourg	Luxembourg	2-0
WC16 November	1977	Wembley	Italy	2-0
22 February	1978	Munich	West Germany	1-2
19 April	1978	Wembley	Brazil	1-1
13 May	1978	Cardiff	Wales	3-1
16 May	1978	Wembley	N Ireland	1-0
20 May	1978	Glasgow	Scotland	1-0
24 May	1978	Wembley	Hungary	4-1
EC20 September	1978	Copenhagen	Denmark	4-3
EC25 October	1978	Dublin	Eire	1-1
29 November	1978	Wembley	Czechoslovakia	1-0
EC 7 February	1979	Wembley	N Ireland	4-0
19 May	1979	Belfast	N Ireland	2-0
23 May	1979	Wembley	Wales	0-0
26 May	1979	Wembley	Scotland	3-1
EC 6 June	1979	Sofia	Bulgaria	3-0
10 June	1979	Stockholm	Sweden	0-0
13 June	1979	Vienna	Austria	3-4
EC 9 September	1979	Wembley	Denmark	1-0
EC17 October	1979	Belfast	N Ireland	5-1
EC22 November	1979	Wembley	Bulgaria	2-0
EC 6 February	1980	Wembley	Eire	2-0
26 March	1980	Barcelona	Spain	2-0
13 May	1980	Wembley	Argentina	3-1
17 May	1980	Wrexham	Wales	1-4
20 May	1980	Wembley	N Ireland	1-1
24 May	1980	Glasgow	Scotland	2-0
31 May	1980	Sydney	Australia	2-1
EC12 June	1980	Turin	Belgium	1-1
EC15 June	1980	Turin	Italy	0-1
EC18 June	1980	Naples	Spain	2-1
WC10 September	1980	Wembley	Norway	4-0
WC15 October	1980	Bucharest	Rumania	1-2
WC19 November	1980	Wembley	Switzerland	2-1
25 March	1981	Wembley	Spain	1-2
WC29 April	1981	Wembley	Rumania	0-0
12 May	1981	Wembley	Brazil	0-1
20 May	1981	Wembley	Wales	0-0
23 May	1981	Wembley	Scotland	0-1
WC30 May	1981	Basle	Switzerland	1-2
WC 6 June	1981	Budapest	Hungary	3-1
WC 9 September	1981	Oslo	Norway	1-2
WC18 November	1981	Wembley	Hungary	1-0
23 February	1982	Wembley	N Ireland	4-0
27 April	1982	Cardiff	Wales	1-0
25 May	1982	Wembley	Holland	2-0
29 May	1982	Glasgow	Scotland	1-0
2 June	1982	Reykjavik	Iceland	1-1
3 June	1982	Helsinki	Finland	4-1
WC16 June	1982	Bilbao	France	3-1
WC20 June	1982	Bilbao	Czechoslovakia	2-0
WC25 June	1982	Bilbao	Kuwait	1-0
WC29 June	1982	Madrid	West Germany	0-0
WC 5 July	1982	Madrid	Spain	0-0
EC22 September	1982	Copenhagen	Denmark	2-2
13 October	1982	Wembley	West Germany	1-2
EC17 November	1982	Salonika	Greece	3-0
EC15 December	1982	Wembley	Luxembourg	9-0
23 February	1983	Wembley	Wales	2-1
EC30 March	1983	Wembley	Greece	0-0

*These four games were all between an England XI and a team of Scots resident in England. The FA does not regard them as official matches

†On each of these days England played two internationals. The FA asked the Corinthian Casuals to provide the teams against Wales, while they themselves selected the sides to play Ireland. Corinthians are the only club side to have represented England in toto

‡This match was abandoned owing to a disaster at the ground. The FA does not regard it as an official match

V – Victory internationals (not regarded as official)

J – Jubilee game (not regarded as official)

WT – War-time internationals (not regarded as official)

WC – World Cup games

ENC – European Nations Cup games

EC – European Championship games

C – Commonwealth tour games. Though billed as 'England' these teams were usually FA Touring XIs. One cap was awarded to each of the players who went on the tour but individual games are not regarded as official internationals

A – Abandoned after 20 minutes owing to torrential rain

successor, Don Revie, steeped in the success of Leeds United, faced a similar problem and England did not reach the last eight of the 1976 European Championship.

Eventually as Revie's squad set out along the qualification route for the 1978 World Cup, the Football League grudgingly agreed to postpone League matches to increase preparation time. Temporarily, at least, the massive withdrawals because of club injuries and commitments were ended—in 1972 Ramsey had lost *nine* of his original squad in such circumstances for the international against Yugoslavia. Revie still faced the problem of making the concession be seen to work, but it made that advertisement for 'young men to play in an international' seem that much further away.

Revie would undoubtedly have suffered the same fate as Ramsey had he not jumped off the ship before it went down. Failure to qualify for the 1978 World Cup finals and Revie's hasty departure to the Middle East left morale at international level at an all-time low. Ron Greenwood's appointment brought muted optimism and some fresh ideas. Club managers working in tandem were given responsibility for nurturing the under-21 and England B sides while Greenwood himself worked in conjunction with Arsenal coach Don Howe. Instead of the big leap into the senior side, there were now a clear series of stepping stones.

After qualification for the 1980 European championship came the next attempt to get England to her first World Cup finals since 1966. Expansion of the competition to 24 countries made it virtually impossible to fail to qualify.

Even then it took a belated decision by the Football League to agree to postpone some Saturday games before vital qualifying matches to clear what was becoming an increasingly rocky path to Spain. With Greenwood's retirement after fulfilling all that could reasonably have been expected of him—qualification for Spain, a robust if uninspiring performance in the finals and England's longest ever run of first-class victories—England moved nearer the era of the soccer supremo. When Bobby Robson took over, he dispensed with the FA's long-serving director of coaching, Allen Wade, and assumed responsibility for that department himself. England now had a manager whose personal influence reached from the international battle grounds right down to playing fields across the country.

Below: *Geoff Hurst is on his way to becoming one of the most famous names in international football; Bobby Moore's 19th minute free-kick is met at the near-post by Hurst and England are back in the 1966 World Cup final with the score at 1-1. It is the least appreciated of England's four goals that day because it came so early and was swamped by the dramas at the end, but it is arguably the most important. It got England back in the game when it might have so easily gone away from them. Fourteen years later Hurst* ***(above)*** *is still a regular visitor at Wembley in the role of chief assistant to the England manager Ron Greenwood (background). England trainer Fred Street is on the right. Hurst's senior role came to an end when Bobby Robson took over from Greenwood as manager and Hurst's own managerial career seemed to have petered out when he left Chelsea in 1981. He will always remain, however, a legend as the first man to score a hat-trick in a World Cup final.*

THE CHALLENGE OF EUROPE

TALK ABOUT EUROPE and you talk about Real Madrid, Ajax, Bayern Munich and Liverpool. These are the teams who have dominated the continent's principal club championship over the last 25 years. In recent seasons English clubs have sprinted to the forefront with Nottingham Forest and Aston Villa cementing a six-year grip on the competition.

Add the early triumphs of Celtic and Manchester United and the picture appears complete. But that would be to overlook the consistency with which British clubs have made an impact in Europe from the very first year official competition in 1955.

True, it took twelve years of Champions' Cup football before Celtic and then United added their names to the winners, but it was London and then Birmingham which made successive final appearances in the old Inter City Fairs Cup between 1955 and 1961. And 1961 coincidentally was the first year of the Cup Winners' Cup and Glasgow Rangers kept the flag flying despite losing the final 4-1 on aggregate to Fiorentina.

The following year, while English soccer was still taking in the shock waves of Ipswich's bold championship victory, the European cupboard went bare. But only for a season. In 1963 FA Cup winners Spurs became the first British club to triumph in Europe when they beat Atletico Madrid 5-1 in the Cup Winners' Cup.

This was a significant victory for two reasons. The 1961 Double winners, who had run Benfica so close in the semi-finals of the Champions' Cup the previous season, achieved their historic win without Dave Mackay, one of the men who so typified their storming, glory glory style. But, perhaps more importantly, Spurs were the first British club to use a real first team squad. They had two goalkeepers in Brown and Hollowbread, three full backs in Baker, Henry and Hopkins, four defenders in Norman, Marchi, Mackay and Blanchflower, and seven forwards: Jones, White, Smith, Greaves, Dyson, Medwin and Allen. It was to set a pattern from which other British clubs would profit.

Spurs' victory wasn't as comfortable as the scoreline suggests. They went in 2-0 up at half-time but a Collar penalty for Madrid put the pressure on until a Dyson cross unexpectedly flew into the net on a gust of wind. In 1964 the holders came face to face with new English Cup-winners Manchester United in the second round. Defeat marked the end of an era for the Double side. Dave Mackay sustained the first of the two broken legs which were to slow his career and Spurs had to wait until 1972 before winning their next European crown, in the UEFA Cup. In 1965 it was West Ham's turn to lift the Cup Winners' Cup with a 2-0 win over TSV Munich 1860 in what was the middle leg of three successive cup-winning Wembley appearances for skipper Bobby Moore.

In the year of England's World Cup win, Liverpool were the beaten Cup Winners' Cup finalists and the following year, Leeds made the first of eight successive Fairs and UEFA Cup final appearances by English clubs. They lost the 1967 final against Dynamo Zagreb but returned to triumph the following year when they beat Ferencvaros over two legs thanks to a solitary goal scored by Mick Jones. Newcastle, Arsenal, Leeds again and then Tottenham and Liverpool in the new-style UEFA competition all won their respective finals before Spurs faltered in the 1974 final against Feijenoord.

The tide that was sweeping clubs to victory in the lesser European competitions finally breached the walls of the premier event in 1967. It may be significant in this context that as clubs like six-times winners Real Madrid and double winners Benfica built up reputations of invincibility, it was often the clubs who beat them who became the new masters of Europe. Benfica succeeded Real Madrid after beating them in the 1962 final, then it was the turn of Milan clubs AC and Inter to inherit the crown. Celtic's one victory in 1967 proved an exception, but they were worthy victors nonetheless. The only British club ever to make a clean sweep of domestic and European honours, Celtic achieved that distinction through a mixture of vitality and good luck. Inter-Milan were without their Spanish inside-left Luis Suarez, who had a leg injury, and without his midfield organization they lacked the heart and stamina to keep up with a younger, fitter Celtic side. The Italians admitted as much when they were forced to switch Facchetti to mark Jimmy Johnstone because international right back Burgnich didn't have the legs to keep up with the mesmerising ball play of the little winger.

Inter went ahead with a sixth minute penalty by Mazzola—and that was probably their undoing. Had they scored a little later, Celtic might not have had time to find a way through the defensive cordon Inter threw around their goal in the hope of holding out. Gemmell struck a ferocious second half equaliser and Chalmers added Celtic's winner.

If Celtic's victory was a hit-and-run affair, the next British win in the European Cup was the result of a crusade which had its roots in the tragedy of Munich ten years earlier. Manchester United, who had gone against the insular wishes of the FA by entering the 1957 competition, where they reached the semi-

Keith Robson scores for West Ham but the 1976 Cup Winners Cup Final against Anderlecht ended in a 4-2 defeat. It was West Ham's second Cup Winners' Final.

EUROPEAN CHAMPION CLUBS' CUP

1955-56 **REAL MADRID**
Paris 12 June 1956 Attendance 38,329
Real Madrid (2) **4** — **Reims** (2) **3**
di Stefano, Rial 2, Marquitos — Leblond, Templin, Hidalgo
Real: Alonso, Atienza, Lesmes, Munoz, Marquitos, Zaggara, Joseito, Marchal, di Stefano, Rial, Gento
Reims: Jacquet, Zimny, Giraudo, Leblond, Jonquet, Siatka, Hidalgo, Glovacki, Kopa, Bliard, Templin

1956-57 **REAL MADRID**
Madrid 30 May 1957 Attendance 125,000
Real Madrid (0) **2** — **Fiorentina** (0) **0**
di Stefano, Gento
Real: Alonso, Torres, Lesmes, Munoz, Marquitos, Zaggara, Kopa, Mateos, di Stefano, Rial, Gento
Fiorentina: Sarti, Magnini, Cervato, Scaramucci, Orzan, Segato, Julinho, Gratton, Virgili, Montuori, Bizzarri

1957-58 **REAL MADRID**
Brussels 29 May 1958 Attendance 67,000
Real Madrid (0) (2) **3** — **AC Milan** (0) (2) **2**
di Stefano, Rial, Gento — Schiaffino, Grillo
Real: Alonso, Atienza, Lesmes, Santisteban, Santamaria, Zaggara, Kopa, Joseito, di Stefano, Rial, Gento
AC Milan: Soldan, Fontana, Beraldo, Bergamaschi, Maldini, Radice, Danova, Liedholm, Schiaffino, Grillo, Cucchiaroni

1958-59 **REAL MADRID**
Stuttgart 3 June 1959 Attendance 80,000
Real Madrid (1) **2** — **Reims** (0) **0**
Mateos, di Stefano
Real: Dominguez, Marquitos, Zaggara, Santisteban, Santamaria, Ruiz, Kopa, Mateos, di Stefano, Rial, Gento
Reims: Colonna, Rodzik, Giraudo, Penverne, Jonquet, Leblond, Lamartine, Bliard, Fontaine, Piantoni, Vincent

1959-60 **REAL MADRID**
Glasgow 18 May 1960 Attendance 127,621
Real Madrid (3) **7** — **Eintracht Frankfurt** (1) **3**
di Stefano 3, Puskas 4 — Kress, Stein 2
Real: Dominguez, Marquitos, Pachin, Vidal, Santamaria, Zaggara, Canario, Del Sol, di Stefano, Puskas, Gento
Eintracht: Loy, Lutz, Hoefer, Weilbacher, Eigenbrodt, Stinka, Kress, Lindner, Stein, Pfaff, Meier

1960-61 **BENFICA**
Berne 31 May 1961 Attendance 33,000
Benfica (2) **3** — **Barcelona** (1) **2**
Aguas, Ramallets (og), Coluna — Kocsis, Czibor
Benfica: Costa Pereira, Joao, Angelo, Neto, Germano, Cruz, Augusto, Santana, Aguas, Coluna, Cavem
Barcelona: Ramallets, Foncho, Gracia, Verges, Gensana, Garay, Kubala, Kocsis, Evaristo, Suarez, Czibor

1961-62 **BENFICA**
Amsterdam 2 May 1962 Attendance 68,000
Benfica (2) **5** — **Real Madrid** (3) **3**
Aguas, Cavem, Coluna, Eusebio 2 (1 pen) — Puskas 3
Benfica: Costa Pereira, Joao, Angelo, Cavem, Germano, Cruz, Augusto, Eusebio, Aguas, Coluna, Simoes
Real: Araquistain, Casado, Miera, Felo, Santamaria, Pachin, Tejada, Del Sol, di Stefano, Puskas, Gento

1962-63 **AC MILAN**
Wembley 22 May 1963 Attendance 45,000
AC Milan (0) **2** — **Benfica** (1) **1**
Altafini 2 — Eusebio
Milan: Ghezzi, David, Trebbi, Benitez, Maldini, Trapattoni, Pivatelli, Dino Sani, Altafini, Rivera, Mora
Benfica: Costa Pereira, Cavem, Cruz, Humberto, Raul, Coluna, Augusto, Santana, Torres, Eusebio, Simoes

1963-64 **INTER MILAN**
Vienna 27 May 1964 Attendance 72,000
Inter Milan (1) **3** — **Real Madrid** (0) **1**
Mazzola 2, Milani — Felo
Inter: Sarti, Burgnich, Facchetti, Tagnin, Guarneri, Picchi, Jair, Mazzola, Milani, Suarez, Corso
Real: Vicente, Isidro, Pachin, Zoco, Santamaria, Muller, Amancio, Felo, di Stefano, Puskas, Gento

1964-65 **INTER MILAN**
Milan 27 May 1965 Attendance 80,000
Inter Milan (1) **1** — **Benfica** (0) **0**
Jair
Inter: Sarti, Burgnich, Facchetti, Bedin, Guarneri, Picchi, Jair, Mazzola, Peiro, Suarez, Corso
Benfica: Costa Pereira, Cavem, Cruz, Neto, Germano, Raul, Augusto, Eusebio, Torres, Coluna, Simoes

1965-66 **REAL MADRID**
Brussels 11 May 1966 Attendance 38,714
Real Madrid (0) **2** — **Partizan Belgrade** (0) **1**
Amancio, Serena — Vasovic
Real: Araquistain, Pachin, Sanchis, Pirri, De Felipe, Zoco, Serena, Amancio, Grosso, Velasquez, Gento
Partizan: Soskic, Jusufi, Migailovic, Becejac, Rasovic, Vasovic, Bajic, Kovacevic, Hasanagic, Galic, Pirmajer

1966-67 **CELTIC**
Lisbon 25 May 1967 Attendance 45,000
Celtic (0) **2** — **Inter Milan** (1) **1**
Gemmell, Chalmers — Mazzola (pen)
Celtic: Simpson, Craig, Gemmell, Murdoch, McNeill, Clark, Johnstone, Wallace, Chalmers, Auld, Lennox
Inter: Sarti, Burgnich, Facchetti, Bedin, Guarneri, Picchi, Domenghini, Mazzola, Cappellini, Biccli, Corso

1967-68 **MANCHESTER UNITED**
Wembley 29 May 1968 Attendance 100,000
Manchester United (0) (1) **4** — **Benfica** (0) (1) **1**
Charlton 2, Best, Kidd — Graca
United: Stepney, Brennan, Dunne, Crerand, Foulkes, Stiles, Best, Kidd, Charlton, Sadler, Aston
Benfica: Henrique, Adolfo, Cruz, Graca, Humberto, Jacinto, Augusto, Eusebio, Torres, Coluna, Simoes

1968-69 **AC MILAN**
Madrid 28 May 1969 Attendance 50,000
AC Milan (2) **4** — **Ajax Amsterdam** (0) **1**
Prati 3, Sormani — Vasovic
Milan: Cudicini, Anquiletti, Schnellinger, Maldera, Rosato, Trapattoni, Hamrin, Lodetti, Sormani, Rivera, Prati
Ajax: Bals, Suurbier (sub Muller), Van Duivenbode, Pronk, Hulsoff, Vasovic, Swart, Cruyff, Danielson, Groot (sub Nuninga), Keizer

1969-70 **FEYENOORD**
Milan 6 May 1970 Attendance 50,000
Feyenoord (1) (1) **2** — **Celtic** (1) (1) **1**
Israel, Kindvall — Gemmell
Feyenoord: Graafland, Romeyns, Laseroms, Israel, Van Duivenbode, Hasil, Jansen, Van Hanegem, Wery, Kindvall, Mouljin (sub Haak)
Celtic: Williams, Hay, Gemmell, Murdoch, McNeill, Brogan, Johnstone, Lennox, Wallace, Auld (sub Connolly), Hughes

1970-71 **AJAX AMSTERDAM**
Wembley 2 June 1971 Attendance 90,000
Ajax Amsterdam (1) **2** — **Panathinaikos** (0) **0**
Van Dijk, Haan
Ajax: Stuy, Vasovic, Suurbier, Hulsoff, Rijinders (sub Haan), Neeskens, Swart (sub Blankenburg), Muhren, Keizer, Van Dijk, Cruyff
Panathinaikos: Economopoulos, Tomaras, Vlahos, Elefetrakis, Kamaras, Sourpis, Grammos, Filokouris, Antoniadis, Domazos, Kapsis

finals, were once again within sight of the final the following year when they were struck down by the air crash which claimed the lives of eight first team players. Having overcome Red Star Belgrade in the quarter-finals, the traumatized United side again went out in the semi-finals, to AC Milan.

By 1968 Matt Busby had reassembled a United side capable of sustaining a challenge in Europe. But once again the semi-finals looked like proving the stumbling block. United's slender 1-0 win in the first leg against Real Madrid seemed insufficient when the home side went 3-1 up in the return. But goals by Sadler and Foulkes sealed an unlikely United victory which brought them back to Wembley for what was virtually a home game against Benfica. That advantage was partially cancelled out by the absence of Denis Law, who missed the final with a knee injury. The teams forsook their traditional red colours, United playing in all-blue and Benfica in all-white, for a final which was the most emotional in British club history. With the score standing at 1-1, United goalkeeper Stepney produced a magnificent save from Eusebio in the closing minutes and so snatched them from the jaws of almost certain defeat. Extra time goals from Best, Charlton and Kidd brought a 4-1 win and England's first European Cup victory. It also brought Busby, the game's best-loved figure, a knighthood.

Following West Ham's 1965 Cup Winners' Cup win, Liverpool and Rangers kept up the British presence in the finals the following two years while the Fairs Cup went on a four-year round-trip of England. Celtic should have added to their 1967 European Cup triumph three years later but inexplicably lost the final to an uninspiring Feijenoord. Another five years passed before Leeds became the next British club to reach the final but on this occasion it was the cream of West Germany's World Cup winners who were their opponents. Bayern Munich won 2-0 to complete the second of their three successive victories.

As Manchester City, Chelsea and Rangers scored consecutive successes in the Cup Winners' Cup in the early Seventies and Leeds became the fourth British club in a row to reach the final, Liverpool were making inroads on the UEFA trophy which were to have remarkable sequels a few years later.

In the 1973 final, they beat Borussia Moenchengladbach 3-2 on aggregate with two goals from Keegan and one from Lloyd. It was the beginning of an era in which the English club were to dominate first the domestic game and then Europe too. Three years later Bill Shankly's team were back in another UEFA Final this time against Bruges. Kennedy, Case and Keegan staged a remarkable second half recovery in the first Anfield leg after Bruges had taken a 2-0 lead. A more resilient Liverpool

1971-72 **AJAX AMSTERDAM**
Rotterdam 31 May 1972 Attendance 67,000
Ajax Amsterdam (0) **2** **Inter Milan** (0) **0**
Cruyff 2
Ajax: Stuy, Suurbier, Blankenburg, Hulshoff, Krol, Neeskens, Haan, Muhren, Swart, Cruyff, Keizer
Inter: Bordon, Burgnich, Bellugi, Oriali, Facchetti, Bedin, Mazzola, Giubertoni (sub Bertini), Jair, Pellicarro, Boninsegna, Frustalupi

1972-73 **AJAX AMSTERDAM**
Belgrade 30 May 1973 Attendance 93,500
Ajax Amsterdam (0) **1** **Juventus** (0) **0**
Rep
Ajax: Stuy, Suurbier, Blankenburg, Hulshoff, Krol, Neeskens, Haan, G. Muhren, Rep, Cruyff, Keizer
Juventus: Zoff, Longobucco, Marchetti, Furino, Morini, Salvadore, Altafini, Causio (sub Cuccureddu), Anastasi, Capello, Bettega (sub Haller)

1973-74 **BAYERN MUNICH**
Brussels 15 May 1974 Attendance 65,000
Bayern Munich (0) (0) **1** **Atletico Madrid** (0) (0) **1**
Schwarzenbeck Luis
Brussels 17 May 1974 Attendance 65,000
Bayern Munich (1) **4** **Atletico Madrid** (0) **0**
Muller 2, Hoeness 2
Bayern Munich: Maier, Hansen, Breitner, Schwarzenbeck, Beckenbauer, Roth, Torstensson (sub Durnberger first match), Zobel, Muller, Hoeness, Kappelmann
Atletico Madrid: Reina, Melo, Capon, Adelardo (sub Benegas second match), Heredia, Eusebio, Luis, Garate, Salcedo (sub Alberto in first match), Ufarte (sub Becerra in both matches), Alberto (Irureta played in first match)

1974-75 **BAYERN MUNICH**
Paris 28 May 1975 Attendance 50,000
Bayern Munich (0) **2** **Leeds United** (0) **0**
Roth, Muller
Bayern Munich: Maier, Durnberger, Andersson (sub Weiss), Schwarzenbeck, Beckenbauer, Roth, Torstensson, Zobel, Muller, Hoeness (sub Wunder), Kappelmann
Leeds United: Stewart, Reaney, F. Gray, Bremner, Madeley, Hunter, Lorimer, Clarke, Jordan, Giles, Yorath (sub E. Gray)

1975-76 **BAYERN MUNICH**
Glasgow 12 May 1,976 Attendance 54,864
Bayern Munich (0) **1** **St. Etienne** (0) **0**
Roth
Bayern Munich: Maier, Hansen, Schwarzenbeck, Beckenbauer, Horsmann, Roth, Durnberger, Kappelmann, Rummenigge, Muller, Hoeness
St. Etienne: Curkovic, Repellini, Piazza, Lopez, Janvion, Bathenay, Santini, Larque, P. Revelli, H. Revelli, Sarramanga (sub Rocheteau)

1976-77 **LIVERPOOL**
Final:
Rome 25.5.77 Attendance 57,000
Liverpool (1) **3** **Borussia Monchengladbach** (0) **1**
McDermott, Smith, Neal (pen) Simonsen
Liverpool: Clemence, Neal, Jones, Smith, Kennedy, Hughes, Keegan, Case, Heighway, Callaghan, McDermott.
Borussia Monchengladbach: Kneib, Vogts, Klinkhammer, Wittkamp, Schaffer, Wohlers (sub Hannes), Bonhoff, Wimmer (sub Kulik), Stielike, Simonsen, Heynckes.

1977-78 **LIVERPOOL**
Wembley 10.5.78 Attendance 92,000
Liverpool (0) **1** **FC Bruges** (0) **0**
Dalglish
Liverpool: Clemence, Neal, Thompson, Hansen, Hughes, McDermott, Kennedy, Souness, Case (sub Heighway), Fairclough, Dalglish
FC Bruges: Jensen, Bastijns, Krieger, Leekens, Maes (sub Volders), Cools, De Cubber, Vandereycken, Ku (sub Sanders), Simoen, Sorensen

1978-79 **NOTTINGHAM FOREST**
Munich 30 May 1979 Attendance 57,500
Nottingham Forest (1) **1** **Malmo** (0) **0**
Francis
Nottm Forest: Shilton, Anderson, Lloyd, Burns, Clark, Francis, McGovern, Bowyer, Robertson, Woodcock, Birtles
Malmo: Moller, Roland Andersson, Jonsson, Magnus Andersson, Erlandsson, Tapper (sub Malmberg), Ljungberg, Prytz, Kinnvall, Hansson (sub Tommy Andersson), Cervin

1979-80 **NOTTINGHAM FOREST**
Madrid 28 May 1980 Attendance 50,000
Nottingham Forest (1) **1** **SV Hamburg** (0) **0**
Robertson
Nottm Forest: Shilton, Anderson, Gray (sub Gunn), McGovern, Lloyd, Burns, O'Neill, Bowyer, Birtles, Mills (sub O'Hare), Robertson
SV Hamburg: Kargus, Kaltz, Nogly, Jakobs, Buljan, Hieronymus (sub Hrubesch), Keegan, Memering, Milewski, Magath, Reimann

1980-81 **LIVERPOOL**
Paris 27 May 1981 Attendance 48,360
Liverpool (0) **1** **Real Madrid** (0) **0**
A. Kennedy
Liverpool: Clemence, Neal, A. Kennedy, Thompson, R. Kennedy, Hansen, Dalglish (sub Case), Lee, Johnson, McDermott, Souness
Real Madrid: Rodriguez, Garcia Cortes, Camacho, Stielike, Sabido (sub Pineda), Del Bosque, Juanito, De Los Santos, Santillana, Navajas, Cunningham

1981-82 **ASTON VILLA**
Rotterdam 26 May 1982 Attendance 46,000
Aston Villa (0) **1** **Bayern Munich** (0) **0**
Withe
Aston Villa: Rimmer (sub Spink), Swain, Williams, Evans, McNaught, Mortimer, Bremner, Shaw, Withe, Cowans, Morley
Bayern Munich: Muller, Dremmler, Horsmann, Weiner, Augenthaler, Kraus (sub Niedermayer), Durnberger, Breitner, Hoeness, Mathy (sub Guttler), Rummenigge

1982-83 **SV HAMBURG**
Athens 25 May 1983 Attendance 80,000
SV Hamburg (1) **1** **Juventus** (0) **0**
Magath
SV Hamburg: Stein, Kaltz, Wehmeyer, Jakobs, Heironymus, Rolff, Milewski, Groh, Hrubesch, Magath, Bastrup
Juventus: Zoff, Gentile, Cabrini, Bonini, Brio, Scirea, Bettega, Tardelli, Rossi (sub Marocchino), Platini, Boniek

performance in the return saw Keegan score in a 1-1 draw and the trophy return to Merseyside.

The significance of the victories over Borussia Moenchengladbach and Bruges became apparent in the run-up to the 1977 and 1978 European Cup Finals. Shankly had retired after Liverpool's 1975 FA Cup win but the continuity which has underpinned the greatest success machine in British soccer history was maintained with the elevation of Bob Paisley from coach to the manager's chair.

Nothing changed except the side's accomplishment in winning more cups for their new boss than they had for their old. Formalities out of the way with a 7-0 aggregate win over Crusaders, Liverpool got down to the real business with a well-earned victory over Turkish side Trabzonspor, overturning a 1-0 away defeat 3-0 in the return. Liverpool had to overcome another 1-0 first leg deficit against French champions Saint Etienne and after winning 3-1 at Anfield, they'd done the hard part of reaching the final. Swiss side Zurich were swept aside in the semifinal 6-1 on aggregate for Liverpool to find themselves up against a team over whom they held a considerable psychological advantage, their UEFA Cup victims Borussia Moenchengladbach.

The Germans were nevertheless a major force. Names like Vogts, Stielike, Bonhof and Simonsen—all of whom played in the UEFA Final—need little introduction today. Liverpool arrived in Rome on the rebound of an FA Cup defeat by Manchester United which ended their quest for the League, Cup and European Cup treble. But as Brian James remarked in his coverage of the final for his book *Journey to Wembley*, when Liverpool slung off their track suit tops, they slung off with them the misery of their FA Cup defeat.

Bonhof gave them a fright when he hit a post from 25 yards with the score 0-0 but a goal after 27 minutes by McDermott put Liverpool deservedly in front. Simonsen—a player whose regular presence in European finals is a tribute in itself—sent another ripple of anxiety through the Liverpool camp with a 60th minute equaliser after a rare mistake by Case. Clemence staved off further cracks appearing in the Liverpool defence with fine saves from Simonsen and Heynkes before Tommy Smith wrote his own Anfield epitaph with a glorious header.

Keegan, who had been locked in battle with his marker Vogts all evening, eventually set the seal on Liverpool's victory by earning a penalty when he went down tackled from behind by the blond West German. A photograph of the incident casts doubt on the correctness of the referee's decision since Vogts can clearly be seen playing the ball. Phil Neal converted the penalty and

EUROPEAN CUP WINNERS CUP FINALS

1960-61 FIORENTINA
First Leg: Glasgow 17.5.61 Attendance 80,000
Rangers (0) 0 **Fiorentina** (1) 2
Milan 2
Second Leg: Florence 27.5.61 Attendance 50,000
Fiorentina (1) 2 **Rangers** (1) 1
Milan, Hamrin — Scott
Rangers: Ritchie, Shearer, Caldow, Davis, Paterson, Baxter, Wilson, McMillan, Scott, Brand, Hume (Millar in second leg)

1961-62 ATLETICO MADRID
Final: Glasgow 10.5.62 Attendance 27,389
Atletico Madrid (1) 1 **Fiorentina** (1) 1
Peiro — Hamrin
Replay: Stuttgart 5.9.62 Attendance 45,000
Atletico Madrid (2) 3 **Fiorentina** (0) 0
Jones, Mendoca, Peiro

1962-63 TOTTENHAM HOTSPUR
Final: Rotterdam 15.5.63 Attendance 25,000
Tottenham Hotspur (2) 5 **Atletico Madrid** (0) 1
Greaves 2, White, Dyson 2 — Collar (pen)
Tottenham Hotspur: Brown, Baker, Henry, Blanchflower, Norman, Marchi, Jones, White, Smith, Greaves, Dyson

1963-64 SPORTING LISBON
Final: Brussels 13.5.64 Attendance 9,000
Sporting Lisbon (1) (3) 3 **MTK Budapest** (1) (3) 3
Figueiredo 2, Dansky (og) — Sandor 2, Kuti
Replay: Antwerp 15.5.64 Attendance 18,000
Sporting Lisbon (1) 1 **MTK Budapest** (0) 0
Morais

1964-65 WEST HAM UNITED
Final: Wembley 19.5.65 Attendance 100,000
West Ham United (0) 2 **TSV Munich 1860** (0) 0
Sealey 2
West Ham United: Standen, Kirkup, Burkett, Peters, Brown, Moore, Sealey, Boyce, Hurst, Dear, Sissons

1965-66 BORUSSIA DORTMUND
Final: Glasgow 5.5.66 Attendance 41,657
Borussia Dortmund (0) (1) 2 **Liverpool** (0) (1) 1
Held, Yeats (og) — Hunt
Liverpool: Lawrence, Lawler, Byrne, Milne, Yeats, Stevenson, Callaghan, Hunt, St John, Smith, Thompson

1966-67 BAYERN MUNICH
Final: Nuremberg 31.5.67 Attendance 69,480
Bayern Munich (0) (0) 1 **Rangers** (0) (0) 0
Roth
Rangers: Martin, Johansen, Provan, Jardine, McKinnon, Greig, Henderson, Smith (A), Hynd, Smith (D), Johnston

1967-68 AC MILAN
Final: Rotterdam 23.5.68
AC Milan (2) 2 **SV Hamburg** (0) 0
Hamrin 2

1968-69 SLOVAN BRATISLAVA
Final: Basle 21.5.69
Slovan Bratislava (3) 3 **Barcelona** (1) 2
Cvetler, Hrivnak, Jan Capkovic — Zaldua, Rexach

1969-70 MANCHESTER CITY
Final: Vienna 29.4.70 Attendance 10,000
Manchester City (2) 2 **Gornik Zabrze** (0) 1
Young, Lee penalty — Oslizlo
Manchester City: Corrigan, Book, Pardoe, Doyle (Bowyer), Booth, Oakes, Heslop, Bell, Lee, Young, Towers

1970-71 CHELSEA
Final: Athens 19.5.71 Attendance 42,000
Chelsea (0) (1) 1 **Real Madrid** (0) (1) 1
Osgood — Zoco
Replay: Athens 21.5.71 Attendance 24,000
Chelsea (2) 2 **Real Madrid** (0) 1
Dempsey, Osgood — Fleitas
Chelsea: *Final:* Bonetti, Boyle, Harris, Hollins (Mulligan), Dempsey, Webb, Weller, Cooke, Osgood (Baldwin), Hudson, Houseman
Replay: Bonetti, Boyle, Harris, Cooke, Dempsey, Webb, Weller, Baldwin, Osgood (Smethurst), Hudson, Houseman

1971-72 RANGERS
Final: Barcelona 24.5.72 Attendance 45,000
Rangers (2) 3 **Moscow Dynamo** (0) 2
Stein, Johnston 2 — Eschtrekov, Makiovic
Rangers: McCloy, Jardine, Mathieson, Greig, Johnstone, Smith, McLean, Conn, Stein, Macdonald, Johnston

1972-73 AC MILAN
Final: Salonika 16.5.73 Attendance 45,000
AC Milan (1) 1 **Leeds United** (0) 0
Chiaguri
Leeds United: Harvey, Reaney, Cherry, Bates, Madeley, Hunter, Lorimer, Jordan, Jones, Gray (F), Yorath (sub McQueen)

Liverpool became the second English club to lift the European crown.

The occasion was summed up in a fan's banner tribute to full-back Joey Jones which encapsulates the best of Merseyside humour: Joey ate the Frogs legs, made the Swiss roll, now he's Munching Gladbach. But there was also a poignant side: the sight of Paisley and Shankly together at the post-match Press conference, Anfield's new master telling the world at large how Liverpool did it, the past master-turned-newspaper columnist cast in the unfamiliar role of being just another member of the audience.

The final was also Keegan's farewell for Liverpool, a £500,000 move to SV Hamburg having already been negotiated. In his place Paisley signed Celtic's Kenny Dalglish who became an instant hero at Anfield with his brilliant ball control and breathtaking goals. Liverpool went into the 1978 European Cup as both holders and League champions again. A bye in the first round was followed by an overwhelming 6-3 aggregate win over Dynamo Dresden. Liverpool hit another six in beating Benfica in the quarter-finals before coming up against Borussia Moenchengladbach for a third time. The Germans won their home leg 2-1 but were imperiously brushed aside at Anfield 3-0. History was repeating itself in an uncanny way, for Liverpool's opponents for this final were FC Bruges—a second repeat final for the Merseysiders.

With a Wembley venue, Liverpool were odds-on favourites to retain the trophy but the game was not the pushover many expected. Indeed it marked the start of a series of tense but extremely dull finals involving British clubs. Bruges, suffering from a spate of injuries, shut up shop and Liverpool won thanks to a solitary goal by Dalglish.

The following season saw the champions of Europe paired in the first round with the new champions of England, Nottingham Forest. It was a pity one had to go out so early in the competition and there were many who had their suspicions about how the pairing came about. Forest won the home leg 2-0 and deposed the holders by keeping them to a goalless draw at Anfield. So Liverpool had become the team to beat, now Forest were en route to becoming the new kings of Europe.

They reached the semi-finals with panache but a 3-3 home draw with Cologne left them with a formidable task. Yet as the return showed, it's never wise to bet against a motivator like Forest manager Brian Clough. Forest won 1-0 in Cologne through an Ian Bowyer goal to earn their first ever place in an European final. For Trevor Francis, transferred from Birmingham the previous winter as Britain's first million pound footballer, the final was his first-ever appearance in Europe. He'd had to sit out earlier rounds in order to qualify.

For Forest, Francis was worth the wait. Seconds before half-time he rose to a superb John Robertson cross to head the only goal of the game. Did that repay a huge slice of Francis's transfer fee, Clough was asked afterwards. No, came the reply, John Robertson was my man of the match and he only cost ten bob.

The following season roles were reversed as Forest entered the competition as holders and Liverpool back in their familiar position of League champions. The two avoided each other in the

1973-74 **FC MAGDEBURG**
Final: Rotterdam 8.5.74 Attendance 5,000
FC Magdeburg (1) **2** **AC Milan** (0) **0**
Lanzi og, Seguin

1974-75 **DYNAMO KIEV**
Final: Basle 14.5.75 Attendance 13,000
Dynamo Kiev (2) **3** **Ferencvaros** (0) **0**
Onischenko (2), Blochin

1975-76 **ANDERLECHT**
Final: Brussels 5.5.76 Attendance 58,000
Anderlecht (1) **4** **West Ham United** (1) **2**
Rensenbrink 2 (1 pen) — Holland, Robson
Van der Elst 2
West Ham United: Day, Coleman, Bonds, T. Taylor, Lampard (sub A. Taylor), McDowell, Brooking, Paddon, Holland, Jennings, Robson

1976-77 **HAMBURG**
Final: Amsterdam 11.5.77 Attendance 65,000
Hamburg (0) **2** **Anderlecht** (0) **0**
Volkert (pen)
Magath

1977-78 **ANDERLECHT**
Final: Paris 3.5.78 Attendance 48,679
Anderlecht (3) **4** **Wien** (0) **0**
Rensenbrink (2)
Van Binst (2)

1978-79 **BARCELONA**
Basle 16 May 1979 Attendance 50,000
Barcelona (2)(2) **4** **Fortuna Dusseldorf** (2)(2) **3** aet
Sanchez, Asensi, Rexach, Krankl — Klaus Allofs, Seel 2

1979-80 **VALENCIA**
Brussels 14 May 1980 Attendance 40,000
Valencia (0) **0** **Arsenal** (0) **0** aet
Valencia won 5-4 on pens
Arsenal: Jennings, Rice, Nelson, Talbot, O'Leary, Young, Brady, Sunderland, Stapleton, Price (sub Hollins), Rix

1980-81 **DYNAMO TBLISI**
Dusseldorf 13 May 1981 Attendance 9,000
Dynamo Tblisi (0) **2** **Carl Zeiss Jena** (0) **1**
Gutsayev, Daraselia — Hoppe

1981-82 **BARCELONA**
Barcelona 12 May 1982 Attendance 100,000
Barcelona (1) **2** **Standard Liege** (1) **1**
Simonsen, Quini — Vandermissen

1982-83 **ABERDEEN**
Gothenburg 11 May 1983 Attendance 17,804
Aberdeen (1) (1) **2** **Real Madrid** (1) (1) **1** aet
Black, Hewitt — Juanito (pen)
Aberdeen: Leighton, Rougvie, McMaster, Cooper, McLeish, Miller, Strachan, Simpson, McGhee, Black (sub Hewitt), Weir
Real Madrid: Augustin, Jean Jose, Camacho, (sub San Jose), Metgod, Bonet, Gallego, Juanito, Angel, Santillana, Stielike, Isidro (sub Salguero)

first round on this occasion but it was of no benefit to Liverpool who fell to the powerful Soviet side Dynamo Tbilisi. Forest ploughed on through a tough series of fixtures, notably against Dynamo Berlin whom they lost against at the City Ground but beat 3-1 away thanks to two goals by Francis, to reach their second consecutive final. But this time there was no Francis. Just as the England player was reaching peak form for the first time in his career, the hard pitches of the English spring caused an achilles tendon injury which kept him out of the game for six months.

Clough told Francis to keep away from the Madrid final for fear that the sight of him on crutches would upset the rest of the squad. The final, which brought Forest up against Kevin Keegan's Hamburg, did little to commend itself to anyone but the most committed Forest fan. An early goal by Robertson, who cut inside Kaltz on the left and scored from 20 yards with his right foot, let Forest sit back on their lead as Keegan became more and more frustrated in his search for an equaliser. After a good first half, he came back looking for the ball and thus hindered rather than helped Hamburg's cause by staying out of the area where he was likely to do any damage. For the third year in succession, the European Cup had been decided by a single goal.

Goals hardly flowed in the Cup Winners' Cup final of 1980 either until Arsenal and Valencia were reduced to a penalty shoot-out. Arsenal had hit the unusually high total of 13 en route but the prospect of a British double in Europe faded when, after a goalless draw, Rix had the unhappy distinction of being the man who missed his spot kick. Arsenal thus gathered the unique record of going through a whole European competition undefeated and still not winning the trophy.

The following year did see the double achieved with Liverpool regaining their European crown from Forest and Ipswich winning the UEFA Cup. This time it was Forest's turn to take a first round knock-out at the hands of CSKA Sofia. But the Bulgarian army side couldn't produce an encore when they met Liverpool in the quarter final, going out 6-1 on aggregate. Liverpool squeezed into their third final thanks to a Ray Kennedy goal in Munich which, with the scores level at 1-1 after a 0-0 draw at Anfield, counted double.

The 1981 final pitted the old masters of Europe against the new. But the Real Madrid vintage of the new decade was poor compared with that of the illustrious fifties. Another dour struggle saw another final decided by one goal, this one coming from Alan Kennedy in the 81st minute. Among the few points of interest was that the opposition again contained an England international though this, like the rest of Laurie Cunningham's Spanish experience, was not the stuff memories are made from.

Liverpool's victory was accomplished with the help of Sammy Lee's hold on Stielike, who once again found himself on the losing side against them. Lee forced the West German international back into his own half and out of the match, a performance like that would have earned most continental youngsters immediate international recognition. Yet it was not until 18 months later, in November 1982, that Lee received his first England cap. Moreover it was the reluctance shown by Ron Greenwood to select young talent which some critics believe was at the root of

the disparity between the performance of British clubs in Europe during the late Seventies and early Eighties and the faltering progress of the national side.

Bobby Robson, who marked his card as a future England manager by guiding Ipswich to such a high level of consistency culminating in their UEFA Cup win over AZ Alkmaar, would soon be putting the theory to the test. When he took over from Greenwood after the 1982 World Cup, Lee was one among several young additions to the England squad.

But 1982 brought a new name on the European Cup. For the sixth year in succession it was British and again it emphasized the paradox of club supremacy and international mediocrity. Aston Villa's triumph was the more remarkable for two reasons: their inexperience in Europe and the events at Villa Park the previous season which had seen the departure of Ron Saunders, the manager who had guided the club to their first championship win in 71 years.

As Liverpool faltered in the quarter-finals against CSKA Sofia, Villa's European novices, under the thoughtful guidance of their former coach, Tony Barton, powered on. Their only two previous campaigns had been short-lived. They had lost a first round UEFA tie in 1975 and two years later reached the quarter-finals. The road to Rotterdam took in Valur in Iceland, Dynamo Berlin,

Left: The first of Nottingham Forest's European Cup triumphs and a glittering prize for captain John McGovern.

FAIRS CUP WINNERS AND FINALS

1955-58 BARCELONA
First Leg: Stamford Bridge 5.3.58 Attendance 45,466
London (1) **2** **Barcelona** (2) **2**
Greaves, Langley (pen) — Tajada, Martinez
Second Leg: Barcelona 1.5.58 Attendance 62,000
Barcelona (3) **6** **London** (0) **0**
Suarez 2, Evaristo 2, Martinez, Verges
London: **First Leg:** Kelsey (Arsenal); Sillett P. (Chelsea), Langley (Fulham); Blanchflower (Spurs), Norman (Spurs), Coote (Brentford); Groves (Arsenal), Greaves (Chelsea), Smith (Spurs), Haynes (Fulham), Robb (Spurs).
Second Leg: Kelsey (Arsenal); Wright (West Ham), Cantwell (West Ham); Blanchflower (Spurs), Brown (West Ham), Bowen (Arsenal); Medwin (Spurs), Groves (Arsenal), Smith (Spurs), Bloomfield (Arsenal), Lewis (Chelsea).

1958-60 BARCELONA
First Leg: Birmingham 29.3.60 Attendance 40,500
Birmingham City (0) **0** **Barcelona** (0) **0**
Second Leg: Barcelona 4.5.60 Attendance 70,000
Barcelona (2) **4** **Birmingham City** (0) **1**
Martinez, Czibor 2, Coll — Hooper

1960-61 AS ROMA
First Leg: Birmingham 27.9.61 Attendance 21,005
Birmingham City (0) **2** **AS Roma** (1) **2**
Hellawell, Orritt — Manfredini 2
Second Leg: Rome 11.10.61 Attendance 60,000
AS Roma (0) **2** **Birmingham City** (0) **0**
Farmer (og), Pestrin

1961-62 VALENCIA
First Leg: Valencia 8.9.62 Attendance 65,000
Valencia **6** **Barcelona** **2**
Second Leg: Barcelona 12.9.62 Attendance 60,000
Barcelona **1** **Valencia** **1**

1962-63 VALENCIA
First Leg: Zagreb 12.6.63 Attendance 40,000
Dynamo Zagreb (1) **1** **Valencia** (0) **2**
Zambata — Waldo, Urtiaga
Second Leg: Valencia 26.6.63 Attendance 55,000
Valencia **2** **Dynamo Zagreb** **0**
Mano, Nunez

1963-64 REAL ZARAGOZA
Final: Barcelona 24.6.64 Attendance 50,000
Real Zaragoza (1) **2** **Valencia** (1) **1**
Villa, Marcelino — Urtiaga

1964-65 FERENCVAROS
Final: Turin 23.6.65 Attendance 25,000
Ferencvaros (1) **1** **Juventus** (0) **0**
Fenyvesi

1965-66 BARCELONA
First Leg: Barcelona 14.9.66 Attendance 70,000
Barcelona (0) **0** **Real Zaragoza** (1) **1**
Canario
Second Leg: Zaragoza 21.9.66 Attendance 70,000
Real Zaragoza (1) **2** **Barcelona** (1) **4**
Marcelino 2 — Pujol 3, Zaballa

1966-67 DYNAMO ZAGREB
First Leg: Zagreb 30.8.67 Attendance 40,000
Dynamo Zagreb (1) **2** **Leeds United** (0) **0**
Cercer 2
Second Leg: Leeds 6.9.67 Attendance 35,604
Leeds United (0) **0** **Dynamo Zagreb** (0) **0**

1967-68 LEEDS UNITED
First Leg: Leeds 7.8.68 Attendance 25,368
Leeds United (1) **1** **Ferencvaros** (0) **0**
Jones
Second Leg: Budapest 11.9.68 Attendance 70,000
Ferencvaros (0) **0** **Leeds United** (0) **0**
Leeds United: Sprake; Reaney, Cooper, Bremner, Charlton, Hunter, Lorimer, Madeley, Jones, Giles (sub Hibbitt), Gray (sub O'Grady).

1968-69 NEWCASTLE UNITED
First Leg: Newcastle 29.5.69 Attendance 60,000
Newcastle United (0) **3** **Ujpest Dozsa** (0) **0**
Moncur 2, Scott
Second Leg: Budapest 11.6.69 Attendance 37,000
Ujpest Dozsa (2) **2** **Newcastle United** (0) **3**
Bene, Gorocs — Moncur, Arentoft, Foggon
Newcastle United: McFaul; Craig, Clark, Gibb, Burton, Moncur, Scott, Robson, Davies, Arentoft, Sinclair. (Foggon substituted for Scott in first leg and for Sinclair in second leg).

1969-70 ARSENAL
First Leg: Brussels 22.4.70 Attendance 37,000
Anderlecht (2) **3** **Arsenal** (0) **1**
Devrindt, Mulder 2 — Kennedy
Second Leg: London 28.4.70 Attendance 51,612
Arsenal (1) **3** **Anderlecht** (0) **0**
Kelly, Radford, Sammels
Arsenal: Wilson; Storey, McNab, Kelly, McLintock, Simpson, Armstrong, Sammels, Radford, George (sub Kennedy in first leg), Graham.

1970-71 LEEDS UNITED
First Leg: Turin 26.5.71 Attendance 65,000
Juventus (0) **0** **Leeds United** (0) **0**
(game abandoned after 51 minutes)
Turin 28.5.71 Attendance 65,000
Juventus (1) **2** **Leeds United** (0) **2**
Bettega, Capello — Madeley, Bates
Second Leg: Leeds 3.6.71 Attendance 42,483
Leeds United (1) **1** **Juventus** (1) **1**
Clarke — Anastasi
Leeds United: Sprake; Reaney, Cooper, Bremner, Charlton, Hunter, Lorimer, Clarke, Jones (sub Bates in first leg), Giles, Madeley (sub Bates in second leg).
(Leeds won on the 'away goals count double' rule).

Dynamo Kiev and Anderlecht, where crowd disturbances by spectators almost lost Villa a hard-earned place in the final.

Villa arrived in Rotterdam very much the underdogs against a Bayern Munich side containing the most potent constituents of the West German World Cup squad. But every underdog has his day and Bayern, admittedly hampered by having European Footballer of the Year Karl-Heinz Rummenigge less than fully fit, failed to take advantage of their domination.

Bayern's lapse was the more astonishing for the fact that Villa lost their goalkeeper, Jimmy Rimmer, after ten minutes and played the rest of the game with their goal in the brave but untested hands of a teenager. Nineteen-year-old Nigel Spink rose to the occasion with a series of crucial saves as Bayern turned the screw on the Villa defence. McNaught and Evans dominated the aerial battle with Rummenigge and the game hinged on one moment of brilliance by Villa winger Tony Morley. Scorer of a brilliant solo match-winner against Anderlecht in the semi-final, Morley sliced through the German defence with the speed of forked lightning and sent over the low cross from which Withe miss-hit Villa's winner. The ball went in off the far post in a better turn of luck than the England centre-forward enjoyed on his international debut against Brazil twelve months earlier, when a similar shot rebounded back into play. Jimmy Rimmer, on the subs' bench for Manchester United in 1968, thus won his second European Cup winners' medal having played only ten minutes out of 180.

Another British victory, the sixth in succession, and the fifth decided by one goal. Application, 90-minute fitness, stamina, the supremacy of British physical attributes over European craft, these are some of the reasons put forward for the reign of Liverpool, Forest and Villa. But the role of the manager must also be taken into account. These victories were symptomatic of the way managers, or in European terms, coaches, have taken over the British game. These are the days of the spy, tactician, organizing general. Perhaps their origins go back to Don Revie and the day of the dossier. After all, didn't Leeds patent the 1-0 win?

UEFA CUP WINNERS AND FINALS

1971-72 TOTTENHAM HOTSPUR
First Leg: Wolverhampton 3.5.72 Attendance 45,000
Wolverhampton Wanderers (0) 1 **Tottenham Hotspur** (0) 2
McCalliog; Chivers 2
Second Leg: Tottenham 17.5.72 Attendance 48,000
Tottenham Hotspur (1) 1 **Wolverhampton Wanderers** (0) 1
Mullery; Wagstaffe
Tottenham Hotspur: Jennings, Kinnear, Knowles, Mullery, England, Beal, Coates (sub Pratt in first leg), Perryman, Chivers, Peters, Gilzean

1972-73 LIVERPOOL
First Leg: Liverpool 10.5.73 Attendance 41,169
Liverpool (3) 3 **Borussia Monchengladbach** (0) 0
Keegan 2, Lloyd
Second Leg: Monchengladbach 23.5.73 Attendance 35,000
Borussia Monchengladbach (2) 2 **Liverpool** (0) 0
Liverpool: Clemence, Lawler, Lindsay, Smith, Lloyd, Hughes, Keegan, Cormack, Toshack, Heighway (sub Hall in first leg, Boersma in second leg), Callaghan

1973-74 FEYENOORD
First Leg: Tottenham 21.5.74 Attendance 46,281
Tottenham Hotspur (1) 2 **Feyenoord** (1) 2
England, Van Daele og; Van Hanegem, De Jong
Second Leg: Rotterdam 29.5.74 Attendance 68,000
Feyenoord (1) 2 **Tottenham Hotspur** (0) 0
Rijsbergen, Ressel

1974-75 BORUSSIA MONCHENGLADBACH
First Leg: Dusseldorf 7.5.75 Attendance 45,000
Borussia Monchengladbach (0) 0 **Twente Enschede** (0) 0
Second Leg: Enschede 21.5.75 Attendance 24,500
Twente Enschede (0) 1 **Borussia Monchengladbach** (2) 5
Drost; Heynckes 3, Simonsen 2 (1 pen.)

1975-76 LIVERPOOL
First Leg: Liverpool 28.4.76 Attendance 56,000
Liverpool (0) 3 **Bruges** (2) 2
Kennedy, Case, Keegan (pen); Lambert, Cools
Second Leg: Bruges 19.5.76 Attendance 32,000
Bruges (1) 1 **Liverpool** (1) 1
Keegan; Lambert (pen)
Liverpool: Clemence, Smith, Neal, Thompson, Kennedy, Hughes, Keegan, Case (Fairclough played in first leg), Heighway, Toshack (sub Case first leg, sub Fairclough second leg), Callaghan

1976-77 JUVENTUS
First Leg: Turin 4.5.77 Attendance 75,000
Juventus (1) 1 **Athletico Bilbao** (0) 0
Tardelli
Second Leg: Bilbao 18.5.77 Attendance 43,000
Athletico Bilbao (1) 2 **Juventus** (1) 1
Irureta, Carlos; Bettega

1977-78 PSV EINDHOVEN
First Leg: Corsica 26.4.78 Attendance 15,000
Bastia (0) 0 **PSV Eindhoven** (0) 0
Second Leg: Eindhoven 9.5.78 Attendance 27,000
PSV Eindhoven (1) 3 **Bastia** (0) 0
W. Van der Kerkhof, Deijkers, Van der Kuylen

1978-79 BORUSSIA MOENCHENGLADBACH
First leg Belgrade 9 May 1979 Attendance 87,500
Red Star Belgrade (1) 1 **Borussia Moenchen.** (0) 1
Sestic; Juristic og
Second leg Dusseldorf 23 May 1979 Attendance 54,000
Borussia Moenchen. (1) 1 **Red Star Belgrade** (0) 0
Simonsen pen

1979-80 EINTRACHT FRANKFURT
First leg Moenchengladbach 7 May 1980 Attendance 25,000
Borussia Moenchen. (1) 3 **Eintracht** (1) 2
Kulik 2, Matthaus; Karger, Holzenbein
Second leg Frankfurt 21 May 1980 Attendance 60,000
Eintracht (0) 1 **Borussia Moenchen.** (0) 0
Schaub
Eintracht won on away goals

1980-81 IPSWICH TOWN
First leg Ipswich 6 May 1981 Attendance 27,532
Ipswich (1) 3 **AZ 67 Alkmaar** (0) 0
Wark pen, Thijssen, Mariner
Second leg Amsterdam 20 May 1981 Attendance 28,500
AZ 67 Alkmaar (3) 4 **Ipswich** (2) 2
Welzl, Metgod, Tol, Jonker; Thijssen, Wark
Ipswich: Cooper, Mills, McCall, Thijssen, Osman, Butcher, Wark, Muhren, Mariner, Brazil, Gates

1981-82 IFK GOTHENBURG
First leg Gothenburg 5 May 1982 Attendance 42,548
IFK Gothenburg (0) 1 **SV Hamburg** (0) 0
Tord Holmgren
Second leg Hamburg 19 May 1982 Attendance 60,000
SV Hamburg (0) 0 **IFK Gothenburg** (1) 3
Corneliusson, Nilsson, Fredriksson pen

1982-83 ANDERLECHT
First leg Brussels 4 May 1983 Attendance 55,000
Anderlecht (1) 1 **Benfica** (1) 0
Brylle
Second leg Lisbon 18 May 1983 Attendance 80,000
Benfica (1) 1 **Anderlecht** (1) 1
Sheu; Lozano

THE WORLD CUP

With just one week of the 1982 World Cup remaining there were only six teams still in contention for the trophy. Three of the four favourites—Brazil, Argentina and Russia—were out and left were West Germany, Italy, France, Poland, England and Northern Ireland. England had already gone ten games undefeated, a 0-0 draw with West Germany coming after a modern record of a nine consecutive wins. Northern Ireland had arrived in Spain after a disastrous build-up and yet had gone on to draw with Yugoslavia and Honduras and then, in probably the best display in her history, beat hosts Spain 1-0 in Valencia. A 2-2 draw with Austria in the second group left the Irish needing to beat France to reach the semi-finals. England, in her turn, needed to defeat Spain by two clear goals to reach the same stage—certainly a possibility as Spain had conceded at least one goal to each of her opponents so far.

Twenty-four hours later the dreams were in tatters. Ireland went out bravely, 4-1 to France, although had an early and entirely legitimate Martin O'Neill goal not been ruled out by the now traditionally incompetent linesman the result might have been different. The only time Northern Ireland had progressed so far, to the quarter-finals in 1958, they had also been beaten by France, 4-0. For England the disappointment was far greater. Not only did they become the one team to fail to score against Spain in the competition, but they struggled to a goalless draw and Kevin Keegan and Trevor Brooking, the heroes of Budapest a year before, missed two easy chances just before the end which would have put their side through.

England hence finished a series which had started so well, and declined thereafter, with two tedious goalless draws. They did, however, manage to go out of the competition undefeated, a distinction they thus now shared with the unlikely company of Scotland (1974), Brazil (1978), and the Cameroons (1982).

For Scotland 1982 yet again reeked of might-have-beens. For the third consecutive tournament they went out at the first stage on goal difference. On each occasion they went home kicking themselves, with myriads of sportswriters crystallizing age-old thoughts about the Scottish urge for self-destruction. In 1974 they had drawn with Brazil and Yugoslavia and had failed because they had been too cautious in defeating Zaire. The 2-0 defeat of the Africans was actually Scotland's first ever win in the World Cup finals, a full 24 years after her first entry. In 1978 they suffered the nightmare of defeat by Peru, an absurd draw with Iran (courtesy of a comical own goal) and then a face-saving defeat of eventual finalists Holland.

In 1982 they would have gone further *if* they had not conceded two goals to New Zealand (though scoring five) or, perhaps, if they had managed slightly better against the defeatable Russians. Another almost comical mix up between Danny McGrain and Willie Miller allowed Shengelia to score Russia's second goal and Souness's late equalizer was not enough. The fact remained that the Scots defence had let them down—of the 24 teams only El Salvador, Chile and New Zealand conceded more goals, though only Brazil and Hungary scored more. A side which had for some time looked the best in the British Isles was off home early yet again. Remarkably, Northern Ireland have still won as many games (three) in the final stages as Scotland and even Wales have a better, 50 per cent, record (one win, three draws and a 1-0 defeat by Brazil).

All in all, the 1982 World Cup was not kind to the Scots. They were originally drawn in the same group as Argentina (the other members would have been Hungary and El Salvador), but a chaotic mix-up by the organizers caused them to be redrawn into an even tougher group. They should certainly have qualified from that original choice—though the World Cup committee must have had the qualities of a fortune teller. If the group had not been redrawn, then the opening match would have featured Scotland and Argentina, an impossibility given the recent conclusion of the Falklands War. As it was, BBC and ITV struck a major blow for freedom and democracy by refusing to show the opening match (Belgium beat Argentina 1-0). Their decision was not entirely comprehensible—no one ever managed to decide what would logically follow if Argentina reached the final—but it perhaps made more sense than the Argentinian televised showing of games including the British teams, where they were described as 'the red-shirted side' or 'the ones with green shorts' throughout.

It was all, perhaps, a reflection of the gradual decline of the appeal, style, sportsmanship and enjoyment in the World Cup—ultimately epitomized by Spain's appalling fouls and their craven acceptance by more-than-dubious referees. Back in 1950, when the home countries had finally condescended to enter a competition then already 20 years old, things were very different. Well, in some ways different and in some ways the same. The Scots rather set the tone for the next few years by refusing to travel to Brazil unless they finished top in the Home International Championship. They didn't, and despite firm and friendly pleas from both England and the organizing committee, the Scots stayed at home.

England probably wished they had too after a 1-0 defeat by the impossibly unfancied United States at Belo Horizonte. England beat Chile 2-0 but lost 1-0 to Spain and were soon home. Four years later the Scots at least managed to reach Switzerland but collapsed in even less dignified fashion when manager Andy Beattie resigned during the competition and his side suffered their second heaviest defeat ever—7-0 to Uruguay. England also went out to the Uruguayans, 4-2, but their's was not a bad performance following a 4-4 draw with Belgium and a 2-0 defeat of their Swiss hosts.

But 1958 was a golden year for the Home Countries when all four reached Sweden. Oddly, it was the Welsh and Irish who reached the quarter-finals. Terry Medwin scored Wales' vital goal against 1954 finalists Hungary to take his country through in a play-off while Northern Ireland twice defeated Czechoslovakia and drew 2-2 with champions West Germany. England went out after a play-off against Russia (though they held Brazil 0-0) while Scotland stumbled to defeats by France and Paraguay (South American teams beginning with P are not the Scots forte) and a draw with Yugoslavia. Wales fought bravely against Brazil in the quarter-finals, losing only 1-0 to a Pele goal, while the injury-struck Irish went out 4-0 to the free-scoring French.

In Chile in 1962 England went alone, beat Argentina and drew with Bulgaria in the qualifying groups but yet again met Brazil and lost 3-1 in the quarter-finals. 1966 and all that is too well documented to need any further coverage here, but 1970 followed the pattern of 1962 and 1966 in that only England actually went to Mexico.

She probably sent her most powerful squad ever and most would argue that the side was better than that of 1966. A very tight 1-0 defeat by Brazil (living forever in the memory as the match of Banks' save and Astle's miss) followed victories over Romania and the Czechs. The disastrous quarter-final was a game in a million. It was England's best performance of the decade, comparable really only with the 1966 semi-final against Portugal. Banks' illness, Bonetti's fumble of Beckenbauer's shot with only a

Trevor Francis comes in for the less than affectionate attentions of West German sweeper Uli Stielike during the England v West Germany clash in Madrid during the 1982 World Cup finals. After an excellent start, which saw three wins in the first qualifying group and a modern-day record of nine consecutive international victories, England proved a great disappointment in the second groups. Her two games, against the Germans and hosts Spain, did not produce a single goal and England went out of the competition, like the Cameroons, undefeated.

few minutes left, Seeler's absolute fluke back-header and Ramsey's unfortunate substitutions were a tragic confluence of misfortune on the world stage. It was not a defeat for which anyone should really be blamed—just proof that a game is never lost until it is won and that luck must still play its part.

The next two World Cups were almost a reaction to the success of 1966 and 1970 as far as England were concerned. For the first times ever she failed to qualify—though on both occasions by the finest of margins against teams destined to finish third and fourth in the finals. The deciding game against Poland at Wembley in 1973 was probably the most exciting seen at international level in Britain in two decades—it had everything, including tragedy, despair and the end of an era, that of Alf Ramsey. In 1978 Italy won in Rome and lost in London, but the group was decided on goal difference and England's inability to score often enough against Luxembourg. Again the Scots went alone, and it was not until 1982 that the Irish made another appearance on the World stage.

Their qualification was singularly unimpressive—nine points from eight games and only six goals scored—but England's was hardly any better. Only a fluke win by the Swiss in Bucharest took England to the World Cup draw at all after appalling defeats in Basel and Oslo, and Ron Greenwood showed his gratitude by wearing a Swiss FA tie at the Madrid draw. When England were drawn (amazingly, as a seed) to play in Bilbao, they had one of the worst recent records in Europe. Of the European sides only Finland, Malta, Norway, Cyprus, Albania, Luxembourg and Turkey had performed less impressively in terms of results in the previous year. And yet England turned over a new leaf after her humiliating defeat in Oslo on 9 September 1981 and won nine consecutive matches. In effect, it was the best run in her history. In 1908-9 there had been ten consecutive wins, but seven of them had been against the then amateur sides of Austria, Hungary and Bohemia. She remained undefeated for over a year (until West Germany won 2-1 at Wembley in October 1982) but this remarkable achievement was somehow overshadowed by the end of that World Cup campaign.

It had started well enough. After 27 seconds Bryan Robson celebrated the fastest goal in World Cup history and England's return to the arena after twelve barren years since Leon and the West Germans. Against eventual (and unlucky) semi-finalists, France, England won convincingly 3-1. They were less sure against Czechoslovakia, winning 2-0 with a gift and an own-goal, but it was good enough. A 1-0 win against Kuwait, via England's best goal of the tournament by Trevor Francis, gave them one of only two 100 per cent records (the other was Brazil's) in the first groups.

After that things deteriorated. A decisive midfield spluttered against West Germany. The decision to play Graham Rix on an Arsenal left-side with Kenny Sansom looked worse by the match. The forwards failed to take their chances and, by the time England realized the match was there for the taking, the chance had gone and England were lucky to stay in at all when a half-fit Rummenigge hit the bar from 25-yards. Germany beat Spain 2-1 and believed they had done enough. They were right. On a despairing Monday night, England spluttered and finally misfired against a demoralized home-side, now out, and just wanting to hide in a corner as soon as possible. Competent displays against Scotland, France and the Czechs were forgotten; the ghost of th Norwegians returned. Kevin Keegan and Trevor Brooking cam on as subs at the end to revive memories of Budapest, but Keega ended his international career with an appalling miss from a cros he would have converted 99 times out of 100 a few years before.

It was all over. Another goalless draw and the disenchantmen of the 1970s was back again, overlaying the brief hopes that ha burst into flame. There was Northern Ireland's performance t celebrate, but a country of one and a half million was never goin to win the World Cup—it was like cheering the giant killer in th third round of the FA Cup.

England and Scotland could at least look forward to 1986 wherever that World Cup was to be held, and reflect, perhaps that no-one had given Italy a chance one month before.

***Below:** The crowning achievement of Irish football history probabl came in Valencia during her 1982 World Cup first group game against hosts Spain. Despite a vicious performance from opponents desperate to win the match, appallingly poor refereeing and Mal Donaghy being sent off, the Irish defeated Spain 1-0 with a Gerry Armstrong goal. The Irish spent much of the match in defence—in this picture John McClelland, Gerry Armstrong, Billy Hamilton and Chris Nicholl fend off Jesus Satrustegui at a corner. Both Armstrong and Hamilton, particularly after his two goals against Austria, became internationally recognized personalities and both featured prominently in many of the 'Best Players of the Tournament' polls afterwards.*

The Clubs

Club information is correct at 1 January 1983 but note that Most League Points section is based on two points for a win system only. In some cases the strips featured are the traditional club colours and do not incorporate such fashions as thin vertical lines, which, like the rash of manufacturers' symbols which appeared on shirts around 1980, are unlikely to be permanent features.

Key

q — qualifying rounds/competition
P — promoted
R — relegated
IIIS — Third Division South
IIIN — Third Division North
C — Football/Scottish League champions
p — preliminary round
L — failed to gain re-election

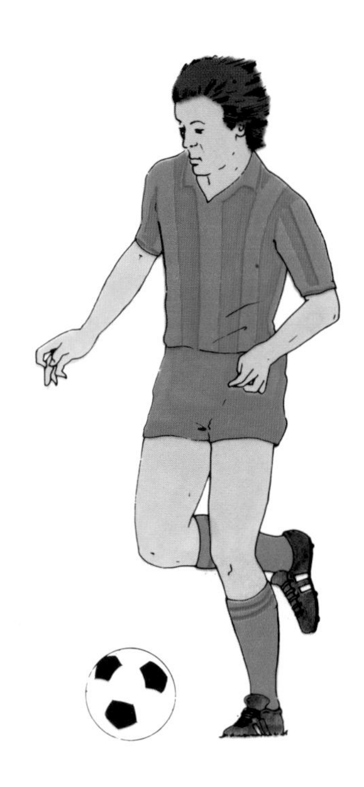

ALDERSHOT

Founded: 1926
Address: Recreation Ground, High Street, Aldershot
Telephone: Aldershot 20211
Ground capacity: 16,000
Playing area: 117 by 76 yards
Record attendance: 19,138 v Carlisle United, FA Cup 4th round replay, 28.1.70
Record victory: 8-1 v Gateshead, Division IV, 1958-59
Record defeat: 0-9 v Bristol City, Division III(S), 28.12.46
Most League points: 56, Division IV, 1972-73
Most League goals: 83, Division IV, 1963-64
League scoring record: 26, John Dungworth, Division IV, 1978-79
Record League aggregate: 172, Jack Howarth, 1965-77
Most League appearances: 450, Len Walker, 1964-76
Most capped player: 1 (10 in all), Peter Scott, Northern Ireland.

THE ALDERSHOT RECORD

	Division & place	*Cup round reached*			
1933	SIII 17	5	1962	IV 7	2
1934	SIII 14	3	1963	IV 11	2
1935	SIII 18	3	1964	IV 9	4
1936	SIII 11	1	1965	IV 18	2
1937	SIII 22	1	1966	IV 17	2
1938	SIII 18	3	1967	IV 10	3
1939	SIII 10	2	1968	IV 9	1
1946		4	1969	IV 15	1
1947	SIII 20	2	1970	IV 6	4
1948	SIII 19	2	1971	IV 13	3
1949	SIII 21	3	1972	IV 17	2
1950	SIII 20	1	1973	IV 4P	2
1951	SIII 18	3	1974	III 8	2
1952	SIII 12	2	1975	III 20	1
1953	SIII 19	1	1976	III 21R	3
1954	SIII 17	2	1977	IV 17	1
1955	SIII 14	2	1978	IV 5	1
1956	SIII 15	3	1979	IV 5	5
1957	SIII 19	1	1980	IV 10	3
1958	SIII 18	3	1981	IV 6	1
1959	IV 22	1	1982	IV 16	2
1960	IV 13	1			
1961	IV 10	4			

ARSENAL

Founded: 1886
Address: Arsenal Stadium, Highbury, London N.5
Telephone: (01) 226 0304
Ground capacity: 60,000
Playing area: 110 by 71 yards
Record attendance: 73,295 v Sunderland, Division 1, 9.3.35
Record victory: 12-0 v Loughborough Town, Division II, 12.3.1900
Record defeat: 0-8 v Loughborough Town, Division II, 12.12.96
Most League points: 66, Division I, 1930-31
Most League goals: 127, Division I, 1930-31
League scoring record: 42, Ted Drake, Division I, 1934-35
Record League aggregate: 150, Cliff Bastin, 1930-1947
Most League appearances: 500, George Armstrong, 1960-1977
Most capped player: 49 Pat Rice, Northern Ireland

FA Cup	*Year*	*Opponents*	*Score*	*Scorers*
Winners	1930	Huddersfield Town	2-0	James, Lambert
	1936	Sheffield United	1-0	Drake
	1950	Liverpool	2-0	Lewis 2
	1971	Liverpool	*2-1	Kelly, George
	1979	Manchester United	3-2	Talbot, Stapleton, Sunderland
Runners-up	1927	Cardiff City	0-1	
	1932	Newcastle United	1-2	John
	1952	Newcastle United	0-1	
	1972	Leeds United	0-1	
	1978	Ipswich Town	0-1	
	1980	West Ham	0-1	
League Cup				
Runners-up	1968	Leeds United	0-1	
	1969	Swindon Town	*1-3	Gould

* – after extra time

THE ARSENAL RECORD

	Division & place	*Cup round reached*			
1890		q	1937	I 3	q-f
1891		1	1938	I 1C	5
1892		1	1939	I 5	3
1893		1	1946		3
1894	II 9	1	1947	I 13	3
1895	II 8	1	1948	I 1C	3
1896	II 7	1	1949	I 5	4
1897	II 10	q	1950	I 6	Winners
1898	II 5	1	1951	I 5	5
1899	II 7	1	1952	I 3	Final
1900	II 8	q	1953	I 1C	q-f
1901	II 7	2	1954	I 12	4
1902	II 4	1	1955	I 9	4
1903	II 3	1	1956	I 5	q-f
1904	II 2P	2	1957	I 5	q-f
1905	I 10	1	1958	I 12	3
1906	I 12	s-f	1959	I 3	5
1907	I 7	s-f	1960	I 13	3
1908	I 14	1	1961	I 11	3
1909	I 6	2	1962	I 10	4
1910	I 18	2	1963	I 7	5
1911	I 10	2	1964	I 8	5
1912	I 10	1	1965	I 13	4
1913	I 20R	2	1966	I 14	3
1914	II 3	1	1967	I 7	5
1915	II 5 P	2	1968	I 9	5
1920	I 11	2	1969	I 4	5
1921	I 9	1	1970	I 12	3
1922	I 17	q-f	1971	I 1C	Winners
1923	I 11	1	1972	I 5	Final
1924	I 19	2	1973	I 2	s-f
1925	I 20	1	1974	I 10	4
1926	I 2	q-f	1975	I 16	q-f
1927	I 11	Final	1976	I 17	3
1928	I 10	s-f	1977	I 8	5
1929	I 9	q-f	1978	I 5	Final
1930	I 14	Winners	1979	I 7	Winners
1931	I 1C	4	1980	I 4	Final
1932	I 2	Final	1981	I 5	3
1933	I 1C	3	1982	I 5	3
1934	I 1C	q-f			
1935	I 1C	q-f			
1936	I 6	Winners			

ASTON VILLA

Founded: 1874
Address: Villa Park, Trinity Road, Birmingham 6
Telephone: (021) 327 6604
Ground capacity: 48,000
Playing area: 115 by 75 yards
Record attendance: 76,588 v Derby County, FA Cup quarter-final, 2.3.46
Record victory: 13-0 v Wednesday Old Alliance, FA Cup 1st round, 30.10.86
Record defeat: 1-8 v Blackburn Rovers, FA Cup 3rd round, 1888-89
Most League points: 70, Division III, 1971-72
Most League goals: 128, Division I, 1930-31
League scoring record: 49, Pongo Waring, Division I, 1930-31
Record League aggregate: 213, Harry Hampton, 1904-1920
and Billy Walker, 1919-1934
Most League appearances: 560, Charlie Aitken, 1961-76
Most capped player: 33 (34 in all), Peter McParland, Northern Ireland

	Year	*Opponents*	*Score*	*Scorers*
FA Cup *Winners*	1887	West Bromwich Albion	2-0	Hodgetts, Hunter
	1895	West Bromwich Albion	1-0	Chatt
	1897	Everton	3-2	Campbell, Wheldon, Crabtree
	1905	Newcastle United	2-0	Hampton 2
	1913	Sunderland	1-0	Barber
	1920	Huddersfield Town	1-0	Kirton
	1957	Manchester United	2-1	McParland 2
Runners-up	1892	West Bromwich Albion	0-3	
	1924	Newcastle United	0-2	
League Cup *Winners*	1961	Rotherham United	A0-2 H3-0	O'Neill, Burrows, McParland
	1975	Norwich City	1-0	Graydon
	1977	Everton	0-0	
		Replay	*1-1	Kenyon og
		Replay	*3-2	Nicholl, Little 2
Runners-up	1963	Birmingham City	A1-3 H0-0	Thomson
	1971	Tottenham Hotspur	0-2	

*after extra time

THE VILLA RECORD

	Division & place	*Cup round reached*
1880		3
1881		4
1882		4
1883		q-f
1884		4
1885		3
1886		2
1887		Winners
1888		1
1889	I 2	q-f
1890	I 8	2
1891	I 9	2
1892	I 4	Final
1893	I 4	1
1894	I 1C	q-f
1895	I 3	Winners
1896	I 1C	1
1897	I 1C	Winners
1898	I 6	1
1899	I 1C	1
1900	I 1C	q-f
1901	I 15	s-f
1902	I 8	1
1903	I 2	s-f
1904	I 5	2
1905	I 4	Winners
1906	I 8	3
1907	I 5	2
1908	I 2	3
1909	I 7	1
1910	I 1C	3
1911	I 2	2
1912	I 6	2
1913	I 2	Winners
1914	I 2	s-f
1915	I 13	2
1920	I 9	Winners
1921	I 10	q-f
1922	I 5	q-f
1923	I 6	1
1924	I 6	Final
1925	I 15	3
1926	I 6	5
1927	I 10	3
1928	I 8	5
1929	I 3	s-f
1930	I 4	q-f
1931	I 2	3
1932	I 5	4
1933	I 2	4
1934	I 13	s-f
1935	I 13	3
1936	I 21R	3
1937	II 9	3
1938	II 1P	s-f
1939	I 12	4
1946		q-f
1947	I 8	3
1948	I 6	3
1949	I 10	4
1950	I 12	3
1951	I 15	4
1952	I 6	3
1953	I 11	q-f
1954	I 13	3
1955	I 6	4
1956	I 20	4
1957	I 10	Winners
1958	I 14	3
1959	I 21R	s-f
1960	II 1P	s-f
1961	I 9	5
1962	I 7	q-f
1963	I 15	4
1964	I 19	3
1965	I 16	5
1966	I 16	3
1967	I 21R	4
1968	II 16	4
1969	II 18	5
1970	II 21R	3
1971	III 4	1
1972	III 1P	1
1973	II 3	3
1974	II 14	5
1975	II 2P	5
1976	I 16	3
1977	I 4	q-f
1978	I 8	3
1979	I 8	3
1980	I 7	q-f
1981	I 1C	3
1982	I 11	5

BARNSLEY

Formed: 1887 (as Barnsley St Peter's)
Address: Oakwell Ground, Grove Street, Barnsley, Yorkshire
Telephone: 0226 295353
Ground capacity: 35,500
Playing area: 111 by 75 yards
Record attendance: 40,255 v Stoke City, FA Cup 5th round, 15.2.36
Record victory: 9-0 v Loughborough Town, Division II, 28.1.1899
9-0 v Accrington Stanley, Division III(N), 3.2.34
Record defeat: 0-9 v Notts County, Division II, 19.11.27
Most League points: 67, Division III(N), 1938-39
Most League goals: 118, Division III(N), 1933-34
League scoring record: 33, Cecil McCormack, Division II, 1950-51
Record League aggregate: 123, Ernest Hine, 1921-1926 and 1934-1938
Most League appearances: 514, Barry Murphy, 1962-1978
Most capped player: 9 (15 in all), Eddie McMorran, Ireland

FA Cup

	Year	*Opponents*	*Score*	*Scorers*
Winners	1912	West Bromwich Albion	0-0	
		Replay	1-0	Tufnell
Runners-up	1910	Newcastle United	1-1	Tufnell
		Replay	0-2	

THE BARNSLEY RECORD

	Division & place	*Cup round reached*
1895		1
1896		p
1897		1
1898		p
1899	II 11	1
1900	II 16	p
1901	II 15	p
1902	II 11	p
1903	II 8	2
1904	II 8	1
1905	II 7	1
1906	II 12	2
1907	II 8	q-f
1908	II 16	1
1909	II 17	1
1910	II 9	Final
1911	II 19	2
1912	II 6	Winners
1913	II 4	2
1914	II 5	1
1915	II 3	1
1920	II 12	2
1921	II 16	1
1922	II 3	3
1923	II 9	2
1924	II 11	1
1925	II 15	2
1926	II 18	1
1927	II 11	4
1928	II 14	3
1929	II 16	3
1930	II 17	3
1931	II 19	5
1932	II 21R	3
1933	NIII 8	3
1934	NIII 1P	1
1935	II 16	3
1936	II 20	q-f
1937	II 14	3
1938	II 21R	4
1939	NIII 1P	3
1946		5
1947	II 10	4
1948	II 12	3
1949	II 9	3
1950	II 13	3
1951	II 15	3
1952	II 20	4
1953	II 22R	4
1954	NIII 2	2
1955	NIII 1P	2
1956	II 18	4
1957	II 19	5
1958	II 14	3
1959	II 22R	3
1960	III 17	1
1961	III 8	q-f
1962	III 20	2
1963	III 18	3
1964	III 20	5
1965	III 24R	2
1966	IV 16	2
1967	IV 16	3
1968	IV 2P	1
1969	III 10	3
1970	III 7	3
1971	III 12	2
1972	III 22R	2
1973	IV 14	1
1974	IV 13	2
1975	IV 15	1
1976	IV 12	1
1977	IV 6	2
1978	IV 7	2
1979	IV 4P	2
1980	III 11	2
1981	III 2P	5
1982	II 6	3

BIRMINGHAM CITY

Founded: 1875
Address: St. Andrew's, Birmingham 9
Telephone: (021) 772 0101
Ground capacity: 44,500 (9,000 seated)
Playing area: 115 by 75 yards
Record attendance: 66,844 v Everton, FA Cup 5th round, 11.2.39
Record victory: 12-0 v Walsall Town Swifts, Division II, 17.12.1892
12-0 v Doncaster Rovers, Division II, 11.4.03
Record defeat: 1-9 v Sheffield Wednesday, Division I, 13.12.30
Most League points: 59, Division II, 1947-48
Most League goals: 103, Division II, 1893-94
League scoring record: 33, Walter Abbott, Division II, 1898-99
Record League aggregate: 249, Joe Bradford, Division I, 1920-35
Most capped player: 28, Malcolm Page, Wales
Most League appearances: 486, Gil Merrick, 1946-60

	Year	*Opponents*	*Score*	*Scorers*
FA Cup				
Runners-up	1931	West Bromwich Albion	1-2	Bradford
	1956	Manchester City	1-3	Kinsey
League Cup				
Winners	1963	Aston Villa	h3-1 a0-0	Leek 2, Bloomfield

THE BIRMINGHAM RECORD

	Division & place	*Cup round reached*
1889*		1
1890		2
1891		d
1892		2
1893	II 1	1
1894	II 2P	1
1895	II 12	1
1896	I 15R	1
1897	II 4	1
1898	II 6	q
1899	II 8	2
1900	II 3	q
1901	II 2P	3
1902	I 17R	p
1903	II 2P	1
1904	I 11	p
1905	I 7	1
1906†	I 7	4
1907	I 9	1
1908	I 20R	1
1909	II 11	1
1910	II 20	1
1911	II 16	1
1912	II 12	1
1913	II 3	3
1914	II 14	3
1915	II 6	3
1920	II 5	3
1921	II 1P	1
1922	II 18	§
1923	I 17	1
1924	I 14	2
1925	I 8	3
1926	I 14	4
1927	I 17	4
1928	I 11	5
1929	I 15	4
1930	I 11	4
1931	I 19	Final
1932	I 9	4
1933	I 13	6
1934	I 20	5
1935	I 19	6
1936	I 12	3
1937	I 11	3
1938	I 18	3
1939	I 21R	5
1946††		s-f
1947	II 3	q-f
1948	II 1P	3
1949	I 17	3
1950	I 22R	3
1951	II 4	s-f
1952	II 3	4
1953	II 6	q-f
1954	II 7	4
1955	II 1P	q-f
1956	I 6	Final
1957	I 12	s-f
1958	I 13	3
1959	I 9	5
1960	I 19	3
1961	I 19	5
1962	I 17	3
1963	I 20	3
1964	I 20	3
1965	I 22R	3
1966	II 10	4
1967	II 10	q-f
1968	II 4	s-f
1969	II 7	5
1970	II 18	3
1971	II 9	3
1972	II 2P	s-f
1973	I 10	3
1974	I 19	4
1975	I 17	s-f
1976	I 19	3
1977	I 13	4
1978	I 11	3
1979	I 21R	3
1980	II 3P	5
1981	I 13	4
1982	I 16	3

* – as Small Heath until 1905
† – as Birmingham until 1945
†† – as Birmingham City
§ – did not enter
d – disqualified for fielding an ineligible player

BLACKBURN ROVERS

Founded: 1875
Address: Ewood Park, Blackburn
Telephone: Blackburn 55432
Ground capacity: 25,000
Playing area: 116 by 72 yards
Record attendance: 61,783 v Bolton Wanderers, FA Cup quarter-final, 2.3.29
Record victory: 11-0 v Rossendale United, FA Cup, 1st round, 25.10.1884
Record defeat: 0-8 v Arsenal, Division I, 25.2.33
Most League points: 60, Division III, 1974-75
Most League goals: 114, Division II, 1954-55
League scoring record: 43, Ted Harper, Division I, 1925-26
Record League aggregate: 140, Tom Briggs, 1952-1958
Most League appearances: 580, Ronnie Clayton, 1950-1969
Most capped player: 41, Bob Crompton, England

FA Cup	*Year*	*Opponents*	*Score*	*Scorers*
Winners	1884	Queen's Park	2-1	Brown, Forrest
	1885	Queen's Park	2-0	Forrest, Brown
	1886	West Bromwich Albion	0-0	
			2-0	Sowerbutts, Brown
	1890	Sheffield Wednesday	6-1	Dewar, Southworth, Lofthouse, Townley 3
	1891	Notts County	3-1	Dewar, Southworth, Townley
	1928	Huddersfield Town	3-1	Roscamp 2, McLean
Runners-up	1882	Old Etonians	0-1	
	1960	Wolverhampton Wanderers	0-3	

THE BLACKBURN RECORD

	Division & place	*Cup round reached*
1880		3
1881		2
1882		Final
1883		2
1884		Winners
1885		Winners
1886		Winners
1887		2
1888		2
1889	I 4	s-f
1890	I 3	Winners
1891	I 6	Winners
1892	I 9	2
1893	I 9	s-f
1894	I 4	s-f
1895	I 5	2
1896	I 8	1
1897	I 14	3
1898	I 15	1
1899	I 6	1
1900	I 4	2
1901	I 9	1
1902	I 4	1
1903	I 16	2
1904	I 15	3
1905	I 13	1
1906	I 9	1
1907	I 12	2
1908	I 14	1
1909	I 4	3
1910	I 3	3
1911	I 12	s-f
1912	I 1C	s-f
1913	I 5	q-f
1914	I 1C	3
1915	I 3	1
1920	I 20	1
1921	I 11	1
1922	I 15	3
1923	I 14	2
1924	I 8	1
1925	I 16	s-f
1926	I 12	4
1927	I 18	3
1928	I 12	Winners
1929	I 7	q-f
1930	I 6	5
1931	I 10	5
1932	I 16	4
1933	I 15	4
1934	I 8	3
1935	I 15	5
1936	I 15	5
1936	I 22R	4
1937	II 12	3
1938	II 16	3
1939	II 1P	q-f
1946		3
1947	I 17	5
1948	I 22R	4
1949	II 14	3
1950	II 16	3
1951	II 6	3
1952	II 14	s-f
1953	II 9	3
1954	II 3	4
1955	II 6	3
1956	II 4	5
1957	II 4	3
1958	II 2P	s-f
1959	I 10	4
1960	I 17	Final
1961	I 18	5
1962	I 16	q-f
1963	I 11	3
1964	I 7	5
1965	I 10	3
1966	I 22R	q-f
1967	II 4	3
1968	II 9	3
1969	II 19	5
1970	II 8	3
1971	II 21R	3
1972	III 10	1
1973	III 3	2
1974	III 13	3
1975	III 1P	3
1976	II 15	3
1977	II 12	5
1978	II 5	4
1979	II 22R	4
1980	III 2P	5
1981	II 4	3
1982	II 10	3

BLACKPOOL

Founded: 1887
Address: Bloomfield Road, Blackpool
Telephone: Blackpool 404331
Ground capacity: 18,000
Playing area: 111 by 73 yards
Record attendance: 39,118 v Manchester United, Division I, 19.4.32
Record victory: 10-0 v Lanerossi Vincenza, Anglo-Italian tournament, 10.6.72
Record defeat: 1-10 v Huddersfield Town, Division I, 13.12.30; v Small Heath, Division II, 2.3.01
Most League points: 58, Division II, 1929-30 & 1967-68
Most League goals: 98, Division II, 1929-30
League scoring record: 45, Jimmy Hampson, Division II, 1929-30
Record League aggregate: 247, Jimmy Hampson, 1927-1938
Most League appearances: 568, Jimmy Armfield, 1952-1971
Most capped player: 43, Jimmy Armfield, England

FA Cup	*Year*	*Opponents*	*Score*	*Scorers*
Winners	1953	Bolton Wanderers	4-3	Mortensen 3, Perry
Runners-up	1948	Manchester United	2-4	Shimwell (pen), Mortensen
	1951	Newcastle United	0-2	

THE BLACKPOOL RECORD

	Division & place	*Cup round reached*
1892		1
1893		1
1894		p
1895		p
1896		1
1897	II 8	1
1898	II 11	p
1899	II 16	2
1900*		p
1901	II 12	p
1902	II 12	p
1903	II 14	q
1904	II 15	p
1905	II 15	1
1906	II 14	3
1907	II 13	1
1908	II 15	1
1909	II 20	2
1910	II 12	1
1911	II 9	1
1912	II 14	2
1913	II 20	1
1914	II 16	1
1915	II 10	1
1920	II 4	2
1921	II 4	2
1922	II 19	1
1923	II 5	1
1924	II 4	2
1925	II 17	q-f
1926	II 6	3
1927	II 9	3
1928	II 19	3
1929	II 8	3
1930	II 1P	4
1931	I 20	4
1932	I 20	3
1933	I 22R	5
1934	II 11	4
1935	II 4	3
1936	II 3	4
1937	II 2P	3
1938	I 12	4
1939	I 15	3
1946		4
1947	I 5	3
1948	I 9	Final
1949	I 16	4
1950	I 7	q-f
1951	I 3	Final
1952	I 9	3
1953	I 7	Winners
1954	I 6	5
1955	I 19	3
1956	I 2	3
1957	I 4	5
1958	I 7	3
1959	I 8	q-f
1960	I 11	4
1961	I 20	3
1962	I 13	3
1963	I 13	3
1964	I 18	3
1965	I 17	3
1966	I 13	3
1967	I 22R	3
1968	II 3	4
1969	II 8	3
1970	II 2P	4
1971	I 22R	4
1972	II 6	3
1973	II 7	3
1974	II 5	3
1975	II 7	3
1976	II 10	4
1977	II 5	3
1978	II 20R	3
1979	III 12	2
1980	III 18	1
1981	III 23R	2
1982	IV 12	4

* – failed to obtain re-election in 1899

BOLTON WANDERERS

Founded: 1874
Address: Burnden Park, Bolton, BL3 2QR
Telephone: Bolton 389200
Ground capacity: 43,000
Playing area: 113 by 76 yards
Record attendance: 69,912 v Manchester City, FA Cup 5th round, 18.2.33
Record victory: 13-0 v Sheffield United, FA Cup 2nd round, 1.2.1890
Record defeat: 0-7 v Manchester City, Division I, 21.3.36
Most League points: 61, Division III, 1972-73
Most League goals: 96, Division II, 1934-35
League scoring record: 38, Joe Smith, Division I, 1920-21
Record League aggregate: 255, Nat Lofthouse, 1946-1961
Most League appearances: 519, Eddie Hopkinson, 1956-1970
Most capped player: 33, Nat Lofthouse, England

FA Cup	*Year*	*Opponents*	*Score*	*Scorers*
Winners	1923	West Ham United	2-0	Jack, J R Smith
	1926	Manchester City	1-0	Jack
	1929	Portsmouth	2-0	Butler, Blackmore
	1958	Manchester United	2-0	Lofthouse (2)
Runners-up	1894	Notts County	1-4	Cassidy
	1904	Manchester City	0-1	
	1953	Blackpool	3-4	Lofthouse, Moir, Bell

THE BOLTON WANDERERS RECORD

	Division & place	*Cup round reached*
1882		2
1883		3
1884		4
1885		q
1886		3
1887		q
1888		q
1889	I 5	q
1890	I 9	s-f
1891	I 5	1
1892	I 3	1
1893	I 5	1
1894	I 13	Final
1895	I 10	q-f
1896	I 4	s-f
1897	I 8	2
1898	I 11	q-f
1899	I 17R	1
1900	II 2P	1
1901	I 10	2
1902	I 12	2
1903	I 18R	1
1904	II 7	Final
1905	II 2P	q-f
1906	I 6	1
1907	I 6	3
1908	I 19R	3
1909	II 1P	1
1910	I 20R	1
1911	II 2P	1
1912	I 4	3
1913	I 8	1
1914	I 6	3
1915	I 17	s-f
1920	I 6	1
1921	I 3	1
1922	I 6	2
1923	I 13	Winners
1924	I 4	2
1925	I 3	2
1926	I 8	Winners
1927	I 4	5
1928	I 7	4
1929	I 14	Winners
1930	I 15	3
1931	I 14	4
1932	I 17	3
1933	I 21R	5
1934	II 3	q-f
1935	II 2P	s-f
1936	I 13	3
1937	I 20	5
1938	I 7	3
1939	I 8	3
1946		s-f
1947	I 18	4
1948	I 17	3
1949	I 14	3
1950	I 16	4
1951	I 8	4
1952	I 5	3
1953	I 14	Final
1954	I 5	q-f
1955	I 18	4
1956	I 8	4
1957	I 9	3
1958	I 15	Winners
1959	I 4	q-f
1960	I 6	4
1961	I 18	4
1962	I 11	3
1963	I 18	3
1964	I 21R	4
1965	II 3	5
1966	II 9	4
1967	II 9	4
1968	II 12	3
1969	II 17	4
1970	II 16	3
1971	II 22R	3
1972	III 8	4
1973	III 1P	5
1974	II 11	4
1975	II 10	3
1976	II 4	5
1977	II 4	3
1978	II 1P	5
1979	I 17	3
1980	I 22R	5
1981	II 18	3
1982	II 19	4

AFC BOURNEMOUTH

Founded: 1899 (as Boscombe)
Address: Dean Court, Bournemouth, Hampshire
Telephone: Bournemouth 35381
Ground capacity: 19,175
Playing area: 112 by 75 yards
Record attendance: 28,799 v Manchester United, FA Cup quarter-final, 2.3.57
Record victory: 11-0 v Margate, FA Cup 1st round, 20.11.71
Record defeat: 0-9 v Lincoln City, Division III, 18.12.82
Most League points: 62, Division III, 1971-72
Most League goals: 88, Division III(S), 1956-57
League scoring record: 42, Ted Macdougall, 1970-71
Record League aggregate: 202, Ron Eyre, 1924-1933
Most League appearances: 412, Ray Bumstead, 1958-1970
Most capped player: 4 (13 in all), Tommy Godwin, Eire

THE BOURNEMOUTH RECORD

	Division & place	*Cup round reached*			
1924	SIII 21	*	1958	SIII 9	2
1925	SIII 20	q	1959	III 12	1
1926	SIII 8	4	1960	III 10	4
1927	SIII 7	3	1961	III 19	3
1928	SIII 14	3	1962	III 3	1
1929	SIII 9	5	1963	III 5	1
1930	SIII 10	3	1964	III 4	1
1931	SIII 10	1	1965	III 11	2
1932	SIII 15	4	1966	III 18	3
1933	SIII 18	1	1967	III 20	2
1934	SIII 21	2	1968	III 12	3
1935	SIII 17	1	1969	III 4	2
1936	SIII 8	3	1970	III 21R	1
1937	SIII 6	3	1971	IV 2P	2
1938	SIII 13	2	1972	III 3	3
1939	SIII 15	3	1973	III 7	3
1946		1	1974	III 11	3
1947	SIII 7	3	1975	III 21R	2
1948	SIII 2	3	1976	IV 6	2
1949	SIII 3	3	1977	IV 13	1
1950	SIII 12	4	1978	IV 17	1
1951	SIII 9	2	1979	IV 18	2
1952	SIII 14	1	1980	IV II	2
1953	SIII 9	1	1981	IV 13	2
1954	SIII 19	2	1982	IV 4P	3
1955	SIII 17	3			
1956	SIII 9	1			
1957	SIII 5	q-f			

* – did not enter

BRADFORD CITY

Founded: 1903
Address: Valley Parade Ground, Bradford BD8 7DY
Telephone: Bradford 306062
Ground capacity: 16,000
Playing area: 110 by 76 yards
Record attendance: 39,146 v Burnley, FA Cup 4th round, 11.3.11
Record victory: 11-1 v Rotherham United, Division III(N), 25.8.28
Record defeat: 1-9 v Colchester United, Division IV, 30.12.61
Most League points: 63, Division III(N), 1928-29
Most League goals: 128, Division III(N), 1928-29
League scoring record: 34, David Layne, Division IV, 1961-62
Record League aggregate: 88, Frank O'Rourke, 1906-13
Most League appearances: 443, Ian Cooper, 1965-1977
Most capped player: 9, H. Hampton, Ireland

FA Cup	*Year*	*Opponents*	*Score*	*Scorers*
Winners	1911	Newcastle United	0-0	
	Replay		1-0	Spiers

THE BRADFORD CITY RECORD

	Division & place	*Cup round reached*			
1904	II 10	p	1950	NIII 19	2
1905	II 8	p	1951	NIII 7	1
1906	II 11	3	1952	NIII 15	2
1907	II 5	3	1953	NIII 16	2
1908	II 1P	1	1954	NIII 5	1
1909	I 18	3	1955	NIII 21	3
1910	I 7	2	1956	NIII 8	2
1911	I 5	Winners	1957	NIII 9	1
1912	I 11	q-f	1958	NIII 3	3
1913	I 13	1	1959	III 11	4
1914	I 9	2	1960	III 19	5
1915	I 10	q-f	1961	III 22R	2
1920	I 15	q-f	1962	IV 5	3
1921	I 15	2	1963	IV 23	3
1922	I 21R	2	1964	IV 5	1
1923	II 15	1	1965	IV 19	1
1924	II 18	1	1966	IV 23	1
1925	II 16	3	1967	IV 11	1
1926	II 16	3	1968	IV 5	2
1927	II 22R	3	1969	IV 4P	1
1928	NIII 6	2	1970	III 10	3
1929	NIII 1P	4	1971	III 19	2
1930	II 18	5	1972	III 24R	1
1931	II 10	4	1973	IV 16	4
1932	II 7	3	1974	IV 8	4
1933	II 11	3	1975	IV 10	1
1934	II 6	3	1976	IV 17	q-f
1935	II 20	4	1977	IV 4P	1
1936	II 12	5	1978	III 22R	1
1937	II 21R	3	1979	IV 15	2
1938	NIII 14	3	1980	IV 5	3
1939	NIII 3	1	1981	IV 14	1
1946		1	1982	IV 2P	1
1947	NIII 5	1			
1948	NIII 14	2			
1949	NIII 22	2			

BRENTFORD

Founded: 1889
Address: Griffin Park, Braemar Road, Brentford, Middlesex TW8 0NT
Telephone: (01) 560 2021
Ground capacity: 37,000
Playing area: 114 by 75 yards
Record attendance: 39,626 v Preston North End, FA Cup quarter-final, 5.3.38
Record victory: 9-0 v Wrexham, Division III, 15.10.63
Record defeat: 0-7 v Swansea Town, Division III(S), 8.11.24
0-7 v Walsall, Division III(S), 19.1.57
Most League points: 62, Division III(S), 1932-33; Division IV, 1962-63
Most League goals: 98, Division IV, 1962-63
League scoring record: 36, John Holliday, Division III(S), 1932-33
Record League aggregate: 153, Jim Towers, 1954-1961
Most League appearances: 514, Ken Coote, 1949-1964
Most capped player: 12, Idris Hopkins, Wales

THE BRENTFORD RECORD

	Division & place	Cup round reached			
1920		1	1956	SIII 6	2
1921	III 21	1	1957	SIII 8	2
1922	SIII 9	1	1958	SIII 2	1
1923	SIII 14	p	1959	III 3	4
1924	SIII 17	p	1960	III 6	2
1925	SIII 21	p	1961	III 17	1
1926	SIII 18	2	1962	III 23R	3
1927	SIII 11	5	1963	IV 1P	1
1928	SIII 12	3	1964	III 16	4
1929	SIII 13	2	1965	III 5	3
1930	SIII 2	1	1966	III 23R	2
1931	SIII 3	4	1967	IV 9	3
1932	SIII 5	4	1968	IV 14	1
1933	SIII 1P	1	1969	IV 11	2
1934	II 4	3	1970	IV 5	1
1935	II 1P	3	1971	IV 14	5
1936	I 5	3	1972	IV 3P	1
1937	I 6	4	1973	III 22R	1
1938	I 6	q-f	1974	IV 19	1
1939	I 18	3	1975	IV 8	2
1946		q-f	1976	IV 18	3
1947	I 21R	4	1977	IV 15	2
1948	II 15	4	1978	IV 4P	2
1949	II 18	q-f	1979	III 10	1
1950	II 9	3	1980	III 19	1
1951	II 9	3	1981	III 9	2
1952	II 10	4	1982	III 8	2
1953	II 17	4			
1954	II 21R	3			
1955	SIII 11	4			

BRIGHTON AND HOVE ALBION

Founded: 1900
Address: Goldstone Ground, Old Shoreham Road, Hove, Sussex
Telephone: Brighton 739535
Ground capacity: 24,000
Playing area: 112 by 75 yards
Record attendance: 36,747 v Fulham, Division II, 27.12.58
Record victory: 10-1 v Wisbech, FA Cup 1st round, 13.11.65
Record defeat: 0-9 v Middlesbrough, Division II, 23.8.58
Most League points: 65, Division III(S), 1955-56, Division III, 1971-72
Most League goals: 112, Division III(S), 1955-56
League scoring record: 32, Peter Ward, Division III, 1976-77
Record League aggregate: 113, Tommy Cook, 1922-29
Most League appearances: 509, Tug Wilson, 1922-36
Most capped player: 13 (16 in all) Mark Lawrenson, Eire

THE BRIGHTON RECORD

	Division & place	Cup round reached			
1906		2	1923	SIII 4	2
1907		1	1924	SIII 5	3
1908		2	1925	SIII 8	2
1909		1	1926	SIII 5	1
1910		1	1927	SIII 4	3
1911		2	1928	SIII 4	2
1912		1	1929	SIII 15	1
1913		2	1930	SIII 5	5
1914		3	1931	SIII 4	4
1915		2	1932	SIII 8	3
1920		p	1933	SIII 12	5
1921	III 18	2	1934	SIII 10	4
1922	SIII 19	2	1935	SIII 9	3

1936	SIII 7	3	1964	IV 8	1
1937	SIII 3	1	1965	IV 1P	1
1938	SIII 5	3	1966	III 15	2
1939	SIII 3	1	1967	III 19	4
1946		5	1968	III 10	2
1947	SIII 17	1	1969	III 12	2
1948	SIII 22	3	1970	III 5	2
1949	SIII 6	1	1971	III 14	3
1950	SIII 8	1	1972	III 2P	2
1951	SIII 13	4	1973	II 22R	3
1952	SIII 5	1	1974	III 19	1
1953	SIII 7	3	1975	III 19	3
1954	SIII 2	2	1976	III 4	3
1955	SIII 6	3	1977	III 2P	1
1956	SIII 2	2	1978	II 4	4
1957	SIII 6	1	1979	II 2P	3
1958	SIII 1P	2	1980	I 15	4
1959	II 12	3	1981	I 19	3
1960	II 14	5	1982	I 13	4
1961	II 16	4			
1962	II 22R	3			
1963	III 22R	1			

BRISTOL CITY

Founded: 1894
Address: Ashton Gate, Bristol BS3 2EJ
Telephone: Bristol 632812
Ground capacity: 30,868
Playing area: 115 by 75 yards
Record attendance: 43, 335 v Preston North End, FA Cup 5th round, 16.2.35
Record victory: 11-0 v Chichester, FA Cup 1st round, 5.11.60
Record defeat: 0-9 v Coventry City, Division III(S), 28.4.34
Most League points: 70, Division III(S), 1954-55
Most League goals: 104, Division III(S), 1926-27
League scoring record: 36, Don Clark, Division III(S), 1946-47
Record League aggregate: 315, John Atyeo, 1951-1966
Most League appearances: 597, John Atyeo, 1951-1966
Most capped player: 26, Billy Wedlock, England

FA Cup	*Year*	*Opponents*	*Score*
Runners-up	1909	Manchester United	0-1

THE CITY RECORD

	Division & place	Cup round reached			
1899		1	1947	SIII 3	2
1900		2	1948	SIII 7	2
1901		q	1949	SIII 16	3
1902	II 6	4q	1950	SIII 15	1
1903	II 4	2	1951	SIII 10	5
1904	II 4	1	1952	SIII 15	2
1905	II 4	2	1953	SIII 5	1
1906	II 1P	1	1954	SIII 3	3
1907	I 2	2	1955	SIII 1P	1
1908	I 10	1	1956	II 11	3
1909	I 8	Final	1957	II 13	5
1910	I 16	2	1958	II 17	5
1911	I 19R	1	1959	II 10	4
1912	II 13	1	1960	II 22R	3
1913	II 16	1	1961	III 14	4
1914	II 8	1	1962	III 6	3
1915	II 13	2	1963	III 14	3
1920	II 8	s-f	1964	III 5	4
1921	II 3	1	1965	III 2P	3
1922	II 22R	1	1966	II 5	3
1923	SIII 1P	2	1967	II 15	5
1924	II 22R	3	1968	II 19	5
1925	SIII 3	2	1969	II 16	3
1926	SIII 4	3	1970	II 14	3
1927	SIII 1P	2	1971	II 19	3
1928	II 12	3	1972	II 8	3
1929	II 20	3	1973	II 5	4
1930	II 20	3	1974	II 16	q-f
1931	II 16	3	1975	II 5	3
1932	II 22R	4	1976	II 2P	3
1933	SIII 15	2	1977	I 18	3
1934	SIII 19	3	1978	I 17	3
1935	SIII 15	5	1979	I 13	4
1936	SIII 13	1	1980	I 20R	3
1937	SIII 16	1	1981	II 21R	5
1938	SIII 2	2	1982	III 23R	4
1939	SIII 8	1			
1946		4			

BRISTOL ROVERS

Founded: 1883
Address: Bristol Stadium, Eastville, Bristol BS5 6NN
Telephone: Bristol 511050
Ground capacity: 12,500
Playing area: 110 by 70 yards
Record attendance: 38,472 v Preston North End, FA Cup 4th round, 30.1.60
Record victory: 15-1 v Weymouth, FA Cup preliminary round, 17.11.1900
Record defeat: 0-12 v Luton Town, Division III(S), 13.4.36
Most League points: 64, Division III(S), 1952-53
Most League goals: 92, Division III(S), 1952-53
League scoring record: 33, Geoff Bradford, Division III(S), 1952-53
Record League aggregate: 245, Geoff Bradford, 1949-1964
Most Leage appearances: 545, Stuart Taylor, 1966-80
Most capped player: 7, Matt O'Mahoney, 6 Eire, 1 Northern Ireland

THE BRISTOL ROVERS RECORD

	Division & place	*Cup round reached*			
1921	III 10	1	1956	II 6	4
1922	SIII 14	q	1957	II 9	4
1923	SIII 13	q	1958	II 10	6
1924	SIII 9	q	1959	II 6	3
1925	SIII 17	1	1960	II 9	4
1926	SIII 19	1	1961	II 17	3
1927	SIII 10	3	1962	II 21R	3
1928	SIII 19	2	1963	III 19	1
1929	SIII 19	2	1964	III 12	4
1930	SIII 20	3	1965	III 6	3
1931	SIII 15	4	1966	III 16	1
1932	SIII 18	2	1967	III 5	3
1933	SIII 9	3	1968	III 15	3
1934	SIII 7	2	1969	III 16	5
1935	SIII 8	3	1970	III 3	2
1936	SIII 17	3	1971	III 6	2
1937	SIII 15	3	1972	III 6	3
1938	SIII 15	1	1973	III 5	1
1939	SIII 22	2	1974	II 2P	3
1946		2	1975	II 19	4
1947	SIII 14	1	1976	II 18	3
1948	SIII 20	4	1977	II 15	3
1949	SIII 5	1	1978	II 18	5
1950	SIII 9	1	1979	II 16	5
1951	SIII 6	6	1980	II 19	3
1952	SIII 7	4	1981	II 22R	4
1953	SIII 1P	3	1982	III 15	1
1954	II 9	3			
1955	II 9	4			

BURNLEY

Founded: 1882
Address: Turf Moor, Burnley, Lancashire
Telephone: Burnley 27777
Ground capacity: 23,000
Playing area: 115 by 73 yards
Record attendance: 54,755 v Huddersfield Town, FA Cup 3rd round, 23.2.24
Record victory: 9-0 v Darwen, Division I, 9.1.1892
9-0 v Crystal Palace, FA Cup 2nd round replay, 1908-09
9-0 v New Brighton, FA Cup 4th round, 26.1.57
Record defeat: 0-10 v Aston Villa, Division I, 29.8.25
0-10 v Sheffield United, Division I, 19.1.29
Most League points: 62, Division II, 1972-73
Most League goals: 102, Division I, 1960-61
League scoring record: 35, George Beel, Division I, 1927-28
Record League aggregate: 178, George Beel, 1923-1932
Most League appearances: 530, Jerry Dawson, 1906-1929
Most capped player: 51 (55 in all), Jimmy McIlroy, Northern Ireland

FA Cup	*Year*	*Opponents*	*Score*	*Scorers*
Winners	1914	Liverpool	1-0	Freeman
Runners-up	1947	Charlton Athletic	0-1	
	1962	Tottenham Hotspur	1-3	Robson

THE BURNLEY RECORD

	Division & place	*Cup round reached*			
1889	I 9	2	1936	II 15	3
1890	I 11	1	1937	II 13	5
1891	I 8	2	1938	II 6	4
1892	I 7	2	1939	II 14	3
1893	I 6	2	1946		3
1894	I 5	1	1947	II 2P	Final
1895	I 9	1	1948	I 3	3
1896	I 10	2	1949	I 15	5
1897	I 16R	1	1950	I 10	5
1898	II 1P	3	1951	I 10	3
1899	I 3	1	1952	I 14	q-f
1900	I 17R	1	1953	I 6	5
1901	II 3	2	1954	I 7	4
1902	II 9	1	1955	I 10	3
1903	II 18	q	1956	I 7	4
1904	II 5	q	1957	I 7	q-f
1905	II 11	q	1958	I 6	4
1906	II 9	1	1959	I 7	q-f
1907	II 7	1	1960	I 1C	q-f
1908	II 7	1	1961	I 4	s-f
1909	II 14	q-f	1962	I 2	Final
1910	II 14	2	1963	I 3	4
1911	II 8	q-f	1964	I 9	q-f
1912	II 3	1	1965	I 12	5
1913	II 2P	s-f	1966	I 3	4
1914	I 12	Winners	1967	I 14	3
1915	I 4	3	1968	I 13	3
1920	I 2	2	1969	I 14	4
1921	I 1C	3	1970	I 14	4
1922	I 3	1	1971	I 21R	3
1923	I 15	1	1972	II 7	3
1924	I 17	s-f	1973	II 1P	3
1925	I 19	1	1974	I 6	s-f
1926	I 20	3	1975	I 10	3
1927	I 5	5	1976	I 21R	3
1928	I 18	3	1977	II 16	4
1929	I 19	4	1978	II 11	4
1930	I 21R	3	1979	II 13	5
1931	II 8	4	1980	II 21R	4
1932	II 19	3	1981	III 8	2
1933	II 19	q-f	1982	III 1P	4
1934	II 13	3			
1935	II 12	s-f			

BURY

Founded: 1885
Address: Gigg Lane, Bury, Lancs
Telephone: (061) 764 4881/2
Ground capacity: 35,000
Playing area: 112 by 72 yards
Record attendance: 35,000 v Bolton, FA Cup 3rd round, 9.1.60
Record victory: 12-1 v Stockton, FA Cup 1st round replay, 1896-97
Record defeat: 0-10 v Blackburn Rovers, FA Cup preliminary round, 1.10.1887
Most League points: 68, Division III, 1960-61
Most League goals: 108, Division III, 1960-61
League scoring record: 35, Craig Madden, Division IV, 1981-82
Record League aggregate: 124, Norman Bullock, 1920-1935
Most League appearances: 506, Norman Bullock, 1920-1935
Most capped player: 11 (14 in all), W Gorman, Republic of Ireland and 4, Northern Ireland

FA Cup	Year	Opponents	Score	Scorers
Winners	1900	Southampton	4-0	McLuckie 2, Wood, Plant
	1903	Derby County	6-0	Ross, Sagar, Leeming 2, Wood, Plant

THE BURY RECORD

	Division & place	*Cup round reached*
1895	II 1P	2
1896	I 11	q-f
1897	I 9	2
1898	I 14	1
1899	I 10	2
1900	I 12	Winners
1901	I 5	2
1902	I 7	q-f
1903	I 8	Winners
1904	I 12	2
1905	I 17	2
1906	I 17	1
1907	I 16	3
1908	I 7	2
1909	I 17	2
1910	I 13	2
1911	I 18	1
1912	I 20R	2
1913	II 11	2
1914	II 10	2
1915	II 11	2
1920	II 5	2
1921	II 11	1
1922	II 11	1
1923	II 6	3
1924	II 2P	1
1925	I 5	1
1926	I 4	4
1927	I 19	3
1928	I 5	4
1929	I 21R	5
1930	II 5	3
1931	II 13	4
1932	II 5	q-f
1933	II 4	4
1934	II 12	4
1935	II 10	3
1936	II 14	4
1937	II 3	4
1938	II 10	4
1939	II 16	3
1946		4
1947	II 17	3
1948	II 20	3
1949	II 12	3
1950	II 18	4
1951	II 20	3
1952	II 17	3
1953	II 20	4
1954	II 17	3
1955	II 13	3
1956	II 16	3
1957	II 21R	3
1958	NIII 4	2
1959	III 10	3
1960	III 7	3
1961	III 1P	1
1962	II 18	3
1963	II 8	4
1964	II 18	4
1965	II 16	3
1966	II 19	3
1967	II 22R	4
1968	III 2P	3
1969	II 21R	3
1970	III 19	1
1971	III 22R	2
1972	IV 8	3
1973	IV 13	1
1974	IV 4P	1
1975	III 14	4
1976	III 13	4
1977	III 7	2
1978	III 15	1
1979	III 19	3
1980	III 21R	5
1981	IV 12	3
1982	IV 9	2

CAMBRIDGE UNITED

Founded: 1919*
Address: Abbey Stadium, Newmarket Road, Cambridge
Telephone: Teversham 2170/3555
Ground capacity: 12,000 (1,200 seated)
Playing area: 115 by 75 yards
Record attendance: †8,691 v Grimsby Town, Division IV, 27.12.71
Record victory: 6-0 v Darlington, Division IV, 18.9.71
Record defeat: 0-6 v Aldershot, Division III, 13.4.74
0-6 v Darlington, Division IV, 28.9.74
Most League points: 65, Division IV, 1976-77
Most League goals: 87, Division IV, 1976-77
League scoring record: 21, Alan Biley, 1977-78
Record League aggregate: 74, Alan Biley, 1975-80
Most League appearances: 297, Steve Fallon, 1975-82
Most capped player: 7 (14 in all), Tom Finney, Northern Ireland
* as Abbey United. Changed name to Cambridge United in 1949
† ground record: 14,000 v Chelsea, Friendly, 1.5.70

THE CAMBRIDGE RECORD

	Division & place	*Cup round reached*
1971	IV 20	2
1972	IV 10	2
1973	IV 3P	1
1974	III 21R	3
1975	IV 6	3
1976	IV 13	1
1977	IV 1P	1
1978	III 2P	2
1979	II 12	3
1980	II 8	4
1981	II 13	3
1982	II 14	3

CARDIFF CITY

Founded: 1899
Address: Ninian Park, Cardiff, CF1 8SX
Telephone: 0222 398636/7/8
Ground capacity: 43,000
Playing area: 114 by 78 yards
Record attendance: *57,800 v Arsenal, Division I, 22.4.53
(***Ground record**: 61,566, Wales v England, 14.10.61)
Record victory: 9-2 v Thames, Division III(S), 6.2.32
Record defeat: 2-11 v Sheffield United, Division I, 1.1.26
Most League points: 66, Division III(S), 1946-47
Most League goals: 93, Division III(S), 1946-47
League scoring record: 31, Stan Richards, Division III(S), 1946-47
Record League aggregate: 127, Len Davies, 1923-1929
Most League appearances: 445, Tom Farquharson, 1922-1935
Most capped player: 39 (41 in all), Alf Sherwood, Wales

FA Cup	Year	Opponents	Score	Scorer
Winners	1927	Arsenal	1-0	Ferguson
Runners-up	1925	Sheffield United	0-1	

THE CARDIFF RECORD

	Division & place	*Cup round reached*
1920		3
1921	II 2P	s-f
1922	I 4	q-f
1923	I 9	3
1924	I 2	q-f
1925	I 11	Final
1926	I 16	4
1927	I 14	Winners
1928	I 6	5
1929	I 22R	3
1930	II 8	4
1931	II 22R	3
1932	SIII 9	3
1933	SIII 19	1
1934	SIII 22	2
1935	SIII 19	1
1936	SIII 20	1
1937	SIII 18	3
1938	SIII 10	3
1939	SIII 13	4
1946		3
1947	SIII 1P	3
1948	II 5	3
1949	II 4	5
1950	II 10	5
1951	II 3	3
1952	II 2P	3
1953	I 12	3
1954	I 10	4
1955	I 20	3
1956	I 17	4
1957	I 21R	4
1958	II 15	5
1959	II 9	4
1960	II 2P	3
1961	I 15	3
1962	I 21R	3
1963	II 10	3
1964	II 15	3
1965	II 13	3
1966	II 20	4
1967	II 20	4
1968	II 13	3
1969	II 5	3
1970	II 7	3
1971	II 3	4
1972	II 19	5
1973	II 20	4
1974	II 17	3
1975	II 21R	3
1976	III 2P	4
1977	II 18	5
1978	II 19	3
1979	II 9	3
1980	II 15	3
1981	II 19	3
1982	II 20R	3

CARLISLE UNITED

Founded: 1904
Address: Brunton Park, Carlisle
Telephone: Carlisle 26237
Ground capacity: 25,000
Playing area: 117 by 78 yards
Record attendance: 27,500 v Birmingham City, FA Cup 3rd round, 5.1.57
Record victory: 8-0 v Hartlepools United, Division III(N), 1.9.28
v Scunthorpe United, Division III(N), 25.12.52
Record defeat: 1-11 v Hull City, Division III(N), 14.1.39
Most League points: 62, Division III(N), 1950-51
Most League goals: 113, Division IV, 1963-64
League scoring record: 42, Jimmy McConnell, Division III(N), 1928-29
Record League aggregate: 126, Jimmy McConnell, 1928-1932
Most League appearances: 465, Alan Ross, 1963-1978
Most capped player: 4, Eric Welsh, Northern Ireland

THE CARLISLE RECORD

	Division & place	*Cup round reached*			
1929	NIII 8	2	1960	IV 19	1
1930	NIII 15	3	1961	IV 19	2
1931	NIII 8	3	1962	IV 4P	3
1932	NIII 18	2	1963	III 23R	3
1933	NIII 19	2	1964	IV 2P	5
1934	NIII 13	2	1965	III 1P	1
1935	NIII 22	1	1966	II 14	4
1936	NIII 13	1	1967	II 3	4
1937	NIII 10	3	1968	II 10	4
1938	NIII 12	1	1969	II 12	3
1939	NIII 19	1	1970	II 12	5
1946		2	1971	II 4	4
1947	NIII 16	3	1972	II 10	3
1948	NIII 9	1	1973	II 18	5
1949	NIII 15	1	1974	II 3P	4
1950	NIII 9	3	1975	I 22R	q-f
1951	NIII 3	3	1976	II 19	3
1952	NIII 7	1	1977	II 20R	4
1953	NIII 9	1	1978	III 13	3
1954	NIII 13	1	1979	III 6	3
1955	NIII 20	2	1980	III 6	4
1956	NIII 21	1	1981	III 19	4
1957	NIII 15	3	1982	III 2P	3
1958	NIII 16	2			
1959	IV 10	2			

CHARLTON ATHLETIC

Founded: 1905
Address: The Valley, Floyd Road, Charlton, London SE7 8AW
Telephone: (01) 858 3711/3712
Ground capacity: 20,000
Playing area: 114 by 78 yards
Record attendance: 75,031 v Aston Villa, FA Cup 5th round, 12.2.38
Record victory: 8-1 v Middlesbrough, Division I, 12.9.53
Record defeat: 1-11 v Aston Villa, Division II, 14.11.59
Most League points: 61, Division III(S), 1934-35
Most League goals: 107, Division II, 1957-58
League scoring record: 32, Ralph Allen, Division III(S), 1934-35
Record League aggregate: 153, Stuart Leary, 1953-62
Most League appearances: 583, Sam Bartram, 1934-56
Most capped player: 19, John Hewie, Scotland

FA Cup	*Year*	*Opponents*	*Score*	*Scorers*
Winners	1947	Burnley	1-0	Duffy
Runners-up	1946	Derby County	1-4	Turner H

THE CHARLTON RECORD

	Division & place	*Cup ound reached*			
1922	SIII 16	q	1957	I 22R	3
1923	SIII 12	4	1958	II 3	4
1924	SIII 14	2	1959	II 8	4
1925	SIII 15	p	1960	II 7	4
1926	SIII 21	3	1961	II 10	3
1927	SIII 13	2	1962	II 15	4
1928	SIII 11	3	1963	II 20	4
1929	SIII 1P	3	1964	II 4	3
1930	II 13	4	1965	II 18	4
1931	II 15	3	1966	II 16	3
1932	II 10	3	1967	II 19	3
1933	II 22R	3	1968	II 15	3
1934	SIII 5	4	1969	II 3	4
1935	SIII 1P	1	1970	II 20	4
1936	II 2P	3	1971	II 20	3
1937	I 2	3	1972	II 21R	3
1938	I 4	5	1973	III 11	3
1939	I 3	3	1974	III 14	1
1946		Final	1975	III 3P	2
1947	I 19	Winners	1976	II 9	5
1948	I 13	5	1977	II 7	3
1949	I 9	3	1978	II 17	3
1950	I 20	4	1979	II 19	4
1951	I 17	3	1980	II 22R	3
1952	I 10	3	1981	III 3P	5
1953	I 5	3	1982	II 13	3
1954	I 9	3			
1955	I 15	3			
1956	I 14	5			

CHELSEA

Founded: 1905
Address: Stamford Bridge, London SW6
Telephone: (01) 385 5545/6
Ground capacity: 45,000
Playing area: 114 by 71 yards
Record attendance: 82,905 v Arsenal, Division I, 12.10.35
Record victory: 13-0 v Jeunesse Hautcharage, 1st Rd European Cup Winners Cup 29.9.71
Record defeat: 1-8 v Wolverhampton Wanderers, Division I, 26.9.53
Most League points: 57, Division II, 1906-07
Most League goals: 98, Division I, 1960-61
League scoring record: 41, Jimmy Greaves, 1960-61
Record League aggregate: 164, Bobby Tambling, 1958-1970
Most League appearances: 655, Ron Harris, 1962-80
Most capped player: 24 (52 in all), Ray Wilkins, England

	Year	Opponents	Score	Scorers
FA Cup				
Winners	1970	Leeds United	*2-2	Houseman, Hutchinson
			*2-1	Osgood, Webb
Runners-up	1915	Sheffield United	0-3	
	1967	Tottenham Hotspur	1-2	Tambling
League Cup				
Winners	1965	Leicester City	H3-2	Tambling, Venables (pen) McCreadie
			A0 0	
Runners up	1972	Stoke City	1 2	Osgood

THE CHELSEA RECORD

Year	Division & place	FA Cup round reached
1906	II 3	3q
1907	II 2P	1
1908	I 13	2
1909	I 11	2
1910	I 19R	2
1911	II 3	s-f
1912	II 2P	2
1913	I 18	2
1914	I 8	1
1915	I 19	Final
1920	I 3	s-f
1921	I 18	q-f
1922	I 9	1
1923	I 19	2
1924	I 21R	1
1925	II 5	1
1926	II 3	4
1927	II 4	q-f
1928	II 3	3
1929	II 9	5
1930	II 2P	3
1931	I 12	q-f
1932	I 12	s-f
1933	I 18	3
1934	I 19	5
1935	I 12	3
1936	I 8	5
1937	I 13	4
1938	I 10	3
1939	I 20	q-f
1946		5
1947	I 15	4
1948	I 18	4
1949	I 13	5
1950	I 13	s-f
1951	I 20	5
1952	I 19	s-f
1953	I 19	5
1954	I 8	3
1955	I 1C	5
1956	I 16	5
1957	I 12	4
1958	I 11	4
1959	I 14	4
1960	I 18	4
1961	I 12	3
1962	I 22R	3
1963	II 2P	5
1964	I 5	4
1965	I 3	s-f
1966	I 5	s-f
1967	I 9	Final
1968	I 6	q-f
1969	I 5	q-f
1970	I 3	Winners
1971	I 6	4
1972	I 7	5
1973	I 12	6
1974	I 17	3
1975	I 21R	4
1976	II 11	5
1977	II 2P	3
1978	I 16	5
1979	I 22R	3
1980	II 4	3
1981	II 12	3
1982	II 12	q-f

CHESTER

Founded: 1884
Address: Sealand Road, Chester, CH1 4LW
Telephone: Chester 371376
Ground capacity: 20,500 (2,100 seated)
Playing area: 114 by 76 yards
Record attendance: 20,500 v Chelsea, FA Cup 3rd round replay, 16.1.52
Record victory: 12-0 v York City, Division III(N), 1.2.36
Record defeat: 2-11 v Oldham Athletic, Division III(N), 19.1.52
Most League points: 56, Division III(N), 1946-47; Division IV, 1964-65
Most League goals: 119, Division IV, 1964-65
League scoring record: 36, Dick Yates, Division III(N), 1946-47
Record League aggregate: 83, Gary Talbot, 1963-1967 and 1968-1970
Most League appearances: 408, Ray Gill, 1951-1962
Most capped player: 9 (30 in all), W Lewis, Wales

THE CHESTER RECORD

Year	Division & place	Cup round reached
1932	NIII 3	2
1933	NIII 4	4
1934	NIII 10	2
1935	NIII 3	3
1936	NIII 2	2
1957	NIII 21	1
1958	NIII 21	2
1959	IV 13	2
1960	IV 20	2
1961	IV 24	1
1962	IV 23	2
1963	IV 21	1
1964	IV 12	2

Year	Division & place	Cup round reached
1937	NIII 3	4
1938	NIII 9	3
1939	NIII 6	4
1946		3
1947	NIII 3	4
1948	NIII 20	4
1949	NIII 18	2
1950	NIII 12	2
1951	NIII 13	1
1952	NIII 19	3
1953	NIII 20	1
1954	NIII 24	1
1955	NIII 24	1
1956	NIII 17	1
1965	IV 8	3
1966	IV 7	3
1967	IV 19	1
1968	IV 22	2
1969	IV 14	2
1970	IV 11	4
1971	IV 5	3
1972	IV 20	1
1973	IV 15	1
1974	IV 7	3
1975	IV 4P	1
1976	III 17	2
1977	III 13	5
1978	III 5	2
1979	III 16	2
1980	III 9	5
1981	III 18	1
1982	III 24R	1

CHESTERFIELD

Founded: 1866
Address: Recreation Ground, Saltergate, Chesterfield, Derbyshire
Telephone: Chesterfield 32318
Ground capacity: 19,750
Playing area: 114 by 72 yards
Record attendance: 30,968 v Newcastle United, Division II, 7.4.39
Record victory: 10-0 v Glossop North End, Division II, 17.1.03
Record defeat: 1-9 v Port Vale, Division II, 24.9.32
Most League points: 64, Division IV, 1969-70
Most League goals: 102, Division III(N), 1930-31
League scoring record: 44, Jimmy Cookson, Division III(N), 1925-26
Record League aggregate: 127, Ernie Moss, 1969-76; 1979-81
Most League appearances: 613, Dave Blakey, 1948-1967
Most capped player: 4 (7 in all), Walter McMillen, Northern Ireland

THE CHESTERFIELD RECORD

Year	Division & place	Cup round reached
1900	II 7	p
1901	II 14	1
1902	II 16	p
1903	II 6	p
1904	II 11	p
1905*	II 5	p
1906*	II 18	2
1907*	II 18	1
1908*	II 19	2
1909*	II 19L	1
1910		1
1911		p
1912		p
1913		1
1914		1
1915		p
1920		p
1921		p
1922	NIII 13	p
1923	NIII 4	p
1924	NIII 3	p
1925	NIII 7	p
1926	NIII 4	3
1927	NIII 7	3
1928	NIII 16	1
1929	NIII 11	3
1930	NIII 4	3
1931	NIII 1P	1
1932	II 17	4
1933	II 21R	5
1934	NIII 2	3
1935	NIII 10	3
1936	NIII 1P	2
1937	II 15	3
1938	II 11	5
1939	II 6	3
1946		3
1947	II 4	4
1948	II 16	3
1949	II 6	3
1950	II 14	5
1951	II 21R	3
1952	NIII 13	2
1953	NIII 12	2
1954	NIII 6	4
1955	NIII 6	1
1956	NIII 6	2
1957	NIII 6	3
1958	NIII 8	1
1959	III 16	3
1960	III 18	1
1961	III 24R	3
1962	IV 19	2
1963	IV 15	2
1964	IV 16	3
1965	IV 12	3
1966	IV 20	1
1967	IV 15	1
1968	IV 7	3
1969	IV 20	3
1970	IV 1P	1
1971	III 5	2
1972	III 13	3
1973	III 16	2
1974	III 5	1
1975	III 15	3
1976	III 15	1
1977	III 18	2
1978	III 9	2
1979	III 20	1
1980	III 4	1
1981	III 5	3
1982	III 11	2

* as Chesterfield Town

COLCHESTER UNITED

Founded: 1937
Address: Layer Road, Colchester, Essex
Telephone: Colchester 74042
Ground capacity: 16,150 (1,205 seated)
Playing area: 110 by 71 yards
Record attendance: 19,072 v Reading, FA Cup 1st round, 27.11.48
Record victory: 9-1 v Bradford City, Division IV, 30.9.61
Record defeat: 0-7 v Leyton Orient, Division III(S), 5.1.52
0-7 v Reading, Division III(S), 18.9.57
Most League points: 60, Division IV, 1973-74
Most League goals: 104, Division IV, 1961-62
League scoring record: 37, Bobby Hunt, Division IV, 1961-62
Record League aggregate: 131, Martyn King, 1959-65
Most League appearances: 536, Mickey Cook, 1969-82
Most capped player: None

THE COLCHESTER RECORD

	Division & & place	Cup round reached
1946		p
1947		1
1948		5
1949		1
1950		p
1951	SIII 16	1
1952	SIII 10	3
1953	SIII 22	3
1954	SIII 23	1
1955	SIII 24	1
1956	SIII 12	1
1957	SIII 3	1
1958	SIII 12	1
1959	III 5	4
1960	III 9	1
1961	III 23R	2
1962	IV 2P	1
1963	III 12	1
1964	III 17	2
1965	III 23R	2
1966	IV 4P	1
1967	III 13	2
1968	III 22R	3
1969	IV 6	2
1970	IV 10	1
1971	IV 6	q-f
1972	IV 11	1
1973	IV 22	2
1974	IV 3P	1
1975	III 11	2
1976	III 22R	1
1977	IV 3P	4
1978	III 8	2
1979	III 7	5
1980	III 5	3
1981	III 22R	3
1982	IV 6	3

COVENTRY CITY

Founded: 1883
Address: Highfield Road, Coventry
Telephone: Coventry 57171
Ground capacity: 20,000 (all seated)
Playing area: 110 by 75 yards
Record attendance: 51,457 v Wolverhampton Wanderers, Division II, 29.4.67
Record victory: 9-0 v Bristol City, Division III(S), 28.4.34
Record defeat: 2-10 v Norwich City, Division III(S), 15.3.30
Most League points: 60, Division IV, 1958-59 & Division III, 1963-64
Most League goals: 108, Division III(S), 1931-32
League scoring record: 49, Clarrie Bourton, Division III(S), 1931-32
Record League aggregate: 171, Clarrie Bourton, 1931-37
Most League appearances: 486, George Curtis, 1956-1970
Most capped player: 21 (48 in all), Dave Clements, Northern Ireland

THE COVENTRY RECORD

	Division & place	Cup round reached
1908		1
1909		q
1910		q-f
1911		3
1912		2
1913		1
1914		4q
1915		6q
1920	II 20	1
1921	II 21	6q
1922	II 20	2
1923	II 18	5q
1924	II 19	1
1925	II 22R	1
1926	NIII 16	1
1927	SIII 15	2
1928	SIII 20	1
1929	SIII 11	1
1930	SIII 6	3
1931	SIII 14	2
1932	SIII 12	1
1933	SIII 6	2
1934	SIII 2	2
1935	SIII 3	3
1936	SIII 1P	1
1937	II 8	5
1938	II 4	3
1939	II 4	3
1946		3
1947	II 8	4
1948	II 10	4
1949	II 16	3
1950	II 12	3
1951	II 7	3
1952	II 21R	4
1953	SIII 6	3
1954	SIII 14	1
1955	SIII 9	3
1956	SIII 8	1
1957	SIII 16	1
1958	SIII 19	2
1959	IV 2P	2
1960	III 5	1
1961	III 15	3
1962	III 14	2
1963	III 4	q-f
1964	III 1P	2
1965	II 10	3
1966	II 3	5
1967	II 1P	3
1968	I 20	4
1969	I 20	4
1970	I 6	3
1971	I 10	3
1972	I 18	4
1973	I 18	6
1974	I 16	5
1975	I 14	4
1976	I 14	4
1977	I 19	4
1978	I 7	3
1979	I 10	3
1980	I 15	4
1981	I 16	5
1982	I 14	q-f

CREWE ALEXANDRA

Founded: 1877
Address: Gresty Road, Crewe, Cheshire
Telephone: Crewe 213014
Ground capacity: 17,000
Playing area: 112 by 74 yards
Record attendance: 20,000 v Tottenham Hotspur, FA Cup 4th round, 30.1.60
Record victory: 8-0 v Rotherham United, Division III(N), 1.10.32
Record defeat: 2-13 v Tottenham Hotspur, FA Cup 4th round replay, 3.2.60
Most League points: 59, Division IV, 1962-63
Most League goals: 95, Division III(N), 1931-32

League scoring record: 34, Terry Harkin, Division IV, 1964-65
Record League aggregate: 126, Bert Swindells, 1928-1937
Most League appearances: 436, Tommy Lowry, 1966-1977
Most capped player: 12 (30 in all), William Lewis, Wales

THE CREWE RECORD

	Division & place	*Cup round reached*
1886		3
1887		p
1888		s-f
1889		1
1890		p
1891		1
1892		1
1893	II 10	p
1894	II 12	p
1895	II 16	p
1896	II 16L	1
1897		p
1898		p
1899		p
1900		p
1901		p
1902		p
1903		p
1904		p
1905		p
1906		1
1907		1
1908		p
1909		p
1910		p
1911		2
1912		1
1913		p
1914		p
1915		p
1920		p
1921		p
1922	NIII 6	p
1923	NIII 6	p
1924	NIII 20	p
1925	NIII 15	p
1926	NIII 11	2
1927	NIII 15	3
1928	NIII 17	4
1929	NIII 9	1
1930	NIII 11	2
1931	NIII 18	2
1932	NIII 6	1
1933	NIII 10	2
1934	NIII 14	1
1935	NIII 13	1
1936	NIII 6	3
1937	NIII 20	3
1938	NIII 8	2
1939	NIII 8	2
1946		1
1947	NIII 8	1
1948	NIII 10	4
1949	NIII 12	3
1950	NIII 7	2
1951	NIII 9	2
1952	NIII 16	1
1953	NIII 10	1
1954	NIII 16	2
1955	NIII 22	1
1956	NIII 24	1
1957	NIII 24	1
1958	NIII 24	1
1959	IV 18	1
1960	IV 14	4
1961	IV 9	4
1962	IV 10	2
1963	IV 3P	2
1964	III 22R	1
1965	IV 10	1
1966	IV 14	4
1967	IV 5	3
1968	IV 4P	1
1969	III 23R	2
1970	IV 15	1
1971	IV 15	2
1972	IV 24	1
1973	IV 21	3
1974	IV 21	1
1975	IV 18	1
1976	IV 16	1
1977	IV 12	1
1978	IV 15	2
1979	**IV 24**	**2**
1980	**IV 23**	**1**
1981	**IV 18**	**1**
1982	**IV 24**	**2**

CRYSTAL PALACE

Founded: 1905
Address: Selhurst Park, SE25 6PU
Telephone: 01-653 4462
Ground capacity: 38,500
Playing area: 112 by 74 yards
Record attendance: 51,482 v Burnley, Division II, 11.5.79
Record victory: 9-0 v Barrow, Division IV, 10.10.59
Record defeat: 4-11 v Manchester City, FA Cup 5th round, 20.2.26
Most League points: 64, Division IV, 1960-61
Most League goals: 110, Division IV, 1960-61
League scoring record: 46, Peter Simpson, Division III(S), 1930-31
Record League aggregate: 154, Peter Simpson, 1930-1936
Most League appearances: 432, Terry Long, 1956-1969
Most capped player: 13, Ian Evans, Wales

THE PALACE RECORD

	Division & place	*Cup round reached*
1921	III 1P	2
1922	II 14	2
1923	II 16	1
1953	SIII 13	2
1954	SIII 22	1
1955	SIII 20	2

1924	II 15	3
1925	II 21R	2
1926	SIII 13	5
1927	SIII 6	1
1928	SIII 5	2
1929	SIII 2	5
1930	SIII 9	3
1931	SIII 2	4
1932	SIII 4	2
1933	SIII 5	1
1934	SIII 12	4
1935	SIII 5	1
1936	SIII 6	2
1937	SIII 14	1
1938	SIII 7	3
1939	SIII 2	1
1946		3
1947	SIII 18	3
1948	SIII 13	3
1949	SIII 22	1
1950	SIII 7	1
1951	SIII 24	1
1952	SIII 19	1
1956	SIII 23	1
1957	SIII 20	3
1958	SIII 14	3
1959	IV 7	3
1960	IV 8	3
1961	IV 2P	2
1962	III 15	3
1963	III 11	2
1964	III 2P	2
1965	II 7	q-f
1966	II 11	3
1967	II 7	3
1968	II 11	3
1969	II 2P	3
1970	I 20	5
1971	I 18	3
1972	I 20	3
1973	I 21R	4
1974	II 20R	3
1975	III 5	2
1976	III 5	s-f
1977	**III 3P**	**3**
1978	**II 9**	**3**
1979	**II 1P**	**5**
1980	**I 13**	**3**
1981	**I 22R**	**3**
1982	**II 15**	**q-f**

DARLINGTON

Founded: 1883
Address: Feethams Ground, Darlington, County Durham
Telephone: Darlington 65097
Ground capacity: 20,000
Playing area: 110 by 74 yards
Record attendance: 21,023 v Bolton Wanderers, League cup 3rd round, 14.11.60
Record victory: 9-2 v Lincoln City, Division III(N), 7.1.28
Record defeat: 0-10 v Doncaster Rovers, Division IV, 25.1.64
Most League points: 59, Division IV, 1965-66
Most League goals: 108, Division III(N), 1929-30
League scoring record: 39, David Brown, Division III(N), 1924-5
Record League aggregate: 74, David Brown, 1923-1926
Most League appearances: 442, Ron Greener, 1955-1967
Most capped player: None

THE DARLINGTON RECORD

	Division & place	*Cup round reached*
1911		3
1912		2
1913		p
1914		p
1915		1
1920		2
1921		1
1922	NIII 2	1
1923	NIII 9	p
1924	NIII 6	1
1925	NIII 1P	1
1926	II 15	2
1927	II 21R	4
1928	NIII 7	3
1929	NIII 19	3
1930	NIII 3	1
1931	NIII 11	1
1932	NIII 11	3
1933	NIII 22	4
1934	NIII 16	1
1935	NIII 5	2
1936	NIII 12	3
1937	NIII 22	4
1938	NIII 19	1
1939	NIII 18	2
1946		2
1947	NIII 17	2
1948	NIII 16	1
1949	NIII 4	3
1950	NIII 17	1
1951	NIII 18	1
1952	NIII 23	1
1953	NIII 21	1
1954	NIII 21	1
1955	NIII 15	3
1956	NIII 15	2
1957	NIII 18	2
1958	NIII 20	5
1959	IV 16	3
1960	IV 15	2
1961	IV 7	2
1962	IV 13	1
1963	IV 12	1
1964	IV 19	1
1965	IV 17	3
1966	IV 2P	2
1967	III 22R	2
1968	IV 16	1
1969	IV 5	2
1970	IV 22	1
1971	IV 12	2
1972	IV 19	2
1973	IV 24	1
1974	IV 20	1
1975	IV 21	2
1976	IV 20	1
1977	IV 11	3
1978	**IV 19**	**1**
1979	**IV 21**	**3**
1980	**IV 22**	**2**
1981	**IV 8**	**1**
1982	**IV 13**	**1**

DERBY COUNTY

Founded: 1884
Address: Baseball Ground, Shaftesbury Crescent, Derby DE3 8NB
Telephone: 0332 40105
Ground capacity: 33,000 (16,000 seated)
Playing area: 110 by 71 yards
Record attendance: 41,826 v Tottenham Hotspur, Division I, 20.9.69
Record victory: 12-0 v Finn Harps, UEFA Cup 3rd round, 15.9.76
Record defeat: 2-11 v Everton, FA Cup 1st round, 18.1.90
Most League points: 63, Division II, 1968-69, Division III(N), 1955-56, 1956-57
Most League goals: 111, Division III(N), 1956-57
League scoring record: 37, Jack Bowers, Division I, 1930-31 and Ray Straw, Division III(N), 1956-57
Record League aggregate: 291, Steve Bloomer, 1892-1906 and 1910-1914
Most League appearances: 486, Kevin Hector, 1966-78; 1980-82
Most capped player: 28, Roy McFarland, England

FA Cup	*Year*	*Opponents*	*Score*	*Scorers*
Winners	1946	Charlton Athletic	*4-1	Stamps 2, Doherty, og
Runners-up	1898	Nottingham Forest	1-3	Bloomer
	1899	Sheffield United	1-4	Boag
	1903	Bury	0-6	

*—after extra time

THE DERBY RECORD

	Division & place	*Cup round reached*			
1885		1	1934	I 4	5
1886		3	1935	I 6	5
1887		2	1936	I 2	q-f
1888		2	1937	I 4	5
1889	I 10	2	1938	I 13	3
1890	I 7	1	1939	I 6	3
1891	I 11	2	1946		Winners
1892	I 10	1	1947	I 14	5
1893	I 13	1	1948	I 4	s-f
1894	I 3	q-f	1949	I 3	q-f
1895	I 15	1	1950	I 11	q-f
1896	I 2	s-f	1951	I 11	4
1897	I 3	s-f	1952	I 17	3
1898	I 10	Final	1953	I 22R	3
1899	I 9	Final	1954	II 18	3
1900	I 6	1	1955	II 22R	3
1901	I 12	1	1956	NIII 2	2
1902	I 6	s-f	1957	NIII 1P	2
1903	I 9	Final	1958	II 16	3
1904	I 14	s-f	1959	II 7	3
1905	I 11	1	1960	II 18	3
1906	I 15	2	1961	II 12	3
1907	I 19R	3	1962	II 16	4
1908	II 6	1	1963	II 18	4
1909	II 5	s-f	1964	II 13	3
1910	II 4	2	1965	II 9	3
1911	II 6	q-f	1966	II 8	3
1912	II 1P	2	1967	II 17	3
1913	I 7	1	1968	II 18	3
1914	I 20R	2	1969	II 1P	3
1915	II 1P	1	1970	I 4	5
1920	I 18	1	1971	I 9	5
1921	I 21R	2	1972	I 1C	5
1922	II 12	1	1973	I 7	6
1923	II 14	s-f	1974	I 3	4
1924	II 3	2	1975	I 1C	5
1925	II 3	1	1976	I 4	s-f
1926	II 2P	4	1977	I 15	q-f
1927	I 12	4	1978	I 12	5
1928	I 4	4	1979	I 19	3
1929	I 6	4	1980	I 21R	3
1930	I 2	4	1981	II 6	3
1931	I 6	3	1982	II 16	3
1932	I 15	5			
1933	I 7	s-f			

DONCASTER ROVERS

Founded: 1879
Address: Belle Vue Ground, Doncaster
Telephone: Doncaster 535281
Ground capacity: 21,150
Playing area: 110 by 77 yards
Record attendance: 37,149 v Hull City, Division III(N), 2.10.48
Record victory: 10-0 v Darlington, Division IV, 25.1.64
Record defeat: 0-12 v Small Heath, Division II, 11.4.03
Most League points: 72, Division III(N), 1946-47
Most League goals: 123, Division III(N), 1946-47
League scoring record: 42, Clarrie Jordan, Division III(N), 1946-47
Record League aggregate: 180, Tom Kettley, 1923-29
Most League appearances: 406, Fred Emery, 1925-1936
Most capped player: 14, Len Graham, Northern Ireland

THE DONCASTER ROVERS RECORD

	Division & place	*Cup round reached*			
1902	II 7	p	1957	II 14	3
1903*	II 16	q	1958	II 22R	3
1905*	II 18	q	1959	III 22R	3
1924	NIII 9	q	1960	IV 17	3
1925	NIII 18	1	1961	IV 11	1
1926	NIII 10	2	1962	IV 21	1
1927	NIII 8	2	1963	IV 16	2
1928	NIII 4	1	1964	IV 14	3
1929	NIII 5	1	1965	IV 9	3
1930	NIII 14	4	1966	IV 1P	1
1931	NIII 15	2	1967	III 23R	1
1932	NIII 15	2	1968	IV 10	3
1933	NIII 6	3	1969	IV 1P	3
1934	NIII 5	1	1970	III 11	2
1935	NIII 1P	1	1971	III 23R	1
1936	II 18	3	1972	IV 12	1
1937	II 22R	3	1973	IV 17	3
1938	NIII 2	3	1974	IV 22	3
1939	NIII 2	4	1975	IV 17	2
1946		1	1976	IV 10	1
1947	NIII 1P	3	1977	IV 8	1
1948	II 21R	3	1978	IV 12	1
1949	NIII 3	1	1979	IV 22	2
1950	NIII 1P	4	1980	IV 12	2
1951	II 11	3	1981	IV 3P	3
1952	II 16	5	1982	III 19	2
1953	II 13	3			
1954	II 12	5			
1955	II 18	5			
1956	II 17	5			

*Doncaster failed to gain re-election. Elected in 1904 and 1923.

EVERTON

Founded: 1878
Address: Goodison Park, Liverpool L4 4EL
Telephone: (051) 521-2020
Ground capacity: 53,091 (25,000 seated)
Playing area: 112 by 78 yards
Record attendance: 78,299 v Liverpool, Division I, 18.8.48
Record victory: 11-2 v Derby County, FA Cup 1st round, 18.1.1890
Record defeat: 4-10 v Tottenham Hotspur, Division I, 11.10.58
Most League points: 66, Division I, 1969-70
Most League goals: 121, Division II, 1930-31
League scoring record: 60, Dixie Dean, Division I, 1927-28
Record League aggregate: 349, Dixie Dean, 1925-1937
Most League appearances: 465, Ted Sagar, 1929-1953
Most capped player: 37 (72 in all), Alan Ball, England

FA Cup	*Year*	*Opponents*	*Score*	*Scorers*
Winners	1906	Newcastle United	1-0	Young
	1933	Manchester City	3-0	Stein, Dean, Dunn
	1966	Sheffield Wednesday	3-2	Trebilcock 2, Temple
Runners-up	1893	Wolverhampton Wanderers	0-1	
	1897	Aston Villa	2-3	Bell, Boyle
	1907	Sheffield Wednesday	1-2	Sharp
	1968	West Bromwich Albion	*0-1	
League Cup				
Runners up	1977	Aston Villa	0-0	
		Replay	*1-1	Latchford
		Replay	*2-3	Latchford, Lyons

*after extra time

THE EVERTON RECORD

	Division & place	*Cup round reached*
1887		1
1888		2
1889	I 8	q
1890	I 2	2
1891	I 1C	1
1892	I 5	1
1893	I 3	Final
1894	I 6	1
1895	I 2	q-f
1896	I 3	q-f
1897	I 7	Final
1898	I 4	s-f
1899	I 4	2
1900	I 11	1
1901	I 7	2
1902	I 2	1
1903	I 12	q-f
1904	I 3	1
1905	I 2	s-f
1906	I 11	Winners
1907	I 3	Final
1908	I 11	q-f
1909	I 2	2
1910	I 10	s-f
1911	I 4	3
1912	I 2	q-f
1913	I 11	q-f
1914	I 15	1
1915	I 1C	s-f
1920	I 16	1
1921	I 7	q-f
1922	I 20	1
1923	I 5	1
1924	I 7	2
1925	I 17	3
1926	I 11	3
1927	I 20	4
1928	I 1C	4
1929	I 18	3
1930	I 22R	4
1931	II 1P	s-f
1932	I 1C	3
1933	I 11	Winners
1934	I 14	3
1935	I 8	q-f
1936	I 16	3
1937	I 17	5
1938	I 14	4
1939	I 1C	q-f
1946		3
1947	I 10	4
1948	I 14	5
1949	I 18	4
1950	I 18	s-f
1951	I 22R	3
1952	II 7	3
1953	II 16	s-f
1954	II 2P	5
1955	I 11	4
1956	I 15	q-f
1957	I 15	5
1958	I 16	4
1959	I 16	5
1960	I 15	3
1961	I 5	3
1962	I 4	5
1963	I 1C	5
1964	I 3	5
1965	I 4	4
1966	I 11	Winners
1967	I 6	q-f
1968	I 5	Final
1969	I 3	s-f
1970	I 1C	3
1971	I 14	s-f
1972	I 15	5
1973	I 17	4
1974	I 7	4
1975	I 4	5
1976	I 11	3
1977	I 9	s-f
1978	I 3	4
1979	I 4	3
1980	I 19	s-f
1981	I 15	q-f
1982	I 8	3

EXETER CITY

Founded: 1904
Address: St. James' Park, Exeter
Telephone: Exeter 54073
Ground capacity: 17,500
Playing area: 114 by 73 yards
Record attendance: 20,984 v Sunderland, FA Cup 6th Rd. replay, 4.3.31
Record victory: 8-1 v Coventry City, Division III(S), 4.12.26
8-1 v Aldershot, Division III(S), 4.5.35
Record defeat: 0-9 v Notts County, Division III(S), 16.10.48, and
0-9 v Northampton Town, Division III(S), 12.4.58
Most League points: 62, Division IV, 1976-77
Most League goals: 88, Division III(S), 1932-33
League scoring record: 34, Fred Whitlow, Division III(S), 1932-33
Record League aggregate: 105, Alan Banks, 1963-66, 1967-1973
Most League appearances: 495, Arnold Mitchell, 1952-66
Most capped player: 1 (17 in all), Dermot Curtis, Eire

THE EXETER CITY RECORD

	Division & place	*Cup round reached*
1909		2
1910		5q
1911		1
1912		4q
1913		4q
1914		2
1915		1
1920		6q
1921	SIII 19	1
1922	SIII 21	5q
1923	SIII 20	5q
1924	SIII 16	2
1925	SIII 7	1
1926	SIII 20	1
1927	SIII 12	3
1928	SIII 8	4
1929	SIII 21	3
1930	SIII 16	1
1931	SIII 13	6
1932	SIII 7	3
1933	SIII 2	1
1934	SIII 9	1
1935	SIII 11	2
1936	SIII 22	1
1937	SIII 21	5
1938	SIII 17	2
1939	SIII 14	1
1946		2
1947	SIII 15	1
1948	SIII 11	1
1949	SIII 12	3
1950	SIII 16	4
1951	SIII 14	4
1952	SIII 23	2
1953	SIII 17	1
1954	SIII 9	1
1955	SIII 22	1
1956	SIII 16	3
1957	SIII 21	1
1958	SIII 24	1
1959	IV 5	1
1960	IV 9	3
1961	IV 21	1
1962	IV 18	1
1963	IV 17	1
1964	IV 4P	2
1965	III 17	2
1966	III 22R	1
1967	IV 14	1
1968	IV 20	2
1969	IV 17	3
1970	IV 18	2
1971	IV 9	1
1972	IV 15	2
1973	IV 8	1
1974	IV 10	1
1975	IV 9	1
1976	IV 7	1
1977	IV 2P	1
1978	III 17	3
1979	III 9	2
1980	III 8	1
1981	III 11	q-f
1982	III 18	1

FULHAM

Founded: 1880
Address: Craven Cottage, Stevenage Road, London SW6
Telephone: (01) 736 5621/6561/2/3
Ground capacity: 20,000
Playing area: 110 by 75 yards
Record attendance: 49,335 v Millwall, Division II, 8.10.38
Record victory: 10-1 v Ipswich Town, Division I, 26.12.63
Record defeat: 0-9 v Wolverhampton Wanderers, Division I, 16.9.59
Most League points: 60, Division II, 1958-59 & Division III, 1970-71
Most League goals: 111, Division III(S), 1931-32
League scoring record: 41, Frank Newton, Division III(S), 1931-32
Record League aggregate: 159, Johnny Haynes, 1952-70
Most League appearances: 598, Johnny Haynes, 1952-70
Most capped player: 56, Johnny Haynes, England

FA Cup	*Year*	*Opponents*	*Score*
Runners-up	1975	West Ham United	0-2

THE FULHAM RECORD

	Division & place	Cup round reached
1904		1
1905		q-f
1906		2
1907		2
1908	II 4	s-f
1909	II 10	2
1910	II 7	2
1911	II 10	1
1912	II 8	q-f
1913	II 9	1
1914	II 11	1
1915	II 12	2
1920	II 6	1
1921	II 9	3
1922	II 7	2
1923	II 10	1
1924	II 20	2
1925	II 12	2
1926	II 19	q-f
1927	II 18	4
1928	II 21R	3
1929	SIII 5	2
1930	SIII 7	4
1931	SIII 9	3
1932	SIII 1P	3
1933	II 3	3
1934	II 16	3
1935	II 7	3
1936	II 9	s-f
1937	II 11	3
1938	II 8	3
1939	II 12	4
1946		3
1947	II 15	3
1948	II 11	q-f
1949	II 1P	3
1950	I 17	3
1951	I 18	q-f
1952	I 22R	3
1953	II 8	3
1954	II 8	4
1955	II 14	3
1956	II 9	4
1957	II 11	4
1958	II 5	s-f
1959	II 2P	4
1960	I 10	4
1961	I 17	3
1962	I 20	s-f
1963	I 16	3
1964	I 15	4
1965	I 20	3
1966	I 20	3
1967	I 19	4
1968	I 22R	4
1969	II 22R	4
1970	III 4	1
1971	III 2P	1
1972	II 20	4
1973	II 9	3
1974	II 13	4
1975	II 9	Final
1976	II 12	3
1977	II 17	3
1978	II 10	3
1979	II 10	4
1980	II 20R	3
1981	III 13	4
1982	III 3P	2

GILLINGHAM

Founded: 1893
Address: Priestfield Stadium, Gillingham, Kent
Telephone: Medway 51854
Ground capacity: 22,000
Playing area: 114 by 75 yards
Record attendance: 23,002 v Queen's Park Rangers, FA Cup 3rd round, 10.1.48
Record victory: 10-1 v Gorleston, FA Cup 1st round, 16.11.57
Record defeat: 2-9 v Nottingham Forest, Division III(S), 18.11.50
Most League points: 62, Division IV, 1973-4
Most League goals: 90, Division IV, 1973-4
League scoring record: 31, Ernie Morgan, Division III(S), 1954-55, Brian Yeo, Division IV, 1973-74
Record League aggregate: 135, Brian Yeo, 1963-75
Most League appearances: 571, John Simpson, 1957-72
Most capped player: 2 (3 in all), Damien Richardson, Eire

THE GILLINGHAM RECORD

	Division & place	Cup round reached
1899*		1
1900		p
1901		p
1902		p
1903		p
1904		p
1905		p
1906		1
1907		2
1908		2
1909		p
1910		p
1911		1
1912		p
1913		1
1914		2
1915		1
1920		1
1921	III 22	p
1922	SIII 18	1
1923	SIII 16	p
1924	SIII 15	1
1925	SIII 13	p
1926	SIII 10	2
1927	SIII 20	2
1928	SIII 16	3
1929	SIII 22	1
1930	SIII 21	1
1931	SIII 16	2
1932	SIII 21	1
1933	SIII 7	2
1934	SIII 17	2
1935	SIII 20	1
1936	SIII 16	2
1937	SIII 11	2
1938†	SIII 22	1
1939		q
1946		q
1947		3
1948		3
1949		q
1950		2
1951	SIII 22	2
1952	SIII 22	2
1953	SIII 20	2
1954	SIII 10	1
1955	SIII 4	2
1956	SIII 10	1
1957	SIII 22	2
1958	SIII 22	3
1959	IV 11	1
1960	IV 7	3
1961	IV 15	3
1962	IV 20	1
1963	IV 5	3
1964	IV 1P	1
1965	III 7	2
1966	III 6	1
1967	III 11	2
1968	III 11	1
1969	III 20	2
1970	III 20	5
1971	III 24R	1
1972	IV 13	3
1973	IV 9	1
1974	IV 2P	1
1975	III 10	1
1976	III 14	2
1977	III 12	1
1978	III 7	2
1979	III 4	1
1980	III 16	1
1981	III 15	2
1982	III 6	4

*New Brompton Excelsior until 1913
†Not re-elected Re-elected 1950

GRIMSBY TOWN

Founded: 1878 (as Grimsby Pelham)
Address: Blundell Park, Cleethorpes, Lincolnshire
Telephone: 0472 691420
Ground capacity: 22,000
Playing area: 111 by 74 yards
Record attendance: 31,657 v Wolves, FA Cup 5th round, 20.2.37
Record victory: 9-2 v Darwen, Division II, 15.4.1899
Record defeat: 1-9 v Arsenal, Division I, 28.1.31
Most League points: 68, Division III(N), 1955-56
Most League goals: 103, Division II, 1933-34
League scoring record: 42, Pat Glover, Division II, 1933-34
Record League aggregate: 182, Pat Glover, 1930-1939
Most League appearances: 448, Keith Jobling, 1953-1969
Most capped player: 7, Pat Glover, Wales

THE GRIMSBY RECORD

	Division & place	Cup round reached
1893	II 4	2
1894	II 5	1
1895	II 5	p
1896	II 3	2
1897	II 3	1
1898	II 12	1
1899	II 10	1
1900	II 6	1
1901	II 1P	p
1902	I 15	1
1903	I 17R	2
1904	II 6	1
1905	II 13	1
1906	II 8	1
1907	II 11	1
1908	II 18	q-f
1909	II 13	1
1910	II 19L	1
1911		3
1912	II 9	p
1913	II 7	1
1914	II 15	1
1915	II 17	1
1920	II 22M	1
1921	III 13	2
1922	NIII 3	1
1923	NIII 14	p
1924	NIII 11	1
1925	NIII 12	p
1926	NIII 1P	3
1927	II 17	3
1928	II 11	3
1929	II 2P	3
1930	I 18	3
1931	I 13	5
1932	I 21R	5
1933	II 13	4
1934	II 1P	4
1935	I 5	3
1936	I 17	s-f
1937	I 11	5
1938	I 20	3
1939	I 10	s-f
1946		3
1947	I 16	4
1948	I 22R	3
1949	II 11	4
1950	II 11	4
1951	II 22R	3
1952	NIII 2	2
1953	NIII 5	3
1954	NIII 17	3
1955	NIII 23	3
1956	NIII 1P	3
1957	II 16	3
1958	II 13	3
1959	II 21R	4
1960	III 4	2
1961	III 6	1
1962	III 2P	1
1963	II 19	3
1964	II 21R	3
1965	III 10	2
1966	III 11	4
1967	III 17	1
1968	III 21R	1
1969	IV 23	1
1970	IV 16	1
1971	IV 19	1
1972	IV 1P	1
1973	III 9	4
1974	III 6	3
1975	III 16	2
1976	III 18	1
1977	III 23R	2
1978	IV 6	3
1979	IV 2P	1
1980	III 1P	3
1981	II 7	3
1982	II 17	5

M—not re-elected to Second Division but invited to join newly formed Third Division.

HALIFAX TOWN

Founded: 1911
Address: Shay Ground, Halifax HX1 2YS
Telephone: Halifax 53423
Ground capacity: 16,500
Playing area: 110 by 70 yards
Record attendance: 36,885 v Tottenham Hotspur, FA Cup 5th round, 14.2.53
Record victory: 7-0 v Bishop Auckland, FA Cup 2nd round replay, 10.1.67
Record defeat: 0-13 v Stockport County, Division III(N), 6.1.34
Most League points: 57, Division IV, 1968-69
Most League goals: 83, Division III(N), 1957-58
League scoring record: 34, Albert Valentine, Division III(N), 1934-35
Record League aggregate: 129, Ernest Dixon, 1922-1930
Most League appearances: 367, John Pickering, 1965-74
Most capped player: 1, Mick Meagan, Eire

THE HALIFAX RECORD

	Division & place	*Cup round reached*
1922	NIII 19	p
1923	NIII 7	1
1924	NIII 14	2
1925	NIII 9	p
1926	NIII 5	1
1927	NIII 4	1
1928	NIII 12	2
1929	NIII 13	1
1930	NIII 21	1
1931	NIII 17	2
1932	NIII 17	3
1933	NIII 15	5
1934	NIII 9	3
1935	NIII 2	1
1936	NIII 17	2
1937	NIII 7	1
1938	NIII 18	1
1939	NIII 12	3
1946		1
1947	NIII 22	2
1948	NIII 21	1
1949	NIII 19	1
1950	NIII 21	1
1951	NIII 22	1
1952	NIII 20	1
1953	NIII 14	5
1954	NIII 23	1
1955	NIII 14	1
1956	NIII 19	2
1957	NIII 11	1
1958	NIII 7	1
1959	III 9	2
1960	III 15	2
1961	III 9	2
1962	III 18	1
1963	III 24R	2
1964	IV 10	1
1965	IV 23	1
1966	IV 15	1
1967	IV 12	3
1968	IV 11	3
1969	IV 2P	4
1970	III 18	1
1971	III 3	1
1972	III 16	1
1973	III 20	2
1974	III 9	2
1975	III 17	2
1976	III 24R	3
1977	IV 21	3
1978	IV 20	1
1979	IV 23	1
1980	IV 18	4
1981	IV 23	1
1982	IV 19	1

HARTLEPOOL UNITED

Founded: 1908
Address: The Victoria Ground, Clarence Road, Hartlepool
Telephone: Hartlepool 72584
Ground capacity: 18,000
Playing area: 113 by 77 yards
Record attendance: 17,426 v Manchester United, FA Cup 3rd round, 5.1.57
Record victory: 10-1 v Barrow, Division IV, 4.4.59
Record defeat: 1-10 v Wrexham, Division IV, 3.3.62
Most League points: 60, Division IV, 1967-68
Most League goals: 90, Division III(N), 1956-57
League scoring record: 28, Bill Robinson, Division III(N), 1927-28
Record League aggregate: 98, Ken Johnson, 1949-1964
Most League appearances: 448, Watty Moore, 1948-1964
Most capped player: 1 (11 in all), Ambrose Fogarty, Eire

THE HARTLEPOOL RECORD

	Division & place	*Cup round reached*
1922	NIII 4	p
1923	NIII 15	p
1924	NIII 21	p
1925	NIII 20	1
1926	NIII 6	p
1927	NIII 17	1
1928	NIII 15	1
1929	NIII 21	1
1930	NIII 8	1
1931	NIII 20	1
1932	NIII 13	1
1933	NIII 14	2
1934	NIII 11	2
1935	NIII 12	2
1936	NIII 8	3
1937	NIII 6	2
1938	NIII 20	2
1939	NIII 21	2
1946		1
1947	NIII 13	2
1948	NIII 19	2
1949	NIII 16	1
1950	NIII 18	2
1951	NIII 16	2
1952	NIII 9	3
1953	NIII 17	2
1954	NIII 18	1
1955	NIII 5	4
1956	NIII 4	3
1957	NIII 2	3
1958	NIII 17	2
1959	IV 19	2
1960	IV 24	1
1961	IV 23	1
1962	IV 22	3
1963	IV 24	1
1964	IV 23	1
1965	IV 15	2
1966	IV 18	3
1967	IV 8	1
1968	IV 3P	1
1969	III 22R	1
1970	IV 23	2
1971	IV 23	1
1972	IV 18	2
1973	IV 20	1
1974	IV 11	1
1975	IV 13	2
1976	IV 14	3
1977	IV 22	1
1978	IV 21	4
1979	IV 13	3
1980	IV 19	1
1981	IV 9	1
1982	IV 14	2

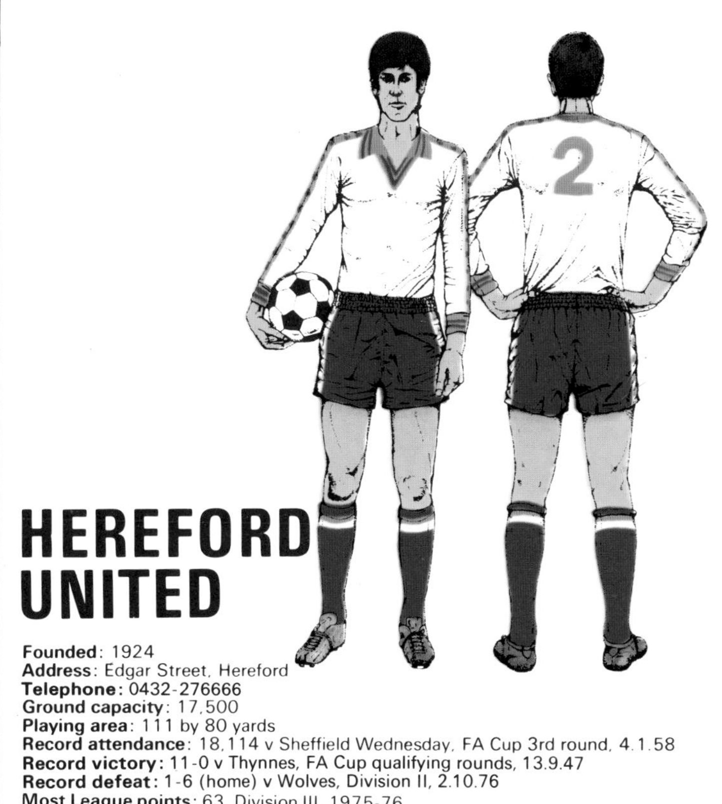

HEREFORD UNITED

Founded: 1924
Address: Edgar Street, Hereford
Telephone: 0432-276666
Ground capacity: 17,500
Playing area: 111 by 80 yards
Record attendance: 18,114 v Sheffield Wednesday, FA Cup 3rd round, 4.1.58
Record victory: 11-0 v Thynnes, FA Cup qualifying rounds, 13.9.47
Record defeat: 1-6 (home) v Wolves, Division II, 2.10.76
Most League points: 63, Division III, 1975-76
Most League goals: 86, Division III, 1975-76
League scoring record: 35, Dixie McNeil, Division III, 1975-76
Record League aggregate: 85, Dixie McNeil, 1974-77
Most League appearances: 240, Tommy Hughes, 1973-82
Most capped player: 1 (7 in all), Brian Evans, Wales

THE HEREFORD RECORD

1973	IV 2P	1
1974	III 18	4
1975	III 12	2
1976	III 1P	3
1977	II 22R	4
1978	III 23R	1
1979	IV 14	1
1980	IV 21	2
1981	IV 22	2
1982	IV 10	4

HUDDERSFIELD TOWN

Founded: 1908
Address: Leeds Road, Huddersfield HD1 6PE
Telephone: Huddersfield 20335/6
Ground capacity: 48,000 (6,200 seated)
Playing area: 115 by 75 yards
Record attendance: 67,037 v Arsenal, FA Cup quarter-final, 27.2.32
Record victory: 10-1 v Blackpool, Division I, 13.12.30
Record defeat: 0-8 v Middlesbrough, Division I, 3.9.50
Most League points: 64, Division II, 1919-20
Most League goals: 101, Division IV, 1979-80
League scoring record: 35, George Brown, Division I, 1925-26, Sam Taylor, Division II, 1919-20
Record League aggregate: 142, George Brown, Division I, 1921-1929
Most League appearances: 520, Billy Smith, 1914-1934
Most capped player: 31 (41 in all), Jimmy Nicholson, Northern Ireland

FA Cup	*Year*	*Opponents*	*Score*	*Scorers*
Winners	1922	Preston North End	1-0	Smith (pen)
Runners-up	1920	Aston Villa	*0-1	
	1928	Blackburn Rovers	1-3	Jackson
	1930	Arsenal	0-2	
	1938	Preston North End	*0-1	

*after extra time

THE HUDDERSFIELD RECORD

	Division & place	*Cup round reached*
1911	II 13	
1912	II 17	1
1913	II 5	2
1914	II 13	2
1915	II 8	1
1920	II 2P	Final
1921	I 17	3
1922	I 14	Winners
1923	I 3	3
1924	I 1C	3
1925	I 1C	1
1926	I 1C	4
1927	I 2	3
1928	I 2	Final
1929	I 16	s-f
1930	I 10	Final
1931	I 5	3
1932	I 4	q-f
1933	I 6	4
1934	I 2	4
1935	I 16	3
1936	I 3	4
1937	I 15	3
1938	I 15	Final
1939	I 19	s-f
1946		3
1947	I 20	3
1948	I 19	3
1949	I 20	4
1950	I 15	3
1951	I 19	5
1952	I 21R	3
1953	II 2P	4
1954	I 3	3
1955	I 12	q-f
1956	I 21R	3
1957	II 12	5
1958	II 9	3
1959	II 14	3
1960	II 6	4
1961	II 20	4
1962	II 7	4
1963	II 6	3
1964	II 12	5
1965	II 8	4
1966	II 4	5
1967	II 6	3
1968	II 14	3
1969	II 6	4
1970	II 1F	3
1971	I 15	4
1972	I 22R	q-f
1973	II 21R	3
1974	III 10	2
1975	III 24R	1
1976	IV 5	4
1977	IV 9	1
1978	IV 11	1
1979	IV 9	1
1980	IV 1P	1
1981	III 4	3
1982	III 17	4

HULL CITY

Founded: 1904
Address: Boothferry Park, Hull HU4 6EU
Telephone: 0482 52195/6
Ground capacity: 42,000 (9,000 seated)
Playing area: 112 by 75 yards
Record attendance: 55,019 v Manchester United, FA Cup quarter-final, 26.2.49
Record victory: 11-1 v Carlisle United, Division III (N), 14.1.39
Record defeat: 0-8 v Wolverhampton Wanderers, Division II, 4.11.11
Most League points: 69, Division III, 1965-66
Most League goals: 109, Division III, 1965-66
League scoring record: 39, Bill McNaughton, Division III (N), 1932-33
Record League aggregate: 195, Chris Chilton, 1960-1971
Most League appearances: 511, Andy Davidson, 1947-1967
Most capped player: 15 (59 in all), Terry Neill, Northern Ireland

THE HULL RECORD

	Division & place	*Cup round reached*
1906	II 5	1
1907	II 9	1
1908	II 8	2
1909	II 4	1
1910	II 3	1
1911	II 5	3
1912	II 7	1
1913	II 12	2
1914	II 7	1
1915	II 7	q-f
1920	II 11	1
1921	II 13	q-f
1922	II 5	2
1923	II 12	1
1924	II 17	1
1925	II 10	3
1926	II 13	3
1927	II 7	5
1928	II 14	3
1929	II 12	3
1930	II 21R	s-f
1931	NIII 6	3
1932	NIII 8	3
1933	NIII 1P	3
1934	II 15	4
1935	II 13	3
1936	II 22R	3
1937	NIII 5	1
1938	NIII 3	3
1939	NIII 7	2
1947	NIII 11	3
1948	NIII 5	3
1949	NIII 1P	q-f
1950	II 7	4
1951	II 10	5
1952	II 18	4
1953	II 18	4
1954	II 15	5
1955	II 19	3
1956	II 22R	3
1957	NIII 8	3
1958	NIII 5	4
1959	III 2P	1
1960	II 21R	3
1961	III 11	3
1962	III 10	2
1963	III 10	3
1964	III 8	3
1965	III 4	2
1966	III 1P	q-f
1967	II 12	3
1968	II 17	3
1969	II 11	3
1970	II 13	3
1971	II 5	q-f
1972	II 12	5
1973	II 13	5
1974	II 9	3
1975	II 8	3
1976	II 14	4
1977	II 14	3
1978	II 22R	3
1979	III 8	2
1980	III 20	1
1981	III 24R	4
1982	IV 8	3

Did not compete in 1946 Cup

IPSWICH TOWN

Founded: 1887
Address: Portman Road, Ipswich, Suffolk IP1 2DA
Telephone: Ipswich 219211
Ground capacity: 38,000
Playing area: 112 by 72 yards
Record attendance: 38,010 v Leeds United, FA Cup 6th round, 8.3.75
Record victory: 10-0 v Floriana, Malta, European Cup, 25.9.62
Record defeat: 1-10 v Fulham, Division I, 26.12.63
Most League points: 64, Division III(S), 1953-54 & 1955-56
Most League goals: 106, Division III(S), 1955-56
League scoring record: 41, Ted Phillips, Division III(S), 1956-57
Record League aggregate: 203, Ray Crawford, 1958-1963 & 1966-1969
Most League appearances: 580, Mick Mills, 1966-82
Most capped player: 47 (53 in all), Allan Hunter, Northern Ireland

FA Cup	*Year*	*Opponents*	*Score*	*Scorer*
Winners	1978	Arsenal	1-0	Osborne

THE IPSWICH RECORD

	Division & place	*Cup round reached*
1939	SIII 7	3
1946		2
1947	SIII 6	2
1948	SIII 4	1
1949	SIII 7	1
1950	SIII 17	3
1951	SIII 8	2
1952	SIII 17	3
1953	SIII 16	3
1954	SIII 1P	5
1955	II 21R	3
1956	SIII 3	1
1957	SIII 1P	3
1958	II 8	4
1959	II 16	5
1960	II 11	3
1961	II 1P	3
1962	I 1C	4
1963	I 17	4
1964	I 22R	4
1965	II 5	4
1966	II 15	3
1967	II 5	5
1968	II 1P	3
1969	I 12	3
1970	I 18	3
1971	I 19	5
1972	I 13	4
1973	I 4	4
1974	I 4	5
1975	I 3	s-f
1976	I 6	4
1977	I 3	4
1978	I 18	Winners
1979	I 6	q-f
1980	I 3	q-f
1981	I 2	s-f
1982	I 2	5

LEEDS UNITED

Founded: 1904†
Address: Elland Road, Leeds LS11 0ES **Telephone**: 0532 716037
Ground capacity: 43,900 **Playing area**: 117 by 76 yards
Record attendance: 57,892 v Sunderland, FA Cup 5th round, 15.3.67
Record victory: 10-0 v Lyn Oslo, European Cup, 1st Rd, 17.9.69
Record defeat: 1-8 v Stoke City, Division I, 27.8.34
Most League points: 67, Division I, 1968-69
Most League goals: 98, Division II, 1927-28
League scoring record: 42, John Charles, 1953-54
Record League aggregate: 154, John Charles, 1949-1957 & 1962
Most League appearances: 629, Jack Charlton, 1953-1973
Most capped player: 54, Billy Bremner, Scotland

FA Cup	**Year**	**Opponents**	**Score**	**Scorers**
Winners	1972	Arsenal	1-0	Clarke
Runners-up	1965	Liverpool	*1-2	Bremner
	1970	Chelsea	*2-2	Charlton, Jones
			*1-2	Jones
	1973	Sunderland	0-1	
League Cup				
Winners	1968	Arsenal	1-0	Cooper

†as Leeds City. Reconstituted as Leeds United 1920 *after extra time

THE LEEDS RECORD

	Division & place	*FA Cup round reached*
1906†	II 6	
1907†	II 10	1
1908†	II 12	1
1909†	II 12	2
1910†	II 17	1
1911†	II 11	1
1912†	II 19	2
1913†	II 6	1
1914†	II 4	2
1915†	II 15	2
1920‡	II	
1921	II 14	1q
1922	II 8	1
1923	II 7	2
1924	II 1P	3
1925	I 18	1
1926	I 19	3
1927	I 21R	4
1928	II 2P	3
1929	I 13	4
1930	I 5	4
1931	I 21R	5
1932	II 2P	3
1933	I 8	5
1934	I 9	3
1935	I 18	4
1936	I 11	5
1937	I 19	3
1938	I 9	4
1939	I 13	4
1946		3
1947	I 22R	3
1948	II 18	3
1949	II 15	3
1950	II 5	q-f
1951	II 5	4
1952	II 6	5
1953	II 10	3
1954	II 10	3
1955	II 4	3
1956	II 2P	3
1957	I 8	3
1958	I 17	3
1959	I 15	3
1960	I 21R	3
1961	II 14	3
1962	II 19	3
1963	II 5	5
1964	II 1P	4
1965	I 2	Final
1966	I 2	4
1967	I 4	s-f
1968	I 4	s-f
1969	I 1C	3
1970	I 2	Final
1971	I 2	5
1972	I 2	Winners
1973	I 3	Final
1974	I 1C	5
1975	I 9	q-f
1976	I 5	4
1977	I 10	s-f
1978	I 9	3
1979	I 5	3
1980	I 11	3
1981	I 9	3
1982	I 20R	4

†as Leeds City
‡Leeds expelled from the League after 8 matches. Fixtures transferred to Port Vale, who finished 13th.

LEICESTER CITY

Founded: 1884
Address: Filbert Street, Leicester
Telephone: Leicester 555000
Ground capacity: 32,000
Playing area: 112 by 75 yards
Record attendance: 47,298 v Tottenham Hotspur, FA Cup 5th round, 18.2.28
Record victory: 10-0 v Portsmouth, Division I, 20.10.28
Record defeat: 0-12 v Nottingham Forest, Division I, 21.4.09
Most League points: 61, Division II, 1956-57
Most League goals: 109, Division II, 1956-57
League scoring record: 44, Arthur Rowley, Division II, 1956-57
Record League aggregate: 262, Arthur Chandler, 1923-1935
Most League appearances: 530, Adam Black, 1919-1935
Most capped player: 37 (73 in all), Gordon Banks, England

	Year	Opponents	Score	Scorers
FA Cup *Runners-up*	1949	Wolverhampton Wanderers	1-3	Griffiths
	1961	Tottenham Hotspur	0-2	
	1963	Manchester United	1-3	Keyworth
	1969	Manchester City	0-1	
League Cup *Winners*	1964	Stoke City	h1-1	Gibson
			a3-2	Stringfellow, Gibson, Riley
Runners-up	1965	Chelsea	a2-3	Appleton, Goodfellow
			h0-0	

THE LEICESTER RECORD

	Division & place	Cup round reached
1894		2
1895	II 4	1
1896	II 8	4q
1897	II 9	4q
1898	II 7	1
1899	II 3	4q
1900	II 5	1
1901	II 11	1
1902	II 14	p
1903	II 15	2q
1904	II 18	4q
1905	II 14	1
1906	II 7	1
1907	II 3	1
1908	II 2P	2
1909	I 20R	2
1910	II 5	q-f
1911	II 15	2
1912	II 10	2
1913	II 15	1
1914	II 18	1
1915	II 19	6q
1920	II 14	3
1921	II 12	1
1922	II 9	3
1923	II 3	2
1924	II 12	1
1925	II 1P	q-f
1926	I 17	3
1927	I 7	1
1928	I 3	5
1929	I 2	5
1930	I 8	3
1931	I 16	3
1932	I 19	5
1933	I 19	3
1934	I 17	s-f
1935	I 21R	4
1936	II 6	5
1937	II 1P	4
1938	I 16	4
1939	I 22R	4
1946		3
1947	II 9	5
1948	II 9	5
1949	II 19	Final
1950	II 15	3
1951	II 14	3
1952	II 5	3
1953	II 5	3
1954	II 1P	q-f
1955	I 21R	3
1956	II 5	4
1957	II 1P	3
1958	I 18	3
1959	I 19	4
1960	I 12	q-f
1961	I 6	Final
1962	I 14	3
1963	I 4	Final
1964	I 11	3
1965	I 18	q-f
1966	I 7	5
1967	I 8	3
1968	I 13	q-f
1969	I 21R	Final
1970	II 3	5
1971	II 1P	q-f
1972	I 12	4
1973	I 16	3
1974	I 9	s-f
1975	I 18	5
1976	I 7	5
1977	I 11	3
1978	I 22R	4
1979	II 17	4
1980	II 1P	3
1981	I 21R	4
1982	II 8	s-f

Founded: 1883
Address: Sincil Bank, Lincoln
Telephone: Lincoln 22224
Ground capacity: 16,225
Playing area: 110 by 75 yards
Record attendance: 23,196 v Derby County, League Cup 4th Rd, 15.11.67
Record victory: 11-1 v Crewe Alexandra, Division III(N), 29.9.51
Record defeat: 3-11 v Manchester City, Division II, 23.3.1895
Most League points: 74, Division IV, 1975-76
Most League goals: 121, Division III(N), 1951-52
League scoring record: 42, Allan Hall, Division III(N), 1931-32
Record League aggregate: 144, Andy Graver, 1950-1954, 1958-1961
Most League appearances: 402, Tony Emery, 1946-1959
Most capped player: 3 (7 in all), David Pugh, Wales
3 (6 in all), Con Moulson, Eire
3, George Moulson, Eire

THE LINCOLN RECORD

	Division & place	Cup round reached
1885		3
1886		1
1887		1
1888		p
1889		p
1890		2
1891		1
1892		p
1893	II 9	p
1894	II 8	p
1895	II 13	q
1896	II 13	p
1897	II 16	p
1898	II 14	p
1899	II 12	p
1900	II 9	p
1901	II 8	p
1902	II 5	2
1903	II 10	1
1904	II 12	q
1905	II 9	1
1906	II 13	2
1907	II 19	2
1908	II 20L	1
1909		1
1910	II 15	p
1911	II 21L	p
1912		2
1913	II 8	p
1914	II 19	1
1915	II 16	1
1920	II 21L	1
1921		2
1922	NIII 14	p
1923	NIII 13	q
1924	NIII 19	p
1925	NIII 8	p
1926	NIII 15	1
1927	NIII 11	3
1928	NIII 2	3
1929	NIII 6	3
1930	NIII 5	2
1931	NIII 2	2
1932	NIII 1P	2
1933	II 18	3
1934	II 22R	3
1935	NIII 4	2
1936	NIII 4	1
1937	NIII 2	2
1938	NIII 7	2
1939	NIII 17	3
1946		2
1947	NIII 12	3
1948	NIII 1P	1
1949	II 22R	3
1950	NIII 4	1
1951	NIII 5	1
1952	NIII 1P	3
1953	II 15	3
1954	II 16	4
1955	II 16	3
1956	II 8	3
1957	II 18	3
1958	II 20	3
1959	II 19	3
1960	II 13	3
1961	II 22R	4
1962	III 22R	1
1963	IV 22	3
1964	IV 11	3
1965	IV 22	3
1966	IV 22	1
1967	IV 24	1
1968	IV 13	1
1969	IV 8	3
1970	IV 8	2
1971	IV 21	3
1972	IV 5	1
1973	IV 10	1
1974	IV 12	1
1975	IV 5	3
1976	IV 1P	4
1977	III 9	3
1978	III 16	1
1979	III 24R	1
1980	IV 7	1
1981	IV 2P	2
1982	III 4	1

L – not re-elected

LINCOLN CITY

LIVERPOOL

Founded: 1892
Address: Anfield Road, Liverpool 4 **Telephone**: (051) 263 2361
Ground capacity: 45,000
Playing area: 110 by 75 yards
Record attendance: 61,905 v Wolverhampton Wanderers, FA Cup 4th Rd, 2.2.52
Record victory: 11-0 v Strömgodset, European Cup Winners Cup, 17.9.74
Record defeat: 1-9 v Birmingham City, Division II, 11.12.54
Most League points: 68, Division I, 1978-79†
Most League goals: 106, Division II, 1895-96
League scoring record: 41, Roger Hunt, Division II, 1961-62
Record League aggregate: 245, Roger Hunt, 1959-1969
Most League appearances: 640, Ian Callaghan, 1960-1978
Most capped player: 54, Emlyn Hughes, England

FA Cup	*Year*	*Opponents*	*Score*	*Scorers*
Winners	1965	Leeds United	*2-1	Hunt, St John
	1974	Newcastle United	3-0	Keegan 2, Heighway
Runners-up	1914	Burnley	0-1	
	1950	Arsenal	0-2	
	1971	Arsenal	*1-2	Heighway
	1977	Manchester United	1-2	Case
League Cup				
Winners	1981	West Ham	1-1*	A. Kennedy
		Replay	2-1	Dalglish, Hansen
	1982	Tottenham	3-1*	Whelan 2, Rush
Runners-up	1978	Nottingham Forest	0-0	
		Replay	0-1	

*After extra time † record under two-points-for-a-win system.

THE LIVERPOOL RECORD

	Division & place	*F.A. Cup round reached*			
1894	II 1P	q-f	1939	I 11	5
1895	I 16R	2	1946		4
1896	II 1P	2	1947	I 1C	s-f
1897	I 5	s-f	1948	I 11	4
1898	I 9	q-f	1949	I 12	5
1899	I 2	s-f	1950	I 8	Final
1900	I 10	2	1951	I 9	3
1901	I 1C	1	1952	I 11	5
1902	I 11	2	1953	I 17	3
1903	I 5	1	1954	I 22R	3
1904	I 17R	1	1955	II 11	5
1905	II 1P	1	1956	II 3	5
1906	I 1C	s-f	1957	II 3	3
1907	I 15	q-f	1958	II 4	q-f
1908	I 8	3	1959	II 4	3
1909	I 16	2	1960	II 3	4
1910	I 2	1	1961	II 3	4
1911	I 13	2	1962	II 1P	5
1912	I 17	2	1963	I 8	s-f
1913	I 12	3	1964	I 1C	q-f
1914	I 16	Final	1965	I 7	Winners
1915	I 14	2	1966	I 1C	3
1920	I 4	q-f	1967	I 5	5
1921	I 4	2	1968	I 3	q-f
1922	I 1C	2	1969	I 2	5
1923	I 1C	3	1970	I 5	q-f
1924	I 12	q-f	1971	I 5	Final
1925	I 4	q-f	1972	I 3	4
1926	I 7	4	1973	I 1C	q-f
1927	I 9	5	1974	I 2	Winners
1928	I 16	4	1975	I 2	4
1929	I 5	4	1976	I 1C	4
1930	I 12	3	1977	I 1C	Final
1931	I 9	3	1978	I 2	3
1932	I 10	q-f	1979	I 1C	s-f
1933	I 14	3	1980	I 1C	s-f
1934	I 18	5	1981	I 5	4
1935	I 7	4	1982	I 1C	5
1936	I 19	4			
1937	I 18	3			
1938	I 11	5			

LUTON TOWN

Founded: 1885
Address: 70 Kenilworth Road, Luton
Telephone: Luton 411622
Ground capacity: 22,601
Playing area: 112 by 72 yards
Record attendance: 30,069 v Blackpool, FA Cup 6th round replay, 4.3.59
Record victory: 12-0 v Bristol Rovers, Division III(S), 13.4.36
Record defeat: 0-9 v Small Heath, Division II, 12.11.1898
Most League points: 66, Division IV, 1967-68
Most League goals: 103, Division III(S), 1936-37
League scoring record: 55, Joe Payne, Division III(S), 1936-37
Record League aggregate: 243, Gordon Turner, 1949-1964
Most League appearances: 494, Bob Morton, 1949-1964
Most capped player: 19, George Cummins, Eire

FA Cup	*Year*	*Opponents*	*Score*	*Scorers*
Runners-up	1959	Nottingham Forest	1-2	Pacey

THE LUTON TOWN RECORD

	Division & place	*Cup round reached*			
1898	II 8	1	1955	II 2P	5
1899	II 15	p	1956	I 10	3
1900	II 17L	p	1957	I 16	3
1921	SIII 9	3	1958	I 8	3
1922	SIII 4	2	1959	I 17	Final
1923	SIII 5	1	1960	I 22R	5
1924	SIII 7	1	1961	II 13	5
1925	SIII 16	1	1962	II 13	3
1926	SIII 7	2	1963	II 22R	3
1927	SIII 8	3	1964	III 18	3
1928	SIII 13	3	1965	III 21R	3
1929	SIII 7	3	1966	IV 6	2
1930	SIII 13	1	1967	IV 17	2
1931	SIII 7	2	1968	IV 1P	2
1932	SIII 6	3	1969	III 3	3
1933	SIII 14	q-f	1970	III 2P	2
1934	SIII 6	3	1971	II 6	3
1935	SIII 4	4	1972	II 13	3
1936	SIII 2	4	1973	II 12	q-f
1937	SIII 1P	4	1974	II 2P	5
1938	II 12	5	1975	I 20R	3
1939	II 7	3	1976	II 7	4
1946		3	1977	II 6	4
1947	II 13	5	1978	II 13	4
1948	II 13	5	1979	II 18	3
1949	II 10	5	1980	II 6	3
1950	II 17	3	1981	II 5	4
1951	II 19	4	1982	II 1P	4
1952	II 8	q-f			
1953	II 3	5			
1954	II 6	3			

MANCHESTER CITY

Founded: 1887
Address: Maine Road, Moss Side, Manchester M14 7WN
Telephone: (061) 226 1191/2
Ground capacity: 52,500
Playing area: 117 by 79 yards
Record attendance: 84,569 v Stoke City, FA Cup quarter-final, 3.3.34
Record victory: 11-3 v Lincoln City, Division II, 23.3.95
Record defeat: 1-9 v Everton, Division I, 3.9.06
Most League points: 62, Division II, 1946-47
Most League goals: 108, Division II, 1926-27
League scoring record: 38, Tom Johnson, Division I, 1928-29
Record League aggregate: 158, Tom Johnson, 1919-1930
Most League appearances: 565, Alan Oakes, 1959-76
Most capped player: 48, Colin Bell, England

FA Cup	*Year*	*Opponents*	*Score*	*Scorers*
Winners	1904	Bolton Wanderers	1-0	Meredith
	1934	Portsmouth	2-1	Tilson, 2
	1956	Birmingham City	3-1	Hayes, Dyson, Johnstone
	1969	Leicester City	1-0	Young
Runners-up	1926	Bolton Wanderers	0-1	
	1933	Everton	0-3	
	1955	Newcastle United	1-3	Johnstone
	1981	Tottenham	*1-1	Hutchison
		Replay	2-3	Mackenzie, Reeves pen.
League Cup				
Winners	1970	West Bromwich Albion	2-1	Doyle, Pardoe
	1976	Newcastle United	2-1	Barnes, Tueart
Runners-up	1974	Wolverhampton Wanderers	1-2	Bell

*after extra time

THE CITY RECORD

	Division & place	*Cup round reached*
1893†	II 5	
1894†	II 13	
1895	II 9	
1896	II 2	
1897	II 6	1
1898	II 3	2
1899	II 1P	2
1900	I 7	1
1901	I 11	1
1902	I 18R	2
1903	II 1P	1
1904	I 2	Winners
1905	I 3	2
1906	I 5	1
1907	I 17	1
1908	I 3	3
1909	I 19R	1
1910	II 1P	q-f
1911	I 17	2
1912	I 15	2
1913	I 6	2
1914	I 13	q-f
1915	I 5	3
1920	I 7	2
1921	I 2	1
1922	I 10	3
1923	I 8	1
1924	I 11	s-f
1925	I 10	1
1926	I 21R	Final
1927	II 3	3
1928	II 1P	5
1929	I 8	3
1930	I 3	5
1931	I 8	3
1932	I 14	s-f
1933	I 16	Final
1934	I 5	Winners
1935	I 4	3
1936	I 9	5
1937	I 1C	q-f
1938	I 21R	q-f
1939	II 5	4
1946		4
1947	II 1P	5
1948	I 10	5
1949	I 7	3
1950	I 21R	3
1951	II 2P	3
1952	I 15	3
1953	I 20	4
1954	I 17	4
1955	I 7	Final
1956	I 4	Winners
1957	I 18	3
1958	I 5	3
1959	I 20	3
1960	I 16	3
1961	I 13	4
1962	I 12	4
1963	I 21R	5
1964	II 6	3
1965	II 11	3
1966	II 1P	q-f
1967	I 15	q-f
1968	I 1C	4
1969	I 13	Winners
1970	I 9	4
1971	I 11	5
1972	I 4	3
1973	I 11	5
1974	I 14	4
1975	I 8	3
1976	I 8	4
1977	I 2	5
1978	I 4	4
1979	I 15	4
1980	I 17	3
1981	I 12	Final
1982	I 10	4

†as Ardwick

MANCHESTER UNITED

Founded: 1878
Address: Old Trafford, Manchester M16 0RA
Telephone: (061) 872 1661/2
Ground capacity: 58,500
Playing area: 116 by 76 yards
Record attendance: *70,504 v Aston Villa, Division I, 27.12.20
Record victory: 10-0 v Anderlecht, European Cup 1956-57
Record defeat: 0-7 v Aston Villa, Division I, 27.12.30
Most League points: 64, Division I, 1956-57
Most League goals: 103, Division I, 1956-57 & Division I, 1958-59
League scoring record: 32, Dennis Viollet, Division I, 1959-60
Record League aggregate: 198, Bobby Charlton, 1956-1973
Most League appearances: 606, Bobby Charlton, 1956-1973
Most capped player: 106, Bobby Charlton, England

FA Cup	*Year*	*Opponents*	*Score*	*Scorers*
Winners	1909	Bristol City	1-0	Turnbull (A)
	1948	Blackpool	4-2	Rowley 2, Pearson, Anderson
	1963	Leicester City	3-1	Herd 2, Law
	1977	Liverpool	2-1	Pearson, Greenhoff, J.
Runners-up	1957	Aston Villa	1-2	Taylor
	1958	Bolton Wanderers	0-2	
	1976	Southampton	0-1	
	1979	**Arsenal**	**2-3**	**McQueen, McIlroy**

*Ground record: 76,962 for Wolverhampton Wanderers v Grimsby Town, FA Cup semi-final, 25.3.39

THE UNITED RECORD

	Division & place	*Cup round reached*
1890÷		1
1891÷		
1892÷		
1893÷	I 16	1
1894÷	I 16R	2
1895÷	II 3	1
1896÷	II 6	2
1897÷	II 2	q-f
1898÷	II 4	2
1899÷	II 4	1
1900÷	II 4	
1901÷	II 10	1
1902÷	II 15	
1903	II 5	2
1904	II 3	2
1905	II 3	
1906	II 2P	q-f
1907	I 8	1
1908	I 1C	q-f
1909	I 13	Winners
1910	I 5	1
1911	I 1C	3
1912	I 13	q-f
1913	I 4	3
1914	I 14	1
1915	I 18	1
1920	I 12	2
1921	I 13	1
1922	I 22R	1
1923	II 4	2
1924	II 14	2
1925	II 2P	1
1926	I 9	s-f
1927	I 15	3
1928	I 19	q-f
1929	I 12	4
1930	I 17	3
1931	I 22R	4
1932	II 12	3
1933	II 6	3
1934	II 20	3
1935	II 5	4
1936	II 1P	4
1937	I 21R	4
1938	II 2P	5
1939	I 14	3
1946		4
1947	I 2	4
1948	I 2	Winners
1949	I 2	s-f
1950	I 4	q-f
1951	I 2	q-f
1952	I 1C	3
1953	I 8	5
1954	I 4	3
1955	I 5	4
1956	I 1C	3
1957	I 1C	Final
1958	I 9	Final
1959	I 2	3
1960	I 7	5
1961	I 7	4
1962	I 15	s-f
1963	I 19	Winners
1964	I 2	s-f
1965	I 1C	s-f
1966	I 4	s-f
1967	I 1C	4
1968	I 2	3
1969	I 11	q-f
1970	I 8	s-f
1971	I 8	3
1972	I 8	4
1973	I 18	3
1974	I 21R	4
1975	II 1P	3
1976	I 3	Final
1977	I 6	Winners
1978	I 10	4
1979	I 9	Final
1980	I 2	3
1981	I 8	4
1982	I 3	3

÷ – as Newton Heath

MANSFIELD TOWN

Founded: 1891 (as Mansfield Wesleyans)
Address: Field Mill Ground, Quarry Lane, Mansfield, Notts.
Telephone: Mansfield 23567
Ground capacity: 23,500
Playing area: 115 by 72 yards
Record attendance: 24,467 v Nottingham Forest, FA Cup 3rd round, 10.1.53
Record victory: 9-2 v Rotherham United, Division III(N), 27.12.32
9-2 v Hounslow Town, FA Cup 1st round replay, 5.11.62
Record defeat: 1-8 v Walsall, Division III(N), 19.1.33
Most League points: 68, Division IV, 1974-75
Most League goals: 108, Division IV, 1962-63
League scoring record: 55, Ted Harston, Division III(N), 1936-37
Record League aggregate: 104, Harry Johnson, 1931-1936
Most League appearances: 417, Don Bradley, 1949-1962
Most capped player: 6, John McClelland, Northern Ireland

THE MANSFIELD RECORD

Year	*Division & place*	*Cup round reached*
1932	SIII 20	1
1933	NIII 16	1
1934	NIII 17	1
1935	NIII 8	3
1936	NIII 19	1
1937	NIII 9	2
1938	SIII 14	3
1939	SIII 16	2
1946		3
1947	SIII 22	1
1948	NIII 8	3
1949	NIII 10	3
1950	NIII 8	2
1951	NIII 2	5
1952	NIII 6	1
1953	NIII 18	3
1954	NIII 7	1
1955	NIII 13	1
1956	NIII 18	2
1957	NIII 16	1
1958	NIII 6	3
1959	III 20	1
1960	III 22R	3
1961	IV 20	2
1962	IV 14	2
1963	IV 4P	3
1964	III 7	1
1965	III 3	2
1966	III 19	1
1967	III 9	4
1968	III 20	1
1969	III 15	q-f
1970	III 6	5
1971	III 7	2
1972	III 21R	2
1973	IV 6	1
1974	IV 17	2
1975	IV 1P	5
1976	III 11	2
1977	III 1P	1
1978	II 21R	3
1979	III 18	1
1980	III 23R	3
1981	IV 7	3
1982	IV 20	1

MIDDLESBROUGH

Founded: 1876
Address: Ayresome Park, Middlesbrough
Telephone: Middlesbrough 819659/815996
Ground capacity: 42,000 (10,200 seated)
Playing area: 115 by 75 yards
Record attendance: 53,596 v Newcastle United, Division I, 27.12.49
Record victory: 9-0 v Brighton, Division II, 23.8.58
Record defeat: 0-9 v Blackburn Rovers, Division II, 6.11.54
Most League points: 65, Division II, 1973-74
Most League goals: 122, Division II, 1926-27
League scoring record: 59, George Camsell, Division II, 1926-27
Record League aggregate: 326, George Camsell, 1925-1939
Most League appearances: 563, Tim Williamson, 1902-1923
Most capped player: 26, Wilf Mannion, England

FA Amateur Cup *Winners*	*Year*	*Opponents*	*Score*	*Scorers*
	1895	Old Carthusians	2-1	Mullen, Nelmes
	1898	Uxbridge	2-1	Bishop, Kempley

THE MIDDLESBROUGH RECORD

Year	*Division & place*	*Cup round reached*
1888		q-f
1889		q
1890		q
1891		q
1892		2
1893		2
1894		1
1895		2
1896		2q
1897		1q
1898		5q
1899		2q
1900	II 14	p
1901	II 6	q-f
1902	II 2P	1
1903	I 13	p
1904	I 10	q-f
1905	I 15	1
1906	I 18	3
1907	I 11	2
1908	I 6	1
1909	I 9	1
1910	I 17	1
1911	I 16	3
1912	I 7	2
1913	I 16	3
1914	I 4	1
1915	I 12	2
1920	I 13	2
1921	I 8	1
1922	I 8	1
1923	I 18	2
1924	I 22R	1
1925	II 13	1
1926	II 10	4
1927	II 1P	5
1928	I 22R	5
1929	II 1P	4
1930	I 16	5
1931	I 7	3
1932	I 18	3
1933	I 17	5
1934	I 16	3
1935	I 20	3
1936	I 14	q-f
1937	I 7	3
1938	I 5	5
1939	I 4	4
1946		5
1947	I 11	q-f
1948	I 16	5
1949	I 19	3
1950	I 9	4
1951	I 6	3
1952	I 18	4
1953	I 13	3
1954	I 21R	3
1955	II 12	3
1956	II 14	4
1957	II 6	4
1958	II 7	4
1959	II 13	3
1960	II 5	3
1961	II 5	3
1962	II 12	5
1963	II 4	4
1964	II 10	3
1965	II 17	5
1966	II 21R	3
1967	III 2P	3
1968	II 6	4
1969	II 4	3
1970	II 4	q-f
1971	II 7	4
1972	II 9	5
1973	II 4	3
1974	II 1P	4
1975	I 7	q-f
1976	I 13	3
1977	I 12	q-f
1978	I 14	q-f
1979	I 12	3
1980	I 9	4
1981	I 14	q-f
1982	I 22R	3

MILLWALL

Founded: 1885
Address: The Den, Cold Blow Lane, New Cross, London SE14 5RH
Telephone: (01) 639 3143
Ground capacity: 32,000
Playing area: 112 by 74 yards
Record attendance: 48,672 v Derby County, FA Cup 5th round, 20.2.37
Record victory: 9-1 v Torquay United, Division III(S), 29.8.27
9-1 v Coventry City, Division III(S), 19.11.27
Record defeat: 1-9 v Aston Villa, FA Cup 4th round, 28.1.46
Most League points: 65, Division III(S), 1927-28; Division III, 1965-66
Most League goals: 127, Division III(S), 1927-28
League scoring record: 37, Dick Parker, Division III(S), 1926-27
Record League aggregate: 79, Derek Possee, 1967-1973
Most League appearances: 523, Barry Kitchener, 1967-1982
Most capped player: 26 (27 in all), Eamonn Dunphy, Eire

THE MILLWALL RECORD

Year	*Division & place*	*Cup round reached*
1895		1
1896		1
1897		1
1898		q
1899		q
1900		s-f
1901		1
1902		p
1903		s-f
1904		1
1905		1
1906		2
1907		2
1908		1
1909		3
1910		1
1911		1
1912		1
1913		1
1914		3
1915		2
1920		1
1921	III 7	1
1922	SIII 12	q-f
1923	SIII 6	2
1924	SIII 3	1
1925	SIII 5	1
1926	SIII 3	5
1927	SIII 3	q-f
1928	SIII 1P	3
1929	II 14	4
1930	II 14	5
1931	II 14	3
1932	II 9	3
1933	II 7	4
1934	II 21R	4
1935	SIII 12	4
1936	SIII 12	3
1937	SIII 8	s-f
1938	SIII 1P	3
1939	II 13	4
1946		4
1947	II 18	3
1948	II 22R	3
1949	SIII 8	2
1950	SIII 22	1
1951	SIII 5	4
1952	SIII 4	2
1953	SIII 2	3
1954	SIII 12	2
1955	SIII 5	3
1956	SIII 22	1
1957	SIII 17	5
1958	SIII 23	2
1959	IV 9	2
1960	IV 5	1
1961	IV 6	1
1962	IV 1P	1
1963	III 16	2
1964	III 21R	1
1965	IV 2P	4
1966	III 2P	2
1967	II 8	3
1968	II 7	3
1969	II 10	4
1970	II 10	3
1971	II 8	3
1972	II 3	4
1973	II 11	5
1974	II 12	3
1975	II 20R	3
1976	III 3P	2
1977	II 10	3
1978	II 16	q-f
1979	II 21R	3
1980	III 14	4
1981	III 16	2
1982	III 9	3

NEWCASTLE UNITED

Founded: 1882
Address: St James' Park, Newcastle-on-Tyne, NE1 4ST
Telephone: (0632) 328361
Ground capacity: 38,000
Playing area: 115 by 75 yards
Record attendance: 68,386 v Chelsea, Division I, 3.9.30
Record victory: 13-0 v Newport County, Division II, 5.10.46
Record defeat: 0-9 v Burton Wanderers, Division II, 15.4.95
Most League points: 57, Division II, 1964-65
Most League goals: 98, Division I, 1951-52
League scoring record: 36, Hughie Gallacher, Division I, 1926-27
Record League aggregate: 178, Jackie Milburn, 1946-1957
Most League appearances: 432, Jim Lawrence, 1904-1922
Most capped player: 40, Alf McMichael, Northern Ireland

FA Cup	*Year*	*Opponents*	*Score*	*Scorers*
Winners	1910	Barnsley	*1-1	Rutherford
			2-0	Shepherd 2 (1 pen)
	1924	Aston Villa	2-0	Harris, Seymour
	1932	Arsenal	2-1	Allen 2
	1951	Blackpool	2-0	Milburn 2
	1952	Arsenal	1-0	Robledo (G)
	1955	Manchester City	3-1	Milburn, Mitchell, Hannah
Runners-up	1905	Aston Villa	0-2	
	1906	Everton	0-1	
	1908	Wolverhampton Wanderers	1-3	Howie
	1911	Bradford City	*0-0	
			0-1	
	1974	Liverpool	0-3	
League Cup				
Runners-up	1976	Manchester City	1-2	Gowling

*After extra time

THE NEWCASTLE RECORD

	Division & place	*Cup round reached*			
1893		1	1938	II 19	3
1894	II 4	2	1939	II 9	5
1895	II 10	2	1946		3
1896	II 5	2	1947	II 5	s-f
1897	II 5	1	1948	II 2P	3
1898	II 2P	2	1949	I 4	3
1899	I 13	2	1950	I 5	4
1900	I 5	2	1951	I 4	Winners
1901	I 6	1	1952	I 8	Winners
1902	I 3	q-f	1953	I 16	4
1903	I 14	1	1954	I 15	5
1904	I 4	1	1955	I 8	Winners
1905	I 1C	Final	1956	I 11	q-f
1906	I 4	Final	1957	I 17	4
1907	I 1C	1	1958	I 19	4
1908	I 4	Final	1959	I 11	3
1909	I 1C	s-f	1960	I 8	3
1910	I 4	Winners	1961	I 21R	q-f
1911	I 8	Final	1962	II 11	3
1912	I 3	1	1963	II 7	4
1913	I 14	q-f	1964	II 8	3
1914	I 11	1	1965	II 1P	3
1915	I 15	q-f	1966	I 15	4
1920	I 8	2	1967	I 20	4
1921	I 5	3	1968	I 10	3
1922	I 7	2	1969	I 9	4
1923	I 4	1	1970	I 7	3
1924	I 9	Winners	1971	I 12	3
1925	I 6	2	1972	I 11	3
1926	I 10	5	1973	I 9	4
1927	I 1C	5	1974	I 15	Final
1928	I 9	3	1975	I 15	4
1929	I 10	3	1976	I 15	q-f
1930	I 19	q-f	1977	I 5	4
1931	I 17	4	1978	I 21R	4
1932	I 11	Winners	1979	II 8	4
1933	I 5	3	1980	II 9	3
1934	I 21R	3	1981	II 11	5
1935	II 6	4	1982	II 9	4
1936	II 8	5			
1937	II 4	3			

NEWPORT COUNTY

Founded: 1912
Address: Somerton Park, Newport, Monmouthshire
Telephone: Newport 277543
Ground capacity: 18,000 (1,200 seated)
Playing area: 110 by 75 yards
Record attendance: 24,268 v Cardiff City, Division III(S), 16.10.37
Record victory: 10-0 v Merthyr Town, Division III(S), 10.4.30
Record defeat: 0-13 v Newcastle United, Division II, 5.10.46
Most League points: 61, Division IV, 1979-80
Most League goals: 85, Division IV, 1964-65
League scoring record: 34, Tudor Martin, Division III(S), 1929-30
Record League aggregate: 99, Reg Parker, 1948-1954
Most League appearances: 530, Ray Wilcox, 1946-1960
Most capped player: 2, Billy Thomas, Wales
2 (4 in all), Jack Nicholls, Wales
2 (9 in all), Freddie Cook, Wales
2 (41 in all), Alf Sherwood, Wales
2, Harold Williams, Wales

THE NEWPORT RECORD

	Division & place	*Cup round reached*			
1920		1	1959	III 17	4
1921	III 15	q	1960	III 13	3
1922	SIII 20	1	1961	III 13	1
1923	SIII 22	p	1962	III 24R	2
1924	SIII 10	q	1963	IV 20	1
1925	SIII 6	p	1964	IV 15	4
1926	SIII 17	2	1965	IV 16	3
1927	SIII 9	1	1966	IV 9	1
1928	SIII 9	1	1967	IV 18	1
1929	SIII 16	2	1968	IV 12	3
1930	SIII 18	2	1969	IV 22	1
1931	SIII 22	2	1970	IV 21	3
1932	*		1971	IV 22	1
1933	SIII 21	2	1972	IV 14	1
1934	SIII 18	2	1973	IV 5	2
1935	SIII 22	1	1974	IV 9	1
1936	SIII 21	1	1975	IV 12	2
1937	SIII 19	2	1976	IV 22	1
1938	SIII 16	3	1977	IV 19	2
1939	SIII 1P	3	1978	IV 16	1
1946		3	1979	IV 8	4
1947	II 22R	3	1980	IV 3P	1
1948	SIII 12	2	1981	III 12	1
1949	SIII 15	5	1982	III 16	1
1950	SIII 21	3			
1951	SIII 11	4			
1952	SIII 6	3			
1953	SIII 15	3			
1954	SIII 15	1			
1955	SIII 19	1			
1956	SIII 19	1			
1957	SIII 12	4			
1958	SIII 11	1			

*Newport were not re-elected in 1931, and took Thames' place in 1932. Did not enter Cup 1931–32.

NORTHAMPTON TOWN

Founded: 1897
Address: County Ground, Abingdon Avenue, Northampton NN1 4PS
Telephone: Northampton 31553
Ground capacity: 17,000 (1,400 seated)
Playing area: 120 by 75 yards
Record attendance: 24,523 v Fulham, Division I, 23.4.66
Record victory: 11-1 v Southend United, Southern League, 30.12.09
10-0 v Walsall, Division III(S), 5.11.27
Record defeat: 0-11 v Southampton, Southern League, 28.12.01
Most League points: 68, Division IV, 1975-76
Most League goals: 109, Division III(S), 1952-53 & Division III, 1962-63
League scoring record: 36, Cliff Holton, Division III, 1961-62
Record League aggregate: 135, Jack English, 1947-1960
Most League appearances: 521, Tommy Fowler, 1946-1961
Most capped player: 12 (16 in all), E Lloyd Davies, Wales

THE NORTHAMPTON RECORD

	Division & place	*Cup round reached*			
1906		1	1951	SIII 21	4
1907		1	1952	SIII 8	1
1908		1	1953	SIII 3	2
1909		1	1954	SIII 5	2
1910		2	1955	SIII 13	1
1911		2	1956	SIII 11	3
1912		3	1957	SIII 14	1
1913		1	1958	SIII 13	4
1914		p	1959	IV 8	2
1915		2	1960	IV 6	1
1920		p	1961	IV 3P	3
1921	III 14	1	1962	III 8	3
1922	SIII 17	2	1963	III 1P	1
1923	SIII 8	p	1964	II 11	3
1924	SIII 8	1	1965	II 2P	3
1925	SIII 9	1	1966	I 21R	3
1926	SIII 12	3	1967	II 21R	3
1927	SIII 18	2	1968	III 17	1
1928	SIII 2	3	1969	III 21R	3
1929	SIII 3	3	1970	IV 14	5
1930	SIII 4	3	1971	IV 7	1
1931	SIII 6	1	1972	IV 21	2
1932	SIII 14	4	1973	IV 23	1
1933	SIII 8	2	1974	IV 5	2
1934	SIII 13	5	1975	IV 16	2
1935	SIII 7	3	1976	IV 2P	1
1936	SIII 15	1	1977	III 22R	1
1937	SIII 7	1	1978	IV 10	2
1938	SIII 9	1	1979	IV 19	1
1939	SIII 17	1	1980	IV 13	1
1946		3	1981	IV 10	1
1947	SIII 13	3	1982	IV 22	2
1948	SIII 14	2			
1949	SIII 20	2			
1950	SIII 2	5			

NORWICH CITY

Founded: 1905
Address: Carrow Road, Norwich NOR 22
Telephone: 0603 612131
Ground capacity: 29,000
Playing area: 114 by 74 yards
Record attendance: 43,984 v Leicester City, FA Cup quarter-final, 30.3.63
Record victory: 10-2 v Coventry City, Division III(S), 15.3.30
Record defeat: 2-10 v Swindon Town, Southern League, 5.9.08
Most League points: 64, Division III(S), 1950-51
Most League goals: 99, Division III(S), 1952-53
League scoring record: 31, Ralph Hunt, Division III(S), 1955-56
Record League aggregate: 122, Johnny Gavin, 1945-1954 & 1955-1958
Most League appearances: 590, Ron Ashman, 1947-1964
Most capped player: 11 (49 in all) Martin O'Neill, Northern Ireland

League Cup	*Year*	*Opponents*	*Score*	*Scorers*
Winners	1962	Rochdale	A3-0 H1-0	Lythgoe 2, Punton Hill
Runners-up	1973	Tottenham Hotspur	0-1	
	1975	Aston Villa	0-1	

THE NORWICH RECORD

	Division & place	*Cup round reached*			
1906		2	1951	SIII 2	5
1907		2	1952	SIII 3	3
1908		2	1953	SIII 4	2
1909		3	1954	SIII 7	5
1910		1	1955	SIII 11	2
1911		2	1956	SIII 7	3
1912		1	1957	SIII 24	1
1913		2	1958	SIII 8	3
1914		1	1959	III 4	s-f
1915		3	1960	III 2P	1
1920		q-f	1961	II 4	5
1921	III 16	1	1962	II 17	5
1922	SIII 15	1	1963	II 11	q-f
1923	SIII 18	1	1964	II 17	3
1924	SIII 11	1	1965	II 6	3
1925	SIII 12	2	1966	II 13	5
1926	SIII 16	1	1967	II 11	5
1927	SIII 16	3	1968	II 9	4
1928	SIII 17	2	1969	II 13	3
1929	SIII 17	3	1970	II 11	3
1930	SIII 8	1	1971	II 10	3
1931	SIII 21	2	1972	II 1P	3
1932	SIII 10	2	1973	I 20	3
1933	SIII 3	1	1974	I 22R	3
1934	SIII 1P	1	1975	II 3P	3
1935	II 14	5	1976	I 10	5
1936	II 11	3	1977	I 16	3
1937	II 17	4	1978	I 13	3
1938	II 14	3	1979	I 16	3
1939	II 21R	3	1980	I 12	3
1946		3	1981	I 20R	4
1947	SIII 21	2	1982	II 3P	5
1948	SIII 21	2			
1949	SIII 9	2			
1950	SIII 11	3			

NOTTINGHAM FOREST

Founded: 1865
Address: City Ground, Nottingham NG2 5FJ
Telephone: Nottingham 868236
Ground capacity: 35,000 (14,200 seated)
Playing area: 115 by 78 yards
Record attendance: 49,946 v Manchester United, Division I, 28.10.67
Record victory: 14-0 v Clapton, FA Cup 1st round, 17.1.1891
Record defeat: 1-9 v Blackburn Rovers, Division II, 10.4.37
Most League points: 70, Division III(S), 1950-51
Most League goals: 110, Division III(S), 1950-51
League scoring record: 36, Wally Ardron, Division III(S), 1950-51
Record League aggregate: 199, Grenville Morris, 1898-1913
Most League appearances: 614, Bob McKinlay, 1951-1970
Most capped player: 36 (49 in all), Martin O'Neill, Northern Ireland

FA Cup	Year	Opponents	Score	Scorers
Winners	1898	Derby County	3-1	Capes 2, McPherson
	1959	Luton Town	2-1	Dwight, Wilson

League Cup	Year	Opponents	Score	Scorers
Winners	1978	Liverpool	0-0	
		Replay	1-0	Robertson (pen)
	1979	Southampton	3-2	Birtles 2, Woodcock
Runners-up	1980	Wolverhampton Wanderers	0-1	

THE FOREST RECORD

	Division & place	*Cup round reached*			
1879		s-f	1931	II 17	3
1880		s-f	1932	II 11	3
1881		2	1933	II 5	3
1882		1	1934	II 17	4
1883		3	1935	II 9	5
1884		2	1936	II 19	4
1885		s-f	1937	II 19	3
1886		3	1938	II 20	4
1887		3	1939	II 20	3
1888		5	1946		3
1889		2	1947	II 11	5
1890		1	1948	II 19	3
1891		q-f	1949	II 21R	3
1892		s-f	1950	SIII 4	2
1893	I 10	2	1951	SIII 1P	2
1894	I 7	q-f	1952	II 4	3
1895	I 7	q-f	1953	II 7	4
1896	I 13	1	1954	II 4	3
1897	I 11	q-f	1955	II 15	5
1898	I 8	Winners	1956	II 7	3
1899	I 11	q-f	1957	II 2P	q-f
1900	I 8	s-f	1958	I 10	4
1901	I 4	2	1959	I 13	Winners
1902	I 5	s-f	1960	I 20	4
1903	I 10	2	1961	I 14	3
1904	I 9	2	1962	I 19	4
1905	I 16	2	1963	I 9	q-f
1906	I 19R	3	1964	I 13	3
1907	II 1P	1	1965	I 5	5
1908	I 9	1	1966	I 18	4
1909	I 14	q-f	1967	I 2	s-f
1910	I 14	3	1968	I 11	4
1911	I 20R	1	1969	I 18	3
1912	II 15	1	1970	I 15	3
1913	II 17	2	1971	I 16	5
1914	II 20	1	1972	I 21R	3
1915	II 18	1	1973	II 14	3
1920	II 18	1	1974	II 7	q-f
1921	II 18	1	1975	II 16	4
1922	II 1P	3	1976	II 8	3
1923	I 20	1	1977	11 3P	4
1924	I 20	1	1978	1 1C	q-f
1925	I 22R	2	1979	I 2	5
1926	II 17	q-f	1980	I 5	4
1927	II 5	4	1981	I 7	q-f
			1982	I 12	3

NOTTS COUNTY

Founded: 1862
Address: Meadow Lane, Nottingham NG2 3HS
Telephone: Nottingham 861155
Ground capacity: 23,680
Playing area: 117 by 76 yards
Record attendance: 47,301 v York City, FA Cup quarter-final, 12.3.55
Record victory: 15-0 v Rotherham United, 1st round FA Cup, 24.10.1885
Record defeat: 1-9 v Aston Villa, Division I, 16.11.1888
1-9 v Blackburn Rovers, Division I, 16.11.1889
1-9 v Portsmouth, Division II, 9.4.27
Most League points: 69, Division IV, 1970-71
Most League goals: 107, Division IV, 1959-60
League scoring record: 39, Tom Keetley, Division III(S), 1930-31
Record League aggregate: 125, Les Bradd, 1967-78
Most League appearances: 564, Albert Iremonger, 1904-1926
Most capped player: 7 (10 in all), Bill Fallon, Republic of Ireland

FA Cup	Year	Opponents	Score	Scorers
Winners	1894	Bolton Wanderers	4-1	Watson, Logan 3
Runners-up	1891	Blackburn Rovers	1-3	Oswald

THE COUNTY RECORD

	Division & place	*Cup round reached*			
1878		1	1931	SIII 1P	4
1879		1	1932	II 16	3
1880		1	1933	II 15	3
1881		3	1934	II 18	3
1882		3	1935	II 22R	3
1883		s-f	1936	SIII 9	3
1884		s-f	1937	SIII 2	1
1885		q-f	1938	SIII 11	4
1886		5	1939	SIII 11	4
1887		q-f	1946		2
1888		q	1947	SIII 12	3
1889	I 11	2	1948	SIII 6	4
1890	I 10	3	1949	SIII 11	4
1891	I 3	Final	1950	SIII 1P	3
1892	I 8	q	1951	II 17	3
1893	I 14R	2	1952	II 15	4
1894	II 3	Winners	1953	II 19	4
1895	II 2	1	1954	II 14	3
1896	II 10	1	1955	II 7	q-f
1897	II 1P	2	1956	II 20	3
1898	I 13	1	1957	II 20	3
1899	I 5	2	1958	II 21R	4
1900	I 15	2	1959	III 23R	1
1901	I 3	2	1960	IV 2P	2
1902	I 13	1	1961	III 5	1
1903	I 15	3	1962	III 13	2
1904	I 13	1	1963	III 7	1
1905	I 18	1	1964	III 24R	2
1906	I 16	1	1965	IV 13	2
1907	I 18	q-f	1966	IV 8	1
1908	I 18	2	1967	IV 20	1
1909	I 15	1	1968	IV 17	1
1910	I 19	1	1969	IV 19	1
1911	I 11	1	1970	IV 7	1
1912	I 16	2	1971	IV 1P	3
1913	I 19R	1	1972	III 4	4
1914	II 1P	1	1973	III 2P	3
1915	I 16	1	1974	II 10	3
1920	I 21R	3	1975	II 14	4
1921	II 6	2	1976	II 5	3
1922	II 13	s-f	1977	II 8	3
1923	II 1P	1	1978	II 15	5
1924	I 10	2	1979	II 6	4
1925	I 9	3	1980	II 17	3
1926	I 22R	5	1981	II 2P	4
1927	II 16	3	1982	I 15	3
1928	II 15	3			
1929	II 5	3			
1930	II 22R	3			

OLDHAM ATHLETIC

Founded: 1894*
Address: Boundary Park, Oldham
Telephone: 061 624 4972
Ground capacity: 26,324
Playing area: 110 by 74 yards
Record attendance: 47,671 v Sheffield Wednesday, FA Cup 4th round, 25.1.30
Record victory: 11-0 v Southport, Division IV, 26.12.62
Record defeat: 4-13 v Tranmere Rovers, Division III(N), 26.12.35
Most League points: 62, Division III, 1973-74
Most League goals: 95, Division IV, 1962-63
League scoring record: 33, Tommy Davis, Division III(N), 1936-37
Record League aggregate: 110, Eric Gemmell, 1947-54
Most League appearances: 525, Ian Wood, 1966-80
Most capped player: 9 (24 in all), Albert Gray, Wales
*as Pine Villa, name changed to Oldham Athletic in 1899

THE OLDHAM RECORD

	Division & place	Cup round reached
1907		2
1908	II 3	2
1909	II 6	1
1910	II 2P	1
1911	I 7	2
1912	I 18	3
1913	I 9	s-f
1914	I 3	1
1915	I 2	q-f
1920	I 17	1
1921	I 19	1
1922	I 19	2
1923	I 22R	1
1924	II 7	2
1925	II 18	1
1926	II 7	3
1927	II 10	3
1928	II 7	4
1929	II 18	3
1930	II 3	4
1931	II 12	3
1932	II 18	3
1933	II 16	3
1934	II 9	4
1935	II 21R	3
1936	NIII 7	2
1937	NIII 4	3
1938	NIII 4	1
1939	NIII 5	1
1946		2
1947	NIII 19	2
1948	NIII 11	2
1949	NIII 6	3
1950	NIII 11	3
1951	NIII 15	3
1952	NIII 4	2
1953	NIII 1P	3
1954	II 22R	3
1955	NIII 10	2
1956	NIII 20	1
1957	NIII 19	2
1958	NIII 15	2
1959	IV 21	3
1960	IV 23	2
1961	IV 12	2
1962	IV 11	4
1963	IV 2P	1
1964	III 9	3
1965	III 20	3
1966	III 20	3
1967	III 10	3
1968	III 16	1
1969	III 24R	1
1970	IV 19	2
1971	IV 3P	1
1972	III 11	1
1973	III 4	1
1974	III 1P	4
1975	II 18	3
1976	II 17	3
1977	II 13	5
1978	II 8	3
1979	II 14	5
1980	II 11	3
1981	II 15	3
1982	II 11	3

THE ORIENT RECORD

	Division & place	Cup round reached
1906*	II 20	1
1907	II 17	q
1908	II 14	p
1909	II 15	1
1910	II 16	1
1911	II 4	1
1912	II 4	1
1913	II 14	1
1914	II 6	2
1915	II 9	1
1920	II 15	1
1921	II 7	1
1922	II 15	1
1923	II 19	1
1924	II 10	1
1925	II 11	1
1926	II 20	q-f
1927	II 20	3
1928	II 20	3
1929	II 22R	4
1930	SIII 12	4
1931	SIII 19	1
1932	SIII 16	2
1933	SIII 20	1
1934	SIII 11	3
1935	SIII 14	2
1936	SIII 14	4
1937	SIII 12	2
1938	SIII 19	2
1939	SIII 20	2
1946		1
1947†	SIII 19	1
1948	SIII 17	1
1949	SIII 19	2
1950	SIII 18	1
1951	SIII 17	1
1952	SIII 16	5
1953	SIII 14	1
1954	SIII 11	q-f
1955	SIII 2	2
1956	SIII 1P	4
1957	II 15	3
1958	II 12	4
1959	II 17	3
1960	II 10	3
1961	II 19	5
1962	II 2P	4
1963	I 22R	5
1964	II 16	4
1965	II 19	3
1966	II 22	3
1967	III 14	2
1968‡	III 18	4
1969	III 18	1
1970	III 1P	1
1971	II 17	4
1972	II 17	q-f
1973	II 15	3
1974	II 4	4
1975	II 12	3
1976	II 13	3
1977	II 19	4
1978	II 14	s-f
1979	II 11	4
1980	II 14	4
1981	II 17	3
1982	II 22R	5

* – as Clapton Orient 1881–1946
† – as Leyton Orient 1946–1968
‡ – as Orient 1968–

ORIENT

Founded: 1881
Address: Leyton Stadium, Brisbane Road, Leyton, London E10 5NE
Telephone: (01) 539 2223/4
Ground capacity: 26,500 (7,171 seated)
Playing area: 110 by 75 yards
Record attendance: 34,345 v West Ham United, FA Cup 4th round, 25.1.64
Record victory: 9-2 v Aldershot, Division III(S), 10.2.34
9-2 v Chester, League Cup 3rd round, 15.10.62
Record defeat: 0-8 v Aston Villa, FA Cup 4th round, 30.1.29
Most League points: 66, Division III(S), 1955-56
Most League goals: 106, Division III(S), 1955-56
League scoring record: 35, Tommy Johnston, Division II, 1957-58
Record League aggregate: 119, Tommy Johnston, 1956-1962
Most League appearances: 430, Peter Allen, 1965-1978
Most capped player: 8 (30 in all), Tony Grealish, Eire

OXFORD UNITED

Founded: 1896*
Address: Manor Ground, Beech Road, Headington, Oxford
Telephone: Oxford 61503
Ground capacity: 17,350
Playing area: 112 by 78 yards
Record attendance: 22,730 v Preston North End, FA Cup quarter-final, 29.2.64
Record victory: 7-1 v Barrow, Division IV, 19.12.64
Record defeat: 0-5 (home) v Nottingham Forest, League Cup 3rd round, 4.10.78
Most League points: 61, Division IV, 1964-65
Most League goals: 87, Division IV, 1964-65
League scoring record: 23, Colin Booth, Division IV, 1964-65
Record League aggregate: 73, Graham Atkinson, 1962-1973
Most League appearances: 480, John Shuker, 1962-1977
Most capped player: 6 (17 in all), Dave Roberts, Wales
*as Headington United. Name changed to Oxford United 25.6.60

THE OXFORD RECORD

	Division & place	Cup round reached
1961		3
1962		1
1963	IV 18	3
1964	IV 18	q-f
1965	IV 4P	1
1966	III 14	1
1967	III 15	1
1968	III 1P	1
1969	II 20	3
1970	II 15	3
1971	II 14	5
1972	II 15	3
1973	II 8	4
1974	II 18	3
1975	II 11	3
1976	II 20R	3
1977	III 17	1
1978	III 18	1
1979	III 11	1
1980	III 17	1
1981	III 14	2
1982	III 5	5

PETERBOROUGH UNITED

Founded: 1934
Address: London Road, Peterborough, PE2 8AL
Telephone: 0733 63947
Ground capacity: 30,000
Playing area: 112 by 76 yards
Record attendance: 30,096 v Swansea Town, FA Cup 5th round, 20.2.65
Record victory: 8-1 v Oldham Athletic, Division IV, 26.11.69
Record defeat: 1-8 v Northampton Town, FA Cup 2nd round, replay, 18.12.46
Most League points: 66, Division IV, 1960-61
Most League goals: 134, Division IV, 1960-61
League scoring record: 52, Terry Bly, Division IV, 1960-61
Record League aggregate: 120, Jim Hall, 1967-75
Most League appearances: 482, Tommy Robson, 1968-81
Most capped player: 8 (21 in all), Tony Millington, Wales

THE PETERBOROUGH RECORD

	Division & place	Cup round reached
1957		4
1958		1
1959		3
1960		4
1961	IV 1P	4
1962	III 5	4
1963	III 6	3
1964	III 10	1
1965	III 8	q-f
1966	III 13	2
1967	III 15	4
1968	III 24 RR	3
1969	IV 18	1
1970	IV 9	4
1971	IV 16	2
1972	IV 8	3
1973	IV 19	3
1974	IV 1P	4
1975	III 7	5
1976	III 10	4
1977	III 16	2
1978	III 4	3
1979	III 21R	1
1980	IV 8	1
1981	IV 5	5
1982	IV 5	3

RR relegated (for illegal payments) Actually finished ninth

PLYMOUTH ARGYLE

Founded: 1886
Address: Home Park, Plymouth, Devon
Telephone: Plymouth 52561/2/3
Ground capacity: 38,000
Playing area: 112 by 75 yards
Record attendance: 43,596 v Aston Villa, Division II, 10.10.36
Record victory: 8-1 v Millwall, Division II, 16.1.32
Record defeat: 0-9 v Stoke City, Division II, 17.12.60
Most League points: 68, Division III(S), 1929-30
Most League goals: 107, Division III(S), 1925-26 and 1951-52
League scoring record: 32, Jack Cock, Division III(S), 1925-26
Record League aggregate: 180, Sammy Black, 1924-1938
Most League appearances: 470, Sammy Black, 1924-1938
Most capped player: 20 (23 in all), Moses Russell, Wales

THE PLYMOUTH RECORD

	Division & place	Cup round reached
1904		1
1905		1
1906		2
1907		1
1908		2
1909		3
1910		1
1911		1
1912		1
1913		2
1914		2
1915		1
1920		3
1921	III 11	3
1922	SIII 2	1
1923	SIII 2	3
1924	SIII 2	1
1925	SIII 2	1
1926	SIII 2	3
1927	SIII 2	3
1928	SIII 3	1
1929	SIII 4	4
1930	SIII 1P	3
1931	II 18	3
1932	II 4	4
1933	II 14	3
1934	II 10	3
1935	II 8	4
1936	II 7	4
1937	II 5	4
1938	II 13	3
1939	II 15	3
1946		3
1947	II 19	3
1948	II 17	3
1949	II 20	3
1950	II 21R	3
1951	SIII 4	3
1952	SIII 1P	1
1953	II 4	5
1954	II 19	4
1955	II 20	3
1956	II 21R	3
1957	SIII 18	2
1958	SIII 3	3
1959	III 1P	3
1960	II 19	3
1961	II 11	3
1962	II 5	4
1963	II 12	3
1964	II 20	3
1965	II 15	4
1966	II 18	4
1967	II 16	3
1968	II 22R	3
1969	III 5	1
1970	III 17	2
1971	III 15	1
1972	III 8	1
1973	III 8	4
1974	III 17	3
1975	III 2P	4
1976	II 16	3
1977	II 21R	3
1978	III 19	3
1979	III 15	1
1980	III 15	1
1981	III 7	3
1982	III 10	1

PORTSMOUTH

Founded: 1898
Address: Fratton Park, Frogmore Road, Portsmouth
Telephone: Portsmouth 731204/5
Ground capacity: 46,000
Playing area: 116 by 73 yards
Record attendance: 51,385 v Derby County, FA Cup quarter-final, 26.2.49
Record victory: 9-1 v Notts County, Division II, 9.4.27
Record defeat: 0-10 v Leicester City, Division I, 20.10.28
Most League points: 65, Division III, 1961-62
Most League goals: 91, Division IV, 1979-80
League scoring record: 40, Billy Haines, Division II, 1926-27
Record League aggregate: 194, Peter Harris, 1946-1960
Most League appearances: 764, Jimmy Dickinson, 1946-1965
Most capped player: 48, Jimmy Dickinson, England

FA Cup	Year	Opponents	Score	Scorers
Winners	1939	Wolverhampton Wanderers	4-1	Parker 2, Barlow, Anderson
Runners-up	1929	Bolton Wanderers	0-2	
	1934	Manchester City	1-2	Rutherford

THE PORTSMOUTH RECORD

	Division & place	*Cup round reached*
1900		1
1901		q-f
1902		q-f
1903		1
1904		1
1905		2
1906		1
1907		2
1908		3
1909		2
1910		2
1911		1
1912		2
1913		1
1914		1
1915		1
1920		1
1921	SIII 12	1
1922	SIII 3	1
1923	SIII 6	1
1924	SIII 1P	1
1925	II 4	2
1926	II 11	3
1927	II 2P	4
1928	I 20	3
1929	I 20	Final
1930	I 13	4
1931	I 4	5
1932	I 8	5
1933	I 9	3
1934	I 10	Final
1935	I 14	4
1936	I 10	3
1937	I 9	3
1938	I 19	4
1939	I 17	Winners
1946		3
1947	I 12	4
1948	I 8	4
1949	I 1C	s-f
1950	I 1C	5
1951	I 7	3
1952	I 4	q-f
1953	I 15	3
1954	I 14	5
1955	I 3	3
1956	I 12	4
1957	I 19	4
1958	I 20	4
1959	I 22R	5
1960	II 20	3
1961	II 21R	3
1962	III 1P	1
1963	II 16	4
1964	II 9	3
1965	II 20	3
1966	II 12	3
1967	II 14	4
1968	II 5	5
1969	II 15	4
1970	II 17	3
1971	II 16	4
1972	II 16	5
1973	II 17	3
1974	II 15	5
1975	II 17	3
1976	II 22R	4
1977	III 20	3
1978	III 24R	2
1979	IV 7	2
1980	IV 4P	3
1981	III 6	1
1982	III 13	1

PORT VALE

Founded: 1876
Address: Vale Park, Hamil Road, Burslem, Stoke-on-Trent
Telephone: Stoke-on-Trent 814134
Ground capacity: 35,000
Playing area: 116 by 76 yards
Record attendance: 50,000 v Aston Villa, FA Cup 5th round, 20.2.60
Record victory: 9-1 v Chesterfield, Division II, 24.9.32
Record defeat: 0-10 v Sheffield United, Division II, 10.12.1892 (home)
0-10 v Notts County, Division II, 26.2.1895
Most League points: 69, Division III(N), 1953-54
Most League goals: 110, Division IV, 1958-59
League scoring record: 38, Wilf Kirkham, Division II, 1926-27
Record League aggregate: 154, Wilf Kirkham, 1923-29, 1931-33
Most League appearances: 761, Roy Sproson, 1950-1972
Most capped player: 7 (18 in all), Sammy Morgan, Northern Ireland

THE PORT VALE RECORD

	Division & place	*Cup round reached*
1893*	II 11	q
1894*	II 7	q
1895*	II 15	q
1896*	II 14L	p
1897*		p
1898*		2
1899*	II 9	1
1900*	II 11	1
1901*	II 9	1
1902*	II 13	1
1903*	II 9	p
1904*	II 13	p
1905*	II 16	2
1906*	II 17	1
1907*	†II 16	2
1908*		p
1909*		p
1910*		p
1911*		p
1912*		p
1913*		p
1914		1
1915		q
1920	§II 13	1
1921	II 17	p
1922	II 18	1
1923	II 17	p
1924	II 16	p
1925	II 8	1
1926	II 8	3
1927	II 8	4
1928	II 9	5
1929	II 21R	3
1930	NIII 1P	2
1931	II 5	4
1932	II 20	4
1933	II 17	3
1934	II 8	3
1935	II 18	3
1936	II 21R	4
1937	NIII 11	3
1938	NIII 15	1
1939	SIII 18	2
1946		3
1947	SIII 10	4
1948	SIII 8	1
1949	SIII 13	1
1950	SIII 13	4
1951	SIII 12	3
1952	SIII 13	1
1953	NIII 2	2
1954	NIII 1P	s-f
1955	II 17	4
1956	II 12	4
1957	II 22R	3
1958	SIII 15	2
1959	IV 1P	1
1960	III 14	5
1961	III 7	3
1962	III 12	5
1963	III 3	4
1964	III 13	4
1965	III 22R	2
1966	IV 19	3
1967	IV 13	2
1968	‡IV 18	1
1969	IV 13	3
1970	IV 4P	2
1971	III 17	1
1972	III 15	3
1973	III 6	3
1974	III 20	3
1975	III 6	1
1976	III 12	2
1977	III 19	5
1978	III 21R	2
1979	IV 16	1
1980	IV 20	1
1981	IV 19	3
1982	IV 7	3

* – As Burslem Port Vale. Name changed in 1913
L – failed to obtain re-election
† – Burslem Port Vale resigned from the League
§ – Port Vale returned to the League, taking over the fixtures and record of Leeds City on 9 October 1919
‡ – Expelled from the League for financial irregularities and therefore technically finished 24th. Obtained re-election immediately.

PRESTON NORTH END

Founded: 1881
Address: Deepdale, Preston PR1 6RU
Telephone: Preston 795919
Ground capacity: 25,000
Playing area: 112 by 78 yards
Record attendance: 42,684 v Arsenal, Division I, 23.4.38
Record victory: 26-0 v Hyde, FA Cup 1st series 1st round, 15.10.1887
Record defeat: 0-7 v Blackpool, Division I, 1.5.48
Most League points: 61, Division III, 1970-71
Most League goals: 100, Division II, 1927-28 & Division I, 1957-58
League scoring record: 37, Ted Harper, Division II, 1932-33
Record League aggregate: 187, Tom Finney, 1946-1960
Most League appearances: 447, Allan Kelly, 1961-75
Most capped player: 76, Tom Finney, England

FA Cup	Year	Opponents	Score	Scorers
Winners	1889	Wolverhampton Wanderers	3-0	Dewhurst, Ross, Thompson
	1938	Huddersfield Town	*1-0	Mutch (pen)
Runners-up	1888	West Bromwich Albion	1-2	Goodall
	1922	Huddersfield Town	0-1	
	1937	Sunderland	1-3	O'Donnell (F)
	1954	West Bromwich Albion	2-3	Morrison, Wayman
	1964	West Ham United	2-3	Holden, Dawson

*after extra time

THE PRESTON RECORD

	Division & place	*Cup round reached*			
1884		4	1935	I 11	q-f
1885		†	1936	I 7	4
1886		3	1937	I 14	Final
1887		s-f	1938	I 3	Winners
1888		Final	1939	I 9	q-f
1889	I 1C	Winners	1946		5
1890	I 1C	q-f	1947	I 7	q-f
1891	I 2	1	1948	I 7	q-f
1892	I 2	q-f	1949	I 21R	4
1893	I 2	s-f	1950	II 6	3
1894	I 14	2	1951	II 1P	4
1895	I 4	2	1952	I 7	3
1896	I 9	1	1953	I 2	4
1897	I 4	q-f	1954	I 11	Final
1898	I 12	1	1955	I 14	4
1899	I 15	2	1956	I 19	3
1900	I 16	q-f	1957	I 3	5
1901	I 17R	1	1958	I 2	3
1902	II 3	1	1959	I 12	5
1903	II 7	2	1960	I 9	q-f
1904	II 1P	2	1961	I 22R	4
1905	I 8	q-f	1962	II 10	q-f
1906	I 2	1	1963	II 17	3
1907	I 14	1	1964	II 3	Final
1908	I 12	1	1965	II 12	4
1909	I 10	2	1966	II 17	q-f
1910	I 12	1	1967	II 13	3
1911	I 14	2	1968	II 20	4
1912	I 19R	1	1969	II 14	4
1913	II 1P	1	1970	II 22R	3
1914	I 19R	3	1971	III 1P	1
1915	II 2P	1	1972	II 18	4
1920	I 19	3	1973	II 19	3
1921	I 16	s-f	1974	II 21R	3
1922	I 16	Final	1975	III 9	3
1923	I 16	2	1976	III 8	2
1924	I 18	1	1977	III 6	2
1925	I 21R	2	1978	III 3P	2
1926	II 12	3	1979	II 7	4
1927	II 6	4	1980	II 10	3
1928	II 4	3	1981	II 20R	3
1929	II 13	3	1982	III 14	1
1930	II 16	3			
1931	II 7	3			
1932	II 13	5			
1933	II 9	3			
1934	II 2P	q-f			

† – Preston expelled by FA

QUEEN'S PARK RANGERS

Founded: 1885
Address: South Africa Road, London W12 7PA
Telephone: (01) 743 0262/3/4/5
Ground capacity: 30,000
Playing area: 112 by 72 yards
Record attendance: 35,353 v Leeds United, Division I, 28.4.74
Record victory: 9-2 v Tranmere Rovers, Division III, 3.12.60
Record defeat: 1-8 v Mansfield Town, Division III, 15.3.65
1-8 v Manchester United, Division I, 12.2.69
Most League points: 67, Division III, 1966-67
Most League goals: 111, Division III, 1961-62
League scoring record: 37, George Goddard, Division III(S), 1929-30
Record League aggregate: 172, George Goddard, 1926-1934
Most League appearances: 519, Tony Ingham, 1950-1963
Most capped player: 26 (56 in all), Don Givens, Eire

FA Cup	*Year*	*Opponents*	*Score*	*Scorers*
Runners-up	1982	Tottenham	*1-1	Fenwick
		Replay	0-1	
League Cup				
Winners	1967	West Bromwich Albion	3-2	Morgan (R), Marsh, Lazarus

*After extra time

THE QPR RECORD

	Division & place	*Cup round reached*			
1900		2	1952	II 22R	3
1901		q	1953	SIII 21	1
1902		q	1954	SIII 18	3
1903		q	1955	SIII 15	1
1904		q	1956	SIII 18	1
1905		q	1957	SIII 10	3
1906		1	1958	SIII 10	2
1907		1	1959	III 13	2
1908		2	1960	III 8	2
1909		1	1961	III 3	2
1910		q-f	1962	III 4	3
1911		1	1963	III 13	3
1912		1	1964	III 15	3
1913		2	1965	III 14	2
1914		q-f	1966	III 3	3
1915		3	1967	III 1P	3
1920		1	1968	II 2P	3
1921	SIII 3	2	1969	I 22R	3
1922	SIII 5	1	1970	II 9	q-f
1923	SIII 11	q-f	1971	II 10	3
1924	SIII 22	1	1972	II 4	3
1925	SIII 19	1	1973	II 2P	5
1926	SIII 22	2	1974	I 8	q-f
1927	SIII 14	*	1975	I 11	5
1928	SIII 10	1	1976	I 2	3
1929	SIII 6	1	1977	I 14	4
1930	SIII 3	3	1978	I 19	5
1931	SIII 8	3	1979	I 20R	3
1932	SIII 13	4	1980	II 5	3
1933	SIII 16	3	1981	II 8	3
1934	SIII 4	3	1982	II 5	Final
1935	SIII 13	2			
1936	SIII 4	1			
1937	SIII 9	3			
1938	SIII 3	2			
1939	SIII 6	3			
1946		5			
1947	SIII 2	3			
1948	SIII 1P	q-f			
1949	II 13	3			
1950	II 20	3			
1951	II 16	3			

* – did not enter

READING

Founded: 1871
Address: Elm Park, Norfolk Road, Reading
Telephone: Reading 57878/9/0
Ground capacity: 27,000 (3,200 seated)
Playing area: 112 by 77 yards
Record attendance: 33,042 v Brentford, FA Cup 5th round, 19.2.27
Record victory: 10-2 v Crystal Palace, Division III S, 4.9.46
Record defeat: 0-18 v Preston North End, FA Cup, 1st round, 27.1.1894
Most League points: 65, Division IV, 1978–79
Most League goals: 112, Division III(S), 1951-52
League scoring record: 39, Ronnie Blackman, Division III(S), 1951-52
Record League aggregate: 156, Ronnie Blackman, 1947-1954
Most League appearances: 471, Steve Death, 1969-82
Most capped player: 8, Pat McConnell, Northern Ireland

THE READING RECORD

	Division & place	Cup round reached
1900		1
1901		3
1902		2
1903		1
1904		1
1905		1
1906		1
1907		1
1908		1
1909		1
1910		1
1911		q
1912		3
1913		3
1914		1
1915		1
1920		1
1921	III 20	1
1922	SIII 13	1
1923	SIII 19	1
1924	SIII 18	1
1925	SIII 14	2
1926	SIII 1P	3
1927	II 14	s-f
1928	II 18	4
1929	II 15	5
1930	II 19	3
1931	II 21R	3
1932	SIII 2	1
1933	SIII 4	3
1934	SIII 3	3
1935	SIII 2	5
1936	SIII 3	3
1937	SIII 5	3
1938	SIII 6	1
1939	SIII 5	1
1946		1
1947	SIII 9	3
1948	SIII 10	3
1949	SIII 2	2
1950	SIII 10	3
1951	SIII 3	3
1952	SIII 2	3
1953	SIII 11	1
1954	SIII 8	1
1955	SIII 18	3
1956	SIII 17	2
1957	SIII 13	3
1958	SIII 5	3
1959	III 6	1
1960	III 11	3
1961	III 18	3
1962	III 7	1
1963	III 20	1
1964	III 6	2
1965	III 13	4
1966	III 8	3
1967	III 4	2
1968	III 5	3
1969	III 14	3
1970	III 8	1
1971	III 21R	3
1972	IV 16	4
1973	IV 7	4
1974	IV 6	2
1975	IV 7	1
1976	IV 3P	1
1977	III 21R	3
1978	IV 8	2
1979	IV 1P	3
1980	III 7	4
1981	III 10	1
1982	III 12	1

ROCHDALE

Founded: 1907
Address: Spotland, Willbutts Lane, Rochdale, Lancashire
Telephone: 0706 44648
Ground capacity: 28,000 (700 seated)
Playing area: 113 by 75 yards
Record attendance: 24,231 v Notts County, FA Cup 2nd round, 10.12.49
Record victory: 8-1 v Chesterfield, Division III(N), 18.12.26
Record defeat: 1-9 v Tranmere, Division III(N), 25.12.31
Most League points: 62, Division III(N), 1923-24
Most League goals: 105, Division III(N), 1926-27
League scoring record: 44, Albert Whitehurst, Division III(N), 1926-27
Record League aggregate: 119, Reg Jenkins, 1964-73
Most League appearances: 317, Graham Smith, 1966-74
Most capped player: None

League Cup	*Year*	*Opponents*	*Score*
Runners-up	1962	Norwich City	h0-3 a0-1

THE ROCHDALE RECORD

	Division & place	Cup round reached
1913		1
1914		p
1915		2
1920		1
1921		1
1922	NIII 20	p
1923	NIII 12	p
1924	NIII 2	p
1925	NIII 6	p
1926	NIII 3	2
1927	NIII 2	1
1928	NIII 13	2
1929	NIII 17	1
1930	NIII 10	1
1931	NIII 21	1
1932	NIII 21	1
1933	NIII 18	1
1934	NIII 22	1
1935	NIII 20	1
1936	NIII 20	1
1937	NIII 18	1
1938	NIII 17	1
1939	NIII 15	1
1946	-	3
1947	NIII 6	3
1948	NIII 12	2
1949	NIII 7	1
1950	NIII 3	2
1951	NIII 11	3
1952	NIII 21	3
1953	NIII 22	1
1954	NIII 19	1
1955	NIII 12	3
1956	NIII 12	1
1957	NIII 13	1
1958	NIII 10	1
1959	III 24R	1
1960	IV 12	2
1961	IV 17	1
1962	IV 12	2
1963	IV 7	1
1964	IV 20	2
1965	IV 6	1
1966	IV 21	2
1967	IV 21	1
1968	IV 19	1
1969	IV 3P	1
1970	III 9	1
1971	III 16	4
1972	III 18	1
1973	III 13	1
1974	III 24R	2
1975	IV 19	2
1976	IV 15	3
1977	IV 18	1
1978	IV 24	1
1979	IV 20	1
1980	IV 24	3
1981	IV 15	1
1982	IV 21	1

ROTHERHAM UNITED

Founded: 1884
Address: Millmoor Ground, Rotherham, Yorkshire
Telephone: Rotherham 562434
Ground capacity: 21,000
Playing area: 115 by 76 yards
Record attendance: 25,000 v Sheffield Wednesday, Division II, 26.1.52
25,000 v Sheffield United, Division II, 13.12.52
Record victory: 8-0 v Oldham Athletic, Division III(N), 26.5.47
Record defeat: 1-11 v Bradford City, Division III(N), 25.8.28
Most League points: 71, Division III(N), 1950-51
Most League goals: 114, Division III(N), 1946-47
League scoring record: 38, Wally Ardron, Division III(N), 1946-47
Record League aggregate: 130, Gladstone Guest, 1946-1956
Most League appearances: 459, Danny Williams, 1946-1962
Most capped player: 6, Harry Millership, Wales

League Cup	*Season*	*Opponents*	*Score*	*Scorers*
Runners-up	1960-61	Aston Villa	H2-0 A0-3	Webster, Kirkman

THE ROTHERHAM RECORD

	Division & place	Cup round reached
1894*	II 14	q
1895*	II 12	q
1896*	II 15	1
1920†	II 17	q
1921†	II 19	q
1922†	II 16	q
1923†	II 21R	1
1924†	NIII 4	q
1925†	NIII 22	q
1926‡	NIII 14	3
1927	NIII 19	1
1928	NIII 14	3
1929	NIII 16	1
1930	NIII 20	3
1931	NIII 14	1
1932	NIII 19	1
1933	NIII 17	1
1934	NIII 21	3
1935	NIII 9	2
1936	NIII 11	2
1937	NIII 17	1
1938	NIII 6	2
1939	NIII 11	1
1946		4
1947	NIII 2	3
1948	NIII 2	3
1949	NIII 2	4
1950	NIII 6	3
1951	NIII 1P	4
1952	II 9	4
1953	II 12	5
1954	II 5	4
1955	II 3	4
1956	II 19	3
1957	II 17	3
1958	II 18	3
1959	II 20	3
1960	II 8	4
1961	II 15	4
1962	II 9	3
1963	II 14	3
1964	II 7	3
1965	II 14	4
1966	II 7	4
1967	II 18	4
1968	II 21R	5
1969	III 11	2
1970	III 14	3
1971	III 8	3
1972	III 5	4
1973	III 21R	2
1974	IV 15	2
1975	IV 3P	3
1976	III 16	2
1977	III 4	3
1978	III 20	3
1979	III 17	3
1980	III 13	2
1981	III 1P	2
1982	II 7	3

* – Rotherham Town, who resigned from the League in 1896
† – Rotherham County elected to the League in 1919
‡ – Rotherham County and Rotherham Town amalgamated to form Rotherham United at the start of the 1925-26 season.

SCUNTHORPE UNITED

Founded: 1904
Address: Old Show Ground, Scunthorpe, South Humberside
Telephone: Scunthorpe 842954/848077
Ground capacity: 25,000
Playing area: 112 by 78 yards
Record attendance: 23,935 v Portsmouth, FA Cup 4th round, 30.1.54
Record victory: 9-0 v Boston United, FA Cup 1st round, 21.11.53
Record defeat: 0-8 v Carlisle United, Division III(N), 25.12.52
Most League points: 66, Division III(N), 1957-58
Most League goals: 88, Division III(N), 1957-58
League scoring record: 31, Barry Thomas, Division II, 1961-62
Record League aggregate: 92, Barry Thomas, 1959-1962, 1964-1966
Most League appearances: 600, Jack Brownsword, 1950-1965
Most capped player: None

THE SCUNTHORPE RECORD

	Division & place	*Cup round reached*			
1951	NIII 12	q	1968	III 23R	2
1952	NIII 14	3	1969	IV 16	1
1953	NIII 15	3	1970	IV 12	5
1954	NIII 3	4	1971	IV 17	3
1955	NIII 3	2	1972	IV 4P	1
1956	NIII 9	4	1973	III 24R	3
1957	NIII 14	2	1974	IV 18	4
1958	NIII 1P	5	1975	IV 24	1
1959	II 18	3	1976	IV 19	1
1960	II 15	4	1977	IV 20	1
1961	II 9	4	1978	IV 14	1
1962	II 4	3	1979	IV 12	1
1963	II 9	3	1980	IV 14	1
1964	II 22R	3	1981	IV 16	2
1965	III 18	1	1982	IV 23	3
1966	III 4	1			
1967	III 18	2			

SHEFFIELD UNITED

Founded: 1889
Address: Bramall Lane, Sheffield S2 4SU
Telephone: 738955/6/7
Ground capacity: 49,000 (15,300 seated)
Playing area: 117 by 75 yards
Record attendance: 68,287 v Leeds United, FA Cup 5th round, 15.2.36
Record victory: 11-2 v Cardiff City, Division 1, 1.1.26
Record defeat: 0-13 v Bolton Wanderers, FA Cup 2nd round, 1.2.90
Most League points: 60, Division II, 1952–53
Most League goals: 102, Division I, 1925–26
League scoring record: 41, Jimmy Dunne, Division I, 1930-31
Record League aggregate: 205, Harry Johnson, 1919-1930
Most League appearances: 629, Joe Shaw, 1948-1966
Most capped player: 25, Billy Gillespie, Northern Ireland

FA Cup	*Year*	*Opponents*	*Score*	*Scorers*
Winners	1899	Derby County	4-1	Bennett, Beers, Almond, Priest
	1902	Southampton	1-1	Common
			2-1	Hedley, Barnes
	1915	Chelsea	3-0	Simmons, Fazackerley, Kitchen
	1925	Cardiff City	1-0	Tunstall
Runners-up	1901	Tottenham Hotspur	2-2	Bennett, Priest
			1-3	Priest
	1936	Arsenal	0-1	

THE UNITED RECORD

	Division & place	*Cup round reached*			
1890		2	1937	II 7	4
1891		1	1938	II 3	4
1892		2	1939	II 2P	5
1893	II 2P	2	1946		4
1894	I 10	1	1947	I 6	q-f
1895	I 6	2	1948	I 12	3
1896	I 12	2	1949	I 22R	4
1897	I 2	1	1950	II 3	4
1898	I 1C	1	1951	II 8	4
1899	I 16	Winners	1952	II 11	q-f
1900	I 2	q-f	1953	II 1P	4
1901	I 14	Final	1954	I 20	3
1902	I 10	Winners	1955	I 13	3
1903	I 4	2	1956	I 22R	5
1904	I 7	q-f	1957	II 7	3
1905	I 6	1	1958	II 6	5
1906	I 13	2	1959	II 3	q-f
1907	I 4	1	1960	II 4	q-f
1908	I 17	1	1961	II 2P	s-f
1909	I 12	1	1962	I 5	q-f
1910	I 6	1	1963	I 10	5
1911	I 9	1	1964	I 12	4
1912	I 14	1	1965	I 19	4
1913	I 15	1	1966	I 9	4
1914	I 10	s-f	1967	I 10	5
1915	I 6	Winners	1968	I 21R	q-f
1920	I 14	2	1969	II 9	3
1921	I 20	1	1970	II 6	4
1922	I 11	1	1971	II 2P	3
1923	I 10	s-f	1972	I 10	3
1924	I 5	1	1973	I 14	4
1925	I 14	Winners	1974	I 13	3
1926	I 5	4	1975	I 6	4
1927	I 8	3	1976	I 22R	3
1928	I 13	s-f	1977	II 11	3
1929	I 11	3	1978	II 12	3
1930	I 20	4	1979	III 20R	3
1931	I 15	5	1980	III 12	2
1932	I 7	4	1981	III 21R	2
1933	I 10	4	1982	IV 1P	1
1934	I 22R	3			
1935	II 11	4			
1936	II 3	Final			

SHEFFIELD WEDNESDAY

Founded: 1867
Address: Hillsborough, Sheffield S6 1SW
Telephone: Sheffield 343123
Ground capacity: 50,174
Playing area: 115 by 75 yards
Record attendance: 72,841 v Manchester City, FA Cup 5th round, 17.2.34
Record victory: 12-0 v Halliwell, FA Cup 1st round, 17.1.1891
Record defeat: 0-10 v Aston Villa, Division I, 5.10.1912
Most League points: 62, Division II, 1958-59
Most League goals: 106, Division II, 1958-59
League scoring record: 46, Derek Dooley, Division II, 1951-52
Record League aggregate: 200, Andy Wilson, 1900-20
Most League appearances: 502, Andy Wilson, 1900-20
Most capped player: 33, Ron Springett, England

FA Cup	*Year*	*Opponents*	*Score*	*Scorers*
Winners	1896	Wolverhampton Wanderers	2-1	Spiksley 2
	1907	Everton	2-1	Stewart, Simpson
	1935	West Bromwich Albion	4-2	Rimmer 2, Palethorpe, Hooper
Runners-up	1890	Blackburn Rovers	1-6	Bennett
	1966	Everton	2-3	McCalliog, Ford

THE WEDNESDAY RECORD

	Division & place	*Cup round reached*
1881		4
1882		s-f
1883		4
1884		2
1885		3
1886		
1887		
1888		q-f
1889		q-f
1890		Final
1891		q-f
1892		q-f
1893	I 12	q-f
1894	I 12	s-f
1895	I 8	s-f
1896	I 7	Winners
1897	I 6	1
1898	I 5	2
1899	I 18R	1
1900	II 1P	2
1901	I 8	1
1902	I 9	1
1903	I 1C	1
1904	I 1C	s-f
1905	I 9	s-f
1906	I 3	q-f
1907	I 13	Winners
1908	I 5	1
1909	I 5	3
1910	I 11	1
1911	I 6	1
1912	I 5	1
1913	I 3	3
1914	I 18	q-f
1915	I 7	3
1920	I 22R	1
1921	II 10	2
1922	II 10	1
1923	II 8	3
1924	II 8	2
1925	II 14	2
1926	II 1P	3
1927	I 16	4
1928	I 14	5
1929*	I 1C	4
1930	I 1C	s-f
1931	I 3	4
1932	I 3	5
1933	I 3	3
1934	I 11	5
1935	I 3	Winners
1936	I 20	4
1937	I 22R	4
1938	II 17	3
1939	II 3	5
1946		5
1947	II 20	5
1948	II 4	4
1949	II 8	4
1950	II 2P	3
1951	I 21R	3
1952	II 1P	3
1953	I 18	3
1954	I 19	s-f
1955	I 22R	4
1956	II 1P	3
1957	I 14	3
1958	I 22R	5
1959	II 1P	3
1960	I 5	s-f
1961	I 2	q-f
1962	I 6	5
1963	I 6	4
1964	I 6	3
1965	I 8	3
1966	I 17	Final
1967	I 11	q-f
1968	I 19	5
1969	I 15	4
1970	I 22R	4
1971	II 15	3
1972	II 14	3
1973	II 10	5
1974	II 19	3
1975	II 22R	3
1976	III 20	3
1977	III 8	1
1978	III 14	2
1979	III 14	3
1980	III 3P	2
1981	II 10	3
1982	II 4	3

*The club officially changed their name to Sheffield Wednesday in the summer of 1929. Before then they were known as The Wednesday.
†Did not enter

SHREWSBURY TOWN

Founded: 1886
Address: Gay Meadow, Shrewsbury, Shropshire
Telephone: Shrewsbury 60111
Ground capacity: 18,000
Playing area: 116 by 76 yards
Record attendance: 18,917 v Walsall, Division III, 26.4.61
Record victory: 7-0 v Swindon Town, Division III(S), 6.5.55
Record defeat: 1-8 v Norwich City, Division III(S), 13.9.52 (home)
1-8 v Coventry City, Division III, 22.10.63
Most League points: 62, Division IV, 1974-75
Most League goals: 101, Division IV, 1958-59
League scoring record: 38, Arthur Rowley, 1958-59
Record League aggregate: 152, Arthur Rowley, 1958-1965
Most League appearances: 370, Ken Mulhearn, 1971-80
Most capped player: 5 (12 in all), Jimmy McLaughlin, Northern Ireland

THE SHREWSBURY RECORD

	Division & place	*Cup round reached*
1951	NIII 20	*
1952	SIII 20	1
1953	SIII 23	4
1954	SIII 21	1
1955	SIII 16	1
1956	SIII 13	2
1957	SIII 9	1
1958	SIII 17	1
1959	IV 4P	2
1960	III 3	1
1961	III 10	3
1962	III 19	4
1963	III 15	3
1964	III 11	1
1965	III 16	5
1966	III 10	5
1967	III 6	3
1968	III 3	3
1969	III 17	1
1970	III 15	2
1971	III 13	2
1972	III 12	3
1973	III 15	2
1974	III 22R	1
1975	IV 2P	1
1976	III 9	3
1977	III 10	3
1978	III 11	3
1979	III 1P	q-f
1980	II 13	3
1981	II 14	4
1982	II 18	q-f

*Shrewsbury withdrew, refusing to play in the qualifying rounds after being elected to the Football League

SOUTHAMPTON

Founded: 1885
Address: The Dell, Milton Road, Southampton SO9 4XX
Telephone: Southampton 39445/39633
Ground capacity: 25,000
Playing area: 110 by 72 yards
Record attendance: 31,044 v Manchester United, Division I, 8.10.69
Record victory: 11-0 v Northampton, Southern League, 28.12.01
Record defeat: 0-8 v Tottenham Hotspur, Division II, 28.3.36
0-8 v Everton, Division I, 20.11.71
Most League points: 61, Division III(S), 1921-22 & Division III, 1959-60
Most League goals: 112, Division III(S), 1957-58
League scoring record: 39, Derek Reeves, Division III, 1959-60
Record League appearances: 182, Mick Channon, 1966-77, 1979-82
Most League appearances: 713, Terry Paine, 1956-74
Most capped player: 45 (46 in all), Mick Channon, England

FA Cup	*Year*	*Opponents*	*Score*	*Scorers*
Winners	1976	Manchester United	1-0	Stokes
Runners-up	1900	Bury	0-4	
	1902	Sheffield United	1-1	Wood
		Replay	1-2	Brown
League Cup				
Runners-up	1979	Nottingham Forest	2-3	Peach, Holmes

THE SOUTHAMPTON RECORD

	Division & place	Cup round reached
1895		1
1896		1
1897		2
1898		s-f
1899		q-f
1900		Final
1901		1
1902		Final
1903		1
1904		2
1905		q-f
1906		q-f
1907		2
1908		s-f
1909		1
1910		2
1911		1
1912		1
1913		1
1914		1
1915		3
1920		1
1921	III 2	3
1922	SIII 1P	2
1923	II 11	q-f
1924	II 5	3
1925	II 7	s-f
1926	II 14	3
1927	II 13	s-f
1928	II 17	3
1929	II 4	3
1930	II 7	3
1931	II 9	3
1932	II 14	3
1933	II 12	3
1934	II 14	3
1935	II 19	4
1936	II 17	3
1937	II 18	3
1938	II 15	3
1939	II 18	3
1946		4
1947	II 14	4
1948	II 3	q-f
1949	II 3	3
1950	II 4	3
1951	II 12	4
1952	II 13	3
1953	II 21R	5
1954	SIII 6	1
1955	SIII 3	2
1956	SIII 14	2
1957	SIII 4	3
1958	SIII 6	2
1959	III 14	3
1960	III 1P	4
1961	II 8	4
1962	II 6	3
1963	II 13	s-f
1964	II 5	3
1965	II 4	4
1966	II 2P	3
1967	I 19	4
1968	I 15	4
1969	I 7	4
1970	I 11	4
1971	I 7	5
1972	I 19	3
1973	I 13	3
1974	I 20R	5
1975	II 13	3
1976	II 6	Winners
1977	II 9	5
1978	II 2P	4
1979	I 14	q-f
1980	I 8	3
1981	I 6	5
1982	I 7	3

THE SOUTHEND RECORD

	Division & place	Cup round reached
1910		2
1911		1
1912		q
1913		1
1914		1
1915		2
1920		1
1921	III 17	3
1922	SIII 22	2
1923	SIII 15	q
1924	SIII 19	2
1925	SIII 10	q
1926	SIII 11	5
1927	SIII 19	2
1928	SIII 7	2
1929	SIII 12	1
1930	SIII 11	2
1931	SIII 5	1
1932	SIII 3	2
1933	SIII 13	4
1934	SIII 16	3
1935	SIII 21	3
1936	SIII 18	3
1937	SIII 10	2
1938	SIII 12	3
1939	SIII 12	4
1946		1
1947	SIII 8	3
1948	SIII 9	1
1949	SIII 18	1
1950	SIII 3	3
1951	SIII 7	1
1952	SIII 9	5
1953	SIII 8	1
1954	SIII 16	2
1955	SIII 10	3
1956	SIII 4	4
1957	SIII 7	4
1958	SIII 7	3
1959	III 8	1
1960	III 12	2
1961	III 20	2
1962	III 16	1
1963	III 8	2
1964	III 14	1
1965	III 12	1
1966	III 21R	3
1967	IV 6	1
1968	IV 6	1
1969	IV 7	4
1970	IV 17	1
1971	IV 18	3
1972	IV 2P	2
1973	III 14	1
1974	III 12	3
1975	III 18	3
1976	III 23R	5
1977	IV 10	3
1978	IV 2P	3
1979	III 13	3
1980	III 22R	2
1981	IV 1P	1
1982	III 7	1

SOUTHEND UNITED

Founded: 1906
Address: Roots Hall Ground, Victoria Avenue, Southend-on-Sea, Essex
Telephone: Southend 40707
Ground capacity: 32,000
Playing area: 110 by 74 yards
Record attendance: 31,033 v Liverpool, FA Cup 3rd round, 10.1.79
Record victory: 10-1 v Golders Green, FA Cup 1st round, 24.11.34
10-1 v Brentwood, FA Cup 2nd round, 2.12.68
Record defeat: 1-11 v Northampton, Southern League, 30.12.09
Most League points: 67, Division IV, 1980-81
Most League goals: 92, Division III(S), 1950-51
League scoring record: 31, Jim Shankly, Division III(S), 1928-29 & Sammy McCrory, Division III(S), 1957-58
Record League aggregate: 122, Roy Hollis, 1953-1960
Most League appearances: 451, Sandy Anderson, 1950-1963
Most capped player: 9, George Mackenzie, Republic of Ireland

STOCKPORT COUNTY

Founded: 1883
Address: Edgeley Park, Stockport, Cheshire
Telephone: 061-480-8888
Ground capacity: 16,500
Playing area: 110 by 75 yards
Record attendance: 27,833 v Liverpool, FA Cup 5th round, 11.2.50
Record victory: 13-0 v Halifax Town, Division III(N), 6.1.34
Record defeat: 1-8 v Chesterfield, Division II, 19.4.02
Most League points: 64, Division IV, 1966-67
Most League goals: 115, Division III(N), 1933-34
League scoring record: 46, Alf Lythgoe, Division III(N), 1933-34
Record League aggregate: 132, Jack Connor, 1951-1956
Most League appearances: 465, Robert Murray, 1952-1963
Most capped player: 1, Harry Hardy, England

THE STOCKPORT RECORD

	Division & place	Cup round reached
1901	II 17	q
1902	II 17	p
1903	II 17	q
1904	II 16	p
1905*		p
1906	II 10	1
1907	II 12	1
1908	II 13	1
1909	II 18	2
1910	II 13	2
1911	II 17	p
1912	II 16	1
1913	II 19	1
1914	II 12	p
1915	II 14	1
1920	II 16	1
1921	II 20R	1
1922	NIII 1P	p
1923	II 20	p
1924	II 13	p
1925	II 19	2
1926	II 22R	3
1927	NIII 6	1
1928	NIII 3	2
1929	NIII 2	3
1930	NIII 2	3
1931	NIII 7	2
1932	NIII 12	1

1933	NIII 3	2	1965	IV 24	4
1934	NIII 3	2	1966	IV 13	2
1935	NIII 7	5	1967	IV 1P	1
1936	NIII 5	1	1968	III 13	1
1937	NIII 1P	1	1969	III 9	3
1938	II 22R	3	1970	III 24R	2
1939	NIII 9	4	1971	IV 11	1
1946		1	1972	IV 23	2
1947	NIII 4	3	1973	IV 11	3
1948	NIII 17	4	1974	IV 24	1
1949	NIII 8	3	1975	IV 20	1
1950	NIII 10	5	1976	IV 21	1
1951	NIII 10	4	1977	IV 14	1
1952	NIII 3	1	1978	IV 18	2
1953	NIII 11	3	1979	IV 17	3
1954	NIII 10	3	1980	IV 16	1
1955	NIII 9	1	1981	IV 20	1
1956	NIII 7	1	1982	IV 18	2
1957	NIII 5	1			
1958	NIII 9	4			
1959	III 21R	3			
1960	IV 10	2			
1961	IV 13	4			
1962	IV 16	1			
1963	IV 19	1			
1964	IV 17	1			

*Failed to gain re-election in 1904. Returned when Divsion II increased from 19 to 20 clubs in 1905

1929	II 6	3	1962	II 8	4
1930	II 11	3	1963	II 1P	3
1931	II 11	3	1964	I 17	5
1932	II 3	5	1965	I 11	4
1933	II 1P	4	1966	I 10	3
1934	I 12	q-f	1967	I 12	3
1935	I 10	3	1968	I 18	4
1936	I 4	5	1969	I 19	5
1937	I 10	4	1970	I 9	4
1938	I 17	4	1971	I 13	s-f
1939	I 7	3	1972	I 17	s-f
1946		q-f	1973	I 15	3
1947	I 4	5	1974	I 5	3
1948	I 15	4	1975	I 5	3
1949	I 11	5	1976	I 12	5
1950	I 19	3	1977	I 21R	3
1951	I 13	5	1978	II 7	3
1952	I 20	4	1979	II 3P	3
1953	I 21R	4	1980	I 18	3
1954	II 11	4	1981	I 11	3
1955	II 5	4	1982	I 18	3
1956	II 13	5			
1957	II 5	3			
1958	II 11	5			
1959	II 5	4			
1960	II 17	3			
1961	II 18	5			

*resigned from League
†name changed to Stoke City in 1925

STOKE CITY

Founded: 1863 (though no recorded reference before 1867)
Address: Victoria Ground, Stoke-on-Trent, Staffordshire
Telephone: 0782 413511
Ground capacity: 35,000
Playing area: 116 by 75 yards
Record attendance: 51,380 v Arsenal, Division I, 29.3.37
Record victory: 10-3 v West Bromwich Albion, Division I, 4.2.37
Record defeat: 0-10 v Preston North End, Division I, 14.9.1889
Most League points: 63, Division III(N), 1926-27
Most League goals: 92, Division III(N), 1926-27
League scoring record: 33, Freddie Steele, Division I, 1936-37
Record League aggregate: 142, Freddie Steele, 1934-1939
Most League appearances: 506, Eric Skeels, 1958-76
Most capped player: 36 (73 in all), Gordon Banks, England

League Cup	*Year*	*Opponents*	*Score*	*Scorers*
Winners	1972	Chelsea	2-1	Conroy, Eastham
Runners-up	1964	Leicester City	1-1	Bebbington
		(aggregate)	2-3	Viollet, Kinnell

THE STOKE CITY RECORD

	Division & place	*Cup round reached*			
1889	I 12	p	1907	I 20R	1
1890	I 12L	q-f	1908*	II 10	q-f
1891		q-f	1909		1
1892	I 13	q-f	1910		1
1893	I 7	1	1911		1
1894	I 11	2	1912		p
1895	I 14	2	1913		1
1896	I 6	q-f	1914		1
1897	I 13	2	1915		p
1898	I 16	2	1920	II 10	1
1899	I 12	s-f	1921	II 20	1
1900	I 9	1	1922	II 2P	3
1901	I 16	1	1923	I 21R	2
1902	I 16	q-f	1924	II 6	1
1903	I 6	q-f	†1925	II 20	1
1904	I 16	1	1926	II 21R	4
1905	I 12	2	1927	NIII 1P	1
1906	I 10	2	1928	II 5	q-f

SUNDERLAND

Founded: 1879
Address: Roker Park Ground, Sunderland, Co. Durham
Telephone: Sunderland 40332
Ground capacity: 47,000
Playing area: 113 by 74 yards
Record attendance: 75,118 v Derby County, FA Cup quarter-final replay, 8.3.33
Record victory: 11-1 v Fairfield, FA Cup 1st round, 2.2.1895
Record defeat: 0-8 v West Ham United, Division I, 19.10.68;
v Watford, Division I, 25.9.82
Most League points: 61, Division II, 1963-64
Most League goals: 109, Division I, 1935-36
League scoring record: 43, David Halliday, Division I, 1928-29
Record League aggregate: 209, Charlie Buchan, 1911-1925
Most League appearances: 537, Jim Montgomery, 1962-1977
Most capped player: 33 (56 in all), Billy Bingham & 33, Martin Harvey, N. Ireland

FA Cup	*Year*	*Opponents*	*Score*	*Scorers*
Winners	1937	Preston North End	3-1	Gurney, Carter, Burbanks
	1973	Leeds United	1-0	Porterfield
Runners-up	1913	Aston Villa	0-1	

THE SUNDERLAND RECORD

	Division & place	*Cup round reached*			
1890		1	1915	I 8	1
1891	I 7	q-f	1920	I 5	3
1892	I 1C	s-f	1921	I 12	1
1893	I 1C	q-f	1922	I 12	1
1894	I 2	2	1923	I 2	2
1895	I 1C	s-f	1924	I 3	1
1896	I 5	2	1925	I 7	2
1897	I 15	2	1926	I 3	5
1898	I 2	1	1927	I 3	3
1899	I 7	2	1928	I 15	4
1900	I 3	2	1929	I 4	3
1901	I 2	1	1930	I 9	5
1902	I 1C	2	1931	I 11	s-f
1903	I 3	1	1932	I 13	4
1904	I 6	1	1933	I 12	q-f
1905	I 5	1	1934	I 6	4
1906	I 14	3	1935	I 2	4
1907	I 10	3	1936	I 1C	3
1908	I 16	1	1937	I 8	Winners
1909	I 3	q-f	1938	I 8	s-f
1910	I 8	3	1939	I 16	5
1911	I 3	1	1946		5
1912	I 8	3	1947	I 9	3
1913	I 1C	Final	1948	I 20	3
1914	I 7	q-f	1949	I 8	4

1950	I 3	4
1951	I 12	q-f
1952	I 12	3
1953	I 9	4
1954	I 18	3
1955	I 4	s-f
1956	I 9	s-f
1957	I 20	4
1958	I 21R	3
1959	II 15	3
1960	II 16	3
1961	II 6	q-f
1962	II 3	4
1963	II 3	5
1964	II 2P	q-f
1965	I 15	4
1966	I 19	3
1967	I 17	5
1968	I 16	3
1969	I 17	3
1970	I 21R	3
1971	II 13	3
1972	II 5	4
1973	II 6	Winners
1974	II 6	3
1975	II 4	4
1976	II 1P	q-f
1977	I 20R	3
1978	II 6	3
1979	II 4	4
1980	II 2P	3
1981	I 17	3
1982	I 19	4

SWANSEA CITY

Founded: 1900 (as Swansea Town)
Address: Vetch Field, Swansea
Telephone: Swansea 474114
Ground capacity: 26,496
Playing area: 110 by 70 yards
Record attendance: 32,796 v Arsenal, FA Cup 4th round, 17.2.68
Record victory: 12-0 v Sliema Wanderers, E.C.W.C., 15.9.82
Record defeat: 1-8 v Fulham, Division II, 22.1.38
Most League points: 62, Division III(S), 1948-49
Most League goals: 90, Division II, 1956-57
League scoring record: 35, Cyril Pearce, Division II, 1931-32
Record League aggregate: 166, Ivor Allchurch, 1949-1958, 1965-1968
Most League appearances: 585, Wilfred Milne, 1919-1937
Most capped player: 42 (68 in all), Ivor Allchurch, Wales

THE SWANSEA RECORD

	Division & place	*Cup round reached*
1921	III 5	2
1922	SIII 10	3
1923	SIII 3	p
1924	SIII 4	2
1925	SIII 1P	2
1926	II 5	s-f
1927	II 12	q-f
1928	II 6	3
1929	II 19	4
1930	II 15	3
1931	II 20	3
1932	II 15	3
1933	II 10	3
1934	II 19	5
1935	II 17	4
1936	II 13	3
1937	II 16	5
1938	II 18	3
1939	II 19	3
1946		3
1947	II 21R	4
1948	SIII 5	3
1949	SIII 1P	2
1950	II 8	4
1951	II 18	3
1952	II 19	5
1953	II 11	3
1954	II 20	4
1955	II 10	5
1956	II 10	3
1957	II 10	3
1958	II 19	3
1959	II 11	3
1960	II 12	4
1961	II 7	5
1962	II 20	3
1963	II 15	4
1964	II 19	s-f
1965	II 22R	5
1966	III 17	1
1967	III 21R	2
1968	IV 15	4
1969	IV 10	3
1970°	IV 3P	3
1971	III 11	4
1972	III 13	4
1973	III 23R	1
1974	IV 14	1
1975	IV 22	1
1976	IV 11	1
1977	IV 5	1
1978	IV 3P	3
1979	III 3P	3
1980	II 12	5
1981	II 3P	3
1982	I 6	3

°Name changed to Swansea City during 1969-70 season

SWINDON TOWN

Founded: 1881
Address: County Ground, Swindon, Wiltshire
Telephone: Swindon 22118
Ground capacity: 26,000 (6,500 seated)
Playing area: 114 by 72 yards
Record attendance: 32,000 v Arsenal, FA Cup 3rd round, 15.1.72
Record victory: 10-1 v Farnham United Brewery, FA Cup 1st round, 28.11.25
Record defeat: 1-10 v Manchester City, FA Cup 4th round replay, 29.1.30
Most League points: 64, Division III, 1968-69
Most League goals: 100, Division III(S), 1926-27
League scoring record: 47, Harry Morris, Division III(S), 1926-27
Record League aggregate: 216, Harry Morris, 1926-1933
Most League appearances: 770, John Trollope, 1960-80
Most capped player: 30 (50 in all), Rod Thomas, Wales

League Cup	*Year*	*Opponents*	*Score*	*Scorers*
Winners	1969	Arsenal	3-1	Smart, Rogers 2

after extra time

THE SWINDON RECORD

	Division & place	*Cup round reached*
1906		1
1907		q
1908		3
1909		1
1910		s-f
1911		q-f
1912		s-f
1913		3
1914		2
1915		1
1920		2
1921	III 4	2
1922	SIII 6	2
1923	SIII 9	1
1924	SIII 6	q-f
1925	SIII 4	1
1926	SIII 6	4
1927	SIII 5	1
1928	SIII 6	4
1929	SIII 10	5
1930	SIII 14	4
1931	SIII 12	1
1932	SIII 17	1
1933	SIII 22	3
1934	SIII 8	3
1935	SIII 16	4
1936	SIII 19	1
1937	SIII 13	2
1938	SIII 8	4
1939	SIII 9	2
1946		1
1947	SIII 4	2
1948	SIII 16	5
1949	SIII 4	3
1950	SIII 14	2
1951	SIII 17	2
1952	SIII 16	5
1953	SIII 18	3
1954	SIII 19	2
1955	SIII 21	1
1956	SIII 24	4
1957	SIII 23	2
1958	SIII 4	1
1959	III 15	2
1960	III 16	1
1961	III 16	2
1962	III 9	1
1963	III 2P	4
1964	II 14	5
1965	II 21R	3
1966	III 7	3
1967	III 8	5
1968	III 9	4
1969	III 2P	3
1970	II 5	q-f
1971	II 12	4
1972	II 11	3
1973	II 16	4
1974	II 22R	3
1975	III 4	4
1976	III 19	3
1977	III 11	4
1978	III 10	3
1979	III 5	4
1980	III 10	4
1981	III 17	2
1982	III 22R	3

TORQUAY UNITED

Founded: 1898
Address: Plainmoor, Torquay, Devon
Telephone: Torquay 38666/7
Ground capacity: 22,000
Playing area: 112 by 74 yards
Record attendance: 21,908 v Huddersfield Town, FA Cup 4th round, 29.1.55
Record victory: 9-0 v Swindon Town, Division III(S), 8.3.52
Record defeat: 2-10 v Fulham, Division III(S), 7.9.31
2-10 v Luton Town, Division III(S), 2.9.33
Most League points: 60, Division IV, 1959-60
Most League goals: 89, Division III(S), 1956-57
League scoring record: 40, 'Sammy' Collins, Division III(S), 1955-56
Record League aggregate: 204, 'Sammy' Collins, 1948-1958
Most League appearances: 443, Dennis Lewis, 1947-1959
Most capped player: None

THE TORQUAY RECORD

	Division & place		*Cup round reached*
1928	SIII	22	Sc
1929	SIII	18	2
1930	SIII	19	1
1931	SIII	11	3
1932	SIII	19	1
1933	SIII	10	2
1934	SIII	20	2
1935	SIII	10	2
1936	SIII	10	2
1937	SIII	20	1
1938	SIII	20	1
1939	SIII	19	2
1946			1
1947	SIII	11	1
1948	SIII	18	3
1949	SIII	9	4
1950	SIII	5	2
1951	SIII	20	1
1952	SIII	11	2
1953	SIII	12	1
1954	SIII	13	1
1955	SII'	8	4
1956	SIII	5	3
1957	SIII	2	3
1958	SIII	21	2
1959	IV	12	3
1960	IV	3P	2
1961	III	12	2
1962	III	21R	2
1963	IV	6	2
1964	IV	6	2
1965	IV	11	3
1966	IV	3P	1
1967	III	7	1
1968	III	4	1
1969	III	6	2
1970	III	13	1
1971	III	10	4
1972	III	23R	3
1973	IV	18	2
1974	IV	16	1
1975	IV	14	1
1976	IV	9	1
1977	IV	16	1
1978	IV	9	1
1979	IV	11	3
1980	IV	9	2
1981	IV	17	3
1982	IV	15	1

Sc—scratched

TOTTENHAM HOTSPUR

Founded: 1882
Address: 748 High Road, Tottenham, London N17
Telephone: (01) 801-3411
Ground capacity: 50,000
Playing area: 110 by 73 yards
Record attendance: 75,038 v Sunderland, FA Cup quarter-final, 5.3.38
Record victory: 13-2 v Crewe Alexandra, FA Cup 4th round, 3.2.60
Record defeat: 0-7 v Liverpool, Division I, 2.9.78
Most League points: 70, Division II, 1919-20
Most League goals: 115, Division I, 1960-61
League scoring record: 37, Jimmy Greaves, Division I, 1962-63
Record League aggregate: 220, Jimmy Greaves, 1961-1970
Most League appearances: 531, Steve Perryman, 1969-82
Most capped player: 66 (95 in all), Pat Jennings, Northern Ireland

	Year	*Opponents*	*Score*	*Scorers*
FA Cup *Winners*	1901	Sheffield United	2-2	Brown 2
			3-1	Cameron, Smith, Brown
	1921	Wolverhampton W	1-0	Dimmock
	1961	Leicester City	2-0	Smith, Dyson
	1962	Burnley	3-1	Greaves, Smith, Blanchflower (pen)
	1967	Chelsea	2-1	Robertson, Saul
	1981	Manchester City	*1-1	Hutchison o.g.
		Replay	3-2	Villa 2, Crooks
	1982	Queen's Park R	*1-1	Hoddle
		Replay	1-0	Hoddle (pen)
League Cup *Winners*	1971	Aston Villa	2-0	Chivers 2
	1973	Norwich City	1-0	Coates
Runners-up	1982	Liverpool	1-3	Archibald

*After extra time

THE SPURS RECORD

	Division & place		*F.A. Cup round reached*
1895			4q
1896			1
1897			3q
1898			2q
1899			q-f
1900			1
1901			Winners
1902			1
1903			q-f
1904			q-f
1905			2
1906			3
1907			3
1908			1
1909	II	2P	3
1910	I	15	3
1911	I	15	2
1912	I	12	1
1913	I	17	2
1914	I	17	2
1915	I	20R	2
1920	II	1P	q-f
1921	I	6	Winners
1922	I	2	s-f
1923	I	12	q-f
1924	I	15	1
1925	I	12	3
1926	I	15	4
1927	I	13	3
1928	I	21R	5
1929	II	10	3
1930	II	12	3
1931	II	3	4
1932	II	8	3
1933	II	2P	4
1934	I	3	5
1935	I	22R	5
1936	II	5	q-f
1937	II	10	q-f
1938	II	5	q-f
1939	II	8	4
1946			3
1947	II	6	3
1948	II	8	s-f
1949	II	5	3
1950	II	1P	5
1951	I	1C	3
1952	I	2	4
1953	I	10	s-f
1954	I	16	q-f
1955	I	16	5
1956	I	18	s-f
1957	I	2	5
1958	I	3	4
1959	I	18	5
1960	I	3	5
1961	I	1C	Winners
1962	I	3	Winners
1963	I	2	3
1964	I	4	3
1965	I	6	5
1966	I	8	5
1967	I	3	Winners
1968	I	7	5
1969	I	6	q-f
1970	I	11	4
1971	I	3	q-f
1972	I	6	q-f
1973	I	8	4
1974	I	11	3
1975	I	19	3
1976	I	9	3
1977	I	22R	3
1978	II	3P	3
1979	I	11	q-f
1980	I	14	q-f
1981	I	10	Winners
1982	I	4	Winners

TRANMERE ROVERS

Founded: 1883
Address: Prenton Park, 14 Prenton Road West, Birkenhead
Telephone: 051 608 3677/4194
Ground capacity: 18,000
Playing area: 112 by 74 yards
Record attendance: 24,424 v Stoke City, FA Cup 4th round, 5.2.72
Record victory: 13-4 v Oldham Athletic, Division III(N), 26.12.35
Record defeat: 1-9 v Tottenham Hotspur, FA Cup 3rd round replay, 14.1.53
Most League points: 60, Division IV, 1964-65
Most League goals: 111, Division III(N), 1930-31
League scoring record: 35, Robert 'Bunny' Bell, Division III(N), 1933-34
Record League aggregate: 104, Robert 'Bunny' Bell, 1931-1936
Most League appearances: 595, Harold Bell, 1946-1964
Most capped player: 3 (4 in all), John Brown, Northern Ireland;
3 (23 in all), Bert Gray, Wales

THE TRANMERE RECORD

	Division & place	*Cup round reached*			
1922	NIII 18	q	1957	NIII 23	1
1923	NIII 16	q	1958	NIII 11	3
1924	NIII 12	p	1959	III 7	2
1925	NIII 21	p	1960	III 20	1
1926	NIII 7	p	1961	III 21R	2
1927	NIII 9	1	1962	IV 15	1
1928	NIII 5	3	1963	IV 8	3
1929	NIII 7	2	1964	IV 7	1
1930	NIII 12	1	1965	IV 5	1
1931	NIII 3	1	1966	IV 5	1
1932	NIII 4	3	1967	IV 4P	2
1933	NIII 11	4	1968	III 19	5
1934	NIII 7	4	1969	III 7	1
1935	NIII 6	2	1970	III 16	4
1936	NIII 3	4	1971	III 18	1
1937	NIII 19	1	1972	III 19	4
1938	NIII 1P	3	1973	III 10	2
1939	II 22R	3	1974	III 16	2
1946		2	1975	III 22R	3
1947	NIII 10	1	1976	IV 4P	1
1948	NIII 18	2	1977	III 14	1
1949	NIII 11	1	1978	III 12	1
1950	NIII 5	2	1979	III 23R	2
1951	NIII 4	2	1980	IV 15	2
1952	NIII 11	4	1981	IV 21	2
1953	NIII 12	3	1982	IV 11	1
1954	NIII 14	3			
1955	NIII 19	1			
1956	NIII 16	2			

WALSALL

Founded: 1888 (as Walsall Town Swifts)
Address: Fellows Park, Walsall, Staffordshire
Telephone: Walsall 22791
Ground capacity: 24,100
Playing area: 113 by 73 yards
Record attendance: 25,453 v Newcastle United, Division II, 29.8.61
Record victory: 10-0 v Darwen, Division II, 4.3.1899
Record defeat: 0-12 v Small Heath, Division II, 17.12.1892
0-12 v Darwen, Division II, 26.12.1896
Most League points: 65, Division IV, 1959-60
Most League goals: 102, Division IV, 1959-60
League scoring record: 40, Gilbert Alsop, Division III(N), 1933-34 & 1934-35
Record League aggregate: 184, Tony Richards, 1954-1963, Colin Taylor, 1958-73
Most League appearances: 467, Colin Harrison, 1964-82
Most capped player: 15 (17 in all), Mick Kearns, Eire

THE WALSALL RECORD

	Division & place	*Cup round reached*			
1893*	II 12	p	1953	SIII 24	1
1894*	II 10	p	1954	SIII 24	3
1895*	II 14L	q	1955	SIII 23	3
1896		p	1956	SIII 20	3
1897	II 12	p	1957	SIII 15	1
1898	II 10	1	1958	SIII 20	1
1899	II 6	p	1959	IV 6	1
1900	II 12	1	1960	IV 1P	2
1901	II 16L	p	1961	III 2P	1
1922	NIII 8	1	1962	II 14	4
1923	NIII 3	p	1963	II 21R	3
1924	NIII 17	p	1964	III 19	1
1925	NIII 19	p	1965	III 19	1
1926	NIII 21	1	1966	III 9	4
1927	NIII 14	3	1967	III 12	3
1928	SIII 18	1	1968	III 7	4
1929	SIII 14	3	1969	III 13	3
1930	SIII 17	4	1970	III 12	3
1931	SIII 17	3	1971	III 20	2
1932	NIII 16	1	1972	III 9	4
1933	NIII 5	4	1973	III 17	2
1934	NIII 4	2	1974	III 15	2
1935	NIII 14	3	1975	III 8	5
1936	NIII 10	3	1976	III 7	1
1937	SIII 17	4	1977	III 15	3
1938	SIII 21	2	1978	III 6	5
1939	SIII 21	5	1979	III 22R	1
1946		1	1980	IV 2P	2
1947	SIII 5	3	1981	III 20	2
1948	SIII 3	3	1982	III 20	2
1949	SIII 14	4			
1950	SIII 19	1			
1951	SIII 15	1			
1952	SIII 24	1			

* as Walsall Town Swifts

WATFORD

Founded: 1891
Address: Vicarage Road, Watford WD1 8ER
Telephone: Watford 49747/8/9
Ground capacity: 28,000
Playing area: 113 by 73 yards
Record attendance: 34,099 v Manchester United, FA Cup 4th round, 3.2.69
Record victory: 10-1 v Lowestoft, FA Cup, 1st round, 27.11.26
Record defeat: 0-10 v Wolverhampton Wanderers, FA Cup 1st round replay, 13.1.12
Most League points: 71, Division IV, 1977-78
Most League goals: 92, Division IV, 1959-60
League scoring record: 42, Cliff Holton, Division IV, 1959-60
Record League aggregate: 144, Tommy Barnett, 1928-1939
Most League appearances: 411, Duncan Welbourne, 1963-74
Most capped player: 15 (42 in all), Gerry Armstrong, Northern Ireland

THE WATFORD RECORD

	Division & place	*Cup round reached*			
1906		2	1933	SIII 11	3
1907		1	1934	SIII 15	1
1908		1	1935	SIII 6	2
1909		1	1936	SIII 5	4
1910		1	1937	SIII 4	1
1911		1	1938	SIII 4	3
1912		1	1939	SIII 4	3
1913		p	1946		4
1914		p	1947	SIII 16	2
1915		p	1948	SIII 15	1
1920		p	1949	SIII 17	1
1921	III 6	2	1950	SIII 6	4
1922	SIII 7	2	1951	SIII 23	1
1923	SIII 10	1	1952	SIII 21	2
1924	SIII 20	3	1953	SIII 10	2
1925	SIII 11	1	1954	SIII 4	1
1926	SIII 15	2	1955	SIII 7	3
1927	SIII 21	2	1956	SIII 20	2
1928	SIII 15	1	1957	SIII 11	2
1929	SIII 8	4	1958	SIII 16	1
1930	SIII 15	2	1959	IV 15	2
1931	SIII 18	5	1960	IV 4P	5
1932	SIII 11	q-f	1961	III 4	3

Year	Division & place	Cup round reached
1962	III 17	3
1963	III 17	4
1964	III 3	2
1965	III 9	1
1966	III 12	2
1967	III 3	3
1968	III 6	3
1969	III 1P	4
1970	II 19	s-f
1971	II 18	4
1972	II 22R	3
1973	III 19	3
1974	III 7	2
1975	III 23R	1
1976	IV 8	1
1977	IV 7	3
1978	IV 1P	3
1979	III 2P	2
1980	II 18	q-f
1981	II 9	4
1982	II 2P	5

WEST BROMWICH ALBION

Founded: 1879
Address: The Hawthorns, West Bromwich, B71 4LF
Telephone: (021) 525-8888
Ground capacity: 38,000 (12,500 seated)
Playing area: 115 by 75 yards
Record attendance: 64,815 v Arsenal, FA Cup quarter-final, 6.3.37
Record victory: 12-0 v Darwen, Division I, 4.4.1892
Record defeat: 3-10 v Stoke City, Division I, 4.2.37
Most League points: 60, Division I, 1919-20
Most League goals: 105, Division II, 1929-30
League scoring record: 39, William G Richardson, Division I, 1935-36
Record League aggregate: 218, Tony Brown, 1963-79
Most League appearances: 574, Tony Brown, 1963-80
Most capped player: 33 (43 in all), Stuart Williams, Wales

FA Cup

	Year	Opponents	Score	Scorers
Winners	1888	Preston North End	2-1	Bayliss, Woodhall
	1892	Aston Villa	3-0	Geddes, Nicholls, Reynolds
	1931	Birmingham City	2-1	W G Richardson 2
	1954	Preston North End	3-2	Allen 2, Griffin
	1968	Everton	*1-0	Astle
Runners-up	1886	Blackburn	0-0	
	replay		0-2	
	1887	Aston Villa	0-2	
	1895	Aston Villa	0-1	
	1912	Barnsley	0-0,	
	replay		0-1	
	1935	Sheffield Wednesday	2-4	Boyes, Sandford

*after extra time

League Cup

	Year	Opponents	Score	Scorers
Winners	1966	West Ham United	(a) 1-2	Astle
			(h) 4-1	Kaye, Brown, Clark (C), Williams
Runners-up	1967	Queen's Park Rangers	2-3	Clark (C) 2
	1970	Manchester City	1-2	Astle

THE ALBION RECORD

Year	Division & place	Cup round reached
1885		q-f
1886		Final
1887		Final
1888		Winners
1889	I 6	s-f
1890	I 5	1
1891	I 12	s-f
1892	I 12	Winners
1893	I 8	1
1894	I 8	1
1895	I 13	Final
1896	I 16	q-f
1897	I 12	2
1898	I 7	q-f
1899	I 14	q-f
1900	I 13	q-f
1901	I 18R	s-f
1902	II 1P	1
1903	I 7	1
1904	I 18R	1
1905	II 10	p
1906	II 4	1
1907	II 4	s-f
1908	II 5	2
1909	II 3	2
1910	II 11	3
1911	II 1P	2
1912	I 9	Final
1913	I 10	1
1914	I 5	3
1915	I 11	1
1920	I 1C	1
1921	I 14	1
1922	I 13	3
1923	I 17	3
1924	I 16	q-f
1925	I 2	q-f
1926	I 13	4
1927	I 22R	3
1928	II 8	3
1929	II 7	q-f
1930	II 6	3
1931	II 2P	Winners
1932	I 6	3
1933	I 4	4
1934	I 7	3
1935	I 9	Final
1936	I 18	4
1937	I 16	s-f
1938	I 22R	4
1939	II 10	4
1946		4
1947	II 7	4
1948	II 7	4
1949	II 2P	q-f
1950	I 14	3
1951	I 16	3
1952	I 13	5
1953	I 4	4
1954	I 2	Winners
1955	I 17	4
1956	I 13	5
1957	I 11	s-f
1958	I 4	q-f
1959	I 5	5
1960	I 4	5
1961	I 10	3
1962	I 9	5
1963	I 14	4
1964	I 10	4
1965	I 14	3
1966	I 6	3
1967	I 13	4
1968	I 8	Winners
1969	I 10	s-f
1970	I 16	3
1971	I 17	4
1972	I 16	3
1973	I 22R	5
1974	II 8	5
1975	II 6	4
1976	II 3P	5
1977	I 7	3
1978	I 6	s-f
1979	I 3	5
1980	I 10	3
1981	I 4	4
1982	I 17	s-f

WEST HAM UNITED

Founded: 1900
Address: Boleyn Ground, Green Street, Upton Park, London E13
Telephone: (01) 472 2740
Ground capacity: 35,500
Playing area: 110 by 72 yards
Record attendance: 42,322 v Tottenham Hotspur, Division I, 17.10.70
Record victory: 8-0 v Rotherham United, Division II, 8.3.58
8-0 v Sunderland, Division I, 19.10.68
Record defeat: 2-8 v Blackburn Rovers, Division I, 26.12.63
Most League points: 66, Division II; 1980-81
Most League goals: 101, Division II, 1957-58
League scoring record: 41, Vic Watson, Division I, 1929-30
Record League aggregate: 306, Vic Watson, 1920-1935
Most League appearances: 545, Bobby Moore, 1958-1974
Most capped player: 108, Bobby Moore, England

FA Cup	Year	Opponents	Score	Scorers
Winners	1964	Preston North End	3-2	Sissons, Hurst, Boyce
	1975	Fulham	2-0	A. Taylor 2
	1980	Arsenal	1-0	Brooking
Runners-up	1923	Bolton Wanderers	0-2	

League Cup

	Year	Opponents	Score	Scorers
Runners-up	1966	West Bromwich Albion	h2-1	Moore, Byrne
			a1-4	Peters
	1981	Liverpool	*1-1	Stewart (pen)
		Replay	1-2	Goddard

*After extra time

THE HAMMERS RECORD

Year	Division & place	Cup round reached
1913		2
1914		3
1915		1
1920	II 7	3
1921	II 5	1
1922	II 4	1
1923	II 2P	Final
1924	I 13	2
1925	I 13	3
1926	I 18	3
1927	I 6	4
1928	I 17	4
1929	I 17	q-f
1930	I 7	q-f
1931	I 18	3
1932	I 22R	4
1933	II 20	s-f
1934	II 7	4
1935	II 3	3
1936	II 4	3
1937	II 6	3
1938	II 9	3
1939	II 11	5
1946		4
1947	II 11	3
1948	II 6	3
1949	II 7	3
1950	II 19	4
1951	II 13	4
1952	II 12	4
1953	II 14	3
1954	II 13	4
1955	II 8	3
1956	II 16	q-f
1957	II 8	4
1958	II 1P	5
1959	I 6	3
1960	I 14	3
1961	I 16	3
1962	I 8	3
1963	I 12	q-f
1964	I 14	Winners
1965	I 9	4
1966	I 12	4
1967	I 16	3
1968	I 12	5
1969	I 8	5
1970	I 17	3
1971	I 20	3
1972	I 14	5
1973	I 6	4
1974	I 18	3
1975	I 13	Winners
1976	I 18	3
1977	I 17	3
1978	I 20R	4
1979	II 5	3
1980	II 7	Winners
1981	II 1P	3
1982	I 9	4

WIGAN ATHLETIC

Founded: 1932*
Address: Springfield Park, Wigan
Telephone: Wigan 44433
Ground capacity: 30,000
Playing area: 117 by 73 yards
Record attendance: 27,500 v Hereford, FA Cup 2nd round, 12.12.53
Record victory: 7-2 v Scunthorpe, Division IV, 12.3.82 (away)
Record defeat: 2-5 (home) v York City, Division IV, 15.9.79
Most League points: 55, Division IV, 1978-79 and 1979-80
Most League goals: 80, Division IV, 1981-82
League scoring record: 19, Les Bradd, Division IV, 1981-82
Record League aggregate: 49, Peter Houghton, 1978-82
Most League appearances: 143, Jeff Wright, 1978-82
Most capped player: None

*Following the disbanding of Wigan Borough in 1931, the first club to resign from the League mid-season. Wigan Athletic were elected to the League at the end of the 1977-78 season.

THE WIGAN RECORD

	Division & place	*Cup round reached*
1979	IV 6	1
1980	IV 6	4
1981	IV 11	1
1982	IV 3P	1

WIMBLEDON

Founded: 1889
Address: Plough Lane, Durensford Road, Wimbledon, London SW19
Telephone: 01-946 6311
Ground capacity: 15,000
Playing area: 110 by 85 yards
Record attendance: 18,000 v H.M.S. Victory, FA Amateur Cup, 23.2.35
Record victory: 7-2 v Windsor and Eton, FA Cup 1st round, 22.11.80
Record defeat: 0-8 v Everton, League Cup 2nd round, 29.8.78
Most League points: 61, Division IV, 1978-79
Most League goals: 78, Division IV, 1978-79
League scoring record, 23, Alan Cork, 1980-81
Record League aggregate: 64, John Leslie, 1977-82
Most League appearances: 211, John Leslie, 1977-82
Most capped player: None

THE WIMBLEDON RECORD

	Division & place	*Cup round reached*
1978	IV 13	1
1979	IV 3P	3
1980	III 24R	2
1981	IV 4P	4
1982	III 21R	2

WOLVERHAMPTON WANDERERS

Founded: 1876 (as St Luke's School, Blakenhall)
Address: Molineux, Wolverhampton, WV1 4QR
Telephone: Wolverhampton 712181
Ground capacity: 41,074
Playing area: 115 by 72 yards
Record attendance: 61,315 v Liverpool, FA Cup 5th round, 11.2.39
Record victory: 14-0 v Crosswell's Brewery, FA Cup qualifying rounds, 13.11.1886
Record defeat: 1-10 v Newton Heath, Division I, 15.10.1892
Most League points: 64, Division I, 1957-58
Most League goals: 115, Division II, 1931-32
League scoring record: 37, Dennis Westcott, Division I, 1946-47
Record League aggregate: 164, Billy Hartill, 1928-1935
Most League appearances: 491, Billy Wright, 1946-1959
Most capped player: 105, Billy Wright, England

FA Cup	*Year*	*Opponents*	*Score*	*Scorers*
Winners	1893	Everton	1-0	Allen
	1908	Newcastle United	3-1	Hunt, Hedley, Harrison on
	1949	Leicester City	3-1	Pye 2, Smyth
	1960	Blackburn Rovers	3-0	McGrath (og), Deeley 2
Runners-up	1889	Preston North End	0-3	
	1896	Sheffield Wednesday	1-2	Black
	1921	Tottenham Hotspur	0-1	
	1939	Portsmouth	1-4	Dorsett
League Cup				
Winners	1974	Manchester City	2-1	Hibbit, Richards
	1980	Nottingham Forest	1-0	Gray

THE WOLVES RECORD

	Division & place	*Cup round reached*			
1884		2	1921	II 15	Final
1885		1	1922	II 17	1
1886		4	1923	II 22R	2
1887		3	1924	NIII 1P	3
1888		3	1925	II 6	1
1889	I 3	Final	1926	II 4	3
1890	I 4	s-f	1927	II 15	q-f
1891	I 4	q-f	1928	II 16	4
1892	I 6	q-f	1929	II 17	3
1893	I 11	Winners	1930	II 9	3
1894	I 9	1	1931	II 4	q-f
1895	I 11	q-f	1932	II 1P	4
1896	I 14	Final	1933	I 20	3
1897	I 10	2	1934	I 15	4
1898	I 3	2	1935	I 17	4
1899	I 8	2	1936	I 15	3
1900	I 4	1	1937	I 5	q-f
1901	I 13	q-f	1938	I 2	4
1902	I 14	1	1939	I 2	Final
1903	I 11	1	1946		4
1904	I 8	2	1947	I 3	4
1905	I 14	2	1948	I 5	4
1906	I 20R	2	1949	I 6	Winners
1907	II 6	1	1950	I 2	5
1908	II 9	Winners	1951	I 14	s-f
1909	II 7	1	1952	I 16	4
1910	II 8	2	1953	I 3	3
1911	II 9	3	1954	I 1C	3
1912	II 5	3	1955	I 2	q-f
1913	II 10	2	1956	I 3	3
1914	II 9	2	1957	I 6	4
1915	II 4	2	1958	I 1C	q-f
1920	II 19	2	1959	I 1C	4

1960	I 2	Winners	1973	I 5	s-f
1961	I 3	3	1974	I 12	3
1962	I 18	4	1975	I 12	3
1963	I 5	3	1976	I 20R	q-f
1964	I 16	3	1977	II 1P	q-f
1965	I 21R	q-f	1978	I 15	4
1966	II 6	5	1979	I 18	s-f
1967	II 2P	4	1980	I 6	5
1968	I 17	3	1981	I 18	s-f
1969	I 16	4	1982	I 21R	3
1970	I 13	3			
1971	I 4	4			
1972	I 9	3			

WREXHAM

Founded: 1873
Address: Racecourse Ground, Mold Road, Wrexham
Telephone: Wrexham (0978) 262129
Ground capacity: 30,000
Playing area: 117 by 75 yards
Record attendance: 34,445 v Manchester United, FA Cup 4th round, 26.1.57
Record victory: 10-1 v Hartlepool, Division IV, 3.3.62
Record defeat: 0-9 v Brentford, Division III, 15.10.63
Most League points: 61, Division IV, 1969-70
61, Division III, 1977-78
Most League goals: 106, Division III(N), 1932-33
League scoring record: 44, Tom Bamford, Division III(N), 1933-34
Record League aggregate: 175, Tom Bamford, 1928-1934
Most League appearances: 592, Arfon Griffiths, 1959-1961, 1962-1979
Most capped player: 28 (51 in all), Dai Davies, Wales

THE WREXHAM RECORD

	Division & place	*Cup round reached*			
1922	NIII 12	2	1957	NIII 12	4
1923	NIII 10	3	1958	NIII 12	1
1924	NIII 16	2	1959	III 18	1
1925	NIII 16	q	1960	III 23R	3
1926	NIII 19	1	1961	IV 16	1
1927	NIII 13	2	1962	IV 3P	3
1928	NIII 11	4	1963	III 9	3
1929	NIII 3	1	1964	III 23R	2
1930	NIII 17	4	1965	IV 14	2
1931	NIII 4	3	1966	IV 24	2
1932	NIII 10	1	1967	IV 7	2
1933	NIII 2	2	1968	IV 8	1
1934	NIII 6	1	1969	IV 9	2
1935	NIII 18	2	1970	IV 2P	4
1936	NIII 18	1	1971	III 9	1
1937	NIII 8	3	1972	III 16	3
1938	NIII 10	2	1973	III 12	2
1939	NIII 14	1	1974	III 4	q-f
1946		3	1975	III 13	1
1947	NIII 7	2	1976	III 6	1
1948	NIII 3	2	1977	III 5	4
1949	NIII 9	1	1978	III 1P	q-f
1950	NIII 20	2	1979	II 15	4
1951	NIII 14	2	1980	II 16	5
1952	NIII 18	2	1981	II 16	5
1953	NIII 3	3	1982	II 21R	4
1954	NIII 8	3			
1955	NIII 18	2			
1956	NIII 14	1			

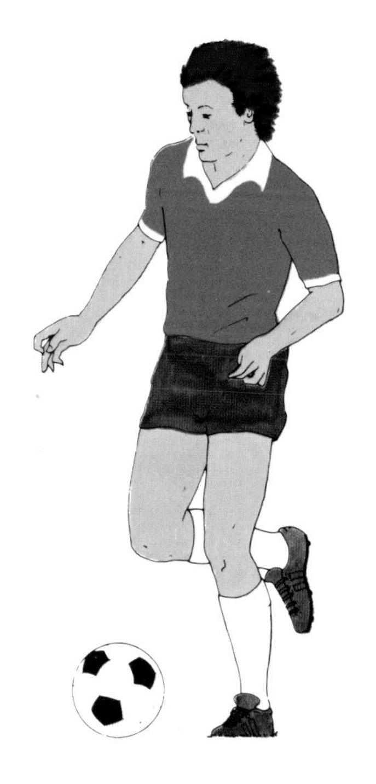

YORK CITY

Founded: 1922
Address: Bootham Crescent, York
Telephone: York 24447
Ground capacity: 16,529
Playing area: 115 by 75 yards
Record attendance: 28,123 v Huddersfield Town, FA Cup 5th round, 5.3.38
Record victory: 9-1 v Southport, Division III(N), 2.2.57
Record defeat: 0-12 v Chester, Division III(N), 1.2.36
Most League points: 62, Division IV, 1964-65
Most League goals: 92, Division III(N), 1954-55
League scoring record: 31, Bill Fenton, Division III(N), 1951-52
31, Alf Bottom, Division III(N), 1955-56
Record League aggregate: 125, Norman Wilkinson, 1954-1966
Most League appearances: 481, Barry Jackson, 1958-1970
Most capped player: 7 (10 in all), Peter Scott, Northern Ireland

THE YORK RECORD

	Division & place	*Cup round reached*			
1930	NIII 6	3	1966	III 24R	1
1931	NIII 12	3	1967	IV 22	2
1932	NIII 10	1	1968	IV 21	1
1933	NIII 20	1	1969	IV 21	3
1934	NIII 12	1	1970	IV 13	4
1935	NIII 15	3	1971	IV 4P	4
1936	NIII 16	1	1972	III 19	2
1937	NIII 12	4	1973	III 18	3
1938	NIII 11	q-f	1974	III 3P	1
1939	NIII 20	3	1975	II 15	3
1946		4	1976	II 21R	4
1947	NIII 15	1	1977	III 24R	2
1948	NIII 13	1	1978	IV 22	1
1949	NIII 14	2	1979	IV 10	4
1950	NIII 22	1	1980	IV 17	2
1951	NIII 17	3	1981	IV 24	1
1952	NIII 10	1	1982	IV 17	2
1953	NIII 4	1			
1954	NIII 22	1			
1955	NIII 4	s-f			
1956	NIII 11	4			
1957	NIII 7	2			
1958	NIII 13	4			
1959	IV 3P	1			
1960	III 21R	3			
1961	IV 5	3			
1962	IV 6	1			
1963	IV 14	3			
1964	IV 22	1			
1965	IV 3P	2			

ABERDEEN

Founded: 1903
Address: Pittodrie Stadium, Aberdeen AB2 1QH
Telephone: 0224 632328/633497
Ground capacity: 24,000 (all seated)
Playing area: 110 by 71 yards
Record attendance: 46,061 v Heart of Midlothian, Scottish Cup 4th round, 13.3.54
Record victory: 13-0 v Peterhead, Scottish Cup 3rd round, 10.2.23
Record defeat: 0-8 v Celtic, Division I, 30.1.65
Most League points: 61, Division I, 1935-36
Most League goals: 96, Division I, 1935-36
League scoring record: 38, Benny Yorston, Division I, 1929-30
Record League aggregate: 160, Harry Yorston, 1950-57
Most capped player: 19, Willie Miller, Scotland

Scottish Cup	*Year*	*Opponents*	*Score*	*Scorers*
Winners	1947	Hibernian	2-1	Hamilton, Williams
	1970	Celtic	3-1	Harper, McKay 2
	1982	Rangers	*4-1	McLeish, McGhee, Strachan, Cooper
Runners-up	1937	Celtic	1-2	Armstrong
	1953	Rangers	1-1 0-1	Yorston
	1954	Celtic	1-2	Buckley
	1959	St Mirren	1-3	Baird
	1967	Celtic	0-2	
	1978	Rangers	1-2	Ritchie
League Cup				
Winners	1946	Rangers	3-2	Baird, Williams, Taylor
	1956	St Mirren	2-1	og, Leggat
	1977	Celtic	2-1	Jarvie, Robb
Runners-up	1947	Rangers	0-4	
	1979	Rangers	1-2	Davidson
	1980	Dundee Utd	0-0	
		Replay	0-3	

*After extra time

THE ABERDEEN RECORD

	Division & place	*Cup round reached*
1906	I 12	2
1907	I 11	2
1908	I 8	s-f
1909	I 8	2
1910	I 4	3
1911	I 2	s-f
1912	I 9	3
1913	I 8	2
1914	I 14	3
1915	I 14	
1916	I 11	
1917	I 20	
1918	†	
1919	†	
1920	I 17	4
1921	I 11	3
1922	I 15	s-f
1923	I 5	4
1924	I 13	s-f
1925	I 15	4
1926	I 11	s-f
1927	I 8	2
1928	I 7	4
1929	I 7	4
1930	I 3	3
1931	I 6	q-f
1932	I 7	1
1933	I 5	2
1934	I 5	q-f
1935	I 6	s-f
1936	I 3	q-f
1937	I 2	Final
1938	I 6	3
1939	I 3	s-f
1947	I 3	Winners
1948	I 10	3
1949	I 13	1
1950	I 8	q-f
1951	I 5	q-f
1952	I 11	q-f
1953	I 11	Final
1954	I 9	Final
1955	I 1C	s-f
1956	I 2	5
1957	I 6	6
1958	I 12	q-f
1959	I 13	Final
1960	I 15	2
1961	I 6	3
1962	I 12	3
1963	I 6	q-f
1964	I 9	3
1965	I 12	1
1966	I 8	s-f
1967	I 4	Final
1968	I 5	2
1969	I 15	s-f
1970	I 8	Winners
1971	I 2	s-f
1972	I 2	q-f
1973	I 4	q-f
1974	I 4	3
1975	I 5	q-f
1976	P 7	4
1977	P 3	4
1978	P 2	Final
1979	P 4	s-f
1980	P 1C	s-f
1981	P 2	4
1982	P 2	Winners

† Aberdeen did not compete

AIRDRIEONIANS

Founded: 1878
Address: Broomfield Park, Airdrie, Lanarkshire
Telephone: Airdrie 62067
Ground capacity: 26,000 (2,000 seated)
Playing area: 112 by 68 yards
Record attendance: 24,000 v Hearts, Scottish Cup 4th round, 8.3.52
Record victory: 15-1 v Dundee Wanderers, Division II, 1.12.1894
Record defeat: 1-11 v Hibernian, Division I, 24.10.59
Most League points: 60, Division II, 1973-74
Most League goals: 107, Division II, 1965-66
League scoring record: 45, H G Yarnall, Division I, 1916-17
Most capped player: 9, Jimmy Crapnell, Scotland

Scottish Cup	*Year*	*Opponents*	*Score*	*Scorers*
Winners	1924	Hibernian	2-0	Russell 2
Runners-up	1975	Celtic	1-3	McCann

THE AIRDRIEONIANS RECORD

	Division & place	*Cup round reached*
1895	II 6	1
1896	II 5	p
1897	II 4	p
1898	II 8	p
1899	II 6	1
1900	II 9	1
1901	II 2	1
1902	II 4	1
1903	II 1P	1
1904	I 12	1
1905	I 4	s-f
1906	I 3	3
1907	I 4	1
1908	I 6	1
1909	I 5	3
1910	I 9	2
1911	I 11	2
1912	I 10	2
1913	I 4	3
1914	I 6	3
1915	I 10	
1916	I 15	
1917	I 4	
1918	I 15	
1919	I 13	
1920	I 7	1
1921	I 10	1
1922	I 16	3
1923	I 2	2
1924	I 2	Winners
1925	I 2	3
1926	I 2	q-f
1927	I 4	2
1928	I 13	3
1929	I 15	3
1930	I 12	3
1931	I 9	2
1932	I 14	s-f
1933	I 18	2
1934	I 18	1
1935	I 14	q-f
1936	I 19R	2
1937	II 4	2
1938	II 3	1
1939	II 4	2
1947	II 2P	1
1948	I 15R	q-f
1949	II 3	1
1950	II 2P	1
1951	I 14	q-f
1952	I 13	q-f
1953	I 14	3
1954	I 15R	1
1955	II 1P	s-f
1956	I 7	q-f
1957	I 11	q-f
1958	I 16	1
1959	I 5	2
1960	I 16	3
1961	I 13	s-f
1962	I 15	1
1963	I 11	2
1964	I 15	3
1965	I 17R	2
1966	II 2P	1
1967	I 13	2
1968	I 13	q-f
1969	I 7	q-f
1970	I 12	2
1971	I 10	s-f
1972	I 15	4
1973	I 18R	q-f
1974	II 1P	3
1975	I 11	Final
1976	I 7	3
1977	I 6	3
1978	I 10	3
1979	I 6	4
1980	I 2P	4
1981	P 7	3
1982	P 10R	3

ALBION ROVERS

Founded: 1881
Address: Cliftonhill Park, Coatbridge, Lanarkshire
Telephone: Coatbridge 32350
Ground capacity: 10,000 (580 seated)
Record attendance: 27,381 v Rangers, Scottish Cup 2nd round, 8.2.36
Record victory: 12-0 v Airdriehill, Scottish Cup 1st round, 3.9.1887
Record defeat: 1-9 v Motherwell, Division I, 2.1.37
Most League points: 54, Division II, 1929-30
Most League goals: 101, Division II, 1929-30
League scoring record: 41, Jim Renwick, Division II, 1932-33
Most capped player: 1, Jock White, Scotland

Scottish Cup

	Year	Opponents	Score	Scorers
Runners-up	1920	Kilmarnock	2-3	Watson, Hillhouse

THE ALBION ROVERS RECORD

	Division & place	Cup round reached
1904	II 9	2
1905	II 8	p
1906	II 3	p
1907	II 6	p
1908	II 9	1
1909	II 10	1
1910	II 9	p
1911	II 3	p
1912	II 11	p
1913	II 9	p
1914	II 2	1
1915	II 9	
1916		
1917		
1918		
1919		
1920	*I 22	Final
1921	I 17	s-f
1922	I 11	2
1923	I 19R	1
1924	II 5	1
1925	II 15	1
1926	II 9	3
1927	II 16	1
1928	II 8	4
1929	II 4	3
1930	II 3	3
1931	II 9	2
1932	II 16	2
1933	II 5	q-f
1934	II 1P	q-f
1935	I 16	2
1936	I 16	2
1937	I 20R	2
1938	II 2P	3
1939	I 16R	1
1947	II 4	3
1948	II 2P	1
1949	I 16R	2
1950	II 11	2
1951	II 8	2
1952	II 14	3
1953	II 16	3
1954	II 7	2
1955	II 11	5
1956	II 17	4
1957	II 5	4
1958	II 17	2
1959	II 10	1
1960	II 10	2
1961	II 17	1
1962	II 18	2
1963	II 7	1
1964	II 9	3
1965	II 11	p
1966	II 7	1
1967	II 8	p
1968	II 8	p
1969	II 7	p
1970	II 11	1
1971	II 7	3
1972	II 18	3
1973	II 18	1
1974	II 17	2
1975	II 12	4
1976	II 9	3
1977	II 6	4
1978	**II 8**	**3**
1979	**II 7**	**1**
1980	**II 4**	**1**
1981	**II 12**	**2**
1982	**II 11**	**3**

*Elected to First Division in 1919

ALLOA ATHLETIC

Founded: 1878
Address: Recreation Ground, Alloa, Clackmannanshire
Telephone: Alloa 722695
Ground capacity: 9,000
Playing area: 110 by 75 yards
Record attendance: 12,800 v Dunfermline, Scottish Cup 3rd round replay, 22.2.39
Record victory: 9-2 v Forfar Athletic, Division II, 18.3.33
Record defeat: 2-11 v Hibernian, League Cup quarter final, 26.9.65
Most League points: 60, Division II, 1921-22
Most League goals: 92, Division II, 1961-62
League scoring record: 49, Wee Crilley, Division II, 1921-22
Most capped player: 1, Jock Hepburn, Scotland

THE ALLOA RECORD

	Division & place	Cup round reached
1920		2
1921		3
1922	II 1P	3
1923	I 20R	1
1924	II 16	2
1925	II 4	2
1926	II 16	2
1927	II 15	3
1928	II 15	3
1929	II 13	1
1930	II 19	1
1931	II 13	2
1932	II 13	1
1933	II 11	1
1934	II 15	2
1935	II 10	1
1936	II 4	1
1937	II 9	1
1938	II 11	1
1939	II 2	q-f
1947	II 5	1
1948	II 12	2
1949	II 14	2
1950	II 16	1
1951	II 16	1
1952	II 7	2
1953	II 9	2
1954	II 11	1
1955	II 15	5
1956	II 13	5
1957	II 15	5
1958	II 8	1
1959	II 13	3
1960	II 13	2
1961	II 11	q-f
1962	II 4	2
1963	II 9	2
1964	II 16	2
1965	II 10	p
1966	II 8	1
1967	II 13	1
1968	II 17	1
1969	II 18	p
1970	II 6	p
1971	II 16	3
1972	II 16	3
1973	II 12	2
1974	II 12	2
1975	II 15	2
1976	II 3	3
1977	II 2P	4
1978	I 13R	3
1979	**II 6**	**3**
1980	**II 14**	**3**
1981	**II 6**	**1**
1982	**II 2P**	**4**

ARBROATH

Founded: 1878
Address: Gayfield Park
Telephone: 02414 72157
Ground capacity: 15,000
Record attendance: 13,510 v Rangers, Scottish Cup 3rd round, 23.2.52
Record victory: 36-0 v Bon Accord, Scottish Cup 1st round, 12.9.85
Record defeat: 0-8 Kilmarnock, Division II, 3.1.49
Most League points: 57, Division II, 1966–67
Most League goals: 87, Division II, 1967–68
League scoring record: 45, Dave Easson, Division II, 1958-59
Record League aggregate: 120, Jimmy Jack, 1966-1971
Most League appearances: 319, Ian Stirling, 1960-1971
Most capped player: 2 (6 in all), Ned Doig, Scotland

THE ARBROATH RECORD

	Division & place	*Cup round reached*
1922	II 16	1
1923	II 20	1
1924	II 17	2
1925	II 5	3
1926	II 10	2
1927	II 19	1
1928	II 10	1
1929	II 3	3
1930	II 9	2
1931	II 15	3
1932	II 11	2
1933	II 10	1
1934	II 3	2
1935	II 2P	1
1936	I 12	1
1937	I 14	2
1938	I 11	1
1939	I 17R	1
1947	II 12	s-f
1948	II 13	2
1949	II 7	1
1950	II 14	1
1951	II 13	1
1952	II 16	3
1953	II 7	1
1954	II 14	2
1955	II 12	5
1956	II 18	5
1957	II 10	5
1958	II 3	2
1959	II 2P	2
1960	I 18R	2
1961	II 12	2
1962	II 6	2
1963	II 6	2
1964	II 3	2
1965	II 7	1
1966	II 6	p
1967	II 3	1
1968	II 2P	2
1969	I 18R	1
1970	II 5	1
1971	II 3	3
1972	II 2P	3
1973	I 15	3
1974	I 13	4
1975	I 18	q-f
1976	I 5	3
1977	I 8	q-f
1978	I 9	3
1979	I 10	3
1980	I 13R	3
1981	II 9	3
1982	II 3	1

AYR UNITED

Founded: 1910
Address: Somerset Park, Ayr, Scotland
Telephone: 0292-263435
Ground capacity: 18,500 (1,500 seated)
Playing area: 111 by 75 yards
Record attendance: 25,225 v Rangers, Division I, 13.9.69
Record victory: 11-1 v Dumbarton, League Cup, 13.8.52
Record defeat: 0-9 v Rangers, Division I, 16.11.29
v Hearts, Division I, 28.2.31
v Third Lanark, Division II, 4.12.54
Most League points: 60 Division II, 1958–59
Most League goals: 122, Division II, 1936–37
League scoring record: 66, J Smith, Division II, 1927–28
Most capped player: 3, Jim Nisbet, Scotland

THE AYR RECORD

	Division & place	*Cup round reached*
1899*	II 8	p
1900*	II 8	p
1901*	II 6	2
1902*	II 8	1
1903*	II 3	2
1904*	II 3	1
1905*	II 5	1
1906*	II 7	p
1907*	II 8	2
1908*	II 3	p
1909*	II 5	1
1910*	II 7	2
1911	II 2	p
1912	II 1	1
1913	II 1P	2
1914	I 10	1
1915	I 5	
1916	I 4	
1917	I 15	
1918	I 18	
1919	I 7	
1920	I 10	3
1921	I 14	3
1922	I 14	2
1923	I 10	3
1924	I 14	q-f
1925	I 19R	2
1926	II 3	1
1927	II 8	1
1928	II 1P	2
1929	I 16	2
1930	I 9	2
1931	I 18	3
1932	I 17	1
1933	I 16	2
1934	I 8	2
1935	I 18	2
1936	I 20R	1
1937	II 1P	1
1938	I 17	q-f
1939	I 14	1
1947	II 11	2
1948	II 10	1
1949	II 9	2
1950	II 13	1
1951	II 3	q-f
1952	II 3	1
1953	II 5	3
1954	II 9	2
1955	II 8	5
1956	II 2P	6
1957	I 18R	5
1958	II 5	1
1959	II 1P	3
1960	I 8	q-f
1961	I 18R	2
1962	II 9	1
1963	II 13	2
1964	II 14	q-f
1965	II 18	1
1966	II 1P	1
1967	I 18R	1
1968	II 5	1
1969	II 2P	2
1970	I 14	1
1971	I 14	3
1972	I 12	4
1973	I 6	s-f
1974	I 7	q-f
1975	I 7	3
1976	P 6	4
1977	P 8	4
1978	P 9R	3
1979	I 4	4
1980	I 3	4
1981	I 6	3
1982	I 6	3

* Ayr FC (combined with Ayr Parkhouse in 1910)
p preliminary round

BERWICK RANGERS

Founded: 1881
Address: Shielfield Park, Tweedmouth, Berwick-on-Tweed, Northumberland
Telephone: 0289-7424/2554
Ground capacity: 10,673 (1,473 seated)
Playing area: 112 by 76 yards
Record attendance: 13,365 v Rangers, Scottish Cup 1st round, 28.1.67
Record victory: 8-1 v Forfar, Division II, 25.12.65
v Vale of Leithen, Scottish Cup Preliminary round, 30.9.67
Record defeat: 1-9 v Dundee Utd, Division II, 21.4.56
v Hamilton, Division I, 2.8.80
Most League points: 54, Division II, 1978-79
Most League goals: 83, Division II, 1961-62
League scoring record: 38, Ken Bowron, Division II, 1963-64
Record League aggregate: 98, Ken Bowron, 1963-1966 & 1968-1969
Most League appearances: 334, Eric Tait, 1970–82

THE BERWICK RECORD

	Division & place	*Cup round reached*
1956	II 14	1
1957	II 18	1
1958	II 19	1
1959	II 10	1
1960	II 9	1
1961	II 11	1
1962	II 8	1
1963	II 17	1
1964	II 12	1
1965	II 8	1
1966	II 11	1
1967	II 10	2
1968	II 14	1
1969	II 16	1
1970	II 9	1
1971	II 13	2
1972	II 13	2
1973	II 9	3
1974	II 6	1
1975	II 10	3
1976	II 11	1
1977	II 8	1
1978	II 4	3
1979	II 1P	4
1980	I 12	q-f
1981	I 14R	3
1982	II 4	2

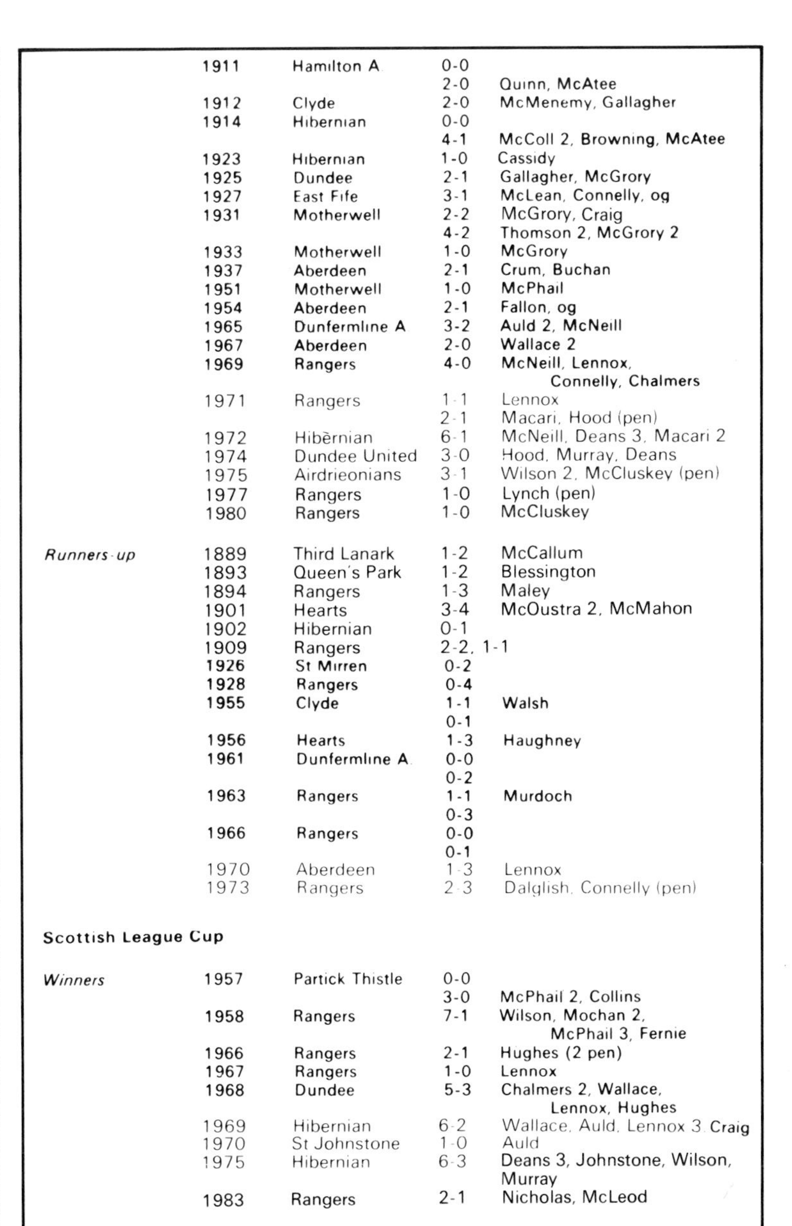

BRECHIN CITY

Founded: 1906
Address: Glebe Park, Brechin, Angus
Telephone: Brechin 2856
Ground capacity: 7,500
Playing area: 110 by 67 yards
Record attendance: 8,123 v Aberdeen, Scottish Cup 3rd round, 3.2.73
Record victory: 12-1 v Thornhill, Scottish Cup, 1st round, 28.1.26
Record defeat: 0-10 v Albion, Division II, 25.1.38
Most League points: 46, Division II, 1981-82
Most League goals: 80, Division II, 1957-58
League scoring record: 26, Willie McIntosh, 1959-60
Most capped player: None

THE BRECHIN RECORD

	Division & place	*Cup round reached*
1924		1
1925		1
1926		3
1927		2
1928		2
1929		2
1930	II 20	1
1931	II 16	1
1932	II 19	1
1933	II 15	1
1934	II 14	2
1935	II 15	3
1936	II 16	1
1937	II 16	1
1938	II 18	1
1939	II 10	1
1947	*	p
1948	*	p
1949	*	p
1950	*	1
1951	*	2
1952	*	1
1953	*	1
1954	*	2
1955	II 16	4
1956	II 6	6
1957	II 6	5
1958	II 7	1
1959	II 5	2
1960	II 12	1
1961	II 14	3
1962	II 19	2
1963	II 19	2
1964	II 15	2
1965	II 19	p
1966	II 16	p
1967	II 20	1
1968	II 16	1
1969	II 17	p
1970	II 14	p
1971	II 19	3
1972	II 15	2
1973	II 19	3
1974	II 19	3
1975	II 17	1
1976	II 13	2
1977	II 13	3
1978	II 14	3
1979	II 11	2
1980	II 7	3
1981	II 4	3
1982	II 5	3

* – Brechin competed in Division 'C'

CELTIC

Founded: 1888
Address: Celtic Park (Parkhead), Glasgow SE
Telephone: (041) 554 2710
Ground capacity: 67,500 (9,000 seated)
Playing area: 115 by 75 yards
Record attendance: 83,500 v Rangers, Division I, 1.1.38
Record defeat: 0-8 v Motherwell, Division I, 30.4.37
Most League points: 67, Division I, 1915–16 & 1921–22
Most League goals: 116, Division I, 1935–36
League scoring record: 50, Jimmy McGrory, Division I, 1935-36
Record League aggregate: 397, Jimmy McGrory, 1922-23 & 1924-1938
Most League appearances: 486, Billy McNeill, 1958–75
Most capped player: 62, Danny McGrain, Scotland

Scottish Cup	*Year*	*Opponents*	*Score*	*Scorers*
Winners	1892	Queen s Park	†5-1	Campbell 2, McMahon 2, og
	1899	Rangers	2-0	Hodge, McMahon
	1900	Queen's Park	4-3	Divers 3, McMahon
	1904	Rangers	3-2	Quinn 3
	1907	Hearts	3-0	Orr (pen), Somers 2
	1908	St Mirren	5-1	Bennett 2, Quinn, Hamilton, Somers
	1911	Hamilton A	0-0	
			2-0	Quinn, McAtee
	1912	Clyde	2-0	McMenemy, Gallagher
	1914	Hibernian	0-0	
			4-1	McColl 2, Browning, McAtee
	1923	Hibernian	1-0	Cassidy
	1925	Dundee	2-1	Gallagher, McGrory
	1927	East Fife	3-1	McLean, Connelly, og
	1931	Motherwell	2-2	McGrory, Craig
			4-2	Thomson 2, McGrory 2
	1933	Motherwell	1-0	McGrory
	1937	Aberdeen	2-1	Crum, Buchan
	1951	Motherwell	1-0	McPhail
	1954	Aberdeen	2-1	Fallon, og
	1965	Dunfermline A	3-2	Auld 2, McNeill
	1967	Aberdeen	2-0	Wallace 2
	1969	Rangers	4-0	McNeill, Lennox, Connelly, Chalmers
	1971	Rangers	1-1	Lennox
			2-1	Macari, Hood (pen)
	1972	Hibernian	6-1	McNeill, Deans 3, Macari 2
	1974	Dundee United	3-0	Hood, Murray, Deans
	1975	Airdrieonians	3-1	Wilson 2, McCluskey (pen)
	1977	Rangers	1-0	Lynch (pen)
	1980	Rangers	1-0	McCluskey
Runners-up	1889	Third Lanark	1-2	McCallum
	1893	Queen's Park	1-2	Blessington
	1894	Rangers	1-3	Maley
	1901	Hearts	3-4	McOustra 2, McMahon
	1902	Hibernian	0-1	
	1909	Rangers	2-2, 1-1	
	1926	St Mirren	0-2	
	1928	Rangers	0-4	
	1955	Clyde	1-1	Walsh
			0-1	
	1956	Hearts	1-3	Haughney
	1961	Dunfermline A	0-0	
			0-2	
	1963	Rangers	1-1	Murdoch
			0-3	
	1966	Rangers	0-0	
			0-1	
	1970	Aberdeen	1-3	Lennox
	1973	Rangers	2-3	Dalglish, Connelly (pen)

Scottish League Cup

	Year	Opponents	Score	Scorers
Winners	1957	Partick Thistle	0-0	
			3-0	McPhail 2, Collins
	1958	Rangers	7-1	Wilson, Mochan 2, McPhail 3, Fernie
	1966	Rangers	2-1	Hughes (2 pen)
	1967	Rangers	1-0	Lennox
	1968	Dundee	5-3	Chalmers 2, Wallace, Lennox, Hughes
	1969	Hibernian	6-2	Wallace, Auld, Lennox 3, Craig
	1970	St Johnstone	1-0	Auld
	1975	Hibernian	6-3	Deans 3, Johnstone, Wilson, Murray
	1983	Rangers	2-1	Nicholas, McLeod
Runners-up	1965	Rangers	1-2	Johnstone
	1971	Rangers	0-1	
	1972	Partick T.	1-4	Dalglish
	1973	Hibernian	1-2	Dalglish
	1974	Dundee	0-1	
	1976	Rangers	0-1	
	1977	Aberdeen	1-2	Dalglish
	1978	Rangers	1-2	Edvaldsson

THE CELTIC RECORD

	Division & place	*Cup round reached*
1889		Final
1890		1
1891	I 3	s f
1892	I 2	Winners
1893	I 1C	Final
1894	I 1C	Final
1895	I 2	3
1896	I 1C	1
1897	I 4	1
1898	I 1C	2
1899	I 3	Winners
1900	I 2	Winners
1901	I 2	Final
1902	I 2	Final
1903	I 5	3
1904	I 3	Winners
1905	I 1C	4
1906	I 1C	3
1907	I 1C	Winners
1908	I 1C	Winners
1909	I 1C	Final
1910	I 1C	4
1911	I 5	Winners
1912	I 2	Winners
1913	I 2	3
1914	I 1C	Winners
1915	I 1C	
1916	I 1C	
1917	I 1C	
1918	I 2	
1919	I 1C	
1920	I 2	3
1921	I 2	3
1922	I 1C	3
1923	I 3	Winners
1924	I 3	1
1925	I 4	Winners
1926	I 1C	Final
1927	I 3	Winners
1928	I 2	Final
1929	I 2	s f
1930	I 4	3
1931	I 2	Winners
1932	I 3	3
1933	I 4	Winners
1934	I 3	4
1935	I 2	4
1936	I 1C	2
1937	I 3	Winners
1938	I 1C	3
1939	I 2	4
1947	I 7	1
1948	I 12	s f
1949	I 6	1
1950	I 4	3
1951	I 7	Winners
1952	I 9	1
1953	I 8	4
1954	I 1C	Winners
1955	I 2	Final
1956	I 5	Final
1957	I 5	s-f
1958	I 3	3
1959	I 6	s f
1960	I 9	s f
1961	I 4	Final
1962	I 3	s f
1963	I 4	Final
1964	I 3	4

1965	I 8	Winners
1966	I 1C	Final
1967	I 1C	Winners
1968	I 1C	1
1969	I 1C	Winners
1970	I 1C	Final
1971	I 1C	Winners
1972	I 1C	Winners
1973	I 1C	Final
1974	I 1C	Winners
1975	I 3	Winners
1976	P 2	3
1977	P 1C	Winners
1978	P 5	4
1979	P 1C	q-f
1980	P 2	Winners
1981	P 1C	s-f
1982	P 1C	4

1961	I 17R	1
1962	II 1P	2
1963	I 17R	2
1964	II 2P	2
1965	I 7	1
1966	I 11	1
1967	I 3	s-f
1968	I 8	2
1969	I 13	2
1970	I 16	1
1971	I 15	4
1972	I 17R	3
1973	II 1P	3
1974	I 15	3
1975	I 16	3
1976	I 14R	3
1977	II 7	3
1978	II 1P	1
1979	I 9	3
1980	I 14R	3
1981	II 8	3
1982	II 1P	3

CLYDE

Founded: 1878
Address: Shawfield Park, Glasgow C.5
Telephone: (041) 647 6329
Ground capacity: 25,000 (2,000 seated)
Playing area: 110 by 70 yards
Record attendance: 52,000 v Rangers, Division I, 21.11.08
Record victory: 11-1 v Cowdenbeath, Division II, 6.10.51
Record defeat: 0-11 v Rangers, Scottish Cup 4th round, 13.11.1880
v Dumbarton, Scottish Cup 4th round, 22.11.1879
Most League points: 64, Division II, 1956-57*
Most League goals: 122, Division II, 1956-57
League scoring record: 32, Bill Boyd, Division I, 1932-33
Most capped player: 12, Tommy Ring, Scotland

Scottish Cup	*Year*	*Opponents*	*Score*	*Scorers*
Winners	1939	Motherwell	4-0	Martin 2, Wallace, Noble
	1955	Celtic	1-1	Robertson
		Replay	1-0	Ring
	1958	Hibernian	1-0	Coyle
Runners-up	1910	Dundee	2-2	Chalmers, Booth
		First replay	0-0	
		Second replay	1-2	Chalmers
	1912	Celtic	0-2	
	1949	Rangers	1-4	Galletly

THE CLYDE RECORD

	Division & place	*Cup round reached*
1892	I 7	p
1893	I 10	1
1894	II 3P	3
1895	I 7	3
1896	I 9	2
1897	I 9	1
1898	I 10	1
1899	I 8	3
1900	I 10R	2
1901	II 4	2
1902	II 12	p
1903	II 12	1
1904	II 2	1
1905	II 1	1
1906	II 2P	1
1907	I 8	1
1908	I 17	p
1909	I 3	s-f
1910	I 5	Final
1911	I 7	q-f
1912	I 3	Final
1913	I 9	s-f
1914	I 9	2
1915	I 17	
1916	I 16	
1917	I 13	
1918	I 17	
1919	I 17	
1920	I 16	1
1921	I 7	2
1922	I 10	3
1923	I 16	1
1924	I 19R	3
1925	II 3	2
1926	II 2P	3
1927	I 17	3
1928	I 15	1
1929	I 17	3
1930	I 11	2
1931	I 12	2
1932	I 13	q-f
1933	I 12	s-f
1934	I 14	1
1935	I 10	2
1936	I 18	s-f
1937	I 10	s-f
1938	I 15	1
1939	I 9	Winners
1947	I 10	1
1948	I 6	3
1949	I 14	Final
1950	I 13	2
1951	I 15R	3
1952	II 1P	2
1953	I 5	q-f
1954	I 8	2
1955	I 7	Winners
1956	I 17R	s-f
1957	II 1P	q-f
1958	I 4	Winners
1959	I 15	2
1960	I 6	s-f

CLYDEBANK

Founded: 1965 (new club)
Address: New Kilbowie Park, Clydebank
Telephone: (041) 952 2887
Ground capacity: 10,000 (all seated)
Playing area: 110 by 68 yards
Record attendance: 14,900 v Hibernian, Scottish Cup 1st round, 10.2.65
Record victory: 8-1 v Arbroath, Division 1, 3.1.77
Record defeat: 1-9 v Galafairydean, Scottish Cup, qualifying round, 15.9.65
Most League points: 58, Division I, 1976-77
Most League goals: 78, Division I, 1978-79
League scoring record: 28, Blair Miller, Division 1, 1978-79

THE CLYDEBANK RECORD

	Division & place	*Cup round reached*
1918	I 9	
1919	I 10	
1920	I 5	
1921	I 20	
1922	I 22R	
1923	II 2P	
1924	I 20R	
1925	II 2P	
1926	I 20R	
1927	II 3	
1928	II 14	
1929	II 16	
1930	II 18	
1931*	II 19	
1965†	II 5	1
1966‡		p
1967§	II 18	p
1968	II 9	p
1969	II 13	p
1970	II 13	2
1971	II 5	3
1972	II 9	4
1973	II 17	1
1974	II 10	3
1975	II 7	4
1976	II 1P	2
1977	I 2P	4
1978	P 10R	3
1979	I 3	4
1980	I 9	3
1981	I 10	q-f
1982	I 4	4

*Old Clydebank disbanded
†East Stirlingshire Clydebank
‡Clydebank juniors
§Clydebank

COWDENBEATH

Founded: 1881
Address: Central Park, Cowdenbeath, Fife, Scotland
Telephone: Cowdenbeath 511205
Ground capacity: 10,000
Playing area: 110 by 70 yards
Record attendance: 25,586 v Rangers, League Cup quarter-final, 21.9.49
Record victory: 12-0 v Johnstone, Scottish Cup 1st round, 21.1.28
Record defeat: 1-11 v Clyde, Division II, 6.10.51
Most League points: 60, Division II, 1938-39
Most League goals: 120, Division II, 1938-39
League scoring record: 40, Willie Devlin, 1925-26
Most capped player: 3, Jim Paterson, Scotland

THE COWDENBEATH RECORD

	Division & place	*Cup round reached*
1906	II 9	p
1907	II 7	1
1908	II 12	p
1909	II 11	p
1910	II 11	p
1911	II 5	p
1912	II 4	p
1913	II 5	p
1914	II 1	p
1915	II 1	
1916		
1917		
1918		
1919		
1920		1
1921		p
1922	II 2	2
1923	II 11	2
1924	II 2P	2
1925	I 5	1
1926	I 7	1
1927	I 7	2
1928	I 9	2
1929	I 13	2
1930	I 16	2
1931	I 7	q-f
1932	I 12	2
1933	I 17	1
1934	I 20R	3
1935	II 12	1
1936	II 10	3
1937	II 6	3
1938	II 6	2
1939	II 1	2
1947	II 14	3
1948	II 5	2
1949	II 13	2
1950	II 5	2
1951	II 11	1
1952	II 8	2
1953	II 13	2
1954	II 13	2
1955	II 14	4
1956	II 7	5
1957	II 3	4
1958	II 6	1
1959	II 14	1
1960	II 19	3
1961	II 8	2
1962	II 14	1
1963	II 8	2
1964	II 17	1
1965	II 12	1
1966	II 10	2
1967	II 6	1
1968	II 12	1
1969	II 12	1
1970	II 2P	p
1971	I 18R	4
1972	II 5	3
1973	II 7	3
1974	II 13	3
1975	II 19	2
1976	II 5	4
1977	II 12	1
1978	II 10	3
1979	II 5	2
1980	II 8	3
1981	II 3	4
1982	II 9	2

DUMBARTON

Founded: 1872 (as Dumbarton Athletic)
Address: Boghead Park, Dumbarton, Strathclyde
Telephone: Dumbarton 62569
Ground capacity: 18,000
Record attendance: 18,000 v Raith Rovers, Scottish Cup quarter-final, 2.3.57
Record victory: 8-0 v Cowdenbeath, Division II, 28.3.64
Record defeat: 1-11 v Ayr United, League Cup, 13.8.52
Most League points: 52, Division II, 1971-72
Most League goals: 101, Division II, 1956-57
League scoring record: 38, Kenny Wilson, Division II, 1971-72
Most capped player: 8, John Lindsay, Scotland
8, James McAulay, Scotland

Scottish Cup	*Year*	*Opponents*	*Score*
Winners	1883	Vale of Leven	2-2
		Replay	2-1
Runners-up	1881	Queen's Park	1-3
	1882	Queen's Park	2-2
		Replay	1-4
	1887	Hibernian	1-2
	1891	Hearts	0-1
	1897	Rangers	1-5

THE DUMBARTON RECORD

	Division & place	*Cup round reached*
1891	I 1C†	Final
1892	I 1C	3
1893	I 7	2
1894	I 5	2
1895	I 10	2
1896	I 10R	1
1897	II 10	Final
1898	*	1
1899	*	1
1900	*	p
1901	*	p
1902	*	p
1903	*	p
1904	*	p
1905	*	p
1906	*	p
1907	II 4	p
1908	II 2	p
1909	II 4	p
1910	II 4	1
1911	II 1	p
1912	II 3	1
1913	II 6E	q-f
1914	I 19	2
1915	I 13	
1916	I 9	
1917	I 10	
1918	I 8	
1919	I 15	
1920	I 11	1
1921	I 21	4
1922	I 20R	1
1923	II 4	1
1924	II 10	1
1925	II 8	2
1926	II 11	q-f
1927	II 18	2
1928	II 11	1
1929	II 14	3
1930	II 16	1
1931	II 10	1
1932	II 12	1
1933	II 9	2
1934	II 6	1
1935	II 16	2
1936	II 18	3
1937	II 15	2
1938	II 7	1
1939	II 11	1
1947	II 13	q-f
1948	II 11	3
1949	II 15	3
1950	II 15	2
1951	II 9	1
1952	II 10	3
1953	II 10	1
1954	II 16L	1
1955	*	4
1956	II 4	4
1957	II 9	q-f
1958	II 4	1
1959	II 4	2
1960	II 6	1
1961	II 10	2
1962	II 17	1
1963	II 12	1
1964	II 6	2
1965	II 14	1
1966	II 12	q-f
1967	II 14	1
1968	II 10	p
1969	II 14	1
1970	II 7	1
1971	II 4	2
1972	II 1P	4
1973	I 16	4
1974	I 10	3
1975	I 14	q-f
1976	I 4	s-f
1977	I 7	3
1978	I 4	q-f
1979	I 7	q-f
1980	I 4	3
1981	I 8	4
1982	I 11	4

† shared jointly with Rangers
* not members of League
E – elected to First Division

DUNDEE

Founded: 1893
Address: Dens Park, Dundee, Angus
Telephone: Dundee 826104
Ground capacity: 22,381 (12,130 seated)
Playing area: 110 by 75 yards
Record attendance: 43,024 v Rangers, Scottish Cup 2nd round, 7.2.53
Record victory: 10-0 v Alloa Athletic, Division II, 8.3.47
10-0 v Dunfermline Athletic, Division II, 22.3.47
Record defeat: 0-11 v Celtic, Division I, 26.10.1895
Most League points: 55, Division I, 1978-79
Most League goals: 113, Division II, 1946-47
League scoring record: 38, David Halliday, Division I, 1923-24
Record League aggregate: 111, Alan Gilzean, 1960-1964
Most League appearances: 341, Doug Cowie, 1947-1961
Most capped player: 24, Alex Hamilton, Scotland

Scottish Cup	*Year*	*Opponents*	*Score*	*Scorers*
Winners	1910	Clyde	2-2	Hunter, Langlands
			0-0	
			2-1	Bellamy, Hunter
Runners-up	1925	Celtic	1-2	McLean (D)
	1952	Motherwell	0-4	
	1964	Rangers	1-3	Cameron
League Cup				
Winners	1952	Rangers	3-2	Flavell, Pattillo, Boyd
	1953	Kilmarnock	2-0	Flavell 2
	1974	Celtic	1-0	Wallace
Runners-up	1968	Celtic	3-5	McLean (G) 2, McLean (J)
	1981	Dundee Utd	0-3	

THE DUNDEE RECORD

Year	Division & place	Cup round reached
1894	I 8	p
1895	I 8	s-f
1896	I 5	2
1897	I 5	q-f
1898	I 7	s-f
1899	I 10	1
1900	I 6	q-f
1901	I 7	q-f
1902	I 9	2
1903	I 2	s-f
1904	I 5	q-f
1905	I 7	1
1906	I 7	1
1907	I 2	2
1908	I 4	2
1909	I 2	2
1910	I 6	Winners
1911	I 6	s-f
1912	I 8	2
1913	I 14	q-f
1914	I 7	2•
1915	I 15	
1916	I 8	
1917	I 16R	
1918†		
1919†		
1920	I 4	2
1921	I 4	q-f
1922	I 4	3
1923	I 7	1-f
1924	I 5	2
1925	I 8	Final
1926	I 10	2
1927	I 5	3
1928	I 14	3
1929	I 18	3
1930	I 14	q-f
1931	I 8	3
1932	I 11	2
1933	I 15	3
1934	I 12	2
1935	I 8	1
1936	I 13	3
1937	I 9	3
1938	I 19R	1
1939	II 6	2
1947	II 1P	q-f
1948	I 4	1
1949	I 2	s-f
1950	I 6	1
1951	I 3	q-f
1952	I 8	Final
1953	I 7	2
1954	I 7	3
1955	I 8	5
1956	I 13	6
1957	I 10	5
1958	I 11	3
1959	I 4	1
1960	I 4	2
1961	I 10	2
1962	I 1C	1
1963	I 9	q-f
1964	I 6	Final
1965	I 6	1
1966	I 9	2
1967	I 6	1
1968	I 9	2
1969	I 9	1
1970	I 6	s-f
1971	I 5	q-f
1972	I 5	4
1973	I 5	s-f
1974	I 5	s-f
1975	I 6	s-f
1976	P 9R	3
1977	I 3	s-f
1978	I 3	3
1979	I 1P	q-f
1980	P 9R	3
1981	I 2P	3
1982	P 8	q-f

† No Second Division

THE DUNDEE UNITED RECORD

Year	Division & place	Cup round reached
1911*	II 8	p
1912*	II 10	p
1913*	II 10	2
1914*	II 4	1
1915*	II 11	
1920*	†	p
1921*	†	p
1922*	II 19	1
1923‡		2
1924	II 9	1
1925	II 1P	2
1926	I 17	1
1927	I 20R	q-f
1928	II 6	2
1929	II 1P	q-f
1930	I 19R	2
1931	II 2P	2
1932	I 19R	3
1933	II 13	2
1934	II 17	1
1935	II 4	3
1936	II 7	2
1937	II 14	1
1938	II 14	2
1939	II 9	2
1947	II 10	1
1948	II 15	2
1949	II 8	2
1950	II 8	2
1951	II 4	1
1952	II 4	3
1953	II 8	1
1954	II 15	1
1955	II 13	4
1956	II 8	5
1957	II 13	6
1958	II 9	2
1959	II 17	2
1960	II 2P	2
1961	I 9	2
1962	I 10	2
1963	I 7	s-f
1964	I 8	1
1965	I 9	2
1966	I 5	2
1967	I 9	s-f
1968	I 11	2
1969	I 5	q-f
1970	I 5	2
1971	I 6	4
1972	I 9	3
1973	I 7	3
1974	I 8	Final
1975	I 4	4
1976	P 8	4
1977	P 4	3
1978	P 3	s-f
1979	P 3	3
1980	P 4	4
1981	P 5	Final
1982	P 4	q-f

*as Dundee Hibernians
† Scottish Second Division not reformed until 1921
‡ Name changed to Dundee United. Dundee Hibernians did not compete in the League 1922-23.

DUNDEE UNITED

Founded: 1910*
Address: Tannadice Park, Dundee, Angus
Telephone: Dundee 86289
Ground capacity: 18,912 (2,204 seated)
Playing area: 110 by 74 yards
Record attendance: 28,000 v Barcelona, Fairs Cup 2nd round, 16.11.66
Record victory: 14-0 v Nithsdale Wanderers, Scottish Cup 1st round, 17.1.31
Record defeat: 1-12 v Motherwell, Division II, 23.1.54
Most League points: 51, Division II, 1928-29
Most League goals: 108, Division II, 1935-36
League scoring record: 41, John Coyle, Division II, 1955-56
Record League aggregate: 202, Peter McKay, 1947-1954
Most League appearances: 587, Doug Smith, 1959-76
Most capped player: 16, David Narey, Scotland
*As Dundee Hibernians. Name changed to Dundee United in 1923

	Year	Opponents	Score	Scorers
Scottish Cup				
Runners-up	1974	Celtic	0-3	
	1981	Rangers	0-0	
		Replay	1-4	Dodds
Scottish League Cup				
Winners	1980	Aberdeen	0-0	
		Replay	3-0	Pettigrew 2, Sturrock
	1981	Dundee	3-0	Dodds, Sturrock 2
Runners-up	1982	Rangers	1-2	Milne

DUNFERMLINE ATHLETIC

Founded: 1885
Address: East End Park, Dunfermline
Telephone: Dunfermline 24295
Ground capacity: 27,000 (3,100 seated)
Playing area: 114 by 72 yards
Record attendance: 27,816 v Celtic, Division I, 30.4.68
Record victory: 11-2 v Stenhousemuir, Division II, 27.9.30
Record defeat: 0-10 v Dundee, Division II, 22.3.47
Most League points: 59, Division II, 1925-26
Most League goals: 120, Division II, 1957-58
League scoring record: 53, Bobby Skinner, Division II, 1925-26
Record League aggregate: 154, Charlie Dickson, 1955-64
Most League appearances: 301, George Peebles, 1956-66
Most capped player: 6 (12 in all), Andy Wilson, Scotland

	Year	Opponents	Score	Scorers
Scottish Cup				
Winners	1961	Celtic	0-0	
			2-0	Thomson, Dickson
	1968	Hearts	3-1	Gardner 2, Lister (pen)
Runners-up	1965	Celtic	2-3	Melrose, McLaughlin
Scottish League Cup				
Runners-up	1950	East Fife	0-3	

	Division & place	Cup round reached
1964	II 4	2
1965	II 9	2
1966	II 4	1
1967	II 5	2
1968	II 3	2
1969	II 3	1
1970	II 10	q-f
1971	II 2P	3
1972	I 16	3
1973	I 9	3
1974	I 17R	3
1975	II 5	3
1976	I 12	3
1977	I 12	q-f
1978	I 14R	3
1979	II 4	3
1980	II 10	3
1981	II 11	3
1982	II 7	2

THE DUNFERMLINE RECORD

	Division & place	*Cup round reached*
1922	II 8	2
1923	II 13	3
1924	II 7	1
1925	II 13	1
1926	II 1P	1
1927	I 18	3
1928	I 20R	4
1929	II 11	1
1930	II 10	1
1931	II 3	1
1932	II 10	q-f
1933	II 3	1
1934	II 2P	1
1935	I 15	q-f
1936	I 10	1
1937	I 19R	1
1938	II 9	1
1939	II 5	3
1947	II 8	1
1948	II 7	2
1949	II 4	1
1950	II 4	3
1951	II 10	1
1952	II 6	3
1953	II 11	1
1954	II 8	2
1955	II 2P	6
1956	I 16	5
1957	I 17R	6
1958	II 2P	3
1959	I 16	q-f
1960	I 13	2
1961	I 12	Winners
1962	I 4	q-f
1963	I 8	3
1964	I 5	s-f
1965	I 3	Final
1966	I 4	s-f
1967	I 8	q-f
1968	I 4	Winners
1969	I 3	2
1970	I 9	1
1971	I 16	4
1972	I 18R	3
1973	II 2P	4
1974	I 16	q-f
1975	I 15	3
1976	I 13R	3
1977	II 3	3
1978	II 3	2
1979	II 2P	3
1980	I 10	4
1981	I 12	3
1982	I 10	3

EAST FIFE

Founded: 1903
Address: Bayview Park, Methil, Fife
Telephone: Leven 26323
Ground capacity: 15,000
Playing area: 110 by 71 yards
Record attendance: 22,515 v Raith Rovers, Division I, 2.1.50
Record victory: 13-2 v Edinburgh City, Division II, 11.12.37
Record defeat: 0-9 v Hearts, Division I, 5.10.57
Most League points: 57, Division II, 1929-30
Most League goals: 114, Division II, 1929-30
League scoring record: 41, Henry Morris, Division II, 1947-48
Most capped player: 5 (8 in all), George Aitken, Scotland

	Year	*Opponents*	*Score*	*Scorers*
Scottish Cup *Winners*	1938	Kilmarnock	1-1	McLeod
		Replay	4-2	McKerrall 2, McLeod Miller
Runners-up	1927	Celtic	1-3	Wood
	1950	Rangers	0-3	
Scottish League Cup *Winners*	1948	Falkirk	0-0	
		Replay	4-1	Duncan 3, Adams
	1950	Dunfermline	3-0	Fleming, Duncan, Morris
	1954	Partick Thistle	3-2	Gardiner, Fleming, Christie

THE EAST FIFE RECORD

	Division & place	*Cup round reached*
1921		3
1922	II 12	1
1923	II 9	3
1924	II 13	2
1925	II 9	1
1926	II 4	1
1927	II 6	Final
1928	II 4	1
1929	II 8	1
1930	II 2P	1
1931	I 20R	1
1932	II 8	1
1933	II 7	1
1934	II 13	1
1935	II 9	1
1936	II 6	1
1937	II 5	3
1938	II 5	Winners
1939	II 3	1
1947	II 3	q-f
1948	II 1P	q-f
1949	I 4	s-f
1950	I 4	Final
1951	I 10	1
1952	I 3	2
1953	I 3	2
1954	I 6	1
1955	I 11	5
1956	I 12	5
1957	I 15	6
1958	I 17R	1
1959	II 8	1
1960	II 18	1
1961	II 13	2
1962	II 10	3
1963	II 11	2

EAST STIRLINGSHIRE

Founded: 1881
Address: Firs Park, Falkirk, Stirlingshire
Telephone: Falkirk 23583
Ground capacity: 12,000
Playing area: 112 by 72 yards
Record attendance: 11,500 v Hibernian, Scottish Cup, 10.2.60
Record victory: 8-2 v Brechin City, Division II, 31.3.62
Record defeat: 1-12 v Dundee Utd, Division II, 13.4.36
Most League points: 55, Division II, 1931-32
Most League goals: 111, Division II, 1931-32
League scoring record: 36, Malcolm Morrison, Division II, 1938-39
Most capped player: 5, Humphrey Jones, Wales

THE EAST STIRLINGSHIRE RECORD

	Division & place	*Cup round reached*
1902	II 9	p
1903	II 8	p
1904	II 6	p
1905	II 9	p
1906	II 12	p
1907	II 11	p
1908	II 5	p
1909	II 9	p
1910	II 8	p
1911	II 7	1
1912	II 9	2
1913	II 3	2
1914	II 8	2
1915	II 4	
1920	†	2
1921	†	3
1922	II 15	3
1923	II 19	1
1924	*	3
1925	II 18	2
1926	II 18	1
1927	II 5	1
1928	II 9	1
1929	II 12	2
1930	II 12	1
1931	II 7	1
1932	II 1P	1
1933	I 20R	1
1934	II 9	3
1935	II 14	1
1936	II 8	1
1937	II 7	1
1938	II 13	1
1939	II 17	1
1947	‡	2
1948	‡	2
1949	‡	1
1950	‡	1
1951	‡	2
1952	‡	1
1953	‡	2
1954	‡	1
1955	‡	4
1956	II 16	4
1957	II 19	4
1958	II 15	1
1959	II 15	1
1960	II 15	3
1961	II 16	1
1962	II 11	2
1963	II 2P	3
1964	I 18R	3
1965††	II 5	p
1966	II 17	1
1967	II 19	p
1968	II 15	1
1969	II 9	2
1970	II 12	p
1971	II 17	2
1972	II 8	1
1973	II 13	2
1974	II 16	1
1975	II 9	3
1976	II 8	1
1977	II 10	3
1978	II 9	2
1979	II 12	2
1980	II 2P	1
1981	I 11	q-f
1982	I 13R	3

* – Did not compete
† – No Second Division
‡ – Competed in Division 'C'
†† – as East Stirlingshire Clydebank

FALKIRK

Founded: 1876
Address: Brockville Park, Falkirk, Scotland
Telephone: Falkirk 24121
Ground capacity: 22,000 (2,750 seated)
Playing area: 100 by 70 yards
Record attendance: 23,100 v Celtic, Scottish Cup 3rd round, 21.2.53
Record victory: 12-1 v Laurieston, Scottish Cup, 2nd round, 23.3.1893
Record defeat: 1-11 v Airdrieonians, Division I, 28.4.51
Most League points: 59, Division II, 1935-36
Most League goals: 132, Division II, 1935-36
League scoring record: 43, Evelyn Morrison, Division I, 1928-29
Most capped player: 14 (15 in all), Alec Parker, Scotland

	Year	Opponents	Score	Scorers
Scottish Cup				
Winners	1913	Raith Rovers	2-0	Robertson, Logan
	1957	Kilmarnock	1-1	Prentice
		Replay	2-1	Merchant, Moran
Scottish League Cup				
Runners-up	1948	East Fife	0-0	
		Replay	1-4	Aikman

THE FALKIRK RECORD

	Division & place	Cup round reached
1902		q-f
1903	II 7	q
1904	II 4	q
1905	II 2P	q
1906	I 13	1
1907	I 5	1
1908	I 2	1
1909	I 9	s-f
1910	I 2	2
1911	I 3	2
1912	I 7	2
1913	I 5	Winners
1914	I 5	1
1915	I 6	
1916	I 12	
1917	I 12	
1918	I 14	
1919	I 16	
1920	I 20	2
1921	I 18	1
1922	I 5	2
1923	I 4	3
1924	I 15	s-f
1925	I 16	3
1926	I 8	3
1927	I 6	s-f
1928	I 10	3
1929	I 11	3
1930	I 7	q-f
1931	I 14	3
1932	I 18	1
1933	I 11	2
1934	I 10	3
1935	I 20R	1
1936	II 1P	s-f
1937	I 7	2
1938	I 4	q-f
1939	I 5	3
1947	I 11	3
1948	I 7	2
1949	I 5	1

	Division & place	Cup round reached
1950	I 14	2
1951	I 16R	1
1952	II 2P	q-f
1953	I 13	3
1954	I 13	2
1955	I 12	7
1956	I 14	5
1957	I 14	Winners
1958	I 10	q-f
1959	I 17R	2
1960	II 8	2
1961	II 2P	1
1962	I 14	1
1963	I 13	1
1964	I 14	q-f
1965	I 16	1
1966	I 10	1
1967	I 14	2
1968	I 15	1
1969	I 17R	1
1970	II 1P	q-f
1971	I 7	3
1972	I 14	3
1973	I 14	4
1974	I 18R	3
1975	II 1	4
1976	I 8	4
1977	I 14R	3
1978	II 5	1
1979	II 3	3
1980	II 1P	1
1981	I 9	4
1982	I 9	3

FORFAR ATHLETIC

Founded: 1884
Address: Station Park, Forfar, Angus
Telephone: Forfar 63576/62817
Ground capacity: 11,800 (850 seated)
Playing area: 115 by 69 yards
Record attendance: 10,800 v Rangers, Scottish Cup 2nd round, 7.2.70
Record victory: 14-1 v Lindertis, Scottish Cup 1st round, 1.9.1888
Record defeat: 2-12 v Kings Park, Division II, 2.1.30
Most League points: 47, Division II, 1968-69
Most League goals: 90, Division II, 1931-32
League scoring record: 45, Davie Kilgour, Division II, 1929-30

THE FORFAR RECORD

	Division & place	Cup round reached
1922	II 14	1
1923	II 15	1
1924	II 14	2
1925	II 20	1
1926	*	2
1927	II 9	2
1928	II 5	2
1929	II 7	1
1930	II 8	2
1931	II 12	1
1932	II 6	1
1933	II 14	1
1934	II 11	2
1935	II 11	1
1936	II 13	1
1937	II 12	1
1938	II 15	2
1939	II 15	1
1947	*	1
1948	*	1
1949	*	1
1950	II 10	1
1951	II 14	1
1952	II 12	1
1953	II 15	2
1954	II 12	2
1955	II 10	5
1956	II 15	5
1957	II 16	4

	Division & place	Cup round reached
1958	II 12	2
1959	II 12	1
1960	II 16	2
1961	II 18	3
1962	II 16	1
1963	II 18	1
1964	II 18	3
1965	II 17	1
1966	II 19	p
1967	II 16	p
1968	II 7	1
1969	II 6	p
1970	II 18	2
1971	II 15	3
1972	II 17	3
1973	II 16	2
1974	II 18	3
1975	II 20	2
1976	II 12	3
1977	II 14	2
1978	II 6	2
1979	II 8	2
1980	II 3	2
1981	II 5	2
1982	II 6	s-f

* – Competed in Division 'C'

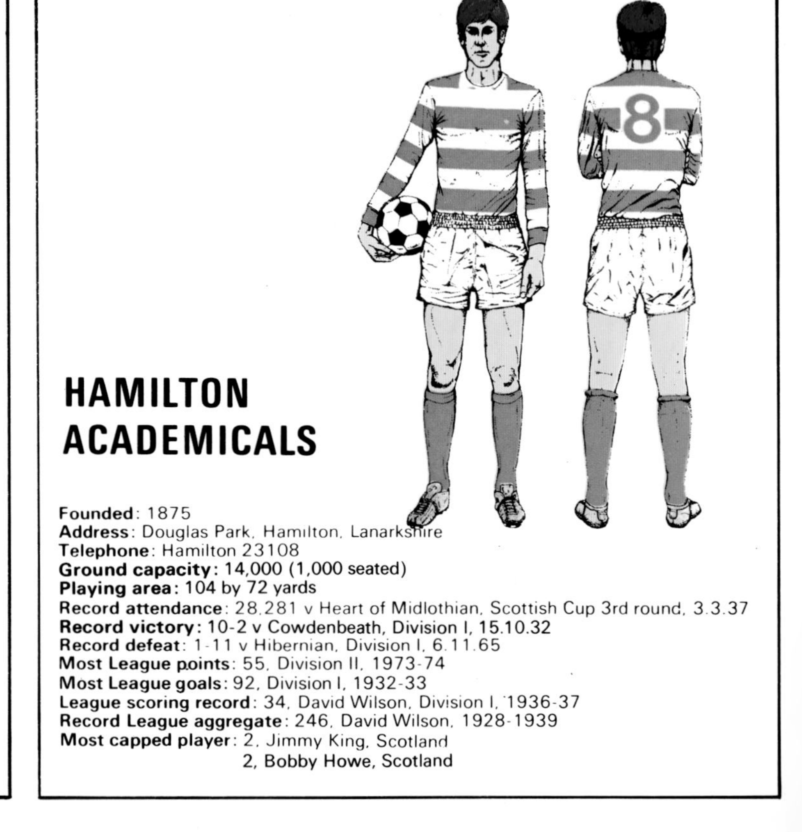

HAMILTON ACADEMICALS

Founded: 1875
Address: Douglas Park, Hamilton, Lanarkshire
Telephone: Hamilton 23108
Ground capacity: 14,000 (1,000 seated)
Playing area: 104 by 72 yards
Record attendance: 28,281 v Heart of Midlothian, Scottish Cup 3rd round, 3.3.37
Record victory: 10-2 v Cowdenbeath, Division I, 15.10.32
Record defeat: 1-11 v Hibernian, Division I, 6.11.65
Most League points: 55, Division II, 1973-74
Most League goals: 92, Division I, 1932-33
League scoring record: 34, David Wilson, Division I, 1936-37
Record League aggregate: 246, David Wilson, 1928-1939
Most capped player: 2, Jimmy King, Scotland
2, Bobby Howe, Scotland

Scottish Cup

	Year	Opponents	Score	Scorer
Runners-up	1911	Celtic	0-0	
			0-2	
	1935	Rangers	1-2	Harrison

THE HAMILTON RECORD

Year	Division & place	Cup round reached
1899	II 5	p
1900	II 7	1
1901	II 9	p
1902	II 5	p
1903	II 6	2
1904	II 1	p
1905	II 3	p
1906	II 4P	2
1907	I 16	p
1908	I 11	1
1909	I 16	1
1910	I 15	p
1911	I 16	Final
1912	I 12	1
1913	I 10	2
1914	I 18	2
1915	I 7	
1916	I 7	
1917	I 11	
1918	I 12	
1919	I 14	
1920	I 21	1
1921	I 15	3
1922	I 18	4
1923	I 18	3
1924	I 12	3
1925	I 13	s-f
1926	I 12	2
1927	I 15	3
1928	I 18	2
1929	I 12	2
1930	I 13	s-f
1931	I 10	2
1932	I 10	s-f
1933	I 8	1
1934	I 11	2
1935	I 4	Final
1936	I 6	1
1937	I 8	q-f
1938	I 13	3
1939	I 7	2
1947	I 16R	1
1948	II 3	1
1949	II 10	1
1950	II 6	1
1951	II 7	2
1952	II 9	2
1953	II 2P	3
1954	I 16R	q-f
1955	II 3	q-f
1956	II 11	5
1957	II 11	6
1958	II 10	1
1959	II 7	3
1960	II 4	1
1961	II 6	3
1962	II 13	2
1963	II 4	3
1964	II 13	2
1965	II 2P	1
1966	I 18R	1
1967	II 4	q-f
1968	II 11	1
1969	II 15	p
1970	II 19	1
1971	II 18	2
1972	II 19	3
1973	II 8	4
1974	II 3	1
1975	II 4	4
1976	I 9	3
1977	I 10	3
1978	I 7	3
1979	I 5	3
1980	I 7	3
1981	I 7	3
1982	I 7	3

HEART OF MIDLOTHIAN

Founded: 1874
Address: Tynecastle Park, Gorgie Road, Edinburgh 11
Telephone: (031) 337 6132
Ground capacity: 23,450 (7,000 seated)
Record attendance: 53,496 v Rangers, Scottish Cup 2nd round, 13.2.32
Record victory: 15-0 v King's Park, Scottish Cup 2nd round, 13.2.37
Record defeat: 1-8 v Vale of Leven, Scottish Cup 3rd round, 1882–83
Most League points: 62, Division I, 1957-58
Most League goals: 132, Division I, 1957-58
League scoring record: 44, Barney Battles, Division I, 1930-31
Record League aggregate: 206, Jimmy Wardhaugh, 1946-1959
Most capped player: 29, Bobby Walker, Scotland

Scottish Cup

	Year	Opponents	Score	Scorers
Winners	1891	Dumbarton	1-0	Mason
	1896	Hibernian	3-1	Baird (pen), King, Michael
	1901	Celtic	4-3	Walker (R), Bell 2, Thomson
	1906	Third Lanark	1-0	Wilson
	1956	Celtic	3-1	Crawford 2, Conn
Runners-up	1903	Rangers	1-1	Walker (R)
			0-0	
			0-2	
	1907	Celtic	0-3	
	1968	Dunfermline Athletic	1-3	Lunn og
	1976	Rangers	1-3	Shaw

Scottish League Cup

	Year	Opponents	Score	Scorers
Winners	1955	Motherwell	4-2	Bauld 3, Wardhaugh
	1959	Partick Thistle	5-1	Bauld 2, Murray 2, Hamilton
	1960	Third Lanark	2-1	Hamilton, Young
	1963	Kilmarnock	1-0	Davidson
Runners-up	1962	Rangers	1-1	Cumming
			1-3	Davidson

THE HEARTS RECORD

Year	Division & place	Cup round reached
1876		2
1877		1
1878		1
1879		4
1880		3
1881		5
1882		1
1883		3
1884		3
1885		2
1886		2
1887		3
1888		4
1889		4
1890		5
1891	I 6	Winners
1892	I 3	3
1893	I 5	3
1894	I 2	1
1895	I 1C	s-f
1896	I 4	Winners
1897	I 1C	2
1898	I 4	3
1899	I 2	1
1900	I 4	s-f
1901	I 10	Winners
1902	I 3	3
1903	I 4	Final
1904	I 2	1
1905	I 8	2
1906	I 2	Winners
1907	I 9	Final
1908	I 12	3
1909	I 12	2
1910	I 12	3
1911	I 14	1
1912	I 4	s-f
1913	I 3	s-f
1914	I 3	2
1915	I 2	
1916	I 6	
1917	I 14	
1918	I 10	
1919	I 6	
1920	I 15	3
1921	I 3	s-f
1922	I 19	3
1923	I 12	2
1924	I 9	4
1925	I 10	2
1926	I 3	3
1927	I 13	1
1928	I 4	3
1929	I 4	1
1930	I 10	s-f
1931	I 5	2
1932	I 8	3
1933	I 3	s-f
1934	I 6	3
1935	I 3	s-f
1936	I 5	1
1937	I 5	3
1938	I 2	1
1939	I 4	3
1947	I 4	q-f
1948	I 9	2
1949	I 8	q-f
1950	I 3	2
1951	I 4	3
1952	I 4	s-f
1953	I 4	s-f
1954	I 2	q-f
1955	I 4	q-f
1956	I 3	Winners
1957	I 2	5
1958	I 1C	3
1959	I 2	2
1960	I 1C	2
1961	I 8	q-f
1962	I 6	3
1963	I 5	2
1964	I 4	3
1965	I 2	q-f
1966	I 7	q-f
1967	I 11	1
1968	I 12	Final
1969	I 8	2
1970	I 4	2
1971	I 11	4
1972	I 6	q-f
1973	I 10	3
1974	I 6	s-f
1975	I 8	q-f
1976	P 5	Final
1977	P 9R	s-f
1978	I 2P	4
1979	P 9R	q-f
1980	I 1P	q-f
1981	P 10R	3
1982	I 3	4

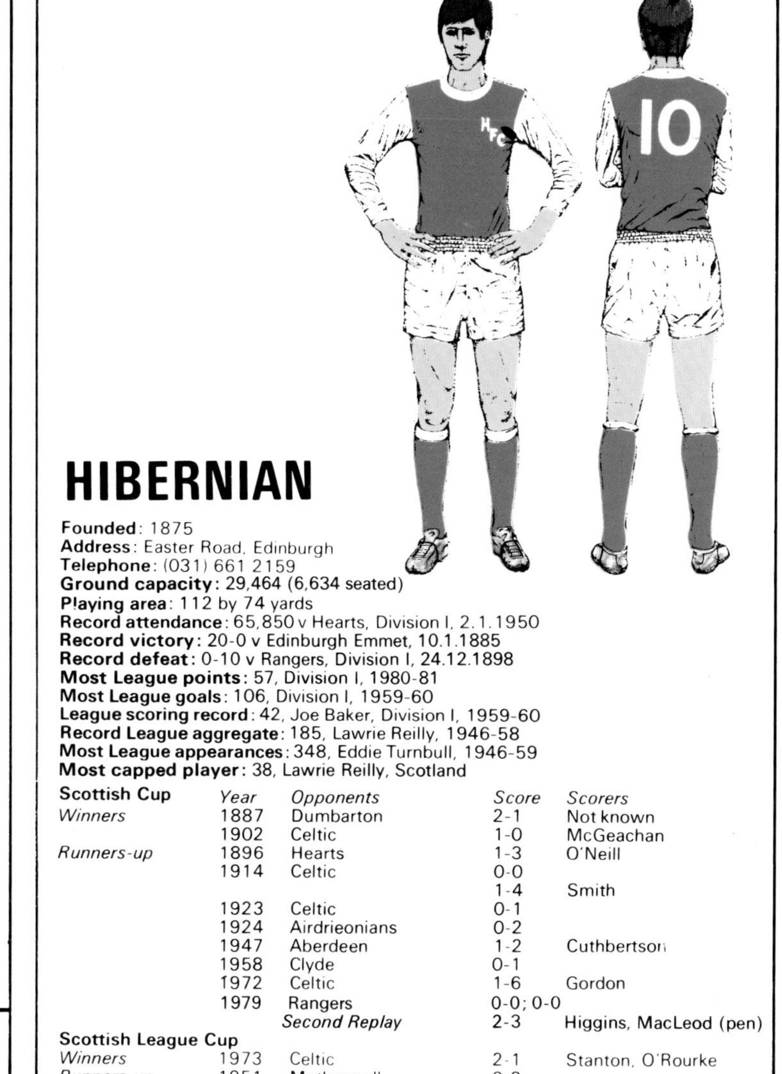

HIBERNIAN

Founded: 1875
Address: Easter Road, Edinburgh
Telephone: (031) 661 2159
Ground capacity: 29,464 (6,634 seated)
Playing area: 112 by 74 yards
Record attendance: 65,850 v Hearts, Division I, 2.1.1950
Record victory: 20-0 v Edinburgh Emmet, 10.1.1885
Record defeat: 0-10 v Rangers, Division I, 24.12.1898
Most League points: 57, Division I, 1980-81
Most League goals: 106, Division I, 1959-60
League scoring record: 42, Joe Baker, Division I, 1959-60
Record League aggregate: 185, Lawrie Reilly, 1946-58
Most League appearances: 348, Eddie Turnbull, 1946-59
Most capped player: 38, Lawrie Reilly, Scotland

Scottish Cup

	Year	Opponents	Score	Scorers
Winners	1887	Dumbarton	2-1	Not known
	1902	Celtic	1-0	McGeachan
Runners-up	1896	Hearts	1-3	O'Neill
	1914	Celtic	0-0	
			1-4	Smith
	1923	Celtic	0-1	
	1924	Airdrieonians	0-2	
	1947	Aberdeen	1-2	Cuthbertson
	1958	Clyde	0-1	
	1972	Celtic	1-6	Gordon
	1979	Rangers	0-0; 0-0	
		Second Replay	2-3	Higgins, MacLeod (pen)

Scottish League Cup

	Year	Opponents	Score	Scorers
Winners	1973	Celtic	2-1	Stanton, O'Rourke
Runners-up	1951	Motherwell	0-3	
	1969	Celtic	2-6	O'Rourke, Stevenson
	1975	Celtic	3-6	Harper 3

THE HIBERNIAN RECORD

	Division & place	*Cup round reached*			
1894	II 1	p	1936	I 17	2
1895	II 1P	2	1937	I 17	2
1896	I 3	Final	1938	I 10	1
1897	I 2	2	1939	I 13	s-f
1898	I 3	q-f	1947	I 2	Final
1899	I 4	2	1948	I 1C	s-f
1900	I 3	2	1949	I 3	q-f
1901	I 3	s-f	1950	I 2	1
1902	I 6	Winners	1951	I 1C	s-f
1903	I 1C	q-f	1952	I 1C	1
1904	I 10	2	1953	I 2	q-f
1905	I 5	1	1954	I 5	3
1906	I 11	q-f	1955	I 5	5
1907	I 12	s-f	1956	I 4	5
1908	I 5	q-f	1957	I 9	5
1909	I 6	1	1958	I 9	Final
1910	I 8	s-f	1959	I 10	q-f
1911	I 9	1	1960	I 7	q-f
1912	I 13	1	1961	I 7	q-f
1913	I 6	3	1962	I 8	1
1914	I 13	Final	1963	I 16	3
1915	I 11		1964	I 10	1
1916	I 19		1965	I 4	s-f
1917	I 17		1966	I 6	2
1918	I 16		1967	I 5	q-f
1919	I 18		1968	I 3	2
1920	I 18	2	1969	I 12	1
1921	I 13	1	1970	I 3	1
1922	I 7	2	1971	I 12	s-f
1923	I 8	Final	1972	I 4	Final
1924	I 7	Final	1973	I 3	4
1925	I 3	1	1974	I 2	q-f
1926	I 16	2	1975	I 2	3
1927	I 9	1	1976	P 3	q-f
1928	I 12	s-f	1977	P 6	4
1929	I 14	1	1978	P 4	4
1930	I 17	3	1979	P 5	Final
1931	I 19R	3	1980	P 10R	s-f
1932	II 7	1	1981	I 1P	q-f
1933	II 1P	q-f	1982	P 6	4
1934	I 16	3			
1935	I 11	3			

KILMARNOCK

Founded: 1869
Address: Rugby Park, Kilmarnock
Telephone: Kilmarnock 25184
Ground capacity: 18,500 (4,200 seated)
Playing area: 115 by 75 yards
Record attendance: 34,246 v Rangers, League Cup, 20.8.63
Record victory: 11-1 v Paisley Academicals, Scottish Cup 1st round, 18.1.30
Record defeat: 1-9 v Celtic, Division I, 13.8.38
Most League points: 58, Division II, 1973-74
Most League goals: 92, Division I, 1962-63
League scoring record: 35, Peerie Cunningham, Division I, 1927-28
Record League aggregate: 102, Jimmy Maxwell, 1931-1934
Most League appearances: 424, Frank Beattie, 1954-1971
Most capped player: 11, Joe Nibloe, Scotland

Scottish Cup	*Year*	*Opponents*	*Score*	*Scorers*
Winners	1920	Albion Rovers	3-2	Culley, J R Smith, Shortt
	1929	Rangers	2-0	Aitken, Williamson
Runners-up	1898	Rangers	0-2	
	1932	Rangers	1-1	Maxwell
			0-3	
	1938	East Fife	1-1	McAvoy
			2-4	Thomson (pen), McGrogan
	1957	Falkirk	1-1	Curlett
			1-2	Curlett
	1960	Rangers	0-2	
Scottish League Cup				
Runners-up	1953	Dundee	0-2	
	1961	Rangers	0-2	
	1963	Hearts	0-1	

THE KILMARNOCK RECORD

	Division & place	*Cup round reached*			
1896	II 4	1	1898	II 1	Final
1897	II 3	s-f	1899	II 1P	q-f

1900	I 5	q-f	1939	I 10	2
1901	I 5	2	1947	I 15R	1
1902	I 7	3	1948	II 6	1
1903	I 9	2	1949	II 11	1
1904	I 14	q-f	1950	II 7	1
1905	I 9	1	1951	II 12	1
1906	I 14	2	1952	II 5	2
1907	I 17	2	1953	II 4	2
1908	I 14	s-f	1954	II 2P	2
1909	I 10	1	1955	I 10	6
1910	I 11	1	1956	I 8	6
1911	I 10	1	1957	I 3	Final
1912	I 16	2	1958	I 5	3
1913	I 11	3	1959	I 8	q-f
1914	I 12	3	1960	I 2	Final
1915	I 12		1961	I 2	2
1916	I 10		1962	I 5	q-f
1917	I 6		1963	I 2	2
1918	I 3		1964	I 2	s-f
1919	I 9		1965	I 1C	q-f
1920	I 9	Winners	1966	I 3	q-f
1921	I 12	2	1967	I 7	1
1922	I 17	2	1968	I 7	1
1923	I 15	2	1969	I 4	q-f
1924	I 16	2	1970	I 7	s-f
1925	I 12	q-f	1971	I 13	q-f
1926	I 9	1	1972	I 11	s-f
1927	I 16	2	1973	I 17R	4
1928	I 8	4	1974	II 2P	3
1929	I 10	Winners	1975	II 12	3
1930	I 8	2	1976	I 2P	q-f
1931	I 11	s-f	1977	P 10R	3
1932	I 9	Final	1978	I 6	q-f
1933	I 14	q-f	1979	I 2P	4
1934	I 7	2	1980	P 8	3
1935	I 9	2	1981	P 9R	4
1936	I 8	2	1982	I 2P	q-f
1937	I 11	1			
1938	I 18	Final			

MEADOWBANK THISTLE

Founded: 1974 (formerly Ferranti Thistle)
Address: Meadowbank Stadium, Edinburgh
Telephone: 031 337 2442
Ground capacity: 16,000 (7,500 seated)
Playing area: 105 by 72 yards
Record attendance: 4,000 v Albion Rovers, Scottish League Cup, 9.8.74
Record victory: 6-1 v Stenhousemuir, Division II, 6.2.82
Record defeat: 0-8 v Hamilton Academicals, Division II, 14.12.74
Most League points: 32, Division II, 1976-77, 1979-80
Most League goals: 43, Division II, 1977–78
League scoring record: 17, John Jobson, Division II, 1979–80

THE MEADOWBANK RECORD

	Division & place	*Cup round reached*			
1975	II 18		1980	II 12	3
1976	II 14	2	1981	II 13	1
1977	II 11	2	1982	II 12	4
1978	II 13	4			
1979	II 14	4			

MONTROSE

Founded: 1879
Address: Links Park, Montrose
Telephone: Montrose 3200
Ground capacity: 9,000
Playing area: 114 by 66 yards
Record attendance: 8,983 v Dundee, Scottish Cup 3rd round, 17.3.73
Record victory: 12-0 v Vale of Leithen, Scottish Cup 2nd round, 4.1.75
Record defeat: 0-13 v Aberdeen Reserves, Division C, 17.3.51
Most League points: 53, Division II, 1974-75
Most League goals: 78, Division II, 1970-71
Most capped player: 2 (6 in all), A Keillor, Scotland

THE MONTROSE RECORD

	Division & place	*Cup round reached*			
1930	II 11	q-f	1962	II 5	2
1931	II 8	3	1963	II 15	2
1932	II 17	1	1964	II 5	1
1933	II 17	2	1965	II 16	1
1934	II 16	1	1966	II 9	1
1935	II 17	1	1967	II 12	p
1936	II 12	1	1968	II 13	p
1937	II 13	1	1969	II 10	2
1938	II 16	1	1970	II 8	1
1939	II 14	2	1971	II 6	2
1947	*	p	1972	II 10	3
1948	*	q-f	1973	II 6	q-f
1949	*	1	1974	II 8	3
1950	*	1	1975	II 3	3
1951	*	1	1976	I 3	q-f
1952	*	1	1977	I 5	3
1953	*	3	1978	I 11	3
1954	*	1	1979	I 13R	3
1955	*	4	1980	II 9	2
1956	II 19	4	1981	II 7	2
1957	II 17	5	1982	II 10	3
1958	II 14	2			
1959	II 19	2			
1960	II 7	2			
1961	II 7	2			

*—Montrose competed in C Division

MORTON

Founded: 1874
Address: Cappielow Park, Greenock
Telephone: Greenock 23571
Ground capacity: 16,400 (6,400 seated)
Playing area: 110 by 71 yards
Record attendance: 23,500 v Rangers, Scottish Cup 3rd round, 21.2.53
Record victory: 11-0 v Carfin Shamrock, Scottish Cup, 13.11.1886
Record defeat: 1-10 v Port Glasgow Ath., Division II, 5.5.1894
Most League points: 69, Division II, 1966-67
Most League goals: 135, Division II, 1963-64
League scoring record: 41, Allan McGraw, Division II, 1963–64
Most capped player: 25, Jimmy Cowan, Scotland

Scottish Cup	*Year*	*Opponents*	*Score*	*Scorers*
Winners	1922	Rangers	1-0	Gourlay
Runners-up	1948	Rangers	1-1	Whyte
		Replay	0-1	
Scottish League Cup				
Runners-up	1964	Rangers	0-5	

THE MORTON RECORD

	Division & place	*Cup round reached*			
1894	II 8	p	1914	I 4	2
1895	II 5	p	1915	I 4	
1896	II 9	1	1916	I 3	
1897	II 5	s-f	1917	I 2	
1898	II 3	2	1918	I 4	
1899	II 7	2	1919	I 3	
1900	II 2E	1	1920	I 6	s-f
1901	I 4	q-f	1921	I 9	2
1902	I 10	1	1922	I 12	Winners
1903	I 12	1	1923	I 14	1
1904	I 11	s-f	1924	I 11	1
1905	I 13	2	1925	I 14	1
1906	I 10	2	1926	I 15	q-f
1907	I 13	2	1927	I 19R	1
1908	I 13	2	1928	II 18	2
1909	I 17	1	1929	II 2P	1
1910	I 17	2	1930	I 18	1
1911	I 13	2	1931	I 16	3
1912	I 6	q-f	1932	I 15	1
1913	I 13	2	1933	I 19R	1

1934	II 5	1	1964	II 1P	2
1935	II 6	2	1965	I 10	2
1936	II 3	q-f	1966	I 17R	1
1937	II 2P	s-f	1967	II 1P	1
1938	I 20R	3	1968	I 6	s-f
1939	II 12E	1	1969	I 10	s-f
1947	I 6	3	1970	I 10	2
1948	I 14	Final	1971	I 8	4
1949	I 15R	3	1972	I 13	4
1950	II 1P	2	1973	I 12	3
1951	I 12	2	1974	I 14	4
1952	I 15R	3	1975	I 17	3
1953	II 6	3	1976	I 11	3
1954	II 5	3	1977	I 4	3
1955	II 9	5	1978	I 1P	q-f
1956	II 9	5	1979	P 7	4
1957	II 4	5	1980	P 6	q-f
1958	II 13	2	1981	P 8	s-f
1959	II 11	3	1982	P 7	3
1960	II 14	1			
1961	II 19	2			
1962	II 3	2			
1963	II 3	1			

E—elected to First Division

MOTHERWELL

Founded: 1885*
Address: Fir Park, Motherwell, Lanarkshire
Telephone: Motherwell 63229
Ground capacity: 22,600 (3,200 seated)
Playing area: 110 by 72 yards
Record attendance: 35,632 v Rangers, Scottish Cup 4th round replay, 12.3.52
Record victory: 12-1 v Dundee United, Division II, 23.1.54
Record defeat: 0-8 v Aberdeen, Division I, 26.3.79
Most League points: 66, Division I, 1931-32
Most League goals: 119, Division I, 1931-32
League scoring record: 52, Bill McFadyen, Division I, 1931-32
Record League aggregate: 283, Hugh Ferguson, 1916-1925
Most League appearances: 626, Bob Ferrier, 1918-1937
Most capped player: 12, George Stevenson, Scotland
*As Wee Alpha. Changed name to Motherwell in 1886.

Scottish Cup	*Year*	*Opponents*	*Score*	*Scorers*
Winners	1952	Dundee	4-0	Watson, Redpath, Humphries, Kelly
Runners-up	1931	Celtic	2-2	Stevenson, McMenemy
			2-4	Murdoch, Stevenson
	1933	Celtic	0-1	
	1939	Clyde	0-4	
	1951	Celtic	0-1	
League Cup				
Winners	1951	Hibernian	3-0	Kelly, Forrest, Watters
Runners-up	1955	Hearts	2-4	Redpath (pen), Bain

THE MOTHERWELL RECORD

	Division & place	*Cup round reached*			
1904	I 13	2	1915	I 18	
1905	I 14	2	1916	I 14	
1906	I 9	1	1917	I 8	
1907	I 10	1	1918	I 5	
1908	I 10	2	1919	I 5	
1909	I 14	2	1920	I 3	1
1910	I 10	3	1921	I 5	q-f
1911	I 17	3	1922	I 13	3
1912	I 14	3	1923	I 13	s-f
1913	I 7	2	1924	I 10	3
1914	I 17	4	1925	I 18	3

1926	I 5	1	1959	I 3	3
1927	I 2	1	1960	I 5	3
1928	I 3	q-f	1961	I 5	q-f
1929	I 3	q-f	1962	I 9	s-f
1930	I 2	3	1963	I 10	2
1931	I 3	Final	1964	I 11	q-f
1932	I 1C	q-f	1965	I 14	s-f
1933	I 2	Final	1966	I 13	2
1934	I 2	s-f	1967	I 10	1
1935	I 7	q-f	1968	I 17R	1
1936	I 4	q-f	1969	II 1P	1
1937	I 4	q-f	1970	I 11	q-f
1938	I 5	q-f	1971	I 9	3
1939	I 12	Final	1972	I 10	q-f
1947	I 8	s-f	1973	I 8	4
1948	I 8	3	1974	I 9	q-f
1949	I 12	2	1975	I 10	s-f
1950	I 10	1	1976	P 4	s-f
1951	I 9	Final	1977	P 7	q-f
1952	I 7	Winners	1978	P 6	4
1953	I 15R	3	1979	P 10R	3
1954	II 1P	s-f	1980	I 6	3
1955	I 15	q-f	1981	I 5	q-f
1956	I 10	5	1982	I 1P	3
1957	I 7	6			
1958	I 8	s-f			

PARTICK THISTLE

Founded: 1876
Address: Firhill Park, Glasgow
Telephone: 041-946 2673
Ground capacity: 36,000 (3,500 seated)
Playing area: 110 by 71 yards
Record attendance: 49,838 v Rangers, Division I, 18.2.22
Record victory: 16-0 v Royal Albert, Scottish Cup 1st round, 17.1.31
Record defeat: 0-10 v Queens Park, Scottish Cup 5th round, 3.12.1881
Most League points: 56, Division II, 1970-71
Most League goals: 91, Division I, 1928-29
League scoring record: 41, Alec Hair, Division I, 1926-27
Most capped player: 51, Alan Rough, Scotland

Scottish Cup	*Year*	*Opponents*	*Score*	*Scorers*
Winners	1921	Rangers	1-0	Blair
Runners-up	1930	Rangers	0-0	
		Replay	1-2	Torbet
Scottish League Cup				
Winners	1972	Celtic	4-1	Rae, Lawrie, McQuade, Bone
Runners-up	1954	East Fife	2-3	Walker, McKenzie
	1957	Celtic	0-0	
		Replay	0-3	
	1959	Hearts	1-5	Smith

THE PARTICK RECORD

	Division & place	*Cup round reached*			
1894	II 5	p	1916	I 5	
1895	II 7	p	1917	I 9	
1896	II 6	p	1918	I 6	
1897	II 1P	1	1919	I 4	
1898	I 8	1	1920	I 13	3
1899	I 9R	q-f	1921	I 6	Winners
1900	II 1P	q-f	1922	I 6	s-f
1901	I 11R	1	1923	I 11	1
1902	II 2P	1	1924	I 8	q-f
1903	I 8	q-f	1925	I 7	3
1904	I 7	1	1926	I 14	3
1905	I 6	q-f	1927	I 11	s-f
1906	I 5	2	1928	I 6	q-f
1907	I 14	1	1929	I 6	2
1908	I 15	2	1930	I 6	Final
1909	I 18	2	1931	I 4	2
1910	I 16	1	1932	I 6	q-f
1911	I 4	2	1933	I 10	3
1912	I 5	1	1934	I 13	2
1913	I 17	3	1935	I 13	2
1914	I 15	q-f	1936	I 9	1
1915	I 8		1937	I 13	3

1938	I 7	3	1965	I 11	2
1939	I 11	1	1966	I 12	1
1947	I 5	1	1967	I 12	2
1948	I 3	3	1968	I 10	q-f
1949	I 11	q-f	1969	I 14	1
1950	I 7	s-f	1970	I 18R	1
1951	I 6	1	1971	II 1P	3
1952	I 6	1	1972	I 7	3
1953	I 9	2	1973	I 13	q-f
1954	I 3	q-f	1974	I 11	4
1955	I 9	5	1975	I 13	3
1956	I 9	q-f	1976	I 1P	4
1957	I 8	5	1977	P 5	3
1958	I 6	2	1978	P 7	s-f
1959	I 9	3	1979	P 8	s-f
1960	I 10	q-f	1980	P 7	q-f
1961	I 11	3	1981	P 6	4
1962	I 7	2	1982	P 9	3
1963	I 3	3			
1964	I 7	3			

QUEEN OF THE SOUTH

Founded: 1919
Address: Palmerston Park, Dumfries
Telephone: Dumfries 4853
Ground capacity: 20,000
Playing area: 111 by 73 yards
Record attendance: 25,000 v Hearts, Scottish Cup 3rd round, 23.2.52
Record victory: 11-1 v Stranraer, Scottish Cup 1st round, 16.1.32
Record defeat: 2-10 v Dundee, Division I, 1.12.62
Most League points: 53, Division II, 1961-62; Division II, 1974-75
Most League goals: 94, Division II, 1959-60
League scoring record: 33, Jimmy Gray, Division II, 1927-28
Most capped player: 3, Billy Houliston, Scotland

THE QUEEN OF THE SOUTH RECORD

	Division & place	*Cup round reached*			
1926	II 17	1	1962	II 2P	2
1927	II 11	1	1963	I 15	q-f
1928	II 12	1	1964	I 17R	2
1929	II 9	2	1965	II 3	1
1930	II 7	2	1966	II 3	2
1931	II 5	1	1967	II 9	1
1932	II 9	2	1968	II 6	2
1933	II 2P	1	1969	II 5	1
1934	I 4	q-f	1970	II 3	1
1935	I 17	1	1971	II 11	3
1936	I 15	3	1972	II 7	3
1937	I 18	q-f	1973	II 11	3
1938	I 16	2	1974	II 4	4
1939	I 6	q-f	1975	II 2	4
1947	I 12	1	1976	I 10	q-f
1948	I 13	3	1977	I 9	q-f
1949	I 10	2	1978	I 12	4
1950	I 15R	s-f	1979	I 14R	3
1951	II 1P	1	1980	II 13	4
1952	I 10	3	1981	II 2P	2
1953	I 10	q-f	1982	I 14R	3
1954	I 10	3			
1955	I 13	5			
1956	I 6	q-f			
1957	I 16	5			
1958	I 15	q-f			
1959	I 18R	1			
1960	II 3	3			
1961	II 5	2			

1947	I 13	3	1968	II 4	p
1948	I 16R	3	1969	II 11	†
1949	II 5	1	1970	II 15	p
1950	II 9	1	1971	II 14	3
1951	II 6	2	1972	II 12	2
1952	II 15	2	1973	II 14	2
1953	II 3	2	1974	II 14	3
1954	II 10	1	1975	II 16	4
1955	II 4	4	1976	II 4	1
1956	II 1P	6	1977	II 5	3
1957	I 13	6	1978	II 7	q-f
1958	I 18R	3	1979	II 13	3
1959	II 18	2	1980	II 5	1
1960	II 11	3	1981	II 1P	1
1961	II 15	1	1982	I 8	q-f
1962	II 12	1			
1963	II 14	3			
1964	II 7	2			
1965	II 4	2			
1966	II 13	1			
1967	II 7	q-f			

(†) - progress in the FA Cup

QUEEN'S PARK

Founded: 1867
Address: Hampden Park, Glasgow
Telephone: 041 632 1275/4090
Ground capacity: 75,000
Playing area: 115 by 75 yards
Record attendance: 97,000 v Rangers, Scottish Cup 2nd round, 18.2.33
(*Ground record*: 149,547, Scotland v England, 17.4.37)
Record victory: 16-0 v St Peter's, Scottish Cup 1st round, 1885-86
Record defeat: 0-9 v Motherwell, Division I, 26.4.30
Most League points: 57, Division II, 1922-23
Most League goals: 100, Division I, 1928-29
League scoring record: 32, Peter Buchanan, Division II, 1962-63
Most capped player: 14, Watty Arnott, Scotland

Scottish Cup

	Year	Opponents	Score
Winners	1874	Clydesdale	2-0
	1875	Renton	3-0
	1876	Third Lanark	1-1
		Replay	2-0
	1880	Thornlibank	3-0
	*1881	Dumbarton	3-1
	1882	Dumbarton	2-2
		Replay	4-1
	†1884	Vale of Leven	
	1886	Renton	3-1
	1890	Vale of Leven	1-1
		Replay	2-1
	1893	Celtic	2-1
Runners-up	‡1892	Celtic	1-5
	1900	Celtic	3-4

*After a protested game which Queen's Park won 2-1
†Queen's Park awarded the cup after Vale of Leven failed to appear
‡After protested game which Celtic won 1-0

FA Cup

			Score	Scorer
Runners up	1884	Blackburn Rovers	1-2	Christie
	1885	Blackburn Rovers	0-2	

THE QUEEN'S PARK RECORD

	Division & place	*Cup round reached*			
1872		(s-f†)	1906	I 16	2
1873		(s-f†)	1907	I 15	s-f
1874		Winners	1908	I 16	q-f
1875		Winners	1909	I 15	q-f
1876		Winners	1910	I 14	q-f
1877		q-f (3†)	1911	I 18	2
1878		3 (1†)	1912	I 17	p
1879		q-f	1913	I 18	3
1880		Winners	1914	I 16	q-f
1881		Winners	1915	I 20	
1882		Winners	1916	I 18	
1883		q-f	1917	I 18	
1884		Winners (Final†)	1918	I 7	
1885		3 (Final†)	1919	I 8	
1886		Winners	1920	I 12	3
1887		s-f	1921	I 19	1
1888		s-f	1922	21R	2
1889		3	1923	II 1P	3
1890		Winners	1924	I 17	3
1891		q-f	1925	I 17	2
1892		Final	1926	I 13	2
1893		Winners	1927	I 12	2
1894		s-f	1928	I 16	s-f
1895		1	1929	I 5	2
1896		q-f	1930	I 15	1
1897		1	1931	I 13	2
1898		q-f	1932	I 16	2
1899		q-f	1933	I 9	2
1900		Final	1934	I 15	2
1901	I 8	2	1935	I 12	2
1902	I 8	q-f	1936	I 14	1
1903	I 10	1	1937	I 15	2
1904	I 8	1	1938	I 12	2
1905	I 12	1	1939	I 19	2

RAITH ROVERS

Founded: 1893
Address: Stark's Park, Pratt Street, Kirkcaldy, Fife
Telephone: Kilcaldy 263514
Ground capacity: 28,000
Playing area: 113 by 67 yards
Record attendance: 32,000 v Herts, Scottish Cup 2nd round, 7.2.53
Record victory: 10-1 v Coldstream, Scottish Cup 2nd round, 13.2.54
Record defeat: 2-11 v Morton, Division II, 18.3.36
Most League points: 59, Division II, 1937-38
Most League goals: 142, Division II, 1937-38
League scoring record: 39, Norman Haywood, Division II, 1937-38
Most capped player: 6, Dave Morris, Scotland

	Year	Opponents	Score
Scottish Cup			
Runners-up	1913	Falkirk	0-2
Scottish League Cup			
Runners-up	1949	Rangers	0-2

THE RAITH ROVERS RECORD

	Division & place	*Cup round reached*			
1903	II 11	p	1930	II 5	1
1904	II 5	p	1931	II 4	1
1905	II 10	p	1932	II 3	2
1906	II 8	p	1933	II 6	1
1907	II 10	q-f	1934	II 8	1
1908	II 1	q-f	1935	II 13	2
1909	II 2	p	1936	II 17	1
1910	II 2P	p	1937	II 8	1
1911	I 15	p	1938	II 1P	q-f
1912	I 15	1	1939	I 20R	1
1913	I 16	Final	1947	II 6	3
1914	I 11	3	1948	II 4	3
1915	I 19		1949	II 1P	2
1916	I 20		1950	I 9	q-f
1917	I 19		1951	I 8	s-f
1918	*		1952	I 5	2
1919	*		1953	I 12	2
1920	I 19	3	1954	I 12	3
1921	I 16	1	1955	I 14	6
1922	I 3	1	1956	I 11	s-f
1923	I 9	q-f	1957	I 4	s-f
1924	I 4	3	1958	I 7	2
1925	I 9	3	1959	I 14	1
1926	I 19R	2	1960	I 11	1
1927	II 2P	1	1961	I 16	3
1928	I 17	2	1962	I 13	3
1929	I 20R	q-f	1963	I 18R	s-f

1964	II	10	1
1965	II	13	p
1966	II	5	p
1967	II	2P	1
1968	I	16	1
1969	I	16	1
1970	I	17R	1
1971	II	8	5
1972	II	11	5
1973	II	3	3
1974	II	5	3
1975	II	13	3
1976	II	2P	4
1977	I	13R	2
1978	II	2P	2
1979	I	11	3
1980	I	5	3
1981	I	4	3
1982	I	12	3

*Raith Rovers did not compete

RANGERS

Founded: 1873
Address: Ibrox Stadium, Glasgow SW1
Telephone: (041) 427 0159
Ground capacity: 44,000 (19,500 seated)
Playing area: 115 by 75 yards
Record attendance: 118,567 v Celtic, Division I, 2.1.39
Record victory: 14-2 v Blairgowrie, Scottish Cup 1st round, 20.1.34
Record defeat: 1-7 v Celtic, League Cup Final, 19.10.57
Most League points: 76, Division I, 1920-21
Most League goals: 118, Division I, 1931-32 & 1933-34
League scoring record: 44, Sam English, Division I, 1931-32
Record League aggregate: 233, Bob McPhail, 1927-1939
Most League appearances: 496, John Greig, 1962-78
Most capped player: 53, George Young, Scotland

Scottish Cup

	Year	*Opponents*	*Score*	*Scorers*
Winners	1894	Celtic	3-1	McCreadie, Barker, McPherson
	1897	Dumbarton	5-1	Miller, Hyslop, McPherson 2, Smith
	1898	Kilmarnock	2-0	Smith, Hamilton
	1903	Heart of Midlothian	1-1	
			0-0	
			2-0	Mackie, Campbell
	1928	Celtic	4-0	Meiklejohn (pen), McPhail, Archibald 2
	1930	Partick Thistle	0-0	
			2-1	Marshall, Craig
	1932	Kilmarnock	1-1	McPhail
			3-0	Fleming, McPhail, English
	1934	St Mirren	5-0	Nicholson 2, McPhail, Smith, Main
	1935	Hamilton	2-1	Smith 2
	1936	Third Lanark	1-0	McPhail
	1948	Morton	1-1	Gillick
			1-0	Williamson
	1949	Clyde	4-1	Young (2 pens), Williamson, Duncanson
	1950	East Fife	3-0	Findlay, Thornton 2
	1953	Aberdeen	1-1	Prentice
			1-0	Simpson
	1960	Kilmarnock	2-0	Millar 2
	1962	St Mirren	2-0	Brand, Wilson
	1963	Celtic	1-1	Brand
			3-0	Wilson, Brand 2,
	1964	Dundee	3-1	Millar 2, Brand
	1966	Celtic	0-0	
			1-0	Johansen
	1973	Celtic	3-2	Parlane, Conn, Forsyth
	1976	Heart of Midlothian	3-1	Johnstone 2, MacDonald
	1978	Aberdeen	2-1	MacDonald, Johnstone
	1979	Hibernian (after 0-0 and 0-0 draws)	3-2	Johnstone 2, Duncan og
	1981	Dundee Utd (after 0-0 draw)	4-1	Cooper, Russell, MacDonald 2
Runners-up	1877	Vale of Leven	0-0	
			1-1	
			2-3	Campbell, McNeil
	1879	Vale of Leven	1-1	Struthers
	1899	Celtic	0-2	
	1904	Celtic	2-3	Speedie 2
	1905	Third Lanark	0-0	
			1-3	
	1909	Celtic	2-2	Gilchrist, Bennett
			1-1	Gordon
	1921	Partick Thistle	0-1	
	1922	Morton	0-1	
	1929	Kilmarnock	0-2	
	1969	Celtic	0-4	
	1971	Celtic	1-1	Johnstone
			1-2	og
	1977	Celtic	0-1	
	1980	Celtic	0-1	
	1982	Aberdeen	1-4	aet MacDonald

Scottish League Cup

Winners	1947	Aberdeen	4-0	Duncanson 2, Williamson, Gillick
	1949	Raith Rovers	2-0	Gillick, Paton
	1961	Kilmarnock	2-0	Brand, Scott
	1962	Heart of Midlothian	1-1	Millar
			3-1	Millar, Brand, McMillan
	1964	Morton	5-0	Forrest 4, Willoughby
	1965	Celtic	2-1	Forrest 2
	1971	Celtic	1-0	Johnstone
	1976	Celtic	1-0	MacDonald
	1978	Celtic	2-1	Cooper, Smith
	1979	Aberdeen	2-1	McMaster og, Jackson
	1982	Dundee Utd	2-1	Cooper, Redford
Runners-up	1952	Dundee	2-3	Findlay, Thornton
	1958	Celtic	1-7	Simpson
	1966	Celtic	1-2	og
	1967	Celtic	0-1	
	1983	Celtic	1-2	Bett

THE RANGERS RECORD

	Division & place		*Cup round reached*
1875			2
1876			2
1877			Final
1878			4
1879			Final
1880			1
1881			q-f
1882			q-f
1883			2
1884			s-f
1885			q-f
1886			1
1887			3
1888			2
1889			2
1890			3
1891	I	1+	1
1892	I	4	4
1893	I	2	3
1894	I	4	Winners
1895	I	3	1
1896	I	2	3
1897	I	3	Winners
1898	I	2	Winners
1899	I	1C	Final
1900	I	1C	s-f
1901	I	1C	1
1902	I	1C	s-f
1903	I	3	Winners
1904	I	4	Final
1905	I	2	Final
1906	I	4	3
1907	I	3	3
1908	I	3	2
1909	I	4	Final
1910	I	3	2
1911	I	1C	3
1912	I	1C	2
1913	I	1C	3
1914	I	2	3
1915	I	3	
1916	I	2	
1917	I	3	
1918	I	1C	
1919	I	2	
1920	I	1C	s-f
1921	I	1C	Final
1922	I	2	Final
1923	I	1C	2
1924	I	1C	3
1925	I	1C	s-f
1926	I	6	s-f
1927	I	1C	q-f
1928	I	1C	Winners
1929	I	1C	Final
1930	I	1C	Winners
1931	I	1C	2
1932	I	2	Winners
1933	I	1C	3
1934	I	1C	Winners
1935	I	1C	Winners
1936	I	2	Winners
1937	I	1C	1
1938	I	3	s-f
1939	I	1C	3
1947	I	1C	3
1948	I	2	Winners
1949	I	1C	Winners
1950	I	1C	Winners
1951	I	2	2
1952	I	2	q-f
1953	I	1C	Winners
1954	I	4	s-f
1955	I	3	6
1956	I	1C	q-f
1957	I	1C	6
1958	I	2	s-f
1959	I	1C	3
1960	I	3	Winners
1961	I	1C	3
1962	I	2	Winners
1963	I	1C	Winners
1964	I	1C	Winners
1965	I	5	q-f
1966	I	2	Winners
1967	I	2	1
1968	I	2	q-f
1969	I	2	Final
1970	I	2	q-f
1971	I	4	Final
1972	I	3	s-f
1973	I	2	Winners
1974	I	3	4
1975	I	1C	3
1976	P	1C	Winners
1977	P	2	Final
1978	P	1C	Winners
1979	P	2	Winners
1980	P	5	Final
1981	P	3	Winners
1982	P	3	Final

+Shared with Dumbarton

ST JOHNSTONE

Founded: 1884
Address: Muirton Park, Perth
Telephone: Perth 26961
Ground capacity: 25,000 (2,500 seated)
Playing area: 115 by 74 yards
Record attendance: 29,972 v Dundee, Scottish Cup 2nd round, 10.2.52
Record victory: 8-1 v Partick Thistle, Scottish League Cup, 16.8.69
Record defeat: 1-10 v Third Lanark, Scottish Cup 1st round, 24.1.03
Most League points: 56, Division II, 1923-24
Most League goals: 102, Division II, 1931-32
League scoring record: 36, Jimmy Benson, Division II, 1931-32
Most capped player: 5: Alex McLaren, Scotland

Scottish League Cup

	Year	Opponents	Score
Runners-up	1970	Celtic	0-1

THE ST JOHNSTONE RECORD

	Division & place	Cup round reached
1912	II 5	1
1913	II 11	3
1914	II 5	1
1915	II 8	
1916		
1917		
1918		
1919		
1920		2
1921		p
1922	II 13	1
1923	II 3	1
1924	II 1P	2
1925	I 11	1
1926	I 18	3
1927	I 14	1
1928	I 11	1
1929	I 9	2
1930	I 20R	2
1931	II 6	2
1932	II 2P	2
1933	I 5	3
1934	I 9	s-f
1935	I 5	q-f
1936	I 7	3
1937	I 12	2
1938	I 8	2
1939	I 8	1
1947	II 9	1
1948	II 9	2
1949	II 6	1
1950	II 3	2
1951	II 5	2
1952	II 11	2
1953	II 14	2
1954	II 6	1
1955	II 7	6
1956	II 3	5
1957	II 12	5
1958	II 11	2
1959	II 6	3
1960	II 1P	1
1961	I 15	1
1962	I 17R	2
1963	II 1P	2
1964	I 13	2
1965	I 13	2
1966	I 14	q-f
1967	I 15	2
1968	I 14	s-f
1969	I 6	q-f
1970	I 13	1
1971	I 3	3
1972	I 8	3
1973	I 11	3
1974	**I 12**	**4**
1975	**I 9**	**4**
1976	**P 10R**	**3**
1977	**I 11**	**3**
1978	**I 8**	**4**
1979	I 12	3
1980	I 11	3
1981	I 3	4
1982	I 5	4

ST MIRREN

Founded: 1876
Address: St Mirren Park, Love Street, Paisley, Renfrewshire
Telephone: 041 840 1337
Ground capacity: 25,800
Playing area: 115 by 74 yards
Record attendance: 47,428 v Celtic, Scottish Cup 4th round, 7.3.25
Record victory: 15-0 v Glasgow University, Scottish Cup 1st round, 30.1.60
Record defeat: 0-9 v Rangers, Division I, 4.12.1897
Most League points: 62, Division II, 1967-68
Most League goals: 114, Division II, 1935-36
League scoring record: 45, Dunky Walker, Division I, 1921-22
Most capped player: 7, Iain Munro, Scotland

Scottish Cup

	Year	Opponents	Score	Scorers
Winners	1926	Celtic	2-0	McCrae, Howieson
	1959	Aberdeen	3-1	Bryceland, Miller, Baker
Runners-up	1908	Celtic	1-5	Cunningham
	1934	Rangers	0-5	
	1962	Rangers	0-2	

Scottish League Cup

	Year	Opponents	Score	Scorers
Runners-up	1956	Aberdeen	1-2	Holmes

THE ST MIRREN RECORD

	Division & place	Cup round reached
1891	I 8	5
1892	I 10	1
1893	I 3	q-f
1894	I 6	2
1895	I 5	2
1896	I 8	2
1897	I 6	2
1898	I 6	2
1899	I 5	2
1900	I 8	1
1901	I 9	s-f
1902	I 5	s-f
1903	I 6	1
1904	I 6	q-f
1905	I 10	q-f
1906	I 8	s-f
1907	I 7	q-f
1908	I 7	Final
1909	I 7	q-f
1910	I 13	2
1911	I 12	1
1912	I 18	1
1913	I 12	q-f
1914	I 20	s-f
1915	I 9	
1916	I 13	
1917	I 7	
1918	I 11	
1919	I 11	
1920	I 14	2
1921	I 22	1
1922	I 8	q-f
1923	I 6	2
1924	I 6	2
1925	I 6	q-f
1926	I 4	Winners
1927	I 10	2
1928	I 5	3
1929	I 8	s-f
1930	I 5	q-f
1931	I 15	s-f
1932	I 5	1
1933	I 7	2
1934	I 17	Final
1935	I 19R	3
1936	II 2P	3
1937	I 16	q-f
1938	I 14	2
1939	I 18	3
1947	I 14	1
1948	I 5	q-f
1949	I 9	2
1950	I 11	1
1951	I 11	1
1952	I 14	2
1953	I 6	2
1954	I 11	1
1955	I 6	5
1956	I 15	6
1957	I 12	q-f
1958	I 13	2
1959	I 7	Winners
1960	I 14	2
1961	I 14	s-f
1962	I 16	Final
1963	I 12	q-f
1964	I 12	3
1965	I 15	1
1966	I 16	1
1967	I 17R	2
1968	II 1P	1
1969	I 11	2
1970	I 15	2
1971	I 17R	4
1972	II 4	4
1973	II 5	3
1974	II 11	3
1975	II 6	2
1976	I 6	3
1977	**I 1P**	**4**
1978	**P 8**	**3**
1979	P 6	4
1980	P 3	4
1981	P 4	3
1982	P 5	s-f

STENHOUSEMUIR

Founded: 1884
Address: Ochilview Park, Stenhousemuir, Scotland
Telephone: Larbert (0324) 562992
Ground capacity: 10,450 (450 seated)
Record attendance: 13,000 v East Fife, Scottish Cup 4th round, 11.3.50
Record victory: 9-2 v Dundee United, Division II, 17.4.37
Record defeat: 2-11 v Dunfermline Athletic, Division II, 27.9.30
Most League points: 50, Division II, 1960-61
Most League goals: 99, Division II, 1960-61
League scoring record: 31, Evelyn Morrison, Division II, 1927-28
Robert Murray, Division II, 1936-37

THE STENHOUSEMUIR RECORD

	Division & place	*Cup round reached*			
1922	II 10	1	1958	II 16	2
1923	II 14	1	1959	II 3	2
1924	II 4	2	1960	II 5	3
1925	II 11	1	1961	II 3	1
1926	II 5	2	1962	II 15	3
1927	II 10	1	1963	II 16	1
1928	II 16	2	1964	II 11	1
1929	II 18	2	1965	II 15	1
1930	II 17	1	1966	II 18	p
1931	II 17	1	1967	II 17	p
1932	II 4	1	1968	II 18	p
1933	II 4	q-f	1969	II 19	1
1934	II 4	1	1970	II 16	p
1935	II 5	1	1971	II 10	2
1936	II 11	2	1972	II 14	1
1937	II 10	1	1973	II 10	2
1938	II 8	2	1974	II 15	2
1939	II 8	1	1975	II 11	1
1947	II 7	1	1976	II 10	3
1948	II 14	1	1977	II 9	1
1949	II 12	q-f	1978	II 12	1
1950	II 12	q-f	1979	II 10	2
1951	II 15	1	1980	II 6	2
1952	II 13	1	1981	II 10	3
1953	II 12	1	1982	II 13	1
1954	II 4	1			
1955	II 6	5			
1956	II 5	q-f			
1957	II 14	5			

p – preliminary round

STIRLING ALBION

Founded: 1945
Address: Annfield Park, Stirling
Telephone: Stirling 3584
Ground capacity: 20,000 (900 seated)
Record attendance: 26,400 v Celtic, Scottish Cup, 4th round, 14.3.59
Record victory: 7-0 v Raith Rovers, Division II, 19.11.47
7-0 v Montrose, Division II, 28.9.57
7-0 v St. Mirren, Division I, 5.3.60 (away)
7-0 v Arbroath, Division II, 11.3.61
Record defeat: 0-9 v Dundee United, Division I, 30.12.67
Most League points: 59, Division II, 1964-65
Most League goals: 105, Division II, 1957-58
League scoring record: 26, Michael Lawson, Division II, 1975-76
Most capped player: None

THE STIRLING ALBION RECORD

	Division & place	*Cup round reached*			
1947		p	1966	I 15	2
1948	II 8	2	1967	I 16	1
1949	II 2P	1	1968	I 18R	1
1950	I 16R	q-f	1969	II 4	1
1951	II 2P	1	1970	II 4	1
1952	I 16R	2	1971	II 12	4
1953	II 1P	2	1972	II 3	2
1954	I 14	3	1973	II 4	4
1955	I 16	5	1974	II 7	4
1956	I 18R	6	1975	II 8	2
1957	II 8	5	1976	II 6	4
1958	II 1P	2	1977	II 1P	3
1959	I 12	q-f	1978	I 5	4
1960	I 17R	2	1979	I 8	3
1961	II 1P	1	1980	I 8	4
1962	I 18R	q-f	1981	I 13R	4
1963	II 10	1	1982	II 8	1
1964	II 19	1			
1965	II 1P	q-f			

STRANRAER

Founded: 1870
Address: Stair Park, Stranraer, Wigtownshire, Scotland
Telephone: Stranraer 3271
Ground capacity: 5,000
Record attendance: 6,500 v Rangers, Scottish Cup 1st round, 24.1.48
Record victory: 7-0 v Brechin City, Division II, 6.2.65
Record defeat: 1-11 v Queen of the South, Scottish Cup 1st round, 16.1.32
Most League points: 44, Division II, 1960-61 and 1971-72
Most League goals: 83, Division II, 1960-61
League scoring record: 27, Derek Frye, Division II, 1977-78
Most capped player: None

THE STRANRAER RECORD

	Division & place	*Cup round reached*			
1956	II 12	4	1971	II 9	3
1957	II 7	5	1972	II 6	2
1958	II 18	2	1973	II 15	4
1959	II 16	2	1974	II 9	2
1960	II 17	1	1975	II 14	2
1961	II 4	2	1976	II 7	2
1962	II 7	3	1977	II 4	2
1963	II 5	1	1978	II 11	2
1964	II 8	2	1979	II 9	2
1965	II 6	p	1980	II 11	2
1966	II 15	1	1981	II 14	2
1967	II 15	p	1982	II 14	1
1968	II 19	p			
1969	II 8	2			
1970	II 17	1			

The Records

Major Competitions: Seasons 1870-1874

FA CUP 1871-72

FIRST ROUND

Clapham Rovers v Upton Park	3-0
Crystal Palace v Hitchin	0-0*
Maidenhead v Great Marlow	2-0
Barnes v Civil Service	2-0
Wanderers v Harrow Chequers (scratched)	wo
Royal Engineers v Reigate Priory (scratched)	wo
Queen's Park	bye
Donington School	bye
Hampstead Heathens	bye

SECOND ROUND

Wanderers v Clapham Rovers	3-1
Crystal Palace v Maidenhead	3-0
Royal Engineers v Hitchin	3-1
Hampstead Heathens v Barnes	2-0
Queen's Park v Donington School (scratched)	wo

THIRD ROUND

Wanderers v Crystal Palace	†*
Royal Engineers v Hampstead Heathens	2-0
Queen's Park	‡bye

†Drawn game for which no score is available.
‡Queen's Park were granted a bye from the third round into the semi-final because of travelling.

SEMI-FINAL

Royal Engineers v Crystal Palace	3-0
Wanderers v Queen's Park (scratched)††	0-0, wo

††Queen's Park could not afford to travel to London for the replay.

FINAL AT KENNINGTON OVAL

Wanderers v Royal Engineers	1-0

*The progress of Crystal Palace and Hitchin into the second round and Crystal Palace and Wanderers into the semi-final round was covered by Rule 8 of the competition whereby in the case of a draw both clubs could compete in the next round.

FA CUP 1872-73

FIRST ROUND

Oxford University v Crystal Palace	3-2
Royal Engineers v Civil Service	3-0
1st Surrey Rifles v Upton Park	2-0
Maidenhead v Great Marlow	1-0
South Norwood v Barnes	1-0
Windsor Home Park v Reigate Priory	4-2
Clapham Rovers v Hitchin (scratched)	wo
Queen's Park	*bye
Wanderers	†bye

*Queen's Park, Glasgow, because of the travelling involved, were awarded byes to the semi-final round.
†This was the only occasion when the Cup holders were excused from taking part until the Final.

SECOND ROUND

Clapham Rovers v Oxford University	0-3
1st Surrey Rifles v Maidenhead	1-3
South Norwood v Windsor Home Park	0-3
Royal Engineers	bye
Queen's Park	bye
Wanderers	bye

THIRD ROUND

Oxford University v Royal Engineers	1-0
Maidenhead v Windsor Home Park	1-0
Queen's Park	bye
Wanderers	bye

FOURTH ROUND

Oxford University v Maidenhead	4-0
Queen's Park	bye
Wanderers	bye

SEMI-FINAL

Oxford University v Queen's Park (scratched)	*wo
Wanderers	bye

*Queen's Park apparently beat Oxford but could not afford to travel to London for the Final.

FINAL AT LILLIE BRIDGE*

Wanderers v Oxford University	2-0

*Wanderers, as Cup holders, had choice of ground.

FA CUP 1873-74

FIRST ROUND

Oxford University v Upton Park	4-0
Barnes v 1st Surrey Rifles	1-0
Cambridge University v South Norwood	1-0
Pilgrims v Great Marlow	1-0
Royal Engineers v Brondesbury	5-0
Uxbridge v Gitanos	3-0
Swifts v Crystal Palace	1-0
Woodford Wells v Reigate Priory	3-0
Sheffield v Shropshire Wanderers	††
Wanderers v Southall (scratched)	wo
Trojans v Farningham (scratched)	wo
Clapham Rovers v A A C (scratched)	wo
Maidenhead v Civil Service (scratched)	wo
High Wycombe v Old Etonians (scratched)	wo

††After two drawn games Sheffield won on the toss of a coin

SECOND ROUND

Oxford University v Barnes	2-1
Clapham Rovers v Cambridge University	4-1
Sheffield v Pilgrims	1-0
Royal Engineers v Uxbridge	2-1
Maidenhead v High Wycombe	1-0
Swifts v Woodford Wells	2-1
Wanderers v Trojans (scratched)	wo

THIRD ROUND

Oxford University v Wanderers	1-0
Clapham Rovers v Sheffield	2-1
Royal Engineers v Maidenhead	7-0
Swifts	bye

SEMI-FINAL

Oxford University v Clapham Rovers	1-0
Royal Engineers v Swifts	2-0

FINAL AT KENNINGTON OVAL

Oxford University v Royal Engineers	2-0

SCOTTISH FA CUP 1873-74

FIRST ROUND

Queen's Park v Dumbreck	7-0
Clydesdale v Granville	6-0
Western v Blythwood	0-1
Alexandria Athletic v Callander	2-0
Eastern v Rovers	4-0
Renton v Kilmarnock	2-0
Dumbarton v Vale of Leven (scratched)	wo
3rd Lanark Rifle Volunteers v Southern (scratched)	wo

SECOND ROUND

Queen's Park v Eastern	1-0
Alexandria Athletic v Blythwood	0-2
Renton v Dumbarton	0-0, 1-0
Clydesdale v 3rd Lanark Rifle Volunteers	1-1, 0-0, 2-0

SEMI-FINAL

Queen's Park v Renton	2-0
Clydesdale v Blythwood	4-0

FINAL AT HAMPDEN PARK

Queen's Park v Clydesdale	2-0

The first FA Cup competitions were far less organised than those a century later. The first winners, Wanderers, won only one game before defeating Royal Engineers in the Final. They received a walk over in the first round, beat Clapham in the second, went through after only drawing in the third and received a walk-over in the semi-final after Queen's Park had been unable to pay for the long journey to London for a replay.
Wanderers' goal in the Final – the first in an FA Cup Final – was scored by M P Betts, who played under the name of A H Chequer, indicating that he had come from Harrow Chequers, who had scratched to Wanderers in the first round. Queen's Park had the same trouble the next year. After defeating Oxford they were unable to travel to the Final and Oxford took their place – thus being one of only three clubs to have reached a Final after losing an earlier match.

Top *Queen's Park in 1874, still undefeated and the first winners of the Scottish Cup.*
Bottom *Royal Engineers in 1872, 7-4 on favourites for the FA Cup, but only runners-up.*

COURTESY OF DR PERCY YOUNG

Major Competitions: Seasons 1875-1877

FA CUP 1874-75

FIRST ROUND

Match	Score
Royal Engineers v Great Marlow	3-0
Cambridge University v Crystal Palace	†2-1
Clapham Rovers v Panthers	3-0
Pilgrims v South Norwood	2-1
Oxford University v Brondesbury	6-0
Wanderers v Farningham	16-0
Barnes v Upton Park	3-0
Old Etonians v Swifts	††3-0
Maidenhead v Hitchin	1-0
Woodford Wells v High Wycombe	1-0
Southall v Leyton	†5-0
Windsor Home Park v Uxbridge (scratched)	wo
Shropshire Wanderers v Sheffield (scratched)	wo
Civil Service v Harrow Chequers (scratched)	wo
Reigate Priory	bye

†Drawn game for which no score is available

SECOND ROUND

Match	Score
Royal Engineers v Cambridge University	5-0
Clapham Rovers v Pilgrims	2-0
Wanderers v Barnes	4-0
Maidenhead v Reigate Priory	2-1
Woodford Wells v Southall	3-0
Oxford University v Windsor Home Park (scratched)	wo
Shropshire Wanderers v Civil Service (scratched)	†wo
Old Etonians	bye

†Drawn game for which no score is available

THIRD ROUND

Match	Score
Royal Engineers v Clapham Rovers	3-2
Oxford University v Wanderers	2-1
Old Etonians v Maidenhead	1-0
Shropshire Wanderers v Woodford Wells	†2-0

†Drawn game for which no score is available

SEMI-FINAL

Match	Score
Royal Engineers v Oxford University	†1-0
Old Etonians v Shropshire Wanderers	1-0

†Drawn game for which no score is available

FINAL AT KENNINGTON OVAL

Match	Score
Royal Engineers v Old Etonians	1-1, 2-0

SCOTTISH FA CUP 1874-75

FIRST ROUND

Match	Score
Helensburgh v 3rd Edinburgh Rifle Volunteers	3-0
Rangers v Oxford	2-0
West End v Star of Leven	3-0
Kilmarnock v Vale of Leven Rovers	4-0
Dumbreck v Alexandria Athletic	5-1
3rd Lanark Rifle Volunteers v Barrhead	1-0
Dumbarton v Arthurlie	3-0
Queen's Park v Western	1-0
Eastern v 23rd Renfrew Rifle Volunteers	3-0
Renton v Blythwood (scratched)	wo
Clydesdale v Vale of Leven (scratched)	wo
Rovers v Hamilton Academicals (scratched)	wo
Standard	bye

SECOND ROUND

Match	Score
Eastern v Kilmarnock	3-0
Renton v Helensburgh	2-0
3rd Lanark Rifle Volunteers v Standard	2-0
Queen's Park v West End	7-0
Clydesdale v Dumbreck	2-0
Dumbarton v Rangers	1-0
Rovers	bye

THIRD ROUND

Match	Score
Renton v Eastern	1-0
Dumbarton v 3rd Lanark Rifle Volunteers	1-0
Queen's Park v Rovers (scratched)	wo
Clydesdale	bye

SEMI-FINAL

Match	Score
Renton v Dumbarton	1-0
Queen's Park v Clydesdale	1-0

FINAL AT HAMPDEN PARK

Match	Score
Queen's Park v Renton	3-0

FA CUP 1875-76

FIRST ROUND

Match	Score
Wanderers v 1st Surrey Rifles	5-0
Crystal Palace v 105th Regiment	†3-0
Upton Park v Southall	1-0
Swifts v Great Marlow	2-0
Royal Engineers v High Wycombe	15-0
Panthers v Woodford Wells	1-0
Reigate Priory v Barnes	1-0
Oxford University v Forest School	6-0
Hertfordshire Rangers v Rochester	4-0
Old Etonians v Pilgrims	4-1
Maidenhead v Ramblers	2-0
Sheffield v Shropshire Wanderers (scratched)	wo
South Norwood v Clydesdale (scratched)	wo
Cambridge University v Civil Service (scratched)	wo
Clapham Rovers v Hitchin (scratched)	wo
Leyton v Harrow Chequers (scratched)	wo

†Drawn game for which no score is available

SECOND ROUND

Match	Score
Wanderers v Crystal Palace	3-0
Swifts v South Norwood	5-0
Reigate Priory v Cambridge University	0-8
Oxford University v Hertfordshire Rangers	8-2
Old Etonians v Maidenhead	8-0
Clapham Rovers v Leyton	12-0
Sheffield v Upton Park (scratched)	wo
Royal Engineers v Panthers (scratched)	wo

THIRD ROUND

Match	Score
Wanderers v Sheffield	2-0
Swifts v Royal Engineers	3-1
Cambridge University v Oxford University	0-4
Old Etonians v Clapham Rovers	1-0

SEMI-FINAL

Match	Score
Wanderers v Swifts	2-1
Oxford University v Old Etonians	0-1

FINAL AT KENNINGTON OVAL

Match	Score
Wanderers v Old Etonians	1-1, 3-0

SCOTTISH FA CUP 1875-76

SECOND ROUND

Match	Score
3rd Edinburgh Rifle Volunteers v Edinburgh Thistle	1-0
Levern v Hamilton Academicals	3-0
Drumpellier v Heart of Midlothian	2-0
Vale of Leven v Renton	3-0
Queen's Park v Northern	5-0
3rd Lanark Rifle Volunteers v Rangers	2-1
Helensburgh v 23rd Renfrew Rifle Volunteers	1-0
Clydesdale v Kilmarnock	6-0
Dumbarton v Renton Thistle	2-1
Western v Sandyford	3-0
Dumbreck v St Andrew's	2-0
Rovers v West End	6-0
Partick Thistle v Towerhill	2-0
Mauchline v Kilbirnie (scratched)	wo

THIRD ROUND

Match	Score
Queen's Park v Clydesdale	2-0
Vale of Leven v Mauchline	6-0
3rd Lanark Rifle Volunteers v Levern	3-0
Dumbreck v Partick Thistle	5-0
Rovers v 3rd Edinburgh Rifle Volunteers	4-0
Western v Helensburgh	2-0
Dumbarton v Drumpellier	5-1

FOURTH ROUND

Match	Score
Queen's Park v Dumbreck	2-0
3rd Lanark Rifle Volunteers v Western	5-0
Vale of Leven v Rovers	2-0
Dumbarton	bye

SEMI-FINAL

Match	Score
Queen's Park v Vale of Leven	3-1
3rd Lanark Rifle Volunteers v Dumbarton	3-0

FINAL AT HAMPDEN PARK

Match	Score
Queen's Park v 3rd Lanark Rifle Volunteers	1-1, 2-0

FA CUP 1876-77

FIRST ROUND

Match	Score
Pilgrims v Ramblers	4-1
Panthers v Wood Grange	3-0
Clapham Rovers v Reigate Priory	5-0
Rochester v Union	5-0
Swifts v Reading Hornets	2-0
Royal Engineers v Old Harrovians	2-1
South Norwood v Saxons	4-1
105th Regiment v 1st Surrey Rifles	3-0
Upton Park v Leyton	7-0
Great Marlow v Hertfordshire Rangers	2-1
Forest School v Gresham	4-1
Wanderers v Saffron Walden (scratched)	wo
Southall v Old Wykehamists (scratched)	wo
Cambridge University v High Wycombe (scratched)	wo
Shropshire Wanderers v Druids (scratched)	wo
Sheffield v Trojans (scratched)	wo
Oxford University v Old Salopians (scratched)	wo
Barnes v Old Etonians (scratched)	wo
Queen's Park	bye

SECOND ROUND

Match	Score
Wanderers v Southall	6-1
Pilgrims v Panthers	1-0
Cambridge University v Clapham Rovers	2-1
Rochester v Swifts	1-0
Royal Engineers v Shropshire Wanderers	3-0
Sheffield v South Norwood	7-0
Oxford University v 105th Regiment	6-1
Upton Park v Barnes	1-0
Great Marlow v Forest School	1-0
Queen's Park	bye

THIRD ROUND

Match	Score
Wanderers v Pilgrims	3-0
Cambridge University v Rochester	4-0
Royal Engineers v Sheffield	1-0
Upton Park v Great Marlow	†1-0
Oxford University v Queen's Park (scratched)	wo

†Drawn game for which no score is available.

FOURTH ROUND

Match	Score
Cambridge University v Royal Engineers	1-0
Oxford University v Upton Park	†1-0
Wanderers	bye

†Drawn game for which no score is available

SEMI-FINAL

Match	Score
Wanderers v Cambridge University	1-0
Oxford University	bye

FINAL AT KENNINGTON OVAL

Match	Score
Wanderers v Oxford University	2-1

SCOTTISH FA CUP 1876-77

FOURTH ROUND

Match	Score
Queen's Park v Northern	4-0
Vale of Leven v Busby	4-0
Lennox v Swifts	4-0
Lancefield v Hamilton	2-0
Rangers v Mauchline	3-0
Ayr Thistle v Partick Thistle (disqualified)	wo

FIFTH ROUND

Match	Score
Rangers v Lennox	3-0
Vale of Leven v Queen's Park	2-1
Ayr Thistle v Lancefield	1-0

SEMI-FINAL

Match	Score
Vale of Leven v Ayr Thistle	9-0
Rangers	bye

FINAL AT HAMPDEN PARK

Match	Score
Vale of Leven v Rangers	0-0, 1-1, 3-2

Queen's Park conceded their first ever goal in the Scottish Cup semi-final against Vale of Leven early in 1876. They had been in existence for almost nine years. Their first ever defeat in Scotland was also at the hands of Vale of Leven on 30 December 1876. The latter won a fifth round Scottish Cup tie 2-1.

FA CUP 1877-78

FIRST ROUND

Wanderers v Panthers	9-1
High Wycombe v Wood Grange	4-0
Great Marlow v Hendon	2-0
Sheffield v Notts County	3-0
Darwen v Manchester	3-1
Pilgrims v Ramblers	†1-0
Druids v Shropshire Wanderers	1-0
Oxford University v Hertfordshire Rangers	5-2
Clapham Rovers v Grantham	2-0
Swifts v Leyton	8-2
Old Harrovians v 105th Regiment	2-0
1st Surrey Rifles v Forest School	1-0
Cambridge University v Southill Park	3-1
Maidenhead v Reading Hornets	10-0
Upton Park v Rochester	3-0
Reading v South Norwood	2-0
Remnants v St Stephens	4-1
Hawks v Minerva	5-2
Barnes v St Marks (scratched)	wo
Royal Engineers v Union (scratched)	wo
Old Foresters v Old Wykehamists (scratched)	wo
Queen's Park	*bye

†Drawn game for which no score is available
*Queen's Park later withdrew

SECOND ROUND

Wanderers v High Wycombe	9-0
Barnes v Great Marlow	3-1
Sheffield v Darwen	1-0
Royal Engineers v Pilgrims	6-0
Oxford University v Old Foresters	1-0
Clapham Rovers v Swifts	4-0
Old Harrovians v 1st Surrey Rifles	6-0
Cambridge University v Maidenhead	4-2
Upton Park v Reading	1-0
Remnants v Hawks	2-0
Druids	bye

THIRD ROUND

Wanderers v Barnes	4-1
Royal Engineers v Druids	8-0
Oxford University v Clapham Rovers	3-2
Old Harrovians v Cambridge University	2-0
Upton Park v Remnants	3-0
Sheffield	bye

FOURTH ROUND

Wanderers v Sheffield	3-0
Royal Engineers v Oxford University	4-2
Old Harrovians v Upton Park	3-1

SEMI-FINAL

Royal Engineers v Old Harrovians	2-1
Wanderers	bye

FINAL AT KENNINGTON OVAL

Wanderers v Royal Engineers	3-1

The first ever Welsh Cup tie was played on Saturday 30 October, 1877, between Druids of Ruabon and Newtown at Newtown. The founder of the Welsh FA, Llewelyn Kenrick, captained Druids that day; they won the game and eventually reached the final to meet Wrexham. Wrexham won 1-0, apparently using a 2-3-5 line up. If that is in fact correct, then it is the first recorded instance of what remained the standard formation for half a century. At the time the Welsh FA had not even purchased a trophy, but when they did it was a magnificent affair which dwarfed the FA Cup.
Because of the dearth of clubs in Wales, the Cup has always been open to English sides. This produced an English winner as early as 1884 when Oswestry defeated Druids 3-2. The situation became a little absurd in 1934, however, with a final replay which is surely unparalleled in any cup competition. The game was between two English clubs – Bristol City and Tranmere Rovers – and was played on an English ground, Chester's Sealand Road. City won 3-0 and it was not until 1948 that the Cup actually returned to a Welsh club.

SCOTTISH FA CUP 1877-78

FOURTH ROUND

Renton v Rovers	4-0
South Western v Glengowan	5-0
Mauchline v Kilbirnie	2-1
Parkgrove v Drumpellier	3-1
3rd Lanark Rifle Volunteers v Govan	7-0
Vale of Leven v Rangers	5-0
Thornliebank v Hibernian	**
Beith v Dundas St Clement's (scratched)	wo
Partick Thistle v Barrhead (disqualified)	wo
Jordanhill	bye
Renfrew	†bye

**After two draws, both teams went through to the next round
†Renfrew, who had earlier been beaten by Barrhead, were reinstated on the latter's disqualification

FIFTH ROUND

Vale of Leven v Jordanhill	10-0
Parkgrove v Partick Thistle	2-1
South Western v Hibernian	3-1
Renton v Thornliebank	2-1
3rd Lanark Rifle Volunteers v Beith	4-0
Mauchline v Renfrew (scratched)	wo

SIXTH ROUND

Vale of Leven v Parkgrove	5-0
3rd Lanark Rifle Volunteers v South Western	2-1
Renton v Mauchline	3-1

SEMI-FINAL

3rd Lanark Rifle Volunteers v Renton	1-0
Vale of Leven	bye

FINAL AT HAMPDEN PARK

Vale of Leven v 3rd Lanark Rifle Volunteers	1-0

SCOTTISH FA CUP 1878-79

FOURTH ROUND

Hibernian v Roy Roy	9-0
3rd Lanark Rifle Volunteers v Renfrew	4-0
Vale of Leven v Govan	11-1
Dumbarton v Portland	6-1
Queen's Park v Mauchline	5-0
Rangers v Alexandria Athletic	3-0
Beith v Kilmarnock Athletic	9-1
Helensburgh v Heart of Midlothian (scratched)	wo
Stonelaw v Thistle (disqualified)	wo
Partick Thistle	bye

FIFTH ROUND

Queen's Park v 3rd Lanark Rifle Volunteers	5-0
Rangers v Partick Thistle	4-0
Helensburgh v Hibernian	2-1
Dumbarton v Stonelaw	9-1
Vale of Leven v Beith	6-1

SIXTH ROUND

Rangers v Queen's Park	1-0
Vale of Leven v Dumbarton	3-1
Helensburgh	bye

SEMI-FINAL

Vale of Leven v Helensburgh	3-0
Rangers	bye

FINAL AT HAMPDEN PARK

Vale of Leven v Rangers	1-1*

*Cup awarded to Vale of Leven. Rangers refused to play the replay within the time allotted by the SFA. Rangers refused to turn up after the SFA had turned down a protest that they had scored a perfectly legitimate second goal in the first game.

The Scottish Cup of 1878-79 saw two scenes unfamiliar a century later. Hearts failed to turn up for their tie at Helensburgh and, later, mighty Rangers refused to play a final replay against Vale of Leven in a fit of pique over a disputed goal.

FA CUP 1878-79

FIRST ROUND

Old Etonians v Wanderers	7-2
Reading v Hendon	1-0
Grey Friars v Great Marlow	2-1
Pilgrims v Brentwood	3-1
Nottingham Forest v Notts County	†1-0
Sheffield v Grantham	†3-1
Old Harrovians v Southill Park	8-0
Oxford University v Wednesbury Strollers	7-0
Royal Engineers v Old Foresters	3-0
Barnes v Maidenhead	†4-0
Upton Park v Saffron Walden	5-0
Forest School v Rochester	4-2
Cambridge University v Hertfordshire Rangers	2-0
Swifts v Hawks	2-1
Romford v Ramblers	3-1
Minerva v 105th Regiment (scratched)	wo
Darwen v Birch (scratched)	wo
Remnants v Unity (scratched)	wo
Panthers v Runnymede (scratched)	†wo
Clapham Rovers v Finchley (scratched)	wo
South Norwood v Leyton (scratched)	wo
Eagley	bye

†Drawn game for which no score is available

SECOND ROUND

Old Etonians v Reading	1-0
Minerva v Grey Friars	3-0
Darwen v Eagley	4-1
Remnants v Pilgrims	6-2
Nottingham Forest v Sheffield	2-0
Old Harrovians v Panthers	3-0
Oxford University v Royal Engineers	4-0
Barnes v Upton Park	3-2
Clapham Rovers v Forest School	10-1
Cambridge University v South Norwood	3-0
Swifts v Romford	3-1

THIRD ROUND

Old Etonians v Minerva	5-2
Darwen v Remnants	3-2
Nottingham Forest v Old Harrovians	2-0
Oxford University v Barnes	2-1
Clapham Rovers v Cambridge University	1-0
Swifts	bye

FOURTH ROUND

Old Etonians v Darwen	5-5, 2-2, 6-2
Nottingham Forest v Oxford University	2-1
Clapham Rovers v Swifts	8-1

SEMI-FINAL

Old Etonians v Nottingham Forest	2-1
Clapham Rovers	bye

FINAL AT KENNINGTON OVAL

Old Etonians v Clapham Rovers	1-0

The 1878-79 Cup season was notable for the arrival of the northern teams. Nottingham Forest became the first northern side to reach the semi-finals (and the only one of the present League clubs to have got so far at the first attempt) but Darwen's displays were more newsworthy. In their fourth round tie against Old Etonians at the Oval, Darwen scored four times in the last 15 minutes to draw 5-5. Etonians refused to play extra time and it took a public subscription to bring Darwen back for a 2-2 draw. A third game was decisive, Etonians winning 6-2 and eventually taking the Cup.
Darwen had in their ranks two Scots – James Love and Fergus Suter – who were reputedly the first of the 'professionals' to find money in their boots. They had come down to Darwen as part of a touring Partick Thistle side, played a friendly, and been persuaded to stay. The tide was on the turn and the days of the gentlemen amateurs almost at an end. Wanderers, after a hat-trick of successes in 1876-78, were defeated in the very first round of the 1878-79 competition by Old Etonians, who went on to become their successors as Cup holders.

Major Competitions: Seasons 1879-80 & 1880-81

FA CUP 1879-80

SECOND ROUND

Clapham Rovers v South Norwood	4-0
Hendon v Mosquitoes	7-1
Wanderers v Old Carthusians	1-0
West End v Hotspurs	1-0
Oxford University v Birmingham	6-0
Aston Villa v Stafford Road Works	3-1
Maidenhead v Henley	3-1
Royal Engineers v Upton Park	4-1
Grey Friars v Gresham	9-0
Nottingham Forest v Turton	6-0
Blackburn Rovers v Darwen	3-1
Sheffield v Sheffield Providence	3-0
Pilgrims v Hertfordshire Rangers (scratched)	wo
Old Harrovians	bye
Old Etonians	bye

THIRD ROUND

Clapham Rovers v Pilgrims	7-0
Old Etonians v Wanderers	3-1
Royal Engineers v Old Harrovians	2-0
Nottingham Forest v Blackburn Rovers	6-0
Oxford University v Aston Villa (scratched)	wo
Hendon	bye
West End	bye
Maidenhead	bye
Grey Friars	bye
Sheffield	bye

FOURTH ROUND

Clapham Rovers v Hendon	2-0
Old Etonians v West End	5-1
Oxford University v Maidenhead	1-0
Royal Engineers v Grey Friars	1-0
Nottingham Forest v Sheffield	*2-2

*Sheffield disqualified for refusing to play extra time

FIFTH ROUND

Clapham Rovers v Old Etonians	1-0
Oxford University v Royal Engineers	†1-0
Nottingham Forest	bye

†Drawn game for which no score is available

SEMI-FINAL

Oxford University v Nottingham Forest	1-0
Clapham Rovers	bye

FINAL AT KENNINGTON OVAL

Clapham Rovers v Oxford University	1-0

F H. AYRES
MANUFACTURER OF
SPORTS & GAMES
1, Aldersgate St., London, E.C.
FOOTBALL'S
THE "INTERNATIONAL."
ASSOCIATION
RUGBY
EVERY REQUISITE
FOR THE GAME.
TESTIMONIAL.
ROVERS' FOOTBALL CLUB.
Dear Sir,
Please forward by return two Association Footballs same as one you sent on trial. Our players consider it a very good one.—Yours truly,
Mr. AYRES. J. B. MITCHELL.
LA CROSSE, HOCKEY, GOLF, BILLIARDS, &c.

Above *The reason Blackburn Rovers won the Cup so often? F H Ayres and Company ran this advertisement regularly for ten years, but 1879-80 was a little premature for it. In their first expedition into the Cup, which was that season, Rovers were rudely dismissed 6-0 by Nottingham Forest, who were at the time on the way to a second consecutive semi-final.*

SCOTTISH FA CUP 1879-80

FOURTH ROUND

South Western v Arbroath	4-0
Pollockshields Athletic v Renfrew	2-1
Dumbarton v Clyde	11-1
Third Lanark v Kirkintilloch	5-1
Rob Roy v Johnstone Athletic	4-2
Thornliebank v Fossilpark	13-0
Mauchline v Hamilton Academicals	2-0
Cambuslang v Plains	3-0
Queen's Park v Strathblane	10-1
Parkgrove v Hibernian	**
Hurlford v Kilbirnie	**

**After two draws both teams went through to the next round

FIFTH ROUND

South Western v Parkgrove	3-2
Dumbarton v Kilbirnie	6-2
Queen's Park v Hurlford	15-1
Thornliebank v Rob Roy	12-0
Pollockshields Athletic v Cambuslang	4-0
Hibernian v Mauchline	2-0
Third Lanark	bye

SIXTH ROUND

Pollockshields Athletic v South Western	6-1
Dumbarton v Hibernian	6-2
Thornliebank v Third Lanark	2-1
Queen's Park	bye

SEMI-FINAL

Queen's Park v Dumbarton	1-0
Thornliebank v Pollockshields Athletic	2-1

FINAL AT CATHKIN PARK

Queen's Park v Thornliebank	3-0

SCOTTISH FA CUP 1880-81

FOURTH ROUND

Heart of Midlothian v Cambridge	3-0
Hurlford v Cartside	3-1
Central v Edinburgh University	1-0
Dumbarton v Glasgow University	9-0
Rangers v Clyde	11-0
Queen's Park v Beith	11-2
St Mirren v Cowlairs	1-0
Arthurlie v South Western (scratched)	wo
Mauchline v Clarkston (scratched)	wo
Vale of Leven v Arbroath (scratched)	wo
Thistle	bye

FIFTH ROUND

Vale of Leven v Thistle	7-1
Dumbarton v St Mirren	5-1
Arthurlie v Heart of Midlothian	4-0
Queen's Park v Mauchline	2-0
Rangers v Hurlford	3-0
Central	bye

SIXTH ROUND

Queen's Park v Central	10-0
Dumbarton v Rangers	3-1
Vale of Leven v Arthurlie	2-0

SEMI-FINAL

Dumbarton v Vale of Leven	2-0
Queen's Park	bye

FINAL AT KINNING PARK

Queen's Park v Dumbarton	2-1*, 3-1

*Dumbarton's protest about spectators on the pitch during the first game was upheld

Old Carthusians defeat of Old Etonians in the 1881 Cup Final was the first leg of a rare double. In 1894 they also won the first Amateur Cup final by defeating Casuals 2-1. In fact this oft repeated 'unique' record is not so: Royal Engineers, FA Cup winners in 1875, later went on to win the Amateur Cup in 1908 as Depot Battalion, Royal Engineers.

FA CUP 1880-81

SECOND ROUND

Old Carthusians v Dreadnought	5-1
Royal Engineers v Pilgrims	1-0
Swifts v Reading	1-0
Upton Park v Weybridge	3-0
Darwen v Sheffield	5-1
The Wednesday v Blackburn Rovers	4-0
Turton v Astley Bridge	3-0
Reading Abbey v Acton	2-1
Great Marlow v West End	4-0
Old Etonians v Hendon	2-0
Grey Friars v Maidenhead	1-0
Stafford Road Works v Grantham	†7-1
Aston Villa v Nottingham Forest	2-1
Notts County	bye
Rangers	bye
Clapham Rovers	bye
Romford	bye
Hertfordshire Rangers	bye

†Drawn game for which no score is available

THIRD ROUND

Royal Engineers v Rangers	6-0
Clapham Rovers v Swifts	2-1
The Wednesday v Turton	2-0
Romford v Reading Abbey	2-0
Old Etonians v Hertfordshire Rangers	3-0
Aston Villa v Notts County	3-1
Old Carthusians	bye
Upton Park	bye
Darwen	bye
Great Marlow	bye
Stafford Road Works	bye
Grey Friars	bye

FOURTH ROUND

Old Carthusians v Royal Engineers	2-1
Clapham Rovers v Upton Park	5-4
Darwen v The Wednesday	5-1
Romford v Great Marlow	2-1
Old Etonians v Grey Friars	4-0
Stafford Road Works v Aston Villa	3-2

FIFTH ROUND

Old Carthusians v Clapham Rovers	4-1
Darwen v Romford	15-0
Old Etonians v Stafford Road Works	2-1

SEMI-FINAL

Old Carthusians v Darwen	4-1
Old Etonians	bye

FINAL AT KENNINGTON OVAL

Old Carthusians v Old Etonians	3-0

The two Scottish Cup finals of 1881 between Queen's Park and Dumbarton resulted in quite unprecedented scenes. The game was played at Rangers' home, Kinning Park, and the crowds were so great that many spent most of the game on the pitch. Because of this Dumbarton protested that Queen's second and winning goal was invalid, the pitch having virtually been invaded, and the SFA ordered a replay. Queen's threatened to withdraw from the Association, but eventually turned out and won 3-1. At the second game the gates had to be closed, the first time that this had happened in Scottish history. This was not really surprising for Dumbarton and Queen's were the Rangers and Celtic of pre-1900 Scotland.

The next year, 1882, there was even more trouble when the two met in the final. The crowd was bad-tempered and there were protests over yet another disputed goal – this time to level at 2-2. Queen's Park went on to win the replay, 4-1, before a record 15,000 crowd, but the two games left a remarkably bitter taste. Up to that point there had been a well-attended friendly every year between the clubs, but this was abandoned . and, indeed, never reinstated. Dumbarton finally won the Cup the following year, beating Vale of Leven, after defeating Queen's Park in the sixth round.

FA CUP 1881-82

SECOND ROUND

Blackburn Rovers v Bolton Wanderers	6-2
Darwen v Accrington	3-1
Turton v Bootle	4-0
Wednesbury Old Alliance v Small Heath Alliance	6-0
Notts County v Wednesbury Strollers	11-1
Staveley v Grantham	3-1
Heeley v Sheffield	4-1
Upton Park v Hanover United	3-1
Hotspur v Reading Abbey	4-1
Reading Minster v Romford	3-1
Swifts v Old Harrovians	7-1
Maidenhead v Acton	2-1
Great Marlow v St Bartholomew's Hospital	2-0
Reading v West End (scratched)	*wo
Old Foresters v Pilgrims	3-1
Old Carthusians v Barnes	7-1
Aston Villa	bye
The Wednesday	bye
Old Etonians	bye
Dreadnought	bye
Royal Engineers	bye

*West End scratched after a drawn game

THIRD ROUND

Darwen v Turton	4-2
Aston Villa v Notts County	**4-1
The Wednesday v Staveley	**5-1
Hotspur v Reading Minster	2-0
Old Etonians v Swifts	3-0
Great Marlow v Dreadnought	2-1
Royal Engineers v Old Carthusians	2-0
Blackburn Rovers	bye
Wednesbury Old Alliance	bye
Heeley	bye
Upton Park	bye
Maidenhead	bye
Reading	bye
Old Foresters	bye

**two drawn games for which no scores are available

FOURTH ROUND

Blackburn Rovers v Darwen	5-1
Wednesbury Old Alliance v Aston Villa	4-2
The Wednesday v Heeley	3-1
Upton Park v Hotspur	5-0
Old Etonians v Maidenhead	6-3
Great Marlow v Reading (scratched)	wo
Old Foresters v Royal Engineers	2-1

FIFTH ROUND

Blackburn Rovers v Wednesbury Old Alliance	3-1
The Wednesday v Upton Park	6-0
Great Marlow v Old Foresters	*1-0
Old Etonians	bye

*drawn game for which no score is available

SEMI-FINAL

Blackburn Rovers v The Wednesday	0-0, 5-1
Old Etonians v Great Marlow	5-0

FINAL AT KENNINGTON OVAL

Old Etonians v Blackburn Rovers	1-0

The 1882 FA Cup Final was the real bridging point between the old 'gentlemen's' football and the new professionalism. It was the first appearance of a northern club – Blackburn Rovers – and the last time a Southern side was to win for 30 years. After the game Lord Kinnaird, the victorious captain, stood on his head in front of the pavillion. He had appeared in 8 Finals and won 5 winners medals, a record that was to be equalled but never surpassed. He also appeared in the following year's Final, when he collected a ninth medal.

Before a first round FA Cup tie against Everton late in 1881, Bootle discovered that they only had eight players. Three spectators were asked to play and Bootle won the tie. In the second round, with a full team, Bootle lost 4-0 to a team called Turton.

SCOTTISH FA CUP 1881-82

FOURTH ROUND

Falkirk v Milton of Campai	3-1
Rangers v Thornliebank	2-0
Clyde v Edinburgh University	3-2
Kilmarnock v Our Boys	9-2
Queen's Park v Johnstone	3-2
Cartvale v Glasgow University	5-4
Hibernian v West Benhar	*8-0
Kilmarnock Athletic v Mauchline	3-2
Partick Thistle v Glasgow Athletic	1-0
Arthurlie v Helensburgh	*1-0
West Calder v Stranraer (scratched)	wo
South Western	bye
Dumbarton	bye
Beith	bye
Vale of Teith	bye
Shotts	bye

*after a drawn game

FIFTH ROUND

Arthurlie v Kilmarnock	4-1
West Calder v Falkirk	4-2
Queen's Park v Partick Thistle	10-0
Shotts v Vale of Teith	5-0
Kilmarnock Athletic v Beith	2-1
Cartvale v Clyde	5-4
Rangers v South Western	†6-4
Dumbarton v Hibernian	†4-1

†after a protested game

SIXTH ROUND

Queen's Park v Shotts	15-0
Kilmarnock Athletic v Arthurlie	5-2
Dumbarton v Rangers	†5-1
Cartvale v West Calder	5-3

†after a protested game

SEMI-FINAL

Queen's Park v Kilmarnock Athletic	3-2
Dumbarton v Cartvale	11-2

FINAL AT CATHKIN PARK

Queen's Park v Dumbarton	2-2, 4-1

SCOTTISH FA CUP 1882-83

FOURTH ROUND

Hurlford v Vale of Teith	3-2
Hibernian v Thistle	2-2, 4-1
Arthurlie v Queen of the South Wanderers	3-1
Dumbarton v Thornliebank	3-0
Queen's Park v Cambuslang	5-0
Lugar Boswell v Renton	5-3
Third Lanark v Dunblane	7-1
Kilmarnock Athletic v Abercorn	5-2
Pollockshields Athletic v Johnstone	3-1
Vale of Leven v Edinburgh University	2-0
Partick Thistle v Glasgow University (scratched)	wo

FIFTH ROUND

Vale of Leven v Lugar Boswell	5-0
Queen's Park v Hurlford	7-2
Arthurlie v Hibernian	†6-0
Third Lanark	bye
Dumbarton	bye
Kilmarnock Athletic	bye
Partick Thistle	bye
Pollockshields Athletic	bye

†after a protested game

SIXTH ROUND

Vale of Leven v Partick Thistle	4-0
Pollockshields Athletic v Third Lanark	5-2
Dumbarton v Queen's Park	3-1
Kilmarnock Athletic v Arthurlie	***1-0

***after three drawn games

SEMI-FINAL

Vale of Leven v Kilmarnock Athletic	*2-0
Dumbarton v Pollockshields Athletic	*5-0

*after a drawn game

FINAL AT HAMPDEN PARK

Dumbarton v Vale of Leven	2-2, 2-1

FA CUP 1882-83

SECOND ROUND

Blackburn Olympic v Lower Darwen	9-1
Darwen Ramblers v Haslingden	3-2
Darwen v Blackburn Rovers	1-0
Druids v Northwich Victoria	5-0
Bolton Wanderers v Liverpool Ramblers	3-0
Eagley v Halliwell	3-1
Old Carthusians v Etonian Ramblers	7-0
Royal Engineers v Reading	8-0
Clapham Rovers v Hanover United	7-1
Windsor v United Hospitals	3-1
Old Etonians v Brentwood	2-1
Swifts v Upton Park	*3-2
Hendon v Chatham	2-1
Great Marlow v Reading Minster (scratched)	wo
Phoenix Bessemer v Grimsby	8-1
The Wednesday v Lockwood Brothers	6-0
Nottingham Forest v Heeley	7-2
Aston Villa v Wednesbury Old Alliance	4-1
Aston Unity v Mitchell's St George's	3-0
Walsall Town v Stafford Road Works	4-1
Church	bye
Old Westminsters	bye
Rochester	bye
South Reading	bye
Notts County	bye

*drawn game for which no score is available

THIRD ROUND

Blackburn Olympic v Darwen Ramblers	8-0
Church v Darwen	*2-0
Druids v Bolton Wanderers	**1-0
Old Carthusians v Old Westminsters	3-2
Clapham Rovers v Windsor	3-0
Old Etonians v Rochester	7-0
Hendon v South Reading	11-1
Notts County v Phoenix Bessemer	*3-2
The Wednesday v Nottingham Forest	*3-2
Aston Villa v Aston Unity	3-1
Eagley	bye
Royal Engineers	bye
Swifts	bye
Great Marlow	bye
Walsall Town	bye

*drawn game for which no score is available
**two drawn games for which no scores are available

FOURTH ROUND

Blackburn Olympic v Church	2-0
Druids v Eagley	2-1
Old Carthusians v Royal Engineers	6-2
Old Etonians v Swifts	2-0
Hendon v Great Marlow	3-0
Notts County v The Wednesday	4-1
Aston Villa v Walsall Town	2-1
Clapham Rovers	bye

FIFTH ROUND

Blackburn Olympic v Druids	4-0
Old Carthusians v Clapham Rovers	5-3
Old Etonians v Hendon	4-2
Notts County v Aston Villa	4-3

SEMI-FINAL

Blackburn Olympic v Old Carthusians	4-0
Old Etonians v Notts County	2-1

FINAL AT KENNINGTON OVAL

Blackburn Olympic v Old Etonians	2-1

Blackburn Olympic, the first winners of the Cup to come from the North of England, and the first overtly professional winners, are perhaps the least known of all successful Cup Finalists. Their star rose suddenly and declined just as quickly. After reaching the semi-final the following season they were never heard of again. Olympic even had a manager, one Jack Hunter, whose earlier career had been with a travelling circus. He took his team away to Blackpool before the Final. Of his players, two were weavers, one a spinner, one a plumber, one a metal worker and two were unemployed other than football. A far cry from Old Etonians, last of the English amateur finalists.

Major Competitions in Season 1883-84

WEST BROMWICH

Albion Football Club.

SEASON TICKET.

1883-1884.

To Admit to all Matches on the

FOUR ACRES,

SITUATE IN SEAGAR STREET.

PRICE :—THREE SHILLINGS.

Above *A West Bromwich Albion season ticket for 1883-84. For one third of the price of admission to the popular side for a single game in 1974, the Throstles fan could watch a whole season's football in the Midlands.*

Top *The first Blackburn Rovers side to win the FA Cup in 1884. Their opponents were the Scots side Queen's Park. If the latter had won they would have completed a remarkable double, for they had already won the Scottish Cup. In fact they returned to Glasgow extremely bitter at the game's refereeing. Under Scottish rules at the time the offside law only required two defenders between the ball and the goal, but English law required three. Queen's scored two goals that would have been allowed in Scotland and felt thoroughly deprived. They were also upset that Blackburn had four full-time professionals, payment of players still being illegal in Scotland.*

FA CUP 1883-84

THIRD ROUND

Blackburn Rovers v Padiham	3-0
Staveley v Lockwood Brothers	1-0
Upton Park v Reading	6-1
Eagley v Preston North End	1-9
Swifts v Clapham Rovers	2-1
Notts County v Grantham	4-1
Bolton Wanderers v Irwell Springs	8-1
Queen's Park v Oswestry	7-1
Aston Villa v Wednesbury Old Alliance	7-4
Wednesbury Town v Derby Midland	1-0
Romford v Brentwood	1-4
Old Foresters	bye
Old Westminsters	bye
Blackburn Olympic	bye
Old Wykehamists	bye
Northwich Victoria	bye

FOURTH ROUND

Blackburn Rovers v Staveley	5-0
Upton Park v Preston North End	1-1, wo*
Swifts v Old Foresters	2-1
Notts County v Bolton Wanderers	2-2, 2-1
Queen's Park v Aston Villa	6-1
Old Westminsters v Wednesbury Town	5-1
Blackburn Olympic v Old Wykehamists	9-1
Brentwood v Northwich Victoria	1-3

*Upton Park protested that Preston paid their players. The FA upheld the protest and disqualified Preston before the replay.

FIFTH ROUND

Blackburn Rovers v Upton Park	3-0
Swifts v Notts County	1-1, 0-1
Queen's Park v Old Westminsters	1-0
Blackburn Olympic v Northwich Victoria	9-1

SEMI-FINAL

Blackburn Rovers v Notts County	1-0
Queen's Park v Blackburn Olympic	4-1

FINAL AT KENNINGTON OVAL

Blackburn Rovers v Queen's Park	2-1

SCOTTISH FA CUP 1883-84

FOURTH ROUND

Mauchline v Royal Albert	4-0
St Bernard's v Thornliebank	2-0
Vale of Leven v Harp	6-0
Pollockshields Athletic v Our Boys	11-0
Dunblane v Rangers	0-6
Kilmarnock Athletic v Cambuslang	2-3
5th KRV v Hibernian	1-8
Partick Thistle v Queen's Park	0-4
Cartvale v Abercorn	4-2
Battlefield v Edinburgh University (scratched)	wo
Arthurlie	bye

FIFTH ROUND

Arthurlie v Vale of Leven	0-0, 1-3
Mauchline v Pollockshields Athletic	2-3
St Bernard's v Rangers	0-3
Queen's Park	bye
Battlefield	bye
Hibernian	bye
Cambuslang	bye
Cartvale	bye

SIXTH ROUND

Cambuslang v Rangers	2-5
Queen's Park v Cartvale	6-1
Vale of Leven v Pollockshields Athletic	4-2
Hibernian v Battlefield	6-1

SEMI-FINAL

Vale of Leven v Rangers	3-0
Hibernian v Queen's Park	1-5

FINAL

Cup awarded to Queen's Park	†

†Vale of Leven wanted to postpone the final because of the illness of two players and the family bereavement of another. But the FA, although sympathetic, decided that was impossible due to other engagements, such as the international against England. Vale did not turn up for the final and the Cup was awarded to Queen's Park.

When Blackburn Rovers reached The Oval for the Cup Final in 1882 they had gone 35 consecutive games without defeat, then recognised to be the longest run of first-class fixtures without setback in English football. Since Darwen defeated them in the first round of the 1880-81 competition, Rovers had won 31 games and drawn four. One of those victories was against mighty Preston North End in the latter's first ever professional game. Blackburn won reasonably convincingly, 16-0.

Major Competitions: Seasons 1884-85 & 1885-86

FA CUP 1884-85

THIRD ROUND

Blackburn Rovers v Witton	6-1
West Bromwich Albion v Aston Villa	††3-0
Druids v Chirk	4-1
Grimsby Town v Lincoln City	1-0
Chatham v Hanover United	2-0
Lower Darwen v Darwen Old Wanderers	4-2
Church v Southport	10-0
Queen's Park v Leek	3-2
Old Wykehamists v Upton Park	2-1
Notts County v Sheffield	9-0
Walsall Swifts v Mitchell's St George's	3-2
Nottingham Forest v The Wednesday	2-1
Swifts v Old Westminsters	2-1
Romford	bye
Old Carthusians	bye
Darwen	bye
Old Etonians	bye
Middlesbrough	bye

††Two drawn games (scores unavailable)

FOURTH ROUND

Blackburn Rovers v Romford	8-0
West Bromwich Albion v Druids	1-0*
Old Carthusians v Grimsby Town	3-0
Chatham v Lower Darwen	1-0
Church v Darwen	3-0
Queen's Park v Old Wykehamists	7-0
Notts County v Walsall Swifts	4-1
Nottingham Forest v Swifts	1-0
Old Etonians v Middlesbrough	5-2

*Druids arrived with only ten men and refused to take the field. West Bromwich therefore scored within five seconds of the kick-off, whereupon Druids decided to take part. This 'goal' is not normally recorded and West Bromwich scored again to 'officially' win 1-0

FIFTH ROUND

Old Carthusians v Chatham	3-0
Blackburn Rovers	bye
West Bromwich Albion	bye
Church	bye
Queen's Park	bye
Notts County	bye
Nottingham Forest	bye
Old Etonians	bye

SIXTH ROUND

Blackburn Rovers v West Bromwich Albion	2-0
Old Carthusians v Church	1-0
Queen's Park v Notts County	2-2, 2-1
Nottingham Forest v Old Etonians	2-0

SEMI-FINAL

Blackburn Rovers v Old Carthusians	5-0
Queen's Park v Nottingham Forest	1-1, 3-0

FINAL AT KENNINGTON OVAL

Blackburn Rovers v Queen's Park	2-0

Blackburn Rovers defeated Queen's Park in both the 1884 and 1885 FA Cup Finals. These remain the only occasions on which the same clubs have contested consecutive Finals. Queen's Park were also the last amateur club to appear in an English Cup Final.
On the way to the 1885 Cup Final Queen's Park defeated both the Nottingham clubs, then considered second only to Blackburn, after a replay. The second semi-final against Nottingham Forest is the only semi-final ever to be played outside England. It was staged at Merchiston Castle School in Edinburgh and it helped Forest set up their remarkable record of having been drawn to play Cup ties in all four home countries. In the first round of the 1888-89 competition they were drawn to play Linfield in Belfast. In fact by the time they arrived Linfield had withdrawn so the game become a friendly instead. No Scottish club ever reached the final again and three years later, the Scottish Football Association banned its members from entering competitions other than its own.

SCOTTISH FA CUP 1884-85

FOURTH ROUND

Hibernian v Ayr	5-1
Morton v Wishaw Swifts	2-1
Vale of Leven v Arthurlie	2-1
Annbank v Queen of the South Wanderers	5-2
Battlefield v Pollockshields Athletic	3-0
Our Boys v West Benhar	3-3, 3-8
Renton v St Mirren	2-1
Rangers v Arbroath	3-4†, 8-1
Dumbarton v Partick Thistle	6-3
Cambuslang v Thornliebank	2-2, 0-0*

†Rangers protested the result and the SFA ordered a replay
*Both teams went through to the next round

FIFTH ROUND

Hibernian v Morton	4-0
Cambuslang v Dumbarton	4-1
Annbank v West Benhar	5-1
Rangers	bye
Renton	bye
Battlefield	bye
Vale of Leven	bye
Thornliebank	bye

SIXTH ROUND

Hibernian v Annbank	5-0
Vale of Leven v Thornliebank	4-3
Renton v Rangers	5-3
Cambuslang v Battlefield	3-1

SEMI-FINAL

Renton v Hibernian	3-2
Vale of Leven v Cambuslang	0-0, 3-1

FINAL AT HAMPDEN PARK

Renton v Vale of Leven	0-0, 3-1

SCOTTISH FA CUP 1885-86

FOURTH ROUND

Dumbarton v Partick Thistle	3-0
Queen of the South Wanderers v Arthurlie	†
Cambuslang v Wishaw Swifts	9-0
Hibernian v Arbroath	5-3
Renton v Cowlairs	4-0
Queen's Park v Airdrieonians	1-0
Third Lanark v Ayr	3-2*, 3-3, 5-1
Abercorn v Strathmore	7-2
Vale of Leven v Harp	6-0
Port Glasgow Athletic	bye

* replayed after Ayr protested
† Arthurlie won the tie. There is no record of the score

FIFTH ROUND

Renton v Vale of Leven	2-2, 3-0
Third Lanark v Port Glasgow Athletic	1-1, 1-1, 4-1
Arthurlie v Queen's Park	1-2
Abercorn v Cambuslang	0-1
Dumbarton v Hibernian	2-2, 3-4

SIXTH ROUND

Hibernian v Cambuslang	3-2
Third Lanark	bye
Renton	bye
Queen's Park	bye

SEMI-FINAL

Hibernian v Renton	0-2
Third Lanark v Queen's Park	0-3

FINAL AT CATHKIN PARK

Queen's Park v Renton	3-1

Rangers were drawn to play Arbroath in the Fourth Round of the 1884-85 Scottish Cup. Having lost 4-3 they sent home a telegram reading 'beaten on a back green'. Having measured the pitch they found it was only 49 yards 2 ft 1 in wide, 11 inches short of the minimum. They protested, the game was replayed, and Rangers won 8-1.

FA CUP 1885-86

THIRD ROUND

Blackburn Rovers v Darwen Old Wanderers	6-1
Staveley v Nottingham Forest	2-1
South Reading v Clapham Rovers*	wo
Burslem Port Vale v Leek (scratched)	wo
Swifts v Old Harrovians*	wo
Church v Rossendale	5-1
South Shore v Halliwell	6-1
Notts County v Notts Rangers	3-0
Wolverhampton Wanderers v Walsall Swifts	2-1
Old Westminsters v Romford	5-1
Preston North End* v Bolton Wanderers	3-2‡
Small Heath Alliance v Derby County	4-2
Davenham v Crewe Alexandra	2-1
Middlesbrough v Grimsby Town	2-1
Brentwood	bye
West Bromwich Albion	bye
Old Carthusians	bye
Redcar	bye

*disqualified
‡Preston disqualified after a protest

FOURTH ROUND

West Bromwich Albion v Wolverhampton Wanderers	3-1
Brentwood v South Reading	3-0
Blackburn Rovers	bye
Staveley	bye
Burslem Port Vale	bye
Swifts	bye
Church	bye
South Shore	bye
Notts County	bye
Old Carthusians	bye
Old Westminsters	bye
Bolton Wanderers	bye
Small Heath Alliance	bye
Davenham	bye
Redcar	bye
Middlesbrough	bye

FIFTH ROUND

Blackburn Rovers v Staveley	7-1
Brentwood v Burslem Port Vale†	wo
Swifts v Church	6-2
South Shore v Notts County	2-1
West Bromwich Albion v Old Carthusians	1-0
Old Westminsters v Bolton Wanderers*	wo
Small Heath Alliance v Davenham	2-1
Redcar v Middlesbrough	2-1

*disqualified
† Burslem Port Vale scratched after one drawn game

SIXTH ROUND

Blackburn Rovers v Brentwood	3-1
Swifts v South Shore	2-1
West Bromwich Albion v Old Westminsters	6-0
Small Heath Alliance v Redcar	2-0

SEMI-FINAL

Blackburn Rovers v Swifts	2-1
West Bromwich Albion v Small Heath Alliance	4-0

FINAL AT KENNINGTON OVAL

Blackburn Rovers v West Bromwich Albion	0-0, 2-0*

*replay at The Racecourse, Derby

The 1886 Cup Final replay, played at The Racecourse, Derby, was the first Final ever played outside London. In winning the game Blackburn Rovers completed a hat-trick of successes never since repeated and were presented with a special shield – which still hangs in their boardroom – to mark the feat. The match is far more famous however, for the performance of the Blackburn captain Jimmy Brown. In his last ever game for the club, Brown dribbled the length of the pitch to score one of the greatest goals in the history of the Cup. In so doing he became the only man ever to score in three consecutive Cup Finals, and, more surprisingly, was immortalized in Arnold Bennett's 'The Card' for the feat.

Major Competitions: Seasons 1886-87 & 1887-88

FA CUP 1886-87†

THIRD ROUND

Aston Villa v Wolverhampton Wanderers	2-2, 3-3, 2-0
Horncastle v Grantham	2-0
Darwen v Bolton Wanderers	4-3
Chirk v Goldenhill (disqualified)	wo
Glasgow Rangers v Cowlairs	3-2
Lincoln City v Gainsborough Trinity	2-2, 1-0
Old Westminsters v Old Etonians	3-0
Partick Thistle v Cliftonville	11-1
Mitchell's St George's v Walsall Town	7-2
Lockwood Brothers v Nottingham Forest	2-1
Notts County v Staveley	3-0
Great Marlow v Dulwich	2-0
Preston North End v Renton	2-0
Old Foresters v Chatham	4-1
Old Carthusians v Caledonians (absent)	wo
Leek v Burslem Port Vale	2-2, 1-1, 3-1
Crewe Alexandra	bye
Swifts	bye
West Bromwich Albion	bye

FOURTH ROUND

Leek v Crewe Alexandra	1-0
Old Foresters v Swifts	2-0
West Bromwich Albion v Mitchell's St George's	1-0
Aston Villa	bye
Horncastle	bye
Darwen	bye
Chirk	bye
Glasgow Rangers	bye
Lincoln City	bye
Old Westminsters	bye
Partick Thistle	bye
Lockwood Brothers	bye
Notts County	bye
Great Marlow	bye
Preston North End	bye
Old Carthusians	bye

FIFTH ROUND

Aston Villa v Horncastle	5-0
Darwen v Chirk	3-1
Glasgow Rangers v Lincoln City	3-0
Old Westminsters v Partick Thistle	1-0
West Bromwich Albion v Lockwood Brothers	2-1*
Notts County v Great Marlow	5-2
Preston North End v Old Foresters	3-0
Old Carthusians v Leek	2-0

*after a disputed game

SIXTH ROUND

Aston Villa v Darwen	3-2
Glasgow Rangers v Old Westminsters	5-1
West Bromwich Albion v Notts County	4-1
Preston North End v Old Carthusians	2-1

SEMI-FINAL

Aston Villa v Glasgow Rangers	3-1
West Bromwich Albion v Preston North End	3-1

FINAL AT KENNINGTON OVAL

Aston Villa v West Bromwich Albion	2-0

†There is some confusion as to the exact specification of the rounds. The *Football Annual for 1887*, edited by the honorary secretary of the Football Association, Charles Alcock, gives seven rounds and a Final. Later historys, such as the official *History of the Cup* give only three rounds and a Final after qualifying matches.

Hibernian's defeat of Dumbarton in the 1887 Scottish Cup final was the first time that an Edinburgh club had won the Scottish Cup. It was also the first and only time that the final was contested at Crosshills. The same year Hibs played and defeated Preston North End at their new ground, Easter Road, in what was billed as the 'Association Football Championship of the World' More remotely Hibernian's success was one of the main promptings for the founding of Celtic in Glasgow.

SCOTTISH FA CUP 1886-87

FIFTH ROUND

Hibernian v Queen of the South Wanderers	7-3
Vale of Leven v Cambuslang Hibernians	2-0
Clyde v Third Lanark	0-0, 2-4
Queen's Park v Cambuslang	1-1, 5-4
Hurlford v Morton	5-1
Kilmarnock v Dunblane	6-0
Port Glasgow Athletic v St Bernard's	6-2
Dumbarton v Harp (scratched)	wo

SIXTH ROUND

Port Glasgow Athletic v Vale of Leven	1-3
Kilmarnock v Queen's Park	0-5
Third Lanark v Hibernian	1-2
Hurlford v Dumbarton	0-0, 2-1*, 1-3

*Hurlford insisted on playing on a frozen pitch; the result was declared null and void by the Scottish FA

SEMI-FINAL

Hibernian v Vale of Leven	3-1
Queen's Park v Dumbarton	1-2

FINAL AT CROSSHILLS

Hibernian v Dumbarton	2-1

Below *The West Bromwich Albion side that won the FA Cup in 1888. It was their third consecutive Final but their first ever success. Billy Bassett is seated, second from the left. After defeating Preston North End at Trent Bridge in the 1887 semi-final, West Bromwich met them again in the actual Final in 1888. To say that Preston were confident is to put it mildly. One of their modest requests was that they might be photographed with the Cup before the game. They explained that they would be dirty afterwards and that this would spoil the picture. The referee, Major Marindin, who controlled eight Finals in all as well as playing in two, suggested that 'Had you not better win it first?' Apparently they had ten good scoring chances to Albion's two, but Albion converted 100% and Preston only 10%. It was called the greatest upset in the history of the Cup, and perhaps remained so until Sunderland defeated Leeds. West Bromwich's inspiration was 5ft 5in Billy Bassett, who went on to win eight consecutive caps against the Scots. Albion went on to beat Aston Villa in a series of three games to become the 'Champions of the Midlands'. Then then went to Scotland to play Scottish Cup winners Renton for the title of 'Champions of the World'. The game was played in a blinding snowstorm and Renton won.*

FA CUP 1887-88†

FIFTH ROUND

West Bromwich Albion v Stoke	4-1
Old Carthusians v Bootle	2-0
Derby Junction v Chirk	1-0
Darwen v Blackburn Rovers	0-3
Nottingham Forest v The Wednesday	2-4
Aston Villa v Preston North End	1-3
Middlesbrough v Old Foresters (scratched)	4-0*
Crewe Alexandra v Derby County	1-0

*Old Foresters protested at the state of the pitch and the FA ordered a replay. Meanwhile, Old Foresters scratched and Middlesbrough thus went through without a second game

SIXTH ROUND

West Bromwich Albion v Old Carthusians	4-2
Derby Junction v Blackburn Rovers	2-1
The Wednesday v Preston North End	1-3
Middlesbrough v Crewe Alexandra	0-2

SEMI-FINAL

West Bromwich Albion v Derby Junction	3-0
Preston North End v Crewe Alexandra	4-0

FINAL AT KENNINGTON OVAL

West Bromwich Albion v Preston North End	2-1

†There is confusion about the exact specification of the rounds. The *Football Annual for 1888* gives seven rounds and a Final, as do newspapers for that year.

SCOTTISH FA CUP 1887-88

FIFTH ROUND

Arbroath v Cowlairs	5-1
Cambuslang v Ayr	10-0
Thistle v Vale of Leven Wanderers	2-9
Abercorn v St Bernard's	9-0
Queen's Park v Partick Thistle	2-0
St Mirren v Renton	2-3
Our Boys v Albion Rovers	4-1
Dundee Wanderers v Carfin Shamrock	5-2

SIXTH ROUND

Abercorn v Arbroath	3-1
Renton v Dundee Wanderers	5-1
Cambuslang v Our Boys	6-0
Queen's Park v Vale of Leven Wanderers	7-1

SEMI-FINAL

Renton v Queen's Park	3-1
Abercorn v Cambuslang	1-1, 1-10

FINAL AT HAMPDEN PARK

Renton v Cambuslang	6-1

FA CUP 1888-89

FIRST ROUND

Grimsby Town v Sunderland Albion	3-1
Bootle v Preston North End	0-3
Halliwell v Crewe Alexandra	2-2, 5-1
Birmingham St George's v Long Eaton Rangers	3-2
Chatham v South Shore	2-1
Nottingham Forest v Linfield (scratched)	2-2, wo*
Small Heath v West Bromwich Albion	2-3
Burnley v Old Westminsters	4-3
Wolverhampton Wanderers v Old Carthusians	4-3
Walsall Town Swifts v Sheffield Heeley	5-1
The Wednesday v Notts Rangers	1-1, 3-0
Notts County v Old Brightonians	2-0
Blackburn Rovers v Accrington	1-1, 5-0
Swifts v Wrexham	3-1
Aston Villa v Witton	3-2
Derby County v Derby Junction	1-0

*Nottingham Forest travelled to Belfast for the replay but Linfield had scratched in the interim and the clubs played a friendly instead

SECOND ROUND

Grimsby Town v Preston North End	0-2
Halliwell v Birmingham St George's	2-3
Chatham v Nottingham Forest	1-1, 2-2, 3-2
West Bromwich Albion v Burnley	5-1
Wolverhampton Wanderers v Walsall Town Swifts	6-1
The Wednesday v Notts County	3-2
Blackburn Rovers v Swifts (scratched)	wo
Aston Villa v Derby County	5-3

THIRD ROUND

Preston North End v Birmingham St George's	2-0
Chatham v West Bromwich Albion	1-10
Wolverhampton Wanderers v The Wednesday	5-0
Blackburn Rovers v Aston Villa	8-1

SEMI-FINAL

Preston North End v West Bromwich Albion	1-0
Wolverhampton Wanderers v Blackburn Rovers	1-1, 3-1

FINAL AT KENNINGTON OVAL

Preston North End v Wolverhampton Wanderers	3-0

SCOTTISH FA CUP 1888-89

FIFTH ROUND

Third Lanark v Abercorn	5-4*, 2-2, 2-2, 3-1
Renton v Arbroath	3-3, 4-0
Celtic v Clyde	0-1†, 9-2
Dumbarton v Mossend Swifts	3-1
St Mirren v Queen of the South Wanderers	3-1
Campsie	bye
Dumbarton Athletic	bye
East Stirlingshire	bye

*Abercorn protested about bad light
†Celtic protested about bad light and the state of the pitch

SIXTH ROUND

Third Lanark v Campsie	6-0
Dumbarton v St Mirren	1-1, 2-2, 2-2, 3-1
Dumbarton Athletic v Renton	1-2
East Stirlingshire v Celtic	1-2

SEMI-FINAL

Dumbarton v Celtic	1-4
Third Lanark v Renton	2-0

FINAL AT HAMPDEN PARK

Third Lanark v Celtic	3-0‡, 2-1

‡The first game was declared unofficial because of a snowstorm. Third Lanark tried to claim the Cup but the SFA ordered a replay.

William Townley scored the first ever Cup Final hat-trick for Blackburn against The Wednesday in the 1890 Final. Rovers won 6-1 to record the highest score in a Final tie. Wednesday arrived for the Final having lost a disputed earlier tie against Notts County.

FOOTBALL LEAGUE 1888-89

		P	W	D	L	F	A	Pts
1	Preston	22	18	4	0	74	15	40
2	Aston Villa	22	12	5	5	61	43	29
3	Wolves	22	12	4	6	50	37	28
4	Blackburn	22	10	6	6	66	45	26
5	Bolton	22	10	2	10	63	59	22
6	WBA	22	10	2	10	40	46	22
7	Accrington	22	6	8	8	48	48	20
8	Everton	22	9	2	11	35	46	20
9	Burnley	22	7	3	12	42	62	17
10	Derby	22	7	2	13	41	60	16
11	Notts County	22	5	2	15	39	73	12
12	Stoke	22	4	4	14	26	51	12

Top *William McGregor of Aston Villa, whose open letter of 2 March 1888 led to the formation of the Football League. A meeting was held at Anderton's Hotel on the eve of the Cup Final (23 March 1888) and the idea was approved in principle. The details were finalized on 17 April at the Royal Hotel in Manchester by the twelve member clubs. With only 22 fixture dates available, other hopefuls—including Sheffield Wednesday and Nottingham Forest—had to be turned down. The League had grown in simple response to the need to guarantee fixtures. While there were only Cup competitions fixtures would always be called off at short notice for replays, and friendlies could never be guaranteed. Because of the uncertainty, spectators were increasingly reluctant to commit themselves to turning up to a match that might never be played—and so emerged McGregor's inevitable solution. Preston were the first winners of the League. Their performance in 1888-89 was unique for they remain the only side in England and Scotland to have gone a whole season without a League or or Cup defeat.*

FOOTBALL LEAGUE 1889-90

		P	W	D	L	F	A	Pts
1	Preston	22	15	3	4	71	30	33
2	Everton	22	14	3	5	65	40	31
3	Blackburn	22	12	3	7	78	41	27
4	Wolves	22	10	5	7	51	38	25
5	WBA	22	11	3	8	47	50	25
6	Accrington	22	9	6	7	53	56	24
7	Derby	22	9	3	10	43	55	21
8	Aston Villa	22	7	5	10	43	51	19
9	Bolton	22	9	1	12	54	65	19
10	Notts County	22	6	5	11	43	51	17
11	Burnley	22	4	5	13	36	65	13
12	Stoke	22	3	4	15	27	69	10

FA CUP 1889-90

FIRST ROUND

Preston North End v Newton Heath	6-1
Lincoln City v Chester	2-0
Bolton Wanderers v Belfast Distillery	10-1
Sheffield United v Burnley	2-1
The Wednesday v Swifts	6-1
Accrington v West Bromwich Albion	3-1
Notts County v Birmingham St George's	4-4, 6-2
South Shore v Aston Villa	2-4
Bootle v Sunderland Albion*	1-3
Derby Midland v Nottingham Forest	3-0
Blackburn Rovers v Sunderland	4-2
Newcastle West End v Grimsby Town	1-2
Wolverhampton Wanderers v Old Carthusians	2-0
Small Heath v Clapton	3-1
Stoke v Old Westminsters	3-0
Everton v Derby County	11-2

*Sunderland Albion were disqualified

SECOND ROUND

Preston North End v Lincoln City	4-0
Bolton Wanderers v Sheffield United	13-0
The Wednesday v Accrington	2-1
Notts County v Aston Villa	4-1
Bootle v Derby Midland	2-1
Blackburn Rovers v Grimsby Town	3-0
Wolverhampton Wanderers v Small Heath	2-1
Stoke v Everton	4-2

THIRD ROUND

Preston North End v Bolton Wanderers	2-3
The Wednesday v Notts County	5-0*, 2-3*, 2-1
Bootle v Blackburn Rovers	0-7
Wolverhampton Wanderers v Stoke	3-2

*replayed after protest on both occasions

SEMI-FINAL

Bolton Wanderers v The Wednesday	1-2
Blackburn Rovers v Wolverhampton Wanderers	1-0

FINAL AT KENNINGTON OVAL

Blackburn Rovers v The Wednesday	6-1

SCOTTISH FA CUP 1889-90

FOURTH ROUND

Aberdeen v Queen's Park	1-13
Airdrieonians v Abercorn	2-3
Grangemouth v Vale of Leven	1-7
Third Lanark v Linthouse	2-0
Lanemark v St Mirren	2-8
Moffat v Carfin Shamrock	4-2
Ayr v Leith Athletic	1-4
Cowdenbeath v Dunblane	†
Hibernian v Queen of the South Wanderers	†
Kilbirnie v East Stirlingshire	†
Heart of Midlothian v Alloa Athletic	†
East End v Cambuslang	†

†No scores are available. The first named team won in each case.

FIFTH ROUND

Queen's Park v St Mirren	1-0
Cowdenbeath v Abercorn	2-8
Vale of Leven v Heart of Midlothian	3-1
East End v Moffat	2-2*
Third Lanark	bye
Hibernian	bye
Leith Athletic	bye
Kilbirnie	bye

*East End won the replay

SIXTH ROUND

Queen's Park v Leith Athletic	1-0
Abercorn v Hibernian	6-2
Vale of Leven v East End	4-0
Third Lanark v Kilbirnie	4-1

SEMI-FINAL

Vale of Leven v Third Lanark	3-0
Queen's Park v Abercorn	2-0

FINAL AT IBROX PARK

Queen's Park v Vale of Leven	1-1, 2-1

FA CUP 1890-91

FIRST ROUND

Middlesbrough Ironopolis v Blackburn Rovers 1-2*, 0-3
Chester v Lincoln City 1-0
Accrington v Bolton Wanderers 2-2, 5-1
Long Eaton Rangers v Wolverhampton Wanderers 2-3
Royal Arsenal v Derby County 1-2
The Wednesday v Halliwell 12-0
Crusaders v Birmingham St George's 0-2
West Bromwich Albion v Old Westminsters (scratched) wo
Darwen v Kidderminster 3-1*, 13-0
Sunderland v Everton 1-0
Clapton v Nottingham Forest 0-14
Sunderland Albion v 93rd Highlanders 2-0
Sheffield United v Notts County 1-9
Burnley v Crewe Alexandra 4-2
Stoke v Preston North End 3-0
Aston Villa v Casuals 13-1
*replayed after protest

SECOND ROUND

Blackburn Rovers v Chester 7-0
Accrington v Wolverhampton Wanderers 2-3
Derby County v The Wednesday 2-3
Birmingham St George's v West Bromwich Albion 0-3
Darwen v Sunderland 0-2
Nottingham Forest v Sunderland Albion 1-1, 0-0, 5-0
Notts County v Burnley 2-1
Stoke v Aston Villa 3-0

THIRD ROUND

Blackburn Rovers v Wolverhampton Wanderers 2-0
The Wednesday v West Bromwich Albion 0-2
Sunderland v Nottingham Forest 4-0
Notts County v Stoke 1-0

SEMI-FINAL

Blackburn Rovers v West Bromwich Albion 3-2
Sunderland v Notts County 3-3, 0-2

FINAL AT KENNINGTON OVAL

Blackburn Rovers v Notts County 3-1

SCOTTISH FA CUP 1890-91

FIFTH ROUND

Dumbarton v 5th KRV 8-0
Heart of Midlothian v Morton 5-1
Royal Albert v Celtic 0-4*, 0-2
St Mirren v Queen's Park 2-3
Abercorn bye
Third Lanark bye
East Stirlingshire bye
Leith Athletic bye
*Crowd invaded the pitch 10 minutes before time and forced a replay, which was played at Ibrox.

SIXTH ROUND

Dumbarton v Celtic 3-0
Heart of Midlothian v East Stirlingshire 3-1
Third Lanark v Queen's Park 1-1, 2-2, 4-1
Leith Athletic v Abercorn 2-3

SEMI-FINAL

Dumbarton v Abercorn 3-1
Heart of Midlothian v Third Lanark 4-1

FINAL AT HAMPDEN PARK

Heart of Midlothian v Dumbarton 1-0

In the first round of the FA Cup in 1890–91, Nottingham Forest beat Clapton 14-0 at Clapton. This remains the highest away win in any English first-class fixture. In the same round Darwen scored 13 against Kidderminster, Villa 13 against Casuals and Sheffield Wednesday 12 against Halliwell. Forest's performance was part of a good day for Nottingham – County also won 9-1 away from home.

FOOTBALL LEAGUE 1890-91

	P	W	D	L	F	A	Pts
1 Everton	22	14	1	7	63	29	29
2 Preston	22	12	3	7	44	23	27
3 Notts County	22	11	4	7	52	35	26
4 Wolves	22	12	2	8	39	50	26
5 Bolton	22	12	1	9	47	34	25
6 Blackburn	22	11	2	9	52	43	24
7 Sunderland	22	10	5	7	51	31	23*
8 Burnley	22	9	3	10	52	63	21
9 Aston Villa	22	7	4	11	45	58	18
10 Accrington	22	6	4	12	28	50	16
11 Derby	22	7	1	14	47	81	15
12 WBA	22	5	2	15	34	57	12

*Two points deducted for fielding Ned Doig against WBA on 20 September 1890 before the League had approved his registration from Arbroath.

SCOTTISH LEAGUE 1890-91

	P	W	D	L	F	A	Pts
1= Dumbarton†	18	13	3	2	61	21	29
1= Rangers†	18	13	3	2	58	25	29
3 Celtic*	18	11	3	4	48	21	21
4 Cambuslang	18	8	4	6	47	42	20
5 Third Lanark*	18	8	3	7	38	39	15
6 Hearts	18	6	2	10	31	37	14
7 Abercorn	18	5	2	11	36	47	12
8 St Mirren	18	5	1	12	39	62	11
9 Vale of Leven	18	5	1	12	27	65	11
10 Cowlairs*	18	3	4	11	24	50	6

†Dumbarton and Rangers drew 2-2 in a play-off and were declared joint Champions.
*Each had four points deducted for infringements.

FOOTBALL LEAGUE 1891-92

	P	W	D	L	F	A	Pts
1 Sunderland	26	21	0	5	93	36	42
2 Preston	26	18	1	7	61	31	37
3 Bolton	26	17	2	7	51	37	36
4 Aston Villa	26	15	0	11	89	56	30
5 Everton	26	12	4	10	49	49	28
6 Wolves	26	11	4	11	59	46	26
7 Burnley	26	11	4	11	49	45	26
8 Notts County	26	11	4	11	55	51	26
9 Blackburn	26	10	6	10	58	65	26
10 Derby	26	10	4	12	46	52	24
11 Accrington	26	8	4	14	40	78	20
12 WBA	26	6	6	14	51	58	18
13 Stoke	26	5	4	17	38	61	14
14 Darwen	26	4	3	19	38	112	11

SCOTTISH LEAGUE 1891-92

	P	W	D	L	F	A	Pts
1 Dumbarton	22	18	1	3	81	26	37
2 Celtic	22	16	3	3	64	19	35
3 Hearts	22	15	4	3	64	36	34
4 Rangers	22	12	2	8	57	49	26
5 Leith	22	12	1	9	52	38	25
6 Third Lanark	22	9	4	9	44	38	22
7 Clyde	22	8	4	10	64	60	20
8 Renton	22	8	4	10	43	41	20
9 Abercorn	22	6	5	11	45	59	17
10 St Mirren	22	4	5	13	43	56	13
11 Cambuslang	22	2	6	14	21	79	10
12 Vale of Leven	22	0	5	17	24	101	5

During the 1890–91 FA Cup quarter-final between Notts County and Stoke at Trent Bridge a shot was punched off the line by County's left-back Hendry with his goalkeeper Toone well beaten. As the laws made no mention of penalties at the time, Stoke had to take a free-kick on the goal-line which Toone smothered easily. County won the match 1-0 and went on to the Final. The incident provoked so much comment that, partially as a result, penalties were introduced by the FA from September 1891. This led to another controversial incident in which Stoke were also the sufferers the next season. During a League game at Aston Villa, Stoke were losing 1-0 when a penalty was awarded them just two minutes from time. The Villa keeper picked up the ball and booted it out of the ground. By the time it had been found the referee had blown for full time. The law was soon changed to allow referees to add on time for penalties. The penalty law was changed again as late as 1892 when players were banned from touching the ball twice – and hence dribbling into the net.

FA CUP 1891-92

FIRST ROUND

Old Westminsters v West Bromwich Albion 2-3
Blackburn Rovers v Derby County 4-1
The Wednesday v Bolton Wanderers 4-1
Small Heath v Royal Arsenal 5-1
Sunderland Albion v Birmingham St George's 4-0
Nottingham Forest v Newcastle East End 2-1
Luton v Middlesbrough 0-3
Preston North End v Middlesbrough Ironopolis 2-2, 6-0
Crewe Alexandra v Wolverhampton Wanderers 2-2, 1-4
Blackpool v Sheffield United 0-3
Aston Villa v Heanor Town 4-1
Bootle v Darwen 0-2
Crusaders v Accrington 1-4
Sunderland v Notts County 4-0
Everton v Burnley 1-3
Stoke v Casuals 3-0

SECOND ROUND

West Bromwich Albion v Blackburn Rovers 3-1
The Wednesday v Small Heath 2-0
Sunderland Albion v Nottingham Forest 0-1
Middlesbrough v Preston North End 1-2
Wolverhampton Wanderers v Sheffield United 3-1
Aston Villa v Darwen 2-0
Accrington v Sunderland 1-3
Burnley v Stoke 1-3

THIRD ROUND

West Bromwich Albion v The Wednesday 2-1
Nottingham Forest v Preston North End 2-0
Wolverhampton Wanderers v Aston Villa 1-3
Sunderland v Stoke 2-2, 4-0

SEMI-FINAL

West Bromwich Albion v Nottingham Forest 1-1, 1-1, 6-2
Aston Villa v Sunderland 4-1

FINAL AT KENNINGTON OVAL

West Bromwich Albion v Aston Villa 3-0

SCOTTISH FA CUP 1891-92

SECOND ROUND

Rangers v Kilmarnock 0-0, 1-1, 3-1
Third Lanark v Dumbarton 1-3
Broxburn Shamrock v Heart of Midlothian 4-5
Annbank v Leith Athletic 2-1
Queen's Park v Bathgate Rovers 6-0
Arbroath v Renton 0-3
Celtic v Kilmarnock Athletic 3-0
Cowlairs v Mid-Annandale 11-2

THIRD ROUND

Celtic v Cowlairs 4-1
Rangers v Annbank 2-0
Renton v Heart of Midlothian 4-4, 1-1, 3-2
Dumbarton v Queen's Park 2-2, 1-4

SEMI-FINAL

Renton v Queen's Park 1-1, 0-3
Celtic v Rangers 5-3

FINAL AT IBROX PARK

Celtic v Queen's Park 1-0*, 5-1
*The final had to be replayed, the first game having been disrupted by an unexpectedly large crowd.

Major Competitions in Season 1892-93

FIRST DIVISION

	P	W	D	L	F	A	Pts
1 Sunderland	30	22	4	4	100	36	48
2 Preston	30	17	3	10	57	39	37
3 Everton	30	16	4	10	74	51	36
4 Aston Villa	30	16	3	11	73	62	35
5 Bolton	30	13	6	11	56	55	32
6 Burnley	30	13	4	13	51	44	30
7 Stoke	30	12	5	13	58	48	29
8 WBA	30	12	5	13	58	69	29
9 Blackburn	30	8	13	9	47	56	29
10 Nottm Forest	30	10	8	12	48	52	28
11 Wolves	30	12	4	14	47	68	28
12 Wednesday	30	12	3	15	55	65	27
13 Derby	30	9	9	12	52	64	27
14 Notts County	30	10	4	16	53	61	24
15 Accrington	30	6	11	13	57	81	23
16 Newton Heath	30	6	6	18	50	85	18

SCOTTISH FA CUP 1892-93

FIRST ROUND

Celtic v Linthouse	3-1
Airdrieonians v Third Lanark	3-6
Cowlairs v Queen's Park	1-4
Clyde v Dumbarton	1-6*
Motherwell v Campsie	9-2†, 6-4
St Mirren v Aberdeen	6-4
Dunblane v Broxburn Shamrock	0-3
Stenhousemuir v Heart of Midlothian	1-1, 0-8
Northern v Leith Athletic	1-3
Royal Albert v Cambuslang	6-1
Abercorn v Renton	6-0
St Bernard's v Queen of South Wanderers	5-1
Rangers v Annbank	7-0
King's Park v Monkcastle	6-1
5th KVR v Camelon	5-3
Albion Rovers v Kilmarnock	1-2

*The invasion of the pitch by the crowd caused the game to be abandoned with 25 minutes left to play. The SFA awarded the tie to Dumbarton.
†After a protest about the size of the pitch the tie was replayed.

SECOND ROUND

Celtic v 5th KVR	7-0
Leith Athletic v St Mirren	0-2
Abercorn v Third Lanark	4-5
St Bernard's v Royal Albert	5-2
Broxburn Shamrock v King's Park	3-0
Heart of Midlothian v Motherwell	4-2
Dumbarton v Rangers	0-1
Kilmarnock v Queen's Park	0-8

THIRD ROUND

Heart of Midlothian v Queen's Park	1-1, 2-5
Celtic v Third Lanark	5-1
St Bernard's v Rangers	3-2
Broxburn Shamrock v St Mirren	4-3

SEMI-FINAL

Queen's Park v Broxburn Shamrock	4-2
Celtic v St Bernard's	5-0

FINAL AT IBROX PARK

Queen's Park v Celtic	2-1

SECOND DIVISION

	P	W	D	L	F	A	Pts
1 Small Heath	22	17	2	3	90	35	36
2 Sheff United	22	16	3	3	62	19	35
3 Darwen	22	14	2	6	60	36	30
4 Grimsby	22	11	1	10	42	41	23
5 Ardwick	22	9	3	10	45	40	21
6 Burton Swifts	22	9	2	11	47	47	20
7 Northwich Vic	22	9	2	11	42	58	20
8 Bootle	22	8	3	11	49	63	19
9 Lincoln	22	7	3	12	45	51	17
10 Crewe	22	6	3	13	42	69	15
11 Burslem PV	22	6	3	13	30	57	15
12 Walsall TS	22	5	3	14	37	75	13

TEST MATCHES 1892-93

Sheffield United 1 Accrington 0
Darwen 3 Notts County 2
Newton Heath 1 Small Heath 1

Play-off
Newton Heath 5 Small Heath 2

Sheffield United and Darwen promoted
Notts County relegated
Accrington resigned from the League

SCOTTISH LEAGUE

	P	W	D	L	F	A	Pts
1 Celtic	18	14	1	3	54	25	29
2 Rangers	18	12	4	2	41	27	28
3 St Mirren	18	9	2	7	40	39	20
4 Third Lanark	18	9	1	8	53	39	19
5 Hearts	18	8	2	8	39	42	18
6 Leith	18	8	1	9	36	31	17
7 Dumbarton	18	8	1	9	35	35	17
8 Renton	18	5	5	8	31	44	15
9 Abercorn	18	5	1	12	35	52	11
10 Clyde	18	2	2	14	25	55	6

1892-93 Champions Sunderland were the second side to be called 'The Team of all the Talents'. They became the first to score 100 goals or more in a single League season. In fact this total was not surpassed until after the First World War though, by then of course teams were playing far more games. Sunderland's winning margin of 11 points over the second club, Preston North End, has been equalled but never beaten in the division since. Aston Villa equalled it in 1897 as did Manchester United in 1956.

FA CUP 1892-93

FIRST ROUND

Everton v West Bromwich Albion	4-1
Nottingham Forest v Casuals	4-0
The Wednesday v Derby County	3-2*, 0-1†, 4-2
Burnley v Small Heath	2-0
Accrington v Stoke	2-1
Preston North End v Burton Swifts	9-2
Marlow v Middlesbrough Ironopolis	1-3
Notts County v Shankhouse	4-0
Wolverhampton Wanderers v Bolton Wanderers	1-1, 2-1
Newcastle United v Middlesbrough	2-3
Darwen v Aston Villa	5-4
Grimsby Town v Stockton	5-0
Blackburn Rovers v Newton Heath	4-0
Loughborough Town v Northwich Victoria	1-2
Blackpool v Sheffield United	1-3
Sunderland v Woolwich Arsenal	6-0

*Replay after protest
† Replay after second protest

SECOND ROUND

Everton v Nottingham Forest	4-2
The Wednesday v Burnley	1-0
Accrington v Preston North End	1-4
Middlesbrough Ironopolis v Notts County	3-2
Wolverhampton Wanderers v Middlesbrough	2-1
Darwen v Grimsby Town	2-0
Blackburn Rovers v Northwich Victoria	4-1
Sheffield United v Sunderland	1-3

THIRD ROUND

Everton v The Wednesday	3-0
Preston North End v Middlesbrough Ironopolis	2-2, 7-0
Wolverhampton Wanderers v Darwen	5-0
Blackburn Rovers v Sunderland	3-0

SEMI-FINAL

Everton v Preston North End	2-2, 0-0, 2-1
Wolverhampton Wanderers v Blackburn Rovers	2-1

FINAL AT FALLOWFIELD (MANCHESTER)

Wolverhampton Wanderers v Everton	1-0

With the introduction of a Second Division in 1892 – in fact the Football League simply absorbed the Football Alliance – a promotion/relegation system of test matches was instituted. This lasted until 1898 when Stoke and Burnley, realising that if they drew their match they would both be in the First Division, contrived a scoreless draw. Suspicions were aroused and a system of two up/two down was introduced.

COLORSPORT

Right *Wolverhampton's 1893 team which won the only Final ever to be played at Fallowfield, Manchester, and the first to be initially contested outside London. An Everton reserve side had beaten the Wolves first team 4-2 the week before, but the underdogs won the real thing with a long-range headed goal from captain Harry Allen. The crowd, officially 45,000 but probably twice that number, broke down the gates and invaded the pitch and the match was played in near chaos.*

On 10 December 1892 Sheffield United defeated Burslem Port Vale 10-0 in a League fixture at Burslem. This remains the biggest away win in any Football League match. A contemporary report commented that: 'The Vale keeper lost his spectacles in the mud.'

Major Competitions in Season 1893-94

FIRST DIVISION

	P	W	D	L	F	A	Pts
1 Aston Villa	30	19	6	5	84	42	44
2 Sunderland	30	17	4	9	72	44	38
3 Derby	30	16	4	10	73	62	36
4 Blackburn	30	16	2	12	69	53	34
5 Burnley	30	15	4	11	61	51	34
6 Everton	30	15	3	12	90	57	33
7 Nottm Forest	30	14	4	12	57	48	32
8 WBA	30	14	4	12	66	59	32
9 Wolves	30	14	3	13	52	63	31
10 Sheff United	30	13	5	12	47	61	31
11 Stoke	30	13	3	14	65	79	29
12 Wednesday	30	9	8	13	48	57	26
13 Bolton	30	10	4	16	38	52	24
14 Preston	30	10	3	17	44	56	23
15 Darwen	30	7	5	18	37	83	19
16 Newton Heath	30	6	2	22	36	72	14

SECOND DIVISION

	P	W	D	L	F	A	Pts
1 Liverpool	28	22	6	0	77	18	50
2 Small Heath	28	21	0	7	103	44	42
3 Notts County	28	18	3	7	70	31	39
4 Newcastle	28	15	6	7	66	39	36
5 Grimsby	28	15	2	11	71	58	32
6 Burton Swifts	28	14	3	11	79	61	31
7 Burslem PV	28	13	4	11	66	64	30
8 Lincoln	28	11	6	11	59	58	28
9 Woolwich A	28	12	4	12	52	55	28
10 Walsall TS	28	10	3	15	51	61	23
11 Md Ironopolis	28	8	4	16	37	72	20
12 Crewe	28	6	7	15	42	73	19
13 Ardwick	28	8	2	18	47	71	18
14 Rotherham Twn	28	6	3	19	44	91	15
15 Northwich Vic	28	3	3	22	30	98	9

TEST MATCHES 1893-94

Preston North End 4 Notts County 0
Small Heath 3 Darwen 1
Liverpool 2 Newton Heath 0

Liverpool and Small Heath promoted
Darwen and Newton Heath relegated

At the beginning of the 1894-95 season Liverpool completed what remained the longest League run without defeat until Leeds broke it in 1969. They had joined the Second Division in 1893 and remained undefeated in the 28-game season. They then won their Test Match to gain promotion to the First, where they drew the first two games before suffering their first ever League defeat by Aston Villa. This was after a run of 31 games.

Aston Villa turned the tables on Sunderland in Season 1893-94 by taking the League Championship with a margin of 6 points. It was the start of an era in which they became the leading club in the land. Over a period of seven years Villa won five Championships and two FA Cup Finals. They also become only the second club to win the double (after Preston North End) in 1897. Yet as recently as 1891 they had finished fourth from bottom and had had to seek re-election to the League.

When the FA made Goodison the venue for the 1894 Cup Final Notts County protested that it was virtually a home tie for Bolton. They won anyway, with Jimmy Logan (seated centre) scoring a hat-trick to equal William Townley's feat of 1890. Only one man, Stan Mortensen in 1953, has done it since.

During the 1893-94 season Everton scored 22 goals in the space of four matches. Jack Southworth claimed 15 of these, including six on the trot against West Bromwich on 30 December 1893. Everton won 7-1.

FA CUP 1893-94

FIRST ROUND

Middlesbrough Ironopolis v Luton Town	2-1
Nottingham Forest v Heanor Town	1-0
Notts County v Burnley	1-0
Stockport County v Burton Wanderers	0-1
Leicester Fosse v South Shore	2-1
Derby County v Darwen	2-0
Newton Heath v Middlesbrough	4-0
West Bromwich Albion v Blackburn Rovers	2-3
Newcastle United v Sheffield United	2-0
Small Heath v Bolton Wanderers	3-4
Liverpool v Grimsby Town	3-0
Preston North End v Reading	18-0
Woolwich Arsenal v The Wednesday	1-2
Stoke v Everton	1-0
Sunderland v Accrington	3-0
Aston Villa v Wolverhampton Wanderers	4-2

SECOND ROUND

Middlesbrough Ironopolis v Nottingham Forest	0-2
Notts County v Burton Wanderers	2-1
Leicester Fosse v Derby County	0-0, 0-3
Newton Heath v Blackburn Rovers	0-0, 1-5
Newcastle United v Bolton Wanderers	1-2
Liverpool v Preston North End	3-2
The Wednesday v Stoke	1-0
Sunderland v Aston Villa	2-2, 1-3

THIRD ROUND

Nottingham Forest v Notts County	1-1, 1-4
Derby County v Blackburn Rovers	1-4
Bolton Wanderers v Liverpool	3-0
The Wednesday v Aston Villa	3-2

SEMI-FINAL

Notts County v Blackburn Rovers	1-0
Bolton Wanderers v The Wednesday	2-1

FINAL AT GOODISON PARK

Notts County v Bolton Wanderers	4-1

SCOTTISH FA CUP 1893-94

FIRST ROUND

Arbroath v Broxburn Shamrock	8-3
St Bernard's v Kilmarnock	3-1
Renton v Grangemouth	7-1
Cambuslang v East Stirlingshire	3-2
Port Glasgow Athletic v Airdrieonians	7-5
Dumbarton v Vale of Leven	2-1
Clyde v King's Park	5-2
Albion Rovers v 2nd Black Watch	6-0
Battlefield v Thistle	3-0
Leith Athletic v Orion	11-2
Queen's Park v Linthouse	5-1
Third Lanark v Inverness Thistle	9-3
Celtic v Hurlford	6-0
Abercorn v 5th KRV	2-1
St Mirren v Heart of Midlothian	1-0
Rangers v Cowlairs	8-0

SECOND ROUND

Abercorn v Battlefield	3-0
Port Glasgow Athletic v Renton	3-1
Queen's Park v Arbroath	3-0
Clyde v Cambuslang	6-0
Rangers v Leith Athletic	2-0
Third Lanark v St Mirren	3-2
Celtic v Albion Rovers	7-0
St Bernard's v Dumbarton	3-1

THIRD ROUND

Third Lanark v Port Glasgow Athletic	2-1
Celtic v St Bernard's	8-1
Clyde v Rangers	0-5
Abercorn v Queen's Park	3-3, 3-3, 0-2

SEMI-FINAL

Third Lanark v Celtic	3-5
Rangers v Queen's Park	1-1, 3-1

FINAL AT HAMPDEN PARK

Rangers v Celtic	3-1

SCOTTISH FIRST DIVISION

	P	W	D	L	F	A	Pts
1 Celtic	18	14	1	3	53	32	29
2 Hearts	18	11	4	3	46	32	26
3 St Bernard's	18	11	1	6	53	41	23
4 Rangers	18	8	4	6	44	30	20
5 Dumbarton	18	7	5	6	32	35	19
6 St Mirren	18	7	3	8	50	46	17
7 Third Lanark	18	7	3	8	37	45	17
8 Dundee	18	6	3	9	43	58	15
9 Leith	18	4	2	12	36	46	10
10 Renton	18	1	2	15	23	52	4

SCOTTISH SECOND DIVISION

	P	W	D	L	F	A	Pts
1 Hibernian	18	13	3	2	83	29	29
2 Cowlairs	18	13	1	4	75	32	27
3 Clyde†	18	11	2	5	51	36	24
4 Motherwell	18	11	1	6	61	46	23
5 Partick	18	10	0	8	56	58	20
6 Port Glasgow	18	9	2	7	52	53	13*
7 Abercorn	18	5	2	11	42	60	12
8 Morton	18	4	1	13	36	62	9
9 Northern	18	3	3	12	29	66	9
10 Thistle	18	2	3	13	31	74	7

*Port Glasgow Athletic had 7 points deducted for fielding an ineligible player
† Clyde promoted to First Division

Below *Notts County, the first Second Division side to win the FA Cup, in 1894.*

COLORSPORT

League Tables 1894-95

FIRST DIVISION

		P	W	D	L	F	A	Pts
1	Sunderland	30	21	5	4	80	37	47
2	Everton	30	18	6	6	82	50	42
3	Aston Villa	30	17	5	8	82	43	39
4	Preston	30	15	5	10	62	46	35
5	Blackburn	30	11	10	9	59	49	32
6	Sheff United	30	14	4	12	57	55	32
7	Nottm Forest	30	13	5	12	50	56	31
8	Wednesday	30	12	4	14	50	55	28
9	Burnley	30	11	4	15	44	56	26
10	Bolton	30	9	7	14	61	62	25
11	Wolves	30	9	7	14	43	63	25
12	Small Heath	30	9	7	14	50	74	25
13	WBA	30	10	4	16	51	66	24
14	Stoke	30	9	6	15	50	67	24
15	Derby	30	7	9	14	45	68	23
16	Liverpool	30	7	8	15	51	70	22

SECOND DIVISION

		P	W	D	L	F	A	Pts
1	Bury	30	23	2	5	78	33	48
2	Notts County	30	17	5	8	75	45	39
3	Newton Heath	30	15	8	7	78	44	38
4	Leicester Fosse	30	15	8	7	72	53	38
5	Grimsby	30	18	1	11	79	52	37
6	Darwen	30	16	4	10	74	43	36
7	Burton Wand	30	14	7	9	67	39	35
8	Woolwich A	30	14	6	10	75	58	34
9	Man City	30	14	3	13	82	72	31
10	Newcastle	30	12	3	15	72	84	27
11	Burton Swifts	30	11	3	16	52	74	25
12	Rotherham T	30	11	2	17	55	62	24
13	Lincoln	30	10	0	20	52	92	20
14	Walsall TS	30	10	0	20	47	92	20
15	Burslem PV	30	7	4	19	39	77	18
16	Crewe	30	3	4	23	26	103	10

FA CUP 1894-95

FIRST ROUND

Aston Villa v Derby County	2-1
Newcastle United v Burnley	2-1
Barnsley St Peter's v Liverpool	1-1, 0-4
Southampton St Mary's v Nottingham Forest	1-4
Sunderland v Fairfield	11-1
Luton Town v Preston North End	0-2
Bolton Wanderers v Woolwich Arsenal	1-0
Bury v Leicester Fosse	4-1
Sheffield United v Millwall Athletic	3-1
Small Heath v West Bromwich Albion	1-2
Darwen v Wolverhampton Wanderers	0-0, 0-2
Newton Heath v Stoke	2-3
The Wednesday v Notts County	5-1
Middlesbrough v Chesterfield	4-0
Southport Central v Everton	0-3
Burton Wanderers v Blackburn Rovers	1-2

SECOND ROUND

Aston Villa v Newcastle United	7-1
Liverpool v Nottingham Forest	0-2
Sunderland v Preston North End	2-0
Bolton Wanderers v Bury	1-0
Sheffield United v West Bromwich Albion	1-1, 1-2
Wolverhampton Wanderers v Stoke	2-0
The Wednesday v Middlesbrough	6-1
Everton v Blackburn Rovers	1-1, 3-2

THIRD ROUND

Aston Villa v Nottingham Forest	6-2
Sunderland v Bolton Wanderers	2-1
West Bromwich Albion v Wolverhampton Wanderers	1-0
The Wednesday v Everton	2-0

SEMI-FINAL

Aston Villa v Sunderland	2-1
West Bromwich Albion v The Wednesday	2-0

FINAL AT CRYSTAL PALACE

Aston Villa v West Bromwich Albion	1-0

SCOTTISH FIRST DIVISION

		P	W	D	L	F	A	Pts
1	Hearts	18	15	1	2	50	18	31
2	Celtic	18	11	4	3	52	31	26
3	Rangers	18	10	2	6	41	26	22
4	Third Lanark	18	10	1	7	51	39	21
5	St Mirren	18	9	1	8	34	36	19
6	St Bernard's	18	8	1	9	39	40	17
7	Clyde	18	8	0	10	40	49	16
8	Dundee	18	6	2	10	28	33	14
9	Leith	18	3	1	14	32	64	7
10	Dumbarton	18	3	1	14	27	58	7

SCOTTISH SECOND DIVISION

		P	W	D	L	F	A	Pts
1	Hibernian†	18	14	2	2	92	27	30
2	Motherwell	18	10	2	6	56	39	22
3	Port Glasgow	18	8	4	6	62	56	20
4	Renton*	17	10	0	7	46	44	20
5	Morton	18	9	1	8	59	63	19
6	Airdrieonians	18	8	2	8	68	45	18
7	Partick	18	8	2	8	50	60	18
8	Abercorn	18	7	3	8	48	65	17
9	Dundee Wand*	17	3	1	13	44	86	9*
10	Cowlairs	18	2	3	13	37	77	7

†Hibernian elected to First Division
*Dundee Wanderers and Renton played each other only once. Dundee were awarded two points when Renton failed to turn up for the return fixture.

TEST MATCHES 1894-95

Bury 1 Liverpool 0
Stoke 3 Newton Heath 0
Derby County 2 Notts County 1
Bury promoted. Liverpool relegated.

SCOTTISH FA CUP 1894-95

FIRST ROUND

St Bernard's v Airdrieonians	4-2
Slamannan Rovers v Renton	2-3*, 0-4
Ayr Parkhouse v Polton Vale	5-2
Clyde v Stevenston Thistle	7-2
Rangers v Heart of Midlothian	1-2
Orion v Dundee	1-5
Kilmarnock v East Stirlingshire	5-1
Raith Rovers v 5th KRV	6-3*, 3-4
Celtic v Queen's Park	4-1
Dumbarton v Galston.	2-1
Leith Athletic v Abercorn	5-1*, 1-4
St Mirren v Battlefield	5-0*, 8-1
Annbank v Third Lanark	6-4
Hibernian v Forfar Athletic	6-1
Motherwell v Mossend Swifts	1-2
Lochee United v King's Park	2-5

*These four ties were replayed after various protests. For example the Slamannan crowd was unruly; Raith Rovers failed to provide goal nets.

SECOND ROUND

St Bernard's v Kilmarnock	3-1
Renton v 5th KRV	6-0
Dundee v St Mirren	2-0
Heart of Midlothian v Abercorn	6-1
Clyde v Annbank	4-2
Ayr Parkhouse v Mossend Swifts	3-1
King's Park v Dumbarton	2-1
Hibernian v Celtic	2-0†, 0-2

†Celtic protested that Hibs fielded an ineligible player and a replay was agreed.

THIRD ROUND

St Bernard's v Clyde	2-1
Ayr Parkhouse v Renton	2-3
Dundee v Celtic	1-0
Heart of Midlothian v King's Park	4-2

SEMI-FINAL

Dundee v Renton	1-1, 3-3, 0-3
Heart of Midlothian v St Bernard's	0-0, 0-1

FINAL AT IBROX PARK

St Bernard's v Renton	2-1

The 1895 Cup Final was the first ever to be held at the Crystal Palace, and it got off to a remarkable start. Within 30 seconds a shot from Bob Chatt had ricocheted off John Devey's knee past the helpless West Bromwich goalkeeper Reader and Villa had won the Cup. Because of confusion at the turnstiles—the crowd of 42,000 was then the largest ever seen in London—many spectators missed the game's only goal, which remains the quickest ever scored in a Cup Final. The match was the third Final between Villa and their neighbours in 8 years; Villa had won 2-0 in 1887 and West Brom 3-0 in 1892, so the aggregate was level at three goals each. They remain the only pair of clubs ever to have met each other in three Finals. Yet another oddity to emerge from this game was that both teams, West Bromwich and Aston Villa, lost the Cup. In the winners' case this was the result of its theft, on 11 September, from below *the window of one William Shillcock, a boot and shoe manufacturer, who was displaying it to help advertise his wares. The Cup was never recovered and Villa were fined £25, which was used to purchase a replica of the original from Vaughton's of Birmingham. The Monday after the Final, meanwhile, Albion played their last League match needing a five-goal victory to avoid the test matches. They beat Wednesday 6-0; allegations of 'fixing' were never substantiated. In 1958 one Harry Burge, then 83, confessed to having stolen the Cup and having melted it down to make half-crowns. It was probably worth about £20.*

HEINEMANN

League Tables 1895-96

FIRST DIVISION

		P	W	D	L	F	A	Pts
1	Aston Villa	30	20	5	5	78	45	45
2	Derby	30	17	7	6	68	35	41
3	Everton	30	16	7	7	66	43	39
4	Bolton	30	16	5	9	49	37	37
5	Sunderland	30	15	7	8	52	41	37
6	Stoke	30	15	0	15	56	47	30
7	Wednesday	30	12	5	13	44	53	29
8	Blackburn	30	12	5	13	40	50	29
9	Preston	30	11	6	13	44	48	28
10	Burnley	30	10	7	13	48	44	27
11	Bury	30	12	3	15	50	54	27
12	Sheff United	30	10	6	14	40	50	26
13	Nottm Forest	30	11	3	16	42	57	25
14	Wolves	30	10	1	19	61	65	21
15	Small Heath	30	8	4	18	39	79	20
16	WBA	30	6	7	17	30	59	19

Below *Fred Spiksley, the Wednesday left-winger who scored both goals in the 2-1 win over Wolverhampton Wanderers which took the FA Cup to Sheffield for the first time. It was also the first time the new Cup, made after the original had been stolen from a Birmingham shop, had been presented.*

SECOND DIVISION

		P	W	D	L	F	A	Pts
1	Liverpool	30	22	2	6	106	32	46
2	Man City	30	21	4	5	63	38	46
3	Grimsby	30	20	2	8	82	38	42
4	Burton Wand	30	19	4	7	69	40	42
5	Newcastle	30	16	2	12	73	50	34
6	Newton Heath	30	15	3	12	66	57	33
7	Woolwich A	30	14	4	12	59	42	32
8	Leicester Fosse	30	14	4	12	57	44	32
9	Darwen	30	12	6	12	72	67	30
10	Notts County	30	12	2	16	57	54	26
11	Burton Swifts	30	10	4	16	39	69	24
12	Loughborough	30	9	5	16	40	67	23
13	Lincoln	30	9	4	17	53	75	22
14	Burslem PV	30	7	4	19	43	78	18
15	Rotherham Tn	30	7	3	20	34	97	17
16	Crewe	30	5	3	22	30	95	13

SCOTTISH FIRST DIVISION

		P	W	D	L	F	A	Pts
1	Celtic	18	15	0	3	64	25	30
2	Rangers	18	11	4	3	57	39	26
3	Hibernian	18	11	2	5	58	39	24
4	Hearts	18	11	0	7	68	36	22
5	Dundee	18	7	2	9	33	42	16
6	Third Lanark	18	7	1	10	47	51	15
7	St Bernard's	18	7	1	10	36	53	15
8	St Mirren	18	5	3	10	31	51	13
9	Clyde	18	4	3	11	39	59	11
10	Dumbarton	18	4	0	14	36	74	8

SCOTTISH SECOND DIVISION

		P	W	D	L	F	A	Pts
1	Abercorn*	18	12	3	3	55	31	27
2	Leith	18	11	1	6	55	37	23
3	Renton	18	9	3	6	40	28	21
4	Kilmarnock	18	10	1	7	45	45	21
5	Airdrieonians	18	7	4	7	48	44	18
6	Partick	18	8	2	8	44	54	18
7	Port Glasgow	18	6	4	8	40	41	16
8	Motherwell	18	5	3	10	31	47	13
9	Morton	18	4	4	10	32	40	12
10	Linthouse	18	5	1	12	25	48	11

*Abercorn elected to First Division

TEST MATCHES 1895-96

Man City 1 WBA 1	Liverpool 2 WBA 0
Small Heath 0 Liverpool 0	Liverpool 4 Small Heath 0
WBA 6 Man City 1	Small Heath 8 Man City 0
Man City 3 Small Heath 0	WBA 2 Liverpool 0

	P	W	D	L	F	A	Pts
Liverpool	4	2	1	1	6	2	5
WBA	4	2	1	1	9	4	5
Small Heath	4	1	1	2	8	7	3
Man City	4	1	1	2	5	15	3

Liverpool promoted. Small Heath relegated.

FA CUP 1895-96

SECOND ROUND

Wolverhampton Wanderers v Liverpool	2-0
Burnley v Stoke	1-1, 1-7
Derby County v Newton Heath	1-1, 5-1
Grimsby Town v West Bromwich Albion	1-1, 0-3
The Wednesday v Sunderland	2-1
Everton v Sheffield United	3-0
Blackpool v Bolton Wanderers	0-2
Newcastle United v Bury	1-3

THIRD ROUND

Wolverhampton Wanderers v Stoke	3-0
Derby County v West Bromwich Albion	1-0
The Wednesday v Everton	4-0
Bolton Wanderers v Bury	2-0

SEMI-FINAL

Wolverhampton Wanderers v Derby County	2-1
The Wednesday v Bolton Wanderers	1-1, 3-1

FINAL AT CRYSTAL PALACE

The Wednesday v Wolverhampton Wanderers	2-1

SCOTTISH FA CUP 1895-96

FIRST ROUND

Blantyre v Heart of Midlothian	1-12
East Stirlingshire v Hibernian	2-3
St Bernard's v Clackmannan	8-1
Renton v Cowdenbeath	1-0
Lochgelly United v Raith Rovers	2-1*, 2-5
Dumbarton v Rangers	1-1, 1-3
Celtic v Queen's Park	2-4
Third Lanark v Leith Athletic	6-0
Annbank v Kilmarnock	3-2
Ayr v Abercorn	3-2
Port Glasgow Athletic v Arthurlie	4-2
St Mirren v Alloa Athletic	7-0
Arbroath v King's Park	5-0
Morton v Dundee	2-3
Clyde v Polton Vale	3-0
St Johnstone v Dundee Wanderers	4-2

*A Lochgelly player, David 'Anderson', was in fact David McLaren of Lochee United and had already appeared for that club in an earlier round. After a protest from Raith the tie was replayed.

SECOND ROUND

Heart of Midlothian v Ayr	5-1
Hibernian v Raith Rovers	6-1
St Bernard's v Annbank	2-0
Renton v Clyde	2-1
Rangers v St Mirren	5-1
Third Lanark v Dundee	4-1
Queen's Park v Port Glasgow Athletic	8-1
Arbroath v St Johnstone	3-1

THIRD ROUND

Heart of Midlothian v Arbroath	4-0
Hibernian v Rangers	3-2
St Bernard's v Queen's Park	3-2
Renton v Third Lanark	3-3, 2-0

SEMI-FINAL

Heart of Midlothian v St Bernard's	1-0
Hibernian v Renton	2-1

FINAL AT LOGIE GREEN, EDINBURGH

Heart of Midlothian v Hibernian	3-1

Above left *John Reynolds, who played at half-back in the England team which defeated Scotland 3-0 at Everton in 1895. Reynolds, though born in Blackburn, had played five times for Ireland during a spell with Distillery in 1890 and 1891. He then moved to West Bromwich, with whom he won a cap for England against Scotland. He then moved to Villa, with whom he won another seven caps. Only one other player, R E Evans, has been known to play for two of the home countries.*

FIRST DIVISION

		P	W	D	L	F	A	Pts
1	Aston Villa	30	21	5	4	73	38	47
2	Sheff United	30	13	10	7	42	29	36
3	Derby	30	16	4	10	70	50	36
4	Preston	30	11	12	7	55	40	34
5	Liverpool	30	12	9	9	46	38	33
6	Wednesday	30	10	11	9	42	37	31
7	Everton	30	14	3	13	62	57	31
8	Bolton	30	12	6	12	40	43	30
9	Bury	30	10	10	10	39	44	30
10	Wolves	30	11	6	13	45	41	28
11	Nottm Forest	30	9	8	13	44	49	26
12	WBA	30	10	6	14	33	56	26
13	Stoke	30	11	3	16	48	59	25
14	Blackburn	30	11	3	16	35	62	25
15	Sunderland	30	7	9	14	34	47	23
16	Burnley	30	6	7	17	43	61	19

SECOND DIVISION

		P	W	D	L	F	A	Pts
1	Notts County	30	19	4	7	92	43	42
2	Newton Heath	30	17	5	8	56	34	39
3	Grimsby	30	17	4	9	66	45	38
4	Small Heath	30	16	5	9	69	47	37
5	Newcastle	30	17	1	12	56	52	35
6	Man City	30	12	8	10	58	50	32
7	Gainsborough	30	12	7	11	50	47	31
8	Blackpool	30	13	5	12	59	56	31
9	Leicester Fosse	30	13	4	13	59	56	30
10	Woolwich A	30	13	4	13	68	70	30
11	Darwen	30	14	0	16	67	61	28
12	Walsall	30	11	4	15	53	69	26
13	Loughborough	30	12	1	17	50	64	25
14	Burton Swifts	30	9	6	15	46	61	24
15	Burton Wand	30	9	2	19	31	67	20
16	Lincoln	30	5	2	23	27	85	12

TEST MATCHES 1896-97

Notts County 1 Sunderland 0
Newton Heath 2 Burnley 0
Burnley 0 Notts County 1
Sunderland 2 Newton Heath 0
Sunderland 0 Notts County 0
Newton Heath 1 Sunderland 1
Burnley 2 Newton Heath 0
Notts County 1 Burnley 1

	P	W	D	L	F	A	Pts
Notts County	4	2	2	0	3	1	6
Sunderland	4	1	2	1	3	2	4
Burnley	4	1	1	2	3	4	3
Newton Heath	4	1	1	2	3	5	3

Notts County promoted
Burnley relegated

FA CUP 1896-97

FIRST ROUND

Aston Villa v Newcastle United	5-0
Small Heath v Notts County	1-2
Preston North End v Manchester City	6-0
Stoke v Glossop North End	5-2
Burnley v Sunderland	0-1
Nottingham Forest v The Wednesday	1-0
Luton Town v West Bromwich Albion	0-1
Liverpool v Burton Swifts	4-3
Everton v Burton Wanderers	5-2
Stockton v Bury	0-0, 1-12
Blackburn Rovers v Sheffield United	2-1
Millwall Athletic v Wolverhampton Wanderers	1-2
Derby County v Barnsley St Peter's	8-1
Bolton Wanderers v Grimsby Town	0-0, 3-3, 3-2
Heanor Town v Southampton St Mary's	1-1, 0-1
Newton Heath v Kettering	5-1

SECOND ROUND

Aston Villa v Notts County	2-1
Preston North End v Stoke	2-1
Sunderland v Nottingham Forest	1-3
West Bromwich Albion v Liverpool	1-2
Everton v Bury	3-0
Blackburn Rovers v Wolverhampton Wanderers	2-1
Derby County v Bolton Wanderers	4-1
Southampton St Mary's v Newton Heath	1-1, 1-3

THIRD ROUND

Aston Villa v Preston North End	1-1, 0-0, 3-2
Nottingham Forest v Liverpool	1-1, 0-1
Everton v Blackburn Rovers	2-0
Derby County v Newton Heath	2-0

SEMI-FINAL

Aston Villa v Liverpool	3-0
Everton v Derby County	3-2

FINAL AT CRYSTAL PALACE

Aston Villa v Everton	3-2

SCOTTISH FA CUP 1896-97

FIRST ROUND

Arthurlie v Celtic	4-2
Third Lanark v Newton Stewart Athletic	8-1
Heart of Midlothian v Clyde	2-0
St Bernard's v Queen's Park	2-1
St Mirren v Renton	5-1
Partick Thistle v Rangers	2-4
Dumbarton v Raith Rovers	2-1
Duncrab Park v Hibernian	1-10
Motherwell v Kilmarnock	3-3, 2-5
Abercorn v Hurlford	4-0
Falkirk v Orion	2-0
Dundee v Inverness Thistle	7-1
Morton v Johnstone	3-1
Blantyre v Bathgate	5-0
Leith Athletic v Dunblane	5-1
Lochgelly United v King's Park	1-2

SECOND ROUND

Arthurlie v Morton	1-5
Kilmarnock v Falkirk	7-3
Third Lanark v Heart of Midlothian	5-2
Dumbarton v Leith Athletic	4-4, 3-3, 3-2
Rangers v Hibernian	3-0
Dundee v King's Park	5-0
St Bernard's v St Mirren	5-0
Abercorn v Blantyre	4-1

THIRD ROUND

Dumbarton v St Bernard's	2-0
Morton v Abercorn	2-2, 3-2
Dundee v Rangers	0-4
Kilmarnock v Third Lanark	3-1

SEMI-FINAL

Morton v Rangers	2-7
Dumbarton v Kilmarnock	4-3

FINAL AT HAMPDEN PARK

Rangers v Dumbarton	5-1

SCOTTISH FIRST DIVISION

		P	W	D	L	F	A	Pts
1	Hearts	18	13	2	3	47	22	28
2	Hibernian	18	12	2	4	50	20	26
3	Rangers	18	11	3	4	64	30	25
4	Celtic	18	10	4	4	42	18	24
5	Dundee	18	10	2	6	38	30	22
6	St Mirren	18	9	1	8	38	29	19
7	St Bernard's	18	7	0	11	32	40	14
8	Third Lanark	18	5	1	12	29	46	11
9	Clyde	18	4	0	14	27	65	8
10	Abercorn	18	1	1	16	21	88	3

SCOTTISH SECOND DIVISION

		P	W	D	L	F	A	Pts
1	Partick†	18	14	3	1	61	28	31
2	Leith	18	13	1	4	54	28	27
3	Kilmarnock	18	10	1	7	44	33	21
4	Airdrieonians	18	10	1	7	48	39	21
5	Morton	18	7	2	9	38	40	16
6	Renton	18	6	2	10	34	40	14
7	Linthouse	18	8	2	8	44	52	14*
8	Port Glasgow	18	4	5	9	39	50	13
9	Motherwell	18	6	1	11	40	55	13
10	Dumbarton	18	2	2	14	27	64	6

*Four points deducted for fielding an ineligible player.
† Partick elected to First Division

The ROYAL RILEY Football, Buttonless, as illustration. Best Selected Quality, Match Size. Each, Post Free, 8/3.
The ROYAL WONDER Football, Buttonless, as Illustration Superior Practice Quality, Full Size. Each, Post Free 6/6.
The CUP-TIE Football, 8 Section. Button Ends. Selected Quality, Match Size, Each, Post Free 7/6.
The CUP-TIE Football, ditto. Size 4, ONLY 7/-.
The SCOT FOOTBALL, Buttonless Pattern, Selected CHROME Waterproof Leather, Match Size only. Post Free, 10/-.
SPECIAL TERMS TO SHOPS. Fully Illustrated List of all Football Goods, Hockey, &c., FREE. Telegrams: "Cricket," Accrington.
E. J. RILEY, Ltd., WILLOW MILLS, ACCRINGTON.

Above *Footballs from Lancashire, as used in the 1890s.*

Left *The Aston Villa side that won the double in 1897. Their eleven point margin over the second League club remains a record and the double was not repeated until the Spurs of 64 years later.*

League Tables 1897-98

FIRST DIVISION

		P	W	D	L	F	A	Pts
1	Sheff United	30	17	8	5	56	31	42
2	Sunderland	30	16	5	9	43	30	37
3	Wolves	30	14	7	9	57	41	35
4	Everton	30	13	9	8	48	39	35
5	Wednesday	30	15	3	12	51	42	33
6	Aston Villa	30	14	5	11	61	51	33
7	WBA	30	11	10	9	44	45	32
8	Nottm Forest	30	11	9	10	47	49	31
9	Liverpool	30	11	6	13	48	45	28
10	Derby	30	11	6	13	57	61	28
11	Bolton	30	11	4	15	28	41	26
12	Preston NE	30	8	8	14	35	43	24
13	Notts County	30	8	8	14	36	46	24
14	Bury	30	8	8	14	39	51	24
15	Blackburn	30	7	10	13	39	54	24
16	Stoke	30	8	8	14	35	55	24

SECOND DIVISION

		P	W	D	L	F	A	Pts
1	Burnley	30	20	8	2	80	24	48
2	Newcastle	30	21	3	6	64	32	45
3	Man City	30	15	9	6	66	36	39
4	Newton Heath	30	16	6	8	64	35	38
5	Woolwich A	30	16	5	9	69	49	37
6	Small Heath	30	16	4	10	58	50	36
7	Leicester Fosse	30	13	7	10	46	35	33
8	Luton	30	13	4	13	68	50	30
9	Gainsborough	30	12	6	12	50	54	30
10	Walsall	30	12	5	13	58	58	29
11	Blackpool	30	10	5	15	49	61	25
12	Grimsby	30	10	4	16	52	62	24
13	Burton Swifts	30	8	5	17	38	69	21
14	Lincoln	30	6	5	19	43	82	17
15	Darwen	30	6	2	22	31	76	14
16	Loughborough	30	6	2	22	24	87	14

SCOTTISH FIRST DIVISION

		P	W	D	L	F	A	Pts
1	Celtic	18	15	3	0	56	13	33
2	Rangers	18	13	3	2	71	15	29
3	Hibernian	18	10	2	6	48	28	22
4	Hearts	18	8	4	6	54	33	20
5	Third Lanark	18	8	2	8	37	38	18
6	St Mirren	18	8	2	8	30	36	18
7	Dundee*	18	5	3	10	29	36	13
8	Partick*	18	6	1	11	34	64	13
9	St Bernard's	18	4	1	13	35	67	9
10	Clyde	18	1	3	14	20	84	5

*Partick Thistle and Dundee played a test match to decide the bottom three and Dundee won 2-0

SCOTTISH SECOND DIVISION

		P	W	D	L	F	A	Pts
1	Kilmarnock	18	14	1	3	64	29	29
2	Port Glasgow	18	12	1	5	66	35	25
3	Morton	18	9	4	5	47	38	22
4	Leith	18	9	2	7	39	38	20
5	Linthouse	18	6	4	8	37	39	16
6	Ayr	18	7	2	9	36	42	16
7	Abercorn	18	6	4	8	33	41	16
8	Airdrieonians	18	6	2	10	44	56	14
9	Hamilton*	18	5	2	11	28	51	12
10	Motherwell	18	3	4	11	31	56	10

*Took the place of Renton, who resigned

COLORSPORT

Left *Ernest 'Nudger' Needham, who led his club, Sheffield United, to the League Championship, the first honour in their history.*

Below *Harry Linacre, the Nottingham Forest goalkeeper and an England cap in the early part of the twentieth century. Linacre came from a great footballing family in Aston-on-Trent, near Derby. His two uncles, Frank and Fred Forman, played in all the 1898-99 season internationals for England and remain the only brothers from the same professional club to have played together for England. They were also Forest regulars, like their nephew, and Frank Forman was captain of the Forest team that won the club's first honour with the FA Cup in 1898. Five days before the Final their opponents and local rivals Derby County had thrashed them 5-0 in a League match. But, despite this and a crippling injury to wing-half Wragg, Forest won the Final 3-1.*

FA CUP 1897-98

FIRST ROUND

Southampton St Mary's v Leicester Fosse	2-1
Preston North End v Newcastle United	1-2
Luton Town v Bolton Wanderers	0-1
Manchester City v Wigan County	2-1
West Bromwich Albion v New Brighton Tower	2-0
Sunderland v The Wednesday	0-1
Nottingham Forest v Grimsby Town	4-0
Long Eaton Rangers v Gainsborough Trinity	0-1
Liverpool v Hucknall St John's	2-0
Newton Heath v Walsall	1-0
Notts County v Wolverhampton Wanderers	0-1
Derby County v Aston Villa	1-0
Burnley v Woolwich Arsenal	3-1
Burslem Port Vale v Sheffield United	1-1, 2-1
Everton v Blackburn Rovers	1-0
Bury v Stoke	1-2

SECOND ROUND

Southampton St Mary's v Newcastle United	1-0
Bolton Wanderers v Manchester City	1-0
West Bromwich Albion v The Wednesday	1-0
Nottingham Forest v Gainsborough Trinity	4-0
Liverpool v Newton Heath	0-0, 2-1
Wolverhampton Wanderers v Derby County	0-1
Burnley v Burslem Port Vale	3-0
Everton v Stoke	0-0, 5-1

THIRD ROUND

Southampton St Mary's v Bolton Wanderers	0-0, 4-0
West Bromwich Albion v Nottingham Forest	2-3
Liverpool v Derby County	1-1, 1-5
Burnley v Everton	1-3

SEMI-FINAL

Southampton St Mary's v Nottingham Forest	1-1, 0-2
Derby County v Everton	3-1

FINAL AT CRYSTAL PALACE

Nottingham Forest v Derby County	3-1

SCOTTISH FA CUP 1897-98

SECOND ROUND

Dundee v St Mirren	2-0
Rangers v Cartvale	12-0
Third Lanark v Celtic	3-2
Kilmarnock v Leith Athletic	9-2
Dundee Wanderers v Ayr Parkhouse	3-6
Hibernian v East Stirlingshire	3-1
Heart of Midlothian v Morton	4-1
St Bernard's v Queen's Park	0-5

THIRD ROUND

Queen's Park v Rangers	1-3
Third Lanark v Hibernian	2-0
Ayr Parkhouse v Kilmarnock	2-7
Dundee v Heart of Midlothian	3-0

SEMI-FINAL

Rangers v Third Lanark	1-1, 2-2, 2-0
Kilmarnock v Dundee	3-2

FINAL AT HAMPDEN PARK

Rangers v Kilmarnock	2-0

TEST MATCHES 1897-98

Newcastle 2 Stoke 1	Blackburn 1 Burnley 3
Burnley 2 Blackburn 0	Stoke 1 Newcastle 0
Newcastle 4 Blackburn 0	Blackburn 4 Newcastle 3
Burnley 0 Stoke 2	Stoke 0 Burnley 0

	P	W	D	L	F	A	Pts
Stoke	4	2	1	1	4	2	5
Burnley	4	2	1	1	5	3	5
Newcastle	4	2	0	2	9	6	4
Blackburn	4	1	0	3	5	12	2

Burnley and Newcastle promoted
No clubs relegated

League Tables 1898-99

FIRST DIVISION

	P	W	D	L	F	A	Pts
1 Aston Villa	34	19	7	8	76	40	45
2 Liverpool	34	19	5	10	49	33	43
3 Burnley	34	15	9	10	45	47	39
4 Everton	34	15	8	11	48	41	38
5 Notts County	34	12	13	9	47	51	37
6 Blackburn	34	14	8	12	60	52	36
7 Sunderland	34	15	6	13	41	41	36
8 Wolves	34	14	7	13	54	48	35
9 Derby	34	12	11	11	62	57	35
10 Bury	34	14	7	13	48	49	35
11 Nottm Forest	34	11	11	12	42	42	33
12 Stoke	34	13	7	14	47	52	33
13 Newcastle	34	11	8	15	49	48	30
14 WBA	34	12	6	16	42	57	30
15 Preston	34	10	9	15	44	47	29
16 Sheff United	34	9	11	14	45	51	29
17 Bolton	34	9	7	18	37	51	25
18 Wednesday	34	8	8	18	32	61	24

SECOND DIVISION

	P	W	D	L	F	A	Pts
1 Man City	34	23	5	6	92	35	52
2 Glossop NE	34	20	6	8	76	38	46
3 Leicester Fosse	34	18	9	7	64	42	45
4 Newton Heath	34	19	5	10	67	43	43
5 New Brighton	34	18	7	9	71	52	43
6 Walsall	34	15	12	7	79	36	42
7 Woolwich A	34	18	5	11	72	41	41
8 Small Heath	34	17	7	10	85	50	41
9 Burslem PV	34	17	5	12	56	34	39
10 Grimsby	34	15	5	14	71	60	35
11 Barnsley	34	12	7	15	52	56	31
12 Lincoln	34	12	7	15	51	56	31
13 Burton Swifts	34	10	8	16	51	70	28
14 Gainsborough	34	10	5	19	56	72	25
15 Luton	34	10	3	21	51	95	23
16 Blackpool	34	8	4	22	49	90	20
17 Loughborough	34	6	6	22	38	92	18
18 Darwen	34	2	5	27	22	141	9

SCOTTISH FIRST DIVISION

	P	W	D	L	F	A	Pts
1 Rangers	18	18	0	0	79	18	36
2 Hearts	18	12	2	4	56	30	26
3 Celtic	18	11	2	5	51	33	24
4 Hibernian	18	10	3	5	42	43	23
5 St Mirren	18	8	4	6	46	32	20
6 Third Lanark	18	7	3	8	33	38	17
7 St Bernard's	18	4	4	10	30	37	12
8 Clyde	18	4	4	10	23	48	12
9 Partick	18	2	2	14	19	58	6
10 Dundee	18	1	2	15	23	65	4

SCOTTISH SECOND DIVISION

	P	W	D	L	F	A	Pts
1 Kilmarnock*	18	14	4	0	73	24	32
2 Leith	18	12	3	3	63	38	27
3 Port Glasgow	18	12	1	5	75	51	25
4 Motherwell	18	7	6	5	41	40	20
5 Hamilton	18	7	1	10	48	58	15
6 Airdrieonians	18	6	3	9	35	46	15
7 Morton	18	6	1	11	36	41	13
8 Ayr	18	5	3	10	35	51	13
9 Linthouse	18	5	1	12	29	62	11
10 Abercorn	18	4	1	13	41	65	9

*Kilmarnock elected to First Division

Below *The Aston Villa side which won the First Division Championship in 1899.*

Second Division Darwen are the only side to have suffered three 10-goal defeats in a single season. In 1898-99 they lost 10-0 to Manchester City, Walsall and Loughborough, all in the space of six weeks. Their 141 goals against was also a record.

Season 1898-99 provided one unique record. Glasgow Rangers won every single game they played in the Scottish League, the only time that this feat has been performed by a British club. Their only defeat in 1898-99 in fact was a shock collapse, 2-0, to Glasgow rivals Celtic in the Scottish Cup final. Only four other clubs — Celtic, Kilmarnock, Preston and Liverpool — have gone a League season without defeat.

FA CUP 1898-99

FIRST ROUND

Everton v Jarrow	3-1
Nottingham Forest v Aston Villa	2-1
Sheffield United v Burnley	2-2, 2-1
Preston North End v Grimsby Town	7-0
West Bromwich Albion v South Shore	8-0
Heanor Town v Bury	0-3
Liverpool v Blackburn Rovers	2-0
Glossop North End v Newcastle United	0-1
Notts County v Kettering Town	2-0
New Brompton v Southampton	0-1
Woolwich Arsenal v Derby County	0-6
Bolton Wanderers v Wolverhampton Wanderers	0-0, 0-1
Small Heath v Manchester City	3-2
Stoke v The Wednesday	2-2, 2-0
Newton Heath v Tottenham Hotspur	1-1, 3-5
Bristol City v Sunderland	2-4

SECOND ROUND

Everton v Nottingham Forest	0-1
Sheffield United v Preston North End	2-2, 2-1
West Bromwich Albion v Bury	2-1
Liverpool v Newcastle United	3-1
Notts County v Southampton	0-1
Derby County v Wolverhampton Wanderers	2-1
Small Heath v Stoke	2-2, 1-2
Tottenham Hotspur v Sunderland	2-1

THIRD ROUND

Nottingham Forest v Sheffield United	0-1
West Bromwich Albion v Liverpool	0-2
Southampton v Derby County	1-2
Stoke v Tottenham Hotspur	4-1

SEMI-FINAL

Sheffield United v Liverpool	2-2, 4-4, 0-1*, 1-0
Derby County v Stoke	3-1

*abandoned

FINAL AT CRYSTAL PALACE

Sheffield United v Derby County	4-1

SCOTTISH FA CUP 1898-99

FIRST ROUND

Queen's Park v Kilsyth Wanderers	4-0
Hibernian v Royal Albert	2-1
6th G R V v Celtic	1-8
St Bernard's v Bo'ness	3-3, 4-2
Port Glasgow Athletic v Renton	3-2
Forfar Athletic v West Calder Swifts	4-5
Irvine v Partick Thistle	0-5
Morton v Annbank	3-1
St Mirren v Leith Athletic	7-1
Third Lanark v Arthurlie	4-1
Orion v Kilmarnock	0-2
East Stirlingshire v Dumbarton	4-1
Rangers v Heart of Midlothian	4-1
Ayr Parkhouse v Dundee	3-1
Clyde v Wishaw Thistle	3-0
Airdrieonians v Arbroath	3-3, 2-3

SECOND ROUND

Queen's Park v Hibernian	5-1
Celtic v St Bernard's	3-0
Port Glasgow Athletic v West Calder Swifts	3-1
Morton v Partick Thistle	2-2, 1-2
Third Lanark v St Mirren	1-2
East Stirlingshire v Kilmarnock	1-1, 0-0, 2-4
Ayr Parkhouse v Rangers	1-4
Clyde v Arbroath	3-1

THIRD ROUND

Celtic v Queen's Park	4-2*, 2-1
Port Glasgow Athletic v Partick Thistle	7-3
Kilmarnock v St Mirren	1-2
Rangers v Clyde	4-0

*abandoned

SEMI-FINAL

Celtic v Port Glasgow Athletic	4-2
St Mirren v Rangers	1-2

FINAL AT HAMPDEN PARK

Celtic v Rangers	2-0

League Tables 1899-1900

FIRST DIVISION

	P	W	D	L	F	A	Pts
1 Aston Villa	34	22	6	6	77	35	50
2 Sheff United	34	18	12	4	63	33	48
3 Sunderland	34	19	3	12	50	35	41
4 Wolves	34	15	9	10	48	37	39
5 Newcastle	34	13	10	11	53	43	36
6 Derby	34	14	8	12	45	43	36
7 Man City	34	13	8	13	50	44	34
8 Nottm Forest	34	13	8	13	56	55	34
9 Stoke	34	10	10	14	37	45	34
10 Liverpool	34	14	5	15	49	45	33
11 Everton	34	13	7	14	47	49	33
12 Bury	34	13	6	15	40	44	32
13 WBA	34	11	8	15	43	51	30
14 Blackburn	34	13	4	17	49	61	30
15 Notts County	34	9	11	14	46	60	29
16 Preston	34	12	4	18	38	48	28
17 Burnley	34	11	5	18	34	54	27
18 Glossop NE	34	4	10	20	31	74	18

SECOND DIVISION

	P	W	D	L	F	A	Pts
1 Wednesday	34	25	4	5	84	22	54
2 Bolton	34	22	8	4	79	25	52
3 Small Heath	34	20	6	8	78	38	46
4 Newton Heath	34	20	4	10	63	27	44
5 Leicester Fosse	34	17	9	8	53	36	43
6 Grimsby	34	17	6	11	67	46	40
7 Chesterfield	34	16	6	12	65	60	38
8 Woolwich A	34	16	4	14	61	43	36
9 Lincoln	34	14	8	12	46	43	36
10 New Brighton	34	13	9	12	66	58	35
11 Burslem PV	34	14	6	14	39	49	34
12 Walsall	34	12	8	14	50	55	32
13 Gainsborough	34	9	7	18	47	75	25
14 Middlesbrough	34	8	8	18	39	69	24
15 Burton Swifts	34	9	6	19	43	84	24
16 Barnsley	34	8	7	19	46	79	23
17 Luton	34	5	8	21	40	75	18
18 Loughborough	34	1	6	27	18	100	8

SCOTTISH FIRST DIVISION

	P	W	D	L	F	A	Pts
1 Rangers	18	15	2	1	68	27	32
2 Celtic	18	9	7	2	46	27	25
3 Hibernian	18	9	6	3	43	24	24
4 Hearts	18	10	3	5	41	24	23
5 Kilmarnock	18	6	6	6	30	37	18
6 Dundee	18	4	7	7	36	40	15
7 Third Lanark	18	5	5	8	31	37	15
8 St Mirren	18	3	6	9	30	46	12
9 St Bernard's	18	4	4	10	29	47	12
10 Clyde	18	2	0	16	25	70	4

The Manchester City keeper, C Williams, scored with a goal-kick against Sunderland on 14 April 1900 when his opposite number, Ned Doig, touched the ball on its way into the net. At that time full-backs used to tap goal-kicks into the keeper's hands and he would punt the ball from the 6-yard semi-circle.

SCOTTISH SECOND DIVISION

	P	W	D	L	F	A	Pts
1 Partick*	18	14	1	3	56	26	29
2 Morton*	18	14	0	4	66	25	28
3 Port Glasgow	18	10	0	8	50	41	20
4 Motherwell	18	9	1	8	38	36	19
5 Leith	18	9	1	8	32	37	19
6 Abercorn	18	7	2	9	46	39	16
7 Hamilton	18	7	1	10	33	46	15
8 Ayr	18	6	2	10	39	48	14
9 Airdrieonians	18	4	3	11	27	49	11
10 Linthouse	18	2	5	11	28	68	9

*Partick Thistle and Morton were elected to the First Division.

Below *Part of the huge crowd at the 1900 Cup Final at Crystal Palace.*

FA CUP 1899-1900

FIRST ROUND

Preston North End v Tottenham Hotspur	1-0
Blackburn Rovers v Portsmouth	0-0, 1-1, 5-0
Nottingham Forest v Grimsby Town	3-0
Sunderland v Derby County	2-2, 3-0
The Wednesday v Bolton Wanderers	1-0
Sheffield United v Leicester Fosse	1-0
Notts County v Chorley	6-0
Burnley v Bury	0-1
Southampton v Everton	3-0
Newcastle United v Reading	2-1
West Bromwich Albion v Walsall	1-1, 6-0
Liverpool v Stoke	0-0, 1-0
Wolverhampton Wanderers v Queen's Park Rangers	1-1, 0-1
Jarrow v Millwall Athletic	0-2
Aston Villa v Manchester City	1-1, 3-1
Bristol City v Stalybridge Rovers	2-1

SECOND ROUND

Preston North End v Blackburn Rovers	1-0
Nottingham Forest v Sunderland	3-0
The Wednesday v Sheffield United	1-1, 0-2
Notts County v Bury	0-0, 0-2
Southampton v Newcastle United	4-1
West Bromwich Albion v Liverpool	1-1, 2-1
Queen's Park Rangers v Millwall Athletic	0-2
Aston Villa v Bristol City	5-1

THIRD ROUND

Preston North End v Nottingham Forest	0-0, 0-1
Sheffield United v Bury	2-2, 0-2
Southampton v West Bromwich Albion	2-1
Millwall Athletic v Aston Villa	1-1, 0-0, 2-1

SEMI-FINAL

Nottingham Forest v Bury	1-1, 2-3
Southampton v Millwall Athletic	0-0, 3-0

FINAL AT CRYSTAL PALACE

Bury v Southampton	4-0

SCOTTISH FA CUP 1899-1900

FIRST ROUND

Rangers v Morton	4-2
Celtic v Bo'ness	7-1
Third Lanark v Raith Rovers	5-1
Heart of Midlothian v St Mirren	0-0, 3-0
Kilmarnock v East Stirlingshire	2-0
Hamilton Academicals v Hibernian	2-3
St Bernard's v Arbroath	1-0
Galston v Partick Thistle	1-2
Forfar Athletic v Motherwell	3-4
Abercorn v Ayr Parkhouse	5-2
Port Glasgow Athletic v Falkirk	7-1
Dundee v Douglas Wanderers	8-0
Maybole v Wishaw Thistle	3-2
Forres Mechanics v Orion	1-1, 1-4
Queen's Park v Leith Athletic	3-0
Airdrieonians v Clyde	0-1

SECOND ROUND

Heart of Midlothian v Hibernian	1-1, 2-1
Dundee v Clyde	3-3, 3-0
Queen's Park v Abercorn	5-1
Rangers v Maybole	12-0
Kilmarnock v Orion	10-0
Partick Thistle v St Bernard's	2-1
Third Lanark v Motherwell	2-1
Port Glasgow Athletic v Celtic	1-5

THIRD ROUND

Rangers v Partick Thistle	6-1
Celtic v Kilmarnock	4-0
Queen's Park v Dundee	1-0
Third Lanark v Heart of Midlothian	1-2

SEMI-FINAL

Rangers v Celtic	1-1, 0-4
Queen's Park v Heart of Midlothian	2-1

FINAL AT IBROX PARK

Celtic v Queen's Park	4-3

League Tables 1900-01

FIRST DIVISION

		P	W	D	L	F	A	Pts
1	Liverpool	34	19	7	8	59	35	45
2	Sunderland	34	15	13	6	57	26	43
3	Notts County	34	18	4	12	54	46	40
4	Nottm Forest	34	16	7	11	53	36	39
5	Bury	34	16	7	11	53	37	39
6	Newcastle	34	14	10	10	42	37	38
7	Everton	34	16	5	13	55	42	37
8	Wednesday	34	13	10	11	52	42	36
9	Blackburn	34	12	9	13	39	47	33
10	Bolton	34	13	7	14	39	55	33
11	Man City	34	13	6	15	48	58	32
12	Derby	34	12	7	15	55	42	31
13	Wolves	34	9	13	12	39	55	31
14	Sheff United	34	12	7	15	35	52	31
15	Aston Villa	34	10	10	14	45	51	30
16	Stoke	34	11	5	18	46	57	27
17	Preston	34	9	7	18	49	75	25
18	WBA	34	7	8	19	35	62	22

SECOND DIVISION

		P	W	D	L	F	A	Pts
1	Grimsby	34	20	9	5	60	33	49
2	Small Heath	34	19	10	5	57	24	48
3	Burnley	34	20	4	10	53	29	44
4	New Brighton	34	17	8	9	57	38	42
5	Glossop NE	34	15	8	11	51	33	38
6	Middlesbrough	34	15	7	12	50	40	37
7	Woolwich A	34	15	6	13	39	35	36
8	Lincoln	34	13	7	14	43	39	33
9	Burslem PV	34	11	11	12	45	47	33
10	Newton Heath	34	14	4	16	42	38	32
11	Leicester Fosse	34	11	10	13	39	37	32
12	Blackpool	34	12	7	15	33	58	31
13	Gainsborough	34	10	10	14	45	60	30
14	Chesterfield	34	9	10	15	46	58	28
15	Barnsley	34	11	5	18	47	60	27
16	Walsall	34	7	13	14	40	56	27
17	Stockport	34	11	3	20	38	68	25
18	Burton Swifts	34	8	4	22	34	66	20

SCOTTISH FIRST DIVISION

		P	W	D	L	F	A	Pts
1	Rangers	20	17	1	2	60	25	35
2	Celtic	20	13	3	4	49	28	29
3	Hibernian	20	9	7	4	29	22	25
4	Morton	20	9	3	8	40	40	21
5	Kilmarnock	20	7	4	9	35	47	18
6	Third Lanark	20	6	6	8	20	29	18
7	Dundee	20	6	5	9	36	35	17
8	Queen's Park	20	7	3	10	33	37	17
9	St Mirren	20	5	6	9	33	43	16
10	Hearts	20	5	4	11	22	30	14
11	Partick	20	4	2	14	28	49	10

SCOTTISH SECOND DIVISION

		P	W	D	L	F	A	Pts
1	St Bernard's	18	10	5	3	41	26	25
2	Airdrieonians	18	11	1	6	46	35	23
3	Abercorn	18	9	3	6	37	33	21
4	Clyde	18	9	2	7	43	35	20
5	Port Glasgow	18	9	1	8	45	44	19
6	Ayr	18	9	0	9	32	34	18
7	E Stirlingshire	18	7	4	7	35	39	18
8	Leith	18	5	3	10	23	33	13
9	Hamilton	18	4	4	10	44	51	12
10	Motherwell	18	4	3	11	26	42	11

Below *The legendary Fatty Foulke, Sheffield United's goalkeeper, fishes the ball out of the net after one of two goals scored against his team in the 1901 Cup Final by Sandy Brown of Tottenham Hotspur. Brown's goals earned the Londoners a 2-2 draw and won him a place in the record books. For Brown had become the first man to score in every round of the competition and the centre-forward's tally of 15 goals—including the one he got in the replay at Bolton—remains a record. Spurs were then members of the Southern League and are the only non-League club to have won the Cup since 1888.*

FA CUP 1900-01

FIRST ROUND

Bolton Wanderers v Derby County	1-0
Reading v Bristol Rovers	2-0
Tottenham Hotspur v Preston North End	1-1, 4-2
The Wednesday v Bury	0-1
Middlesbrough v Newcastle United	3-1
Kettering Town v Chesterfield Town	1-1, 2-1
Woolwich Arsenal v Blackburn Rovers	2-0
West Bromwich Albion v Manchester City	1-0
Notts County v Liverpool	2-0
Wolverhampton Wanderers v New Brighton Tower	5-1
Sunderland v Sheffield United	1-2
Southampton v Everton	1-3
Stoke v Small Heath	1-1, 1-2
Newton Heath v Burnley	0-0, 1-7
Aston Villa v Millwall Athletic	5-0
Nottingham Forest v Leicester Fosse	5-1

SECOND ROUND

Bolton Wanderers v Reading	0-1
Tottenham Hotspur v Bury	2-1
Middlesbrough v Kettering Town	5-0
Woolwich Arsenal v West Bromwich Albion	0-1
Notts County v Wolverhampton Wanderers	2-3
Sheffield United v Everton	2-0
Small Heath v Burnley	1-0
Aston Villa v Nottingham Forest	0-0, 3-1

THIRD ROUND

Reading v Tottenham Hotspur	1-1, 0-3
Middlesbrough v West Bromwich Albion	0-1
Wolverhampton Wanderers v Sheffield United	0-4
Small Heath v Aston Villa	0-0, 0-1

SEMI-FINAL

Tottenham Hotspur v West Bromwich Albion	4-0
Sheffield United v Aston Villa	2-2, 3-0

FINAL AT CRYSTAL PALACE

Tottenham Hotspur v Sheffield United	2-2, 3-1*

*replay at Bolton

SCOTTISH FA CUP 1900-01

FIRST ROUND

Dundee Wanderers v Abercorn	0-3
Celtic v Rangers	1-0
Third Lanark v Douglas Wanderers	5-0
Kilmarnock v Airdrieonians	3-2
St Mirren v Kilwinning Eglinton	10-0
Morton v Bo'ness	10-0
Dundee v Arthurlie	3-1
Stenhousemuir v Queen's Park	1-3
St Bernard's v Partick Thistle	5-0
Heart of Midlothian v Mossend Swifts	7-0
Ayr v Orion	2-2, 3-1
Port Glasgow Athletic v Newton Stewart Athletic	9-1
Hibernian v Dumbarton	7-0
Royal Albert v St Johnstone	1-1, 2-2, 2-0
Forfar Athletic v Leith Athletic	0-4
Clyde v East Stirlingshire	6-0

SECOND ROUND

Clyde v Dundee	3-5
Heart of Midlothian v Queen's Park	2-1
Royal Albert v Hibernian	1-1, 0-1
Ayr v St Mirren	1-3
Celtic v Kilmarnock	6-0
Third Lanark v Abercorn	1-1, 1-0
Morton v St Bernard's	3-1
Leith Athletic v Port Glasgow Athletic	0-3

THIRD ROUND

Dundee v Celtic	0-1
St Mirren v Third Lanark	0-0, 1-1, 3-3, 1-0
Port Glasgow Athletic v Heart of Midlothian	1-5
Hibernian v Morton	2-0

SEMI-FINAL

Heart of Midlothian v Hibernian	1-1, 2-1
St Mirren v Celtic	0-1

FINAL AT IBROX PARK

Heart of Midlothian v Celtic	4-3

League Tables 1901-02

FIRST DIVISION

		P	W	D	L	F	A	Pts
1	Sunderland	34	19	6	9	50	35	44
2	Everton	34	17	7	10	53	35	41
3	Newcastle	34	14	9	11	48	34	37
4	Blackburn	34	15	6	13	52	48	36
5	Nottm Forest	34	13	9	12	43	43	35
6	Derby	34	13	9	12	39	41	35
7	Bury	34	13	8	13	44	38	34
8	Aston Villa	34	13	8	13	42	40	34
9	Wednesday	34	13	8	13	48	52	34
10	Sheff United	34	13	7	14	53	48	33
11	Liverpool	34	10	12	12	42	38	32
12	Bolton	34	12	8	14	51	56	32
13	Notts County	34	14	4	16	51	57	32
14	Wolves	34	13	6	15	46	57	32
15	Grimsby	34	13	6	15	44	60	32
16	Stoke	34	11	9	14	45	55	31
17	Small Heath	34	11	8	15	47	45	30
18	Man City	34	11	6	17	42	58	28

SECOND DIVISION

		P	W	D	L	F	A	Pts
1	WBA	34	25	5	4	82	29	55
2	Middlesbrough	34	23	5	6	90	24	51
3	Preston NE	34	18	6	10	71	32	42
4	Woolwich A	34	18	6	10	50	26	42
5	Lincoln	34	14	13	7	45	35	41
6	Bristol City	34	17	6	11	52	35	40
7	Doncaster	34	13	8	13	49	58	34
8	Glossop NE	34	10	12	12	36	40	32
9	Burnley	34	10	10	14	41	45	30
10	Burton United	34	11	8	15	46	54	30
11	Barnsley	34	12	6	16	51	63	30
12	Burslem PV	34	10	9	15	43	59	29
13	Blackpool	34	11	7	16	40	56	29
14	Leicester Fosse	34	12	5	17	38	56	29
15	Newton Heath	34	11	6	17	38	53	28
16	Chesterfield	34	11	6	17	47	68	28
17	Stockport	34	8	7	19	36	72	23
18	Gainsborough	34	4	11	19	30	80	19

SCOTTISH FIRST DIVISION

		P	W	D	L	F	A	Pts
1	Rangers	18	13	2	3	43	29	28
2	Celtic	18	11	4	3	38	28	26
3	Hearts	18	10	2	6	32	21	22
4	Third Lanark	18	7	5	6	30	26	19
5	St Mirren	18	8	3	7	29	28	19
6	Hibernian	18	6	4	8	36	24	16
7	Kilmarnock	18	5	6	7	21	25	16
8	Queen's Park	18	5	4	9	21	32	14
9	Dundee	18	4	5	9	16	31	13
10	Morton	18	1	5	12	18	40	7

SCOTTISH SECOND DIVISION

		P	W	D	L	F	A	Pts
1	Port Glasgow*	22	14	4	4	71	31	32
2	Partick*	22	14	3	5	55	26	31
3	Motherwell	22	12	2	8	50	44	26
4	Airdrieonians	22	10	5	7	40	32	25
5	Hamilton	22	11	3	8	45	40	25
6	St Bernard's	22	10	2	10	30	30	22
7	Leith	22	9	3	10	34	38	21
8	Ayr	22	8	5	9	27	33	21
9	E Stirlingshire	22	8	3	11	36	46	19
10	Arthurlie	22	6	5	11	32	42	17
11	Abercorn	22	4	5	13	27	57	13
12	Clyde	22	5	3	14	22	50	13

*Elected to First Division

On 5 April 1902, England met Scotland in an International Championship match at Ibrox Park, Glasgow. The day produced the worst disaster the game had known.

The ground was full by kick-off time, and latecomers, anxious not to miss too much of the game, made a dash from the packed East terrace to the West terrace. They charged up the staircases to the top, and settled to watch the match. Heavy rain was falling. Suddenly, rows of steel pylons at the back and front of the terrace shook and a yawning gap 70 feet by 14 feet wide appeared. People literally dropped through to the ground below, and others followed and fell on top of them. Officially, 25 were killed, 24 dangerously injured, 153 injured, and 172 slightly injured. The match ended 1-1, but was deleted from international records, and later replayed at Birmingham.

Top *The Aston Villa forwards attack Sunderland's goal in March 1902. Before the start of the following season, the curved line marking the goal area was replaced by the six-yard box.*

Bottom *'Fatty' Foulke, Sheffield United's 21-stone goalkeeper, prepares to gather a tentative shot from the old-style lines during the 1902 Cup Final.*

FA CUP 1901-02

FIRST ROUND

Tottenham Hotspur v Southampton	1-1, 2-2, 1-2
Liverpool v Everton	2-2, 2-0
Bury v West Bromwich Albion	5-1
Walsall v Burnley	1-0
Glossop North End v Nottingham Forest	1-3
Manchester City v Preston North End	1-1, 0-0, 4-2*
Stoke v Aston Villa	2-2, 2-1
Bristol Rovers v Middlesbrough	1-1, 1-0
Northampton Town v Sheffield United	0-2
Wolverhampton Wanderers v Bolton Wanderers	0-2
Woolwich Arsenal v Newcastle United	0-2
The Wednesday v Sunderland	0-1
Blackburn Rovers v Derby County	0-2
Lincoln City v Oxford City	0-0, 4-0
Portsmouth v Grimsby Town	1-1, 2-0
Notts County v Reading	1-2

*At Preston. Preston won the toss for choice of ground.

SECOND ROUND

Southampton v Liverpool	4-1
Walsall v Bury	0-5
Manchester City v Nottingham Forest	0-2
Bristol Rovers v Stoke	0-1
Sheffield United v Bolton Wanderers	2-1
Newcastle United v Sunderland	1-0
Lincoln City v Derby County	1-3
Reading v Portsmouth	0-1

THIRD ROUND

Bury v Southampton	2-3
Nottingham Forest v Stoke	2-0
Newcastle United v Sheffield United	1-1, 1-2
Derby County v Portsmouth	0-0, 6-3

SEMI-FINAL

Southampton v Nottingham Forest	3-1
Sheffield United v Derby County	1-1, 1-1, 1-0

FINAL AT CRYSTAL PALACE

Sheffield United v Southampton	1-1, 2-1†

†replay at Crystal Palace

SCOTTISH FA CUP 1901-02

FIRST ROUND

Arbroath v Kilwinning Eglinton (scratched)	wo
Third Lanark v Morton	0-0, 3-2
St Mirren v Airdrieonians	1-0
Ayr v Dundee	0-0, 0-2
Arthurlie v Port Glasgow Athletic	1-1, 1-3
Celtic v Thornliebank	3-0
Rangers v Johnstone	6-1
Queen's Park v Maxwelltown Volunteers	7-0
Partick Thistle v Kilmarnock	0-4
Falkirk	bye
Forfar Athletic	bye
Heart of Midlothian	bye
Hibernian	bye
Inverness Caledonian	bye
St Bernard's	bye
Stenhousemiur	bye

SECOND ROUND

Heart of Midlothian v Third Lanark	4-1
St Mirren v Stenhousemuir	6-0
Arbroath v Celtic	2-3
Rangers v Inverness Caledonian	5-1
Kilmarnock v Dundee	2-0
Falkirk v St Bernard's	2-0
Forfar Athletic v Queen's Park	1-4
Port Glasgow Athletic v Hibernian	1-5

THIRD ROUND

Falkirk v St Mirren	0-1
Heart of Midlothian v Celtic	1-1, 1-2
Hibernian v Queen's Park	7-1
Rangers v Kilmarnock	2-0

SEMI-FINAL

Rangers v Hibernian	0-2
St Mirren v Celtic	2-3

FINAL AT CELTIC PARK,

Hibernian v Celtic	1-0

League Tables 1902-03

FIRST DIVISION

		P	W	D	L	F	A	Pts
1	Wednesday	34	19	4	11	54	36	42
2	Aston Villa	34	19	3	12	61	40	41
3	Sunderland	34	16	9	9	51	36	41
4	Sheff United	34	17	5	12	58	44	39
5	Liverpool	34	17	4	13	68	49	38
6	Stoke	34	15	7	12	46	38	37
7	WBA	34	16	4	14	54	53	36
8	Bury	34	16	3	15	54	43	35
9	Derby	34	16	3	15	50	47	35
10	Nottm Forest	34	14	7	13	49	47	35
11	Wolves	34	14	5	15	48	57	33
12	Everton	34	13	6	15	45	47	32
13	Middlesbrough	34	14	4	16	41	50	32
14	Newcastle	34	14	4	16	41	51	32
15	Notts County	34	12	7	15	41	49	31
16	Blackburn	34	12	5	17	44	63	29
17	Grimsby	34	8	9	17	43	62	25
18	Bolton	34	8	3	23	37	73	19

SECOND DIVISION

		P	W	D	L	F	A	Pts
1	Man City	34	25	4	5	95	29	54
2	Small Heath	34	24	3	7	74	36	51
3	Woolwich A	34	20	8	6	66	30	48
4	Bristol City	34	17	8	9	59	38	42
5	Man United	34	15	8	11	53	38	38
6	Chesterfield	34	14	9	11	67	40	37
7	Preston	34	13	10	11	56	40	36
8	Barnsley	34	13	8	13	55	51	34
9	Burslem PV	34	13	8	13	57	62	34
10	Lincoln	34	12	6	16	46	53	30
11	Glossop NE	34	11	7	16	43	58	29
12	Gainsborough	34	11	7	16	41	59	29
13	Burton United	34	11	7	16	39	59	29
14	Blackpool	34	9	10	15	44	59	28
15	Leicester Fosse	34	10	8	16	41	65	28
16	Doncaster	34	9	7	18	35	72	25
17	Stockport	34	7	6	21	39	74	20
18	Burnley	34	6	8	20	30	77	20

SCOTTISH FIRST DIVISION

		P	W	D	L	F	A	Pts
1	Hibernian	22	16	5	1	48	18	37
2	Dundee	22	13	5	4	31	12	31
3	Rangers	22	12	5	5	56	30	29
4	Hearts	22	11	6	5	46	27	28
5	Celtic	22	8	10	4	36	30	26
6	St Mirren	22	7	8	7	39	40	22
7	Third Lanark	22	8	5	9	34	27	21
8	Partick	22	6	7	9	34	50	19
9	Kilmarnock	22	6	4	12	24	43	16
10	Queen's Park	22	5	5	12	33	48	15
11	Port Glasgow	22	3	5	14	26	49	11
12	Morton	22	2	5	15	22	55	9

SCOTTISH SECOND DIVISION

		P	W	D	L	F	A	Pts
1	Airdrieonians*	22	15	5	2	43	19	35
2	Motherwell*	22	12	4	6	44	35	28
3	Ayr	22	12	3	7	34	24	27
4	Leith	22	11	5	6	43	41	27
5	St Bernard's	22	12	2	8	45	32	26
6	Hamilton	22	11	1	10	44	35	23
7	Falkirk	22	8	7	7	39	37	23
8	E Stirlingshire	22	9	3	10	46	41	21
9	Arthurlie	22	6	8	8	34	46	20
10	Abercorn	22	5	2	15	35	58	12
11	Raith	22	3	5	14	34	55	11
12	Clyde	22	2	7	13	22	40	11

*elected to First Division

Bury on the attack against Derby County on their way to the record win, 6-0, in an FA Cup Final.

CONWAY PICTURE LIBRARY

FA CUP 1902-03

FIRST ROUND

Tottenham Hotspur v West Bromwich Albion	0-0, 2-0
Bolton Wanderers v Bristol City	0-5
Aston Villa v Sunderland	4-1
Barnsley v Lincoln City	2-0
Woolwich Arsenal v Sheffield United	1-3
Bury v Wolverhampton Wanderers	1-0
Grimsby Town v Newcastle United	2-1
Notts County v Southampton	0-0, 2-2, 2-1
Derby County v Small Heath	2-1
Blackburn Rovers v The Wednesday	0-0, 1-0
Nottingham Forest v Reading	0-0, 6-3
Glossop North End v Stoke	2-3
Millwall Athletic v Luton Town	3-0
Preston North End v Manchester City	3-1
Everton v Portsmouth	5-0
Manchester United v Liverpool	2-1

SECOND ROUND

Tottenham Hotspur v Bristol City	1-0
Aston Villa v Barnsley	4-1
Sheffield United v Bury	0-1
Grimsby Town v Notts County	0-2
Derby County v Blackburn Rovers	2-0
Nottingham Forest v Stoke	0-0, 0-2
Millwall Athletic v Preston North End	4-1
Everton v Manchester United	3-1

THIRD ROUND

Tottenham Hotspur v Aston Villa	2-3
Bury v Notts County	1-0
Derby County v Stoke	3-0
Millwall Athletic v Everton	1-0

SEMI-FINAL

Aston Villa v Bury	0-3
Derby County v Millwall Athletic	3-0

FINAL AT CRYSTAL PALACE

Bury v Derby County	6-0

SCOTTISH FA CUP 1902-03

FIRST ROUND

Celtic v St Mirren	0-0, 1-1, 4-0
St Johnstone v Third Lanark	1-10
Nithsdale Wanderers v Orion	1-0
Queen's Park v Motherwell	1-2
Abercorn v Douglas Wanderers	2-2, 1-3
Vale of Leven v Partick Thistle	0-4
Hamilton Academicals v Airdrieonians	5-0
Arbroath v Kilmarnock	1-3
Leith Athletic v Broxburn United	4-1
St Bernard's v Port Glasgow Athletic	1-2
Rangers v Auchterarder Thistle	7-0
Clyde v Heart of Midlothian	1-2
Hibernian v Morton	7-0
Ayr v Camelon	2-0
Dundee v Barholm Rovers	wo
Stenhousemuir v Inverness Caledonian	wo

SECOND ROUND

Celtic v Port Glasgow Athletic	2-0
Hamilton Academicals v Third Lanark	2-2, 1-3
Stenhousemuir v Douglas Wanderers	6-1
Motherwell v Partick Thistle	0-2
Dundee v Nithsdale Wanderers	7-0
Rangers v Kilmarnock	4-0
Ayr v Heart of Midlothian	2-4
Hibernian v Leith Athletic	4-1

THIRD ROUND

Celtic v Rangers	0-3
Dundee v Hibernian	0-0, 0-0, 1-0
Heart of Midlothian v Third Lanark	2-1
Stenhousemuir v Partick Thistle	3-0

SEMI-FINAL

Stenhousemuir v Rangers	1-4
Dundee v Heart of Midlothian	0-0, 0-1

FINAL AT CELTIC PARK

Rangers v Heart of Midlothian	1-1, 0-0, 2-0

FIRST DIVISION

		P	W	D	L	F	A	Pts
1	Wednesday	34	20	7	7	48	28	47
2	Man City	34	19	6	9	71	45	44
3	Everton	34	19	5	10	59	32	43
4	Newcastle	34	18	6	10	58	45	42
5	Aston Villa	34	17	7	10	70	48	41
6	Sunderland	34	17	5	12	63	49	39
7	Sheff United	34	15	8	11	62	57	38
8	Wolves	34	14	8	12	44	66	36
9	Nottm Forest	34	11	9	14	57	57	31
10	Middlesbrough	34	9	12	13	46	47	30
11	Small Heath	34	11	8	15	39	52	30
12	Bury	34	7	15	12	40	53	29
13	Notts County	34	12	5	17	37	61	29
14	Derby	34	9	10	15	58	60	28
15	Blackburn	34	11	6	17	48	60	28
16	Stoke	34	10	7	17	54	57	27
17	Liverpool	34	9	8	17	49	62	26
18	WBA	34	7	10	17	36	60	24

SECOND DIVISION

		P	W	D	L	F	A	Pts
1	Preston	34	20	10	4	62	24	50
2	Woolwich A	34	21	7	6	91	22	49
3	Man United	34	20	8	6	65	33	48
4	Bristol City	34	18	6	10	73	41	42
5	Burnley	34	15	9	10	50	55	39
6	Grimsby	34	14	8	12	50	49	36
7	Bolton	34	12	10	12	59	41	34
8	Barnsley	34	11	10	13	38	57	32
9	Gainsborough	34	14	3	17	53	60	31
10	Bradford City	34	12	7	15	45	59	31
11	Chesterfield	34	11	8	15	37	45	30
12	Lincoln	34	11	8	15	41	58	30
13	Burslem PV	34	10	9	15	54	52	29
14	Burton United	34	11	7	16	45	61	29
15	Blackpool	34	11	5	18	40	67	27
16	Stockport	34	8	11	15	40	72	27
17	Glossop NE	34	10	6	18	57	64	26
18	Leicester Fosse	34	6	10	18	42	82	22

SCOTTISH FIRST DIVISION

		P	W	D	L	F	A	Pts
1	Third Lanark	26	20	3	3	61	26	43
2	Hearts	26	18	3	5	62	34	39
3	Celtic	26	18	2	6	68	27	38
4	Rangers	26	16	6	4	80	33	38
5	Dundee	26	13	2	11	54	45	28
6	St Mirren	26	11	5	10	45	38	27
7	Partick	26	10	7	9	46	41	27
8	Queen's Park	26	6	9	11	28	47	21
9	Port Glasgow	26	8	4	14	32	49	20
10	Hibernian	26	7	5	14	29	40	19
11	Morton	26	7	4	15	32	53	18
12	Airdrieonians	26	7	4	15	32	62	18
13	Motherwell	26	6	3	17	26	61	15
14	Kilmarnock	26	4	5	17	24	63	13

SCOTTISH SECOND DIVISION

		P	W	D	L	F	A	Pts
1	Hamilton	22	16	5	1	56	19	37
2	Clyde	22	12	5	5	51	36	29
3	Ayr	22	11	6	5	33	30	28
4	Falkirk	22	11	4	7	50	34	26
5	Raith	22	8	5	9	40	38	21
6	E Stirlingshire	22	8	5	9	35	40	21
7	Leith	22	8	4	10	42	40	20
8	St Bernard's	22	9	2	11	31	43	20
9	Albion*	22	8	5	9	47	37	19
10	Abercorn	22	6	4	12	38	55	16
11	Arthurlie	22	5	5	12	37	50	15
12	Ayr Parkhouse	22	3	4	15	23	61	10

*Two points deducted for fielding an unregistered player.

Below *The Manchester City side that won the FA Cup in 1903-04. Seated in the centre is the captain and great Welsh right-winger, Billy Meredith of Chirk.*

At Bradford, Sheffield FC, the oldest football club in the world, won their first and only honour when they beat Ealing 3-1 in the 1904 Amateur Cup final.

MANCHESTER CITY FOOTBALL CLUB.

WINNERS OF ENGLISH CUP, 1903-4.

RUNNERS-UP, FOOTBALL LEAGUE, 1903-4. ◆ JOINT HOLDERS MANCHESTER CUP, 1903-4.

RADIO TIMES HULTON PICTURE LIBRARY

FA CUP 1903-04

FIRST ROUND

Manchester City v Sunderland	3-2
Woolwich Arsenal v Fulham	1-0
Millwall Athletic v Middlesbrough	0-2
Preston North End v Grimsby Town	1-0
Plymouth Argyle v The Wednesday	2-2, 0-2
Notts County v Manchester United	3-3, 1-2
Everton v Tottenham Hotspur	1-2
Stoke v Aston Villa	2-3
Reading v Bolton Wanderers	1-1, 2-3
Southampton v Burslem Port Vale	3-0
Bristol City v Sheffield United	1-3
Bury v Newcastle United	2-1
Portsmouth v Derby County	2-5
Stockton v Wolverhampton Wanderers	1-4
Blackburn Rovers v Liverpool	3-1
West Bromwich Albion v Nottingham Forest	1-1, 1-3

SECOND ROUND

Woolwich Arsenal v Manchester City	0-2
Preston North End v Middlesbrough	0-3
The Wednesday v Manchester United	6-0
Tottenham Hotspur v Aston Villa	0-1*, 1-0
Bolton Wanderers v Southampton	4-1
Bury v Sheffield United	1-2
Derby County v Wolverhampton Wanderers	2-2, 2-2, 1-0
Blackburn Rovers v Nottingham Forest	3-1

*The Tottenham crowd invaded the pitch when Villa were leading 1-0 and the game was abandoned. Tottenham were fined £350 and the FA ordered the return to be played at Villa Park.

THIRD ROUND

Manchester City v Middlesbrough	0-0, 3-1
Tottenham Hotspur v The Wednesday	1-1, 0-2
Sheffield United v Bolton Wanderers	0-2
Derby County v Blackburn Rovers	2-1

SEMI-FINAL

Manchester City v The Wednesday	3-0
Bolton Wanderers v Derby County	1-0

FINAL AT CRYSTAL PALACE

Manchester City v Bolton Wanderers	1-0

SCOTTISH FA CUP 1903-04

FIRST ROUND

Abercorn v Maxwelltown Volunteers	2-2, 1-1, 2-1
Nithsdale Wanderers v Kilmarnock	2-2, 1-1, 1-2
Clyde v Arbroath	2-2, 0-4
Rangers v Heart of Midlothian	3-2
Dundee v Queen's Park	3-0
Hibernian v Airdrieonians	2-1
Motherwell v Partick Thistle	2-1
Ayr v St Mirren	0-2
St Johnstone v Hearts of Beath	2-0
Albion Rovers v Kilwinning Eglinton	2-1
St Bernard's v West Calder Swifts	1-1, 3-3, 2-1
Port Glasgow Athletic v Leith Athletic	1-2
Alloa Athletic v Aberdour	2-1
Third Lanark v Newton Stewart Athletic (scratched)	wo
Celtic v Stanley (scratched)	wo
Morton v Dalbeattie Star (scratched)	wo

SECOND ROUND

Kilmarnock v Albion Rovers	2-2, 1-0
St Bernard's v Celtic	0-4
Dundee v Abercorn	4-0
Third Lanark v Alloa Athletic	3-1
Hibernian v Rangers	1-2
Leith Athletic v Motherwell	3-1
Morton v Arbroath	2-0
St Mirren v St Johnstone	4-0

THIRD ROUND

Celtic v Dundee	1-1, 0-0, 5-0
Third Lanark v Kilmarnock	3-0
St Mirren v Rangers	0-1
Leith Athletic v Morton	1-3

SEMI-FINAL

Celtic v Third Lanark	2-1
Rangers v Morton	3-0

FINAL AT HAMPDEN PARK

Celtic v Rangers	3-2

League Tables 1904-05

FIRST DIVISION

		P	W	D	L	F	A	Pts
1	Newcastle	34	23	2	9	72	33	48
2	Everton	34	21	5	8	63	36	47
3	Man City	34	20	6	8	66	37	46
4	Aston Villa	34	19	4	11	63	43	42
5	Sunderland	34	16	8	10	60	44	40
6	Sheff United	34	19	2	13	64	56	40
7	Small Heath	34	17	5	12	54	38	39
8	Preston	34	13	10	11	42	37	36
9	Wednesday	34	14	5	15	61	57	33
10	Woolwich A	34	12	9	13	36	40	33
11	Derby	34	12	8	14	37	48	32
12	Stoke	34	13	4	17	40	58	30
13	Blackburn	34	11	5	18	40	51	27
14	Wolves	34	11	4	19	47	73	26
15	Middlesbrough	34	9	8	17	36	56	26
16	Nottm Forest	34	9	7	18	40	61	25
17	Bury	34	10	4	20	47	67	24
18	Notts County	34	5	8	21	36	69	18

SECOND DIVISION

		P	W	D	L	F	A	Pts
1	Liverpool	34	27	4	3	93	25	58
2	Bolton	34	27	2	5	87	32	56
3	Man United	34	24	5	5	81	30	53
4	Bristol City	34	19	4	11	66	45	42
5	Chesterfield	34	14	11	9	44	35	39
6	Gainsborough	34	14	8	12	61	58	36
7	Barnsley	34	14	5	15	38	56	33
8	Bradford City	34	12	8	14	45	49	32
9	Lincoln	34	12	7	15	42	40	31
10	WBA	34	13	4	17	56	48	30
11	Burnley	34	12	6	16	43	52	30
12	Glossop NE	34	10	10	14	37	46	30
13	Grimsby	34	11	8	15	33	46	30
14	Leicester Fosse	34	11	7	16	40	55	29
15	Blackpool	34	9	10	15	36	48	28
16	Burslem PV	34	10	7	17	47	72	27
17	Burton United	34	8	4	22	30	84	20
18	Doncaster	34	3	2	29	23	81	8

SCOTTISH FIRST DIVISION

		P	W	D	L	F	A	Pts
1	Celtic*	26	18	5	3	68	31	41
2	Rangers	26	19	3	4	83	28	41
3	Third Lanark	26	14	7	5	60	28	35
4	Airdrieonians	26	11	5	10	38	45	27
5	Hibernian	26	9	8	9	39	39	26
6	Partick	26	12	2	12	36	56	26
7	Dundee	26	10	5	11	38	32	25
8	Hearts	26	11	3	12	46	44	25
9	Kilmarnock	26	9	5	12	29	45	23
10	St Mirren	26	9	4	13	33	36	22
11	Port Glasgow	26	8	5	13	30	51	21
12	Queen's Park	26	6	8	12	28	45	20
13	Morton	26	7	4	15	27	50	18
14	Motherwell	26	6	2	18	28	53	14

*Celtic won a deciding match against Rangers

SCOTTISH SECOND DIVISION

		P	W	D	L	F	A	Pts
1	Clyde	22	13	6	3	38	22	32
2	Falkirk*	22	12	4	6	31	25	28
3	Hamilton	22	12	3	7	40	22	27
4	Leith	22	10	4	8	36	26	24
5	Ayr	22	11	1	10	46	37	23
6	Arthurlie	22	9	5	8	37	42	23
7	Aberdeen*	22	7	7	8	36	26	21
8	Albion	22	8	4	10	38	53	20
9	E Stirlingshire	22	7	5	10	38	38	19
10	Raith	22	9	1	12	30	34	19
11	Abercorn	22	8	1	13	31	45	17
12	St Bernard's	22	3	5	14	23	54	11

*Aberdeen and Falkirk were elected to the First Division

FA CUP 1904-05

FIRST ROUND

Lincoln City v Manchester City	1-2
Bolton Wanderers v Bristol Rovers	1-1, 3-0
Middlesbrough v Tottenham Hotspur	1-1, 0-1
Newcastle United v Plymouth Argyle	1-1, 1-1, 2-0
Woolwich Arsenal v Bristol City	0-0, 0-1
Derby County v Preston North End	0-2
Blackburn Rovers v The Wednesday	1-2
Small Heath v Portsmouth	0-2
Stoke v Grimsby Town	2-0
Liverpool v Everton	1-1, 1-2
Sunderland v Wolverhampton Wanderers	1-1, 0-1
Southampton v Millwall Athletic	3-1
Aston Villa v Leicester Fosse	5-1
Bury v Notts County	1-0
Fulham v Reading	0-0, 0-0, 1-0
Nottingham Forest v Sheffield United	2-0

SECOND ROUND

Manchester City v Bolton Wanderers	1-2
Tottenham Hotspur v Newcastle United	1-1, 0-4
Bristol City v Preston North End	0-0, 0-1
The Wednesday v Portsmouth	2-1
Stoke v Everton	0-4
Wolverhampton Wanderers v Southampton	2-3
Aston Villa v Bury	3-2
Fulham v Nottingham Forest	1-0

THIRD ROUND

Bolton Wanderers v Newcastle United	0-2
Preston North End v The Wednesday	1-1, 0-3
Everton v Southampton	4-0
Aston Villa v Fulham	5-0

SEMI-FINAL

Newcastle United v The Wednesday	1-0
Everton v Aston Villa	1-1, 1-2

FINAL AT CRYSTAL PALACE

Aston Villa v Newcastle United	2-0

SCOTTISH FA CUP 1904-05

FIRST ROUND

Rangers v Ayr	2-1
Dundee v Heart of Midlothian	1-3
Dumfries v Celtic	1-2
Port Glasgow Athletic v Stranraer	3-0
Airdrieonians v St Johnstone	7-0
Aberdeen v Queen's Park	2-1
St Mirren v Clyde	1-0
Third Lanark v Leith Athletic	4-1
Morton v Renton	2-0
Kilmarnock v Beith	2-2, 1-3
Bathgate v Arbroath	2-1
Arthurlie v Motherwell	0-0, 0-1
Hibernian v Partick Thistle	1-1, 2-4
Kirkcaldy United v Crieff Morrisonians	3-1
Cowdenbeath v 6th GRV	6-0
Lochgelly United v Inverness Caledonian	5-1

SECOND ROUND

Celtic v Lochgelly United	3-0
Aberdeen v Bathgate	1-1, 6-1
Kirkcaldy United v Partick Thistle	0-1
Morton v Rangers	0-6
Airdrieonians v Port Glasgow Athletic	3-0
Motherwell v Third Lanark	0-1
St Mirren v Heart of Midlothian	1-0
Beith v Cowdenbeath	4-0

THIRD ROUND

St Mirren v Airdrieonians	0-0, 1-3
Rangers v Beith	5-1
Celtic v Partick Thistle	3-0
Third Lanark v Aberdeen	4-1

SEMI-FINAL

Celtic v Rangers	0-2
Airdrieonians v Third Lanark	1-2

FINAL AT HAMPDEN PARK

Third Lanark v Rangers	0-0, 3-1

Doncaster Rovers had a disastrous spell in the Second Division and were voted out of the League in 1905 after gaining the fewest number of points (8) ever won by a League club in a single season. Not one of those 8 was won away from home. This equalled Loughborough Town's dreadful 1899-1900 season when they also accumulated just 8 points. Loughborough, however, established a record by winning only one of their 34 League games.

Below *The only known panoramic view of Crystal Palace during a Cup Final. The event was played there from 1895 to 1914 but, apart from the small stands on the right, there was little accommodation available. The Crystal Palace itself, which had been moved from Hyde Park after the Great Exhibition of the 1850s, was on the hill above the funfair to the right. The 1905 Final attracted over 100,000 spectators, only the second time in history an English football match had drawn a six-figure crowd. Some fans can be seen clinging on to trees on the left as Aston Villa play Newcastle United.*

RADIO TIMES HULTON PICTURE LIBRARY/ROY FLOOKS

FIRST DIVISION

		P	W	D	L	F	A	Pts
1	Liverpool	38	23	5	10	79	46	51
2	Preston NE	38	17	13	8	54	39	47
3	Wednesday	38	18	8	12	63	52	44
4	Newcastle	38	18	7	13	74	48	43
5	Man City	38	19	5	14	73	54	43
6	Bolton	38	17	7	14	81	67	41
7	Birmingham	38	17	7	14	65	59	41
8	Aston Villa	38	17	6	15	72	56	40
9	Blackburn	38	16	8	14	54	52	40
10	Stoke	38	16	7	15	54	55	39
11	Everton	38	15	7	16	70	66	37
12	Woolwich A	38	15	7	16	62	64	37
13	Sheff United	38	15	6	17	57	62	36
14	Sunderland	38	15	5	18	61	70	35
15	Derby	38	14	7	17	39	58	35
16	Notts County	38	11	12	15	55	71	34
17	Bury	38	11	10	17	57	74	32
18	Middlesbrough	38	10	11	17	56	71	31
19	Nottm Forest	38	13	5	20	58	79	31
20	Wolves	38	8	7	23	58	99	23

SECOND DIVISION

		P	W	D	L	F	A	Pts
1	Bristol City	38	30	6	2	83	28	66
2	Man United	38	28	6	4	90	28	62
3	Chelsea	38	22	9	7	90	37	53
4	WBA	38	22	8	8	79	36	52
5	Hull	38	19	6	13	67	54	44
6	Leeds City	38	17	9	12	59	47	43
7	Leicester Fosse	38	15	12	11	53	48	42
8	Grimsby	38	15	10	13	46	46	40
9	Burnley	38	15	8	15	42	53	38
10	Stockport	38	13	9	16	44	56	35
11	Bradford City	38	13	8	17	46	60	34
12	Barnsley	38	12	9	17	60	62	33
13	Lincoln	38	12	6	20	69	72	30
14	Blackpool	38	10	9	19	37	62	29
15	Gainsborough	38	12	4	22	44	57	28
16	Glossop NE	38	10	8	20	49	71	28
17	Burslem PV	38	12	4	22	49	82	28
18	Chesterfield	38	10	8	20	40	72	28
19	Burton United	38	10	6	22	34	67	26
20	Clapton Orient	38	7	7	24	35	78	21

SCOTTISH FIRST DIVISION

		P	W	D	L	F	A	Pts
1	Celtic	30	24	1	5	76	19	49
2	Hearts	30	18	7	5	64	27	43
3	Airdrieonians	30	15	8	7	53	31	38
4	Rangers	30	15	7	8	58	48	37
5	Partick	30	15	6	9	44	40	36
6	Third Lanark	30	16	2	12	62	39	34
7	Dundee	30	11	12	7	40	33	34
8	St Mirren	30	13	5	12	41	37	31
9	Motherwell	30	9	8	13	50	62	26
10	Morton	30	10	6	14	35	54	26
11	Hibernian	30	10	5	15	35	40	25
12	Aberdeen	30	8	8	14	36	48	24
13	Falkirk	30	9	5	16	52	68	23
14	Kilmarnock	30	8	4	18	46	68	20
15	Port Glasgow	30	6	8	16	38	68	20
16	Queen's Park	30	5	4	21	39	87	14

SCOTTISH SECOND DIVISION

		P	W	D	L	F	A	Pts
1	Leith	22	15	4	3	46	21	34
2	Clyde*	22	11	9	2	37	21	31
3	Albion	22	12	3	7	48	29	27
4	Hamilton*	22	12	2	8	45	34	26
5	St Bernard's	22	9	4	9	42	34	22
6	Arthurlie	22	10	2	10	42	43	22
7	Ayr	22	9	3	10	43	51	21
8	Raith	22	6	7	9	36	42	19
9	Cowdenbeath	22	7	3	12	27	39	17
10	Abercorn	22	6	5	11	29	45	17
11	Vale of Leven	22	6	4	12	34	49	16
12	E Stirlingshire	22	1	10	11	26	47	12

*Elected to First Division

Below *The Everton team that won the club's first ever FA Cup in 1906.*

COLORSPORT

FA CUP 1905-06

SECOND ROUND

Woolwich Arsenal v Watford	3-0
Sunderland v Gainsborough Trinity	1-1, 3-0
Manchester United v Norwich City	3-0
Aston Villa v Plymouth Argyle	0-0, 5-1
Derby County v Newcastle United	0-0, 1-2
Blackpool v Sheffield United	2-1
Tottenham Hotspur v Reading	3-2
Stoke v Birmingham	0-1
Chesterfield Town v Everton	0-3
Bradford City v Wolverhampton Wanderers	5-0
The Wednesday v Millwall Athletic	1-1, 3-0
Fulham v Nottingham Forest	1-3
Barnsley v Liverpool	0-1
Brentford v Lincoln City	3-0
New Brompton v Southampton	0-0, 0-1
Brighton v Middlesbrough	1-1, 1-1, 1-3

THIRD ROUND

Woolwich Arsenal v Sunderland	5-0
Manchester United v Aston Villa	5-1
Newcastle United v Blackpool	5-0
Tottenham Hotspur v Birmingham	1-1, 0-2
Everton v Bradford City	1-0
The Wednesday v Nottingham Forest	4-1
Liverpool v Brentford	2-0
Southampton v Middlesbrough	6-1

FOURTH ROUND

Manchester United v Woolwich Arsenal	2-3
Birmingham v Newcastle United	2-2, 0-3
Everton v The Wednesday	4-3
Liverpool v Southampton	3-0

SEMI-FINAL

Woolwich Arsenal v Newcastle United	0-2
Everton v Liverpool	2-0

FINAL AT CRYSTAL PALACE

Everton v Newcastle United	1-0

SCOTTISH FA CUP 1905-06

FIRST ROUND

Dundee v Celtic	1-2
Kilmarnock v Clyde	2-1
Beith v Inverness Thistle	2-0
Third Lanark v Galston	5-0
Forfar Athletic v Queen's Park	0-4
Falkirk v Hibernian	1-2
Leith Athletic v Partick Thistle	1-2
Heart of Midlothian v Nithsdale Wanderers	4-1
Motherwell v Hamilton Academicals	2-3
Airdrieonians v Maxwelltown Volunteers	9-2
Aberdeen v Dunfermline Athletic	3-0
Morton v Lochgelly United	4-3
St Mirren v Black Watch	7-2
Arthurlie v Rangers	1-7
Arbroath v Bo'ness	1-4
Port Glasgow Athletic v Dunblane	6-1

SECOND ROUND

Aberdeen v Rangers	2-3
Hibernian v Partick Thistle	1-1, 1-1, 2-1
Beith v Heart of Midlothian	0-3
Celtic v Bo'ness	3-0
Third Lanark v Hamilton Academicals	2-2, 3-1
St Mirren v Morton	3-1
Kilmarnock v Port Glasgow Athletic	2-2, 0-0, 0-0, 0-1
Queen's Park v Airdrieonians	1-2

THIRD ROUND

Celtic v Heart of Midlothian	1-2
Airdrieonians v St Mirren	0-0, 0-2
Port Glasgow Athletic v Rangers	1-0
Hibernian v Third Lanark	1-2

SEMI-FINAL

St Mirren v Third Lanark	1-1, 0-0, 0-1
Port Glasgow Athletic v Heart of Midlothian	0-2

FINAL AT IBROX PARK

Heart of Midlothian v Third Lanark	1-0

League Tables 1906-07

FIRST DIVISION

	P	W	D	L	F	A	Pts
1 Newcastle	38	22	7	9	74	46	51
2 Bristol City	38	20	8	10	66	47	48
3 Everton	38	20	5	13	70	46	45
4 Sheff United	38	17	11	10	57	55	45
5 Aston Villa	38	19	6	13	78	52	44
6 Bolton	38	18	8	12	59	47	44
7 Woolwich A	38	20	4	14	66	59	44
8 Man United	38	17	8	13	53	56	42
9 Birmingham	38	15	8	15	52	52	38
10 Sunderland	38	14	9	15	65	66	37
11 Middlesbrough	38	15	6	17	56	63	36
12 Blackburn	38	14	7	17	56	59	35
13 Wednesday	38	12	11	15	49	60	35
14 Preston	38	14	7	17	44	57	35
15 Liverpool	38	13	7	18	64	65	33
16 Bury	38	13	6	19	58	68	32
17 Man City	38	10	12	16	53	77	32
18 Notts County	38	8	15	15	46	50	31
19 Derby	38	9	9	20	41	59	27
20 Stoke	38	8	10	20	41	64	26

SECOND DIVISION

	P	W	D	L	F	A	Pts
1 Nottm Forest	38	28	4	6	74	36	60
2 Chelsea	38	26	5	7	80	34	57
3 Leicester Fosse	38	20	8	10	62	39	48
4 WBA	38	21	5	12	83	45	47
5 Bradford City	38	21	5	12	70	53	47
6 Wolves	38	17	7	14	66	53	41
7 Burnley	38	17	6	15	62	47	40
8 Barnsley	38	15	8	15	73	55	38
9 Hull	38	15	7	16	65	57	37
10 Leeds City	38	13	10	15	55	63	36
11 Grimsby	38	16	3	19	57	62	35
12 Stockport	38	12	11	15	42	52	35
13 Blackpool	38	11	11	16	33	51	33
14 Gainsborough	38	14	5	19	45	72	33
15 Glossop NE	38	13	6	19	53	79	32
16 Burslem PV	38	12	7	19	60	83	31
17 Clapton Orient	38	11	8	19	45	67	30
18 Chesterfield	38	11	7	20	50	66	29
19 Lincoln	38	12	4	22	46	73	28
20 Burton United	38	8	7	23	34	68	23

SCOTTISH FIRST DIVISION

	P	W	D	L	F	A	Pts
1 Celtic	34	23	9	2	80	30	55
2 Dundee	34	18	12	4	53	26	48
3 Rangers	34	19	7	8	69	33	45
4 Airdrieonians	34	18	6	10	59	44	42
5 Falkirk	34	17	7	10	73	58	41
6 Third Lanark	34	15	9	10	57	48	39
7 St Mirren	34	12	13	9	50	44	37
8 Clyde	34	15	6	13	47	52	36
9 Hearts	34	11	13	10	47	43	35
10 Motherwell	34	12	9	13	45	49	33
11 Aberdeen	34	10	10	14	48	55	30
12 Hibernian	34	10	10	14	40	49	30
13 Morton	34	11	6	17	41	50	28
14 Partick Thistle	34	9	8	17	40	60	26
15 Queen's Park	34	9	6	19	51	66	24
16 Hamilton	34	8	5	21	40	64	21
17 Kilmarnock	34	8	5	21	40	72	21
18 Port Glasgow	34	7	7	20	30	67	21

SCOTTISH SECOND DIVISION

	P	W	D	L	F	A	Pts
1 St Bernard's	22	14	4	4	41	24	32
2 Vale of Leven	22	13	1	8	54	35	27
3 Arthurlie	22	12	3	7	50	39	27
4 Dumbarton	22	11	3	8	52	35	25
5 Leith	22	10	4	8	40	35	24
6 Albion	22	10	3	9	43	36	23
7 Cowdenbeath	22	10	5	7	36	39	23*
8 Ayr	22	7	6	9	34	38	20
9 Abercorn	22	5	7	10	29	47	17
10 Raith	22	6	4	12	39	47	16
11 E Stirlingshire	22	6	4	12	37	48	16
12 Ayr Parkhouse	22	5	2	15	32	64	12

*two points deducted for an irregularity

FA CUP 1906-07

SECOND ROUND

Burslem Port Vale v Notts County	2-2, 0-5
Blackburn Rovers v Tottenham Hotspur	1-1, 1-1, 1-2
West Bromwich Albion v Norwich City	1-0
Derby County v Lincoln City	1-0
Fulham v Crystal Palace	0-0, 0-1
Brentford v Middlesbrough	1-0
West Ham United v Everton	1-2
Bolton Wanderers v Aston Villa	2-0
Woolwich Arsenal v Bristol City	2-1
Bristol Rovers v Millwall	3-0
Barnsley v Portsmouth	1-0
Bury v New Brompton	1-0
Oldham Athletic v Liverpool	0-1
Bradford City v Accrington Stanley	1-0
Southampton v The Wednesday	1-1, 1-3
Luton Town v Sunderland	0-0, 0-1

THIRD ROUND

Notts County v Tottenham Hotspur	4-0
West Bromwich Albion v Derby County	2-0
Crystal Palace v Brentford	1-1, 1-0
Everton v Bolton Wanderers	0-0, 3-0
Woolwich Arsenal v Bristol Rovers	1-0
Barnsley v Bury	1-0
Liverpool v Bradford City	1-0
The Wednesday v Sunderland	0-0, 1-0

FOURTH ROUND

West Bromwich Albion v Notts County	3-1
Crystal Palace v Everton	1-1, 0-4
Barnsley v Woolwich Arsenal	1-2
The Wednesday v Liverpool	1-0

SEMI-FINAL

West Bromwich Albion v Everton	1-2
Woolwich Arsenal v The Wednesday	1-3

FINAL AT CRYSTAL PALACE

The Wednesday v Everton	2-1

Below *A plate produced by The Wednesday to commemorate winning the Cup in 1907.*

SCOTTISH FA CUP 1906-07

FIRST ROUND

Third Lanark v St Johnstone	4-1
Falkirk v Rangers	1-2
Heart of Midlothian v Airdrieonians	0-0, 2-0
Dumfries v Port Glasgow Athletic	2-2, 0-2
Maxwelltown Volunteers v Morton	0-3
Ayr v Cowdenbeath	2-0
Raith Rovers v Aberdeen University	5-1
Arbroath v Queen's Park	1-1, 0-4
Renton v St Bernard's	0-0, 1-1, 2-0
Aberdeen v Johnstone	0-0, 1-2
Celtic v Clyde	2-1
Arthurlie v St Mirren	1-2
Partick Thistle v Dundee	2-2, 1-5
Galston v Motherwell	2-1
Kilmarnock v Clachnacuddin	4-0

SECOND ROUND

Queen's Park v Third Lanark	3-1
Raith Rovers v Ayr	4-0
St Mirren v Port Glasgow Athletic	4-1
Morton v Celtic	0-0, 1-1, 1-2
Hibernian v Johnstone	1-1, 5-0
Galston v Rangers	0-4
Kilmarnock v Heart of Midlothian	0-0, 1-2
Renton v Dundee	1-0

THIRD ROUND

Rangers v Celtic	0-3
St Mirren v Hibernian	1-1, 0-2
Queen's Park v Renton	4-1
Heart of Midlothian v Raith Rovers	2-2, 1-0

SEMI-FINAL

Celtic v Hibernian	0-0, 0-0, 3-0
Heart of Midlothian v Queen's Park	1-0

FINAL AT HAMPDEN PARK

Celtic v Heart of Midlothian	3-0

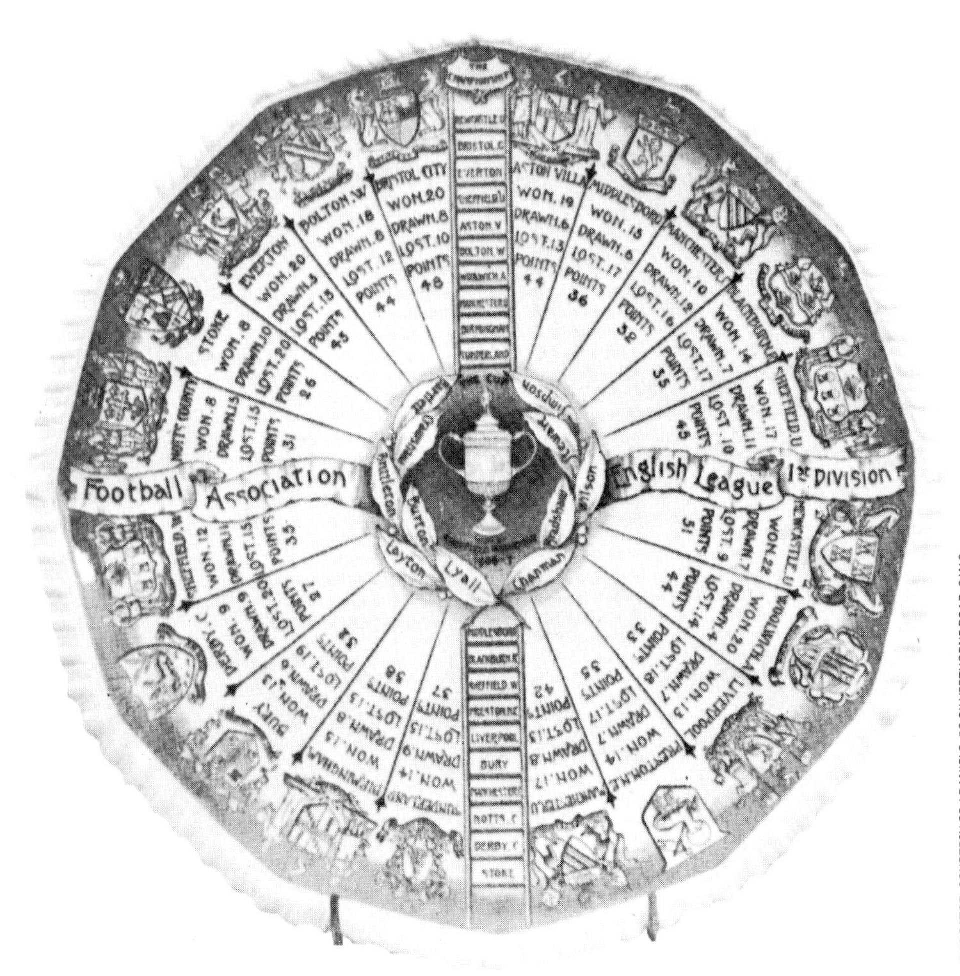

C PROCTOR: COURTESY OF J DANIELS, 20 SILVERTHORNE ROAD, S.W.8

League Tables 1907-08

FIRST DIVISION

	P	W	D	L	F	A	Pts
1 Man United	38	23	6	9	81	48	52
2 Aston Villa	38	17	9	12	77	59	43
3 Man City	38	16	11	11	62	54	43
4 Newcastle	38	15	12	11	65	54	42
5 Wednesday	38	19	4	15	73	64	42
6 Middlesbrough	38	17	7	14	54	45	41
7 Bury	38	14	11	13	58	61	39
8 Liverpool	38	16	6	16	68	61	38
9 Nottm Forest	38	13	11	14	59	62	37
10 Bristol City	38	12	12	14	58	61	36
11 Everton	38	15	6	17	58	64	36
12 Preston	38	12	12	14	47	53	36
13 Chelsea	38	14	8	16	53	62	36
14 Blackburn*	38	12	12	14	51	63	36
15 Woolwich A*	38	12	12	14	51	63	36
16 Sunderland	38	16	3	19	78	75	35
17 Sheff United	38	12	11	15	52	58	35
18 Notts County	38	13	8	17	39	51	34
19 Bolton	38	14	5	19	52	58	33
20 Birmingham	38	9	12	17	40	60	30

*equal

SECOND DIVISION

	P	W		L	F	A	Pts
1 Bradford City	38	24	6	8	90	42	54
2 Leicester Fosse	38	21	10	7	72	47	52
3 Oldham	38	22	6	10	76	42	50
4 Fulham	38	22	5	11	82	49	49
5 WBA	38	19	9	10	61	39	47
6 Derby	38	21	4	13	77	45	46
7 Burnley	38	20	6	12	67	50	46
8 Hull	38	21	4	13	73	62	46
9 Wolves	38	15	7	16	50	45	37
10 Stoke	38	16	5	17	57	52	37
11 Gainsborough	38	14	7	17	47	71	35
12 Leeds City	38	12	8	18	53	65	32
13 Stockport	38	12	8	18	48	67	32
14 Clapton Orient	38	11	10	17	40	65	32
15 Blackpool	38	11	9	18	51	58	31
16 Barnsley	38	12	6	20	54	68	30
17 Glossop NE	38	11	8	19	54	74	30
18 Grimsby	38	11	8	19	43	71	30
19 Chesterfield	38	6	11	21	46	92	23
20 Lincoln	38	9	3	26	46	83	21

SCOTTISH FIRST DIVISION

	P	W	D	L	F	A	Pts
1 Celtic	34	24	7	3	86	27	55
2 Falkirk	34	22	7	5	102	40	51
3 Rangers	34	21	8	5	74	40	50
4 Dundee	34	20	8	6	70	27	48
5 Hibernian	34	17	8	9	55	42	42
6 Airdrieonians	34	18	5	11	58	41	41
7 St Mirren	34	13	10	11	50	59	36
8 Aberdeen	34	13	9	12	45	44	35
9 Third Lanark	34	13	7	14	45	50	33
10 Motherwell	34	12	7	15	61	53	31
11 Hamilton	34	10	8	16	54	65	28
12 Hearts	34	11	6	17	50	62	28
13 Morton	34	9	9	16	43	66	27
14 Kilmarnock	34	6	13	15	38	61	25
15 Partick	34	8	9	17	43	69	25
16 Queen's Park	34	7	8	19	54	84	22
17 Clyde	34	5	8	21	36	75	18
18 Port Glasgow	34	5	7	22	39	98	17

SCOTTISH SECOND DIVISION

	P	W	D	L	F	A	Pts
1 Raith	22	14	2	6	37	23	30
2 Dumbarton	22	12	5	5	49	32	27*
3 Ayr	22	11	5	6	40	33	27
4 Abercorn	22	9	5	8	33	30	23
5 E Stirlingshire	22	9	5	8	30	32	23
6 Ayr Parkhouse	22	11	0	11	38	38	22
7 Leith	22	8	5	9	41	40	21
8 St Bernard's	22	8	5	9	31	32	21
9 Albion	22	7	5	10	36	48	19
10 Vale of Leven	22	5	8	9	25	31	18
11 Arthurlie	22	6	5	11	33	45	17
12 Cowdenbeath	22	5	4	13	26	35	14

*Two points deducted for a registration irregularity

Below *Wednesday goalkeeper Lyell, well backed up by his defence, repulses a Chelsea attack in a First Division match. It was Chelsea's first ever season in the First Division.*

RADIO TIMES HULTON PICTURE LIBRARY

FA CUP 1907-08

SECOND ROUND

Wolverhampton Wanderers v Bury	2-0
Swindon Town v Queen's Park Rangers	2-1
Stoke v Gainsborough Trinity	1-1, 2-2, 3-1
Portsmouth v Leicester Fosse	1-0
Notts County v Bolton Wanderers	1-1, 1-2
Oldham Athletic v Everton	0-0, 1-6
Southampton v West Bromwich Albion	1-0
Bristol Rovers v Chesterfield Town	2-0
Newcastle United v West Ham United	2-0
Liverpool v Brighton	1-1, 3-0
Grimsby Town v Carlisle United	6-2
Plymouth Argyle v Crystal Palace	2-3
Manchester City v New Brompton	1-1, 2-1
Norwich City v Fulham	1-2
Manchester United v Chelsea	1-0
Aston Villa v Hull City	3-0

THIRD ROUND

Wolverhampton Wanderers v Swindon Town	2-0
Portsmouth v Stoke	0-1
Bolton Wanderers v Everton	3-3, 1-3
Southampton v Bristol Rovers	2-0
Newcastle United v Liverpool	3-1
Grimsby Town v Crystal Palace	1-0
Manchester City v Fulham	1-1, 1-3
Aston Villa v Manchester United	0-2

FOURTH ROUND

Stoke v Wolverhampton Wanderers	0-1
Everton v Southampton	0-0, 2-3
Newcastle United v Grimsby Town	5-1
Fulham v Manchester United	2-1

SEMI-FINAL

Wolverhampton Wanderers v Southampton	2-0
Newcastle United v Fulham	6-0

FINAL AT CRYSTAL PALACE

Wolverhampton Wanderers v Newcastle United	3-1

SCOTTISH FA CUP 1907-08

FIRST ROUND

Falkirk v Rangers	2-2, 1-4
Heart of Midlothian v St Johnstone	2-1
Celtic v Peebles Rovers	4-0
Hibernian v Abercorn	5-1
St Bernard's v Queen's Park	1-1, 1-1, 0-1
Aberdeen v Albion Rovers	3-0
Dumfries v Motherwell	0-4
Partick Thistle v Bo'ness	4-0
Port Glasgow Athletic v Ayr Parkhouse	7-1
Dunblane v Elgin City	8-3
Kilmarnock v Hamilton Academicals	2-1
Raith Rovers v Inverness Thistle	2-0
Galston v Uphall	wo
St Mirren v Third Lanark	3-1
Morton v Vale of Atholl	7-1
Airdrieonians v Dundee	0-1

SECOND ROUND

Motherwell v St Mirren	2-2, 0-2
Heart of Midlothian v Port Glasgow Athletic	4-0
Rangers v Celtic	1-2
Partick Thistle v Raith Rovers	1-1, 1-2
Queen's Park v Galston	6-2
Kilmarnock v Dunblane	3-0
Hibernian v Morton	3-0
Aberdeen v Dundee	0-0, 2-2, 3-1

THIRD ROUND

Aberdeen v Queen's Park	3-1
Raith Rovers v Celtic	0-3
Hibernian v Kilmarnock	0-1
St Mirren v Heart of Midlothian	1-0*, 3-1

*abandoned

SEMI-FINAL

Aberdeen v Celtic	0-1
Kilmarnock v St Mirren	0-0, 0-2

FINAL AT HAMPDEN PARK

Celtic v St Mirren	5-1

League Tables 1908-09

FIRST DIVISION

		P	W	D	L	F	A	Pts
1	Newcastle	38	24	5	9	65	41	53
2	Everton	38	18	10	10	82	57	46
3	Sunderland	38	21	2	15	78	63	44
4	Blackburn	38	14	13	11	61	50	41
5	Wednesday	38	17	6	15	67	61	40
6	Woolwich A	38	14	10	14	52	49	38
7	Aston Villa	38	14	10	14	58	56	38
8	Bristol City	38	13	12	13	45	58	38
9	Middlesbrough	38	14	9	15	59	53	37
10	Preston	38	13	11	14	48	44	37
11	Chelsea	38	14	9	15	56	61	37
12	Sheff United	38	14	9	15	51	59	37
13	Man United	38	15	7	16	58	68	37
14	Nottm Forest	38	14	8	16	66	57	36
15	Notts County	38	14	8	16	51	48	36
16	Liverpool	38	15	6	17	57	65	36
17	Bury	38	14	8	16	63	77	36
18	Bradford City	38	12	10	16	47	47	34
19	Man City	38	15	4	19	67	69	34
20	Leicester Fosse	38	8	9	21	54	102	25

SECOND DIVISION

		P	W	D	L	F	A	Pts
1	Bolton	38	24	4	10	59	28	52
2	Tottenham	38	20	11	7	67	32	51
3	WBA	38	19	13	6	56	27	51
4	Hull	38	19	6	13	63	39	44
5	Derby	38	16	11	11	55	41	43
6	Oldham	38	17	6	15	55	43	40
7	Wolves	38	14	11	13	56	48	39
8	Glossop NE	38	15	8	15	57	53	38
9	Gainsborough	38	15	8	15	49	70	38
10	Fulham	38	13	11	14	58	48	37
11	Birmingham	38	14	9	15	58	61	37
12	Leeds City	38	14	7	17	43	53	35
13	Grimsby	38	14	7	17	41	54	35
14	Burnley	38	13	7	18	51	58	33
15	Clapton Orient	38	12	9	17	37	49	33
16	Bradford PA	38	13	6	19	51	59	32
17	Barnsley	38	11	10	17	48	57	32
18	Stockport	38	14	3	21	39	71	31
19	Chesterfield	38	11	8	19	37	67	30
20	Blackpool	38	9	11	18	46	68	29

FA CUP 1908-09

SECOND ROUND

Manchester United v Everton	1-0
Blackburn Rovers v Chelsea	2-1
Tottenham Hotspur v Fulham	1-0
Crystal Palace v Burnley	0-0, 0-9
Newcastle United v Blackpool	2-1
Leeds City v West Ham United	1-1, 1-2
Preston North End v Sunderland	1-2
West Bromwich Albion v Bradford City	1-2
Bristol City v Bury	2-2, 1-0
Liverpool v Norwich City	2-3
Stockport County v Glossop North End	1-1, 0-1
Portsmouth v The Wednesday	2-2, 0-3
Leicester Fosse v Derby County	0-2
Plymouth Argyle v Exeter City	2-0
Nottingham Forest v Brentford	1-0
Woolwich Arsenal v Millwall Athletic	1-1, 0-1

THIRD ROUND

Manchester United v Blackburn Rovers	6-1
Tottenham Hotspur v Burnley	0-0, 1-3
West Ham United v Newcastle United	0-0, 1-2
Bradford City v Sunderland	0-1
Bristol City v Norwich City	2-0
The Wednesday v Glossop North End	0-1
Derby County v Plymouth Argyle	1-0
Nottingham Forest v Millwall Athletic	3-1

FOURTH ROUND

Burnley v Manchester United	1-0*, 2-3
Newcastle United v Sunderland	2-2, 3-0
Glossop North End v Bristol City	0-0, 0-1
Derby County v Nottingham Forest	3-0

*abandoned

SEMI-FINAL

Manchester United v Newcastle United	1-0
Bristol City v Derby County	1-1, 2-1

FINAL AT CRYSTAL PALACE

Manchester United v Bristol City	1-0

SCOTTISH FIRST DIVISION

		P	W	D	L	F	A	Pts
1	Celtic	34	23	5	6	71	24	51
2	Dundee	34	22	6	6	70	32	50
3	Clyde	34	21	6	7	61	37	48
4	Rangers	34	19	7	8	91	38	45
5	Airdrieonians	34	16	9	9	67	46	41
6	Hibernian	34	16	7	11	40	32	39
7	St Mirren	34	15	6	13	53	45	36
8	Aberdeen	34	15	6	13	61	53	36
9	Falkirk	34	13	7	14	58	56	33
10	Kilmarnock	34	13	7	14	47	61	33
11	Third Lanark	34	11	10	13	56	49	32
12	Hearts	34	12	8	14	54	49	32
13	Port Glasgow	34	10	8	16	39	52	28
14	Motherwell	34	11	6	17	47	73	28
15	Queen's Park	34	6	13	15	42	65	25
16	Hamilton	34	6	12	16	42	72	24
17	Morton	34	8	7	19	39	90	23
18	Partick	34	2	4	28	38	102	8

SCOTTISH SECOND DIVISION

		P	W	D	L	F	A	Pts
1	Abercorn	22	13	5	4	40	18	31
2	Raith	22	11	6	5	46	22	28
3	Vale of Leven	22	12	4	6	39	25	28
4	Dumbarton	22	10	5	7	34	34	25
5	Ayr	22	10	3	9	43	36	23
6	Leith	22	10	3	9	37	33	23
7	Ayr Parkhouse	22	8	5	9	29	31	21
8	St Bernard's	22	9	3	10	34	37	21
9	E Stirlingshire	22	9	3	10	28	34	21
10	Albion	22	9	2	11	37	48	20
11	Cowdenbeath	22	4	4	14	19	42	12
12	Arthurlie	22	5	1	16	29	55	11

Below *After a 1-1 draw, 1908 League Champions Manchester United, beat Queen's Park Rangers, the Southern League winners, 4-0 in September to become the first holders of* **inset** *the Charity Shield.*

RADIO TIMES HULTON PICTURE LIBRARY

SCOTTISH FA CUP 1908-09

SECOND ROUND

Third Lanark v Aberdeen	4-1
Clyde v Hibernian	1-0
Airdrieonians v Heart of Midlothian	2-0
St Mirren v Beith	3-0
Dundee v Rangers	0-0, 0-1
Queen's Park v Partick Thistle	3-0
Motherwell v Falkirk	1-3
Celtic v Port Glasgow Athletic	4-0

THIRD ROUND

Celtic v Airdrieonians	3-1
Third Lanark v Falkirk	1-2
Clyde v St Mirren	3-1
Rangers v Queen's Park	1-0

SEMI-FINAL

Falkirk v Rangers	0-1
Celtic v Clyde	0-0, 2-0

FINAL AT HAMPDEN PARK

Rangers v Celtic	2-2, 1-1†

†Some newspapers had suggested that, if the first replay ended level, extra-time would be played. The rules, in fact, stated that extra-time could only be played after a third game. When the players left the field some sections of the crowd obviously felt cheated and started protesting. This led to a full-scale riot with pay-boxes burned and hundreds injured. Rangers and Celtic both refused to play a third game as a result, threatening that one or other would simply scratch, and the Scottish FA agreed that the Cup would be withheld.

In April 1909 Leicester Fosse, already relegated to the Second Division, were beaten 12-0 by neighbours Nottingham Forest in one of the last games of the season. As this was a record Division One score, and as those two points confirmed Forest's place in the First Division, a League Commission inquiry examined the circumstances surrounding the match. Their finding was quite simply that the Leicester Fosse players had been celebrating the wedding of a colleague the day before the game was played.

Broxburn and Beith met five times in a first-round Scottish Cup tie. The last three games were played on three consecutive days, Beith finally winning 4-2 on a Friday. The following day they met St Mirren in the next round, their fourth game in four days. They lost . . .

League Tables 1909-10

FIRST DIVISION

	P	W	D	L	F	A	Pts
1 Aston Villa	38	23	7	8	84	42	53
2 Liverpool	38	21	6	11	78	57	48
3 Blackburn	38	18	9	11	73	55	45
4 Newcastle	38	19	7	12	70	56	45
5 Man United	38	19	7	12	69	61	45
6 Sheff United	38	16	10	12	62	41	42
7 Bradford City	38	17	8	13	64	47	42
8 Sunderland	38	18	5	15	66	51	41
9 Notts County	38	15	10	13	67	59	40
10 Everton	38	16	8	14	51	56	40
11 Wednesday	38	15	9	14	60	63	39
12 Preston	38	15	5	18	52	58	35
13 Bury	38	12	9	17	62	66	33
14 Nottm Forest	38	11	11	16	54	72	33
15 Tottenham	38	11	10	17	53	69	32
16 Bristol City	38	12	8	18	45	60	32
17 Middlesbrough	38	11	9	18	56	73	31
18 Woolwich A	38	11	9	18	37	67	31
19 Chelsea	38	11	7	20	47	70	29
20 Bolton	38	9	6	23	44	71	24

SECOND DIVISION

	P	W	D	L	F	A	Pts
1 Man City	38	23	8	7	81	40	54
2 Oldham	38	23	7	8	79	39	53
3 Hull City	38	23	7	8	80	46	53
4 Derby	38	22	9	7	72	47	53
5 Leicester Fosse	38	20	4	14	79	58	44
6 Glossop NE	38	18	7	13	64	57	43
7 Fulham	38	14	13	11	51	43	41
8 Wolves	38	17	6	15	64	63	40
9 Barnsley	38	16	7	15	62	59	39
10 Bradford PA	38	17	4	17	64	59	38
11 WBA	38	16	5	17	58	56	37
12 Blackpool	38	14	8	16	50	52	36
13 Stockport	38	13	8	17	50	47	34
14 Burnley	38	14	6	18	62	61	34
15 Lincoln	38	10	11	17	42	69	31
16 Clapton Orient	38	12	6	20	37	60	30
17 Leeds City	38	10	7	21	46	80	27
18 Gainsborough	38	10	6	22	33	75	26
19 Grimsby	38	9	6	23	50	77	24
20 Birmingham	38	8	7	23	42	78	23

SCOTTISH FIRST DIVISION

	P	W	D	L	F	A	Pts
1 Celtic	34	24	6	4	63	22	54
2 Falkirk	34	22	8	4	71	28	52
3 Rangers	34	20	6	8	70	35	46
4 Aberdeen	34	16	8	10	44	29	40
5 Clyde	34	14	9	11	47	40	37
6 Dundee	34	14	8	12	52	44	36
7 Third Lanark	34	13	8	13	62	44	34
8 Hibernian	34	14	6	14	33	40	34
9 Airdrieonians	34	12	9	13	46	57	33
10 Motherwell	34	12	8	14	59	60	32
11 Kilmarnock	34	12	8	14	53	60	32
12 Hearts	34	12	7	15	59	50	31
13 St Mirren	34	13	5	16	49	58	31
14 Queen's Park	34	12	6	16	54	74	30
15 Hamilton	34	11	6	17	50	67	28
16 Partick	34	8	10	16	47	59	26
17 Morton	34	11	3	20	38	60	25
18 Port Glasgow	34	3	5	26	25	95	11

SCOTTISH SECOND DIVISION

	P	W	D	L	F	A	Pts
1 Leith	22	13	7	2	44	19	33
2 Raith*	22	14	5	3	36	21	33
3 St Bernard's	22	12	3	7	43	31	27
4 Dumbarton	22	9	5	8	44	38	23
5 Abercorn	22	7	8	7	38	40	22
6 Vale of Leven	22	8	5	9	36	38	21
7 Ayr	22	9	3	10	37	40	21
8 E Stirlingshire	22	9	2	11	38	43	20
9 Albion	22	7	5	10	34	39	19
10 Arthurlie	22	6	5	11	34	47	17
11 Cowdenbeath	22	7	3	12	22	34	17
12 Ayr Parkhouse	22	4	3	15	27	43	11

*Elected to First Division

Below *In 1910 Newcastle were the last club to win the second FA Cup. The design had been pirated for a minor competition and the old Cup was presented to Lord Kinnaird.*

COLORSPORT

FA CUP 1909-10

SECOND ROUND

Newcastle United v Fulham	4-0
Bradford City v Blackburn Rovers	1-2
Leicester Fosse v Bury	3-2
Stockport County v Leyton	0-2
Swindon Town v Burnley	2-0
Chelsea v Tottenham Hotspur	0-1
Southampton v Manchester City	0-5
Aston Villa v Derby County	6-1
Bristol Rovers v Barnsley	0-4
Bristol City v West Bromwich Albion	1-1, 2-4
Southend United v Queen's Park Rangers	0-0, 2-3
Wolverhampton Wanderers v West Ham United	1-5
Everton v Woolwich Arsenal	5-0
Sunderland v Bradford Park Avenue	3-1
Portsmouth v Coventry City	0-1
Northampton Town v Nottingham Forest	0-0, 0-1

THIRD ROUND

Newcastle United v Blackburn Rovers	3-1
Leicester Fosse v Leyton	1-0
Swindon Town v Tottenham Hotspur	3-2
Aston Villa v Manchester City	1-2
Barnsley v West Bromwich Albion	1-0
Queen's Park Rangers v West Ham United	1-1, 1-0
Everton v Sunderland	2-0
Coventry City v Nottingham Forest	3-1

FOURTH ROUND

Newcastle United v Leicester Fosse	3-0
Swindon Town v Manchester City	2-0
Barnsley v Queen's Park Rangers	1-0
Coventry City v Everton	0-2

SEMI-FINAL

Newcastle United v Swindon Town	2-0
Barnsley v Everton	0-0, 3-0

FINAL AT CRYSTAL PALACE

Newcastle United v Barnsley	1-1, 2-0*

*Replay at Goodison Park

SCOTTISH FA CUP 1909-10

FIRST ROUND

Rangers v Inverness Thistle	3-1
Queen's Park v Kirkcaldy United	0-0, 6-0
St Mirren v Elgin City	8-0
Kilmarnock v Third Lanark	0-0, 0-2
Dumbarton v Celtic	1-2
Morton v Partick Thistle	4-3
Airdrieonians v Douglas Wanderers	6-0
Leith Athletic v Clyde	0-1
Motherwell v Forfar Athletic	1-0
Bathgate v Heart of Midlothian	0-4
Hamilton v Hibernian	0-0, 0-2
Falkirk v Port Glasgow Athletic	3-0
Dundee v Beith	1-1, 1-0
Ayr v Alloa Athletic	3-2
Aberdeen v Bo'ness	3-0
East Fife v Hurlford	4-1

SECOND ROUND

Motherwell v Morton	3-0
Dundee v Falkirk	3-0
Clyde v Rangers	2-0
St Mirren v Heart of Midlothian	2-2, 0-0, 0-4
Ayr v Hibernian	0-1
Celtic v Third Lanark	3-1
Aberdeen v Airdrieonians	3-0
East Fife v Queen's Park	2-3

THIRD ROUND

Hibernian v Heart of Midlothian	0-1*, 1-0
Celtic v Aberdeen	2-1
Queen's Park v Clyde	2-2, 2-2, 1-2
Motherwell v Dundee	1-3

*abandoned

SEMI-FINAL

Clyde v Celtic	3-1
Hibernian v Dundee	0-0, 0-0, 0-1

FINAL AT IBROX PARK

Dundee v Clyde	2-2, 0-0, 2-1

League Tables 1910-11

FIRST DIVISION

		P	W	D	L	F	A	Pts
1	Man United	38	22	8	8	72	40	52
2	Aston Villa	38	22	7	9	69	41	51
3	Sunderland	38	15	15	8	67	48	45
4	Everton	38	19	7	12	50	36	45
5	Bradford City	38	20	5	13	51	42	45
6	Wednesday	38	17	8	13	47	48	42
7	Oldham	38	16	9	13	44	41	41
8	Newcastle	38	15	10	13	61	43	40
9	Sheff United	38	15	8	15	49	43	38
10	Woolwich A	38	13	12	13	41	49	38
11	Notts County	38	14	10	14	37	45	38
12	Blackburn	38	13	11	14	62	54	37
13	Liverpool	38	15	7	16	53	53	37
14	Preston	38	12	11	15	40	49	35
15	Tottenham	38	13	6	19	52	63	32
16	Middlesbrough	38	11	10	17	49	63	32
17	Man City	38	9	13	16	43	58	31
18	Bury	38	9	11	18	43	71	29
19	Bristol City	38	11	5	22	43	66	27
20	Nottm Forest	38	9	7	22	55	75	25

SECOND DIVISION

		P	W	D	L	F	A	Pts
1	WBA	38	22	9	7	67	41	53
2	Bolton	38	21	9	8	69	40	51
3	Chelsea	38	20	9	9	71	35	49
4	Clapton Orient	38	19	7	12	44	35	45
5	Hull	38	14	16	8	55	39	44
6	Derby	38	17	8	13	73	52	42
7	Blackpool	38	16	10	12	49	38	42
8	Burnley	38	13	15	10	45	45	41
9	Wolves	38	15	8	15	51	52	38
10	Fulham	38	15	7	16	52	48	37
11	Leeds City	38	15	7	16	58	56	37
12	Bradford PA	38	14	9	15	53	55	37
13	Huddersfield	38	13	8	17	57	58	34
14	Glossop NE	38	13	8	17	48	62	34
15	Leicester Fosse	38	14	5	19	52	62	33
16	Birmingham	38	12	8	18	42	64	32
17	Stockport	38	11	8	19	47	79	30
18	Gainsborough	38	9	11	18	37	55	29
19	Barnsley	38	7	14	17	52	62	28
20	Lincoln	38	7	10	21	28	72	24

SCOTTISH FIRST DIVISION

		P	W	D	L	F	A	Pts
1	Rangers	34	23	6	5	90	34	52
2	Aberdeen	34	19	10	5	53	28	48
3	Falkirk	34	17	10	7	65	42	44
4	Partick	34	17	8	9	50	41	42
5	Celtic	34	15	11	8	48	18	41
6	Dundee	34	18	5	11	54	42	41
7	Clyde	34	14	11	9	45	36	39
8	Third Lanark	34	16	7	11	59	53	39
9	Hibernian	34	15	6	13	44	48	36
10	Kilmarnock	34	12	10	12	43	45	34
11	Airdrieonians	34	12	9	13	49	53	33
12	St Mirren	34	12	7	15	46	57	31
13	Morton	34	9	11	14	49	51	29
14	Hearts	34	8	8	18	42	59	24
15	Raith	34	7	10	17	36	56	24
16	Hamilton	34	8	5	21	31	60	21
17	Motherwell	34	8	4	22	37	66	20
18	Queen's Park	34	5	4	25	28	80	14

SCOTTISH SECOND DIVISION

		P	W	D	L	F	A	Pts
1	Dumbarton	22	15	1	6	55	31	31
2	Ayr	22	12	3	7	52	36	27
3	Albion	22	10	5	7	27	21	25
4	Leith	22	9	6	7	42	43	24
5	Cowdenbeath	22	9	5	8	31	27	23
6	St Bernard's	22	10	2	10	36	39	22
7	E Stirlingshire	22	7	6	9	28	35	20
8	Port Glasgow	22	8	3	11	27	32	19
9	Dundee Hibs	22	7	5	10	29	36	19
10	Arthurlie	22	7	5	10	26	33	19
11	Abercorn	22	9	1	12	39	50	19
12	Vale of Leven	22	4	8	10	22	31	16

Below *Bradford City defend in depth as Newcastle threaten their goal in the 1911 Cup Final at Crystal Palace. The game, which ended 0-0, was the Tynesiders' fifth appearance at Crystal Palace in seven years.*

RADIO TIMES HULTON PICTURE LIBRARY

FA CUP 1910-11

SECOND ROUND

Bradford City v Norwich City	2-1
Crewe Alexandra v Grimsby Town	1-5
Burnley v Barnsley	2-0
Brighton v Coventry City	0-0, 0-2
Blackburn Rovers v Tottenham Hotspur	0-0, 2-0
Middlesbrough v Leicester Fosse	0-0, 2-1
West Ham United v Preston North End	3-0
Manchester United v Aston Villa	2-1
Newcastle United v Northampton Town	1-1, 1-0†
Hull City v Oldham Athletic	1-0
Derby County v West Bromwich Albion	2-0
Everton v Liverpool	2-1
Chesterfield Town v Chelsea	1-4
Wolverhampton Wanderers v Manchester City	1-0
Swindon Town v Woolwich Arsenal	1-0
Darlington v Bradford Park Avenue	2-1

† Both games played at Newcastle. Northampton sold their rights to a replay at home for £900.

THIRD ROUND

Bradford City v Grimsby Town	1-0
Burnley v Coventry City	5-0
Middlesbrough v Blackburn Rovers	0-3
West Ham United v Manchester United	2-1
Newcastle United v Hull City	3-2
Derby County v Everton	5-0
Wolverhampton Wanderers v Chelsea	0-2
Darlington v Swindon Town	0-3

FOURTH ROUND

Bradford City v Burnley	1-0
West Ham United v Blackburn Rovers	2-3
Newcastle United v Derby County	4-0
Chelsea v Swindon Town	3-1

SEMI-FINAL

Bradford City v Blackburn Rovers	3-0
Newcastle United v Chelsea	3-0

FINAL AT CRYSTAL PALACE

Bradford City v Newcastle United	0-0, 1-0*

*Replay at Old Trafford

SCOTTISH FA CUP 1910-11

FIRST ROUND

Aberdeen v Brechin City	3-0
Airdrieonians v Bo'ness	2-0
Celtic v St Mirren	2-0
Heart of Midlothian v Clyde	1-1, 0-1
Dundee v Hibernian	2-1
Leith Athletic v Falkirk	2-2, 1-4
Forfar Athletic v 5th KOSB	3-0
Galston v Lochgelly United	8-0
Rangers v Kilmarnock	2-1
East Stirlingshire v Morton	1-4
Third Lanark v Hamilton Academicals	0-1
Inverness Thistle v Johnstone	0-1
Motherwell v Annbank	5-0
Nithsdale Wanderers v Inverness Caledonian	3-1
Partick Thistle v St Bernard's	7-2
Stanley v Queen's Park	1-6

SECOND ROUND

Aberdeen v Airdrieonians	1-0
Clyde v Queen's Park	4-1
Partick Thistle v Dundee	0-3
Forfar Athletic v Falkirk	2-0
Celtic v Galston	1-0
Rangers v Morton	3-0
Hamilton Academicals v Johnstone	1-1, 3-1
Nithsdale Wanderers v Motherwell	0-0, 0-1

THIRD ROUND

Aberdeen v Forfar Athletic	6-0
Celtic v Clyde	1-0
Dundee v Rangers	2-1
Hamilton Academicals v Motherwell	2-1

SEMI-FINAL

Celtic v Aberdeen	1-0
Hamilton Academicals v Dundee	3-2

FINAL AT IBROX PARK

Celtic v Hamilton Academicals	0-0, 2-1

League Tables 1911-12

FIRST DIVISION

	P	W	D	L	F	A	Pts
1 Blackburn	38	20	9	9	60	43	49
2 Everton	38	20	6	12	46	42	46
3 Newcastle	38	18	8	12	64	50	44
4 Bolton	38	20	3	15	54	43	43
5 Wednesday	38	16	9	13	69	49	41
6 Aston Villa	38	17	7	14	76	63	41
7 Middlesbrough	38	16	8	14	56	45	40
8 Sunderland	38	14	11	13	58	51	39
9 WBA	38	15	9	14	43	47	39
10 Woolwich A	38	15	8	15	55	59	38
11 Bradford City	38	15	8	15	46	50	38
12 Tottenham	38	14	9	15	53	53	37
13 Man United	38	13	11	14	45	60	37
14 Sheff United	38	13	10	15	63	56	36
15 Man City	38	13	9	16	56	58	35
16 Notts County	38	14	7	17	46	63	35
17 Liverpool	38	12	10	16	49	55	34
18 Oldham	38	12	10	16	46	54	34
19 Preston	38	13	7	18	40	57	33
20 Bury	38	6	9	23	32	59	21

SECOND DIVISION

	P	W	D	L	F	A	Pts
1 Derby	38	23	8	7	74	28	54
2 Chelsea	38	24	6	8	64	34	54
3 Burnley	38	22	8	8	77	41	52
4 Clapton Orient	38	21	3	14	61	44	45
5 Wolves	38	16	10	12	57	33	42
6 Barnsley	38	15	12	11	45	42	42
7 Hull	38	17	8	13	54	51	42
8 Fulham	38	16	7	15	66	58	39
9 Grimsby	38	15	9	14	48	55	39
10 Leicester Fosse	38	15	7	16	49	66	37
11 Bradford PA	38	13	9	16	44	45	35
12 Birmingham	38	14	6	18	55	59	34
13 Bristol City	38	14	6	18	41	60	34
14 Blackpool	38	13	8	17	32	52	34
15 Nottm Forest	38	13	7	18	46	48	33
16 Stockport	38	11	11	16	47	54	33
17 Huddersfield	38	13	6	19	50	64	32
18 Glossop NE	38	8	12	18	42	56	28
19 Leeds City	38	10	8	20	50	78	28
20 Gainsborough	38	5	13	20	30	64	23

SCOTTISH FIRST DIVISION

	P	W	D	L	F	A	Pts
1 Rangers	34	24	3	7	86	34	51
2 Celtic	34	17	11	6	58	33	45
3 Clyde	34	19	4	11	56	32	42
4 Hearts	34	16	8	10	54	40	40
5 Partick	34	16	8	10	47	40	40
6 Morton	34	14	9	11	44	44	37
7 Falkirk	34	15	6	13	46	43	36
8 Dundee	34	13	9	12	52	41	35
9 Aberdeen	34	14	7	13	44	44	35
10 Airdrieonians	34	12	8	14	40	41	32
11 Third Lanark	34	12	7	15	40	57	31
12 Hamilton	34	11	8	15	32	44	30
13 Hibernian	34	12	5	17	44	47	29
14 Motherwell	34	11	5	18	34	44	27
15 Raith	34	9	9	16	39	59	27
16 Kilmarnock	34	11	4	19	38	60	26
17 Queen's Park	34	8	9	17	29	53	25
18 St Mirren	34	7	10	17	32	59	24

SCOTTISH SECOND DIVISION

	P	W	D	L	F	A	Pts
1 Ayr	22	16	3	3	54	24	35
2 Abercorn	22	13	4	5	43	22	30
3 Dumbarton	22	13	1	8	47	31	27
4 Cowdenbeath	22	12	2	8	39	31	26
5 St Johnstone	22	10	4	8	29	27	24
6 St Bernard's	22	9	5	8	38	36	23
7 Leith	22	9	4	9	31	34	22
8 Arthurlie	22	7	5	10	26	30	19
9 E Stirlingshire	22	7	3	12	21	31	17
10 Dundee Hibs	22	5	5	12	21	41	15
11 Vale of Leven	22	6	1	15	19	37	13
12 Albion	22	6	1	15	26	50	13

Below *Spurs entertain the Football League champions, Blackburn Rovers, at White Hart Lane. Bob Crompton (right of goalkeeper), Blackburn's captain, watches anxiously as his keeper is challenged by a Tottenham forward.*

RADIO TIMES HULTON PICTURE LIBRARY

FA CUP 1911-12

SECOND ROUND
Coventry City v Manchester United 1-5
Aston Villa v Reading 1-1, 0-1
Derby County v Blackburn Rovers 1-2
Wolverhampton Wanderers v Lincoln City 2-1
Leeds City v West Bromwich Albion 0-1
Crystal Palace v Sunderland 0-0, 0-1
Fulham v Liverpool 3-0
Darlington v Northampton Town 1-1, 0-2
Swindon Town v Notts County 2-0
Middlesbrough v West Ham United 1-1, 1-2
Everton v Bury 1-1, 6-0
Manchester City v Oldham Athletic 0-1
Bradford City v Chelsea 2-0
Bradford Park Avenue v Portsmouth 2-0
Barnsley v Leicester Fosse 1-0
Bolton Wanderers v Blackpool 1-0

THIRD ROUND
Reading v Manchester United 1-1, 0-3
Blackburn Rovers v Wolverhampton Wanderers 3-2
Sunderland v West Bromwich Albion 1-2
Fulham v Northampton Town 2-1
West Ham United v Swindon Town 1-1, 0-4
Oldham Athletic v Everton 0-2
Bradford Park Avenue v Bradford City 0-1
Bolton Wanderers v Barnsley 1-2

FOURTH ROUND
Manchester United v Blackburn Rovers 1-1, 2-4
West Bromwich Albion v Fulham 3-0
Swindon Town v Everton 2-1
Barnsley v Bradford City 0-0, 0-0, 0-0, 3-2

SEMI-FINAL
Blackburn Rovers v West Bromwich Albion 0-0, 0-1
Swindon Town v Barnsley 0-0, 0-1

FINAL AT CRYSTAL PALACE
Barnsley v West Bromwich Albion 0-0, 1-0*
*Replay at Bramall Lane

SCOTTISH FA CUP 1911-12

FIRST ROUND
St Mirren v Aberdeen 3-3, 0-4
Raith Rovers v Airdrieonians 0-0, 1-3
Armadale v Peterhead 2-1
Broxburn Athletic v Beith 6-0
Celtic v Dunfermline Athletic 1-0
Clyde v Abercorn 2-0
Partick Thistle v Dundee 2-2, 0-3
East Stirlingshire v Dumbarton 3-1
Falkirk v King's Park 2-2, 6-1
Rangers v Stenhousemuir 3-0
Morton v Clachnacuddin 2-0
Hibernian v Heart of Midlothian 1-1, 0-0, 1-2
Kilmarnock v Hamilton Academicals 1-0
Leith v Ayr United 3-0
St Johnstone v Motherwell 0-2
Third Lanark v Renton 5-0

SECOND ROUND
Aberdeen v Armadale 3-0
Celtic v East Stirlingshire 3-0
Clyde v Rangers 3-1
Heart of Midlothian v Dundee 1-0
Leith Athletic v Kilmarnock 0-2
Falkirk v Morton 0-0, 1-3
Motherwell v Airdrieonians 5-1
Third Lanark v Broxburn Athletic 6-1

THIRD ROUND
Aberdeen v Celtic 2-2, 0-2
Kilmarnock v Clyde 1-6
Morton v Heart of Midlothian 0-1
Third Lanark v Motherwell 3-1

SEMI-FINAL
Celtic v Heart of Midlothian 3-0
Clyde v Third Lanark 3-1

FINAL AT IBROX PARK
Celtic v Clyde 2-0

League Tables 1912-13

FIRST DIVISION

		P	W	D	L	F	A	Pts
1	Sunderland	38	25	4	9	86	43	54
2	Aston Villa	38	19	12	7	86	52	50
3	Wednesday	38	21	7	10	75	55	49
4	Man United	38	19	8	11	69	43	46
5	Blackburn	38	16	13	9	79	43	45
6	Man City	38	18	8	12	53	37	44
7	Derby	38	17	8	13	69	66	42
8	Bolton	38	16	10	12	62	63	42
9	Oldham	38	14	14	10	50	55	42
10	WBA	38	13	12	13	57	50	38
11	Everton	38	15	7	16	48	54	37
12	Liverpool	38	16	5	17	61	71	37
13	Bradford City	38	12	11	15	50	60	35
14	Newcastle	38	13	8	17	47	47	34
15	Sheff United	38	14	6	18	56	70	34
16	Middlesbrough	38	11	10	17	55	69	32
17	Tottenham	38	12	6	20	45	72	30
18	Chelsea	38	11	6	21	51	73	28
19	Notts County	38	7	9	22	28	56	23
20	Woolwich A	38	3	12	23	26	74	18

SECOND DIVISION

		P	W	D	L	F	A	Pts
1	Preston	38	19	15	4	56	33	53
2	Burnley	38	21	8	9	88	53	50
3	Birmingham	38	18	10	10	59	44	46
4	Barnsley	38	19	7	12	57	47	45
5	Huddersfield	38	17	9	12	66	40	43
6	Leeds City	38	15	10	13	70	64	40
7	Grimsby	38	15	10	13	51	50	40
8	Lincoln	38	15	10	13	50	52	40
9	Fulham	38	17	5	16	65	55	39
10	Wolves	38	14	10	14	56	54	38
11	Bury	38	15	8	15	53	57	38
12	Hull	38	15	6	17	60	56	36
13	Bradford PA	38	14	8	16	60	60	36
14	Clapton Orient	38	10	14	14	34	47	34
15	Leicester Fosse	38	13	7	18	50	65	33
16	Bristol City	38	9	15	14	46	72	33
17	Nottm Forest	38	12	8	18	58	59	32
18	Glossop NE	38	12	8	18	49	68	32
19	Stockport	38	8	10	20	56	78	26
20	Blackpool	38	9	8	21	39	69	26

FA CUP 1912-13

SECOND ROUND

Aston Villa v West Ham United	5-0
Crystal Palace v Bury	2-0
Bradford Park Avenue v Wolverhampton Wanderers	3-0
Chelsea v The Wednesday	1-1, 0-6
Oldham Athletic v Nottingham Forest	5-1
Plymouth Argyle v Manchester United	0-2
Brighton v Everton	0-0, 0-1
Bristol Rovers v Norwich City	1-1, 2-2, 1-0
Sunderland v Manchester City	2-0
Huddersfield Town v Swindon Town	1-2
Hull City v Newcastle United	0-0, 0-3
Woolwich Arsenal v Liverpool	1-4
Burnley v Gainsborough Trinity	4-1
Middlesbrough v Queen's Park Rangers	3-2
Barnsley v Blackburn Rovers	2-3
Reading v Tottenham Hotspur	1-0

THIRD ROUND

Aston Villa v Crystal Palace	5-0
Bradford Park Avenue v The Wednesday	2-1
Oldham Athletic v Manchester United	0-0, 2-1
Bristol Rovers v Everton	0-4
Sunderland v Swindon Town	4-2
Liverpool v Newcastle United	1-1, 0-1
Burnley v Middlesbrough	3-1
Reading v Blackburn Rovers	1-2

FOURTH ROUND

Bradford Park Avenue v Aston Villa	0-5
Everton v Oldham Athletic	0-1
Sunderland v Newcastle United	0-0, 2-2, 3-0
Blackburn Rovers v Burnley	0-1

SEMI-FINAL

Aston Villa v Oldham Athletic	1-0
Sunderland v Burnley	0-0, 3-2

FINAL AT CRYSTAL PALACE

Aston Villa v Sunderland	1-0

SCOTTISH FIRST DIVISION

		P	W	D	L	F	A	Pts
1	Rangers	34	24	5	5	76	41	53
2	Celtic	34	22	5	7	53	28	49
3	Hearts	34	17	7	10	71	43	41
4	Airdrieonians	34	15	11	8	64	46	41
5	Falkirk	34	14	12	8	56	38	40
6	Hibernian	34	16	5	13	63	54	37
7	Motherwell	34	12	13	9	47	39	37
8	Aberdeen	34	14	9	11	47	40	37
9	Clyde	34	13	9	12	41	44	35
10	Hamilton	34	12	8	14	44	47	32
11	Kilmarnock	34	10	11	13	37	54	31
12	St Mirren	34	10	10	14	50	60	30
13	Morton	34	11	7	16	50	59	29
14	Dundee	34	8	13	13	33	46	29
15	Third Lanark	34	8	12	14	31	41	28
16	Raith	34	8	10	16	46	60	26
17	Partick	34	10	4	20	40	55	24
18	Queen's Park	34	5	3	26	34	88	13

SCOTTISH SECOND DIVISION

		P	W	D	L	F	A	Pts
1	Ayr*	26	13	8	5	45	19	34
2	Dunfermline	26	13	7	6	45	27	33
3	E Stirlingshire	26	12	8	6	43	27	32
4	Abercorn	26	12	7	7	33	31	31
5	Cowdenbeath	26	12	6	8	36	27	30
6	Dumbarton*	26	12	5	9	39	30	29
7	St Bernard's	26	12	3	11	36	34	27
8	Johnstone	26	9	6	11	31	43	24
9	Albion	26	10	3	13	38	40	23
10	Dundee Hibs	26	6	10	10	34	43	22
11	St Johnstone	26	7	7	12	29	38	21
12	Vale of Leven	26	8	5	13	28	45	21
13	Arthurlie	26	7	5	14	37	49	19
14	Leith	26	5	8	13	26	47	18

*Ayr United and Dumbarton were elected to the First Division. Nevertheless, no clubs were demoted from the First Division.

SCOTTISH FA CUP 1912-13

SECOND ROUND

Ayr United v Airdrieonians	0-2
Celtic v Arbroath	4-0
East Stirlingshire v Clyde	1-1, 0-0, 0-1
Dumbarton v Aberdeen	2-1
Dundee v Thornhill	5-0
Morton v Falkirk	2-2, 1-3
Hamilton Academicals v Rangers	1-1, 0-2
Heart of Midlothian v Dunfermline Athletic	3-1
Hibernian v Motherwell	0-0, 1-1, 2-1
Kilmarnock v Abercorn	5-1
Partick Thistle v Inverness Caledonian	4-1
Aberdeen University v Peebles Rovers	0-3
Queen's Park v Dundee Hibernians	4-2
Raith Rovers v Broxburn United	5-0
St Johnstone v East Fife	3-0
St Mirren v Third Lanark	0-0, 2-0

THIRD ROUND

Celtic v Peebles Rovers	3-0
Clyde v Queen's Park	1-0
Dumbarton v St Johnstone	1-0
Partick Thistle v Dundee	0-1
Rangers v Falkirk	1-3
Kilmarnock v Heart of Midlothian	0-2
Raith Rovers v Hibernian	2-2, 1-0
St Mirren v Airdrieonians	1-0

FOURTH ROUND

Clyde v Dundee	1-1, 0-0, 2-1
Falkirk v Dumbarton	1-0
Celtic v Heart of Midlothian	0-1
Raith Rovers v St Mirren	2-1

SEMI-FINAL

Falkirk v Heart of Midlothian	1-0
Raith Rovers v Clyde	1-1, 1-0

FINAL AT CELTIC PARK

Falkirk v Raith Rovers	2-0

RADIO TIMES HULTON PICTURE LIBRARY

Above *Aston Villa's one goal victory over Oldham in the semi-final of the FA Cup meant that for the only time in the history of the competition the Finalists – Villa and Sunderland – were also the clubs that finished first and second in the League. Here, a Villa attack against Oldham comes to nothing but Villa did win the Cup, 1-0.*

League Tables 1913-14

FIRST DIVISION

		P	W	D	L	F	A	Pts
1	Blackburn	38	20	11	7	78	42	51
2	Aston Villa	38	19	6	13	65	50	44
3	Oldham	38	17	9	12	55	45	43
4	Middlesbrough	38	19	5	14	77	60	43
5	WBA	38	15	13	10	46	42	43
6	Bolton	38	16	10	12	65	52	42
7	Sunderland	38	17	6	15	63	52	40
8	Chelsea	38	16	7	15	46	55	39
9	Bradford City	38	12	14	12	40	40	38
10	Sheff United	38	16	5	17	63	60	37
11	Newcastle	38	13	11	14	39	48	37
12	Burnley	38	12	12	14	61	53	36
13	Man City	38	14	8	16	51	53	36
14	Man United	38	15	6	17	52	62	36
15	Everton	38	12	11	15	46	55	35
16	Liverpool	38	14	7	17	46	62	35
17	Tottenham	38	12	10	16	50	62	34
18	Wednesday	38	13	8	17	53	70	34
19	Preston	38	12	6	20	52	69	30
20	Derby	38	8	11	19	55	71	27

SECOND DIVISION

		P	W	D	L	F	A	Pts
1	Notts County	38	23	7	8	77	36	53
2	Bradford PA	38	23	3	12	71	47	49
3	Arsenal	38	20	9	9	54	38	49
4	Leeds City	38	20	7	11	76	46	47
5	Barnsley	38	19	7	12	51	45	45
6	Clapton Orient	38	16	11	11	47	35	43
7	Hull	38	16	9	13	53	37	41
8	Bristol City	38	16	9	13	52	50	41
9	Wolves	38	18	5	15	51	52	41
10	Bury	38	15	10	13	39	40	40
11	Fulham	38	16	6	16	46	43	38
12	Stockport	38	13	10	15	55	57	36
13	Huddersfield	38	13	8	17	47	53	34
14	Birmingham	38	12	10	16	48	60	34
15	Grimsby	38	13	8	17	42	58	34
16	Blackpool	38	9	14	15	33	44	32
17	Glossop NE	38	11	6	21	51	67	28
18	Leicester Fosse	38	11	4	23	45	61	26
19	Lincoln	38	10	6	22	36	66	26
20	Nottm Forest	38	7	9	22	37	76	23

SCOTTISH FIRST DIVISION

		P	W	D	L	F	A	Pts
1	Celtic	38	30	5	3	81	14	65
2	Rangers	38	27	5	6	79	31	59
3	Hearts	38	23	8	7	70	29	54
4	Morton	38	26	2	10	76	51	54
5	Falkirk	38	20	9	9	69	51	49
6	Airdrieonians	38	18	12	8	72	43	48
7	Dundee	38	19	5	14	64	53	43
8	Third Lanark	38	13	10	15	42	51	36
9	Clyde	38	11	11	16	46	46	33
10	Ayr	38	13	7	18	58	74	33
11	Raith	38	13	6	19	56	57	32
12	Kilmarnock	38	11	9	18	48	68	31
13	Hibernian	38	12	6	20	58	75	30
14	Aberdeen	38	10	10	18	38	55	30
15	Partick	38	10	9	19	37	51	29
16	Queen's Park	38	10	9	19	52	84	29
17	Motherwell	38	11	6	21	49	66	28
18	Hamilton	38	11	6	21	46	65	28
19	Dumbarton	38	10	7	21	45	87	27
20	St Mirren	38	8	6	24	38	73	22

SCOTTISH SECOND DIVISION

		P	W	D	L	F	A	Pts
1	Cowdenbeath	22	13	5	4	34	17	31
2	Albion	22	10	7	5	38	33	27
3	Dunfermline	22	11	4	7	46	28	26
4	Dundee Hibs	22	11	4	7	36	31	26
5	St Johnstone	22	9	5	8	48	38	23
6	Abercorn	22	10	3	9	32	32	23
7	St Bernard's	22	8	6	8	39	31	22
8	E Stirlingshire	22	7	8	7	40	36	22
9	Arthurlie	22	8	4	10	35	37	20
10	Leith	22	5	9	8	31	37	19
11	Vale of Leven	22	5	3	14	23	47	13
12	Johnstone	22	4	4	14	20	55	12

Below *September 1913 and Woolwich Arsenal play Hull at Highbury. It had been a rush removal to what were then the grounds of a theological college, and in Arsenal's first match there, earlier in the month, the players washed in bowls of water, while an injured player was taken away on a milk-cart.*

RADIO TIMES HULTON PICTURE LIBRARY

FA CUP 1913-14

SECOND ROUND

Sheffield United v Bradford Park Avenue	3-1
Millwall Athletic v Bradford City	1-0
Manchester City v Tottenham Hotspur	2-1
Blackburn Rovers v Bury	2-0
Burnley v Derby County	3-2
Bolton Wanderers v Swindon Town	4-2
Sunderland v Plymouth Argyle	2-1
Glossop North End v Preston North End	0-1
Exeter City v Aston Villa	1-2
Leeds City v West Bromwich Albion	0-2
Wolverhampton Wanderers v The Wednesday	1-1, 0-1
Brighton v Clapton Orient	3-1
Liverpool v Gillingham	2-0
West Ham United v Crystal Palace	2-0
Swansea Town v Queen's Park Rangers	1-2
Birmingham v Huddersfield Town	1-0

THIRD ROUND

Millwall Athletic v Sheffield United	0-4
Blackburn Rovers v Manchester City	1-2
Burnley v Bolton Wanderers	3-0
Sunderland v Preston North End	2-0
Aston Villa v West Bromwich Albion	2-1
The Wednesday v Brighton	3-0
West Ham United v Liverpool	1-1, 1-5
Birmingham v Queen's Park Rangers	1-2

FOURTH ROUND

Manchester City v Sheffield United	0-0, 0-0, 0-1
Sunderland v Burnley	0-0, 1-2
The Wednesday v Aston Villa	0-1
Liverpool v Queen's Park Rangers	2-1

SEMI-FINAL

Sheffield United v Burnley	0-0, 0-1
Aston Villa v Liverpool	0-2

FINAL AT CRYSTAL PALACE

Burnley v Liverpool	1-0

SCOTTISH FA CUP 1913-14

SECOND ROUND

Aberdeen v Albion Rovers	4-1
Airdrieonians v Dundee Hibernian	5-0
Broxburn United v Dumfries	5-1
Celtic v Clyde	0-0, 2-0
Morton v Hibernian	1-1, 1-2
East Stirlingshire v Forfar Athletic	1-1, 0-2
Kilmarnock v Hamilton Academicals	3-1
Leith Athletic v Motherwell	1-1, 2-5
Partick Thistle v Nithsdale Wanderers	1-0
Forres Mechanics v Peebles Rovers	0-4
Queen's Park v Arthurlie	1-0
Raith Rovers v Heart of Midlothian	2-0
Rangers v Alloa Athletic	5-0
St Mirren v Dundee	2-1
Kirkcaldy United v Stevenston United	0-4
Third Lanark v Dumbarton	2-0

THIRD ROUND

Forfar Athletic v Celtic	0-5
Hibernian v Rangers	2-1
Broxburn United v Motherwell	0-2
Kilmarnock v Partick Thistle	1-4
Airdrieonians v Queen's Park	1-1, 1-2
Aberdeen v St Mirren	1-2
Stevenston United v Peebles Rovers	3-2
Third Lanark v Raith Rovers	4-1

FOURTH ROUND

Motherwell v Celtic	1-3
Queen's Park v Hibernian	1-3
St Mirren v Partick Thistle	1-0
Third Lanark v Stevenston United	1-1, 0-0, 1-0

SEMI-FINAL

Celtic v Third Lanark	2-0
Hibernian v St Mirren	3-1

FINAL AT IBROX PARK

Celtic v Hibernian	0-0, 4-1

FIRST DIVISION 1914-15

		P	W	D	L	F	A	Pts
1	Everton	38	19	8	11	76	47	46
2	Oldham	38	17	11	10	70	56	45
3	Blackburn	38	18	7	13	83	61	43
4	Burnley	38	18	7	13	61	47	43
5	Man City	38	15	13	10	49	39	43
6	Sheff United	38	15	13	10	49	41	43
7	Wednesday	38	15	13	10	61	54	43
8	Sunderland	38	18	5	15	81	72	41
9	Bradford PA	38	17	7	14	69	65	41
10	Bradford City	38	13	14	11	55	49	40
11	WBA	38	15	10	13	49	43	40
12	Middlesbrough	38	13	12	13	62	74	38
13	Aston Villa	38	13	11	14	62	72	37
14	Liverpool*	38	14	9	15	65	75	37
15	Newcastle	38	11	10	17	46	48	32
16	Notts County	38	9	13	16	41	57	31
17	Bolton	38	11	8	19	68	84	30
18	Man United*	38	9	12	17	46	62	30
19	Chelsea	38	8	13	17	51	65	29
20	Tottenham	38	8	12	18	57	90	28

*A commission concluded that the Manchester United–Liverpool game on 2 April 1915 had been 'fixed' but the result (2-0) was allowed to stand. No points were deducted.

SCOTTISH DIVISION 'A' 1914-15

		P	W	D	L	F	A	Pts
1	Celtic	38	30	5	3	91	25	65
2	Hearts	38	27	7	4	83	32	61
3	Rangers	38	23	4	11	74	47	50
4	Morton	38	18	12	8	74	48	48
5	Ayr	38	20	8	10	55	40	48
6	Falkirk	38	16	7	15	48	48	39
7	Hamilton	38	16	6	16	60	55	38
8	Partick	38	15	8	15	56	58	38
9	St Mirren	38	14	8	16	56	65	36
10	Airdrieonians	38	14	7	17	54	60	35
11	Hibernian	38	12	11	15	59	66	35
12	Kilmarnock	38	15	4	19	55	59	34
13	Dumbarton	38	13	8	17	51	66	34
14	Aberdeen	38	11	11	16	39	52	33
15	Dundee	38	12	9	17	43	61	33
16	Third Lanark	38	10	12	16	51	57	32
17	Clyde	38	12	6	20	44	59	30
18	Motherwell	38	10	10	18	49	66	30
19	Raith	38	9	10	19	53	68	28
20	Queen's Park	38	4	5	29	27	90	13

SECOND DIVISION 1914-15

		P	W	D	L	F	A	Pts
1	Derby	38	23	7	8	71	33	53
2	Preston	38	20	10	8	61	42	50
3	Barnsley	38	22	3	13	51	51	47
4	Wolves	38	19	7	12	77	52	45
5	Birmingham	38	17	9	12	62	39	43
6	Arsenal	38	19	5	14	69	41	43
7	Hull	38	19	5	14	65	54	43
8	Huddersfield	38	17	8	13	61	42	42
9	Clapton Orient	38	16	9	13	50	48	41
10	Blackpool	38	17	5	16	58	57	39
11	Bury	38	15	8	15	61	56	38
12	Fulham	38	15	7	16	53	47	37
13	Bristol City	38	15	7	16	62	56	37
14	Stockport	38	15	7	16	54	60	37
15	Leeds City	38	14	4	20	65	64	32
16	Lincoln	38	11	9	18	46	65	31
17	Grimsby	38	11	9	18	48	76	31
18	Nottm Forest	38	10	9	19	43	77	29
19	Leicester Fosse	38	10	4	24	47	88	24
20	Glossop NE	38	6	6	26	31	87	18

SCOTTISH DIVISION 'B' 1914-15

		P	W	D	L	F	A	Pts
1	Cowdenbeath	26	16	5	5	49	17	37
2	Leith	26	15	7	4	54	31	37
3	St Bernard's	26	18	1	7	66	34	37
4	E Stirlingshire	26	13	5	8	53	46	31
5	Clydebank	26	13	4	9	68	37	30
6	Dunfermline	26	13	2	11	49	39	28
7	Johnstone	26	11	5	10	41	52	27
8	St Johnstone	26	10	6	10	56	53	26
9	Albion	26	9	7	10	37	42	25
10	Lochgelly	26	9	3	14	44	60	21
11	Dundee Hibs	26	8	3	15	48	61	19
12	Abercorn	26	5	7	14	35	65	17
13	Arthurlie	26	6	4	16	36	66	16
14	Vale of Leven	26	4	5	17	33	66	13

WINNERS 1914-15

Southern League Watford
Central League Huddersfield Town
Irish Cup Linfield
Irish League Belfast Celtic
Welsh Cup Wrexham

FA CUP 1914-15

FIRST ROUND

Blackpool v Sheffield United	1-2
Liverpool v Stockport County	3-0
Bradford Park Avenue v Portsmouth	1-0
Bury v Plymouth Argyle	1-1, 2-1
Croydon Common v Oldham Athletic	0-3
Rochdale v Gillingham	2-0
Birmingham v Crystal Palace	2-2, 3-0
Brighton v Lincoln City	2-1
Bolton Wanderers v Notts County	2-1
Millwall Athletic v Clapton Orient	2-1
Burnley v Huddersfield Town	3-1
Bristol Rovers v Southend United	0-0, 0-3
Hull City v West Bromwich Albion	1-0
Grimsby Town v Northampton Town	0-3
Southampton v Luton Town	3-0
South Shields v Fulham	1-2
Chelsea v Swindon	1-1, 5-2
Arsenal v Merthyr Town	3-0
Preston North End v Manchester City	0-0, 0-3
Aston Villa v Exeter City	2-0
West Ham United v Newcastle United	2-2, 2-3
Swansea Town v Blackburn Rovers	1-0
The Wednesday v Manchester United	1-0
Reading v Wolverhampton Wanderers	0-1
Everton v Barnsley	3-0
Bristol City v Cardiff City	2-0
Queen's Park Rangers v Glossop North End	2-1
Derby County v Leeds City	1-2
Darlington v Bradford City	0-1
Middlesbrough v Goole Town	9-3
Nottingham Forest v Norwich City	1-4
Tottenham Hotspur v Sunderland	2-1

SECOND ROUND

Sheffield United v Liverpool	1-0
Bury v Bradford Park Avenue	0-1
Oldham Athletic v Rochdale	3-0
Brighton v Birmingham	0-0*, 0-3
Bolton Wanderers v Millwall Athletic	0-0*, 2-2*, 4-1
Burnley v Southend United	6-0
Hull City v Northampton Town	2-1
Fulham v Southampton	2-3*
Chelsea v Arsenal	1-0
Manchester City v Aston Villa	1-0
Newcastle United v Swansea Town	1-1*, 2-0
The Wednesday v Wolverhampton Wanderers	2-0
Everton v Bristol City	4-0
Queen's Park Rangers v Leeds City	1-0
Bradford City v Middlesbrough	1-0
Norwich City v Tottenham Hotspur	3-2

THIRD ROUND

Sheffield United v Bradford Park Avenue	1-0*
Birmingham v Oldham Athletic	2-3
Bolton Wanderers v Burnley	2-1*
Southampton v Hull City	2-2*, 0-4
Manchester City v Chelsea	0-1
The Wednesday v Newcastle United	1-2
Queen's Park Rangers v Everton	1-2
Bradford City v Norwich City	1-1*, 0-0*, 2-0

FOURTH ROUND

Oldham Athletic v Sheffield United	0-0*, 0-3
Bolton Wanderers v Hull City	4-2
Chelsea v Newcastle United	1-1*, 1-0
Bradford City v Everton	0-2

SEMI-FINAL

Sheffield United v Bolton Wanderers	2-1
Chelsea v Everton	2-0

FINAL AT OLD TRAFFORD

Sheffield United v Chelsea	3-0

*Extra time played

Left *A heatwave in London during August 1914 prompts this St John's Ambulance man to supply the crowd with drinking water.*

There was such a rush of games at the end of season 1915-16 that Celtic played two League games on 15 April. They beat Raith Rovers 6-0 and, in the evening, Motherwell 3-1.

WINNERS 1915-16

Lancashire Regional Tournament Manchester City
Lancashire Tournament Northern Division Burnley
Lancashire Tournament Southern Division Manchester City
Midland Regional Tournament Nottingham Forest
Midland Tournament Southern Division Nottingham Forest
Midland Tournament Northern Division Leeds City
Midland Tournament Midland Division Grimsby Town
London Combination Chelsea
London Supplementary Tournament 'A' Chelsea
London Supplementary Tournament 'B' West Ham United
South Western Combination Portsmouth
Irish Cup Linfield

WINNERS 1916-17

Lancashire Regional Tournament Liverpool
Lancashire Subsidiary Tournament Rochdale
Midland Regional Tournament Leeds City
Midland Subsidiary Tournament Bradford PA
London Combination West Ham United
Irish Cup Glentoran
Belfast and District League Glentoran

WINNERS 1917-18

Lancashire Regional Tournament Stoke
Lancashire Subsidiary Tournament Liverpool
Midland Regional Tournament Leeds City
Midland Subsidiary Tournament Grimsby Town
League Championship Play-off Leeds City
London Combination Chelsea
Irish Cup Belfast Celtic
Belfast and District League Linfield

WINNERS 1918-19

Lancashire Regional Tournament Everton
Lancashire Subsidiary Tournament 'A' Blackpool
Lancashire Subsidiary Tournament 'B' Oldham Athletic
Lancashire Subsidiary Tournament 'C' Manchester City
Lancashire Subsidiary Tournament 'D' Liverpool
Midland Regional Tournament Nottingham Forest
Midland Subsidiary Tournament 'A' Sheffield United
Midland Subsidiary Tournament 'B' Birmingham
Midland Subsidiary Tournament 'C' Bradford PA
Midland Subsidiary Tournament 'D' Hull City
League Championship Play-off Nottingham Forest
London Combination Brentford
Irish Cup Linfield

SCOTTISH LEAGUE 1915-16

		P	W	D	L	F	A	Pts
1	Celtic	38	32	3	3	116	23	67
2	Rangers	38	25	6	7	87	39	56
3	Morton*	37	22	7	8	83	35	51
4	Ayr	38	20	8	10	72	45	48
5	Partick	38	19	8	11	65	41	46
6	Hearts*	37	20	6	11	66	45	46
7	Hamilton	38	19	3	16	68	76	41
8	Dundee	38	18	4	16	57	49	40
9	Dumbarton	38	13	11	14	53	64	37
10	Kilmarnock	38	12	11	15	46	49	35
11	Aberdeen	38	11	12	15	51	64	34
12	Falkirk	38	12	9	17	45	61	33
13	St Mirren	38	13	4	21	50	67	30
14	Motherwell	38	11	8	19	55	81	30
15	Airdrieonians	38	11	8	19	44	71	30
16	Clyde	38	11	7	20	49	71	29
17	Third Lanark	38	9	11	18	38	56	29
18	Queen's Park	38	11	6	21	53	100	28
19	Hibernian	38	9	7	22	44	70	25
20	Raith	38	9	5	24	30	65	23

*Morton and Hearts only played each other once.

SCOTTISH LEAGUE 1916-17

		P	W	D	L	F	A	Pts
1	Celtic	38	27	10	1	77	17	64
2	Morton	38	24	6	8	72	39	54
3	Rangers	38	24	5	9	68	32	53
4	Airdrieonians	38	21	8	9	71	38	50
5	Third Lanark	38	19	11	8	53	37	49
6	Kilmarnock	38	18	7	13	69	45	43
7	St Mirren	38	15	10	13	49	43	40
8	Motherwell	38	16	6	16	57	58	38
9	Partick	38	14	7	17	44	43	35
10	Dumbarton	38	12	11	15	56	73	35
11	Hamilton	38	13	9	16	54	73	35
12	Falkirk	38	12	10	16	57	57	34
13	Clyde	38	10	14	14	41	51	34
14	Hearts	38	14	4	20	44	59	32
15	Ayr	38	12	7	19	46	59	31
16	Dundee	38	13	4	21	58	71	30
17	Hibernian	38	10	10	18	57	72	30
18	Queen's Park	38	11	7	20	56	81	29
19	Raith	38	8	7	23	42	91	23
20	Aberdeen	38	7	7	24	36	68	21

SCOTTISH LEAGUE 1917-18

		P	W	D	L	F	A	Pts
1	Rangers	34	25	6	3	66	24	56
2	Celtic	34	24	7	3	66	26	55
3	Kilmarnock	34	19	5	10	69	41	43
4	Morton	34	17	9	8	53	42	43
5	Motherwell	34	16	9	9	70	51	41
6	Partick	34	14	12	8	51	37	40
7	Queen's Park	34	14	6	14	64	63	34
8	Dumbarton	34	13	8	13	48	49	34
9	Clydebank	34	14	5	15	55	56	33
10	Hearts	34	14	4	16	41	58	32
11	St Mirren	34	11	7	16	42	50	29
12	Hamilton	34	11	6	17	52	63	28
13	Third Lanark	34	10	7	17	56	62	27
14	Falkirk	34	9	9	16	38	58	27
15	Airdrieonians	34	10	6	18	46	58	26
16	Hibernian	34	8	9	17	42	57	25
17	Clyde	34	9	2	23	37	72	20
18	Ayr	34	5	9	20	32	61	19

SCOTTISH LEAGUE 1918-19

		P	W	D	L	F	A	Pts
1	Celtic	34	26	6	2	70	22	58
2	Rangers	34	26	5	3	86	16	57
3	Morton	34	18	11	5	76	38	47
4	Partick	34	17	7	10	62	43	41
5	Motherwell	34	14	10	10	51	40	38
6	Hearts	34	14	9	11	59	52	37
7	Ayr	34	14	9	11	57	53	37
8	Queen's Park	34	15	5	14	59	57	35
9	Kilmarnock	34	14	7	13	61	59	35
10	Clydebank	34	12	8	14	52	65	32
11	St Mirren	34	10	12	12	43	55	32
12	Third Lanark	34	11	9	14	60	60	31
13	Airdrieonians	34	9	11	14	45	54	29
14	Hamilton	34	11	5	18	49	75	27
15	Dumbarton	34	7	8	19	31	57	22
16	Falkirk	34	6	8	20	46	72	20
17	Clyde	34	7	6	21	45	75	20
18	Hibernian	34	5	4	25	28	87	14

Right *George Utley leads Sheffield United out for their semi-final FA Cup tie with Bolton Wanderers in 1915. United won 2-1, going on to the only Final this century initially played outside London. That Final, in which they beat Chelsea 3-0, was played at Old Trafford, and has always been known as the 'Khaki Final' because of the large number of soldiers in the crowd.*

The only first-class game in English football played without spectators was the 1915 Bradford City-Norwich second Cup replay. Questions had been raised in the Commons about British-made shells failing to explode in France. The Government decided that the people making the shells were being distracted, and banned football matches during working hours in the vicinity of munitions factories. The game, at Lincoln, was played behind locked doors.

League Tables 1919-20

FIRST DIVISION

	P	W	D	L	F	A	Pts
1 WBA	42	28	4	10	104	47	60
2 Burnley	42	21	9	12	65	59	51
3 Chelsea	42	22	5	15	56	51	49
4 Liverpool	42	19	10	13	59	44	48
5 Sunderland	42	22	4	16	72	59	48
6 Bolton	42	19	9	14	72	65	47
7 Man City	42	18	9	15	71	62	45
8 Newcastle	42	17	9	16	44	39	43
9 Aston Villa	42	18	6	18	75	73	42
10 Arsenal	42	15	12	15	56	58	42
11 Bradford PA	42	15	12	15	60	63	42
12 Man United	42	13	14	15	54	50	40
13 Middlesbrough	42	15	10	17	61	65	40
14 Sheff United	42	16	8	18	59	69	40
15 Bradford City	42	14	11	17	54	63	39
16 Everton	42	12	14	16	69	68	38
17 Oldham	42	15	8	19	49	52	38
18 Derby	42	13	12	17	47	57	38
19 Preston	42	14	10	18	57	73	38
20 Blackburn	42	13	11	18	64	77	37
21 Notts County	42	12	12	18	56	74	36
22 Wednesday	42	7	9	26	28	64	23

SECOND DIVISION

	P	W	D	L	F	A	Pts
1 Tottenham	42	32	6	4	102	32	70
2 Huddersfield	42	28	8	6	97	38	64
3 Birmingham	42	24	8	10	85	34	56
4 Blackpool	42	21	10	11	65	47	52
5 Bury	42	20	8	14	60	44	48
6 Fulham	42	19	9	14	61	50	47
7 West Ham	42	19	9	14	47	40	47
8 Bristol City	42	13	17	12	46	43	43
9 South Shields	42	15	12	15	58	48	42
10 Stoke	42	18	6	18	60	54	42
11 Hull	42	18	6	18	78	72	42
12 Barnsley	42	15	10	17	61	55	40
13 Port Vale*	42	16	8	18	59	62	40
14 Leicester	42	15	10	17	41	61	40
15 Clapton Orient	42	16	6	20	51	59	38
16 Stockport	42	14	9	19	52	61	37
17 Rotherham Co	42	13	8	21	51	83	34
18 Nottm Forest	42	11	9	22	43	73	31
19 Wolves	42	10	10	22	55	80	30
20 Coventry	42	9	11	22	35	73	29
21 Lincoln	42	9	9	24	44	101	27
22 Grimsby	42	10	5	27	34	75	25

*Leeds City were expelled from the League on 4 October 1919, when their record was P8 W4 D2 L2 F17 A10 Pts10. Port Vale took over their remaining fixtures

SCOTTISH LEAGUE

	P	W	D	L	F	A	Pts
1 Rangers	42	31	9	2	106	25	71
2 Celtic	42	29	10	3	89	31	68
3 Motherwell	42	23	11	8	73	53	57
4 Dundee	42	22	6	14	79	65	50
5 Clydebank	42	20	8	14	78	54	48
6 Morton	42	16	13	13	71	48	45
7 Airdrieonians	42	17	10	15	57	43	44
8 Third Lanark	42	16	11	15	57	62	43
9 Kilmarnock	42	20	3	19	59	74	43
10 Ayr	42	15	10	17	72	69	40
11 Dumbarton	42	13	13	16	57	65	39
12 Queen's Park	42	14	10	18	67	73	38
13 Partick	42	13	12	17	51	62	38
14 St Mirren	42	15	8	19	63	81	38
15 Hearts	42	14	9	19	57	72	37
16 Clyde	42	14	9	19	64	71	37
17 Aberdeen	42	11	13	18	46	64	35
18 Hibernian	42	13	7	22	60	79	33
19 Raith	42	11	10	21	61	82	32
20 Falkirk	42	10	11	21	45	74	31
21 Hamilton	42	11	7	24	56	86	29
22 Albion	42	10	7	25	42	77	27

SCOTTISH FA CUP 1919-20

FIRST ROUND

Cowdenbeath v Aberdeen 0-1
Albion Rovers v Dykehead 0-0, 2-1
Dunfermline Harp v Alloa Athletic 0-0, 0-1
Armadale v Clyde 1-0
Dundee v Airdrieonians 1-0
East Fife v Arthurlie 4-0
East Stirlingshire v Thornhill 6-0
St Bernard's v Bathgate 2-0
Heart of Midlothian v Nithsdale Wanderers 5-1
Galston v Hibernian 0-0, 1-2
Lochgelly United v Clachnacuddin 2-0
Morton v Forfar Athletic 4-0
Partick Thistle v Motherwell 3-1
Queen's Park v Hamilton Academicals 2-0
Rangers v Dumbarton 0-0, 1-0
Royal Albert v Forres Mechanics 7-0
Stevenston United v St Mirren 1-2
Third Lanark v Inverness Caledonian 4-1

SECOND ROUND

Aberdeen v Gala Fairydean 2-0
Albion Rovers v Huntingtower (scratched) wo
Armadale v Hibernian 1-0
Ayr United v St Mirren 2-1
Broxburn United v Queen of the South Wanderers 1-0
Dundee v Celtic 1-3
St Bernard's v Bathgate 2-0
Heart of Midlothian v Falkirk 2-0
Alloa Athletic v Kilmarnock 0-2
Lochgelly United v Royal Albert 2-1
St Johnstone v Morton 1-1, 3-5
Partick Thistle v East Fife 5-0
Queen's Park v Vale of Leithen 3-0
Raith Rovers v East Stirlingshire 0-0, 1-1, 0-0, 4-0
Rangers v Arbroath 5-0
Third Lanark v Vale of Leven 2-1

THIRD ROUND

Aberdeen v Heart of Midlothian 1-0
St Bernard's v Albion Rovers 1-1, 1-4
Ayr United v Armadale 1-1, 0-1
Celtic v Partick Thistle 2-0
Kilmarnock v Queen's Park 4-1
Raith Rovers v Morton 2-2, 0-3
Rangers v Broxburn United 3-0
Lochgelly United v Third Lanark 0-3

FOURTH ROUND

Albion Rovers v Aberdeen 2-1
Morton v Third Lanark 3-0
Armadale v Kilmarnock 1-2
Rangers v Celtic 1-0

SEMI-FINAL

Kilmarnock v Morton 3-2
Albion Rovers v Rangers 0-0, 1-1, 2-0

FINAL AT HAMPDEN PARK

Kilmarnock v Albion Rovers 3-2

FA CUP 1919-20

FIRST ROUND

Aston Villa v Queen's Park Rangers 2-1
Port Vale v Manchester United 1-2
Sunderland v Hull City 6-2
Thorneycroft's Wanderers v Burnley 0-0, 0-5
Bristol Rovers v Tottenham Hotspur 1-4
West Stanley v Gillingham 3-1
Southampton v West Ham United 0-0, 1-3
Bury v Stoke 2-0
Bolton Wanderers v Chelsea 0-1
Fulham v Swindon Town 1-2
Newport County v Leicester City 0-0, 0-2
Manchester City v Clapton Orient 4-1
Bradford Park Avenue v Nottingham Forest 3-0
Castleford Town v Hednesford Town 2-0
Notts County v Millwall Athletic 2-0
Middlesbrough v Lincoln City 4-1
Grimsby Town v Bristol City 1-2
Arsenal v Rochdale 4-2
Cardiff City v Oldham Athletic 2-0
Blackburn Rovers v Wolverhampton Wanderers 2-2, 0-1
Bradford City v Portsmouth 2-2*, 2-0
Sheffield United v Southend United 3-0
Preston North End v Stockport County 3-1
Blackpool v Derby County 0-0, 4-1
Huddersfield Town v Brentford 5-1
Newcastle United v Crystal Palace 2-0
Plymouth Argyle v Reading 2-0
West Bromwich Albion v Barnsley 0-1
South Shields v Liverpool 1-1, 0-2
Luton Town v Coventry City 2-2, 1-0
Birmingham v Everton 2-0
Darlington v The Wednesday 0-0, 2-0

*abandoned

SECOND ROUND

Manchester United v Aston Villa 1-2
Burnley v Sunderland 1-1, 0-2
Tottenham Hotspur v West Stanley 4-0
West Ham United v Bury 6-0
Chelsea v Swindon Town 4-0
Leicester City v Manchester City 3-0
Bradford Park Avenue v Castleford Town 3-2
Notts County v Middlesbrough 1-0
Bristol City v Arsenal 1-0
Wolverhampton Wanderers v Cardiff City 1-2
Bradford City v Sheffield United 2-1
Preston North End v Blackpool 2-1
Newcastle United v Huddersfield Town 0-1
Plymouth Argyle v Barnsley 4-1
Luton Town v Liverpool 0-2
Birmingham v Darlington 4-0

THIRD ROUND

Aston Villa v Sunderland 1-0
Tottenham Hotspur v West Ham United 3-0
Chelsea v Leicester City 3-0
Notts County v Bradford Park Avenue 3-4
Bristol City v Cardiff City 2-1
Preston North End v Bradford City 0-3
Huddersfield Town v Plymouth Argyle 3-1
Liverpool v Birmingham 2-0

FOURTH ROUND

Tottenham Hotspur v Aston Villa 0-1
Chelsea v Bradford Park Avenue 4-1
Bristol City v Bradford City 2-0
Huddersfield Town v Liverpool 2-1

SEMI-FINAL

Aston Villa v Chelsea 3-1
Huddersfield Town v Bristol City 2-1

FINAL AT STAMFORD BRIDGE

Aston Villa v Huddersfield Town 1-0

Far left *Billy Walker, the Aston Villa forward whose two goals in Villa's 3-1 win over Chelsea in the FA Cup semi-final saved the Football Association an embarrassing situation. If Chelsea had won they would have played the Final on their own ground, Stamford Bridge. This was against the rules of the competition but arrangements were too far advanced to be changed.*

FIRST DIVISION

	P	W	D	L	F	A	Pts
1 Burnley	42	23	13	6	79	36	59
2 Man City	42	24	6	12	70	50	54
3 Bolton	42	19	14	9	77	53	52
4 Liverpool	42	18	15	9	63	35	51
5 Newcastle	42	20	10	12	66	45	50
6 Tottenham	42	19	9	14	70	48	47
7 Everton	42	17	13	12	66	55	47
8 Middlesbrough	42	17	12	13	53	53	46
9 Arsenal	42	15	14	13	59	63	44
10 Aston Villa	42	18	7	17	63	70	43
11 Blackburn	42	13	15	14	57	59	41
12 Sunderland	42	14	13	15	57	60	41
13 Man United	42	15	10	17	64	68	40
14 WBA	42	13	14	15	54	58	40
15 Bradford City	42	12	15	15	61	63	39
16 Preston	42	15	9	18	61	65	39
17 Huddersfield	42	15	9	18	42	49	39
18 Chelsea	42	13	13	16	48	58	39
19 Oldham	42	9	15	18	49	86	33
20 Sheff United	42	6	18	18	42	68	30
21 Derby	42	5	16	21	32	58	26
22 Bradford PA	42	8	8	26	43	76	24

SECOND DIVISION

	P	W	D	L	F	A	Pts
1 Birmingham	42	24	10	8	79	38	58
2 Cardiff	42	24	10	8	59	32	58
3 Bristol City	42	19	13	10	49	29	51
4 Blackpool	42	20	10	12	54	42	50
5 West Ham	42	19	10	13	51	30	48
6 Notts County	42	18	11	13	55	40	47
7 Clapton Orient	42	16	13	13	43	42	45
8 South Shields	42	17	10	15	61	46	44
9 Fulham	42	16	10	16	43	47	42
10 Wednesday	42	15	11	16	48	48	41
11 Bury	42	15	10	17	45	49	40
12 Leicester	42	12	16	14	39	46	40
13 Hull	42	10	20	12	43	53	40
14 Leeds	42	14	10	18	40	45	38
15 Wolves	42	16	6	20	49	66	38
16 Barnsley	42	10	16	16	48	50	36
17 Port Vale	42	11	14	17	43	49	36
18 Nottm Forest	42	12	12	18	48	55	36
19 Rotherham Co	42	12	12	18	37	53	36
20 Stoke	42	12	11	19	46	56	35
21 Coventry	42	12	11	19	39	70	35
22 Stockport	42	9	12	21	42	75	30

THIRD DIVISION

	P	W	D	L	F	A	Pts
1 Crystal Palace	42	24	11	7	70	34	59
2 Southampton	42	19	16	7	64	28	54
3 QPR	42	22	9	11	61	32	53
4 Swindon	42	21	10	11	73	49	52
5 Swansea	42	18	15	9	56	45	51
6 Watford	42	20	8	14	59	44	48
7 Millwall Ath	42	18	11	13	42	30	47
8 Merthyr Town	42	15	15	12	60	49	45
9 Luton	42	16	12	14	61	56	44
10 Bristol Rovers	42	18	7	17	68	57	43
11 Plymouth	42	11	21	10	35	34	43
12 Portsmouth	42	12	15	15	46	48	39
13 Grimsby	42	15	9	18	49	59	39
14 Northampton	42	15	8	19	59	75	38
15 Newport	42	14	9	19	43	64	37
16 Norwich	42	10	16	16	44	53	36
17 Southend	42	14	8	20	44	61	36
18 Brighton	42	14	8	20	42	61	36
19 Exeter	42	10	15	17	39	54	35
20 Reading	42	12	7	23	42	59	31
21 Brentford	42	9	12	21	42	67	30
22 Gillingham	42	8	12	22	34	74	28

SCOTTISH LEAGUE

	P	W	D	L	F	A	Pts
1 Rangers	42	35	6	1	91	24	76
2 Celtic	42	30	6	6	86	35	66
3 Hearts	42	20	10	12	74	49	50
4 Dundee	42	19	11	12	54	48	49
5 Motherwell	42	19	10	13	75	51	48
6 Partick	42	17	12	13	53	39	46
7 Clyde	42	21	3	18	63	62	45
8 Third Lanark	42	19	6	17	74	61	44
9 Morton	42	15	14	13	66	58	44
10 Airdrieonians	42	17	9	16	71	64	43
11 Aberdeen	42	14	14	14	53	54	42
12 Kilmarnock	42	17	8	17	62	68	42
13 Hibernian	42	16	9	17	58	57	41
14 Ayr	42	14	12	16	62	69	40
15 Hamilton	42	14	12	16	44	57	40
16 Raith	42	16	5	21	54	58	37
17 Albion	42	11	12	19	57	68	34
18 Falkirk	42	11	12	19	54	72	34
19 Queen's Park	42	11	11	20	45	80	33
20 Clydebank	42	7	14	21	47	72	28
21 Dumbarton	42	10	4	28	41	89	24
22 St Mirren	42	7	4	31	43	92	18

RADIO TIMES HULTON PICTURE LIBRARY

Burnley's Championship side which went 30 games without defeat in 1920-21.

FA CUP 1920-21

SECOND ROUND

Southend United v Blackpool 1-0
Tottenham Hotspur v Bradford City 4-0
Notts County v Aston Villa 0-0, 0-1
Bradford Park Avenue v Huddersfield Town 0-1
Crystal Palace v Hull City 0-2
Burnley v Queen's Park Rangers 4-2
South Shields v Luton Town 0-4
Preston North End v Watford 4-1
Everton v The Wednesday 1-1, 1-0
Newcastle United v Liverpool 1-0
Lincoln City v Fulham 0-0, 0-1
Derby County v Wolverhampton Wanderers 1-1, 0-1
Grimsby Town v Southampton 1-3
Brighton v Cardiff City 0-0, 0-1
Swansea Town v Plymouth Argyle 1-2
Swindon Town v Chelsea 0-2

THIRD ROUND

Southend United v Tottenham Hotspur 1-4
Aston Villa v Huddersfield Town 2-0
Hull City v Burnley 3-0
Luton Town v Preston North End 2-3
Everton v Newcastle United 3-0
Fulham v Wolverhampton Wanderers 0-1
Southampton v Cardiff City 0-1
Plymouth Argyle v Chelsea 0-0, 0-0, 1-2

FOURTH ROUND

Tottenham Hotspur v Aston Villa 1-0
Hull City v Preston North End 0-0, 0-1
Everton v Wolverhampton Wanderers 0-1
Cardiff City v Chelsea 1-0

SEMI-FINAL

Tottenham Hotspur v Preston North End 2-1
Wolverhampton Wanderers v Cardiff City 0-0, 3-1

FINAL AT STAMFORD BRIDGE

Tottenham Hotspur v Wolverhampton Wanderers 1-0

SCOTTISH FA CUP 1920-21

SECOND ROUND

Kilmarnock v Aberdeen 1-2
Albion Rovers v Mid-Annandale 3-1
Clydebank v Alloa Athletic 0-0, 1-1, 0-1
Bo'ness v Armadale 0-0, 0-2
Ayr United v Dykehead 4-0
Vale of Leven v Celtic 0-3
Dumbarton v Elgin City 3-0
Dundee v Stenhousemuir 1-0
Stevenston United v East Fife 0-0, 1-2
East Stirlingshire v Solway Star 5-1
Broxburn United v Hamilton Academicals 1-2
Clyde v Heart of Midlothian 0-0, 1-1, 2-3
Motherwell v Renton 3-0
Queen of the South v Nithsdale Wanderers 1-3
Partick Thistle v Hibernian 0-0, 0-0, 1-0
Rangers v Morton 2-0

THIRD ROUND

Armadale v Albion Rovers 0-0, 0-0, 2-2, 0-2
East Fife v Celtic 1-3
Dumbarton v Nithsdale Wanderers 5-0
Aberdeen v Dundee 1-1, 0-0, 0-2
Hamilton Academicals v Heart of Midlothian 0-1
Motherwell v Ayr United 1-1, 1-1, 3-1
East Stirlingshire v Partick Thistle 1-2
Rangers v Alloa Athletic 0-0, 4-1

FOURTH ROUND

Dundee v Albion Rovers 0-2
Celtic v Heart of Midlothian 1-2
Partick Thistle v Motherwell 0-0, 2-2, 2-1
Dumbarton v Rangers 0-3

SEMI-FINAL

Partick v Heart of Midlothian 0-0, 0-0, 2-0
Rangers v Albion Rovers 4-1

FINAL AT CELTIC PARK

Partick Thistle v Rangers 1-0

League Tables 1921-22

FIRST DIVISION

	P	W	D	L	F	A	Pts
1 Liverpool	42	22	13	7	63	36	57
2 Tottenham	42	21	9	12	65	39	51
3 Burnley	42	22	5	15	72	54	49
4 Cardiff	42	19	10	13	61	53	48
5 Aston Villa	42	22	3	17	74	55	47
6 Bolton	42	20	7	15	68	59	47
7 Newcastle	42	18	10	14	59	45	46
8 Middlesbrough	42	16	14	12	79	69	46
9 Chelsea	42	17	12	13	40	43	46
10 Man City	42	18	9	15	65	70	45
11 Sheff United	42	15	10	17	59	54	40
12 Sunderland	42	16	8	18	60	62	40
13 WBA	42	15	10	17	51	63	40
14 Huddersfield	42	15	9	18	53	54	39
15 Blackburn	42	13	12	17	54	57	38
16 Preston	42	13	12	17	42	65	38
17 Arsenal	42	15	7	20	47	56	37
18 Birmingham	42	15	7	20	48	60	37
19 Oldham	42	13	11	18	38	50	37
20 Everton	42	12	12	18	57	55	36
21 Bradford City	42	11	10	21	48	72	32
22 Man United	42	8	12	22	41	73	28

SECOND DIVISION

	P	W	D	L	F	A	Pts
1 Nottm Forest	42	22	12	8	51	30	56
2 Stoke	42	18	16	8	60	44	52
3 Barnsley	42	22	8	12	67	52	52
4 West Ham	42	20	8	14	52	39	48
5 Hull	42	19	10	13	51	41	48
6 South Shields	42	17	12	13	43	38	46
7 Fulham	42	18	9	15	57	38	45
8 Leeds	42	16	13	13	48	38	45
9 Leicester	42	14	17	11	39	34	45
10 Wednesday	42	15	14	13	47	50	44
11 Bury	42	15	10	17	54	55	40
12 Derby	42	15	9	18	60	64	39
13 Notts County	42	12	15	15	47	51	39
14 Crystal Palace	42	13	13	16	45	51	39
15 Clapton Orient	42	15	9	18	43	50	39
16 Rotherham Co	42	14	11	17	32	43	39
17 Wolves	42	13	11	18	44	49	37
18 Port Vale	42	14	8	20	43	57	36
19 Blackpool	42	15	5	22	44	57	35
20 Coventry	42	12	10	20	51	60	34
21 Bristol City	42	12	9	21	37	58	33
22 Bradford PA	42	12	9	21	46	62	33

FA CUP 1921-22

SECOND ROUND

Crystal Palace v Millwall Athletic	0-0, 0-2
Southend United v Swansea Town	0-1
Swindon Town v Blackburn Rovers	0-1
Brighton v Huddersfield Town	0-0, 0-2
Aston Villa v Luton Town	1-0
Northampton Town v Stoke	2-2, 0-3
Liverpool v West Bromwich Albion	0-1
Bradford City v Notts County	1-1, 1-1, 0-1
Bradford Park Avenue v Arsenal	2-3
Leicester City v Fulham	2-0
Barnsley v Oldham Athletic	3-1
Preston North End v Newcastle United	3-1
Southampton v Cardiff City	1-1, 0-2
Nottingham Forest v Hull City	3-0
Bolton Wanderers v Manchester City	1-3
Tottenham Hotspur v Watford	1-0

THIRD ROUND

Millwall Athletic v Swansea Town	4-0
Blackburn Rovers v Huddersfield Town	1-1, 0-5
Stoke v Aston Villa	0-0, 0-4
West Bromwich Albion v Notts County	1-1, 0-2
Arsenal v Leicester City	3-0
Barnsley v Preston North End	1-1, 0-3
Cardiff City v Nottingham Forest	4-1
Tottenham Hotspur v Manchester City	2-1

FOURTH ROUND

Huddersfield Town v Millwall Athletic	3-0
Notts County v Aston Villa	2-2, 4-3
Arsenal v Preston North End	1-1, 1-2
Cardiff City v Tottenham Hotspur	1-1, 1-2

SEMI-FINAL

Huddersfield Town v Notts County	3-1
Preston North End v Tottenham Hotspur	2-1

FINAL AT STAMFORD BRIDGE

Huddersfield Town v Preston North End	1-0

THIRD DIVISION (NORTH)

	P	W	D	L	F	A	Pts
1 Stockport	38	24	8	6	60	21	56
2 Darlington	38	22	6	10	81	37	50
3 Grimsby	38	21	8	9	72	47	50
4 Hartlepools	38	17	8	13	52	39	42
5 Accrington	38	19	3	16	73	57	41
6 Crewe	38	18	5	15	60	56	41
7 Stalybridge Cel	38	18	5	15	62	63	41
8 Walsall	38	18	3	17	66	65	39
9 Southport	38	14	10	14	55	44	38
10 Ashington	38	17	4	17	59	66	38
11 Durham City	38	17	3	18	68	67	37
12 Wrexham	38	14	9	15	51	56	37
13 Chesterfield	38	16	3	19	48	67	35
14 Lincoln	38	14	6	18	48	59	34
15 Barrow	38	14	5	19	42	54	33
16 Nelson	38	13	7	18	48	66	33
17 Wigan Borough	38	11	9	18	46	72	31
18 Tranmere	38	9	11	18	51	61	29
19 Halifax	38	10	9	19	56	76	29
20 Rochdale	38	11	4	23	52	77	26

THIRD DIVISION (SOUTH)

	P	W	D	L	F	A	Pts
1 Southampton	42	23	15	4	68	21	61
2 Plymouth	42	25	11	6	63	24	61
3 Portsmouth	42	18	17	7	62	39	53
4 Luton	42	22	8	12	64	35	52
5 QPR	42	18	13	11	53	44	49
6 Swindon	42	16	13	13	72	60	45
7 Watford	42	13	18	11	54	48	44
8 Aberdare Ath	42	17	10	15	57	51	44
9 Brentford	42	16	11	15	52	43	43
10 Swansea	42	13	15	14	50	47	41
11 Merthyr Town	42	17	6	19	45	56	40
12 Millwall Ath	42	10	18	14	38	42	38
13 Reading	42	14	18	10	40	47	38
14 Bristol Rovers	42	14	10	18	52	67	38
15 Norwich	42	12	13	17	50	62	37
16 Charlton	42	13	11	18	43	56	37
17 Northampton	42	13	11	18	47	71	37
18 Gillingham	42	14	8	20	47	60	36
19 Brighton	42	13	9	20	45	51	35
20 Newport	42	11	12	19	44	61	34
21 Exeter	42	11	12	19	38	59	34
22 Southend	42	8	11	23	34	74	27

SCOTTISH FA CUP 1921-22

SECOND ROUND

Aberdeen v Queen's Park	1-1, 2-1
Cowdenbeath v Airdrieonians	0-0, 1-4
Vale of Leven v Alloa Athletic	0-0, 0-1
Bathgate v Falkirk	1-0
Celtic v Third Lanark	1-0
Clyde v Bo'ness	5-1
Royal Albert v Dundee	0-1
East Stirlingshire v Dunfermline Athletic	2-1
Morton v Clydebank	1-1, 3-1
Hamilton Academicals v King's Park	4-1
Broxburn United v Heart of Midlothian	2-2, 2-2, 1-3
Motherwell v Hibernian	3-2
Ayr United v Partick Thistle	0-1
Inverness Citadel v Queen of the South	2-2, 1-2
Albion Rovers v Rangers	1-1, 0-4
Kilmarnock v St Mirren	1-4

THIRD ROUND

Aberdeen v Dundee	3-0
Morton v Clyde	4-1
Celtic v Hamilton Academicals	1-3
Motherwell v Alloa Athletic	1-0
Partick Thistle v Bathgate	3-0
Queen of the South v East Stirlingshire	2-0
Heart of Midlothian v Rangers	0-4
St Mirren v Airdrieonians	3-0

FOURTH ROUND

Hamilton Academicals v Aberdeen	0-0, 0-2
Motherwell v Morton	1-2
Partick Thistle v Queen of the South	1-0
Rangers v St Mirren	1-1, 2-0

SEMI-FINAL

Morton v Aberdeen	3-1
Rangers v Partick Thistle	2-0

FINAL AT HAMPDEN PARK

Morton v Rangers	1-0

SCOTTISH FIRST DIVISION

	P	W	D	L	F	A	Pts
1 Celtic	42	27	13	2	83	20	67
2 Rangers	42	28	10	4	83	26	66
3 Raith	42	19	13	10	66	43	51
4 Dundee	42	19	11	12	57	40	49
5 Falkirk	42	16	17	9	48	38	49
6 Partick	42	20	8	14	57	53	48
7 Hibernian	42	16	14	12	55	44	46
8 St Mirren	42	17	12	13	71	61	46
9 Third Lanark	42	17	12	13	58	52	46
10 Clyde	42	16	12	14	60	51	44
11 Albion	42	17	10	15	55	51	44
12 Morton	42	16	10	16	58	57	42
13 Motherwell	42	16	7	19	63	58	39
14 Ayr	42	13	12	17	55	63	38
15 Aberdeen	42	13	9	20	48	54	35
16 Airdrieonians	42	12	11	19	46	56	35
17 Kilmarnock	42	13	9	20	56	83	35
18 Hamilton	42	9	16	17	51	62	34
19 Hearts	42	11	10	21	50	60	32
20 Dumbarton*	42	10	10	22	46	81	30
21 Queen's Park*	42	9	10	23	38	82	28
22 Clydebank*	42	6	8	28	34	103	20

* Three clubs relegated to Second Division

SCOTTISH SECOND DIVISION

	P	W	D	L	F	A	Pts
1 Alloa*	38	26	8	4	81	32	60
2 Cowdenbeath	38	19	9	10	56	30	47
3 Armadale	38	20	5	13	64	49	45
4 Vale of Leven	38	17	10	11	56	43	44
5 Bathgate	38	16	11	11	56	41	43
6 Bo'ness	38	16	7	15	57	49	39
7 Broxburn	38	14	11	13	43	43	39
8 Dunfermline	38	14	10	14	56	42	38
9 St Bernard's	38	15	8	15	50	49	38
10 Stenhousemuir	38	14	10	14	50	51	38
11 Johnstone	38	14	10	14	46	59	38
12 East Fife	38	15	7	16	55	54	37
13 St Johnstone	38	12	11	15	41	52	35
14 Forfar	38	11	12	15	44	53	34
15 E Stirlingshire	38	12	10	16	43	60	34
16 Arbroath	38	11	11	16	45	56	33
17 King's Park	38	10	12	16	47	65	32
18 Lochgelly Utd	38	11	9	18	46	56	31
19 Dundee Hibs	38	10	8	20	47	65	28
20 Clackmannan	38	10	7	21	41	75	27

* Only Alloa promoted

On Boxing Day 1921, Aston Villa's winning goal in their Division One fixture with Sheffield United was a spectacular 30-yard header. Frank Barson, Villa's centre-half, was the man responsible. Another Villa player, Billy Walker, had also done the unusual in a League match that season. In November, he had scored three penalties against Bradford City—a record for one game.

Jimmy Evans, Southend United's full-back, scored a total of 10 goals in the Third Division South in 1921-22. All were from penalties, and meant that Evans became the first full-back to finish a season as a club's top League scorer.

The Scottish Second Division restarted in 1921-22, with promotion by position.

League Tables 1922-23

FIRST DIVISION

		P	W	D	L	F	A	Pts
1	Liverpool	42	26	8	8	70	31	60
2	Sunderland	42	22	10	10	72	54	54
3	Huddersfield	42	21	11	10	60	32	53
4	Newcastle	42	18	12	12	45	37	48
5	Everton	42	20	7	15	63	59	47
6	Aston Villa	42	18	10	14	64	51	46
7	WBA	42	17	11	14	58	49	45
8	Man City	42	17	11	14	50	49	45
9	Cardiff	42	18	7	17	73	59	43
10	Sheff United	42	16	10	16	68	64	42
11	Arsenal	42	16	10	16	61	62	42
12	Tottenham	42	17	7	18	50	50	41
13	Bolton	42	14	12	16	50	58	40
14	Blackburn	42	14	12	16	47	62	40
15	Burnley	42	16	6	20	58	59	38
16	Preston	42	13	11	18	60	64	37
17	Birmingham	42	13	11	18	41	57	37
18	Middlesbrough	42	13	10	19	57	63	36
19	Chelsea	42	9	18	15	45	53	36
20	Nottm Forest	42	13	8	21	41	70	34
21	Stoke	42	10	10	22	47	67	30
22	Oldham	42	10	10	22	35	65	30

THIRD DIVISION (SOUTH)

		P	W	D	L	F	A	Pts
1	Bristol City	42	24	11	7	66	40	59
2	Plymouth	42	23	7	12	61	29	53
3	Swansea	42	22	9	11	78	45	53
4	Brighton	42	20	11	11	52	34	51
5	Luton	42	21	7	14	68	49	49
6	Portsmouth	42	19	8	15	58	52	46
7	Millwall Ath	42	14	18	10	45	40	46
8	Northampton	42	17	11	14	54	44	45
9	Swindon	42	17	11	14	62	56	45
10	Watford	42	17	10	15	57	54	44
11	QPR	42	16	10	16	54	49	42
12	Charlton	42	14	14	14	55	51	42
13	Bristol Rovers	42	13	16	13	35	36	42
14	Brentford	42	13	12	17	41	51	38
15	Southend	42	12	13	17	49	54	37
16	Gillingham	42	15	7	20	51	59	37
17	Merthyr Town	42	11	14	17	39	48	36
18	Norwich	42	13	10	19	51	71	36
19	Reading	42	10	14	18	36	55	34
20	Exeter	42	13	7	22	47	84	33
21	Aberdare Ath	42	9	11	22	42	70	29
22	Newport	42	8	11	23	40	70	27

SCOTTISH FIRST DIVISION

		P	W	D	L	F	A	Pts
1	Rangers	38	23	9	6	67	29	55
2	Airdrieonians	38	20	10	8	58	38	50
3	Celtic	38	19	8	11	52	39	46
4	Falkirk	38	14	17	7	44	32	45
5	Aberdeen	38	15	12	11	46	34	42
6	St Mirren	38	15	12	11	54	44	42
7	Dundee	38	17	7	14	51	45	41
8	Hibernian	38	17	7	14	45	40	41
9	Raith	38	13	13	12	31	43	39
10	Ayr	38	13	12	13	43	44	38
11	Partick	38	14	9	15	51	48	37
12	Hearts	38	11	15	12	51	50	37
13	Motherwell	38	13	10	15	59	60	36
14	Morton	38	12	11	15	44	47	35
15	Kilmarnock	38	14	7	17	57	66	35
16	Clyde	38	12	9	17	36	44	33
17	Third Lanark	38	11	8	19	40	59	30
18	Hamilton	38	11	7	20	43	59	29
19	Albion	38	8	10	20	38	64	26
20	Alloa	38	6	11	21	27	52	23

In Division Two, 1922-23, Southampton had an uneventful season, finishing in the middle of the table. But their final record is something of a curiosity. It reads, P42, W14, D14, L14, F40, A40, Pts42.

Liverpool won the League Championship for the second successive season.

SECOND DIVISION

		P	W	D	L	F	A	Pts
1	Notts County	42	23	7	12	46	34	53
2	West Ham	42	20	11	11	63	38	51
3	Leicester	42	21	9	12	65	44	51
4	Man United	42	17	14	11	51	36	48
5	Blackpool	42	18	11	13	60	43	47
6	Bury	42	18	11	13	55	46	47
7	Leeds	42	18	11	13	43	36	47
8	Wednesday	42	17	12	13	54	47	46
9	Barnsley	42	17	11	14	62	51	45
10	Fulham	42	16	12	14	43	32	44
11	Southampton	42	14	14	14	40	40	42
12	Hull	42	14	14	14	43	45	42
13	South Shields	42	15	10	17	35	44	40
14	Derby	42	14	11	17	46	50	39
15	Bradford City	42	12	13	17	41	45	37
16	Crystal Palace	42	13	11	18	54	62	37
17	Port Vale	42	14	9	19	39	51	37
18	Coventry	42	15	7	20	46	63	37
19	Clapton Orient	42	12	12	18	40	50	36
20	Stockport	42	14	8	20	43	58	36
21	Rotherham Co	42	13	9	20	44	63	35
22	Wolves	42	9	9	24	42	77	27

THIRD DIVISION (NORTH)

		P	W	D	L	F	A	Pts
1	Nelson	38	24	3	11	61	41	51
2	Bradford PA	38	19	9	10	67	38	47
3	Walsall	38	19	8	11	51	44	46
4	Chesterfield	38	19	7	12	68	52	45
5	Wigan Borough	38	18	8	12	64	39	44
6	Crewe	38	17	9	12	48	38	43
7	Halifax	38	17	7	14	53	46	41
8	Accrington	38	17	7	14	59	65	41
9	Darlington	38	15	10	13	59	46	40
10	Wrexham	38	14	10	14	38	48	38
11	Stalybridge Cel	38	15	6	17	42	47	36
12	Rochdale	38	13	10	15	42	53	36
13	Lincoln	38	13	10	15	39	55	36
14	Grimsby	38	14	5	19	55	52	33
15	Hartlepools	38	10	12	16	48	54	32
16	Tranmere	38	12	8	18	49	59	32
17	Southport	38	12	7	19	32	46	31
18	Barrow	38	13	4	21	50	60	30
19	Ashington	38	11	8	19	51	77	30
20	Durham City	38	9	10	19	43	59	28

SCOTTISH SECOND DIVISION

		P	W	D	L	F	A	Pts
1	Queen's Park	38	24	9	5	73	31	57
2	Clydebank	38	21	10	7	69	29	52
3	St Johnstone	38	19	12	7	60	39	48*
4	Dumbarton	38	17	8	13	61	40	42
5	Bathgate	38	16	9	13	67	55	41
6	Armadale	38	15	11	12	63	52	41
7	Bo'ness	38	12	17	9	48	46	41
8	Broxburn	38	14	12	12	40	43	40
9	East Fife	38	16	7	15	48	42	39
10	Lochgelly	38	16	5	17	41	64	37
11	Cowdenbeath	38	16	6	16	56	52	36*
12	King's Park	38	14	6	18	46	60	34
13	Dunfermline	38	11	11	16	47	44	33
14	Stenhousemuir	38	13	7	18	53	67	33
15	Forfar	38	13	7	18	51	73	33
16	Johnstone	38	13	6	19	41	62	32
17	Vale of Leven	38	11	8	19	50	59	30
18	St Bernard's	38	8	15	15	39	50	29*
19	E Stirlingshire	38	10	8	20	48	69	28
20	Arbroath	38	8	12	18	45	69	28

*Two points deducted for fielding an ineligible player.

The most goals a player has scored in an FA Cup game and yet finished on the losing side is seven. Billy Minter of St Albans City scored seven times against Dulwich Hamlet in a replayed Fourth Round qualifying tie on 22 November 1922. But despite poor Minter's monumental contribution, his side eventually lost the match 8-7.

FA CUP 1922-23

SECOND ROUND

Bolton Wanderers v Leeds United	3-1
Millwall Athletic v Huddersfield Town	0-0, 0-3
Charlton Athletic v Preston North End	2-0
West Bromwich Albion v Sunderland	2-1
Middlesbrough v Sheffield United	1-1, 0-3
Wolverhampton Wanderers v Liverpool	0-2
Wigan Borough v Queen's Park Rangers	2-4
South Shields v Blackburn Rovers	0-0, 1-0
Bury v Stoke	3-1
Chelsea v Southampton	0-0, 0-1
Brighton v West Ham United	1-1, 0-1
Plymouth Argyle v Bradford Park Avenue	4-1
Bristol City v Derby County	0-3
The Wednesday v Barnsley	2-1
Tottenham Hotspur v Manchester United	4-0
Leicester City v Cardiff City	0-1

THIRD ROUND

Huddersfield Town v Bolton Wanderers	1-1, 0-1
Charlton Athletic v West Bromwich Albion	1-0
Liverpool v Sheffield United	1-2
Queen's Park Rangers v South Shields	3-0
Bury v Southampton	0-0, 0-1
West Ham United v Plymouth Argyle	2-0
Derby County v The Wednesday	1-0
Cardiff City v Tottenham Hotspur	2-3

FOURTH ROUND

Charlton Athletic v Bolton Wanderers	0-1
Queen's Park Rangers v Sheffield United	0-1
Southampton v West Ham United	1-1, 1-1, 0-1
Tottenham Hotspur v Derby County	0-1

SEMI-FINAL

Bolton Wanderers v Sheffield United	1-0
West Ham United v Derby County	5-2

FINAL

Bolton Wanderers v West Ham United	2-0

SCOTTISH FA CUP 1922-23

SECOND ROUND

Airdrieonians v Aberdeen	1-1, 0-2
Ayr United v Rangers	2-0
Bo'ness v Heart of Midlothian	3-2
Celtic v Hurlford	4-0
Dundee v St Bernard's	0-0, 3-2
Dunfermline Athletic v Clydebank	1-0
Hibernian v Peebles Rovers	0-0, 3-0
Kilmarnock v East Fife	1-1, 0-1
Johnstone v Falkirk	0-1
Hamilton Academicals v King's Park	1-0
Motherwell v St Mirren	2-1
Dundee Hibernians v Nithsdale Wanderers	0-1
Peterhead v Galston	1-0
Queen's Park v Bathgate	1-1, 2-0
Raith Rovers v Cowdenbeath	2-0
Vale of Leven v Third Lanark	2-2, 1-2

THIRD ROUND

Aberdeen v Peterhead	13-0
Bo'ness v Nithsdale Wanderers	2-0
Celtic v East Fife	2-1
Dundee v Hamilton Academicals	0-0, 1-0
Hibernian v Queen's Park	2-0
Motherwell v Falkirk	3-0
Dunfermline Athletic v Raith Rovers	0-3
Third Lanark v Ayr United	2-0

FOURTH ROUND

Celtic v Raith Rovers	1-0
Hibernian v Aberdeen	2-0
Motherwell v Bo'ness	4-2
Dundee v Third Lanark	0-0, 1-1, 0-1

SEMI-FINAL

Celtic v Motherwell	2-0
Hibernian v Third Lanark	1-0

FINAL AT HAMPDEN PARK

Celtic v Hibernian	1-0

League Tables 1923-24

FIRST DIVISION

1 Huddersfield	42	23	11	8	60	33	57
2 Cardiff	42	22	13	7	61	34	57
3 Sunderland	42	22	9	11	71	54	53
4 Bolton	42	18	14	10	68	34	50
5 Sheff United	42	19	12	11	69	49	50
6 Aston Villa	42	18	13	11	52	37	49
7 Everton	42	18	13	11	62	53	49
8 Blackburn	42	17	11	14	54	50	45
9 Newcastle	42	17	10	15	60	54	44
10 Notts County	42	14	14	14	44	49	42
11 Man City	42	15	12	15	54	71	42
12 Liverpool	42	15	11	16	49	48	41
13 West Ham	42	13	15	14	40	43	41
14 Birmingham	42	13	13	16	41	49	39
15 Tottenham	42	12	14	16	50	56	38
16 WBA	42	12	14	16	51	62	38
17 Burnley	42	12	12	18	55	60	36
18 Preston	42	12	10	20	52	67	34
19 Arsenal	42	12	9	21	40	63	33
20 Nottm Forest	42	10	12	20	42	64	32
21 Chelsea	42	9	14	19	31	53	32
22 Middlesbrough	42	7	8	27	37	60	22

SECOND DIVISION

	P	W	D	L	F	A	Pts
1 Leeds	42	21	12	9	61	35	54
2 Bury	42	21	9	12	63	35	51
3 Derby	42	21	9	12	75	42	51
4 Blackpool	42	18	13	11	72	47	49
5 Southampton	42	17	14	11	52	31	48
6 Stoke	42	14	18	10	44	42	46
7 Oldham	42	14	17	11	45	52	45
8 Wednesday	42	16	12	14	54	51	44
9 South Shields	42	17	10	15	49	50	44
10 Clapton Orient	42	14	15	13	40	36	43
11 Barnsley	42	16	11	15	57	61	43
12 Leicester	42	17	8	17	64	54	42
13 Stockport	42	13	16	13	44	52	42
14 Man United	42	13	14	15	52	44	40
15 Crystal Palace	42	13	13	16	53	65	39
16 Port Vale	42	13	12	17	50	66	38
17 Hull	42	10	17	15	46	51	37
18 Bradford City	42	11	15	16	35	48	37
19 Coventry	42	11	13	18	52	68	35
20 Fulham	42	10	14	18	45	56	34
21 Nelson	42	10	13	19	40	74	33
22 Bristol City	42	7	15	20	32	65	29

THIRD DIVISION (SOUTH)

	P	W	D	L	F	A	Pts
1 Portsmouth	42	24	11	7	87	30	59
2 Plymouth	42	23	9	10	70	34	55
3 Millwall Ath	42	22	10	10	64	38	54
4 Swansea	42	22	8	12	60	48	52
5 Brighton	42	21	9	12	68	37	51
6 Swindon	42	17	13	12	58	44	47
7 Luton	42	16	14	12	50	44	46
8 Northampton	42	17	11	14	64	47	45
9 Bristol Rovers	42	15	13	14	52	46	43
10 Newport	42	17	9	16	56	64	43
11 Norwich	42	16	8	18	60	59	40
12 Aberdare Ath	42	12	14	16	45	58	38
13 Merthyr Town	42	11	16	15	45	65	38
14 Charlton	42	11	15	16	38	45	37
15 Gillingham	42	12	13	17	43	58	37
16 Exeter	42	15	7	20	37	52	37
17 Brentford	42	14	8	20	54	71	36
18 Reading	42	13	9	20	51	57	35
19 Southend	42	12	10	20	53	84	34
20 Watford	42	9	15	18	45	54	33
21 Bournemouth	42	11	11	20	40	65	33
22 QPR	42	11	9	22	37	77	31

THIRD DIVISION (NORTH)

	P	W	D	L	F	A	Pts
1 Wolves	42	24	15	3	76	27	63
2 Rochdale	42	25	12	5	60	26	62
3 Chesterfield	42	22	10	10	70	39	54
4 Rotherham Co	42	23	6	13	70	43	52
5 Bradford PA	42	21	10	11	69	43	52
6 Darlington	42	20	8	14	70	53	48
7 Southport	42	16	14	12	44	42	46
8 Ashington	42	18	8	16	59	61	44
9 Doncaster	42	15	12	15	59	53	42
10 Wigan Borough	42	14	14	14	55	53	42
11 Grimsby	42	14	13	15	49	47	41
12 Tranmere	42	13	15	14	51	60	41
13 Accrington	42	16	8	18	48	61	40
14 Halifax	42	15	10	17	42	59	40
15 Durham City	42	15	9	18	59	60	39
16 Wrexham	42	10	18	14	37	44	38
17 Walsall	42	14	8	20	44	59	36
18 New Brighton	42	11	13	18	40	53	35
19 Lincoln	42	10	12	20	48	59	32
20 Crewe	42	7	13	22	32	58	27
21 Hartlepools	42	7	11	24	33	70	25
22 Barrow	42	8	9	25	35	80	25

SCOTTISH FIRST DIVISION

	P	W	D	L	F	A	Pts
1 Rangers	38	25	9	4	72	22	59
2 Airdrieonians	38	20	10	8	72	46	50
3 Celtic	38	17	12	9	56	33	46
4 Raith	38	18	7	13	56	38	43
5 Dundee	38	15	13	10	70	57	43
6 St Mirren	38	15	12	11	53	45	42
7 Hibernian	38	15	11	12	66	52	41
8 Partick	38	15	9	14	58	55	39
9 Hearts	38	14	10	14	61	50	38
10 Motherwell	38	15	7	16	58	63	37
11 Morton	38	16	5	17	48	54	37
12 Hamilton	38	15	6	17	52	57	36
13 Aberdeen	38	13	10	15	37	41	36
14 Ayr	38	12	10	16	38	60	34
15 Falkirk	38	13	6	19	46	53	32
16 Kilmarnock	38	12	8	18	48	65	32
17 Queen's Park	38	11	9	18	43	60	31
18 Third Lanark	38	11	8	19	54	78	30
19 Clyde	38	10	9	19	40	70	29
20 Clydebank	38	10	5	23	42	71	25

The first player to have scored two goals for each side in a single Football League game is Sammy Wynne of Oldham. In the Division Two match with Manchester United on 6 October 1923, Wynne scored for his own side with a free-kick and a penalty, but also put two through his own goal. Those four goals probably give poor Wynne the dubious record for the most goals scored by a full-back in one League game.

SCOTTISH SECOND DIVISION

	P	W	D	L	F	A	Pts
1 St Johnstone	38	22	12	4	79	33	56
2 Cowdenbeath	38	23	9	6	78	33	55
3 Bathgate	38	16	12	10	58	49	44
4 Stenhousemuir	38	16	11	11	58	45	43
5 Albion	38	15	12	11	67	53	42
6 King's Park	38	16	10	12	67	56	42
7 Dunfermline	38	14	11	13	52	45	39
8 Johnstone	38	16	7	15	60	56	39
9 Dundee United	38	12	15	11	41	41	39
10 Dumbarton	38	17	5	16	55	58	39
11 Armadale	38	16	6	16	56	63	38
12 Bo'ness	38	13	11	14	45	52	37
13 East Fife	38	14	9	15	54	47	37
14 Forfar	38	14	7	17	43	68	35
15 Broxburn	38	13	8	17	50	56	34
16 Alloa	38	14	6	18	44	53	34
17 Arbroath	38	12	8	18	49	51	32
18 St Bernard's	38	11	10	17	49	54	32
19 Vale of Leven	38	11	9	18	41	67	31
20 Lochgelly	38	4	4	30	20	86	12

A Birch, Chesterfield's goalkeeper, set a League goalscoring record for a keeper in 1923-24. Birch, who played in every one of his club's Division Three North fixtures, scored from five penalties.

During the Third Division North match between Crewe and Bradford Park Avenue on 8 March 1924, four penalties were awarded in five minutes, a League record.

FA CUP 1923-24

SECOND ROUND

Derby County v Newcastle United 2-2, 2-2, 2-2, 3-5
Exeter City v Watford 0-0, 0-1
Southampton v Blackpool 3-1
Bolton Wanderers v Liverpool 1-4
Manchester City v Halifax Town 2-2, 0-0, 3-0
Brighton v Everton 5-2
Cardiff City v Arsenal 1-0
The Wednesday v Bristol City 1-1, 0-2
Swansea Town v Aston Villa 0-2
West Ham United v Leeds United 1-1, 0-1
West Bromwich Albion v Corinthians 5-0
Charlton Athletic v Wolverhampton Wanderers 0-0, 0-1
Swindon Town v Oldham Athletic 2-0
Crystal Palace v Notts County 0-0, 0-0, 0-0, 2-1
Burnley v Fulham 0-0, 1-0
Manchester United v Huddersfield Town 0-3

THIRD ROUND

Watford v Newcastle United 0-1
Southampton v Liverpool 0-0, 0-2
Brighton v Manchester City 1-5
Cardiff City v Bristol City 3-0
Aston Villa v Leeds United 3-0
West Bromwich Albion v Wolverhampton Wanderers 1-1, 2-0
Crystal Palace v Swindon Town 1-2
Burnley v Huddersfield Town 1-0

FOURTH ROUND

Newcastle United v Liverpool 1-0
Manchester City v Cardiff City 0-0, 1-0
West Bromwich Albion v Aston Villa 0-2
Swindon Town v Burnley 1-1, 1-3

SEMI-FINAL

Newcastle United v Manchester City 2-0
Aston Villa v Burnley 3-0

FINAL

Newcastle United v Aston Villa 2-0

SCOTTISH FA CUP 1923-24

SECOND ROUND

Airdrieonians v St Johnstone 4-0
Forfar Athletic v Motherwell 1-3
Ayr United v Kilmarnock 1-0
Clydebank v Arbroath 4-0
Falkirk v East Fife 2-0
Queen's Park v Armadale 3-1
Heart of Midlothian v Galston 6-0
Clyde v Vale of Leven 2-0
Cowdenbeath v Aberdeen 0-2
East Stirlingshire v Mid-Annandale 1-0
St Bernard's v Stenhousemuir 0-0, 0-0, 2-0
Dundee v Raith Rovers 0-0, 0-1
Hibernian v Alloa Athletic 1-1, 5-0
St Mirren v Rangers 0-1
Partick Thistle v Bo'ness 3-0
Hamilton Academicals v Queen of the South 2-1

THIRD ROUND

Motherwell v Airdrieonians 0-5
Clydebank v Ayr United 2-3
Falkirk v Queen's Park 0-0, 2-0
Heart of Midlothian v Clyde 3-1
Aberdeen v East Stirlingshire 2-0
Raith Rovers v St Bernard's 0-1
Rangers v Hibernian 1-2
Partick Thistle v Hamilton Academicals 1-1, 2-1

FOURTH ROUND

Airdrieonians v Ayr United 1-1, 0-0, 1-0
Heart of Midlothian v Falkirk 1-2
Aberdeen v St Bernard's 3-0
Hibernian v Partick Thistle 2-2, 1-1, 2-1

SEMI-FINAL

Airdrieonians v Falkirk 2-1
Aberdeen v Hibernian 0-0, 0-0, 0-1

FINAL AT IBROX PARK

Airdrieonians v Hibernian 2-0

FIRST DIVISION

		P	W	D	L	F	A	Pts
1	Huddersfield	42	21	16	5	69	28	58
2	WBA	42	23	10	9	58	34	56
3	Bolton	42	22	11	9	76	34	55
4	Liverpool	42	20	10	12	63	55	50
5	Bury	42	17	15	10	54	51	49
6	Newcastle	42	16	16	10	61	42	48
7	Sunderland	42	19	10	13	64	51	48
8	Birmingham	42	17	12	13	49	53	46
9	Notts County	42	16	13	13	42	31	45
10	Man City	42	17	9	16	76	68	43
11	Cardiff	42	16	11	15	56	51	43
12	Tottenham	42	15	12	15	52	43	42
13	West Ham	42	15	12	15	62	60	42
14	Sheff United	42	13	13	16	55	63	39
15	Aston Villa	42	13	13	16	58	71	39
16	Blackburn	42	11	13	18	53	66	35
17	Everton	42	12	11	19	40	60	35
18	Leeds	42	11	12	19	46	59	34
19	Burnley	42	11	12	19	46	75	34
20	Arsenal	42	14	5	23	46	58	33
21	Preston	42	10	6	26	37	74	26
22	Nottm Forest	42	6	12	24	29	65	24

SECOND DIVISION

		P	W	D	L	F	A	Pts
1	Leicester	42	24	11	7	90	32	59
2	Man United	42	23	11	8	57	23	57
3	Derby	42	22	11	9	71	36	55
4	Portsmouth	42	15	18	9	58	50	48
5	Chelsea	42	16	15	11	51	37	47
6	Wolves	42	20	6	16	55	51	46
7	Southampton	42	13	18	11	40	36	44
8	Port Vale	42	17	8	17	48	56	42
9	South Shields	42	12	17	13	42	38	41
10	Hull	42	15	11	16	50	49	41
11	Clapton Orient	42	14	12	16	42	42	40
12	Fulham	42	15	10	17	41	56	40
13	Middlesbrough	42	10	19	13	36	44	39
14	Wednesday	42	15	8	19	50	56	38
15	Barnsley	42	13	12	17	46	59	38
16	Bradford City	42	13	12	17	37	50	38
17	Blackpool	42	14	9	19	65	61	37
18	Oldham	42	13	11	18	35	51	37
19	Stockport	42	13	11	18	37	57	37
20	Stoke	42	12	11	19	34	46	35
21	Crystal Palace	42	12	10	20	38	54	34
22	Coventry	42	11	9	22	45	84	31

THIRD DIVISION (SOUTH)

		P	W	D	L	F	A	Pts
1	Swansea	42	23	11	8	68	35	57
2	Plymouth	42	23	10	9	77	38	56
3	Bristol City	42	22	9	11	60	41	53
4	Swindon	42	20	11	11	66	38	51
5	Millwall Ath	42	18	13	11	58	38	49
6	Newport	42	20	9	13	62	42	49
7	Exeter	42	19	9	14	59	48	47
8	Brighton	42	19	8	15	59	45	46
9	Northampton	42	20	6	16	51	44	46
10	Southend	42	19	5	18	51	61	43
11	Watford	42	17	9	16	38	47	43
12	Norwich	42	14	13	15	53	51	41
13	Gillingham	42	13	14	15	35	44	40
14	Reading	42	14	10	18	37	38	38
15	Charlton	42	13	12	17	46	48	38
16	Luton	42	10	17	15	49	57	37
17	Bristol Rovers	42	12	13	17	42	49	37
18	Aberdare Ath	42	14	9	19	54	67	37
19	QPR	42	14	8	20	42	63	36
20	Bournemouth	42	13	8	21	40	58	34
21	Brentford	42	9	7	26	38	91	25
22	Merthyr Town	42	8	5	29	35	77	21

THIRD DIVISION (NORTH)

		P	W	D	L	F	A	Pts
1	Darlington	42	24	10	8	78	33	58
2	Nelson	42	23	7	12	79	50	53
3	New Brighton	42	23	7	12	75	50	53
4	Southport	42	22	7	13	59	37	51
5	Bradford PA	42	19	12	11	84	42	50
6	Rochdale	42	21	7	14	75	53	49
7	Chesterfield	42	17	11	14	60	44	45
8	Lincoln	42	18	8	16	53	58	44
9	Halifax	42	16	11	15	56	52	43
10	Ashington	42	16	10	16	68	76	42
11	Wigan Borough	42	15	11	16	62	65	41
12	Grimsby	42	15	9	18	60	60	39
13	Durham City	42	13	13	16	50	68	39
14	Barrow	42	16	7	19	51	74	39
15	Crewe	42	13	13	16	53	78	39
16	Wrexham	42	15	8	19	53	61	38
17	Accrington	42	15	8	19	60	72	38
18	Doncaster	42	14	10	18	54	65	38
19	Walsall	42	13	11	18	44	53	37
20	Hartlepools	42	12	11	19	45	63	35
21	Tranmere	42	14	4	24	59	78	32
22	Rotherham Co	42	7	7	28	42	88	21

SCOTTISH FIRST DIVISION

		P	W	D	L	F	A	Pts
1	Rangers	38	25	10	3	77	27	60
2	Airdrieonians	38	25	7	6	85	31	57
3	Hibernian	38	22	8	8	78	43	52
4	Celtic	38	18	8	12	76	43	44
5	Cowdenbeath	38	16	10	12	76	65	42
6	St Mirren	38	18	4	16	65	63	40
7	Partick	38	14	10	14	60	61	38
8	Dundee	38	14	8	16	48	55	36
9	Raith	38	14	8	16	52	60	36
10	Hearts	38	12	11	15	65	69	35
11	St Johnstone	38	12	11	15	56	71	35
12	Kilmarnock	38	12	9	17	53	64	33
13	Hamilton	38	15	3	20	50	63	33
14	Morton	38	12	9	17	46	69	33
15	Aberdeen	38	11	10	17	46	56	32
16	Falkirk	38	12	8	18	44	54	32
17	Queen's Park	38	12	8	18	50	71	32
18	Motherwell	38	10	10	18	55	64	30
19	Ayr	38	11	8	19	43	65	30
20	Third Lanark	38	11	8	19	53	84	30

SCOTTISH SECOND DIVISION

		P	W	D	L	F	A	Pts
1	Dundee United	38	20	10	8	58	44	50
2	Clydebank	38	20	8	10	65	42	48
3	Clyde	38	20	7	11	72	39	47
4	Alloa	38	17	11	10	57	33	45
5	Arbroath	38	16	10	12	47	46	42
6	Bo'ness	38	16	9	13	71	48	41
7	Broxburn	38	16	9	13	48	54	41
8	Dumbarton	38	15	10	13	45	44	40
9	East Fife	38	17	5	16	66	58	39
10	King's Park	38	15	8	15	54	46	38
11	Stenhousemuir	38	15	7	16	51	58	37
12	Arthurlie	38	14	8	16	56	60	36
13	Dunfermline	38	14	7	17	62	57	35
14	Armadale	38	15	5	18	55	62	35
15	Albion	38	15	5	18	46	61	35
16	Bathgate	38	12	10	16	58	74	34
17	St Bernard's	38	14	4	20	52	70	32
18	E Stirlingshire	38	11	8	19	58	72	30
19	Johnstone	38	12	4	22	53	85	28
20	Forfar	38	10	7	21	46	67	27

Merthyr Town, who finished bottom of the Third Division South, suffered 29 defeats in their 42 matches, the greatest number ever lost in a single season in that division.

Manchester United conceded only 23 goals in their 42 Second Division matches. This is the lowest number of goals ever recorded against a club in that division.

Arthur Chandler, of Second Division champions Leicester City, not only led that division's scoring lists with 33 goals, but also established a record by finding the net in sixteen consecutive League games.

Huddersfield, in winning their second consecutive Championship, did not concede more than two goals in any League game.

FA CUP 1924-25

SECOND ROUND

Cardiff City v Fulham	1-0
Notts County v Norwich City	4-0
Hull City v Crystal Palace	3-2
Newcastle United v Leicester City	2-2, 0-1
Bradford Park Avenue v Blackpool	1-1, 1-2
Nottingham Forest v West Ham United	0-2
Tottenham Hotspur v Bolton Wanderers	1-1, 1-0
Blackburn Rovers v Portsmouth	0-0, 0-0, 1-0
Southampton v Brighton	1-0
Barnsley v Bradford City	0-3
Birmingham v Stockport County	1-0
Bristol City v Liverpool	0-1
West Bromwich Albion v Preston North End	2-0
Swansea Town v Aston Villa	1-3
Sunderland v Everton	0-0, 1-2
Sheffield United v The Wednesday	3-2

THIRD ROUND

Notts County v Cardiff City	0-2
Hull City v Leicester City	1-1, 1-3
West Ham United v Blackpool	1-1, 0-3
Tottenham Hotspur v Blackburn Rovers	2-2, 1-3
Southampton v Bradford City	2-0
Liverpool v Birmingham	2-1
West Bromwich Albion v Aston Villa	1-1, 2-1
Sheffield United v Everton	1-0

FOURTH ROUND

Cardiff City v Leicester City	2-1
Blackburn Rovers v Blackpool	1-0
Southampton v Liverpool	1-0
Sheffield United v West Bromwich Albion	2-0

SEMI-FINAL

Cardiff City v Blackburn Rovers	3-1
Sheffield United v Southampton	2-0

FINAL

Sheffield United v Cardiff City	1-0

SCOTTISH FA CUP 1924-25

SECOND ROUND

Celtic v Alloa Athletic	2-1
Vale of Leven v Solway Star	2-2, 3-3, 1-2
St Mirren v Ayr United	1-0
Partick Thistle v Dundee United	5-1
Montrose v Rangers	0-2
Arbroath v Clyde	3-0
Kilmarnock v Heart of Midlothian	2-1
Dykehead v Peebles Rovers	3-1
Dundee v Lochgelly United	2-1
Airdrieonians v Queen's Park	4-0
Royal Albert v Broxburn United	1-3
Falkirk v Dumbarton	2-0
Hamilton Academicals v East Stirlingshire	4-0
Raith Rovers v Bo'ness	0-0, 3-1
Armadale v Aberdeen	1-1, 0-2
Motherwell v Arthurlie	2-0

THIRD ROUND

Celtic v Solway Star	2-0
St Mirren v Partick Thistle	2-0
Rangers v Arbroath	5-3
Kilmarnock v Dykehead	5-3
Dundee v Airdrieonians	3-1
Broxburn United v Falkirk	2-1
Hamilton Academicals v Raith Rovers	1-0
Aberdeen v Motherwell	0-0, 2-1

FOURTH ROUND

St Mirren v Celtic	0-0, 1-1, 0-1
Kilmarnock v Rangers	1-2
Dundee v Broxburn United	1-0
Aberdeen v Hamilton Academicals	0-2

SEMI-FINAL

Celtic v Rangers	5-0
Dundee v Hamilton Academicals	1-1, 2-0

FINAL

Celtic v Dundee	2-1

League Tables 1925-26

FIRST DIVISION

	P	W	D	L	F	A	Pts
1 Huddersfield	42	23	11	8	92	60	57
2 Arsenal	42	22	8	12	87	63	52
3 Sunderland	42	21	6	15	96	80	48
4 Bury	42	20	7	15	85	77	47
5 Sheff United	42	19	8	15	102	82	46
6 Aston Villa	42	16	12	14	86	76	44
7 Liverpool	42	14	16	12	70	63	44
8 Bolton	42	17	10	15	75	76	44
9 Man United	42	19	6	17	66	73	44
10 Newcastle	42	16	10	16	84	75	42
11 Everton	42	12	18	12	72	70	42
12 Blackburn	42	15	11	16	91	80	41
13 WBA	42	16	8	18	79	78	40
14 Birmingham	42	16	8	18	66	81	40
15 Tottenham	42	15	9	18	66	79	39
16 Cardiff	42	16	7	19	61	76	39
17 Leicester	42	14	10	18	70	80	38
18 West Ham	42	15	7	20	63	76	37
19 Leeds	42	14	8	20	64	76	36
20 Burnley	42	13	10	19	85	108	36
21 Man City	42	12	11	19	89	100	35
22 Notts County	42	13	7	22	54	74	33

SECOND DIVISION

	P	W	D	L	F	A	Pts
1 Wednesday	42	27	6	9	88	48	60
2 Derby	42	25	7	10	77	42	57
3 Chelsea	42	19	14	9	76	49	52
4 Wolves	42	21	7	14	84	60	49
5 Swansea	42	19	11	12	77	57	49
6 Blackpool	42	17	11	14	76	69	45
7 Oldham	42	18	8	16	74	62	44
8 Port Vale	42	19	6	17	79	69	44
9 South Shields	42	18	8	16	74	65	44
10 Middlesbrough	42	21	2	19	77	68	44
11 Portsmouth	42	17	10	15	79	74	44
12 Preston	42	18	7	17	71	84	43
13 Hull	42	16	9	17	63	61	41
14 Southampton	42	15	8	19	63	63	38
15 Darlington	42	14	10	18	72	77	38
16 Bradford City	42	13	10	19	47	66	36
17 Nottm Forest	42	14	8	20	51	73	36
18 Barnsley	42	12	12	18	58	84	36
19 Fulham	42	11	12	19	46	77	34
20 Clapton Orient	42	12	9	21	50	65	33
21 Stoke	42	12	8	22	54	77	32
22 Stockport	42	8	9	25	51	97	25

THIRD DIVISION (NORTH)

	P	W	D	L	F	A	Pts
1 Grimsby	42	26	9	7	91	40	61
2 Bradford PA	42	26	8	8	101	43	60
3 Rochdale	42	27	5	10	104	58	59
4 Chesterfield	42	25	5	12	100	54	55
5 Halifax	42	17	11	14	53	50	45
6 Hartlepools	42	18	8	16	82	73	44
7 Tranmere	42	19	6	17	73	83	44
8 Nelson	42	16	11	15	89	71	43
9 Ashington	42	16	11	15	70	62	43
10 Doncaster	42	16	11	15	80	72	43
11 Crewe	42	17	9	16	63	61	43
12 New Brighton	42	17	8	17	69	67	42
13 Durham City	42	18	6	18	63	70	42
14 Rotherham	42	17	7	18	69	92	41
15 Lincoln	42	17	5	20	66	82	39
16 Coventry	42	16	6	20	73	82	38
17 Wigan Borough	42	13	11	18	68	74	37
18 Accrington	42	17	3	22	81	105	37
19 Wrexham	42	11	10	21	63	92	32
20 Southport	42	11	10	21	62	92	32
21 Walsall	42	10	6	26	58	107	26
22 Barrow	42	7	4	31	50	98	18

THIRD DIVISION (SOUTH)

	P	W	D	L	F	A	Pts
1 Reading	42	23	11	8	77	52	57
2 Plymouth	42	24	8	10	107	67	56
3 Millwall	42	21	11	10	73	39	53
4 Bristol City	42	21	9	12	72	51	51
5 Brighton	42	19	9	14	84	73	47
6 Swindon	42	20	6	16	69	64	46
7 Luton	42	18	7	17	80	75	43
8 Bournemouth	42	17	9	16	75	91	43
9 Aberdare	42	17	8	17	74	66	42
10 Gillingham	42	17	8	17	53	49	42
11 Southend	42	19	4	19	78	73	42
12 Northampton	42	17	7	18	82	80	41
13 Crystal Palace	42	19	3	20	75	79	41
14 Merthyr Town	42	14	11	17	69	75	39
15 Watford	42	15	9	18	73	89	39
16 Norwich	42	15	9	18	58	73	39
17 Newport	42	14	10	18	64	74	38
18 Brentford	42	16	6	20	69	94	38
19 Bristol Rovers	42	15	6	21	66	69	36
20 Exeter	42	15	5	22	72	70	35
21 Charlton	42	11	13	18	48	68	35
22 QPR	42	6	9	27	37	84	21

SCOTTISH FIRST DIVISION

	P	W	D	L	F	A	Pts
1 Celtic	38	25	8	5	97	40	58
2 Airdrieonians	38	23	4	11	95	54	50
3 Hearts	38	21	8	9	87	56	50
4 St Mirren	38	20	7	11	62	52	47
5 Motherwell	38	19	8	11	67	46	46
6 Rangers	38	19	6	13	79	55	44
7 Cowdenbeath	38	18	6	14	87	68	42
8 Falkirk	38	14	14	10	61	57	42
9 Kilmarnock	38	17	7	14	79	77	41
10 Dundee	38	14	9	15	47	59	37
11 Aberdeen	38	13	10	15	49	54	36
12 Hamilton	38	13	9	16	68	79	35
13 Queen's Park	38	15	4	19	70	81	34
14 Partick	38	10	13	15	64	73	33
15 Morton	38	12	7	19	57	84	31
16 Hibernian	38	12	6	20	72	77	30
17 Dundee United	38	11	6	21	52	74	28
18 St Johnstone	38	9	10	19	43	78	28
19 Raith	38	11	4	23	46	81	26
20 Clydebank	38	7	8	23	55	92	22

SCOTTISH SECOND DIVISION

	P	W	D	L	F	A	Pts
1 Dunfermline	38	26	7	5	109	43	59
2 Clyde	38	24	5	9	87	51	53
3 Ayr	38	20	12	6	77	39	52
4 East Fife	38	20	9	9	98	73	49
5 Stenhousemuir	38	19	10	9	74	52	48
6 Third Lanark	38	19	8	11	72	47	46
7 Arthurlie	38	17	5	16	81	75	39
8 Bo'ness	38	17	5	16	65	70	39
9 Albion	38	16	6	16	78	71	38
10 Arbroath	38	17	4	17	80	73	38
11 Dumbarton	38	14	10	14	54	78	38
12 Nithsdale	38	15	7	16	79	82	37
13 King's Park	38	14	9	15	67	73	37
14 St Bernard's	38	15	5	18	86	82	35
15 Armadale	38	14	5	19	82	101	33
16 Alloa	38	11	8	19	54	63	30
17 Queen of the S	38	10	8	20	64	88	28
18 E Stirlingshire	38	10	7	21	59	89	27
19 Bathgate	38	7	6	25	60	105	20
20 Broxburn	38	4	6	28	55	126	14

Manchester City had a distressing end to the 1925-26 season. After losing the Cup Final 1-0 to Bolton, City went to Newcastle for their last League game. They missed a penalty, lost 3-2, and were relegated. Had they scored from the penalty they would have remained in the First Division. City thus became the first club to reach the Cup Final and be relegated in the same season.

Huddersfield created a League record by playing 18 consecutive First Division games away from home without defeat. This run lasted from 15 November 1924 to 14 November 1925 and included 12 wins.

Louis Page scored a double hat-trick in his first game as centre-forward for Burnley, against Birmingham, on 10 April 1926.

FA CUP 1925-26

FOURTH ROUND

Bournemouth v Bolton Wanderers	2-2, 2-6
South Shields v Birmingham	2-1
Nottingham Forest v Swindon Town	2-0
Southend United v Derby County	4-1
Swansea Town v Stoke City	6-3
Bury v Millwall	3-3, 0-2
Arsenal v Blackburn Rovers	3-1
West Bromwich Albion v Aston Villa	1-2
Manchester City v Huddersfield Town	4-0
Crystal Palace v Chelsea	2-1
Clapton Orient v Middlesbrough	4-2
Cardiff City v Newcastle United	0-2
Tottenham Hotspur v Manchester United	2-2, 0-2
Sheffield United v Sunderland	1-2
Fulham v Liverpool	3-1
Notts County v New Brighton	2-0

FIFTH ROUND

Bolton Wanderers v South Shields	3-0
Southend United v Nottingham Forest	0-1
Millwall v Swansea Town	0-1
Aston Villa v Arsenal	1-1, 0-2
Manchester City v Crystal Palace	11-4
Clapton Orient v Newcastle United	2-0
Sunderland v Manchester United	3-3, 1-2
Notts County v Fulham	0-1

SIXTH ROUND

Nottingham Forest v Bolton Wanderers	2-2, 0-0, 0-1
Swansea Town v Arsenal	2-1
Clapton Orient v Manchester City	1-6
Fulham v Manchester United	1-2

SEMI-FINAL

Bolton Wanderers v Swansea Town	3-0
Manchester City v Manchester United	3-0

FINAL

Bolton Wanderers v Manchester City	1-0

SCOTTISH FA CUP 1925-26

SECOND ROUND

Arbroath v St Mirren	0-0, 0-3
Partick Thistle v King's Park	4-1
Hibernian v Airdrieonians	2-3
Bo'ness v Bathgate	1-1, 1-3
Rangers v Stenhousemuir	1-0
Falkirk v Montrose	5-1
Morton v Raith Rovers	3-1
Albion Rovers v Peebles Rovers	1-1, 4-0
Celtic v Hamilton Academicals	4-0
Alloa Athletic v Heart of Midlothian	2-5
Forfar Athletic v Dumbarton	2-2, 1-4
Arthurlie v Clyde	2-2, 0-1
Aberdeen v Dundee	0-0, 3-0
St Johnstone v Queen's Park	7-2
Third Lanark v Leith Athletic	6-1
Solway Star v Brechin City	0-3

THIRD ROUND

St Mirren v Partick Thistle	2-1
Bathgate v Airdrieonians	2-5
Falkirk v Rangers	0-2
Morton v Albion Rovers	1-0
Heart of Midlothian v Celtic	0-4
Dumbarton v Clyde	3-0
Aberdeen v St Johnstone	2-2, 1-0
Third Lanark v Brechin City	4-0

FOURTH ROUND

St Mirren v Airdrieonians	2-0
Morton v Rangers	0-4
Celtic v Dumbarton	6-1
Third Lanark v Aberdeen	1-1, 0-3

SEMI-FINAL

St Mirren v Rangers	1-0
Celtic v Aberdeen	1-0

FINAL

St Mirren v Celtic	2-0

League Tables 1926-27

FIRST DIVISION

		P	W	D	L	F	A	Pts
1	Newcastle	42	25	6	11	96	58	56
2	Huddersfield	42	17	17	8	76	60	51
3	Sunderland	42	21	7	14	98	70	49
4	Bolton	42	19	10	13	84	62	48
5	Burnley	42	19	9	14	91	80	47
6	West Ham	42	19	8	15	86	70	46
7	Leicester	42	17	12	13	85	70	46
8	Sheff United	42	17	10	15	74	86	44
9	Liverpool	42	18	7	17	69	61	43
10	Aston Villa	42	18	7	17	81	83	43
11	Arsenal	42	17	9	16	77	86	43
12	Derby	42	17	7	18	86	73	41
13	Tottenham	42	16	9	17	76	78	41
14	Cardiff	42	16	9	17	55	65	41
15	Man United	42	13	14	15	52	64	40
16	Wednesday	42	15	9	18	75	92	39
17	Birmingham	42	17	4	21	64	73	38
18	Blackburn	42	15	8	19	77	96	38
19	Bury	42	12	12	18	68	77	36
20	Everton	42	12	10	20	64	90	34
21	Leeds	42	11	8	23	69	88	30
22	WBA	42	11	8	23	65	86	30

SECOND DIVISION

		P	W	D	L	F	A	Pts
1	Middlesbrough	42	27	8	7	122	60	62
2	Portsmouth	42	23	8	11	87	49	54
3	Man City	42	22	10	10	108	61	54
4	Chelsea	42	20	12	10	62	52	52
5	Nottm Forest	42	18	14	10	80	55	50
6	Preston	42	20	9	13	63	52	49
7	Hull	42	20	7	15	63	52	47
8	Port Vale	42	16	13	13	88	78	45
9	Blackpool	42	18	8	16	95	80	44
10	Oldham	42	19	6	17	74	84	44
11	Barnsley	42	17	9	16	88	87	43
12	Swansea	42	16	11	15	68	72	43
13	Southampton	42	15	12	15	60	62	42
14	Reading	42	16	8	18	64	72	40
15	Wolves	42	14	7	21	73	75	35
16	Notts County	42	15	5	22	70	96	35
17	Grimsby	42	11	12	19	74	91	34
18	Fulham	42	13	8	21	58	92	34
19	South Shields	42	11	11	20	71	96	33
20	Clapton Orient	42	12	7	23	60	96	31
21	Darlington	42	12	6	24	79	98	30
22	Bradford City	42	7	9	26	50	88	23

THIRD DIVISION (NORTH)

		P	W	D	L	F	A	Pts
1	Stoke	42	27	9	6	92	40	63
2	Rochdale	42	26	6	10	105	65	58
3	Bradford PA	42	24	7	11	101	59	55
4	Halifax	42	21	11	10	70	53	53
5	Nelson	42	22	7	13	104	75	51
6	Stockport	42	22	7	13	93	69	49*
7	Chesterfield	42	21	5	16	92	68	47
8	Doncaster	42	18	11	13	81	65	47
9	Tranmere	42	19	8	15	85	67	46
10	New Brighton	42	18	10	14	79	67	46
11	Lincoln	42	15	12	15	90	78	42
12	Southport	42	15	9	18	80	85	39
13	Wrexham	42	14	10	18	65	73	38
14	Walsall	42	14	10	18	68	81	38
15	Crewe	42	14	9	19	71	81	37
16	Ashington	42	12	12	18	60	90	36
17	Hartlepools	42	14	6	22	66	81	34
18	Wigan Borough	42	11	10	21	66	83	32
19	Rotherham	42	10	12	20	70	92	32
20	Durham City	42	12	6	24	58	105	30
21	Accrington	42	10	7	25	62	98	27
22	Barrow	42	7	8	27	34	117	22

*Two points deducted for fielding Joe Smith without FA permission on 26 March 1927.

THIRD DIVISION (SOUTH)

		P	W	D	L	F	A	Pts
1	Bristol City	42	27	8	7	104	54	62
2	Plymouth	42	25	10	7	95	61	60
3	Millwall	42	23	10	9	89	51	56
4	Brighton	42	21	11	10	79	50	53
5	Swindon	42	21	9	12	100	85	51
6	Crystal Palace	42	18	9	15	84	81	45
7	Bournemouth	42	18	8	16	78	66	44
8	Luton	42	15	14	13	68	66	44
9	Newport	42	19	6	17	57	71	44
10	Bristol Rovers	42	16	9	17	78	80	41
11	Brentford	42	13	14	15	70	61	40
12	Exeter	42	15	10	17	76	73	40
13	Charlton	42	16	8	18	60	61	40
14	QPR	42	15	9	18	65	71	39
15	Coventry	42	15	7	20	71	86	37
16	Norwich	42	12	11	19	59	71	35
17	Merthyr Town	42	13	9	20	63	80	35
18	Northampton	42	15	5	22	59	83	35
19	Southend	42	14	6	22	64	77	34
20	Gillingham	42	11	10	21	54	72	32
21	Watford	42	12	8	22	57	87	32
22	Aberdare Ath	42	9	7	26	62	101	25

SCOTTISH FIRST DIVISION

		P	W	D	L	F	A	Pts
1	Rangers	38	23	10	5	85	41	56
2	Motherwell	38	23	5	10	81	52	51
3	Celtic	38	21	7	10	101	55	49
4	Airdrieonians	38	18	9	11	97	64	45
5	Dundee	38	17	9	12	77	51	43
6	Falkirk	38	16	10	12	77	60	42
7	Cowdenbeath	38	18	6	14	74	60	42
8	Aberdeen	38	13	14	11	73	72	40
9	Hibernian	38	16	7	15	62	71	39
10	St Mirren	38	16	5	17	78	76	37
11	Partick	38	15	6	17	89	74	36
12	Queen's Park	38	15	6	17	74	84	36
13	Hearts	38	12	11	15	65	64	35
14	St Johnstone	38	13	9	16	55	69	35
15	Hamilton	38	13	9	16	60	85	35
16	Kilmarnock	38	12	8	18	54	71	32
17	Clyde	38	10	9	19	54	85	29
18	Dunfermline	38	10	8	20	53	85	28
19	Morton	38	12	4	22	56	101	28
20	Dundee United	38	7	8	23	56	101	22

The highest number of goals scored by a recognized half-back in a League match is three. T McDonald of Newcastle grabbed a hat-trick against Cardiff on Christmas Day 1926.

SCOTTISH SECOND DIVISION

		P	W	D	L	F	A	Pts
1	Bo'ness	38	23	10	5	86	41	56
2	Raith	38	21	7	10	92	52	49
3	Clydebank	38	18	9	11	94	75	45
4	Third Lanark	38	17	10	11	67	48	44
5	E Stirlingshire	38	18	8	12	93	75	44
6	East Fife	38	19	4	15	103	91	42
7	Arthurlie	38	18	5	15	90	83	41
8	Ayr	38	13	15	10	67	68	41
9	Forfar	38	15	7	16	66	79	37
10	Stenhousemuir	38	12	12	14	69	75	36
11	Queen of the S	38	16	4	18	72	80	36
12	King's Park	38	13	9	16	76	75	35
13	St Bernard's	38	14	6	18	70	77	34
14	Armadale	38	12	10	16	69	78	34
15	Alloa	38	11	11	16	70	78	33
16	Albion	38	11	11	16	74	87	33
17	Bathgate	38	13	7	18	76	98	33
18	Dumbarton	38	13	6	19	69	84	32
19	Arbroath	38	13	6	19	64	82	32
20	Nithsdale	38	7	9	22	59	100	23

Middlesbrough's George Camsell established an individual scoring record with his 59 Second Division goals in 1926-27. William Dean beat it by just one the following season, 1927-28. Camsell also established a record for the number of League hat-tricks in a season with his nine in 1926-27.

FA CUP 1926-27

FOURTH ROUND

Chelsea v Accrington Stanley	7-2
Fulham v Burnley	0-4
Leeds United v Bolton Wanderers	0-0, 0-3
Darlington v Cardiff City	0-2
The Wednesday v South Shields	1-1, 0-1
Barnsley v Swansea Town	1-3
Reading v Portsmouth	3-1
West Ham United v Brentford	1-1, 0-2
Port Vale v Arsenal	2-2, 0-1
Liverpool v Southport	3-1
Wolverhampton Wanderers v Nottingham Forest	2-0
Hull City v Everton	1-1, 2-2, 3-2
Derby County v Millwall	0-2
Preston North End v Middlesbrough	0-3
Southampton v Birmingham	4-1
Corinthians v Newcastle United	1-3

FIFTH ROUND

Chelsea v Burnley	2-1
Bolton Wanderers v Cardiff City	0-2
South Shields v Swansea Town	2-2, 1-2
Reading v Brentford	1-0
Arsenal v Liverpool	2-0
Wolverhampton Wanderers v Hull City	1-0
Millwall v Middlesbrough	3-2
Southampton v Newcastle United	2-1

SIXTH ROUND

Chelsea v Cardiff City	0-0, 2-3
Swansea Town v Reading	1-3
Arsenal v Wolverhampton Wanderers	2-1
Millwall v Southampton	0-0, 0-2

SEMI-FINAL

Cardiff City v Reading	3-0
Arsenal v Southampton	2-1

FINAL

Cardiff City v Arsenal	1-0

SCOTTISH FA CUP 1926-27

SECOND ROUND

Buckie Thistle v Beith	2-0
Bo'ness v Cowdenbeath	2-1
Kilmarnock v Dundee	1-1, 1-5
Brechin City v Celtic	3-6
Falkirk v Queen's Park	6-3
Mid-Annandale v Forfar Athletic	3-0
Rangers v St Mirren	6-0
Hamilton Academicals v Clydebank	5-1
Alloa Athletic v Dumbarton	1-1, 4-0
St Bernard's v Arthurlie	0-3
East Fife v Aberdeen	1-1, 2-1
Dunfermline Athletic v Airdrieonians	2-1
Elgin City v Clyde	2-4
Partick Thistle v King's Park	4-2
Dundee United v Vale of Leven	4-1
Broxburn United v Montrose	2-2, 0-1

THIRD ROUND

Buckie Thistle v Bo'ness	0-3
Dundee v Celtic	2-4
Falkirk v Mid-Annandale	3-0
Rangers v Hamilton Academicals	4-0
Alloa Athletic v Arthurlie	0-0, 0-3
East Fife v Dunfermline Athletic	2-0
Clyde v Partick Thistle	0-1
Dundee United v Montrose	2-2, 3-1

FOURTH ROUND

Bo'ness v Celtic	2-5
Falkirk v Rangers	2-2, 1-0
Arthurlie v East Fife	0-3
Partick Thistle v Dundee United	5-0

SEMI-FINAL

Celtic v Falkirk	1-0
East Fife v Partick Thistle	2-1

FINAL

Celtic v East Fife	3-1

League Tables 1927-28

FIRST DIVISION

		P	W	D	L	F	A	Pts
1	Everton	42	20	13	9	102	66	53
2	Huddersfield	42	22	7	13	91	68	51
3	Leicester	42	18	12	12	96	72	48
4	Derby	42	17	10	15	96	83	44
5	Bury	42	20	4	18	80	80	44
6	Cardiff	42	17	10	15	70	80	44
7	Bolton	42	16	11	15	81	66	43
8	Aston Villa	42	17	9	16	78	73	43
9	Newcastle	42	15	13	14	79	81	43
10	Arsenal	42	13	15	14	82	86	41
11	Birmingham	42	13	15	14	70	75	41
12	Blackburn	42	16	9	17	66	78	41
13	Sheff United	42	15	10	17	79	86	40
14	Wednesday	42	13	13	16	81	78	39
15	Sunderland	42	15	9	18	74	76	39
16	Liverpool	42	13	13	16	84	87	39
17	West Ham	42	14	11	17	81	88	39
18	Burnley	42	16	7	19	82	98	39
19	Man United	42	16	7	19	72	87	39
20	Portsmouth	42	16	7	19	66	90	39
21	Tottenham	42	15	8	19	74	86	38
22	Middlesbrough	42	11	15	16	81	88	37

SECOND DIVISION

		P	W	D	L	F	A	Pts
1	Man City	42	25	9	8	100	59	59
2	Leeds	42	25	7	10	98	49	57
3	Chelsea	42	23	8	11	75	45	54
4	Preston	42	22	9	11	100	66	53
5	Stoke	42	22	8	12	78	59	52
6	Swansea	42	18	12	12	75	63	48
7	Oldham	42	19	8	15	75	51	46
8	WBA	42	17	12	13	90	70	46
9	Port Vale	42	18	8	16	68	57	44
10	Nottm Forest	42	15	10	17	83	84	40
11	Grimsby	42	14	12	16	69	83	40
12	Bristol City	42	15	9	18	76	79	39
13	Hull	42	12	15	15	41	54	39
14	Barnsley	42	14	11	17	65	85	39
15	Notts County	42	13	12	17	68	74	38
16	Wolves	42	13	10	19	63	91	36
17	Southampton	42	14	7	21	68	77	35
18	Reading	42	11	13	18	53	75	35
19	Blackpool	42	13	8	21	83	101	34
20	Clapton Orient	42	11	12	19	55	85	34
21	Fulham	42	13	7	22	68	89	33
22	South Shields	42	7	9	26	56	111	23

THIRD DIVISION (SOUTH)

		P	W	D	L	F	A	Pts
1	Millwall	42	30	5	7	127	50	65
2	Northampton	42	23	9	10	102	64	55
3	Plymouth	42	23	7	12	85	54	53
4	Brighton	42	19	10	13	81	69	48
5	Crystal Palace	42	18	12	12	79	72	48
6	Swindon	42	19	9	14	90	69	47
7	Southend	42	20	6	16	80	64	46
8	Exeter	42	17	12	13	70	60	46
9	Newport	42	18	9	15	81	84	45
10	QPR	42	17	9	16	72	71	43
11	Charlton	42	15	13	14	60	70	43
12	Brentford	42	16	8	18	76	74	40
13	Luton	42	16	7	19	94	87	39
14	Bournemouth	42	13	12	17	72	79	38
15	Watford	42	14	10	18	68	78	38
16	Gillingham	42	13	11	18	62	81	37
17	Norwich	42	10	16	16	66	70	36
18	Walsall	42	12	9	21	75	101	33
19	Bristol Rovers	42	14	4	24	67	93	32
20	Coventry	42	11	9	22	67	96	31
21	Merthyr Town	42	9	13	20	53	91	31
22	Torquay	42	8	14	20	53	103	30

THIRD DIVISION (NORTH)

		P	W	D	L	F	A	Pts
1	Bradford PA	42	27	9	6	101	45	63
2	Lincoln	42	24	7	11	91	64	55
3	Stockport	42	23	8	11	89	51	54
4	Doncaster	42	23	7	12	80	44	53
5	Tranmere	42	22	9	11	105	72	53
6	Bradford City	42	18	12	12	85	60	48
7	Darlington	42	21	5	16	89	74	47
8	Southport	42	20	5	17	79	70	45
9	Accrington	42	18	8	16	76	67	44
10	New Brighton	42	14	14	14	72	62	42
11	Wrexham	42	18	6	18	64	67	42
12	Halifax	42	13	15	14	73	71	41
13	Rochdale	42	17	7	18	74	77	41
14	Rotherham	42	14	11	17	65	69	39
15	Hartlepools	42	16	6	20	69	81	38
16	Chesterfield	42	13	10	19	71	78	36
17	Crewe	42	12	10	20	77	86	34
18	Ashington	42	11	11	20	77	103	33
19	Barrow	42	10	11	21	54	102	31
20	Wigan Borough	42	10	10	22	56	97	30
21	Durham City	42	11	7	24	53	100	29
22	Nelson	42	10	6	26	76	136	26

SCOTTISH FIRST DIVISION

		P	W	D	L	F	A	Pts
1	Rangers	38	26	8	4	109	36	60
2	Celtic	38	23	9	6	93	39	55
3	Motherwell	38	23	9	6	92	46	55
4	Hearts	38	20	7	11	89	50	47
5	St Mirren	38	18	8	12	77	76	44
6	Partick	38	18	7	13	85	67	43
7	Aberdeen	38	19	5	14	71	61	43
8	Kilmarnock	38	15	10	13	68	78	40
9	Cowdenbeath	38	16	7	15	66	68	39
10	Falkirk	38	16	5	17	76	69	37
11	St Johnstone	38	14	8	16	66	67	36
12	Hibernian	38	13	9	16	73	75	35
13	Airdrieonians	38	12	11	15	59	69	35
14	Dundee	38	14	7	17	65	80	35
15	Clyde	38	10	11	17	46	72	31
16	Queen's Park	38	12	6	20	69	80	30
17	Raith	38	11	7	20	60	89	29
18	Hamilton	38	11	6	21	67	86	28
19	Bo'ness	38	9	8	21	48	86	26
20	Dunfermline	38	4	4	30	41	126	12

SCOTTISH SECOND DIVISION

		P	W	D	L	F	A	Pts
1	Ayr	38	24	6	8	117	60	54
2	Third Lanark	38	18	9	11	99	66	45
3	King's Park	38	16	12	10	84	68	44
4	East Fife	38	18	7	13	87	73	43
5	Forfar	38	18	7	13	83	73	43
6	Dundee United	38	17	9	12	81	73	43
7	Arthurlie	38	18	4	16	84	90	40
8	Albion	38	17	4	17	79	69	38
9	E Stirlingshire	38	14	10	14	84	76	38
10	Arbroath	38	16	4	18	84	86	36
11	Dumbarton	38	16	4	18	66	72	36
12	Queen of the S	38	15	6	17	92	106	36
13	Leith	38	13	9	16	76	71	35
14	Clydebank	38	16	3	19	78	80	35
15	Alloa	38	12	11	15	72	76	35
16	Stenhousemuir	38	15	5	18	75	81	35
17	St Bernard's	38	15	5	18	75	101	35
18	Morton	38	13	8	17	65	82	34
19	Bathgate	38	10	11	17	62	81	31
20	Armadale	38	8	8	22	53	112	24

On 3 March 1928 Ronnie Dix became the youngest person to score in the League. Dix, aged 15 years and 180 days, scored for Bristol Rovers against Norwich in a Division Three South match. Dix had made his League debut just seven days earlier against Charlton.

Dixie Dean's 60 goals in 39 League games for Everton set a League scoring record.

1927-28 saw the keenest relegation struggle in the League's history. Of the last nine clubs in Division One, seven finished the season with 39 points, one had 38, and one 37. Spurs and Middlesbrough were demoted. Spurs' 38 points meant that they were relegated with the highest number of points ever secured by a club removed from either the First or Second Division.

FA CUP 1927-28

FOURTH ROUND

Exeter City v Blackburn Rovers 2-2, 1-3
Port Vale v New Brighton 3-0
Bury v Manchester United 1-1, 0-1
Wrexham v Birmingham 1-3
Arsenal v Everton 4-3
Aston Villa v Crewe Alexandra 3-0
Sunderland v Manchester City 1-2
Stoke City v Bolton Wanderers 4-2
Huddersfield Town v West Ham United 2-1
Southport v Middlesbrough 0-3
Reading v Leicester City 0-1
Tottenham Hotspur v Oldham Athletic 3-0
Sheffield United v Wolverhampton Wanderers 3-1
Swindon Town v The Wednesday 1-2
Derby County v Nottingham Forest 0-0, 0-2
Cardiff City v Liverpool 2-1

FIFTH ROUND

Blackburn Rovers v Port Vale 2-1
Manchester United v Birmingham 1-0
Arsenal v Aston Villa 4-1
Manchester City v Stoke City 0-1
Huddersfield Town v Middlesbrough 4-0
Leicester City v Tottenham Hotspur 0-3
The Wednesday v Sheffield United 1-1, 1-4
Nottingham Forest v Cardiff City 2-1

SIXTH ROUND

Blackburn Rovers v Manchester United 2-0
Arsenal v Stoke City 4-1
Huddersfield Town v Tottenham Hotspur 6-1
Sheffield United v Nottingham Forest 3-0

SEMI-FINAL

Blackburn Rovers v Arsenal 1-0
Huddersfield Town v Sheffield United 2-2, 0-0, 1-0

FINAL

Blackburn Rovers v Huddersfield Town 3-1

SCOTTISH FA CUP 1927-28

SECOND ROUND

Rangers v Cowdenbeath 4-2
Armadale v King's Park 2-4
Brechin City v Albion Rovers 1-4
Airdrieonians v Hamilton Academicals 2-1
Third Lanark v Hibernian 0-2
Ayr United v Falkirk 2-4
Dunfermline Athletic v Leith Amateurs 3-1
Dundee United v Dundee 3-3, 0-1
Keith v Celtic 1-6
Stenhousemuir v Alloa Athletic 1-2
Motherwell v Raith Rovers 2-2, 2-1
Heart of Midlothian v Forres Mechanics 7-0
Queen's Park v Morton 4-1
Forfar Athletic v Kilmarnock 1-2
Partick Thistle v Nithsdale Wanderers 4-0
St Mirren v Vale of Atholl 5-1

THIRD ROUND

Rangers v King's Park 3-1
Albion Rovers v Airdrieonians 3-1
Hibernian v Falkirk 0-0, 1-0
Dundee v Dunfermline Athletic 1-2
Celtic v Alloa Athletic 2-0
Heart of Midlothian v Motherwell 1-2
Kilmarnock v Queen's Park 4-4, 0-1
St Mirren v Partick Thistle 0-5

FOURTH ROUND

Albion Rovers v Rangers 0-1
Dunfermline Athletic v Hibernian 0-4
Motherwell v Celtic 0-2
Queen's Park v Partick Thistle 1-0

SEMI-FINAL

Rangers v Hibernian 3-0
Celtic v Queen's Park 2-1

FINAL

Rangers v Celtic 4-0

League Tables 1928-29

FIRST DIVISION

	P	W	D	L	F	A	Pts
1 Wednesday	42	21	10	11	86	62	52
2 Leicester	42	21	9	12	96	67	51
3 Aston Villa	42	23	4	15	98	81	50
4 Sunderland	42	20	7	15	93	75	47
5 Liverpool	42	17	12	13	90	64	46
6 Derby	42	18	10	14	86	71	46
7 Blackburn	42	17	11	14	72	63	45
8 Man City	42	18	9	15	95	86	45
9 Arsenal	42	16	13	13	77	72	45
10 Newcastle	42	19	6	17	70	72	44
11 Sheff United	42	15	11	16	86	85	41
12 Man United	42	14	13	15	66	76	41
13 Leeds	42	16	9	17	71	84	41
14 Bolton	42	14	12	16	73	80	40
15 Birmingham	42	15	10	17	68	77	40
16 Huddersfield	42	14	11	17	70	61	39
17 West Ham	42	15	9	18	86	96	39
18 Everton	42	17	4	21	63	75	38
19 Burnley	42	15	8	19	81	103	38
20 Portsmouth	42	15	6	21	56	80	36
21 Bury	42	12	7	23	62	99	31
22 Cardiff	42	8	13	21	43	59	29

SECOND DIVISION

	P	W	D	L	F	A	Pts
1 Middlesbrough	42	22	11	9	92	57	55
2 Grimsby	42	24	5	13	82	61	53
3 Bradford PA	42	22	4	16	88	70	48
4 Southampton	42	17	14	11	74	60	48
5 Notts County	42	19	9	14	78	65	47
6 Stoke	42	17	12	13	74	51	46
7 WBA	42	19	8	15	80	79	46
8 Blackpool	42	19	7	16	92	76	45
9 Chelsea	42	17	10	15	64	65	44
10 Tottenham	42	17	9	16	75	81	43
11 Nottm Forest	42	15	12	15	71	70	42
12 Hull	42	13	14	15	58	63	40
13 Preston	42	15	9	18	78	79	39
14 Millwall	42	16	7	19	71	86	39
15 Reading	42	15	9	18	63	86	39
16 Barnsley	42	16	6	20	69	66	38
17 Wolves	42	15	7	20	77	81	37
18 Oldham	42	16	5	21	54	75	37
19 Swansea	42	13	10	19	62	75	36
20 Bristol City	42	13	10	19	58	72	36
21 Port Vale	42	15	4	23	71	86	34
22 Clapton Orient	42	12	8	22	45	72	32

THIRD DIVISION (SOUTH)

	P	W	D	L	F	A	Pts
1 Charlton	42	23	8	11	86	60	54
2 Crystal Palace	42	23	8	11	81	67	54
3 Northampton	42	20	12	10	96	57	52
4 Plymouth	42	20	12	10	83	51	52
5 Fulham	42	21	10	11	101	71	52
6 QPR	42	19	14	9	82	61	52
7 Luton	42	19	11	12	89	73	49
8 Watford	42	19	10	13	79	74	48
9 Bournemouth	42	19	9	14	84	77	47
10 Swindon	42	15	13	14	75	72	43
11 Coventry	42	14	14	14	62	57	42
12 Southend	42	15	11	16	80	75	41
13 Brentford	42	14	10	18	56	60	38
14 Walsall	42	13	12	17	73	79	38
15 Brighton	42	16	6	20	58	76	38
16 Newport	42	13	9	20	69	86	35
17 Norwich	42	14	6	22	69	81	34
18 Torquay	42	14	6	22	66	84	34
19 Bristol Rovers	42	13	7	22	60	79	33
20 Merthyr Town	42	11	8	23	55	103	30
21 Exeter	42	9	11	22	67	88	29
22 Gillingham	42	10	9	23	43	83	29

THIRD DIVISION (NORTH)

	P	W	D	L	F	A	Pts
1 Bradford City	42	27	9	6	128	43	63
2 Stockport	42	28	6	8	111	58	62
3 Wrexham	42	21	10	11	91	69	52
4 Wigan Borough	42	21	9	12	82	49	51
5 Doncaster	42	20	10	12	76	66	50
6 Lincoln	42	21	6	15	91	67	48
7 Tranmere	42	22	3	17	79	77	47
8 Carlisle	42	19	8	15	86	77	46
9 Crewe	42	18	8	16	80	68	44
10 South Shields	42	18	8	16	83	74	44
11 Chesterfield	42	18	5	19	71	77	41
12 Southport	42	16	8	18	75	85	40
13 Halifax	42	13	13	16	63	62	39
14 New Brighton	42	15	9	18	64	71	39
15 Nelson	42	17	5	20	77	90	39
16 Rotherham	42	15	9	18	60	77	39
17 Rochdale	42	13	10	19	79	96	36
18 Accrington	42	13	8	21	68	82	34
19 Darlington	42	13	7	22	64	88	33
20 Barrow	42	10	8	24	64	93	28
21 Hartlepools	42	10	6	26	59	112	26
22 Ashington	42	8	7	27	45	115	23

SCOTTISH FIRST DIVISION

	P	W	D	L	F	A	Pts
1 Rangers	38	30	7	1	107	32	67
2 Celtic	38	22	7	9	67	44	51
3 Motherwell	38	20	10	8	85	66	50
4 Hearts	38	19	9	10	91	57	47
5 Queen's Park	38	18	7	13	100	69	43
6 Partick Thistle	38	17	7	14	91	70	41
7 Aberdeen	38	16	8	14	81	69	40
8 St Mirren	38	16	8	14	78	74	40
9 St Johnstone	38	14	10	14	57	70	38
10 Kilmarnock	38	14	8	16	79	74	36
11 Falkirk	38	14	8	16	68	86	36
12 Hamilton	38	13	9	16	58	83	35
13 Cowdenbeath	38	14	5	19	55	69	33
14 Hibernian	38	13	6	19	54	62	32
15 Airdrieonians	38	12	7	19	56	65	31
16 Ayr	38	12	7	19	65	84	31
17 Clyde	38	12	6	20	47	71	30
18 Dundee	38	9	11	18	58	68	29
19 Third Lanark	38	10	6	22	71	102	26
20 Raith	38	9	6	23	52	105	24

SCOTTISH SECOND DIVISION

	P	W	D	L	F	A	Pts
1 Dundee United	36	24	3	9	99	55	51
2 Morton	36	21	8	7	85	49	50
3 Arbroath	36	19	9	8	90	60	47
4 Albion	36	18	8	10	95	67	44
5 Leith	36	18	7	11	78	56	43
6 St Bernard's	36	16	9	11	77	55	41
7 Forfar	35	14	10	11	69	75	38
8 East Fife	35	15	6	14	88	77	36
9 Queen of the S	36	16	4	16	86	79	36
10 Bo'ness	35	15	5	15	62	62	35
11 Dunfermline	36	13	7	16	66	72	33
12 E Stirlingshire	36	14	4	18	71	75	32
13 Alloa	36	12	7	17	64	77	31
14 Dumbarton	36	11	9	16	59	78	31
15 King's Park	36	8	13	15	60	84	29
16 Clydebank	36	11	5	20	70	86	27
17 Arthurlie*	32	9	7	16	51	73	25
18 Stenhousemuir	35	9	6	20	52	90	24
19 Armadale	36	8	7	21	47	99	23

*Arthurlie resigned towards the end of the season—but their record was allowed to stand.

The worst kind of record

During the 1928-29 season, Rotherham United became only the second side to have had at least 10 goals scored against them in more than one Football League game in the same season. Rotherham, of Division Three North, first lost 11-1 at Bradford City on 25 August 1928, and then 10-1 away to South Shields on 16 March 1929.

The Scottish team in the Football League

In the First Division, the record for fielding a side containing the most Scotsmen belongs to Newcastle United. In the Newcastle side that faced Leeds United on 6 October 1928, only Wood, the centre-half, came from outside Scotland. In 1955-56 Accrington went one better by fielding a team of 11 Scots in several Third Division North fixtures.

FA CUP 1928-29

FOURTH ROUND

Blackburn Rovers v Derby County	1-1, 3-0
Manchester United v Bury	0-1
Leicester City v Swansea Town	1-0
Liverpool v Bolton Wanderers	0-0, 2-5
West Bromwich Albion v Middlesbrough	1-0
Plymouth Argyle v Bradford Park Avenue	0-1
Huddersfield Town v Leeds United	3-0
Millwall v Crystal Palace	0-0, 3-5
Chelsea v Birmingham	1-0
Portsmouth v Bradford City	2-0
Bournemouth v Watford	6-4
West Ham United v Corinthians	3-0
Reading v The Wednesday	1-0
Aston Villa v Clapton Orient	0-0, 8-0
Burnley v Swindon Town	3-3, 2-3
Arsenal v Mansfield Town	2-0

FIFTH ROUND

Blackburn Rovers v Bury	1-0
Leicester City v Bolton Wanderers	1-2
West Bromwich Albion v Bradford Park Avenue	6-0
Huddersfield Town v Crystal Palace	5-2
Chelsea v Portsmouth	1-1, 0-1
Bournemouth v West Ham United	1-1, 1-3
Reading v Aston Villa	1-3
Swindon Town v Arsenal	0-0, 0-1

SIXTH ROUND

Blackburn Rovers v Bolton Wanderers	1-1, 1-2
West Bromwich Albion v Huddersfield Town	1-1, 1-2
Portsmouth v West Ham United	3-2
Aston Villa v Arsenal	1-0

SEMI-FINAL

Bolton Wanderers v Huddersfield Town	3-1
Portsmouth v Aston Villa	1-0

FINAL

Bolton Wanderers v Portsmouth	2-0

SCOTTISH FA CUP 1928-29

SECOND ROUND

Celtic v East Stirlingshire	3-0
Murrayfield Amateurs v Arbroath	1-1, 2-5
Cowdenbeath v Airdrieonians	0-0, 2-3
St Johnstone v Motherwell	2-3
Bathgate v Raith Rovers	1-1, 2-5
Fraserburgh v Dumbarton	0-3
Albion Rovers v Clackmannan	8-1
Kilmarnock v Bo'ness	3-2
Rangers v Partick Thistle	5-1
Clyde v Hamilton Academicals	1-1, 2-1
Dundee v Brechin City	6-1
Stenhousemuir v Dundee United	1-1, 0-2
Aberdeen v Queen's Park	4-0
Queen of the South v Falkirk	1-2
Ayr United v Armadale	5-1
Third Lanark v St Mirren	0-1

THIRD ROUND

Celtic v Arbroath	4-1
Airdrieonians v Motherwell	1-1, 1-3
Raith Rovers v Dumbarton	3-2
Albion Rovers v Kilmarnock	0-1
Clyde v Rangers	0-2
Dundee v Dundee United	1-1, 0-1
Falkirk v Aberdeen	3-5
Ayr United v St Mirren	0-2

FOURTH ROUND

Celtic v Motherwell	0-0, 2-1
Raith Rovers v Kilmarnock	2-3
Rangers v Dundee United	3-1
St Mirren v Aberdeen	4-3

SEMI-FINAL

Celtic v Kilmarnock	0-1
Rangers v St Mirren	3-2

FINAL

Kilmarnock v Rangers	2-0

League Tables 1929-30

FIRST DIVISION

		P	W	D	L	F	A	Pts
1	Sheff Wed	42	26	8	8	105	57	60
2	Derby	42	21	8	13	90	82	50
3	Man City	42	19	9	14	91	81	47
4	Aston Villa	42	21	5	16	92	83	47
5	Leeds	42	20	6	16	79	63	46
6	Blackburn	42	19	7	16	99	93	45
7	West Ham	42	19	5	18	86	79	43
8	Leicester	42	17	9	16	86	90	43
9	Sunderland	42	18	7	17	76	80	43
10	Huddersfield	42	17	9	16	63	69	43
11	Birmingham	42	16	9	17	67	62	41
12	Liverpool	42	16	9	17	63	79	41
13	Portsmouth	42	15	19	17	66	62	40
14	Arsenal	42	14	11	17	78	66	39
15	Bolton	45	15	9	18	74	74	39
16	Middlesbrough	42	16	6	20	82	84	38
17	Man United	42	15	8	19	67	88	38
18	Grimsby	42	15	7	20	73	89	37
19	Newcastle	42	15	7	20	71	92	37
20	Sheff United	42	15	6	21	91	96	36
21	Burnley	42	14	8	20	79	97	36
22	Everton	42	12	11	19	80	92	35

SECOND DIVISION

		P	W	D	L	F	A	Pts
1	Blackpool	42	27	4	11	98	67	58
2	Chelsea	42	22	11	9	74	46	55
3	Oldham	42	21	11	10	90	51	53
4	Bradford PA	42	19	12	11	91	70	50
5	Bury	42	22	5	15	78	67	49
6	WBA	42	21	5	16	105	73	47
7	Southampton	42	17	11	14	77	76	45
8	Cardiff	42	18	8	16	61	59	44
9	Wolves	42	16	9	17	77	79	41
10	Nottm Forest	42	13	15	14	55	69	41
11	Stoke	42	16	8	18	74	72	40
12	Tottenham	42	15	9	18	59	61	39
13	Charlton	42	14	11	17	59	63	39
14	Millwall	42	12	15	15	57	73	39
15	Swansea	42	14	9	19	57	61	37
16	Preston	42	13	11	18	65	80	37
17	Barnsley	42	14	8	20	56	71	36
18	Bradford City	42	12	12	18	60	77	36
19	Reading	42	12	11	19	54	67	35
20	Bristol City	42	13	9	20	61	83	35
21	Hull	42	14	7	21	51	78	35
22	Notts County	42	9	15	18	54	70	33

THIRD DIVISION (SOUTH)

		P	W	D	L	F	A	Pts
1	Plymouth	42	30	8	4	98	38	68
2	Brentford	42	28	5	9	94	44	61
3	QPR	42	21	9	12	80	68	51
4	Northampton	42	21	8	13	82	58	50
5	Brighton	42	21	8	13	87	63	50
6	Coventry	42	19	9	14	88	73	47
7	Fulham	42	18	11	13	87	83	47
8	Norwich	42	18	10	14	88	77	46
9	Crystal Palace	42	17	12	13	81	74	46
10	Bournemouth	42	15	13	14	72	61	43
11	Southend	42	15	13	14	69	59	43
12	Clapton Orient	42	14	13	15	55	62	41
13	Luton	42	14	12	16	64	78	40
14	Swindon	42	13	12	17	73	83	38
15	Watford	42	15	8	19	60	73	38
16	Exeter	42	12	11	19	67	73	35
17	Walsall	42	13	8	21	71	78	34
18	Newport	42	12	10	20	74	85	34
19	Torquay	42	10	11	21	64	94	31
20	Bristol Rovers	42	11	8	23	67	93	30
21	Gillingham	42	11	8	23	51	80	30
22	Merthyr Town	42	6	9	27	60	135	21

THIRD DIVISION (NORTH)

		P	W	D	L	F	A	Pts
1	Port Vale	42	30	7	5	103	37	67
2	Stockport	42	28	7	7	106	44	63
3	Darlington	42	22	6	14	108	73	50
4	Chesterfield	42	22	6	14	76	56	50
5	Lincoln	42	17	14	11	83	61	48
6	York	42	15	16	11	77	64	46
7	South Shields	42	18	10	14	77	74	46
8	Hartlepools	42	17	11	14	81	74	45
9	Southport	42	15	13	14	81	74	43
10	Rochdale	42	18	7	17	89	91	43
11	Crewe	42	17	8	17	82	71	42
12	Tranmere	42	16	9	17	83	86	41
13	New Brighton	42	16	8	18	69	79	40
14	Doncaster	42	15	9	18	62	69	39
15	Carlisle	42	16	7	19	90	101	39
16	Accrington	42	14	9	19	84	81	37
17	Wrexham	42	13	8	21	67	88	34
18	Wigan Borough	42	13	7	22	60	88	33
19	Nelson	42	13	7	22	51	80	33
20	Rotherham	42	11	8	23	67	113	30
21	Halifax	42	10	8	24	44	79	28
22	Barrow	42	11	5	26	41	98	27

SCOTTISH FIRST DIVISION

		P	W	D	L	F	A	Pts
1	Rangers	38	28	4	6	94	32	60
2	Motherwell	38	25	5	8	104	48	55
3	Aberdeen	38	23	7	8	85	61	53
4	Celtic	38	22	5	11	88	46	49
5	St Mirren	38	18	5	15	73	56	41
6	Partick	38	16	9	13	72	61	41
7	Falkirk	38	16	9	13	62	64	41
8	Kilmarnock	38	15	9	14	77	73	39
9	Ayr	38	16	6	16	70	92	38
10	Hearts	38	14	9	15	69	69	37
11	Clyde	38	13	11	14	64	69	37
12	Airdrieonians	38	16	4	18	60	66	36
13	Hamilton	38	14	7	17	76	81	35
14	Dundee	38	14	6	18	51	58	34
15	Queen's Park	38	15	4	19	67	80	34
16	Cowdenbeath	38	13	7	18	64	74	33
17	Hibernian	38	9	11	18	45	62	29
18	Morton	38	10	7	21	67	95	27
19	Dundee United	38	7	8	23	56	109	22
20	St Johnstone	38	6	7	25	48	96	19

SCOTTISH SECOND DIVISION

		P	W	D	L	F	A	Pts
1	Leith Athletic	38	23	11	4	92	42	57
2	East Fife	38	26	5	7	114	58	57
3	Albion	38	24	6	8	101	60	54
4	Third Lanark	38	23	6	9	92	53	52
5	Raith	38	18	8	12	94	67	44
6	King's Park	38	17	8	13	109	80	42
7	Queen of the S	38	18	6	14	65	63	42
8	Forfar	38	18	5	15	98	95	41
9	Arbroath	38	16	7	15	83	87	39
10	Dunfermline	38	16	6	16	99	85	38
11	Montrose	38	14	10	14	79	87	38
12	E Stirlingshire	38	16	4	18	83	75	36
13	Bo'ness	38	15	4	19	67	95	34
14	St Bernard's	38	13	6	19	65	65	32
15	Armadale	38	13	5	20	56	91	31
16	Dumbarton	38	14	2	22	77	95	30
17	Stenhousemuir	38	11	5	22	75	108	27
18	Clydebank	38	7	10	21	66	92	24
19	Alloa	38	9	6	23	55	104	24
20	Brechin	38	7	4	27	57	125	18

Jim Barrett of West Ham United made his international debut for England against Northern Ireland on 19 October 1929. After only eight minutes he was injured and carried off, and as he never played for England again, his became the shortest international career on record.

Sheffield Wednesday won the League Championship for the second successive season.

Albert Geldard of Bradford Park Avenue became the youngest footballer to play in the League when, aged 15 years and 158 days, he played against Millwall in a Division Two match on 16 September 1929.

Joe Bambrick's six goals in Northern Ireland's 7-0 win over Wales in February 1930 made him the highest individual scorer in an international match between Home Countries.

FA CUP 1929-30

FOURTH ROUND

West Ham United v Leeds United	4-1
Millwall v Doncaster Rovers	4-0
Arsenal v Birmingham	2-2, 1-0
Middlesbrough v Charlton Athletic	1-1, 1-1, 1-0
Hull City v Blackpool	3-1
Swindon Town v Manchester City	1-1, 1-10
Newcastle United v Clapton Orient	3-1
Portsmouth v Brighton	0-1
Aston Villa v Walsall	3-1
Blackburn Rovers v Everton	4-1
Huddersfield Town v Sheffield United	2-1
Wrexham v Bradford City	0-0, 1-2
Nottingham Forest v Fulham	2-1
Sunderland v Cardiff City	2-1
Oldham Athletic v Sheffield Wednesday	3-4
Derby County v Bradford Park Avenue	1-1, 1-2

FIFTH ROUND

West Ham United v Millwall	4-1
Middlesbrough v Arsenal	0-2
Manchester City v Hull City	1-2
Newcastle United v Brighton	3-0
Aston Villa v Blackburn Rovers	4-1
Huddersfield Town v Bradford City	2-1
Sunderland v Nottingham Forest	2-2, 1-3
Sheffield Wednesday v Bradford Park Avenue	5-1

SIXTH ROUND

West Ham United v Arsenal	0-3
Newcastle United v Hull City	1-1, 0-1
Aston Villa v Huddersfield Town	1-2
Nottingham Forest v Sheffield Wednesday	2-2, 1-3

SEMI-FINAL

Arsenal v Hull City	2-2, 1-0
Huddersfield Town v Sheffield Wednesday	2-1

FINAL

Arsenal v Huddersfield Town	2-0

SCOTTISH FA CUP 1929-30

SECOND ROUND

Rangers v Cowdenbeath	2-2, 3-0
Motherwell v Clyde	3-0
Montrose v Citadel	3-1
Albion Rovers v Beith	2-1
Dundee v St Johnstone	4-1
Airdrieonians v Murrayfield Amateurs	8-3
Heart of Midlothian v St Bernard's	0-0, 5-1
Ayr United v Hibernian	1-3
Forfar Athletic v St Mirren	0-0, 0-3
Celtic v Arbroath	5-0
Hamilton Academicals v Kilmarnock	4-2
Vale of Leithen v King's Park	2-7
Falkirk v Queen of the South	1-1, 4-3
Leith Athletic v Clachnacuddin	2-0
Dundee United v Partick Thistle	0-3
Aberdeen v Nithsdale Wanderers	5-1

THIRD ROUND

Motherwell v Rangers	2-5
Albion Rovers v Montrose	2-2, 1-3
Dundee v Airdrieonians	0-0, 0-0, 1-0
Hibernian v Heart of Midlothian	1-3
Celtic v St Mirren	1-3
Hamilton Academicals v King's Park	4-0
Falkirk v Leith Athletic	0-0, 1-1, 1-1, 1-0
Partick Thistle v Aberdeen	3-2

FOURTH ROUND

Rangers v Montrose	3-0
Dundee v Heart of Midlothian	2-2, 0-4
St Mirren v Hamilton Academicals	3-4
Partick Thistle v Falkirk	3-1

SEMI-FINAL

Rangers v Heart of Midlothian	4-1
Partick Thistle v Hamilton Academicals	3-1

FINAL

Rangers v Partick Thistle	0-0, 2-1

League Tables 1930-31

FIRST DIVISION

		P	W	D	L	F	A	Pts
1	Arsenal	42	28	10	4	127	59	66
2	Aston Villa	42	25	9	8	128	78	59
3	Sheff Wed	42	22	8	12	102	75	52
4	Portsmouth	42	18	13	11	84	67	49
5	Huddersfield	42	18	12	12	81	65	48
6	Derby	42	18	10	14	94	79	46
7	Middlesbrough	42	19	8	15	98	90	46
8	Man City	42	18	10	14	75	70	46
9	Liverpool	42	15	12	15	86	85	42
10	Blackburn	42	17	8	17	83	84	42
11	Sunderland	42	16	9	17	89	85	41
12	Chelsea	42	15	10	17	64	67	40
13	Grimsby	42	17	5	20	82	87	39
14	Bolton	42	15	9	18	68	81	39
15	Sheff United	42	14	10	18	78	84	38
16	Leicester	42	16	6	20	80	95	38
17	Newcastle	42	15	6	21	78	87	36
18	West Ham	42	14	8	20	79	94	36
19	Birmingham	42	13	10	19	55	70	36
20	Blackpool	42	11	10	21	71	125	32
21	Leeds	42	12	7	23	68	81	31
22	Man United	42	7	8	27	53	115	22

SECOND DIVISION

		P	W	D	L	F	A	Pts
1	Everton	42	28	5	9	121	66	61
2	WBA	42	22	10	10	83	49	54
3	Tottenham	42	22	7	13	88	55	51
4	Wolves	42	21	5	16	84	67	47
5	Port Vale	42	21	5	16	67	61	47
6	Bradford PA	42	18	10	14	97	66	46
7	Preston	42	17	11	14	83	64	45
8	Burnley	42	17	11	14	81	77	45
9	Southampton	42	19	6	17	74	62	44
10	Bradford City	42	17	10	15	61	63	44
11	Stoke	42	17	10	15	64	71	44
12	Oldham	42	16	10	16	61	72	42
13	Bury	42	19	3	20	75	82	41
14	Millwall	42	16	7	19	71	80	39
15	Charlton	42	15	9	18	59	86	39
16	Bristol City	42	15	8	19	54	82	38
17	Nottm Forest	42	14	9	19	80	85	37
18	Plymouth	42	14	8	20	76	84	36
19	Barnsley	42	13	9	20	59	79	35
20	Swansea	42	12	10	20	51	74	34
21	Reading	42	12	6	24	72	96	30
22	Cardiff	42	8	9	25	47	87	25

THIRD DIVISION (SOUTH)

		P	W	D	L	F	A	Pts
1	Notts County	42	24	11	7	97	46	59
2	Crystal Palace	42	22	7	13	107	71	51
3	Brentford	42	22	6	14	90	64	50
4	Brighton	42	17	15	10	68	53	49
5	Southend	42	22	5	15	76	60	49
6	Northampton	42	18	12	12	77	59	48
7	Luton	42	19	8	15	76	51	46
8	QPR	42	20	3	19	82	75	43
9	Fulham	42	18	7	17	77	75	43
10	Bournemouth	42	15	13	14	72	73	43
11	Torquay	42	17	9	16	80	84	43
12	Swindon	42	18	6	18	89	94	42
13	Exeter	42	17	8	17	84	90	42
14	Coventry	42	16	9	17	75	65	41
15	Bristol Rovers	42	16	8	18	75	92	40
16	Gillingham	42	14	10	18	61	76	38
17	Walsall	42	14	9	19	78	95	37
18	Watford	42	14	7	21	72	75	35
19	Clapton Orient	42	14	7	21	63	91	35
20	Thames	42	13	8	21	54	93	34
21	Norwich	42	10	8	24	47	76	28
22	Newport	42	11	6	25	69	111	28

THIRD DIVISION (NORTH)

		P	W	D	L	F	A	Pts
1	Chesterfield	42	26	6	10	102	57	58
2	Lincoln	42	25	7	10	102	59	57
3	Tranmere	42	24	6	12	111	74	54
4	Wrexham	42	21	12	9	94	62	54
5	Southport	42	22	9	11	88	56	53
6	Hull	42	20	10	12	99	55	50
7	Stockport	42	20	9	13	77	61	49
8	Carlisle	42	20	5	17	98	81	45
9	Gateshead	42	16	13	13	71	73	45
10	Wigan Borough	42	19	5	18	76	86	43
11	Darlington	42	16	10	16	71	59	42
12	York	42	18	6	18	85	82	42
13	Accrington	42	15	9	18	84	108	39
14	Rotherham	42	13	12	17	81	83	38
15	Doncaster	42	13	11	18	65	65	37
16	Barrow	42	15	7	20	68	89	37
17	Halifax	42	13	9	20	55	89	35
18	Crewe	42	14	6	22	66	93	34
19	New Brighton	42	13	7	22	49	76	33
20	Hartlepools	42	12	6	24	67	86	30
21	Rochdale	42	12	6	24	62	107	30
22	Nelson	42	6	7	29	43	113	19

SCOTTISH FIRST DIVISION

		P	W	D	L	F	A	Pts
1	Rangers	38	27	6	5	96	29	60
2	Celtic	38	24	10	4	101	34	58
3	Motherwell	38	24	8	6	102	42	56
4	Partick	38	24	5	9	76	44	53
5	Hearts	38	19	6	13	90	63	44
6	Aberdeen	38	17	7	14	79	63	41
7	Cowdenbeath	38	17	7	14	58	65	41
8	Dundee	38	17	5	16	65	63	39
9	Airdrieonians	38	17	5	16	59	66	39
10	Hamilton	38	16	5	17	59	57	37
11	Kilmarnock	38	15	5	18	59	60	35
12	Clyde	38	15	4	19	60	87	34
13	Queen's Park	38	13	7	18	71	72	33
14	Falkirk	38	14	4	20	77	87	32
15	St Mirren	38	11	8	19	49	72	30
16	Morton	38	11	7	20	58	83	29
17	Leith	38	8	11	19	52	85	27
18	Ayr	38	8	11	19	53	92	27
19	Hibernian	38	9	7	22	49	81	25
20	East Fife	38	8	4	26	45	113	20

SCOTTISH SECOND DIVISION

		P	W	D	L	F	A	Pts
1	Third Lanark	38	27	7	4	107	42	61
2	Dundee United	38	21	8	9	93	54	50
3	Dunfermline	38	20	7	11	83	50	47
4	Raith	38	20	6	12	93	72	46
5	Queen of the S	38	18	6	14	83	66	42
6	St Johnstone	38	18	6	14	76	64	42
7	E Stirlingshire	38	17	7	14	85	74	41
8	Montrose	38	19	3	16	75	90	41
9	Albion	38	14	11	13	80	83	39
10	Dumbarton	38	15	8	15	73	72	38
11	St Bernard's	38	14	9	15	85	66	37
12	Forfar	38	15	6	17	78	83	36
13	Alloa	38	15	5	18	65	87	35
14	King's Park	38	14	6	18	78	70	34
15	Arbroath	38	15	4	19	83	94	34
16	Brechin	38	13	7	18	52	84	33
17	Stenhousemuir	38	13	6	19	78	98	32
18	Armadale	38	13	2	23	74	99	28
19	Clydebank	38	10	2	26	61	108	22
20	Bo'ness	38	9	4	25	54	100	22

The outstanding example of each member of a forward line scoring in a single game was when all five Everton forwards scored against Charlton Athletic at the Valley in an 18 minute spell. The Everton forwards were Stein, Dean, Dunn, Critchley and Johnson. The match, a Division Two League fixture played on 7 February 1931, ended as a convincing 7-0 victory for the Merseysiders, who went on to win the Division Two Championship.

The famous occasion when a referee was 'sent off' occurred in the annual Sheffield versus Glasgow match on 22 September 1930. Sheffield were playing in white shirts and black shorts, and the referee, Mr J Thomson of Burnbank, wore a white shirt without a jacket. When Sheffield's captain, Jimmy Seed, found that he was passing to the referee in error, he asked him to stop the game and put on a jacket. Mr Thomson obliged.

FA CUP 1930-31

FOURTH ROUND

Birmingham v Port Vale	2-0
Watford v Brighton	2-0
Chelsea v Arsenal	2-1
Blackburn Rovers v Bristol Rovers	5-1
Bolton Wanderers v Sunderland	1-1, 1-3
Sheffield United v Notts County	4-1
Bury v Exeter City	1-2
Leeds United v Newcastle United	4-1
Crystal Palace v Everton	0-6
Grimsby Town v Manchester United	1-0
Southport v Blackpool	2-1
Bradford Park Avenue v Burnley	2-0
Brentford v Portsmouth	0-1
West Bromwich Albion v Tottenham Hotspur	1-0
Barnsley v Sheffield Wednesday	2-1
Bradford City v Wolverhampton Wanderers	0-0, 2-4

FIFTH ROUND

Birmingham v Watford	3-0
Chelsea v Blackburn Rovers	3-0
Sunderland v Sheffield United	2-1
Exeter City v Leeds United	3-1
Everton v Grimsby Town	5-3
Southport v Bradford Park Avenue	1-0
Portsmouth v West Bromwich Albion	0-1
Barnsley v Wolverhampton Wanderers	1-3

SIXTH ROUND

Birmingham v Chelsea	2-2, 3-0
Sunderland v Exeter City	1-1, 4-2
Everton v Southport	9-1
West Bromwich Albion v Wolverhampton Wanderers	1-1, 2-1

SEMI-FINAL

Birmingham v Sunderland	2-0
Everton v West Bromwich Albion	0-1

FINAL

West Bromwich Albion v Birmingham	2-1

SCOTTISH FA CUP 1930-31

SECOND ROUND

Dundee United v Celtic	2-3
Queen's Park v Morton	0-1
Aberdeen v Partick Thistle	1-1, 3-0
Rangers v Dundee	1-2
Kilmarnock v Heart of Midlothian	3-2
Montrose v Civil Service Strollers	2-0
Bo'ness v Alloa Athletic	4-2
Murrayfield Amateurs v Ayr United	0-1
Motherwell v Albion Rovers	4-1
Hamilton Academicals v Hibernian	2-2, 2-5
Cowdenbeath v St Johnstone	1-1, 4-0
King's Park v St Bernard's	1-1, 0-1
St Mirren v Clyde	3-1
Inverness Caledonian v Falkirk	2-7
Third Lanark v Airdrieonians	1-0
Arbroath v Edinburgh City	1-0

THIRD ROUND

Morton v Celtic	1-4
Dundee v Aberdeen	1-1, 0-2
Montrose v Kilmarnock	0-3
Bo'ness v Ayr United	1-0
Hibernian v Motherwell	0-3
Cowdenbeath v St Bernard's	3-0
St Mirren v Falkirk	2-0
Third Lanark v Arbroath	4-2

FOURTH ROUND

Celtic v Aberdeen	4-0
Bo'ness v Kilmarnock	1-1, 0-5
Cowdenbeath v Motherwell	0-1
Third Lanark v St Mirren	1-1, 0-3

SEMI-FINAL

Celtic v Kilmarnock	3-0
Motherwell v St Mirren	1-0

FINAL

Celtic v Motherwell	2-2, 4-2

League Tables 1931-32

FIRST DIVISION

		P	W	D	L	F	A	Pts
1	Everton	42	26	4	12	116	64	56
2	Arsenal	42	22	10	10	90	48	54
3	Sheff Wed	42	22	6	14	96	82	50
4	Huddersfield	42	19	10	13	80	63	48
5	Aston Villa	42	19	8	15	104	72	46
6	WBA	42	20	6	16	77	55	46
7	Sheff United	42	20	6	16	80	75	46
8	Portsmouth	42	19	7	16	62	62	45
9	Birmingham	42	18	8	16	78	67	44
10	Liverpool	42	19	6	17	81	93	44
11	Newcastle	42	18	6	18	80	87	42
12	Chelsea	42	16	8	18	69	73	40
13	Sunderland	42	15	10	17	67	73	40
14	Man City	42	13	12	17	83	73	38
15	Derby	42	14	10	18	71	75	38
16	Blackburn	42	16	6	20	89	95	38
17	Bolton	42	17	4	21	72	80	38
18	Middlesbrough	42	15	8	19	64	89	38
19	Leicester	42	15	7	20	74	94	37
20	Blackpool	42	12	9	21	65	102	33
21	Grimsby	42	13	6	23	67	98	32
22	West Ham	42	12	7	23	62	107	31

SECOND DIVISION

		P	W	D	L	F	A	Pts
1	Wolves	42	24	8	10	115	49	56
2	Leeds	42	22	10	10	78	54	54
3	Stoke	42	19	14	9	69	48	52
4	Plymouth	42	20	9	13	100	66	49
5	Bury	42	21	7	14	70	58	49
6	Bradford PA	42	21	7	14	72	63	49
7	Bradford City	42	16	13	13	80	61	45
8	Tottenham	42	16	11	15	87	78	43
9	Millwall	42	17	9	16	61	61	43
10	Charlton	42	17	9	16	61	66	43
11	Nottm Forest	42	16	10	16	77	72	42
12	Man United	42	17	8	17	71	72	42
13	Preston	42	16	10	16	75	77	42
14	Southampton	42	17	7	18	66	77	41
15	Swansea	42	16	7	19	73	75	39
16	Notts County	42	13	12	17	75	75	38
17	Chesterfield	42	13	11	18	64	86	37
18	Oldham	42	13	10	19	62	84	36
19	Burnley	42	13	9	20	59	87	35
20	Port Vale	42	13	7	22	58	89	33
21	Barnsley	42	12	9	21	55	91	33
22	Bristol City	42	6	11	25	39	78	23

THIRD DIVISION (SOUTH)

		P	W	D	L	F	A	Pts
1	Fulham	42	24	9	9	111	62	57
2	Reading	42	23	9	10	97	67	55
3	Southend	42	21	11	10	77	53	53
4	Crystal Palace	42	20	11	11	74	63	51
5	Brentford	42	19	10	13	68	52	48
6	Luton	42	20	7	15	95	70	47
7	Exeter	42	20	7	15	77	62	47
8	Brighton	42	17	12	13	73	58	46
9	Cardiff	42	19	8	15	87	73	46
10	Norwich	42	17	12	13	76	67	46
11	Watford	42	19	8	15	81	79	46
12	Coventry	42	18	8	16	108	97	44
13	QPR	42	15	12	15	79	73	42
14	Northampton	42	16	7	19	69	69	39
15	Bournemouth	42	13	12	17	70	78	38
16	Clapton Orient	42	12	11	19	77	90	35
17	Swindon	42	14	6	22	70	84	34
18	Bristol Rovers	42	13	8	21	65	92	34
19	Torquay	42	12	9	21	72	106	33
20	Mansfield	42	11	10	21	75	108	32
21	Gillingham	42	10	8	24	40	82	28
22	Thames	42	7	9	26	53	109	23

THIRD DIVISION (NORTH)

		P	W	D	L	F	A	Pts
1	Lincoln	40	26	5	9	106	47	57
2	Gateshead	40	25	7	8	94	48	57
3	Chester	40	21	8	11	78	60	50
4	Tranmere	40	19	11	10	107	58	49
5	Barrow	40	24	1	15	86	59	49
6	Crewe	40	21	6	13	95	66	48
7	Southport	40	18	10	12	58	53	46
8	Hull	40	20	5	15	82	53	45
9	York	40	18	7	15	76	81	43
10	Wrexham	40	18	7	15	64	69	43
11	Darlington	40	17	4	19	66	69	38
12	Stockport	40	13	11	16	55	53	37
13	Hartlepools	40	16	5	19	78	100	37
14	Accrington	40	15	6	19	75	80	36
15	Doncaster	40	16	4	20	59	80	36
16	Walsall	40	16	3	21	57	85	35
17	Halifax	40	13	8	19	61	87	34
18	Carlisle	40	11	11	18	64	79	33
19	Rotherham	40	14	4	22	63	72	32
20	New Brighton	40	8	8	24	38	76	24
21	Rochdale	40	4	3	33	48	135	11
22	Wigan Borough resigned from the League							

SCOTTISH FIRST DIVISION

		P	W	D	L	F	A	Pts
1	Motherwell	38	30	6	2	119	31	66
2	Rangers	38	28	5	5	118	42	61
3	Celtic	38	20	8	10	94	50	48
4	Third Lanark	38	21	4	13	92	81	46
5	St Mirren	38	20	4	14	77	56	44
6	Partick	38	19	4	15	58	59	42
7	Aberdeen	38	16	9	13	57	49	41
8	Hearts	38	17	5	16	63	61	39
9	Kilmarnock	38	16	7	15	68	70	39
10	Hamilton	38	16	6	16	84	65	38
11	Dundee	38	14	10	14	61	72	38
12	Cowdenbeath	38	15	8	15	66	78	38
13	Clyde	38	13	9	16	58	70	35
14	Airdrieonians	38	13	6	19	74	81	32
15	Morton	38	12	7	19	78	87	31
16	Queen's Park	38	13	5	20	59	79	31
17	Ayr	38	11	7	20	70	90	29
18	Falkirk	38	11	5	22	70	76	27
19	Dundee United	38	6	7	25	40	118	19
20	Leith	38	6	4	28	46	137	16

SCOTTISH SECOND DIVISION

		P	W	D	L	F	A	Pts
1	E Stirlingshire	38	26	3	9	111	55	55
2	St Johnstone	38	24	7	7	102	52	55
3	Raith	38	20	6	12	83	65	46
4	Stenhousemuir	38	19	8	11	88	76	46
5	St Bernard's	38	19	7	12	81	62	45
6	Forfar	38	19	7	12	90	79	45
7	Hibernian	38	18	8	12	73	52	44
8	East Fife	38	18	5	15	107	77	41
9	Queen of the S	38	18	5	15	99	91	41
10	Dunfermline	38	17	6	15	78	73	40
11	Arbroath	38	17	5	16	82	78	39
12	Dumbarton	38	14	10	14	70	68	38
13	Alloa	38	14	7	17	73	74	35
14	Bo'ness	38	15	4	19	70	103	34
15	King's Park	38	14	5	19	97	93	33
16	Albion	38	13	2	23	81	104	28
17	Montrose	38	11	6	21	60	96	28
18	Armadale	38	10	5	23	68	102	25
19	Brechin	38	9	7	22	52	97	25
20	Edinburgh City	38	5	7	26	78	146	17

There is thought to have been only one League game without a corner kick. That was a Division One match between Newcastle United and Portsmouth, 5 December 1931, which ended as it began, 0-0.

On 26 October 1931, Wigan Borough became the first League club to resign during a season. Their record was expunged.

Rochdale break all the wrong records

Rochdale had a grim season in Division Three North. They set a League record by losing 17 games in succession: on 7 November 1931, they beat New Brighton 3-2, but then failed to gain another point until their 1-1 draw with the same team on 9 March 1932. Their 33 defeats in 40 matches were also a record for the division.

FA CUP 1931-32

FOURTH ROUND

Huddersfield Town v Queen's Park Rangers	5-0
Preston North End v Wolverhampton Wanderers	2-0
Portsmouth v Aston Villa	1-1, 1-0
Arsenal v Plymouth Argyle	4-2
Bury v Sheffield United	3-1
Sunderland v Stoke City	1-1, 1-1, 1-2
Manchester City v Brentford	6-1
Derby County v Blackburn Rovers	3-2
Chesterfield v Liverpool	2-4
Grimsby Town v Birmingham	2-1
Sheffield Wednesday v Bournemouth	7-0
Chelsea v West Ham United	3-1
Newcastle United v Southport	1-1, 1-1, 9-0
Port Vale v Leicester City	1-2
Watford v Bristol City	2-1
Bradford Park Avenue v Northampton Town	4-2

FIFTH ROUND

Huddersfield Town v Preston North End	4-0
Portsmouth v Arsenal	0-2
Bury v Stoke City	3-0
Manchester City v Derby County	3-0
Liverpool v Grimsby Town	1-0
Sheffield Wednesday v Chelsea	1-1, 0-2
Newcastle United v Leicester City	3-1
Watford v Bradford Park Avenue	1-0

SIXTH ROUND

Huddersfield Town v Arsenal	0-1
Bury v Manchester City	3-4
Liverpool v Chelsea	0-2
Newcastle United v Watford	5-0

SEMI-FINAL

Arsenal v Manchester City	1-0
Chelsea v Newcastle United	1-2

FINAL

Newcastle United v Arsenal	2-1

SCOTTISH FA CUP 1931-32

SECOND ROUND

Raith Rovers v Rangers	0-5
Heart of Midlothian v Cowdenbeath	4-1
Queen's Park v Motherwell	0-2
St Johnstone v Celtic	2-4
Hamilton Academicals v Armadale	5-2
Clyde v Arbroath	1-0
Edinburgh City v St Bernard's	2-3
Kilmarnock v Albion Rovers	2-0
Queen of the South v Dundee United	2-2, 1-1, 1-2
Dunfermline Athletic v Dundee	1-0
Airdrieonians v King's Park	2-2, 3-1
Bo'ness v Partick Thistle	2-2, 1-5

THIRD ROUND

Heart of Midlothian v Rangers	0-1
Motherwell v Celtic	2-0
Clyde v St Bernard's	2-0
Dundee United v Kilmarnock	1-1, 0-3
Hamilton Academicals	bye
Dunfermline Athletic	bye
Airdrieonians	bye
Partick Thistle	bye

FOURTH ROUND

Rangers v Motherwell	2-0
Clyde v Hamilton Academicals	0-2
Dunfermline Athletic v Kilmarnock	1-3
Airdrieonians v Partick Thistle	4-1

SEMI-FINAL

Rangers v Hamilton Academicals	5-2
Kilmarnock v Airdrieonians	3-2

FINAL

Rangers v Kilmarnock	1-1, 3-0

League Tables 1932-33

FIRST DIVISION

		P	W	D	L	F	A	Pts
1	Arsenal	42	25	8	9	118	61	58
2	Aston Villa	42	23	8	11	92	67	54
3	Sheff Wed	42	21	9	12	80	68	51
4	WBA	42	20	9	13	83	70	49
5	Newcastle	42	22	5	15	71	63	49
6	Huddersfield	42	18	11	13	66	53	47
7	Derby	42	15	14	13	76	69	44
8	Leeds	42	15	14	13	59	62	44
9	Portsmouth	42	18	7	17	74	76	43
10	Sheff United	42	17	9	16	74	80	43
11	Everton	42	16	9	17	81	74	41
12	Sunderland	42	15	10	17	63	80	40
13	Birmingham	42	14	11	17	57	57	39
14	Liverpool	42	14	11	17	79	84	39
15	Blackburn	42	14	10	18	76	102	38
16	Man City	42	16	5	21	68	71	37
17	Middlesbrough	42	14	9	19	63	73	37
18	Chelsea	42	14	7	21	63	73	35
19	Leicester	42	11	13	18	75	89	35
20	Wolves	42	13	9	20	80	96	35
21	Bolton	42	12	9	21	78	92	33
22	Blackpool	42	14	5	23	69	85	33

SECOND DIVISION

		P	W	D	L	F	A	Pts
1	Stoke	42	25	6	11	78	39	56
2	Tottenham	42	20	15	7	96	51	55
3	Fulham	42	20	10	12	78	65	50
4	Bury	42	20	9	13	84	59	49
5	Nottm Forest	42	17	15	10	67	59	49
6	Man United	42	15	13	14	71	68	43
7	Millwall	42	16	11	15	59	57	43
8	Bradford PA	42	17	8	17	77	71	42
9	Preston	42	16	10	16	74	70	42
10	Swansea	42	19	4	19	50	54	42
11	Bradford City	42	14	13	15	65	61	41
12	Southampton	42	18	5	19	66	66	41
13	Grimsby	42	14	13	15	79	84	41
14	Plymouth	42	16	9	17	63	67	41
15	Notts County	42	15	10	17	67	78	40
16	Oldham	42	15	8	19	67	80	38
17	Port Vale	42	14	10	18	66	79	38
18	Lincoln	42	12	13	17	72	87	37
19	Burnley	42	11	14	17	67	79	36
20	West Ham	42	13	9	20	75	93	35
21	Chesterfield	42	12	10	20	61	84	34
22	Charlton	42	12	7	23	60	91	31

FA CUP 1932-33

FOURTH ROUND

Burnley v Sheffield United 3-1
Darlington v Chesterfield 0-2
Bolton Wanderers v Grimsby Town 2-1
Manchester City v Walsall 2-0
Southend United v Derby County 2-3
Aldershot v Millwall 1-0
Aston Villa v Sunderland 0-3
Blackpool v Huddersfield Town 2-0
Everton v Bury 3-1
Tranmere Rovers v Leeds United 0-0, 0-4
Chester v Halifax Town 0-0, 2-3
Luton Town v Tottenham Hotspur 2-0
Brighton v Bradford Park Avenue 2-1
West Ham United v West Bromwich Albion 2-0
Middlesbrough v Stoke City 4-1
Birmingham v Blackburn Rovers 3-0

FIFTH ROUND

Burnley v Chesterfield 1-0
Bolton Wanderers v Manchester City 2-4
Derby County v Aldershot 2-0
Sunderland v Blackpool 1-0
Everton v Leeds United 2-0
Halifax Town v Luton Town 0-2
Brighton v West Ham United 2-2, 0-1
Middlesbrough v Birmingham 0-0, 0-3

SIXTH ROUND

Burnley v Manchester City 0-1
Derby County v Sunderland 4-4, 1-0
Everton v Luton Town 6-0
West Ham United v Birmingham 4-0

SEMI-FINAL

Manchester City v Derby County 3-2
Everton v West Ham United 2-1

FINAL

Everton v Manchester City 3-0

THIRD DIVISION (SOUTH)

		P	W	D	L	F	A	Pts
1	Brentford	42	26	10	6	90	49	62
2	Exeter	42	24	10	8	88	48	58
3	Norwich	42	22	13	7	88	55	57
4	Reading	42	19	13	10	103	71	51
5	Crystal Palace	42	19	8	15	78	64	46
6	Coventry	42	19	6	17	106	77	44
7	Gillingham	42	18	8	16	72	61	44
8	Northampton	42	18	8	16	76	66	44
9	Bristol Rovers	42	15	14	13	61	56	44
10	Torquay	42	16	12	14	72	67	44
11	Watford	42	16	12	14	66	63	44
12	Brighton	42	17	8	17	66	65	42
13	Southend	42	15	11	16	65	82	41
14	Luton	42	13	13	16	78	78	39
15	Bristol City	42	12	13	17	83	90	37
16	QPR	42	13	11	18	72	87	37
17	Aldershot	42	13	10	19	61	72	36
18	Bournemouth	42	12	12	18	60	81	36
19	Cardiff	42	12	7	23	69	99	31
20	Clapton Orient	42	8	13	21	59	93	29
21	Newport	42	11	7	24	61	105	29
22	Swindon	42	9	11	22	60	105	29

THIRD DIVISION (NORTH)

		P	W	D	L	F	A	Pts
1	Hull	42	26	7	9	100	45	59
2	Wrexham	42	24	9	9	106	51	57
3	Stockport	42	21	12	9	99	58	54
4	Chester	42	22	8	12	94	66	52
5	Walsall	42	19	10	13	75	58	48
6	Doncaster	42	17	14	11	77	79	48
7	Gateshead	42	19	9	14	78	67	47
8	Barnsley	42	19	8	15	92	80	46
9	Barrow	42	18	7	17	60	60	43
10	Crewe	42	20	3	19	80	84	43
11	Tranmere	42	17	8	17	70	66	42
12	Southport	42	17	7	18	70	67	41
13	Accrington	42	15	10	17	78	76	40
14	Hartlepools	42	16	7	19	87	116	39
15	Halifax	42	15	8	19	71	90	38
16	Mansfield	42	14	7	21	84	100	35
17	Rotherham	42	14	6	22	60	84	34
18	Rochdale	42	13	7	22	58	80	33
19	Carlisle	42	13	7	22	51	75	33
20	York	42	13	6	23	72	92	32
21	New Brighton	42	11	10	21	63	88	32
22	Darlington	42	10	8	24	66	109	28

SCOTTISH FIRST DIVISION

		P	W	D	L	F	A	Pts
1	Rangers	38	26	10	2	113	43	62
2	Motherwell	38	27	5	6	114	53	59
3	Hearts	38	21	8	9	84	51	50
4	Celtic	38	20	8	10	75	44	48
5	St Johnstone	38	17	10	11	70	57	44
6	Aberdeen	38	18	6	14	85	58	42
7	St Mirren	38	18	6	14	73	60	42
8	Hamilton	38	18	6	14	92	78	42
9	Queen's Park	38	17	7	14	78	79	41
10	Partick	38	17	6	15	75	55	40
11	Falkirk	38	15	6	17	70	70	36
12	Clyde	38	15	5	18	69	75	35
13	Third Lanark	38	14	7	17	70	80	35
14	Kilmarnock	38	13	9	16	72	86	35
15	Dundee	38	12	9	17	58	74	33
16	Ayr	38	13	4	21	62	96	30
17	Cowdenbeath	38	10	5	23	65	111	25
18	Airdrieonians	38	10	3	25	55	102	23
19	Morton	38	6	9	23	49	97	21
20	E Stirlingshire	38	7	3	28	55	115	17

Reduced to ten men after 10 minutes, Wales did well to beat Scotland 5-2 at Tynecastle, Edinburgh, in October 1932. It was their first win on Scottish soil since 1906.

Everton capped a memorable three seasons by winning the FA Cup. In 1931-32, they were League champions, the season before, they had won the Second Division Championship.

SCOTTISH SECOND DIVISION

		P	W	D	L	F	A	Pts
1	Hibernian	34	25	4	5	80	29	54
2	Queen of the S	34	20	9	5	93	59	49
3	Dunfermline	34	20	7	7	89	44	47
4	Stenhousemuir	34	18	6	10	67	58	42
5	Albion	34	19	2	13	82	57	40
6	Raith	34	16	4	14	83	67	36
7	East Fife	34	15	4	15	85	71	34
8	King's Park	34	13	8	13	85	80	34
9	Dumbarton	34	14	6	14	69	67	34
10	Arbroath	34	14	5	15	65	62	33
11	Alloa	34	14	5	15	60	58	33
12	St Bernard's	34	13	6	15	67	64	32
13	Dundee United	34	14	4	16	65	67	32
14	Forfar	34	12	4	18	68	87	28
15	Brechin	34	11	4	19	65	95	26
16	Leith	34	10	5	19	43	81	25
17	Montrose	34	8	5	21	63	89	21
18	Edinburgh City	34	4	4	26	39	133	12

The international Rangers

Towards the end of 1932-33, Glasgow Rangers had 13 internationals on their books. They were: Archibald, Brown, Craig, Fleming, Gray, T Hamilton, McPhail, Marshall, Meiklejohn and Morton, all Scotsmen, and English, R Hamilton and McDonald, who were Irish internationals. This considerable array of Scots and Irish talent helped Rangers finish the season at the top of the Scottish First Division, three points clear of Motherwell.

SCOTTISH FA CUP 1932-33

SECOND ROUND

Celtic v Falkirk 2-0
Partick Thistle v Ayr United 1-1, 2-0
Albion Rovers v Dumbarton 2-1
Heart of Midlothian v Airdrieonians 6-1
St Johnstone v Dundee United 4-3
Hibernian v Aberdeen 1-1, 1-0
Motherwell v Montrose 7-1
Dundee v Bo'ness 4-0
Kilmarnock v St Mirren 1-0
Rangers v Queen's Park 1-1, 1-1, 3-1
Clyde v Leith Athletic 1-1, 5-0
Stenhousemuir v Third Lanark 2-0

THIRD ROUND

Celtic v Partick Thistle 2-1
Heart of Midlothian v St Johnstone 2-0
Motherwell v Dundee 5-0
Kilmarnock v Rangers 1-0
Albion Rovers bye
Hibernian bye
Clyde bye
Stenhousemuir bye

FOURTH ROUND

Celtic v Albion Rovers 1-1, 3-1
Heart of Midlothian v Hibernian 2-0
Motherwell v Kilmarnock 3-3, 8-3
Clyde v Stenhousemuir 3-2

SEMI-FINAL

Celtic v Heart of Midlothian 0-0, 2-1
Motherwell v Clyde 2-0

FINAL

Celtic v Motherwell 1-0

League Tables 1933-34

FIRST DIVISION

		P	W	D	L	F	A	Pts
1	Arsenal	42	25	9	8	75	47	59
2	Huddersfield	42	23	10	9	90	61	56
3	Tottenham	42	21	7	14	79	56	49
4	Derby	42	17	11	14	68	54	45
5	Man City	42	17	11	14	65	72	45
6	Sunderland	42	16	12	14	81	56	44
7	WBA	42	17	10	15	78	70	44
8	Blackburn	42	18	7	17	74	81	43
9	Leeds	42	17	8	17	75	66	42
10	Portsmouth	42	15	12	15	52	55	42
11	Sheff Wed	42	16	9	17	62	67	41
12	Stoke	42	15	11	16	58	71	41
13	Aston Villa	42	14	12	16	78	75	40
14	Everton	42	12	16	14	62	63	40
15	Wolves	42	14	12	16	74	86	40
16	Middlesbrough	42	16	7	19	68	80	39
17	Leicester	42	14	11	17	59	74	39
18	Liverpool	42	14	10	18	79	87	38
19	Chelsea	42	14	8	20	67	69	36
20	Birmingham	42	12	12	18	54	56	36
21	Newcastle	42	10	14	18	68	77	34
22	Sheff United	42	12	7	23	58	101	31

SECOND DIVISION

		P	W	D	L	F	A	Pts
1	Grimsby	42	27	5	10	103	59	59
2	Preston	42	23	6	13	71	52	52
3	Bolton	42	21	9	12	79	55	51
4	Brentford	42	22	7	13	85	60	51
5	Bradford PA	42	23	3	16	86	67	49
6	Bradford City	42	20	6	16	73	67	46
7	West Ham	42	17	11	14	78	70	45
8	Port Vale	42	19	7	16	60	55	45
9	Oldham	42	17	10	15	72	60	44
10	Plymouth	42	15	13	14	69	70	43
11	Blackpool	42	15	13	14	62	64	43
12	Bury	42	17	9	16	70	73	43
13	Burnley	42	18	6	18	60	72	42
14	Southampton	42	15	8	19	54	58	38
15	Hull	42	13	12	17	52	68	38
16	Fulham	42	15	7	20	48	67	37
17	Nottm Forest	42	13	9	20	73	74	35
18	Notts County	42	12	11	19	53	62	35
19	Swansea	42	10	15	17	51	60	35
20	Man United	42	14	6	22	59	85	34
21	Millwall	42	11	11	20	39	68	33
22	Lincoln	42	9	8	25	44	75	26

THIRD DIVISION (NORTH)

		P	W	D	L	F	A	Pts
1	Barnsley	42	27	8	7	118	61	62
2	Chesterfield	42	27	7	8	86	43	61
3	Stockport	42	24	11	7	115	52	59
4	Walsall	42	23	7	12	97	60	53
5	Doncaster	42	22	9	11	83	61	53
6	Wrexham	42	23	5	14	102	73	51
7	Tranmere	42	20	7	15	84	63	47
8	Barrow	42	19	9	14	116	94	47
9	Halifax	42	20	4	18	80	91	44
10	Chester	42	17	6	19	89	86	40
11	Hartlepools	42	16	7	19	89	93	39
12	York	42	15	8	19	71	74	38
13	Carlisle	42	15	8	19	66	81	38
14	Crewe	42	15	6	21	81	97	36
15	New Brighton	42	14	8	20	62	87	36
16	Darlington	42	13	9	20	70	101	35
17	Mansfield	42	11	12	19	81	88	34
18	Southport	42	8	17	17	63	90	33
19	Gateshead	42	12	9	21	76	110	33
20	Accrington	42	13	7	22	65	101	33
21	Rotherham	42	10	8	24	53	91	28
22	Rochdale	42	9	6	27	53	103	24

THIRD DIVISION (SOUTH)

		P	W	D	L	F	A	Pts
1	Norwich	42	25	11	6	88	49	61
2	Coventry	42	21	12	9	100	54	54
3	Reading	42	21	12	9	82	50	54
4	QPR	42	24	6	12	70	51	54
5	Charlton	42	22	8	12	83	56	52
6	Luton	42	21	10	11	83	61	52
7	Bristol Rovers	42	20	11	11	77	47	51
8	Swindon	42	17	11	14	64	68	45
9	Exeter	42	16	11	15	68	57	43
10	Brighton	42	15	13	14	68	60	43
11	Clapton Orient	42	16	10	16	75	69	42
12	Crystal Palace	42	16	9	17	71	67	41
13	Northampton	42	14	12	16	71	78	40
14	Aldershot	42	13	12	17	52	71	38
15	Watford	42	15	7	20	71	63	37
16	Southend	42	12	10	20	51	74	34
17	Gillingham	42	11	11	20	75	96	33
18	Newport	42	8	17	17	49	70	33
19	Bristol City	42	10	13	19	58	85	33
20	Torquay	42	13	7	22	53	93	33
21	Bournemouth	42	9	9	24	60	102	27
22	Cardiff	42	9	6	27	57	105	24

SCOTTISH FIRST DIVISION

		P	W	D	L	F	A	Pts
1	Rangers	38	30	6	2	118	41	66
2	Motherwell	38	29	4	5	97	45	62
3	Celtic	38	18	11	9	78	53	47
4	Queen of the S	38	21	3	14	75	78	45
5	Aberdeen	38	18	8	12	90	57	44
6	Hearts	38	17	10	11	86	59	44
7	Kilmarnock	38	17	9	12	73	64	43
8	Ayr	38	16	10	12	87	92	42
9	St Johnstone	38	17	6	15	74	53	40
10	Falkirk	38	16	6	16	73	68	38
11	Hamilton	38	15	8	15	65	79	38
12	Dundee	38	15	6	17	68	64	36
13	Partick	38	14	5	19	73	78	33
14	Clyde	38	10	11	17	56	70	31
15	Queen's Park	38	13	5	20	65	85	31
16	Hibernian	38	12	3	23	51	69	27
17	St Mirren	38	9	9	20	46	75	27
18	Airdrieonians	38	10	6	22	59	103	26
19	Third Lanark	38	8	9	21	62	103	25
20	Cowdenbeath	38	5	5	28	58	118	15

SCOTTISH SECOND DIVISION

		P	W	D	L	F	A	Pts
1	Albion	34	20	5	9	74	47	45
2	Dunfermline	34	20	4	10	90	52	44
3	Arbroath	34	20	4	10	83	53	44
4	Stenhousemuir	34	18	4	12	70	73	40
5	Morton	34	17	5	12	67	64	39
6	Dumbarton	34	17	3	14	67	68	37
7	King's Park	34	14	8	12	78	70	36
8	Raith	34	15	5	14	71	55	35
9	E Stirlingshire	34	14	7	13	65	74	35
10	St Bernard's	34	15	4	15	75	56	34
11	Forfar	34	13	7	14	77	71	33
12	Leith	34	12	8	14	63	60	32
13	East Fife	34	12	8	14	71	76	32
14	Brechin	34	13	5	16	60	70	31
15	Alloa	34	11	9	14	55	68	31
16	Montrose	34	11	4	19	53	81	26
17	Dundee United	34	10	4	20	81	88	24
18	Edinburgh City	34	4	6	24	37	111	14

The record number of goals scored by a conventional half-back in a Football League game is three. The record was set in 1926 by a Newcastle player, T McDonald, and equalled against Wolves on 21 April 1934 by another Newcastle player, W Imrie.

In June 1934, Stanley Rous was appointed secretary of the Football Association.

S Milton had surely one of the unhappiest Football League debuts on record. A goalkeeper, Milton was picked to play in that position for Halifax Town against Stockport County in a Third Division North League match on 6 January 1934. Milton was faced with a Stockport attack in fine fettle, and he had to retrieve the ball from his net 13 times, an unenviable record. The score—13-0—also set a record, for the highest score in a League match.

FA CUP 1933-34

FOURTH ROUND

Portsmouth v Grimsby Town	2-0
Bury v Swansea Town	1-1, 0-3
Liverpool v Tranmere Rovers	3-1
Brighton v Bolton Wanderers	1-1, 1-6
Workington v Preston North End	1-2
Huddersfield Town v Northampton Town	0-2
Birmingham v Charlton Athletic	1-0
Millwall v Leicester City	3-6
Aston Villa v Sunderland	7-2
Tottenham Hotspur v West Ham United	4-1
Derby County v Wolverhampton Wanderers	3-0
Arsenal v Crystal Palace	7-0
Stoke City v Blackpool	3-0
Chelsea v Nottingham Forest	1-1, 3-0
Oldham Athletic v Sheffield Wednesday	1-1, 1-6
Hull City v Manchester City	2-2, 1-4

FIFTH ROUND

Swansea Town v Portsmouth	0-1
Liverpool v Bolton Wanderers	0-3
Preston North End v Northampton Town	4-0
Birmingham v Leicester City	1-2
Tottenham Hotspur v Aston Villa	0-1
Arsenal v Derby County	1-0
Stoke City v Chelsea	3-1
Sheffield Wednesday v Manchester City	2-2, 0-2

SIXTH ROUND

Bolton Wanderers v Portsmouth	0-3
Preston North End v Leicester City	0-1
Arsenal v Aston Villa	1-2
Manchester City v Stoke City	1-0

SEMI-FINAL

Portsmouth v Leicester City	4-1
Manchester City v Aston Villa	6-1

FINAL

Manchester City v Portsmouth	2-1

SCOTTISH FA CUP 1933-34

SECOND ROUND

Third Lanark v Rangers	0-3
Queen's Park v Heart of Midlothian	1-2
Hibernian v Alloa Athletic	6-0
Aberdeen v Dundee	2-0
Vale of Leithen v St Johnstone	1-3
Cowdenbeath v St Bernard's	2-1
Brechin City v St Mirren	0-4
Ayr United v Celtic	2-3
Hamilton Academicals v Falkirk	2-4
Albion Rovers v Kilmarnock	2-1
Ross County v Galston	3-1
Partick Thistle v Motherwell	3-3, 1-2
East Stirlingshire v Arbroath	1-1, 3-0
Queen of the South	bye

THIRD ROUND

Rangers v Heart of Midlothian	0-0, 2-1
Hibernian v Aberdeen	0-1
Queen of the South v Cowdenbeath	3-0
Celtic v Falkirk	3-1
Albion Rovers v Ross County	6-1
Motherwell v East Stirlingshire	5-0
St Johnstone	bye
St Mirren	bye

FOURTH ROUND

Rangers v Aberdeen	1-0
St Johnstone v Queen of the South	2-0
St Mirren v Celtic	2-0
Albion Rovers v Motherwell	1-1, 0-6

SEMI-FINAL

Rangers v St Johnstone	1-0
St Mirren v Motherwell	3-1

FINAL

Rangers v St Mirren	5-0

League Tables 1934-35

FIRST DIVISION

	P	W	D	L	F	A	Pts
1 Arsenal	42	23	12	7	115	46	58
2 Sunderland	42	19	16	7	90	51	54
3 Sheff Wed	42	18	13	11	70	64	49
4 Man City	42	20	8	14	82	67	48
5 Grimsby	42	17	11	14	78	60	45
6 Derby	42	18	9	15	81	66	45
7 Liverpool	42	19	7	16	85	88	45
8 Everton	42	16	12	14	89	88	44
9 WBA	42	17	10	15	83	83	44
10 Stoke	42	18	6	18	71	70	42
11 Preston	42	15	12	15	62	67	42
12 Chelsea	42	16	9	17	73	82	41
13 Aston Villa	42	14	13	15	74	88	41
14 Portsmouth	42	15	10	17	71	72	40
15 Blackburn	42	14	11	17	66	78	39
16 Huddersfield	42	14	10	18	76	71	38
17 Wolves	42	15	8	19	88	94	38
18 Leeds	42	13	12	17	75	92	38
19 Birmingham	42	13	10	19	63	81	36
20 Middlesbrough	42	10	14	18	70	91	34
21 Leicester	42	12	9	21	61	86	33
22 Tottenham	42	10	10	22	54	93	30

SECOND DIVISION

	P	W	D	L	F	A	Pts
1 Brentford	42	26	9	7	93	48	61
2 Bolton	42	26	4	12	96	48	56
3 West Ham	42	26	4	12	80	63	56
4 Blackpool	42	21	11	10	79	57	53
5 Man United	42	23	4	15	76	55	50
6 Newcastle	42	22	4	16	89	68	48
7 Fulham	42	17	12	13	76	56	46
8 Plymouth	42	19	8	15	75	64	46
9 Nottm Forest	42	17	8	17	76	70	42
10 Bury	42	19	4	19	62	73	42
11 Sheff United	42	16	9	17	79	70	41
12 Burnley	42	16	9	17	63	73	41
13 Hull	42	16	8	18	63	74	40
14 Norwich	42	14	11	17	71	61	39
15 Bradford PA	42	11	16	15	55	63	38
16 Barnsley	42	13	12	17	60	83	38
17 Swansea	42	14	8	20	56	67	36
18 Port Vale	42	11	12	19	55	74	34
19 Southampton	42	11	12	19	46	75	34
20 Bradford City	42	12	8	22	50	68	32
21 Oldham	42	10	6	26	56	95	26
22 Notts County	42	9	7	26	46	97	25

THIRD DIVISION (SOUTH)

	P	W	D	L	F	A	Pts
1 Charlton	42	27	7	8	103	52	61
2 Reading	42	21	11	10	89	65	53
3 Coventry	42	21	9	12	86	50	51
4 Luton	42	19	12	11	92	60	50
5 Crystal Palace	42	19	10	13	86	64	48
6 Watford	42	19	9	14	76	49	47
7 Northampton	42	19	8	15	65	67	46
8 Bristol Rovers	42	17	10	15	73	77	44
9 Brighton	42	17	9	16	69	62	43
10 Torquay	42	18	6	18	81	75	42
11 Exeter	42	16	9	17	70	75	41
12 Millwall	42	17	7	18	57	62	41
13 QPR	42	16	9	17	63	72	41
14 Clapton Orient	42	15	10	17	65	65	40
15 Bristol City	42	15	9	18	52	68	39
16 Swindon	42	13	12	17	67	78	38
17 Bournemouth	42	15	7	20	54	71	37
18 Aldershot	42	13	10	19	50	75	36
19 Cardiff	42	13	9	20	62	82	35
20 Gillingham	42	11	13	18	55	75	35
21 Southend	42	11	9	22	65	78	31
22 Newport	42	10	5	27	54	112	25

THIRD DIVISION (NORTH)

	P	W	D	L	F	A	Pts
1 Doncaster	42	26	5	11	87	44	57
2 Halifax	42	25	5	12	76	67	55
3 Chester	42	20	14	8	91	58	54
4 Lincoln	42	22	7	13	87	58	51
5 Darlington	42	21	9	12	80	59	51
6 Tranmere	42	20	11	11	74	55	51
7 Stockport	42	22	3	17	90	72	47
8 Mansfield	42	19	9	14	75	62	47
9 Rotherham	42	19	7	16	86	73	45
10 Chesterfield	42	17	10	15	71	52	44
11 Wrexham	42	16	11	15	76	69	43
12 Hartlepools	42	17	7	18	80	78	41
13 Crewe	42	14	11	17	66	86	39
14 Walsall	42	13	10	19	81	72	36
15 York	42	15	6	21	76	82	36
16 New Brighton	42	14	8	20	59	76	36
17 Barrow	42	13	9	20	58	87	35
18 Accrington	42	12	10	20	63	89	34
19 Gateshead	42	13	8	21	58	96	34
20 Rochdale	42	11	11	20	53	71	33
21 Southport	42	10	12	20	55	85	32
22 Carlisle	42	8	7	27	51	102	23

SCOTTISH FIRST DIVISION

	P	W	D	L	F	A	Pts
1 Rangers	38	25	5	8	96	46	55
2 Celtic	38	24	4	10	92	45	52
3 Hearts	38	20	10	8	87	51	50
4 Hamilton	38	19	10	9	87	67	48
5 St Johnstone	38	18	10	10	66	46	46
6 Aberdeen	38	17	10	11	68	54	44
7 Motherwell	38	15	10	13	83	64	40
8 Dundee	38	16	8	14	63	63	40
9 Kilmarnock	38	16	6	16	76	68	38
10 Clyde	38	14	10	14	71	69	38
11 Hibernian	38	14	8	16	59	70	36
12 Queen's Park	38	13	10	15	61	80	36
13 Partick	38	15	5	18	61	68	35
14 Airdrieonians	38	13	7	18	64	72	33
15 Dunfermline	38	13	5	20	56	96	31
16 Albion	38	10	9	19	62	77	29
17 Queen of the S	38	11	7	20	52	72	29
18 Ayr	38	12	5	21	61	112	29
19 St Mirren	38	11	5	22	49	70	27
20 Falkirk	38	9	6	23	58	82	24

The famous occasion when a player headed a goal from a penalty-kick took place on 5 January 1935. Anfield was the setting for a North-South clash between Liverpool and Arsenal. In the course of the game, Arsenal were awarded a penalty which their full-back, Eddie Hapgood, elected to take. Liverpool's goalkeeper, Riley, fisted Hapgood's spot-kick back out, and Hapgood headed home the rebound. Arsenal won the match 2-0.

SCOTTISH SECOND DIVISION

	P	W	D	L	F	A	Pts
1 Third Lanark	34	23	6	5	94	43	52
2 Arbroath	34	23	4	7	78	42	50
3 St Bernard's	34	20	7	7	103	47	47
4 Dundee United	34	18	6	10	105	65	42
5 Stenhousemuir	34	17	5	12	86	80	39
6 Morton	34	17	4	13	88	64	38
7 King's Park	34	18	2	14	86	71	38
8 Leith	34	16	5	13	69	71	37
9 East Fife	34	16	3	15	79	73	35
10 Alloa	34	12	10	12	68	61	34
11 Forfar	34	13	8	13	77	73	34
12 Cowdenbeath	34	13	6	15	84	75	32
13 Raith	34	13	3	18	68	73	29
14 E Stirlingshire	34	11	7	16	57	76	29
15 Brechin	34	10	6	18	51	98	26
16 Dumbarton	34	9	4	21	60	105	22
17 Montrose	34	7	6	21	58	105	20
18 Edinburgh City	34	3	2	29	45	134	8

The record gate for an English League match was broken on 23 February 1935, when 77,582 people paid to see Manchester City play Arsenal at Maine Road, Manchester. Season-ticket holders brought the total number of spectators present to 80,000.

S Raleigh, Gillingham's centre-forward, died from concussion sustained in a match with Brighton, 1 December 1934.

FA CUP 1934-35

FOURTH ROUND

Wolverhampton Wanderers v Sheffield Wednesday 1-2
Norwich City v Leeds United 3-3, 2-1
Reading v Millwall 1-0
Leicester City v Arsenal 0-1
Southampton v Birmingham 0-3
Blackburn Rovers v Liverpool 1-0
Nottingham Forest v Manchester United 0-0, 3-0
Burnley v Luton Town 3-1
Plymouth Argyle v Bolton Wanderers 1-4
Tottenham Hotspur v Newcastle United 2-0
Derby County v Swansea Town 3-0
Sunderland v Everton 1-1, 4-6
Swindon Town v Preston North End 0-2
Portsmouth v Bristol City 0-0, 0-2
Bradford City v Stockport County 0-0, 2-3
West Bromwich Albion v Sheffield United 7-1

FIFTH ROUND

Norwich City v Sheffield Wednesday 0-1
Reading v Arsenal 0-1
Blackburn Rovers v Birmingham 1-2
Nottingham Forest v Burnley 0-0, 0-3
Tottenham Hotspur v Bolton Wanderers 1-1, 1-1, 0-2
Everton v Derby County 3-1
Bristol City v Preston North End 0-0, 0-5
Stockport County v West Bromwich Albion 0-5

SIXTH ROUND

Sheffield Wednesday v Arsenal 2-1
Burnley v Birmingham 3-2
Everton v Bolton Wanderers 1-2
West Bromwich Albion v Preston North End 1-0

SEMI-FINAL

Sheffield Wednesday v Burnley 3-0
Bolton Wanderers v West Bromwich Albion 1-1, 0-2

FINAL

Sheffield Wednesday v West Bromwich Albion 4-2

SCOTTISH FA CUP 1934-35

SECOND ROUND

Motherwell v Morton 7-1
Rangers v Third Lanark 2-0
St Mirren v Forfar Athletic 3-0
Airdrieonians v Rosyth Dockyard 1-0
Ayr United v King's Park 1-1, 2-2, 4-4, 1-2
Heart of Midlothian v Kilmarnock 2-0
Dundee United v Queen's Park 6-3
Aberdeen v Albion Rovers 4-0
Hibernian v Clachnacuddin 7-1
Celtic v Partick Thistle 1-1, 3-1
Brechin City v Raith Rovers 1-1, 4-2
Clyde v Hamilton Academicals 3-3, 3-6
St Johnstone v Dumbarton 4-0
Buckie Thistle bye

THIRD ROUND

Rangers v St Mirren 1-0
Airdrieonians v King's Park 6-2
Heart of Midlothian v Dundee United 2-2, 4-2
Aberdeen v Hibernian 0-0, 1-1, 3-2
Brechin City v Hamilton Academicals 2-4
Buckie Thistle v St Johnstone 0-1
Motherwell bye
Celtic bye

FOURTH ROUND

Motherwell v Rangers 1-4
Airdrieonians v Heart of Midlothian 2-3
Aberdeen v Celtic 3-1
Hamilton Academicals v St Johnstone 3-0

SEMI-FINAL

Rangers v Heart of Midlothian 1-1, 2-0
Aberdeen v Hamilton Academicals 1-2

FINAL

Rangers v Hamilton Academicals 2-1

League Tables 1935-36

FIRST DIVISION

		P	W	D	L	F	A	Pts
1	Sunderland	42	25	6	11	109	74	56
2	Derby	42	18	12	12	61	52	48
3	Huddersfield	42	18	12	12	59	56	48
4	Stoke	42	20	7	15	57	57	47
5	Brentford	42	17	12	13	81	60	46
6	Arsenal	42	15	15	12	78	48	45
7	Preston	42	18	8	16	67	64	44
8	Chelsea	42	15	13	14	65	72	43
9	Man City	42	17	8	17	68	60	42
10	Portsmouth	42	17	8	17	54	67	42
11	Leeds	42	15	11	16	66	64	41
12	Birmingham	42	15	11	16	61	63	41
13	Bolton	42	14	13	15	67	76	41
14	Middlesbrough	42	15	10	17	84	70	40
15	Wolves	42	15	10	17	77	76	40
16	Everton	42	13	13	16	89	89	39
17	Grimsby	42	17	5	20	65	73	39
18	WBA	42	16	6	20	89	88	38
19	Liverpool	42	13	12	17	60	64	38
20	Sheff Wed	42	13	12	17	63	77	38
21	Aston Villa	42	13	9	20	81	110	35
22	Blackburn	42	12	9	21	55	96	33

SECOND DIVISION

		P	W	D	L	F	A	Pts
1	Man United	42	22	12	8	85	43	56
2	Charlton	42	22	11	9	85	58	55
3	Sheff United	42	20	12	10	79	50	52
4	West Ham	42	22	8	12	90	68	52
5	Tottenham	42	18	13	11	91	55	49
6	Leicester	42	19	10	13	79	57	48
7	Plymouth	42	20	8	14	71	57	48
8	Newcastle	42	20	6	16	88	79	46
9	Fulham	42	15	14	13	76	52	44
10	Blackpool	42	18	7	17	93	72	43
11	Norwich	42	17	9	16	72	65	43
12	Bradford City	42	15	13	14	55	65	43
13	Swansea	42	15	9	18	67	76	39
14	Bury	42	13	12	17	66	84	38
15	Burnley	42	12	13	17	50	59	37
16	Bradford PA	42	14	9	19	62	84	37
17	Southampton	42	14	9	19	47	65	37
18	Doncaster	42	14	9	19	51	71	37
19	Nottm Forest	42	12	11	19	69	76	35
20	Barnsley	42	12	9	21	54	80	33
21	Port Vale	42	12	8	22	56	106	32
22	Hull	42	5	10	27	47	111	20

THIRD DIVISION (SOUTH)

		P	W	D	L	F	A	Pts
1	Coventry	42	24	9	9	102	45	57
2	Luton	42	22	12	8	81	45	56
3	Reading	42	26	2	14	87	62	54
4	QPR	42	22	9	11	84	53	53
5	Watford	42	20	9	13	80	54	49
6	Crystal Palace	42	22	5	15	96	74	49
7	Brighton	42	18	8	16	70	63	44
8	Bournemouth	42	16	11	15	60	56	43
9	Notts County	42	15	12	15	60	57	42
10	Torquay	42	16	9	17	62	62	41
11	Aldershot	42	14	12	16	53	61	40
12	Millwall	42	14	12	16	58	71	40
13	Bristol City	42	15	10	17	48	59	40
14	Clapton Orient	42	16	6	20	55	61	38
15	Northampton	42	15	8	19	62	90	38
16	Gillingham	42	14	9	19	66	77	37
17	Bristol Rovers	42	14	9	19	69	95	37
18	Southend	42	13	10	19	61	62	36
19	Swindon	42	14	8	20	64	73	36
20	Cardiff	42	13	10	19	60	73	36
21	Newport	42	11	9	22	60	111	31
22	Exeter	42	8	11	23	59	93	27

THIRD DIVISION (NORTH)

		P	W	D	L	F	A	Pts
1	Chesterfield	42	24	12	6	92	39	60
2	Chester	42	22	11	9	100	45	55
3	Tranmere	42	22	11	9	93	58	55
4	Lincoln	42	22	10	8	91	51	53
5	Stockport	42	20	8	14	65	49	48
6	Crewe	42	19	9	14	80	76	47
7	Oldham	42	18	9	15	86	73	45
8	Hartlepools	42	15	12	15	57	61	42
9	Accrington	42	17	8	17	63	72	42
10	Walsall	42	16	9	17	79	59	41
11	Rotherham	42	16	9	17	69	66	41
12	Darlington	42	17	6	19	74	79	40
13	Carlisle	42	14	12	16	56	62	40
14	Gateshead	42	13	14	15	56	76	40
15	Barrow	42	13	12	17	58	65	38
16	York	42	13	12	17	62	95	38
17	Halifax	42	15	7	20	57	61	37
18	Wrexham	42	15	7	20	66	75	37
19	Mansfield	42	14	9	19	80	91	37
20	Rochdale	42	10	13	19	58	88	33
21	Southport	42	11	9	22	48	90	31
22	New Brighton	42	9	6	27	43	102	24

SCOTTISH FIRST DIVISION

		P	W	D	L	F	A	Pts
1	Celtic	38	32	2	4	115	33	66
2	Rangers	38	27	7	4	110	43	61
3	Aberdeen	38	26	9	3	96	50	61
4	Motherwell	38	18	12	8	77	58	48
5	Hearts	38	20	7	11	88	55	47
6	Hamilton	38	15	7	16	77	74	37
7	St Johnstone	38	15	7	16	70	81	37
8	Kilmarnock	38	14	7	17	69	64	35
9	Partick	38	12	10	16	64	72	34
10	Dunfermline	38	13	8	17	73	92	34
11	Third Lanark	38	14	5	19	63	71	33
12	Arbroath	38	11	11	16	46	69	33
13	Dundee	38	11	10	17	67	80	32
14	Queen's Park	38	11	10	17	58	75	32
15	Queen of the S	38	11	9	18	54	72	31
16	Albion	38	13	4	21	69	92	30
17	Hibernian	38	11	7	20	56	82	29
18	Clyde	38	10	8	20	63	84	28
19	Airdrieonians	38	9	9	20	68	91	27
20	Ayr	38	11	3	24	53	98	25

SCOTTISH SECOND DIVISION

		P	W	D	L	F	A	Pts
1	Falkirk	34	28	3	3	132	34	59
2	St Mirren	34	25	2	7	114	41	52
3	Morton	34	21	6	7	117	60	48
4	Alloa	34	19	6	9	65	51	44
5	St Bernard's	34	18	4	12	106	78	40
6	East Fife	34	16	6	12	86	79	38
7	Dundee United	34	16	5	13	108	81	37
8	E Stirlingshire	34	13	8	13	70	75	34
9	Leith	34	15	3	16	67	77	33
10	Cowdenbeath	34	13	5	16	76	77	31
11	Stenhousemuir	34	13	3	18	59	78	29
12	Montrose	34	13	3	18	58	82	29
13	Forfar	34	10	7	17	60	81	27
14	King's Park	34	11	5	18	55	109	27
15	Edinburgh City	34	8	9	17	57	83	25
16	Brechin	34	8	6	20	57	96	22
17	Raith	34	9	3	22	60	96	21
18	Dumbarton	34	5	6	23	52	121	16

The loneliness of long-distance football

On Good Friday, 10 April 1936, Swansea Town defeated Plymouth by two goals to one in a Second Division match at Home Park, Plymouth. The following day, Swansea met Newcastle at St James' Park, Newcastle, losing 2-0. Between the two games, Swansea travelled 400 miles, a record distance for a League club to travel between games played on consecutive days.

Footballing fatality

James Thorpe, Sunderland's goalkeeper, died a few days after his team had met Chelsea on 1 February 1936. His death was due to diabetes, but a coroner's jury found that the illness had been accelerated by rough usage of the goalkeeper. They criticized the referee (who was not called as a witness), and urged all referees to exercize stricter control. An FA commission later exonerated the referee, adding that he had acted totally in accordance with his instructions.

FA CUP 1935-36

FOURTH ROUND

Liverpool v Arsenal	0-2
Sheffield Wednesday v Newcastle United	1-1, 1-3
Tranmere Rovers v Barnsley	2-4
Stoke City v Manchester United	0-0, 2-0
Port Vale v Grimsby Town	0-4
Manchester City v Luton Town	2-1
Middlesbrough v Clapton Orient	3-0
Leicester City v Watford	6-3
Fulham v Blackpool	5-2
Chelsea v Plymouth Argyle	4-1
Bradford City v Blackburn Rovers	3-1
Derby County v Nottingham Forest	2-0
Preston North End v Sheffield United	0-0, 0-2
Leeds United v Bury	2-1*, 3-2
Tottenham Hotspur v Huddersfield Town	1-0
Bradford Park Avenue v West Bromwich Albion	1-1, 1-1, 2-0

*abandoned

FIFTH ROUND

Newcastle United v Arsenal	3-3, 0-3
Barnsley v Stoke City	2-1
Grimsby Town v Manchester City	3-2
Middlesbrough v Leicester City	2-1
Chelsea v Fulham	0-0, 2-3
Bradford City v Derby County	0-1
Sheffield United v Leeds United	3-1
Bradford Park Avenue v Tottenham Hotspur	0-0, 1-2

SIXTH ROUND

Arsenal v Barnsley	4-1
Grimsby Town v Middlesbrough	3-1
Fulham v Derby County	3-0
Sheffield United v Tottenham Hotspur	3-1

SEMI-FINAL

Arsenal v Grimsby Town	1-0
Fulham v Sheffield United	1-2

FINAL

Arsenal v Sheffield United	1-0

SCOTTISH FA CUP 1935-36

SECOND ROUND

Aberdeen v King's Park	6-0
Celtic v St Johnstone	1-2
Dalbeattie Star v St Mirren	0-1
Albion Rovers v Rangers	1-3
Clyde v Hibernian	4-1
Dundee v Airdrieonians	2-1
Cowdenbeath v Dundee United	5-3
Motherwell v St Bernard's	3-0
Falkirk v Kilmarnock	1-1, 3-1
Dunfermline Athletic v Galston	5-2
Morton v Stenhousemuir	3-0
Elgin City v Queen of the South	0-3
Third Lanark v Leith Athletic	2-0
Dumbarton	bye

THIRD ROUND

Aberdeen v St Johnstone	1-1, 1-0
St Mirren v Rangers	1-2
Clyde v Dundee	1-1, 3-0
Cowdenbeath v Motherwell	1-3
Morton v Queen of the South	2-0
Third Lanark v Dumbarton	8-0
Falkirk	bye
Dunfermline Athletic	bye

FOURTH ROUND

Aberdeen v Rangers	0-1
Clyde v Motherwell	3-2
Falkirk v Dunfermline Athletic	5-0
Morton v Third Lanark	3-5

SEMI-FINAL

Rangers v Clyde	3-0
Falkirk v Third Lanark	1-3

FINAL

Rangers v Third Lanark	1-0

League Tables 1936-37

FIRST DIVISION

		P	W	D	L	F	A	Pts
1	Man City	42	22	13	7	107	61	57
2	Charlton	42	21	12	9	58	49	54
3	Arsenal	42	18	16	8	80	49	52
4	Derby	42	21	7	14	96	90	49
5	Wolves	42	21	5	16	84	67	47
6	Brentford	42	18	10	14	82	78	46
7	Middlesbrough	42	19	8	15	74	71	46
8	Sunderland	42	19	6	17	89	87	44
9	Portsmouth	42	17	10	15	62	66	44
10	Stoke	42	15	12	15	72	57	42
11	Birmingham	42	13	15	14	64	60	41
12	Grimsby	42	17	7	18	86	81	41
13	Chelsea	42	14	13	15	52	55	41
14	Preston	42	14	13	15	56	67	41
15	Huddersfield	42	12	15	15	62	64	39
16	WBA	42	16	6	20	77	98	38
17	Everton	42	14	9	19	81	78	37
18	Liverpool	42	12	11	19	62	84	35
19	Leeds	42	15	4	23	60	80	34
20	Bolton	42	10	14	18	43	66	34
21	Man United	42	10	12	20	55	78	32
22	Sheff Wed	42	9	12	21	53	69	30

SECOND DIVISION

		P	W	D	L	F	A	Pts
1	Leicester	42	24	8	10	89	57	56
2	Blackpool	42	24	7	11	88	53	55
3	Bury	42	22	8	12	74	55	52
4	Newcastle	42	22	5	15	80	56	49
5	Plymouth	42	18	13	11	71	53	49
6	West Ham	42	19	11	12	73	55	49
7	Sheff United	42	18	10	14	66	54	46
8	Coventry	42	17	11	14	66	54	45
9	Aston Villa	42	16	12	14	82	70	44
10	Tottenham	42	17	9	16	88	66	43
11	Fulham	42	15	13	14	71	61	43
12	Blackburn	42	16	10	16	70	62	42
13	Burnley	42	16	10	16	57	61	42
14	Barnsley	42	16	9	17	50	64	41
15	Chesterfield	42	16	8	18	84	89	40
16	Swansea	42	15	7	20	50	65	37
17	Norwich	42	14	8	20	63	71	36
18	Nottm Forest	42	12	10	20	68	90	34
19	Southampton	42	11	12	19	53	77	34
20	Bradford PA	42	12	9	21	52	88	33
21	Bradford City	42	9	12	21	54	94	30
22	Doncaster	42	7	10	25	30	84	24

THIRD DIVISION (NORTH)

		P	W	D	L	F	A	Pts
1	Stockport	42	23	14	5	84	39	60
2	Lincoln	42	25	7	10	103	57	57
3	Chester	42	22	9	11	87	57	53
4	Oldham	42	20	11	11	77	59	51
5	Hull	42	17	12	13	68	69	46
6	Hartlepools	42	19	7	16	75	69	45
7	Halifax	42	18	9	15	68	63	45
8	Wrexham	42	16	12	14	71	57	44
9	Mansfield	42	18	8	16	91	76	44
10	Carlisle	42	18	8	16	65	68	44
11	Port Vale	42	17	10	15	58	64	44
12	York	42	16	11	15	79	70	43
13	Accrington	42	16	9	17	76	69	41
14	Southport	42	12	13	17	73	87	37
15	New Brighton	42	13	11	18	55	70	37
16	Barrow	42	13	10	19	70	86	36
17	Rotherham	42	14	7	21	78	91	35
18	Rochdale	42	13	9	20	69	86	35
19	Tranmere	42	12	9	21	71	88	33
20	Crewe	42	10	12	20	55	83	32
21	Gateshead	42	11	10	21	63	98	32
22	Darlington	42	8	14	20	66	96	30

THIRD DIVISION (SOUTH)

		P	W	D	L	F	A	Pts
1	Luton	42	27	4	11	103	53	58
2	Notts County	42	23	10	9	74	52	56
3	Brighton	42	24	5	13	74	43	53
4	Watford	42	19	11	12	85	60	49
5	Reading	42	19	11	12	76	60	49
6	Bournemouth	42	20	9	13	65	59	49
7	Northampton	42	20	6	16	85	68	46
8	Millwall	42	18	10	14	64	54	46
9	QPR	42	18	9	15	73	52	45
10	Southend	42	17	11	14	78	67	45
11	Gillingham	42	18	8	16	52	66	44
12	Clapton Orient	42	14	15	13	52	52	43
13	Swindon	42	14	11	17	75	73	39
14	Crystal Palace	42	13	12	17	62	61	38
15	Bristol Rovers	42	16	4	22	71	80	36
16	Bristol City	42	15	6	21	58	70	36
17	Walsall	42	13	10	19	62	84	36
18	Cardiff	42	14	7	21	54	87	35
19	Newport	42	12	10	20	67	98	34
20	Torquay	42	11	10	21	57	80	32
21	Exeter	42	10	12	20	59	88	32
22	Aldershot	42	7	9	26	50	89	23

SCOTTISH FIRST DIVISION

		P	W	D	L	F	A	Pts
1	Rangers	38	26	9	3	88	32	61
2	Aberdeen	38	23	8	7	89	44	54
3	Celtic	38	22	8	8	89	58	52
4	Motherwell	38	22	7	9	96	54	51
5	Hearts	38	24	3	11	99	60	51
6	Third Lanark	38	20	6	12	79	61	46
7	Falkirk	38	19	6	13	98	66	44
8	Hamilton	38	18	5	15	91	96	41
9	Dundee	38	12	15	11	58	69	39
10	Clyde	38	16	6	16	59	70	38
11	Kilmarnock	38	14	9	15	60	70	37
12	St Johnstone	38	14	8	16	74	68	36
13	Partick	38	11	12	15	73	68	34
14	Arbroath	38	13	5	20	57	84	31
15	Queen's Park	38	9	12	17	51	77	30
16	St Mirren	38	11	7	20	68	81	29
17	Hibernian	38	6	13	19	54	83	25
18	Queen of the S	38	8	8	22	49	95	24
19	Dunfermline	38	5	11	22	65	98	21
20	Albion	38	5	6	27	53	116	16

SCOTTISH SECOND DIVISION

		P	W	D	L	F	A	Pts
1	Ayr	34	25	4	5	122	49	54
2	Morton	34	23	5	6	110	42	51
3	St Bernard's	34	22	4	8	102	51	48
4	Airdrieonians	34	18	8	8	85	60	44
5	East Fife	34	15	8	11	76	51	38
6	Cowdenbeath	34	14	10	10	75	59	38
7	E Stirlingshire	34	18	2	14	81	78	38
8	Raith	34	16	4	14	72	66	36
9	Alloa	34	13	7	14	64	65	33
10	Stenhousemuir	34	14	4	16	82	86	32
11	Leith	34	13	5	16	62	65	31
12	Forfar	34	11	8	15	73	89	30
13	Montrose	34	11	6	17	65	100	28
14	Dundee United	34	9	9	16	72	97	27
15	Dumbarton	34	11	5	18	57	83	27
16	Brechin	34	8	9	17	64	98	25
17	King's Park	34	11	3	20	61	106	25
18	Edinburgh City	34	2	3	29	42	120	7

Ted Harston of Mansfield Town set a record for goals scored in a season in Division Three North. In the 41 games he played during the season, Harston found the net 55 times.

On 30 January 1937, there was not one away win in all the 35 FA Cup and League matches played.

On 17 April 1937, 149,547 people watched Scotland beat England 3-1 at Hampden Park in the last match of the Home Championship. This was both a British and a world record attendance. The receipts totalled £24,303. Seven days later, at the same ground, 144,303 people paid £11,000 to watch Celtic triumph 2-1 over Aberdeen in the Scottish Cup final. Both the attendance and the receipts broke all previous records for the Scottish Cup final.

FA CUP 1936-37

FOURTH ROUND

Luton Town v Sunderland	2-2, 1-3
Swansea Town v York City	0-0, 3-1
Grimsby Town v Walsall	5-1
Wolverhampton Wanderers v Sheffield United	2-2, 2-1
Millwall v Chelsea	3-0
Derby County v Brentford	3-0
Bolton Wanderers v Norwich City	1-1, 2-1
Manchester City v Accrington Stanley	2-0
Tottenham Hotspur v Plymouth Argyle	1-0
Everton v Sheffield Wednesday	3-0
Preston North End v Stoke City	5-1
Exeter City v Leicester City	3-1
Coventry City v Chester	2-0
West Bromwich Albion v Darlington	3-2
Burnley v Bury	4-1
Arsenal v Manchester United	5-0

FIFTH ROUND

Sunderland v Swansea Town	3-0
Grimsby Town v Wolverhampton Wanderers	1-1, 2-6
Millwall v Derby County	2-1
Bolton Wanderers v Manchester City	0-5
Everton v Tottenham Hotspur	1-1, 3-4
Preston North End v Exeter City	5-3
Coventry City v West Bromwich Albion	2-3
Burnley v Arsenal	1-7

SIXTH ROUND

Wolverhampton Wanderers v Sunderland	1-1, 2-2, 0-4
Millwall v Manchester City	2-0
Tottenham Hotspur v Preston North End	1-3
West Bromwich Albion v Arsenal	3-1

SEMI-FINAL

Sunderland v Millwall	2-1
Preston North End v West Bromwich Albion	4-1

FINAL

Sunderland v Preston North End	3-1

SCOTTISH FA CUP 1936-37

SECOND ROUND

Inverness Caledonian v East Fife	1-6
Albion Rovers v Celtic	2-5
Duns v Dumbarton	2-0
Falkirk v Motherwell	0-3
St Mirren v Brechin City	1-0
Cowdenbeath v Solway Star	9-1
Clyde v St Johnstone	3-1
Dundee v Queen's Park	2-0
Hamilton Academicals v Hibernian	2-1
Heart of Midlothian v King's Park	15-0
Aberdeen v Third Lanark	4-2
Partick Thistle v Arbroath	4-1
Queen of the South v Airdrieonians	2-0
Morton	bye

THIRD ROUND

East Fife v Celtic	0-3
Duns v Motherwell	2-5
St Mirren v Cowdenbeath	1-0
Clyde v Dundee	0-0, 1-0
Hamilton Academicals v Heart of Midlothian	2-1
Morton v Partick Thistle	1-1, 2-1
Aberdeen	bye
Queen of the South	bye

FOURTH ROUND

Celtic v Motherwell	4-4, 2-1
St Mirren v Clyde	0-3
Hamilton Academicals v Aberdeen	1-2
Morton v Queen of the South	4-1

SEMI-FINAL

Celtic v Clyde	2-0
Aberdeen v Morton	2-0

FINAL

Celtic v Aberdeen	2-1

FIRST DIVISION

	P	W	D	L	F	A	Pts
1 Arsenal	42	21	10	11	77	44	52
2 Wolves	42	20	11	11	72	49	51
3 Preston	42	16	17	9	64	44	49
4 Charlton	42	16	14	12	65	51	46
5 Middlesbrough	42	19	8	15	72	65	46
6 Brentford	42	18	9	15	69	59	45
7 Bolton	42	15	15	12	64	60	45
8 Sunderland	42	14	16	12	55	57	44
9 Leeds	42	14	15	13	64	69	43
10 Chelsea	42	14	13	15	65	65	41
11 Liverpool	42	15	11	16	65	71	41
12 Blackpool	42	16	8	18	61	66	40
13 Derby	42	15	10	17	66	87	40
14 Everton	42	16	7	19	79	75	39
15 Huddersfield	42	17	5	20	55	68	39
16 Leicester	42	14	11	17	54	75	39
17 Stoke	42	13	12	17	58	59	38
18 Birmingham	42	10	18	14	58	62	38
19 Portsmouth	42	13	12	17	62	68	38
20 Grimsby	42	13	12	17	51	68	38
21 Man City	42	14	8	20	80	77	36
22 WBA	42	14	8	20	74	91	36

SECOND DIVISION

	P	W	D	L	F	A	Pts
1 Aston Villa	42	25	7	10	73	35	57
2 Man United	42	22	9	11	82	50	53
3 Sheff United	42	22	9	11	73	56	53
4 Coventry	42	20	12	10	66	45	52
5 Tottenham	42	19	6	17	76	54	44
6 Burnley	42	17	10	15	54	54	44
7 Bradford PA	42	17	9	16	69	56	43
8 Fulham	42	16	11	15	61	57	43
9 West Ham	42	14	14	14	53	52	42
10 Bury	42	18	5	19	63	60	41
11 Chesterfield	42	16	9	17	63	63	41
12 Luton	42	15	10	17	89	86	40
13 Plymouth	42	14	12	16	57	65	40
14 Norwich	42	14	11	17	56	75	39
15 Southampton	42	15	9	18	55	77	39
16 Blackburn	42	14	10	18	71	80	38
17 Sheff Wed	42	14	10	18	49	56	38
18 Swansea	42	13	12	17	45	73	38
19 Newcastle	42	14	8	20	51	58	36
20 Nottm Forest	42	14	8	20	47	60	36
21 Barnsley	42	11	14	17	50	64	36
22 Stockport	42	11	9	22	43	70	31

FA CUP 1937-38

FOURTH ROUND

Preston North End v Leicester City 2-0
Wolverhampton Wanderers v Arsenal 1-2
Barnsley v Manchester United 2-2, 0-1
Brentford v Portsmouth 2-1
Manchester City v Bury 3-1
Luton Town v Swindon Town 2-1
Charlton Athletic v Leeds United 2-1
Aston Villa v Blackpool 4-0
Everton v Sunderland 0-1
Bradford Park Avenue v Stoke City 1-1, 2-1
Chesterfield v Burnley 3-2
New Brighton v Tottenham Hotspur 0-0, 2-5
York City v West Bromwich Albion 3-2
Nottingham Forest v Middlesbrough 1-3
Sheffield United v Liverpool 1-1, 0-1
Huddersfield Town v Notts County 1-0

FIFTH ROUND

Arsenal v Preston North End 0-1
Brentford v Manchester United 2-0
Luton Town v Manchester City 1-3
Charlton Athletic v Aston Villa 1-1, 2-2, 1-4
Sunderland v Bradford Park Avenue 1-0
Chesterfield v Tottenham Hotspur 2-2, 1-2
York City v Middlesbrough 1-0
Liverpool v Huddersfield Town 0-1

SIXTH ROUND

Brentford v Preston North End 0-3
Aston Villa v Manchester City 3-2
Tottenham Hotspur v Sunderland 0-1
York City v Huddersfield Town 0-0, 1-2

SEMI-FINAL

Preston North End v Aston Villa 2-1
Sunderland v Huddersfield Town 1-3

FINAL

Preston North End v Huddersfield Town 1-0

THIRD DIVISION (NORTH)

	P	W	D	L	F	A	Pts
1 Tranmere	42	23	10	9	81	41	56
2 Doncaster	42	21	12	9	74	49	54
3 Hull	42	20	13	9	80	43	53
4 Oldham	42	19	13	10	67	46	51
5 Gateshead	42	20	11	11	84	59	51
6 Rotherham	42	20	10	12	68	56	50
7 Lincoln	42	19	8	15	66	50	46
8 Crewe	42	18	9	15	71	53	45
9 Chester	42	16	12	14	77	72	44
10 Wrexham	42	16	11	15	58	63	43
11 York	42	16	10	16	70	68	42
12 Carlisle	42	15	9	18	57	67	39
13 New Brighton	42	15	8	19	60	61	38
14 Bradford City	42	14	10	18	66	69	38
15 Port Vale	42	12	14	16	65	73	38
16 Southport	42	12	14	16	53	82	38
17 Rochdale	42	13	11	18	67	78	37
18 Halifax	42	12	12	18	44	66	36
19 Darlington	42	11	10	21	54	79	32
20 Hartlepools	42	10	12	20	53	80	32
21 Barrow	42	11	10	21	41	71	32
22 Accrington	42	11	7	24	45	75	29

THIRD DIVISION (SOUTH)

	P	W	D	L	F	A	Pts
1 Millwall	42	23	10	9	83	37	56
2 Bristol City	42	21	13	8	68	40	55
3 QPR	42	22	9	11	80	47	53
4 Watford	42	21	11	10	73	43	53
5 Brighton	42	21	9	12	64	44	51
6 Reading	42	20	11	11	71	63	51
7 Crystal Palace	42	18	12	12	67	47	48
8 Swindon	42	17	10	15	49	49	44
9 Northampton	42	17	9	16	51	57	43
10 Cardiff	42	15	12	15	67	54	42
11 Notts County	42	16	9	17	50	50	41
12 Southend	42	15	10	17	70	68	40
13 Bournemouth	42	14	12	16	56	57	40
14 Mansfield	42	15	9	18	62	67	39
15 Bristol Rovers	42	13	13	16	46	61	39
16 Newport	42	11	16	15	43	52	38
17 Exeter	42	13	12	17	57	70	38
18 Aldershot	42	15	5	22	39	59	35
19 Clapton Orient	42	13	7	22	42	61	33
20 Torquay	42	9	12	21	38	73	30
21 Walsall	42	11	7	24	52	88	29
22 Gillingham	42	10	6	26	36	77	26

SCOTTISH FA CUP 1937-38

SECOND ROUND

Rangers v Queen of the South 3-1
Falkirk v St Mirren 3-2
Ross County v Albion Rovers 2-5
Larbert Amateurs v Morton 2-3
Queen's Park v Ayr United 1-1, 1-2
Celtic v Nithsdale Wanderers 5-0
St Bernard's v King's Park 1-1, 4-3
Stenhousemuir v Motherwell 1-1, 1-6
Hamilton Academicals v Forfar Athletic 5-1
Raith Rovers v Edinburgh City 9-2
Partick Thistle v Cowdenbeath 1-0
Aberdeen v St Johnstone 5-1
East Fife v Dundee United 5-0
Kilmarnock bye

THIRD ROUND

Falkirk v Albion Rovers 4-0
Morton v Ayr United 1-1, 1-4
Celtic v Kilmarnock 1-2
Motherwell v Hamilton Academicals 2-0
Partick Thistle v Raith Rovers 1-2
East Fife v Aberdeen 1-1, 2-1
Rangers bye
St Bernard's bye

FOURTH ROUND

Falkirk v Rangers 1-2
Kilmarnock v Ayr United 1-1, 5-0
St Bernard's v Motherwell 3-1
East Fife v Raith Rovers 2-2, 3-2

SEMI-FINAL

Rangers v Kilmarnock 3-4
St Bernard's v East Fife 1-1, 1-1, 1-2

FINAL

Kilmarnock v East Fife 1-1, 2-4

SCOTTISH FIRST DIVISION

	P	W	D	L	F	A	Pts
1 Celtic	38	27	7	4	114	42	61
2 Hearts	38	26	6	6	90	50	58
3 Rangers	38	18	13	7	75	49	49
4 Falkirk	38	19	9	10	82	52	47
5 Motherwell	38	17	10	11	78	69	44
6 Aberdeen	38	15	9	14	74	59	39
7 Partick	38	15	9	14	68	70	39
8 St Johnstone	38	16	7	15	78	81	39
9 Third Lanark	38	11	13	14	68	73	35
10 Hibernian	38	11	13	14	57	65	35
11 Arbroath	38	11	13	14	58	79	35
12 Queen's Park	38	11	12	15	59	74	34
13 Hamilton	38	13	7	18	81	76	33
14 St Mirren	38	14	5	19	58	66	33
15 Clyde	38	10	13	15	68	78	33
16 Queen of the S	38	11	11	16	58	71	33
17 Ayr	38	9	15	14	66	85	33
18 Kilmarnock	38	12	9	17	65	91	33
19 Dundee	38	13	6	19	70	74	32
20 Morton	38	6	3	29	64	127	15

The only Second Division Scottish club to win the Scottish Cup is East Fife, who achieved this distinction in 1937-38. East Fife, who had two players on loan because of injuries to their regular players, took part in five replays during the course of the competition. This included the final, when after a 1-1 draw, East Fife disposed of Kilmarnock by four goals to two.

SCOTTISH SECOND DIVISION

	P	W	D	L	F	A	Pts
1 Raith	34	27	5	2	142	54	59
2 Albion	34	20	8	6	97	50	48
3 Airdrieonians	34	21	5	8	100	53	47
4 St Bernard's	34	20	5	9	75	49	45
5 East Fife	34	19	5	10	104	61	43
6 Cowdenbeath	34	17	9	8	115	71	43
7 Dumbarton	34	17	5	12	85	66	39
8 Stenhousemuir	34	17	5	12	87	78	39
9 Dunfermline	34	17	5	12	82	76	39
10 Leith	34	16	5	13	71	56	37
11 Alloa	34	11	4	19	78	106	26
12 King's Park	34	11	4	19	64	96	26
13 E Stirlingshire	34	9	7	18	55	95	25
14 Dundee United	34	9	5	20	69	104	23
15 Forfar	34	8	6	20	67	100	22
16 Montrose	34	7	8	19	56	88	22
17 Edinburgh City	34	7	3	24	77	135	17
18 Brechin	34	5	2	27	53	139	12

During the season, Jimmy Richardson, the Millwall inside-right, appeared in all three divisions of the Football League, playing with Huddersfield, Newcastle and Millwall.

Raith Rovers, with 142 goals from 34 games, amassed the highest aggregate of goals in a League season in British League football. On their way to this record, they set another, by losing only two of their League matches, the second fewest in any post-1919 division.

FIRST DIVISION

		P	W	D	L	F	A	Pts
1	Everton	42	27	5	10	88	52	59
2	Wolves	42	22	11	9	88	39	55
3	Charlton	42	22	6	14	75	59	50
4	Middlesbrough	42	20	9	13	93	74	49
5	Arsenal	42	19	9	14	55	41	47
6	Derby	42	19	8	15	66	55	46
7	Stoke	42	17	12	13	71	68	46
8	Bolton	42	15	15	12	67	58	45
9	Preston	42	16	12	14	63	59	44
10	Grimsby	42	16	11	15	61	69	43
11	Liverpool	42	14	14	14	62	63	42
12	Aston Villa	42	15	11	16	71	60	41
13	Leeds	42	16	9	17	59	67	41
14	Man United	42	11	16	15	57	65	38
15	Blackpool	42	12	14	16	56	68	38
16	Sunderland	42	13	12	17	54	67	38
17	Portsmouth	42	12	13	17	47	70	37
18	Brentford	42	14	8	20	53	74	36
19	Huddersfield	42	12	11	19	58	64	35
20	Chelsea	42	12	9	21	64	80	33
21	Birmingham	42	12	8	22	62	84	32
22	Leicester	42	9	11	22	48	82	29

SECOND DIVISION

		P	W	D	L	F	A	Pts
1	Blackburn	42	25	5	12	94	60	55
2	Sheff United	42	20	14	8	69	41	54
3	Sheff Wed	42	21	11	10	88	59	53
4	Coventry	42	21	8	13	62	45	50
5	Man City	42	21	7	14	96	72	49
6	Chesterfield	42	20	9	13	69	52	49
7	Luton	42	22	5	15	82	66	49
8	Tottenham	42	19	9	14	67	62	47
9	Newcastle	42	18	10	14	61	48	46
10	WBA	42	18	9	15	89	72	45
11	West Ham	42	17	10	15	70	52	44
12	Fulham	42	17	10	15	61	55	44
13	Millwall	42	14	14	14	64	53	42
14	Burnley	42	15	9	18	50	56	39
15	Plymouth	42	15	8	19	49	55	38
16	Bury	42	12	13	17	65	74	37
17	Bradford PA	42	12	11	19	61	82	35
18	Southampton	42	13	9	20	56	82	35
19	Swansea	42	11	12	19	50	83	34
20	Nottm Forest	42	10	11	21	49	82	31
21	Norwich	42	13	5	24	50	91	31
22	Tranmere	42	6	5	31	39	99	17

THIRD DIVISION (SOUTH)

		P	W	D	L	F	A	Pts
1	Newport	42	22	11	9	58	45	55
2	Crystal Palace	42	20	12	10	71	52	52
3	Brighton	42	19	11	12	68	49	49
4	Watford	42	17	12	13	62	51	46
5	Reading	42	16	14	12	69	59	46
6	QPR	42	15	14	13	68	49	44
7	Ipswich	42	16	12	14	62	52	44
8	Bristol City	42	16	12	14	61	63	44
9	Swindon	42	18	8	16	72	77	44
10	Aldershot	42	16	12	14	53	66	44
11	Notts County	42	17	9	16	59	54	43
12	Southend	42	16	9	17	61	64	41
13	Cardiff	42	15	11	16	61	65	41
14	Exeter	42	13	14	15	65	82	40
15	Bournemouth	42	13	13	16	52	58	39
16	Mansfield	42	12	15	15	44	62	39
17	Northampton	42	15	8	19	51	58	38
18	Port Vale	42	14	9	19	52	58	37
19	Torquay	42	14	9	19	54	70	37
20	Clapton Orient	42	11	13	18	53	55	35
21	Walsall	42	11	11	20	68	69	33
22	Bristol Rovers	42	10	13	19	55	61	33

THIRD DIVISION (NORTH)

		P	W	D	L	F	A	Pts
1	Barnsley	42	30	7	5	94	34	67
2	Doncaster	42	21	14	7	87	47	56
3	Bradford City	42	22	8	12	89	56	52
4	Southport	42	20	10	12	75	54	50
5	Oldham	42	22	5	15	76	59	49
6	Chester	42	20	9	13	88	70	49
7	Hull	42	18	10	14	83	74	46
8	Crewe	42	19	6	17	82	70	44
9	Stockport	42	17	9	16	91	77	43
10	Gateshead	42	14	14	14	74	67	42
11	Rotherham	42	17	8	17	64	64	42
12	Halifax	42	13	16	13	52	54	42
13	Barrow	42	16	9	17	66	65	41
14	Wrexham	42	17	7	18	66	79	41
15	Rochdale	42	15	9	18	92	82	39
16	New Brighton	42	15	9	18	68	73	39
17	Lincoln	42	12	9	21	66	92	33
18	Darlington	42	13	7	22	62	92	33
19	Carlisle	42	13	7	22	64	111	33
20	York	42	12	8	22	66	92	32
21	Hartlepools	42	12	7	23	55	94	31
22	Accrington	42	7	6	29	49	103	20

SCOTTISH FIRST DIVISION

		P	W	D	L	F	A	Pts
1	Rangers	38	25	9	4	112	55	59
2	Celtic	38	20	8	10	99	53	48
3	Aberdeen	38	20	6	12	91	61	46
4	Hearts	38	20	5	13	98	70	45
5	Falkirk	38	19	7	12	73	63	45
6	Queen of the S	38	17	9	12	69	64	43
7	Hamilton	38	18	5	15	67	71	41
8	St Johnstone	38	17	6	15	85	82	40
9	Clyde	38	17	5	16	78	70	39
10	Kilmarnock	38	15	9	14	73	86	39
11	Partick Thistle	38	17	4	17	74	87	38
12	Motherwell	38	16	5	17	82	86	37
13	Hibernian	38	14	7	17	68	69	35
14	Ayr	38	13	9	16	76	83	35
15	Third Lanark	38	12	8	18	80	96	32
16	Albion	38	12	6	20	65	90	30
17	Arbroath	38	11	8	19	54	75	30
18	St Mirren	38	11	7	20	57	80	29
19	Queen's Park	38	11	5	22	57	83	27
20	Raith	38	10	2	26	65	99	22

SCOTTISH SECOND DIVISION

		P	W	D	L	F	A	Pts
1	Cowdenbeath	34	28	4	2	120	45	60
2	Alloa	34	22	4	8	91	46	48
3	East Fife	34	21	6	7	99	61	48
4	Airdrieonians	34	21	5	8	85	57	47
5	Dunfermline	34	18	5	11	99	78	41
6	Dundee	34	15	7	12	99	63	37
7	St Bernard's	34	15	6	13	79	79	36
8	Stenhousemuir	34	15	5	14	74	69	35
9	Dundee United	34	15	3	16	78	69	33
10	Brechin	34	11	9	14	82	106	31
11	Dumbarton	34	9	12	13	68	76	30
12	Morton	34	11	6	17	74	88	28
13	King's Park	34	12	2	20	87	92	26
14	Montrose	34	10	5	19	82	96	25
15	Forfar	34	11	3	20	74	138	25
16	Leith	34	10	4	20	57	83	24
17	E Stirlingshire	34	9	4	21	89	130	22
18	Edinburgh	34	6	4	24	58	119	16

Dixie Dean goes West

On 25 January 1939, Dixie Dean, the most prolific goalscorer of the time, left Notts County and English football to join Sligo Rovers in Eire. In April of that year, he played centre-forward for Sligo in the FA of Ireland Cup final against Shelbourne. The game ended in a 1-1 draw, and Sligo lost the replay 1-0.

1938-39 was the last season when players went unidentified. In 1939-40, players wore numbers in League games for the first time.

In Division Two, Tranmere Rovers lost 31 of their 42 League games, a Division Two record. Wolves set a First Division record in 1938-39 by conceding only 39 goals in 42 games, a record under the new offside rule. Barnsley also set a record—in Division Three North—letting in only 34 goals in 42 games.

FA CUP 1938-39

FOURTH ROUND

Portsmouth v West Bromwich Albion 2-0
West Ham United v Tottenham Hotspur 3-3, 1-1, 2-1
Preston North End v Aston Villa 2-0
Cardiff City v Newcastle United 0-0, 1-4
Leeds United v Huddersfield Town 2-4
Notts County v Walsall 0-0, 0-4
Middlesbrough v Sunderland 0-2
Blackburn Rovers v Southend United 4-2
Wolverhampton Wanderers v Leicester City 5-1
Liverpool v Stockport County 5-1
Everton v Doncaster Rovers 8-0
Birmingham v Chelmsford City 6-0
Chelsea v Fulham 3-0
Sheffield Wednesday v Chester 1-1, 1-1, 2-0
Sheffield United v Manchester City 2-0
Millwall v Grimsby Town 2-2, 2-3

FIFTH ROUND

Portsmouth v West Ham United 2-0
Newcastle United v Preston North End 1-2
Huddersfield Town v Walsall 3-0
Sunderland v Blackburn Rovers 1-1, 0-0, 0-1
Wolverhampton Wanderers v Liverpool 4-1
Birmingham v Everton 2-2, 1-2
Chelsea v Sheffield Wednesday 1-1, 0-0, 3-1
Sheffield United v Grimsby Town 0-0, 0-1

SIXTH ROUND

Portsmouth v Preston North End 1-0
Huddersfield Town v Blackburn Rovers 1-1, 2-1
Wolverhampton Wanderers v Everton 2-0
Chelsea v Grimsby Town 0-1

SEMI-FINAL

Portsmouth v Huddersfield Town 2-1
Wolverhampton Wanderers v Grimsby Town 5-0

FINAL

Portsmouth v Wolverhampton Wanderers 4-1

SCOTTISH FA CUP 1938-39

SECOND ROUND

Dundee v Clyde 0-0, 0-1
Rangers v Hamilton Academicals 2-0
Blairgowrie v Buckie Thistle 3-3, 1-4
Third Lanark v Cowdenbeath 3-0
Dunfermline Athletic v Duns 2-0
Hibernian v Kilmarnock 3-1
Falkirk v Airdrieonians 7-0
Aberdeen v Queen's Park 5-1
Queen of the South v Babcock & Wilcox 5-0
Heart of Midlothian v Elgin City 14-1
Montrose v Celtic 1-7
Edinburgh City v St Mirren 1-3
Dundee United v Motherwell 1-5
Alloa Athletic bye

THIRD ROUND

Rangers v Clyde 1-4
Buckie Thistle v Third Lanark 0-6
Dunfermline Athletic v Alloa Athletic 1-1, 2-3
Falkirk v Aberdeen 2-3
Heart of Midlothian v Celtic 2-2, 1-2
Motherwell v St Mirren 4-2
Hibernian bye
Queen of the South bye

FOURTH ROUND

Clyde v Third Lanark 1-0
Hibernian v Alloa Athletic 3-1
Aberdeen v Queen of the South 2-0
Motherwell v Celtic 3-1

SEMI-FINAL

Clyde v Hibernian 1-0
Aberdeen v Motherwell 1-1, 1-3

FINAL

Clyde v Motherwell 4-0

FIRST DIVISION 1939-40

	P	W	D	L	F	A	Pts
Blackpool	3	3	0	0	5	2	6
Sheff United	3	2	1	0	3	1	5
Arsenal	3	2	1	0	8	4	5
Liverpool	3	2	0	1	6	3	4
Everton	3	1	2	0	5	4	4
Bolton	3	2	0	1	6	5	4
Charlton	3	2	0	1	3	4	4
Derby	3	2	0	1	3	3	4
Man United	3	1	1	1	5	3	3
Chelsea	3	1	1	1	4	4	3
Stoke	3	1	1	1	7	4	3
Brentford	3	1	1	1	3	3	3
Leeds	3	1	1	1	2	4	3
Grimsby	3	1	1	1	2	4	3
Sunderland	3	1	0	2	6	7	2
Aston Villa	3	1	0	2	3	3	2
Wolverhampton	3	0	2	1	3	4	2
Huddersfield	3	1	0	2	2	3	2
Preston	3	0	2	1	0	2	2
Portsmouth	3	1	0	2	3	5	2
Blackburn	3	0	1	2	3	5	1
Middlesbrough	3	0	1	2	3	8	1

SECOND DIVISION 1939-40

	P	W	D	L	F	A	Pts
Luton	3	2	1	0	7	1	5
Birmingham	3	2	1	0	5	1	5
West Ham	3	2	0	1	5	4	4
Coventry	3	1	2	0	8	6	4
Leicester	3	2	0	1	6	5	4
Nottm Forest	3	2	0	1	5	5	4
Plymouth	3	2	0	1	4	3	4
Tottenham	3	1	2	0	6	5	4
WBA	3	1	1	1	8	8	3
Bury	3	1	1	1	4	5	3
Newport	3	1	1	1	5	4	3
Millwall	3	1	1	1	5	4	3
Man City	3	1	1	1	6	5	3
Southampton	3	1	0	2	5	6	2
Swansea	3	1	0	2	5	11	2
Barnsley	3	1	0	2	7	8	2
Chesterfield	2	1	0	1	2	2	2
Newcastle	3	1	0	2	8	6	2
Sheff Wed	3	1	0	2	3	5	2
Bradford	3	0	1	2	2	7	1
Fulham	3	0	1	2	3	6	1
Burnley	2	0	1	1	1	3	1

THIRD DIVISION (NORTH) 1939-40

	P	W	D	L	F	A	Pts
Accrington	3	3	0	0	6	1	6
Halifax	3	2	1	0	6	1	5
Darlington	3	2	1	0	5	2	5
Chester	3	2	1	0	5	2	5
Rochdale	3	2	0	1	2	2	4
New Brighton	3	2	0	1	4	5	4
Tranmere	3	1	1	1	6	6	3
Rotherham	3	1	1	1	5	6	3
Wrexham	3	1	1	1	3	2	3
Lincoln	3	1	1	1	6	7	3
Crewe	2	1	1	0	3	0	3
Oldham	3	1	0	2	3	5	2
Doncaster	3	1	0	2	4	5	2
Gateshead	3	1	0	2	6	7	2
Southport	3	0	2	1	4	5	2
Hull	2	0	2	0	3	3	2
Hartlepools	3	0	2	1	1	4	2
Barrow	3	0	2	1	4	5	2
Carlisle	2	1	0	1	3	3	2
York	3	0	1	2	3	5	1
Bradford City	3	0	1	2	3	6	1
Stockport	2	0	0	2	0	5	0

THIRD DIVISION (SOUTH) 1939-40

	P	W	D	L	F	A	Pts
Reading	3	2	1	0	8	2	5
Exeter	3	2	1	0	5	3	5
Cardiff	3	2	0	1	5	5	4
Crystal Palace	3	2	0	1	8	9	4
Brighton	3	1	2	0	5	4	4
Ipswich	3	1	2	0	5	3	4
Notts County	2	2	0	0	6	3	4
Southend	3	1	1	1	3	3	3
Bristol City	3	1	1	1	5	5	3
Clapton Orient	3	0	3	0	3	3	3
Mansfield	3	1	1	1	8	8	3
Norwich	3	1	1	1	4	4	3
Torquay	3	0	3	0	4	4	3
Bournemouth	3	1	1	1	13	4	3
Walsall	3	1	1	1	3	3	3
Northampton	3	1	0	2	2	12	2
QPR	3	0	2	1	4	5	2
Watford	3	0	2	1	4	5	2
Bristol Rovers	3	0	1	2	2	7	1
Port Vale	2	0	1	1	0	1	1
Aldershot	3	0	1	2	3	4	1
Swindon	3	0	1	2	2	4	1

SCOTTISH DIVISION 'A' 1939-40

	P	W	D	L	F	A	Pts
Rangers	5	4	1	0	14	3	9
Falkirk	5	4	0	1	20	10	8
Aberdeen	5	3	0	2	9	9	6
Celtic	5	3	0	2	7	7	6
Hearts	5	2	2	1	13	9	6
Partick Thistle	5	2	2	1	7	7	6
Motherwell	5	2	1	2	14	12	5
Hamilton	5	2	1	1	7	11	5
Third Lanark	5	2	1	2	9	8	5
Queen of the S	5	2	1	2	10	9	5
Albion	5	2	1	2	12	7	5
St Mirren	5	1	3	1	8	8	5
Kilmarnock	5	2	1	2	10	9	5
Hibernian	5	2	0	3	11	13	4
Alloa	5	2	0	3	8	13	4
Arbroath	5	2	0	3	9	9	4
St Johnstone	5	2	0	3	7	8	4
Ayr	5	2	0	3	10	17	4
Clyde	5	1	0	4	10	14	2
Cowdenbeath	5	1	0	4	6	14	2

SCOTTISH DIVISION 'B' 1939-40

	P	W	D	L	F	A	Pts
Dundee	4	3	1	0	13	5	7
Dunfermline	4	2	2	0	10	5	6
King's Park	4	2	2	0	11	7	6
East Fife	4	2	1	1	12	6	5
Queen's Park	4	1	3	0	7	5	5
Stenhousemuir	4	2	1	1	6	5	5
Dundee United	4	2	1	1	8	7	5
Dumbarton	4	2	1	1	9	9	5
E Stirlingshire	4	1	2	1	7	7	4
St Bernard's	4	1	2	1	7	7	4
Airdrieonians	4	2	0	2	7	8	4
Edinburgh	4	1	1	2	9	8	3
Montrose	4	1	1	2	7	8	3
Raith	4	1	1	2	8	12	3
Morton	4	1	1	2	4	7	3
Leith	4	1	0	3	4	7	2
Brechin	4	0	2	2	3	8	2
Forfar	4	0	0	4	7	18	0

Above *When War broke out, the 1939-40 football season had hardly got under way. The tables above show the state of each division when the League programme was halted. Goal average has not been calculated, as at such an early stage in the season, the figures presented in these hitherto unpublished tables serve as a guide to each team's performance, rather than a means of listing the teams in order.*

The Englishman who played for Wales
Stanley Mortensen made his war-time international debut against his own country. At Wembley, on 25 September 1943, England played Wales. Mortensen was reserve for England, but when the injured Welsh left-half, Ivor Powell, was unable to resume after the interval, it was agreed by both sides that Mortensen should take Powell's place. The game ended in an 8-3 victory for England.

WINNERS 1939-40

League Cup West Ham United
Midland League Wolverhampton Wanderers
North East League Huddersfield Town
North West League Bury
South 'A' League Arsenal
South 'B' League Queen's Park Rangers
South 'C' League Tottenham Hotspur
South 'D' League Crystal Palace
West League Stoke City
South West League Plymouth Argyle
East Midland League Chesterfield
Scottish Emergency Cup Rangers
Scottish Regional League West & South Rangers
Scottish Regional League East & North Falkirk
Irish FA Cup Ballymena United
FA of Ireland Cup (Eire) Shamrock Rovers
League of Ireland (Eire) St James' Gate

WINNERS 1940-41

League Cup Preston North End
Football League South Watford
Northern Regional League Preston North End
Southern Regional League Crystal Palace
London Cup Reading
Lancashire Cup Manchester United
Midland Cup Leicester City
Combined Cities Cup Middlesbrough
Western Regional Cup Bristol City
Scottish Southern League Cup Rangers
Scottish Summer Cup Hibernian
Scottish Southern League Rangers
Irish FA Cup Belfast Celtic
FA of Ireland Cup (Eire) Cork United
League of Ireland (Eire) Cork United

WINNERS 1941-42

League Cup Wolverhampton Wanderers
League North Blackpool
League South Leicester City
London Cup Brentford
London League Arsenal
Scottish Southern League Cup Rangers
Scottish Summer Cup Rangers
Scottish Southern League Rangers
Scottish North Eastern League 1st series Rangers
Scottish North Eastern League 2nd series Aberdeen
Irish FA Cup Linfield
FA of Ireland Cup (Eire) Dundalk
League of Ireland (Eire) Cork United

WINNERS 1942-43

League North Cup Blackpool
League North Blackpool
League South Cup Arsenal
League South Arsenal
League West Cup Swansea Town
League West Lovells Athletic
Scottish Southern League Cup Rangers
Scottish Summer Cup St Mirren
Scottish Southern League Rangers
Scottish North Eastern League 1st series Aberdeen
Scottish North Eastern League 2nd series Aberdeen
Irish FA Cup Belfast Celtic
FA of Ireland Cup (Eire) Drumcondra
League of Ireland (Eire) Cork United

WINNERS 1943-44

League North Cup Aston Villa
League North Blackpool
League South Cup Charlton Athletic
League South Tottenham Hotspur
League West Cup Bath City
League West Lovells Athletic
Scottish Southern League Cup Hibernian
Scottish Summer Cup Motherwell
Scottish Southern League Rangers
Scottish North Eastern League 1st series Raith Rovers
Scottish North Eastern League 2nd series Aberdeen
Irish FA Cup Belfast Celtic
FA of Ireland Cup (Eire) Shamrock Rovers
League of Ireland (Eire) Shelbourne

WINNERS 1944-45

League North Cup Bolton Wanderers
League North Huddersfield Town
League South Cup Chelsea
League South Tottenham Hotspur
League West Cup Bath City
League West Cardiff City
Scottish Southern League Cup Rangers
Scottish Summer Cup Partick Thistle
Scottish Southern League Rangers
Scottish North Eastern League 1st series Dundee
Scottish North Eastern League 2nd series Aberdeen
Irish FA Cup Linfield
FA of Ireland Cup (Eire) Shamrock Rovers
League of Ireland (Eire) Cork United

WINNERS 1945-46

League North Sheffield United
League South Birmingham City
League Three North Cup Rotherham United
League Three North (West) Accrington Stanley
League Three North (East) Rotherham United
League Three South Cup Bournemouth
League Three South (North) Queen's Park Rangers
League Three South (South) Crystal Palace
Scottish Southern League 'A' Rangers
Scottish Southern League 'B' Dundee
Scottish Victory Cup Rangers
Irish FA Cup Linfield
FA of Ireland Cup (Eire) Drumcondra
League of Ireland (Eire) Cork United

SCOTTISH SOUTHERN LEAGUE CUP 1945-46 (LEAGUE CUP)

SECTION WINNERS

Division A	Division B
1 Heart of Midlothian	1 East Fife
2 Rangers	2 Ayr United
3 Aberdeen	3 Airdrieonians
4 Clyde	4 Dundee

QUARTER-FINAL

Aberdeen v Ayr United	2-0
Airdrieonians v Clyde	1-0
Heart of Midlothian v East Fife	3-0
Rangers v Dundee	3-1

SEMI-FINAL

Aberdeen v Airdrieonians	2-2, 5-3
Rangers v Hearts	2-1

FINAL

Aberdeen v Rangers	3-2

LEADING GOALSCORERS (ENGLAND) 1939-46

Albert Stubbins, Newcastle United	226
Jock Dodds, Blackpool	221
Tommy Lawton, Everton, Tranmere Rovers, Aldershot and Chelsea	212

FA CUP 1945-46

THIRD ROUND (two legs)

Stoke City v Burnley	3-1, 1-2
Huddersfield Town v Sheffield United	1-1, 0-2
Mansfield Town v Sheffield Wednesday	0-0, 0-5
Chesterfield v York City	1-1, 2-3
Bolton Wanderers v Blackburn Rovers	1-0, 3-1
Chester v Liverpool	0-2, 1-2
Wrexham v Blackpool	1-4, 1-4
Leeds United v Middlesbrough	4-4, 2-7
Accrington Stanley v Manchester United	2-2, 1-5
Preston North End v Everton	2-1, 2-2
Charlton Athletic v Fulham	3-1, 1-2
Lovells Athletic v Wolverhampton Wanderers	2-4, 1-8
Southampton v Newport County	4-3, 2-1
Queen's Park Rangers v Crystal Palace	0-0, 0-0*, 1-0
Bristol City v Swansea Town	5-1, 2-2
Tottenham Hotspur v Brentford	2-2, 0-2
Chelsea v Leicester City	1-1, 2-0
West Ham United v Arsenal	6-0, 0-1
Northampton Town v Millwall	2-2, 0-3
Coventry City v Aston Villa	2-1, 0-2
Norwich City v Brighton	1-2, 1-4
Aldershot v Plymouth Argyle	2-0, 1-0
Luton Town v Derby County	0-6, 0-3
Cardiff City v West Bromwich Albion	1-1, 0-4
Newcastle United v Barnsley	4-2, 0-3
Rotherham United v Gateshead	2-2, 2-0
Bradford Park Avenue v Port Vale	2-1, 1-1
Manchester City v Barrow	6-2, 2-2
Grimsby Town v Sunderland	1-3, 1-2
Bury v Rochdale	3-3, 4-2
Birmingham City v Portsmouth	1-0, 0-0
Nottingham Forest v Watford	1-1, 1-1*, 0-1

*abandoned

FOURTH ROUND (two legs)

Stoke City v Sheffield United	2-0, 2-3
Sheffield Wednesday v York City	5-1, 6-1
Bolton Wanderers v Liverpool	5-0, 0-2
Blackpool v Middlesbrough	3-2, 2-3, 0-1
Manchester United v Preston North End	1-0, 1-3
Charlton Athletic v Wolverhampton Wanderers	5-2, 1-1
Southampton v Queen's Park Rangers	0-1, 3-4
Bristol City v Brentford	2-1, 0-5
Chelsea v West Ham United	2-0, 0-1
Millwall v Aston Villa	2-4, 1-9
Brighton v Aldershot	3-0, 4-1
Derby County v West Bromwich Albion	1-0, 3-1
Barnsley v Rotherham United	3-0, 1-2
Bradford Park Avenue v Manchester City	1-3, 8-2
Sunderland v Bury	3-1, 4-5
Birmingham City v Watford	5-0, 1-1

FIFTH ROUND (two legs)

Stoke City v Sheffield Wednesday	2-0, 0-0
Bolton Wanderers v Middlesbrough	1-0, 1-1
Preston North End v Charlton Athletic	1-1, 0-6
Queen's Park Rangers v Brentford	1-3, 0-0
Chelsea v Aston Villa	0-1, 0-1
Brighton v Derby County	1-4, 0-6
Barnsley v Bradford Park Avenue	0-1, 1-1
Sunderland v Birmingham City	1-0, 1-3

SIXTH ROUND (two legs)

Stoke City v Bolton Wanderers	0-2, 0-0
Charlton Athletic v Brentford	6-3, 3-1
Aston Villa v Derby County	3-4, 1-1
Bradford Park Avenue v Birmingham City	2-2, 0-6

SEMI-FINAL

Bolton Wanderers v Charlton Athletic	0-2
Derby County v Birmingham City	1-1, 4-0

FINAL

Derby County v Charlton Athletic	4-1

TOPIX

TOPIX

Top *In 1945 Jack Tinn, manager of Portsmouth, proudly shows Field Marshal Montgomery the FA Cup won by Portsmouth six years earlier. There was no FA Cup competition during the War, so Pompey held the Cup until the competition restarted in 1945-46.*

Above *A shot by Duncan, deflected by Charlton's Bert Turner, enters the net for Derby's first goal in the 1946 Cup Final. During this game, the ball burst. Oddly enough, the chances of this happening were discussed in a BBC broadcast shortly before the game, and the referee, Mr E D Smith of Cumberland, remarked that it was a million-to-one chance. Even more curiously, the ball also burst when Derby played Charlton in a League match just five days after their Wembley meeting.*

League Tables 1946-47

FIRST DIVISION

	P	W	D	L	F	A	Pts
1 Liverpool	42	25	7	10	84	52	57
2 Man United	42	22	12	8	95	54	56
3 Wolves	42	25	6	11	98	56	56
4 Stoke	42	24	7	11	90	53	55
5 Blackpool	42	22	6	14	71	70	50
6 Sheff United	42	21	7	14	89	75	49
7 Preston	42	18	11	13	76	74	47
8 Aston Villa	42	18	9	15	67	53	45
9 Sunderland	42	18	8	16	65	66	44
10 Everton	42	17	9	16	62	67	43
11 Middlesbrough	42	17	8	17	73	68	42
12 Portsmouth	42	16	9	17	66	60	41
13 Arsenal	42	16	9	17	72	70	41
14 Derby	42	18	5	19	73	79	41
15 Chelsea	42	16	7	19	69	84	39
16 Grimsby	42	13	12	17	61	82	38
17 Blackburn	42	14	8	20	45	53	36
18 Bolton	42	13	8	21	57	69	34
19 Charlton	42	11	12	19	57	71	34
20 Huddersfield	42	13	7	22	53	79	33
21 Brentford	42	9	7	26	45	88	25
22 Leeds	42	6	6	30	45	90	18

SECOND DIVISION

	P	W	D	L	F	A	Pts
1 Man City	42	26	10	6	78	35	62
2 Burnley	42	22	14	6	65	29	58
3 Birmingham	42	25	5	12	74	33	55
4 Chesterfield	42	18	14	10	58	44	50
5 Newcastle	42	19	10	13	95	62	48
6 Tottenham	42	17	14	11	65	53	48
7 WBA	42	20	8	14	88	75	48
8 Coventry	42	16	13	13	66	59	45
9 Leicester	42	18	7	17	69	64	43
10 Barnsley	42	17	8	17	84	86	42
11 Nottm Forest	42	15	10	17	69	74	40
12 West Ham	42	16	8	18	70	76	40
13 Luton	42	16	7	19	71	73	39
14 Southampton	42	15	9	18	69	76	39
15 Fulham	42	15	9	18	63	74	39
16 Bradford PA	42	14	11	17	65	77	39
17 Bury	42	12	12	18	80	78	36
18 Millwall	42	14	8	20	56	79	36
19 Plymouth	42	14	5	23	79	96	33
20 Sheff Wed	42	12	8	22	67	88	32
21 Swansea	42	11	7	24	55	83	29
22 Newport	42	10	3	29	61	133	23

THIRD DIVISION (NORTH)

	P	W	D	L	F	A	Pts
1 Doncaster	42	33	6	3	123	40	72
2 Rotherham	42	29	6	7	114	53	64
3 Chester	42	25	6	11	95	51	56
4 Stockport	42	24	2	16	78	53	50
5 Bradford City	42	20	10	12	62	47	50
6 Rochdale	42	19	10	13	80	64	48
7 Wrexham	42	17	12	13	65	51	46
8 Crewe	42	17	9	16	70	74	43
9 Barrow	42	17	7	18	54	62	41
10 Tranmere	42	17	7	18	66	77	41
11 Hull	42	16	8	18	49	53	40
12 Lincoln	42	17	5	20	86	87	39
13 Hartlepools	42	15	9	18	64	73	39
14 Gateshead	42	16	6	20	62	72	38
15 York	42	14	9	19	67	81	37
16 Carlisle	42	14	9	19	70	93	37
17 Darlington	42	15	6	21	68	80	36
18 New Brighton	42	14	8	20	57	77	36
19 Oldham	42	12	8	22	55	80	32
20 Accrington	42	14	4	24	56	92	32
21 Southport	42	7	11	24	53	85	25
22 Halifax	42	8	6	28	43	92	22

THIRD DIVISION (SOUTH)

	P	W	D	L	F	A	Pts
1 Cardiff	42	30	6	6	93	30	66
2 QPR	42	23	11	8	74	40	57
3 Bristol City	42	20	11	11	94	56	51
4 Swindon	42	19	11	12	84	73	49
5 Walsall	42	17	12	13	74	59	46
6 Ipswich	42	16	14	12	61	53	46
7 Bournemouth	42	18	8	16	72	54	44
8 Southend	42	17	10	15	71	60	44
9 Reading	42	16	11	15	83	74	43
10 Port Vale	42	17	9	16	68	63	43
11 Torquay	42	15	12	15	52	61	42
12 Notts County	42	15	10	17	63	63	40
13 Northampton	42	15	10	17	72	75	40
14 Bristol Rovers	42	16	8	18	59	69	40
15 Exeter	42	15	9	18	60	69	39
16 Watford	42	17	5	20	61	76	39
17 Brighton	42	13	12	17	54	72	38
18 Crystal Palace	42	13	11	18	49	62	37
19 Leyton Orient	42	12	8	22	54	75	32
20 Aldershot	42	10	12	20	48	78	32
21 Norwich	42	10	8	24	64	100	28
22 Mansfield	42	9	10	23	48	96	28

SCOTTISH DIVISION 'A'

	P	W	D	L	F	A	Pts
1 Rangers	30	21	4	5	76	26	46
2 Hibernian	30	19	6	5	69	33	44
3 Aberdeen	30	16	7	7	58	41	39
4 Hearts	30	16	6	8	52	43	38
5 Partick Thistle	30	16	3	11	74	59	35
6 Morton	30	12	10	8	58	45	34
7 Celtic	30	13	6	11	53	55	32
8 Motherwell	30	12	5	13	58	54	29
9 Third Lanark	30	11	6	13	56	64	28
10 Clyde	30	9	9	12	55	65	27
11 Falkirk	30	8	10	12	62	61	26
12 Queen of the S	30	9	8	13	44	69	26
13 Queen's Park	30	8	6	16	47	60	22
14 St Mirren	30	9	4	17	47	65	22
15 Kilmarnock	30	6	9	15	44	66	21
16 Hamilton	30	2	7	21	38	85	11

SCOTTISH DIVISION 'B'

	P	W	D	L	F	A	Pts
1 Dundee	26	21	3	2	113	30	45
2 Airdrieonians	26	19	4	3	78	38	42
3 East Fife	26	12	7	7	58	39	31
4 Albion	26	10	7	9	50	54	27
5 Alloa	26	11	5	10	51	57	27
6 Raith	26	10	6	10	45	52	26
7 Stenhousemuir	26	8	7	11	43	53	23
8 Dunfermline	26	10	3	13	50	72	23
9 St Johnstone	26	9	4	13	45	47	22
10 Dundee United	26	9	4	13	53	60	22
11 Ayr	26	9	2	15	56	73	20
12 Arbroath	26	7	6	13	42	63	20
13 Dumbarton	26	7	4	15	41	54	18
14 Cowdenbeath	26	6	6	14	44	77	18

When Italy beat Hungary 3-2 on 11 May 1947, a record ten members of the victorious Italian team came from Juventus.

Hull City used 42 players in the Third Division North, 1946-47. This was only the third time in the history of the League that such a large pool of players had been used in one season by a single club.

Cardiff equalled a Division Three South record by winning 30 of their 42 matches. By contrast, Leeds set a First Division record by losing 30 of their 42 matches.

Doncaster Rovers enjoyed an enormously successful season in winning the Third Division North championship in 1946-47. They set four League records during the course of the season. Their points total (72) was the highest number of points ever won by a club in any division of the League; that total included 37 points won away from home, also a League record. By winning 18 of their 21 away games, Doncaster established a third League record, for the most games won away from home and, in all, Doncaster Rovers won 33 of their 42 Division Three North games to set another League record. They also equalled the record for the division by losing just three matches during the season.

FA CUP 1946-47

FOURTH ROUND

West Bromwich Albion v Charlton Athletic	1-2
Blackburn Rovers v Port Vale	2-0
Preston North End v Barnsley	6-0
Sheffield Wednesday v Everton	2-1
Newcastle United v Southampton	3-1
Brentford v Leicester City	0-0, 0-0, 1-4
Wolverhampton Wanderers v Sheffield United	0-0, 0-2
Chester v Stoke City	0-0, 2-3
Burnley v Coventry City	2-0
Luton Town v Swansea Town	2-0
Middlesbrough v Chesterfield	2-1
Manchester United v Nottingham Forest	0-2
Liverpool v Grimsby Town	2-0
Chelsea v Derby County	2-2, 0-1
Birmingham City v Portsmouth	1-0
Bolton Wanderers v Manchester City	3-3, 0-1

FIFTH ROUND

Charlton Athletic v Blackburn Rovers	1-0
Sheffield Wednesday v Preston North End	0-2
Newcastle United v Leicester City	1-1, 2-1
Stoke City v Sheffield United	0-1
Luton Town v Burnley	0-0, 0-3
Nottingham Forest v Middlesbrough	2-2, 2-6
Liverpool v Derby County	1-0
Birmingham City v Manchester City	5-0

SIXTH ROUND

Charlton Athletic v Preston North End	2-1
Sheffield United v Newcastle United	0-2
Middlesbrough v Burnley	1-1, 0-1
Liverpool v Birmingham City	4-1

SEMI-FINAL

Charlton Athletic v Newcastle United	4-0
Burnley v Liverpool	0-0, 1-0

FINAL

Charlton Athletic v Burnley	1-0

SCOTTISH FA CUP 1946-47

SECOND ROUND

Aberdeen v Ayr United	8-0
East Fife v East Stirlingshire	5-1
Morton	bye
Dundee	bye
Albion Rovers	bye
Arbroath	bye
Raith Rovers	bye
Heart of Midlothian	bye
Cowdenbeath	bye
Hibernian	bye
Rangers	bye
Dumbarton	bye
Third Lanark	bye
Motherwell	bye
Falkirk	bye
Queen's Park	bye

THIRD ROUND

Morton v Aberdeen	1-1, 1-2
Dundee v Albion Rovers	3-0
Arbroath v Raith Rovers	5-4
Heart of Midlothian v Cowdenbeath	2-0
Rangers v Hibernian	0-0, 0-2
Dumbarton v Third Lanark	2-0
Falkirk v Motherwell	0-0, 0-1
East Fife v Queen's Park	3-1

FOURTH ROUND

Dundee v Aberdeen	1-2
Arbroath v Heart of Midlothian	2-1
Hibernian v Dumbarton	2-0
East Fife v Motherwell	0-2

SEMI-FINAL

Aberdeen v Arbroath	2-0
Hibernian v Motherwell	2-0

FINAL

Aberdeen v Hibernian	2-1

League Tables 1947-48

FIRST DIVISION

		P	W	D	L	F	A	Pts
1	Arsenal	42	23	13	6	81	32	59
2	Man United	42	19	14	9	81	48	52
3	Burnley	42	20	12	10	56	43	52
4	Derby	42	19	12	11	77	57	50
5	Wolves	42	19	9	14	83	70	47
6	Aston Villa	42	19	9	14	65	57	47
7	Preston	42	20	7	15	67	68	47
8	Portsmouth	42	19	7	16	68	50	45
9	Blackpool	42	17	10	15	57	41	44
10	Man City	42	15	12	15	52	47	42
11	Liverpool	42	16	10	16	65	61	42
12	Sheff United	42	16	10	16	65	70	42
13	Charlton	42	17	6	19	57	66	40
14	Everton	42	17	6	19	52	66	40
15	Stoke	42	14	10	18	41	55	38
16	Middlesbrough	42	14	9	19	71	73	37
17	Bolton	42	16	5	21	46	58	37
18	Chelsea	42	14	9	19	53	71	37
19	Huddersfield	42	12	12	18	51	60	36
20	Sunderland	42	13	10	19	56	67	36
21	Blackburn	42	11	10	21	54	72	32
22	Grimsby	42	8	6	28	45	111	22

SECOND DIVISION

		P	W	D	L	F	A	Pts
1	Birmingham	42	22	15	5	55	24	59
2	Newcastle	42	24	8	10	72	41	56
3	Southampton	42	21	10	11	71	53	52
4	Sheff Wed	42	20	11	11	66	53	51
5	Cardiff	42	18	11	13	61	58	47
6	West Ham	42	16	14	12	55	53	46
7	WBA	42	18	9	15	63	58	45
8	Tottenham	42	15	14	13	56	43	44
9	Leicester	42	16	11	15	60	57	43
10	Coventry	42	14	13	15	59	52	41
11	Fulham	42	15	10	17	47	46	40
12	Barnsley	42	15	10	17	62	64	40
13	Luton	42	14	12	16	56	59	40
14	Bradford PA	42	16	8	18	68	72	40
15	Brentford	42	13	14	15	44	61	40
16	Chesterfield	42	16	7	19	54	55	39
17	Plymouth	42	9	20	13	40	58	38
18	Leeds	42	14	8	20	62	72	36
19	Nottm Forest	42	12	11	19	54	60	35
20	Bury	42	9	16	17	58	68	34
21	Doncaster	42	9	11	22	40	66	29
22	Millwall	42	9	11	22	44	74	29

THIRD DIVISION (SOUTH)

		P	W	D	L	F	A	Pts
1	QPR	42	26	9	7	74	37	61
2	Bournemouth	42	24	9	9	76	35	57
3	Walsall	42	21	9	12	70	40	51
4	Ipswich	42	23	3	16	67	61	49
5	Swansea	42	18	12	12	70	52	48
6	Notts County	42	19	8	15	68	59	46
7	Bristol City	42	18	7	17	77	65	43
8	Port Vale	42	16	11	15	63	54	43
9	Southend	42	15	13	14	51	58	43
10	Reading	42	15	11	16	56	58	41
11	Exeter	42	15	11	16	55	63	41
12	Newport	42	14	13	15	61	73	41
13	Crystal Palace	42	13	13	16	49	49	39
14	Northampton	42	14	11	17	58	72	39
15	Watford	42	14	10	18	57	79	38
16	Swindon	42	10	16	16	41	46	36
17	Leyton Orient	42	13	10	19	51	73	36
18	Torquay	42	11	13	18	63	62	35
19	Aldershot	42	10	15	17	45	67	35
20	Bristol Rovers	42	13	8	21	71	75	34
21	Norwich	42	13	8	21	61	76	34
22	Brighton	42	11	12	19	43	73	34

THIRD DIVISION (NORTH)

		P	W	D	L	F	A	Pts
1	Lincoln	42	26	8	8	81	40	60
2	Rotherham	42	25	9	8	95	49	59
3	Wrexham	42	21	8	13	74	54	50
4	Gateshead	42	19	11	12	75	57	49
5	Hull	42	18	11	13	59	48	47
6	Accrington	42	20	6	16	62	59	46
7	Barrow	42	16	13	13	49	40	45
8	Mansfield	42	17	11	14	57	51	45
9	Carlisle	42	18	7	17	88	77	43
10	Crewe	42	18	7	17	61	63	43
11	Oldham	42	14	13	15	63	64	41
12	Rochdale	42	15	11	16	48	72	41
13	York	42	13	14	15	65	60	40
14	Bradford City	42	15	10	17	65	66	40
15	Southport	42	14	11	17	60	63	39
16	Darlington	42	13	13	16	54	70	39
17	Stockport	42	13	12	17	63	67	38
18	Tranmere	42	16	4	22	54	72	36
19	Hartlepools	42	14	8	20	51	73	36
20	Chester	42	13	9	20	64	67	35
21	Halifax	42	7	13	22	43	76	27
22	New Brighton	42	8	9	25	38	81	25

SCOTTISH DIVISION 'A'

		P	W	D	L	F	A	Pts
1	Hibernian	30	22	4	4	86	27	48
2	Rangers	30	21	4	5	64	28	46
3	Partick	30	16	4	10	61	42	36
4	Dundee	30	15	3	12	67	51	33
5	St Mirren	30	13	5	12	54	58	31
6	Clyde	30	12	7	11	52	57	31
7	Falkirk	30	10	10	10	55	48	30
8	Motherwell	30	13	3	14	45	47	29
9	Hearts	30	10	8	12	37	42	28
10	Aberdeen	30	10	7	13	45	45	27
11	Third Lanark	30	10	6	14	56	73	26
12	Celtic	30	10	5	15	41	56	25
13	Queen of the S	30	10	5	15	49	74	25
14	Morton	30	9	6	15	47	43	24
15	Airdrieonians	30	7	7	16	39	78	21
16	Queen's Park	30	9	2	19	45	75	20

SCOTTISH DIVISION 'B'

		P	W	D	L	F	A	Pts
1	East Fife	30	25	3	2	103	36	53
2	Albion	30	19	4	7	58	49	42
3	Hamilton	30	17	6	7	75	45	40
4	Raith	30	14	6	10	83	66	34
5	Cowdenbeath	30	12	8	10	56	53	32
6	Kilmarnock	30	13	4	13	72	62	30
7	Dunfermline	30	13	3	14	72	71	29
8	Stirling	30	11	6	13	85	66	28
9	St Johnstone	30	11	5	14	69	63	27
10	Ayr	30	9	9	12	59	61	27
11	Dumbarton	30	9	7	14	66	79	25
12	Alloa	30	10	6	14	53	77	24*
13	Arbroath	30	10	3	17	55	62	23
14	Stenhousemuir	30	6	11	13	53	83	23
15	Dundee United	30	10	2	18	58	88	22
16	Leith	30	6	7	17	45	84	19

*Two points deducted for fielding unregistered players.

In the 1947-48 FA Cup, Manchester United were drawn in turn against six Division One clubs. This was the first instance of this happening to any club. The teams United met were, in order, Aston Villa, Liverpool, Charlton Athletic, Preston North End, and Blackpool, whom they beat 4-2 in the Final.

Quick off the mark

William Sharp, of Partick Thistle, scored against Queen of the South just seven seconds after the Scottish Division 'A' match had kicked off on 20 December 1947.

Tommy Lawton became the first Third Division player since World War Two to represent England in the International Championship. Lawton, of Notts County, played at centre-forward in England's 2-0 win over Scotland at Hampden Park on 10 April 1948.

In January 1948, 83,260 people watched Manchester United play Arsenal in a First Division match at Maine Road, Manchester. This was a record for a League match.

FA CUP 1947-48

FOURTH ROUND

Queen's Park Rangers v Stoke City	3-0
Luton Town v Coventry City	3-2
Brentford v Middlesbrough	1-2
Crewe Alexandra v Derby County	0-3
Manchester United v Liverpool	3-0
Charlton Athletic v Stockport County	3-0
Manchester City v Chelsea	2-0
Portsmouth v Preston North End	1-3
Fulham v Bristol Rovers	5-2
Wolverhampton Wanderers v Everton	1-1, 2-3
Blackpool v Chester	4-0
Colchester United v Bradford Park Avenue	3-2
Southampton v Blackburn Rovers	3-2
Swindon Town v Notts County	1-0
Tottenham Hotspur v West Bromwich Albion	3-1
Leicester City v Sheffield Wednesday	2-1

FIFTH ROUND

Queen's Park Rangers v Luton Town	3-1
Middlesbrough v Derby County	1-2
Manchester United v Charlton Athletic	2-0
Manchester City v Preston North End	0-1
Fulham v Everton	1-1, 1-0
Blackpool v Colchester United	5-0
Southampton v Swindon Town	3-0
Tottenham Hotspur v Leicester City	5-2

SIXTH ROUND

Queen's Park Rangers v Derby County	1-1, 0-5
Manchester United v Preston North End	4-1
Fulham v Blackpool	0-2
Southampton v Tottenham Hotspur	0-1

SEMI-FINAL

Derby County v Manchester United	1-3
Blackpool v Tottenham Hotspur	3-1

FINAL

Manchester United v Blackpool	4-2

SCOTTISH FA CUP 1947-48

SECOND ROUND

Rangers v Leith Athletic	4-0
Partick Thistle v Dundee United	4-3
East Fife v St Johnstone	5-1
Peterhead v Dumbarton	1-2
Hibernian v Arbroath	4-0
Nithsdale Wanderers v Aberdeen	0-5
St Mirren v East Stirlingshire	2-0
Clyde v Dunfermline Athletic	2-1
Morton v Falkirk	3-2
Queen's Park v Deveronvale	8-2
Airdrieonians v Heart of Midlothian	2-1
Stirling Albion v Raith Rovers	2-4
Celtic v Cowdenbeath	3-0
Motherwell v Third Lanark	1-0
Montrose v Duns	2-0
Alloa Athletic v Queen of the South	0-1

THIRD ROUND

Rangers v Partick Thistle	3-0
Dumbarton v East Fife	0-1
Hibernian v Aberdeen	4-2
St Mirren v Clyde	2-1
Morton v Queen's Park	3-0
Airdrieonians v Raith Rovers	3-0
Celtic v Motherwell	1-0
Montrose v Queen of the South	2-1

FOURTH ROUND

Rangers v East Fife	1-0
Hibernian v St Mirren	3-1
Airdrieonians v Morton	0-3
Celtic v Montrose	4-0

SEMI-FINAL

Rangers v Hibernian	1-0
Morton v Celtic	1-0

FINAL

Rangers v Morton	1-1, 1-0

FIRST DIVISION

		P	W	D	L	F	A	Pts
1	Portsmouth	42	25	8	9	84	42	58
2	Man United	42	21	11	10	77	44	53
3	Derby	42	22	9	11	74	55	53
4	Newcastle	42	20	12	10	70	56	52
5	Arsenal	42	18	13	11	74	44	49
6	Wolves	42	17	12	13	79	66	46
7	Man City	42	15	15	12	47	51	45
8	Sunderland	42	13	17	12	49	58	43
9	Charlton	42	15	12	15	63	67	42
10	Aston Villa	42	16	10	16	60	76	42
11	Stoke	42	16	9	17	66	68	41
12	Liverpool	42	13	14	15	53	43	40
13	Chelsea	42	12	14	16	69	68	38
14	Bolton	42	14	10	18	59	68	38
15	Burnley	42	12	14	16	43	50	38
16	Blackpool	42	11	16	15	54	67	38
17	Birmingham	42	11	15	16	36	38	37
18	Everton	42	13	11	18	41	63	37
19	Middlesbrough	42	11	12	19	46	57	34
20	Huddersfield	42	12	10	20	40	69	34
21	Preston	42	11	11	20	62	75	33
22	Sheff United	42	11	11	20	57	78	33

SECOND DIVISION

		P	W	D	L	F	A	Pts
1	Fulham	42	24	9	9	77	37	57
2	WBA	42	24	8	10	69	39	56
3	Southampton	42	23	9	10	69	36	55
4	Cardiff	42	19	13	10	62	47	51
5	Tottenham	42	17	16	9	72	44	50
6	Chesterfield	42	15	17	10	51	45	47
7	West Ham	42	18	10	14	56	58	46
8	Sheff Wed	42	15	13	14	63	56	43
9	Barnsley	42	14	12	16	62	61	40
10	Luton	42	14	12	16	55	57	40
11	Grimsby	42	15	10	17	72	76	40
12	Bury	42	17	6	19	67	76	40
13	QPR	42	14	11	17	44	62	39
14	Blackburn	42	15	8	19	53	63	38
15	Leeds	42	12	13	17	55	63	37
16	Coventry	42	15	7	20	55	64	37
17	Bradford PA	42	13	11	18	65	78	37
18	Brentford	42	11	14	17	42	53	36
19	Leicester	42	10	16	16	62	79	36
20	Plymouth	42	12	12	18	49	64	36
21	Nottm Forest	42	14	7	21	50	54	35
22	Lincoln	42	8	12	22	53	91	28

THIRD DIVISION (SOUTH)

		P	W	D	L	F	A	Pts
1	Swansea	42	27	8	7	87	34	62
2	Reading	42	25	5	12	77	50	55
3	Bournemouth	42	22	8	12	69	48	52
4	Swindon	42	18	15	9	64	56	51
5	Bristol Rovers	42	19	10	13	61	51	48
6	Brighton	42	15	18	9	55	55	48
7	Ipswich	42	18	9	15	78	77	45
8	Millwall	42	17	11	14	63	64	45
9	Torquay	42	17	11	14	65	70	45
10	Norwich	42	16	12	14	67	49	44
11	Notts County	42	19	5	18	102	68	43
12	Exeter	42	15	10	17	63	76	40
13	Port Vale	42	14	11	17	51	54	39
14	Walsall	42	15	8	19	56	64	38
15	Newport	42	14	9	19	68	92	37
16	Bristol City	42	11	14	17	44	62	36
17	Watford	42	10	15	17	41	54	35
18	Southend	42	9	16	17	41	46	34
19	Leyton Orient	42	11	12	19	58	80	34
20	Northampton	42	12	9	21	51	62	33
21	Aldershot	42	11	11	20	48	59	33
22	Crystal Palace	42	8	11	23	38	76	27

THIRD DIVISION (NORTH)

		P	W	D	L	F	A	Pts
1	Hull	42	27	11	4	93	28	65
2	Rotherham	42	28	6	8	90	46	62
3	Doncaster	42	20	10	12	53	40	50
4	Darlington	42	20	6	16	83	74	46
5	Gateshead	42	16	13	13	69	58	45
6	Oldham	42	18	9	15	75	67	45
7	Rochdale	42	18	9	15	55	53	45
8	Stockport	42	16	11	15	61	56	43
9	Wrexham	42	17	9	16	56	62	43
10	Mansfield	42	14	14	14	52	48	42
11	Tranmere	42	13	15	14	46	57	41
12	Crewe	42	16	9	17	52	74	41
13	Barrow	42	14	12	16	41	48	40
14	York	42	15	9	18	74	74	39
15	Carlisle	42	14	11	17	60	77	39
16	Hartlepools	42	14	10	18	45	58	38
17	New Brighton	42	14	8	20	46	58	36
18	Chester	42	11	13	18	57	56	35
19	Halifax	42	12	11	19	45	62	35
20	Accrington	42	12	10	20	55	64	34
21	Southport	42	11	9	22	45	64	31
22	Bradford City	42	10	9	23	48	77	29

SCOTTISH DIVISION 'A'

		P	W	D	L	F	A	Pts
1	Rangers	30	20	6	4	63	32	46
2	Dundee	30	20	5	5	71	48	45
3	Hibernian	30	17	5	8	75	52	39
4	East Fife	30	16	3	11	64	46	35
5	Falkirk	30	12	8	10	70	54	32
6	Celtic	30	12	7	11	48	40	31
7	Third Lanark	30	13	5	12	56	52	31
8	Hearts	30	12	6	12	64	54	30
9	St Mirren	30	13	4	13	51	47	30
10	Queen of the S	30	11	8	11	47	53	30
11	Partick	30	9	9	12	50	63	27
12	Motherwell	30	10	5	15	44	49	25
13	Aberdeen	30	7	11	12	39	48	25
14	Clyde	30	9	6	15	50	67	24
15	Morton	30	7	8	15	39	51	22
16	Albion	30	3	2	25	30	105	8

SCOTTISH DIVISION 'B'

		P	W	D	L	F	A	Pts
1	Raith	30	20	2	8	80	44	42
2	Stirling	30	20	2	8	71	47	42
3	Airdrieonians	30	16	9	5	76	42	41
4	Dunfermline	30	16	9	5	80	58	41
5	Queen's Park	30	14	7	9	66	49	35
6	St Johnstone	30	14	4	12	58	51	32
7	Arbroath	30	12	8	10	62	56	32
8	Dundee United	30	10	7	13	60	67	27
9	Ayr	30	10	7	13	51	70	27
10	Hamilton	30	9	8	13	48	57	26
11	Kilmarnock	30	9	7	14	58	61	25
12	Stenhousemuir	30	8	8	14	50	54	24
13	Cowdenbeath	30	9	5	16	53	58	23
14	Alloa	30	10	3	17	42	85	23
15	Dumbarton	30	8	6	16	52	79	22
16	E Stirlingshire	30	6	6	18	38	67	18

On Saturday 18 September 1948, there were 9 drawn games in Division One of the Football League, a record for any division of the League in a single day.

In both Divisions One and Two, the tally of goals scored during the season was 1303.

Portsmouth, 1948-49 League champions, and Swansea, who finished top of Division Three South, both completed the season without a home defeat. At Fratton Park, Portsmouth won 18 games and drew 3, while Swansea won 20 and drew one at Vetch Field.

Three honours for Bromley

Bromley won the FA Amateur Cup by beating Romford 1-0 at Wembley; they also won the Kent Amateur Cup with the highest score recorded in the final: 9-1. Bromley completed a magnificent season by capturing the Athenian League championship. George Brown, their centre-forward, scored 100 goals during the season. These included a 7, a 6, two 5's, three 4's and five hat-tricks.

In Scotland, Rangers became the first side to achieve the treble, winning the League, the Scottish Cup and the League Cup.

FA CUP 1948-49

FOURTH ROUND

Manchester United v Bradford Park Avenue 1-1, 1-1, 5-0
Yeovil Town v Sunderland 2-1
Hull City v Grimsby Town 3-2
Stoke City v Blackpool 1-1, 1-0
Wolverhampton Wanderers v Sheffield United 3-0
Liverpool v Notts County 1-0
West Bromwich Albion v Gateshead 3-1
Chelsea v Everton 2-0
Leicester City v Preston North End 2-0
Luton Town v Walsall 4-0
Brentford v Torquay United 1-0
Burnley v Rotherham United 1-0
Portsmouth v Sheffield Wednesday 2-1
Newport County v Huddersfield Town 3-3, 3-1
Derby County v Arsenal 1-0
Cardiff City v Aston Villa 2-1

FIFTH ROUND

Manchester United v Yeovil Town 8-0
Hull City v Stoke City 2-0
Wolverhampton Wanderers v Liverpool 3-1
West Bromwich Albion v Chelsea 3-0
Leicester City v Luton Town 5-5, 5-3
Brentford v Burnley 4-2
Portsmouth v Newport County 3-2
Derby County v Cardiff City 2-1

SIXTH ROUND

Hull City v Manchester United 0-1
Wolverhampton Wanderers v West Bromwich Albion 1-0
Leicester City v Brentford 2-0
Portsmouth v Derby County 2-1

SEMI-FINAL

Manchester United v Wolverhampton Wanderers 1-1, 0-1
Leicester City v Portsmouth 3-1

FINAL

Wolverhampton Wanderers v Leicester City 3-1

SCOTTISH FA CUP 1948-49

SECOND ROUND

Motherwell v Rangers 0-3
Partick Thistle v Queen of the South 3-0
Cowdenbeath v East Fife 1-2
Hibernian v Raith Rovers 1-1, 4-3
Clyde v Alloa Athletic 3-1
Ayr United v Morton 0-2
Stenhousemuir v Albion Rovers 5-1
Dundee v St Mirren 0-0, 2-1
Heart of Midlothian v Third Lanark 3-1
Dumbarton v Dundee United 1-1, 3-1

THIRD ROUND

Clyde v Morton 2-0
Heart of Midlothian v Dumbarton 3-0
Rangers bye
Partick Thistle bye
East Fife bye
Hibernian bye
Stenhousemuir bye
Dundee bye

FOURTH ROUND

Rangers v Partick Thistle 4-0
Hibernian v East Fife 0-2
Stenhousemuir v Clyde 0-1
Heart of Midlothian v Dundee 2-4

SEMI-FINAL

Rangers v East Fife 3-0
Clyde v Dundee 2-2, 2-1

FINAL

Rangers v Clyde 4-1

FIRST DIVISION

	P	W	D	L	F	A	Pts
1 Portsmouth	42	22	9	11	74	38	53
2 Wolves	42	20	13	9	76	49	53
3 Sunderland	42	21	10	11	83	62	52
4 Man United	42	18	14	10	69	44	50
5 Newcastle	42	19	12	11	77	55	50
6 Arsenal	42	19	11	12	79	55	49
7 Blackpool	42	17	15	10	46	35	49
8 Liverpool	42	17	14	11	64	54	48
9 Middlesbrough	42	20	7	15	59	48	47
10 Burnley	42	16	13	13	40	40	45
11 Derby	42	17	10	15	69	61	44
12 Aston Villa	42	15	12	15	61	61	42
13 Chelsea	42	12	16	14	58	65	40
14 WBA	42	14	12	16	47	53	40
15 Huddersfield	42	14	9	19	52	73	37
16 Bolton	42	10	14	18	45	59	34
17 Fulham	42	10	14	18	41	54	34
18 Everton	42	10	14	18	42	66	34
19 Stoke	42	11	12	19	45	75	34
20 Charlton	42	13	6	23	53	65	32
21 Man City	42	8	13	21	36	68	29
22 Birmingham	42	7	14	21	31	67	28

SECOND DIVISION

	P	W	D	L	F	A	Pts
1 Tottenham	42	27	7	8	81	35	61
2 Sheff Wed	42	18	16	8	67	48	52
3 Sheff United	42	19	14	9	68	49	52
4 Southampton	42	19	14	9	64	48	52
5 Leeds	42	17	13	12	54	45	47
6 Preston	42	18	9	15	60	49	45
7 Hull	42	17	11	14	64	72	45
8 Swansea	42	17	9	16	53	49	43
9 Brentford	42	15	13	14	44	49	43
10 Cardiff	42	16	10	16	41	44	42
11 Grimsby	42	16	8	18	74	73	40
12 Coventry	42	13	13	16	55	55	39
13 Barnsley	42	13	13	16	64	67	39
14 Chesterfield	42	15	9	18	43	47	39
15 Leicester	42	12	15	15	55	65	39
16 Blackburn	42	14	10	18	55	60	38
17 Luton	42	10	18	14	41	51	38
18 Bury	42	14	9	19	60	65	37
19 West Ham	42	12	12	18	53	61	36
20 QPR	42	11	12	19	40	57	34
21 Plymouth	42	8	16	18	44	65	32
22 Bradford PA	42	10	11	21	51	77	31

THIRD DIVISION (SOUTH)

	P	W	D	L	F	A	Pts
1 Notts County	42	25	8	9	95	50	58
2 Northampton	42	20	11	11	72	50	51
3 Southend	42	19	13	10	66	48	51
4 Nottm Forest	42	20	9	13	67	39	49
5 Torquay	42	19	10	13	66	63	48
6 Watford	42	16	13	13	45	35	45
7 Crystal Palace	42	15	14	13	55	54	44
8 Brighton	42	16	12	14	57	69	44
9 Bristol Rovers	42	19	5	18	51	51	43
10 Reading	42	17	8	17	70	64	42
11 Norwich	42	16	10	16	65	63	42
12 Bournemouth	42	16	10	16	57	56	42
13 Port Vale	42	15	11	16	47	42	41
14 Swindon	42	15	11	16	59	62	41
15 Bristol City	42	15	10	17	60	61	40
16 Exeter	42	14	11	17	63	75	39
17 Ipswich	42	12	11	19	57	86	35
18 Leyton Orient	42	12	11	19	53	85	35
19 Walsall	42	9	16	17	61	62	34
20 Aldershot	42	13	8	21	48	60	34
21 Newport	42	13	8	21	67	98	34
22 Millwall	42	14	4	24	55	63	32

THIRD DIVISION (NORTH)

	P	W	D	L	F	A	Pts
1 Doncaster	42	19	17	6	66	38	55
2 Gateshead	42	23	7	12	87	54	53
3 Rochdale	42	21	9	12	68	41	51
4 Lincoln	42	21	9	12	60	39	51
5 Tranmere	42	19	11	12	51	48	49
6 Rotherham	42	19	10	13	80	59	48
7 Crewe	42	17	14	11	68	55	48
8 Mansfield	42	18	12	12	66	54	48
9 Carlisle	42	16	15	11	68	51	47
10 Stockport	42	19	7	16	55	52	45
11 Oldham	42	16	11	15	58	63	43
12 Chester	42	17	6	19	70	79	40
13 Accrington	42	16	7	19	57	62	39
14 New Brighton	42	14	10	18	45	63	38
15 Barrow	42	14	9	19	47	53	37
16 Southport	42	12	13	17	51	71	37
17 Darlington	42	11	13	18	56	69	35
18 Hartlepools	42	14	5	23	52	79	33
19 Bradford City	42	12	8	22	61	76	32
20 Wrexham	42	10	12	20	39	54	32
21 Halifax	42	12	8	22	58	85	32
22 York	42	9	13	20	52	70	31

SCOTTISH DIVISION 'A'

	P	W	D	L	F	A	Pts
1 Rangers	30	22	6	2	58	26	50
2 Hibernian	30	22	5	3	86	34	49
3 Hearts	30	20	3	7	86	40	43
4 East Fife	30	15	7	8	58	43	37
5 Celtic	30	14	7	9	51	50	35
6 Dundee	30	12	7	11	49	46	31
7 Partick Thistle	30	13	3	14	55	45	29
8 Aberdeen	30	11	4	15	48	56	26
9 Raith	30	9	8	13	45	54	26
10 Motherwell	30	10	5	15	53	58	25
11 St Mirren	30	8	9	13	42	49	25
12 Third Lanark	30	11	3	16	44	62	25
13 Clyde	30	10	4	16	56	73	24
14 Falkirk	30	7	10	13	48	72	24
15 Queen of the S	30	5	6	19	31	63	16
16 Stirling	30	6	3	21	38	77	15

SCOTTISH DIVISION 'B'

	P	W	D	L	F	A	Pts
1 Morton	30	20	7	3	77	33	47
2 Airdrieonians	30	19	6	5	79	40	44
3 Dunfermline	30	16	4	10	71	57	36
4 St Johnstone	30	15	6	9	64	56	36
5 Cowdenbeath	30	16	3	11	63	56	35
6 Hamilton	30	14	6	10	57	44	34
7 Kilmarnock	30	14	5	11	50	43	33
8 Dundee United	30	14	5	11	74	56	33
9 Queen's Park	30	12	7	11	63	59	31
10 Forfar	30	11	8	11	53	56	30
11 Albion	30	10	7	13	49	61	27
12 Stenhousemuir	30	8	8	14	54	72	24
13 Ayr	30	8	6	16	53	80	22
14 Arbroath	30	5	9	16	47	69	19
15 Dumbarton	30	6	4	20	39	62	16
16 Alloa	30	5	3	22	47	96	13

Charlie Mortimore scored 15 goals for Aldershot in Division Three South during 1949-50. These made Mortimore the club's top scorer for the season, and meant that he became the second amateur to head a League club's scoring list since the First World War.

England lose to America

On 28 June 1950, an amazing scoreline came out of Brazil. For at Belo Horizonte, the United States had beaten England 1-0.

On 16 July 1950, 199,854 people watched the World Cup Final in Rio de Janeiro, the official record crowd for any football match.

The Third Division was extended from 44 to 48 clubs as a result of the clamour by minor professional clubs for first-class status. The League management committee proposed the enlargement of each section of the Third Division by two clubs, and this proposal was adopted at the 1950 AGM.

FA CUP 1949-50

FOURTH ROUND

Arsenal v Swansea Town	2-1
Burnley v Port Vale	2-1
Leeds United v Bolton Wanderers	1-1, 3-2
Charlton Athletic v Cardiff City	1-1, 0-2
Chelsea v Newcastle United	3-0
Chesterfield v Middlesbrough	3-2
Watford v Manchester United	0-1
Portsmouth v Grimsby Town	5-0
Liverpool v Exeter City	3-1
Stockport County v Hull City	0-0, 2-0
Blackpool v Doncaster Rovers	2-1
Wolverhampton Wanderers v Sheffield United	0-0, 4-3
West Ham United v Everton	1-2
Tottenham Hotspur v Sunderland	5-1
Bury v Derby County	2-2, 2-5
Bournemouth v Northampton Town	1-1, 1-2

FIFTH ROUND

Arsenal v Burnley	2-0
Leeds United v Cardiff City	3-1
Chesterfield v Chelsea	1-1, 0-3
Manchester United v Portsmouth	3-3, 3-1
Stockport County v Liverpool	1-2
Wolverhampton Wanderers v Blackpool	0-0, 0-1
Everton v Tottenham Hotspur	1-0
Derby County v Northampton Town	4-2

SIXTH ROUND

Arsenal v Leeds United	1-0
Chelsea v Manchester United	2-0
Liverpool v Blackpool	2-1
Derby County v Everton	1-2

SEMI-FINAL

Arsenal v Chelsea	2-2, 1-0
Liverpool v Everton	2-0

FINAL

Arsenal v Liverpool	2-0

SCOTTISH FA CUP 1949-50

SECOND ROUND

Rangers v Cowdenbeath	8-0
Raith Rovers v Clyde	3-2
Queen of the South v Morton	1-1, 3-0
Aberdeen v Heart of Midlothian	3-1
Celtic v Third Lanark	1-1, 4-1
Partick Thistle v Dundee United	5-0
Stirling Albion v Dumbarton	2-2, 1-1, 6-2
Stenhousemuir v St Johnstone	2-2, 4-2
Dunfermline Athletic v Albion Rovers	2-1
Falkirk v East Fife	2-3

THIRD ROUND

Celtic v Aberdeen	0-1
Dunfermline Athletic v Stenhousemuir	1-4
Rangers	bye
Raith Rovers	bye
Queen of the South	bye
Partick Thistle	bye
Stirling Albion	bye
East Fife	bye

FOURTH ROUND

Rangers v Raith Rovers	1-1, 1-1, 2-0
Queen of the South v Aberdeen	3-3, 2-1
Partick Thistle v Stirling Albion	5-1
Stenhousemuir v East Fife	0-3

SEMI-FINAL

Rangers v Queen of the South	1-1, 3-0
Partick Thistle v East Fife	1-2

FINAL

Rangers v East Fife	3-0

John Charles, Leeds United's centre-half, became Wales' youngest ever international when, on 8 March 1950, at the age of 18 years and 71 days, he played against Northern Ireland.

League Tables 1950-51

FIRST DIVISION

	P	W	D	L	F	A	Pts
1 Tottenham	42	25	10	7	82	44	60
2 Man United	42	24	8	10	74	40	56
3 Blackpool	42	20	10	12	79	53	50
4 Newcastle	42	18	13	11	62	53	49
5 Arsenal	42	19	9	14	73	56	47
6 Middlesbrough	42	18	11	13	76	65	47
7 Portsmouth	42	16	15	11	71	68	47
8 Bolton	42	19	7	16	64	61	45
9 Liverpool	42	16	11	15	53	59	43
10 Burnley	42	14	14	14	48	43	42
11 Derby	42	16	8	18	81	75	40
12 Sunderland	42	12	16	14	63	73	40
13 Stoke	42	13	14	15	50	59	40
14 Wolves	42	15	8	19	74	61	38
15 Aston Villa	42	12	13	17	66	68	37
16 WBA	42	13	11	18	53	61	37
17 Charlton	42	14	9	19	63	80	37
18 Fulham	42	13	11	18	52	68	37
19 Huddersfield	42	15	6	21	64	92	36
20 Chelsea	42	12	8	22	53	65	32
21 Sheff Wed	42	12	8	22	64	83	32
22 Everton	42	12	8	22	48	86	32

SECOND DIVISION

	P	W	D	L	F	A	Pts
1 Preston	42	26	5	11	91	49	57
2 Man City	42	19	14	9	89	61	52
3 Cardiff	42	17	16	9	53	45	50
4 Birmingham	42	20	9	13	64	53	49
5 Leeds	42	20	8	14	63	55	48
6 Blackburn	42	19	8	15	65	66	46
7 Coventry	42	19	7	16	75	59	45
8 Sheff United	42	16	12	14	72	62	44
9 Brentford	42	18	8	16	75	74	44
10 Hull	42	16	11	15	74	70	43
11 Doncaster	42	15	13	14	64	68	43
12 Southampton	42	15	13	14	66	73	43
13 West Ham	42	16	10	16	68	69	42
14 Leicester	42	15	11	16	68	58	41
15 Barnsley	42	15	10	17	74	68	40
16 QPR	42	15	10	17	71	82	40
17 Notts County	42	13	13	16	61	60	39
18 Swansea	42	16	4	22	54	77	36
19 Luton	42	9	14	19	57	70	32
20 Bury	42	12	8	22	60	86	32
21 Chesterfield	42	9	12	21	44	69	30
22 Grimsby	42	8	12	22	61	95	28

THIRD DIVISION (NORTH)

	P	W	D	L	F	A	Pts
1 Rotherham	46	31	9	6	103	41	71
2 Mansfield	46	26	12	8	78	48	64
3 Carlisle	46	25	12	9	79	50	62
4 Tranmere	46	24	11	11	83	62	59
5 Lincoln	46	25	8	13	89	58	58
6 Bradford PA	46	23	8	15	90	72	54
7 Bradford City	46	21	10	15	90	63	52
8 Gateshead	46	21	8	17	84	62	50
9 Crewe	46	19	10	17	61	60	48
10 Stockport	46	20	8	18	63	63	48
11 Rochdale	46	17	11	18	69	62	45
12 Scunthorpe	46	13	18	15	58	57	44
13 Chester	46	17	9	20	62	64	43
14 Wrexham	46	15	12	19	55	71	42
15 Oldham	46	16	8	22	73	73	40
16 Hartlepools	46	16	7	23	64	66	39
17 York	46	12	15	19	66	77	39
18 Darlington	46	13	13	20	59	77	39
19 Barrow	46	16	6	24	51	76	38
20 Shrewsbury	46	15	7	24	43	74	37
21 Southport	46	13	10	23	56	72	36
22 Halifax	46	11	12	23	50	69	34
23 Accrington	46	11	10	25	42	101	32
24 New Brighton	46	11	8	27	40	90	30

THIRD DIVISION (SOUTH)

	P	W	D	L	F	A	Pts
1 Nottm Forest	46	30	10	6	110	40	70
2 Norwich	46	25	14	7	82	45	64
3 Reading	46	21	15	10	88	53	57
4 Plymouth	46	24	9	13	85	55	57
5 Millwall	46	23	10	13	80	57	56
6 Bristol Rovers	46	20	15	11	64	42	55
7 Southend	46	21	10	15	92	69	52
8 Ipswich	46	23	6	17	69	58	52
9 Bournemouth	46	22	7	17	65	57	51
10 Bristol City	46	20	11	15	64	59	51
11 Newport	46	19	9	18	77	70	47
12 Port Vale	46	16	13	17	60	65	45
13 Brighton	46	13	17	16	71	79	43
14 Exeter	46	18	6	22	62	85	42
15 Walsall	46	15	10	21	52	62	40
16 Colchester	46	14	12	20	63	76	40
17 Swindon	46	18	4	24	55	67	40
18 Aldershot	46	15	10	21	56	88	40
19 Leyton Orient	46	15	8	23	53	75	38
20 Torquay	46	14	9	23	64	81	37
21 Northampton	46	10	16	20	55	67	36
22 Gillingham	46	13	9	24	69	101	35
23 Watford	46	9	11	26	54	88	29
24 Crystal Palace	46	8	11	27	33	84	27

SCOTTISH DIVISION 'A'

	P	W	D	L	F	A	Pts
1 Hibernian	30	22	4	4	78	26	48
2 Rangers	30	17	4	9	64	37	38
3 Dundee	30	15	8	7	47	30	38
4 Hearts	30	16	5	9	72	45	37
5 Aberdeen	30	15	5	10	61	50	35
6 Partick Thistle	30	13	7	10	57	48	33
7 Celtic	30	12	5	13	48	46	29
8 Raith	30	13	2	15	52	52	28
9 Motherwell	30	11	6	13	58	65	28
10 East Fife	30	10	8	12	48	66	28
11 St Mirren	30	9	7	14	35	51	25
12 Morton	30	10	4	16	47	59	24
13 Third Lanark	30	11	2	17	40	51	24
14 Airdrieonians	30	10	4	16	52	67	24
15 Clyde	30	8	7	15	37	57	23
16 Falkirk	30	7	4	19	35	81	18

SCOTTISH DIVISION 'B'

	P	W	D	L	F	A	Pts
1 Queen of the S	30	21	3	6	69	35	45
2 Stirling	30	21	3	6	78	44	45
3 Ayr	30	15	6	9	64	40	36
4 Dundee United	30	16	4	10	78	58	36
5 St Johnstone	30	14	5	11	68	53	33
6 Queen's Park	30	13	7	10	56	53	33
7 Hamilton	30	12	8	10	65	49	32
8 Albion	30	14	4	12	56	51	32
9 Dumbarton	30	12	5	13	52	53	29
10 Dunfermline	30	12	4	14	58	73	28
11 Cowdenbeath	30	12	3	15	61	57	27
12 Kilmarnock	30	8	8	14	44	49	24
13 Arbroath	30	8	5	17	46	78	21
14 Forfar	30	9	3	18	43	76	21
15 Stenhousemuir	30	9	2	19	51	80	20
16 Alloa	30	7	4	19	58	98	18

In their first season in the Football League, Scunthorpe United conceded only nine goals in their 23 home matches in Division Three North. In their 23 away games in the same division, Hartlepools United scored only nine times, failing to break a duck in their last 11 fixtures.

Nottingham Forest won the Third Division South championship with a record points total for that division—70.

Billingham Synthonia did not concede a single goal at home in their Northern League programme, though they scored 44.

On 15 November 1950, Leslie Compton, the Arsenal centre-half, played in that position for England against Wales. It was Compton's first international appearance, and at 38 years and 2 months, he is credited with making the oldest international debut in the Home Championship.

FA CUP 1950-51

FOURTH ROUND

Newcastle United v Bolton Wanderers 3-2
Stoke City v West Ham United 1-0
Luton Town v Bristol Rovers 1-2
Hull City v Rotherham United 2-0
Wolverhampton Wanderers v Aston Villa 3-1
Preston North End v Huddersfield Town 0-2
Sunderland v Southampton 2-0
Newport County v Norwich City 0-2
Blackpool v Stockport County 2-1
Sheffield United v Mansfield Town 0-0, 1-2
Exeter City v Chelsea 1-1, 0-2
Millwall v Fulham 0-1
Derby County v Birmingham City 1-3
Bristol City v Brighton 1-0
Manchester United v Leeds United 4-0
Arsenal v Northampton Town 3-2

FIFTH ROUND

Stoke City v Newcastle United 2-4
Bristol Rovers v Hull City 3-0
Wolverhampton Wanderers v Huddersfield Town 2-0
Sunderland v Norwich City 3-1
Blackpool v Mansfield Town 2-0
Chelsea v Fulham 1-1, 0-3
Birmingham City v Bristol City 2-0
Manchester United v Arsenal 1-0

SIXTH ROUND

Newcastle United v Bristol Rovers 0-0, 3-1
Sunderland v Wolverhampton Wanderers 1-1, 1-3
Blackpool v Fulham 1-0
Birmingham City v Manchester United 1-0

SEMI-FINAL

Newcastle United v Wolverhampton Wanderers 0-0, 2-1
Blackpool v Birmingham City 0-0, 2-1

FINAL

Blackpool v Newcastle United 0-2

SCOTTISH FA CUP 1950-51

SECOND ROUND

Celtic v Duns 4-0
East Stirlingshire v Heart of Midlothian 1-5
Aberdeen v Third Lanark 4-0
St Johnstone v Dundee 1-3
Raith Rovers v Brechin City 5-2
Morton v Airdrieonians 3-3, 1-2
Albion Rovers v Clyde 0-2
Rangers v Hibernian 2-3
Queen's Park v Ayr United 1-3
Motherwell v Hamilton Academicals 4-1

THIRD ROUND

Heart of Midlothian v Celtic 1-2
Airdrieonians v Clyde 4-0
Aberdeen bye
Dundee bye
Raith Rovers bye
Hibernian bye
Ayr United bye
Motherwell bye

FOURTH ROUND

Celtic v Aberdeen 3-0
Dundee v Raith Rovers 1-2
Airdrieonians v Hibernian 0-3
Ayr United v Motherwell 2-2, 1-2

SEMI-FINAL

Celtic v Raith Rovers 3-2
Hibernian v Motherwell 2-3

FINAL

Celtic v Motherwell 1-0

League Tables 1951-52

FIRST DIVISION

		P	W	D	L	F	A	Pts
1	Man United	42	23	11	8	95	52	57
2	Tottenham	42	22	9	11	76	51	53
3	Arsenal	42	21	11	10	80	61	53
4	Portsmouth	42	20	8	14	68	58	48
5	Bolton	42	19	10	13	65	61	48
6	Aston Villa	42	19	9	14	79	70	47
7	Preston	42	17	12	13	74	54	46
8	Newcastle	42	18	9	15	98	73	45
9	Blackpool	42	18	9	15	64	64	45
10	Charlton	42	17	10	15	68	63	44
11	Liverpool	42	12	19	11	57	61	43
12	Sunderland	42	15	12	15	70	61	42
13	WBA	42	14	13	15	74	77	41
14	Burnley	42	15	10	17	56	63	40
15	Man City	42	13	13	16	58	61	39
16	Wolves	42	12	14	16	73	73	38
17	Derby	42	15	7	20	63	80	37
18	Middlesbrough	42	15	6	21	64	88	36
19	Chelsea	42	14	8	20	52	72	36
20	Stoke	42	12	7	23	49	88	31
21	Huddersfield	42	10	8	24	49	82	28
22	Fulham	42	8	11	23	58	77	27

SECOND DIVISION

		P	W	D	L	F	A	Pts
1	Sheff Wed	42	21	11	10	100	66	53
2	Cardiff	42	20	11	11	72	54	51
3	Birmingham	42	21	9	12	67	56	51
4	Nottm Forest	42	18	13	11	77	62	49
5	Leicester	42	19	9	14	78	64	47
6	Leeds	42	18	11	13	59	57	47
7	Everton	42	17	10	15	64	58	44
8	Luton	42	16	12	14	77	78	44
9	Rotherham	42	17	8	17	73	71	42
10	Brentford	42	15	12	15	54	55	42
11	Sheff United	42	18	5	19	90	76	41
12	West Ham	42	15	11	16	67	77	41
13	Southampton	42	15	11	16	61	73	41
14	Blackburn	42	17	6	19	54	63	40
15	Notts County	42	16	7	19	71	68	39
16	Doncaster	42	13	12	17	55	60	38
17	Bury	42	15	7	20	67	69	37
18	Hull	42	13	11	18	60	70	37
19	Swansea	42	12	12	18	72	76	36
20	Barnsley	42	11	14	17	59	72	36
21	Coventry	42	14	6	22	59	82	34
22	QPR	42	11	12	19	52	81	34

THIRD DIVISION (SOUTH)

		P	W	D	L	F	A	Pts
1	Plymouth	46	29	8	9	107	53	66
2	Reading	46	29	3	14	112	60	61
3	Norwich	46	26	9	11	89	50	61
4	Millwall	46	23	12	11	74	53	58
5	Brighton	46	24	10	12	87	63	58
6	Newport	46	21	12	13	77	76	54
7	Bristol Rovers	46	20	12	14	89	53	52
8	Northampton	46	22	5	19	93	74	49
9	Southend	46	19	10	17	75	66	48
10	Colchester	46	17	12	17	56	77	46
11	Torquay	46	17	10	19	86	98	44
12	Aldershot	46	18	8	20	78	89	44
13	Port Vale	46	14	15	17	50	66	43
14	Bournemouth	46	16	10	20	69	75	42
15	Bristol City	46	15	12	19	58	69	42
16	Swindon	46	14	14	18	51	68	42
17	Ipswich	46	16	9	21	63	74	41
18	Leyton Orient	46	16	9	21	55	68	41
19	Crystal Palace	46	15	9	22	61	80	39
20	Shrewsbury	46	13	10	23	62	86	36
21	Watford	46	13	10	23	57	81	36
22	Gillingham	46	11	13	22	71	81	35
23	Exeter	46	13	9	24	65	86	35
24	Walsall	46	13	5	28	55	94	31

THIRD DIVISION (NORTH)

		P	W	D	L	F	A	Pts
1	Lincoln	46	30	9	7	121	52	69
2	Grimsby	46	29	8	9	96	45	66
3	Stockport	46	23	13	10	74	40	59
4	Oldham	46	24	9	13	90	61	57
5	Gateshead	46	21	11	14	66	49	53
6	Mansfield	46	22	8	16	73	60	52
7	Carlisle	46	19	13	14	62	57	51
8	Bradford PA	46	19	12	15	74	64	50
9	Hartlepools	46	21	8	17	71	65	50
10	York	46	18	13	15	73	52	49
11	Tranmere	46	21	6	19	76	71	48
12	Barrow	46	17	12	17	57	61	46
13	Chesterfield	46	17	11	18	65	66	45
14	Scunthorpe	46	14	16	16	65	74	44
15	Bradford City	46	16	10	20	61	68	42
16	Crewe	46	17	8	21	63	82	42
17	Southport	46	15	11	20	53	71	41
18	Wrexham	46	15	9	22	63	73	39
19	Chester	46	15	9	22	72	85	39
20	Halifax	46	14	7	25	61	97	35
21	Rochdale	46	11	13	22	47	79	35
22	Accrington	46	10	12	24	61	92	32
23	Darlington	46	11	9	26	64	103	31
24	Workington	46	11	7	28	50	91	29

SCOTTISH DIVISION 'A'

		P	W	D	L	F	A	Pts
1	Hibernian	30	20	5	5	92	36	45
2	Rangers	30	16	9	5	61	31	41
3	East Fife	30	17	3	10	71	49	37
4	Hearts	30	14	7	9	69	53	35
5	Raith	30	14	5	11	43	42	33
6	Partick	30	12	7	11	48	51	31
7	Motherwell	30	12	7	11	51	57	31
8	Dundee	30	11	6	13	53	52	28
9	Celtic	30	10	8	12	52	55	28
10	Queen of the S	30	10	8	12	50	60	28
11	Aberdeen	30	10	7	13	65	58	27
12	Third Lanark	30	9	8	13	51	62	26
13	Airdrieonians	30	11	4	15	54	69	26
14	St Mirren	30	10	5	15	43	58	25
15	Morton	30	9	6	15	49	56	24
16	Stirling	30	5	5	20	36	99	15

SCOTTISH DIVISION 'B'

		P	W	D	L	F	A	Pts
1	Clyde	30	19	6	5	100	45	44
2	Falkirk	30	18	7	5	80	34	43
3	Ayr	30	17	5	8	55	45	39
4	Dundee United	30	16	5	9	75	60	37
5	Kilmarnock	30	16	2	12	62	48	34
6	Dunfermline	30	15	2	13	74	65	32
7	Alloa	30	13	6	11	55	49	32
8	Cowdenbeath	30	12	8	10	66	67	32
9	Hamilton	30	12	6	12	47	51	30
10	Dumbarton	30	10	8	12	51	57	28
11	St Johnstone	30	9	7	14	62	68	25
12	Forfar	30	10	4	16	59	97	24
13	Stenhousemuir	30	8	6	16	57	74	22
14	Albion	30	6	10	14	39	57	22
15	Queen's Park	30	8	4	18	40	62	20
16	Arbroath	30	6	4	20	40	83	16

An Englishman from Wales

The first player to appear in an England representative side while not attached to an English club was Charlie Rutter, Cardiff City's right-back. Rutter played for the England 'B' side against the Netherlands 'B' side in Amsterdam, March 1952. England won the match—a kind of forerunner to the Under-23 international games—1-0.

Freddie Steele's move from Mansfield to Port Vale on 28 December 1951 was the first case of a player-manager being transferred from one Football League club to another.

Billy Foulkes of Newcastle United scored with his first kick in his first international appearance for Wales, against England at Cardiff in October 1951.

FA CUP 1951-52

FOURTH ROUND

Tottenham Hotspur v Newcastle United	0-3
Swansea Town v Rotherham United	3-0
Notts County v Portsmouth	1-3
Middlesbrough v Doncaster Rovers	1-4
Blackburn Rovers v Hull City	2-0
Gateshead v West Bromwich Albion	0-2
Burnley v Coventry City	2-0
Liverpool v Wolverhampton Wanderers	2-1
Arsenal v Barnsley	4-0
Birmingham City v Leyton Orient	0-1
Luton Town v Brentford	2-2, 0-0, 3-2
Swindon Town v Stoke City	1-1, 1-0
Chelsea v Tranmere Rovers	4-0
Leeds United v Bradford Park Avenue	2-0
West Ham United v Sheffield United	0-0, 2-4
Southend United v Bristol Rovers	2-1

FIFTH ROUND

Swansea Town v Newcastle United	0-1
Portsmouth v Doncaster Rovers	4-0
Blackburn Rovers v West Bromwich Albion	1-0
Burnley v Liverpool	2-0
Leyton Orient v Arsenal	0-3
Luton Town v Swindon Town	3-1
Leeds United v Chelsea	1-1, 1-1, 1-5
Southend United v Sheffield United	1-2

SIXTH ROUND

Portsmouth v Newcastle United	2-4
Blackburn Rovers v Burnley	3-1
Luton Town v Arsenal	2-3
Sheffield United v Chelsea	0-1

SEMI-FINAL

Newcastle United v Blackburn Rovers	0-0, 2-1
Arsenal v Chelsea	1-1, 3-0

FINAL

Newcastle United v Arsenal	1-0

SCOTTISH FA CUP 1951-52

SECOND ROUND

St Mirren v Motherwell	2-3
Clyde v Dunfermline Athletic	3-4
Rangers v Elgin City	6-1
Cowdenbeath v Arbroath	1-4
Heart of Midlothian v Raith Rovers	1-0
St Johnstone v Queen of the South	2-2, 1-3
Airdrieonians v East Fife	2-1
Clachnacuddin v Morton	1-2
Wigtown & Bladnoch v Dundee	1-7
Alloa Athletic v Berwick Rangers	0-0, 1-4
Aberdeen v Kilmarnock	2-1
Leith Athletic v Dundee United	1-4
Hamilton Academicals v Third Lanark	1-1, 0-4
Albion Rovers v Stranraer	1-1, 4-3
Falkirk v Stirling Albion	3-3, 2-1
Dumbarton v Queen's Park	1-0

THIRD ROUND

Dunfermline Athletic v Motherwell	1-1, 0-4
Arbroath v Rangers	0-2
Queen of the South v Heart of Midlothian	1-3
Airdrieonians v Morton	4-0
Dundee v Berwick Rangers	1-0
Dundee United v Aberdeen	2-2, 2-3
Albion Rovers v Third Lanark	1-3
Dumbarton v Falkirk	1-3

FOURTH ROUND

Rangers v Motherwell	1-1, 1-2
Airdrieonians v Heart of Midlothian	2-2, 4-6
Dundee v Aberdeen	4-0
Third Lanark v Falkirk	1-0

SEMI-FINAL

Motherwell v Heart of Midlothian	1-1, 1-1, 3-1
Dundee v Third Lanark	2-0

FINAL

Motherwell v Dundee	4-0

League Tables 1952-53

FIRST DIVISION

	P	W	D	L	F	A	Pts
1 Arsenal	42	21	12	9	97	64	54
2 Preston	42	21	12	9	85	60	54
3 Wolves	42	19	13	10	86	63	51
4 WBA	42	21	8	13	66	60	50
5 Charlton	42	19	11	12	77	63	49
6 Burnley	42	18	12	12	67	52	48
7 Blackpool	42	19	9	14	71	70	47
8 Man United	42	18	10	14	69	72	46
9 Sunderland	42	15	13	14	68	82	43
10 Tottenham	42	15	11	16	78	69	41
11 Aston Villa	42	14	13	15	63	61	41
12 Cardiff	42	14	12	16	54	46	40
13 Middlesbrough	42	14	11	17	70	77	39
14 Bolton	42	15	9	18	61	69	39
15 Portsmouth	42	14	10	18	74	83	38
16 Newcastle	42	14	9	19	59	70	37
17 Liverpool	42	14	8	20	61	82	36
18 Sheff Wed	42	12	11	19	62	72	35
19 Chelsea	42	12	11	19	56	66	35
20 Man City	42	14	7	21	72	87	35
21 Stoke	42	12	10	20	53	66	34
22 Derby	42	11	10	21	59	74	32

SECOND DIVISION

	P	W	D	L	F	A	Pts
1 Sheff United	42	25	10	7	97	55	60
2 Huddersfield	42	24	10	8	84	33	58
3 Luton	42	22	8	12	84	49	52
4 Plymouth	42	20	9	13	65	60	49
5 Leicester	42	18	12	12	89	74	48
6 Birmingham	42	19	10	13	71	66	48
7 Nottm Forest	42	18	8	16	77	67	44
8 Fulham	42	17	10	15	81	71	44
9 Blackburn	42	18	8	16	68	65	44
10 Leeds	42	14	15	13	71	63	43
11 Swansea	42	15	12	15	78	81	42
12 Rotherham	42	16	9	17	75	74	41
13 Doncaster	42	12	16	14	58	64	40
14 West Ham	42	13	13	16	58	60	39
15 Lincoln	42	11	17	14	64	71	39
16 Everton	42	12	14	16	71	75	38
17 Brentford	42	13	11	18	59	76	37
18 Hull	42	14	8	20	57	69	36
19 Notts County	42	14	8	20	60	88	36
20 Bury	42	13	9	20	53	81	35
21 Southampton	42	10	13	19	68	85	33
22 Barnsley	42	5	8	29	47	108	18

THIRD DIVISION (NORTH)

	P	W	D	L	F	A	Pts
1 Oldham	46	22	15	9	77	45	59
2 Port Vale	46	20	18	8	67	35	58
3 Wrexham	46	24	8	14	86	66	56
4 York	46	20	13	13	60	45	53
5 Grimsby	46	21	10	15	75	59	52
6 Southport	46	20	11	15	63	60	51
7 Bradford PA	46	19	12	15	75	61	50
8 Gateshead	46	17	15	14	76	60	49
9 Carlisle	46	18	13	15	82	68	49
10 Crewe	46	20	8	18	70	68	48
11 Stockport	46	17	13	16	82	69	47
12 Chesterfield*	46	18	11	17	65	63	47
13 Tranmere*	46	21	5	20	65	63	47
14 Halifax	46	16	15	15	68	68	47
15 Scunthorpe	46	16	14	16	62	56	46
16 Bradford City	46	14	18	14	75	80	46
17 Hartlepools	46	16	14	16	57	61	46
18 Mansfield	46	16	14	16	55	62	46
19 Barrow	46	16	12	18	66	71	44
20 Chester	46	11	15	20	64	85	37
21 Darlington	46	14	6	26	58	96	34
22 Rochdale	46	14	5	27	62	83	33
23 Workington	46	11	10	25	55	91	32
24 Accrington	46	8	11	27	39	89	27

*Equal

THIRD DIVISION (SOUTH)

	P	W	D	L	F	A	Pts
1 Bristol Rovers	46	26	12	8	92	46	64
2 Millwall	46	24	14	8	82	44	62
3 Northampton	46	26	10	10	109	70	62
4 Norwich	26	25	10	11	99	55	60
5 Bristol City	46	22	15	9	95	61	59
6 Coventry	46	19	12	15	77	62	50
7 Brighton	46	19	12	15	81	75	50
8 Southend	46	18	13	15	69	74	49
9 Bournemouth	46	19	9	18	74	69	47
10 Watford	46	15	17	14	62	63	47
11 Reading	46	19	8	19	69	64	46
12 Torquay	46	18	9	19	87	88	45
13 Crystal Palace	46	15	13	18	66	82	43
14 Leyton Orient	46	16	10	20	68	73	42
15 Newport	46	16	10	20	70	82	42
16 Ipswich	46	13	15	18	60	69	41
17 Exeter	46	13	14	19	61	71	40
18 Swindon	46	14	12	20	64	79	40
19 Aldershot	46	12	15	19	61	77	39
20 Gillingham	46	12	15	19	55	74	39
21 QPR	46	12	15	19	61	82	39
22 Colchester	46	12	14	20	59	76	38
23 Shrewsbury	46	12	12	22	68	91	36
24 Walsall	46	7	10	29	56	118	24

SCOTTISH DIVISION 'A'

	P	W	D	L	F	A	Pts
1 Rangers	30	18	7	5	80	39	43
2 Hibernian	30	19	5	6	93	51	43
3 East Fife	30	16	7	7	72	48	39
4 Hearts	30	12	6	12	59	50	30
5 Clyde	30	13	4	13	78	78	30
6 St Mirren	30	11	8	11	52	58	30
7 Dundee	30	9	11	8	44	37	29
8 Celtic	30	11	7	12	51	54	29
9 Partick	30	10	9	11	55	63	29
10 Queen of the S	30	10	8	12	43	61	28
11 Aberdeen	30	11	5	14	64	68	27
12 Raith Rovers	30	9	8	13	47	53	26
13 Falkirk	30	11	4	15	53	63	26
14 Airdrieonians	30	10	6	14	53	75	26
15 Motherwell	30	10	5	15	57	80	25
16 Third Lanark	30	8	4	18	52	75	20

SCOTTISH DIVISION 'B'

	P	W	D	L	F	A	Pts
1 Stirling	30	20	4	6	64	43	44
2 Hamilton	30	20	3	7	72	40	43
3 Queen's Park	30	15	7	8	70	46	37
4 Kilmarnock	30	17	2	11	74	48	36
5 Ayr	30	17	2	11	76	56	36
6 Morton	30	15	3	12	79	57	33
7 Arbroath	30	13	7	10	52	57	33
8 Dundee United	30	12	5	13	52	56	29
9 Alloa	30	12	5	13	63	68	29
10 Dumbarton	30	11	6	13	58	67	28
11 Dunfermline	30	9	9	12	51	58	27
12 Stenhousemuir	30	10	6	14	56	65	26
13 Cowdenbeath	30	8	7	15	37	54	23
14 St Johnstone	30	8	6	16	41	63	22
15 Forfar	30	8	4	18	54	88	20
16 Albion	30	5	4	21	44	77	14

A Division One match between Aston Villa and Sunderland in September 1952 produced a remarkable goal. It was scored by Peter Aldis, the Aston Villa full-back, who headed the ball into Sunderland's net from 35 yards. This goal, Aldis's first in the League, is reckoned to give Aldis the distance record for a headed goal in League football.

The footballing parson

The only post-War Football League professional who was also a parson was the Reverend Norman Hallam. A Methodist minister, Hallam was right-half for Port Vale in 1952-53. He later played for Barnsley and then Halifax before joining the Midland League club, Goole Town.

FA CUP 1952-53

FOURTH ROUND

Blackpool v Huddersfield Town	1-0
Shrewsbury Town v Southampton	1-4
Arsenal v Bury	6-2
Burnley v Sunderland	2-0
Preston North End v Tottenham Hotspur	2-2, 0-1
Halifax Town v Stoke City	1-0
Sheffield United v Birmingham City	1-1, 1-3
Chelsea v West Bromwich Albion	1-1, 0-0, 1-1, 4-0
Bolton Wanderers v Notts County	1-1, 2-2, 1-0
Manchester City v Luton Town	1-1, 1-5
Hull City v Gateshead	1-2
Plymouth Argyle v Barnsley	1-0
Everton v Nottingham Forest	4-1
Manchester United v Walthamstow Avenue	1-1, 5-2
Aston Villa v Brentford	0-0, 2-1
Newcastle United v Rotherham United	1-3

FIFTH ROUND

Blackpool v Southampton	1-1, 2-1
Burnley v Arsenal	0-2
Halifax Town v Tottenham Hotspur	0-3
Chelsea v Birmingham City	0-4
Luton Town v Bolton Wanderers	0-1
Plymouth Argyle v Gateshead	0-1
Everton v Manchester United	2-1
Rotherham United v Aston Villa	1-3

SIXTH ROUND

Arsenal v Blackpool	1-2
Birmingham City v Tottenham Hotspur	1-1, 2-2, 0-1
Gateshead v Bolton Wanderers	0-1
Aston Villa v Everton	0-1

SEMI-FINAL

Blackpool v Tottenham Hotspur	2-1
Bolton Wanderers v Everton	4-3

FINAL

Blackpool v Bolton Wanderers	4-3

SCOTTISH FA CUP 1952-53

SECOND ROUND

Dundee v Rangers	0-2
Cowdenbeath v Morton	0-1
Forfar Athletic v Falkirk	2-4
Stirling Albion v Celtic	1-1, 0-3
Raith Rovers v Heart of Midlothian	0-1
St Johnstone v Montrose	1-2
Berwick Rangers v Queen of the South	2-3
Albion Rovers v East Stirlingshire	2-0
Partick Thistle v Clyde	0-2
Buckie Thistle v Ayr United	1-5
Wigtown & Bladnoch v Third Lanark	1-3
Hamilton Academicals v Kilmarnock	2-2, 2-0
Airdrieonians v East Fife	3-0
Hibernian v Queen's Park	4-2
Alloa Athletic v Motherwell	0-2
Aberdeen v St Mirren	2-0

THIRD ROUND

Morton v Rangers	1-4
Falkirk v Celtic	2-3
Heart of Midlothian v Montrose	3-1
Queen of the South v Albion Rovers	2-0
Clyde v Ayr United	8-3
Third Lanark v Hamilton Academicals	1-0
Airdrieonians v Hibernian	0-4
Aberdeen v Motherwell	5-5, 6-1

FOURTH ROUND

Rangers v Celtic	2-0
Heart of Midlothian v Queen of the South	2-1
Clyde v Third Lanark	1-2
Hibernian v Aberdeen	1-1, 0-2

SEMI-FINAL

Rangers v Heart of Midlothian	2-1
Third Lanark v Aberdeen	1-1, 1-2

FINAL

Aberdeen v Rangers	1-1, 0-1

FIRST DIVISION

		P	W	D	L	F	A	Pts
1	Wolves	42	25	7	10	96	56	57
2	WBA	42	22	9	11	86	63	53
3	Huddersfield	42	20	11	11	78	61	51
4	Man United	42	18	12	12	73	58	48
5	Bolton	42	18	12	12	75	60	48
6	Blackpool	42	19	10	13	80	69	48
7	Burnley	42	21	4	17	78	67	46
8	Chelsea	42	16	12	14	74	68	44
9	Charlton	42	19	6	17	75	77	44
10	Cardiff	42	18	8	16	51	71	44
11	Preston	42	19	5	18	87	58	43
12	Arsenal	42	15	13	14	75	73	43
13	Aston Villa	42	16	9	17	70	68	41
14	Portsmouth	42	14	11	17	81	89	39
15	Newcastle	42	14	10	18	72	77	38
16	Tottenham	42	16	5	21	65	76	37
17	Man City	42	14	9	19	62	77	37
18	Sunderland	42	14	8	20	81	89	36
19	Sheff Wed	42	15	6	21	70	91	36
20	Sheff United	42	11	11	20	69	90	33
21	Middlesbrough	42	10	10	22	60	91	30
22	Liverpool	42	9	10	23	68	97	28

SECOND DIVISION

		P	W	D	L	F	A	Pts
1	Leicester	42	23	10	9	97	60	56
2	Everton	42	20	16	6	92	58	56
3	Blackburn	42	23	9	10	86	50	55
4	Nottm Forest	42	20	12	10	86	59	52
5	Rotherham	42	21	7	14	80	67	49
6	Luton	42	18	12	12	64	59	48
7	Birmingham	42	18	11	13	78	58	47
8	Fulham	42	17	10	15	98	85	44
9	Bristol Rovers	42	14	16	12	64	58	44
10	Leeds	42	15	13	14	89	81	43
11	Stoke	42	12	17	13	71	60	41
12	Doncaster	42	16	9	17	59	63	41
13	West Ham	42	15	9	18	67	69	39
14	Notts County	42	13	13	16	54	74	39
15	Hull	42	16	6	20	64	66	38
16	Lincoln	42	14	9	19	65	83	37
17	Bury	42	11	14	17	54	72	36
18	Derby	42	12	11	19	64	82	35
19	Plymouth	42	9	16	17	65	82	34
20	Swansea	42	13	8	21	58	82	34
21	Brentford	42	10	11	21	40	78	31
22	Oldham	42	8	9	25	40	89	25

THIRD DIVISION (SOUTH)

		P	W	D	L	F	A	Pts
1	Ipswich	46	27	10	9	82	51	64
2	Brighton	46	26	9	11	86	61	61
3	Bristol City	46	25	6	15	88	66	56
4	Watford	46	21	10	15	85	69	52
5	Northampton	46	20	11	15	82	55	51
6	Southampton	46	22	7	17	76	63	51
7	Norwich	46	20	11	15	73	66	51
8	Reading	46	20	9	17	86	73	49
9	Exeter	46	20	8	18	68	58	48
10	Gillingham	46	19	10	17	61	66	48
11	Leyton Orient	46	18	11	17	79	73	47
12	Millwall	46	19	9	18	74	77	47
13	Torquay	46	17	12	17	81	88	46
14	Coventry	46	18	9	19	61	56	45
15	Newport	46	19	6	21	61	81	44
16	Southend	46	18	7	21	69	71	43
17	Aldershot	46	17	9	20	74	86	43
18	QPR	46	16	10	20	60	68	42
19	Bournemouth	46	16	8	22	67	70	40
20	Swindon	46	15	10	21	67	70	40
21	Shrewsbury	46	14	12	20	65	76	40
22	Crystal Palace	46	14	12	20	60	86	40
23	Colchester	46	10	10	26	50	78	30
24	Walsall	46	9	8	29	40	87	26

THIRD DIVISION (NORTH)

		P	W	D	L	F	A	Pts
1	Port Vale	46	26	17	3	74	21	69
2	Barnsley	46	24	10	12	77	57	58
3	Scunthorpe	46	21	15	10	77	56	57
4	Gateshead	46	21	13	12	74	55	55
5	Bradford City	46	22	9	15	60	55	53
6	Chesterfield	46	19	14	13	76	64	52
7	Mansfield	46	20	11	15	88	67	51
8	Wrexham	46	21	9	16	81	68	51
9	Bradford PA	46	18	14	14	77	68	50
10	Stockport	46	18	11	17	77	67	47
11	Southport	46	17	12	17	63	60	46
12	Barrow	46	16	12	18	72	71	44
13	Carlisle	46	14	15	17	83	71	43
14	Tranmere	46	18	7	21	59	70	43
15	Accrington	46	16	10	20	66	74	42
16	Crewe	46	14	13	19	49	67	41
17	Grimsby	46	16	9	21	51	77	41
18	Hartlepools	46	13	14	19	59	65	40
19	Rochdale	46	15	10	21	59	77	40
20	Workington	46	13	14	19	59	80	40
21	Darlington	46	12	14	20	50	71	38
22	York	46	12	13	21	64	86	37
23	Halifax	46	12	10	24	44	73	34
24	Chester	46	11	10	25	48	67	32

SCOTTISH DIVISION 'A'

		P	W	D	L	F	A	Pts
1	Celtic	30	20	3	7	72	29	43
2	Hearts	30	16	6	8	70	45	38
3	Partick	30	17	1	12	76	54	35
4	Rangers	30	13	8	9	56	35	34
5	Hibernian	30	15	4	11	72	51	34
6	East Fife	30	13	8	9	55	45	34
7	Dundee	30	14	6	10	46	47	34
8	Clyde	30	15	4	11	64	67	34
9	Aberdeen	30	15	3	12	66	51	33
10	Queen of the S	30	14	4	12	72	53	32
11	St Mirren	30	12	4	14	44	54	28
12	Raith	30	10	6	14	56	60	26
13	Falkirk	30	9	7	14	47	61	25
14	Stirling	30	10	4	16	39	62	24
15	Airdrieonians	30	5	5	20	41	92	15
16	Hamilton	30	4	3	23	29	94	11

SCOTTISH DIVISION 'B'

		P	W	D	L	F	A	Pts
1	Motherwell	30	21	3	6	109	43	45
2	Kilmarnock	30	19	4	7	71	39	42
3	Third Lanark	30	13	10	7	78	48	36
4	Stenhousemuir	30	14	8	8	66	58	36
5	Morton	30	15	3	12	85	65	33
6	St Johnstone	30	14	3	13	80	71	31
7	Albion	30	12	7	11	55	63	31
8	Dunfermline	30	11	9	10	48	57	31
9	Ayr	30	11	8	11	50	56	30
10	Queen's Park	30	9	9	12	56	51	27
11	Alloa	30	7	10	13	50	72	24
12	Forfar	30	10	4	16	38	69	24
13	Cowdenbeath	30	9	5	16	67	81	23
14	Arbroath	30	8	7	15	53	67	23
15	Dundee United	30	8	6	16	54	79	22
16	Dumbarton	30	7	8	15	51	92	22

Since the offside rule was changed in 1925, the record number of League games which a club has played in any one season without conceding a goal is 30. Port Vale, with their unpopular yet effective brand of defensive football, set this record in Division Three North, 1953-54. That season, Vale lost but three games, also a record for that division, conceding just 21 goals, a League record.

Stalemate
On 9 January 1954, 15 of the 32 Third Round FA Cup ties played that day ended as draws, a record for the FA Cup competition.

A post-war record Scottish FA Cup win away from home was set on 13 February 1954. Then, in the Second Round, Raith Rovers crumpled Coldstream 10-1.

FA CUP 1953-54

FOURTH ROUND

West Bromwich Albion v Rotherham United 4-0
Burnley v Newcastle United 1-1, 0-1
Blackburn Rovers v Hull City 2-2, 1-2
Manchester City v Tottenham Hotspur 0-1
Leyton Orient v Fulham 2-1
Plymouth Argyle v Doncaster Rovers 0-2
Cardiff City v Port Vale 0-2
West Ham United v Blackpool 1-1, 1-3
Sheffield Wednesday v Chesterfield 0-0, 4-2
Everton v Swansea Town 3-0
Headington United v Bolton Wanderers 2-4
Scunthorpe United v Portsmouth 1-1, 2-2, 0-4
Arsenal v Norwich City 1-2
Stoke City v Leicester City 0-0, 1-3
Lincoln City v Preston North End 0-2
Ipswich Town v Birmingham City 1-0

FIFTH ROUND

West Bromwich Albion v Newcastle United 3-2
Hull City v Tottenham Hotspur 1-1, 0-2
Leyton Orient v Doncaster Rovers 3-1
Port Vale v Blackpool 2-0
Sheffield Wednesday v Everton 3-1
Bolton Wanderers v Portsmouth 0-0, 2-1
Norwich City v Leicester City 1-2
Preston North End v Ipswich Town 6-1

SIXTH ROUND

West Bromwich Albion v Tottenham Hotspur 3-0
Leyton Orient v Port Vale 0-1
Sheffield Wednesday v Bolton Wanderers 1-1, 2-0
Leicester City v Preston North End 1-1, 2-2, 1-3

SEMI-FINAL

West Bromwich Albion v Port Vale 2-1
Sheffield Wednesday v Preston North End 0-2

FINAL

West Bromwich Albion v Preston North End 3-2

SCOTTISH FA CUP 1953-54

SECOND ROUND

Falkirk v Celtic 1-2
Stirling Albion v Arbroath 0-0, 3-1
Brechin City v Hamilton Academicals 2-3
Morton v Cowdenbeath 4-0
Tarff Rovers v Partick Thistle 1-9
Peebles Rovers v Buckie Thistle 1-1, 2-7
Motherwell v Dunfermline Athletic 5-2
Coldstream v Raith Rovers 1-10
Third Lanark v Deveronvale 7-2
Rangers v Kilmarnock 2-2, 3-1
Berwick Rangers v Ayr United 5-1
Albion Rovers v Dundee 1-1, 0-4
Queen of the South v Forfar Athletic 3-0
Fraserburgh v Heart of Midlothian 0-3
Hibernian v Clyde 7-0
Duns v Aberdeen 0-8

THIRD ROUND

Stirling Albion v Celtic 3-4
Hamilton Academicals v Morton 2-0
Partick Thistle v Buckie Thistle 5-3
Motherwell v Raith Rovers 4-1
Third Lanark v Rangers 0-0, 4-4, 2-3
Berwick Rangers v Dundee 3-0
Queen of the South v Heart of Midlothian 1-2
Hibernian v Aberdeen 1-3

FOURTH ROUND

Hamilton Academicals v Celtic 1-2
Partick Thistle v Motherwell 1-1, 1-2
Rangers v Berwick Rangers 4-0
Aberdeen v Heart of Midlothian 3-0

SEMI-FINAL

Celtic v Motherwell 2-2, 3-1
Rangers v Aberdeen 0-6

FINAL

Aberdeen v Celtic 1-2

League Tables 1954-55

FIRST DIVISION

	P	W	D	L	F	A	Pts
1 Chelsea	42	20	12	10	81	57	52
2 Wolves	42	19	10	13	89	70	48
3 Portsmouth	42	18	12	12	74	62	48
4 Sunderland	42	15	18	9	64	54	48
5 Man United	42	20	7	15	84	74	47
6 Aston Villa	42	20	7	15	72	73	47
7 Man City	42	18	10	14	76	69	46
8 Newcastle	42	17	9	16	89	77	43
9 Arsenal	42	17	9	16	69	63	43
10 Burnley	42	17	9	16	51	48	43
11 Everton	42	16	10	16	62	68	42
12 Huddersfield	42	14	13	15	63	68	41
13 Sheff United	42	17	7	18	70	86	41
14 Preston	42	16	8	18	83	64	40
15 Charlton	42	15	10	17	76	75	40
16 Tottenham	42	16	8	18	72	73	40
17 WBA	42	16	8	18	76	96	40
18 Bolton	42	13	13	16	62	69	39
19 Blackpool	42	14	10	18	60	64	38
20 Cardiff	42	13	11	18	62	76	37
21 Leicester	42	12	11	19	74	86	35
22 Sheff Wed	42	8	10	24	63	100	26

SECOND DIVISION

	P	W	D	L	F	A	Pts
1 Birmingham	42	22	10	10	92	47	54
2 Luton	42	23	8	11	88	53	54
3 Rotherham	42	25	4	13	94	64	54
4 Leeds	42	23	7	12	70	53	53
5 Stoke	42	21	10	11	69	46	52
6 Blackburn	42	22	6	14	114	79	50
7 Notts County	42	21	6	15	74	71	48
8 West Ham	42	18	10	14	74	70	46
9 Bristol Rovers	42	19	7	16	75	70	45
10 Swansea	42	17	9	16	86	83	43
11 Liverpool	42	16	10	16	92	96	42
12 Middlesbrough	42	18	6	18	73	82	42
13 Bury	42	15	11	16	77	72	41
14 Fulham	42	14	11	17	76	79	39
15 Nottm Forest	42	16	7	19	58	62	39
16 Lincoln	42	13	10	19	68	79	36
17 Port Vale	42	12	11	19	48	71	35
18 Doncaster	42	14	7	21	58	95	35
19 Hull	42	12	10	20	44	69	34
20 Plymouth	42	12	7	23	57	82	31
21 Ipswich	42	11	6	25	57	92	28
22 Derby	42	7	9	26	53	82	23

THIRD DIVISION (SOUTH)

	P	W	D	L	F	A	Pts
1 Bristol City	46	30	10	6	101	47	70
2 Leyton Orient	46	26	9	11	89	47	61
3 Southampton	46	24	11	11	75	51	59
4 Gillingham	46	20	15	11	77	66	55
5 Millwall	46	20	11	15	72	68	51
6 Brighton	46	20	10	16	76	63	50
7 Watford	46	18	14	14	71	62	50
8 Torquay	46	18	12	16	82	82	48
9 Coventry	46	18	11	17	67	59	47
10 Southend	46	17	12	17	83	80	46
11 Brentford	46	16	14	16	82	82	46
12 Norwich	46	18	10	18	60	60	46
13 Northampton	46	19	8	19	73	81	46
14 Aldershot	46	16	13	17	75	71	45
15 QPR	46	15	14	17	69	75	44
16 Shrewsbury	46	16	10	20	70	78	42
17 Bournemouth	46	12	18	16	57	65	42
18 Reading	46	13	15	18	65	73	41
19 Newport	46	11	16	19	60	73	38
20 Crystal Palace	46	11	16	19	52	80	38
21 Swindon	46	11	15	20	46	64	37
22 Exeter	46	11	15	20	47	73	37
23 Walsall	46	10	14	22	75	86	34
24 Colchester	46	9	13	24	53	91	31

THIRD DIVISION (NORTH)

	P	W	D	L	F	A	Pts
1 Barnsley	46	30	5	11	86	46	65
2 Accrington	46	25	11	10	96	67	61
3 Scunthorpe	46	23	12	11	81	53	58
4 York	46	24	10	12	92	63	58
5 Hartlepools	46	25	5	16	64	49	55
6 Chesterfield	46	24	6	16	81	70	54
7 Gateshead	46	20	12	14	65	69	52
8 Workington	46	18	14	14	68	55	50
9 Stockport	46	18	12	16	84	70	48
10 Oldham	46	19	10	17	74	68	48
11 Southport	46	16	16	14	47	44	48
12 Rochdale	46	17	14	15	69	66	48
13 Mansfield	46	18	9	19	65	71	45
14 Halifax	46	15	13	18	63	67	43
15 Darlington	46	14	14	18	62	73	42
16 Bradford PA	46	15	11	20	56	70	41
17 Barrow	46	17	6	23	70	89	40
18 Wrexham	46	13	12	21	65	77	38
19 Tranmere	46	13	11	22	55	70	37
20 Carlisle	46	15	6	25	78	89	36
21 Bradford City	46	13	10	23	47	55	36
22 Crewe	46	10	14	22	68	91	34
23 Grimsby	46	13	8	25	47	78	34
24 Chester	46	12	9	25	44	77	33

SCOTTISH DIVISION 'A'

	P	W	D	L	F	A	Pts
1 Aberdeen	30	24	1	5	73	26	49
2 Celtic	30	19	8	3	76	37	46
3 Rangers	30	19	3	8	67	33	41
4 Hearts	30	16	7	7	74	45	39
5 Hibernian	30	15	4	11	64	54	34
6 St Mirren	30	12	8	10	55	54	32
7 Clyde	30	11	9	10	59	50	31
8 Dundee	30	13	4	13	48	48	30
9 Partick Thistle	30	11	7	12	49	61	29
10 Kilmarnock	30	10	6	14	46	58	26
11 East Fife	30	9	6	15	51	62	24
12 Falkirk	30	8	8	14	42	54	24
13 Queen of the S	30	9	6	15	38	56	24
14 Raith	30	10	3	17	49	57	23
15 Motherwell	30	9	4	17	42	62	22
16 Stirling	30	2	2	26	29	105	6

SCOTTISH DIVISION 'B'

	P	W	D	L	F	A	Pts
1 Airdrieonians	30	18	10	2	103	61	46
2 Dunfermline	30	19	4	7	72	40	42
3 Hamilton	30	17	5	8	74	51	39
4 Queen's Park	30	15	5	10	65	36	35
5 Third Lanark	30	13	7	10	63	49	33
6 Stenhousemuir	30	12	8	10	70	51	32
7 St Johnstone	30	15	2	13	60	51	32
8 Ayr	30	14	4	12	61	73	32
9 Morton	30	12	5	13	58	69	29
10 Forfar	30	11	6	13	63	80	28
11 Albion	30	8	10	12	50	69	26
12 Arbroath	30	8	8	14	55	72	24
13 Dundee United	30	8	6	16	55	70	22
14 Cowdenbeath	30	8	5	17	55	72	21
15 Alloa	30	7	6	17	51	75	20
16 Brechin	30	8	3	19	53	89	19

A combined effort

Stan Milburn and Jack Froggatt, both Leicester City defenders, are officially recorded as 'sharing one own goal' on 18 December 1954. In the Division One game with Chelsea at Stamford Bridge, Froggatt and Milburn were involved in a misunderstanding in front of goal, and simultaneously booted the ball into the Leicester net, thus sharing the blame. Chelsea won the game by three goals to one.

Stoke City and Bury created an endurance record for an FA Cup match when they met five times in the Third Round in January 1955. Altogether they played for 9 hours and 22 minutes before Stoke won 3-2 at Old Trafford.

On 2 April 1955, Duncan Edwards of Manchester United became the youngest ever England international when, aged 18 years six months, he played against Scotland.

FA CUP 1954-55

FOURTH ROUND

Everton v Liverpool	0-4
Torquay United v Huddersfield Town	0-1
Hartlepools United v Nottingham Forest	1-1, 1-2
Newcastle United v Brentford	3-2
Sheffield Wednesday v Notts County	1-1, 0-1
Bristol Rovers v Chelsea	1-3
Bishop Auckland v York City	1-3
Tottenham Hotspur v Port Vale	4-2
Swansea Town v Stoke City	3-1
Preston North End v Sunderland	3-3, 0-2
Wolverhampton Wanderers v Arsenal	1-0
West Bromwich Albion v Charlton Athletic	2-4
Birmingham City v Bolton Wanderers	2-1
Doncaster Rovers v Aston Villa	0-0, 2-2, 1-1, 0-0, 3-1
Rotherham United v Luton Town	1-5
Manchester City v Manchester United	2-0

FIFTH ROUND

Liverpool v Huddersfield Town	0-2
Nottingham Forest v Newcastle United	1-1, 2-2, 1-2
Notts County v Chelsea	1-0
York City v Tottenham Hotspur	3-1
Swansea Town v Sunderland	2-2, 0-1
Wolverhampton Wanderers v Charlton Athletic	4-1
Birmingham City v Doncaster Rovers	2-1
Luton Town v Manchester City	0-2

SIXTH ROUND

Huddersfield Town v Newcastle United	1-1, 0-2
Notts County v York City	0-1
Sunderland v Wolverhampton Wanderers	2-0
Birmingham City v Manchester City	0-1

SEMI-FINAL

Newcastle United v York City	1-1, 2-0
Sunderland v Manchester City	0-1

FINAL

Newcastle United v Manchester City	3-1

SCOTTISH FA CUP 1954-55

FIFTH ROUND

Clyde v Albion Rovers	3-0
Morton v Raith Rovers	1-3
Ayr United v Inverness Caledonian	1-1, 2-4
Heart of Midlothian v Hibernian	5-0
Stirling Albion v Aberdeen	0-6
Dundee v Rangers	0-0, 0-1
Airdrieonians v Forfar Athletic	4-3
Dunfermline Athletic v Partick Thistle	4-2
Third Lanark v Queen of the South	2-1
Forres Mechanics v Motherwell	3-4
East Fife v Kilmarnock	1-2
Alloa Athletic v Celtic	2-4
Arbroath v St Johnstone	0-4
Hamilton Academicals v St Mirren	2-1
Falkirk v Stenhousemuir	4-0
Buckie Thistle v Inverness Thistle	2-0

SIXTH ROUND

Clyde v Raith Rovers	3-1
Inverness Caledonian v Falkirk	0-7
Buckie Thistle v Heart of Midlothian	0-6
Aberdeen v Rangers	2-1
Airdrieonians v Dunfermline Athletic	7-0
Third Lanark v Motherwell	1-3
Celtic v Kilmarnock	1-1, 1-0
St Johnstone v Hamilton Academicals	0-1

SEVENTH ROUND

Clyde v Falkirk	5-0
Aberdeen v Heart of Midlothian	1-1, 2-0
Airdrieonians v Motherwell	4-1
Celtic v Hamilton Academicals	2-1

SEMI-FINAL

Aberdeen v Clyde	2-2, 0-1
Airdrieonians v Celtic	2-2, 0-2

FINAL

Celtic v Clyde	1-1, 0-1

League Tables 1955-56

FIRST DIVISION

	P	W	D	L	F	A	Pts
1 Man United	42	25	10	7	83	51	60
2 Blackpool	42	20	9	13	86	62	49
3 Wolves	42	20	9	13	89	65	49
4 Man City	42	18	10	14	82	69	46
5 Arsenal	42	18	10	14	60	61	46
6 Birmingham	42	18	9	15	75	57	45
7 Burnley	42	18	8	16	64	54	44
8 Bolton	42	18	7	17	71	58	43
9 Sunderland	42	17	9	16	80	95	43
10 Luton	42	17	8	17	66	64	42
11 Newcastle	42	17	7	18	85	70	41
12 Portsmouth	42	16	9	17	78	85	41
13 WBA	42	18	5	19	58	70	41
14 Charlton	42	17	6	19	75	81	40
15 Everton	42	15	10	17	55	69	40
16 Chelsea	42	14	11	17	64	77	39
17 Cardiff	42	15	9	18	55	69	39
18 Tottenham	42	15	7	20	61	71	37
19 Preston	42	14	8	20	73	72	36
20 Aston Villa	42	11	13	18	52	69	35
21 Huddersfield	42	14	7	21	54	83	35
22 Sheff United	42	12	9	21	63	77	33

SECOND DIVISION

	P	W	D	L	F	A	Pts
1 Sheff Wed	42	21	13	8	101	62	55
2 Leeds	42	23	6	13	80	60	52
3 Liverpool	42	21	6	15	85	63	48
4 Blackburn	42	21	6	15	84	65	48
5 Leicester	42	21	6	15	94	78	48
6 Bristol Rovers	42	21	6	15	84	70	48
7 Nottm Forest	42	19	9	14	68	63	47
8 Lincoln	42	18	10	14	79	65	46
9 Fulham	42	20	6	16	89	79	46
10 Swansea	42	20	6	16	83	81	46
11 Bristol City	42	19	7	16	80	64	45
12 Port Vale	42	16	13	13	60	58	45
13 Stoke	42	20	4	18	71	62	44
14 Middlesbrough	42	16	8	18	76	78	40
15 Bury	42	16	8	18	86	90	40
16 West Ham	42	14	11	17	74	69	39
17 Doncaster	42	12	11	19	69	96	35
18 Barnsley	42	11	12	19	47	84	34
19 Rotherham	42	12	9	21	56	75	33
20 Notts County	42	11	9	22	55	82	31
21 Plymouth	42	10	8	24	54	87	28
22 Hull	42	10	6	26	53	97	26

THIRD DIVISION (NORTH)

	P	W	D	L	F	A	Pts
1 Grimsby	46	31	6	9	76	29	68
2 Derby	46	28	7	11	110	55	63
3 Accrington	46	25	9	12	92	57	59
4 Hartlepools	46	26	5	15	81	60	57
5 Southport	46	23	11	12	66	53	57
6 Chesterfield	46	25	4	17	94	66	54
7 Stockport	46	21	9	16	90	61	51
8 Bradford City	46	18	13	15	78	64	49
9 Scunthorpe	46	20	8	18	75	63	48
10 Workington	46	19	9	18	75	63	47
11 York	46	19	9	18	85	72	47
12 Rochdale	46	17	13	16	66	84	47
13 Gateshead	46	17	11	18	77	84	45
14 Wrexham	46	16	10	20	66	73	42
15 Darlington	46	16	9	21	60	73	41
16 Tranmere	46	16	9	21	59	84	41
17 Chester	46	13	14	19	52	82	40
18 Mansfield	46	14	11	21	84	81	39
19 Halifax	46	14	11	21	66	76	39
20 Oldham	46	10	18	18	76	86	38
21 Carlisle	46	15	8	23	71	95	38
22 Barrow	46	12	9	25	61	83	33
23 Bradford PA	46	13	7	26	61	122	33
24 Crewe	46	9	10	27	50	105	28

THIRD DIVISION (SOUTH)

	P	W	D	L	F	A	Pts
1 Leyton Orient	46	29	8	9	106	49	66
2 Brighton	46	29	7	10	112	50	65
3 Ipswich	46	25	14	7	106	60	64
4 Southend	46	21	11	14	88	80	53
5 Torquay	46	20	12	14	86	63	52
6 Brentford	46	19	14	13	69	66	52
7 Norwich	46	19	13	14	86	82	51
8 Coventry	46	20	9	17	73	60	49
9 Bournemouth	46	19	10	17	63	51	48
10 Gillingham	46	19	10	17	69	71	48
11 Northampton	46	20	7	19	67	71	47
12 Colchester	46	18	11	17	76	81	47
13 Shrewsbury	46	17	12	17	69	66	46
14 Southampton	46	18	8	20	91	81	44
15 Aldershot	46	12	16	18	70	90	40
16 Exeter	46	15	10	21	58	77	40
17 Reading	46	15	9	22	70	79	39
18 QPR	46	14	11	21	64	86	39
19 Newport	46	15	9	22	58	79	39
20 Walsall	46	15	8	23	68	84	38
21 Watford	46	13	11	22	52	85	37
22 Millwall	46	15	6	25	83	100	36
23 Crystal Palace	46	12	10	24	54	83	34
24 Swindon	46	8	14	24	34	78	30

SCOTTISH LEAGUE 'A'

	P	W	D	L	F	A	Pts
1 Rangers	34	22	8	4	85	27	52
2 Aberdeen	34	18	10	6	87	50	46
3 Hearts	34	19	7	8	99	47	45
4 Hibernian	34	19	7	8	86	50	45
5 Celtic	34	16	9	9	55	39	41
6 Queen of the S	34	16	5	13	69	73	37
7 Airdrieonians	34	14	8	12	85	96	36
8 Kilmarnock	34	12	10	12	52	45	34
9 Partick Thistle	34	13	7	14	62	60	33
10 Motherwell	34	11	11	12	53	59	33
11 Raith	34	12	9	13	58	75	33
12 East Fife	34	13	5	16	61	69	31
13 Dundee	34	12	6	16	56	65	30
14 Falkirk	34	11	6	17	58	75	28
15 St Mirren	34	10	7	17	57	70	27
16 Dunfermline	34	10	6	18	42	82	26
17 Clyde	34	8	6	20	50	74	22
18 Stirling	34	4	5	25	23	82	13

SCOTTISH LEAGUE 'B'

	P	W	D	L	F	A	Pts
1 Queen's Park	36	23	8	5	78	28	54
2 Ayr	36	24	3	9	103	55	51
3 St Johnstone	36	21	7	8	86	45	49
4 Dumbarton	36	21	5	10	83	62	47
5 Stenhousemuir	36	20	4	12	82	54	44
6 Brechin	36	18	6	12	60	56	42
7 Cowdenbeath	36	16	7	13	80	85	39
8 Dundee United	36	12	14	10	78	65	38
9 Morton	36	15	6	15	71	69	36
10 Third Lanark	36	16	3	17	80	64	35
11 Hamilton	36	13	7	16	86	84	33
12 Stranraer	36	14	5	17	77	92	33
13 Alloa	36	12	7	17	67	73	31
14 Berwick	36	11	9	16	52	77	31
15 Forfar	36	10	9	17	62	75	29
16 E Stirlingshire	36	9	10	17	66	94	28
17 Albion	36	8	11	17	58	82	27
18 Arbroath	36	10	6	20	47	67	26
19 Montrose	36	4	3	29	44	133	11

Accrington Stanley set a League record early in the 1955-56 season by fielding a side composed entirely of Scottish-born players. During the season, this team appeared several times. Indeed, all but four of the first-team squad of 19 players the club used that season in the Third Division North were born in Scotland.

On 3 September 1955, Wolves beat Cardiff 9-1 away from home to equal the Division One record away win. Curiously, later in the season, Cardiff won 2-0 at Wolves.

All four countries in the Home Championship finished level with three points, the first time this had ever happened.

FA CUP 1955-56

FOURTH ROUND

Leyton Orient v Birmingham City	0-4
West Bromwich Albion v Portsmouth	2-0
Charlton Athletic v Swindon Town	2-1
Arsenal v Aston Villa	4-1
Fulham v Newcastle United	4-5
Leicester City v Stoke City	3-3, 1-2
Bolton Wanderers v Sheffield United	1-2
York City v Sunderland	0-0, 1-2
Bristol Rovers v Doncaster Rovers	1-1, 0-1
Tottenham Hotspur v Middlesbrough	3-1
West Ham United v Cardiff City	2-1
Barnsley v Blackburn Rovers	0-1
Port Vale v Everton	2-3
Burnley v Chelsea	1-1, 1-1, 2-2, 0-0, 0-2
Liverpool v Scunthorpe United	3-3, 2-1
Southend United v Manchester City	0-1

FIFTH ROUND

West Bromwich Albion v Birmingham City	0-1
Charlton Athletic v Arsenal	0-2
Newcastle United v Stoke City	2-1
Sheffield United v Sunderland	0-0, 0-1
Doncaster Rovers v Tottenham Hotspur	0-2
West Ham United v Blackburn Rovers	0-0, 3-2
Everton v Chelsea	1-0
Manchester City v Liverpool	0-0, 2-1

SIXTH ROUND

Arsenal v Birmingham City	1-3
Newcastle United v Sunderland	0-2
Tottenham Hotspur v West Ham United	3-3, 2-1
Manchester City v Everton	2-1

SEMI-FINAL

Birmingham City v Sunderland	3-0
Tottenham Hotspur v Manchester City	0-1

FINAL

Manchester City v Birmingham City	3-1

SCOTTISH FA CUP 1955-56

FIFTH ROUND

Heart of Midlothian v Forfar Athletic	3-0
Stirling Albion v St Johnstone	2-1
Rangers v Aberdeen	2-1
Dundee v Dundee United	2-2, 3-0
Hibernian v Raith Rovers	1-1, 1-3
Motherwell v Queen's Park	0-2
Partick Thistle v Alloa Athletic	2-0
Brechin City v Arbroath	1-1, 3-2
Falkirk v Kilmarnock	0-3
Queen of the South v Cowdenbeath	3-1
East Fife v Stenhousemuir	1-3
Clyde v Dunfermline Athletic	5-0
St Mirren v Third Lanark	6-0
Airdrieonians v Hamilton Academicals	7-1
Ayr United v Berwick Rangers	5-2
Morton v Celtic	0-2

SIXTH ROUND

Heart of Midlothian v Stirling Albion	5-0
Dundee v Rangers	0-1
Raith Rovers v Queen's Park	2-2, 2-1
Partick Thistle v Brechin City	3-1
Kilmarnock v Queen of the South	2-2, 0-2
Stenhousemuir v Clyde	0-1
St Mirren v Airdrieonians	4-4, 1-3
Ayr United v Celtic	0-3

SEVENTH ROUND

Heart of Midlothian v Rangers	4-0
Raith Rovers v Partick Thistle	2-1
Queen of the South v Clyde	2-4
Celtic v Airdrieonians	2-1

SEMI-FINAL

Heart of Midlothian v Raith Rovers	0-0, 3-0
Celtic v Clyde	2-0

FINAL

Heart of Midlothian v Celtic	3-1

FIRST DIVISION

	P	W	D	L	F	A	Pts
1 Man United	42	28	8	6	103	54	64
2 Tottenham	42	22	12	8	104	56	56
3 Preston	42	23	10	9	84	56	56
4 Blackpool	42	22	9	11	93	65	53
5 Arsenal	42	21	8	13	85	69	50
6 Wolves	42	20	8	14	94	70	48
7 Burnley	42	18	10	14	56	50	46
8 Leeds	42	15	14	13	72	63	44
9 Bolton	42	16	12	14	65	65	44
10 Aston Villa	42	14	15	13	65	55	43
11 WBA	42	14	14	14	59	61	42
12 Birmingham*	42	15	9	18	69	69	39
13 Chelsea*	42	13	13	16	73	73	39
14 Sheff Wed	42	16	6	20	82	88	38
15 Everton	42	14	10	18	61	79	38
16 Luton	42	14	9	19	58	76	37
17 Newcastle	42	14	8	20	67	87	36
18 Man City	42	13	9	20	78	88	35
19 Portsmouth	42	10	13	19	62	92	33
20 Sunderland	42	12	8	22	67	88	32
21 Cardiff	42	10	9	23	53	88	29
22 Charlton	42	9	4	29	62	120	22

*Equal

SECOND DIVISION

	P	W	D	L	F	A	Pts
1 Leicester	42	25	11	6	109	67	61
2 Nottm Forest	42	22	10	10	94	55	54
3 Liverpool	42	21	11	10	82	54	53
4 Blackburn	42	21	10	11	83	75	52
5 Stoke	42	20	8	14	83	58	48
6 Middlesbrough	42	19	10	13	84	60	48
7 Sheff United	42	19	8	15	87	76	46
8 West Ham	42	19	8	15	59	63	46
9 Bristol Rovers	42	18	9	15	81	67	45
10 Swansea	42	19	7	16	90	90	45
11 Fulham	42	19	4	19	84	76	42
12 Huddersfield	42	18	6	18	68	74	42
13 Bristol City	42	16	9	17	74	79	41
14 Doncaster	42	15	10	17	77	77	40
15 Leyton Orient	42	15	10	17	66	84	40
16 Grimsby	42	17	5	20	61	62	39
17 Rotherham	42	13	11	18	74	75	37
18 Lincoln	42	14	6	22	54	80	34
19 Barnsley	42	12	10	20	59	89	34
20 Notts County	42	9	12	21	58	86	30
21 Bury	42	8	9	25	60	96	25
22 Port Vale	42	8	6	28	57	101	22

THIRD DIVISION (SOUTH)

	P	W	D	L	F	A	Pts
1 Ipswich	46	25	9	12	101	54	59
2 Torquay	46	24	11	11	89	64	59
3 Colchester	46	22	14	10	84	56	58
4 Southampton	46	22	10	14	76	52	54
5 Bournemouth	46	19	14	13	88	62	52
6 Brighton	46	19	14	13	86	65	52
7 Southend	46	18	12	16	73	65	48
8 Brentford	46	16	16	14	78	76	48
9 Shrewsbury	46	15	18	13	72	79	48
10 QPR	46	18	11	17	61	60	47
11 Watford	46	18	10	18	72	75	46
12 Newport	46	16	13	17	65	62	45
13 Reading	46	18	9	19	80	81	45
14 Northampton	46	18	9	19	66	73	45
15 Walsall	46	16	12	18	80	74	44
16 Coventry	46	16	12	18	74	84	44
17 Millwall	46	16	12	18	64	84	44
18 Plymouth	46	16	11	19	68	73	43
19 Aldershot	46	15	12	19	79	92	42
20 Crystal Palace	46	11	18	17	62	75	40
21 Exeter	46	12	13	21	61	79	37
22 Gillingham	46	12	13	21	54	85	37
23 Swindon	46	15	6	25	66	96	36
24 Norwich	46	8	15	23	61	94	31

THIRD DIVISION (NORTH)

	P	W	D	L	F	A	Pts
1 Derby	46	26	11	9	111	53	63
2 Hartlepools	46	25	9	12	90	63	59
3 Accrington	46	25	8	13	95	64	58
4 Workington	46	24	10	12	93	63	58
5 Stockport	46	23	8	15	91	75	54
6 Chesterfield	46	22	9	15	96	79	53
7 York	46	21	10	15	75	61	52
8 Hull	46	21	10	15	84	69	52
9 Bradford City	46	22	8	16	78	68	52
10 Barrow	46	21	9	16	76	62	51
11 Halifax	46	21	7	18	65	70	49
12 Wrexham	46	19	10	17	97	74	48
13 Rochdale	46	18	12	16	65	65	48
14 Scunthorpe	46	15	15	16	71	69	45
15 Carlisle	46	16	13	17	76	85	45
16 Mansfield	46	17	10	19	91	90	44
17 Gateshead	46	17	10	19	72	90	44
18 Darlington	46	17	8	21	82	95	42
19 Oldham	46	12	15	19	66	74	39
20 Bradford PA	46	16	3	27	66	93	35
21 Chester	46	10	13	23	55	84	33
22 Southport	46	10	12	24	52	94	32
23 Tranmere	46	7	13	26	51	91	27
24 Crewe	46	6	9	31	43	110	21

SCOTTISH FIRST DIVISION

	P	W	D	L	F	A	Pts
1 Rangers	34	26	3	5	96	48	55
2 Hearts	34	24	5	5	81	48	53
3 Kilmarnock	34	16	10	8	57	39	42
4 Raith	34	16	7	11	84	58	39
5 Celtic	34	15	8	11	58	43	38
6 Aberdeen	34	18	2	14	79	59	38
7 Motherwell	34	16	5	13	72	66	37
8 Partick Thistle	34	13	8	13	53	51	34
9 Hibernian	34	12	9	13	69	56	33
10 Dundee	34	13	6	15	55	61	32
11 Airdrieonians	34	13	4	17	77	89	30
12 St Mirren	34	12	6	16	58	72	30
13 Queen's Park	34	11	7	16	55	59	29
14 Falkirk	34	10	8	16	51	70	28
15 East Fife	34	10	6	18	59	82	26
16 Queen of the S	34	10	5	19	54	96	25
17 Dunfermline	34	9	6	19	54	74	24
18 Ayr	34	7	5	22	48	89	19

SCOTTISH SECOND DIVISION

	P	W	D	L	F	A	Pts
1 Clyde	36	29	6	1	122	39	64
2 Third Lanark	36	24	3	9	105	51	51
3 Cowdenbeath	36	20	5	11	87	65	45
4 Morton	36	18	7	11	81	70	43
5 Albion	36	18	6	12	98	80	42
6 Brechin	36	15	10	11	72	68	40
7 Stranraer	36	15	10	11	79	77	40
8 Stirling	36	17	5	14	81	64	39
9 Dumbarton	36	17	4	15	101	70	38
10 Arbroath	36	17	4	15	79	57	38
11 Hamilton	36	14	8	14	69	68	36
12 St Johnstone	36	14	6	16	79	80	34
13 Dundee United	36	14	6	16	75	80	34
14 Stenhousemuir	36	13	6	17	71	81	32
15 Alloa	36	11	5	20	66	99	27
16 Forfar	36	9	5	22	75	100	23
17 Montrose	36	7	7	22	54	124	21
18 Berwick	36	7	6	23	58	114	20
19 E Stirlingshire	36	5	7	24	56	121	17

New man in charge
On 1 January 1957, Alan Hardaker became secretary to the Football League. Hardaker, once an amateur footballer with Hull City, had been assistant secretary since 1951.

After beating Scunthorpe United 2-1, on 19 September 1956, Crewe Alexandra of the Third Division North did not win again until they beat Bradford City 1-0 on 13 April 1957, a League record of 30 games without a win.

FA CUP 1956-57

FOURTH ROUND

Middlesbrough v Aston Villa	2-3
Bristol City v Rhyl	3-0
Burnley v New Brighton	9-0
Huddersfield Town v Peterborough United	3-1
Newport County v Arsenal	0-2
Bristol Rovers v Preston North End	1-4
Blackpool v Fulham	6-2
West Bromwich Albion v Sunderland	4-2
Wrexham v Manchester United	0-5
Everton v West Ham United	2-1
Wolverhampton Wanderers v Bournemouth	0-1
Tottenham Hotspur v Chelsea	4-0
Southend United v Birmingham City	1-6
Millwall v Newcastle United	2-1
Cardiff City v Barnsley	0-1
Portsmouth v Nottingham Forest	1-3

FIFTH ROUND

Aston Villa v Bristol City	2-1
Huddersfield Town v Burnley	1-2
Preston North End v Arsenal	3-3, 1-2
Blackpool v West Bromwich Albion	0-0, 1-2
Manchester United v Everton	1-0
Bournemouth v Tottenham Hotspur	3-1
Millwall v Birmingham City	1-4
Barnsley v Nottingham Forest	1-2

SIXTH ROUND

Burnley v Aston Villa	1-1, 0-2
West Bromwich Albion v Arsenal	2-2, 2-1
Bournemouth v Manchester United	1-2
Birmingham City v Nottingham Forest	0-0, 1-0

SEMI-FINAL

Aston Villa v West Bromwich Albion	2-2, 1-0
Manchester United v Birmingham City	2-0

FINAL

Aston Villa v Manchester United	2-1

SCOTTISH FA CUP 1956-57

FIFTH ROUND

Berwick Rangers v Falkirk	1-2
Hibernian v Aberdeen	3-4
Dundee v Clyde	0-0, 1-2
Queen's Park v Brechin City	3-0
Inverness Caledonian v Raith Rovers	2-3
Stenhousemuir v Dundee United	1-1, 0-4
Queen of the South v Dumbarton	2-2, 2-4
Stirling Albion v Motherwell	1-2
Dunfermline Athletic v Morton	3-0
St Mirren v Partick Thistle	1-1, 2-2, 5-1
Heart of Midlothian v Rangers	0-4
Forres Mechanics v Celtic	0-5
Hamilton Academicals v Alloa Athletic	2-2, 5-3
Stranraer v Airdrieonians	1-2
East Fife v St Johnstone	4-0
Kilmarnock v Ayr United	1-0

SIXTH ROUND

Falkirk v Aberdeen	3-1
Queen's Park v Clyde	1-1, 0-2
Raith Rovers v Dundee United	7-0
Motherwell v Dumbarton	1-3
St Mirren v Dunfermline Athletic	1-0
Celtic v Rangers	4-4, 2-0
Hamilton Academicals v Airdrieonians	1-2
East Fife v Kilmarnock	0-0, 0-2

SEVENTH ROUND

Falkirk v Clyde	2-1
Dumbarton v Raith Rovers	0-4
Celtic v St Mirren	2-1
Kilmarnock v Airdrieonians	3-1

SEMI-FINAL

Falkirk v Raith Rovers	2-2, 2-0
Celtic v Kilmarnock	1-1, 1-3

FINAL

Falkirk v Kilmarnock	1-1, 2-1

League Tables 1957-58

FIRST DIVISION

		P	W	D	L	F	A	Pts
1	Wolves	42	28	8	6	103	47	64
2	Preston	42	26	7	9	100	51	59
3	Tottenham	42	21	9	12	93	77	51
4	WBA	42	18	14	10	92	70	50
5	Man City	42	22	5	15	104	100	49
6	Burnley	42	21	5	16	80	74	47
7	Blackpool	42	19	6	17	80	67	44
8	Luton	42	19	6	17	69	63	44
9	Man United	42	16	11	15	85	75	43
10	Nottm Forest	42	16	10	16	69	63	42
11	Chelsea	42	15	12	15	83	79	42
12	Arsenal	42	16	7	19	73	85	39
13	Birmingham	42	14	11	17	76	89	39
14	Aston Villa	42	16	7	19	73	86	39
15	Bolton	42	14	10	18	65	87	38
16	Everton	42	13	11	18	65	75	37
17	Leeds	42	14	9	19	51	63	37
18	Leicester	42	14	5	23	91	112	33
19	Newcastle	42	12	8	22	73	81	32
20	Portsmouth	42	12	8	22	73	88	32
21	Sunderland	42	10	12	20	54	97	32
22	Sheff Wed	42	12	7	23	69	92	31

SECOND DIVISION

		P	W	D	L	F	A	Pts
1	West Ham	42	23	11	8	101	54	57
2	Blackburn	42	22	12	8	93	57	56
3	Charlton	42	24	7	11	107	69	55
4	Liverpool	42	22	10	10	79	54	54
5	Fulham	42	20	12	10	97	59	52
6	Sheff United	42	21	10	11	75	50	52
7	Middlesbrough	42	19	7	16	83	74	45
8	Ipswich	42	16	12	14	68	69	44
9	Huddersfield	42	14	16	12	63	66	44
10	Bristol Rovers	42	17	8	17	85	80	42
11	Stoke	42	18	6	18	75	73	42
12	Leyton Orient	42	18	5	19	77	79	41
13	Grimsby	42	17	6	19	86	83	40
14	Barnsley	42	14	12	16	70	74	40
15	Cardiff	42	14	9	19	63	77	37
16	Derby	42	14	8	20	60	81	36
17	Bristol City	42	13	9	20	63	88	35
18	Rotherham	42	14	5	23	65	101	33
19	Swansea	42	11	9	22	72	99	31
20	Lincoln	42	11	9	22	55	82	31
21	Notts County	42	12	6	24	44	80	30
22	Doncaster	42	8	11	23	56	88	27

THIRD DIVISION (NORTH)

		P	W	D	L	F	A	Pts
1	Scunthorpe	46	29	8	9	88	50	66
2	Accrington	46	25	9	12	83	61	59
3	Bradford City	46	21	15	10	73	49	57
4	Bury	46	23	10	13	94	62	56
5	Hull	46	19	15	12	78	67	53
6	Mansfield	46	22	8	16	100	92	52
7	Halifax	46	20	11	15	83	69	51
8	Chesterfield	46	18	15	13	71	69	51
9	Stockport	46	18	11	17	74	67	47
10	Rochdale	46	19	8	19	79	67	46
11	Tranmere	46	18	10	18	82	76	46
12	Wrexham	46	17	12	17	61	63	46
13	York	46	17	12	17	68	76	46
14	Gateshead	46	15	15	16	68	76	45
15	Oldham	46	14	17	15	72	84	45
16	Carlisle	46	19	6	21	80	78	44
17	Hartlepools	46	16	12	18	73	76	44
18	Barrow	46	13	15	18	66	74	41
19	Workington	46	14	13	19	72	81	41
20	Darlington	46	17	7	22	78	89	41
21	Chester	46	13	13	20	73	81	39
22	Bradford PA	46	13	11	22	68	95	37
23	Southport	46	11	6	29	52	88	28
24	Crewe	46	8	7	31	47	93	23

THIRD DIVISION (SOUTH)

		P	W	D	L	F	A	Pts
1	Brighton	46	24	12	10	88	64	60
2	Brentford	46	24	10	12	82	56	58
3	Plymouth	46	25	8	13	67	48	58
4	Swindon	46	21	15	10	79	50	57
5	Reading	46	21	13	12	79	51	55
6	Southampton	46	22	10	14	112	72	54
7	Southend	46	21	12	13	90	58	54
8	Norwich	46	19	15	12	75	70	53
9	Bournemouth	46	21	9	16	81	74	51
10	QPR	46	18	14	14	64	65	50
11	Newport	46	17	14	15	73	67	48
12	Colchester	46	17	13	16	77	79	47
13	Northampton	46	19	6	21	87	79	44
14	Crystal Palace	46	15	13	18	70	72	43
15	Port Vale	46	16	10	20	67	58	42
16	Watford	46	13	16	17	59	77	42
17	Shrewsbury	46	15	10	21	49	71	40
18	Aldershot	46	12	16	18	59	89	40
19	Coventry	46	13	13	20	61	81	39
20	Walsall	46	14	9	23	61	75	37
21	Torquay	46	11	13	22	49	74	35
22	Gillingham	46	13	9	24	52	81	35
23	Millwall	46	11	9	26	63	91	31
24	Exeter	46	11	9	26	57	99	31

SCOTTISH FIRST DIVISION

		P	W	D	L	F	A	Pts
1	Hearts	34	29	4	1	132	29	62
2	Rangers	34	22	5	7	89	49	49
3	Celtic	34	19	8	7	84	47	46
4	Clyde	34	18	6	10	84	61	42
5	Kilmarnock	34	14	9	11	60	55	37
6	Partick Thistle	34	17	3	14	69	71	37
7	Raith Rovers	34	14	7	13	66	56	35
8	Motherwell	34	12	8	14	68	67	32
9	Hibernian	34	13	5	16	59	60	31
10	Falkirk	34	11	9	14	64	82	31
11	Dundee	34	13	5	16	49	65	31
12	Aberdeen	34	14	2	18	68	76	30
13	St Mirren	34	11	8	15	59	66	30
14	Third Lanark	34	13	4	17	69	88	30
15	Queen of the S	34	12	5	17	61	72	29
16	Airdrieonians	34	13	2	19	71	92	28
17	East Fife	34	10	3	21	45	88	23
18	Queen's Park	34	4	1	29	41	114	9

SCOTTISH SECOND DIVISION

		P	W	D	L	F	A	Pts
1	Stirling Albion	36	25	5	6	105	48	55
2	Dunfermline	36	24	5	7	120	42	53
3	Arbroath	36	21	5	10	89	72	47
4	Dumbarton	36	20	4	12	92	57	44
5	Ayr	36	18	6	12	98	81	42
6	Cowdenbeath	36	17	8	11	100	85	42
7	Brechin	36	16	8	12	80	81	40
8	Alloa	36	15	9	12	88	78	39
9	Dundee United	36	12	9	15	81	77	33
10	Hamilton	36	12	9	15	70	79	33
11	St Johnstone	36	12	9	15	67	85	33
12	Forfar	36	13	6	17	70	71	32
13	Morton	36	12	8	16	77	83	32
14	Montrose	36	13	6	17	55	72	32
15	E Stirlingshire	36	12	5	19	55	79	29
16	Stenhousemuir	36	12	5	19	68	98	29
17	Albion	36	12	5	19	53	79	29
18	Stranraer	36	9	7	20	54	83	25
19	Berwick	36	5	5	26	37	109	15

In Moscow on 18 May 1958, England played the USSR for the first time ever.

Before the start of the 1957-58 season, it was decided that four Divisions would be introduced in 1958-59. So at the end of the season, the top halves of both Third Divisions formed the new Division Three, and the rest of the teams made up Division Four.

Have boots, will travel
Tony McNamara, a right-winger, played in all four divisions of the Football League inside twelve months. On 12 October 1957, he played his last game for Everton in Division One, and on 27 September 1958 he made his debut for Bury in Division Three. In between, he played in Division Two for Liverpool, and in the Fourth Division for Crewe.

FA CUP 1957-58

FOURTH ROUND

Everton v Blackburn Rovers 1-2
Cardiff City v Leyton Orient 4-1
Liverpool v Northampton Town 3-1
Newcastle United v Scunthorpe United 1-3
Wolverhampton Wanderers v Portsmouth 5-1
Chelsea v Darlington 3-3, 1-4
Stoke City v Middlesbrough 3-1
York City v Bolton Wanderers 0-0, 0-3
Manchester United v Ipswich Town 2-0
Sheffield Wednesday v Hull City 4-3
West Bromwich Albion v Nottingham Forest 3-3, 5-1
Tottenham Hotspur v Sheffield United 0-3
Bristol Rovers v Burnley 2-2, 3-2
Notts County v Bristol City 1-2
West Ham United v Stockport County 3-2
Fulham v Charlton Athletic 1-1, 2-0

FIFTH ROUND

Cardiff City v Blackburn Rovers 0-0, 1-2
Scunthorpe United v Liverpool 0-1
Wolverhampton Wanderers v Darlington 6-1
Bolton Wanderers v Stoke City 3-1
Manchester United v Sheffield Wednesday 3-0
Sheffield United v West Bromwich Albion 1-1, 1-4
Bristol City v Bristol Rovers 3-4
West Ham United v Fulham 2-3

SIXTH ROUND

Blackburn Rovers v Liverpool 2-1
Bolton Wanderers v Wolverhampton Wanderers 2-1
West Bromwich Albion v Manchester United 2-2, 0-1
Fulham v Bristol Rovers 3-1

SEMI-FINAL

Blackburn Rovers v Bolton Wanderers 1-2
Manchester United v Fulham 2-2, 5-3

FINAL

Bolton Wanderers v Manchester United 2-0

SCOTTISH FA CUP 1957-58

SECOND ROUND

Celtic v Stirling Albion 7-2
Clyde v Arbroath 4-0
Falkirk v St Johnstone 6-3
Montrose v Buckie Thistle 2-2, 1-4
Motherwell v Partick Thistle 2-2, 4-0
Inverness Caledonian v Stenhousemuir 5-2
Morton v Aberdeen 0-1
Raith Rovers v Dundee 0-1
Forfar Athletic v Rangers 1-9
St Mirren v Dunfermline Athletic 1-4
Queen of the South v Stranraer 7-0
Kilmarnock v Vale of Leithen 7-0
Dundee United v Hibernian 0-0, 0-2
Heart of Midlothian v Albion Rovers 4-1
Third Lanark v Lossiemouth 6-1
Queen's Park v Fraserburgh 7-2

THIRD ROUND

Clyde v Celtic 2-0
Buckie Thistle v Falkirk 1-2
Inverness Caledonian v Motherwell 0-7
Dundee v Aberdeen 1-3
Dunfermline Athletic v Rangers 1-2
Kilmarnock v Queen of the South 2-2, 0-3
Heart of Midlothian v Hibernian 3-4
Third Lanark v Queen's Park 5-3

FOURTH ROUND

Clyde v Falkirk 2-1
Motherwell v Aberdeen 2-1
Queen of the South v Rangers 3-4
Hibernian v Third Lanark 3-2

SEMI-FINAL

Clyde v Motherwell 3-2
Rangers v Hibernian 2-2, 1-2

FINAL

Clyde v Hibernian 1-0

League Tables 1958-59

FIRST DIVISION

	P	W	D	L	F	A	Pts
1 Wolves	42	28	5	9	110	49	61
2 Man United	42	24	7	11	103	66	55
3 Arsenal	42	21	8	13	88	68	50
4 Bolton	42	20	10	12	79	66	50
5 WBA	42	18	13	11	88	68	49
6 West Ham	42	21	6	15	85	70	48
7 Burnley	42	19	10	13	81	70	48
8 Blackpool	42	18	11	13	66	49	47
9 Birmingham	42	20	6	16	84	68	46
10 Blackburn	42	17	10	15	76	70	44
11 Newcastle	42	17	7	18	80	80	41
12 Preston	42	17	7	18	70	77	41
13 Nottm Forest	42	17	6	19	71	74	40
14 Chelsea	42	18	4	20	77	98	40
15 Leeds	42	15	9	18	57	74	39
16 Everton	42	17	4	21	71	87	38
17 Luton	42	12	13	17	68	71	37
18 Tottenham	42	13	10	19	85	95	36
19 Leicester	42	11	10	21	67	98	32
20 Man City	42	11	9	22	64	95	31
21 Aston Villa	42	11	8	23	58	87	30
22 Portsmouth	42	6	9	27	64	112	21

SECOND DIVISION

	P	W	D	L	F	A	Pts
1 Sheff Wed	42	28	6	8	106	48	62
2 Fulham	42	27	6	9	96	61	60
3 Sheff United	42	23	7	12	82	48	53
4 Liverpool	42	24	5	13	87	62	53
5 Stoke	42	21	7	14	72	58	49
6 Bristol Rovers	42	18	12	12	80	64	48
7 Derby	42	20	8	14	74	71	48
8 Charlton	42	18	7	17	92	90	43
9 Cardiff	42	18	7	17	65	65	43
10 Bristol City	42	17	7	18	74	70	41
11 Swansea	42	16	9	17	79	81	41
12 Brighton	42	15	11	16	74	90	41
13 Middlesbrough	42	15	10	17	87	71	40
14 Huddersfield	42	16	8	18	62	55	40
15 Sunderland	42	16	8	18	64	75	40
16 Ipswich	42	17	6	19	62	77	40
17 Leyton Orient	42	14	8	20	71	78	36
18 Scunthorpe	42	12	9	21	55	84	33
19 Lincoln	42	11	7	24	63	93	29
20 Rotherham	42	10	9	23	42	82	29
21 Grimsby	42	9	10	23	62	90	28
22 Barnsley	42	10	7	25	55	91	27

THIRD DIVISION

	P	W	D	L	F	A	Pts
1 Plymouth	46	23	16	7	89	59	62
2 Hull	46	26	9	11	90	55	61
3 Brentford	46	21	15	10	76	49	57
4 Norwich	46	22	13	11	89	62	57
5 Colchester	46	21	10	15	71	67	52
6 Reading	46	21	8	17	78	63	50
7 Tranmere	46	21	8	17	82	67	50
8 Southend	46	21	8	17	85	80	50
9 Halifax	46	21	8	17	80	77	50
10 Bury	46	17	14	15	69	58	48
11 Bradford City	46	18	11	17	84	76	47
12 Bournemouth	46	17	12	17	69	69	46
13 QPR	46	19	8	19	74	77	46
14 Southampton	46	17	11	18	88	80	45
15 Swindon	46	16	13	17	59	57	45
16 Chesterfield	46	17	10	19	67	64	44
17 Newport	46	17	9	20	69	68	43
18 Wrexham	46	14	14	18	63	77	42
19 Accrington	46	15	12	19	71	87	42
20 Mansfield	46	14	13	19	73	98	41
21 Stockport	46	13	10	23	65	78	36
22 Doncaster	46	14	5	27	50	90	33
23 Notts County	46	8	13	25	55	96	29
24 Rochdale	46	8	12	26	37	79	28

FOURTH DIVISION

	P	W	D	L	F	A	Pts
1 Port Vale	46	26	12	8	110	58	64
2 Coventry	46	24	12	10	84	47	60
3 York	46	21	18	7	73	52	60
4 Shrewsbury	46	24	10	12	101	63	58
5 Exeter	46	23	11	12	87	61	57
6 Walsall	46	21	10	15	95	64	52
7 Crystal Palace	46	20	12	14	90	71	52
8 Northampton	46	21	9	16	85	78	51
9 Millwall	46	20	10	16	76	69	50
10 Carlisle	46	19	12	15	62	65	50
11 Gillingham	46	20	9	17	82	77	49
12 Torquay	46	16	12	18	78	77	44
13 Chester	46	16	12	18	72	84	44
14 Bradford PA	46	18	7	21	75	77	43
15 Watford	46	16	10	20	81	79	42
16 Darlington	46	13	16	17	66	68	42
17 Workington	46	12	17	17	63	78	41
18 Crewe	46	15	10	21	70	82	40
19 Hartlepools	46	15	10	21	74	88	40
20 Gateshead	46	16	8	22	56	85	40
21 Oldham	46	16	4	26	59	84	36
22 Aldershot	46	14	7	25	63	97	35
23 Barrow	46	9	10	27	51	104	28
24 Southport	46	7	12	27	41	86	26

SCOTTISH FIRST DIVISION

	P	W	D	L	F	A	Pts
1 Rangers	34	21	8	5	92	51	50
2 Hearts	34	21	6	7	92	51	48
3 Motherwell	34	18	8	8	83	50	44
4 Dundee	34	16	9	9	61	51	41
5 Airdrie	34	15	7	12	64	62	37
6 Celtic	34	14	8	12	70	53	36
7 St Mirren	34	14	7	13	71	74	35
8 Kilmarnock	34	13	8	13	58	51	34
9 Partick Thistle	34	14	6	14	59	66	34
10 Hibernian	34	13	6	15	68	70	32
11 Third Lanark	34	11	10	13	74	83	32
12 Stirling	34	11	8	15	54	64	30
13 Aberdeen	34	12	5	17	63	66	29
14 Raith	34	10	9	15	60	70	29
15 Clyde	34	12	4	18	62	66	28
16 Dunfermline	34	10	8	16	68	87	28
17 Falkirk	34	10	7	17	58	79	27
18 Queen of the S	34	6	6	22	38	101	18

SCOTTISH SECOND DIVISION

	P	W	D	L	F	A	Pts
1 Ayr United	36	28	4	4	115	48	60
2 Arbroath	36	23	5	8	86	59	51
3 Stenhousemuir	36	20	6	10	87	68	46
4 Dumbarton	36	19	7	10	94	61	45
5 Brechin	36	16	10	10	79	65	42
6 St Johnstone	36	15	10	11	54	44	40
7 Hamilton	36	15	8	13	76	62	38
8 East Fife	36	15	8	13	83	81	38
9 Berwick	36	16	6	14	63	66	38
10 Albion	36	14	7	15	84	79	35
11 Morton	36	13	8	15	68	85	34
12 Forfar	36	12	9	15	73	87	33
13 Alloa	36	12	7	17	76	81	31
14 Cowdenbeath	36	13	5	18	67	79	31
15 E Stirlingshire	36	10	8	18	50	77	28
16 Stranraer	36	8	11	17	63	76	27
17 Dundee United	36	9	7	20	62	86	25
18 Queen's Park	36	9	6	21	53	80	24
19 Montrose	36	6	6	24	49	96	18

Beginning with the game against France on 3 October 1951, Billy Wright made a world record 70 consecutive appearances for England, ending on 8 May 1959 with the match against the USA. In the Home Championship, he had a record run of 25 games between April 1951 and April 1959.

Denis Law became Scotland's youngest international, when on 18 October 1958, he played against Wales aged just 18 years and 236 days.

The most away wins in any division of the League on a single day is eight, in Division 3, 27 September 1958.

FA CUP 1958-59

FOURTH ROUND

Nottingham Forest v Grimsby Town	4-1
Birmingham City v Fulham	1-1, 3-2
Wolverhampton W v Bolton W	1-2
Preston North End v Bradford City	3-2
Charlton Athletic v Everton	2-2, 1-4
Chelsea v Aston Villa	1-2
Blackburn Rovers v Burnley	1-2
Accrington Stanley v Portsmouth	0-0, 1-4
Colchester United v Arsenal	2-2, 0-4
Worcester City v Sheffield United	0-2
Tottenham Hotspur v Newport County	4-1
Norwich City v Cardiff City	3-2
Bristol City v Blackpool	1-1, 0-1
West Bromwich Albion v Brentford	2-0
Stoke City v Ipswich Town	0-1
Leicester City v Luton Town	1-1, 1-4

FIFTH ROUND

Birmingham City v Nottm Forest	1-1, 1-1, 0-5
Bolton W v Preston North End	2-2, 1-1, 1-0
Everton v Aston Villa	1-4
Burnley v Portsmouth	1-0
Arsenal v Sheffield United	2-2, 0-3
Tottenham Hotspur v Norwich City	1-1, 0-1
Blackpool v West Bromwich Albion	3-1
Ipswich Town v Luton Town	2-5

SIXTH ROUND

Nottingham Forest v Bolton Wanderers	2-1
Aston Villa v Burnley	0-0, 2-0
Sheffield United v Norwich City	1-1, 2-3
Blackpool v Luton Town	1-1, 0-1

SEMI-FINAL

Nottingham Forest v Aston Villa	1-0
Norwich City v Luton Town	1-1, 0-1

FINAL

Nottingham Forest v Luton Town	2-1

SCOTTISH FA CUP 1958-59

SECOND ROUND

St Mirren v Peebles Rovers	10-0
Airdrieonians v Motherwell	2-7
Montrose v Dunfermline Athletic	0-1
Ayr United v Stranraer	3-0
Fraserburgh v Stirling Albion	3-4
Babcock & Wilcox v Morton	0-5
Celtic v Clyde	1-1, 4-3
Rangers v Heart of Midlothian	3-2
Dundee United v Third Lanark	0-4
Brechin City v Alloa Athletic	3-3, 1-3
Hibernian v Falkirk	3-1
Stenhousemuir v Partick Thistle	1-3
St Johnstone v Queen's Park	3-1
Aberdeen v Arbroath	3-0
Coldstream v Hamilton Academicals	0-4
Dumbarton v Kilmarnock	2-8

THIRD ROUND

St Mirren v Motherwell	3-2
Dunfermline Athletic v Ayr United	2-1
Stirling Albion v Morton	3-1
Celtic v Rangers	2-1
Third Lanark v Alloa Athletic	3-2
Hibernian v Partick Thistle	4-1
St Johnstone v Aberdeen	1-2
Hamilton Academicals v Kilmarnock	0-5

FOURTH ROUND

St Mirren v Dunfermline Athletic	2-1
Stirling Albion v Celtic	1-3
Third Lanark v Hibernian	2-1
Aberdeen v Kilmarnock	3-1

SEMI-FINAL

St Mirren v Celtic	4-0
Third Lanark v Aberdeen	1-1, 0-1

FINAL

St Mirren v Aberdeen	3-1

League Tables 1959-60

FIRST DIVISION

	P	W	D	L	F	A	Pts
1 Burnley	42	24	7	11	85	61	55
2 Wolves	42	24	6	12	106	67	54
3 Tottenham	42	21	11	10	86	50	53
4 WBA	42	19	11	12	83	57	49
5 Sheff Wed	42	19	11	12	80	59	49
6 Bolton	42	20	8	14	59	51	48
7 Man United	42	19	7	16	102	80	45
8 Newcastle	42	18	8	16	82	78	44
9 Preston	42	16	12	14	79	76	44
10 Fulham	42	17	10	15	73	80	44
11 Blackpool	42	15	10	17	59	71	40
12 Leicester	42	13	13	16	66	75	39
13 Arsenal	42	15	9	18	68	80	39
14 West Ham	42	16	6	20	75	91	38
15 Man City	42	17	3	22	78	84	37
16 Everton	42	13	11	18	73	78	37
17 Blackburn	42	16	5	21	60	70	37
18 Chelsea	42	14	9	19	76	91	37
19 Birmingham	42	13	10	19	63	80	36
20 Nottm Forest	42	13	9	20	50	74	35
21 Leeds	42	12	10	20	65	92	34
22 Luton	42	9	12	21	50	73	30

SECOND DIVISION

	P	W	D	L	F	A	Pts
1 Aston Villa	42	25	9	8	89	43	59
2 Cardiff	42	23	12	7	90	62	58
3 Liverpool	42	20	10	12	90	66	50
4 Sheff United	42	19	12	11	68	51	50
5 Middlesbrough	42	19	10	13	90	64	48
6 Huddersfield	42	19	9	14	73	52	47
7 Charlton	42	17	13	12	90	87	47
8 Rotherham	42	17	13	12	61	60	47
9 Bristol Rovers	42	18	11	13	72	78	47
10 Leyton Orient	42	15	14	13	76	61	44
11 Ipswich	42	19	6	17	78	68	44
12 Swansea	42	15	10	17	82	84	40
13 Lincoln	42	16	7	19	75	78	39
14 Brighton	42	13	12	17	67	76	38
15 Scunthorpe	42	13	10	19	57	71	36
16 Sunderland	42	12	12	18	52	65	36
17 Stoke	42	14	7	21	66	83	35
18 Derby	42	14	7	21	61	77	35
19 Plymouth	42	13	9	20	61	89	35
20 Portsmouth	42	10	12	20	59	77	32
21 Hull	42	10	10	22	48	76	30
22 Bristol City	42	11	5	26	60	97	27

THIRD DIVISION

	P	W	D	L	F	A	Pts
1 Southampton	46	26	9	11	106	75	61
2 Norwich	46	24	11	11	82	54	59
3 Shrewsbury	46	18	16	12	97	75	52
4 Coventry	46	21	10	15	78	63	52
5 Grimsby	46	18	16	12	87	70	52
6 Brentford	46	21	9	16	78	61	51
7 Bury	46	21	9	16	64	51	51
8 QPR	46	18	13	15	73	54	49
9 Colchester	46	18	11	17	83	74	47
10 Bournemouth	46	17	13	16	72	72	47
11 Reading	46	18	10	18	84	77	46
12 Southend	46	19	8	19	76	74	46
13 Newport	46	20	6	20	80	79	46
14 Port Vale	46	19	8	19	80	79	46
15 Halifax	46	18	10	18	70	72	46
16 Swindon	46	19	8	19	69	78	46
17 Barnsley	46	15	14	17	65	66	44
18 Chesterfield	46	18	7	21	71	84	43
19 Bradford City	46	15	12	19	66	74	42
20 Tranmere	46	14	13	19	72	75	41
21 York	46	13	12	21	57	73	38
22 Mansfield	46	15	6	25	81	112	36
23 Wrexham	46	14	8	24	68	101	36
24 Accrington	46	11	5	30	57	123	27

FOURTH DIVISION

	P	W	D	L	F	A	Pts
1 Walsall	46	28	9	9	102	60	65
2 Notts County	46	26	8	12	107	69	60
3 Torquay	46	26	8	12	84	58	60
4 Watford	46	24	9	13	92	67	57
5 Millwall	46	18	17	11	84	61	53
6 Northampton	46	22	9	15	85	63	53
7 Gillingham	46	21	10	15	74	69	52
8 Crystal Palace	46	19	12	15	84	64	50
9 Exeter	46	19	11	16	80	70	49
10 Stockport	46	19	11	16	58	54	49
11 Bradford PA	46	17	15	14	70	68	49
12 Rochdale	46	18	10	18	65	60	46
13 Aldershot	46	18	9	19	77	74	45
14 Crewe	46	18	9	19	79	88	45
15 Darlington	46	17	9	20	63	73	43
16 Workington	46	14	14	18	68	60	42
17 Doncaster	46	16	10	20	69	76	42
18 Barrow	46	15	11	20	77	87	41
19 Carlisle	46	15	11	20	51	66	41
20 Chester	46	14	12	20	59	77	40
21 Southport	46	10	14	22	48	92	34
22 Gateshead	46	12	9	25	58	86	33
23 Oldham	46	8	12	26	41	83	28
24 Hartlepools	46	10	7	29	59	109	27

SCOTTISH FIRST DIVISION

	P	W	D	L	F	A	Pts
1 Hearts	34	23	8	3	102	51	54
2 Kilmarnock	34	24	2	8	67	45	50
3 Rangers	34	17	8	9	72	38	42
4 Dundee	34	16	10	8	70	49	42
5 Motherwell	34	16	8	10	71	61	40
6 Clyde	34	15	9	10	77	69	39
7 Hibernian	34	14	7	13	106	85	35
8 Ayr	34	14	6	14	65	73	34
9 Celtic	34	12	9	13	73	59	33
10 Partick Thistle	34	14	4	16	54	78	32
11 Raith Rovers	34	14	3	17	64	62	31
12 Third Lanark	34	13	4	17	75	83	30
13 Dunfermline	34	10	9	15	72	80	29
14 St Mirren	34	11	6	17	78	86	28
15 Aberdeen	34	11	6	17	54	72	28
16 Airdrieonians	34	11	6	17	56	80	28
17 Stirling Albion	34	7	8	19	55	72	22
18 Arbroath	34	4	7	23	38	106	15

SCOTTISH SECOND DIVISION

	P	W	D	L	F	A	Pts
1 St Johnstone	36	24	5	7	87	47	53
2 Dundee United	36	22	6	8	90	45	50
3 Queen of the S	36	21	7	8	94	52	49
4 Hamilton	36	21	6	9	91	62	48
5 Stenhousemuir	36	20	4	12	86	67	44
6 Dumbarton	36	18	7	11	67	53	43
7 Montrose	36	19	5	12	60	52	43
8 Falkirk	36	15	9	12	77	43	39
9 Berwick	36	16	5	15	62	55	37
10 Albion	36	14	8	14	71	78	36
11 Queen's Park	36	17	2	17	65	79	36
12 Brechin	36	14	6	16	66	66	34
13 Alloa	36	13	5	18	70	85	31
14 Morton	36	10	8	18	67	79	28
15 E Stirlingshire	36	10	8	18	68	82	28
16 Forfar	36	10	8	18	53	84	28
17 Stranraer	36	10	3	23	53	79	23
18 East Fife	36	7	6	23	50	87	20
19 Cowdenbeath	36	6	2	28	42	124	14

An expensive agreement
In July 1959, the Football League established the copyright on their fixture lists. As a result, the Pools Promoters agreed to pay the League a minimum of £245,000 each year for 10 years. In return, the Pools firms were to be allowed to reprint the fixtures on their coupons.

Cliff Holton of Watford, the 1959-60 Football League leading goalscorer, became the only player since the War to notch two hat-tricks in League matches in successive days. On Good Friday, 15 April 1960, Holton scored three times against Chester. A day later, he hit three more against Gateshead.

FA CUP 1959-60

FOURTH ROUND

Wolverhampton v Charlton Athletic	2-1
Huddersfield Town v Luton Town	0-1
Leicester City v Fulham	2-1
West Bromwich Albion v Bolton Wanderers	2-0
Bristol Rovers v Preston North End	3-3, 1-5
Rotherham United v Brighton	1-1, 1-1, 0-6
Scunthorpe United v Port Vale	0-1
Chelsea v Aston Villa	1-2
Sheffield United v Nottingham Forest	3-0
Southampton v Watford	2-2, 0-1
Liverpool v Manchester United	1-3
Sheffield Wednesday v Peterborough United	2-0
Bradford City v Bournemouth	3-1
Swansea Town v Burnley	0-0, 1-2
Crewe Alexandra v Tottenham Hotspur	2-2, 2-13
Blackburn Rovers v Blackpool	1-1, 3-0

FIFTH ROUND

Luton Town v Wolverhampton	1-4
Leicester City v West Bromwich Albion	2-1
Preston North End v Brighton	2-1
Port Vale v Aston Villa	1-2
Sheffield United v Watford	3-2
Manchester United v Sheffield Wednesday	0-1
Bradford City v Burnley	2-2, 0-5
Tottenham Hotspur v Blackburn Rovers	1-3

SIXTH ROUND

Leicester City v Wolverhampton Wanderers	1-2
Aston Villa v Preston North End	2-0
Sheffield United v Sheffield Wednesday	0-2
Burnley v Blackburn Rovers	3-3, 0-2

SEMI-FINAL

Wolverhampton Wanderers v Aston Villa	1-0
Sheffield Wednesday v Blackburn Rovers	1-2

FINAL

Wolverhampton Wanderers v Blackburn Rovers	3-0

SCOTTISH FA CUP 1959-60

SECOND ROUND

Rangers v Arbroath	2-0
Dunfermline Athletic v Stenhousemuir	2-3
E Stirlingshire v Inverness Caledonian	2-2, 4-1
Hibernian v Dundee	3-0
Elgin City v Forfar Athletic	5-1
St Mirren v Celtic	1-1, 4-4, 2-5
Dundee United v Partick Thistle	2-2, 1-4
Stirling Albion v Queen of the South	3-3, 1-5
Peebles Rovers v Ayr United	1-6
Alloa Athletic v Airdrieonians	1-5
Aberdeen v Clyde	0-2
Montrose v Queen's Park	2-2, 1-1, 1-2
Eyemouth United v Albion Rovers	1-0
Cowdenbeath v Falkirk	1-0
Motherwell v Keith	6-0
Heart of Midlothian v Kilmarnock	1-1, 1-2

THIRD ROUND

Stenhousemuir v Rangers	0-3
East Stirlingshire v Hibernian	0-3
Elgin City v Celtic	1-2
Partick Thistle v Queen of the South	3-2
Ayr United v Airdrieonians	4-2
Clyde v Queen's Park	6-0
Eyemouth United v Cowdenbeath	3-0
Kilmarnock v Motherwell	2-0

FOURTH ROUND

Rangers v Hibernian	3-2
Celtic v Partick Thistle	2-0
Ayr United v Clyde	0-2
Eyemouth United v Kilmarnock	1-2

SEMI-FINAL

Rangers v Celtic	1-1, 4-1
Clyde v Kilmarnock	0-2

FINAL

Rangers v Kilmarnock	2-0

League Tables 1960-61

FIRST DIVISION

	P	W	D	L	F	A	Pts
1 Tottenham	42	31	4	7	115	55	66
2 Sheff Wed	42	23	12	7	78	47	58
3 Wolves	42	25	7	10	103	75	57
4 Burnley	42	22	7	13	102	77	51
5 Everton	42	22	6	14	87	69	50
6 Leicester	42	18	9	15	87	70	45
7 Man United	42	18	9	15	88	76	45
8 Blackburn	42	15	13	14	77	76	43
9 Aston Villa	42	17	9	16	78	77	43
10 WBA	42	18	5	19	67	71	41
11 Arsenal	42	15	11	16	77	85	41
12 Chelsea	42	15	7	20	98	100	37
13 Man City	42	13	11	18	79	90	37
14 Nottm Forest	42	14	9	19	62	78	37
15 Cardiff	42	13	11	18	60	85	37
16 West Ham	42	13	10	19	77	88	36
17 Fulham	42	14	8	20	72	95	36
18 Bolton	42	12	11	19	58	73	35
19 Birmingham	42	14	6	22	62	84	34
20 Blackpool	42	12	9	21	68	73	33
21 Newcastle	42	11	10	21	86	109	32
22 Preston	42	10	10	22	43	71	30

SECOND DIVISION

	P	W	D	L	F	A	Pts
1 Ipswich	42	26	7	9	100	55	59
2 Sheff United	42	26	6	10	81	51	58
3 Liverpool	42	21	10	11	87	58	52
4 Norwich	42	20	9	13	70	53	49
5 Middlesbrough	42	18	12	12	83	74	48
6 Sunderland	42	17	13	12	75	60	47
7 Swansea	42	18	11	13	77	73	47
8 Southampton	42	18	8	16	84	81	44
9 Scunthorpe	42	14	15	13	69	64	43
10 Charlton	42	16	11	15	97	91	43
11 Plymouth	42	17	8	17	81	82	42
12 Derby	42	15	10	17	80	80	40
13 Luton	42	15	9	18	71	70	39
14 Leeds	42	14	10	18	75	83	38
15 Rotherham	42	12	13	17	65	64	37
16 Brighton	42	14	9	19	61	75	37
17 Bristol Rovers	42	15	7	20	73	92	37
18 Stoke	42	12	12	18	51	59	36
19 Leyton Orient	42	14	8	20	55	78	36
20 Huddersfield	42	13	9	20	62	71	35
21 Portsmouth	42	11	11	20	64	91	33
22 Lincoln	42	8	8	26	48	95	24

THIRD DIVISION

	P	W	D	L	F	A	Pts
1 Bury	46	30	8	8	108	45	68
2 Walsall	46	28	6	12	98	60	62
3 QPR	46	25	10	11	93	60	60
4 Watford	46	20	12	14	85	72	52
5 Notts County	46	21	9	16	82	77	51
6 Grimsby	46	20	10	16	77	69	50
7 Port Vale	46	17	15	14	96	79	49
8 Barnsley	46	21	7	18	83	80	49
9 Halifax	46	16	17	13	71	78	49
10 Shrewsbury	46	15	16	15	83	75	46
11 Hull	46	17	12	17	73	73	46
12 Torquay	46	14	17	15	75	83	45
13 Newport	46	17	11	18	81	90	45
14 Bristol City	46	17	10	19	70	68	44
15 Coventry	46	16	12	18	80	83	44
16 Swindon	46	14	15	17	62	55	43
17 Brentford	46	13	17	16	56	70	43
18 Reading	46	14	12	20	72	83	40
19 Bournemouth	46	15	10	21	58	76	40
20 Southend	46	14	11	21	60	76	39
21 Tranmere	46	15	8	23	79	115	38
22 Bradford City	46	11	14	21	65	87	36
23 Colchester	46	11	11	24	68	101	33
24 Chesterfield	46	10	12	24	67	87	32

FOURTH DIVISION

	P	W	D	L	F	A	Pts
1 Peterborough	46	28	10	8	134	65	66
2 Crystal Palace	46	29	6	11	110	69	64
3 Northampton	46	25	10	11	90	62	60
4 Bradford PA	46	26	8	12	84	74	60
5 York	46	21	9	16	80	60	51
6 Millwall	46	21	8	17	97	86	50
7 Darlington	46	18	13	15	78	70	49
8 Workington	46	21	7	18	74	76	49
9 Crewe	46	20	9	17	61	67	49
10 Aldershot	46	18	9	19	79	69	45
11 Doncaster	46	19	7	20	76	78	45
12 Oldham	46	19	7	20	79	88	45
13 Stockport	46	18	9	19	57	66	45
14 Southport	46	19	6	21	69	67	44
15 Gillingham	46	15	13	18	64	66	43
16 Wrexham	46	17	8	21	62	56	42
17 Rochdale	46	17	8	21	60	66	42
18 Accrington	46	16	8	22	74	88	40
19 Carlisle	46	13	13	20	61	79	39
20 Mansfield	46	16	6	24	71	78	38
21 Exeter	46	14	10	22	66	94	38
22 Barrow	46	13	11	22	52	79	37
23 Hartlepools	46	12	8	26	71	103	32
24 Chester	46	11	9	26	61	104	31

SCOTTISH FIRST DIVISION

	P	W	D	L	F	A	Pts
1 Rangers	34	23	5	6	88	46	51
2 Kilmarnock	34	21	8	5	77	45	50
3 Third Lanark	34	20	2	12	100	80	42
4 Celtic	34	15	9	10	64	46	39
5 Motherwell	34	15	8	11	70	57	38
6 Aberdeen	34	14	8	12	72	72	36
7 Hibernian	34	15	4	15	66	69	34
8 Hearts	34	13	8	13	51	53	34
9 Dundee United	34	13	7	14	60	58	33
10 Dundee	34	13	6	15	61	53	32
11 Partick Thistle	34	13	6	15	59	69	32
12 Dunfermline	34	12	7	15	65	81	31
13 Airdrieonians	34	10	10	14	61	71	30
14 St Mirren	34	11	7	16	53	58	29
15 St Johnstone	34	10	9	15	47	63	29
16 Raith Rovers	34	10	7	17	46	67	27
17 Clyde	34	6	11	17	55	77	23
18 Ayr	34	5	12	17	51	81	22

SCOTTISH SECOND DIVISION

	P	W	D	L	F	A	Pts
1 Stirling Albion	36	24	7	5	89	37	55
2 Falkirk	36	24	6	6	100	40	54
3 Stenhousemuir	36	24	2	10	99	69	50
4 Stranraer	36	19	6	11	83	55	44
5 Queen of the S	36	20	3	13	77	52	43
6 Hamilton	36	17	7	12	84	80	41
7 Montrose	36	19	2	15	75	65	40
8 Cowdenbeath	36	17	6	13	71	65	40
9 Berwick	36	14	9	13	62	69	37
10 Dumbarton	36	15	5	16	78	82	35
11 Alloa	36	13	7	16	78	68	33
12 Arbroath	36	13	7	16	56	76	33
13 East Fife	36	14	4	18	70	80	32
14 Brechin	36	9	9	18	60	78	27
15 Queen's Park	36	10	6	20	61	87	26
16 E Stirlingshire	36	9	7	20	59	100	25
17 Albion	36	9	6	21	60	89	24
18 Forfar	36	10	4	22	65	98	24
19 Morton	36	5	11	20	56	93	21

Tottenham began the season with 11 consecutive wins, a record, and ended it having won 31 of their 42 games, a First Division record. Spurs' 16 away wins—including an unequalled 8 in a row—was another First Division record. Spurs also equalled Arsenal's Division One record points total of 66.

Burnley were fined £1000 by the Football League for fielding ten reserves in a League match against Chelsea.

The maximum wage restrictions were removed and Johnny Haynes of Fulham became the first British footballer to earn £100 a week.

FA CUP 1960-61

FOURTH ROUND

Leicester City v Bristol City	5-1
Birmingham City v Rotherham United	4-0
Huddersfield Town v Barnsley	1-1, 0-1
Luton Town v Manchester City	3-1
Newcastle United v Stockport County	4-0
Stoke City v Aldershot	0-0, 0-0, 3-0
Sheffield United v Lincoln City	3-1
Bolton Wanderers v Blackburn Rovers	3-3, 0-4
Southampton v Leyton Orient	0-1
Sheffield Wednesday v Manchester United	1-1, 7-2
Brighton v Burnley	3-3, 0-2
Swansea Town v Preston North End	2-1
Scunthorpe United v Norwich City	1-4
Liverpool v Sunderland	0-2
Peterborough United v Aston Villa	1-1, 1-2
Tottenham Hotspur v Crewe Alexandra	5-1

FIFTH ROUND

Birmingham City v Leicester City	1-1, 1-2
Barnsley v Luton Town	1-0
Newcastle United v Stoke City	3-1
Sheffield United v Blackburn Rovers	2-1
Leyton Orient v Sheffield Wednesday	0-2
Burnley v Swansea Town	4-0
Norwich City v Sunderland	0-1
Aston Villa v Tottenham Hotspur	0-2

SIXTH ROUND

Leicester City v Barnsley	0-0, 2-1
Newcastle United v Sheffield United	1-3
Sheffield Wednesday v Burnley	0-0, 0-2
Sunderland v Tottenham Hotspur	1-1, 0-5

SEMI-FINAL

Leicester City v Sheffield United	0-0, 0-0, 2-0
Burnley v Tottenham Hotspur	0-3

FINAL

Leicester City v Tottenham Hotspur	0-2

SCOTTISH FA CUP 1960-61

SECOND ROUND

Buckie Thistle v Raith Rovers	0-2
Celtic v Montrose	6-0
Queen of the South v Hamilton Academicals	0-2
Hibernian v Peebles Rovers	15-1
Brechin City v Duns	5-3
Ayr United v Airdrieonians	0-0, 1-3
Cowdenbeath v Motherwell	1-4
Dundee v Rangers	1-5
East Fife v Partick Thistle	1-3
Kilmarnock v Heart of Midlothian	1-2
Dundee United v St Mirren	0-1
Third Lanark v Arbroath	5-2
Aberdeen v Deveronvale	4-2
Stranraer v Dunfermline Athletic	1-3
Alloa Athletic v Dumbarton	2-0
Forfar Athletic v Morton	2-0

THIRD ROUND

Raith Rovers v Celtic	1-4
Hamilton Academicals v Hibernian	0-4
Brechin City v Airdrieonians	0-3
Motherwell v Rangers	2-2, 5-2
Partick Thistle v Heart of Midlothian	1-2
St Mirren v Third Lanark	3-3, 8-0
Aberdeen v Dunfermline Athletic	3-6
Alloa Athletic v Forfar Athletic	2-1

FOURTH ROUND

Celtic v Hibernian	1-1, 1-0
Motherwell v Airdrieonians	0-1
Heart of Midlothian v St Mirren	0-1
Dunfermline Athletic v Alloa Athletic	4-0

SEMI-FINAL

Celtic v Airdrieonians	4-0
Dunfermline Athletic v St Mirren	0-0, 1-0

FINAL

Celtic v Dunfermline Athletic	0-0, 0-2

League Tables 1961-62

FIRST DIVISION

	P	W	D	L	F	A	Pts
1 Ipswich	42	24	8	10	93	67	56
2 Burnley	42	21	11	10	101	67	53
3 Tottenham	42	21	10	11	88	69	52
4 Everton	42	20	11	11	88	54	51
5 Sheff United	42	19	9	14	61	69	47
6 Sheff Wed	42	20	6	16	72	58	46
7 Aston Villa	42	18	8	16	65	56	44
8 West Ham	42	17	10	15	76	82	44
9 WBA	42	15	13	14	83	67	43
10 Arsenal	42	16	11	15	71	72	43
11 Bolton	42	16	10	16	62	66	42
12 Man City	42	17	7	18	78	81	41
13 Blackpool	42	15	11	16	70	75	41
14 Leicester	42	17	6	19	72	71	40
15 Man United	42	15	9	18	72	75	39
16 Blackburn	42	14	11	17	50	58	39
17 Birmingham	42	14	10	18	65	81	38
18 Wolves	42	13	10	19	73	86	36
19 Nottm Forest	42	13	10	19	63	79	36
20 Fulham	42	13	7	22	66	74	33
21 Cardiff	42	9	14	19	50	81	32
22 Chelsea	42	9	10	23	63	94	28

SECOND DIVISION

	P	W	D	L	F	A	Pts
1 Liverpool	42	27	8	7	99	43	62
2 Leyton Orient	42	22	10	10	69	40	54
3 Sunderland	42	22	9	11	85	50	53
4 Scunthorpe	42	21	7	14	86	71	49
5 Plymouth	42	19	8	15	75	75	46
6 Southampton	42	18	9	15	77	62	45
7 Huddersfield	42	16	12	14	67	59	44
8 Stoke	42	17	8	17	55	57	42
9 Rotherham	42	16	9	17	70	76	41
10 Preston	42	15	10	17	55	57	40
11 Newcastle	42	15	9	18	64	58	39
12 Middlesbrough	42	16	7	19	76	72	39
13 Luton	42	17	5	20	69	71	39
14 Walsall	42	14	11	17	70	75	39
15 Charlton	42	15	9	18	69	75	39
16 Derby	42	14	11	17	68	75	39
17 Norwich	42	14	11	17	61	70	39
18 Bury	42	17	5	20	52	76	39
19 Leeds	42	12	12	18	50	61	36
20 Swansea	42	12	12	18	61	83	36
21 Bristol Rovers	42	13	7	22	53	81	33
22 Brighton	42	10	11	21	42	86	31

THIRD DIVISION

	P	W	D	L	F	A	Pts
1 Portsmouth	46	27	11	8	87	47	65
2 Grimsby	46	28	6	12	80	56	62
3 Bournemouth	46	21	17	8	69	45	59
4 QPR	46	24	11	11	111	73	59
5 Peterborough	46	26	6	14	107	82	58
6 Bristol City	46	23	8	15	94	72	54
7 Reading	46	22	9	15	77	66	53
8 Northampton	46	20	11	15	85	57	51
9 Swindon	46	17	15	14	78	71	49
10 Hull	46	20	8	18	67	54	48
11 Bradford PA	46	20	7	19	80	78	47
12 Port Vale	46	17	11	18	65	58	45
13 Notts County	46	17	9	20	67	74	43
14 Coventry	46	16	11	19	64	71	43
15 Crystal Palace	46	14	14	18	83	80	42
16 Southend	46	13	16	17	57	69	42
17 Watford	46	14	13	19	63	74	41
18 Halifax	46	15	10	21	62	84	40
19 Shrewsbury	46	13	12	21	73	84	38
20 Barnsley	46	13	12	21	71	95	38
21 Torquay	46	15	6	25	76	100	36
22 Lincoln	46	9	17	20	57	87	35
23 Brentford	46	13	8	25	53	93	34
24 Newport	46	7	8	31	46	102	22

FOURTH DIVISION

	P	W	D	L	F	A	Pts
1 Millwall	44	23	10	11	87	62	56
2 Colchester	44	23	9	12	104	71	55
3 Wrexham	44	22	9	13	96	56	53
4 Carlisle	44	22	8	14	64	63	52
5 Bradford City	44	21	9	14	94	86	51
6 York	44	20	10	14	84	53	50
7 Aldershot	44	22	5	17	81	60	49
8 Workington	44	19	11	14	69	70	49
9 Barrow	44	17	14	13	74	58	48
10 Crewe	44	20	6	18	79	70	46
11 Oldham	44	17	12	15	77	70	46
12 Rochdale	44	19	7	18	71	71	45
13 Darlington	44	18	9	17	61	73	45
14 Mansfield	44	19	6	19	77	66	44
15 Tranmere	44	20	4	20	70	81	44
16 Stockport	44	17	9	18	70	69	43
17 Southport	44	17	9	18	61	71	43
18 Exeter	44	13	11	20	62	77	37
19 Chesterfield	44	14	9	21	70	87	37
20 Gillingham	44	13	11	20	73	94	37
21 Doncaster	44	11	7	26	60	85	29
22 Hartlepools	44	8	11	25	52	101	27
23 Chester	44	7	12	25	54	96	26

24 Accrington Stanley resigned from the League

SCOTTISH FIRST DIVISION

	P	W	D	L	F	A	Pts
1 Dundee	34	25	4	5	80	46	54
2 Rangers	34	22	7	5	84	31	51
3 Celtic	34	19	8	7	81	37	46
4 Dunfermline	34	19	5	10	77	46	43
5 Kilmarnock	34	16	10	8	74	58	42
6 Hearts	34	16	6	12	54	49	38
7 Partick Thistle	34	16	3	15	60	55	35
8 Hibernian	34	14	5	15	58	72	33
9 Motherwell	34	13	6	15	65	62	32
10 Dundee United	34	13	6	15	70	71	32
11 Third Lanark	34	13	5	16	59	60	31
12 Aberdeen	34	10	9	15	60	73	29
13 Raith Rovers	34	10	7	17	51	73	27
14 Falkirk	34	11	4	19	45	68	26
15 Airdrieonians	34	9	7	18	57	78	25
16 St Mirren	34	10	5	19	52	80	25
17 St Johnstone	34	9	7	18	35	61	25
18 Stirling Albion	34	6	6	22	34	76	18

SCOTTISH SECOND DIVISION

	P	W	D	L	F	A	Pts
1 Clyde	36	15	4	7	108	47	54
2 Queen of the S	36	24	5	7	78	33	53
3 Morton	36	19	6	11	78	64	44
4 Alloa	36	17	8	11	92	78	42
5 Montrose	36	15	11	10	63	50	41
6 Arbroath	36	17	7	12	66	59	41
7 Stranraer	36	14	11	11	61	62	39
8 Berwick	36	16	6	14	83	70	38
9 Ayr	36	15	8	13	71	63	38
10 East Fife	36	15	7	14	60	59	37
11 E Stirlingshire	36	15	4	17	70	81	34
12 Queen's Park	36	12	9	15	64	62	33
13 Hamilton	36	14	5	17	78	79	33
14 Cowdenbeath	36	11	9	16	65	77	31
15 Stenhousemuir	36	13	5	18	69	86	31
16 Forfar	36	11	8	17	68	76	30
17 Dumbarton	36	9	10	17	49	66	28
18 Albion	36	10	5	21	42	74	25
19 Brechin	36	5	2	29	44	123	12

Triple success
Only once since the War have three players hit hat-tricks for one side in the same League match. Ron Barnes, Roy Ambler and Wyn Davies did this in Wrexham's 10-1 thrashing of Hartlepools in a Fourth Division game on 3 March 1962.

The England player from the Third Division
Johnny Byrne, the Crystal Palace inside-right, became only the third footballer from the Third Division, to appear for England (v Ireland, 22 November 1961) in the Home Championship since the War.

FA CUP 1961-62

FOURTH ROUND

Burnley v Leyton Orient	1-1, 1-0
Everton v Manchester City	2-0
Peterborough United v Sheffield United	1-3
Norwich City v Ipswich Town	1-1, 2-1
Fulham v Walsall	2-2, 2-0
Sunderland v Port Vale	0-0, 1-3
Stoke City v Blackburn Rovers	0-1
Shrewsbury Town v Middlesbrough	2-2, 1-5
Oldham Athletic v Liverpool	1-2
Preston North End v Weymouth	2-0
Manchester United v Arsenal	1-0
Nottingham Forest v Sheffield Wednesday	0-2
Aston Villa v Huddersfield Town	2-1
Charlton Athletic v Derby County	2-1
Wolverhampton Wanderers v West Bromwich Albion	1-2
Plymouth Argyle v Tottenham Hotspur	1-5

FIFTH ROUND

Burnley v Everton	3-1
Sheffield United v Norwich City	3-1
Fulham v Port Vale	1-0
Blackburn Rovers v Middlesbrough	2-1
Liverpool v Preston North End	0-0, 0-0, 0-1
Manchester United v Sheffield Wednesday	0-0, 2-0
Aston Villa v Charlton Athletic	2-1
West Bromwich Albion v Tottenham Hotspur	2-4

SIXTH ROUND

Sheffield United v Burnley	0-1
Fulham v Blackburn Rovers	2-2, 1-0
Preston North End v Manchester United	0-0, 1-2
Tottenham Hotspur v Aston Villa	2-0

SEMI-FINAL

Burnley v Fulham	1-1, 2-1
Manchester United v Tottenham Hotspur	1-3

FINAL

Burnley v Tottenham Hotspur	1-3

SCOTTISH FA CUP 1961-62

SECOND ROUND

Rangers v Arbroath	6-0
Clyde v Aberdeen	2-2, 3-10
Brechin City v Kilmarnock	1-6
Dumbarton v Ross County	2-3
Stirling Albion v Partick Thistle	3-1
East Fife v Albion Rovers	1-0
Stranraer v Montrose	0-0, 1-0
Motherwell v St Johnstone	4-0
Vale of Leithen v Heart of Midlothian	0-5
Morton v Celtic	1-3
Hamilton Academicals v Third Lanark	0-2
Inverness Caledonian v East Stirlingshire	3-0
Dunfermline Athletic v Wigtown	9-0
Queen of the South v Stenhousemuir	0-2
Alloa Athletic v Raith Rovers	1-2
Dundee v St Mirren	0-1

THIRD ROUND

Aberdeen v Rangers	2-2, 5-1
Kilmarnock v Ross County	7-0
Stirling Albion v East Fife	4-1
Stranraer v Motherwell	1-3
Heart of Midlothian v Celtic	3-4
Third Lanark v Inverness Caledonian	6-1
Dunfermline Athletic v Stenhousemuir	0-0, 3-0
Raith Rovers v St Mirren	1-1, 0-4

FOURTH ROUND

Kilmarnock v Rangers	2-4
Stirling Albion v Motherwell	0-6
Celtic v Third Lanark	4-4, 4-0
Dunfermline Athletic v St Mirren	0-1

SEMI-FINAL

Rangers v Motherwell	3-1
Celtic v St Mirren	1-3

FINAL

Rangers v St Mirren	2-0

League Tables 1962-63

FIRST DIVISION

		P	W	D	L	F	A	Pts
1	Everton	42	25	11	6	84	42	61
2	Tottenham	42	23	9	10	111	62	55
3	Burnley	42	22	10	10	78	57	54
4	Leicester	42	20	12	10	79	53	52
5	Wolves	42	20	10	12	93	65	50
6	Sheff Wed	42	19	10	13	77	63	48
7	Arsenal	42	18	10	14	86	77	46
8	Liverpool	42	17	10	15	71	59	44
9	Nottm Forest	42	17	10	15	67	69	44
10	Sheff United	42	16	12	14	58	60	44
11	Blackburn	42	15	12	15	79	71	42
12	West Ham	42	14	12	16	73	69	40
13	Blackpool	42	13	14	15	58	64	40
14	WBA	42	16	7	19	71	79	39
15	Aston Villa	42	15	8	19	62	68	38
16	Fulham	42	14	10	18	50	71	38
17	Ipswich	42	12	11	19	59	78	35
18	Bolton	42	15	5	22	55	75	35
19	Man United	42	12	10	20	67	81	34
20	Birmingham	42	10	13	19	63	90	33
21	Man City	42	10	11	21	58	102	31
22	Leyton Orient	42	6	9	27	37	81	21

SECOND DIVISION

		P	W	D	L	F	A	Pts
1	Stoke	42	20	13	9	73	50	53
2	Chelsea	42	24	4	14	81	42	52
3	Sunderland	42	20	12	10	84	55	52
4	Middlesbrough	42	20	9	13	86	85	49
5	Leeds	42	19	10	13	79	53	48
6	Huddersfield	42	17	14	11	63	50	48
7	Newcastle	42	18	11	13	79	59	47
8	Bury	42	18	11	13	51	47	47
9	Scunthorpe	42	16	12	14	57	59	44
10	Cardiff	42	18	7	17	83	73	43
11	Southampton	42	17	8	17	72	67	42
12	Plymouth	42	15	12	15	76	73	42
13	Norwich	42	17	8	17	80	79	42
14	Rotherham	42	17	6	19	67	74	40
15	Swansea	42	15	9	18	51	72	39
16	Portsmouth	42	13	11	18	63	79	37
17	Preston	42	13	11	18	59	74	37
18	Derby	42	12	12	18	61	72	36
19	Grimsby	42	11	13	18	55	66	35
20	Charlton	42	13	5	24	62	94	31
21	Walsall	42	11	9	22	53	89	31
22	Luton	42	11	7	24	61	84	29

THIRD DIVISION

		P	W	D	L	F	A	Pts
1	Northampton	46	26	10	10	109	60	62
2	Swindon	46	22	14	10	87	56	58
3	Port Vale	46	23	8	15	72	58	54
4	Coventry	46	18	17	11	83	69	53
5	Bournemouth	46	18	16	12	63	46	52
6	Peterborough	46	20	11	15	93	75	51
7	Notts County	46	19	13	14	73	74	51
8	Southend	46	19	12	15	75	77	50
9	Wrexham	46	20	9	17	84	83	49
10	Hull	46	19	10	17	74	69	48
11	Crystal Palace	46	17	13	16	68	58	47
12	Colchester	46	18	11	17	73	93	47
13	QPR	46	17	11	18	85	76	45
14	Bristol City	46	16	13	17	100	92	45
15	Shrewsbury	46	16	12	18	83	81	44
16	Millwall	46	15	13	18	82	87	43
17	Watford	46	17	8	21	82	85	42
18	Barnsley	46	15	11	20	63	74	41
19	Bristol Rovers	46	15	11	20	70	88	41
20	Reading	46	16	8	22	74	78	40
21	Bradford PA	46	14	12	20	79	97	40
22	Brighton	46	12	12	22	58	84	36
23	Carlisle	46	13	9	24	61	89	35
24	Halifax	46	9	12	25	64	106	30

FOURTH DIVISION

		P	W	D	L	F	A	Pts
1	Brentford	46	27	8	11	98	64	62
2	Oldham	46	24	11	11	95	60	59
3	Crewe	46	24	11	11	86	58	59
4	Mansfield	46	24	9	13	108	69	57
5	Gillingham	46	22	13	11	71	49	57
6	Torquay	46	20	16	10	75	56	56
7	Rochdale	46	20	11	15	67	59	51
8	Tranmere	46	20	10	16	81	67	50
9	Barrow	46	19	12	15	82	80	50
10	Workington	46	17	13	16	76	68	47
11	Aldershot	46	15	17	14	73	69	47
12	Darlington	46	19	6	21	72	87	44
13	Southport	46	15	14	17	72	106	44
14	York	46	16	11	19	67	62	43
15	Chesterfield	46	13	16	17	70	64	42
16	Doncaster	46	14	14	18	64	77	42
17	Exeter	46	16	10	20	57	77	42
18	Oxford	46	13	15	18	70	71	41
19	Stockport	46	15	11	20	56	70	41
20	Newport	46	14	11	21	76	90	39
21	Chester	46	15	9	22	51	66	39
22	Lincoln	46	13	9	24	68	89	35
23	Bradford City	46	11	10	25	64	93	32
24	Hartlepools	46	7	11	28	56	104	25

SCOTTISH FIRST DIVISION

		P	W	D	L	F	A	Pts
1	Rangers	34	25	7	2	94	28	57
2	Kilmarnock	34	20	8	6	92	40	48
3	Partick Thistle	34	20	6	8	66	44	46
4	Celtic	34	19	6	9	76	44	44
5	Hearts	34	17	9	8	85	59	43
6	Aberdeen	34	17	7	10	70	47	41
7	Dundee United	34	15	11	8	67	52	41
8	Dunfermline	34	13	8	13	50	47	34
9	Dundee	34	12	9	13	60	49	33
10	Motherwell	34	10	11	13	60	63	31
11	Airdrieonians	34	14	2	18	52	76	30
12	St Mirren	34	10	8	16	52	72	28
13	Falkirk	34	12	3	19	54	69	27
14	Third Lanark	34	9	8	17	56	68	26
15	Queen of the S	34	10	6	18	36	75	26
16	Hibernian	34	8	9	17	47	67	25
17	Clyde	34	9	5	20	49	83	23
18	Raith	34	2	5	27	35	118	9

SCOTTISH SECOND DIVISION

		P	W	D	L	F	A	Pts
1	St Johnstone	36	25	5	6	83	37	55
2	E Stirlingshire	36	20	9	7	80	50	49
3	Morton	36	23	2	11	100	49	48
4	Hamilton	36	18	8	10	69	56	44
5	Stranraer	36	16	10	10	81	70	42
6	Arbroath	36	18	4	14	74	51	40
7	Albion	36	18	2	16	72	79	38
8	Cowdenbeath	36	15	7	14	72	61	37
9	Alloa	36	15	6	15	57	56	36
10	Stirling	36	16	4	16	74	75	36
11	East Fife	36	15	6	15	60	69	36
12	Dumbarton	36	15	4	17	64	64	34
13	Ayr	36	13	8	15	68	77	34
14	Queen's Park	36	13	6	17	66	72	32
15	Montrose	36	13	5	18	57	70	31
16	Stenhousemuir	36	13	5	18	54	75	31
17	Berwick	36	11	7	18	57	77	29
18	Forfar	36	9	5	22	73	99	23
19	Brechin	36	3	3	30	39	113	9

Terrible winter disrupts the football programme

The winter of 1962-63 broke all previous records for postponements and abandoned matches due to bad weather. For six weeks, the football programme was wrecked by impossible playing conditions and over 400 League and Cup games were postponed or abandoned in England, Wales and Scotland. The worst-hit day—in fact the worst-hit ever, except for the War years—in England and Scotland was 9 February. Then, 57 games were called off through snow and ice, and only seven were completed. As a result of the severe winter, the football season was extended.

FA CUP 1962-63

FOURTH ROUND

Leicester City v Ipswich Town	3-1
Leyton Orient v Derby County	3-0
Manchester City v Bury	1-0
Norwich City v Newcastle United	5-0
Arsenal v Sheffield Wednesday	2-0
Burnley v Liverpool	1-1, 1-2
West Ham United v Swansea Town	1-0
Swindon Town v Everton	1-5
West Bromwich Albion v Nottingham Forest	0-0, 1-2
Middlesbrough v Leeds United	0-2
Southampton v Watford	3-1
Port Vale v Sheffield United	1-2
Portsmouth v Coventry City	1-1, 2-2, 1-2
Gravesend v Sunderland	1-1, 2-5
Charlton Athletic v Chelsea	0-3
Manchester United v Aston Villa	1-0

FIFTH ROUND

Leicester City v Leyton Orient	1-0
Manchester City v Norwich City	1-2
Arsenal v Liverpool	1-2
West Ham United v Everton	1-0
Nottingham Forest v Leeds United	3-0
Southampton v Sheffield United	1-0
Coventry City v Sunderland	2-1
Manchester United v Chelsea	2-1

SIXTH ROUND

Norwich City v Leicester City	0-2
Liverpool v West Ham United	1-0
Nottingham Forest v Southampton	1-1, 3-3, 0-5
Coventry City v Manchester United	1-3

SEMI-FINAL

Leicester City v Liverpool	1-0
Southampton v Manchester United	0-1

FINAL

Leicester City v Manchester United	1-3

SCOTTISH FA CUP 1962-63

SECOND ROUND

Airdrieonians v Rangers	0-6
East Stirlingshire v Motherwell	1-0
Dundee v Montrose	8-0
Brechin City v Hibernian	0-2
Queen's Park v Alloa Athletic	5-1
Ayr United v Dundee United	1-2
Kilmarnock v Queen of the South	0-0, 0-1
Hamilton Academicals v Nairn County	1-1, 2-1
East Fife v Third Lanark	1-1, 0-2
Raith Rovers v Clyde	3-2
St Johnstone v Aberdeen	1-2
Cowdenbeath v Dunfermline Athletic	2-3
Berwick Rangers v St Mirren	1-3
Partick Thistle v Arbroath	1-1, 2-2, 3-2
Gala Fairydean v Duns	1-1, 2-1
Celtic v Heart of Midlothian	3-1

THIRD ROUND

Rangers v East Stirlingshire	7-2
Dundee v Hibernian	1-0
Queen's Park v Dundee United	1-1, 1-3
Queen of the South v Hamilton Academicals	3-0
Third Lanark v Raith Rovers	0-1
Aberdeen v Dunfermline Athletic	4-0
St Mirren v Partick Thistle	1-1, 1-0
Celtic v Gala Fairydean	6-0

FOURTH ROUND

Dundee v Rangers	1-1, 2-3
Dundee United v Queen of the South	1-1, 1-1, 4-0
Raith Rovers v Aberdeen	2-1
St Mirren v Celtic	0-1

SEMI-FINAL

Rangers v Dundee United	5-2
Raith Rovers v Celtic	2-5

FINAL

Rangers v Celtic	1-1, 3-0

FIRST DIVISION

	P	W	D	L	F	A	Pts
1 Liverpool	42	26	5	11	92	45	57
2 Man United	42	23	7	12	90	62	53
3 Everton	42	21	10	11	84	64	52
4 Tottenham	42	22	7	13	97	81	51
5 Chelsea	42	20	10	12	72	56	50
6 Sheff Wed	42	19	11	12	84	67	49
7 Blackburn	42	18	10	14	89	65	46
8 Arsenal	42	17	11	14	90	82	45
9 Burnley	42	17	10	15	71	64	44
10 WBA	42	16	11	15	70	61	43
11 Leicester	42	16	11	15	61	58	43
12 Sheff United	42	16	11	15	61	64	43
13 Nottm Forest	42	16	9	17	64	68	41
14 West Ham	42	14	12	16	69	74	40
15 Fulham	42	13	13	16	58	65	39
16 Wolves	42	12	15	15	70	80	39
17 Stoke	42	14	10	18	77	78	38
18 Blackpool	42	13	9	20	52	73	35
19 Aston Villa	42	11	12	19	62	71	34
20 Birmingham	42	11	7	24	54	92	29
21 Bolton	42	10	8	24	48	80	28
22 Ipswich	42	9	7	26	56	121	25

SECOND DIVISION

	P	W	D	L	F	A	Pts
1 Leeds	42	24	15	3	71	34	63
2 Sunderland	42	25	11	6	81	37	61
3 Preston	42	23	10	9	79	54	56
4 Charlton	42	19	10	13	76	70	48
5 Southampton	42	19	9	14	100	73	47
6 Man City	42	18	10	14	84	66	46
7 Rotherham	42	19	7	16	90	78	45
8 Newcastle	42	20	5	17	74	69	45
9 Portsmouth	42	16	11	15	79	70	43
10 Middlesbrough	42	15	11	16	67	52	41
11 Northampton	42	16	9	17	58	60	41
12 Huddersfield	42	15	10	17	57	64	40
13 Derby	42	14	11	17	56	67	39
14 Swindon	42	14	10	18	57	69	38
15 Cardiff	42	14	10	18	56	81	38
16 Leyton Orient	42	13	10	19	54	72	36
17 Norwich	42	11	13	18	64	80	35
18 Bury	42	13	9	20	57	73	35
19 Swansea	42	12	9	21	63	74	33
20 Plymouth	42	8	16	18	45	67	32
21 Grimsby	42	9	14	19	47	75	32
22 Scunthorpe	42	10	10	22	52	82	30

THIRD DIVISION

	P	W	D	L	F	A	Pts
1 Coventry	46	22	16	8	98	61	60
2 Crystal Palace	46	23	14	9	73	51	60
3 Watford	46	23	12	11	79	59	58
4 Bournemouth	46	24	8	14	79	58	56
5 Bristol City	46	20	15	11	84	64	55
6 Reading	46	21	10	15	79	62	52
7 Mansfield	46	20	11	15	76	62	51
8 Hull	46	16	17	13	73	68	49
9 Oldham	46	20	8	18	73	70	48
10 Peterborough	46	18	11	17	75	70	47
11 Shrewsbury	46	18	11	17	73	80	47
12 Bristol Rovers	46	19	8	19	91	79	46
13 Port Vale	46	16	14	16	53	49	46
14 Southend	46	15	15	16	77	78	45
15 QPR	46	18	9	19	76	78	45
16 Brentford	46	15	14	17	87	80	44
17 Colchester	46	12	19	15	70	68	43
18 Luton	46	16	10	20	64	80	42
19 Walsall	46	13	14	19	59	76	40
20 Barnsley	46	12	15	19	68	94	39
21 Millwall	46	14	10	22	53	67	38
22 Crewe	46	11	12	23	50	77	34
23 Wrexham	46	13	6	27	75	107	32
24 Notts County	46	9	9	28	45	92	27

FOURTH DIVISION

	P	W	D	L	F	A	Pts
1 Gillingham	46	23	14	9	59	30	60
2 Carlisle	46	25	10	11	113	58	60
3 Workington	46	24	11	11	76	52	59
4 Exeter	46	20	18	8	62	37	58
5 Bradford City	46	25	6	15	76	62	56
6 Torquay	46	20	11	15	80	54	51
7 Tranmere	46	20	11	15	85	73	51
8 Brighton	46	19	12	15	71	52	50
9 Aldershot	46	19	10	17	83	78	48
10 Halifax	46	17	14	15	77	77	48
11 Lincoln	46	19	9	18	67	75	47
12 Chester	46	19	8	19	65	60	46
13 Bradford PA	46	18	9	19	75	81	45
14 Doncaster	46	15	12	19	70	75	42
15 Newport	46	17	8	21	64	73	42
16 Chesterfield	46	15	12	19	57	71	42
17 Stockport	46	15	12	19	50	68	42
18 Oxford	46	14	13	19	59	63	41
19 Darlington	46	14	12	20	66	93	40
20 Rochdale	46	12	15	19	56	59	39
21 Southport	46	15	9	22	63	88	39
22 York	46	14	7	25	52	66	35
23 Hartlepools	46	12	9	25	54	93	33
24 Barrow	46	6	18	22	51	93	30

SCOTTISH FIRST DIVISION

	P	W	D	L	F	A	Pts
1 Rangers	34	25	5	4	85	31	55
2 Kilmarnock	34	22	5	7	77	40	49
3 Celtic	34	19	9	6	89	34	47
4 Hearts	34	19	9	6	74	40	47
5 Dunfermline	34	18	9	7	64	33	45
6 Dundee	34	20	5	9	94	50	45
7 Partick Thistle	34	15	5	14	55	54	35
8 Dundee United	34	13	8	13	65	49	34
9 Aberdeen	34	12	8	14	53	53	32
10 Hibernian	34	12	6	16	59	66	30
11 Motherwell	34	9	11	14	51	62	29
12 St Mirren	34	12	5	17	44	74	29
13 St Johnstone	34	11	6	17	54	70	28
14 Falkirk	34	11	6	17	54	84	28
15 Airdrieonians	34	11	4	19	52	97	26
16 Third Lanark	34	9	7	18	47	74	25
17 Queen of the S	34	5	6	23	40	92	16
18 E Stirlingshire	34	5	2	27	37	91	12

SCOTTISH SECOND DIVISION

	P	W	D	L	F	A	Pts
1 Morton	36	32	3	1	135	37	67
2 Clyde	36	22	9	5	81	44	53
3 Arbroath	36	20	6	10	79	46	46
4 East Fife	36	16	13	7	92	57	45
5 Montrose	36	19	6	11	79	57	44
6 Dumbarton	36	16	6	14	67	59	38
7 Queen's Park	36	17	4	15	57	54	38
8 Stranraer	36	16	6	14	71	73	38
9 Albion	36	12	12	12	67	71	36
10 Raith	36	15	5	16	70	61	35
11 Stenhousemuir	36	15	5	16	83	75	35
12 Berwick	36	10	10	16	68	84	30
13 Hamilton	36	12	6	18	65	81	30
14 Ayr	36	12	5	19	58	83	29
15 Brechin	36	10	8	18	61	98	28
16 Alloa	36	11	5	20	64	92	27
17 Cowdenbeath	36	7	11	18	46	72	25
18 Forfar	36	6	8	22	57	104	20
19 Stirling	36	6	8	22	47	99	20

On 12 October 1963, Tottenham Hotspur had seven players on international duty in the Home Championship, a record. Norman, Greaves and Smith were in the England side that met Wales. The Welsh team included Spurs' brilliant winger, Cliff Jones. Scotland paraded Brown, Mackay and White against Ireland.

Quick off the mark

The fastest goal in first-class football was scored by Jim Fryatt of Bradford Park Avenue on 25 April 1964. Just four seconds after the kick-off, Tranmere Rovers found themselves a goal down. Though a fantastic time, referee R. J. Simon's stop-watch confirmed it.

FA CUP 1963-64

FOURTH ROUND

West Ham United v Leyton Orient	1-1, 3-0
Aldershot v Swindon Town	1-2
Burnley v Newport County	2-1
Chelsea v Huddersfield Town	1-2
Sunderland v Bristol City	6-1
Leeds United v Everton	1-1, 0-2
Barnsley v Bury	2-1
Manchester United v Bristol Rovers	4-1
Ipswich Town v Stoke City	1-1, 0-1
Sheffield United v Swansea Town	1-1, 0-4
West Bromwich Albion v Arsenal	3-3, 0-2
Liverpool v Port Vale	0-0, 2-1
Oxford United v Brentford	2-2, 2-1
Blackburn Rovers v Fulham	2-0
Bedford Town v Carlisle United	0-3
Bolton Wanderers v Preston North End	2-2, 1-2

FIFTH ROUND

West Ham United v Swindon Town	3-1
Burnley v Huddersfield Town	3-0
Sunderland v Everton	3-1
Barnsley v Manchester United	0-4
Stoke City v Swansea Town	2-2, 0-2
Arsenal v Liverpool	0-1
Oxford United v Blackburn Rovers	3-1
Carlisle United v Preston North End	0-1

SIXTH ROUND

West Ham United v Burnley	3-2
Manchester United v Sunderland	3-3, 2-2, 5-1
Liverpool v Swansea Town	1-2
Oxford United v Preston North End	1-2

SEMI-FINAL

West Ham United v Manchester United	3-1
Swansea Town v Preston North End	1-2

FINAL

West Ham United v Preston North End	3-2

SCOTTISH FA CUP 1963-64

SECOND ROUND

Rangers v Duns	9-0
Partick Thistle v St Johnstone	2-0
Morton v Celtic	1-3
Alloa Athletic v Airdrieonians	1-3
East Fife v East Stirlingshire	0-1
Dunfermline Athletic v Fraserburgh	7-0
Aberdeen v Queen's Park	1-1, 2-1
Buckie Thistle v Ayr United	1-3
Hamilton Academicals v Kilmarnock	1-3
Albion Rovers v Arbroath	4-3
St Mirren v Stranraer	2-0
Falkirk v Berwick Rangers	2-2, 5-1
Motherwell v Dumbarton	4-1
Queen of the South v Heart of Midlothian	0-3
Clyde v Forfar Athletic	2-2, 2-3
Brechin City v Dundee	2-9

THIRD ROUND

Rangers v Partick Thistle	3-0
Celtic v Airdrieonians	4-1
East Stirlingshire v Dunfermline Athletic	1-6
Aberdeen v Ayr United	1-2
Kilmarnock v Albion Rovers	2-0
St Mirren v Falkirk	0-1
Motherwell v Heart of Midlothian	3-3, 2-1
Dundee v Forfar Athletic	6-1

FOURTH ROUND

Rangers v Celtic	2-0
Dunfermline Athletic v Ayr United	7-0
Kilmarnock v Falkirk	2-1
Dundee v Motherwell	1-1, 4-2

SEMI-FINAL

Rangers v Dunfermline Athletic	1-0
Kilmarnock v Dundee	0-4

FINAL

Rangers v Dundee	3-1

League Tables 1964-65

FIRST DIVISION

	P	W	D	L	F	A	Pts
1 Man United	42	26	9	7	89	39	61
2 Leeds	42	26	9	7	83	52	61
3 Chelsea	42	24	8	10	89	54	56
4 Everton	42	17	15	10	69	60	49
5 Nottm Forest	42	17	13	12	71	67	47
6 Tottenham	42	19	7	16	87	71	45
7 Liverpool	42	17	10	15	67	73	44
8 Sheff Wed	42	16	11	15	57	55	43
9 West Ham	42	19	4	19	82	71	42
10 Blackburn	42	16	10	16	83	79	42
11 Stoke	42	16	10	16	67	66	42
12 Burnley	42	16	10	16	70	70	42
13 Arsenal	42	17	7	18	69	75	41
14 WBA	42	13	13	16	70	65	39
15 Sunderland	42	14	9	19	64	74	37
16 Aston Villa	42	16	5	21	57	82	37
17 Blackpool	42	12	11	19	67	78	35
18 Leicester	42	11	13	18	69	85	35
19 Sheff United	42	12	11	19	50	64	35
20 Fulham	42	11	12	19	60	78	34
21 Wolves	42	13	4	25	59	89	30
22 Birmingham	42	8	11	23	64	96	27

SECOND DIVISION

	P	W	D	L	F	A	Pts
1 Newcastle	42	24	9	9	81	45	57
2 Northampton	42	20	16	6	66	50	56
3 Bolton	42	20	10	12	80	58	50
4 Southampton	42	17	14	11	83	63	48
5 Ipswich	42	15	17	10	74	67	47
6 Norwich	42	20	7	15	61	57	47
7 Crystal Palace	42	16	13	13	55	51	45
8 Huddersfield	42	17	10	15	53	51	44
9 Derby	42	16	11	15	84	79	43
10 Coventry	42	17	9	16	72	70	43
11 Man City	42	16	9	17	63	62	41
12 Preston	42	14	13	15	76	81	41
13 Cardiff	42	13	14	15	64	57	40
14 Rotherham	42	14	12	16	70	69	40
15 Plymouth	42	16	8	18	63	79	40
16 Bury	42	14	10	18	60	66	38
17 Middlesbrough	42	13	9	20	70	76	35
18 Charlton	42	13	9	20	64	75	35
19 Leyton Orient	42	12	11	19	50	72	35
20 Portsmouth	42	12	10	20	56	77	34
21 Swindon	42	14	5	23	63	81	33
22 Swansea	42	11	10	21	62	84	32

THIRD DIVISION

	P	W	D	L	F	A	Pts
1 Carlisle	46	25	10	11	76	53	60
2 Bristol City	46	24	11	11	92	55	59
3 Mansfield	46	24	11	11	95	61	59
4 Hull	46	23	12	11	91	57	58
5 Brentford	46	24	9	13	83	55	57
6 Bristol Rovers	46	20	15	11	82	58	55
7 Gillingham	46	23	9	14	70	50	55
8 Peterborough	46	22	7	17	85	74	51
9 Watford	46	17	16	13	71	64	50
10 Grimsby	46	16	17	13	68	67	49
11 Bournemouth	46	18	11	17	72	63	47
12 Southend	46	19	8	19	78	71	46
13 Reading	46	16	14	16	70	70	46
14 QPR	46	17	12	17	72	80	46
15 Workington	46	17	12	17	58	69	46
16 Shrewsbury	46	15	12	19	76	84	42
17 Exeter	46	12	17	17	51	52	41
18 Scunthorpe	46	14	12	20	65	72	40
19 Walsall	46	15	7	24	55	80	37
20 Oldham	46	13	10	23	61	83	36
21 Luton	46	11	11	24	51	94	33
22 Port Vale	46	9	14	23	41	76	32
23 Colchester	46	10	10	26	50	89	30
24 Barnsley	46	9	11	26	54	90	29

FOURTH DIVISION

	P	W	D	L	F	A	Pts
1 Brighton	46	26	11	9	102	57	63
2 Millwall	46	23	16	7	78	45	62
3 York	46	28	6	12	91	56	62
4 Oxford	46	23	15	8	87	44	61
5 Tranmere	46	27	6	13	99	56	60
6 Rochdale	46	22	14	10	74	53	58
7 Bradford PA	46	20	17	9	86	62	57
8 Chester	46	25	6	15	119	81	56
9 Doncaster	46	20	11	15	84	72	51
10 Crewe	46	18	13	15	90	81	49
11 Torquay	46	21	7	18	70	70	49
12 Chesterfield	46	20	8	18	58	70	48
13 Notts County	46	15	14	17	61	73	44
14 Wrexham	46	17	9	20	84	92	43
15 Hartlepools	46	15	13	18	61	85	43
16 Newport	46	17	8	21	85	81	42
17 Darlington	46	18	6	22	84	87	42
18 Aldershot	46	15	7	24	64	84	37
19 Bradford City	46	12	8	26	70	88	32
20 Southport	46	8	16	22	58	89	32
21 Barrow	46	12	6	28	59	105	30
22 Lincoln	46	11	6	29	58	99	28
23 Halifax	46	11	6	29	54	103	28
24 Stockport	46	10	7	29	44	87	27

SCOTTISH FIRST DIVISION

	P	W	D	L	F	A	Pts
1 Kilmarnock	34	22	6	6	62	33	50
2 Hearts	34	22	6	6	90	49	50
3 Dunfermline	34	22	5	7	83	36	49
4 Hibernian	34	21	4	9	75	47	46
5 Rangers	34	18	8	8	78	35	44
6 Dundee	34	15	10	9	86	63	40
7 Clyde	34	17	6	11	64	58	40
8 Celtic	34	16	5	13	76	57	37
9 Dundee United	34	15	6	13	59	51	36
10 Morton	34	13	7	14	54	54	33
11 Partick Thistle	34	11	10	13	57	58	32
12 Aberdeen	34	12	8	14	59	75	32
13 St Johnstone	34	9	11	14	57	62	29
14 Motherwell	34	10	8	16	45	54	28
15 St Mirren	34	9	6	19	38	70	24
16 Falkirk	34	7	7	20	43	85	21
17 Airdrieonians	34	5	4	25	48	110	14
18 Third Lanark	34	3	1	30	22	99	7

SCOTTISH SECOND DIVISION

	P	W	D	L	F	A	Pts
1 Stirling Albion	36	26	7	3	84	31	59
2 Hamilton	36	21	8	7	86	53	50
3 Queen of the S	36	16	13	7	84	50	45
4 Queen's Park	36	17	9	10	57	41	43
5 ES Clydebank	36	15	10	11	64	50	40
6 Stranraer	36	17	6	13	74	64	40
7 Arbroath	36	13	13	10	56	51	39
8 Berwick	36	15	9	12	73	70	39
9 East Fife	36	15	7	14	78	77	37
10 Alloa	36	14	8	14	71	81	36
11 Albion	36	14	5	17	56	60	33
12 Cowdenbeath	36	11	10	15	55	62	32
13 Raith	36	9	14	13	54	61	32
14 Dumbarton	36	13	6	17	55	67	32
15 Stenhousemuir	36	11	8	17	49	74	30
16 Montrose	36	10	9	17	80	91	29
17 Forfar	36	9	7	20	63	89	25
18 Ayr	36	9	6	21	49	67	24
19 Brechin	36	6	7	23	53	102	19

Gillingham set a record for an undefeated run of home matches including Cup and League Cup games. From 9 April 1963, Gillingham had gone 52 games—48 of them in the League—at their Priestfield Stadium without a defeat, before losing 1-0 to Exeter on 10 April 1965.

Stan Lynn, Birmingham City's full-back, scored 10 goals (8 from penalties) and ended the 1964-65 season as his club's top League goal-scorer. Only one other full-back—Jimmy Evans of Southend United in 1921-2—has achieved this distinction among Football League clubs.

FA CUP 1964-65

FOURTH ROUND

Liverpool v Stockport County 1-1, 2-0
Preston North End v Bolton Wanderers 1-2
Leicester City v Plymouth Argyle 5-0
Charlton Athletic v Middlesbrough 1-1, 1-2
West Ham United v Chelsea 0-1
Tottenham Hotspur v Ipswich Town 5-0
Peterborough United v Arsenal 2-1
Swansea Town v Huddersfield Town 1-0
Wolverhampton Wanderers v Rotherham United 2-2, 3-0
Sheffield United v Aston Villa 0-2
Stoke City v Manchester United 0-0, 0-1
Reading v Burnley 1-1, 0-1
Southampton v Crystal Palace 1-2
Sunderland v Nottingham Forest 1-3
Millwall v Shrewsbury Town 1-2
Leeds United v Everton 1-1, 2-1

FIFTH ROUND

Bolton Wanderers v Liverpool 0-1
Middlesbrough v Leicester City 0-3
Chelsea v Tottenham Hotspur 1-0
Peterborough United v Swansea Town 0-0, 2-0
Aston Villa v Wolverhampton Wanderers 1-1, 0-0, 1-3
Manchester United v Burnley 2-1
Crystal Palace v Nottingham Forest 3-1
Leeds United v Shrewsbury Town 2-0

SIXTH ROUND

Leicester City v Liverpool 0-0, 0-1
Chelsea v Peterborough United 5-1
Wolverhampton Wanderers v Manchester United 3-5
Crystal Palace v Leeds United 0-3

SEMI-FINAL

Liverpool v Chelsea 2-0
Manchester United v Leeds United 0-0, 0-1

FINAL

Leeds United v Liverpool 1-2

SCOTTISH FA CUP 1964-65

FIRST ROUND

St Mirren v Celtic 0-3
Dumbarton v Queen's Park 0-0, 1-2
Aberdeen v East Fife 0-0, 0-1
Kilmarnock v Cowdenbeath 5-0
Motherwell v Stenhousemuir 3-2
St Johnstone v Dundee 1-0
Clyde v Morton 0-4
Falkirk v Heart of Midlothian 0-3
Hibernian v E S Clydebank 1-1, 2-0
Ayr United v Partick Thistle 1-1, 1-7
Forfar Athletic v Dundee United 0-3
Rangers v Hamilton Academicals 3-0
Stirling Albion v Arbroath 2-1
Airdrieonians v Montrose 7-3
Inverness Caledonian v Third Lanark 1-5
Queen of the South v Dunfermline Athletic 0-2

SECOND ROUND

Queen's Park v Celtic 0-1
East Fife v Kilmarnock 0-0, 0-3
Motherwell v St Johnstone 1-0
Morton v Heart of Midlothian 3-3, 0-2
Hibernian v Partick Thistle 5-1
Dundee United v Rangers 0-2
Stirling Albion v Airdrieonians 1-1, 2-0
Third Lanark v Dunfermline Athletic 1-1, 2-2, 2-4

THIRD ROUND

Celtic v Kilmarnock 3-2
Motherwell v Heart of Midlothian 1-0
Hibernian v Rangers 2-1
Dunfermline Athletic v Stirling Albion 2-0

SEMI-FINAL

Celtic v Motherwell 2-2, 3-0
Hibernian v Dunfermline Athletic 0-2

FINAL

Celtic v Dunfermline Athletic 3-2

League Tables 1965-66

FIRST DIVISION

	P	W	D	L	F	A	Pts
1 Liverpool	42	26	9	7	79	34	61
2 Leeds	42	23	9	10	79	38	55
3 Burnley	42	24	7	11	79	47	55
4 Man United	42	18	15	9	84	59	51
5 Chelsea	42	22	7	13	65	53	51
6 WBA	42	19	12	11	91	69	50
7 Leicester	42	21	7	14	80	65	49
8 Tottenham	42	16	12	14	75	66	44
9 Sheff United	42	16	11	15	56	59	43
10 Stoke	42	15	12	15	65	64	42
11 Everton	42	15	11	16	56	62	41
12 West Ham	42	15	9	18	70	83	39
13 Blackpool	42	14	9	19	55	65	37
14 Arsenal	42	12	13	17	62	75	37
15 Newcastle	42	14	9	19	50	63	37
16 Aston Villa	42	15	6	21	69	80	36
17 Sheff Wed	42	14	8	20	56	66	36
18 Nottm Forest	42	14	8	20	56	72	36
19 Sunderland	42	14	8	20	51	72	36
20 Fulham	42	14	7	21	67	85	35
21 Northampton	42	10	13	19	55	92	33
22 Blackburn	42	8	4	30	57	88	20

SECOND DIVISION

	P	W	D	L	F	A	Pts
1 Man City	42	22	15	5	76	44	59
2 Southampton	42	22	10	10	85	56	54
3 Coventry	42	20	13	9	73	53	53
4 Huddersfield	42	19	13	10	62	36	51
5 Bristol City	42	17	17	8	63	48	51
6 Wolves	42	20	10	12	87	61	50
7 Rotherham	42	16	14	12	75	74	46
8 Derby	42	16	11	15	71	68	43
9 Bolton	42	16	9	17	62	59	41
10 Birmingham	42	16	9	17	70	75	41
11 Crystal Palace	42	14	13	15	47	52	41
12 Portsmouth	42	16	8	18	74	78	40
13 Norwich	42	12	15	15	52	52	39
14 Carlisle	42	17	5	20	60	63	39
15 Ipswich	42	15	9	18	58	66	39
16 Charlton	42	12	14	16	61	70	38
17 Preston	42	11	15	16	62	70	37
18 Plymouth	42	12	13	17	54	63	37
19 Bury	42	14	7	21	62	76	35
20 Cardiff	42	12	10	20	71	91	34
21 Middlesbrough	42	10	13	19	58	86	33
22 Leyton Orient	42	5	13	24	38	80	23

THIRD DIVISION

	P	W	D	L	F	A	Pts
1 Hull	46	31	7	8	109	62	69
2 Millwall	46	27	11	8	76	43	65
3 QPR	46	24	9	13	95	65	57
4 Scunthorpe	46	21	11	14	80	67	53
5 Workington	46	19	14	13	67	57	52
6 Gillingham	46	22	8	16	62	54	52
7 Swindon	46	19	13	14	74	48	51
8 Reading	46	19	13	14	70	63	51
9 Walsall	46	20	10	16	77	64	50
10 Shrewsbury	46	19	11	16	73	64	49
11 Grimsby	46	17	13	16	68	62	47
12 Watford	46	17	13	16	55	51	47
13 Peterborough	46	17	12	17	80	66	46
14 Oxford	46	19	8	19	70	74	46
15 Brighton	46	16	11	19	67	65	43
16 Bristol Rovers	46	14	14	18	64	64	42
17 Swansea	46	15	11	20	81	96	41
18 Bournemouth	46	13	12	21	38	56	38
19 Mansfield	46	15	8	23	59	89	38
20 Oldham	46	12	13	21	55	81	37
21 Southend	46	16	4	26	54	83	36
22 Exeter	46	12	11	23	53	79	35
23 Brentford	46	10	12	24	48	69	32
24 York	46	9	9	28	53	106	27

FOURTH DIVISION

	P	W	D	L	F	A	Pts
1 Doncaster	46	24	11	11	85	54	59
2 Darlington	46	25	9	12	72	53	59
3 Torquay	46	24	10	12	72	49	58
4 Colchester	46	23	10	13	70	47	56
5 Tranmere	46	24	8	14	93	66	56
6 Luton	46	24	8	14	90	70	56
7 Chester	46	20	12	14	79	70	52
8 Notts County	46	19	12	15	61	53	50
9 Newport	46	18	12	16	75	75	48
10 Southport	46	18	12	16	68	69	48
11 Bradford PA	46	21	5	20	102	92	47
12 Barrow	46	16	15	15	72	76	47
13 Stockport	46	18	6	22	71	70	42
14 Crewe	46	16	9	21	61	63	41
15 Halifax	46	15	11	20	67	75	41
16 Barnsley	46	15	10	21	74	78	40
17 Aldershot	46	15	10	21	75	84	40
18 Hartlepools	46	16	8	22	63	75	40
19 Port Vale	46	15	9	22	48	59	39
20 Chesterfield	46	13	13	20	62	78	39
21 Rochdale	46	16	5	25	71	87	37
22 Lincoln	46	13	11	22	57	82	37
23 Bradford City	46	12	13	21	63	94	37
24 Wrexham	46	13	9	24	72	104	35

SCOTTISH FIRST DIVISION

	P	W	D	L	F	A	Pts
1 Celtic	34	27	3	4	106	30	57
2 Rangers	34	25	5	4	91	29	55
3 Kilmarnock	34	20	5	9	73	46	45
4 Dunfermline	34	19	6	9	94	55	44
5 Dundee United	34	19	5	10	79	51	43
6 Hibernian	34	16	6	12	81	55	38
7 Hearts	34	13	12	9	56	48	38
8 Aberdeen	34	15	6	13	61	54	36
9 Dundee	34	14	6	14	61	61	34
10 Falkirk	34	15	1	18	48	72	31
11 Clyde	34	13	4	17	62	64	30
12 Partick Thistle	34	10	10	14	55	64	30
13 Motherwell	34	12	4	18	52	69	28
14 St Johnstone	34	9	8	17	58	81	26
15 Stirling Albion	34	9	8	17	40	68	26
16 St Mirren	34	9	4	21	44	82	22
17 Morton	34	8	5	21	42	84	21
18 Hamilton	34	3	2	29	27	117	8

SCOTTISH SECOND DIVISION

	P	W	D	L	F	A	Pts
1 Ayr	36	22	9	5	78	37	53
2 Airdrieonians	36	22	6	8	107	56	50
3 Queen of the S	36	18	11	7	83	53	47
4 East Fife	36	20	4	12	72	55	44
5 Raith	36	16	11	9	71	43	43
6 Arbroath	36	15	13	8	72	52	43
7 Albion	36	18	7	11	58	54	43
8 Alloa	36	14	10	12	65	65	38
9 Montrose	36	15	7	14	67	63	37
10 Cowdenbeath	36	15	7	14	69	68	37
11 Berwick	36	12	11	13	69	58	35
12 Dumbarton	36	14	7	15	63	61	35
13 Queen's Park	36	13	7	16	62	65	33
14 Third Lanark	36	12	8	16	55	65	32
15 Stranraer	36	9	10	17	64	83	28
16 Brechin	36	10	7	19	52	92	27
17 E Stirlingshire	36	9	5	22	59	91	23
18 Stenhousemuir	36	6	7	23	47	93	19
19 Forfar	36	7	3	26	61	120	17

On 1 January 1966, while they were beating Aldershot 3-2 in a Division Four game, Chester lost both their full-backs, Ray Jones and Bryn Jones, with broken legs.

The World Cup final receipts—£204,805—were a world record for a football match.

At the start of the season, Manchester United had 15 internationals on their staff. They were: Pat Dunne, Harry Gregg, Shay Brennan, Noel Cantwell, Pat Crerand, Bill Foulkes, Denis Law, Nobby Stiles, Tony Dunne, George Best, David Herd, John Connelly, Bobby Charlton, Graham Moore, and David Sadler, then an amateur cap.

FA CUP 1965-66

FOURTH ROUND

Bedford Town v Everton 0-3
Crewe Alexandra v Coventry City 1-1, 1-4
Manchester City v Grimsby Town 2-0
Birmingham City v Leicester City 1-2
Manchester United v Rotherham United 0-0, 1-0
Wolverhampton Wanderers v Sheffield United 3-0
Bolton Wanderers v Preston North End 1-1, 2-3
Tottenham Hotspur v Burnley 4-3
Chelsea v Leeds United 1-0
Shrewsbury Town v Carlisle United 0-0, 1-1, 4-3
Hull City v Nottingham Forest 2-0
Southport v Cardiff City 2-0
Norwich City v Walsall 3-2
West Ham United v Blackburn Rovers 3-3, 1-4
Plymouth Argyle v Huddersfield Town 0-2
Newcastle United v Sheffield Wednesday 1-2

FIFTH ROUND

Everton v Coventry City 3-0
Manchester City v Leicester City 2-2, 1-0
Wolverhampton Wanderers v Manchester United 2-4
Preston North End v Tottenham Hotspur 2-1
Chelsea v Shrewsbury Town 3-2
Hull City v Southport 2-0
Norwich City v Blackburn Rovers 2-2, 2-3
Huddersfield Town v Sheffield Wednesday 1-2

SIXTH ROUND

Manchester City v Everton 0-0, 0-0, 0-2
Preston North End v Manchester United 1-1, 1-3
Chelsea v Hull City 2-2, 3-1
Blackburn Rovers v Sheffield Wednesday 1-2

SEMI-FINAL

Everton v Manchester United 1-0
Chelsea v Sheffield Wednesday 0-2

FINAL

Everton v Sheffield Wednesday 3-2

SCOTTISH FA CUP 1965-66

FIRST ROUND

Celtic v Stranraer 4-0
Dundee v East Fife 9-1
Heart of Midlothian v Clyde 2-1
Hibernian v Third Lanark 4-3
Stirling Albion v Queen's Park 3-1
Dunfermline Athletic v Partick Thistle 3-1
Morton v Kilmarnock 1-1, 0-3
East Stirlingshire v Motherwell 0-0, 1-4
Dumbarton v Montrose 2-1
Queen of the South v Albion Rovers 3-0
Hamilton Academicals v Aberdeen 1-3
Dundee United v Falkirk 0-0, 2-1
Cowdenbeath v St Mirren 1-0
Ayr United v St Johnstone 1-1, 0-1
Alloa Athletic v Ross County 3-5
Rangers v Airdrieonians 5-1

SECOND ROUND

Dundee v Celtic 0-2
Heart of Midlothian v Hibernian 2-1
Stirling Albion v Dunfermline Athletic 0-0, 1-4
Kilmarnock v Motherwell 5-0
Dumbarton v Queen of the South 1-0
Aberdeen v Dundee United 5-0
Cowdenbeath v St Johnstone 3-3, 0-3
Ross County v Rangers 0-2

THIRD ROUND

Celtic v Heart of Midlothian 3-3, 3-1
Dunfermline Athletic v Kilmarnock 2-1
Dumbarton v Aberdeen 0-3
Rangers v St Johnstone 2-0

SEMI-FINAL

Celtic v Dunfermline Athletic 2-0
Aberdeen v Rangers 0-0, 1-2

FINAL

Celtic v Rangers 0-0, 0-1

FIRST DIVISION

	P	W	D	L	F	A	Pts
1 Man United	42	24	12	6	84	45	60
2 Nottm Forest	42	23	10	9	64	41	56
3 Tottenham	42	24	8	10	71	48	56
4 Leeds	42	22	11	9	62	42	55
5 Liverpool	42	19	13	10	64	47	51
6 Everton	42	19	10	13	65	46	48
7 Arsenal	42	16	14	12	58	47	46
8 Leicester	42	18	8	16	78	71	44
9 Chelsea	42	15	14	13	67	62	44
10 Sheff United	42	16	10	16	52	59	42
11 Sheff Wed	42	14	13	15	56	47	41
12 Stoke	42	17	7	18	63	58	41
13 WBA	42	16	7	19	77	73	39
14 Burnley	42	15	9	18	66	76	39
15 Man City	42	12	15	15	43	52	39
16 West Ham	42	14	8	20	80	84	36
17 Sunderland	42	14	8	20	58	72	36
18 Fulham	42	11	12	19	71	83	34
19 Southampton	42	14	6	22	74	92	34
20 Newcastle	42	12	9	21	39	81	33
21 Aston Villa	42	11	7	24	54	85	29
22 Blackpool	42	6	9	27	41	76	21

SECOND DIVISION

	P	W	D	L	F	A	Pts
1 Coventry	42	23	13	6	74	43	59
2 Wolves	42	25	8	9	88	48	58
3 Carlisle	42	23	6	13	71	54	52
4 Blackburn	42	19	13	10	56	46	51
5 Ipswich	42	17	16	9	70	54	50
6 Huddersfield	42	20	9	13	58	46	49
7 Crystal Palace	42	19	10	13	61	55	48
8 Millwall	42	18	9	15	49	58	45
9 Bolton	42	14	14	14	64	58	42
10 Birmingham	42	16	8	18	70	66	40
11 Norwich	42	13	14	15	49	55	40
12 Hull	42	16	7	19	77	72	39
13 Preston	42	16	7	19	65	67	39
14 Portsmouth	42	13	13	16	59	70	39
15 Bristol City	42	12	14	16	56	62	38
16 Plymouth	42	14	9	19	59	58	37
17 Derby	42	12	12	18	68	72	36
18 Rotherham	42	13	10	19	61	70	36
19 Charlton	42	13	9	20	49	53	35
20 Cardiff	42	12	9	21	61	87	33
21 Northampton	42	12	6	24	47	84	30
22 Bury	42	11	6	25	49	83	28

THIRD DIVISION

	P	W	D	L	F	A	Pts
1 QPR	46	26	15	5	103	38	67
2 Middlesbrough	46	23	9	14	87	64	55
3 Watford	46	20	14	12	61	46	54
4 Reading	46	22	9	15	76	57	53
5 Bristol Rovers	46	20	13	13	76	67	53
6 Shrewsbury	46	20	12	14	77	62	52
7 Torquay	46	21	9	16	73	54	51
8 Swindon	46	20	10	16	81	59	50
9 Mansfield	46	20	9	17	84	79	49
10 Oldham	46	19	10	17	80	63	48
11 Gillingham	46	15	16	15	58	62	46
12 Walsall	46	18	10	18	65	72	46
13 Colchester	46	17	10	19	76	73	44
14 Leyton Orient	46	13	18	15	58	68	44
15 Peterborough	46	14	15	17	66	71	43
16 Oxford	46	15	13	18	61	66	43
17 Grimsby	46	17	9	20	61	68	43
18 Scunthorpe	46	17	8	21	58	73	42
19 Brighton	46	13	15	18	61	71	41
20 Bournemouth	46	12	17	17	39	57	41
21 Swansea	46	12	15	19	85	89	39
22 Darlington	46	13	11	22	47	81	37
23 Doncaster	46	12	8	26	58	117	32
24 Workington	46	12	7	27	55	89	31

FOURTH DIVISION

	P	W	D	L	F	A	Pts
1 Stockport	46	26	12	8	69	42	64
2 Southport	46	23	13	10	69	42	59
3 Barrow	46	24	11	11	76	54	59
4 Tranmere	46	22	14	10	66	43	58
5 Crewe	46	21	12	13	70	55	54
6 Southend	46	22	9	15	70	49	53
7 Wrexham	46	16	20	10	76	62	52
8 Hartlepools	46	22	7	17	66	64	51
9 Brentford	46	18	13	15	58	56	49
10 Aldershot	46	18	12	16	72	57	48
11 Bradford City	46	19	10	17	74	62	48
12 Halifax	46	15	14	17	59	68	44
13 Port Vale	46	14	15	17	55	58	43
14 Exeter	46	14	15	17	50	60	43
15 Chesterfield	46	17	8	21	60	63	42
16 Barnsley	46	13	15	18	60	64	41
17 Luton	46	16	9	21	59	73	41
18 Newport	46	12	16	18	56	63	40
19 Chester	46	15	10	21	54	78	40
20 Notts County	46	13	11	22	53	72	37
21 Rochdale	46	13	11	22	53	75	37
22 York	46	12	11	23	65	79	35
23 Bradford PA	46	11	13	22	52	79	35
24 Lincoln	46	9	13	24	58	82	31

SCOTTISH FIRST DIVISION

	P	W	D	L	F	A	Pts
1 Celtic	34	26	6	2	111	33	58
2 Rangers	34	24	7	3	92	31	55
3 Clyde	34	20	6	8	64	48	46
4 Aberdeen	34	17	8	9	72	38	42
5 Hibernian	34	19	4	11	72	49	42
6 Dundee	34	16	9	9	74	51	41
7 Kilmarnock	34	16	8	10	59	46	40
8 Dunfermline	34	14	10	10	72	52	38
9 Dundee United	34	14	9	11	68	62	37
10 Motherwell	34	10	11	13	59	60	31
11 Hearts	34	11	8	15	39	48	30
12 Partick Thistle	34	9	12	13	49	68	30
13 Airdrieonians	34	11	6	17	41	53	28
14 Falkirk	34	11	4	19	33	70	26
15 St Johnstone	34	10	5	19	53	73	25
16 Stirling	34	5	9	20	31	85	19
17 St Mirren	34	4	7	23	25	81	15
18 Ayr	34	1	7	26	20	86	9

SCOTTISH SECOND DIVISION

	P	W	D	L	F	A	Pts
1 Morton	38	33	3	2	113	20	69
2 Raith	38	27	4	7	95	44	58
3 Arbroath	38	25	7	6	75	32	57
4 Hamilton	38	18	8	12	74	60	44
5 East Fife	38	19	4	15	70	63	42
6 Cowdenbeath	38	16	8	14	70	55	40
7 Queen's Park	38	15	10	13	78	68	40
8 Albion	38	17	6	15	66	62	40
9 Queen of the S	38	15	9	14	84	76	39
10 Berwick	38	16	6	16	63	55	38
11 Third Lanark	38	13	8	17	67	78	34
12 Montrose	38	13	8	17	63	77	34
13 Alloa	38	15	4	19	55	74	34
14 Dumbarton	38	12	9	17	56	64	33
15 Stranraer	38	13	7	18	57	73	33
16 Forfar	38	12	3	23	74	106	27
17 Stenhousemuir	38	9	9	20	62	104	27
18 Clydebank	38	8	8	22	59	92	24
19 E Stirlingshire	38	7	10	21	44	87	24
20 Brechin	38	8	7	23	58	93	23

A great year for Celtic
Celtic won the Scottish League, Cup and League Cup, the Glasgow Cup, and became the first British club to win the European Cup, thus completing a remarkable grand slam.

More directors than players
When Workington increased their board of directors by the addition of a 13th member in October 1966, they found themselves with more directors than full-time players.

FA CUP 1966-67

FOURTH ROUND

Brighton & Hove Albion v Chelsea	1-1, 0-4
Fulham v Sheffield United	1-1, 1-3
Manchester United v Norwich City	1-2
Sheffield Wednesday v Mansfield Town	4-0
Sunderland v Peterborough United	7-1
Leeds United v West Bromwich Albion	5-0
Cardiff City v Manchester City	1-1, 1-3
Ipswich Town v Carlisle United	2-0
Rotherham United v Birmingham City	0-0, 1-2
Bolton Wanderers v Arsenal	0-0, 0-3
Tottenham Hotspur v Portsmouth	3-1
Bristol City v Southampton	1-0
Nottingham Forest v Newcastle United	3-0
Swindon Town v Bury	2-1
Wolverhampton Wanderers v Everton	1-1, 1-3
Liverpool v Aston Villa	1-0

FIFTH ROUND

Chelsea v Sheffield United	2-0
Norwich City v Sheffield Wednesday	1-3
Sunderland v Leeds United	1-1, 1-1, 1-2
Manchester City v Ipswich Town	1-1, 3-0
Birmingham City v Arsenal	1-0
Tottenham Hotspur v Bristol City	2-0
Nottingham Forest v Swindon Town	0-0, 1-1, 3-0
Everton v Liverpool	1-0

SIXTH ROUND

Chelsea v Sheffield Wednesday	1-0
Leeds United v Manchester City	1-0
Birmingham City v Tottenham Hotspur	0-0, 0-6
Nottingham Forest v Everton	3-2

SEMI-FINAL

Chelsea v Leeds United	1-0
Tottenham Hotspur v Nottingham Forest	2-1

FINAL

Chelsea v Tottenham Hotspur	1-2

SCOTTISH FA CUP 1966-67

FIRST ROUND

Celtic v Arbroath	4-0
Elgin City v Ayr United	2-0
Queen's Park v Raith Rovers	3-2
Stirling Albion v Airdrieonians	1-2
Morton v Clyde	0-1
Motherwell v East Fife	0-1
St Mirren v Cowdenbeath	1-1, 2-0
Inverness Caledonian v Hamilton Academicals	1-3
Heart of Midlothian v Dundee United	0-3
Falkirk v Alloa Athletic	3-1
Partick Thistle v Dumbarton	3-0
Kilmarnock v Dunfermline Athletic	2-2, 0-1
Hibernian v Brechin City	2-0
Berwick Rangers v Rangers	1-0
St Johnstone v Queen of the South	4-0
Aberdeen v Dundee	5-0

SECOND ROUND

Celtic v Elgin City	7-0
Queen's Park v Airdrieonians	1-1, 2-1
Clyde v East Fife	4-1
St Mirren v Hamilton Academicals	0-1
Dundee United v Falkirk	1-0
Partick Thistle v Dunfermline Athletic	1-1, 1-5
Hibernian v Berwick Rangers	1-0
St Johnstone v Aberdeen	0-5

THIRD ROUND

Celtic v Queen's Park	5-3
Clyde v Hamilton Academicals	0-0, 5-1
Dundee United v Dunfermline Athletic	1-0
Hibernian v Aberdeen	1-1, 0-3

SEMI-FINAL

Celtic v Clyde	0-0, 2-0
Dundee United v Aberdeen	0-1

FINAL

Celtic v Aberdeen	2-0

League Tables 1967-68

FIRST DIVISION

		P	W	D	L	F	A	Pts
1	Man City	42	26	6	10	86	43	58
2	Man United	42	24	8	10	89	55	56
3	Liverpool	42	22	11	9	71	40	55
4	Leeds	42	22	9	11	71	41	53
5	Everton	42	23	6	13	67	40	52
6	Chelsea	42	18	12	12	62	68	48
7	Tottenham	42	19	9	14	70	59	47
8	WBA	42	17	12	13	75	62	46
9	Arsenal	42	17	10	15	60	56	44
10	Newcastle	42	13	15	14	54	67	41
11	Nottm Forest	42	14	11	17	52	64	39
12	West Ham	42	14	10	18	73	69	38
13	Leicester	42	13	12	17	64	69	38
14	Burnley	42	14	10	18	64	71	38
15	Sunderland	42	13	11	18	51	61	37
16	Southampton	42	13	11	18	66	83	37
17	Wolves	42	14	8	20	66	75	36
18	Stoke	42	14	7	21	50	73	35
19	Sheff Wed	42	11	12	19	51	63	34
20	Coventry	42	9	15	18	51	71	33
21	Sheff United	42	11	10	21	49	70	32
22	Fulham	42	10	7	25	56	98	27

SECOND DIVISION

		P	W	D	L	F	A	Pts
1	Ipswich	42	22	15	5	79	44	59
2	QPR	42	25	8	9	67	36	58
3	Blackpool	42	24	10	8	71	43	58
4	Birmingham	42	19	14	9	83	51	52
5	Portsmouth	42	18	13	11	68	55	49
6	Middlesbrough	42	17	12	13	60	54	46
7	Millwall	42	14	17	11	62	50	45
8	Blackburn	42	16	11	15	56	49	43
9	Norwich	42	16	11	15	60	65	43
10	Carlisle	42	14	13	15	58	52	41
11	Crystal Palace	42	14	11	17	56	56	39
12	Bolton	42	13	13	16	60	63	39
13	Cardiff	42	13	12	17	60	66	38
14	Huddersfield	42	13	12	17	46	61	38
15	Charlton	42	12	13	17	63	68	37
16	Aston Villa	42	15	7	20	54	64	37
17	Hull	42	12	13	17	58	73	37
18	Derby	42	13	10	19	71	78	36
19	Bristol City	42	13	10	19	48	62	36
20	Preston	42	12	11	19	43	65	35
21	Rotherham	42	10	11	21	42	76	31
22	Plymouth	42	9	9	24	38	72	27

THIRD DIVISION

		P	W	D	L	F	A	Pts
1	Oxford	46	22	13	11	69	47	57
2	Bury	46	24	8	14	91	66	56
3	Shrewsbury	46	20	15	11	61	49	55
4	Torquay	46	21	11	14	60	56	53
5	Reading	46	21	9	16	70	60	51
6	Watford	46	21	8	17	74	50	50
7	Walsall	46	19	12	15	74	61	50
8	Barrow	46	21	8	17	65	54	50
9	Swindon	46	16	17	13	74	51	49
10	Brighton	46	16	16	14	57	55	48
11	Gillingham	46	18	12	16	59	63	48
12	Bournemouth	46	16	15	15	56	51	47
13	Stockport	46	19	9	18	70	75	47
14	Southport	46	17	12	17	65	65	46
15	Bristol Rovers	46	17	9	20	72	78	43
16	Oldham	46	18	7	21	60	65	43
17	Northampton	46	14	13	19	58	72	41
18	Leyton Orient	46	12	17	17	46	62	41
19	Tranmere	46	14	12	20	62	74	40
20	Mansfield	46	12	13	21	51	67	37
21	Grimsby	46	14	9	23	52	69	37
22	Colchester	46	9	15	22	50	87	33
23	Scunthorpe	46	10	12	24	56	87	32
24	Peterborough	46	20	10	16	79	67	31†

†Peterborough had 19 points deducted for offering irregular bonuses to their players. They were automatically demoted to the Fourth Division.

FOURTH DIVISION

		P	W	D	L	F	A	Pts
1	Luton	46	27	12	7	87	44	66
2	Barnsley	46	24	13	9	68	46	61
3	Hartlepools	46	25	10	11	60	46	60
4	Crewe	46	20	18	8	74	49	58
5	Bradford City	46	23	11	12	72	51	57
6	Southend	46	20	14	12	77	58	54
7	Chesterfield	46	21	11	14	71	50	53
8	Wrexham	46	20	13	13	72	53	53
9	Aldershot	46	18	17	11	70	55	53
10	Doncaster	46	18	15	13	66	56	51
11	Halifax	46	15	16	15	52	49	46
12	Newport	46	16	13	17	58	63	45
13	Lincoln	46	17	9	20	71	68	43
14	Brentford	46	18	7	21	61	64	43
15	Swansea	46	16	10	20	63	77	42
16	Darlington	46	12	17	17	47	53	41
17	Notts County	46	15	11	20	53	79	41
18	Port Vale	46	12	15	19	61	72	39†
19	Rochdale	46	12	14	20	51	72	38
20	Exeter	46	11	16	19	45	65	38
21	York	46	11	14	21	65	68	36
22	Chester	46	9	14	23	57	78	32
23	Workington	46	10	11	25	54	87	31
24	Bradford PA	46	4	15	27	30	82	23

†Port Vale were expelled from the League at the end of the season for making unauthorised payments. They were re-elected immediately.

SCOTTISH FIRST DIVISION

		P	W	D	L	F	A	Pts
1	Celtic	34	30	3	1	106	24	63
2	Rangers	34	28	5	1	93	34	61
3	Hibernian	34	20	5	9	67	49	45
4	Dunfermline	34	17	5	12	64	41	39
5	Aberdeen	34	16	5	13	63	48	37
6	Morton	34	15	6	13	57	53	36
7	Kilmarnock	34	13	8	13	59	57	34
8	Clyde	34	15	4	15	55	55	34
9	Dundee	34	13	7	14	62	59	33
10	Partick Thistle	34	12	7	15	51	67	31
11	Dundee United	34	10	11	13	53	72	31
12	Hearts	34	13	4	17	56	61	30
13	Airdrieonians	34	10	9	15	45	58	29
14	St Johnstone	34	10	7	17	43	52	27
15	Falkirk	34	7	12	15	36	50	26
16	Raith Rovers	34	9	7	18	58	86	25
17	Motherwell	34	6	7	21	40	66	19
18	Stirling Albion	34	4	4	26	29	105	12

SCOTTISH SECOND DIVISION

		P	W	D	L	F	A	Pts
1	St Mirren	36	27	8	1	100	23	62
2	Arbroath	36	24	5	7	87	34	53
3	East Fife	36	21	7	8	71	47	49
4	Queen's Park	36	20	8	8	76	47	48
5	Ayr	36	18	6	12	69	48	42
6	Queen of the S	36	16	6	14	73	57	38
7	Forfar	36	14	10	12	57	63	38
8	Albion	36	14	9	13	62	55	37
9	Clydebank	36	13	8	15	62	73	34
10	Dumbarton	36	11	11	14	63	74	33
11	Hamilton	36	13	7	16	49	58	33
12	Cowdenbeath	36	12	8	16	57	62	32
13	Montrose	36	10	11	15	54	64	31
14	Berwick	36	13	4	19	34	54	30
15	E Stirlingshire	36	9	10	17	61	74	28
16	Brechin	36	8	12	16	45	62	28
17	Alloa	36	11	6	19	42	69	28
18	Stenhousemuir	36	7	6	23	34	93	20
19	Stranraer	36	8	4	24	41	80	20

FA CUP 1967–68

FOURTH ROUND

Carlisle United v Everton	0-2
Coventry City v Tranmere Rovers	1-1, 0-2
Aston Villa v Rotherham United	0-1
Manchester City v Leicester City	0-0, 3-4
Leeds United v Nottingham Forest	2-1
Middlesbrough v Bristol City	1-1, 1-2
Stoke City v West Ham United	0-3
Sheffield United v Blackpool	2-1
Swansea Town v Arsenal	0-1
Birmingham City v Leyton Orient	3-0
Sheffield Wednesday v Swindon Town	2-1
Chelsea v Norwich City	1-0
Fulham v Portsmouth	0-0, 0-1
West Bromwich Albion v Southampton	1-1, 3-2
Tottenham Hotspur v Preston North End	3-1
Walsall v Liverpool	0-0, 2-5

FIFTH ROUND

Everton v Tranmere Rovers	2-0
Rotherham United v Leicester City	1-1, 0-2
Leeds United v Bristol City	2-0
West Ham United v Sheffield United	1-2
Arsenal v Birmingham City	1-1, 1-2
Sheffield Wednesday v Chelsea	2-2, 0-2
Portsmouth v West Bromwich Albion	1-2
Tottenham Hotspur v Liverpool	1-1, 1-2

SIXTH ROUND

Everton v Leicester City	3-1
Leeds United v Sheffield United	1-0
Birmingham City v Chelsea	1-0
West Bromwich Albion v Liverpool	0-0, 1-1, 2-1

SEMI-FINAL

Everton v Leeds United	1-0
West Bromwich Albion v Birmingham City	2-0

FINAL

Everton v West Bromwich Albion	0-1

SCOTTISH FA CUP 1967–68

FIRST ROUND

Rangers v Hamilton Academicals	3-1
Cowdenbeath v Dundee	0-1
Dundee United v St. Mirren	3-1
Heart of Midlothian v Brechin City	4-1
East Fife v Alloa Athletic	3-0
Morton v Falkirk	4-0
Elgin City v Forfar Athletic	3-1
Ayr United v Arbroath	0-2
Celtic v Dunfermline Athletic	0-2
Aberdeen v Raith Rovers	1-1, 1-0
Partick Thistle v Kilmarnock	0-0, 2-1
Clyde v Berwick Rangers	2-0
Motherwell v Airdrieonians	1-1, 0-1
East Stirlingshire v Hibernian	3-5
St Johnstone v Hawick Royal Albert	3-0
Queen of the South v Stirling Albion	1-1, 3-1

SECOND ROUND

Dundee v Rangers	1-1, 1-4
Dundee United v Heart of Midlothian	5-6
East Fife v Morton	0-0, 2-5
Elgin City v Arbroath	2-0
Dunfermline Athletic v Aberdeen	2-1
Partick Thistle v Clyde	3-2
Airdrieonians v Hibernian	1-0
St Johnstone v Queen of the South	5-2

THIRD ROUND

Rangers v Heart of Midlothian	1-1, 0-1
Morton v Elgin City	2-1
Dunfermline Athletic v Partick Thistle	1-0
St Johnstone v Airdrieonians	2-1

SEMI-FINAL

Heart of Midlothian v Morton	1-1, 2-1
Dunfermline Athletic v St Johnstone	1-1, 2-1

FINAL

Dunfermline Athletic v Heart of Midlothian	3-1

League Tables 1968-69

FIRST DIVISION

	P	W	D	L	F	A	Pts
1 Leeds	42	27	13	2	66	26	67
2 Liverpool	42	25	11	6	63	24	61
3 Everton	42	21	15	6	77	36	57
4 Arsenal	42	22	12	8	56	27	56
5 Chelsea	42	20	10	12	73	53	50
6 Tottenham	42	14	17	11	61	51	45
7 Southampton	42	16	13	13	57	48	45
8 West Ham	42	13	18	11	66	50	44
9 Newcastle	42	15	14	13	61	55	44
10 WBA	42	16	11	15	64	67	43
11 Man United	42	15	12	15	57	53	42
12 Ipswich	42	15	11	16	59	60	41
13 Man City	42	15	10	17	64	55	40
14 Burnley	42	15	9	18	55	82	39
15 Sheff Wed	42	10	16	16	41	54	36
16 Wolves	42	10	15	17	41	58	35
17 Sunderland	42	11	12	19	43	67	34
18 Nottm Forest	42	10	13	19	45	57	33
19 Stoke	42	9	15	18	40	63	33
20 Coventry	42	10	11	21	46	64	31
21 Leicester	42	9	12	21	39	68	30
22 QPR	42	4	10	28	39	95	18

SECOND DIVISION

	P	W	D	L	F	A	Pts
1 Derby	42	26	11	5	65	32	63
2 Crystal Palace	42	22	12	8	70	47	56
3 Charlton	42	18	14	10	61	52	50
4 Middlesbrough	42	19	11	12	58	49	49
5 Cardiff	42	20	7	15	67	54	47
6 Huddersfield	42	17	12	13	53	46	46
7 Birmingham	42	18	8	16	73	59	44
8 Blackpool	42	14	15	13	51	41	43
9 Sheff United	42	16	11	15	61	50	43
10 Millwall	42	17	9	16	57	49	43
11 Hull	42	13	16	13	59	52	42
12 Carlisle	42	16	10	16	46	49	42
13 Norwich	42	15	10	17	53	56	40
14 Preston	42	12	15	15	38	44	39
15 Portsmouth	42	12	14	16	58	58	38
16 Bristol City	42	11	16	15	46	53	38
17 Bolton	42	12	14	16	55	67	38
18 Aston Villa	42	12	14	16	37	48	38
19 Blackburn	42	13	11	18	52	63	37
20 Oxford	42	12	9	21	34	55	33
21 Bury	42	11	8	23	51	80	30
22 Fulham	42	7	11	24	40	81	25

THIRD DIVISION

	P	W	D	L	F	A	Pts
1 Watford	46	27	10	9	74	34	64
2 Swindon	46	27	10	9	71	35	64
3 Luton	46	25	11	10	74	38	61
4 Bournemouth	46	21	9	16	60	45	51
5 Plymouth	46	17	15	14	53	49	49
6 Torquay	46	18	12	16	54	46	48
7 Tranmere	46	19	10	17	70	68	48
8 Southport	46	17	13	16	71	64	47
9 Stockport	46	16	14	16	67	68	46
10 Barnsley	46	16	14	16	58	63	46
11 Rotherham	46	16	13	17	56	50	45
12 Brighton	46	16	13	17	72	65	45
13 Walsall	46	14	16	16	50	49	44
14 Reading	46	15	13	18	67	66	43
15 Mansfield	46	16	11	19	58	62	43
16 Bristol Rovers	46	16	11	19	63	71	43
17 Shrewsbury	46	16	11	19	51	67	43
18 Orient	46	14	14	18	51	58	42
19 Barrow	46	17	8	21	56	75	42
20 Gillingham	46	13	15	18	54	63	41
21 Northampton	46	14	12	20	54	61	40
22 Hartlepool	46	10	19	17	40	70	39
23 Crewe	46	13	9	24	52	76	35
24 Oldham	46	13	9	24	50	83	35

FOURTH DIVISION

	P	W	D	L	F	A	Pts
1 Doncaster	46	21	17	8	65	38	59
2 Halifax	46	20	17	9	53	37	57
3 Rochdale	46	18	20	8	68	35	56
4 Bradford City	46	18	20	8	65	46	56
5 Darlington	46	17	18	11	62	45	52
6 Colchester	46	20	12	14	57	53	52
7 Southend	46	19	13	14	78	61	51
8 Lincoln	46	17	17	12	54	52	51
9 Wrexham	46	18	14	14	61	52	50
10 Swansea	46	19	11	16	58	54	49
11 Brentford	46	18	12	16	64	65	48
12 Workington	46	15	17	14	40	43	47
13 Port Vale	46	16	14	16	46	46	46
14 Chester	46	16	13	17	76	66	45
15 Aldershot	46	19	7	20	66	66	45
16 Scunthorpe	46	18	8	20	61	60	44
17 Exeter	46	16	11	19	66	65	43
18 Peterborough	46	13	16	17	60	57	42
19 Notts County	46	12	18	16	48	57	42
20 Chesterfield	46	13	15	18	43	50	41
21 York	46	14	11	21	53	75	39
22 Newport	46	11	14	21	49	74	36
23 Grimsby	46	9	15	22	47	69	33
24 Bradford PA	46	5	10	31	32	106	20

SCOTTISH FIRST DIVISION

	P	W	D	L	F	A	Pts
1 Celtic	34	23	8	3	89	32	54
2 Rangers	34	21	7	6	81	32	49
3 Dunfermline	34	19	7	8	63	45	45
4 Kilmarnock	34	15	14	5	50	32	44
5 Dundee United	34	17	9	8	61	49	43
6 St Johnstone	34	16	5	13	66	59	37
7 Airdrieonians	34	13	11	10	46	44	37
8 Hearts	34	14	8	12	52	54	36
9 Dundee	34	10	12	12	47	48	32
10 Morton	34	12	8	14	58	68	32
11 St Mirren	34	11	10	13	40	54	32
12 Hibernian	34	12	7	15	60	59	31
13 Clyde	34	9	13	12	35	50	31
14 Partick Thistle	34	9	10	15	39	53	28
15 Aberdeen	34	9	8	17	50	59	26
16 Raith	34	8	5	21	45	67	21
17 Falkirk	34	5	8	21	33	69	18
18 Arbroath	34	5	6	23	41	82	16

SCOTTISH SECOND DIVISION

	P	W	D	L	F	A	Pts
1 Motherwell	36	30	4	2	112	23	64
2 Ayr	36	23	7	6	82	31	53
3 East Fife	36	21	6	9	82	45	48
4 Stirling	36	21	6	9	67	40	48
5 Queen of the S	36	20	7	9	75	41	47
6 Forfar	36	18	7	11	71	56	47
7 Albion	36	19	5	12	60	56	43
8 Stranraer	36	17	7	12	57	45	41
9 E Stirlingshire	36	17	5	14	70	62	39
10 Montrose	36	15	4	17	59	71	34
11 Queen's Park	36	13	7	16	50	59	33
12 Cowdenbeath	36	12	5	19	54	67	29
13 Clydebank	36	6	15	15	52	67	27
14 Dumbarton	36	11	5	20	46	69	27
15 Hamilton	36	8	8	20	37	72	24
16 Berwick	36	7	9	20	42	70	23
17 Brechin	36	8	6	22	40	78	22
18 Alloa	36	7	7	22	45	79	21
19 Stenhousemuir	36	6	6	24	55	125	18

On 6 May 1969 only 7,843 people were at Hampden Park to see Northern Ireland play Scotland, then the smallest ever crowd at a full home international. There were on average more people at each of Fourth Division Lincoln City's games during the same season.

On 24 August 1968 the main stand at Nottingham Forest's ground caught fire during the game with Leeds and was completely destroyed. Police evacuated the 34,000 crowd and Forest played out the year on neighbouring Notts County's pitch, three hundred yards away.

FA CUP 1968–69

FOURTH ROUND

Newcastle United v Manchester City	0-0, 0-2
Blackburn Rovers v Portsmouth	4-0
Tottenham Hotspur v Wolverhampton Wanderers	2-1
Southampton v Aston Villa	2-2, 1-2
Sheffield Wednesday v Birmingham City	2-2, 1-2
Manchester United v Watford	1-1, 2-0
Bolton Wanderers v Bristol Rovers	1-2
Coventry City v Everton	0-2
West Bromwich Albion v Fulham	2-1
Arsenal v Charlton Athletic	2-0
Preston North End v Chelsea	0-0, 1-2
Stoke City v Halifax Town	1-1, 3-0
Mansfield Town v Southend United	2-1
Huddersfield v West Ham United	0-2
Liverpool v Burnley	2-1
Millwall v Leicester City	0-1

FIFTH ROUND

Manchester City v Blackburn Rovers	4-1
Tottenham Hotspur v Aston Villa	3-2
Birmingham City v Manchester United	2-2, 2-6
Bristol Rovers v Everton	0-1
West Bromwich Albion v Arsenal	1-0
Chelsea v Stoke City	3-2
Mansfield Town v West Ham United	3-0
Liverpool v Leicester City	0-0, 0-1

SIXTH ROUND

Manchester City v Tottenham Hotspur	1-0
Manchester United v Everton	0-1
Chelsea v West Bromwich Albion	1-2
Mansfield Town v Leicester City	0-1

SEMI-FINAL

Manchester City v Everton	1-0
West Bromwich Albion v Leicester City	0-1

FINAL

Leicester City v Manchester City	0-1

SCOTTISH FA CUP 1968–69

FIRST ROUND

Rangers v Hibernian	1-0
Dundee v Hearts	1-2
Dumbarton v St Mirren	0-1
Stenhousemuir v Airdrieonians	0-3
Aberdeen v Berwick Rangers	3-0
Raith Rovers v Dunfermline Athletic	0-2
Montrose v Cowdenbeath	1-0
Kilmarnock v Glasgow University	6-0
Dundee United v Queen's Park	2-1
Ayr United v Queen of the South	1-0
Stranraer v East Fife	3-1
Falkirk v Morton	1-2
East Stirlingshire v Stirling Albion	2-0
St Johnstone v Arbroath	3-2
Motherwell v Clyde	1-1, 1-2
Partick Thistle v Celtic	3-3, 1-8

SECOND ROUND

Rangers v Hearts	2-0
St Mirren v Airdrieonians	1-1, 1-3
Aberdeen v Dunfermline Athletic	2-2, 2-0
Montrose v Kilmarnock	1-1, 1-4
Dundee United v Ayr United	6-2
Stranraer v Morton	1-3
East Stirlingshire v St Johnstone	1-1, 0-3
Clyde v Celtic	0-0, 0-3

THIRD ROUND

Rangers v Airdrieonians	1-0
Aberdeen v Kilmarnock	0-0, 3-0
Dundee United v Morton	2-3
Celtic v St Johnstone	3-2

SEMI-FINAL

Rangers v Aberdeen	6-1
Morton v Celtic	1-4

FINAL

Celtic v Rangers	4-0

League Tables 1969-70

FIRST DIVISION

		P	W	D	L	F	A	Pts
1	Everton	42	29	8	5	72	34	66
2	Leeds	42	21	15	6	84	49	57
3	Chelsea	42	21	13	8	70	50	55
4	Derby	42	22	9	11	64	37	53
5	Liverpool	42	20	11	11	65	42	51
6	Coventry	42	19	11	12	58	48	49
7	Newcastle	42	17	13	12	57	35	47
8	Man United	42	14	17	11	66	61	45
9	Stoke	42	15	15	12	56	52	45
10	Man City	42	16	11	15	55	48	43
11	Tottenham	42	17	9	16	54	55	43
12	Arsenal	42	12	18	12	51	49	42
13	Wolves	42	12	16	14	55	57	40
14	Burnley	42	12	15	15	56	61	39
15	Nottm Forest	42	10	18	14	50	71	38
16	WBA	42	14	9	19	58	66	37
17	West Ham	42	12	12	18	51	60	36
18	Ipswich	42	10	11	21	40	63	31
19	Southampton	42	6	17	19	46	67	29
20	Crystal Palace	42	6	15	21	34	68	27
21	Sunderland	42	6	14	22	30	68	26
22	Sheff Wed	42	8	9	25	40	71	25

SECOND DIVISION

		P	W	D	L	F	A	Pts
1	Huddersfield	42	24	12	6	68	37	60
2	Blackpool	42	20	13	9	56	45	53
3	Leicester	42	19	13	10	64	50	51
4	Middlesbrough	42	20	10	12	55	45	50
5	Swindon	42	17	16	9	57	47	50
6	Sheff United	42	22	5	15	73	38	49
7	Cardiff	42	18	13	11	61	41	49
8	Blackburn	42	20	7	15	54	50	47
9	QPR	42	17	11	14	66	57	45
10	Millwall	42	15	14	13	56	56	44
11	Norwich	42	16	11	15	49	46	43
12	Carlisle	42	14	13	15	58	56	41
13	Hull	42	15	11	16	72	70	41
14	Bristol City	42	13	13	16	54	50	39
15	Oxford	42	12	15	15	35	42	39
16	Bolton	42	12	12	18	54	61	36
17	Portsmouth	42	13	9	20	66	80	35
18	Birmingham	42	11	11	20	51	78	33
19	Watford	42	9	13	20	44	57	31
20	Charlton	42	7	17	18	35	76	31
21	Aston Villa	42	8	13	21	36	62	29
22	Preston	42	8	12	22	43	63	28

THIRD DIVISION

		P	W	D	L	F	A	Pts
1	Orient	46	25	12	9	67	36	62
2	Luton	46	23	14	9	77	43	60
3	Bristol Rovers	46	20	16	10	80	59	56
4	Fulham	46	20	15	11	81	55	55
5	Brighton	46	23	9	14	57	43	55
6	Mansfield	46	21	11	14	70	49	53
7	Barnsley	46	19	15	12	68	59	53
8	Reading	46	21	11	14	87	77	53
9	Rochdale	46	18	10	18	69	60	46
10	Bradford City	46	17	12	17	57	50	46
11	Doncaster	46	17	12	17	52	54	46
12	Walsall	46	17	12	17	54	67	46
13	Torquay	46	14	17	15	62	59	45
14	Rotherham	46	15	14	17	62	54	44
15	Shrewsbury	46	13	18	15	62	63	44
16	Tranmere	46	14	16	16	56	72	44
17	Plymouth	46	16	11	19	56	64	43
18	Halifax	46	14	15	17	47	63	43
19	Bury	46	15	11	20	75	80	41
20	Gillingham	46	13	13	20	52	64	39
21	Bournemouth	46	12	15	19	48	71	39
22	Southport	46	14	10	22	48	66	38
23	Barrow	46	8	14	24	46	81	30
24	Stockport	46	6	11	29	27	71	23

FOURTH DIVISION

		P	W	D	L	F	A	Pts
1	Chesterfield	46	27	10	9	77	32	64
2	Wrexham	46	26	9	11	84	49	61
3	Swansea	46	21	18	7	66	45	60
4	Port Vale	46	20	19	7	61	33	59
5	Brentford	46	20	16	10	58	39	56
6	Aldershot	46	20	13	13	78	65	53
7	Notts County	46	22	8	16	73	62	52
8	Lincoln	46	17	16	13	66	52	50
9	Peterborough	46	17	14	15	77	69	48
10	Colchester	46	17	14	15	64	63	48
11	Chester	46	21	6	19	58	66	48
12	Scunthorpe	46	18	10	18	67	65	46
13	York	46	16	14	16	55	62	46
14	Northampton	46	16	12	18	64	55	44
15	Crewe	46	16	12	18	51	51	44
16	Grimsby	46	14	15	17	54	58	43
17	Southend	46	15	10	21	59	85	40
18	Exeter	46	14	11	21	57	59	39
19	Oldham	46	13	13	20	60	65	39
20	Workington	46	12	14	20	46	64	38
21	Newport	46	13	11	22	53	74	37
22	Darlington	46	13	10	23	53	73	36
23	Hartlepool	46	10	10	26	42	82	30
24	Bradford P A	46	6	11	29	41	96	23

SCOTTISH FIRST DIVISION

		P	W	D	L	F	A	Pts
1	Celtic	34	27	3	4	96	33	57
2	Rangers	34	19	7	8	67	40	45
3	Hibernian	34	19	6	9	65	40	44
4	Hearts	34	13	12	9	50	36	38
5	Dundee United	34	16	6	12	62	64	38
6	Dundee	34	15	6	13	49	44	36
7	Kilmarnock	34	13	10	11	62	57	36
8	Aberdeen	34	14	7	13	55	45	35
9	Dunfermline	34	15	5	14	45	45	35
10	Morton	34	13	9	12	52	52	35
11	Motherwell	34	11	10	13	49	51	32
12	Airdrieonians	34	12	8	14	59	64	32
13	St Johnstone	34	11	9	14	50	62	31
14	Ayr	34	12	6	16	37	52	30
15	St Mirren	34	8	9	17	39	54	25
16	Clyde	34	9	7	18	34	56	25
17	Raith	34	5	11	18	32	67	21
18	Partick Thistle	34	5	7	22	41	82	17

SCOTTISH SECOND DIVISION

		P	W	D	L	F	A	Pts
1	Falkirk	36	25	6	5	94	34	56
2	Cowdenbeath	36	24	7	5	81	35	55
3	Queen of the S	36	22	6	8	72	49	50
4	Stirling	36	18	10	8	70	40	46
5	Arbroath	36	20	4	12	76	39	44
6	Alloa	36	19	5	12	62	41	43
7	Dumbarton	36	17	6	13	55	46	40
8	Montrose	36	15	7	14	57	55	37
9	Berwick	36	15	5	16	67	55	35
10	East Fife	36	15	4	17	59	63	34
11	Albion	36	14	5	17	53	64	33
12	E Stirlingshire	36	14	5	17	58	75	33
13	Clydebank	36	10	10	16	47	65	30
14	Brechin	36	11	6	19	47	74	28
15	Queen's Park	36	10	6	20	38	62	26
16	Stenhousemuir	36	10	6	20	47	89	26
17	Stranraer	36	9	7	20	56	75	25
18	Forfar	36	11	1	24	55	83	23
19	Hamilton	36	8	4	24	42	92	20

Leeds go marching on

Leeds United established a new First Division record for the number of consecutive League games played without a defeat. They completed a run of 34 home and away matches without losing a single game. Their unbeaten run finally ended on 30 August 1969 when they lost 3-2 to Everton, the club that was to take the League title from them.

Six of the Best

George Best scored a record number of goals in a Cup tie, notching six for Manchester United in their 8-2 win over Fourth Division Northampton Town in the fifth round of the FA Cup. Best's team-mate Denis Law, when with Manchester City, once scored six goals in a fourth round tie at Luton, but the match was abandoned and Luton won the replay.

FA CUP 1969–70

FOURTH ROUND

Chelsea v Burnley	2-2, 3-1
Tottenham Hotspur v Crystal Palace	0-0, 0-1
Charlton Athletic v Queen's Park Rangers	2-3
Derby County v Sheffield United	3-0
Watford v Stoke City	1-0
Gillingham v Peterborough United	5-1
Liverpool v Wrexham	3-1
Southampton v Leicester City	1-1, 2-4
Tranmere Rovers v Northampton Town	0-0, 1-2
Manchester United v Manchester City	3-0
Carlisle United v Aldershot	2-2, 4-1
Middlesbrough v York City	4-1
Swindon Town v Chester	4-2
Sheffield Wednesday v Scunthorpe United	1-2
Blackpool v Mansfield Town	0-2
Sutton United v Leeds United	0-6

FIFTH ROUND

Chelsea v Crystal Palace	4-1
Queen's Park Rangers v Derby County	1-0
Watford v Gillingham	2-1
Liverpool v Leicester City	0-0, 2-0
Northampton Town v Manchester United	2-8
Carlisle United v Middlesbrough	1-2
Swindon Town v Scunthorpe United	3-1
Mansfield Town v Leeds United	0-2

SIXTH ROUND

Queen's Park Rangers v Chelsea	2-4
Watford v Liverpool	1-0
Manchester United v Middlesbrough	1-1, 2-1
Swindon Town v Leeds United	0-2

SEMI-FINAL

Chelsea v Watford	5-1
Manchester United v Leeds United	0-0, 0-0, 0-1

THIRD PLACE PLAY-OFF

Manchester United v Watford	2-0

FINAL

Chelsea v Leeds United	2-2, 2-1

SCOTTISH FA CUP 1969–70

FIRST ROUND

Celtic v Dunfermline Athletic	2-1
Dundee United v Ayr United	1-0
Dumbarton v Forfar Athletic	1-2
Rangers v Hibernian	3-1
East Fife v Raith Rovers	3-0
Morton v Queen of the South	2-0
Albion Rovers v Dundee	1-2
Airdrieonians v Hamilton Academicals	5-0
Motherwell v St Johnstone	2-1
Stranraer v Inverness Caledonian	2-5
Kilmarnock v Partick Thistle	3-0
Montrose v Heart of Midlothian	1-1, 0-1
Falkirk v Tarff Rovers	3-0
St Mirren v Stirling Albion	2-0
Arbroath v Clydebank	1-2
Clyde v Aberdeen	0-4

SECOND ROUND

Celtic v Dundee United	4-0
Forfar Athletic v Rangers	0-7
East Fife v Morton	1-0
Dundee v Airdrieonians	3-0
Motherwell v Inverness Caledonian	3-1
Kilmarnock v Heart of Midlothian	2-0
Falkirk v St Mirren	2-1
Aberdeen v Clydebank	2-1

THIRD ROUND

Celtic v Rangers	3-1
East Fife v Dundee	0-1
Motherwell v Kilmarnock	0-1
Falkirk v Aberdeen	0-1

SEMI-FINAL

Celtic v Dundee	2-1
Kilmarnock v Aberdeen	0-1

FINAL

Celtic v Aberdeen	1-3

League Tables 1970-71

FIRST DIVISION

	P	W	D	L	F	A	Pts
1 Arsenal	42	29	7	6	71	29	65
2 Leeds	42	27	10	5	72	30	64
3 Tottenham	42	19	14	9	54	33	52
4 Wolves	42	22	8	12	64	54	52
5 Liverpool	42	17	17	8	42	24	51
6 Chelsea	42	18	15	9	52	42	51
7 Southampton	42	17	12	13	56	44	46
8 Man United	42	16	11	15	65	66	43
9 Derby	42	16	10	16	56	54	42
10 Coventry	42	16	10	16	37	38	42
11 Man City	42	12	17	13	47	42	41
12 Newcastle	42	14	13	15	44	46	41
13 Stoke	42	12	13	17	44	48	37
14 Everton	42	12	13	17	54	60	37
15 Huddersfield	42	11	14	17	40	49	36
16 Nottm Forest	42	14	8	20	42	61	36
17 WBA	42	10	15	17	58	75	35
18 Crystal Palace	42	12	11	19	39	57	35
19 Ipswich	42	12	10	20	42	48	34
20 West Ham	42	10	14	18	47	60	34
21 Burnley	42	7	13	22	29	63	27
22 Blackpool	42	4	15	23	34	66	23

SECOND DIVISION

	P	W	D	L	F	A	Pts
1 Leicester	42	23	13	6	57	30	59
2 Sheff United	42	21	14	7	73	39	56
3 Cardiff	42	20	13	9	64	41	53
4 Carlisle	42	20	13	9	65	43	53
5 Hull	42	19	13	10	54	41	51
6 Luton	42	18	13	11	62	43	49
7 Middlesbrough	42	17	14	11	60	43	48
8 Millwall	42	19	9	14	59	42	47
9 Birmingham	42	17	12	13	58	48	46
10 Norwich	42	15	14	13	54	52	44
11 QPR	42	16	11	15	58	53	43
12 Swindon	42	15	12	15	61	51	42
13 Sunderland	42	15	12	15	52	54	42
14 Oxford	42	14	14	14	41	48	42
15 Sheff Wed	42	12	12	18	51	69	36
16 Portsmouth	42	10	14	18	46	61	34
17 Orient	42	9	16	17	29	51	34
18 Watford	42	10	13	19	38	60	33
19 Bristol City	42	10	11	21	46	64	31
20 Charlton	42	8	14	20	41	65	30
21 Blackburn	42	6	15	21	37	69	27
22 Bolton	42	7	10	25	35	74	24

THIRD DIVISION

	P	W	D	L	F	A	Pts
1 Preston	46	22	17	7	63	39	61
2 Fulham	46	24	12	10	68	41	60
3 Halifax	46	22	12	12	74	55	56
4 Aston Villa	46	19	15	12	54	46	53
5 Chesterfield	46	17	17	12	66	38	51
6 Bristol Rovers	46	19	13	14	69	50	51
7 Mansfield	46	18	15	13	64	62	51
8 Rotherham	46	17	16	13	64	60	50
9 Wrexham	46	18	13	15	72	65	49
10 Torquay	46	19	11	16	54	57	49
11 Swansea	46	15	16	15	59	56	46
12 Barnsley	46	17	11	18	49	52	45
13 Shrewsbury	46	16	13	17	58	62	45
14 Brighton	46	14	16	16	50	47	44
15 Plymouth	46	12	19	15	63	63	43
16 Rochdale	46	14	15	17	61	68	43
17 Port Vale	46	15	12	19	52	59	42
18 Tranmere	46	10	22	14	45	55	42
19 Bradford City	46	13	14	19	49	62	40
20 Walsall	46	14	11	21	51	57	39
21 Reading	46	14	11	21	48	85	39
22 Bury	46	12	13	21	52	60	37
23 Doncaster	46	13	9	24	45	66	35
24 Gillingham	46	10	13	23	42	67	33

FOURTH DIVISION

	P	W	D	L	F	A	Pts
1 Notts County	46	30	9	7	89	36	69
2 Bournemouth	46	24	12	10	81	46	60
3 Oldham	46	24	11	11	88	63	59
4 York	46	23	10	13	78	54	56
5 Chester	46	24	7	15	69	55	55
6 Colchester	46	21	12	13	70	54	54
7 Northampton	46	19	13	14	63	59	51
8 Southport	46	21	6	19	63	57	48
9 Exeter	46	17	14	15	67	68	48
10 Workington	46	18	12	16	48	49	48
11 Stockport	46	16	14	16	49	65	46
12 Darlington	46	17	11	18	58	57	45
13 Aldershot	46	14	17	15	66	71	45
14 Brentford	46	18	8	20	66	62	44
15 Crewe	46	18	8	20	75	76	44
16 Peterborough	46	18	7	21	70	71	43
17 Scunthorpe	46	15	13	18	56	61	43
18 Southend	46	14	15	17	53	66	43
19 Grimsby	46	18	7	21	57	71	43
20 Cambridge	46	15	13	18	51	66	43
21 Lincoln	46	13	13	20	70	71	39
22 Newport	46	10	8	28	55	85	28
23 Hartlepool	46	8	12	26	34	74	28
24 Barrow	46	7	8	31	51	90	22

SCOTTISH FIRST DIVISION

	P	W	D	L	F	A	Pts
1 Celtic	34	25	6	3	89	23	56
2 Aberdeen	34	24	6	4	68	18	54
3 St Johnstone	34	19	6	9	59	44	44
4 Rangers	34	16	9	9	58	34	41
5 Dundee	34	14	10	10	53	45	38
6 Dundee United	34	14	8	12	53	54	36
7 Falkirk	34	13	9	12	46	53	35
8 Morton	34	13	8	13	44	44	34
9 Motherwell	34	13	8	13	43	47	34
10 Airdrieonians	34	13	8	13	60	65	34
11 Hearts	34	13	7	14	41	40	33
12 Hibernian	34	10	10	14	47	53	30
13 Kilmarnock	34	10	8	16	43	67	28
14 Ayr	34	9	8	17	37	54	26
15 Clyde	34	8	10	16	33	59	26
16 Dunfermline	34	6	11	17	44	56	23
17 St Mirren	34	7	9	18	38	56	23
18 Cowdenbeath	34	7	3	24	33	77	17

SCOTTISH SECOND DIVISION

	P	W	D	L	F	A	Pts
1 Partick Thistle	36	23	10	3	78	26	56
2 East Fife	36	22	7	7	86	44	51
3 Arbroath	36	19	8	9	80	52	46
4 Dumbarton	36	19	6	11	87	46	44
5 Clydebank	36	17	8	11	57	43	42
6 Montrose	36	17	7	12	78	64	41
7 Albion	36	15	9	12	53	52	39
8 Raith	36	15	9	12	62	62	39
9 Stranraer	36	14	8	14	54	52	36
10 Stenhousemuir	36	14	8	14	64	70	36
11 Queen of the S	36	13	9	14	50	56	35
12 Stirling	36	12	8	16	61	61	32
13 Berwick	36	10	10	16	42	60	30
14 Queen's Park	[illegible]	13	4	19	51	72	30
15 Forfar	36	9	11	16	63	75	29
16 Alloa	36	9	11	16	56	86	29
17 E Stirlingshire	36	9	9	18	57	86	27
18 Hamilton	36	8	7	21	50	79	23
19 Brechin	36	6	7	23	30	73	19

The unnecessary goalkeeper

One of the strangest events in all football annals happened on 12 May 1971. In the course of the England–Malta game the ball did not cross the England goal-line once and the England goalkeeper, Gordon Banks, did not receive the ball direct from a Maltese player at any time during the game.

A pools punter's best friend

In the 1970-71 season, Tranmere Rovers of the Third Division broke Plymouth Argyle's 50-year-old record by drawing 22 of their 46 League matches, the most ever tied in a single season. In actual fact, Plymouth's drawn percentage was higher as they played 42 and tied 21 games in the 1920-21 season.

FA CUP 1970–71

FOURTH ROUND

Liverpool v Swansea City	3-0
York City v Southampton	3-3, 2-3
Carlisle United v Tottenham Hotspur	2-3
Nottingham Forest v Orient	1-1, 1-0
Everton v Middlesbrough	3-0
Derby County v Wolverhampton Wanderers	2-1
Rochdale v Colchester United	3-3, 0-5
Leeds United v Swindon Town	4-0
Hull City v Blackpool	2-0
Cardiff City v Brentford	0-2
Stoke City v Huddersfield Town	3-3, 0-0, 1-0
West Bromwich Albion v Ipswich Town	1-1, 0-3
Leicester City v Torquay United	3-0
Oxford United v Watford	1-1, 2-1
Chelsea v Manchester City	0-3
Portsmouth v Arsenal	1-1, 2-3

FIFTH ROUND

Liverpool v Southampton	1-0
Tottenham Hotspur v Nottingham Forest	2-1
Everton v Derby County	1-0
Colchester United v Leeds United	3-2
Hull City v Brentford	2-1
Stoke City v Ipswich Town	0-0, 1-0
Leicester City v Oxford United	1-1, 3-1
Manchester City v Arsenal	1-2

SIXTH ROUND

Liverpool v Tottenham Hotspur	0-0, 1-0
Everton v Colchester United	5-0
Hull City v Stoke City	2-3
Leicester City v Arsenal	0-0, 0-1

SEMI-FINAL

Liverpool v Everton	2-1
Stoke City v Arsenal	2-2, 0-2

THIRD PLACE PLAY-OFF

Stoke City v Everton	3-2

FINAL

Liverpool v Arsenal	1-2

SCOTTISH FA CUP 1970–71

THIRD ROUND

Celtic v Queen of the South	5-1
Hibernian v Forfar Athletic	8-1
East Fife v St Mirren	1-1, 1-1, 1-3
St Johnstone v Raith Rovers	2-2, 3-4
Clyde v Brechin City	2-0
Airdrieonians v Alloa Athletic	1-1, 2-0
Rangers v Falkirk	3-0
Aberdeen v Elgin City	5-0
Dundee v Partick Thistle	1-0
Clachnacuddin v Cowdenbeath	0-3
Clydebank v Dundee United	0-0, 1-5
Stirling Albion v Motherwell	3-1
Dunfermline v Arbroath	3-1
Morton v Ayr United	2-0
Queen's Park v Kilmarnock	0-1
Heart of Midlothian v Stranraer	3-0

FOURTH ROUND

Dundee United v Aberdeen	1-1, 0-2
Raith Rovers v Clyde	1-1, 2-0
Morton v Kilmarnock	1-2
Cowdenbeath v Airdrieonians	0-4
St Mirren v Rangers	1-3
Dundee v Stirling Albion	2-0
Celtic v Dunfermline	1-1, 1-0
Heart of Midlothian v Hibernian	1-2

FIFTH ROUND

Rangers v Aberdeen	1-0
Hibernian v Dundee	1-0
Celtic v Raith Rovers	7-1
Kilmarnock v Airdrieonians	2-3

SEMI-FINAL

Hibernian v Rangers	0-0, 1-2
Celtic v Airdrieonians	3-3, 2-0

FINAL

Rangers v Celtic	1-1, 1-2

League Tables 1971-72

FIRST DIVISION

	P	W	D	L	F	A	Pts
1 Derby	42	24	10	8	69	33	58
2 Leeds	42	24	9	9	73	31	57
3 Liverpool	42	24	9	9	64	30	57
4 Man City	42	23	11	8	77	45	57
5 Arsenal	42	22	8	12	58	40	52
6 Tottenham	42	19	13	10	63	42	51
7 Chelsea	42	18	12	12	58	49	48
8 Man United	42	19	10	13	69	61	48
9 Wolves	42	18	11	13	65	57	47
10 Sheff United	42	17	12	13	61	60	46
11 Newcastle	42	15	11	16	49	52	41
12 Leicester	42	13	13	16	41	46	39
13 Ipswich	42	11	16	15	39	53	38
14 West Ham	42	12	12	18	47	51	36
15 Everton	42	9	18	15	37	48	36
16 WBA	42	12	11	19	42	54	35
17 Stoke	42	10	15	17	39	56	35
18 Coventry	42	9	15	18	44	67	33
19 Southampton	42	12	7	23	52	80	31
20 Crystal Palace	42	8	13	21	39	65	29
21 Nottm Forest	42	8	9	25	47	81	25
22 Huddersfield	42	6	13	23	27	59	25

SECOND DIVISION

	P	W	D	L	F	A	Pts
1 Norwich	42	21	15	6	60	36	57
2 Birmingham	42	19	18	5	60	31	56
3 Millwall	42	19	17	6	64	46	55
4 QPR	42	20	14	8	57	28	54
5 Sunderland	42	17	16	9	67	57	50
6 Blackpool	42	20	7	15	70	50	47
7 Burnley	42	20	6	16	70	55	46
8 Bristol City	42	18	10	14	61	49	46
9 Middlesbrough	42	19	8	15	50	48	46
10 Carlisle	42	17	9	16	61	57	43
11 Swindon	42	15	12	15	47	47	42
12 Hull	42	14	10	18	49	53	38
13 Luton	42	10	18	14	43	48	38
14 Sheff Wed	42	13	12	17	51	58	38
15 Oxford	42	12	14	16	43	55	38
16 Portsmouth	42	12	13	17	59	68	37
17 Orient	42	14	9	19	50	61	37
18 Preston	42	12	12	18	52	58	36
19 Cardiff	42	10	14	18	56	69	34
20 Fulham	42	12	10	20	45	68	34
21 Charlton	42	12	9	21	55	77	33
22 Watford	42	5	9	28	24	75	19

THIRD DIVISION

	P	W	D	L	F	A	Pts
1 Aston Villa	46	32	6	8	85	32	70
2 Brighton	46	27	11	8	82	47	65
3 Bournemouth	46	23	16	7	73	37	62
4 Notts County	46	25	12	9	74	44	62
5 Rotherham	46	20	15	11	69	52	55
6 Bristol Rovers	46	21	12	13	75	56	54
7 Bolton	46	17	16	13	51	41	50
8 Plymouth	46	20	10	16	74	64	50
9 Walsall	46	15	18	13	62	57	48
10 Blackburn	46	19	9	18	54	57	47
11 Oldham	46	17	11	18	59	63	45
12 Shrewsbury	46	17	10	19	73	65	44
13 Chesterfield	46	18	8	20	57	57	44
14 Swansea	46	17	10	19	46	59	44
15 Port Vale	46	13	15	18	43	59	41
16 Wrexham	46	16	8	22	59	63	40
17 Halifax	46	13	12	21	48	61	38
18 Rochdale	46	12	13	21	57	83	37
19 York	46	12	12	22	57	66	36
20 Tranmere	46	10	16	20	50	71	36
21 Mansfield	46	8	20	18	41	63	36
22 Barnsley	46	9	18	19	32	64	36
23 Torquay	46	10	12	24	41	69	32
24 Bradford City	46	11	10	25	45	77	32

FOURTH DIVISION

	P	W	D	L	F	A	Pts
1 Grimsby	46	28	7	11	88	56	63
2 Southend	46	24	12	10	81	55	60
3 Brentford	46	24	11	11	76	44	59
4 Scunthorpe	46	22	13	11	56	37	57
5 Lincoln	46	21	14	11	77	59	56
6 Workington	46	16	19	11	50	34	51
7 Southport	46	18	14	14	66	46	50
8 Peterborough	46	17	16	13	82	64	50
9 Bury	46	19	12	15	73	59	50
10 Cambridge	46	17	14	15	62	60	48
11 Colchester	46	19	10	17	70	69	48
12 Doncaster	46	16	14	16	56	63	46
13 Gillingham	46	16	13	17	61	67	45
14 Newport	46	18	8	20	60	72	44
15 Exeter	46	16	11	19	61	68	43
16 Reading	46	17	8	21	56	76	42
17 Aldershot	46	9	22	15	48	54	40
18 Hartlepool	46	17	6	23	58	69	40
19 Darlington	46	14	11	21	64	82	39
20 Chester	46	10	18	18	47	56	38
21 Northampton	46	12	13	21	66	79	37
22 Barrow	46	13	11	22	40	71	37
23 Stockport	46	9	14	23	55	87	32
24 Crewe	46	10	9	27	43	69	29

SCOTTISH FIRST DIVISION

	P	W	D	L	F	A	Pts
1 Celtic	34	28	4	2	96	28	60
2 Aberdeen	34	21	8	5	80	26	50
3 Rangers	34	21	2	11	71	38	44
4 Hibernian	34	19	6	9	62	34	44
5 Dundee	34	14	13	7	59	38	41
6 Hearts	34	13	13	8	53	49	39
7 Partick	34	12	10	12	53	54	34
8 St Johnstone	34	12	8	14	52	58	32
9 Dundee United	34	12	7	15	55	70	31
10 Motherwell	34	11	7	16	49	69	29
11 Kilmarnock	34	11	6	17	49	64	28
12 Ayr	34	9	10	15	40	58	28
13 Morton	34	10	7	17	46	52	27
14 Falkirk	34	10	7	17	44	60	27
15 Airdrieonians	34	7	12	15	44	76	26
16 East Fife*	34	5	15	14	34	61	25
17 Clyde	34	7	10	17	33	66	24
18 Dunfermline	34	7	9	18	31	50	23

SCOTTISH SECOND DIVISION

	P	W	D	L	F	A	Pts
1 Dumbarton	36	24	4	8	89	51	52
2 Arbroath	36	22	8	6	71	41	52
3 Stirling	36	21	8	7	75	37	50
4 St Mirren	36	24	2	10	84	47	50
5 Cowdenbeath	36	19	10	7	69	28	48
6 Stranraer	36	18	8	10	70	62	44
7 Queen of the S	36	17	9	10	56	38	43
8 E Stirlingshire	36	17	7	12	60	58	41
9 Clydebank	36	14	11	11	60	52	39
10 Montrose	36	15	6	15	73	54	36
11 Raith	36	13	8	15	56	56	34
12 Queen's Park	36	12	9	15	47	61	33
13 Berwick	36	14	4	18	53	50	32
14 Stenhousemuir	36	10	8	18	41	58	28
15 Brechin	36	8	7	21	41	79	23
16 Alloa	36	9	4	23	41	75	22
17 Forfar	36	6	9	21	32	84	21
18 Albion	36	7	6	23	36	61	20
19 Hamilton	36	4	8	24	31	93	16

Mansfield Town did not score a League goal at home until the 23rd minute of their game against Plymouth Argyle on 18 December 1971. This unrewarded period of 833 minutes of Third Division football at Field Mill is thought to constitute a record-breaking start to any Football League club's season. Mansfield still lost the game 3-2.

Aldershot drew 22 of their Fourth Division fixtures to equal Tranmere Rovers' record of the 1970-71 season. Both Tranmere and Aldershot, however, played 46 games that season and their achievement does not, therefore, compare in percentage terms with Plymouth's feat of 1920-21. That year Argyle drew 21 of their 42 League games.

FA CUP 1971-72

FOURTH ROUND

Liverpool v Leeds United	0-0, 0-2
Cardiff City v Sunderland	1-1, 1-1, 3-1
Everton v Walsall	2-1
Tottenham Hotspur v Rotherham United	2-0
Birmingham City v Ipswich Town	1-0
Portsmouth v Swansea City	2-0
Huddersfield Town v Fulham	3-0
Hereford United v West Ham United	0-0, 1-3
Preston North End v Manchester United	0-2
Millwall v Middlesbrough	2-2, 1-2
Tranmere Rovers v Stoke City	2-2, 0-2
Coventry City v Hull City	0-1
Leicester City v Orient	0-2
Chelsea v Bolton Wanderers	3-0
Derby County v Notts County	6-0
Reading v Arsenal	1-2

FIFTH ROUND

Cardiff City v Leeds United	0-2
Everton v Tottenham Hotspur	0-2
Birmingham City v Portsmouth	3-1
Huddersfield Town v West Ham United	4-2
Manchester United v Middlesbrough	0-0, 3-0
Stoke City v Hull City	4-1
Orient v Chelsea	3-2
Derby County v Arsenal	2-2, 0-0, 0-1

SIXTH ROUND

Leeds United v Tottenham Hotspur	2-1
Birmingham City v Huddersfield Town	3-1
Manchester United v Stoke City	1-1, 1-2
Orient v Arsenal	0-1

SEMI-FINAL

Leeds United v Birmingham City	3-0
Arsenal v Stoke City	1-1, 2-1

FINAL

Leeds United v Arsenal	1-0

SCOTTISH FA CUP 1971-72

THIRD ROUND

Celtic v Albion Rovers	5-0
Dundee v Queen of the South	3-0
Heart of Midlothian v St Johnstone	2-0
Clydebank v East Fife	1-1, 1-0
Dumbarton v Hamilton Academicals	3-1
Raith Rovers v Dunfermline Athletic	2-0
Elgin City v Inverness Caledonian	3-1
Kilmarnock v Alloa Athletic	5-1
Clyde v Ayr United	0-1
Motherwell v Montrose	2-0
Forfar Athletic v St Mirren	0-1
Falkirk v Rangers	2-2, 0-2
Dundee United v Aberdeen	0-4
Morton v Cowdenbeath	1-0
Arbroath v Airdrieonians	1-3
Partick Thistle v Hibernian	0-2

FOURTH ROUND

Celtic v Dundee	4-0
Heart of Midlothian v Clydebank	4-0
Dumbarton v Raith Rovers	0-3
Elgin City v Kilmarnock	1-4
Ayr United v Motherwell	0-0, 1-2
St Mirren v Rangers	1-4
Aberdeen v Morton	1-0
Hibernian v Airdrieonians	2-0

FIFTH ROUND

Celtic v Heart of Midlothian	1-1, 1-0
Raith Rovers v Kilmarnock	1-3
Motherwell v Rangers	2-2, 2-4
Hibernian v Aberdeen	2-0

SEMI-FINAL

Celtic v Kilmarnock	3-1
Rangers v Hibernian	1-1, 0-2

FINAL

Celtic v Hibernian	6-1

FIRST DIVISION

	P	W	D	L	F	A	Pts
1 Liverpool	42	25	10	6	72	42	60
2 Arsenal	42	23	11	8	57	43	57
3 Leeds	42	21	11	10	77	45	53
4 Ipswich	42	17	14	11	55	45	48
5 Wolves	42	18	11	13	66	54	47
6 West Ham	42	17	12	13	67	53	46
7 Derby	42	19	8	15	56	54	46
8 Tottenham	42	16	13	13	58	48	45
9 Newcastle	42	16	13	13	60	51	45
10 Birmingham	42	15	12	15	53	54	42
11 Man City	42	15	11	16	57	60	41
12 Chelsea	42	13	14	15	49	51	40
13 Southampton	42	11	18	13	47	52	40
14 Sheff United	42	15	10	17	51	59	40
15 Stoke	42	14	10	18	61	56	38
16 Leicester	42	10	17	15	40	46	37
17 Everton	42	13	11	18	41	49	37
18 Man United	42	12	13	17	44	60	37
19 Coventry	42	13	9	20	40	55	35
20 Norwich	42	11	10	21	36	63	32
21 Crystal Palace	42	9	12	21	41	58	30
22 WBA	42	9	10	23	38	62	28

SECOND DIVISION

	P	W	D	L	F	A	Pts
1 Burnley	42	24	14	4	72	35	62
2 QPR	42	24	13	5	81	37	61
3 Aston Villa	42	18	14	10	51	47	50
4 Middlesbrough	42	17	13	12	46	43	47
5 Bristol City	42	17	12	13	63	51	46
6 Sunderland	42	17	12	13	59	49	46
7 Blackpool	42	18	10	14	56	51	46
8 Oxford	42	19	7	16	52	43	45
9 Fulham	42	16	12	14	58	49	44
10 Sheff Wed	42	17	10	15	59	55	44
11 Millwall	42	16	10	16	55	47	42
12 Luton	42	15	11	16	44	53	41
13 Hull	42	14	12	16	64	59	40
14 Nottm Forest	42	14	12	16	47	52	40
15 Orient	42	12	12	18	49	53	36
16 Swindon	42	10	16	16	46	60	36
17 Portsmouth	42	12	11	19	42	59	35
18 Carlisle	42	11	12	19	50	52	34
19 Preston	42	11	12	19	37	64	34
20 Cardiff	42	11	11	20	43	58	33
21 Huddersfield	42	8	17	17	36	56	33
22 Brighton	42	8	13	21	46	83	29

THIRD DIVISION

	P	W	D	L	F	A	Pts
1 Bolton	46	25	11	10	73	39	61
2 Notts County	46	23	11	12	67	47	57
3 Blackburn	46	20	15	11	57	47	55
4 Oldham	46	19	16	11	72	54	54
5 Bristol Rovers	46	20	13	13	77	56	53
6 Port Vale	46	21	11	14	56	69	53
7 Bournemouth	46	17	16	13	66	44	50
8 Plymouth	46	20	10	16	74	66	50
9 Grimsby	46	20	8	18	67	61	48
10 Tranmere	46	15	16	15	56	52	46
11 Charlton	46	17	11	18	69	67	45
12 Wrexham	46	14	17	15	55	54	45
13 Rochdale	46	14	17	15	48	54	45
14 Southend	46	17	10	19	61	54	44
15 Shrewsbury	46	15	14	17	46	54	44
16 Chesterfield	46	17	9	20	57	61	43
17 Walsall	46	18	7	21	56	66	43
18 York	46	13	15	18	42	46	41
19 Watford	46	12	17	17	43	48	41
20 Halifax	46	13	15	18	43	53	41
21 Rotherham	46	17	7	22	51	65	41
22 Brentford	46	15	7	24	51	69	37
23 Swansea	46	14	9	23	51	73	37
24 Scunthorpe	46	10	10	26	33	72	30

FOURTH DIVISION

	P	W	D	L	F	A	Pts
1 Southport	46	36	10	10	71	48	62
2 Hereford	46	23	12	11	56	38	58
3 Cambridge	46	20	17	9	67	57	57
4 Aldershot	46	22	12	12	60	38	56
5 Newport	46	22	12	12	64	44	56
6 Mansfield	46	20	14	12	78	51	54
7 Reading	46	17	18	11	51	38	52
8 Exeter	46	18	14	14	57	51	50
9 Gillingham	46	19	11	16	63	58	49
10 Lincoln	46	16	16	14	64	57	48
11 Stockport	46	18	12	16	53	53	48
12 Bury	46	14	18	14	58	51	46
13 Workington	46	17	12	17	59	61	46
14 Barnsley	46	14	16	16	58	60	44
15 Chester	46	14	15	17	61	52	43
16 Bradford	46	16	11	19	61	65	43
17 Doncaster	46	15	12	19	49	58	42
18 Torquay	46	12	17	17	44	47	41
19 Peterborough	46	14	13	19	71	76	41
20 Hartlepool	46	12	17	17	34	49	41
21 Crewe	46	9	18	19	38	61	36
22 Colchester	46	10	11	25	48	76	31
23 Northampton	46	10	11	25	40	73	31
24 Darlington	46	7	15	24	42	85	29

SCOTTISH FIRST DIVISION

	P	W	D	L	F	A	Pts
1 Celtic	34	26	5	3	93	28	57
2 Rangers	34	26	4	4	74	30	56
3 Hibernian	34	19	7	8	74	33	45
4 Aberdeen	34	16	11	7	61	34	43
5 Dundee	34	17	9	8	68	43	43
6 Ayr	34	16	8	10	50	51	40
7 Dundee United	34	17	5	12	56	51	39
8 Motherwell	34	11	9	14	38	48	31
9 East Fife	34	11	8	15	46	54	30
10 Hearts	34	12	6	16	39	50	30
11 St Johnstone	34	10	9	15	52	67	29
12 Morton	34	10	8	16	47	53	28
13 Partick	34	10	8	16	40	53	28
14 Falkirk	34	7	12	15	38	56	26
15 Arbroath	34	9	8	17	39	63	26
16 Dumbarton	34	6	11	17	43	72	23
17 Kilmarnock	34	7	8	19	40	71	22
18 Airdrieonians	34	4	8	22	34	75	16

SCOTTISH SECOND DIVISION

	P	W	D	L	F	A	Pts
1 Clyde	36	23	10	3	68	28	56
2 Dunfermline	36	23	6	7	95	32	52
3 Raith	36	19	9	8	73	42	47
4 Stirling	36	19	9	8	70	39	47
5 St Mirren	36	19	7	10	79	50	45
6 Montrose	36	18	8	10	82	58	44
7 Cowdenbeath	36	14	10	12	57	53	38
8 Hamilton	36	16	6	14	67	63	38
9 Berwick	36	16	5	15	45	54	37
10 Stenhousemuir	36	14	8	14	44	41	36
11 Queen of the S	36	13	8	15	45	52	34
12 Alloa	36	11	11	14	45	49	33
13 E Stirlingshire	36	12	8	16	52	69	32
14 Queen's Park	36	9	12	15	44	61	30
15 Stranraer	36	13	4	19	56	78	30
16 Forfar	36	10	9	17	38	66	29
17 Clydebank	36	9	6	21	48	72	21
18 Albion	36	5	8	23	35	83	18
19 Brechin	36	5	4	27	46	99	14

Arsenal's defeat in the semi-final at Hillsborough prevented them from becoming the first club this century to appear in three consecutive Cup Finals. It also prevented the first 'repeat' Cup Final of the twentieth century as Leeds were their 1972 opponents.

Sunderland, by defeating Leeds 1-0 in the 1973 Cup Final became only the fifth Second Division side to win the FA Cup. On the way they defeated three of the previous holders – Manchester City, Arsenal and Leeds for a remarkably memorable win.

FA CUP 1972-73

FOURTH ROUND

Arsenal v Bradford City	2-0
Bolton Wanderers v Cardiff City	2-2, 1-1, 1-0
Carlisle United v Sheffield United	2-1
Chelsea v Ipswich Town	2-0
Coventry City v Grimsby Town	1-0
Derby County v Tottenham Hotspur	1-1, 5-3
Everton v Millwall	0-2
Hull City v West Ham United	1-0
Leeds United v Plymouth Argyle	2-1
Liverpool v Manchester City	0-0, 0-2
Newcastle United v Luton Town	0-2
Oxford United v Queen's Park Rangers	0-2
Sheffield Wednesday v Crystal Palace	1-1, 1-1, 3-2
Sunderland v Reading	1-1, 3-1
West Bromwich Albion v Swindon Town	2-0
Wolverhampton Wanderers v Bristol City	1-0

FIFTH ROUND

Bolton Wanderers v Luton Town	0-1
Carlisle United v Arsenal	1-2
Coventry City v Hull City	3-0
Derby County v Queen's Park Rangers	4-2
Leeds United v West Bromwich Albion	2-0
Manchester City v Sunderland	2-2, 1-3
Sheffield Wednesday v Chelsea	1-2
Wolverhampton Wanderers v Millwall	1-0

SIXTH ROUND

Chelsea v Arsenal	2-2, 1-2
Derby County v Leeds United	0-1
Sunderland v Luton Town	2-0
Wolverhampton Wanderers v Coventry City	2-0

SEMI-FINAL

Arsenal v Sunderland	1-2
Leeds United v Wolverhampton Wanderers	1-0

FINAL

Leeds United v Sunderland	0-1

SCOTTISH FA CUP 1972-73

THIRD ROUND

Ayr United v Inverness Thistle	3-0
Berwick Rovers v Falkirk	1-3
Brechin City v Aberdeen	2-4
Celtic v East Fife	4-1
Clyde v Montrose	1-1, 2-4
Dumbarton v Cowdenbeath	4-1
Dunfermline Athletic v Dundee	0-3
Elgin City v Hamilton Academicals	0-1
Heart of Midlothian v Airdrieonians	0-0 1-3
Hibernian v Morton	2-0
Kilmarnock v Queen of the South	2-1
Motherwell v Raith Rovers	2-1
Rangers v Dundee United	1-0
St Mirren v Partick Thistle	0-1
Stirling Albion v Arbroath	3-3, 1-0
Stranraer v St Johnstone	1-1, 2-1

FOURTH ROUND

Ayr United v Stirling Albion	2-1
Dumbarton v Partick Thistle	2-2, 1-3
Kilmarnock v Airdrieonians	0-1
Montrose v Hamilton Academicals	2-2, 1-0
Motherwell v Celtic	0-4
Rangers v Hibernian	1-1, 2-1
Stranraer v Dundee	2-9
Aberdeen v Falkirk	3-1

FIFTH ROUND

Celtic v Aberdeen	0-0, 1-0
Montrose v Dundee	1-4
Partick Thistle v Ayr United	1-5
Rangers v Airdrieonians	2-0

SEMI-FINAL

Ayr United v Rangers	0-2
Celtic v Dundee	0-0, 3-0

FINAL

Celtic v Rangers	2-3

League Tables 1973-74

FIRST DIVISION

		P	W	D	L	F	A	Pts
1	Leeds	42	24	14	4	66	31	62
2	Liverpool	42	22	13	7	52	31	57
3	Derby	42	17	14	11	52	42	48
4	Ipswich	42	18	11	13	67	58	47
5	Stoke	42	15	16	11	54	42	46
6	Burnley	42	16	14	12	56	53	46
7	Everton	42	16	12	14	50	48	44
8	QPR	42	13	17	12	56	52	43
9	Leicester	42	13	16	13	51	41	42
10	Arsenal	42	14	14	14	49	51	42
11	Tottenham	42	14	14	14	45	50	42
12	Wolves	42	13	15	14	49	49	41
13	Sheff United	42	14	12	16	44	49	40
14	Man City†	42	14	12	16	39	46	40
15	Newcastle	42	13	12	17	49	48	38
16	Coventry	42	14	10	18	43	54	38
17	Chelsea	42	12	13	17	56	60	37
18	West Ham	42	11	15	16	55	60	37
19	Birmingham	42	12	13	17	52	64	37
20	Southampton*	42	11	14	17	47	68	36
21	Man United*†	42	10	12	20	38	48	32
22	Norwich*	42	7	15	20	37	62	29

* Three clubs relegated.
† Game at Old Trafford abandoned after 86 minutes. Manchester City, who were leading 1-0, awarded both points.

SECOND DIVISION

		P	W	D	L	F	A	Pts
1	Middlesbrough*	42	27	11	4	77	30	65
2	Luton*	42	19	12	11	64	51	50
3	Carlisle*	42	20	9	13	61	48	49
4	Orient	42	15	18	9	55	42	48
5	Blackpool	42	17	13	12	57	40	47
6	Sunderland	42	19	9	14	58	44	47
7	Nottm Forest	42	15	15	12	57	43	45
8	WBA	42	14	16	12	48	45	44
9	Hull	42	13	17	12	46	47	43
10	Notts County	42	15	13	14	55	60	43
11	Bolton	42	15	12	15	44	40	42
12	Millwall	42	14	14	14	51	51	42
13	Fulham	42	16	10	16	39	43	42
14	Aston Villa	42	13	15	14	48	45	41
15	Portsmouth	42	14	12	16	45	62	40
16	Bristol City	42	14	10	18	47	54	38
17	Cardiff	42	10	16	16	49	62	36
18	Oxford	42	10	16	16	35	46	36
19	Sheff Wed	42	12	11	19	51	63	35
20	Crystal Palace‡	42	11	12	19	43	56	34
21	Preston‡§	42	9	14	19	40	62	31
22	Swindon‡	42	7	11	24	36	72	25

* Three clubs promoted.
‡ Three clubs relegated.
§ Preston had one point deducted for fielding an ineligible player.

THIRD DIVISION

		P	W	D	L	F	A	Pts
1	Oldham‡	46	25	12	9	83	47	62
2	Bristol Rovers‡	46	22	17	7	65	33	61
3	York‡	46	21	19	6	67	38	61
4	Wrexham	46	22	12	12	63	43	56
5	Chesterfield	46	21	14	11	55	42	56
6	Grimsby	46	18	15	13	67	50	51
7	Watford	46	19	12	15	64	56	50
8	Aldershot	46	19	11	16	65	52	49
9	Halifax	46	14	21	11	48	51	49
10	Huddersfield	46	17	13	16	56	55	47
11	Bournemouth	46	16	15	15	54	58	47
12	Southend	46	16	14	16	62	62	46
13	Blackburn	46	18	10	18	62	64	46
14	Charlton	46	19	8	19	66	73	46
15	Walsall	46	16	13	17	57	48	45
16	Tranmere	46	15	15	16	50	44	45
17	Plymouth	46	17	10	19	59	54	44
18	Hereford	46	14	15	17	53	57	43
19	Brighton	46	16	11	19	52	58	43
20	Port Vale	46	14	14	18	52	58	42
21	Cambridge*	46	13	9	24	48	81	35
22	Shrewsbury*	46	10	11	25	41	62	31
23	Southport*	46	6	16	24	35	82	28
24	Rochdale*	46	2	17	27	38	94	21

‡ Three clubs promoted.
* Four clubs relegated.

FOURTH DIVISION

		P	W	D	L	F	A	Pts
1	Peterborough*	46	27	11	8	75	38	65
2	Gillingham*	46	25	12	9	90	49	62
3	Colchester*	46	24	12	10	73	36	60
4	Bury*	46	24	11	11	81	49	59
5	Northampton	46	20	13	13	63	48	53
6	Reading	46	16	19	11	58	37	51
7	Chester	46	17	15	14	54	55	49
8	Bradford	46	17	14	15	58	52	48
9	Newport‡	46	16	14	16	56	65	45
10	Exeter†	45	18	8	19	58	55	44
11	Hartlepool	46	16	12	18	48	47	44
12	Lincoln	46	16	12	18	63	67	44
13	Barnsley	46	17	10	19	58	64	44
14	Swansea	46	16	11	19	45	46	43
15	Rotherham	46	15	13	18	56	58	43
16	Torquay	46	13	17	16	52	57	43
17	Mansfield	46	13	17	16	62	69	43
18	Scunthorpe†	45	14	12	19	47	64	42
19	Brentford	46	12	16	18	48	50	40
20	Darlington	46	13	13	20	40	62	39
21	Crewe	46	14	10	22	43	71	38
22	Doncaster	46	12	11	23	47	80	35
23	Workington	46	11	13	22	43	74	35
24	Stockport	46	7	20	19	44	69	34

† Exeter failed to turn up for their fixture at Scunthorpe and the latter were awarded both points.
‡ Newport had one point deducted for fielding an ineligible player.
* Four clubs promoted.

SCOTTISH FIRST DIVISION

		P	W	D	L	F	A	Pts
1	Celtic	34	23	7	4	82	27	53
2	Hibernian	34	20	9	5	75	42	49
3	Rangers	34	21	6	7	67	34	48
4	Aberdeen	34	13	16	5	46	26	42
5	Dundee	34	16	7	11	67	48	39
6	Hearts	34	14	10	10	54	43	38
7	Ayr	34	15	8	11	44	40	38
8	Dundee United	34	15	7	12	55	51	37
9	Motherwell	34	14	7	13	45	40	35
10	Dumbarton	34	11	7	16	43	58	29
11	Partick	34	9	10	15	33	46	28
12	St Johnstone	34	9	10	15	41	60	28
13	Arbroath	34	10	7	17	52	69	27
14	Morton	34	8	10	16	37	49	26
15	Clyde	34	8	9	17	29	65	25
16	Dunfermline	34	8	8	18	43	65	24
17	East Fife	34	9	6	19	26	51	24
18	Falkirk	34	4	14	16	33	58	22

SCOTTISH SECOND DIVISION

		P	W	D	L	F	A	Pts
1	Airdrieonians	36	28	4	4	102	25	60
2	Kilmarnock	36	26	6	4	96	44	58
3	Hamilton	36	24	7	5	68	38	55
4	Queen of the S	36	20	7	9	73	41	47
5	Raith	36	18	9	9	69	48	45
6	Berwick	36	16	13	7	53	35	45
7	Stirling	36	17	6	13	76	50	40
8	Montrose	36	15	7	14	71	64	37
9	Stranraer	36	14	8	14	64	70	36
10	Clydebank	36	13	8	15	47	48	34
11	St Mirren	36	12	10	14	62	66	34
12	Alloa	36	15	4	17	47	58	34
13	Cowdenbeath	36	11	9	16	59	85	31
14	Queen's Park	36	12	4	20	42	64	28
15	Stenhousemuir	36	11	5	20	44	59	27
16	E Stirlingshire	36	9	5	22	47	73	23
17	Albion	36	7	6	23	38	72	20
18	Forfar	36	5	6	25	42	94	16
19	Brechin	36	5	4	27	33	99	14

FA CUP 1973-74

FOURTH ROUND

Arsenal v Aston Villa	1-1, 0-2
Coventry City v Derby County	0-0, 1-0
Everton v West Bromwich Albion	0-0, 0-1
Fulham v Leicester City	1-1, 1-2
Hereford United v Bristol City	0-1
Liverpool v Carlisle United	0-0, 2-0
Luton Town v Bradford City	3-0
Manchester United v Ipswich Town	0-1
Newcastle United v Scunthorpe United	1-1, 3-0
Nottingham Forest v Manchester City	4-1
Oldham Athletic v Burnley	1-4
Peterborough United v Leeds United	1-4
Portsmouth v Orient	0-0, 1-1, 2-0
Queen's Park Rangers v Birmingham City	2-0
Southampton v Bolton Wanderers	3-3, 2-0
Wrexham v Middlesbrough	1-0

FIFTH ROUND

Bristol City v Leeds United	1-1, 1-0
Burnley v Aston Villa	1-0
Coventry City v Queen's Park Rangers	0-0, 2-3
Liverpool v Ipswich Town	2-0
Luton Town v Leicester City	0-4
Nottingham Forest v Portsmouth	1-0
Southampton v Wrexham	0-1
West Bromwich Albion v Newcastle United	0-3

SIXTH ROUND

Bristol City v Liverpool	0-1
Burnley v Wrexham	1-0
Newcastle United v Nottingham Forest	4-3*, 0-0, 1-0
Queen's Park Rangers v Leicester City	0-2

*FA ordered replay because of crowd invasion. Second and third games both played at Goodison Park.

SEMI-FINAL

Burnley v Newcastle United	0-2
Leicester City v Liverpool	0-0, 1-3

FINAL

Liverpool v Newcastle United	3-0

SCOTTISH FA CUP 1973-74

THIRD ROUND

Aberdeen v Dundee	0-2
Arbroath v Dumbarton	1-0
Celtic v Clydebank	6-1
Cowdenbeath v Ayr United	0-5
Dundee United v Airdrieonians	4-1
Falkirk v Dunfermline Athletic	2-2, 0-1
Forfar Athletic v St Johnstone	1-6
Heart of Midlothian v Clyde	3-1
Hibernian v Kilmarnock	5-2
Montrose v Stirling Albion	1-1, 1-3
Motherwell v Brechin City	2-0
Partick Thistle v Ferranti Thistle	6-1
Queen of the South v East Fife	1-0
Raith Rovers v Morton	2-2, 0-0, 0-1
Rangers v Queen's Park	8-0
Stranraer v St Mirren	1-1, 1-1, 3-2

FOURTH ROUND

Arbroath v Motherwell	1-3
Celtic v Stirling Albion	6-1
Dundee United v Morton	1-0
Dunfermline Athletic v Queen of the South	1-0
Heart of Midlothian v Partick Thistle	1-1, 4-1
Rangers v Dundee	0-3
St Johnstone v Hibernian	1-3
Stranraer v Ayr United	1-7

FIFTH ROUND

Celtic v Motherwell	2-2, 1-0
Dunfermline Athletic v Dundee United	1-1, 0-4
Heart of Midlothian v Ayr United	1-1, 2-1
Hibernian v Dundee	3-3, 0-3

SEMI-FINAL

Celtic v Dundee	1-0
Heart of Midlothian v Dundee United	1-1, 2-4

FINAL

Celtic v Dundee United	3-0

League Tables 1974-75

FIRST DIVISION

		P	W	D	L	F	A	Pts
1	Derby	42	21	11	10	67	49	53
2	Liverpool	42	20	11	11	60	39	51
3	Ipswich	42	23	5	14	66	44	51
4	Everton	42	16	18	8	56	42	50
5	Stoke	42	17	15	10	64	48	49
6	Sheff United	42	18	13	11	58	51	49
7	Middlesbrough	42	18	12	12	54	40	48
8	Man City	42	18	10	14	54	54	46
9	Leeds	42	16	13	13	57	49	45
10	Burnley	42	17	11	14	68	67	45
11	QPR	42	16	10	16	54	54	42
12	Wolverhampton	42	14	11	17	57	54	39
13	West Ham	42	13	13	16	58	59	39
14	Coventry	42	12	15	15	51	62	39
15	Newcastle	42	15	9	18	59	72	39
16	Arsenal	42	13	11	18	47	49	37
17	Birmingham	42	14	9	19	53	61	37
18	Leicester	42	12	12	18	46	60	36
19	Tottenham	42	13	8	21	52	63	34
20	Luton	42	11	11	20	47	65	33
21	Chelsea	42	9	15	18	42	72	33
22	Carlisle	42	12	5	25	43	59	29

SECOND DIVISION

		P	W	D	L	F	A	Pts
1	Man United	42	26	9	7	66	30	61
2	Aston Villa	42	25	8	9	69	32	58
3	Norwich	42	20	13	9	58	37	53
4	Sunderland	42	19	13	10	65	35	51
5	Bristol City	42	21	8	13	47	33	50
6	WBA	42	18	9	15	54	42	45
7	Blackpool	42	14	17	11	38	33	45
8	Hull	42	15	14	13	40	53	44
9	Fulham	42	13	16	13	44	39	42
10	Bolton	42	15	12	15	45	41	42
11	Oxford	42	15	12	15	41	51	42
12	Orient	42	11	20	11	28	39	42
13	Southampton	42	15	11	16	53	54	41
14	Notts County	42	12	16	14	49	59	40
15	York	42	14	10	18	51	55	38
16	Nottm Forest	42	12	14	16	43	55	38
17	Portsmouth	42	12	13	17	44	54	37
18	Oldham	42	10	15	17	40	48	35
19	Bristol Rovers	42	12	11	19	42	64	35
20	Millwall	42	10	12	20	44	56	32
21	Cardiff	42	9	14	19	36	62	32
22	Sheff Wed	42	5	11	26	29	64	21

THIRD DIVISION

		P	W	D	L	F	A	Pts
1	Blackburn	46	22	16	8	68	45	60
2	Plymouth	46	24	11	11	79	58	59
3	Charlton Ath	46	22	11	13	76	61	55
4	Swindon	46	21	11	14	64	58	53
5	Crystal Palace	46	18	15	13	66	57	51
6	Port Vale	46	18	15	13	61	54	51
7	Peterborough	46	19	12	15	47	53	50
8	Walsall	46	18	13	15	67	52	49
9	Preston NE	46	19	11	16	63	56	49
10	Gillingham	46	17	14	15	65	60	48
11	Colchester	46	17	13	16	70	63	47
12	Hereford	46	16	14	16	64	66	46
13	Wrexham	46	15	15	16	65	55	45
14	Bury	46	16	12	18	53	50	44
15	Chesterfield	46	16	12	18	62	66	44
16	Grimsby	46	15	13	18	55	64	43
17	Halifax	46	13	17	16	49	65	43
18	Southend	46	13	16	17	46	51	42
19	Brighton	46	16	10	20	56	64	42
20	Aldershot	46	14	11	21	53	63	38*
21	Bournemouth	46	13	12	21	44	58	38
22	Tranmere	46	14	9	23	55	57	37
23	Watford	46	10	17	19	52	75	37
24	Huddersfield	46	11	10	25	47	76	32

*One point deducted for playing unregistered player.

FOURTH DIVISION

		P	W	D	L	F	A	Pts
1	Mansfield	46	28	12	6	90	40	68
2	Shrewsbury	46	26	10	10	80	43	62
3	Rotherham	46	22	15	9	71	41	59
4	Chester	46	23	11	12	64	38	57
5	Lincoln	46	21	15	10	79	48	57
6	Cambridge	46	20	14	12	62	44	54
7	Reading	46	21	10	15	63	47	52
8	Brentford	46	18	13	15	53	45	49
9	Exeter	46	19	11	16	60	63	49
10	Bradford	46	17	13	16	56	51	47
11	Southport	46	15	17	14	56	56	47
12	Newport	46	19	9	18	68	75	47
13	Hartlepool	46	16	11	19	52	62	43
14	Torquay	46	14	14	18	46	61	42
15	Barnsley	46	15	11	20	62	65	41
16	Northampton	46	15	11	20	67	73	41
17	Doncaster	46	14	12	20	65	79	40
18	Crewe	46	11	18	17	34	47	40
19	Rochdale	46	13	13	20	59	75	39
20	Stockport	46	12	14	20	43	70	38
21	Darlington	46	13	10	23	54	67	36
22	Swansea	46	15	6	25	26	73	36
23	Workington	46	10	11	25	46	66	31
24	Scunthorpe	46	7	15	24	41	78	29

SCOTTISH FIRST DIVISION

		P	W	D	L	F	A	Pts
1	Rangers	34	25	6	3	86	33	56
2	Hibernian	34	20	9	5	69	37	49
3	Celtic	34	20	5	9	81	41	45
4	Dundee United	34	19	7	8	72	43	41
5	Aberdeen	34	16	9	9	66	43	38
6	Dundee	34	16	6	12	48	42	36
7	Ayr	34	14	8	12	50	61	35
8	Hearts	34	11	13	10	47	52	34
9	St Johnstone	34	11	12	11	41	44	33
10	Motherwell	34	14	5	15	52	57	31
11	Airdrie	34	11	9	14	43	55	31
12	Kilmarnock	34	8	15	11	52	68	31
13	Partick	34	10	10	14	48	62	30
14	Dumbarton	34	7	10	17	44	55	24
15	Dumfermline	34	7	9	18	46	66	23
16	Clyde	34	6	10	18	40	63	22
17	Morton	34	6	10	18	31	62	22
18	Arbroath	34	5	7	22	34	66	17

SCOTTISH SECOND DIVISION

		P	W	D	L	F	A	Pts
1	Falkirk	38	26	2	10	76	29	54
2	Queen of the S	38	23	7	8	77	33	53
3	Montrose	38	23	7	8	70	37	53
4	Hamilton	38	21	7	10	69	30	49
5	East Fife	38	20	9	11	57	42	47
6	St Mirren	38	19	8	11	74	52	46
7	Clydebank	38	18	8	12	50	40	44
8	Stirling	38	17	9	12	67	55	43
9	Berwick	38	17	6	15	53	49	40
10	E. Stirlingshire	38	16	8	14	56	52	40
11	Stenhousemuir	38	14	11	13	52	42	39
12	Albion	38	16	7	15	72	64	39
13	Raith	38	14	9	15	48	44	37
14	Stranraer	38	12	11	15	47	69	35
15	Alloa	38	11	11	16	49	56	33
16	Queen's Park	38	10	10	18	41	54	30
17	Brechin	38	9	7	22	44	85	25
18	Meadowbank	38	9	5	24	26	87	23
19	Cowdenbeath	38	5	12	22	39	78	21
20	Forfar	38	1	7	30	27	102	9

FA CUP 1974-75

FOURTH ROUND

Queens Park Rangers v Notts County	3-0
Aston Villa v Sheffield United	4-1
Bury v Mansfield Town	1-2
Carlisle United v West Bromwich Albion	3-2
Chelsea v Birmingham City	0-1
Coventry City v Arsenal	1-1, 3-0
Ipswich Town v Liverpool	1-0
Leatherhead v Leicester City	2-3
Leeds United v Wimbledon	0-0, 1-0
Middlesbrough v Sunderland	3-1
Plymouth Argyle v Everton	1-3
Stafford Rangers v Peterborough United	1-2
Walsall v Newcastle United	1-0
West Ham United v Swindon Town	1-1, 2-1
Derby County v Bristol Rovers	2-0
Fulham v Nottingham Forest	0-0, 1-1, 1-1, 2-1

FIFTH ROUND

Arsenal v Leicester City	0-0, 1-0
Birmingham City v Walsall	2-1
Everton v Fulham	1-2
Ipswich Town v Aston Villa	3-2
Mansfield Town v Carlisle United	0-1
Peterborough United v Middlesbrough	1-1, 2-0
West Ham United v Queen's Park Rangers	2-1
Derby County v Leeds United	0-1

SIXTH ROUND

Arsenal v West Ham United	0-2
Birmingham City v Middlesbrough	1-0
Carlisle United v Fulham	0-1
Ipswich Town v Leeds United	0-0, 1-1, 0-0, 3-2

SEMI-FINAL

Fulham v Birmingham City	1-1, 1-0
West Ham United v Ipswich Town	0-0, 2-1

FINAL

Fulham v West Ham United	0-2

SCOTTISH FA CUP 1974-75

THIRD ROUND

Aberdeen v Rangers	1-1, 2-1
Arbroath v East Stirling	1-0
Ayr United v Queen's Park	1-2
Clyde v Dundee	0-1
Hibernian v Celtic	0-2
Inverness Caledonian v Albion Rovers	0-1
Motherwell v Partick Thistle	0-0, 1-0
Queen of the South v Raith Rovers	2-0
Montrose v Hamilton Academicals	0-0, 0-3
Airdrieonians v Morton	0-0, 3-0
Clydebank v Dunfermline Athletic	2-1
Dumbarton v Inverness Clachnacuddin	2-1
Heart of Midlothian v Kilmarnock	2-0
St. Johnstone v East Fife	1-0
Ross County v Falkirk	1-5
Dundee United v Berwick Rangers	1-1, 1-0

FOURTH ROUND

Airdrieonians v Falkirk	2-0
Arbroath v Albion Rovers	2-0
Celtic v Clydebank	4-1
Hamilton Academicals v Dumbarton	0-1
Motherwell v Queen's Park	4-0
Queen of the South v Heart of Midlothian	0-2
St. Johnstone v Dundee	0-1
Dundee United v Aberdeen	0-1

FIFTH ROUND

Aberdeen v Motherwell	0-1
Arbroath v Airdrieonians	2-2, 0-3
Dumbarton v Celtic	1-2
Heart of Midlothian v Dundee	1-1, 2-3

SEMI-FINAL

Celtic v Dundee	1-0
Airdrieonians v Motherwell	1-1, 1-0

FINAL

Airdrieonians v Celtic	1-3

League Tables 1975-76

FIRST DIVISION

		P	W	D	L	F	A	Pts
1	Liverpool	42	23	14	5	66	31	60
2	QPR	42	24	11	7	67	33	59
3	Man United	42	23	10	10	68	42	56
4	Derby	42	21	11	10	75	58	53
5	Leeds	42	21	9	12	65	46	51
6	Ipswich	42	16	14	12	54	48	46
7	Leicester	42	13	19	10	48	51	45
8	Man City	42	16	12	15	64	46	43
9	Tottenham	42	14	15	13	63	63	43
10	Norwich	42	16	10	16	58	58	42
11	Everton	42	15	12	15	60	66	42
12	Stoke	42	15	11	16	48	50	41
13	Middlesbrough	42	15	10	17	46	45	40
14	Coventry	42	13	14	15	47	57	40
15	Newcastle	42	15	9	18	71	62	39
16	Aston Villa	42	11	17	14	51	59	39
17	Arsenal	42	13	10	19	47	53	36
18	West Ham	42	13	10	19	48	71	36
19	Birmingham	42	13	7	22	57	75	33
20	Wolverhampton	42	10	10	22	51	68	30
21	Burnley	42	9	10	23	43	66	28
22	Sheff United	42	6	10	26	33	82	22

THIRD DIVISION

		P	W	D	L	F	A	Pts
1	Hereford	46	26	11	9	86	55	63
2	Cardiff	46	22	13	11	69	48	57
3	Millwall	46	20	16	10	54	43	56
4	Brighton	46	22	9	15	78	53	53
5	Crystal Palace	46	18	17	11	61	46	53
6	Wrexham	46	20	12	14	66	55	52
7	Walsall	46	18	14	14	74	61	50
8	Preston	46	19	10	17	62	57	48
9	Shrewsbury	46	19	10	17	61	59	48
10	Peterborough	46	15	18	13	63	63	48
11	Mansfield	46	16	15	15	58	52	47
12	Port Vale	46	15	16	15	55	54	46
13	Bury	46	14	16	16	51	46	44
14	Chesterfield	46	17	9	20	69	69	43
15	Gillingham	46	12	19	15	58	68	43
16	Rotherham	46	15	12	19	54	65	42
17	Chester	46	15	12	19	53	62	42
18	Grimsby	46	15	10	21	62	74	40
19	Swindon	46	16	8	22	62	75	40
20	Sheff Wed	46	12	16	18	48	59	40
21	Aldershot	46	13	13	20	59	75	39
22	Colchester	46	12	14	20	41	65	38
23	Southend	46	12	13	21	65	75	37
24	Halifax	46	11	13	22	41	61	35

FOURTH DIVISION

		P	W	D	L	F	A	Pts
1	Lincoln	46	32	10	4	111	39	74
2	Northampton	46	29	10	7	87	40	68
3	Reading	46	24	12	10	70	51	60
4	Tranmere	46	24	10	12	89	55	58
5	Huddersfield	46	21	14	11	55	41	56
6	Bournemouth	46	20	12	14	57	48	52
7	Exeter	46	18	14	14	56	47	50
8	Watford	46	22	6	18	62	62	50
9	Torquay	46	18	14	14	55	63	50
10	Doncaster	46	19	11	16	75	69	49
11	Swansea	46	16	15	15	66	57	47
12	Barnsley	46	14	16	16	52	48	44
13	Cambridge	46	14	15	17	58	62	43
14	Hartlepool	46	16	10	20	62	78	42
15	Rochdale	46	12	18	16	40	54	42
16	Crewe	46	13	15	18	58	57	41
17	Bradford	46	12	17	17	63	65	41
18	Brentford	46	14	13	19	56	60	41
19	Scunthorpe	46	14	10	22	50	59	38
20	Darlington	46	14	10	22	48	57	38
21	Stockport	46	13	12	21	43	76	38
22	Newport	46	13	9	24	57	90	35
23	Southport	46	8	10	28	41	57	26
24	Workington	46	7	7	32	30	87	27

SECOND DIVISION

		P	W	D	L	F	A	Pts
1	Sunderland	42	24	8	10	67	36	56
2	Bristol City	42	19	15	8	59	35	53
3	WBA	42	20	13	9	50	33	53
4	Bolton	42	20	12	10	64	38	52
5	Notts County	42	19	11	12	60	41	49
6	Southampton	42	21	7	14	66	50	49
7	Luton	42	19	10	13	61	51	48
8	Nottm Forest	42	17	12	13	55	40	46
9	Charlton	42	15	12	15	61	72	42
10	Blackpool	42	14	14	14	40	49	42
11	Chelsea	42	12	16	14	53	54	40
12	Fulham	42	13	14	15	45	47	40
13	Orient	42	13	14	15	37	39	40
14	Hull	42	14	11	17	45	49	39
15	Blackburn	42	12	14	16	45	50	38
16	Plymouth	42	13	12	17	48	54	38
17	Oldham	42	13	12	17	57	68	38
18	Bristol Rovers	42	11	16	15	38	50	38
19	Carlisle	42	12	13	17	45	59	37
20	Oxford	42	11	11	20	39	59	33
21	York	42	10	8	24	39	71	28
22	Portsmouth	42	9	7	26	32	61	25

SCOTTISH PREMIER DIVISION

		P	W	D	L	F	A	Pts
1	Rangers	36	23	8	5	59	24	54
2	Celtic	36	21	6	9	71	42	48
3	Hibernian	36	20	7	9	58	40	43
4	Motherwell	36	16	8	12	57	49	40
5	Hearts	36	13	9	14	39	44	35
6	Ayr	36	14	5	17	46	59	33
7	Aberdeen	36	11	10	15	49	50	32
8	Dundee United	36	12	8	16	46	48	32
9	Dundee	36	11	10	15	49	62	32
10	St Johnstone	36	3	5	28	29	79	11

SCOTTISH FIRST DIVISION

		P	W	D	L	F	A	Pts
1	Partick Thistle	26	17	7	2	47	19	40
2	Kilmarnock	26	16	3	7	44	29	40
3	Montrose	26	12	6	8	53	43	35
4	Dumbarton	26	12	4	10	53	46	29
5	Arbroath	26	11	4	11	41	39	29
6	St Mirren	26	9	8	9	37	37	25
7	Airdrieonians	26	7	11	8	44	41	25
8	Falkirk	26	10	5	11	38	35	24
9	Hamilton	26	7	10	9	37	37	24
10	Queen of the S	26	9	6	11	41	47	23
11	Morton	26	7	9	10	31	40	19
12	East Fife	26	8	7	11	39	53	18
13	Dunfermline	26	5	10	11	30	51	17
14	Clyde	26	5	4	17	34	52	16

SCOTTISH SECOND DIVISION

		P	W	D	L	F	A	Pts
1	Clydebank	26	17	6	3	44	13	40
2	Raith	26	15	10	1	45	22	40
3	Alloa	26	14	7	5	44	28	35
4	Queen's Park	26	10	9	7	41	33	29
5	Cowdenbeath	26	11	7	8	44	43	29
6	Stirling Albion	26	9	7	10	39	32	25
7	Stranraer	26	11	3	12	49	43	25
8	East Stirling	26	8	8	10	33	33	24
9	Albion	26	7	10	9	35	38	24
10	Stenhousemuir	26	9	5	12	39	44	23
11	Berwick	26	7	5	14	32	44	19
12	Forfar	26	4	10	12	28	48	18
13	Brechin	26	6	5	15	28	51	17
14	Meadowbank T	26	5	6	15	24	53	16

FA CUP 1975-76

FOURTH ROUND

Bradford City v Tooting & Mitcham United	3-1
Charlton Athletic v Portsmouth	1-1, 3-0
Coventry City v Newcastle United	1-1, 0-5
Derby County v Liverpool	1-0
Huddersfield Town v Bolton Wanderers	0-1
Ipswich Town v Wolverhampton Wanderers	0-0, 0-1
Leeds United v Crystal Palace	0-1
Leicester City v Bury	1-0
Manchester United v Peterborough United	3-1
Norwich City v Luton Town	2-0
Southampton v Blackpool	3-1
Southend United v Cardiff City	2-1
Stoke City v Manchester City	1-0
Sunderland v Hull City	1-0
West Bromwich Albion v Lincoln City	3-2
York City v Chelsea	0-2

FIFTH ROUND

Bolton Wanderers v Newcastle United	3-3, 0-0, 1-2
Chelsea v Crystal Palace	2-3
Derby County v Southend United	1-0
Leicester City v Manchester United	1-2
Norwich City v Bradford City	1-2
Stoke City v Sunderland	0-0, 1-2
West Bromwich Albion v Southampton	1-1, 0-4
Wolverhampton Wanderers v Charlton Athletic	3-0

SIXTH ROUND

Bradford City v Southampton	0-1
Derby County v Newcastle United	4-2
Manchester Utd v Wolverhampton Wanderers	1-1, 3-2
Sunderland v Crystal Palace	0-1

SEMI-FINAL

Manchester United v Derby County	2-0
Southampton v Crystal Palace	2-0

FINAL

Southampton v Manchester United	1-0

SCOTTISH FA CUP 1975-76

THIRD ROUND

Albion Rovers v Partick Thistle	1-2
Alloa Athletic v Aberdeen	0-4
Ayr United v Airdrieonians	4-2
Cowdenbeath v St Mirren	3-0
Dumbarton v Keith	2-0
Dundee v Falkirk	1-2
Dundee United v Hamilton Academicals	4-0
Heart of Midlothian v Clyde	2-2, 1-0
Hibernian v Dunfermline Athletic	3-2
Motherwell v Celtic	3-2
Morton v Montrose	1-3
Queen of the South v St Johnstone	3-2
Raith Rovers v Arbroath	1-0
Rangers v East Fife	3-0
Stenhousemuir v Kilmarnock	1-1, 0-1
Stirling Albion v Forfar Athletic	2-1

FOURTH ROUND

Ayr United v Queen of the South	2-2, 4-5
Cowdenbeath v Motherwell	0-2
Heart of Midlothian v Stirling Albion	3-0
Hibernian v Dundee United	1-1, 2-0
Kilmarnock v Falkirk	3-1
Montrose v Raith Rovers	2-1
Partick Thistle v Dumbarton	0-0, 0-1
Rangers v Aberdeen	4-1

FIFTH ROUND

Dumbarton v Kilmarnock	2-1
Montrose v Heart of Midlothian	2-2, 2-2, 1-2
Motherwell v Hibernian	2-2, 1-1, 2-1
Queen of the South v Rangers	0-3

SEMI-FINAL

Motherwell v Rangers	2-3
Dumbarton v Heart of Midlothian	0-0, 0-3

FINAL

Heart of Midlothian v Rangers	1-3

League Tables 1976-77

FIRST DIVISION

		P	W	D	L	F	A	Pts
1	Liverpool	42	23	11	8	62	33	57
2	Man City	42	21	14	7	60	34	56
3	Ipswich	42	22	8	12	66	39	56
4	Aston Villa	42	22	7	13	76	50	51
5	Newcastle	42	18	13	11	64	49	49
6	Man United	42	18	11	13	71	62	47
7	WBA	42	16	13	13	62	56	45
8	Arsenal	42	16	11	15	64	59	43
9	Everton	42	14	14	14	62	64	42
10	Leeds	42	15	12	15	48	51	42
11	Leicester	42	12	18	12	47	60	42
12	Middlesbrough	42	14	13	15	40	45	41
13	Birmingham	42	13	12	17	63	61	38
14	QPR	42	13	12	17	47	52	38
15	Derby	42	9	19	14	50	55	37
16	Norwich	42	14	9	19	47	64	37
17	West Ham	42	11	14	17	46	65	36
18	Bristol City	42	11	13	18	38	48	35
19	Coventry	42	10	15	17	48	59	35
20	Sunderland	42	11	12	19	46	54	34
21	Stoke	42	10	14	18	28	51	34
22	Tottenham	42	12	9	21	48	72	33

SECOND DIVISION

		P	W	D	L	F	A	Pts
1	Wolves	42	22	13	7	84	45	57
2	Chelsea	42	21	13	8	73	53	55
3	Nottm Forest	42	21	10	11	77	43	52
4	Bolton	42	10	11	11	74	54	51
5	Blackpool	42	17	17	8	58	42	51
6	Luton	42	23	6	15	67	48	48
7	Charlton	42	16	16	10	71	58	48
8	Notts County	42	19	10	13	65	60	48
9	Southampton	42	17	10	15	72	67	44
10	Millwall	42	17	13	14	57	53	43
11	Sheff United	42	14	12	16	54	63	40
12	Blackburn	42	15	9	18	42	54	39
13	Oldham	42	14	10	18	52	64	38
14	Hull	42	10	17	15	45	53	37
15	Bristol Rovers	42	12	13	17	53	68	37
16	Burnley	42	11	14	17	46	64	36
17	Fulham	42	11	13	18	44	61	35
18	Cardiff	42	12	10	20	56	67	34
19	Orient	42	9	16	17	37	55	34
20	Carlisle	42	11	12	19	49	75	34
21	Plymouth	42	8	16	18	46	65	32
22	Hereford	42	8	15	19	57	78	31

THIRD DIVISION

		P	W	D	L	F	A	Pts
1	Mansfield	46	28	8	10	78	33	64
2	Brighton	46	25	11	10	83	39	61
3	Crystal Palace	46	23	13	10	68	40	59
4	Rotherham	46	22	15	9	69	44	59
5	Wrexham	46	24	10	12	80	54	58
6	Preston	46	21	12	13	64	43	54
7	Bury	46	23	8	15	64	59	54
8	Sheff Wed	46	22	9	15	65	55	53
9	Lincoln	46	25	14	13	77	70	52
10	Shrewsbury	46	18	11	17	65	59	47
11	Swindon	46	15	15	16	68	75	45
12	Gillingham	46	14	12	18	55	64	44
13	Chester	46	18	8	20	48	58	44
14	Tranmere	46	13	17	16	51	53	43
15	Walsall	46	13	15	18	57	65	41
16	Peterborough	46	13	15	18	55	65	41
17	Oxford	46	12	15	19	55	65	39
18	Chesterfield	46	14	10	22	56	64	38
19	Port Vale	46	11	16	19	47	71	38
20	Portsmouth	46	11	14	21	43	70	35
21	Reading	46	13	9	24	49	73	35
22	Northampton	46	13	8	25	60	75	34
23	Grimsby	46	12	9	25	45	69	33
24	York	46	10	12	24	50	89	32

FOURTH DIVISION

		P	W	D	L	F	A	Pts
1	Cambridge	46	26	13	7	87	40	65
2	Exeter	46	25	12	9	70	46	62
3	Colchester	46	25	9	12	77	43	59
4	Bradford	46	23	13	10	71	51	59
5	Swansea	46	25	8	13	82	68	58
6	Barnsley	46	23	9	14	62	39	55
7	Watford	46	18	15	13	67	55	51
8	Doncaster	46	21	9	16	61	65	51
9	Huddersfield	46	19	12	15	60	49	50
10	Southend	46	15	19	12	52	45	49
11	Darlington	46	18	13	15	59	64	49
12	Crewe	46	19	11	16	47	60	49
13	Bournemouth	46	15	18	13	55	44	48
14	Stockport	46	13	19	14	53	57	45
15	Brentford	46	18	7	21	77	76	43
16	Torquay	46	17	9	20	59	67	43
17	Aldershot	46	16	11	19	45	59	43
18	Rochdale	46	13	12	21	50	59	38
19	Newport	46	14	10	22	42	58	38
20	Scunthorpe	46	13	11	22	49	73	37
21	Halifax	46	11	14	21	47	58	36
22	Hartlepool	46	10	12	24	77	73	32
23	Southport	46	3	19	24	53	77	25
24	Workington	46	4	11	31	41	102	19

SCOTTISH PREMIER DIVISION

		P	W	D	L	F	A	Pts
1	Celtic	36	23	9	4	79	39	55
2	Rangers	36	18	10	8	62	37	46
3	Aberdeen	36	16	11	9	56	42	43
4	Dundee United	36	16	9	11	54	45	41
5	Partick Thistle	36	11	13	12	40	44	35
6	Hibernian	36	8	18	10	34	35	34
7	Motherwell	36	10	11	14	57	50	32
8	Ayr	36	11	8	17	44	68	30
9	Hearts	36	7	13	16	49	66	27
10	Kilmarnock	36	4	9	23	32	71	17

SCOTTISH FIRST DIVISION

		P	W	D	L	F	A	Pts
1	St Mirren	39	25	12	2	91	38	62
2	Clydebank	39	24	10	5	89	38	58
3	Dundee	39	21	9	9	90	55	51
4	Morton	39	20	10	9	77	52	50
5	Montrose	39	16	9	14	61	62	41
6	Airdrieonians	39	13	12	14	63	58	38
7	Dumbarton	39	14	9	16	63	68	37
8	Arbroath	39	17	3	19	46	62	37
9	Queen of the S	39	11	13	15	58	65	35
10	Hamilton	39	11	14	18	44	55	32
11	St Johnstone	39	8	13	18	44	64	29
12	East Fife	39	8	13	18	40	71	29
13	Raith	39	8	11	20	45	68	27
14	Falkirk	39	6	8	25	36	85	20

SCOTTISH SECOND DIVISION

		P	W	D	L	F	A	Pts
1	Stirling	39	22	11	6	59	29	55
2	Alloa	39	19	13	7	73	45	51
3	Dunfermline	39	20	10	11	52	36	50
4	Stranraer	39	20	6	13	74	53	46
5	Queens Park	39	17	11	11	65	51	45
6	Albion	39	15	12	12	74	60	42
7	Clyde	39	15	11	13	68	65	41
8	Berwick	39	13	10	16	37	51	36
9	Stenhousemuir	39	15	5	19	38	49	35
10	E Stirlingshire	39	12	8	19	47	63	32
11	Meadowbank	39	8	16	15	41	57	32
12	Cowdenbeath	39	13	5	21	45	64	31
13	Brechin	39	7	12	20	57	77	26
14	Forfar	39	7	10	22	43	68	24

FA CUP 1976-77

FOURTH ROUND

Arsenal v Coventry	3-1
Aston Villa v West Ham	3-0
Birmingham v Leeds	1-2
Blackburn v Orient	3-0
Cardiff v Wrexham	3-2
Chester v Luton	1-0
Colchester v Derby	1-1, 0-1
Ipswich v Wolverhampton Wanderers	2-2, 0-1
Liverpool v Carlisle	3-0
Manchester United v Queen's Park Rangers	1-0
Middlesbrough v Hereford	4-0
Northwich Victoria v Oldham	1-3*
Port Vale v Burnley	2-1
Swindon v Everton	2-2, 1-2
Nottingham Forest v Southampton	3-3, 1-2
Newcastle v Manchester City	1-3

FIFTH ROUND

Aston Villa v Port Vale	3-0
Cardiff v Everton	1-2
Derby v Blackburn	3-1
Leeds v Manchester City	1-0
Liverpool v Oldham	3-1
Middlesbrough v Arsenal	4-1
Southampton v Manchester United	2-2, 1-2
Wolverhampton Wanderers v Chester	1-0

SIXTH ROUND

Everton v Derby	2-0
Liverpool v Middlesbrough	2-0
Manchester United v Aston Villa	2-1
Wolverhampton Wanderers v Leeds	0-1

SEMI-FINALS

Everton v Liverpool (both games at Maine Rd)	2-2, 0-3
Leeds v Manchester United (at Hillsborough)	1-2

FINAL

Liverpool v Manchester United	1-2

*played at Maine Rd.

SCOTTISH FA CUP 1976-77

THIRD ROUND

Airdrie v Celtic	1-1, 0-5
Arbroath v Brechin	1-0
Dunfermline v Aberdeen	0-1
East Fife v Clyde	2-1
East Stirling v Albion	0-3
Heart of Midlothian v Dumbarton	1-1, 1-0
Morton v Ayr United	0-1
Motherwell v Kilmarnock	3-0
Queen's Park v Alloa	0-0, 0-1
Queen of the South v Montrose	3-2
Rangers v Falkirk	3-1
St Mirren v Dundee	4-1
Stirling Albion v Elgin City	1-1, 2-3
St Johnstone v Dundee	1-1, 2-4
Hamilton v Clydebank	0-0, 0-3
Hibernian v Partick Thistle	3-0

FOURTH ROUND

Arbroath v Hibernian	1-1, 2-1
Dundee v Aberdeen	0-0, 2-1
East Fife v Albion	2-1
Heart of Midlothian v Clydebank	1-0
Motherwell v St Mirren	2-1
Queen of the South v Alloa	2-1
Rangers v Elgin City	3-0
Celtic v Ayr United	1-1, 3-1

FIFTH ROUND

Celtic v Queen of the South	5-1
Heart of Midlothian v East Fife	0-0, 3-1
Rangers v Motherwell	2-0
Arbroath v Dundee	1-3

SEMI-FINALS

Celtic v Dundee	2-0
Rangers v Heart of Midlothian	2-0

FINAL

Celtic v Rangers	1-0

League Tables 1977-78

FIRST DIVISION

		P	W	D	L	F	A	Pts
1	Nottm Forest	42	25	14	3	69	24	64
2	Liverpool	42	24	9	9	65	34	57
3	Everton	42	22	11	9	76	45	55
4	Man City	42	20	12	10	74	51	52
5	Arsenal	42	21	10	11	60	37	52
6	WBA	42	18	14	10	62	53	50
7	Coventry	42	18	12	12	75	62	48
8	Aston Villa	42	18	10	14	57	42	46
9	Leeds	42	18	10	14	63	53	46
10	Man United	42	16	10	16	67	63	42
11	Birmingham	42	16	9	17	55	60	41
12	Derby	42	14	13	15	54	59	41
13	Norwich	42	11	18	13	52	66	40
14	Middlesbrough	42	12	15	15	42	54	39
15	Wolves	42	12	12	18	51	64	36
16	Chelsea	42	11	14	17	46	69	36
17	Bristol City	42	11	13	18	49	53	35
18	Ipswich	42	11	13	18	47	61	35
19	QPR	42	9	15	18	47	64	33
20	West Ham	42	12	8	22	52	69	32
21	Newcastle	42	6	10	26	42	78	22
22	Leicester	42	5	12	25	26	70	22

SECOND DIVISION

		P	W	D	L	F	A	Pts
1	Bolton	42	24	10	8	63	33	58
2	Southampton	42	22	13	7	70	39	57
3	Tottenham	42	20	16	6	83	49	56
4	Brighton	42	22	12	8	63	38	56
5	Blackburn	42	16	13	13	56	60	45
6	Sunderland	42	14	16	12	67	59	44
7	Stoke	42	16	10	16	53	49	42
8	Oldham	42	13	16	13	54	58	42
9	Crystal Palace	42	13	15	14	50	47	41
10	Fulham	42	14	13	15	49	49	41
11	Burnley	42	15	10	17	56	64	40
12	Sheff United	42	16	8	18	62	73	40
13	Luton	42	14	10	18	54	52	38
14	Orient	42	10	18	14	43	49	38
15	Notts County	42	11	16	15	54	62	38
16	Millwall	42	12	14	16	49	57	38
17	Charlton	42	13	12	17	55	68	38
18	Bristol Rovers	42	13	12	17	61	77	38
19	Cardiff	42	13	12	17	51	71	38
20	Blackpool	42	12	13	17	59	60	37
21	Mansfield	42	10	11	21	49	69	31
22	Hull	42	8	12	22	34	52	28

THIRD DIVISION

		P	W	D	L	F	A	Pts
1	Wrexham	46	23	15	8	78	45	61
2	Cambridge	46	23	12	11	72	51	58
3	Preston	46	20	16	10	63	38	56
4	Peterborough	46	20	16	10	47	33	56
5	Chester	46	16	22	8	59	56	54
6	Walsall	46	18	17	11	61	50	53
7	Gillingham	46	15	20	11	67	60	50
8	Colchester	46	15	18	13	55	44	48
9	Chesterfield	46	17	14	15	58	49	48
10	Swindon	46	16	16	14	67	60	48
11	Shrewsbury	46	16	15	15	63	57	47
12	Tranmere	46	16	15	15	57	52	47
13	Carlisle	46	14	19	13	59	59	47
14	Sheff Wed	46	15	16	15	50	52	46
15	Bury	46	13	19	14	62	56	45
16	Lincoln	46	15	15	16	53	61	45
17	Exeter	46	15	14	17	49	59	44
18	Oxford	46	13	14	19	64	67	40
19	Plymouth	46	11	17	18	61	68	39
20	Rotherham	46	13	13	20	51	68	39
21	Port Vale	46	8	20	18	46	67	36
22	Bradford	46	12	10	24	56	86	34
23	Hereford	46	9	14	23	34	60	32
24	Portsmouth	46	7	17	22	31	75	31

FOURTH DIVISION

		P	W	D	L	F	A	Pts
1	Watford	46	30	11	5	85	38	71
2	Southend	46	25	10	11	66	39	60
3	Swansea	46	23	10	13	87	47	56
4	Brentford	46	21	14	11	86	54	56
5	Aldershot	46	19	16	11	67	47	54
6	Grimsby	46	21	11	14	57	51	53
7	Barnsley	46	18	14	14	61	49	50
8	Reading	46	18	14	14	55	52	50
9	Torquay	46	16	15	15	57	56	47
10	Northampton	46	17	13	16	63	68	47
11	Huddersfield	46	15	15	16	63	55	45
12	Doncaster	46	14	17	15	52	65	45
13	Wimbledon	46	14	16	16	66	67	44
14	Scunthorpe	46	14	16	16	50	55	44
15	Crewe	46	15	14	17	50	69	44
16	Newport	46	16	11	19	65	73	43
17	Bournemouth	46	14	15	17	41	51	43
18	Stockport	46	16	10	20	56	56	42
19	Darlington	46	14	13	19	52	59	41
20	Halifax	46	10	21	15	52	62	41
21	Hartlepool	46	15	7	24	51	84	37
22	York	46	12	12	22	50	69	36
23	Southport	46	6	19	21	52	76	31
24	Rochdale	46	8	8	30	43	85	24

SCOTTISH PREMIER DIVISION

		P	W	D	L	F	A	Pts
1	Rangers	36	24	7	5	76	39	55
2	Aberdeen	36	22	9	5	68	29	53
3	Dundee United	36	16	8	12	42	32	40
4	Hibernian	36	15	7	14	51	43	37
5	Celtic	36	15	6	15	63	54	36
6	Motherwell	36	13	7	16	45	52	33
7	Partick	36	14	5	17	52	64	33
8	St Mirren	36	11	8	17	52	63	30
9	Ayr	36	9	6	21	36	68	24
10	Clydebank	36	6	7	23	23	64	19

SCOTTISH FIRST DIVISION

		P	W	D	L	F	A	Pts
1	Morton	39	25	8	6	85	42	58
2	Hearts	39	24	10	5	77	42	58
3	Dundee	39	25	7	7	91	44	57
4	Dumbarton	39	16	17	6	65	48	49
5	Stirling	39	15	12	12	60	52	42
6	Kilmarnock	39	14	12	13	52	46	40
7	Hamilton	39	12	12	15	54	56	36
8	St Johnstone	39	15	6	18	52	64	36
9	Arbroath	39	11	13	15	42	55	35
10	Airdrieonians	39	12	10	17	50	64	34
11	Montrose	39	10	9	20	55	71	29
12	Queen of the S	39	8	13	18	44	68	29
13	Alloa	39	8	8	23	44	84	24
14	East Fife	39	4	11	24	39	74	19

SCOTTISH SECOND DIVISION

		P	W	D	L	F	A	Pts
1	Clyde	39	21	11	7	71	32	53
2	Raith	39	19	15	5	63	38	53
3	Dunfermline	39	18	12	9	64	41	48
4	Berwick	39	16	16	7	68	51	48
5	Falkirk	39	15	14	10	51	46	44
6	Forfar	39	17	8	14	61	55	42
7	Queen's Park	39	13	15	11	52	51	41
8	Albion	39	16	8	15	68	68	40
9	East Stirling	39	15	8	16	55	65	38
10	Cowdenbeath	39	13	8	18	75	78	34
11	Stranraer	39	13	7	19	54	59	33
12	Stenhousemuir	39	10	10	19	43	67	30
13	Meadowbank	39	6	10	23	43	89	22
14	Brechin	39	7	6	26	45	73	20

FA CUP 1977-78

FOURTH ROUND

Arsenal v Wolverhampton Wanderers	2-1
Bolton Wanderers v Mansfield Town	1-0
Brighton & Hove Albion v Notts County	1-2
Bristol Rovers v Southampton	2-0
Chelsea v Burnley	6-2
Derby County v Birmingham City	2-1
Ipswich v Hartlepool	4-1
Manchester United v West Bromwich Albion	1-1, 2-3
Middlesbrough v Everton	3-2
Millwall v Luton Town	4-0
Newcastle United v Wrexham	2-2, 1-4
Nottingham Forest v Manchester City	2-1
Orient v Blackburn Rovers	3-1
Stoke City v Blyth Spartans	2-3
Walsall v Leicester City	1-0
West Ham United v Queen's Park Rangers	1-1, 1-6

FIFTH ROUND

Arsenal v Walsall	4-1
Bristol Rovers v Ipswich	2-2, 0-3
Derby County v West Bromwich Albion	2-3
Orient v Chelsea	0-0, 2-1
Middlesbrough v Bolton Wanderers	2-0
Millwall v Notts County	2-1
Queen's Park Rangers v Nottingham Forest	1-1, 1-3
Wrexham v Blyth Spartans	1-1, 2-1

SIXTH ROUND

Middlesbrough v Orient	0-0, 1-2
Millwall v Ipswich	1-6
West Bromwich Albion v Nottingham Forest	2-0
Wrexham v Arsenal	2-3

SEMI-FINALS

Arsenal v Orient	3-0
Ipswich v West Bromwich Albion	3-1

FINAL

Arsenal v Ipswich	0-1

SCOTTISH FA CUP 1977-78

THIRD ROUND

Aberdeen v Ayr United	2-0
Albion Rovers v Morton	0-1
Airdrieonians v Heart of Midlothian	2-3
Arbroath v Motherwell	0-4
Berwick Rangers v Rangers	2-4
Celtic v Dundee	2-1
Dumbarton v Alloa Athletic	2-1
Hamilton Academicals v Dundee United	1-4
Hibernian v East Fife	4-0
Meadowbank v Inverness Caledonia	2-1
Partick Thistle v Cowdenbeath	1-1, 1-0
Queen of the South v Montrose	2-2, 3-1
St Johnstone v Brechin City	1-0
St Mirren v Kilmarnock	1-2
Stirling Albion v Clydebank	0-0 (abandoned), 3-0
Vale of Leithen v Queen's Park	0-1

FOURTH ROUND

Aberdeen v St Johnstone	3-0
Celtic v Kilmarnock	1-1, 0-1
Dumbarton v Heart of Midlothian	1-0
Dundee United v Queen of the South	3-0
Morton v Meadowbank	3-0
Motherwell v Queen's Park	1-3
Rangers v Stirling Albion	1-0
Hibernian v Partick Thistle	0-0, 1-2

FIFTH ROUND

Aberdeen v Morton	2-2, 2-1
Dundee United v Queen's Park	2-0
Partick Thistle v Dumbarton	2-1
Rangers v Kilmarnock	4-1

SEMI-FINALS

Aberdeen v Partick Thistle	4-2
Rangers v Dundee United	2-0

FINAL

Rangers v Aberdeen	2-1

FIRST DIVISION

		P	W	D	L	F	A	Pts
1	Liverpool	42	30	8	4	85	16	68
2	Nottm Forest	42	21	18	3	61	26	60
3	WBA	42	24	11	7	72	35	59
4	Everton	42	17	17	8	52	40	51
5	Leeds	42	18	14	10	70	52	50
6	Ipswich	42	20	9	13	63	49	49
7	Arsenal	42	17	14	11	61	48	48
8	Aston Villa	42	15	16	11	59	49	46
9	Man United	42	15	15	12	60	63	45
10	Coventry	42	14	16	12	58	68	44
11	Tottenham	42	13	15	14	48	61	41
12	Middlesbrough	42	15	10	17	57	50	40
13	Bristol City	42	15	10	17	47	51	40
14	Southampton	42	12	16	14	47	53	40
15	Man City	42	13	13	16	58	56	39
16	Norwich	42	7	23	12	51	57	37
17	Bolton	42	12	11	19	54	75	35
18	Wolves	42	13	8	21	44	68	34
19	Derby	42	10	11	21	44	71	31
20	QPR	42	6	13	23	45	73	25
21	Birmingham	42	6	10	26	37	64	22
22	Chelsea	42	5	10	27	44	92	20

SECOND DIVISION

		P	W	D	L	F	A	Pts
1	Crystal Palace	42	19	19	4	51	24	57
2	Brighton	42	23	10	9	72	39	56
3	Stoke	42	20	16	6	58	31	56
4	Sunderland	42	22	11	9	70	44	55
5	West Ham	42	18	14	10	70	39	50
6	Notts County	42	14	16	12	48	60	44
7	Preston	42	12	18	12	59	57	42
8	Newcastle	42	17	8	17	51	55	42
9	Cardiff	42	16	10	16	56	70	42
10	Fulham	42	13	15	14	50	47	41
11	Orient	42	15	10	17	51	51	40
12	Cambridge	42	12	16	14	44	52	40
13	Burnley	42	14	12	16	51	62	40
14	Oldham	42	13	13	16	52	61	39
15	Wrexham	42	12	14	16	45	42	38
16	Bristol Rovers	42	14	10	18	48	60	38
17	Leicester	42	10	17	15	43	52	37
18	Luton	42	13	10	19	60	57	36
19	Charlton	42	11	13	18	60	69	35
20	Sheff United	42	11	12	19	52	69	34
21	Millwall	42	11	10	21	42	61	32
22	Blackburn	42	10	10	22	41	72	30

THIRD DIVISION

		P	W	D	L	F	A	Pts
1	Shrewsbury	46	21	19	6	61	41	61
2	Watford	46	24	12	10	83	52	60
3	Swansea	46	24	12	10	83	61	60
4	Gillingham	46	21	17	8	65	42	59
5	Swindon	46	25	7	14	74	52	57
6	Carlisle	46	15	22	9	53	42	52
7	Colchester	46	17	17	12	60	55	51
8	Hull	46	19	11	16	66	61	49
9	Exeter	46	17	15	14	61	56	49
10	Brentford	46	19	9	18	53	49	47
11	Oxford	46	14	18	14	44	50	46
12	Blackpool	46	18	9	19	61	59	45
13	Southend	46	15	15	16	51	49	45
14	Sheff Wed	46	13	19	14	53	53	45
15	Plymouth	46	15	14	17	67	68	44
16	Chester	46	14	16	16	57	61	44
17	Rotherham	46	17	10	19	49	55	44
18	Mansfield	46	12	19	15	51	52	43
19	Bury	46	11	20	15	59	65	42
20	Chesterfield	46	13	14	19	51	65	40
21	Peterborough	46	11	14	21	44	63	36
22	Walsall	46	10	12	24	56	71	32
23	Tranmere	46	6	16	24	45	78	28
24	Lincoln	46	7	11	28	41	88	25

FOURTH DIVISION

		P	W	D	L	F	A	Pts
1	Reading	46	26	13	7	76	35	65
2	Grimsby	46	26	9	11	82	49	61
3	Wimbledon	46	25	11	10	78	46	61
4	Barnsley	46	24	13	9	73	42	61
5	Aldershot	46	20	17	9	63	47	57
6	Wigan	46	21	13	12	63	48	55
7	Portsmouth	46	20	12	14	62	48	52
8	Newport	46	21	10	15	66	55	52
9	Huddersfield	46	18	11	17	57	53	47
10	York	46	18	11	17	51	55	47
11	Torquay	46	19	8	19	58	65	46
12	Scunthorpe	46	17	11	18	54	60	45
13	Hartlepool	46	13	18	15	57	66	44
14	Hereford	46	15	13	18	53	53	43
15	Bradford C.	46	17	9	20	62	68	43
16	Port Vale	46	14	14	18	57	70	42
17	Stockport	46	14	12	20	58	60	40
18	Bournemouth	46	14	11	21	47	48	39
19	Northampton	46	15	9	22	64	76	39
20	Rochdale	46	15	9	22	47	64	39
21	Darlington	46	11	15	20	49	66	37
22	Doncaster	46	13	11	22	50	73	37
23	Halifax	46	9	8	29	39	72	26
24	Crewe	46	6	14	26	43	90	26

SCOTTISH PREMIER DIVISION

		P	W	D	L	F	A	Pts
1	Celtic	36	21	6	9	61	37	48
2	Rangers	36	18	9	9	52	35	45
3	Dundee United	36	18	8	10	56	37	44
4	Aberdeen	36	13	14	9	59	36	40
5	Hibernian	36	12	13	11	44	48	37
6	St Mirren	36	15	6	15	45	41	36
7	Morton	36	12	12	12	52	53	36
8	Partick	36	13	8	15	42	39	34
9	Hearts	36	8	7	21	49	71	23
10	Motherwell	36	5	7	24	33	86	17

SCOTTISH FIRST DIVISION

		P	W	D	L	F	A	Pts
1	Dundee	39	24	7	8	68	36	55
2	Kilmarnock	39	22	10	7	72	35	54
3	Clydebank	39	24	6	9	78	50	54
4	Ayr	39	21	5	13	71	52	47
5	Hamilton	39	17	9	13	62	60	43
6	Airdrieonians	39	16	8	15	72	61	40
7	Dumbarton	39	14	11	14	58	49	39
8	Stirling A.	39	13	9	17	43	55	35
9	Clyde	39	13	8	18	54	65	34
10	Arbroath	39	11	11	17	50	61	33
11	Raith	39	12	8	19	47	55	32
12	St Johnstone	39	10	11	18	57	66	31
13	Montrose	39	8	9	22	55	92	25
14	Queen of the S	39	8	8	23	43	93	24

SCOTTISH SECOND DIVISION

		P	W	D	L	F	A	Pts
1	Berwick	39	22	10	7	82	44	54
2	Dunfermline	39	19	14	6	66	40	52
3	Falkirk	39	19	12	8	66	37	50
4	East Fife	39	17	9	13	64	53	43
5	Cowdenbeath	39	16	10	13	63	58	42
6	Alloa	39	16	9	14	57	62	41
7	Albion	39	15	10	14	57	56	40
8	Forfar	39	13	12	14	55	52	38
9	Stranraer	39	18	2	19	52	66	38
10	Stenhousemuir	39	12	8	19	54	58	32
11	Brechin	39	9	14	16	49	65	32
12	E Stirlingshire	39	12	8	19	61	87	32
13	Queen's Park	39	8	12	19	46	57	28
14	Meadowbank	39	8	8	23	37	74	24

FA CUP 1978-79

FOURTH ROUND

Arsenal v Notts County	2-0
Ipswich v Orient	0-0, 2-0
Newcastle v Wolverhampton W	1-1, 0-1
Nottingham Forest v York City	3-1
Shrewsbury v Manchester City	2-0
Crystal Palace v Bristol City	3-0
Aldershot v Swindon	2-1
Liverpool v Blackburn	1-0
Newport v Colchester	0-0, 0-1
Fulham v Manchester United	1-1, 0-1
Bristol Rovers v Charlton Athletic	1-0
Preston v Southampton	0-1
Tottenham v Wrexham	3-3, 3-2
Burnley v Sunderland	1-1, 3-0
West Bromwich Albion v Leeds	3-3, 2-0
Oldham v Leicester	3-1

FIFTH ROUND

Nottingham Forest v Arsenal	0-1
West Bromwich Albion v Southampton	1-1, 1-2
Aldershot v Shrewsbury	2-2, 1-3
Crystal Palace v Wolverhampton W	0-1
Liverpool v Burnley	3-0
Ipswich Town v Bristol Rovers	6-1
Oldham v Tottenham	0-1
Colchester United v Manchester United	0-1

QUARTER-FINALS

Southampton v Arsenal	1-1, 0-2
Wolverhampton W v Shrewsbury	1-1, 3-1
Ipswich v Liverpool	0-1
Tottenham v Manchester United	1-1, 0-2

SEMI-FINALS

Arsenal v Wolverhampton W	2-0
Manchester United v Liverpool	2-2, 1-0

FINAL

Arsenal v Manchester United	3-2

SCOTTISH FA CUP 1978-79

THIRD ROUND

Arbroath v Airdrieonians	0-1
East Fife v Berwick Rangers	0-1
Hamilton v Aberdeen	0-2
Raith Rovers v Heart of Midlothian	0-2
Dunfermline Athletic v Hibernian	1-1, 0-2
Clyde v Kilmarnock	1-5
Clydebank v Queen's Park	3-3, 1-0
Meadowbank v Spartans	2-1
Montrose v Celtic	2-4
Ayr United v Queen of the South	4-0
Rangers v Motherwell	3-1
Dumbarton v Alloa	1-0
Morton v St Johnstone	1-1, 4-2
Stirling Albion v Partick Thistle	0-2
Dundee v Falkirk	1-0
Dundee United v St Mirren	0-2

FOURTH ROUND

Aberdeen v Ayr United	6-2
Meadowbank v Hibernian	0-6
Rangers v Kilmarnock	1-1, 1-0
Dumbarton v Clydebank	3-1
Partick Thistle v Airdrieonians	3-0
Celtic v Berwick	3-0
Dundee v St Mirren	4-1
Heart of Midlothian v Morton	1-1, 1-0

QUARTER-FINALS

Rangers v Dundee	6-3
Dumbarton v Partick Thistle	0-1
Aberdeen v Celtic	1-1, 2-1
Hibernian v Heart of Midlothian	2-1

SEMI-FINALS

Partick Thistle v Rangers	0-0, 0-1
Aberdeen v Hibernian	1-2

FINAL

Rangers v Hibernian	0-0, 0-0, 3-2

League Tables 1979–80

FIRST DIVISION

		P	W	D	L	F	A	Pts
1	Liverpool	42	25	10	7	81	30	60
2	Man United	42	24	10	8	65	35	58
3	Ipswich	42	22	9	11	68	39	53
4	Arsenal	42	18	16	8	52	36	52
5	Nottm Forest	42	20	8	14	63	43	48
6	Wolves	42	19	9	14	58	47	47
7	Aston Villa	42	16	14	12	51	50	46
8	Southampton	42	18	9	15	65	53	45
9	Middlesbrough	42	16	12	14	50	44	44
10	WBA	42	11	19	12	54	50	41
11	Leeds	42	13	14	15	46	50	40
12	Norwich	42	13	14	15	58	66	40
13	Crystal Palace	42	12	16	14	41	50	40
14	Tottenham	42	15	10	17	52	62	40
15	Coventry	42	16	7	19	56	66	39
16	Brighton	42	11	15	16	47	57	37
17	Man City	42	12	13	17	43	66	37
18	Stoke	42	13	10	19	44	58	36
19	Everton	42	9	17	16	43	51	35
20	Bristol City	42	9	13	20	37	66	31
21	Derby	42	11	8	23	47	67	30
22	Bolton	42	5	15	22	38	73	25

SECOND DIVISION

		P	W	D	L	F	A	Pts
1	Leicester	42	21	13	8	58	38	55
2	Sunderland	42	21	12	9	69	42	54
3	Birmingham	42	21	11	10	58	38	53
4	Chelsea	42	23	7	12	66	52	53
5	QPR	42	18	13	11	75	53	49
6	Luton	42	16	17	9	66	45	49
7	West Ham	42	20	7	15	54	43	47
8	Cambridge	42	14	16	12	61	53	44
9	Newcastle	42	15	14	13	53	49	44
10	Preston	42	12	19	11	56	52	43
11	Oldham	42	16	11	15	49	53	43
12	Swansea	42	17	9	16	48	53	43
13	Shrewsbury	42	18	5	19	60	53	41
14	Orient	42	12	17	13	48	54	41
15	Cardiff	42	16	8	18	41	48	40
16	Wrexham	42	16	6	20	40	49	38
17	Notts County	42	11	15	16	51	52	37
18	Watford	42	12	13	17	39	46	37
19	Bristol Rovers	42	11	13	18	50	64	35
20	Fulham	42	11	7	24	42	74	29
21	Burnley	42	6	15	21	39	73	27
22	Charlton	42	6	10	26	39	78	22

THIRD DIVISION

		P	W	D	L	F	A	Pts
1	Grimsby	46	26	10	10	73	42	62
2	Blackburn	46	25	9	12	58	36	59
3	Sheff Wed	46	21	16	9	81	47	58
4	Chesterfield	46	23	11	12	71	46	57
5	Colchester	46	20	12	14	64	56	52
6	Carlisle	46	18	12	16	66	56	48
7	Reading	46	16	16	14	66	65	48
8	Exeter	46	19	10	17	60	68	48
9	Chester	46	17	13	16	49	57	47
10	Swindon	46	19	8	19	71	63	46
11	Barnsley	46	16	14	16	53	56	46
12	Sheff United	46	18	10	18	60	66	46
13	Rotherham	46	18	10	18	58	66	46
14	Millwall	46	16	13	17	65	59	45
15	Plymouth	46	16	12	18	59	55	44
16	Gillingham	46	14	14	18	49	51	42
17	Oxford	46	14	13	19	57	62	41
18	Blackpool	46	15	11	20	62	74	41
19	Brentford	46	15	11	20	59	73	41
20	Hull	46	12	16	18	51	69	40
21	Bury	46	16	7	23	45	59	39
22	Southend	46	14	10	22	47	58	38
23	Mansfield	46	10	16	20	47	58	36
24	Wimbledon	46	10	14	22	52	81	34

FOURTH DIVISION

		P	W	D	L	F	A	Pts
1	Huddersfield	46	27	12	7	101	48	66
2	Walsall	46	23	18	5	75	47	64
3	Newport	46	27	7	12	83	50	61
4	Portsmouth	46	24	12	10	91	49	60
5	Bradford	46	24	12	10	77	50	60
6	Wigan	46	21	13	12	76	61	55
7	Lincoln	46	18	17	11	64	42	53
8	Peterborough	46	21	10	15	58	47	52
9	Torquay	46	15	17	14	70	69	47
10	Aldershot	46	16	13	17	62	53	45
11	Bournemouth	46	13	18	15	52	51	44
12	Doncaster	46	15	14	17	62	63	44
13	Northampton	46	16	12	18	51	66	44
14	Scunthorpe	46	14	15	17	58	75	43
15	Tranmere	46	14	13	19	50	56	41
16	Stockport	46	14	12	20	48	72	40
17	York	46	14	11	21	65	82	39
18	Halifax	46	13	13	20	46	72	39
19	Hartlepool	46	14	10	22	59	64	38
20	Port Vale	46	12	12	22	56	70	36
21	Hereford	46	11	14	21	38	52	36
22	Darlington	46	9	17	20	50	74	35
23	Crewe	46	11	13	22	35	68	35
24	Rochdale	46	7	13	26	33	79	27

SCOTTISH PREMIER DIVISION

		P	W	D	L	F	A	Pts
1	Aberdeen	36	19	10	7	68	36	48
2	Celtic	36	18	11	7	61	38	47
3	St Mirren	36	15	12	9	56	49	42
4	Dundee United	36	12	13	11	43	30	37
5	Rangers	36	15	7	14	50	46	37
6	Morton	36	14	8	14	51	46	36
7	Partick	36	11	14	11	43	47	36
8	Kilmarnock	36	11	11	14	36	52	33
9	Dundee	36	10	6	20	47	73	26
10	Hibernian	36	6	6	24	29	67	18

SCOTTISH FIRST DIVISION

		P	W	D	L	F	A	Pts
1	Hearts	39	20	13	6	58	39	53
2	Airdrie	39	21	9	9	78	47	51
3	Ayr	39	16	12	11	64	51	44
4	Dumbarton	39	19	6	14	59	51	44
5	Raith	39	14	15	10	59	46	43
6	Motherwell	39	16	11	12	59	48	43
7	Hamilton	39	15	10	14	60	59	40
8	Stirling	39	13	13	13	40	40	39
9	Clydebank	39	14	8	17	58	57	36
10	Dunfermline	39	11	13	15	39	57	35
11	St Johnstone	39	12	10	17	57	74	34
12	Berwick	39	8	15	16	57	64	31
13	Arbroath	39	9	10	20	50	79	28
14	Clyde	39	6	13	20	43	69	25

SCOTTISH SECOND DIVISION

		P	W	D	L	F	A	Pts
1	Falkirk	39	19	12	8	65	35	50
2	E Stirlingshire	39	21	7	11	55	40	49
3	Forfar	39	19	8	12	63	51	46
4	Albion	39	16	12	11	73	56	44
5	Queen's Park	39	16	9	14	59	47	41
6	Stenhousemuir	39	16	9	14	56	51	41
7	Brechin	39	15	10	14	61	59	40
8	Cowdenbeath	39	14	12	13	54	52	40
9	Montrose	39	14	10	15	60	63	38
10	East Fife	39	12	9	18	45	57	33
11	Stranraer	39	12	8	19	51	65	32
12	Meadowbank	39	12	8	19	42	70	32
13	Queen of the S	39	11	9	19	51	69	31
14	Alloa	39	11	7	21	44	64	29

FA CUP 1979-80

FOURTH ROUND

Arsenal v Brighton	2-0
Birmingham v Middlesbrough	2-1
Blackburn v Coventry	1-0
Bolton v Halifax	2-0
Bradford v Ipswich	1-2
Bury v Burnley	1-0
Cambridge v Aston Villa	1-1, 1-4
Carlisle v Wrexham	0-0, 1-3
Chester v Millwall	2-0
Everton v Wigan	3-0
Nottingham Forest v Liverpool	0-2
Orient v West Ham	2-3
Swansea v Reading	4-1
Swindon v Tottenham Hotspur	0-0, 1-2
Watford v Harlow	4-3
Wolverhampton W v Norwich	1-1, 3-2

FIFTH ROUND

West Ham v Swansea	2-0
Blackburn v Aston Villa	1-1, 0-1
Ipswich v Chester	2-1
Everton v Wrexham	5-2
Liverpool v Bury	2-0
Tottenham Hotspur v Birmingham	3-1
Wolverhampton W v Watford	0-3
Bolton v Arsenal	1-1, 0-3

QUARTER-FINALS

West Ham v Aston Villa	1-0
Everton v Ipswich	2-1
Tottenham Hotspur v Liverpool	0-1
Watford v Arsenal	1-2

SEMI-FINALS

West Ham v Everton	1-1, 1-0
Arsenal v Liverpool	0-0, 1-1, 1-1, 1-0

FINAL

West Ham v Arsenal	1-0

SCOTTISH FA CUP 1979-80

THIRD ROUND

Arbroath v Aberdeen	1-1, 0-5
Berwick v Peterhead	3-1
Celtic v Raith Rovers	2-1
Clyde v Rangers	2-2, 0-2
Clydebank v Stirling Albion	1-1, 1-1, 0-1
Dumbarton v Ayr United	1-2
Hamilton v Keith	2-3
Meadowbank v Hibernian	0-1
Morton v Cowdenbeath	1-0
Queen of the South v Motherwell	2-0
St Mirren v Brechin City	3-1
Airdrieonians v St Johnstone	3-1
Alloa v Heart of Midlothian	0-1
Dundee United v Dundee	5-1
Dunfermline v Buckie Thistle	2-0
Kilmarnock v Partick Thistle	0-1

FOURTH ROUND

Aberdeen v Airdrieonians	8-0
Celtic v St Mirren	1-1, 3-2
Heart of Midlothian v Stirling Albion	2-0
Keith v Berwick	1-2
Morton v Dunfermline	5-0
Queen of the South v Partick Thistle	1-3
Rangers v Dundee United	1-0
Hibernian v Ayr United	2-0

QUARTER-FINALS

Celtic v Morton	2-0
Berwick Rangers v Hibernian	0-0, 0-1
Partick Thistle v Aberdeen	1-2
Rangers v Heart of Midlothian	6-1

SEMI-FINALS

Celtic v Hibernian	5-0
Aberdeen v Rangers	0-1

FINAL

Celtic v Rangers	1-0

League Tables 1980–81

FIRST DIVISION

		P	W	D	L	F	A	Pts
1	Aston Villa	42	26	8	8	72	40	60
2	Ipswich	42	23	10	9	77	43	56
3	Arsenal	42	19	15	8	61	45	53
4	WBA	42	20	12	10	60	42	52
5	Liverpool	42	17	17	8	62	46	51
6	Southampton	42	20	10	12	76	56	50
7	Nottm Forest	42	19	12	11	62	45	50
8	Man United	42	15	18	9	51	36	48
9	Leeds	42	17	10	15	39	47	44
10	Tottenham	42	14	15	13	70	68	43
11	Stoke	42	12	18	12	51	60	42
12	Man City	42	14	11	17	56	59	39
13	Birmingham	42	13	12	17	50	61	38
14	Middlesbrough	42	16	5	21	53	51	37
15	Everton	42	13	10	19	55	58	36
16	Coventry	42	13	10	19	48	68	36
17	Sunderland	42	14	7	21	58	53	35
18	Wolves	42	13	9	20	47	55	35
19	Brighton	42	14	7	21	54	67	35
20	Norwich	42	13	7	22	49	73	33
21	Leicester	42	13	6	23	40	67	32
22	Crystal Palace	42	6	7	29	47	83	19

SECOND DIVISION

		P	W	D	L	F	A	Pts
1	West Ham	42	28	10	4	79	29	66
2	Notts County	42	18	17	7	49	38	53
3	Swansea	42	18	14	10	64	44	50
4	Blackburn	42	16	18	8	42	29	50
5	Luton	42	18	12	12	61	46	48
6	Derby	42	15	15	12	57	52	45
7	Grimsby	42	15	15	12	44	42	45
8	QPR	42	15	13	14	56	46	43
9	Watford	42	16	11	15	50	45	43
10	Sheff Wed	42	17	8	17	53	51	42
11	Newcastle	42	14	14	14	30	45	42
12	Chelsea	42	14	12	16	46	41	40
13	Cambridge	42	17	6	17	53	65	40
14	Shrewsbury	42	11	17	14	46	47	39
15	Oldham	42	12	15	15	39	48	39
16	Wrexham	42	12	14	16	43	45	38
17	Orient	42	13	12	17	52	56	38
18	Bolton	42	14	10	18	61	66	38
19	Cardiff	42	12	12	18	44	60	36
20	Preston	42	11	14	17	41	62	36
21	Bristol City	42	7	16	19	29	51	30
22	Bristol Rovers	42	5	13	24	34	65	23

THIRD DIVISION

		P	W	D	L	F	A	Pts
1	Rotherham	46	24	13	9	62	32	61
2	Barnsley	46	21	17	8	72	45	59
3	Charlton	46	25	9	12	63	44	59
4	Huddersfield	46	21	14	11	71	40	56
5	Chesterfield	46	23	10	13	72	48	56
6	Portsmouth	46	22	9	15	55	47	53
7	Plymouth	46	19	14	13	56	44	52
8	Burnley	46	18	14	14	60	48	50
9	Brentford	46	14	19	13	52	49	47
10	Reading	46	18	10	18	62	62	46
11	Exeter	46	16	13	17	62	66	45
12	Newport	46	15	13	18	64	61	43
13	Fulham	46	15	13	18	57	64	43
14	Oxford	46	13	17	16	39	47	43
15	Gillingham	46	12	18	16	48	58	42
16	Millwall	46	14	14	18	43	60	42
17	Swindon	46	13	15	18	51	56	41
18	Chester	46	15	11	20	41	48	41
19	Carlisle	46	14	13	19	57	70	41
20	Walsall	46	13	15	18	59	74	41
21	Sheff United	46	14	13	19	65	62	40
22	Colchester	46	14	11	21	45	65	39
23	Blackpool	46	9	14	23	45	75	32
24	Hull	46	8	16	22	40	71	32

FOURTH DIVISION

		P	W	D	L	F	A	Pts
1	Southend	46	30	7	9	79	31	67
2	Lincoln	46	25	15	6	66	25	65
3	Doncaster	46	22	12	12	59	49	56
4	Wimbledon	46	23	9	14	64	46	55
5	Peterborough	46	17	18	11	68	54	52
6	Aldershot	46	18	14	14	43	41	50
7	Mansfield	46	20	9	17	58	44	49
8	Darlington	46	19	11	16	65	59	49
9	Hartlepool	46	20	9	17	64	61	49
10	Northampton	46	18	13	15	65	67	49
11	Wigan	46	18	11	17	51	55	47
12	Bury	46	17	11	18	70	62	45
13	Bournemouth	46	16	13	17	47	48	45
14	Bradford	46	14	16	16	53	60	44
15	Rochdale	46	14	15	17	60	70	43
16	Scunthorpe	46	11	20	15	60	69	42
17	Torquay	46	18	5	23	55	63	41
18	Crewe	46	13	14	19	48	61	40
19	Port Vale	46	12	15	19	57	68	39
20	Stockport	46	16	7	23	44	57	39
21	Tranmere	46	13	10	23	59	73	36
22	Hereford	46	11	13	22	38	62	35
23	Halifax	46	11	12	23	44	71	34
24	York	46	12	9	25	47	66	33

SCOTTISH PREMIER DIVISION

		P	W	D	L	F	A	Pts
1	Celtic	36	26	4	6	84	37	56
2	Aberdeen	36	19	11	6	61	26	49
3	Rangers	36	16	12	8	60	32	44
4	St Mirren	36	18	8	10	56	47	44
5	Dundee United	36	17	9	10	66	42	43
6	Partick	36	10	10	16	32	48	30
7	Airdrieonians	36	10	9	17	36	55	29
8	Morton	36	10	8	18	36	58	28
9	Kilmarnock	36	5	9	22	23	65	19
10	Hearts	36	6	6	24	27	71	18

SCOTTISH FIRST DIVISION

		P	W	D	L	F	A	Pts
1	Hibernian	39	24	9	6	67	24	57
2	Dundee	39	22	8	9	64	40	52
3	St Johnstone	39	20	11	8	64	45	51
4	Raith	39	20	10	9	49	32	50
5	Motherwell	39	19	11	9	65	51	49
6	Ayr	39	17	11	11	59	42	45
7	Hamilton	39	15	7	17	61	57	37
8	Dumbarton	39	13	11	15	49	50	37
9	Falkirk	39	13	8	18	39	52	34
10	Clydebank	39	10	13	16	48	59	33
11	E Stirlingshire	39	6	17	16	41	56	29
12	Dunfermline	39	10	7	22	41	58	27
13	Stirling	39	6	11	22	18	48	23
14	Berwick	39	5	12	22	31	82	22

SCOTTISH SECOND DIVISION

		P	W	D	L	F	A	Pts
1	Queen's Park	39	16	18	5	62	43	50
2	Queen of the S	39	16	14	9	66	53	46
3	Cowdenbeath	39	18	9	12	63	48	45
4	Brechin	39	15	14	10	52	46	44
5	Forfar	39	17	9	13	63	57	43
6	Alloa	39	15	12	12	61	54	42
7	Montrose	39	16	8	15	66	55	40
8	Clyde	39	14	12	13	68	63	40
9	Arbroath	39	13	12	14	58	54	38
10	Stenhousemuir	39	13	11	15	63	58	37
11	East Fife	39	10	15	14	44	53	35
12	Albion	39	13	9	17	59	72	34
13	Meadowbank	39	11	7	21	42	64	29
14	Stranraer	39	7	8	24	36	83	22

FA CUP 1980-81

FOURTH ROUND

Barnsley v Enfield	1-1, 3-0
Carlisle v Bristol City	1-1, 0-5
Coventry v Birmingham	3-2
Everton v Liverpool	2-1
Fulham v Charlton	1-2
Leicester v Exeter	1-1, 1-3
Manchester City v Norwich	6-0
Middlesbrough v West Bromwich Albion	1-0
Newcastle v Luton	2-1
Nottingham Forest v Manchester United	1-0
Notts County v Peterborough	0-1
Shrewsbury v Ipswich	0-0, 0-3
Tottenham v Hull	2-0
Watford v Wolverhampton W	1-1, 1-2
Wrexham v Wimbledon	2-1
Southampton v Bristol Rovers	3-1

FIFTH ROUND

Ipswich v Charlton	2-0
Middlesbrough v Barnsley	2-1
Newcastle v Exeter	1-1, 0-4
Nottingham Forest v Bristol City	2-1
Peterborough v Manchester City	0-1
Southampton v Everton	0-0, 0-1
Tottenham v Coventry	3-1
Wolverhampton W v Wrexham	3-1

QUARTER-FINALS

Tottenham Hotspur v Exeter	2-0
Middlesbrough v Wolverhampton W	1-1, 1-3
Nottingham Forest v Ipswich	3-3, 0-1
Everton v Manchester City	2-2, 1-3

SEMI-FINALS

Tottenham Hotspur v Wolverhampton W	2-2, 3-0
Ipswich v Manchester City	0-1

FINAL

Tottenham Hotspur v Manchester City	1-1, 3-2

SCOTTISH FA CUP 1980-81

THIRD ROUND

Airdrieonians v Rangers	0-5
Arbroath v Cowdenbeath	1-1, 0-4
Berwick v Celtic	0-2
Brechin v Dundee United	1-2
Buckie Thistle v Stirling Albion	1-3
East Fife v Clydebank	0-0, 4-5
East Stirling v Inverness Thistle	4-1
Falkirk v Dundee	1-0
Hamilton v St Johnstone	0-3
Hibernian v Dunfermline	1-1, 2-1
Kilmarnock v Ayr United	2-1
Morton v Heart of Midlothian	0-0, 3-1
Partick Thistle v Clyde	2-2, 4-2
Raith Rovers v Aberdeen	1-2
St Mirren v Dumbarton	0-2
Stenhousemuir v Motherwell	1-1, 1-2

FOURTH ROUND

Celtic v Stirling Albion	3-0
Cowdenbeath v East Stirlingshire	1-2
Dundee United v Partick Thistle	1-0
Hibernian v Falkirk	1-0
Kilmarnock v Clydebank	0-0, 1-1, 0-1
Morton v Aberdeen	1-0
Motherwell v Dumbarton	2-1
St Johnstone v Rangers	3-3, 1-3

QUARTER-FINALS

Dundee United v Motherwell	6-1
Rangers v Hibernian	3-1
Celtic v East Stirlingshire	2-0
Morton v Clydebank	0-0, 6-0

SEMI-FINALS

Morton v Rangers	1-2
Celtic v Dundee United	0-0, 2-3

FINAL

Rangers v Dundee United	0-0, 4-1

FIRST DIVISION

		P	W	D	L	F	A	Pts
1	Liverpool	42	26	9	7	80	32	87
2	Ipswich	42	26	5	11	75	53	83
3	Man United	42	22	12	8	59	29	78
4	Tottenham	42	20	11	11	67	48	71
5	Arsenal	42	20	11	11	48	37	71
6	Swansea	42	21	6	15	58	51	69
7	Southampton	42	19	9	14	72	67	66
8	Everton	42	17	13	12	56	50	64
9	West Ham	42	14	16	12	66	57	58
10	Man City	42	15	13	14	49	50	58
11	Aston Villa	42	15	12	15	55	53	57
12	Nottm Forest	42	15	12	15	42	48	57
13	Brighton	42	13	13	16	43	52	52
14	Coventry	42	13	11	18	56	62	50
15	Notts County	42	13	8	21	45	69	47
16	Birmingham	42	10	14	18	53	61	44
17	WBA	42	11	11	20	46	57	44
18	Stoke	42	12	8	22	44	63	44
19	Sunderland	42	11	11	20	38	58	44
20	Leeds	42	10	12	20	39	61	42
21	Wolves	42	10	10	22	32	63	40
22	Middlesbrough	42	8	15	19	34	52	39

SECOND DIVISION

		P	W	D	L	F	A	Pts
1	Luton	42	25	13	4	86	46	88
2	Watford	42	23	11	8	76	42	80
3	Norwich	42	22	5	15	64	50	71
4	Sheff Wed	42	20	10	12	55	51	70
5	QPR	42	21	6	15	65	43	69
6	Barnsley	42	19	10	13	59	41	67
7	Rotherham	42	20	7	15	66	54	67
8	Leicester	42	18	12	12	56	48	66
9	Newcastle	42	18	8	16	52	50	62
10	Blackburn	42	16	11	15	47	43	59
11	Oldham	42	15	14	13	50	51	59
12	Chelsea	42	15	12	15	60	60	57
13	Charlton	42	13	12	17	50	65	51
14	Cambridge	42	13	9	20	48	53	48
15	Crystal Palace	42	13	9	20	34	45	48
16	Derby	42	12	12	18	53	68	48
17	Grimsby	42	11	13	18	53	65	46
18	Shrewsbury	42	11	3	18	37	57	46
19	Bolton	42	13	7	22	39	61	46
20	Cardiff	42	12	8	22	45	61	44
21	Wrexham	42	11	11	20	40	56	44
22	Orient	42	10	9	23	39	61	39

THIRD DIVISION

		P	W	D	L	F	A	Pts
1	Burnley	46	21	17	8	66	49	80
2	Carlisle	46	23	11	12	65	50	80
3	Fulham	46	21	15	10	77	51	78
4	Lincoln	46	21	14	11	66	40	77
5	Oxford	46	19	14	13	63	49	71
6	Gillingham	46	20	11	15	64	56	71
7	Southend	46	18	15	13	63	51	69
8	Brentford	46	19	11	16	56	47	68
9	Millwall	46	18	13	15	62	62	67
10	Plymouth	46	18	11	17	64	56	65
11	Chesterfield	46	18	10	18	67	58	64
12	Reading	46	17	11	18	67	75	62
13	Portsmouth	46	14	19	13	56	51	61
14	Preston	46	16	13	17	50	56	61
15	Bristol Rovers*	46	18	9	19	58	65	61
16	Newport	46	14	16	16	54	54	58
17	Huddersfield	46	15	12	19	64	59	57
18	Exeter	46	16	9	21	71	84	57
19	Doncaster	46	13	17	16	55	68	56
20	Walsall	46	13	14	19	51	55	53
21	Wimbledon	46	14	11	21	61	75	53
22	Swindon	46	13	13	20	55	71	52
23	Bristol City	46	11	13	22	40	65	46
24	Chester	46	7	11	28	36	78	32

* Two points deducted by League.

FOURTH DIVISION

		P	W	D	L	F	A	Pts
1	Sheff United	46	27	15	4	94	41	96
2	Bradford	46	26	13	7	88	45	91
3	Wigan	46	26	13	7	80	46	91
4	Bournemouth	46	23	19	4	62	30	88
5	Peterborough	46	24	10	12	71	57	82
6	Colchester	46	20	12	14	82	57	72
7	Port Vale	46	18	16	12	56	49	70
8	Hull	46	19	12	15	70	61	69
9	Bury	46	17	17	12	80	59	68
10	Hereford	46	16	19	11	64	58	67
11	Tranmere	46	14	18	14	51	56	60
12	Blackpool	46	15	13	18	66	60	58
13	Darlington	46	15	13	18	61	62	58
14	Hartlepool	46	13	16	17	73	84	55
15	Torquay	46	14	13	19	47	59	55
16	Aldershot	46	13	15	18	57	68	54
17	York	46	14	8	24	69	91	50
18	Stockport	46	12	13	21	48	67	49
19	Halifax	46	9	22	15	51	72	49
20	Mansfield*	46	13	10	23	63	81	47
21	Rochdale	46	10	16	20	50	62	46
22	Northampton	46	11	9	26	57	84	42
23	Scunthorpe	46	9	15	22	43	79	42
24	Crewe	46	6	9	31	29	84	27

* Two points deducted by League.

SCOTTISH PREMIER DIVISION

		P	W	D	L	F	A	Pts
1	Celtic	36	24	7	5	79	33	55
2	Aberdeen	36	23	7	6	71	29	53
3	Rangers	36	16	11	9	57	45	43
4	Dundee United	36	15	10	11	61	38	40
5	St Mirren	36	14	9	13	49	52	37
6	Hibernian	36	11	14	11	48	40	36
7	Morton	36	9	12	15	31	54	30
8	Dundee	36	11	4	21	46	72	26
9	Partick	36	6	10	20	35	59	22
10	Airdrieonians	36	5	8	23	31	76	18

SCOTTISH FIRST DIVISION

		P	W	D	L	F	A	Pts
1	Motherwell	39	26	9	4	92	36	61
2	Kilmarnock	39	17	17	5	60	29	51
3	Hearts	39	21	8	10	65	37	50
4	Clydebank	39	19	8	12	61	53	46
5	St Johnstone	39	17	8	14	69	60	42
6	Ayr	39	15	12	12	56	50	42
7	Hamilton	39	16	8	15	52	49	40
8	Queen's Park	39	13	10	16	41	41	36
9	Falkirk	39	11	14	14	49	52	36
10	Dunfermline	39	11	14	14	46	56	36
11	Dumbarton	39	13	9	17	49	61	35
12	Raith	39	11	7	21	31	59	29
13	E Stirlingshire	39	7	10	22	38	77	24
14	Queen of the S	39	4	10	25	44	93	18

SCOTTISH SECOND DIVISION

		P	W	D	L	F	A	Pts
1	Clyde	39	24	11	4	79	38	59
2	Alloa	39	19	12	8	66	42	50
3	Arbroath	39	20	10	9	62	50	50
4	Berwick	39	20	8	11	66	38	48
5	Brechin	39	18	10	11	61	43	46
6	Forfar	39	15	15	9	59	35	45
7	East Fife	39	14	9	16	48	51	37
8	Stirling	39	12	11	16	39	44	35
9	Cowdenbeath	39	11	13	15	51	57	35
10	Montrose	39	12	8	19	49	74	32
11	Albion	39	13	5	21	52	74	31
12	Meadowbank	39	10	10	19	49	62	30
13	Stenhousemuir	39	11	6	22	41	65	28
14	Stranraer	39	7	6	26	36	85	20

FA CUP 1981-82

FOURTH ROUND

Tottenham Hotspur v Leeds United	1-0
Bristol City v Aston Villa	0-1
Chelsea v Wrexham	0-0, 1-1, 2-1
Sunderland v Liverpool	0-3
Hereford v Leicester	0-1
Watford v West Ham	2-0
Shrewbury v Burnley	1-0
Luton v Ipswich	0-3
Gillingham v West Bromwich Albion	0-1
Norwich v Doncaster Rovers	2-1
Manchester City v Coventry	1-3
Brighton v Oxford United	0-3
Crystal Palace v Bolton	1-0
Huddersfield v Orient	1-1, 0-2
Newcastle v Grimsby	1-2
Blackpool v Queen's Park Rangers	0-0, 1-5

FIFTH ROUND

Tottenham Hotspur v Aston Villa	1-0
Chelsea v Liverpool	2-0
Leicester v Watford	2-0
Shrewbury v Ipswich	2-1
West Bromwich Albion v Norwich	1-0
Coventry v Oxford United	4-0
Crystal Palace v Orient	0-0, 1-0
Queen's Park Rangers v Grimsby	3-1

QUARTER-FINALS

Chelsea v Tottenham Hotspur	2-3
Leicester v Shrewsbury	5-2
West Bromwich Albion v Coventry	2-0
Queen's Park Rangers v Crystal Palace	1-0

SEMI-FINALS

Tottenham Hotspur v Leicester	2-0
West Bromwich Albion v Queen's Park Rangers	0-1

FINAL

Tottenham Hotspur v Queen's Park Rangers	1-1, 1-0

SCOTTISH FA CUP 1981-82

THIRD ROUND

Motherwell v Aberdeen	0-1
Celtic v Queen of the South	4-0
Kilmarnock v Montrose	1-0
Gala Fairydean v St Johnstone	1-2
Clydebank v Dunfermline	2-1
St Mirren v Morton	2-1
Brechin v Dundee United	2-4
Hibernian v Falkirk	2-0
Airdrieonians v Queen's Park	1-2
Alloa Athletic v Ayr United	2-1
East Stirlingshire v Heart of Midlothian	1-4
Hamilton v Forfar Athletic	0-0, 2-3
Dundee v Raith Rovers	1-0
Clyde v Meadowbank	2-2, 2-4
Partick Thistle v Dumbarton	1-2
Rangers v Albion Rovers	6-2

FOURTH ROUND

Aberdeen v Celtic	1-0
Kilmarnock v St Johnstone	3-1
Clydebank v St Mirren	0-2
Dundee United v Hibernian	1-1, 1-1, 3-0
Queen's Park v Alloa Athletic	2-0
Heart of Midlothian v Forfar Athletic	0-1
Dundee v Meadowbank	3-0
Rangers v Dumbarton	4-0

QUARTER-FINALS

Aberdeen v Kilmarnock	4-2
St Mirren v Dundee United	1-0
Queen's Park v Forfar Athletic	1-2
Rangers v Dundee	2-0

SEMI-FINALS

Aberdeen v St Mirren	1-1, 3-2
Forfar Athletic v Rangers	0-0, 2-3

FINAL

Aberdeen v Rangers	4-1

League Tables 1982–83

FIRST DIVISION

	P	W	D	L	F	A	Pts
1 Liverpool	42	24	10	8	87	37	82
2 Watford	42	22	5	15	74	57	71
3 Man United	42	19	13	8	56	38	70
4 Tottenham	42	20	9	13	65	50	69
5 Nottm Forest	42	20	9	13	62	50	69
6 Aston Villa	42	21	5	16	62	50	68
7 Everton	42	18	10	14	66	48	64
8 West Ham	42	20	4	18	68	62	64
9 Ipswich	42	15	13	14	64	50	58
10 Arsenal	42	16	10	16	58	56	58
11 WBA	42	15	12	15	51	49	57
12 Southampton	42	15	12	15	54	58	57
13 Stoke	42	16	9	17	53	64	57
14 Norwich	42	14	12	16	52	58	54
15 Sunderland	42	12	14	16	48	61	50
16 Notts County	42	15	7	21	55	71	52
17 Birmingham	42	12	15	16	40	55	50
18 Luton	42	12	13	17	65	84	49
19 Coventry	42	13	9	20	48	59	48
20 Man City	42	13	8	21	47	70	47
21 Swansea	42	10	11	21	51	69	41
22 Brighton	42	9	13	20	38	67	40

SECOND DIVISION

	P	W	D	L	F	A	Pts
1 QPR	42	26	7	9	77	36	85
2 Wolves	42	20	15	7	68	44	75
3 Leicester	42	20	10	12	72	44	70
4 Fulham	42	20	9	13	64	47	69*
5 Newcastle	42	18	13	11	75	53	67
6 Sheff Wed	42	16	15	11	60	47	63
7 Oldham	42	14	19	9	64	47	61
8 Leeds	42	13	21	8	51	46	60
9 Shrewsbury	42	15	14	13	48	48	59
10 Barnsley	42	14	15	13	57	55	57
11 Blackburn	42	15	12	15	58	58	57
12 Cambridge	42	13	12	17	42	60	51
13 Derby	42	10	19	13	49	58	49*
14 Carlisle	42	12	12	18	68	70	48
15 Crystal Palace	42	12	12	18	43	52	48
16 Middlesbrough	42	11	15	16	46	67	48
17 Charlton	42	13	9	20	63	86	48
18 Chelsea	42	11	14	17	51	61	47
19 Grimsby	42	12	11	19	45	70	47
20 Rotherham	42	10	15	17	45	68	45
21 Burnley	42	12	8	22	56	66	44
22 Bolton	42	11	11	20	42	61	44

*Game between Derby and Fulham abandoned after 88 minutes but result allowed to stand at 1-0.

THIRD DIVISION

	P	W	D	L	F	A	Pts
1 Portsmouth	46	27	10	9	74	41	91
2 Cardiff	46	25	11	10	76	50	86
3 Huddersfield	46	23	13	10	84	49	82
4 Newport	46	23	9	14	76	54	78
5 Oxford	46	22	12	12	71	53	78
6 Lincoln	46	23	7	16	77	51	76
8 Bristol Rovers	46	22	9	15	84	57	75
8 Plymouth	46	19	8	19	61	66	65
9 Brentford	46	18	10	18	88	77	64
10 Walsall	46	17	13	16	64	63	64
11 Sheff United	46	19	7	20	62	64	64
12 Bradford City	46	16	13	17	68	69	61
13 Gillingham	46	16	13	17	58	59	61
14 Bournemouth	46	16	13	17	59	68	61
15 Southend	46	15	14	17	66	65	59
16 Preston	46	15	13	18	60	69	58
17 Millwall	46	14	13	19	64	78	55
18 Wigan	46	15	9	22	60	72	54
19 Exeter	46	14	12	20	81	104	54
20 Orient	46	15	9	22	64	88	54
21 Reading	46	12	17	17	63	80	53
21 Wrexham	46	12	15	19	57	76	51
23 Doncaster	46	9	11	26	57	97	38
24 Chesterfield	46	8	13	25	44	68	37

FOURTH DIVISION

	P	W	D	L	F	A	Pts
1 Wimbledon	46	29	11	6	96	45	98
2 Hull	46	25	15	6	75	34	90
3 Port Vale	46	26	10	10	67	34	88
4 Scunthorpe	46	23	14	9	71	42	83
5 Bury	46	24	12	11	76	44	81
6 Colchester	46	24	9	13	75	55	81
7 York	46	22	13	11	88	58	79
8 Swindon	46	19	11	16	61	54	68
9 Peterborough	46	17	13	16	58	52	64
10 Mansfield	46	16	13	17	61	70	61
11 Halifax	46	16	12	18	59	66	60
12 Torquay	46	17	7	22	56	65	58
13 Chester	46	15	11	20	55	60	56
14 Bristol City	46	13	17	16	59	70	56
15 Northampton	46	14	12	20	67	75	54
16 Stockport	46	14	12	20	60	79	54
17 Darlington	46	13	13	20	61	71	52
18 Aldershot	46	12	15	19	61	82	51
19 Tranmere	46	13	11	22	49	71	50
20 Rochdale	46	11	16	19	55	73	49
21 Blackpool	46	13	12	21	55	74	49
22 Hartlepool	46	13	9	24	46	76	48
23 Crewe	46	11	8	27	53	71	41
24 Hereford	46	11	8	27	43	79	41

SCOTTISH PREMIER DIVISION

	P	W	D	L	F	A	Pts
1 Dundee United	36	24	8	4	90	35	56
2 Celtic	36	25	5	6	90	36	55
3 Aberdeen	36	25	5	6	76	24	55
4 Rangers	36	13	12	11	52	41	38
5 St Mirren	36	11	12	13	47	51	34
6 Dundee	36	9	11	16	42	53	29
7 Hibernian	36	11	7	18	35	51	29
8 Motherwell	36	11	5	20	39	73	27
9 Morton	36	6	8	22	30	74	20
10 Kilmarnock	36	3	11	22	28	91	17

SCOTTISH FIRST DIVISION

	P	W	D	L	F	A	Pts
1 St Johnstone	39	25	5	9	59	37	55
2 Hearts	39	22	10	7	79	38	54
3 Clydebank	39	20	10	9	72	49	50
4 Partick	39	20	9	10	66	45	49
5 Airdrie	39	16	7	16	62	46	39
6 Alloa	39	14	11	14	52	52	39
7 Falkirk	39	15	6	18	45	55	36
8 Dumbarton	39	13	10	16	50	59	36
9 Hamilton	39	11	12	16	54	66	34
10 Raith	39	13	8	18	64	63	34
11 Clyde	39	14	6	19	55	66	34
12 Ayr	39	12	8	19	45	61	32
13 Dunfermline	39	7	17	15	39	69	31
14 Queen's Park	39	16	11	22	44	80	23

SCOTTISH SECOND DIVISION

	P	W	D	L	F	A	Pts
1 Brechin	39	21	3	5	77	38	55
2 Meadowbank	39	23	8	8	64	45	54
3 Arbroath	39	21	7	11	78	51	49
4 Forfar	39	18	12	9	58	37	48
5 Stirling A	39	18	10	11	57	41	46
6 East Fife	39	16	11	12	68	43	43
7 Queen of the S	39	17	7	15	75	56	42
8 Cowdenbeath	39	13	12	14	55	53	38
9 Berwick	39	13	10	16	47	60	36
10 Albion	39	14	6	19	55	66	34
11 Stenhousemuir	39	7	14	18	43	66	29
12 Stranraer	39	10	6	23	46	79	27
13 E Stirling	39	7	9	23	43	79	23
14 Montrose	39	8	6	25	37	86	22

FA CUP 1982-83

FOURTH ROUND

Luton Town v Manchester United	0-2
Derby County v Chelsea	2-1
Tottenham Hotspur v WBA	2-1
Everton v Shrewsbury Town	2-1
Aston Villa v Wolverhampton Wanderers	1-0
Watford v Fulham	1-1, 2-1
Middlesbrough v Notts County	2-0
Arsenal v Leeds United	1-1, 1-1, 2-1
Torquay United v Sheffield Wednesday	2-3
Cambridge United v Barnsley	1-0
Crystal Palace v Birmingham	1-0
Burnley v Swindon Town	3-1
Coventry City v Norwich City	2-2, 1-2
Ipswich Town v Grimsby Town	2-0
Liverpool v Stoke City	2-0
Brighton v Manchester City	4-0

FIFTH ROUND

Derby County v Manchester United	0-1
Everton v Tottenham Hotspur	2-0
Aston Villa v Watford	4-1
Middlesbrough v Arsenal	1-1, 1-2
Cambridge United v Sheffield Wednesday	1-2
Crystal Palace v Burnley	0-0, 0-1
Norwich City v Ipswich Town	1-0
Liverpool v Brighton	1-2

QUARTER-FINALS

Manchester United v Everton	1-0
Arsenal v Aston Villa	2-0
Burnley v Sheffield Wednesday	1-1, 0-5
Brighton v Norwich City	1-0

SEMI-FINALS

Manchester United v Arsenal	2-1
Brighton v Sheffield Wednesday	2-1

FINAL

Manchester United v Brighton	2-2, 4-0

SCOTTISH FA CUP 1982-83

FOURTH ROUND

Aberdeen v Dundee	1-0
Albion Rovers v Airdrie	0-3
Celtic v Dunfermline	3-0
Hearts v East Fife	2-1
Morton v St Mirren	0-2
Partick Thistle v Clyde	2-2, 1-1*, 6-0
Queen's Park v St Johnstone	1-0
Rangers v Forfar	2-1

*abandoned in 13th minute, of extra time.

QUARTER-FINALS

Airdrie v St Mirren	0-5
Celtic v Hearts	4-1
Partick Thistle v Aberdeen	1-2
Queen's Park v Rangers	1-2

SEMI-FINALS

Aberdeen v Celtic	1-0
Rangers v St Mirren	1-1, 1-0

FINAL

Aberdeen v Rangers	1-0